Signs of Life in the U.S.A.

Eighth Edition

Signs of Life in the U.S.A.

Readings on Popular Culture for Writers

Sonia Maasik

University of California, Los Angeles

Jack Solomon

California State University, Northridge

BEDFORD/ST. MARTIN'S   Boston ◆ New York

For Bedford/St. Martin's

Vice President, Editorial, Macmillan Higher Education Humanities: Edwin Hill
Editorial Director for English and Music: Karen S. Henry
Publisher for Composition, Business and Technical Writing and Developmental Writing: Leasa Burton
Executive Editor: John Sullivan
Senior Developmental Editor: Adam Whitehurst
Editorial Assistant: Kathleen Wisneski
Senior Production Editor: Jessica Gould
Senior Production Supervisor: Lisa McDowell
Executive Marketing Manager: Jane Helms
Copy Editor: Jennifer Greenstein
Director of Rights and Permissions: Hilary Newman
Senior Art Director: Anna Palchik
Cover Design: Marine Miller
Cover Art/Cover Photo: Simon Evans, *Everything I Have*, 2008. Pen, paper, Scotch tape, correction fluid, and ink-jet prints of personal inventory, 60¼ × 40⅛ in., 153.04 × 101.92 cm © Simon Evans / Courtesy James Cohan Gallery, New York/Shanghai
Composition: Cenveo Publisher Services
Printing and Binding: LSC Communications

2 1 0 9 8 7
f e d c b a

For information, write: Bedford/St. Martin's, 75 Arlington Street, Boston, MA 02116 (617-399-4000)

ISBN: 978-1-319-12679-7

Acknowledgments

Preface for Instructors

The more things change, the more they . . . intensify. For in the years since the publication of the seventh edition of *Signs of Life in the U.S.A.*, two profound interventions in American history — the Great Recession and the Digital Revolution — have only increased their influence on American culture and consciousness. Years of diminishing opportunities, of un- and under-employment, stagnant wages, and economic disruption persistently erode the national spirit, even as the explosive growth of digital technology continues its transformation of our culture into a vast social network: an always-on virtual society that has recast Marshall McLuhan's global village into a global hive. And there is little reason to believe that either of these forces will be abating in the foreseeable future.

In the midst of such interventions, the role of popular culture in our lives has equally intensified. No longer a mere cultural embellishment or ornament, popular culture now permeates almost everything we do even as it reflects back to us what we are becoming as a society and who we are. With digital technology blurring beyond recognition the line between everyday life and entertainment, transforming the traditional work spaces of school and office into virtual play stations and shopping malls, if we wish to understand America today we must learn to think critically about the vast panoply of entertainments and commodities that were once condescendingly dismissed as elements of "mass culture." And that is what *Signs of Life in the U.S.A.* has always been designed to teach your students to do.

Then and Now

The importance of thinking critically about popular culture has not always been apparent to the academic world. When the first edition of *Signs of Life* appeared, the study of popular culture was still embroiled in the "culture wars" of the late 1980s and early 1990s, a struggle for academic legitimacy in which the adherents of popular cultural studies ultimately prevailed. Since then, more and more scholars and teachers have come to recognize the importance of understanding what Michel de Certeau has called "the practice of everyday life" and the value of using popular culture as a thematic ground for educating students in critical thinking and writing. Once excluded from academic study on the basis of a naturalized distinction between "high" and "low" culture, which contemporary cultural analysis has shown to be historically contingent, popular culture has come to be an accepted part of the curriculum, widely studied in freshman composition classrooms as well as in upper-division undergraduate courses and graduate seminars.

But recognition of the importance that popular culture has assumed in our society has not been restricted to the academy. Increasingly, Americans are realizing that American culture and popular culture are virtually one and the same, and that whether we are looking at our political system, our economy, or simply our national consciousness, the power of popular culture to shape our lives is strikingly apparent. That is why, unlike most other popular cultural texts, *Signs of Life* adopts an interpretive approach — semiotics — that is explicitly designed to analyze that intersection of ideology and entertainment that we call *popular culture*. We continue to make semiotics the guiding methodology behind *Signs of Life* because semiotics helps us, and our students, avoid the common pitfalls of uncritical celebration or simple trivia swapping.

The Critical Method: Semiotics

The reception of the first seven editions of this text has demonstrated that the semiotic approach to popular culture has indeed found a place in America's composition classrooms. Composition instructors have seen that students feel a certain sense of ownership toward the products of popular culture and that using popular culture as a focus can help students overcome the sometimes alienating effects of traditional academic subject matter. At the same time, the semiotic method has helped instructors teach their students how to analyze the popular cultural phenomena that they enjoy writing about, and through these methods students have learned the critical thinking and writing skills that their composition classes are designed to impart.

Reflecting the broad academic interest in cultural studies, we've assumed an inclusive definition of *popular culture*. The seven chapters in *Signs of Life in the U.S.A.* embrace everything from the marketing and consumption of the products of mass production to the television programs and movies that entertain us. We have chosen semiotics as our approach because it has struck us that while students enjoy assignments that ask them to look at popular cultural phenomena, they often have trouble distinguishing between an argued interpretive analysis and the simple expression of an opinion. Some textbooks, for example, suggest assignments that involve analyzing a TV show or film, but they don't always tell a student how to do that. The semiotic method provides that guidance.

As a conceptual framework, semiotics teaches students to formulate cogent, well-supported interpretations. It emphasizes the examination of assumptions and of the way language shapes our apprehension of the world. And, because semiotics focuses on how beliefs are formulated within a social and political context (rather than just judging or evaluating those beliefs), it's ideal for discussing sensitive or politically charged issues. As an approach used in literature, media studies, anthropology, art and design coursework, sociology, law, and market research (to name only some of its more prominent field applications), semiotics has a cross-disciplinary appeal that makes it ideal for a writing class of students from a variety of majors and disciplines. We recognize that semiotics has a reputation for being highly technical or theoretical; rest assured that *Signs of Life* does not require students or instructors to have a technical knowledge of semiotics. We've provided clear and accessible introductions that explain what students need to know.

We also recognize that adopting a theoretical approach may be new to some instructors, so we've designed the book to allow instructors to use semiotics with their students as much or as little as they wish. The book does not obligate instructors or students to spend a lot of time with semiotics — although we do hope you'll find the approach intriguing and provocative.

The Editorial Apparatus

With its emphasis on popular culture, *Signs of Life* should generate lively class discussion and inspire many kinds of writing and thinking activities. The general introduction provides an overall framework for the book, acquainting students with the semiotic method they can use to interpret the topics raised in each chapter. It is followed by the section "Writing about Popular Culture" that not only provides a brief introduction to this topic but also features three sample student essays that demonstrate different approaches to writing critical essays on popular cultural topics. The introduction concludes with "Conducting Research and Citing Sources," a section to help your students properly document the research they've done for their writing assignments, including three articles that guide students in the appropriate use of the Internet as a research tool.

Each chapter starts with a frontispiece, a provocative visual image related to the chapter's topic, and an introduction that suggests ways to "read" the topic, provides model interpretations, and links the issues raised by the reading selections. Every chapter introduction contains three types of boxed questions designed to stimulate student thinking on the topic. The Exploring the Signs questions invite students to reflect on an issue in a journal entry or other prewriting activity, while the Discussing the Signs questions trigger class activities such as debates, discussions, or small-group work. Reading Online questions invite students to explore the chapter's topic on the Internet, both for research purposes and for texts to analyze.

Two sorts of assignments accompany each reading. The Reading the Text questions help students comprehend the selections, asking them to identify important concepts and arguments, explain key terms, and relate main ideas to one another and to the evidence presented. The Reading the Signs questions are writing and activity prompts designed to produce clear analytic thinking and strong persuasive writing; they often make connections among reading selections from different chapters. Most assignments call for analytic essays, while some invite journal responses, in-class debates, group work, or other creative activities. Complementing the readings in each chapter are images that serve as visual texts to be discussed. We also include a glossary of semiotic terms, which can serve as a ready reference to key words and concepts used in the chapter introductions. Finally, the Instructor's Manual (*Editors' Notes for Signs of Life in the U.S.A.*) provides suggestions for organizing your syllabus, encouraging student responses to the readings, and using popular culture and semiotics in the writing class.

What's New in the Eighth Edition

Popular culture evolves at a rapid pace, and the substantial revision required for the eighth edition of *Signs of Life in the U.S.A.* reflects this essential mutability. First, we have updated our readings, including more than twenty-five new selections focusing on issues and trends that have emerged since the last edition of this book. We have also updated the exemplary topics in our introductions, which are used to model the critical assignments that follow, and have adjusted the focus of some chapters to reflect the changing conditions of students' lives and the ways they consume popular culture. Two new chapters, "Heroes and Villains: Encoding Our Conflicts" and "My Selfie, My Self: Ma(s)king Identity in the New Millennium," explore the ways in which the conflicts and contradictions in American society are reflected in video entertainments awash in heroes, antiheroes, and villains, even as our sense of our selves is being reshaped in an era of online profiling and self-advertising.

From the beginning, *Signs of Life in the U.S.A.* has been based on the premise that in a postindustrial, McLuhanesque world, the image has come to supplant the printed word in American, and global, culture. That is yet another of the reasons we chose semiotics, which provides a rational basis for the critical analysis of images as the guiding methodology for every edition of our book. Each edition of *Signs of Life* has accordingly included images for critical analysis; the eighth edition continues this tradition. The images included in the text supplement the readings, offering a visual perspective designed to enhance the critical understanding modeled by the texts. Yet the images are not meant to replace the texts — we strongly believe that while the semiotic interpretation of images can help students hone their writing skills, it should not be a substitute for learning critical thinking through the analysis of written texts.

At the same time, the way that students consume images has been revolutionized by digital and mobile technologies, and *Signs of Life in the U.S.A.* reflects this new reality both through the offering of an e-book version of the main text and through LaunchPad Solo for *Signs of Life in the U.S.A.*, a collection of digital resources referenced throughout the print book that includes reading and writing tutorials, quizzing on rhetorical and grammatical topics, and e-readings — from vintage TV ads and films to documentary clips that elaborate on the topics covered by the reading selections. LaunchPad Solo for *Signs of Life in the U.S.A.* is available as a free package.

Even as we revise this text to reflect current trends, popular culture continues to evolve. The inevitable gap between the pace of editing and publishing, on the one hand, and the flow of popular culture, on the other, need not affect the use of popular culture in the classroom, however. The readings in the text, and the semiotic method we propose, are designed to show students how to analyze and write critical essays about any topic they choose. They can choose a topic that appeared before they were born, or they can turn to the latest box-office or prime-time hit to appear after the publication of this edition of *Signs of Life in the U.S.A.* Facebook and Twitter may well have been replaced by such more recent sites as Snapchat, Pinterest, and Instagram within the life span of this edition (indeed, Facebook obliterated MySpace shortly after the publication of the sixth edition of this book), but such changes are opportunities for further analysis, not obstacles. To put it another way, the practice of everyday life may itself be filled with evanescent fads and trends, but daily life is not itself a fad. As the vital texture of our lived experience, popular culture provides a stable background against which students of every generation can test their critical skills.

Acknowledgments

The vastness of the terrain of popular culture has enabled many users of the seventh edition of this text to make valuable suggestions for the eighth edition. We have incorporated many such suggestions and thank all for their comments on our text. We are also grateful to those reviewers who examined the book in depth: Anna Alessi, Saddleback Community College; Suzanne Arakawa, California State University — San Bernardino; Nick Brittin, Lake Michigan College; Mary Ann Bushman, Illinois Wesleyan University; Jane Christensen,

University of Nebraska at Kearney; Amy Corey, Gonzaga University; Patricia Cullinan, Truckee Meadows Community College; Nicole Denner, Stetson University; Sarah Duerden, Arizona State University; Catherine Gillis, Napa Valley College; Lynda Glennon, Rollins College; Christi Hein, Colorado Mesa University; Shawne Johnson, Community College of Philadelphia; Terry Krueger, Central Oregon Community College; David McCracken, Coker College; Laurie Vickroy, Bradley University; Chris Warnick, College of Charleston; Edward Wesp, Western New England University; Paula White, Community College of Philadelphia; Eve Wiederhold, George Mason University; Joshua Woodfork, American University; and John Ziebell, Florida State College Jacksonville.

If we have not included something you'd like to work on, you may still direct your students to it, using this text as a guide, not as a set of absolute prescriptions. The practice of everyday life includes the conduct of a classroom, and we want all users of the eighth edition of *Signs of Life in the U.S.A.* to feel free to pursue that practice in whatever way best suits their interests and aims.

Once again, we wish to thank heartily the people at Bedford/St. Martin's who have enabled us to make this new edition a reality. We especially want to thank our editor, Adam Whitehurst, a real partner in our work who brings to the eighth edition of *Signs of Life* both a fresh perspective and a storehouse of creative energy that, in the tradition of our collaboration with Bedford's editors, has left its own imprint on the book. Jessica Gould ably guided our manuscript through the rigors of production, while Kathleen Wisneski handled the numerous questions and details that arose during textbook development. Susan Doheny expertly researched and obtained permissions for art, and Margaret Gorenstein cleared text permissions. Our thanks go as well to Jennifer Greenstein for her fine copyediting of this book.

Get the most out of your course with *Signs of Life in the U.S.A.*

Bedford/St. Martin's offers resources and format choices that help you and your students get even more out of your book and course. To learn more about or to order any of the following products, contact your Bedford/St. Martin's sales representative, e-mail sales support (**sales_support@bfwpub .com**), or visit the Web site at **macmillanhighered.com/signsoflife/catalog**.

LAUNCHPAD SOLO FOR SIGNS OF LIFE IN THE U.S.A.*: WHERE STUDENTS LEARN*

LaunchPad Solo provides engaging content and new ways to get the most out of your course. Get **unique, book-specific materials** in a fully customizable course space; then assign and mix our resources with yours. Visit **macmillanhighered.com/signsoflife8e**.

- **Curated content** — including readings, videos, tutorials, and more — is **easy to adapt and assign** by adding your own materials and mixing them with our high-quality multimedia content and ready-made assessment options, such as **LearningCurve** adaptive quizzing. LaunchPad Solo for *Signs of Life in the U.S.A.* lets students make connections between their reading and real pop culture artifacts, including TV commercials and film clips.

- LaunchPad Solo also provides access to a **gradebook** that provides a clear window on the performance of your whole class, individual students, and even individual assignments.

- A **streamlined interface** helps students focus on what's due, and social commenting tools let them **engage**, make connections, and learn from one another.

To get the most out of your course, order LaunchPad Solo for *Signs of Life in the U.S.A.* packaged with the print book **at no additional charge**. (LaunchPad Solo for *Signs of Life in the U.S.A.* can also be purchased on its own.) An activation code is required. To order LaunchPad Solo for *Signs of Life in the U.S.A.* with the print book, use ISBN 978-1-319-01383-7.

CHOOSE FROM ALTERNATIVE FORMATS OF SIGNS OF LIFE IN THE U.S.A.

Bedford/St. Martin's offers a range of affordable formats, allowing students to choose the one that works best for them. For details, visit **macmillanhighered.com/signsoflife/catalog**.

- **Paperback.** To order the paperback edition, use ISBN 978-1-4576-7025-1.

- *Bedford e-Book to Go.* A portable, downloadable e-book is available at about half the price of the print book. To order the *Bedford e-Book to Go*, use ISBN 978-1-4576-7084-8.

- **Other popular e-book formats.** For details, visit **macmillanhighered.com/ebooks**.

PACKAGE WITH ANOTHER BEDFORD/ST. MARTIN'S TITLE AND SAVE

Get the most value for your students by packaging *Signs of Life in the U.S.A.* with a Bedford/St. Martin's handbook or any other Bedford/St. Martin's title for a significant discount. To order, please request a package ISBN from your sales representative or e-mail sales support (**salessupport@bfwpub.com**).

SELECT VALUE PACKAGES

Add value to your text by packaging one of the following resources with *Signs of Life in the U.S.A.* To learn more about package options for any of the following products, contact your Bedford/St. Martin's sales representative or visit **macmillanhighered.com/signsoflife/catalog**.

LearningCurve for Readers and Writers, Bedford/St. Martin's adaptive quizzing program, quickly learns what students already know and helps them practice what they don't yet understand. Gamelike quizzing motivates students to engage with their course, and reporting tools help teachers discern their students' needs. *LearningCurve for Readers and Writers* can be packaged with *Signs of Life in the U.S.A.* at a significant discount. An activation code is required. To order *LearningCurve* packaged with the print book, contact your sales representative for a package ISBN. For details, visit **learningcurveworks.com.**

i-series. This popular series presents multimedia tutorials in a flexible format — because there are things you can't do in a book.

- *ix visualizing composition 2.0* helps students put into practice key rhetorical and visual concepts. To order *ix visualizing composition* packaged with the print book, contact your sales representative for a package ISBN.

- *i-claim: visualizing argument* offers a new way to see argument — with six multimedia tutorials, an illustrated glossary, and a wide array of multimedia arguments. To order *i-claim: visualizing argument* packaged with the print book, contact your sales representative for a package ISBN.

Portfolio Keeping, **Third Edition, by Nedra Reynolds and Elizabeth Davis,** provides all the information students need to use the portfolio method successfully in a writing course. *Portfolio Teaching*, a companion guide for instructors, provides the practical information instructors and writing program administrators need to use the portfolio method successfully in a writing course. To order *Portfolio Keeping* packaged with the print book, contact your sales representative for a package ISBN.

MAKE LEARNING FUN WITH RE:WRITING 3
bedfordstmartins.com/rewriting

New open online resources with videos and interactive elements engage students in new ways of writing. You'll find tutorials about using common digital writing tools, an interactive peer review game, Extreme Paragraph Makeover, and more — all for free and for fun. Visit **bedfordstmartins.com/rewriting**.

INSTRUCTOR RESOURCES
macmillanhighered.com/signsoflife/catalog

You have a lot to do in your course. Bedford/St. Martin's wants to make it easy for you to find the support you need — and to get it quickly.

Editors' Notes for Signs of Life in the U.S.A. is available as a PDF that can be downloaded from the Bedford/St. Martin's online catalog at the URL above. In addition to chapter overviews and teaching tips, the instructor's manual includes a sample syllabus, assignment and course organization ideas, and additional advice using semiotics in your writing course.

Teaching Central offers the entire list of Bedford/St. Martin's print and online professional resources in one place. You'll find landmark reference works, sourcebooks on pedagogical issues, award-winning collections, and practical advice for the classroom — all free for instructors. Visit **macmillanhighered .com/teachingcentral**.

Bits collects creative ideas for teaching a range of composition topics in an easily searchable blog format and includes "Teaching Popular Culture Semiotics," the blog by *Signs of Life in the U.S.A.* author Jack Solomon. A community of teachers — leading scholars, authors, and editors — discuss revision, research, grammar and style, technology, peer review, and much more. Take, use, adapt, and pass the ideas around. Then, come back to the site to comment or share your own suggestion. Visit **bedfordbits.com**.

Contents

e LaunchPad Solo for *Signs of Life in the U.S.A.* takes advantage of what the Web can do, at
macmillanhighered.com/signsoflife8e.

FORD MOTOR COMPANY: *Two-Ford Freedom* [VINTAGE ADVERTISEMENT] 🅮

Portfolio of Advertisements
  Bose
  Buffalo Exchange
  California Walnuts
  Johnson's Baby
  Limbo
  Sanuk
  Shinola

Chapter 3.
Video Dreams: *Television and Cultural Forms*   255

NICK SERPE: *Reality Pawns: The New Money TV*   268

> "On *Storage Wars*, naked economic warfare takes a . . . central role, but the family unit and flights of whimsy intervene to prevent the characters from looking like complete sociopaths."

┌─ PAIRED READINGS: SOUTHERN WOMAN

CLAIRE MIYE STANFORD: *You've Got the Wrong Song:* Nashville *and Country Music Feminism*   276

> "As a show . . . *Nashville*—in its unapologetically pure focus on female characters, its self-aware examination of the struggles of female artists, and its critique of male-dominated industries—is one of the most feminist television shows on television."

MICHELLE DEAN: *Here Comes the Hillbilly, Again*   283

> "Hillbilly stereotypes have always made it easier for middle-class whites to presume that racism is the exclusive province of 'that kind' of person."

CARL MATHESON: The Simpsons, *Hyper-Irony, and the Meaning of Life*   287

> "The lifeblood of *The Simpsons*, and its astonishing achievement, is the pace of cruelty and ridicule that it has managed to sustain for over a decade."

NATASHA SIMONS: Mad Men *and the Paradox of the Past*   300

> "Conservatives and liberals just can't help but see *Mad Men* differently: the former with apprehension, the latter with anticipation."

🄴 macmillanhighered.com/signsoflife8e

Chapter 7.
My Selfie, My Self: Ma(s)king Identity in the
New Millennium *491*

🄴 macmillanhighered.com/signsoflife8e

Signs of Life in the U.S.A.

POPULAR SIGNS

*Or, Everything You Always
Knew about American Culture
(but Nobody Asked)*

Dawn of the Living Droid

"HARDER. BETTER. FASTER. STRANGER."

With these words, Marvel Comics introduced its new series, *Avengers A.I.*, in 2013, the same year that *Iron Man 3* busted the box office, Daft Punk's *Random Access Memories* topped the charts, and Google Glass became available in a $1,500 version for selected consumers.

And so, even as *World War Z* and *The Walking Dead* continued to demonstrate that the reign of the undead was far from over, American popular culture began to show signs of the advent of a new empire of the unliving, of intelligent machines whose long-anticipated arrival would push the world ever closer to the apocalyptic event that futurists have called "the Singularity": that posthuman moment when human intelligence will be surpassed by artificial intelligence and humanity itself will be replaced by robotic androids.

Now, whether the Singularity ever comes to pass (frankly, we are skeptical), it appears that after years of fascination with the living dead—first with vampires and then with zombies, who completed their migration from the margins of fantasy fiction to pop culture's center stage in the first decade of the new millennium—American popular culture is now preparing a similar movement for the figures of the cyborg and the android. This emergence of the man-machine—as with the zombies and vampires before him—is not an overnight occurrence (Iron Man, for example, was created half a century ago, and the Six Million Dollar Man was a creation of the 1970s), but it is picking up steam as we write these words. While you might easily assume that this development is natural and inevitable and has no particular significance, there is actually quite a lot of cultural meaning behind it. One of the purposes of this book is to help you find such meanings.

Indeed, the foundational principle of *Signs of Life in the U.S.A.* is that human behavior has meaning and that popular culture is particularly meaningful and should never simply be taken for granted. Treating popular cultural behavior as a system of **signs**, this book will teach you how to read — or interpret — these signs, while at the same time teaching you the critical thinking skills necessary to write strong university-level arguments. Accordingly, each chapter in this book focuses upon a particular segment of American popular culture and, through readings, images, and assignments, guides you through the process that will help you analyze the significance of the full range of our everyday lives, behaviors, and entertainments. We will return shortly in this Introduction to the prevalence of such inhuman, or even posthuman, figures as androids, zombies, and vampires as a prominent example of a popular cultural sign, but first we will look at just what we mean by the term "popular culture" and why it is important to think critically about it.

From Folk to Fab

Traditionally, popular or "low" culture constituted the culture of the masses. It was set apart from "high" culture, which included classical music and literature, the fine arts and philosophy, and the elite learning that was the province of the ruling classes who had the money and leisure necessary to attain it — and who were often the direct patrons of high art and its creators. Low culture, for its part, had two main sides. One side, most notoriously illustrated by the violent entertainments of the Roman Empire (such as gladiatorial contests, public executions, and feeding Christians to lions) continues to be a sure crowd-pleaser to this day, as demonstrated by the widespread popularity of violent, erotic, and/or vulgar entertainment (can you spell *Jackass*?). The other side, which we can call "popular" in the etymological sense of being of the people, overlaps with what we now call "folk culture." Quietly existing alongside high culture, folk culture expressed the experience and creativity of the masses in the form of ballads, agricultural festivals, fairy tales, feasts, folk art, folk music, and so on. Self-produced by amateur performers, folk culture is exemplified by neighbors gathering on a modest Appalachian front porch to play their guitars, banjos, dulcimers, zithers, mandolins, and fiddles to perform, for their own entertainment, ballads and songs passed down from generation to generation.

Folk culture, of course, still exists. But for the past two hundred years it has been dwindling, with increasing rapidity, as it becomes overwhelmed by a different kind of popular culture, a commercialized culture that, while still including elements of both the folk and the vulgar traditions, represents the outcome of a certain historical evolution. This culture, the popular culture that is most familiar today and that is the topic of this book, is a commercial, for-profit culture aimed at providing entertainment to a mass audience. Corporate

AP Photo/Richard Drew

Traditional high culture: Deborah Voigt in performance at the Metropolitan Opera in New York.

rather than communal, it has transformed entertainment into a commodity to be marketed alongside all the other products in a consumer society.

The forces that transformed the low culture of the past into contemporary popular culture arose in the industrial revolution of the late eighteenth century and its accompanying urbanization of European and American society. Along with the rise of corporate capitalism and the advent of electronic technologies, these four, essentially interrelated, historical forces — industrialization, urbanization, capitalism, and electronic technology — shaped the emergence of the mass cultural marketplace of entertainments that we know today. To see how this happened, let's begin with the industrial revolution.

Prior to the industrial revolution, most Europeans and Americans lived in scattered agricultural settlements. While traveling entertainers in theatrical troupes and circuses might have visited the larger of these settlements, most people, especially those with little money, had little access to professional entertainment and so had to produce their own entertainment. But with the industrial revolution, masses of people who had made their living through agriculture were compelled to leave their rural communities and move to the industrial towns and cities where employment could increasingly be found. Populations began to concentrate in urban centers as the rural countryside emptied, leading to the development of mass societies.

With the emergence of mass society came the development of **mass culture**. For just as mass societies are governed by centralized systems of governance (as the huge expanse of the United States is governed by a federal government concentrated in Washington, DC), so, too, are mass cultures entertained by culture industries concentrated in a few locations (as the film and TV industries are concentrated in Hollywood and its immediate environs). Thanks to the invention of such technologies as the cinema, the phonograph, and the radio at the end of the nineteenth century, and of television and digital technology in the mid to late twentieth century, the means to disseminate centrally produced mass entertainments to a mass society became possible. Thus, whether you live in Boston or Boise, New York or Nebraska, the entertainment you enjoy is produced in the same few locations and is the same entertainment (TV programs, movies, DVDs, or Netflix series) no matter where you consume it. This growth of mass culture has been fundamentally shaped by the growth of a capitalist economic system in America, which has ensured that mass culture would develop as a for-profit industry.

To get a better idea of how the whole process unfolded, let's go back to that Appalachian front porch. Before electricity and urbanization, folks living in the backwoods of rural America needed to make their music themselves if they wanted music. They had no radios, phonographs, CD players, iPods, iPads, smartphones, or even electricity, and theaters with live performers were hard to get to and expensive. Under such conditions, the Appalachian region developed a vibrant folk musical culture. But as people started to move to places like Pittsburgh and Detroit, where the steel and auto industries began to offer employment in the late nineteenth and early twentieth centuries, the conditions under which neighbors could produce their own music decayed, for the communal conditions under which folk culture thrived were broken down by the mass migration to the cities. At the same time, the need to produce one's own music declined as folks who had once plucked their own guitars and banjos could simply turn on their radios or purchase records to listen to professional musicians perform for them. Those musicians were contracted by recording companies that were in business to turn a profit, and their music, in turn, could be heard on the radio because corporate sponsors provided the advertising that made (and still makes) commercial radio broadcasting possible.

Thus, the folk music of the American countryside became *country music*. An amalgamation of the traditional songs that a predominantly Scots-Irish immigrant population brought over from the British Isles with such American

AP Photo

Traditional folk culture in transition: Bill Monroe is known as the father of
bluegrass music.

traditions as "white" gospel music, cowboy songs, and rock 'n' roll, contemporary "country" preserves the rural working-class perspective of folk music
even as it is performed by wealthy professionals. (Country music's working-
class roots explain why it is so often filled with the broken romances and
broken-down cars of the poor.)

So the performance of folk music, which had once been an amateur,
do-it-yourself activity, became a professional, for-profit industry with passive consumers paying for their entertainment either by directly purchasing a commodity (for example, a CD) or by listening to the advertising that
encouraged them to purchase the products that sponsored their favorite radio
programs. It is still possible, of course, to make one's own music, but most
people find it easier and perhaps more aesthetically pleasing to listen to a
professional recording. Today we are, in effect, constantly being trained to be
the sort of passive consumers who keep the whole consumer-capitalist system going. Without that consumption, the economy might totally collapse.

This is hardly an exaggeration, for postindustrial capitalism is making
popular culture all the more dominant in our society with every passing year.
With the American economy turning further away from industrial production

and increasingly toward the production and consumption of entertainment (including sports), entertainment has been moving from the margins of our cultural consciousness — as a mere form of play or recreation — to its center as a major buttress of our economy. A constant bombardment of advertising (which, after all, is the driving force behind the financing of digital media, just as it was for radio and television a generation or two ago) continually prods us to consume the entertainments that our economy produces. That bombardment has been so successful that our whole cultural consciousness is changing: We are becoming more concerned with play than with work, even while *at* work. (Tell the truth now: Do you ever tweet, or post something to Tumblr or Instagram, during class?)

The result of the centuries-long process we have sketched above is the kind of culture we have today: an *entertainment culture* in which all aspects of society, including politics and the traditional elite arts, are linked by a common imperative to entertain. Indeed, as traditional high culture shrinks in social importance and becomes part of what might be called a museum culture (which is quietly marginalized and mostly ignored), popular culture itself has assumed its own "high" and "low" strata, with television programs like *Mad Men* and *Game of Thrones* enjoying a kind of high cultural status, while *Here Comes Honey Boo Boo* profitably entertains at the low end.

Congressman Paul Ryan poses with *Duck Dynasty* stars Willie and Korie Robertson at the 2014 State of the Union address.

Jewel Samad

Pop Culture Goes to College

Far from being a mere recreational frivolity, a leisure activity that our society could easily dispense with, popular cultural entertainment today constitutes the essential texture of our everyday lives. From the way we entertain ourselves to the goods and services that we produce and consume, we are enveloped in a popular cultural environment that we can neither do without nor escape, even if we wanted to. To see this, just try to imagine a world without cloud computing, TV, movies, sports, music, shopping malls, or advertising. The study of popular culture has accordingly taken a prominent place in American higher education — not least in American composition classrooms, which have taken the lead in incorporating popular culture into academic study, both because of the subject's inherent interest value and because of its profound familiarity to most students. Your own expertise in popular culture means not only that you may know more about a given topic than your instructor but that you can use that knowledge as a basis for learning the critical thinking and writing skills that your composition class is intended to teach you.

Signs of Life in the U.S.A., then, is designed to let you exploit your knowledge of popular culture so that you may grow into a better writer, whatever the subject. You can interpret the popularity of a TV program like *The Walking Dead*, for example, in the same manner as you would interpret, say, a short story, because *The Walking Dead*, too, constitutes a kind of sign. A sign is something, anything, that carries a meaning. The familiar red sign at an intersection, for instance, means exactly what it says: "Stop." But it also carries the implied message ". . . or risk getting a ticket or into an accident." Words, too, are signs: you read them to figure out what they mean. You were trained to read such signs, but that training began so long ago that you may well take your ability to read for granted. Nevertheless, all your life you have been encountering and interpreting other sorts of signs. Although you were never formally taught to read them, you know what they mean anyway. Take the way you wear your hair. When you get your hair cut, you are not simply removing hair; you are making a statement, sending a message about yourself. It's the same for both men and women. Why was your hair short last year and long this year? Aren't you saying something with the scissors? In this way, you make your hairstyle into a sign that sends a message about your identity. You are surrounded by such signs. Just look at your classmates.

The world of signs could be called a kind of text, the text of America's popular culture. We want you to think of *Signs of Life in the U.S.A.* as a window onto that text. What you read in this book's essays and Chapter Introductions should lead you to study and analyze the world around you for yourself. Let the selections guide you to your own interpretations, your own readings, of the text of America.

In this edition of *Signs of Life in the U.S.A.*, we have chosen seven "windows" that look out onto separate, but often interrelated, segments of the American scene. In each chapter, we have included essays that help you think about a specific popular cultural topic and guide you to locate and analyze related examples of your own. Each chapter also includes an Introduction written to alert you to the kinds of signs you will find there, along with model analyses and advice on how to go about interpreting the topic that the chapter raises.

We have designed *Signs of Life in the U.S.A.* to reflect the many ways in which culture shapes our sense of reality and of ourselves, from the products we buy to the way culture, through such media as television and the movies, constructs our personal identities. This text thus introduces you to both the entertainment side and the ideological side of popular culture—and shows how the two sides are mutually dependent. Indeed, one of the major lessons you can learn from this book is how to find the ideological underpinnings of some of the most apparently innocent entertainments and consumer goods.

Signs of Life in the U.S.A., accordingly, begins with a chapter called "Consuming Passions." Because America is a consumer culture, the environment in which the galaxy of popular signs functions is, more often than not, a consumerist one. This is true not only for obvious consumer products like clothes and cars but for traditionally nonconsumer items such as political candidates, who are often marketed like any other product. It is difficult to find anything in contemporary America that is not affected somehow by our consumerist ethos or by consumerism's leading promoter, the advertiser. Thus, the second chapter, "Brought to You B(u)y," explores the world of advertising, for advertising provides the grease, so to speak, that lubricates the engine of America's consumer culture. Because television and film are the sources of many of our most significant cultural products, we include a chapter on each. Chapters on the digital cloud, American heroes and villains, and personal identity round out our survey of everyday life.

Throughout, the book invites you to go out and select your own "texts" for analysis (an advertisement, a film, a fashion fad, a TV show, and so on). Here's where your own experience is particularly valuable, because it has made you familiar with many different kinds of popular signs and their backgrounds, as well as with the particular popular cultural system or environment to which they belong.

The seven "windows" you will find in *Signs of Life in the U.S.A.* are all intended to reveal the common intersections of entertainment and ideology that can be found in contemporary American life. Often what seems to be simply entertainment, like an action-adventure movie, can actually be quite political (consider the Native American response to *The Lone Ranger*), while what *is* political can be cast as entertainment as well—as in *House of Cards*. The point is that little in American life is merely entertainment; indeed, just about everything we do has a meaning, often a profound one.

The Semiotic Method

To find this meaning, to interpret and write effectively about the signs of popular culture, you need a method, and part of the purpose of this book is to introduce such a method to you. Without a methodology for interpreting signs, writing about them could become little more than producing descriptive reviews or opinion pieces. Although nothing is wrong with writing descriptions and opinions, one of your goals in your writing class is to learn how to write academic essays — that is, analytical essays that present theses or arguments that are well supported by evidence. The method we use in this book — a method known as **semiotics** — is especially well suited for analyzing popular culture. Whether or not you're familiar with this word, you already practice sophisticated semiotic analyses every day of your life. Reading this page is an act of semiotic decoding (words and letters are signs that must be interpreted), but so is figuring out just what a friend means by wearing a particular shirt or dress. For a semiotician (one who practices semiotic analysis), a shirt, a haircut, a TV image, anything at all, can be taken as a sign, as a message to be decoded and analyzed to discover its meaning. Every cultural activity leaves a trace of meaning for semioticians, a kind of blip on the semiotic Richter scale that remains for them to read, just as geologists "read" the earth for signs of earthquakes, volcanic activity, and other geological phenomena.

Many who hear the word *semiotics* for the first time assume that it is the name of a new and forbidding subject. But in truth, the study of signs is neither new nor forbidding. Its modern form took shape in the late nineteenth and early twentieth centuries through the writings and lectures of two men. Charles Sanders Peirce (1839–1914) was an American philosopher who first coined the word *semiotics*, while Ferdinand de Saussure (1857–1913) was a Swiss linguist whose lectures became the foundation for what he called *semiology* (which was later developed under the rubric of linguistic *structuralism*). Without knowing of each other's work, Peirce and Saussure established the fundamental principles that modern semioticians or semiologists — the terms are essentially interchangeable — have developed into the contemporary study of semiotics.

Reduced to its simplest principles, the semiotic method carries on Saussure's argument that the meaning of a sign lies, in part, in the fact that it can be *differentiated* from any other sign within the **system**, or **code**, to which it belongs. For example, in the traffic code, being able to distinguish the difference between green, red, and amber lights is essential to understanding the meaning of a traffic signal. But that's not all there is to it, because it is only within the code that green, red, and amber signify "go," "stop," and "caution." So in order to interpret a traffic signal correctly, you need to be able to *associate* any particular red light you see with all other red traffic lights under the concept "stop" that the code assigns to it, and any green light with all other green lights under the concept "go," and so on.

But outside of the traffic code, the same colors can have very different meanings, always depending upon the system in which they appear. For example, in the codes of American politics, green signifies not only a political party but an entire worldview in support of environmentalist policies, while red, rather paradoxically, can signify either communist sympathies or the conservative politics of the so-called "red states," depending upon the context. Amber, for its part, has no significance within the codes of American politics.

The fact that the color red has gained a new significance in the codes of American politics demonstrates the fact that systems, and the meanings encoded within them, can change—an important principle when you are interpreting popular cultural signs, because their meanings are constantly changing, unlike the more or less fixed signs of the traffic code. Here is where Peirce's contribution comes in, because while Saussure's structural semiology is static in its interpretational orientation, Peircean semiotics is dynamic, situating signs within *history* and thus enabling us to trace the ways in which meaning shifts and changes with time.

But neither Saussure nor Peirce applied their methodologies to popular cultural signs, so to complete our description of the semiotic method, we must turn to the work of French semiologist Roland Barthes (1915–1980), who, in his book *Mythologies* (1957), pioneered the semiotic analysis of everything from professional wrestling to striptease, toys, and plastics. It was Barthes, too, who established the political dimensions of semiotic analysis, revealing how phenomena that may look like mere entertainments can hold profound political or ideological significance. Since "politics" is something of a dirty word in our society, Barthes's politicization of pop culture may make you feel a little uneasy at first. You may even think that to find political meaning in popular culture is tantamount to reading something into it that isn't really there. But consider the way people responded to *Batman: The Dark Knight Rises* in 2012. Many conservative commentators were upset that the villain of the movie was named Bane—they insisted that this was an allusion to Bain Capital, the former employer of then–presidential candidate Mitt Romney. For them, the movie was a piece of liberal propaganda. Conversely, liberal commentators saw Bane's revolution as an insidious allusion to the Occupy Wall Street movement and complained that it demonized a legitimate desire for greater economic equality.

In other words, the political interpretation of popular culture, even when it is not conducted under the name of semiotics, is already a part of our culture. The semiotic method simply makes it explicit, pointing out that all social behavior is political because it always reflects some subjective or group interest. Such interests are encoded in the ideologies that express the values and opinions of those who hold them. Politics, then, is just another name for the clash of ideologies that takes place in any complex society where the interests of those who belong to it constantly compete with one another.

While not all popular cultural signs are politically controversial, careful analysis can uncover some set of political values within them, although those values may be subtly concealed behind an apparently apolitical facade. Indeed, the political values that guide our social behavior are often concealed behind images that don't look political at all. But that is because we have to look beyond what a popular cultural sign **denotes**, or directly shows, to what it **connotes**, or indirectly suggests. The **denotation** of a sign is its first level of meaning, and you have to be able to understand that meaning before you can move to the next level. The **connotation** of a sign takes you to its political or cultural significance.

Take, for instance, the depiction of the "typical" American family in the classic TV sitcoms of the 1950s and 1960s, which denoted images of happy, docile housewives in suburban middle-class families. At the time, most viewers did not look beyond their denotation, so to them those images looked "normal" or natural—the way families and women were supposed to be. The shows didn't seem a bit ideological. But to a feminist semiotician, the old sitcoms were in fact highly political, because from a feminist viewpoint the happy housewives they presented were really images designed to convince women that their place was in the home, not in the workplace competing with men. Such images—or signs—did not reflect reality; they reflected, rather, the interests of a patriarchal, male-centered society. That, in effect, was their connotation. If you disagree, then ask yourself why programs were called *Father Knows Best, Bachelor Father*, and *My Three Sons*, but not *My Three Daughters*. And why did few of the women characters have jobs or ever seem to leave the house? Of course, there was *I Love Lucy*, but wasn't Lucy a screwball whose husband, Ricky, had to rescue her from one crisis after another?

Such an interpretation reflects what the English cultural theorist Stuart Hall (1932–2014) called an *oppositional* reading. Such a reading of a cultural text like a sitcom challenges the "preferred reading," which would simply take the program at face value, accepting its representation of family life as normative and natural. The oppositional reading, on the other hand, proposes an interpretation that resists the normative view, seeking to uncover a political subtext that often contradicts any particular intended "message." The fact that so many cultural signifiers *appear* normative and natural, as transparent images of an apolitical social reality, can make oppositional reading look

The popular television show *Leave It to Beaver* (1957–1963) exemplified traditional family values of the 1950s.

The Kobal Collection at Art Resource, NY

"unnatural," or like "reading into" your topic a meaning that isn't there. After all, isn't a sitcom simply a trivial entertainment that distracts viewers from the concerns of everyday life? But given the commercial foundation of our popular culture, the fact that something is entertaining is itself significant, because only those scripts that are calculated to be popular with a mass audience make it to the screen (whether digital, "silver," or TV). In other words, popular culture appeals to audience desire, and so the fact that something is entertaining raises a fundamental semiotic question: *Why* is it entertaining, and what does that say about those who are entertained by it?

Abduction and Overdetermination

You may think that a semiotic analysis resembles sociological interpretation, and indeed cultural semiotics and sociology do not significantly differ. The differences are largely methodological. Sociology tends to be highly statistical in its methodology, often working with case studies, surveys, and other quantifiable evidence. Cultural semiotics primarily works by looking at broad patterns of behavior and seeking what Charles Sanders Peirce called *abductive* explanations for them. **Abduction** is the process of arriving at an interpretation by seeking the most plausible explanation for something. No one can absolutely prove a semiotic interpretation, but the more material you can bring into your systems of related and differentiated signifiers, the more convincing your movement from denotation to connotation will be.

As you build up your interpretation of a cultural signifier, you can often find more than one explanation for it. Is that a problem? Are you just having trouble deciding on a single argument? No, because cultural signs are usually **overdetermined**: That is, they can have more than one cause or explanation (another word for this is *polysemous*). This is especially true for what we consider "rich" cultural signs, ones that have had a long-standing effect on our tastes and habits. As we will see in the analysis that follows, the popularity of the "unliving" is especially overdetermined, with many interpretive explanations converging. Indeed, the more causes behind a cultural phenomenon, the more popular it is likely to be.

Interpreting Popular Signs: Androids and Zombies and Vampires, Oh My!

The essential approach to interpreting popular cultural signs is to *situate signs within systems of related phenomena with which they can be associated and differentiated.* Being attuned to the history that provides the background for a sign is also essential. To see how this works in practice, let's return now to those unliving protagonists of so many currently popular entertainments.

Now, the fact that vampires peaked in the first decade of the twenty-first century and were overtaken by zombies (who are very likely to have peaked and similarly declined by the time this book is published) not only is *not* a reason to dismiss them as yesterday's fad but, quite conversely, raises a number of interesting questions in itself: Why *did* vampires become so popular in the 1990s and 2000s? Why did zombies take over? And why does it appear that androids are next in line?

To answer such questions, let's first ask another very basic one: What do vampires, zombies, and androids all denote? There is a very simple answer to this question: *unliving humanoids* (there are, of course, some differences between them that we will return to shortly, but this is their basic common ground). The task of a semiotic interpretation is to move from such a denotational significance to a connotational one, and in order to do that, we must determine whether the popularity of all three of these beings reveals any pattern or system.

The fact that vampires, zombies, and androids all denote unliving humanoids provides us with the basis for such a system because it enables us to *associate* them together in a single category. So in what kind of stories do we find unliving humanoids as characters? This one is easy: in *fantasy* stories — stories that, like fairy tales, are about things that are not found in ordinary reality. Ordinary reality is the subject of a very different variety of story called *literary realism*, and this *difference* is highly significant. To see this significance, however, we have to turn to some history.

A little research will reveal that until the latter part of the 1960s, fantasy stories in America (including fairy tales, science fiction, cartoon superheroes, and horror tales) were regarded as kid's stuff: something for B movies, comic books, Sunday matinees, and children's literature. Literary realism, on the other hand, was for grown-ups. This distinction effectively marginalized fantasy as nonserious and trivial; thus, the relation between fantasy and literary realism was not unlike the traditional relation between low culture and high culture.

But with the appearance of Gene Roddenberry's *Star Trek* in 1966, along with the popular revival of J. R. R. Tolkien's *Lord of the Rings* trilogy and *The Hobbit* at the same time, the hierarchical relationship between realism and fantasy began to change. Add to this the appearance of George Romero's *Night of the Living Dead* (1968) and the makings of a cultural revolution were at hand, a revolution that was sealed in the 1970s with the enormous successes of George Lucas's *Star Wars* (1977) and Anne Rice's *Interview with the Vampire* (1976). Suddenly fantasy wasn't mere kid's stuff anymore.

This shift of fantasy from marginal to central cultural status has only intensified in the decades since it began, with realism being increasingly marginalized in a popular culture dominated by the many descendants of Tolkien, Roddenberry, Romero, Lucas, and Rice. Thus, we now have a striking historical difference to consider.

So let's ask: Is there any possible significance in this shift from realism to fantasy? To answer this question, we can go back to the years in which it all began, the decade when America's baby-boom generation first began to come of age. The first generation in history to be raised on television, the boomers were provided with a source of constant daily entertainment heavy on children's fantasy. As a result, they were responsible for the creation of the *youth culture* that has been inherited, and enhanced, by every succeeding generation in America, from Gen X to the millennials. And it is within the context of an emerging youth culture that we can situate the rise of fantasy.

The values of a youth culture include not only a preference for prolonging childhood and clinging to the physical appearance of being young, but also a desire to maintain the tastes of childhood, which include a strong attraction to the sort of fantasies with which the young have been traditionally raised. These fantasies provide an alternative to the realities of adult life: the dull grind of making a living, of raising families rather than having adventures, of not being free to do whatever one likes. In other words, we can abductively argue that the triumph of fantasy connotatively signifies a culture-wide rejection of the realities of everyday life in America, a disillusionment (or simple boredom) with what ordinary experience has to offer and a desire to escape into the imaginative fairylands of infancy.

But while this can explain why such fantasy figures as vampires, zombies, and androids are so popular today in mainstream entertainment, it doesn't explain why zombies surpassed vampires in popularity in the second decade of the new millennium, or why androids are a likely contender to supplant zombies in the near future (with such films as *Her* and a remade *Robocop* leading the way, along with TV's *Almost Human*). And here is where overdetermination comes in, because the popularity of vampires, zombies, and androids is not *solely* explained by the rise of fantasy in American youth culture; there are other determinants as well, specific to each. The way in which an overdetermined set of phenomena can branch out into further systems with their own meanings is one of the key elements of a semiotic analysis.

It would be beyond the scope of this Introduction to provide a separate interpretation of all three of these figures (a full analysis of vampires, for its part, would focus on their transition from hideous monsters to romantic and sympathetic lovers and high schoolers, and you can find an interpretation of zombies in Chapter 3). But to show how the differences within a system lead to further semiotic meanings, let's return to androids for a moment. The key difference between androids and the other fantasy figures we have looked at is that androids are machines while the others are, in some way or another, biological. That is, if vampires and zombies denote the "living dead," androids aren't alive at all—they are only "powered on or off." But there is a more important difference to consider here: Unlike zombies and vampires, who don't exist and won't ever exist, androids are actually close to existing. What is science fiction or mere fantasy today could be reality in some not so very distant future.

The development of androids was a lot farther off in the days of R2-D2, C-3PO, HAL 9000, and Roy Batty, as was the prospect of real biomechanical men like Iron Man and the Six Million Dollar Man. But now, with Google Glass portending the arrival of real-life vision-enhanced Riddicks (the protagonist in a series of Vin Diesel films), and AI researchers coming ever closer to the creation of independently functioning intelligent machines by downloading human

The poster for the film *Her* (2013).

minds into computers, the android/cyborg is transitioning from fantasy to real possibility, a prospect at once glamorously exciting and naggingly worrisome.

In short, when we situate the android in the larger context of the growing dominance of technology in our lives, an abductively plausible interpretation emerges. That is, as "socializing" becomes "social networking," university classes become massive open online courses (MOOCs), cars become self-propelled robots, and the Singularity comes ever closer to arrival, the line between human and machine is becoming blurred. With our lives increasingly being conducted via cloud computing, just who we are as human beings is becoming less and less clear. In such an environment, we should not be surprised to see a host of androids storming the center stage of popular culture both as superheroes and as perplexed not-quite-humans who resent their

The poster for the film reboot of *Robocop*.

subservience to their creators, signifying at once a fascination with a looming brave new world of posthuman existence and a nervousness over what it all may lead to.

The Classroom Connection

This analysis of androids in popular culture could be extended further, but we will leave that for you to consider for yourself. The key point is that while the popularity of any particular fantasy characters, like androids or zombies, is evanescent, what such characters *signify* is not. The vampire fad is still significant, even if vampires today are old hat. The zombie fad is significant and will remain so after it has passed. All the fads of an ever-shifting popular cultural terrain remain significant, just as all the historical events in an ever-changing world are significant. In fact, performing a popular cultural analysis is essentially equivalent to writing interpretive history, but it is an interpretive history of the present.

Thus, semiotic analyses of popular culture are not different from the more conventional interpretive analyses you will be asked to perform in your college writing career. It is in the nature of all critical thinking to make connections and mark differences in order to go beyond the surface of a text or issue toward a meaning. The skills you already have as an interpreter of the popular signs around you—of images, objects, and forms of behavior—are the same skills that you develop as a writer of critical essays that present an argued point of view and the evidence to defend it.

Because most of us tend to identify closely with our favorite popular cultural phenomena and have strong opinions about them, it can be difficult to adopt the same sort of analytic perspective toward popular culture that we do toward, say, texts assigned in a literature class. Still, that is what you should do in a semiotic interpretation: You need to set your aesthetic or fan-related opinions aside in order to pursue an interpretive argument with evidence to support it. Note how in our interpretation of the android story we didn't say whether or not we like it: Our concern was with what it might mean within a larger cultural context. It is not difficult to express an aesthetic opinion or a statement of personal preference, but that isn't the goal of analytic writing and critical thinking. Analytic writing requires that you marshal supporting evidence, just as a lawyer needs evidence to argue a case. So by learning to write analyses of our culture, by searching for supporting evidence to underpin your interpretive take on modern life, you are also learning to write critical arguments.

"But how," you (and perhaps your instructor) may ask, "can I know that a semiotic interpretation is right?" Good question—it is commonly asked by those who fear that a semiotic analysis might read too much into a subject. But then, it can also be asked of the writer of any interpretive essay, and the answer in each case is the same. No one can absolutely *prove* the truth of an argument in the human sciences; what you can do is *persuade* your audience by including pertinent evidence in an abductive reasoning process. In analyzing popular culture, that evidence comes from your knowledge of the system to which the object you are interpreting belongs. The more you know about the system, the more convincing your interpretations will be. And that is true whether you are writing about popular culture or about more traditional academic subjects.

Of Myths and Men

As we have seen, in a semiotic analysis we do not search for the meanings of things in the things themselves. Rather, we find meaning in the way we can relate things together through association and differentiation, moving from objective denotation to culturally subjective connotation. Such a movement commonly takes us from the realm of mere facts to the world of cultural values. But while values often *feel* like facts, from a semiotic perspective, they derive from cultural systems that semioticians call *cultural mythologies*.

A cultural **mythology** is not some fanciful story from the past; indeed, if the word *mythology* seems confusing because of its traditional association with such stories, you may prefer to use the term "value system" or "ideology." Consider the value system that governs our traditional thinking about gender roles. Have you ever noticed how our society presumes that it is primarily the role of women — adult daughters — to take care of aging and infirm parents? If you want to look at the matter from a physiological perspective, it might seem that men would be better suited to the task: In a state of nature, men are physically stronger and so would seem to be the natural protectors of the aged. And yet, though our cultural mythology holds that men should protect the nuclear family, it tends to assign to women the care of extended families. It is culture that decides here, not nature.

But while cultural mythologies guide our behavior, they are subject to change. You may have already experienced a transitional phase in the myths surrounding courtship behavior. In the past, the gender myths that formed the rules of the American dating game held that it is the role of the male to initiate proceedings (he calls) and for the female to react (she waits for the call). Similarly, the rules once held that it is invariably the responsibility of the male to plan the evening and pay the tab. These rules are changing, aren't they? Can you describe the rules that now govern courtship behavior?

A cultural mythology or value system, then, is a kind of lens that governs the way we view our world. Think of it this way: Say you were born with rose-tinted eyeglasses permanently attached over your eyes, but you didn't know they were there. Because the world would *look* rose colored to you, you would presume that it *is* rose colored. You wouldn't wonder whether the world might look otherwise through different lenses. But in the world there are other kinds of eyeglasses with different lenses, and reality does look different to those who wear them. Those lenses are cultural mythologies, and no culture can claim to have the one set of glasses that reveals things as they really are.

The principle that meaning is not culture-blind, that it is conditioned by systems of ideology and belief that are codified differently by different cultures, is a foundational semiotic judgment. Human beings, in other words, construct their own social realities, so who gets to do the constructing becomes very important. Every contest over a cultural code is, accordingly, a contest for power, but the contest is usually masked because the winner generally defines its mythology as the truth, as what is most natural or reasonable. Losers in the contest become objects of scorn and are quickly marginalized and declared unnatural, deviant, or even insane. The stakes are high as myth battles myth, with truth itself as the highest prize.

This does not mean that you must abandon your own beliefs when conducting a semiotic analysis, only that you cannot take them for granted and must be prepared to argue for them. We want to assure you that semiotics will not tell you what to think and believe. It *does* assume that what you believe reflects some cultural system or other and that no cultural system can claim absolute validity or superiority. The readings and Chapter Introductions in this book contain their own values and ideologies, and if you wish to challenge those values, you can begin by exposing the myths that they may take for granted.

Thus, everything in this book reflects a political point of view. If you hold a different view, it is not enough to presuppose the innate superiority of your own perspective—to claim that one writer is being political while you are simply telling the truth. This may sound heretical precisely because human beings operate within cultural mythologies whose political invisibility is guaranteed by the system. No mythology, that is to say, begins with "This is just a political construct or interpretation." Every mythology begins, "This is the truth." It is very difficult to imagine, from within the mythology, any alternatives. Indeed, as you read this book, you may find it upsetting to see that some traditional beliefs—such as "proper" roles of men and women—are socially constructed and not absolute. But the outlines of the mythology, the bounding (and binding) frame, can be discerned only by first seeing that it *is* a mythology, a constructive scaffolding upon which our consciousness and desires are constituted.

Getting Started

Mythology, like culture, is not static, and so the semiotician must always keep his or her eye on the clock, so to speak. History and the passing of time are constant factors in a constantly changing world. Since the earlier editions of this book, American popular culture has moved on. In this edition, we have tried to reflect those changes, but inevitably, further changes will occur in the time it takes for this book to appear on your class syllabus. That such changes occur is part of the excitement of the semiotic enterprise: There is always something new to consider and interpret. What does not change is the nature of semiotic interpretation: Whatever you choose to analyze in the realm of American popular culture, the semiotic approach will help you understand it.

It's your turn now. Start asking questions, pushing, probing. That's what critical thinking and writing are all about, but this time you're part of the question. Arriving at answers is the fun part here, but answers aren't the basis of analytic thinking: Questions are. You always begin with a question, a query, a hypothesis, something to explore. If you already knew the answer, there would be no point in conducting the analysis. We encourage you to explore the almost-infinite variety of questions that the readings in this book raise. Many come equipped with their own "answers," but you may (indeed you will and should) find that such answers raise further questions. To help you ask those questions, keep in mind the elemental principles of semiotics that we have just explored:

1. Cultural semiotics treats human behavior itself—not what people say about their behavior but what they actually do—as **signs**.
2. The meaning of signs can be found not in themselves but in their relationships (both differences and associations) with other signs within a

system. To interpret an individual sign, then, you must determine the general system to which it belongs.

3. Things have both **denotative** meanings (what they *are*) and **connotative** meanings (what they *suggest as signs*); semiotics moves beyond the denotative surface to the connotative significance.

4. Arriving at the connotative significance of a sign involves both **abduction** (a search for the most likely explanation or interpretation) and **overdetermination** (the multiple causes behind a cultural phenomenon).

5. What we call social "reality" is a human construct, the product of cultural **mythologies** or value systems that intervene between our minds and the world we experience. Such cultural myths reflect the values and ideological interests of their builders, not the laws of nature or logic.

Perhaps our first principle could be more succinctly phrased, "Behavior is meaningful," and our second, "Everything is connected," while our third advises, "Don't take things at face value." More simply, always ask yourself, whenever you are interpreting something, "What's going on here?" In short, question *everything*. And one more reminder: Signs are like weather vanes, they point in response to invisible historical winds. We invite you now to start looking at the weather.

WRITING ABOUT POPULAR CULTURE

Throughout this book, you will find readings on popular culture that you can use as models for your own writing or as subjects to which you may respond, assignments for writing critical essays on popular culture, and advice to help you analyze a wide variety of cultural phenomena. As you approach these readings and assignments, you may find it helpful to review the following suggestions for writing critical essays — whether on popular culture or on any subject — as well as some examples of student essays written in response to assignments based on *Signs of Life in the U.S.A.* Mastering the skills summarized and exemplified here should enable you to write the kinds of papers you will be assigned throughout your college career.

As you prepare to write a critical essay on popular culture, remember that you are already an expert in your subject. After all, simply by actively participating in everyday life, you have accumulated a vast store of knowledge about what makes our culture tick. Just think of all you know about movies, or the thousands upon thousands of ads you've seen, or the many unwritten "rules" governing courtship behavior among your circle of friends. Your very expertise in popular culture, ironically, may create a challenge simply because you may take your knowledge for granted. It might not seem that your knowledge can "count" as material for a college-level assignment, and it might not even occur to you to use it in an essay. You should certainly draw on your own knowledge, but to write a strong essay, you need to do more than just go along with the "flow" of your subject as you live it; instead, you need to consider it from a critical distance.

Using Active Reading Strategies

The first step in developing a strong essay about any topic happens well before you sit down to write: You need to make sure you understand accurately the reading selections that your instructor has assigned. You want to engage in *active* reading—that is, you want to get more than just the "drift" of a passage. Skimming a selection may give you a rough idea of the author's point, but your understanding of it is also likely to be partial, superficial, or even downright wrong. And that's not a solid start to writing a good paper!

Active reading techniques can help you understand the nuances of how an author constructs his or her argument accurately and precisely. You should question, summarize, agree with, and/or refute the author's claims. In other words, try to have a kind of *conversation* with the author. Studies have shown that such interactive learning simply works better than passive learning; if you read actively, you'll gain knowledge at a higher rate and retain it longer. With any reading selection, it can be helpful to read at least twice: first, to gain a general sense of the author's ideas and, second, to study more specifically how those ideas work together to form an argument. To do this, you can use some formal discovery techniques, or what are called *heuristics*. One of the most famous heuristics is the journalist's "five Ws and an H": who, what, where, when, why, and how. By asking these questions, a reporter can quickly unearth the essential details of a breaking story and draft a clear account of it. For your purposes, you can apply the following questions to reading selections you will discuss in your own essays.

Active Reading Questions

- What is the *author's primary argument*? Can you identify a *thesis statement*, or is the thesis implied?
- What *key terms* are fundamental to that argument? If you are not familiar with the fundamental vocabulary of the selection, be sure to check a dictionary or encyclopedia for the word's meaning.
- What *evidence* does the author provide to support the argument? Is it relevant and specific? Does the author cite reliable, authoritative sources?
- What *underlying assumptions* shape the author's position? Does the author consider alternative points of view (counterarguments)?

---

e macmillanhighered.com/signsoflife
LearningCurve > Critical Reading
Tutorials > Critical Reading: Active Reading Strategies

- What *style* and *tone* does the author adopt?
- What is the *genre* of the piece? You need to identify what kind of writing you are responding to, because different kinds have different purposes and goals. A personal narrative, for instance, expresses the writer's experiences and beliefs, but you shouldn't expect it to present a complete argument supported by documentation.
- Who is the *intended readership* of this selection, and does it affect the author's reasoning or evidence?

As you read, write *annotations*, or notes, in your book. Doing so will help you both remember and analyze what you read. A pencil is probably the best memory aid ever invented. No one, not even the most experienced and perceptive reader, remembers everything—and let's face it, not everything that you read is worth remembering. Writing annotations as you read will lead you back to important points. And annotating helps you start analyzing a reading—long before you start writing an essay—rather than uncritically accepting what's on the page. If you are using an electronic version of this text, you can do the same with the highlight and annotate tools available in most e-readers.

There's yet another reason to annotate what you read: You can use the material you've identified as the starting point for your journal notes and essays, and since it doesn't take long to circle a word or jot a note in the margin, you can save a great deal of time in the long run. We suggest that you *not* use a highlighter. While using a highlighter is better than using nothing—it can at least help you mark key points—writing *words* in your book goes much further in helping you analyze what you read. We've seen entire pages bathed in fluorescent-yellow highlighter, and that's of doubtful use in identifying the important stuff. Of course, if you simply can't bring yourself to mark up your book, write on sticky notes instead and put those in the margins.

So as you read, circle key words, note transitions between ideas, jot definitions of unfamiliar terms (you can probably guess their meaning from the context or look them up later), underline phrases or terms to research on a search engine such as Google, write short summaries of important points, or simply note where you're confused or lost with a question mark or a *huh?!* In fact, figuring out exactly what parts you do and don't understand is one of the best ways to tackle a difficult reading. Frequently, the confusing bits turn out to be the most interesting—and sometimes the most important. Responding to what you read *as* you read will help you become a more active reader—and will ultimately help you become a stronger writer.

Signs of Life in the U.S.A. frequently asks you to respond to a reading selection in a *journal* or *reading log*, sometimes directly and sometimes indirectly, as in suggestions that you write a letter to the author of a selection. In doing so, you're taking a first step in articulating your response to the issues and to the author's presentation of them. In asking you to keep a journal or a reading log, your instructor will probably be less concerned with your writing style than with your comprehension of assigned readings and your thoughtful responses to them. Let's say you're asked to write your response to Jessica Hagedorn's "Asian Women in Film: No Joy, No Luck" in Chapter 4. You should first think through exactly what Hagedorn is saying—what her point is—by asking the questions listed on pages 22–23 and by reviewing your annotations. Then consider how you feel about her essay. If you agree with Hagedorn's contention that films perpetuate outmoded stereotypes of Asian women, why do you feel that way? Can you think of films Hagedorn does not mention that reflect the gendered patterns she observes? Or do you know of films that represent Asian female characters positively? Suppose you're irritated by Hagedorn's argument: Again, why do you feel that way? Your aim in jotting all this down is not to produce a draft of an essay. It's to play with your own ideas, see where they lead, and even just help you decide what your ideas are in the first place.

Prewriting Strategies

Before you start writing, you'll find it useful to spend some time generating your ideas freely and openly: Your goal at this point is to develop as many ideas as possible, even ones that you might not actually use in your essay. Writing instructors call this process *prewriting*, and it's a step you should take when writing on any subject in any class, not just in your writing class. This textbook includes many suggestions for how you can develop your ideas; even if your instructor doesn't require you to use all of them, you can try them on your own.

These strategies will work when you are asked to respond to a particular reading or image. Sometimes, though, you may be asked to write about a more general subject. Your instructor may ask you to brainstorm ideas or to freewrite in response to an issue. You can use both strategies in your journal or on your own as you start working on an essay. *Brainstorming* is simply amassing as many relevant (and even some irrelevant) ideas as possible. Let's say your instructor asks you to brainstorm a list of popular toys used by girls and boys in preparation for an essay about the gendered designs of children's toys. Try to list your thoughts freely, jotting down whatever comes to mind. Don't censor yourself at this point. That is, don't worry if something is really a game rather than a toy, or if both boys and girls play with it, or if it is really an adult toy. Later on you can throw out ideas that don't fit. What you'll be left with is a rich list of examples that you can then study and analyze. *Freewriting* works much the same way and is particularly useful when you're not sure how you feel about an issue. Sit down and just start writing or typing, and don't stop until you've written for at least ten or fifteen minutes. Let your ideas wander around your subject, working associatively, following their own path. As with brainstorming, you may produce some irrelevant ideas, but you may also arrive at a sharper picture of your beliefs.

If your instructor asks you to create your own topic, you might wonder, "Where should I start?" Suppose you need to analyze an aspect of the film industry but can't decide on a focus. Here, the Internet might help. You could explore a resource such as filmsite.org, a site divided into categories such as History, Genres, and Reviews. These categories can lead you to more specific links, such as "Film History by Decade" and "Film Reviews by Decade." With so many to choose from, you're bound to find something that interests you. In effect, you can go online to engage in *electronic brainstorming* about your topic.

One cautionary note: When going online to brainstorm, be sure to *evaluate the appropriateness of your sources* (see p. 60). Many sites are commercial and are therefore intended more to sell a product or image than to provide reliable information. In addition, since anyone with the technological know-how can set up a Web site, some sites amount to little more than personal expression and need to be evaluated for their reliability, accuracy, and authenticity. Scrutinize the sites you use carefully: Is the author an authority in the field? Does the site identify the author, at least by name and e-mail address? (Be wary of fully anonymous sites.) Does the site contain interesting and relevant links? If you find an advocacy site, one that openly advances a special interest, does the site's bias interfere with the accuracy of its information? Asking such questions can help ensure that your electronic brainstorming is fruitful and productive. If you are unsure of the validity of a site, you might want to check with your instructor.

You can also strengthen your argument if you consider the *history* of your subject. You might think this requires a lot of library research, but research may not be necessary if you are already familiar with the social and cultural history of your topic. If you know, for instance, that the baggy pants so popular among teens until recently were once ubiquitous among street-gang members, you know an important historical detail that goes a long way toward explaining their significance. Depending on your assignment, you might want to expand on your own historical knowledge and collect additional data about your topic, perhaps through surveys and interviews. If you're analyzing gendered patterns of courtship rituals, for instance, you could interview some people from different age groups, as well as both genders, to get a sense of how such patterns have evolved over time. The material you gather through such interviews will be raw data, and you'll want to do more than just "dump" the information into your essay. Instead, see this material as an original body of evidence that you'll sort through (you probably won't use every scrap of information), study, and interpret in its own right.

Not all prewriting activities need be solitary, of course. In fact, *Signs of Life* includes lots of suggestions that ask you to work with other students, either in your class or across campus. We suggest such *group work* because much academic work is collaborative and collegial. A scientist conducting research, for instance, often works with a team; in addition, he or she may present preliminary findings at colloquia or conferences and may call or e-mail a colleague at another school to try out some ideas. There's no reason you can't benefit from the social nature of academic thinking as well. But be aware that such in-class group work is by no means "busywork." The goal, rather, is to help you develop and shape your understanding of the issues and your attitudes toward them. If you're asked to study with three classmates how a product is packaged, for instance, you're starting to test Thomas Hine's thesis in "What's in a Package" (Chapter 1), seeing how it applies or doesn't apply and benefiting from your peers' insights. By discussing the package with your peers, you are articulating, perhaps for the first time, what it might mean and so are taking the first step toward writing a more formal analysis (especially if you receive feedback and comments from your class). Similarly, if you stage an in-class debate over whether multitasking is "healthy" or dangerous, you're amassing a storehouse of arguments, counterarguments, and evidence to consider when you write your own essay that either supports or refutes S. Craig Watkins's argument in "Fast Entertainment and Multitasking in an Always-On World" (Chapter 5). As with other prewriting strategies, you may not directly use every idea generated in conversation with your classmates, but that's OK. You should find yourself better able to sort through and articulate the ideas that you do find valuable.

Developing Strong Arguments about Popular Culture

We expect that students will write many different sorts of papers in response to the selections in this book. You may write personal experience narratives, semiotic analyses, opinion pieces, research papers, and many others. We'd like to focus here on writing analytic essays because the experience of analyzing popular culture may seem different from that of analyzing other subjects. Occasionally we've had students who feel reluctant to analyze popular culture because they think that analysis requires them to trash their subject, and they don't want to write a "negative" essay about what may be their favorite film or TV program. Or a few students may feel uncertain because "it's all subjective." Since most people have opinions about popular culture, they say, how can any one essay be stronger than another?

While these concerns are understandable, they needn't be an obstacle to writing a strong analytic paper — whether on popular culture or any other topic. To avoid overt subjectivity, you should begin by setting aside your own personal tastes when writing an analysis, not because your preferences are unimportant, but because you need to be aware of your own attitudes and observations about your topic. An analysis of, say, *The Big Bang Theory* is not

[e] macmillanhighered.com/signsoflife
LearningCurve > Topic Sentences and Supporting Details; Topics and Main Ideas

the same as a paper that explains "why I like (or dislike) this TV program." Instead, an analysis would explain how it works, what cultural beliefs and viewpoints underlie it, what its significance is, and so forth. And such a paper would not necessarily be positive or negative; it would seek to explain *how* the elements of the show work together to have a particular effect on its audience. If your instructor asks you to write a critical analysis or a critical argument, he or she is requesting neither a hit job nor a celebration of your topic.

For most of your college essays, you will probably be asked to make sure that your paper has a clear *thesis*. A thesis statement lays out the argument you intend to make and provides a scope for your essay. If you think of your thesis as a road map that your paper will follow, you might find that it is easier to structure your paper. A thesis for an essay on popular culture should follow the usual guidelines for any academic essay: It should make a debatable, interesting assertion (as opposed to a statement of fact or a truism); it should be demonstrable through the presentation of specific evidence; it should have a clear focus and scope; and it should spark your readers' interest. Additionally, a strong thesis statement will help you overcome any anxieties you might have about writing a strong analysis, because a good thesis statement, rather than merely offering a simple opinion on your topic, also explains how you came to hold that opinion. The thesis statements in the sample papers that begin on page 34 are annotated to help you see how they function in academic writing.

When your paper has a strong thesis, subjectivity becomes even less of a problem. That's because your analysis should be grounded in concrete demonstration. You're not simply presenting a personal opinion about your subject; rather, you're presenting a central insight about its significance, and you need to demonstrate it with logical, specific evidence. It's that evidence that will take your essay out of the category of being "merely subjective." You should start with your own opinion, but you will want to add to it lots of support that shows the legitimacy of that opinion. Does that sound familiar? It should, because that's what you need to do in any analytic essay, no matter what your subject matter happens to be.

When writing about popular culture, students sometimes wonder what sort of evidence they should use to support their points. Your instructor will probably give you guidelines for each assignment, but we'll provide some suggestions here. Start with your subject itself. You'll find it's useful to view your subject—whether it's an ad, a film, or anything else—as a text that you can "read" closely. That's what you would do if you were asked to analyze a poem: You would read it carefully, studying individual words, images, rhythm, and so forth, and those details would support whatever claims you wanted to make about the poem. Read your pop culture subject with the same care. If your instructor asks you to analyze a television series, you should look at the details: What actors appear in the series, and what are their roles? What "story" does the program tell about its characters and the world in which they live? Is there anything missing from this world that you would expect to find? What are the *connotative* meanings behind the surface signs? Your answers to such questions could form the basis for the evidence that your essay needs.

Conducting a Semiotic Analysis

In an essay focused on a semiotic analysis, you can probe a wider range of questions about your subject that can yield even more specific evidence and arguments. You can start with some basic questions that we ask throughout the Chapter Introductions in this book, and which we summarize in the list below. Now let's apply these questions to an example, the TV series *House*, still popular and significant, even though it is now in reruns.

DENOTATIVE MEANINGS

What is a simple, literal description of your subject? You need to make sure you understand this before looking for "deeper meanings," because if you misunderstand the factual status of your subject, you will probably get derailed in your analysis. In the case of *House*, we find a story of a medical genius who, though he is his hospital's most successful diagnostician, is also

---

Questions for Conducting a Semiotic Analysis

- What is the **denotative** meaning of your subject? In other words, determine a factual definition of exactly what it is.
- What is your topic's **connotative** significance? To determine that, situate your subject in a system of related signs.
- What **associated** signs belong to that system?
- What **differences** do you see in those signs?
- What **abductive** explanation do you have for your observations? What is the most likely explanation for the patterns that you see?

---

e macmillanhighered.com/signsoflife
Need help editing for common grammar mistakes?
LearningCurve > Commas; Fragments; Run-ons and Comma Splices; Active and Passive Voice; Appropriate Language; Subject-Verb Agreement

rude, nasty, and practically dysfunctional in his personal life, suffering from an addiction to Vicodin and almost constant depression. The plots of *House* tend to exemplify the series's slogan, "Everybody lies," and often depict House's patients or their families as liars with dark secrets that they are concealing and that House eventually uncovers. Clearly, if we were to misidentify *House* as a documentary, we'd misconstrue it as a scathing political exposé of the U.S. medical system — but that doesn't feel right. *House* is no exposé.

CONNOTATIVE MEANINGS AND A SYSTEM OF RELATED SIGNS

After determining your subject's denotation, you must locate your subject within a larger system in order to determine its connotative meaning. Recall that a system is the network of related signs to which your topic belongs and that identifying the system helps to reveal its significance. This may sound hard to do, but it is through identifying a system that you can draw on your own vast knowledge of popular culture. So, in our analysis of *House*, we need to move from our denotative understanding of the series to its connotative significance. In order to make this move, we need to identify a system of related signs. In the case of *House*, this entails identifying programs with which it is similar. In other words, to what genre of television programming does *House* belong? What conventions, goals, and motifs do shows in this genre share? What is the history of the genre? *House*, of course, belongs to the medical drama genre, which is distinct from, say, situation comedy, even though *House* does have certain comic elements that would allow us to classify it as a medical *dramedy*. The history of TV medical drama includes such programs as *Dr. Kildare* and *Ben Casey* in the 1960s; *Marcus Welby, M.D.,* and *Quincy, M.E.,* in the 1970s; *St. Elsewhere* and *ER* in the 1980s and beyond; and *Grey's Anatomy* and *Nip/Tuck* in recent years. All these programs can be associated with *House* and testify to the enduring popularity of the genre. (Indeed, long before television, an old joke had it that the most certain formula to follow in writing a best seller was to write a book about Abraham Lincoln's doctor's dog.)

DIFFERENCES WITHIN THE SYSTEM

But while the associations between these television series demonstrate a popular interest in doctors and medical stories, there is still a striking difference to consider, a kind of dividing line marked by the series *St. Elsewhere*. Until *St. Elsewhere*, the main character in a medical series was a benevolent healer whose own personal life beyond the hospital was generally not a part of the story line (there were exceptions: Dr. Kildare once had a patient with whom he fell in love; Ben Casey had a somewhat edgy nature; and Jack Klugman's Quincy — a forensic pathologist whose mystery-solving abilities anticipate those of Gregory House — had plenty of attitude). But all in all, the physician protagonists of the earlier series maintained a general profile of almost superhuman benevolence; they were "official heroes," in Robert B. Ray's terms (see "The Thematic Paradigm," p. 450), caring for the innocent victims of disease.

St. Elsewhere changed that, and from that program onward (especially as developed by ER), the flaws in the lives and personalities of the main characters, the doctors, became much more prominent. The doctors were, in short, much more humanized—a shift in characterization that has led to the caustic, sometimes dysfunctional and lawbreaking, Dr. House.

ABDUCTIVE EXPLANATIONS

At this point, we are ready to start interpreting, seeking abductive explanations for the shift. We can begin with the construction of another system, this time looking at the larger context of other television genres. If we look at this system, we can find in situation comedies, crime series, Westerns, and many other genres a shift similar to the one in the history of medical dramas. The difference between the family sitcoms of the 1950s and 1960s and those of the 1980s and beyond is well known, taking us from the happy families of the Cleavers and the Nelsons to the dysfunctional Bundys and Griffins. Similarly, it is a long way from Dick Tracy and Dragnet's Joe Friday to the callous cops of The Wire. And it is a long way from Gunsmoke to Justified. Many other such differences could be mentioned, but we'll move on to our abductive interpretation.

The post–St. Elsewhere medical drama reflects a broader trend in American entertainment away from squeaky-clean television protagonists to more "realistically" flawed ones, heroes who definitely have feet of clay. This trend reflects a cultural shift whose beginning can be found in the cultural revolution of the 1960s, when American mass culture began a long process of disillusionment. After the Vietnam War and Watergate, increasingly cynical Americans were no longer predisposed to believe in absolute human perfection, preferring a more "realistic" depiction of human beings with all their flaws visible.

Thus, we can now see House as part of a larger cultural trend in which the once-cherished, even revered, figure of the physician has been pulled off the pedestal and brought to earth along with everyone else. Heroes are still heroes (after all, Gregory House is just plain smarter than anyone else around him), but they are more like ordinary folks. They misbehave, get cranky, break rules. Even the victims of misfortune (patients in a medical drama) have been degraded, appearing no longer as the objects of our sympathy but as flawed people with dark secrets. Everybody lies. No one is innocent. To the disillusioned, House, with its all-too-human hero and cast, is an entertaining, if cynical, vision of the way things are—or at least of the way that large numbers of viewers think they are. Doctors (and cops, families, cowboys, and everyone else) have warts too, and, as a sort of anti–Marcus Welby, Gregory House entertains his audience by not being afraid to show his flaws to the world.

Reading Visual Images Actively

Signs of Life in the U.S.A. includes many visual images, in many cases with accompanying questions for analysis. In analyzing images, you will develop the ability to identify specific telling details and evidence—a talent useful no matter what your subject matter may be. Because the semiotic method lends itself especially well to visual analysis, it is an excellent means for honing this ability. Here are some questions to consider as you look at images.

Questions for Analyzing Images

- What is the **appearance of the image**? Is it black and white? Color? Glossy? Consider how the form in which the image is expressed affects its message. If an image is composed of primary colors, does it look fun and lively, for instance?

- What **kind of image** is it? Is it abstract, does it represent an actual person or place, or is it a combination of the two? If people are represented, who are they?

- Who is the intended **audience** for the image? Is it an artistic photograph or a commercial work, such as an advertisement? If it is an ad, to what kind of person is it directed? Where is the ad placed? If it is in a magazine, consider the audience for the publication.

- What **emotions** does the image convey? Overall, is it serious, sad, funny? Is that expression of emotion, in your opinion, intentional? What emotional associations do you have with the image?

- If the image includes more than one element, what is the most prominent element in the **composition**? A particular section? A logo? Any writing? A person or group of people? A product? How does each part contribute to the whole?

- Where does the image's **layout** lead your eye? Are you drawn to any specific part? What is the order in which you look at the various parts? Does any particular section immediately jump out?

- Does the image include **text**? If so, how do the image and the text relate to one another?

- Does the image call for a **response**? For instance, does it suggest that you purchase a product? If so, what claims does it make?

To see how we can apply these questions, let's look at a sample analysis of an advertisement for Lee jeans (see image on p. 32).

Appearance: Although this image is reproduced here in black and white, it originally appeared in color. The colors are muted, however, almost sepia-toned, and thus suggest an old-fashioned look.

Kind of image: This is a fairly realistic image, with a patina of rural nostalgia. A solitary woman, probably in her twenties or thirties, but perhaps older, is set against an empty natural expanse. She has a traditional hairstyle evocative of the 1950s or early 1960s and leads an old-fashioned bicycle with a wicker basket attached.

Audience: The intended audience for this jeans ad is most likely a woman in her late twenties or older. We see only the model's back, so she is faceless. That allows the viewer to project herself into the scene, and the nostalgic look suggests that the viewer could imagine herself at a younger time in her life. Note that the product is "stretch" jeans. There's no suggestion here, although it is often made in ads for other brands, that the jeans will enhance a woman's sexual appeal; rather, the claim is that the jeans are practical — and will fit a body beyond the teen years. Note the sensible hairstyle and shoes. For an interesting contrast, you might compare this ad to one for Diesel jeans.

Emotion: The woman's body language suggests individuality and determination; she's literally "going it alone." She's neither posing for nor aware of the viewer, suggesting that "what you see is what you get." And, perhaps, she doesn't particularly care what you think.

Composition and layout: The layout of the ad is carefully designed to lead your eye: The hill slopes down from top right toward middle left, and the bike draws your eye from bottom right to mid-left, with both lines converging on the product, the jeans. For easy readability, the text is included at the top against the blank sky.

Text: The message, "The things that give a woman substance will never appear on any 'what's in/what's out' list," suggests that Lee jeans are a product for women who aren't interested in following trends, but rather want a good, old-fashioned value — "substance," not frivolity.

Response: The manufacturer of Lee jeans would prefer, naturally, that the viewer of the ad buy the product. The viewer would identify with the woman wearing the jeans in the advertisement and be convinced that these practical (if not particularly cutting-edge) jeans would be a good purchase.

In sum, most fashion ads stress the friends (and often, mates) you will attract if you buy the product, but this ad presents "a road not taken," suggesting the American ideology of marching to the beat of a different drummer, the kind of old-fashioned individualism that brings to mind Robert Frost and Henry David Thoreau. The pastoral surroundings and the "old painting" effect echo artists such as Andrew Wyeth and Norman Rockwell. All these impressions connote lasting American values (rural, solid, middle American) that are meant to be associated with anti-trendiness and enduring qualities, such as individualism and practicality. And these impressions suggest the advertisers carefully and effectively kept the ad's semiotic messages in mind as they designed it.

Reading Essays about Popular Culture

In your writing course, it's likely that your instructor will ask you to work in groups with other students, perhaps reviewing each other's rough drafts. You'll find many benefits to this activity. Not only will you receive more feedback on your own in-progress work, but you will see other students' ideas and approaches to an assignment and develop an ability to evaluate academic writing. For the same reasons, we're including three sample student essays that satisfy assignments about popular culture. You may agree or disagree with the authors' views, and you might have responded to the assigned topics differently; that's fine. We've selected these essays because they differ in style, focus, and purpose and thus suggest different approaches to their assignments — approaches that might help you as you write your own essays about popular culture. We've annotated the essays to point out various argumentative, organizational, and rhetorical strategies. As you read the essays and the annotations, ask why the authors chose these strategies and how you might incorporate some of the same strategies into your own writing.

Essay 1

In this essay, Amy Lin of UCLA argues that the Barbie doll, and all its associated products and marketing, essentially is a means for engendering a consumerist ethos in young girls who are the toy's fans. To do so, Lin relies on a range of sources, including articles in *Signs of Life in the U.S.A.*, academic and journalistic sources, and a corporate Web site that presents the panoply of Barbie products. Notice that Lin does not treat toysrus.com as a source of unbiased information about the products (that would amount to taking promotional material at face value); rather, she analyzes the Web site as evidence for her larger argument about consumerism. As you read Lin's essay, study how she uses her sources and integrates them into her own discussion.

Barbie: Queen of Dolls and Consumerism

In my closet, a plastic bag contains five Barbie dolls. A cardboard box beside my nightstand holds yet another, and one more
box contains a Ken doll. Under my bed we find my Barbies' traveling
walk-in closet, equipped with a light-up vanity and foldout chair
and desk. We also find Doctor Barbie along with the baby, sticker
Band-Aids, and sounding stethoscope with which she came. Under
my sister's bed are their furniture set, including sofas, loveseats,
flower vases, and a coffee table. A Tupperware container holds Ken's
pants, dress shirts, and special boots (whose spurs make patterns
when rolled in ink) in addition to Barbie's excess clothing that did
not fit in the walk-in closet. In a corner of my living room sits the
special holiday edition Barbie, outfitted in a gown, fur stole, and
holly headband.

*Amy's intro-
duction is
a visual
anecdote
that illustrates
her argument
about
consumption.*

These plastic relics prove that, as a young girl, I, like many
other females, fell into the waiting arms of the Mattel Corporation. Constantly feeding the public with newer, shinier toys, the
Barbie enterprise illustrates America's propensity for consumerism. Upon close examination, Barbie products foster materialism in
young females through both their overwhelmingly large selection
and their ability to create a financially carefree world for children,
sending the message that excessive consumption is acceptable. This
consequently perpetuates the misassumption that "the American
economy [is] an endlessly fertile continent whose boundaries never
need be reached" (Shames 81) among the American youth.

*Amy articu-
lates her
thesis and
refers to
Laurence
Shames's
article as a
context.*

Search the term "Barbie" at toysrus.com, and you will receive
286 items in return — more than enough to create a blur of pinkish-
purple as you scroll down the Web page. The Barbie enterprise
clearly embraces "the observation that 'no natural boundary seems
to be set to the efforts of man'" (Shames 78). In other words,
humankind is, in all ways, ambitious; people will keep creating,
buying, and selling with the belief that these opportunities will
always be available. This perfectly describes the mentality of those
behind Barbie products, as new, but unnecessary, Barbie merchandise is put on shelves at an exorbitant rate. At toysrus.com, for
example, a variety of four different mermaids, eleven fairies, and two
"merfairies" — products from the "Fairytopia-Mermaidia" line — find
their place among the search results (*Toys*). Instead of inventing

*The corporate
Web site is
used not as
a source of
objective
information
but as evi-
dence to
support the
thesis.*

a more original or educational product, Mattel merges the mermaid world with the fairy world into "Fairytopia-Mermaidia," demonstrating the company's lack of innovation and care for its young consumers' development. Thus the corporation's main motivation reveals itself: profit. Another prime example found among the search results is the "Barbie: 12 Dancing Princesses Horse Carriage" (*Toys*), a more recent product in the Barbie family. The carriage, "in its original form, . . . can seat six princess dolls but . . . can expand to hold all 12 dolls at once" (*Toys*). The dolls, of course, do not come with it, forcing the child to buy at least one for the carriage to even be of any use. But that child will see the glorious picture of the carriage filled with all twelve dolls (which are inevitably on the box), and she will want to buy the remaining eleven. In addition, the product description states that the carriage "is inspired by the upcoming DVD release, Barbie in *The 12 Dancing Princesses*" (*Toys*). Essentially, one Mattel creation inspires another, meaning that the DVD's sole purpose is to give Mattel an excuse to create and market more useless merchandise.

Much of this, however, may have to do with branding, a strategy manufacturers utilize that ultimately results in "consumers transfer[ring] a favorable or unfavorable image from one product to others from the same brand" (Neuhaus and Taylor 419). In accordance with this strategy, all Barbie products must maintain

Amy moves to the larger marketing context.

a certain similarity so as not to "'confuse' potential customers . . . and thereby reduce demand for the products" (Sappington and Wernerfelt 280). This explains the redundancy found in much of Mattel's Barbie merchandise, since the sudden manufacturing of a radically different product could encourage the migration of consumers to another brand. But given that Barbie has become "the alpha doll" (Talbot 74) for girls in today's popular culture, young female consumers clearly associate only good things with Barbie. And who can blame them? Barbie has become a tradition handed down from mother to daughter or a rite of passage that most girls go through. In this way, excessive consumption and the effects of branding are handed down as well, as Barbie dolls are essentially their physical manifestations.

With a company as driven to produce and sell products as Mattel, consumers can expect to find increasingly ridiculous items on toy store shelves. One such product found at toysrus.com is "Barbie and Tanner" (*Toys*), Tanner being Barbie's dog. The doll and dog come with brown pellets that function both as dog food and dog waste, a "special magnetic scooper[,] and trash can" (*Toys*). Upon telling any post-Barbie-phase female about this product, she will surely look amazed and ask, "Are you kidding me?" Unfortunately, Tanner's movable "mouth, ears, head and tail" (*Toys*) and "soft[,] . . . fuzzy" coat will most likely blind children to the product's absurdity, instead enchanting them into purchasing the product. Another particularly hilarious item is the "Barbie Collector Platinum Label Pink Grapefruit Obsession" (*Toys*). The doll wears a "pink, charmeuse mermaid gown with deep pink chiffon wedges sewn into the flared skirt and adorned with deep pink bands that end in bows under the bust and at the hip" (*Toys*). And "as a . . . special surprise, [the] doll's head is scented with the striking aroma of pink grapefruit" (*Toys*). Finally, the doll is described as "an ideal tribute to [the] delightful [grapefruit] flavor" (*Toys*). The consumer will find it difficult to keep a straight face as he or she reads through the description, as it essentially describes a doll dedicated to a scent. The doll's randomness shows Mattel's desperation for coming out with new products. Eager to make profit, Barbie's designers, it seems, make dolls according to whatever whim that happens to cross their minds.

The para-graph includes a rich array of concrete, specific detail.

In the quest to make profit by spreading the consumerist mind-set, Barbie products even manage to commodify culture. Nowadays, Barbie dolls come in a variety of ethnicities. Take, for example, the "Diwali Festival Doll" from the "Barbie Dolls of the World" (*Toys*) line. Except for the traditional Indian apparel and dark hair, however, the doll could easily be mistaken for Caucasian. And what about Barbie's multiracial doll friends? They are reduced to mere accessories — disposable and only supplementary to Barbie, the truly important figure. Therefore, despite Mattel's attempts at identifying with a larger group of girls, an undeniable "aura of blondness still [clings] to the Mattel doll" (Talbot 82) because its attempts aim more toward creating a larger customer base than anything else.

Amy develops her argument by considering the cultural and ethnic angle.

But enough of dolls. Mattel has grown so large that it can expand its products beyond Barbie's mini-world. Consumers can easily find Barbie brand tennis shoes, rain boots, slippers, bicycles, and helmets. Many of Barbie's non-doll products even reflect the various fads among America's youth, such as video games, skate-boards, scooters, guitars, and dance mats (in accordance with the

A quick, short transi-tion moves the reader to a broader consideration of Mattel's promotion of materialism.

popularity of the game, Dance Dance Revolution). Anne Parducci, Mattel's senior VP of Barbie Marketing, claims Mattel does this because it "want[s] to make sure . . . [it] capture[s] girls in the many ways they are spending their time now and in the future," that it "want[s] Barbie to represent a lifestyle brand for girls, not just a brand of toys" (Edut). This phenomenon, however, can simply be seen as Mattel trying to "infiltrat[e] girls' lives everywhere they go" (Edut). Either way, Mattel's actions allow materialism to develop at an early age, especially since it makes the latest "it" items more accessible to children. Those behind Barbie figure that if children are going to buy into the latest trends anyway, they might as well buy them from Mattel.

Amy allows for a counter-argument but then refutes it.

Since Barbie products promote the attitude of keeping up with society's crazes, they create a carefree fantasy world for children, obscuring the fact that Mattel's motivation is making money. The company knows that if it enchants children, those children will in turn convince their parents to buy the products for them. The company also knows that commercials are its best opportunities to do this. One recent Mattel commercial advertises the "Let's Dance Genevieve" doll, a doll also inspired by *The 12 Dancing Princesses* DVD that interacts with its owner in three ways: the doll "can dance to music for the girl," "teach the girl dance moves by demonstrating and using speech prompts," and "follow along with the girl's dance moves using special bracelets and a shoe accessory" (*Toys*). Girls dressed in ballerina attire give overly joyous reactions to the doll's behaviors, making the doll seem remarkably advanced when, really, the doll can only raise its arms and legs. In addition, computer graphic scenes from the movie run seamlessly into scenes of the girls playing with the doll, and one of these girls is even transposed onto a clip of the movie. This blurs the lines of reality and fantasy, encouraging young viewers to think that if they own the doll, they, too, can feel like "dancing princesses," that somehow the doll can trans-port its owner into a fairy-tale world. In actuality, young females will likely tire of the doll within weeks. The commercial even resorts to flattery, describing the doll and its owner as "two beau-tiful dancers." Finally, the commercial ends with inspirational lyr-ics, singing, "You can shine." This sort of "vaguely girl-positive" advertising only "wrap[s] the Mattel message — buy our products now!" (Edut). Together, all these advertising elements add up to a highly desirable product among young girls.

Barbie undoubtedly increases the materialistic tendencies in children, specifically females, Barbie's target audience. After all, since "Barbie dolls need new clothes and accessories more often than boys' action figures do," "young girls learn . . . very early" to "assume consumer roles" (Katz). Interestingly, "Barbie was an early rebel against the domesticity that dominated the lives of baby-boom mothers," as she shows no "car[e] for babies or children" or "visible ties to parents" (Cross 773). But ironically, instead of "[teaching] girls to shed [such] female stereotypes," Barbie simply created a new stereotype for females — the shopa-holic persona — because "she prompted [young girls] to associate the freedom of being an adult with carefree consumption" (Cross 774). So the overall effect of Barbie's presence in children's lives is increased expectations for material possessions. Or, in other words, Barbie products cause "catalog-induced anxiety," a condi-tion that can occur "from [viewing] catalogs themselves or from other forms of public exposure of the lives of the rich or cel-ebrated, . . . mak[ing] what a typical person possesses seem paltry, even if the person is one of the many . . . living well by objective standards" (Easterbrook 404, 405). Given that Barbie is a fictitious character, Mattel can make her as beautiful, hip, and rich as it pleases. But what happens when little girls begin comparing their lives to that of Barbie? They think, "If Barbie gets to have such amenities, so should I." And toys like the "Barbie Hot Tub Party Bus" (*Target*) do not help the situation. The product description reads that the bus contains "all the comforts of home like a flat screen TV, dinette table, and beds" (*Target*). Children will inevita-bly expect these luxuries that, for Barbie, are merely givens in her doll utopia, causing discontent when they discover they cannot have everything they want. It may even reach the point where, "as . . . more material things become available and fail to" satisfy children, "material abundance . . . [can] have the perverse effect of instilling unhappiness — because it will never be possible to have everything that economics can create" (Easterbrook 402).

For my long-forgotten Barbie dolls, as for those of many older females, the dream house has stopped growing. In fact, the house has been demolished, leaving my dolls homeless. But this does not

References to Gary Cross's article buttress the essay's argu-ment.

Amy invokes Gregg Easterbrook as she explores the long-term implications of Mattel's promotion of consumerism.

Amy signals closure by coming full circle, returning to her opening anecdote.

mean that women have escaped the effects of years of Barbie play as they have temporarily escaped the clutches of Mattel. (I say temporarily because even if a woman has outgrown Barbie, Mattel will suck her back in through her daughters, nieces, goddaughters, and granddaughters.) Since Barbie preaches the admissibility of hyperconsumption to females at a young age, women, unsurprisingly, "engage in an estimated 80% of all consumer spending" (Katz). Women, conditioned from all those trips to the toy store looking for the perfect party dress for Barbie or the perfect convertible to take her to that party, still find themselves doing this — just on a larger scale — in shopping malls. But perhaps men's consumerism is catching up. The recent "proliferation of metrosexuals" signals a rise in "straight young men whose fashion and grooming tastes have crossed over into areas once reserved for feminine consumption" (St. John 177, 174). Mattel, too, takes part in this phenomenon through the "reintroduc[tion] [of] the Ken doll," which now possesses a "new metrosexual look" (Talbot 79). Well, one thing is certain: Mattel continues its expansive construction on Barbie's ever-costly dream mansion, and knows that millions of little girls will do the same.

By considering men's consumer habits and male dolls, Amy ends with a refreshing twist.

Works Cited

Cross, Gary. "Barbie, G.I. Joe, and Play in the 1960s." Maasik and Solomon, pp. 772-78.

Easterbrook, Gregg. "The Progress Paradox." Maasik and Solomon, pp. 400–407.

Edut, Ophira. "Barbie Girls Rule?" *Bitch: Feminist Response to Pop Culture,* 31 Jan. 1999, p. 16.

Katz, Phyllis A., and Margaret Katz. "Purchasing Power: Spending for Change." *Iris,* 30 Apr. 2000, p. 36.

Maasik, Sonia, and Jack Solomon, editors. *Signs of Life in the U.S.A.: Readings on Popular Culture for Writers,* 7th ed., Bedford/St. Martin's, 2012.

Neuhaus, Colin F., and James R. Taylor. "Variables Affecting Sales of Family-Branded Products." *Journal of Marketing Research,* vol. 4, no. 9, 1972, pp. 419–22.

Sappington, David E. M., and Birger Wernerfelt. "To Brand or Not
   to Brand? A Theoretical and Empirical Question." *Journal of
   Business*, vol. 58, no. 3, 1985, pp. 279-93.

Shames, Laurence. "The More Factor." Maasik and Solomon, pp. 76-82.

St. John, Warren. "Metrosexuals Come Out." Maasik and Solomon,
   pp. 174-77.

Talbot, Margaret. "Little Hotties: Barbie's New Rivals." *The New
   Yorker*, 4 Dec. 2006, pp. 74+.

Target. Target Brands, Inc., 2006. www.target.com. Accessed
   14 Nov. 2006.

Toys "R" Us. Geoffrey LLC, 2006. www.toysrus.com. Accessed
   14 Nov. 2006.

Essay 2

Exemplifying a semiotic approach, Rose Sorooshian, a student at California State University, Northridge, explores the social and cultural conditions that led *The Walking Dead* to become one of America's most popular TV programs. The show became a hit not *despite* the difficult economic times in which it aired, she concludes, but *because* of those troubled times. Here, Sorooshian provides a fine reading of how a television program can be an articulate and potent sign of its time.

The Walking 99 Percent: An Analysis of *The Walking Dead*
in the Context of the 2008 Recession

   People have lost their homes and their jobs, and their standards of living are falling. People are fighting to survive, and these catastrophic events are not their fault. Yet somehow these events are affecting people more than they could possibly have imagined. This description could be the premise of the popular television show *The Walking Dead*, based on the series of graphic novels by the same name. Set in Georgia, the show follows Sheriff Rick Grimes, his wife, and their son, as well as a group of other survivors as they struggle to stay alive and maintain their humanity in the midst of a zombie apocalypse. However, this description also matches a real-life disaster that began in the United States in 2008 known as the Great Recession. A report from a Pew Research Center Survey describes the recent recession:

Of the 13 recessions that the American public has endured since the Great Depression of 1929–33, none has presented a more punishing combination of length, breadth and depth than this one. A new Pew Research survey finds that 30 months after it began, the Great Recession has led to a downsizing of Americans' expectations about their retirements and their children's future; a new frugality in their spending and borrowing habits; and a concern that it could take several years, at a minimum, for their house values and family finances to recover. (Taylor)

Rose locates The Walking Dead *in the historical context of the Great Recession.*

She poses a focusing question about the show's cultural significance.

Coming after a period of relatively stable economic times, the economic shock has created a great deal of fear and anger. And Americans are flocking to watch *The Walking Dead* in droves because they sense the parallels between the Great Recession and a zombie apocalypse. Though there have been cult-classic zombie movies in the past, never before has a zombie television show been so fervently embraced by such a widespread audience. What is the secret of its mainstream appeal, and what does the extreme popularity of *The Walking Dead* say about modern American society?

One reason this show is so popular among a diverse audience is that today's TV viewers feel a strong connection between the characters' attempts to live through a zombie apocalypse and their own attempts to cope with modern life and, especially, their recent economic struggles. The zombie apocalypse depicted in *The Walking Dead* shares many similarities with the economic recession that America has been suffering since 2008. Both events affected everyone in the country, and not just a particular group. During both, people lost

Rose links the characters' struggles with Americans' economic woes.

homes, jobs, and a certain standard of living. People feel like they are fighting just to survive and, most significantly, that this catastrophe is not their fault, is beyond their control, and is destroying their lives. Many feel that the government in some way caused it, should have prevented it, and should take responsibility for fixing it.

Another reason for *The Walking Dead*'s popularity is that it appeals to people who are highly critical of government entities such as politicians, the military, and government agencies. This mistrust is reflected in one of the ways the show departs from previous zombie movies. In most zombie movies, the protagonists' challenge is something like "hold on until morning." That is, they have a set amount of time they need to survive and then the government (the military) will save them. Or, sometimes the challenge is to arrive at a certain location where the government will take care of them. However, in *The Walking Dead*, no encounter with any government entity ends well. At the outset of the show, Rick is told that if he can make it to Atlanta, the CDC (Centers for Disease Control) has a base there that can help him. However, when he arrives, he finds the city overrun with zombies, and when Rick and his companions, including his wife and son, eventually do find the CDC compound, it quickly becomes clear that the government will not be rescuing anyone. All but one of the workers have either fled or committed suicide. The government has failed to devise a cure for the virus that is creating the zombies, and the building safety protocols almost kill off the main cast of characters. In the end, one of their group members and the last surviving CDC worker decide to stay behind in the gas explosion that destroys the building, killing themselves instead of continuing the struggle of living in the post-apocalyptic world. That indicates how completely hopeless people are feeling. In *The Walking Dead*, there is no magic cure, no government to come to their rescue, no military to save them. They are on their own. This parallel to the current economic environment is striking. People feel abandoned by and afraid of their own government, left to fend for themselves.

A comparison with other zombie movies points to a difference within the system.

Finally, the show's popularity spans across all demographics because it is set in a total fantasy world open to one's own interpretation. In other words, viewers can choose to think of the "bad guys," those responsible for the zombie apocalypse, as representing whomever they think are the bad guys in real life. As Leslie Savan states:

> Most of us watch because it's a terrific, suspenseful soap opera. But *TWD* also comes packed with a central metaphor—the zombie apocalypse—that can be used to explain just about every political point of view, whether right or left, pro-NRA or pro-gun control, small- or big-government, even pro-sequester or pro-stimulus.

The Walking Dead airs on AMC, a TV channel that also broadcasts two other top-rated dramas: *Mad Men* and *Breaking Bad*. On the surface, these three shows could hardly seem more different.

While *The Walking Dead* is a fairly standard horror show, *Mad Men* is a historical workplace drama set in the 1950s through 1960s in which most of the high-intensity moments come from whether or not an advertising deal will work out. And unlike both *Mad Men* and *The Walking Dead*, *Breaking Bad* is a modern-day reality show about a high school chemistry teacher who is diagnosed with terminal cancer and then begins dealing methamphetamine and becomes a drug lord. Although these three shows differ, they share the same attraction that makes them so popular today: All are chillingly realistic in their depiction of blood, guts, and a lot of naked skin. And this kind of realism is not exclusive to these three shows; most top television programs recently have followed this pattern, including comedies as well as dramas. *The Office*, *Parks and Recreation*, and *30 Rock* are three popular comedies that also present realistic portrayals of characters and situations. This becomes even more apparent in current fantasy and horror programs, including *The Walking Dead*, *Game of Thrones*, *Once upon a Time*, *Supernatural*, and *True Blood*, to name just a few. These shows tend to be very realistic in spite of their otherworldly concepts. Gone are the days of *Star Trek*'s shiny view of the future in which everything is clean and silver and everyone wears a uniform. TV's fantasy worlds are no longer clean, fun, or nice. They are dirty, trying, harsh places where people are cruel and life is difficult. In other words, they are just like reality but with zombies and vampires. People living through extremely difficult times, worrying about losing their jobs and their homes, can identify with the fear that monsters are threatening them. It seems very real to them, and they want their shows to display the same nitty-gritty realism they face in their lives. Anything less would seem superficial and irrelevant.

Rose connects The Walking Dead *to other related TV programs.*

This realism also applies to the characters. Most of the protagonists of previous decades were good, upstanding people: doctors, lawyers, fathers, and heroes. They were men, primarily, who did what they knew was right and stood for truth and justice. These days, however, those types of characters are viewed as old-fashioned, one-dimensional, and frankly silly. Instead, today's protagonists are flawed, sometimes immoral, characters, most of whom the average viewer would not want to meet. Viewers identify with complex characters with a lot of wiggle room in their moral structures, such as a serial killer with a conscience, murderers who are

The focus narrows to an interpretation of the characters.

also great fathers, sheriffs who disregard the law, and vampires who love and protect. According to Stephen Garrett in "Why We Love TV's Antiheroes," "The heroes of today are radically different from those of two or three decades ago. They have evolved to represent a radically changed world" (319). Garrett goes on to state that in the past the difference between good and evil was clear, or, as he puts it, "There were never better baddies than the Nazis, and the causes, as well as the purposes, of the Second World War were crystal clear" (319). But now, Garrett explains, our wars are much less cut-and-dried. Conflicts now have "an element of moral ambiguity built into them" (319). Is it any wonder that, given such a change in our national moral compass, we would want television heroes who are likewise morally ambiguous? Gone are the days of the father charac-ter who comes home at five o'clock to pick up his pipe, listen to the problems of the wife and children, and lay down a simple solution. Gone are the days of the doctors who can cure all ills, the lawyers who always follow the law, and the police officers who adhere firmly to their moral codes. Characters now must exist in some kind of moral gray area, or else they will seem irrelevant to today's view-ers. *The Walking Dead* fills that need quite well.

Zombies are a popular cultural phenomenon right now. *The Walking Dead, Warm Bodies*, plus countless zombie events such as zombie walks and runs in which large groups of people get together and dress as zombies, all point to a societal fascination with the concept of zombies. In fact, people seem interested in all kinds of undead beings. Vampires are, arguably, the most popular fantasy "creatures" right now, although contemporary vampires are no longer the monsters they once were. Vampires have become more human, more sympathetic, and much more sexy. Ever since another TV series, *Buffy the Vampire Slayer*, introduced the character of Angel as a sexy, brooding vampire with a soul, and with whom the title character, Buffy, was destined to fall in love, vampires have changed from bloodsucking monsters to bloodsucking heroes. As stated in *Signs of Life in the U.S.A.*, "To put it simply: Vampires are hot. From *True Blood* to *Twilight*, *The Vampire Diaries* to *The Gates*, contemporary popular culture is awash in vampire stories" (Maasik and Solomon 1). However, though vampires are still intensely popu-lar, there appears to also be a continuing strong market for other types of supernatural monster drama, such as zombies.

Rose locates the show in the larger context of supernatural monster dramas.

The zombie movie has been a popular genre for decades, and the movie *Night of the Living Dead*, written and directed by George A. Romero, made zombie movies a staple of Hollywood. *The Walking Dead* has taken that popularity to a new level, however, because people facing their own fears and struggles seem to respond to the extremely realistic portrayal of the struggle of humans against zombies, who are, of course, a terrifying and perverted form of humans themselves. They reflect people's feelings of powerlessness and fear that they, their community, or their government will be "taken over" by evildoers. As Lee Roberts states, "The attraction of some to the zombie and the genre of films in which they appear represents an inner desire to place blame for society's misgivings on the establishment, i.e., big business, big government, etc., and use the zombie as the most logical outcome if the establishment were to be left unchecked by a complacent population" (Roberts).

Although *The Walking Dead*'s appeal may be that viewers strongly identify with characters who are fighting a battle against terrifying unknown forces, people who are insecure and fearful often cling to the known and even return to traditional behaviors and values. In a return to outdated gender roles, *The Walking Dead* portrays women as powerless and ineffective and men as strong and competent. Perhaps this indicates a desire on the part of the audience to go back to the 1950s, a more optimistic era when Americans had great hopes of increasing affluence and an always-increasing standard of living, but it also means a return to a time when women were weak and subservient to men.

She argues that the show appeals to traditional values and explains why.

In this show, what little power the women may have is frequently stripped away. In a show in which characters rely heavily on weapons, the women lack the training to use them, but the men are portrayed as fully competent with various weapons and prevent the women from obtaining or holding on to them. In the second season, one of the male characters, Dale, decides that it is no longer prudent for Andrea, a young woman, to carry a gun. Although Dale holds no real authority over her and the gun is legally hers, Andrea barely protests Dale's confiscation of the gun. In fact, the only real fight she gives is asking for Shane, another male character, to back her up. Shane sides with Dale, saying that until everyone is trained in the use of guns, the fewer they have "floating around camp," the better ("What Lies Ahead"). Andrea accepts this with little argument. So, in a traditional and patriarchal way, the men get to decide who has the weapons and the men generally carry the weapons and protect the women and children. For a show set in a contemporary setting, this is strikingly old-fashioned. In addition, females in the show are generally incompetent. Andrea, while still in possession of her gun, does not know how to clean it herself and, when attacked by a zombie, has the entire thing in pieces. Instead of successfully staying quiet and hidden, she attracts the zombie's attention and must rely on Dale's weapon in order to save herself. Lori often says things that are viewed by the other characters as weak or ignorant. When the group stumbles upon a veritable gold mine of supplies in the form of a pileup of old cars, Lori emotionally tries to persuade them not to use the supplies by saying "This is a graveyard" ("What Lies Ahead"). The others simply ignore her (female) sentimentality. When hiding from a group of zombies, it is Sophia, a young girl, not Carl, her male counterpart, who attracts the attention of two zombies and has to run off into the woods to hide. And then only the male characters go out to search for her.

Specific details support her claim about traditional values.

Overall, this show reinforces very strong, traditional gender roles. The women are soft-spoken, weak, and mothering. They do not carry weapons, they are ineffectual fighters, and they require almost constant protection by the men. They worry about clothes and hygiene in spite of the terrors surrounding them. The show goes so far as to show a group of women washing clothes and gossiping while a man looks on as protection. The men, on the other hand, are strong and capable. They carry guns and other weapons and can take care of themselves (and the women). They rarely require help from others and never from a woman. They are the doers—they come up with the plans and put them into action. The women are carried along in their wake. Without the men, the women would not last a day. Without the women, the men would have a much easier time surviving. In a time when many people feel somewhat uncertain about gender roles, the show roots itself securely in a more comfortable (for some, anyway) past.

Both the Great Depression and the Great Recession began after years of economic prosperity, and the 2008 recession was the worst economic downturn since the Great Depression. But the entertainment choices during the 1930s were very different from

Rose returns to history as her essay draws to a close.

those today. During the 1930s, Shirley Temple, a precocious child star, was the number one box office hit, and many found her movies to offer a temporary break from the misery and fear of the depressed economic state. "President Franklin Delano Roosevelt proclaimed that 'as long as our country has Shirley Temple, we will be all right'" ("Shirley Temple Black"). But now people seem to be looking for something else in their entertainment, immersing themselves in a terrifying zombie apocalypse. Why is this? Is it due to differences between the Great Depression and the Great Recession? According to National Public Radio, "Even though both events were momentous enough to earn the word 'great' as a modifier, they really are not comparable, according to recent research by economist Mark Vaughan, a fellow at the Weidenbaum Center on the Economy at Washington University in St. Louis" (qtd. in Geewax). Vaughn goes on to explain that the recent recession "pales in magnitude" with the Great Depression: "The Great Depression was painful in ways we can scarcely imagine now because we have grown so accustomed to having a government-funded safety net" (qtd. in Geewax).

In the 1930s, the public did not initially blame the government for the unemployment problem: This was prior to the passage of the Employment Act of 1946, which made the government responsible for maintaining high employment. In 2008, on the other hand, people felt betrayed and blamed the government and big business for the recession. During the Great Depression, people looked to entertainment as an escape from the frustrations of everyday life, while people today are, instead, looking for characters they can identify with as suffering victims being let down by the establishment and forced to take things into their own hands.

Rose encapsulates her answer to her opening question about the show's popularity.

The Walking Dead is a fairly well-written show with good acting and generally good special effects, and it tugs at emotional heartstrings and keeps the audience on the edge of their seats. But more than that, the show managed to come on the scene at just the perfect time when Americans were angry with government, angry with the establishment, and looking for a way to vent their frustrations. *The Walking Dead* is generic enough that all Americans can relate to it and, therefore, they can use it as a way to vicariously fight the recession without actually stepping out of their front doors.

Works Cited

Garrett, Stephen. "Why We Love TV's Antiheroes." Maasik and
    Solomon, pp. 318-21.
Geewax, Marilyn. "Did the Great Recession Bring Back the 1930s?"
    NPR, 11 July 2012, 6 May 2013, www.npr.org/2012/07/11/
    155991507/did-the-great-recession-bring-back-the-1930s.
Maasik, Sonia, and Jack Solomon, editors. *Signs of Life in the U.S.A.:
    Readings on Popular Culture for Writers,* 7th ed., Bedford/
    St. Martin's, 2012.
Roberts, Lee. "Zombie Movie History: A Reference for Zombie
    Masters." *Best Horror Movies*, 2012, besthorrormovies.com.
    Accessed 6 May 2013.
Savan, Leslie. "Whose Side Is *The Walking Dead* On?" *The Nation*,
    7 Apr. 2013, www.thenation.com/article/whose-side-walking
    -dead/. Accessed 6 May 2013.
"Shirley Temple Black." *The John F. Kennedy Center for the
    Performing Arts*, www.kennedy-center.org/. Accessed 6 May
    2013.
Taylor, Paul, editor. "How the Great Recession Has Changed Life in
    America." *Pew Research Social & Demographic Trends*, 30 June
    2010, www.pewsocialtrends.org/2010/06/30/how-the-great
    -recession-has-changed-life-in-america/. Accessed 6 May 2013.
"*The Walking Dead* (Season 1)." *Wikipedia,* 30 Apr. 2013,
    en.wikipedia.org/wiki/The_Walking_Dead_(season_1).
    Accessed 6 May 2013.
"What Lies Ahead." *The Walking Dead*, Directed by Ernest Dickerson
    and Gwyneth Horder-Payton. AMC, 16 Oct. 2011.

Essay 3

In this essay, first-year UCLA student Ryan Kim explores the representation of Asians in film, focusing on *Gran Torino*. He notices that, at first glance, the film seems to depart from some typical ethnic stereotypes. However, using Michael Omi's "In Living Color: Race and American Culture" (p. 538) as a critical framework, Kim interprets *Gran Torino*'s representation of both Asians and whites, finding that the film ultimately reinforces conventional stereotypes. As you read Kim's essay, note his movement between "first glance" readings of the film and his deeper analysis based on Omi's essay.

A Reading of *Gran Torino*

Despite advancements made toward racial equality, racial discrimination still persists in America; as professor Michael Omi explains, "Film and television have been notorious in disseminating images of racial minorities which establish for audiences what these groups look like, how they behave, and in essence, 'who they are'" (629). In films, the Western genre has been especially harmful in its perpetuation of stereotypes, as in it, "the humanity of whites is contrasted with the brutality and treachery of nonwhites" and this notion of "white superiority" reveals certain "intriguing trends" (Omi 630). These trends are often contradictory and target many minority groups, including Asians. According to the documentary *Dragon Lady*, the stereotyping of Asians in film may have roots in historical events, but these portrayals can be inaccurate. The 2008 film *Gran Torino* attempts to combat these trends by providing a seemingly more accurate representation of the Hmong, a Southeast Asian ethnic group. However, the film's attempt at a realistic portrayal is undermined by the perpetuation of "the docile Asian" stereotype, double standards, insensitive motifs of white superiority, and the sexualization of Asian women commonly seen in older films.

A brief overview of the film will highlight the most significant details for this analysis. *Gran Torino* follows the life of Walt Kowalski and his Hmong neighbors in a Michigan ghetto. Kowalski, a hardened "tough guy" veteran, is weighed down by his misdeeds during the Korean War, and he wrestles with the guilt. He is stern, traditional, and judgmental. Thao Vang Lor, Walt's next-door neighbor, is a fairly quiet and unconfident Hmong teenager. Both Walt and his family consider him somewhat womanly, as he is notably subordinate to his sister and mother. Unlike Thao, his older sister Sue is loud and confident, and is the first Hmong person toward whom Walt shows any goodwill. The film's main antagonists, Thao's gangster cousin, Spider, and his friend Smokie are brash, villainous, and relatively unintelligent. Throughout the movie, they bully Thao because he refuses to join their gang.

The heart of the story begins after Thao fails to steal Walt's car during a gang initiation. As a form of apology, Thao is forced to work for Walt, who teaches Thao how to be a man, by forcing him

Ryan articulates his thesis about the film's representation of Asians up front.

He provides a précis of the film, focusing on details relevant to his thesis.

to perform difficult yard work. Thao develops and grows more confident as the film progresses, finding a job and even asking a girl out on a date. However, he is constantly harassed by Spider and his gang, who do not appreciate him rejecting their invitations. Taking matters into his own hands, Walt pummels Smokie. In response, Smokie and Spider kidnap Sue, perform a drive-by shooting at the Vang Lor residence, and beat and rape Sue. Infuriated, Thao pushes Walt to seek vengeance with him. However, Walt locks Thao in his basement and goes to the gangster hangout unarmed. Knowing that his days were already numbered after receiving the results from his medical tests, Walt sacrifices himself to put the gangsters behind bars to protect Thao and Sue.

Gran Torino does differ from past films that made little distinction among Asian minorities by humanizing the Hmong as a unique group. After a large influx of new immigrants, many racial stereotypes were created, and the idea of "outsider" races was created (Omi 629). This insider-outsider mentality made differences between nonwhite ethnic groups somewhat irrelevant; as a result, many nonwhite ethnic groups were categorized together, particularly different Asian groups. Older films presented different Asian minorities as homogenous. Unlike those films, *Gran Torino* makes sure the audience is aware that the Hmong characters are "Hmong" and not simply "Asian." Additionally, it attempts to educate the audience about the Hmong's role in the Vietnam War. In a scene where Sue and Walt converse, Sue informs Walt that the Hmong fought with the United States in the war but were persecuted after the United States pulled out. This message from the filmmakers demonstrates an earnest attempt to avoid grouping Asians into one group as older films did.

Ryan locates Gran Torino *within the context of other films that stereotype Asian characters.*

The movie also attempts to subvert moral distinctions based on class. Walt considers himself superior to the Hmong, which showcases the perception of class based on race. Walt, a bigoted white man, considers himself more civilized than ethnic minorities. His offensive terms and jokes are indicative of this attitude, and he places himself higher on the social hierarchy. This distinction created between classes because of race exhibits a prevalent habit of the entertainment industry. As Michael Parenti illustrates, "The entertainment media present working people not only as unlettered and uncouth but also as less desirable and less moral than other

He extends his argument by considering class difference.

people" (421). All of the Hmong in the film live in the ghetto and are most likely poor. It is surprising, then, that the film depicts the Hmong as more moral than Walt. Walt's unabashed racism contrasts with Sue and Thao's attitude toward him, because they seem to accept him regardless. But despite the film's efforts to present the Hmong as a moral and unique ethnic group, *Gran Torino* ultimately portrays old-Hollywood Asian stereotypes and harmful motifs.

Walt's blatantly racist epithets demonstrate the same stereotypical portrayals of Asians and notions of white superiority commonly seen in film. Walt's racism is an example of "overt racism," blatant examples of racial discrimination (Omi 627). As Omi suggests, racial stereotypes "underscore white 'superiority' by reinforcing the traits, habits, and predispositions of nonwhites which demonstrate their 'inferiority'" (630). Throughout the film, Walt maliciously calls the Hmong "barbarians, chinks, gooks, and swamp rats." Despite becoming close to Sue and Thao, Walt never ceases to use his favorite racial slurs. This habit can be easily seen when he interacts with Thao, purposely mispronouncing his name as "Toad" and calling him a "zipperhead." While these epithets are designed to be satirical and humorously mocking of bigots, they suggest that Walt has more power and authority than the Hmong. The film does nothing to counter this arrangement. Thao, as well as the other Hmong, never seem to be offended, and they never retaliate. They allow Walt to continue with his offensive mannerisms. The docility of the Hmong perpetuates the stereotype that Asians are passive and meek, and this stereotype is juxtaposed against Walt's ascendency while "underscoring" his white superiority over them.

Ryan uses Michael Omi's article to enhance his analysis of racial representation.

In many older Hollywood films, white men would conquer territories in political turmoil, bring "order" to the region, and impart their way of life onto the natives; *Gran Torino* privileges the same Eurocentric worldview through Walt's protection of the Hmong. Walt becomes a guardian to the broken Hmong community, as it appears unable to resolve its own problems. Throughout the entire film, Thao and Sue meet adversity and Walt resolves the problem. In the beginning of the film, Walt prevents Thao from being abducted by Spider. Later, he magically appears in time to save Sue from being harassed and possibly kidnapped by African American thugs. Walt is inevitably the one who sacrifices himself to lock up Spider, Smokie, and the gangsters. It also appears that the Hmong need

Walt to perform even basic household tasks, as the entire neighborhood was in shambles until Walt steps in to fix it. Inferior because
of their inability to help themselves, the Hmong become a modern
parallel to the barbarians in the old Westerns. This further demonstrates that *Gran Torino* is cut from the same cloth as the other
Hollywood films.

   The "good-bad variant" described by Omi is ever-present in
Gran Torino, demonstrating the film's failure to treat race progres-
sively. The "good-bad variant" is when a film attempts to compensate for negative racial stereotypes by providing a counterexample:
This attempt leads to the creation of a "good" racial character and
a "bad" one. Omi explains that such distinctions simply make the
"good" character "exist as a foil to underscore the intelligence,
courage, and virility of the white male hero" (631). At a cursory
glance, it seems the film is trying to subvert older stereotypes about
Asians by comparing Thao to the Hmong gangsters. Thao, one of
the "good characters," like the other Hmong, is initially passive
and noticeably nonthreatening. He perpetuates the stereotype that
Asians are docile and a "model minority." Ruthless and unforgiving,
the "bad Asians," Spider and Smokie, are dangerous "sinister criminals." The gangsters are much like the "barbarians" in Westerns.
Unlike the gangsters, Thao develops, eventually subverting the
docility stereotype by becoming more assertive and confident under
Walt's tutelage. *Gran Torino* appears to be adding another level of
dimension to the Hmong by providing differing and contradictory
images of them. Unfortunately, Thao is simply another "good character" acting as a foil to a white protagonist. He manages to discard
his old characteristics only with Walt's help, and even then, he is
simply embodying Walt's "white characteristics." By doing this, the
film inadvertently becomes another racially insensitive piece of
visual media, much like films before it.

   Walt's tutelage of Thao also harkens back to older films
through the usage of masculine and feminine stereotypes. Hmong
men are mostly absent from the film, and when they do appear,
they seem unable to raise their own sons. Sue describes Hmong boys
as lacking in direction and being jail bound. Walt inevitably takes it
upon himself to teach Thao "how to be a man," specifically, a white
man. Thao performs feats of manual labor that "toughen him up"
and he learns about tool usage. Walt also teaches Thao how to "talk

*He again
extends his
discussion by
addressing
male gender
roles.*

like a real man" by taking him to his Italian barber. This "man talk" is an exchange of insults, racial slurs, and "manly" small talk. With these "masculine" skills under his belt, Thao finds a job at a construction site. This character shift links masculinity to being white, and Thao "becomes a man" when he learns how to be "white." Soon after, he develops the gumption to ask a girl out on a date. Before Thao becomes "white," he appears almost completely uninterested in girls. In fact, Walt had to lecture him for not taking initiative with Youa, the girl Thao eventually asks out. Thao only discovers success in his "masculine" endeavors by emulating Walt, revealing a notion of the superiority of white masculinity over Asian masculinity. Nothing in the movie challenges this. Sue even admits that Walt is Thao's biggest father figure, because her late father was "too traditional." Walt tells her that he is old-fashioned as well. Sue, however, argues, "But you're an American." Sue is admitting that traditional American values are better than Asian ones. In a racial context, the film depicts masculinity as being white.

He follows up with female gender roles.

The portrayal of Asian women in *Gran Torino* also reveals the film's link to older films. As Jessica Hagedorn explains, Asian women in film have been mostly "decorative, invisible, or one-dimensional" (403). Asian women were thus hypersexualized in old Hollywood, according to *Slaying the Dragon*, and the Hmong women in *Gran Torino* are just as one-dimensional as the Asian women in the films of old. For example, Youa as a character is very underdeveloped: She speaks very few lines, and her role is only to act as a stepping-stone for Thao's development as a man. In this way, Youa is defined as a goal rather than a person; this in turn subtly sexually objectifies her, as she becomes nothing more than an "object of desire" (Hagedorn 403). Although Sue does not obviously conform to any Asian stereotype, even she is sexualized. When she is harassed by the African American thugs, they explicitly sexualize her because of race, and they speak to her in extremely derogatory and lewd terms.

Ryan closes by lamenting Gran Torino's representation of Asians.

While *Gran Torino* was well-intentioned and was meant to bring a neglected and misunderstood ethnic group to the spotlight, it has merely perpetuated racially insensitive motifs and has spread racism further. It successfully avoids some of the mistakes of older films by humanizing the Hmong in giving them a distinct identity and moral high ground. However, the film uses or reinvents older motifs. The lack of initiative by the Hmong indicates a persistence of the docile Asian stereotype in the film. Additionally, the film entertains white superiority by using Thao as a foil for Walt, promoting "white" characteristics and ways of life, while Sue and Youa are sexualized—just as Asian women in film have been since old Hollywood. These stereotypes began with the initial contact of Western and Eastern cultures yet still persist today, despite the rich mixing of cultures that occurs across our modern society.

Works Cited

Hagedorn, Jessica. "Asian Women in Film: No Joy, No Luck." Maasik
    and Solomon, pp. 396–404.

Maasik, Sonia, and Jack Solomon, editors. *Signs of Life in the U.S.A.:*
    Readings on Popular Culture for Writers, 7th ed., Bedford/
    St. Martin's, 2012.

Omi, Michael. "In Living Color: Race and American Culture." Maasik
    and Solomon, pp. 625–35.

Parenti, Michael. "Class and Virtue." Maasik and Solomon,
    pp. 421–23.

Slaying the Dragon. Directed by Deborah Gee, performance by Herb
    Wong, Asian Women United of California, 2011.

CONDUCTING RESEARCH AND CITING SOURCES

Your instructor may ask you to use secondary sources to support your analyses of popular culture. These sources may include a wide variety of published materials, from other essays (such as those featured in this book) to interviews you conduct to YouTube videos. When you write about popular culture, a host of sources are available to you to help lend weight to your arguments as well as help you develop fresh thinking about your topic.

The Internet age has afforded us innovative research opportunities, and with a wealth of information at your fingertips, it is up to you, the writer, to learn to determine which sources you should trust and which you should be suspicious of. As always, the library is a great place to begin. Research librarians continue to be excellent resources not only for finding sources for your papers, but for learning best practices for conducting research. It is more than likely that they are aware of resources at your disposal that you haven't considered, from academic databases like EBSCOhost to library catalogs to film and video archives.

The following selections offer additional help for conducting academically sound research online.

e macmillanhighered.com/signsoflife
Tutorials > Working with Sources > Do I Need to Cite This?

SCOTT JASCHIK
A Stand against Wikipedia

Increasingly, college faculty are concerned about the widespread use of Wikipedia in student research and writing. The problem, as faculty see it, is twofold. First, there is the problem of reliability. Wikipedia does strive to provide reliable information, but given the wide-open nature of the site — anyone can contribute — ensuring accuracy is not really possible. This leads to student work that can disseminate misinformation. Second, even where Wikipedia is accurate (and it can be an accurate source of information), it is, after all, an encyclopedia, and while encyclopedic sources may be suitable for background information, students performing college-level research should seek primary sources and academic-level secondary sources that they find on their own. The following article from insidehighered.com surveys the problems with Wikipedia as a research source as seen by college faculty from a number of universities.

As Wikipedia has become more and more popular with students, some professors have become increasingly concerned about the online, reader-produced encyclopedia.

While plenty of professors have complained about the lack of accuracy or completeness of entries, and some have discouraged or tried to bar students from using it, the history department at Middlebury College is trying to take a stronger, collective stand. It voted this month to bar students from citing the Web site as a source in papers or other academic work. All faculty members will be telling students about the policy and explaining why material on Wikipedia — while convenient — may not be trustworthy. "As educators, we are in the business of reducing the dissemination of misinformation," said Don Wyatt, chair of the department. "Even though Wikipedia may have some value, particularly from the value of leading students to citable sources, it is not itself an appropriate source for citation," he said.

The department made what Wyatt termed a consensus decision on the issue after discussing problems professors were seeing as students cited incorrect information from Wikipedia in papers and on tests. In one instance, Wyatt said, a professor noticed several students offering the same incorrect information, from Wikipedia. There was some discussion in the department of trying to ban students from using Wikipedia, but Wyatt said that didn't seem appropriate. Many Wikipedia entries have good bibliographies, Wyatt said. And any absolute ban would just be ignored. "There's the issue of freedom of access," he said. "And I'm not in the business of promulgating unenforceable edicts."

Wyatt said that the department did not specify punishments for citing Wikipedia, and that the primary purpose of the policy was to educate, not to be punitive. He said he doubted that a paper would be rejected for having a single Wikipedia footnote, but that students would be told that they shouldn't do so, and that multiple violations would result in reduced grades or even a failure. "The important point that we wish to communicate to all students taking courses and submitting work in our department in the future is that they cite Wikipedia at their peril," he said. He stressed that the objection of the department to Wikipedia wasn't its online nature, but its unedited nature, and he said students need to be taught to go for quality information, not just convenience.

The frustrations of Middlebury faculty members are by no means unique. 5 Last year, Alan Liu, a professor of English at the University of California at Santa Barbara, adopted a policy that Wikipedia "is not appropriate as the primary or sole reference for anything that is central to an argument, complex, or controversial." Liu said that it was too early to tell what impact his policy is having. In explaining his rationale — which he shared with an e-mail list — he wrote that he had "just read a paper about the relation between structuralism, deconstruction, and postmodernism in which every reference was to the Wikipedia articles on those topics with no awareness that there was any need to read a primary work or even a critical work."

Wikipedia officials agree — in part — with Middlebury's history department. "That's a sensible policy," Sandra Ordonez, a spokeswoman, said in an e-mail interview. "Wikipedia is the ideal place to start your research and get a global picture of a topic; however, it is not an authoritative source. In fact, we recommend that students check the facts they find in Wikipedia against other sources. Additionally, it is generally good research practice to cite an original source when writing a paper, or completing an exam. It's usually not advisable, particularly at the university level, to cite an encyclopedia." Ordonez acknowledged that, given the collaborative nature of Wikipedia writing and editing, "there is no guarantee an article is 100 percent correct," but she said that the site is shifting its focus from growth to improving quality, and that the site is a great resource for students. "Most articles are continually being edited and improved upon, and most contributors are real lovers of knowledge who have a real desire to improve the quality of a particular article," she said.

Experts on digital media said that the Middlebury history professors' reaction was understandable and reflects growing concern among faculty members about the accuracy of what students find online. But some worry that bans on citing Wikipedia may not deal with the underlying issues.

Roy Rosenzweig, director of the Center for History and New Media at George Mason University, did an analysis of the accuracy of Wikipedia for the *Journal of American History*, and he found that in many entries, Wikipedia was as accurate as or more accurate than more traditional encyclopedias. He said that the quality of material was inconsistent, and that biographical entries were generally well done, while more thematic entries were much less so. Like Ordonez, he said the real problem is one of college students using encyclopedias when they should be using more advanced sources. "College students shouldn't be citing encyclopedias in their papers," he said. "That's not what college is about. They either should be using primary sources or serious secondary sources."

In the world of college librarians, a major topic of late has been how to guide students in the right direction for research, when Wikipedia and similar sources are so easy. Some of those who have been involved in these discussions said that the Middlebury history department's action pointed to the need for more outreach to students. Lisa Hinchliffe, head of the undergraduate library and coordinator of information literacy at the University of Illinois at Urbana-Champaign, said that earlier generations of students were in fact taught when it was appropriate (or not) to consult an encyclopedia and why for many a paper they would never even cite a popular magazine or nonscholarly work. "But it was a relatively constrained landscape," and students didn't have easy access to anything equivalent to Wikipedia, she said. "It's not that students are being lazy today. It's a much more complex environment."

When she has taught, and spotted footnotes to sources that aren't appropriate, she's considered that "a teachable moment," Hinchliffe said. She said that she would be interested to see how Middlebury professors react when they get the first violations of their policy, and said she thought there could be positive discussions about why sources are or aren't good ones. That kind of teaching, she said, is important "and can be challenging." 10

Steven Bell, associate librarian for research and instructional services at Temple University, said of the Middlebury approach: "I applaud the effort for wanting to direct students to good quality resources," but he said he would go about it in a different way. "I understand what their concerns are. There's no question that [on Wikipedia and similar sites] some things are great and some things are questionable. Some of the pages could be by eighth graders," he said. "But to simply say 'don't use that one' might take students in the wrong direction from the perspective of information literacy."

Students face "an ocean of information" today, much of it of poor quality, so a better approach would be to teach students how to "triangulate" a source like Wikipedia, so they could use other sources to tell whether a given entry could be trusted. "I think our goal should be to equip students with the critical thinking skills to judge."

PATTI S. CARAVELLO
Judging Quality on the Web

When you conduct research on the Internet, you'll find a dizzying range of sources, from academic journals to government Web sites, from newspapers and popular magazines to blogs, wikis, and social networking and file-sharing sites. Having a plethora of sources at hand with just the click of a mouse has been a boon to researchers in all fields. But the very democratic basis of the Internet that makes all this information so readily available creates a challenge, for it comes with no guarantees of quality control. Indeed, it is incumbent upon you, the researcher, to determine the reliability of the Web sources that you use. The following article from the UCLA Library's Web site, "Judging Quality on the Web," lists criteria that will allow you to evaluate the usefulness and reliability of Internet sources.

Even after refining a query in a search engine, a researcher often retrieves a huge number of Web sites. It is essential to know how to evaluate Web sites for the same reasons you would evaluate a periodical article or a book: *to ascertain whether you can rely on the information, to identify its inherent biases or limitations, and to see how or whether it fits into your overall research strategy.*

A good (useful, reliable) Web site:

1. Clearly states the author and/or organizational **source** of the information
   Your task:
   - Consider the qualifications, other works, and organizational affiliation of the author
   - Look up the organization which produced the Web site (if it's unfamiliar) to identify its credentials, viewpoint, or agenda
   - If the source is an E-journal, discover whether it is refereed (reviewed by scholars before it is accepted for publication)

2. Clearly states the **date** the material was written and the date the site was last revised
   Your task:
   - If the information is not current enough for your purposes or the date is not given, look elsewhere

3. Provides **accurate** data whose parameters are clearly defined
    Your task:
    - Compare the data found on the Web site with data found in other sources (encyclopedias, reference books, articles, etc.) for accuracy, completeness, recency
    - Ask a librarian about other important sources to check for this information

4. Provides the **type and level** of information you need
    Your task:
    - Decide whether the level of detail and comprehensiveness, the treatment of the topic (e.g., scholarly or popular), and the graphics or other features are acceptable
    - If the site does not provide the depth of coverage you need, look elsewhere

5. Keeps **bias** to a minimum, and clearly indicates point of view
    Your task:
    - Be aware that producing a Web page does not require the checking and review that publishing a scholarly book requires; you might have retrieved nothing but someone's personal opinion on the topic
    - Appealing graphics can distract you from noticing even overt bias, so heighten your skepticism and examine the evidence (source, date, accuracy, level, links)

6. Provides live **links** to related high-quality Web sites
    Your task:
    - Click on several of the links provided to see if they are active (or if they give an "error" message indicating the links are not being maintained) and to see if they are useful
    - Check to see if the criteria are stated for selecting the links

7. In the case of **commercial** sites, keeps advertising separate from content, and does not let advertisers determine content
    Your task:
    - Look at the Web address: Sites that are commercial have *.com* in their addresses and might have advertising or offer to sell something. The *.com* suffix is also found in news sites (e.g., newspapers, TV networks) and personal pages (sites created by individuals who

have purchased a domain name but who may or may not have a commercial or institutional affiliation)

8. Is clearly organized and **designed** for ease of use
    Your task:
    - Move around the page to see if its organization makes sense and it is easy to return to the top or to the sections you need
    - Decide whether the graphics enhance the content or detract from it

TRIP GABRIEL

For Students in Internet Age, No Shame in Copy and Paste

The Internet is an invaluable source for information about popular culture, both because of its instant accessibility and because of its ability to keep pace with the rapid turnover in popular fashions and trends in a way that print-technology publication never can. But, as is so often the case with the Internet, there is a downside to the matter. Because, as Trip Gabriel observes in this feature that originally appeared in the *New York Times*, "concepts of intellectual property, copyright, and originality are under assault in the unbridled exchange of online information," the result is a pandemic of inadvertent, and sometimes deliberate, plagiarism. Certainly in an era of group-oriented writing—as on Wikipedia—traditional notions of individual authorship are being deconstructed, which makes it all the more important that students learn in their writing classes what the conventions for documentation are and why they are still necessary. Trip Gabriel is a longtime reporter, and former Styles editor, at the *New York Times*.

At Rhode Island College, a freshman copied and pasted from a Web site's frequently asked questions page about homelessness—and did not think he needed to credit a source in his assignment because the page did not include author information.

At DePaul University, the tip-off to one student's copying was the purple shade of several paragraphs he had lifted from the Web; when confronted by a writing tutor his professor had sent him to, he was not defensive—he just wanted to know how to change purple text to black.

And at the University of Maryland, a student reprimanded for copying from Wikipedia in a paper on the Great Depression said he thought its entries — unsigned and collectively written — did not need to be credited since they counted, essentially, as common knowledge.

Professors used to deal with plagiarism by admonishing students to give credit to others and to follow the style guide for citations, and pretty much left it at that.

But these cases — typical ones, according to writing tutors and officials responsible for discipline at the three schools who described the plagiarism — suggest that many students simply do not grasp that using words they did not write is a serious misdeed.

It is a disconnect that is growing in the Internet age as concepts of intellectual property, copyright and originality are under assault in the unbridled exchange of online information, say educators who study plagiarism.

Digital technology makes copying and pasting easy, of course. But that is the least of it. The Internet may also be redefining how students — who came of age with music file-sharing, Wikipedia and Web-linking — understand the concept of authorship and the singularity of any text or image.

"Now we have a whole generation of students who've grown up with information that just seems to be hanging out there in cyberspace and doesn't seem to have an author," said Teresa Fishman, director of the Center for Academic Integrity at Clemson University. "It's possible to believe this information is just out there for anyone to take."

Professors who have studied plagiarism do not try to excuse it — many are champions of academic honesty on their campuses — but rather try to understand why it is so widespread.

In surveys from 2006 to 2010 by Donald L. McCabe, a co-founder of the Center for Academic Integrity and a business professor at Rutgers University, about 40 percent of 14,000 undergraduates admitted to copying a few sentences in written assignments.

Perhaps more significant, the number who believed that copying from the Web constitutes "serious cheating" is declining — to 29 percent on average in recent surveys from 34 percent earlier in the decade.

Sarah Brookover, a senior at the Rutgers campus in Camden, N.J., said many of her classmates blithely cut and paste without attribution.

"This generation has always existed in a world where media and intellectual property don't have the same gravity," said Ms. Brookover, who at 31 is older than most undergraduates. "When you're sitting at your computer, it's the same machine you've downloaded music with, possibly illegally, the same machine you streamed videos for free that showed on HBO last night."

Ms. Brookover, who works at the campus library, has pondered the differences between researching in the stacks and online. "Because you're not walking into a library, you're not physically holding the article, which takes you closer to 'this doesn't belong to me,'" she said. Online, "everything can belong to you really easily."

A University of Notre Dame anthropologist, Susan D. Blum, disturbed by   15 the high rates of reported plagiarism, set out to understand how students view authorship and the written word, or "texts" in Ms. Blum's academic language.

She conducted her ethnographic research among 234 Notre Dame undergraduates. "Today's students stand at the crossroads of a new way of conceiving texts and the people who create them and who quote them," she wrote last year in the book *My Word!: Plagiarism and College Culture*, published by Cornell University Press.

Ms. Blum argued that student writing exhibits some of the same qualities of pastiche that drive other creative endeavors today — TV shows that constantly reference other shows or rap music that samples from earlier songs.

In an interview, she said the idea of an author whose singular effort creates an original work is rooted in Enlightenment ideas of the individual. It is buttressed by the Western concept of intellectual property rights as secured by copyright law. But both traditions are being challenged.

"Our notion of authorship and originality was born, it flourished, and it may be waning," Ms. Blum said.

She contends that undergraduates are less interested in cultivating a   20 unique and authentic identity — as their 1960s counterparts were — than in trying on many different personas, which the Web enables with social networking.

"If you are not so worried about presenting yourself as absolutely unique, then it's O.K. if you say other people's words, it's O.K. if you say things you don't believe, it's O.K. if you write papers you couldn't care less about because they accomplish the task, which is turning something in and getting a grade," Ms. Blum said, voicing student attitudes. "And it's O.K. if you put words out there without getting any credit."

The notion that there might be a new model young person, who freely borrows from the vortex of information to mash up a new creative work, fueled a brief brouhaha earlier this year with Helene Hegemann, a German teenager whose best-selling novel about Berlin club life turned out to include passages lifted from others.

Instead of offering an abject apology, Ms. Hegemann insisted, "There's no such thing as originality anyway, just authenticity." A few critics rose to her defense, and the book remained a finalist for a fiction prize (but did not win).

That theory does not wash with Sarah Wilensky, a senior at Indiana University, who said that relaxing plagiarism standards "does not foster creativity, it fosters laziness."

"You're not coming up with new ideas if you're grabbing and mixing and   25 matching," said Ms. Wilensky, who took aim at Ms. Hegemann in a column in her student newspaper headlined "Generation Plagiarism."

"It may be increasingly accepted, but there are still plenty of creative people — authors and artists and scholars — who are doing original work," Ms. Wilensky said in an interview. "It's kind of an insult that that ideal is gone, and now we're left only to make collages of the work of previous generations."

In the view of Ms. Wilensky, whose writing skills earned her the role of informal editor of other students' papers in her freshman dorm, plagiarism has nothing to do with trendy academic theories.

The main reason it occurs, she said, is because students leave high school unprepared for the intellectual rigors of college writing.

"If you're taught how to closely read sources and synthesize them into your own original argument in middle and high school, you're not going to be tempted to plagiarize in college, and you certainly won't do so unknowingly," she said.

At the University of California, Davis, of the 196 plagiarism cases referred 30 to the disciplinary office last year, a majority did not involve students ignorant of the need to credit the writing of others.

Many times, said Donald J. Dudley, who oversees the discipline office on the campus of 32,000, it was students who intentionally copied — knowing it was wrong — who were "unwilling to engage the writing process."

"Writing is difficult, and doing it well takes time and practice," he said.

And then there was a case that had nothing to do with a younger generation's evolving view of authorship. A student accused of plagiarism came to Mr. Dudley's office with her parents, and the father admitted that he was the one responsible for the plagiarism. The wife assured Mr. Dudley that it would not happen again.

Synthesizing and Citing Sources

One of the questions you might ask yourself as you write is, "How many sources do I need?" Your instructor may give you guidance, but questions of exactly when you need to employ the support of other authors is up to you. Synthesis in academic writing refers to the incorporation of sources into your writing. As you develop your arguments, you will want to look at your sources and consider how what they say interacts with your own opinions. Do you see any similarities between what you want to write and what your sources say, or will you be faced with the task of discussing how your sources don't see your topic the way you do? Think of your paper as a conversation between you and your sources. As you write, ask yourself where you and

e macmillanhighered.com/signsoflife
LearningCurve > Working with Sources (MLA)
Tutorials > How to Cite an Article in MLA Style; How to Cite a Book in MLA Style; How to Cite a Database in MLA Style; How to Cite a Web Site in MLA Style

your sources agree and disagree, and make sure you account for this in your paper. You might want to ask yourself the following questions:

- Have I used my sources as evidence to support any claims I'm making?
- Have I considered any counterarguments?
- Have I taken care to characterize my sources in a way that is fair and accurate?
- When I have finished my draft, have I reconsidered my thesis in light of the source material I've used? Do I need to change my thesis to reflect any new discoveries I've made?

Finally, you will want to make sure you have properly documented any sources you use in your papers. When you write an essay and use another author's work — whether you use the author's exact words or paraphrase them — you need to cite that source for your readers. In most humanities courses, writers use the system of documentation developed by the Modern Language Association (MLA). This system indicates a source in two ways: (1) notations that briefly identify the sources in the body of your essay and (2) notations that give fuller bibliographic information about the sources at the end of your essay. The notations for some commonly used types of sources are illustrated in this chapter. For documenting other sources, consult a writing handbook or the *MLA Handbook*, Eighth Edition (Modern Language Association of America, 2016).

In-Text Citations

In the body of your essay, you should signal to your reader that you've used a source and indicate, in parentheses, where your reader can find the source in your list of works cited. You don't need to repeat the author's name in both your writing and in the parenthetical note.

SOURCE WITH ONE AUTHOR

Patrick Goldstein asserts that "Talk radio has pumped up the volume of our public discourse and created a whole new political language — perhaps the prevailing political language" (16).

SOURCE WITH TWO OR THREE AUTHORS

Researchers have found it difficult to study biker subcultures because, as one team describes the problem, "it was too dangerous to take issue with outlaws on their own turf" (Hooper and Moore 368).

INDIRECT SOURCE

In discussing the baby mania trend, *Time* claimed, "Career women are opting for pregnancy and they are doing it in style" (qtd. in Faludi 106).

List of Works Cited

At the end of your essay, include a list of all the sources you have cited in parenthetical notations. This list, alphabetized by author, should provide full publication information for each source; you should indicate the date you accessed any online sources.

The first line of each entry should begin flush left. Subsequent lines should be indented half an inch (or five spaces) from the left margin. Double-space the entire list, both between and within entries.

Nonelectronic Sources

BOOK BY ONE AUTHOR

Weisman, Alan. *The World without Us*. Thomas Dunne Books, 2007.

BOOK BY TWO OR MORE AUTHORS

Collins, Ronald K. L., and David M. Skover. *The Death of Discourse*. Westview, 1996.

(Note that only the first author's name is reversed.)

WORK IN AN ANTHOLOGY

Corbett, Julia B. "A Faint Green Sell: Advertising and the Natural World." *Signs of Life in the U.S.A.: Readings on Popular Culture for Writers*. 8th edition, edited by Sonia Maasik and Jack Solomon, Bedford/St. Martin's, 2015, pp. 235-52.

ARTICLE IN A WEEKLY MAGAZINE

Lacayo, Richard. "How Does '80s Art Look Now?" *Time,* 28 Mar. 2005, pp. 58+.

(A plus sign is used to indicate that the article is not printed on consecutive pages; otherwise, a page range should be given: *16–25*, for example.)

ARTICLE IN A MONTHLY MAGAZINE

Judd, Elizabeth. "After School." *The Atlantic,* June 2005, p. 118.

ARTICLE IN A JOURNAL

Hooper, Columbus B., and Johnny Moore. "Women in Outlaw Motorcycle Gangs." *Journal of Contemporary Ethnography,* vol. 18, no. 4, 1990, pp. 363-87.

PERSONAL INTERVIEW

Chese, Charlie. Personal interview. 28 Sept. 2014.

Electronic Sources

FILM OR DVD

Hachi: A Dog's Tale. Directed by Lasse Hallström, performance by Richard Gere,
  Stage 6 Films, 2009.

No Country for Old Men. Directed by Ethan and Joel Coen, 2007. Buena Vista Home
  Entertainment, 2008.

TELEVISION PROGRAM

"Collateral Damage." *CSI: Miami.* Performance by David Caruso, KBAK, Bakersfield,
  4 May 2009.

SOUND RECORDING

Adams, Ryan. *Cold Roses.* Lost Highway, 2005.

E-MAIL

Katt, Susie. "Interpreting the Mall." Message to the author, 29 Sept. 2014.

ARTICLE IN AN ONLINE REFERENCE BOOK

"Gender." *Britannica Online,* 22 Oct. 2013, www.britannica.com/topic/gender
  -grammar. Accessed 30 May 2014.

  (Note that the first date indicates when the information was posted; the
second indicates the date of access.)

ARTICLE IN AN ONLINE JOURNAL

Schaffer, Scott. "Disney and the Imagineering of Histories." *Postmodern Culture,*
  vol. 6, no. 3, 1996, pmc.iath.virginia.edu/. Accessed 26 Aug. 2014.

ARTICLE IN AN ONLINE MAGAZINE

Rosenberg, Scott. "Don't Link or I'll Sue!" *Salon,* 12 Aug. 1999, www.salon
  .com/1999/08/12/deep_links/. Accessed 13 Aug. 2014.

ONLINE BOOK

James, Henry. *The Bostonians,* 1886. *The Henry James Scholar's Guide to Web Sites,*
  Aug. 1999, www2.newpaltz.edu/~hathaway/. Accessed 15 Oct. 2014.

ONLINE POEM

Frost, Robert. "The Road Not Taken." *Mountain Interval,* 1915. *Project Bartleby Archive,* Mar. 1995, www.bartleby.com/119/1.html. Accessed 13 Aug. 2014.

PROFESSIONAL WEB SITE

National Council of Teachers of English. *National Council of Teachers of English,* Jan. 2014, www.ncte.org/. Accessed 6 July 2014.

PERSONAL HOME PAGE

Stallman, Richard. Home page. Mar. 2008, stallman.org/. Accessed 4 Mar. 2014.

POSTING TO A DISCUSSION LIST

Yen, Jessica. "Quotations within Parentheses (Study Measures)." *Copyediting-L,* 18 Mar. 2016, list.indiana.edu/sympa/arc/copyediting-l/2016-03/msg00492 .html.

ONLINE SCHOLARLY PROJECT

Barlow, Michael, editor. *Corpus Linguistics,* Apr. 1998, report.rice.edu/sir/www.ruf .rice.edu/~barlow/corpus.html. Accessed 13 Aug. 2010.

WORK FROM A DATABASE SERVICE

Cullather, Nick. "The Third Race." *Diplomatic History,* vol. 33, no 3, 2009, pp. 507-12. *Academic OneFile,* infotrac.galegroup.com/. Accessed 1 May 2009.

YOUTUBE OR OTHER ONLINE VIDEO

YouTube, 7 Aug. 2010, www.youtube.com/watch?v=VKsVSBhSwJg. Accessed 12 Feb. 2011.

PHOTOGRAPH OR WORK OF ART

Warhol, Andy. *Black Bean.* 1968, Whitney Museum of American Art, *whitney.org.* Accessed 26 Aug. 2014.

CONSUMING PASSIONS

The Culture of American Consumption

The CCI

The CCI is one of the most avidly watched broadcasts in America, and, no, it isn't a television crime series. Based on the monthly Consumer Confidence Survey, as issued by the Conference Board (a private, nonprofit organization that, in its own words, "is a global, independent business membership and research association working in the public interest"), the Consumer Confidence Index charts the mood of American consumers. When it goes up, the stock market goes up; when it goes down, the stock market goes down with it.

What does this have to do with popular culture? The short answer is "everything" because American popular culture is grounded in consumption, whether we are looking at the direct purchase of goods and services; the enjoyment of music, movies, and television; or simply the use of your iPhone or other digital devices and all that such devices offer you. That is why your Facebook profile, Tumblr microblog, Google searches, and Twitter account are free; it is why traditional network television and traditional radio are free as well. All such media are free because they are underwritten by advertising and marketing expenditures made by companies that want to sell you something. While movies, for their part, are usually not free, they themselves are commodities to be consumed through the purchase of tickets, DVDs, cable subscriptions, Netflix or Red Box accounts, and so on. Music, too, is a commodity, whether consumed via download, CD, or vinyl (yes, there has been a small resurgence of that most venerable of music technologies). In short, American popular culture is grounded in a consumer society, and that is why this chapter appears first in this book.

At the same time, people in consumer societies use their possessions to communicate with one another, which is to say that consumer goods aren't simply objects, they're **signs**—from the out-and-out status symbols whose purpose is to convey your place in the social hierarchy, to the clothes you wear, the music you listen to, and even the smartphone you choose to purchase. Like all signs, they get their meaning from the cultural **systems**, or **codes**, within which they appear, and their meanings can change as history reworks the systems that define them. To see how, let's look at a consumer trend that has been in fashion for a number of years now and looks to continue for a number of years more.

The Skinny on Skinny Jeans

Once again, it all begins with a *difference*: baggy versus skinny.

From the 1980s through the 1990s and into the early 2000s, baggy jeans were the jean fashion of choice for many young Americans, especially boys and men. That changed sometime early in the new millennium, when decidedly tight skinny jeans exploded into popularity for both men and women. In itself, such a difference would appear to be meaningless, but when systematically situated within the history of blue jeans and the meanings that jeans have conveyed over the years, this difference becomes significant—in fact, very complicatedly significant.

So let's look at some history. Blue jeans first appeared in the nineteenth century when Levi Strauss tailored durable denim cloth into trousers for workers in the California gold fields. As such, their **denotation** was simply the pants themselves. But given their use by men engaged in heavy manual labor, those trousers came to **connote**, or signify, "working-class clothing," with cowboys being the most glamorous of their wearers. By the 1950s, however, blue jeans began to bear an additional class significance as "casual wear" for middle-class Americans; but whether they connoted working-class or casual middle-class wear, blue jeans were still regarded as unsuitable for formal middle-class attire either in school or on the job.

But during the countercultural revolution of the 1960s, American baby boomers self-consciously adopted blue jeans as a kind of uniform in defiance of middle-class proscriptions, often wearing them as a sign of solidarity with the working class. Jeans became so identified with the counterculture that Charles Reich, in his popular 1970 book *The Greening of America*, argued that denim bell-bottoms were a symbol of the Age of Aquarius, signifying a free and freewheeling new generation.

Eventually, as happens so often in American consumer culture, what was once a symbol of defiance settled down into a simple fashion statement, and by the 1970s, blue jeans signified little more than "fashionable clothing." This opened the way for designer jeans, like Jordache and Chic, which were worn very tight by both men and women and were styled to enhance their sex appeal.

In the 1970s, however, blue jeans also assumed a new significance as members of some punk rock and New Wave bands introduced a new jeans alternative. The album jacket art for Blondie's record *Parallel Lines* provides a good illustration: The male band members all wear narrowly tailored black jeans that taper down tightly at the ankle. What is more, one member of the group wears bright red Converse sneakers, while another wears one black Converse sneaker and one red one. The look is "hipster" rather than sexy,

---

Discussing the Signs of Consumer Culture

On the board, list in categories the fashion styles worn by members of the class. Be sure to note details, such as styles of shoes, jewelry, backpacks, or sunglasses, as well as broader trends. Next, discuss what the clothing choices say about individuals. What messages are people sending about their personal identity? Do individual students agree with the class's interpretations of their clothing choices? Can any distinctions be made by gender, age, or ethnicity? Then discuss what the fashion styles worn by the whole class say: Is a group identity projected by class members?

recalling one of the Beat fashions of fifties-era bohemianism, and, as we shall see in a moment, has important resonances with today's skinny jeans trend.

Meanwhile, in the 1980s extravagantly oversized, or baggy, jeans entered into denim's history as part of the hip-hop scene. Taking the place of the loose sweats popular during the break-dancing era, baggy jeans were a signifier of the evolution of rap/hip-hop toward its gangsta incarnation. Part of a uniform that then included backward-facing ball caps and untied Nikes, baggy jeans were often worn "sagging." The gangsta-inflected fashion system within which baggy jeans signified soon was supplemented by a parallel, but different, system when white American youth adopted (or adapted) rap/hip-hop styles for themselves — as when skateboarders appropriated baggy jeans for their own use, and grunge fashion included an ensemble that combined Doc Martens with baggy cutoffs. This turn to oversized jeans among a diverse group of consumers created a national fashion system that endured for well over twenty years, signifying what can best be called "attitude" on the part of their wearers — until the whole thing simmered down into just another teen fashion without any real significance, as so often happens with fashions originally intended to be subversive.

All of which takes us to the present. In the early 2000s, the look that Blondie had resurrected from the 1950s came to be adopted by various post-punk, indie, and otherwise "alternative" bands. So skinny jeans entered the fashion system big time, assuming a new connotative significance, one very different from the "flower child" meanings of the patched-jeans sixties, the "grunge" inflections of the early nineties, and the "street gang" connotations of the baggy era. In short, skinny jeans became "hip," where hip meant "coffee shop–indie / alternative hipster." But just as baggy jeans came eventually to signify little more than "youth fashion item," so, too, have skinny jeans become so pervasive today that they have lost much of their "hipster" connotation and usually signify nothing more than "I'm wearing what everyone else is wearing."

Yet, not quite. Because, as you may have already noted for yourself, there is a racial component to the recent history of blue jeans that we have not addressed yet. That angle on the matter becomes quite obvious when you consider the racial connotations of "alternative" versus "hip-hop" culture. Alternative culture has a "white" association; hip-hop is a code of black America. These associations became quite obvious in 2009 when rappers New Boyz released a video called "You're a Jerk" — a single from their significantly titled album *Skinny Jeanz and a Mic*. Highlighting both skinny jeans and brightly colored sneakers, this video initially attracted some very angry commentary on YouTube. Since these comments aren't reprintable here, let's just say that along with the positive fan responses, in 2009 there were a lot of hostile accusations that the New Boyz were "murdering" hip-hop.

The crux of the matter goes back to those baggy jeans, which became such an enduring signifier of African American street culture. One may say that it was a question of authenticity, with "skinny rather than baggy" signifying to some black consumers a kind of fashion betrayal. Interviews with the members of New Boyz and other figures in the jerkin' scene in 2009 clearly indicate that they were quite aware of what they were doing, for while they retained many of the signifiers of hip-hop culture through their rapping, their wearing of baseball caps (though adjusted their own way), and their wearing of sagging skinny jeans, they explicitly distinguished themselves from the gangsta subculture, speaking to interviewers at the time of the "positive" attractions of elements such as entrepreneurialism. Given that their skinny jeans had their origins in such white-coded fashions as punk (significantly, a hairstyle seen among jerkers was called the "frohawk") and New Wave, the New Boyz were thus not only adopting a white-coded fashion statement but also reversing a certain trend in the history of American youth culture that usually features white youth adopting and adapting the signifiers of black youth. Hence the hostile reaction. Indeed, several years ago, one fan of skinny jeans remarked to a reporter that he swapped his skinny jeans for baggy ones before returning home in order to avoid getting into trouble in his neighborhood.

But that was then, and fashion history rolls on. A survey of the more recent YouTube comments accompanying the "New Boyz 'You're a Jerk' OFFICIAL Music Video HD Extended" version reveals that the whole matter has lost its sting. One commenter places it in the "distant" past ("my daddy use to always try to do this dance lols whole house be shakin"), while another simply says "wonderful." But still, one quietly unhappy holdover from the old days remarks: "I am still angry at them for introducing dudes to skinny pants . . . sigh," he (or she) writes. Black consumer or white, then, skinny jeans appear to have crossed over into a simple fashion statement, all (or at least most) passion spent.

Disposable Decades

When analyzing a consumer sign, you will often find yourself referring to particular decades (as we have above) in which certain popular fads and trends were prominent, because the decade in which a given style appears may be an essential key to the system that explains it. Have you ever wondered why American cultural trends seem to change with every decade, why it is so easy to speak of the sixties or the seventies or the eighties and immediately recognize the popular styles that dominated each decade? Have you ever looked at the style of a friend and thought, "Oh, she's so seventies"? Can you place platform shoes or bell-bottoms at the drop of a hat? A change in the calendar always seems to herald a change in style in a consuming culture. But why?

The decade-to-decade shift in America's pop cultural and consumer identity goes back a good number of years. It is still easy, for example, to distinguish F. Scott Fitzgerald's Jazz Age twenties from John Steinbeck's wrathful thirties. The fifties, an especially connotative decade, raise images of ducktail haircuts and poodle skirts, drive-in culture and Elvis, family sitcoms and white-bread innocence, while the sixties are remembered for acid rock, hippies, the student revolution, and back-to-the-land communes. We remember the seventies as a pop cultural era divided among disco, Nashville, and preppiedom, with John Travolta, truckers, and Skippy and Muffy as dominant pop icons. The boom-boom eighties gave us Wall Street glitz and the yuppie invasion. Indeed, each decade since World War I — which, not accidentally, happens to coincide roughly with the rise of modern advertising and mass production — seems to carry its own consumerist style.

It's no accident that the decade-to-decade shift in consumer styles coincides with the advent of modern advertising and mass production, because it was mass production that created a need for constant consumer turnover in the first place. Mass production, that is, promotes stylistic change because with so many products being produced, a market must be created to consume all of them, and this means constantly consuming *more*. To get consumers to keep buying all the new stuff, you have to convince them that the stuff they already have is passé. Why else do fashion designers completely change their lines each year? Why do car manufacturers annually change their color schemes and body shapes when the previous year's model seemed good enough? Why did the Apple iPhone 5c come out in so many colors? The new colors and designs aren't simply functional improvements (though they are marketed as such); they are inducements to go out and replace what you already have to avoid appearing out of fashion. Just think: If you could afford to buy any car or phone you want, what would it be? Would your choice a few years ago have been the same?

Mass production, then, creates consumer societies based on the constant creation of new products that are intended to be disposed of with the next product year. But something happened along the way to the establishment of our consumer culture: We began to value consumption more than production. Shoppers storm the doors as the Christmas shopping season begins earlier and earlier every year. Listen to the economic news: Consumption, not production, is relied upon to carry America out of its economic downturns. When Americans stop buying, our economy grinds to a halt. Consumption lies at the center of our

---

Exploring the Signs of Consumer Culture

"You are what you buy." In your journal, freewrite on the importance of consumer products in your life. How do you respond to being told your identity is equivalent to the products you buy? Do you resist the notion? Do you recall any instances when you have felt lost without a favorite object? How do you communicate your sense of self to others through objects, whether clothing, books, food, home decor, electronic goods, or something else?

economic system now, constituting some two-thirds of our economic activity, and the result has been a transformation in the very way we view ourselves.

A Tale of Two Cities

It has not always been thus in America, however. Once, Americans prided themselves on their productivity. In 1914, for example, the poet Carl Sandburg boasted of a Chicago that was "Hog Butcher for the World, / Tool maker, Stacker of Wheat, / Player with Railroads and the Nation's Freight Handler." One wonders what Sandburg would think of the place today. From the South Side east to the industrial suburb of Gary, Indiana, Chicago's once-proud mills and factories rust in the winter wind. At the Chicago Mercantile Exchange, trade today is in commodity futures, not commodities.

Meanwhile, a few hundred miles to the northwest, Bloomington, Minnesota, buzzes with excitement. For there stands the Mall of America, a colossus of consumption so large that it contains within its walls a seven-acre Nickelodeon Universe theme park, with lots of room to spare. You can find almost anything you want in the Mall of America, but most of what you will find won't have been manufactured in America. The proud tag "Made in the U.S.A." is an increasingly rare item.

It's a long way from Sandburg's Chicago to the Mall of America, a trip that traverses America's shift from a producer to a consumer economy. This shift is not simply economic; it is behind a cultural transformation that is shaping a new mythology in which we define ourselves, our hopes, and our desires.

Ask yourself right now what your own goals are in going to college. Do you envision a career in law, or medicine, or banking and finance? Do you want to be a teacher, an advertising executive, or a civil servant? Or maybe you are preparing for a career in an Internet-related field. If you've considered any of these careers, you are contemplating what are known as service jobs. While essential to society, none of them actually produces anything. If you've given thought to going into some facet of manufacturing, on the other hand, you are unusual because America offers increasingly fewer opportunities in that area and little prestige. The prestigious jobs are in law and medicine and in high-tech operations like Google and Facebook, a fact that is easy to take for granted. But ask yourself: Does it have to be so?

To live in a consumer culture is not simply a matter of shopping or career choice, however; it is also a matter of being. Often aligned with the preeminent American mythology of personal freedom, the freedom to consume *what* you want *whenever* you want it has become — thanks in large part to the advent of mobile digital technology — a defining value of modern American life: a human right, not a mere pleasure or convenience. You are what you buy, and what you buy fulfills what you are. And in case you forget this, a constant drumbeat of advertising and marketing schemes exhorts you to go out and buy something, replacing the freedom to march to the beat of a different drummer with the freedom to buy.

When the Going Gets Tough, the Tough Go Shopping

In a cultural system where our identities are displayed in the products we buy, it accordingly behooves us to pay close attention to what we consume and why. From the cars we drive to the clothes we wear, we are enmeshed in a web of consumption. As students, you are probably freer to choose the images you wish to project through the products you consume than most other demographic groups in America. This claim may sound paradoxical: After all, don't working adults have more money than starving students? Yes, generally. But the working world places severe restrictions on the choices employees can make in their clothing and grooming styles, and even automobile choice may be restricted (real estate agents, for example, can't escort their clients around town in Kia Souls). Corporate business wear, for all its variations, still revolves around a central core of necktied and dark-hued sobriety, regardless of the gender of the wearer. On campus, however, you can be pretty much whatever you want to be, which is why your own daily life provides you with a particularly rich field of consumer signs to read and decode.

So go to it. By the time you finish reading this book, a lot will have changed. Look around. Start reading the signs.

The Readings

As this chapter's lead-off essay, Laurence Shames's "The More Factor" offers a historical context for American consumer culture, relating America's frontier history to our ever-expanding desire for more goods and services. Anne

---

Reading Consumer Culture Online

Log on to one of the many home shopping networks or auction sites. You might try QVC (www.QVC.com), Shop at Home (www.shopathome .com), or eBay (www.ebay.com). Analyze both the products sold and the way they are marketed. Who is the target audience for the network you're studying, and what images and values are used to attract this market? How does the marketing compare with nonelectronic sales pitches, such as displays in shopping malls and magazines or TV advertising? Does the electronic medium affect your behavior as a consumer, or does the time pressure of an electronic auction affect your behavior as well? How do you account for any differences in electronic and traditional marketing strategies?

Norton and Malcolm Gladwell follow with a paired set of readings on the ways in which retailers seek to maximize sales by designing the shopping experience to influence consumers' buying behavior, with Norton providing semiotic analyses of shopping malls and mail-order catalogs and Gladwell reporting on the measures that brick-and-mortar-store managers take to encourage spending. Next, Jon Mooallem explores the world of self-storage facilities in an era when consumption is outstripping many Americans' ability to house all their stuff. Stephanie Clifford and Quentin Hardy's *Business Day* article reports on the ways in which even brick-and-mortar shops are now tracking customers' behavior by monitoring their smartphone signals, while Thomas Hine takes us into the low-tech world of packaging, revealing how a simple package can be a complex sign system used in the front lines of marketing. James A. Roberts's survey of status consumption and the paradox of diminishing returns provides a piquant counterpoint to Phyllis M. Japp and Debra K. Japp's rhetorical analysis of the "voluntary simplicity movement," a consumer phenomenon that manages to commodify the desire not to be addicted to consumption. Steve McKevitt then analyzes the ways in which technology and psychology come together in the consumer marketplace. The chapter concludes with Thomas Frank's revelation of how corporate America has turned consumption into a hip signifier of inauthentic rebellion: a "commodification of dissent."

LAURENCE SHAMES
The More Factor

A bumper sticker popular in the 1980s read, "Whoever dies with the most toys wins." In this selection from *The Hunger for More: Searching for Values in an Age of Greed* (1989), Laurence Shames shows how the great American hunger for more — more toys, more land, more opportunities — is an essential part of our history and character, stemming from the frontier era when the horizon alone seemed the only limit to American desire. The author of *The Big Time: The Harvard Business School's Most Successful Class and How It Shaped America* (1986) and the holder of a Harvard MBA, Shames is a journalist who has contributed to such publications as *Playboy*, *Vanity Fair*, *Manhattan, inc.*, and *Esquire.* He currently is working full-time on writing fiction and screenplays, with his most recent publications including *Florida Straits* (1992), *Sunburn* (1995), *Welcome to Paradise* (1999), *The Naked Detective* (2000), *Not Fade Away* (2003, with Peter Barton), and *Shot on Location* (2013).

1

Americans have always been optimists, and optimists have always liked to speculate. In Texas in the 1880s, the speculative instrument of choice was towns, and there is no tale more American than this.

What people would do was buy up enormous tracts of parched and vacant land, lay out a Main Street, nail together some wooden sidewalks, and start slapping up buildings. One of these buildings would be called the Grand Hotel and would have a saloon complete with swinging doors. Another might be dubbed the New Academy or the Opera House. The developers would erect a flagpole and name a church, and once the workmen had packed up and moved on, the towns would be as empty as the sky.

But no matter. The speculators, next, would hire people to pass out handbills in the Eastern and Midwestern cities, tracts limning the advantages of relocation to "the Athens of the South" or "the new plains Jerusalem." When persuasion failed, the builders might resort to bribery, paying people's moving costs and giving them houses, in exchange for nothing but a pledge to stay until a certain census was taken or a certain inspection made. Once the nose count was completed, people were free to move on, and there was in fact a contingent of folks who made their living by keeping a cabin on skids and dragging it for pay from one town to another.

macmillanhighered.com/signsoflife
How does materialism affect us psychologically?
e-readings > **Gene Brockhoff**, *Shop 'til You Drop* [video]

The speculators' idea, of course, was to lure the railroad. If one could create a convincing semblance of a town, the railroad might come through it, and a real town would develop, making the speculators staggeringly rich. By these devices a man named Sanborn once owned Amarillo.[1]

But railroad tracks are narrow and the state of Texas is very, very wide.   5
For every Wichita Falls or Lubbock there were a dozen College Mounds or Belchervilles,[2] bleached, unpeopled burgs that receded quietly into the dust, taking with them large amounts of speculators' money.

Still, the speculators kept right on bucking the odds and depositing empty towns in the middle of nowhere. Why did they do it? Two reasons — reasons that might be said to summarize the central fact of American economic history and that go a fair way toward explaining what is perhaps the central strand of the national character.

The first reason was simply that the possible returns were so enormous as to partake of the surreal, to create a climate in which ordinary logic and prudence did not seem to apply. In a boom like that of real estate when the railroad barreled through, long shots that might pay one hundred thousand to one seemed worth a bet.

The second reason, more pertinent here, is that there was a presumption that America would *keep* on booming — if not forever, then at least longer than it made sense to worry about. There would always be another gold rush, another Homestead Act, another oil strike. The next generation would always ferret out opportunities that would be still more lavish than any that had gone before. America *was* those opportunities. This was an article not just of faith, but of strategy. You banked on the next windfall, you staked your hopes and even your self-esteem on it, and this led to a national turn of mind that might usefully be thought of as the habit of more.

A century, maybe two centuries, before anyone had heard the term *baby boomer*, much less *yuppie*, the habit of more had been instilled as the operative truth among the economically ambitious. The habit of more seemed to suggest that there was no such thing as getting wiped out in America. A fortune lost in Texas might be recouped in Colorado. Funds frittered away on grazing land where nothing grew might flood back in as silver. There was always a second chance, or always seemed to be, in this land where growth was destiny and where expansion and purpose were the same.

The key was the frontier, not just as a matter of acreage, but as idea. Vast,   10
varied, rough as rocks, America was the place where one never quite came to the end. Ben Franklin explained it to Europe even before the Revolutionary War had finished: America offered new chances to those "who, in their own

---

[1]For a fuller account of railroad-related land speculation in Texas, see F. Stanley, *Story of the Texas Panhandle Railroads* (Borger, Tex.: Hess Publishing Co., 1976).

[2]T. Lindsay Baker, *Ghost Towns of Texas* (Norman, Okla.: University of Oklahoma Press, 1986).

Countries, where all the Lands [were] fully occupied . . . could never [emerge] from the poor Condition wherein they were born."[3]

So central was this awareness of vacant space and its link to economic promise that Frederick Jackson Turner, the historian who set the tone for much of the twentieth century's understanding of the American past, would write that it was "not the constitution, but free land . . . [that] made the democratic type of society in America."[4] Good laws mattered; an accountable government mattered; ingenuity and hard work mattered. But those things were, so to speak, an overlay on the natural, geographic America that was simply *there*, and whose vast and beckoning possibilities seemed to generate the ambition and the sometimes reckless liberty that would fill it. First and foremost, it was open space that provided "the freedom of the individual to rise under conditions of social mobility."[5]

Open space generated not just ambition, but metaphor. As early as 1835, Tocqueville was extrapolating from the fact of America's emptiness to the observation that "no natural boundary seems to be set to the efforts of man."[6] Nor was any limit placed on what he might accomplish, since, in that heyday of the Protestant ethic, a person's rewards were taken to be quite strictly proportionate to his labors.

Frontier; opportunity; more. This has been the American trinity from the very start. The frontier was the backdrop and also the raw material for the streak of economic booms. The booms became the goad and also the justification for the myriad gambles and for Americans' famous optimism. The optimism, in turn, shaped the schemes and visions that were sometimes noble, sometimes appalling, always bold. The frontier, as reality and as symbol, is what has shaped the American way of doing things and the American sense of what's worth doing.

But there has been one further corollary to the legacy of the frontier, with its promise of ever-expanding opportunities: Given that the goal — a realistic goal for most of our history — was *more*, Americans have been somewhat backward in adopting values, hopes, ambitions that have to do with things *other than* more. In America, a sense of quality has lagged far behind a sense of scale. An ideal of contentment has yet to take root in soil traditionally more hospitable to an ideal of restless striving. The ethic of decency has been upstaged by the ethic of success. The concept of growth has been applied almost exclusively to things that can be measured, counted, weighed. And the hunger for those things that are unmeasurable but fine — the sorts of accomplishment that cannot be undone by circumstance or a shift in social fashion, the kind of serenity that cannot be shattered by tomorrow's headline — has gone largely unfulfilled, and even unacknowledged.

[3]Benjamin Franklin, "Information to Those Who Would Remove to America," in *The Autobiography and Other Writings* (New York: Penguin Books, 1986), 242.

[4]Frederick Jackson Turner, *The Frontier in American History* (Melbourne, Fla.: Krieger, 1976 [reprint of 1920 edition]), 293.

[5]Ibid., 266.

[6]Tocqueville, *Democracy in America*.

2

If the supply of more went on forever, perhaps that wouldn't matter very   15
much. Expansion could remain a goal unto itself, and would continue to
generate a value system based on bulk rather than on nuance, on quantities
of money rather than on quality of life, on "progress" itself rather than on
a sense of what the progress was for. But what if, over time, there was less
more to be had?

That is the essential situation of America today.

Let's keep things in proportion: The country is not running out of wealth,
drive, savvy, or opportunities. We are not facing imminent ruin, and neither
panic nor gloom is called for. But there have been ample indications over the
past two decades that we are running out of more.

Consider productivity growth — according to many economists, the single
most telling and least distortable gauge of changes in real wealth. From 1947
to 1965, productivity in the private sector (adjusted, as are all the following
figures, for inflation) was advancing, on average, by an annual 3.3 percent.
This means, simply, that each hour of work performed by a specimen American worker contributed 3.3 cents worth or more to every American dollar every year; whether we saved it or spent it, that increment went into a
national kitty of ever-enlarging aggregate wealth. Between 1965 and 1972,
however, the "more-factor" decreased to 2.4 percent a year, and from 1972
to 1977 it slipped further, to 1.6 percent. By the early 1980s, productivity
growth was at a virtual standstill, crawling along at 0.2 percent for the five
years ending in 1982.[7] Through the middle years of the 1980s, the numbers
rebounded somewhat — but by then the gains were being neutralized by the
gargantuan carrying costs on the national debt.[8]

Inevitably, this decline in the national stockpile of more held consequences for the individual wallet.[9] During the 1950s, Americans' average
hourly earnings were humping ahead at a gratifying 2.5 percent each year. By
the late seventies, that figure stood just where productivity growth had come
to stand, at a dispiriting 0.2 cents on the dollar. By the first half of the eighties, the Reagan "recovery" notwithstanding, real hourly wages were actually
moving backward — declining at an average annual rate of 0.3 percent.

Compounding the shortage of more was an unfortunate but crucial demo-   20
graphic fact. Real wealth was nearly ceasing to expand just at the moment

[7]These figures are taken from the Council of Economic Advisers, *Economic Report of the President*, February 1984, 267.

[8]For a lucid and readable account of the meaning and implications of our reservoir
of red ink, see Lawrence Malkin, *The National Debt* (New York: Henry Holt and Co., 1987).
Through no fault of Malkin's, many of his numbers are already obsolete, but his explanation
of who owes what to whom, and what it means, remains sound and even entertaining in a
bleak sort of way.

[9]The figures in this paragraph and the next are from "The Average Guy Takes It on the
Chin," *New York Times*, 13 July 1986, sec. 3.

when the members of that unprecedented population bulge known as the baby boom were entering what should have been their peak years of income expansion. A working man or woman who was thirty years old in 1949 could expect to see his or her real earnings burgeon by 63 percent by age forty. In 1959, a thirty-year-old could still look forward to a gain of 49 percent by his or her fortieth birthday.

But what about the person who turned thirty in 1973? By the time that worker turned forty, his or her real earnings had shrunk by a percentage point. For all the blather about yuppies with their beach houses, BMWs, and radicchio salads, and even factoring in those isolated tens of thousands making ludicrous sums in consulting firms or on Wall Street, the fact is that between 1979 and 1983 real earnings of all Americans between the ages of twenty-five and thirty-four actually declined by 14 percent.[10] The *New York Times*, well before the stock market crash put the kibosh on eighties confidence, summed up the implications of this downturn by observing that "for millions of bread-winners, the American dream is becoming the impossible dream."[11]

Now, it is not our main purpose here to detail the ups and downs of the American economy. Our aim, rather, is to consider the effects of those ups and downs on people's goals, values, sense of their place in the world. What happens at that shadowy juncture where economic prospects meld with personal choice? What sorts of insights and adjustments are called for so that economic ups and downs can be dealt with gracefully?

Fact one in this connection is that, if America's supply of more is in fact diminishing, American values will have to shift and broaden to fill the gap where the expectation of almost automatic gains used to be. Something more durable will have to replace the fat but fragile bubble that had been getting frailer these past two decades and that finally popped—a tentative, partial pop—on October 19, 1987. A different sort of growth—ultimately, a growth in responsibility and happiness—will have to fulfill our need to believe that our possibilities are still expanding.

The transition to that new view of progress will take some fancy stepping, because, at least since the end of World War II, simple economic growth has stood, in the American psyche, as the best available substitute for the literal frontier. The economy has *been* the frontier. Instead of more space, we have had more money. Rather than measuring progress in terms of geographical expansion, we have measured it by expansion in our standard of living. Economics has become the metaphor on which we pin our hopes of open space and second chances.

The poignant part is that the literal frontier did not pass yesterday: it has not existed for a hundred years. But the frontier's promise has become so much a part of us that we have not been willing to let the concept die. We have kept the frontier mythology going by invocation, by allusion, by hype.

[10]See, for example, "The Year of the Yuppie," *Newsweek*, 31 December 1984, 16.
[11]"The Average Guy."

It is not a coincidence that John F. Kennedy dubbed his political program the New Frontier. It is not mere linguistic accident that makes us speak of Frontiers of Science or of psychedelic drugs as carrying one to Frontiers of Perception. We glorify fads and fashions by calling them Frontiers of Taste. Nuclear energy has been called the Last Frontier; solar energy has been called the Last Frontier. Outer space has been called the Last Frontier; the oceans have been called the Last Frontier. Even the suburbs, those blandest and least adventurous of places, have been wryly described as the crabgrass frontier.[12]

What made all these usages plausible was their being linked to the image of the American economy as an endlessly fertile continent whose boundaries never need be reached, a domain that could expand in perpetuity, a gigantic playing field that would never run out of room and on which the game would get forever bigger and more filled with action. This was the frontier that would not vanish.

It is worth noting that people in other countries (with the possible exception of that other America, Australia) do not talk about frontier this way. In Europe, and in most of Africa and Asia, "frontier" connotes, at worst, a place of barbed wire and men with rifles, and at best, a neutral junction where one changes currency while passing from one fixed system into another. Frontier, for most of the world's people, does not suggest growth, expanse, or opportunity.

For Americans, it does, and always has. This is one of the things that sets America apart from other places and makes American attitudes different from those of other people. It is why, from *Bonanza* to the Sierra Club, the notion or even the fantasy of empty horizons and untapped resources has always evoked in the American heart both passion and wistfulness. And it is why the fear that the economic frontier — our last, best version of the Wild West — may finally be passing creates in us not only money worries but also a crisis of morale and even of purpose.

3

It might seem strange to call the 1980s an era of nostalgia. The decade, after 30 all, has been more usually described in terms of coolness, pragmatism, and a blithe innocence of history. But the eighties, unawares, were nostalgic for frontiers; and the disappointment of that nostalgia had much to do with the time's greed, narrowness, and strange want of joy. The fear that the world may not be a big enough playground for the full exercise of one's energies and yearnings, and worse, the fear that the playground is being fenced off and will no longer expand — these are real worries and they have had consequences. The eighties were an object lesson in how people play the game when there is an awful and unspoken suspicion that the game is winding down.

[12]With the suburbs again taking on a sort of fascination, this phrase was resurrected as the title of a 1985 book — *Crabgrass Frontier: The Suburbanization of America*, by Kenneth T. Jackson (Oxford University Press).

It was ironic that the yuppies came to be so reviled for their vaunting ambition and outsized expectations, as if they'd invented the habit of more, when in fact they'd only inherited it the way a fetus picks up an addiction in the womb. The craving was there in the national bloodstream, a remnant of the frontier, and the baby boomers, described in childhood as "the luckiest generation,"[13] found themselves, as young adults, in the melancholy position of wrestling with a two-hundred-year dependency on a drug that was now in short supply.

True, the 1980s raised the clamor for more to new heights of shrillness, insistence, and general obnoxiousness, but this, it can be argued, was in the nature of a final binge, the storm before the calm. America, though fighting the perception every inch of the way, was coming to realize that it was not a preordained part of the natural order that one should be richer every year. If it happened, that was nice. But who had started the flimsy and pernicious rumor that it was normal?

READING THE TEXT

1. Summarize in a paragraph how, according to Shames, the frontier functions as a symbol of American consciousness.
2. What does Shames mean when he says, "Open space generated not just ambition, but metaphor" (para. 12)?
3. What connections does Shames make between America's frontier history and consumer behavior?
4. Why does Shames term the 1980s "an era of nostalgia" (para. 30)?
5. Characterize Shames's attitude toward the American desire for more. How does his tone reveal his personal views on his subject?

READING THE SIGNS

1. Shames asserts that Americans have been influenced by the frontier belief "that America would *keep* on booming" (para. 8). Do you feel that this belief continues to be influential into the twenty-first century? Write an essay arguing for your position.
2. Shames claims that, because of the desire for more, "the ethic of decency has been upstaged by the ethic of success" (para. 14). In class, form teams and debate the validity of Shames's claim.
3. **CONNECTING TEXTS** Read or review Steve McKevitt's "Everything Now" (p. 143). Using Maslow's hierarchy of needs (p. 147), write an essay illustrating, refuting, or complicating the proposition that "the hunger for more" is driven by the fact that "our *needs* have been fulfilled and so, for the first time ever, we have an economy that is almost entirely devoted to the business of satisfying our *wants* instead" (para. 3).
4. In an essay, argue for or refute the proposition that the "hunger for more" that Shames describes is a universal human trait, not simply an American one.

[13]Thomas Hine, *Populuxe* (New York: Alfred A. Knopf, 1986), 15.

ANNE NORTON
The Signs of Shopping

Shopping malls are more than places to shop, just as mail-order catalogs are more than simple lists of goods. Both malls and catalogs are coded systems that not only encourage us to buy but, more profoundly, help us construct our very sense of identity, as in the J. Peterman catalog that "constructs the reader as a man of rugged outdoor interests, taste, and money." In this selection from *Republic of Signs* (1993), Anne Norton, a professor of political science at the University of Pennsylvania, analyzes the many ways in which malls, catalogs, and home shopping networks sell you what they want by telling you who you are. Norton's other books include *Alternative Americas* (1986), *Reflections on Political Identity* (1988), *Ninety-Five Theses on Politics, Culture, and Method* (2003), *Leo Strauss and the Politics of American Empire* (2004), and *On the Muslim Question* (2013).

Shopping at the Mall

The mall has been the subject of innumerable debates. Created out of the modernist impulse for planning and the centralization of public activity, the mall has become the distinguishing sign of suburban decentralization, springing up in unplanned profusion. Intended to restore something of the lost unity of city life to the suburbs, the mall has come to export styles and strategies to stores at the urban center. Deplored by modernists, it is regarded with affection only by their postmodern foes. Ruled more by their content than by their creators' avowed intent, the once sleek futurist shells have taken on a certain aura of postmodern playfulness and popular glitz.

The mall is a favorite subject for the laments of cultural conservatives and others critical of the culture of consumption. It is indisputably the cultural locus of commodity fetishism. It has been noticed, however, by others of a less condemnatory disposition that the mall has something of the mercado, or the agora, about it. It is both a place of meeting for the young and one of the rare places where young and old go together. People of different races and classes, different occupations, different levels of education meet there. As M. Pressdee and John Fiske note, however, though the mall appears to be a public place, it is not. Neither freedom of speech nor freedom of assembly is permitted there. Those who own and manage malls restrict what comes within their confines. Controversial displays, by stores or customers or the plethora of organizations and agencies that present themselves in the open spaces of the mall, are not permitted. These seemingly public spaces conceal a pervasive private authority.

The mall exercises its thorough and discreet authority not only in the regulation of behavior but in the constitution of our visible, inaudible, public discourse. It is the source of those commodities through which we speak of our identities, our opinions, our desires. It is a focus for the discussion of style among peripheral consumers. Adolescents, particularly female adolescents, are inclined to spend a good deal of time at the mall. They spend, indeed, more time than money. They acquire not simple commodities (they may come home with many, few, or none) but a well-developed sense of the significance of those commodities. In prowling the mall they embed themselves in a lexicon of American culture. They find themselves walking through a dictionary. Stores hang a variety of identities on their racks and mannequins. Their window displays provide elaborate scenarios conveying not only what the garment is but what the garment means.

A display in the window of Polo provides an embarrassment of semiotic riches. Everyone, from the architecture critic at the *New York Times* to kids in the hall of a Montana high school, knows what *Ralph Lauren* means. The polo mallet and the saddle, horses and dogs, the broad lawns of Newport, Kennebunkport, old photographs in silver frames, the evocation of age, of ancestry and Anglophilia, of indolence and the Ivy League, evoke the upper class. Indian blankets and buffalo plaids, cowboy hats and Western saddles, evoke a past distinct from England but nevertheless determinedly Anglo. The supposedly arcane and suspect arts of deconstruction are deployed easily, effortlessly, by the readers of these cultural texts.

Walking from one window to another, observing one another, shoppers, 5 especially the astute and observant adolescents, acquire a facility with the language of commodities. They learn not only words but a grammar. Shop windows employ elements of sarcasm and irony, strategies of inversion and allusion. They provide models of elegant, economical, florid, and prosaic expression. They teach composition.

The practice of shopping is, however, more than instructive. It has long been the occasion for women to escape the confines of their homes and enjoy the companionship of other women. The construction of woman's role as one of provision for the needs of the family legitimated her exit. It provided an occasion for women to spend long stretches of time in the company of their friends, without the presence of their husbands. They could exchange information and reflections, ask advice, and receive support. As their daughters grew, they would be brought increasingly within this circle, included in shopping trips and lunches with their mothers. These would form, reproduce, and restructure communities of taste.

The construction of identity and the enjoyment of friendship outside the presence of men was thus effected through a practice that constructed women as consumers and subjected them to the conventions of the marketplace. Insofar as they were dependent on their husbands for money, they were dependent on their husbands for the means to the construction of their identities. They could not represent themselves through commodities without the funds men provided, nor could they, without money, participate in the community of women that was realized in "going shopping." Their identities were made contingent not only on the possession of property but on the recognition of dependence.

Insofar as shopping obliges dependent women to recognize their dependence, it also opens up the possibility of subversion.[1] The housewife who shops for pleasure takes time away from her husband, her family, and her house and claims it for herself. Constantly taught that social order and her private happiness depend on intercourse between men and women, she chooses the company of women instead. She engages with women in an activity marked as feminine, and she enjoys it. When she spends money, she exercises an authority over property that law and custom may deny her. If she has no resources independent of her husband, this may be the only authority over property she is able to exercise. When she buys things her husband does not approve — or does not know of — she further subverts an order that leaves control over property in her husband's hands.[2]

Her choice of feminine company and a feminine pursuit may involve additional subversions. As Fiske and Pressdee recognize, shopping without buying and shopping for bargains have a subversive quality. This is revealed, in a form that gives it additional significance, when a saleswoman leans forward and tells a shopper, "Don't buy that today, it will be on sale on Thursday." Here solidarity of gender (and often of class) overcome, however partially and briefly, the imperatives of the economic order.

Shoppers who look, as most shoppers do, for bargains, and salespeople who warn shoppers of impending sales, see choices between commodities as something other than the evidence and the exercise of freedom. They see covert direction and exploitation; they see the withholding of information and the manipulation of knowledge. They recognize that they are on enemy terrain and that their shopping can be, in Michel de Certeau's[3] term, a "guerrilla raid." This recognition in practice of the presence of coercion in choice challenges the liberal conflation of choice and consent.

Shopping at Home

Shopping is an activity that has overcome its geographic limits. One need no longer go to the store to shop. Direct mail catalogues, with their twenty-four-hour

---

[1] Nuanced and amusing accounts of shopping as subversion are provided in John Fiske's analyses of popular culture, particularly *Reading the Popular* (Boston: Unwin Hyman [now Routledge], 1989), pp. 13–42.

[2] See R. Bowlby, *Just Looking: Consumer Culture in Dreiser, Gissing, and Zola* (London: Methuen, 1985), p. 22, for another discussion and for an example of the recommendation of this strategy by Elizabeth Cady Stanton in the 1850s.

[3] **Michel de Certeau** (1925–1986) French social scientist and semiotician who played an important role in the development of contemporary cultural studies. –EDS.

phone numbers for ordering, permit people to shop where and when they please. An activity that once obliged one to go out into the public sphere, with its diverse array of semiotic messages, can now be done at home. An activity that once obliged one to be in company, if not in conversation, with one's compatriots can now be conducted in solitude.

The activity of catalogue shopping, and the pursuit of individuality, are not, however, wholly solitary. The catalogues invest their commodities with vivid historical and social references. The J. Peterman catalogue, for example, constructs the reader as a man of rugged outdoor interests, taste, and money.[4] He wears "The Owner's Hat" or "Hemingway's Cap," a leather flight jacket or the classic "Horseman's Duster," and various other garments identified with the military, athletes, and European imperialism. The copy for "The Owner's Hat" naturalizes class distinctions and, covertly, racism:

> Some of us work on the plantation.
> Some of us own the plantation.
> Facts are facts.
> This hat is for those who own the plantation.[5]

Gender roles are strictly delineated. The copy for a skirt captioned "Women's Legs" provides a striking instance of the construction of the gaze as male, of women as the object of the gaze:

> Just when you think you see something, a shape you think you recognize, it's gone and then it begins to return and then it's gone and of course you can't take your eyes off it.
> Yes, the long slow motion of women's legs. Whatever happened to those things at carnivals that blew air up into girls' skirts and you could spend hours watching.[6]

"You," of course, are male. There is also the lace blouse captioned "Mystery": "lace says yes at the same time it says no."[7] Finally, there are notes of imperialist nostalgia: the Shepherd's Hotel (Cairo) bathrobe and white pants for "the bush" and "the humid hell-holes of Bombay and Calcutta."[8]

---

[4]I have read several of these. I cite *The J. Peterman Company Owner's Manual No. 5*, from the J. Peterman Company, 2444 Palumbo Drive, Lexington, Ky. 40509.

[5]Ibid., p. 5. The hat is also identified with the Canal Zone, "successfully bidding at Beaulieu," intimidation, and LBOs. Quite a hat. It might be argued against my reading that the J. Peterman Company also offers the "Coal Miner's Bag" and a mailbag. However, since the descriptive points of reference on color and texture and experience for these bags are such things as the leather seats of Jaguars, and driving home in a Bentley, I feel fairly confident in my reading.

[6]Ibid., p. 3. See also pp. 15 and 17 for instances of women as the object of the male gaze. The identification of the gaze with male sexuality is unambiguous here as well.

[7]Ibid., p. 17.

[8]Ibid., pp. 7, 16, 20, 21, 37, and 50.

It may no longer be unforgivable to say that the British left a few good things behind in India and in Kenya, Singapore, Borneo, etc., not the least of which was their Englishness.[9]

As Paul Smith observes, in his reading of their catalogues, the Banana Republic has also made capital out of imperial nostalgia.[10]

The communities catalogues create are reinforced by shared mailing lists. The constructed identities are reified and elaborated in an array of semiotically related catalogues. One who orders a spade or a packet of seeds will be constructed as a gardener and receive a deluge of catalogues from plant and garden companies. The companies themselves may expand their commodities to appeal to different manifestations of the identities they respond to and construct. Smith and Hawken, a company that sells gardening supplies with an emphasis on aesthetics and environmental concern, puts out a catalogue in which a group of people diverse in age and in their ethnicity wear the marketed clothes while gardening, painting, or throwing pots. Williams-Sonoma presents its catalogue not as a catalogue of things for cooking but as "A Catalog for Cooks." The catalogue speaks not to need but to the construction of identity.

The Nature Company dedicates its spring 1990 catalogue "to trees," 15 endorses Earth Day, and continues to link itself to the Nature Conservancy through posters and a program in which you buy a tree for a forest restoration project. Here, a not-for-profit agency is itself commodified, adding to the value of the commodities offered in the catalogue.[11] In this catalogue, consumption is not merely a means for the construction and representation of the self, it is also a means for political action. Several commodities are offered as "A Few Things You Can Do" to save the earth: a string shopping bag, a solar battery recharger, a home newspaper recycler. Socially conscious shopping is a liberal practice in every sense. It construes shopping as a form of election, in which one votes for good commodities or refuses one's vote to candidates whose practices are ethically suspect. In this respect, it reveals its adherence to the same ideological presuppositions that structure television's Home Shopping Network and other cable television sales shows.

Both politically informed purchasing and television sales conflate the free market and the electoral process. Dollars are identified with votes, purchases with endorsements. Both offer those who engage in them the possibility to "talk back" to manufacturers. In television sales shows this ability to talk back is both more thoroughly elaborated and more thoroughly exploited. Like the "elections" on MTV that invite viewers to vote for their favorite video by calling a number on their telephones, they permit those who watch to respond,

[9]Ibid., p. 20.

[10]Paul Smith, "Visiting the Banana Republic," in *Universal Abandon?* ed. Andrew Ross for *Social Text* (Minneapolis: University of Minnesota Press, 1988), pp. 128–48.

[11]*The Nature Company Catalog*, The Nature Company, P.O. Box 2310, Berkeley, Calif. 94702, Spring 1990. See pp. 1–2 and order form insert between pp. 18 and 19. Note also the entailed donation to Designs for Conservation on p. 18.

to speak, and to be heard by the television. Their votes, of course, cost money. On MTV, as in the stores, you can buy as much speech as you can afford. On the Home Shopping Network, the purchase of speech becomes complicated by multiple layers and inversions.

Each commodity is introduced. It is invested by the announcer with a number of desirable qualities. The value of these descriptions of the commodities is enhanced by the construction of the announcer as a mediator not only between the commodity and the consumer but between the salespeople and the consumer. The announcer is not, the format suggests, a salesperson (though of course the announcer is). He or she is an announcer, describing goods that others have offered for sale. Television claims to distinguish itself by making objects visible to the eyes, but it is largely through the ears that these commodities are constructed. The consumer, in purchasing the commodity, purchases the commodity, what the commodity signifies, and, as we say, "buys the salesperson's line." The consumer may also acquire the ability to speak on television. Each purchase is recorded and figures as a vote in a rough plebiscite, confirming the desirability of the object. Although the purchase figures are announced as if they were confirming votes, it is, of course, impossible to register one's rejection of the commodity. Certain consumers get a little more (or rather less) for their money. They are invited to explain the virtue of the commodity — and their purchase — to the announcer and the audience. The process of production, of both the consumers and that which they consume, continues in this apology for consumption.

The semiotic identification of consumption as an American activity, indeed, a patriotic one, is made with crude enthusiasm on the Home Shopping Network and other video sales shows. Red, white, and blue figure prominently in set designs and borders framing the television screen. The Home Shopping Network presents its authorities in an office conspicuously adorned with a picture of the Statue of Liberty.[12] Yet the messages that the Home Shopping Network sends its customers — that you can buy as much speech as you can afford, that you are recognized by others in accordance with your capacity to consume — do much to subvert the connection between capitalism and democracy on which this semiotic identification depends.

READING THE TEXT

1. What does Norton mean when she claims that the suburban shopping mall appears to be a public place but in fact is not?
2. What is Norton's interpretation of Ralph Lauren's Polo stores?
3. How is shopping a subversive activity for women, according to Norton?

---

[12]This moment from the Home Shopping Network was generously brought to my attention, on videotape, by Peter Bregman, a student in my American Studies class of fall 1988, at Princeton University.

4. How do mail-order catalogs create communities of shoppers, in Norton's view?

5. What are the political messages sent by the Home Shopping Network, as Norton sees them, and how are they communicated?

READING THE SIGNS

1. Visit a local shopping mall, and study the window displays, focusing on stores intended for one group of consumers (teenagers, for example, or children). Then write an essay in which you analyze how the displays convey what the stores' products "mean."

2. Bring a few product catalogs to class, and in small groups compare the kinds of consumer "constructed" by the cultural images and allusions in the catalogs. Do you note any patterns associated with gender, ethnicity, or age group? Report your group's interpretations to the whole class.

3. Interview five women of different age groups about their motivations and activities when they shop in a mall. Use your results as evidence in an essay in which you support, refute, or complicate Norton's assertion that shopping constitutes a subversive activity for women.

4. Watch an episode of the Home Shopping Network or a similar program, and write a semiotic analysis of the ways in which products are presented to consumers.

5. Select a single mail-order catalog, and write a detailed semiotic interpretation of the identity it constructs for its market.

6. Visit the Web site for a major chain store (for instance, www.urbanoutfitters.com), and study how the site "moves" the consumer through it. How does the site induce you to consume?

UNDERSTANDING SHOPPING

MALCOLM GLADWELL
The Science of Shopping

Ever wonder why the season's hottest new styles at stores like the Gap are usually displayed on the right at least fifteen paces in from the front entrance? It's because that's where shoppers are most likely to see them as they enter the store, gear down from the walking pace of a mall corridor, and adjust to the shop's spatial environment. Ever wonder how shop managers know this sort of thing? It's because, as Malcolm Gladwell reports here, they hire consultants like Paco Underhill, a "retail anthropologist" and "urban geographer" whose studies (often aided by hidden cameras) of shopping behavior have become valuable guides to store managers looking for the best ways to move the goods. Does this feel just a little Orwellian? Read on. A staff writer for the *New Yorker*, in which this selection first appeared, Gladwell has also written *The Tipping Point* (2000), *Blink: The Power of Thinking without Thinking* (2005), *Outliers: The Story of Success* (2008), *What the Dog Saw: And Other Adventures* (2009 compilation of *New Yorker* articles), and *David and Goliath* (2013).

Human beings walk the way they drive, which is to say that Americans tend to keep to the right when they stroll down shopping-mall concourses or city sidewalks. This is why in a well-designed airport travellers drifting toward their gate will always find the fast-food restaurants on their left and the gift shops on their right: people will readily cross a lane of pedestrian traffic to satisfy their hunger but rarely to make an impulse buy of a T-shirt or a magazine. This is also why Paco Underhill tells his retail clients to make sure that their window displays are canted, preferably to both sides but especially to the left, so that a potential shopper approaching the store on the inside of the sidewalk — the shopper, that is, with the least impeded view of the store window — can see the display from at least twenty-five feet away.

Of course, a lot depends on how fast the potential shopper is walking. Paco, in his previous life, as an urban geographer in Manhattan, spent a great deal of time thinking about walking speeds as he listened in on the great debates of the nineteen-seventies over whether the traffic lights in midtown should be timed to facilitate the movement of cars or to facilitate the movement of pedestrians and so break up the big platoons that move down Manhattan sidewalks. He knows that the faster you walk the more your peripheral vision narrows, so you become unable to pick up visual cues as quickly as someone who is just ambling along. He knows, too, that people who walk fast take a surprising amount of time to slow down — just as it takes a good stretch of road to change gears with a stick-shift automobile. On the basis of his research, Paco estimates the human downshift period to be anywhere from twelve to twenty-five feet, so if you own a store, he says, you never want to be next door to a bank: potential shoppers speed up when they walk past a bank (since there's nothing to look at), and by the time they slow down they've walked right past your business. The downshift factor also means that when potential shoppers enter a store it's going to take them from five to fifteen paces to adjust to the light and refocus and gear down from walking speed to shopping speed — particularly if they've just had to navigate a treacherous parking lot or hurry to make the light at Fifty-seventh and Fifth.

Paco calls that area inside the door the Decompression Zone, and something he tells clients over and over again is never, ever put anything of value in that zone — not shopping baskets or tie racks or big promotional displays — because no one is going to see it. Paco believes that, as a rule of thumb, customer interaction with any product or promotional display in the Decompression Zone will increase at least thirty percent once it's moved to the back edge of the zone, and even more if it's placed to the right, because another of the fundamental rules of how human beings shop is that upon entering a store — whether it's Nordstrom or K Mart, Tiffany or the Gap — the shopper invariably and reflexively turns to the right. Paco believes in the existence of the Invariant Right because he has actually verified it. He has put cameras in stores trained directly on the doorway, and if you go to his office, just above Union Square, where videocassettes and boxes of Super-eight film from all his work over the years are stacked in plastic Tupperware containers practically up to the ceiling, he can show you reel upon reel of grainy entryway video — customers striding in the door, downshifting, refocusing, and then, again and again, making that little half turn.

Paco Underhill is a tall man in his mid-forties, partly bald, with a neatly trimmed beard and an engaging, almost goofy manner. He wears baggy khakis and shirts open at the collar, and generally looks like the academic he might have been if he hadn't been captivated, twenty years ago, by the ideas of the urban anthropologist William Whyte. It was Whyte who pioneered the use of time-lapse photography as a tool of urban planning, putting cameras in parks and the plazas in front of office buildings in midtown Manhattan, in order to determine what distinguished a public space that worked from one that didn't. As a Columbia undergraduate, in 1974, Paco heard a lecture on Whyte's work and, he recalls, left the room "walking on air." He immediately read everything Whyte had written. He emptied his bank account to buy cameras and film and make his own home movie, about a pedestrian mall in Poughkeepsie. He took his "little exercise" to Whyte's advocacy group, the Project for Public Spaces, and was offered a job. Soon, however, it dawned on Paco that Whyte's ideas could be taken a step further — that the same techniques he used to establish why a plaza worked or didn't work could also be used to determine why a store worked or didn't work. Thus was born the field of retail anthropology, and, not long afterward, Paco founded Envirosell, which in just over fifteen years has counselled some of the most familiar names in American retailing, from Levi Strauss to Kinney, Starbucks, McDonald's, Blockbuster, Apple Computer, AT&T, and a number of upscale retailers that Paco would rather not name.

When Paco gets an assignment, he and his staff set up a series of video 5 cameras throughout the test store and then back the cameras up with Envirosell staffers — trackers, as they're known — armed with clipboards. Where the cameras go and how many trackers Paco deploys depends on exactly what the store wants to know about its shoppers. Typically, though, he might use six cameras and two or three trackers, and let the study run for two or three days, so that at the end he would have pages and pages of carefully annotated tracking sheets and anywhere from a hundred to five hundred hours of film. These days, given the expansion of his business, he might tape fifteen thousand hours in a year, and, given that he has been in operation since the late seventies, he now has well over a hundred thousand hours of tape in his library.

Even in the best of times, this would be a valuable archive. But today, with the retail business in crisis, it is a gold mine. The time per visit that the average American spends in a shopping mall was sixty-six minutes last year — down from seventy-two minutes in 1992 — and is the lowest number ever recorded. The amount of selling space per American shopper is now more than double what it was in the mid-seventies, meaning that profit margins have never been narrower, and the costs of starting a retail business — and of failing — have never been higher. In the past few years, countless dazzling new retailing temples have been built along Fifth and Madison Avenues — Barneys, Calvin Klein, Armani, Valentino, Banana Republic, Prada, Chanel, NikeTown, and on and on — but it is an explosion of growth based on no more than a hunch, a hopeful multimillion-dollar gamble that the way to break through is to provide the shopper with spectacle and more spectacle. "The arrogance is gone," Millard Drexler, the president and C.E.O. of the Gap, told me. "Arrogance makes failure. Once you think you know the answer, it's almost always over." In such a competitive environment, retailers don't just want to know how shoppers behave in their stores. They *have* to know. And who better to ask than Paco Underhill, who in the past decade and a half has analyzed tens of thousands of hours of shopping videotape and, as a result, probably knows more about the strange habits and quirks of the species *Emptor americanus* than anyone else alive?

Paco is considered the originator, for example, of what is known in the trade as the butt-brush theory — or, as Paco calls it, more delicately, *le facteur bousculade* — which holds that the likelihood of a woman's being converted from a browser to a buyer is inversely proportional to the likelihood of her being brushed on her behind while she's examining merchandise. Touch — or brush or bump or jostle — a woman on the behind when she has stopped to look at an item, and she will bolt. Actually, calling this a theory is something of a misnomer, because Paco doesn't offer any explanation for why women react that way, aside from venturing that they are "more sensitive back there." It's really an observation, based on repeated and close analysis of his videotape library, that Paco has transformed into a retailing commandment: A women's product that requires extensive examination should never be placed in a narrow aisle.

Paco approaches the problem of the Invariant Right the same way. Some retail thinkers see this as a subject crying out for interpretation and speculation. The design guru Joseph Weishar, for example, argues, in his magisterial *Design for Effective Selling Space*, that the Invariant Right is a function of the fact that we "absorb and digest information in the left part of the brain" and "assimilate and logically use this information in the right half," the result being that we scan the store from left to right and then fix on an object to the right "essentially at a 45 degree angle from the point that we enter." When I asked Paco about this interpretation, he shrugged, and said he thought the reason was simply that most people are right-handed. Uncovering the fundamentals of "why" is clearly not a pursuit that engages him much. He is not a theoretician but an empiricist, and for him the important thing is that in amassing his huge library of in-store time-lapse photography he has gained enough hard evidence to know how often and under what circumstances the Invariant Right is expressed and how to take advantage of it.

What Paco likes are facts. They come tumbling out when he talks, and, because he speaks with a slight hesitation — lingering over the first syllable in, for example, "re-tail" or "de-sign" — he draws you in, and you find yourself truly hanging on his words. "We have reached a historic point in American history," he told me in our very first conversation. "Men, for the first time, have begun to buy their own underwear." He then paused to let the comment sink in, so that I could absorb its implications, before he elaborated: "Which means that we have to *totally* rethink the way we sell that product." In the parlance of Hollywood scriptwriters, the best endings must be surprising and yet inevitable; and the best of Paco's pronouncements take the same shape. It would never have occurred to me to wonder about the increasingly critical role played by touching — or, as Paco calls it, petting — clothes in the course of making the decision to buy them. But then I went to the Gap and to Banana Republic and saw people touching, and fondling and, one after another, buying shirts and sweaters laid out on big wooden tables, and what Paco told me — which was no doubt based on what he had seen on his videotapes — made perfect sense: that the reason the Gap and Banana Republic have tables is not merely that sweaters and shirts look better there, or that tables fit into the warm and relaxing residential feeling that the Gap and Banana Republic are trying to create in their stores, but that tables invite — indeed, symbolize — touching. "Where do we eat?" Paco asks. "We eat, we pick up food, on tables."

Paco produces for his clients a series of carefully detailed studies, totalling 10 forty to a hundred and fifty pages, filled with product-by-product breakdowns

Sports apparel for sale at a NikeTown store in Chicago.

© Cathy Melloan Resources/PhotoEdit

and bright-colored charts and graphs. In one recent case, he was asked by a major clothing retailer to analyze the first of a new chain of stores that the firm planned to open. One of the things the client wanted to know was how successful the store was in drawing people into its depths, since the chances that shoppers will buy something are directly related to how long they spend shopping, and how long they spend shopping is directly related to how deep they get pulled into the store. For this reason, a supermarket will often put dairy products on one side, meat at the back, and fresh produce on the other side, so that the typical shopper can't just do a drive-by but has to make an entire circuit of the store, and be tempted by everything the supermarket has to offer. In the case of the new clothing store, Paco found that ninety-one percent of all shoppers penetrated as deep as what he called Zone 4, meaning more than three-quarters of the way in, well past the accessories and shirt racks and belts in the front, and little short of the far wall, with the changing rooms and the pants stacked on shelves. Paco regarded this as an extraordinary figure, particularly for a long, narrow store like this one, where it is not unusual for the rate of penetration past, say, Zone 3 to be under fifty percent. But that didn't mean the store was perfect — far from it. For Paco, all kinds of questions remained.

Purchasers, for example, spent an average of eleven minutes and twenty-seven seconds in the store, nonpurchasers two minutes and thirty-six seconds. It wasn't that the nonpurchasers just cruised in and out: in those two minutes and thirty-six seconds, they went deep into the store and examined an average of 3.42 items. So why didn't they buy? What, exactly, happened to cause some browsers to buy and other browsers to walk out the door?

Then, there was the issue of the number of products examined. The purchasers were looking at an average of 4.81 items but buying only 1.33 items. Paco found this statistic deeply disturbing. As the retail market grows more cut-throat, store owners have come to realize that it's all but impossible to increase the number of customers coming in, and have concentrated instead on getting the customers they do have to buy more. Paco thinks that if you can sell someone a pair of pants you must also be able to sell that person a belt, or a pair of socks, or a pair of underpants, or even do what the Gap does so well: sell a person a complete outfit. To Paco, the figure 1.33 suggested that the store was doing something very wrong, and one day when I visited him in his office he sat me down in front of one of his many VCRs to see how he looked for the 1.33 culprit.

It should be said that sitting next to Paco is a rather strange experience. "My mother says that I'm the best-paid spy in America," he told me. He laughed, but he wasn't entirely joking. As a child, Paco had a nearly debilitating stammer, and, he says, "since I was never that comfortable talking I always relied on my eyes to understand things." That much is obvious from the first moment you meet him: Paco is one of those people who looks right at you, soaking up every nuance and detail. It isn't a hostile gaze, because Paco isn't hostile at all. He has a big smile, and he'll call you "chief" and use your first name a lot and generally act as if he knew you well. But that's the awkward thing: He has looked at you so closely that you're sure he does know you well, and you, meanwhile, hardly know him at all.

This kind of asymmetry is even more pronounced when you watch his shopping videos with him, because every movement or gesture means something to Paco—he has spent his adult life deconstructing the shopping experience—but nothing to the outsider, or, at least, not at first. Paco had to keep stopping the video to get me to see things through his eyes before I began to understand. In one sequence, for example, a camera mounted high on the wall outside the changing rooms documented a man and a woman shopping for a pair of pants for what appeared to be their daughter, a girl in her midteens. The tapes are soundless, but the basic steps of the shopping dance are so familiar to Paco that, once I'd grasped the general idea, he was able to provide a running commentary on what was being said and thought. There is the girl emerging from the changing room wearing her first pair. There she is glancing at her reflection in the mirror, then turning to see herself from the back. There is the mother looking on. There is the father—or, as fathers are known in the trade, the "wallet carrier"—stepping forward and pulling up the jeans. There's the girl trying on another pair. There's the primp again. The twirl. The mother. The wallet carrier. And then again, with another pair. The full sequence lasted twenty minutes, and at the end came the take-home lesson, for which Paco called in one of his colleagues, Tom Moseman, who had supervised the project.

"This is a very critical moment," Tom, a young, intense man wearing 15 little round glasses, said, and he pulled up a chair next to mine. "She's saying, 'I don't know whether I should wear a belt.' Now here's the salesclerk. The girl says to him, 'I need a belt,' and he says, 'Take mine.' Now there he is taking her back to the full-length mirror."

A moment later, the girl returns, clearly happy with the purchase. She wants the jeans. The wallet carrier turns to her, and then gestures to the salesclerk. The wallet carrier is telling his daughter to give back the belt. The girl gives back the belt. Tom stops the tape. He's leaning forward now, a finger jabbing at the screen. Beside me, Paco is shaking his head. I don't get it—at least, not at first—and so Tom replays that last segment. The wallet carrier tells the girl to give back the belt. She gives back the belt. And then, finally, it dawns on me why this store has an average purchase number of only 1.33. "Don't you see?" Tom said. "*She wanted the belt.* A great opportunity to make an add-on sale . . . *lost!*"

Should we be afraid of Paco Underhill? One of the fundamental anxieties of the American consumer, after all, has always been that beneath the pleasure and the frivolity of the shopping experience runs an undercurrent of manipulation, and that anxiety has rarely seemed more justified than today. The practice of prying into the minds and habits of American consumers is now a multibillion-dollar business. Every time a product is pulled across a supermarket checkout scanner, information is recorded, assembled, and sold to a market-research firm for analysis. There are companies that put tiny cameras inside frozen-food cases in supermarket aisles; market-research firms that feed census data and behavioral statistics into algorithms and come out with complicated maps of the American consumer; anthropologists who sift through the garbage of carefully targeted households to analyze their true consumption patterns; and endless rounds of highly organized focus groups and questionnaire takers and phone surveyors. That some people are now tracking our every shopping move with video cameras seems in many respects the last straw: Paco's movies are, after all, creepy. They look like the surveillance videos taken during convenience-store holdups—hazy and soundless and slightly warped by the angle of the lens. When you watch them, you find yourself waiting for something bad to happen, for someone to shoplift or pull a gun on a cashier.

The more time you spend with Paco's videos, though, the less scary they seem. After an hour or so, it's no longer clear whether simply by watching people shop—and analyzing their every move—you can learn how to control them. The shopper that emerges from the videos is not pliable or manipulable. The screen shows people filtering in and out of stores, petting and moving on, abandoning their merchandise because checkout lines are too long, or leaving a store empty-handed because they couldn't fit their stroller into the aisle between two shirt racks. Paco's shoppers are fickle and headstrong, and are quite unwilling to buy anything unless conditions are perfect—unless the belt is presented at *exactly* the right moment. His theories of the butt-brush and petting and the Decompression Zone and the Invariant Right seek not to make shoppers conform to the desires of sellers but to make sellers conform to the desires of shoppers. What Paco is teaching his clients is a kind of slavish devotion to the shopper's every whim. He is teaching them humility.

READING THE TEXT

1. Summarize in your own words the ways that retailers use spatial design to affect the consumer's behavior and buying habits.

2. What is Gladwell's tone in this selection, and what does it reveal about his attitudes toward the retail industry's manipulation of customers?

3. What is the effect on the reader of Gladwell's description of Paco Underhill's background and physical appearance?

4. Why does Paco Underhill's mother say that he is "the best-paid spy in America" (para. 13)?

READING THE SIGNS

1. **CONNECTING TEXTS** Visit a local store or supermarket, and study the spatial design. How many of the design strategies that Gladwell describes do you observe, and how do they affect customers' behavior? Use your observations as the basis for an essay interpreting the store's spatial design. To develop your ideas further, consult Anne Norton's "The Signs of Shopping" (p. 87).

2. In class, form teams and debate the proposition that the surveillance of consumers by retail anthropologists is manipulative and unethical.

3. Visit the Web site of a major retailer (such as www.abercrombieandfitch.com or www.gap.com). How is the online "store" designed to encourage consuming behavior?

4. Write an essay in response to Gladwell's question "Should we be afraid of Paco Underhill?" (para. 17).

Credit Card Barbie

READING THE SIGNS

1. Why might girls enjoy playing with a Barbie who shops rather than engaging her in some other kind of activity?

2. Do you think that having Barbie use a credit card to purchase cosmetics has an effect on the girls who play with the doll? If so, what are those effects?

JON MOOALLEM
The Self-Storage Self

The Great Recession emptied a lot of homes as their owners were cast in to the abyss of foreclosure, but in doing so it filled a lot of storage facilities with the piles of things — some of them mere junk, some of them priceless possessions — that most of us accumulate in our lives. In this feature article for the *New York Times Magazine*, Jon Mooallem visits some of the ordinary folk who have found themselves needing self-storage units in the wake of broken careers, broken engagements, broken marriages, or simply disrupted lives. And the things they hold on to, paying sizable fees to store stuff that often appears to be little better than trash, may be surprising—until we remember that our possessions are an important measure of our lives. Jon Mooallem is a contributing writer for the *New York Times Magazine* and is the author of *Wild Ones: A Sometimes Dismaying, Weirdly Reassuring Story about Looking at People Looking at Animals in America* (2013).

Statewide Self Storage spreads out near Highway 4 in Antioch, Calif., a suburban community between San Francisco and Sacramento. It's a phalanx of long, low-slung buildings separated by wide driveways and lined with red doors. The complex houses 453 storage units and is wedged between a car dealership and a Costco.

It was the last afternoon in May, and the sun seared all the concrete and corrugated steel. Statewide's gate opened, and a man named Jimmy Sloan made for the far corner of the property. Sloan, who dresses and styles his hair like James Dean, is a part-owner of the Harley-Davidson repair shop nearby. He rolled open the door of a 10-by-30-foot unit, the largest Statewide offers. It was his ex-fiancée's but still leased under his name, and packed with, among other things, a particleboard shelving unit, some wicker items, a microwave oven, a box labeled "Mickey's Hornet Neon," a floor lamp, a television and a wooden child's bed standing on its end on a desk. It was hard to tell how deep the inventory went. "She hasn't seen most of this stuff in six years," Sloan said.

For five years, he stored most of it above the garage of his house. But he had to borrow on the house to keep the bike shop running, and last year, feeling in over his head, he opted to sell the house and downsize before he fell behind and risked foreclosure. "Pretty much got out of that house at zero — didn't make a penny on it," he told me with the kind of ascetic pride that wouldn't have made any sense before our economically crippled era. Sloan's fiancée insisted he rent a storage unit and move everything over the garage into it for her. So he did. Then they split up.

He kept paying the rent on the unit for almost a year — $217 every month. But Sloan finally lost his patience and told her: "You know, we're not even together anymore. This stuff's gotta go." Everything here, he told me, was worth less than what he had paid to store it. "Storage is always a bad investment, any way you look at it," he said. The rent was her responsibility now. But the former future Mrs. Jimmy Sloan never paid Statewide. By now, it seemed likely that the managers would end up auctioning off the contents of the unit in accordance with state law. That was fine with Jimmy Sloan. But he wanted to get in first and make sure that his late father's collection of hunting knives and die-cast toy tractors, which he'd lost track of, weren't mixed in there. And so, to regain access, he'd just walked into the office and paid Statewide what was owed: $460. He'd counted out the cash unresentfully, like a man retrieving his dog from a neighbor's house for the 10th or 11th time.

"That stuff is Happy Meal junk," he now said, pointing to a see-through 5 Rubbermaid bin in the storage unit's brickwork of boxes. It was full of brightly colored plastic toys and a pair of hot pink sunglasses that belonged to his ex-fiancée's children. "The kids broke it, played with it once. It wasn't even for Christmas," he said.

Sloan had not started rummaging for his dad's knife and tractor collections in earnest; he was still pecking at the concretion's surface, not tunneling into it. But already he'd found a Marilyn Monroe poster and a souvenir road sign for James Dean Boulevard and set them near the door. They were his, from his old living room. He had forgotten about them and wanted to take them home. Soon, he peeled back the top of a huge bin. Inside, I could see a VHS cassette of "American Pie" and a black-and-white toy football with the logo of the Oakland Raiders. "Look at that!" Sloan said suddenly. "A Raider football!" He put it next to the poster and the road sign. Apparently it, too, was just appealing enough to hang on to.

The Self Storage Association, a nonprofit trade group, estimates that since the onset of the recession, occupancies at storage facilities nationwide are down, on average, about 2 or 3 percent. It's not a cataclysmic drop but enough to disorient an industry that has always considered itself recession-resistant, if not outright recession-proof. But the collapsing economy created an opportunity, and in some cases an ultimatum, for Americans to reassess the raft of obligations and the loads of stuff we accumulated before things went wrong. We've been making difficult decisions, and for a lot of us, that has involved rolling up the door of a storage unit and carting property in or out. The storage industry's expansion in the first flush years of this decade was both enabled by, and helped enable, the extreme consumption that defined America then. The people coming through the gates now are defining who we will be when this turmoil is over.

The first modern self-storage facilities opened in the 1960s, and for two decades storage remained a low-profile industry, helping people muddle through what it terms "life events." For the most part, storage units were meant to temporarily absorb the possessions of those in transition: moving, marrying or divorcing, or dealing with a death in the family. And the late 20th century turned out to be a golden age of life events in America, with peaking divorce rates and a rush of second- and third-home buying. At the same time, the first baby boomers were left to face down the caches of heirlooms and clutter in their parents' basements.

Across America, from 2000 to 2005, upward of 3,000 self-storage facilities went up every year. Somehow, Americans managed to fill that brand-new empty space. It raises a simple question: where was all that stuff before? "A lot of it just comes down to the great American propensity toward accumulating stuff," [industry veteran Tom] Litton explained. Between 1970 and 2008, real disposable personal income per capita doubled, and by 2008 we were spending nearly all of it — all but 2.7 percent — each year. Meanwhile, the price of much of what we were buying plunged. Even by the early '90s, American families had, on average, twice as many possessions as they did 25 years earlier. By 2005, according to the Boston College sociologist Juliet B. Schor, the average consumer purchased one new piece of clothing every five and a half days.

Schor has been hacking intrepidly through the jumble of available data 10 quantifying the last decade's consumption spree. Between 1998 and 2005, she found, the number of vacuum cleaners coming into the country every year more than doubled. The number of toasters, ovens and coffeemakers tripled. A 2006 U.C.L.A. study found middle-class families in Los Angeles "battling a nearly universal overaccumulation of goods." Garages were clogged. Toys and outdoor furniture collected in the corners of backyards. "The home-goods storage crisis has reached almost epic proportions," the authors of the study wrote. A new kind of customer was being propelled, hands full, into self-storage.

Consider our national furniture habit. In an unpublished paper, Schor writes that "anecdotal evidence suggests an 'Ikea effect.'" We've spent more on furniture even as prices have dropped, thereby amassing more of it. The amount entering the United States from overseas doubled between 1998 and 2005, reaching some 650 million pieces a year. Comparing Schor's data with E.P.A. data on municipal solid waste shows that the rate at which we threw out old furniture rose about one-thirteenth as fast during roughly the same period. In other words, most of that new stuff — and any older furniture it displaced — is presumably still knocking around somewhere. In fact, some seven million American households now have at least one piece of furniture in their storage units. Furniture is the most commonly stored thing in America.

The marketing consultant Derek Naylor told me that people stockpile furniture while saving for bigger or second homes but then, in some cases, "they don't want to clutter up their new home with all the things they have in storage." So they buy new, nicer things and keep paying to store the old ones anyway. Clem Tang, a spokesman for Public Storage, explains: "You say, 'I paid $1,000 for this table a couple of years ago. I'm not getting rid of it, or selling it for 10 bucks at a garage sale. That's like throwing away $1,000.'" It's not a surprising response in a society replacing things at such an accelerated rate — this inability to see our last table as suddenly worthless, even though we've just been out shopping for a new one as though it were.

"My parents were Depression babies," Litton told me, "and what they taught me was, it's the accumulation of things that defines you as an American, and to throw anything away was being wasteful." The self-storage industry reconciles these opposing values: paying for storage is, paradoxically, thrifty. "That propensity toward consumption is what fueled the world's economy," Litton said. The self-storage industry almost had to expand; it grew along with the volume of container ships reaching our ports.

By 2007, a full 15 percent of customers told the Self Storage Association they were storing items that they "no longer need or want." It was the third-most-popular use for a unit and was projected to grow to 25 percent of renters the following year. The line between necessity and convenience — between temporary life event and permanent lifestyle — totally blurred. "There's a lot of junk stored in our properties," Ronald L. Havner Jr., Public Storage's chief executive, told a symposium in New York. But really, there's no way of knowing exactly who is still [storing their possessions], what they've got locked up and how they feel about it — and, more important, how those complicated feelings might change if the psychology of the American consumer is substantially reshaped in a recovery.

Tom Litton, for example, still keeps four storage units himself, at two facil- 15 ities, all of them 10-by-30 units. I asked what's inside. "I have a canoe, I have a vending machine, I have a drill press," Litton began. His old lawn mower was in one. (He got a bigger, riding lawn mower when he bought a ranch in wine country.) "I've got some of my old clothes that I probably wouldn't wear anyway," he continued, and some trophies from college. "I also have some old cassette tapes that I produced." The cassettes are like audiobooks, he explained — tutorials on how to get into the storage industry and succeed. He made them before the storage-facility building boom ended a couple of years ago. "They didn't sell," Litton said, "so they're all in storage now."

One afternoon in late May, a woman slouched inside one of Statewide's narrow hallways, reorganizing the innards of her unit. She said her name was Elizabeth — no last name given, since, as she told me, "this is not a high-self-esteem moment." Most everything here belonged to Elizabeth's parents, who entered assisted living last year, and she needed to clear it out to cut expenses. She was keeping an eye out for particular family memorabilia, but otherwise it was a long, beleaguering purge. "Just stuff? Like my mother's kitchen stuff?" she told me. "Whatever."

Boxed haphazardly inside the closet-size space was, as she put it, 53 years of married life. An empty pill bottle and an egg carton lingered on the little bit of visible floor space. "I got rid of all the furniture," Elizabeth said, except her own drafting table, which, she pointed out, had wound up against the rear wall. She was an architect, accomplished but out of work ("Architecture is dead, dead, dead, dead," she explained) and was attacking this project with a conspicuously architect-ish methodology.

She had brought with her dozens of new, perfectly uniform white boxes, each bearing the Harry Potter logo in one of several colors. They lined the hallway behind her, still flattened. "When the books come out, there's just hundreds and hundreds of these boxes at every bookstore," she said. "I just went around and got them." She repacked and erected a tidy column of Harry Potter boxes in one corner of the unit. She turned a few others, tops folded inward, into a kind of bookshelf. "This was when *The Half-Blood Prince* came out," Elizabeth said. "They stack really nicely." She was going to transfer these boxes, full of the few things worth saving, into a storage unit she recently rented in a nearby town. That unit housed most of what Elizabeth owned. Forced to leave her parents' old house and unable to afford a place of her own, she had moved in with a friend about eight months ago. As far as the storage industry was concerned, then, all the contemporaneous chaos of Elizabeth's and her parents' lives ultimately amounted to a wash: one old unit was being vacated, one new one was being rented.

In fact, since last year, owners around the country have reported quickening rates of both move-outs and move-ins, making any occupancy rate — the industry's fundamental yardstick — feel kind of arbitrary, like the momentary averaging-out of a blur of activity, with no single, dominant trend (or maybe even logic) behind it. At Statewide, for example, those like Elizabeth renting smaller units — traditionally the backbone of the business — have been steadily leaving. "All I hear is, 'I can't afford it anymore,'" says Joe Dopart, who manages Statewide along with his daughter Amy and his wife, Evie, a retired schoolteacher. At the same time, though, Statewide's larger units — mostly empty for years — are now completely full. "Every single one, practically, has a foreclosure in it," Amy told me. Others were being rented by endangered businesses, like a coffee shop and a tea room whose owners were forced to shutter their storefronts in Antioch's struggling historic downtown and move everything into storage while they plotted their next moves.

The upshot, while this traffic runs both ways in the background, is that [20] Statewide has remained about 88 percent full — about two or three points lower than last summer, right in line with the national estimate. But that may obscure a more meaningful shift. By shaking up the composition of renters, and their reasons for renting, the recession could be quietly tilting the character of American storage closer to what it was originally: a pragmatic solution to a sudden loss of space, rather than a convenient way of dealing with, or putting off dealing with, an excess of stuff.

Of course, some people don't fit entirely into one category or the other. I found people who had been foreclosed on at most of the storage places I hung around at, and I met many more who were forced to walk away from places they were renting. Among them were two teenage brothers, Luis Jaramillo and Nikolas Aceves, in the city of Stockton, an hour from Sacramento, whose family was about to scatter to relatives' houses in surrounding towns. And Jason Williams, a 38-year-old father of three who was filling a unit with furniture before he and his family moved in with his stepmother.

On one of my first mornings at Statewide, Evie Dopart introduced me to Danielle Johnson, who worked at Dollar Tree and was also studying criminal justice. After her husband left to serve in Iraq, she couldn't afford the rent on their house in Oakland. So she locked everything but her clothes and schoolbooks in storage and moved in with her grandma. "It's O.K.," she assured me, "I'll get another one someday." She meant another house. That was a year ago. Her husband was now stationed in Kentucky, but if Johnson pulled out of school to join him, she would have to repay her student loans immediately and would end up with nothing. "Well," she told me, "I'm just going to finish, and I'll have my degree. He can wait." She seemed incapable of not putting a good face on the situation. "Actually," she told me and Evie, "it's kind of cool living with Grandma. Home-cooked meals are awesome, and no one makes them like Grandma does."

"Your family's Italian, right?" Evie asked.

"No, we're redneck, though," Johnson said with a big smile. "And I mean rednecks make some really good food. Gosh! My grandma's biscuits and gravy are screaming."

Virtually no one I asked, at any level of the business, took seriously the 25 idea that this recession would produce a sea change in who uses self-storage and why. In an industry whose freewheeling success has been so closely tied to the evolving character and prosperity of our society, it can be hard to even talk about storage's future without getting philosophical or patriotic.

"I really think there's a spirit that things will turn around," Jim Chiswell, a Virginia-based consultant to the industry, told me. "I believe that my children—and both my children are proving it already—they're going to have more at the end of their lifetimes, and more success, than I've had. And so will their children. I don't believe the destiny of this country as a beacon of freedom and hope is over. And I believe there will be more growth, and more people wanting to have things and collect things." Tom Litton put it another way: "The good news is that your age group"—I'm 31—"has the same propensity for accumulating crap that I have. You guys got introduced to it in college, and you actually think you really need storage. You see storage the way that we all see cable and Internet access."

Maybe the recession really is making American consumers serious about scaling back, about decluttering and de-leveraging. But there are upward of 51,000 storage facilities across this country—more than seven times the number of Starbucks. Storage is part of our national infrastructure now. And all it is, is empty space: something Americans have always colonized and cap-italized on in good times, and retreated into to regroup when things soured. It's tough to imagine a product more malleable to whatever turns our indi-vidual life stories take, wherever we're collectively heading.

But where are we now? Of all the storage units I toured, one sticks out as being most emblematic of this particular moment. It belonged to Terry Wal-lace, a 59-year-old veteran with white streaks in his hair and a broad, shaggy moustache who, when I stumbled across his 10-by-30 at a Storage PRO in Stockton, was sitting in a leather office chair, working at his desk under the open door, like a notary in a storefront. Some open mail and a Herman Wouk novel were pushed aside, and the desk was covered with stacks of quarters, the ones celebrating the 50 states. Wallace was sorting them, state by state, into empty prescription-pill bottles. "I've got 'em all," he said, astounded. "I've got all 50." Then he invited me in.

A folded-up Nordic Track leaned against the desk, and a bucket of fire axes sat behind him. (After serving as a helicopter mechanic in Vietnam, Wallace worked as a back-country firefighter in Yosemite.) But otherwise, the unit looked warehouselike. Stacked, labeled boxes stretched down either side of the deep, rectangular space with a snug but passable aisle between. This was everything Wallace owned, except the truck parked outside. A year ago, he was living in an apartment in Carson City, Nev., funneling the entire $1,200 he collected in retirement benefits and disability directly into his rent and alimony payments every month. "So I started doing a lot of credit-card stuff," he said. Soon he was $30,000 in debt.

Wallace hated living in a city anyway, "so because of my debt crisis and 30 my marriage crisis and everything, I moved everything into storage and I just live out of my truck," he told me, resting his hands on his gut. That was June 15, 2008. At first, he rented a second unit across the way and spent a few months sorting, giving away items he didn't need to an organization for homeless veterans. "You can call me homeless," he told me. "But I'm not goofing around. I've got money, but I just want to get this debt down."

It was like a cleansing: the storage unit cost about $200 a month. But aside from gas, truck payments and food (he had several boxes of meals-ready-to-eat stocked here), it was his only major expense. He had cut out rent, cable, phone and electricity, and purged all the unnecessary fees from his bank statements. For the last year, he had been camping a lot and driving around the West visit-ing ex-firefighter friends. He saw a woman in Antioch occasionally. "It's feeling good," he said, "and it's working. That's the thing: it's working. Debts are down to almost zippo right now." He figured he'd be done by Thanksgiving.

For a decade at least, storage has been a mechanism allowing Americans to live beyond our means. Wallace was using his unit as a center of gravity, to pull his financial life back within reach. He had even started saving, he told me, and was looking into a small condo in a suburb near Lake Tahoe. "It's not my style or anything," he said; he'd prefer something more secluded—bigger, and with land. "But I could do that." He missed sleeping in his own bed.

He also missed his music collection—and the books and rare coins he had collected. Also, his pins. "Little pins, like flag pins," he explained. "I've got veterans pins, and I've got Rose Parade pins, and pins that I got at fairs." He missed his stuff. "Hey," he said as I left. "I'll call you when I'm getting ready to load the truck."

READING THE TEXT

1. How does Mooallem's opening anecdote about repair-shop owner Jimmy Sloan's visit to his Statewide Self Storage unit set a tone for the rest of the selection?

2. According to Mooallem, how has the Great Recession affected the self-storage industry?

3. Synthesize in your own words the various reasons that customers rely upon self-storage facilities.

4. What does sociologist Juliet B. Schor mean by the "Ikea effect" (para. 11)?

5. What does storage industry consultant Tom Litton mean by saying young people have "the same propensity for accumulating crap that I have. . . . [They] see storage the way that we all see cable and Internet access" (para. 26)?

READING THE SIGNS

1. In a journal entry, contemplate your own and/or your family's possessions. If you needed to scale back what you own, how would you decide what to dispose of, keep, store, or sell? What would your choices indicate about your priorities and interests?

2. **CONNECTING TEXTS**   Write an essay in which you evaluate the validity of Tom Litton's claim that "it's the accumulation of things that defines you as an American" (para. 13). To develop your ideas, consult Laurence Shames's "The More Factor" (p. 80) and the Introduction to Chapter 1, "Consuming Passions: The Culture of American Consumption" (p. 71).

3. **CONNECTING TEXTS**   In "Everything Now" (p. 143), Steve McKevitt argues that our current consumption habits are "enormously wasteful: a huge and unnecessary drain on the world's dwindling natural resources" (para. 22). In an essay, write an argument that assesses the extent to which Americans' propensity for accumulating material objects contributed to that drain. Does storing items actually reduce the need to produce more, or does it serve to enable the production of more waste?

4. Despite the economic woes suffered by many of the people interviewed in this article, industry consultant Tom Litton remains confident about America's economic future. What is the basis of his confidence? Write an essay in which you demonstrate, refute, or modify his position.

STEPHANIE CLIFFORD AND QUENTIN HARDY

Attention, Shoppers: Store Is Tracking Your Cell

Between the scandal over the National Security Administration's global surveillance and the periodic flaps over Facebook's privacy policies, most people today are aware that their Internet activities are being monitored. But the news that we are being tracked via smartphone Wi-Fi signals when we are simply walking around while shopping in a brick-and-mortar store is something else again. As this report from the *New York Times* Business Day section by Stephanie Clifford and Quentin Hardy suggests, a lot of people aren't happy about it. "Way over the line," expresses one consumer in a post, ironically enough, to a Facebook account. Maybe that person is already receiving unsolicited ads for things that go over the line. Stephanie Clifford and Quentin Hardy are writers for the *New York Times*.

Like dozens of other brick-and-mortar retailers, Nordstrom wanted to learn more about its customers—how many came through the doors, how many were repeat visitors—the kind of information that e-commerce sites like Amazon have in spades. So last fall the company started testing new technology that allowed it to track customers' movements by following the Wi-Fi signals from their smartphones.

But when Nordstrom posted a sign telling customers it was tracking them, shoppers were unnerved. "We did hear some complaints," said Tara Darrow, a spokeswoman for the store. Nordstrom ended the experiment in May, she said, in part because of the comments.

Nordstrom's experiment is part of a movement by retailers to gather data about in-store shoppers' behavior and moods, using video surveillance and signals from their cellphones and apps to learn information as varied as their sex, how many minutes they spend in the candy aisle and how long they look at merchandise before buying it. All sorts of retailers—including national chains, like Family Dollar, Cabela's and Mothercare, a British company, and specialty stores like Benetton and Warby Parker—are testing these technologies and using them to decide on matters like changing store layouts and offering customized coupons.

But while consumers seem to have no problem with cookies, profiles and other online tools that let e-commerce sites know who they are and how they shop, some bristle at the physical version, at a time when government surveillance—of telephone calls, Internet activity and Postal Service deliveries—is front and center because of the leaks by Edward J. Snowden. "Way over the line," one consumer posted to Facebook in response to a local news story about Nordstrom's efforts at some of its stores. Nordstrom says the counts were made anonymous. Technology specialists, though, say the tracking is worrisome. "The idea that you're being stalked in a store is, I think, a bit creepy, as opposed to, it's only a cookie — they don't really know who I am," said Robert Plant, a computer information systems professor at the University of Miami School of Business Administration, noting that consumers can rarely control or have access to this data.

Some consumers wonder how the information is used. "The creepy thing isn't the privacy violation, it's how much they can infer," said Bradley Voytek, a neuroscientist who had stopped in at Philz Coffee in Berkeley, Calif. Philz uses technology from Euclid Analytics, of Palo Alto, Calif., the company that worked on the Nordstrom experiment, to measure the signals between a smartphone and a Wi-Fi antenna to count how many people walk by a store and how many enter.

Still, physical retailers argue that they are doing nothing more than what is routinely done online. "Brick-and-mortar stores have been disadvantaged compared with online retailers, which get people's digital crumbs," said Guido Jouret, the head of Cisco's emerging technologies group, which supplies tracking cameras to stores. Why, Mr. Jouret asked, should physical stores not "be able to tell if someone who didn't buy was put off by prices, or was just coming in from the cold?" The companies that provide this technology offer a wide range of services.

One, RetailNext, uses video footage to study how shoppers navigate, determining, say, that men spend only one minute in the coat department, which may help a store streamline its men's outerwear layout. It also differentiates men from women, and children from adults. RetailNext, based in San Jose, Calif., adds data from shoppers' smartphones to deduce even more specific patterns. If a shopper's phone is set to look for Wi-Fi networks, a store that offers Wi-Fi can pinpoint where the shopper is in the store, within a 10-foot radius, even if the shopper does not connect to the network, said Tim Callan, RetailNext's chief marketing officer. The store can also recognize returning shoppers, because mobile devices send unique identification codes when they search for networks. That means stores can now tell how repeat customers behave and the average time between visits. RetailNext also uses data to map customers' paths; perhaps the shopper is 70 percent likely to go right immediately, or 14 percent likely to linger at a display, Mr. Callan said.

Brickstream uses video information to watch shoppers. The company, based near Atlanta, sells a $1,500 stereoscopic camera that separates adults from children, and counts people in different parts of a store to determine which aisles are popular and how many cash registers to open. "Watching where people go in a store is like watching how they looked at a second or third Web page" on an online retailer, said Ralph Crabtree, Brickstream's chief technical officer.

Cameras have become so sophisticated, with sharper lenses and data-processing, that companies can analyze what shoppers are looking at, and even what their mood is. For example, Realeyes, based in London, which analyzes facial cues for responses to online ads, monitors shoppers' so-called happiness levels in stores and their reactions at the register. Synqera, a start-up in St. Petersburg, Russia, is selling software for checkout devices or computers that tailors marketing messages to a customer's gender, age and mood, measured by facial recognition. "If you are an angry man of 30, and it is Friday evening, it may offer you a bottle of whiskey," said Ekaterina Savchenko, the company's head of marketing.

Nomi, of New York, uses Wi-Fi to track customers' behavior in a store, 10 but goes one step further by matching a phone with an individual. When a shopper has volunteered some personal information, either by downloading a retailer's app or providing an e-mail address when using in-store Wi-Fi, Nomi pulls up a profile of that customer — the number of recent visits, what products that customer was looking at on the Web site last night, purchase history. The store then has access to that profile.

"I walk into Macy's, Macy's knows that I just entered the store, and they're able to give me a personalized recommendation through my phone the moment I enter the store," said Corey Capasso, Nomi's president. "It's literally bringing the Amazon experience into the store." Nomi then uses Wi-Fi signals to follow the customer throughout the store, adding to the information it maintains. "If I'm going and spending 20 minutes in the shoe section, that means I'm highly interested in buying a pair of shoes," Mr. Capasso said, and the store might send a coupon for sneakers.

If these methods seem intrusive, at least some consumers seem happy to trade privacy for deals. Placed, a company based in Seattle, has an app that asks consumers where they are in a store in exchange for cash and prepaid gift cards from Amazon and Google Play, among others. More than 500,000 people have downloaded the app since last August, said a company spokeswoman, Sarah Radwanick, providing information like gender, age and income, and agreeing to be tracked over GPS, Wi-Fi and cellular networks. Placed then sells the data to store owners, online retailers and app developers.

"I would just love it if a coupon pops up on my phone," said Linda Vertiieb, 30, a blogger in Philadelphia, who said that she was not aware of the tracking methods, but that the idea did not bother her. Stores are "trying to sell, so that makes sense," she said.

READING THE TEXT

1. Summarize in your own words the various strategies retailers use to track store customers electronically.

2. According to Clifford and Hardy, what use do stores make of the information gleaned by electronic tracking of shoppers?

3. What objections do technology experts voice to the electronic tracking of shoppers? What objections do consumers voice?

4. How do retailers defend the practice of tracking shoppers electronically?

5. What concerns does electronic tracking raise about personal privacy?

READING THE SIGNS

1. In your journal, reflect on whether you agree with Professor Robert Plant's claim that "the idea that you're being [electronically] stalked in a store is . . . a bit creepy" (para. 4).

2. In an argumentative essay, support, oppose, or complicate retailers' justification that store tracking simply levels the playing field with online retailers.

3. **CONNECTING TEXTS** Both Malcolm Gladwell's "The Science of Shopping" (p. 93) and this selection describe ways in which retailers use surveillance strategies to learn more about consumers' behavior. Write an essay in which you evaluate the ethics of such strategies. To what extent do the techniques described in these essays cross an unwritten standard of acceptable intrusiveness? Are there ways in which the public can benefit from these techniques?

THOMAS HINE
What's in a Package

What's in a package? According to Thomas Hine, a great deal, perhaps even more than what is actually inside the package. From the cereal boxes you find in the supermarket to the perfume bottles sold at Tiffany's, the shape and design of the packages that contain just about every product we consume have been carefully calculated to stimulate consumption. Indeed, as Hine explains in this excerpt from *The Total Package: The Evolution and Secret Meanings of Boxes, Bottles, Cans, and Tubes* (1995), "for manufacturers, packaging is the crucial final payoff to a marketing campaign." A former architecture and design critic for the *Philadelphia Inquirer*, Hine has published *Populuxe* (1986), on American design and culture; *Facing Tomorrow* (1991), on past and current attitudes toward the future; *The Rise and Fall of the American Teenager: A New History of the American Adolescent Experience* (1999); *I Want That! How We All Became Shoppers* (2002); and *The Great Funk: Falling Apart and Coming Together (on a Shag Rug) in the Seventies* (2007).

When you put yourself behind a shopping cart, the world changes. You become an active consumer, and you are moving through environments—the supermarket, the discount store, the warehouse club, the home center—that have been made for you.

During the thirty minutes you spend on an average trip to the supermarket, about thirty thousand different products vie to win your attention and ultimately to make you believe in their promise. When the door opens, automatically, before you, you enter an arena where your emotions and your appetites are in play, and a walk down the aisle is an exercise in self-definition. Are you a good parent, a good provider? Do you have time to do all you think you should, and would you be interested in a shortcut? Are you worried about your health and that of those you love? Do you care about the environment? Do you appreciate the finer things in life? Is your life what you would like it to be? Are you enjoying what you've accomplished? Wouldn't you really like something chocolate?

Few experiences in contemporary life offer the visual intensity of a Safeway, a Krogers, a Pathmark, or a Piggly Wiggly. No marketplace in the world—not Marrakesh or Calcutta or Hong Kong—offers so many different goods with such focused salesmanship as your neighborhood supermarket, where you're exposed to a thousand different products a minute. No wonder it's tiring to shop.

There are, however, some major differences between the supermarket and a traditional marketplace. The cacophony of a traditional market has given way to programmed, innocuous music, punctuated by enthusiastically intoned commercials. A stroll through a traditional market offers an array of sensuous aromas; if you are conscious of smelling something in a super-market, there is a problem. The life and death matter of eating, expressed in traditional markets by the sale of vegetables with stems and roots and by hanging animal carcasses, is purged from the supermarket, where food is processed somewhere else, or at least trimmed out of sight.

But the most fundamental difference between a traditional market and   5 the places through which you push your cart is that in a modern retail setting nearly all the selling is done without people. The product is totally dissociated from the personality of any particular person selling it—with the possible exception of those who appear in its advertising. The supermarket purges sociability, which slows down sales. It allows manufacturers to control the way they present their products to the world. It replaces people with packages.

Packages are an inescapable part of modern life. They are omnipresent and invisible, deplored and ignored. During most of your waking moments, there are one or more packages within your field of vision. Packages are so ubiquitous that they slip beneath conscious notice, though many packages are designed so that people will respond to them even if they're not paying attention.

Once you begin pushing the shopping cart, it matters little whether you are in a supermarket, a discount store, or a warehouse club. The important thing is that you are among packages: expressive packages intended to engage your emotions, ingenious packages that make a product useful, informative packages that help you understand what you want and what you're getting. Historically, packages are what made self-service retailing possible, and in turn such stores increased the number and variety of items people buy. Now a world without packages is unimaginable.

Packages lead multiple lives. They preserve and protect, allowing people to make use of things that were produced far away, or a while ago. And they are potently expressive. They assure that an item arrives unspoiled, and they help those who use the item feel good about it.

We share our homes with hundreds of packages, mostly in the bathroom and kitchen, the most intimate, body-centered rooms of the house. Some packages—a perfume flacon, a ketchup bottle, a candy wrapper, a beer can—serve as permanent landmarks in people's lives that outlast homes, careers, or spouses. But packages embody change, not just in their age-old promise that their contents are new and improved, but in their attempt to respond to changing tastes and achieve new standards of convenience. Packages record changing hairstyles and changing lifestyles. Even social policy issues are reflected. Nearly unopenable tamperproof seals and other forms of closures testify to the fragility of the social contract, and the susceptibility of the great mass of people to the destructive acts of a very few. It was a mark of rising environmental consciousness when containers recently began to make a novel promise: "less packaging."

For manufacturers, packaging is the crucial final payoff to a marketing campaign. Sophisticated packaging is one of the chief ways people find the confidence to buy. It can also give a powerful image to products and commodities that are in themselves characterless. In many cases, the shopper has been prepared for the shopping experience by lush, colorful print advertisements, thirty-second television minidramas, radio jingles, and coupon promotions. But the package makes the final sales pitch, seals the commitment, and gets itself placed in the shopping cart. Advertising leads consumers into temptation. Packaging is the temptation. In many cases it is what makes the product possible. 10

But the package is also useful to the shopper. It is a tool for simplifying and speeding decisions. Packages promise, and usually deliver, predictability. One reason you don't think about packages is that you don't need to. The candy bar, the aspirin, the baking powder, or the beer in the old familiar package may, at times, be touted as new and improved, but it will rarely be very different.

You put the package into your cart, or not, usually without really having focused on the particular product or its many alternatives. But sometimes you do examine the package. You read the label carefully, looking at what the product promises, what it contains, what it warns. You might even look at the package itself and judge whether it will, for example, reseal to keep a product fresh. You might consider how a cosmetic container will look on your dressing table, or you might think about whether someone might have tampered with it or whether it can be easily recycled. The possibility of such scrutiny is one of the things that make each detail of the package so important.

The environment through which you push your shopping cart is extraordinary because of the amount of attention that has been paid to the packages that line the shelves. Most contemporary environments are landscapes of inattention. In housing developments, malls, highways, office buildings, even furniture, design ideas are few and spread very thin. At the supermarket, each box and jar, stand-up pouch and squeeze bottle, each can and bag and tube and spray has been very carefully considered. Designers have worked and reworked the design on their computers and tested mock-ups on the store shelves. Refinements are measured in millimeters.

All sorts of retail establishments have been redefined by packaging. Drugs and cosmetics were among the earliest packaged products, and most drugstores now resemble small supermarkets. Liquor makers use packaging to add a veneer of style to the intrinsic allure of intoxication, and some sell their bottle rather than the drink. It is no accident that vodka, the most characterless of spirits, has the highest-profile packages. The local gas station sells sandwiches and soft drinks rather than tires and motor oil, and in turn, automotive products have been attractively repackaged for sales at supermarkets, warehouse clubs, and home centers.

With its thousands of images and messages, the supermarket is as visu- 15 ally dense, if not as beautiful, as a Gothic cathedral. It is as complex and as predatory as a tropical rain forest. It is more than a person can possibly take in during an ordinary half-hour shopping trip. No wonder a significant percentage of people who need to wear eyeglasses don't wear them when they're shopping, and some researchers have spoken of the trancelike state that pushing a cart through this environment induces. The paradox here is that the visual intensity that overwhelms shoppers is precisely the thing that makes the design of packages so crucial. Just because you're not looking at a package doesn't mean you don't see it. Most of the time, you see far more than a container and a label. You see a personality, an attitude toward life, perhaps even a set of beliefs.

The shopper's encounter with the product on the shelf is, however, only the beginning of the emotional life cycle of the package. The package is very important in the moment when the shopper recognizes it either as an old friend or a new temptation. Once the product is brought home, the package seems to disappear, as the quality or usefulness of the product it contains becomes paramount. But in fact, many packages are still selling even at home, enticing those who have bought them to take them out of the cupboard, the closet, or the refrigerator and consume their contents. Then once the product has been used up, and the package is empty, it becomes suddenly visible once more. This time, though, it is trash that must be discarded or recycled. This instant of disposal is the time when people are most aware of packages. It is a negative moment, like the end of a love affair, and what's left seems to be a horrid waste.

The forces driving package design are not primarily aesthetic. Market researchers have conducted surveys of consumer wants and needs, and consultants have studied photographs of families' kitchen cupboards and medicine chests to get a sense of how products are used. Test subjects have been tied into pieces of heavy apparatus that measure their eye movement, their blood pressure or body temperature, when subjected to different packages. Psychologists get people to talk about the packages in order to get a sense of their innermost feelings about what they want. Government regulators and private health and safety advocates worry over package design and try to make it truthful. Stock-market analysts worry about how companies are managing their "brand equity," that combination of perceived value and consumer loyalty that is expressed in advertising but embodied in packaging. The retailer is paying attention to the packages in order to weed out the ones that don't sell or aren't sufficiently profitable. The use of supermarket scanners generates information on the profitability of every cubic inch of the store. Space on the supermarket shelf is some of the most valuable real estate in the world, and there are always plenty of new packaged products vying for display.

Packaging performs a series of disparate tasks. It protects its contents from contamination and spoilage. It makes it easier to transport and store goods. It provides uniform measuring of contents. By allowing brands to be created and standardized, it makes advertising meaningful and large-scale distribution possible. Special kinds of packages, with dispensing caps, sprays, and other convenience features, make products more usable. Packages serve as symbols both of their contents and of a way of life. And just as they can very powerfully communicate the satisfaction a product offers, they are equally potent symbols of wastefulness once the product is gone.

Most people use dozens of packages each day and discard hundreds of them each year. The growth of mandatory recycling programs has made people increasingly aware of packages, which account in the United States for about forty-three million tons, or just under 30 percent of all refuse discarded. While forty-three million tons of stuff is hardly insignificant, repeated surveys have shown that the public perceives that far more than 30 percent — indeed, nearly all — their garbage consists of packaging. This perception creates a political problem for the packaging industry, but it also demonstrates the power of packaging. It is symbolic. It creates an emotional relationship. Bones and wasted food (thirteen million tons), grass clippings and yard waste (thirty-one million tons), or even magazines and newspapers (fourteen million tons) do not feel as wasteful as empty vessels that once contained so much promise.

Packaging is a cultural phenomenon, which means that it works differently 20 in different cultures. The United States has been a good market for packages since it was first settled and has been an important innovator of packaging technology and culture. Moreover, American packaging is part of an international culture of modernity and consumption. At its deepest level, the culture of American packaging deals with the issue of surviving among strangers in a new world. This is an emotion with which anyone who has been touched by modernity can identify. In lives buffeted by change, people seek the safety and reassurance that packaged products offer. American packaging, which has always sought to appeal to large numbers of diverse people, travels better than that of most other cultures.

But the similar appearance of supermarkets throughout the world should not be interpreted as the evidence of a single, global consumer culture. In fact, most companies that do business internationally redesign their packages for each market. This is done partly to satisfy local regulations and adapt to available products and technologies. But the principal reason is that people in different places have different expectations and make different uses of packaging.

The United States and Japan, the world's two leading industrial powers, have almost opposite approaches to packaging. Japan's is far more elaborate than America's, and it is shaped by rituals of respect and centuries-old traditions of wrapping and presentation. Packaging is explicitly recognized as an expression of culture in Japan and largely ignored in America. Japanese packaging is designed to be appreciated; American packaging is calculated to be unthinkingly accepted.

Foods that only Japanese eat—even relatively humble ones like refrigerated prepared fish cakes—have wrappings that resemble handmade paper or leaves. Even modestly priced refrigerated fish cakes have beautiful wrappings in which traditional design accommodates a scannable bar code. Such products look Japanese and are unambiguously intended to do so. Products that are foreign, such as coffee, look foreign, even to the point of having only Roman lettering and no Japanese lettering on the can. American and European companies are sometimes able to sell their packages in Japan virtually unchanged, because their foreignness is part of their selling power. But Japanese exporters hire designers in each country to repackage their products. Americans— whose culture is defined not by refinements and distinctions but by inclusiveness—want to think about the product itself, not its cultural origins.

We speak glibly about global villages and international markets, but problems with packages reveal some unexpected cultural boundaries. Why are Canadians willing to drink milk out of flexible plastic pouches that fit into reusable plastic holders, while residents of the United States are believed to be so resistant to the idea that they have not even been given the opportunity to do so? Why do Japanese consumers prefer packages that contain two tennis balls and view the standard U.S. pack of three to be cheap and undesirable? Why do Germans insist on highly detailed technical specifications on packages of videotape, while Americans don't? Why do Swedes think that blue is masculine, while the Dutch see the color as feminine? The answers lie in unquestioned habits and deep-seated imagery, a culture of containing, adorning, and understanding that no sharp marketer can change overnight.

There is probably no other field in which designs that are almost a century 25 old—Wrigley's gum, Campbell's soup, Hershey's chocolate bar—remain in production only subtly changed and are understood to be extremely valuable corporate assets. Yet the culture of packaging, defined by what people are buying and selling every day, keeps evolving, and the role nostalgia plays is very small.

For example, the tall, glass Heinz ketchup bottle has helped define the American refrigerator skyline for most of the twentieth century (even though it is generally unnecessary to refrigerate ketchup). Moreover, it provides the tables of diners and coffee shops with a vertical accent and a token of hospitality, the same qualities projected by candles and vases of flowers in more upscale eateries. The bottle has remained a fixture of American life, even though it has always been a nuisance to pour the thick ketchup through the little hole. It seemed not to matter that you have to shake and shake the bottle, impotently, until far too much ketchup comes out in one great scarlet plop. Heinz experimented for years with wide-necked jars and other sorts of bottles, but they never caught on.

Then in 1992 a survey of consumers indicated that more Americans believed that the plastic squeeze bottle is a better package for ketchup than the glass bottle. The survey did not offer any explanations for this change of preference, which has been evolving for many years as older people for whom the tall bottle is an icon became a less important part of the sample. Could it be that the difficulty of using the tall bottle suddenly became evident to those born after 1960? Perhaps the tall bottle holds too little ketchup. There is a clear trend toward buying things in larger containers, in part because lightweight plastics have made them less costly for manufacturers to ship and easier for consumers to use. This has happened even as the number of people in an average American household has been getting smaller. But houses, like packages, have been getting larger. Culture moves in mysterious ways.

The tall ketchup bottle is still preferred by almost half of consumers, so it is not going to disappear anytime soon. And the squeeze bottle does contain visual echoes of the old bottle. It is certainly not a radical departure. In Japan, ketchup and mayonnaise are sold in cellophane-wrapped plastic bladders that would certainly send Americans into severe culture shock. Still, the tall bottle's loss of absolute authority is a significant change. And its ultimate disappearance would represent a larger change in most people's visual environment than would the razing of nearly any landmark building.

But although some package designs are pleasantly evocative of another time, and a few appear to be unchanging icons in a turbulent world, the reason they still exist is because they still work. Inertia has historically played a role in creating commercial icons. Until quite recently, it was time-consuming and expensive to make new printing plates or to vary the shape or material of a container. Now computerized graphics and rapidly developing technology in the package-manufacturing industries make a packaging change easier than in the past, and a lot cheaper to change than advertising, which seems a far more evanescent medium. There is no constituency of curators or preservationists to protect the endangered package. If a gum wrapper manages to survive nearly unchanged for ninety years, it's not because any expert has determined that it is an important cultural expression. Rather, it's because it still helps sell a lot of gum.

———

So far, we've been discussing packaging in its most literal sense: designed 30
containers that protect and promote products. Such containers have served
as the models for larger types of packaging, such as chain restaurants,
supermarkets, theme parks, and festival marketplaces. . . . Still, it is impossible to ignore a broader conception of packaging that is one of the preoc-
cupations of our time. This concerns the ways in which people construct and
present their personalities, the ways in which ideas are presented and dif-
fused, the ways in which political candidates are selected and public policies
formulated. We must all worry about packaging ourselves and everything we
do, because we believe that nobody has time to really pay attention.

Packaging strives at once to offer excitement and reassurance. It promises something newer and better, but not necessarily different. When we talk
about a tourist destination, or even a presidential contender, being packaged,
that's not really a metaphor. The same projection of intensified ordinariness,
the same combination of titillation and reassurance, are used for laundry
detergents, theme parks, and candidates alike.

The imperative to package is unavoidable in a society in which people
have been encouraged to see themselves as consumers not merely of toothpaste and automobiles, but of such imponderables as lifestyle, government,
and health. The marketplace of ideas is not an agora, where people haggle,
posture, clash, and come to terms with one another. Rather, it has become
a supermarket, where values, aspirations, dreams, and predictions are presented with great sophistication. The individual can choose to buy them, or
leave them on the shelf.

In such a packaged culture, the consumer seems to be king. But people
cannot be consumers all the time. If nothing else, they must do something to
earn the money that allows them to consume. This, in turn, pressures people
to package themselves in order to survive. The early 1990s brought economic
recession and shrinking opportunities to all the countries of the developed
world. Like products fighting for their space on the shelf, individuals have had
to re-create, or at least represent, themselves in order to seem both desirable
and safe. Moreover, many jobs have been reconceived to depersonalize individuals and to make them part of a packaged service experience.

These phenomena have their own history. For decades, people have
spoken of writing resumes in order to package themselves for a specific opportunity. Thomas J. Watson Jr., longtime chairman of IBM, justified his company's famously conservative and inflexible dress code — dark suits, white
shirts, and rep ties for all male employees — as "self-packaging," analogous
to the celebrated product design, corporate imagery, and packaging done for
the company by Elliot Noyes and Paul Rand. You can question whether IBM's
employees were packaging themselves or forced into a box by their employer.
Still, anyone who has ever dressed for success was doing a packaging job.

Since the 1950s, there have been discussions of packaging a candidate 35
to respond to what voters are telling the pollsters who perform the same

tasks as market researchers do for soap or shampoo. More recently, such discussions have dominated American political journalism. The packaged candidate, so he and his handlers hope, projects a message that, like a Diet Pepsi, is stimulating without being threatening. Like a Weight Watchers frozen dessert bar, the candidate's contradictions must be glazed over and, ultimately, comforting. Aspects of the candidate that are confusing or viewed as extraneous are removed, just as stems and sinew are removed from packaged foods. The package is intended to protect the candidate; dirt won't stick. The candidate is uncontaminated, though at a slight remove from the consumer-voter.

People profess to be troubled by this sort of packaging. When we say a person or an experience is "packaged," we are complaining of a sense of excessive calculation and a lack of authenticity. Such a fear of unreality is at least a century old; it arose along with industrialization and rapid communication. Now that the world is more competitive, and we all believe we have less time to consider things, the craft of being instantaneously appealing has taken on more and more importance. We might say, cynically, that the person who appears "packaged" simply doesn't have good packaging.

Still, the sense of uneasiness about encountering packaged people in a packaged world is real, and it shouldn't be dismissed. Indeed, it is a theme of contemporary life, equally evident in politics, entertainment, and the supermarket. Moreover, public uneasiness about the phenomenon of packaging is compounded by confusion over a loss of iconic packages and personalities.

Producers of packaged products have probably never been as nervous as they became during the first half of the 1990s. Many of the world's most famous brands were involved in the merger mania of the 1980s, which produced debt-ridden companies that couldn't afford to wait for results either from their managers or their marketing strategies. At the same time, the feeling was that it was far too risky to produce something really new. The characteristic response was the line extension — "dry" beer, "lite" mayonnaise, "ultra" detergent. New packages have been appearing at a rapid pace, only to be changed whenever a manager gets nervous or a retailer loses patience.

The same skittishness is evident in the projection of public personalities as the clear, if synthetic, images of a few decades ago have lost their sharpness and broken into a spectrum of weaker, reflected apparitions. Marilyn Monroe, for example, had an image that was, Jayne Mansfield notwithstanding, unique and well defined. She was luscious as a Hershey's bar, shapely as a Coke bottle. But in a world where Coke can be sugar free, caffeine free, and cherry flavored (and Pepsi can be clear!), just one image isn't enough for a superstar. Madonna is available as Marilyn or as a brunette, a Catholic schoolgirl, or a bondage devotee. Who knows what brand extension will come next? Likewise, John F. Kennedy and Elvis Presley had clear, carefully projected images. But Bill Clinton is defined largely by evoking memories of both. As our commercial civilization seems to have lost the power to amuse or convince us in new and exciting ways, formerly potent packages are recycled and devalued. That has left the door open for such phenomena as generic cigarettes, President's Choice cola, and H. Ross Perot.

This cultural and personal packaging both fascinates and infuriates. There 40 is something liberating in its promise of aggressive self-creation, and something terrifying in its implication that everything must be subject to the ruthless discipline of the marketplace. People are at once passive consumers of their culture and aggressive packagers of themselves, which can be a stressful and lonely combination.

READING THE TEXT

1. How does Hine compare a supermarket with a traditional marketplace?
2. What does Hine mean when he asserts that modern retailing "replaces people with packages" (para. 5)?
3. How does packaging stimulate the desire to buy, according to Hine?
4. How do Americans' attitudes toward packaging compare with those of the Japanese, according to Hine?

READING THE SIGNS

1. Bring one product package to class; preferably, all students should bring items from a few similar product categories (personal hygiene, say, or bottled water). In class, give a brief presentation in which you interpret your package. After all the students have presented, compare the different messages the packages send to consumers.
2. Visit a popular retail store, such as Urban Outfitters or Victoria's Secret, and study the ways the store uses packaging to create, as Hine puts it, "a personality, an attitude toward life" (para. 15). Be thorough in your observations, studying everything from the store's bags to perfume or cologne packages to clothing labels. Use your findings as evidence for an essay in which you analyze the image the store creates for itself and its customers.
3. In your journal, write an entry in which you explore your motives for purchasing a product simply because you liked the package. What did you like about the package, and how did it contribute to your sense of identity?
4. Visit a store with an explicit political theme, such as the Body Shop or Whole Foods, and write a semiotic analysis of the packaging you see in the store.
5. Study the packages that are visible to a visitor to your home, and write an analysis of the messages those packages might send to the visitor.

JAMES A. ROBERTS
The Treadmill of Consumption

Once, "keeping up with the Joneses" was a neighborhood affair; now, thanks to modern mass media, it's a matter of "keeping up with the Kardashians" — that is, competing with the rich and famous in a never-ending spiral of status consumption. James A. Roberts's analysis of the compulsion to signify "social power through conspicuous consumption" is a sobering read for anyone who has ever gone into debt just to have a snazzier cell phone, like GoldVish's million-dollar white-gold and diamond offering. A professor of marketing at Baylor University, Roberts is the author of *Shiny Objects: Why We Spend Money We Don't Have in Search of Happiness We Can't Buy* (2011), from which this selection is taken.

Using material possessions to exhibit status is commonplace in today's consumer culture. We may not know our neighbors, but we feel compelled to make sure they know that we're people of value. As humans we rely on visual cues such as material possessions to convey our status to others and to ascertain the status of people we don't know. The quest for status symbols influences both kids and adults, although the objects we choose to display may differ with age. (Cell phones may be an exception that spans all age groups.)

For young people, cell phones are seen as necessities, not luxuries. A teen or even preteen without a cell phone feels set apart, on the outside looking in. This is in part because cell phones are a way to stay tightly connected with others (text messaging "blind," with cell phone in the pocket, is one of my favorites); however, cell phones are also important fashion statements and social props. For young people, cell phones are second only to cars as symbols of independence. Many teens see cell phones as an extension of their personality, and phone manufacturers and service providers, knowing this, give them many options to express their inner selves — ways to personalize their ringtone, change their "wallpaper," and customize their "skin," for example, as well as add many apps and accessories.

Adults, especially men, are also susceptible to the status appeal of cell phones. Researchers in the United Kingdom studied the use of cell phones after reading newspaper stories about nightclubs in South America that required patrons to check their phones at the door. Club managers found, the stories reported, that many checked phones were props — not working cell phones. To learn more about whether and how people were using their cell phones as social props, the researchers studied cell phone use in upscale pubs in the UK. What they found is most interesting: men and women used their cell phones in different manners. While women would leave their phone in their purse until they needed it, men were more likely to take their phone out of their pocket or briefcase and place it on the counter or table in view of all. Furthermore, like peacocks strutting with their plumage in full display to attract a mate, men spent more time tinkering with and displaying their phone when the number of men relative to women in the pub increased.[1]

As long as consumers attempt to signal their social power through conspicuous consumption, the levels required to make a visible statement of power will continue to rise. If person A buys a new car, person B has to buy a better car to compete; and then person A has to buy a boat as well—and so on. But once basic needs are met there's no additional happiness with additional purchases. The process of moving ahead materially without any real gain in satisfaction is often called "the treadmill of consumption." That treadmill is a barrier to raising your level of happiness, because it causes you to quickly adapt to good things by taking them for granted.

Research has shown that humans are very flexible. We tend to get used to new circumstances in our lives—including financial circumstances, both good and bad—and we make such mental shifts quickly. Economic gains or losses do give us pleasure or pain, but the effects wear off quickly. When our situation improves, having more money or possessions almost instantaneously becomes the new "normal." As our store of material possessions grows, so do our expectations.   5

Many researchers have likened this process to drug addiction, where the addict continually needs more and more of the drug of choice to achieve an equivalent "high." This means that acquiring more possessions doesn't take us any closer to happiness; it just speeds up the treadmill. I regret to say that there is a great deal of evidence supporting the existence—and potential harm—of the treadmill of consumption.

If the treadmill didn't exist, people with more possessions would be happier than those "less fortunate" souls who own less. But this simply isn't the case. The "less fortunate" are, for the most part, just as happy as those with more stuff. Big purchases and the piling up of material possessions hold little sway over happiness. Probably the most discouraging proof for this statement can be found in the study of lottery winners. An integral component of the shiny-objects ethos is quick riches. What better way to catapult yourself past your neighbors than to strike it rich with the lottery, right? If you foresee nothing but a lifetime of fun and sun for lottery winners, you're wrong. A study of twenty winners found that they were no happier a few years after their good fortune; in fact, some were even less happy than before they bought their winning ticket.[2] If the lottery can't pull us out of our current torpor, what hope is there for a raise at work, a flat-screen (plasma) television, an iPhone, or a new car (surely the new Lexus would be an exception)?

Consuming for Status

One important reason that consumers buy products is to satisfy social needs. Many of us spend a large proportion of our disposable income on so-called status items, and this trend is on the rise as we continue to embrace the shiny-objects ethos. "Wait a minute," some of you might be saying; "hasn't the current economic crisis stemmed the tide of status consumption?" My response to that question is that it never has in the past. Sure, we might mind our financial p's and q's during the actual crisis, but we have always returned to our profligate ways once we've navigated our way through the economic doldrums.

You need look no further back than the early 2000s, when the Internet bubble burst and the stock market tanked. It wasn't long until our spending picked up again, and with a renewed vengeance. That's precisely what brought us where we are today. Similar economic corrections in the 1970s, '80s, and '90s produced the same results: we tightened our financial belts only to loosen them when the clouds receded. It's really a lot like yo-yo dieting. Each time after we fall off the financial wagon we're a little worse off than the time before. Apparently as consumers we tend to suffer from short-term memory loss!

Pursuing materialistic ideals is a competitive and comparative process — hence the expression "keeping up with the Joneses." And today, with daily twenty-four/seven media coverage of the lifestyles of the rich and famous, our competition is no longer limited to our neighborhood. Bill and Melinda Gates and the sultan of Brunei have replaced Joe and Irma down the street as our points of reference. To achieve a position of social power or status, one must exceed this expanding community norm. Even the superrich aren't happy. There's always someone with a bigger home or fancier yacht — or, heaven forbid, a prettier wife. Yes, we even use other humans as chattel in our attempt to secure our position in the social hierarchy! The result of all this social posturing is no end to our wants and little improvement in our satisfaction, despite an ever-increasing consumption of goods. And Madison Avenue knows it: after price, status is the principal theme of most advertising.

Status consumption has been defined as "the motivational process by which individuals strive to improve their social standing through conspicuous consumption of consumer products that confer or symbolize status to the individual and to surrounding significant others."[3] It is our attempt as consumers to gain the respect, consideration, and envy from those around us. Status consumption is the heart and soul of the consumer culture, which revolves around our attempts to signal our comparative degree of social power through conspicuous consumption. If you don't buy into status consumption yourself, you certainly know people who do. They go by many names, but "social climbers" and "status seekers" will do for now. Climbers and seekers work to surround

Can You Hear Me Now?

I thought I had found the ultimate status symbol when I came across Motorola's new $2,000 Aura cell phone. The avant-garde Aura sports 700-plus individual components, a stainless-steel housing, and a front plate that takes the manufacturer a month to create. Add to this list the world's first handset with a circular display (great color and resolution!), a sixty-two-carat sapphire crystal lens, a multimedia player, stereo Bluetooth, and much, much more.

My amazement over Motorola's Aura was short-lived, however. I lost interest when I heard about the $1 million — yes, $1 million — cell phone from GoldVish (a Swiss company). The phone is made of eighteen-carat white gold and is covered with diamonds. Bluetooth? Of course. How about a two-gigabyte memory, eight-megapixel camera, MP3 player, worldwide FM radio, and e-mail access? Not to worry if a million is a bit rich for you: GoldVish has made available several other phones for around $25,000 — no doubt delivered in plain brown-paper packaging to avoid any embarrassment associated with buying a cheaper model.[4]

themselves with visible evidence of the superior rank they claim or aspire to. Most of us, to some degree, are concerned with our social status, and we try to make sure others are aware of it as well.

Status consumption began in the United States as a way for members of the upper crust to flaunt their wealth to each other. Over the past century the practice has trickled down to the lower rungs of the economic ladder. People are willing to go into debt to buy certain products and brands — let's say a $2,500 Jimmy Choo handbag — because these status symbols represent power in our consumer culture. Cars, for example, are an expensive but easy way to tell the world you've made it; there's no mistaking which are the most expensive. The problem is that nearly everyone else is upgrading to the latest model as well, so no real increase in status occurs — another example of the treadmill of consumption. Fortunately — note the irony there — our consumer culture, with its vast array of products, allows us many other opportunities to confer status upon ourselves. Media mogul Ted Turner put it this way: "Life is a game. Money is how we keep score."[5]

Status consumers are willing to pay premium prices for products that are perceived to convey status and prestige. A high-end Patek Philippe watch is a good example of a product that is — and is blatantly marketed as — a quintessential status symbol. One of Patek's advertising slogans is, "You never really own a Patek Philippe. You merely look after it for the next generation." Trust me; you're buying it for yourself. Despite the manufacturer's claims to the contrary, a Patek Philippe does not keep better time than the myriad of cheaper alternatives on the market; on the contrary, it serves primarily as an unambiguous symbol of status. To many people, owning a Patek signals that you've made it. To me, however, it sends the signal that you've forgone a golden opportunity to do good with the money spent so lavishly on a very expensive watch. It's a zero-sum game no matter how much money you make.

And, of course, Patek Philippe watches are only one of a myriad of examples I could use to document our preoccupation with status consumption. What about Lucky Jeans, bling (it's shiny), Hummer automobiles (maybe one of the more blatant cries for help), iPhones, fifty-two-inch plasma TVs, $3,000 Chihuahua lap dogs (think Paris Hilton), McMansions, expensive rims for your car tires, anything couture, Gulfstream jets, Abercrombie & Fitch and Hollister clothes (for teens and preteens) — even drinking water! No consumer product category has been left untouched. Even the most banal, everyday products have been branded — think $2,000 fountain pens.

Today, status is conveyed more often through ownership of status products   15 than through personal, occupational, or family reputation. This is particularly true in large, impersonal metropolitan areas, where people can no longer depend on their behavior or reputation to convey their status and position in society.

NOTES

[1]John E. Lycett and Robin I. M. Dunbar, "Mobile Phones as Lekking Devices among Human Males," *Human Nature* 11, no. 1 (2000): 93–104.

[2]Philip Brickman et al., "Lottery Winners and Accident Victims: Is Happiness Relative?" *Journal of Personality and Social Psychology* 36, no. 8 (1978): 917–27.

[3]Jacqueline Eastman et al., "The Relationship between Status Consumption and Materialism: A Cross Cultural Comparison of Chinese, Mexican, and American Students," *Journal of Marketing Theory and Practice*, Winter 1997, 52–66, 58.

[4]Darren Murph, "Motorola Intros Avant-Garde $2,000 Aura, Markets It Like a Rolex," October 21, 2008, www.endgadget.com, accessed October 21, 2008.

[5]Ted Turner quote, www.quotegarden.com, accessed November 15, 2009.

READING THE TEXT

1. Define in your own words what Roberts means by "the treadmill of consumption."

2. How have the mass media affected the desire for status symbols, according to Roberts?

3. What explanation does Roberts give for his claim that economic downturns have a minimal effect on the pursuit of material goods?

4. In your own words, explain Roberts's concept of the "shiny-objects ethos" (para. 7).

READING THE SIGNS

1. In your journal, explore what items count as status symbols in your own circle of friends (these do not need to be the sort of high-end items that Roberts
mentions but could be particular brands of jeans, handbags, shoes, or electronic devices). What appeal do these items have for you? Does acquiring
them make you happy? If so, how long does that feeling last? If not, why not?

2. **CONNECTING TEXTS**   Roberts assumes that the treadmill of consumption is irre-
versible, that we will inevitably "continue to embrace the shiny-objects ethos"
(para. 8). Discuss this assumption in class. If you agree, what evidence can
you advance to support Roberts's claim? If you do not, what economic or
social evidence can you find to refute his belief? Use the class discussion
as a springboard for your own essay on this topic. To develop your ideas,
you might consult Laurence Shames's "The More Factor" (p. 80) and Steve
McKevitt's "Everything Now" (p. 143).

3. In what ways does television, especially reality TV programming, encourage
the shiny-objects ethos? Select one show, such as *Keeping Up with the Kardashians*, and analyze the way in which it stimulates the desire to buy products that convey prestige and status.

PHYLLIS M. JAPP AND DEBRA K. JAPP

Purification through Simplification: Nature, the Good Life, and Consumer Culture

One of the greatest paradoxes of American culture is its simultaneous devotion to rampant consumerism and its celebration of rural
simplicity as the ideal model for "the good life." And as Phyllis M.
Japp and Debra K. Japp argue in this reading, these two contradictory impulses come together in the "voluntary simplicity movement." Selecting the Home and Garden network's reality TV series
The Good Life as an apt expression of the movement and subjecting
it to an in-depth rhetorical analysis, they find a similar theme in each
episode — people "who have left highly paid, highly stressed jobs in
the city and relocated to a more natural environment to live a simpler and therefore better life" — with a similar outcome: "Voluntary
simplicity . . . appears to reinforce dictates of simple living while
wrapped firmly within commodity culture, defining it primarily as a
psychological search for self-actualization in which nature becomes
a resource for purchase." Phyllis M. Japp was a professor emerita
in the Department of Communication Studies at the University of

Nebraska–Lincoln and was the coeditor, with Mark Meister, of *Enviropop: Studies in Environmental Rhetoric and Popular Culture* (2002), from which this essay is taken. Debra K. Japp is a professor of communications studies at St. Cloud State University.

The search for the good life is a major theme in human societies, from Aristotle to the present. In its current incarnation in late twentieth century America, the term represents dual and contradictory visions. Since the beginning of the nation, two major myths of the good life have developed simultaneously. The first is the belief in happiness and fulfillment through technology, the availability and acquisition of wealth and possessions, upward social mobility, and political influence. Existing alongside and countering this mythos has been the belief that happiness and fulfillment are found in a life of simplicity, one with the minimum of possessions, a life that does not seek wealth or influence but finds joy in connection to nature and service to others. As Shi (1985) notes, "From colonial days, the image of America as a spiritual commonwealth and a republic of virtue has survived alongside the more tantalizing vision of America as a cornucopia of economic opportunities and consumer delights" (p. 277). If these are the two poles in the definition of the good life, there have been many variations over the years, as each era has engaged the tension between having less and having more.

In times of prosperity and unchecked consumption, when it seems as if the "more is better" mentality has gained complete control, a growing sense of unease and guilt seems to draw the "less is more" rhetoric into focus and odes to a simpler mode of life appear.

In popular culture, the opposing visions of the good life are integrated into advertising, entertainment, and popular literature. For example, a Sears advertising campaign informs consumers that Sears stands ready to supply the "good life at a great price, guaranteed" as we view clothing, appliances, and other commodities supposedly essential to the quality of life. Alternately, the state of Nebraska's advertising slogan is "Nebraska — The Good Life," invoking visions of endless sky and bountiful prairies, a place where life is simple and nature revered. Note that however contradictory these visions are in many respects, nature in some form is necessary to their fulfillment. In the first version, nature must provide the resources utilized to manufacture the endless list of commodities now necessary to living the good life, the SUVs and fuel to run them, the lumber for bigger and bigger homes, the land that can be converted to golf courses and resorts where one can vacation in style. In the second version, nature is a spiritual and psychological resource, a retreat from the frantic pace of urban life, a reassurance in the healing powers of the earth. . . .

If the "more is better" mythos uses nature as raw material to develop and maintain the commodities necessary for the good life, the "less is more" mythos finds the real meaning of life in the human connection to natural environments.

Nature plays a central role in this vision of life. Shi (1985) observes: "Contact with nature, whether the virgin wilderness, the plowed field, or the Arcadian retreat, meant turning away from the artificiality of modern civilization to more abiding realities. God and goodness always seemed more accessible in the woods than in the city. Moreover, the countryside offered fresh air and a stimulus to strenuous activity" (p. 195). And Kenneth Burke (1984b) concurs: "The most basic support of all, the Earth, is perhaps the deepest source of reestablishment for bewildered sophisticates who, having lost all sense of a moral fountainhead, would restore themselves by contact with the 'telluric'" (p. 205).

While simple living has been a consistent theme since the beginning of ₅ the republic, it remains an abstraction that can be shaped to fit a variety of conditions and purposes. As Shi (1985) notes, "the precise meaning of the simple life has never been fixed"; rather, it has always been represented by "a shifting cluster of ideas, sentiments, and activities" (p. 3). Staple ingredients in the traditional recipe have included "a hostility toward luxury and a suspicion of riches, a reverence for nature and a preference for rural over urban ways of life and work, a desire for personal self-reliance through frugality and diligence, a nostalgia for the past and a skepticism toward the claims of modernity, conscientious rather than conspicuous consumption, and an aesthetic taste for the plain and functional" (Shi, 1985, p. 3). Thus the concept survives as both an "enduring myth" and as "an actual way of living" for at least a few citizens in each era (Shi, 1985, p. 279). In a technologically oriented commodity culture, we argue, this long-standing tradition of frugal living is transformed by an inescapable dependence on, and embrace of, products and services that have come to be defined as necessities of life. The reverence for nature is transformed into consumption as well, as the natural environment becomes yet another commodity, to be owned or appropriated as part of the simple lifestyle. Thus the rhetoric of simple living is inescapably infiltrated with the attitudes and orientations of consumption.

Burke and Environmental Rhetoric

Kenneth Burke looms as an important figure in many works on environmental rhetoric. He is well suited to be the patron theorist of environmental criticism for several reasons. First, Burke lived the life of an environmentalist, rejecting a life revolving around commodities for one closely in touch with the earth, the seasons, the rhythms of nature. Burks (1991) notes that Burke "seems to have despised consumerism and capitalism's promotion of it throughout his adult life" (p. 224). His lifestyle (Burke called himself an "agro-bohemian" with "Garden of Eden plumbing") testified to his rejection of consumer values and his need for engagement with nature (Burks, 1991, p. 224). Second, the environment is a theme that runs through his writings. Examples of the barnyard, the wren, the hapless fish with a faulty orientation, references to walking down the road, gardening, and the weather not only permeate his work but provided him inspiration to develop his critical perspective. Third, Burke's theory of symbolic action, his "tools" for deconstructing rhetoric, is ideal for discovering nuances in cultural artifacts. These tools are especially useful for the investigation of popular culture, for it is clear that what we desire, buy, eat, and wear, and where and how we choose to live are symbolic responses that articulate, support, and/or challenge the power structures of cultural institutions.

While Burke makes a number of specific references to the good life, the concept implicitly pervades his thought and energizes much of his terminology. Indeed, one could argue that a subtext of Burke's corpus could be the search for the good life, with attendant warnings about those motivational patterns that placed such in peril. Writing in the 1930s, Burke was traumatized by the Depression, by economic threats to the quality of life. By the 1960s he feared that nuclear war, the technology of destruction, could destroy all that we valued in life. He increasingly believed that environmental pollution, exacerbated and excused by consumer culture, stood poised to destroy any hope of a good life lived in tune with nature. Although he personally chose a life of simplicity, he was aware that the accumulation of possessions was the definition that most citizens embraced. Thus what is examined here, the cultural tension between the simple life of "less" and the commodified life of "more," is a tension also evident in Burke from *Counterstatement* (1968) to his last essays.

"Voluntary Simplicity": A Variation on *The Good Life*

A recent trend in contemporary popular culture is often termed "voluntary simplicity." This current variation on the theme of simple living is described in how-to books, films, television programming, and magazines. A recent bibliography of over 160 recent books, posted on a simple living Web site, includes such titles as *Circle of Simplicity: Return to the Good Life*, *101 Ways to Simplify Your Life*, *Six Weeks to a Simpler Life Style*, and *Skills for Simple Living*. Two simple living magazines have been recently launched, *Real Simple* and *Simplycity*. As *USA Today* observes in reviewing the magazines, "The simple life now comes with instructions" (Horovitz, 2000, p. 1A). Certainly there is much variation evident within this theme. Some advocate a complete lifestyle change and rejection of consumer values; others seek to downsize and de-stress within present circumstances. For still others, simplicity is a stylistic trend that determines which new home décor to purchase and what sort of vacation to take.

The vast amount of self-help literature surrounding this movement calls to mind Burke's (1973b) assertion that the people who consume such literature often have no intention of actually doing what is advocated. Reading is not the *prelude to*, but the *substitute for*, action; vicarious, armchair experience is less threatening than facing the decisions necessary for change

(Burke, 1973b, pp. 298–299). Certainly the widespread popularity of simple living ideas seems to have made little difference in the consumption styles of most of the population.

The theme of voluntary simplicity holds an especially powerful appeal for middle-class professionals torn between the need for more and the need for less as they try to manage the complexity of their lives. As with most calls for change, however, the desire for simple, painless maxims drives this massive quantity of literature. Irony abounds as self-styled experts in simplicity write books, circulate newspapers and magazines, develop Web sites, and travel the country presenting symposiums, consuming fuel and resources in the process, thereby reinforcing the importance of money, space, mobility, and other non-simple practices. The irony is reinforced as the media technology that has developed around the desire for wealth, that is the proliferation of materials, seminars, books, and guides advising people how to get rich, is now employed to help people simplify their lives. In the case study to follow, the television program *The Good Life* depends upon a complex media organization and a profusion of technology, including the equipment required to film a television series, although such is carefully kept out of camera range, rendering invisible its intrusion on the pristine natural settings in which the program is usually filmed.

Equally ironic is that this effort at simplicity must be *voluntary*, the result of a choice to renounce affluence and artificiality. The poor, who live lives of enforced rather than voluntary simplicity, are deprived of the moral value of such lives, voluntary simplicity being the prerogative of those "free to choose their standard of living" rather than the sordid poverty of those on the lower socioeconomic rungs of the hierarchy (Shi, 1985, p. 7). "Selective indulgence" is the theme of much of the current literature. As MonDesire (2000) notes, "The nostalgic urge for a simple life by and large emanates from people who've never had to duck a landlord on the first of the month, never had to wait in the rain for a packed city bus that rides on by, never had to slide the money for a half-gallon of milk under the narrow slot in a grocery store's bullet-proof window" (p. 19A).

Overall, the simple life appears dictated by personal needs and is framed almost entirely in the desire for fulfillment and personal growth. Converts do not renounce consumerism for religious reasons, for political dedication, or as a result of an environmental conscience. The quest is personal not political; secular rather than religious; self- instead of other-centered. As defined by the oxymoronic *Simple Life Corporation*, the concept means a journey, an awakening to self and one's inner needs, the removal of things that distract one from "finding" oneself, including not only possessions but activities, relationships, and duties. A *Cathy* cartoon strip neatly sums up the ironies. The script reads: "The simple life: Discard the day planner, disconnect call waiting, unplug the TV, cancel all subscriptions, say 'no' to invitations, clear closets and cupboards of everything but the bare essentials, and travel to a cool, quiet place that inspires possibility. The Mall" (Guisewite, 2000).

HGTV's *The Good Life*

A variety of texts could be used to exemplify the rhetoric of voluntary sim-plicity, for example, Internet Web sites, books, advice columns, sermons, and instructional seminars, for it is the interaction of these aspects of popu-lar culture that constructs and supports the ideologies of simple living. For this essay, a Home and Garden network (HGTV) half-hour series entitled *The Good Life* was chosen and the analysis included more than twenty episodes aired over a period of two years. Although the stories vary — there are for-mer lawyers, professors, journalists, models, executives, importers, even oil riggers — they are all variations on a theme. All articulate a core vision of what it means to live the good life. The stories, in fact, are strikingly similar despite the assurance that the good life is different for every individual. In these dra-matic presentations the cultural drama of "less is more" plays out against its counter, "more is better." The stories are introduced as examples of people ("people just like you and me" the narrator assures us) who have left highly paid, highly stressed jobs in the city and relocated to a more natural environ-ment to live a simpler and therefore better life. The verbal and visual dramas provide standard, mutually reinforcing formulas as viewers follow the stories of people who have changed their lives, following their dreams to the good life. Although viewers experience visual and verbal dramas simultaneously, in this essay visual and verbal dramas are each considered first as a sepa-rate domain of meaning, and then considered together to point out how each complements the other as they construct the meanings of *The Good Life*.

The Verbal Drama of *The Good Life*

The verbal drama of *The Good Life* is a classic example of Burke's dramatis-tic process of guilt, repentance, and redemption. This well-known cycle of cleansing, drawn from religious rhetoric, is appropriated by Burke as a critical strategy for understanding how both social and personal change takes place symbolically. In this drama, conflicts of motives construct hierarchies, which in turn create various sorts of guilt. These shortcomings, when recognized, require change or redemption. Burke argues this process as fundamental to human communication. Thus in any situation, a critic can profitably look for the guilt, that is, the shortcoming, inadequacy, inconsistency, need for closure, that is the impetus for communicating. In the inevitable socioeconomic hierar-chies, those with more are guilty of their excesses, those with less, of their lack of prestige or attainments; and each must seek to be redeemed via explana-tion and justification. In any social structure characterized by hierarchies, says Burke (1966), "Those 'Up' are guilty of not being 'Down,' those 'Down' are certainly guilty of not being 'Up'" (p. 15). These are not necessarily conscious emotions or explicit rhetorical strategies but are inherent motives or "patterns of action" that drive explanations, justifications, comparisons, identifications, divisions. In *The Good Life*, these implicit motives become an explicit motif or narrative form.

The Good Life features such salvation stories as its fundamental script. 15
Participants guilty of the sin of overwork at high-stress professions and refugees from frantic urban lifestyles repent of their erring ways and seek redemption. Nature is, as we will see, the primary agency of purification. Thus each episode of *The Good Life* turns on a conversion experience, as overworked suburbanites discover that something is missing in their lives and embrace change. At the root of their desires is a need for purification, through nature, from the guilt of consumerism. They repent, turn from their current way of life, and become new people, born again to a supposedly simpler existence, closer to nature, and implicitly, closer to God. Edye Ellis, the host and guru of the program, serves as an evangelist for this lifestyle change, exhorting others to follow in the footsteps of those whose conversion story was featured in this week's program. As with the self-help genre that infuses this portrayal, there is the "before and after" theme characteristic of any narrative of change (weight loss, addiction recovery, relational renewal, or political or religious conversions, to mention a few examples). The story each week follows the standard form of conversion testimony, from guilt to repentance to redemption.

Establishing guilt. The narrative begins with attention to the pathology of the participants' old way of life, by implication a "bad life." They describe their former lives as filled with stress, complexity, urban crowding, and long daily commutes, as they recount long hours on the job, mourn their disconnect from nature, and describe familial relationships in peril. The resulting self-diagnosis is described as a loss of self, identity, and meaning. They are no longer satisfied with the success they sought, the prestige gained, or the possessions accumulated by climbing the ladder to the top of their professions. "There must be something better" is the mantra of these seeking souls. For example, a former university dean tells of the day he discovered that he "had everything he wanted but didn't want anything he had" and vowed to quit his job and change his life.

Evincing repentance. The conversion always involves *risk* as well as renunciation. Penitents must pay the price by taking an economic or social risk, giving up something, either something *actual* (e.g., a high salary, social prestige) or *potential* (e.g., the chance for advancement). The "no pain, no gain" formula is reminiscent of the stories of risk-taking in pursuit of wealth. The definitions of risk, however, are comfortingly middle class, attractive to those who know they can somehow recover what may be lost. Thus they risk investing their savings in a business, in a move from a familiar location, by leaving their circle of friends, by choosing to live in a smaller space, or by making do with fewer possessions in their quest for something better. Although there is an attempt to maintain suspense, risk remains little more than a minor and temporary challenge to their middle-class values and identities. For example, a former journalist risks his savings to open a bakery in a small town, a

Texas landscaper invests his life savings to convert a rural hotel to a bed-and-breakfast, a Chicago lawyer abandons his practice to open a restaurant.

Seeking redemption. Once willingness to risk is established, the redemptive moment of the narrative occurs, a turning point of almost mystical quality. Some penitents drive down a country road and find at the end a location where they are "meant to be." Or they may discover a small town and feel instantly as if they were born there. Almost always this redemptive moment involves some contact with the earth, or with nature in some form. This mystical moment is also a pivotal point at which penitents can surrender and embrace the salvation of the good life or draw back from the risk and remain doomed to its alternative. Following the muse involves, above all, the search for a location where a good life is possible. Few manage the conversion without some physical move, most frequently from urban to rural, large town to small town.

Thus, communion with nature is essential to the good life, whether from a cabin in the woods, a farm, the rural charm of a small town, or even a tranquil garden in a suburban backyard. Also essential to the conversion experience is a new occupation compatible with the conversion values. Work in some form is essential; few remain idle. Entrepreneurship is especially attractive, satisfying the yearning to be one's own boss, control one's own time. Artistry is likewise a key to the good life (writing, crafting, achieving creative fulfillment, and frequently making money from the endeavor). The new occupation or avocation often requires some contact with the earth, from growing one's own food to using natural products to make beautiful and artistic creations.

A constant redemptive theme is the search for ideal relationships, for people with whom one can live the good life. Some converts bring intact families in need of renewal via simplicity; some seek change because of broken relationships and look for new, like-minded friends and/or life partners. Problems in previous relationships are linked to the values and practices of the old life (to date we have seen no programs about those whose relationships have broken up as a result of converting to the simple life). The search for self is paramount, however. As the old life is stripped away, as old locations, occupations, and relationships are replaced, the unique authentic self of the convert is revealed, hidden below the artificiality of the old life. The needs that were ignored in the complexity of urban professional life can now thrive and grow. Hidden skills and talents are uncovered: a professor discovers he is an artist, a former model becomes a world-class chef, others find amazing abilities to sculpt, create music, take prize-winning photographs.

Bearing witness. The final turn of the salvation drama is the evangelical responsibility of the convert. All participants devoutly affirm that they are now living the good life, lives of "deep fulfillment" as one declares. To a person, they express no regrets or nostalgia for the life left behind. The gains are far greater than the losses, the satisfaction worth the risk. They encourage others to make the same choice, again emphasizing choice and reinforcing the voluntary nature of their life change. The host completes the narrative with an altar call for conversion as she addresses viewers directly: "You too can have the good life." Like these inspiring stories, renewal begins "one step at a time."

Nature's role as commodity is evident in the consumerist attitude of selecting and owning an appropriate natural setting or backdrop for living the simple life. Control of life choices remains central; the stories turn on the volunteerist motive. The centrality of voluntary choice is significant. It implies that what has been surrendered can, if desired, be reappropriated. Participants stress they could have continued, even succeeded, in their former circumstances but chose to change their lives, always for personal and relational reasons. Thus choice implies a way out if the rigors of simple living are too great and smoothes a path back into the former lifestyle. The factors that support the ability to choose simplicity (money, education, social class) are also the very attributes necessary to success in a consumer society; thus these important qualities remain the property of the individual, to be played out as desires dictate. The sense of entitlement or ownership of nature as well as the implicit dependence on the attributes of consumerism continue to reinforce the orientations of the "old life," undermining the claims of conversion to simplicity.

The Visual Drama of *The Good Life*

In this analysis of the visual drama of *The Good Life*, another dimension of Burke's dramatism is used, focusing on how various elements are presented visually as the substance or grounding of the good life. Burke's pentad is built upon the concept of substance, the symbolically constructed foundation or basis on which various aspects of the drama are played out. Burke (1973a) identifies five major orientations that compel the human drama—scene, act, agent, agency, and purpose (pp. 21–23). Humans use symbol systems to constitute their situations and contexts, their identities and differences, their shared pasts and futures, their needs, goals, desires. In the process, they construct compelling explanations of the human condition—narratives of human agency, of the constraining power of natural conditions, of being bound or liberated by ideas, of individual desire or cooperative action that overpowers restraints. Burke (1973a) argues that these orientations and the tensions among them, e.g. the struggle between the power of will (agent) and the power of situation (scene), are necessary to any well-rounded explanation of "what people are doing and why they are doing it" (p. xv). This perspective seems ideal for exploring the visual drama of *The Good Life* because of the overwhelming visual power of the physical settings as the essence or substance of the good life. We concentrate on the primacy of the scenic in the visualizations of the good life but the other terms are ever-present and inevitably accessed in understandings of the visual drama presented in the program.

Nature as scene. The visual drama powerfully constructs the scenic dimension of the good life, both the foundational substance that grounds this life and the context, that is, the physical spaces or places in which the good life can be lived. Nature is a major component of both the grounding and the setting of a good life. But this scene is not raw and unruly nature. It is a nature ordered, controlled, and structured into the perfect setting for the values and qualities of the good life. This nature of pristine mountains, meadows, streams, and oceans is a nature without heat, humidity, drought, cold, damp, mosquitoes, snakes, storms, or blight. Thus the camera pans over beautiful views, bountiful gardens, wildlife, forests, landscaped lawns, even occasional swimming pools and guest houses. Nature here is a visual feast, with shots carefully chosen to exclude power lines, cellular towers, jet contrails, litter, dams, encroaching urbanization, highways, and other visual blights from human development. Likewise the cameras, trucks, and other equipment necessary to filming are carefully kept out of camera range, as noted above, ignoring the irony that their presence destroys the very tranquility they are attempting to capture.

As the scene of the good life is visualized, it is done in true Burkean fashion by referencing what it "is not" in order to substantiate what it "is." Shots of the "old life" of stress and complexity, pollution and gridlock, are juxtaposed with those of the "new life." Nature thus is instantiated as both the substance that generates the good life and the setting or scene in which such a life is possible. (Of course, by implication, the scenes of the old life become places where a good life is not possible.) 25

Style as scene. There is another component to the scene, however, overlapping and extending the emphasis on nature. If the good life is grounded in nature, it is also rooted in the stylistic, an element necessary to separate the middle-class good life from the inadvertent and unavoidable simplicity of poverty and lower-class existence. Burke (1984b) defines style as a moral dimension of symbolizing that involves doing or being "right," that is, appropriate to the situation. It is "an elaborate set of prescriptions and proscriptions for 'doing the right thing' . . . a complex schema of what-goes-with-what carried through all the subtleties of manner and attitudes" (pp. 268–269). Those scenes and agents imbued with style determine the "correct" use of commodities. While most folks dress themselves, set their tables, and decorate their homes, to do so with style requires a knowledge of the nuances of social correctness as well as a flair for originality within the bounds of appropriateness. Thus style is an option for those with money and good taste, setting them apart from those who must take whatever is available at a price they can afford.

In *The Good Life*, nature as chief commodity must be stylized, made appropriate to the scene. Just as the natural beauty of the outdoors is configured into an aesthetic backdrop for the good life, the interiors of the simple but tasteful abodes are charmingly decorated with arts, crafts, and fabrics that utilize nature in elegant and artistic ways. Edye Ellis, the host of the program and the Martha Stewart of simple living, provides an enduring aura of taste, elegance, and aesthetic appeal. Cameras linger on Edye as she poses with flower arrangements, room décor, gardens, beautiful views, and tasteful accessories that embed style into the substance of the good life.

"Doing" nature with style: Constructing agents. Thus, these two components, nature and style, combine to produce the grounding for the good life. The scene, however, requires agents appropriate to that scene, generated by and imbued with its qualities. As Burke (1973a) explains: "It is a principle of drama that the nature of acts and agents should be consistent with the nature of the scene" (p. 3). As the verbal narrative stresses, converts to the good life must experience a rebirth, a reawakening of appreciation for nature and their own artistic abilities. The visual drama chronicles this rebirth. We see photos of the subjects as children, growing up, engaging as adults in the "bad life," juxtaposed with shots of new converts enjoying the good life. The visual connection between "what I was and what I am" constructs a new identity forged by their identification with the scene.

As noted above, converts to the good life almost always discover hidden artistic talents that can only now be developed. Abilities to paint, sculpt, photograph, decorate, or do crafts emerge as if by magic, as the substance of the good life draws these forth from participants. They thus possess the necessary style to be appropriate agents in the good life drama, style being a latent quality called forth by their participation in the scene. We often see participants actually constructing, physically and metaphorically, their placement in the new location. Often at the end of the program, the camera integrates agent and scene, as it lingers on converts engaged in the daily routines of the good life, for example, walking in the woods or by a lake, taking in a natural panorama from a deck, working in the garden, creating artistic objects from natural products, tastefully decorating their homes, or taking photographs of nature. The visual message is: "This is the good life and we now belong here, we have grown from and are now situated in this place, like the mountains and trees that surround us."

The snake in the garden: Commodity as agency. The visual drama has another 30 component, however, one that challenges and ultimately overpowers the Edenic visions of the good life, infusing both scene and agent with the values of commodity culture—advertising. According to Burke (1973a), agency is the manner or means by which action is possible (p. xv). Advertising thus is implicitly the agency or means by which a good life is possible. As with all television programming, advertising is a vital ingredient of the program, and becomes part of the visual flow of meaning. The viewer can validly assume that the products advertised are by implication those necessary for, or at least compatible with, the good life. Television programming constructs a flow of meaning, evoking "subtle associations between aspects of the show and the commodity" presented in the commercials (Budd, Craig, & Steinman, 1999, pp. 153–154). Thus as visuals of nature are juxtaposed with repeated ads for luxury automobiles, vacation cruises, and investment opportunities, the program implicitly argues that expensive commodities, consumed with style, are essential to the good life. In fact, these commodities and the wealth they imply are instantiated as

Speed Bump

the agency or means through which the good life is attained, making this a life framed by, surrounded by, and energized by consumer culture.

Style therefore is the essential quality that links nature and consumer culture. Living with nature appropriately requires style, just as style requires appreciation of the finest commodities that only money can purchase. The good life, then, uses consumption (with style) as agency to bridge the fundamental disjunction that has always rested at the heart of this culture's vision of the good life, the term that connects the "less is more" and "more is better" versions of the good life. As visualized in this program, the good life apparently means being able to drive up to your rural abode in your new Lexus, booking a Caribbean cruise from your rustic living room when you need a break from simplicity, and taking it for granted that you have a right to consume both nature and commodities as long as you do it with style.

Interaction of the Visual and Verbal Dramas of *The Good Life*

Obviously the verbal and visual dramas are interdependent, both needed to define the good life. If one considers the verbal narrative the dominant narrative—and that is only because our tools for dealing with words are more familiar — the visual narrative reduces and expands, abstracts and concretizes the verbal. Together the verbal and the visual dramas reside in the tensions between stability and change. If the verbal drama is the story of change, of agential choice shaping, molding, creating the desired environments for one's salvation, the visual drama privileges scenic power, as stable, enduring nature embraces the prodigal, restores those who dwell therein to the timeless serenity of the universe. The incompleteness of each makes space for the other; in their contradictions lies satisfactory completion.

The verbal drama of choice includes no admission that the lifestyle of consumption being renounced bears any responsibility for misuse of nature. The visual narrative presents a static, ever-stable natural beauty, for example, pristine mountains, streams, and meadows unaffected by human excess and mismanagement. As noted, nature is visual artwork, purchased and now possessed via the risks taken. In no sense is it an active entity. This visualization of nature energizes the verbal, temporal drama of human quest. The eternal ever-present backdrop of nature becomes an object of desire in the temporal formula, placed back in eternal timelessness at the end. Each narrative (spatial and temporal) supports and constrains the other. The visual reduces nature to an aesthetic that complements the verbal drama's definition of nature as a choice of lifestyle, implying that a beautiful environment exists to satisfy human desires but failing to assign any responsibility for preserving that environment.

HGTV's *The Good Life* is one example, among many, of current visions of simple living. It is particularly striking because it embeds so many values in one compact package and presents so many seemingly oppositional ideas in a coherent verbal and visual narrative; this version of the good life provides vicarious atonement, offers the chance to reform without serious sacrifice. Its pathology is that it allows no serious economic, social, or environmental issues to emerge. It reduces complex, potentially tragic consequences of policies and practices to matters of individual preference, stylistic choices, aesthetic visions. Here the good life is about following one's own dream, discovering one's inner self. It is individualized as the freedom to "do what I want, when I want," as a number of participants observe. There are no stories of failure, no acknowledgment of social responsibility, no sympathy for those who cannot choose. It maintains the myth of infinite possibility for all, defining simplicity not as a moral alternative or environmental necessity but as a trendy lifestyle, allowing the viewer to forget that only the fortunate few can choose to leave a mess they have helped to create and maintain for a flight to rural, unspoiled areas.

By implication, the good life takes place in select localities, in rural, [35] sparsely populated, attractive, and relatively unspoiled places such as the slopes of the Rockies, the foothills of the Appalachians, the ocean, lakefront, or bayou, in quaint New England towns, in other rural and unspoiled beauty spots of the nation. The visual component strengthens the aesthetic and grounds it in nature in ways the verbal cannot. Most examples presented in *The Good Life* require money, influence, and taste as the converts attempt to create a lifestyle of elegance and beauty in a new setting. Great emphasis is placed on improving communication in families and relationships; nature is the mystique that makes this possible. The work ethic is retained but relocated to include contact with nature. Each episode ends with an altar call, "You too can have the good life."

Thus, the good life utilizes natural environments as a stage-set for a lifestyle that continues to valorize commodity culture. Nature, in fact, is the foremost commodity; in order to live the good life it must be purchased, modified, and controlled. Nature and simplicity must be managed with the same skills and dedication that former professional careers were managed. As Burke (1973b) observes, the vision of the good life was built around the

> ideal of the "live-wire" salesman, with culture taken to mean the maximum purchase of manufactured commodities. . . . Out of books, out of delightful moments in one's personal life, out of sporadic voyages, out of *vacational* experiences as distinct from *vocational* ones, people got visions of a noncompetitive structure of living, a "good life" involving gentle surroundings, adequate physical outlets, the pursuit of knowledge, etc., and the very slogans of the commercial ethic assured them that they were "entitled" to all this. (p. 248)

Conclusion

Voluntary simplicity in 2002, then, appears to reinforce the dictates of simple living while wrapped firmly within commodity culture, defining it primarily as a psychological search for self-actualization in which nature becomes a resource for purchase. It calls us not to change our ways but to dabble in self-fulfillment, while continuing on our present course of overconsumption and self-indulgence. By reducing the issues to individual conversion experiences, there is no need for national repentance, for a brake on conspicuous and wasteful consumption of resources. As this example illustrates, the simple life discourse is framed in and contained by assumptions and connections to consumption. It is constructed in the language of a consumer society. It is not a call for change but a powerful endorsement of the status quo. The cultural myth of success, the "divine right" to consume the world's resources, the unwillingness to acknowledge that the environment is not merely a backdrop or stage-set for our consumption of goods and enactment of trendy lifestyles, makes many current odes to simplicity, the "less is more" narratives, merely alternate versions of the "more is better" stories.

One program from one genre of popular culture—television entertainment—says little except when, as with *The Good Life*, its assumptions and expectations are deeply embedded in American culture. The program draws from and reinforces the powers of consumerism and the inevitable subsuming of environmental concerns to consumerist values. When these same assumptions, expectations, and values are evident across various genres of popular culture, they become an uncritical and unconscious dimension of our cultural reality. Popular culture thus implicitly assures us that we are entitled to a good life, whether one of economic complexity or voluntary simplicity, and offers us nature for sale, an environment to be purchased and used in the search for personal fulfillment.

REFERENCES

Budd, M., Craig, S., & Steinman, C. (1999). *Consuming environments: Television and commercial culture*. New Brunswick, NJ: Rutgers University Press.
Burke, K. (1966). *Language as symbolic action*. Berkeley, CA: University of California Press.
Burke, K. (1973a). *Grammar of motives*. 2nd ed. Berkeley, CA: University of California Press.
Burke, K. (1973b). *Philosophy of literary form*. 3rd ed. Berkeley, CA: University of California Press.
Burke, K. (1984a). *Attitudes toward history*. 4th ed. Berkeley, CA: University of California Press.
Burke, K. (1984b). *Permanence and change*. 4th ed. Berkeley, CA: University of California Press.
Burks, D. (1991). Kenneth Burke: The agro-bohemian "Marxoid." *Communication Studies, 42,* 219–233.
Dudgeon, C. (Executive producer). *The Good Life*. Knoxville, TN: Home and Garden Television (HGTV). Retrieved from http://www.hgtv.com
Guisewite, C. (2000, June 24). *Cathy* [Cartoon]. *Omaha World Herald*.
Horovitz, B. (2000, June 1). Simplesells: Chic back-to-basics explosion carries hefty load of irony. *USA Today,* p.1A + .
MonDesire, D. (2000, June 9). How hard should we strive for simple life? *USA Today,* p. 19A.
Shi, D. E. (1985). *The simple life: Plain living and high thinking in American culture*. New York, NY: Oxford.

READING THE TEXT

1. What are the two major myths of the good life in American culture, according to Japp and Japp? What belief do Americans hold that contradicts the two major myths?

2. Summarize in your own words rhetorician Kenneth Burke's theory of symbolic action and how it applies to the HGTV program *The Good Life*.

3. How does American popular culture reflect, or mediate, the contradictory tendencies in Americans' views of the good life, according to the article?

4. What is the "voluntary simplicity movement," and how is it represented in *The Good Life*?

5. What are the "visual" and "verbal" dramas of *The Good Life*?

READING THE SIGNS

1. Visit a site such as TVrage.com or Hulu that archives TV programs, and watch a later episode of *The Good Life*. In an essay, analyze the narrative the episode tells about the featured participant. To what extent does it conform to the salvation formula that Japp and Japp claim is typical of the show? If it deviates, how does it do so, and what alternative narrative is created for the participant?

2. Analyze a magazine such as *Real Simple* or a TV program such as *Simple Living with Wanda Urbanska*. To what extent does your subject "reinforce the dictates of simple living while wrapped firmly within commodity culture" (para. 37)?

3. Read Jon Krakauer's *Into the Wild*, which narrates the ultimately fatal journey of Chris McCandless into the Alaska wilderness, and write an essay that analyzes the protagonist's experiment with "voluntary simplicity." Does he engage in a genuine rejection of material culture and embrace of nature or, as some critics have noted, does he turn living in nature into something of a self-indulgent competitive sport?

4. Write an analysis of the contradictions you find in green marketing campaigns that present the possession of consumer goods as ways to achieve the simple life. To develop your ideas, consult Julia B. Corbett's "A Faint Green Sell: Advertising and the Natural World" (p. 235).

5. Compare and contrast Japp and Japp's critique of the voluntary simplicity movement's use of nature with Thomas Frank's analysis of the countercultural pose of much current advertising (see "Commodify Your Dissent," p. 150). In what ways do the authors see nature and countercultural beliefs as being co-opted by consumer culture?

6. When describing the convention of "style as scene," Japp and Japp claim that "while most folks dress themselves, set their tables, and decorate their homes, to do so with style requires a knowledge of the nuances of social correctness as well as a flair for originality within the bounds of appropriateness" (para. 26). Analyze an issue of *Martha Stewart Living*. To what extent does the publication replicate Japp and Japp's indictment of media that simply present a visual drama of the good life?

STEVE McKEVITT

Everything Now

Paradoxically, although today people in developed societies have more consumer choices, 24/7 access to a global cornucopia of goods, and (thanks to generous credit availability) more sheer *stuff*, many report feelings of unhappiness, especially when it comes to the stress triggered by working to pay for all that stuff. But while work indeed contributes to that unhappiness, Steve McKevitt argues in this selection that much of it can be credited to massive marketing campaigns designed to convince us that if we only buy this product or that service, we will be happy. Combining psychology with the technological ability to bombard us around the clock with clever advertisements designed to convince us that our every *want* is actually a *need*, current marketing strategies keep us unhappy in order to move the goods. A marketing consultant and author whose books include *City Slackers* (2006) and *Everything Now* (2013, from where this selection comes), McKevitt is chairman of Golden, "an ideas agency."

> You can never get enough of what you don't need to make you happy.
> — ERIC HOFFER, philosopher and social writer

What do you want?

Whether you are looking for motor cars, mobile phones, holidays or simply what to have for lunch, the range of options available to you can be genuinely overwhelming. With nothing more than a broadband Internet connection, you can enjoy immediate and unfettered access to millions of books, newspapers and magazines; thousands of movies and TV shows and almost the entire canon of recorded music. Many lifetimes' worth of content, all of it available at the click of a mouse. Whatever it is you want, you can have it. Everything Now.

We are living through a time of endless choices and unlimited convenience. We now take for granted the ubiquity of goods and services that can be instantly accessed, but the 24/7 society we live in — where everything is available practically all the time — is a recent achievement. Everything Now did not happen by chance or overnight. It is the culmination of a deliberate and concerted 30-year drive to increase choice and convenience for everyone. Those of us lucky enough to be living in the developed world today are, on average, healthier, wealthier, longer lived and better educated than at any other point in history. Our *needs* have been fulfilled and so, for the first time ever, we have an economy that is almost entirely devoted to the business of satisfying our *wants* instead. The question is: with so much effort dedicated to giving us what we want, why aren't we happier or, at the very least, worrying less and enjoying life more? . . .

People do not buy technology, what they buy is functionality. Consumers do not purchase stereos, DVD players and mobile phones because they want the items for themselves, but because they want to listen to music, watch movies, and keep in touch with family and friends. The same is true of computers. But in this case there is much more functionality, so people end up buying computers for many different reasons—to work, play games, browse the Internet, edit movies, create magazines and so on. To do this they need to run software. To gain a competitive edge within a crowded market, software publishers were creating products crammed with features and optimised to run most effectively on the fastest machines available at the time of their release.

This was especially true for computer games, which, because of their rich graphics, placed the heaviest demands upon the hardware. If consumers wanted to derive the most functionality from the latest software—in the case of my games, experience the smoothest animation, highest resolution and most spectacular visuals—they would need the fastest computer, which would almost certainly contain one of [Intel's] microprocessors.

However, as Intel's business model demonstrated, it would only be the fastest computer for a maximum of three months. The pace of this process was so rapid that [Intel VP of Marketing] Manfred could be confident that even the best computer available today would not be able to cope with the latest software being published three years hence. The pursuit of functionality—our games—could be used to force consumers to invest in Intel's new technology. Intel was not only creating faster microprocessors, it was also creating the demand for them.

Intel may be a master of the art, but it is certainly not the only company in the business of inventing wants as well as products. Manfred is correct: wants are very different to needs. "Want versus Need" is one of the most basic concepts in economics. A need is something we have to have—like food, sleep or water. A want is something we would like to have—like a Big Mac, a Tempur mattress or a bottle of Evian. You might think that you cannot survive without your BlackBerry or your BMW, but you can. It might even be the case that you do need a phone to carry out your work and a car to get around in, but what brand it is and, to a large extent, what features it has are really just wants.

Needs are rational and permanent. We have always needed—and will always need—food, water and shelter. The solution may change, but the problem is always the same, you can't create new needs. Wants, on the other hand, are emotional, ephemeral and ever changing. Just because you want something today doesn't mean you will want it tomorrow, always want it, or ever want it again. For example, back in 1981, everybody wanted a Rubik's Cube, it was the world's most popular toy, but it is unlikely to ever repeat this feat in the future. This transience creates an opportunity for anyone who is trying to sell us something—whether that's a product, a service or even an idea—and they can invent wants for us as well as the means to assuage them.

In 1976, a year with one of the hottest summers on record, almost nobody drank bottled water in the UK (unless they went on holiday "abroad"); we spent less than £200,000 on just 3 million litres of the stuff. Today, each of us drinks an average of 33 litres per year, spending a total of £1.4 billion. We do this despite the fact that tap water is essentially an identical product that is as widely and freely available as it was in 1976.

Manufacturing wants for things like bottled water is what keeps us in 10
a permanent state of dissatisfaction, because only by making us unhappy
with what we have today is it possible to persuade us to pay for something
that will make us happy tomorrow. In the case of bottled water, its success
depended on us becoming dissatisfied with drinking tap water. The basis
of this dissatisfaction is usually emotional rather than rational, it doesn't
require hard evidence—all that is needed, perhaps, is promoting a notion
that bottled water tastes better or using language to suggest it is somehow
healthier than tap water. In Intel's case, the continual introduction of new
microprocessors means that purchasing a new computer will only briefly
appease the existing want for maximum functionality. Likewise, once upon
a time, you may have yearned for an iPhone Mk1, but now, several upgrades
later with that model nothing more than a distant memory, you've become
dissatisfied with your current handset, and can't wait for the opportunity to
forsake it for next year's version. It is simple and, as ever-increasing sales of
bottled water, personal computers and mobile phones testifies, it has been
extremely effective.

Maslow's Hierarchy of Needs is a theory of developmental psychology
which describes the phases of human growth. It is often portrayed as a pyramid, with the biggest, most basic needs at the bottom (air, food, water), then
safety issues (health, employment, property), moving up through relationships
and esteem (achievement, confidence, respect), reaching self-actualisation at
the top (morality, creativity and problem solving).

Maslow believed that these needs play a major role in motivating behav-
iours in Western societies where the individual is paramount. Basic biological, physiological and safety needs will always take priority over the need
for respect or self-expression, but once they have been satisfied, the needs
higher up the pyramid become increasingly important. As one set of needs is
assuaged, focus moves to those on the next level up the pyramid. Everything
Now is an extreme example of an individualistic society, hence our tendency
is to be egocentric, focusing on the improvement of one's self and circumstances, with self-actualisation at the zenith.

For example, tackling obesity and associated issues of low self-esteem is
a priority in the UK and USA, where food is cheap and plentiful, but in places
where food is expensive and in short supply, these problems simply don't
exist. There are few branches of Weight Watchers in the Third World and no
need, at present, for Western governments to develop famine-relief strategies
to feed their own people. . . .

Yes we are still innovating, but we are doing so in small steps, not the
giant leaps we once were. [John] Smart makes a very interesting observation
about the areas in which innovation is taking place:

> Certain types of innovation saturation might now appear to be occur-
> ring because our accelerating technological productivity is beginning to
> intersect with an effectively fixed number of human needs . . . We may
> observe that as the world develops and we all climb higher on Maslow's

Figure 1. Maslow's Hierarchy of Needs

hierarchy of relatively fixed needs, those who already have sufficient housing, transportation, etc., are now pursuing innovations on the most abstract, virtual, and difficult-to-quantify levels, like social interaction, status, entertainment, and self-esteem.

It is because we don't really need anything anymore that the focus of inno-   15 vation has itself turned to addressing our wants instead. As Maslow demonstrates, once needs are taken care of, wants can be just as powerful drivers. This is all well and good if we know what it is that we want, but most of the time we don't. Nor do the things we want necessarily have to be good, either for ourselves or for the rest of society. Some people want to smoke, to take drugs or, as a more extreme example, to commit crimes. Needs require rational decision-making. However, the evidence is that decisions about wants are driven entirely by our emotions and these feelings can be so strong that they cause us to overrule or simply ignore rational objections. This combination makes us highly suggestible: easily persuaded by things that engage our sympathies, willing to be told what it is that we want, and then to act upon that information, regardless of the consequences. We should also consider that the people empathising with us — the ones engaging our sympathies and then telling us what it is that we want — are often trying to hawk us a solution as well.

You can find examples of this everywhere. Just look at an everyday product, like toothpaste. We need toothpaste to ensure our teeth and gums remain healthy. On average, people with healthy teeth live longer and tend to lead healthier lives than those who lose their teeth prematurely. Visit your local supermarket and you'll find around 120 different brands of toothpaste to choose from. Some promise fresher breath, others whiter teeth, others healthier gums. There will be brands for sensitive teeth, for people with fillings or cavities, there will be gels, pastes and powders, but despite this welter of options, each and every one will be virtually identical chemically; essentially the same thing, packaged and positioned in dozens of slightly different ways. The same is true whatever the category, from soap to soap operas. Scratch beneath the surface of Everything Now's apparently endless choice at any point and what you will find is hundreds of virtually identical products. Toothpaste is really just toothpaste.

Nobody needs to have 120 different varieties of intrinsically indistinguishable products like toothpaste or soap to choose from, and you may argue that nobody wants them either, but these "choices" are offered in a much more subtle way. Where once there was a category called soap, now there are soaps for dry skin, greasy skin, sensitive skin; there is strong soap, gentle soap; soap in a bar, in a bottle, in a jar or from a dispenser; liquid soap, foam soap, hard soap, scented soap, simple soap, plain soap, soft soap and soap on a rope. Now all you have to do is choose one.

Things can't go on like this. And that's not some liberal cri de coeur, I mean it literally: they can't. Whatever your views are on climate change, you have to at least concede that we are not going to be able to rely on fossil fuels forever. If we carry on at the current rate of consumption—some 85 million barrels of oil a day, burning through the fossil record at the rate of 20 million years, every year—then we're going to run out sooner rather than later. Well, I'm all for screwing in low-energy light bulbs, buying locally produced peas and only drinking European wine, if that's what it takes to save the planet, yet I can't help thinking that, in the face of the thousands of freight carriers that are making their way to these shores slowly, but inexorably, from China and India to deliver their precious cargoes of Christmas cracker gifts and trinkets, these Herculean efforts might not suffice!

And even if we do discover substantial new reserves of oil and gas to ensure we can be supplied with miniature screwdriver sets and mini playing cards for the next 200 years, there still aren't enough resources for everyone to live as wastefully as we do in the developed world. We are currently using 1.5 times the world's gross annual product every year, which requires us to draw on an inevitably limited and dwindling stockpile of natural resources to make up the shortfall. But even as we burn through 50 percent more than we produce, over-fishing, over-farming, over-watering and deforesting as we go, competition for these diminishing resources is increasing as the huge economies in Brazil, Russia, India and China (the so-called BRIC nations) and those in the rest of Southern Asia and South America become stronger. This means that even if those miniature screwdriver sets are still available, they're going to be a lot more expensive. And I do mean a lot more. Economists expect food prices to double in the next 20 years in real terms. Remember, this is the case even if we ignore climate change, which, I'll concede, is a bit like ignoring a herd of elephants in your living room. . . .

The world we live in today no longer needs either stone knappers or rocket-scientists. It requires people to work out how the music industry can make money from file sharing; how Sunday newspaper executives can convince new readers that 500,000 words of content is worth the price of a cup of coffee; how TV channels can survive without relying on advertising revenue. It needs marketers and creative thinkers who can persuade millions of other people that This Brand is exclusively for them, that the next version of this film/TV/video game franchise is really the best one ever, or that some website helps us get closer to the things we love. It needs people who can develop products that are slightly better than the previous version, who can identify tiny gaps in crowded markets, who can think up new ways to package, deliver or sell the same things. It needs people who can find innovative ways of managing finance, who can manipulate the money markets, exploit political boundaries and economic loopholes, who can persuade people to leverage their assets, or to liquidate, re-mortgage, plough-back or reinvest, or just to keep their capital moving. But most of all it needs people who can work out ways of getting all of the above to us as soon as we want it. And of course, we want it now.

Inventors are innovating as much now as they ever have, it's just that they are solving problems that won't necessarily be rewarded with patents. The inventors are busy doing other things. Not necessarily brilliant things either. For every iPad there is a Chicken Nugget—but both are, in their own way, elegant solutions to problems people didn't know that they had.

Everything Now is enormously wasteful: a huge and unnecessary drain on the world's dwindling natural resources. By skewing our motivation it has entirely displaced the process of innovation. This is the real cost of changing our focus to wants instead of needs. Everything Now is making it almost impossible for us to address any genuinely big problems we face in the long term. We are not just demand-led, but are busily creating the demands themselves. We have become so obsessed with inventing and meeting the wants of the individual in the short term that attention has become diverted from the real challenges of meeting fundamental human needs of the future: energy and food supply, changing climate, population growth and the sustainable use of natural resources.

SOURCES

Bott, David (Director of Innovation Programmes, UK Government Technology Strategy Board), "Challenge = Opportunity" The 9th Roberts Lecture, University of Sheffield, 18 October 2011

Davies, John, "Debt Facts and Figures July 2011," Credit Action, July 2011

Purdy, L., "The Dissatisfaction Syndrome," Publicis, May 2002

READING THE TEXT

1. Summarize in your own words the distinctions between "wants" and "needs," according to McKevitt.

2. What is the logic behind Maslow's hierarchy of needs?

3. How does the marketing of products such as computers and bottled water convince consumers that these items are "needs," not "wants," as McKevitt explains?

4. After describing the world of "Everything Now," McKenna says, "Things can't go on like this. . . . I mean it literally: they can't" (para. 18). Why does he believe this?

5. What effect has the wide variety of consumer choices had on the relative happiness of people today, according to McKevitt?

READING THE SIGNS

1. In your journal, write your own response to McKevitt's opening quotation from Eric Hoffer: "You can never get enough of what you don't need to make you happy."

2. In class, make a list of all the consumer products that you and your classmates need, and then a list of what you want. What differences, if any, are there between the lists? If you have difficulty categorizing a product as a need or a want, how do you explain that difficulty?

3. **CONNECTING TEXTS**   Using McKevitt's selection as a critical perspective, write an essay analyzing the results of the University of Maryland research study described in "Students Addicted to Social Media" (p. 403). Do you think the students reported on in that selection would categorize their electronic devices as needs or wants? Where would you locate those devices on Maslow's hierarchy of needs?

4. Study current advertisements (either print or online) for bottled water. Do today's ads reflect McKevitt's claim that "only by making us unhappy with what we have today is it possible to persuade us to pay for something that will make us happy tomorrow" (para. 10)?

THOMAS FRANK

Commodify Your Dissent

"Sometimes You Gotta Break the Rules." "This is different. Different is good." "The Line Has Been Crossed." "Resist the Usual." If you are guessing that these defiant declarations must come from the Che Guevara/Jack Kerouac Institute of World Revolution and Extreme Hipness, you're in for a surprise, because they are actually advertising slogans for such corporations as Burger King, Arby's, Toyota, Clash Clear Malt, and Young & Rubicam. Just why huge corporations are aping the language of the Beats and the 1960s counterculture is the centerpiece of Thomas Frank's thesis that the countercultural idea has become "an official aesthetic of consumer society." Commodifying the decades-long youth habit of dissenting against corporate America, corporate America has struck back by adopting the very attitudes that once meant revolution, Frank believes, thus turning to its own capitalist uses the postures of rebellion. Indeed, when Apple can persuade you to buy a computer because its guy is just plain *cooler* than some IBM nerd, there may be no way out. Frank is the author of *Commodify Your Dissent: Salvos from the Baffler* (with Matt Weiland, 1997), from which this selection is taken; *The Conquest of Cool: Business Culture, Counterculture, and the Rise of Hip Consumerism* (1998); *One Market under God: Extreme Capitalism, Market Populism, and the End of Economic Democracy* (2001); *What's the Matter with Kansas?: How Conservatives Won the Heart of America* (2005); *The Wrecking Crew: How Conservatives Rule* (2008); and *Pity the Billionaire: The Hard-Times Swindle and the Unlikely Comeback of the Right* (2012).

The public be damned! I work for my stockholders.
— WILLIAM H. VANDERBILT, 1879

Break the rules. Stand apart. Keep your head. Go with your heart.
— TV commercial for Vanderbilt perfume, 1994

Capitalism is changing, obviously and drastically. From the moneyed pages of the *Wall Street Journal* to TV commercials for airlines and photocopiers we hear every day about the new order's globe-spanning, cyber-accumulating ways. But our notion about what's wrong with American life and how the figures responsible are to be confronted haven't changed much in thirty years. Call it, for convenience, the "countercultural idea." It holds that the paramount ailment of our society is conformity, a malady that has variously been described as overorganization, bureaucracy, homogeneity, hierarchy, logocentrism, technocracy, the Combine, the Apollonian.[1] We all know what it is and what it does. It transforms humanity into "organization man," into "the man in the gray flannel suit." It is "Moloch[2] whose mind is pure machinery," the "incomprehensible prison" that consumes "brains and imagination." It is artifice, starched shirts, tailfins, carefully mowed lawns, and always, always, the consciousness of impending nuclear destruction. It is a stiff, militaristic order that seeks to suppress instinct, to forbid sex and pleasure, to deny basic human impulses and individuality, to enforce through a rigid uniformity a meaningless plastic consumerism.

As this half of the countercultural idea originated during the 1950s, it is appropriate that the evils of conformity are most conveniently summarized with images of 1950s suburban correctness. You know, that land of sedate

[1]**Apollonian** An allusion to the god Apollo, a term for rational consciousness. –EDS.
[2]**Moloch** An ancient idol to whom children were sacrificed, used by Allen Ginsberg as a symbol for industrial America in his poem "Howl." –EDS.

music, sexual repression, deference to authority, Red Scares, and smiling white people standing politely in line to go to church. Constantly appearing as a symbol of arch-backwardness in advertising and movies, it is an image we find easy to evoke.

The ways in which this system are to be resisted are equally well understood and agreed-upon. The Establishment demands homogeneity; we revolt by embracing diverse, individual lifestyles. It demands self-denial and rigid adherence to convention; we revolt through immediate gratification, instinct uninhibited, and liberation of the libido and the appetites. Few have put it more bluntly than Jerry Rubin did in 1970: "Amerika says: Don't! The yippies say: Do It!" The countercultural idea is hostile to any law and every establishment. "Whenever we see a rule, we must break it," Rubin continued. "Only by breaking rules do we discover who we are." Above all rebellion consists of a sort of Nietzschean antinomianism,[3] an automatic questioning of rules, a rejection of whatever social prescriptions we've happened to inherit. Just Do It is the whole of the law.

The patron saints of the countercultural idea are, of course, the Beats, whose frenzied style and merry alienation still maintain a powerful grip on the American imagination. Even forty years after the publication of *On the Road*, the works of Kerouac, Ginsberg, and Burroughs remain the sine qua non of dissidence, the model for aspiring poets, rock stars, or indeed anyone who feels vaguely artistic or alienated. That frenzied sensibility of pure experience, life on the edge, immediate gratification, and total freedom from moral restraint, which the Beats first propounded back in those heady days when suddenly everyone could have their own TV and powerful V-8, has stuck with us through all the intervening years and become something of a permanent American style. Go to any poetry reading and you can see a string of junior Kerouacs go through the routine, upsetting cultural hierarchies by pushing themselves to the limit, straining for that gorgeous moment of original vice when Allen Ginsberg first read "Howl" in 1955 and the patriarchs of our fantasies recoiled in shock. The Gap may have since claimed Ginsberg and *USA Today* may run feature stories about the brilliance of the beloved Kerouac, but the rebel race continues today regardless, with ever-heightening shit-references calculated to scare Jesse Helms, talk about sex and smack that is supposed to bring the electricity of real life, and ever-more determined defiance of the repressive rules and mores of the American 1950s — rules and mores that by now we know only from movies.

But one hardly has to go to a poetry reading to see the countercultural 5 idea acted out. Its frenzied ecstasies have long since become an official aesthetic of consumer society, a monotheme of mass as well as adversarial culture. Turn on the TV and there it is instantly: the unending drama of consumer unbound and in search of an ever-heightened good time, the inescapable rock 'n' roll soundtrack, dreadlocks and ponytails bounding into Taco Bells, a drunken, swinging-camera epiphany of tennis shoes, outlaw soda pops, and

---

[3]**Nietzschean antinomianism** An allusion to the German philosopher Friedrich Nietzsche's challenging of conventional Christian morality. –Eds.

mind-bending dandruff shampoos. Corporate America, it turns out, no longer speaks in the voice of oppressive order that it did when Ginsberg moaned in 1956 that *Time* magazine was

> always telling me about responsibility. Business-
> men are serious. Movie producers are serious.
> Everybody's serious but me.

Nobody wants you to think they're serious today, least of all Time Warner. On the contrary: the Culture Trust is now our leader in the Ginsbergian search for kicks upon kicks. Corporate America is not an oppressor but a sponsor of fun, provider of lifestyle accoutrements, facilitator of carnival, our slang-speaking partner in the quest for that ever-more apocalyptic orgasm. The countercultural idea has become capitalist orthodoxy, its hunger for transgression upon transgression now perfectly suited to an economic-cultural regime that runs on ever-faster cyclings of the new; its taste for self-fulfillment and its intolerance for the confines of tradition now permitting vast latitude in consuming practices and lifestyle experimentation.

Consumerism is no longer about "conformity" but about "difference." Advertising teaches us not in the ways of puritanical self-denial (a bizarre notion on the face of it), but in orgiastic, never-ending self-fulfillment. It counsels not rigid adherence to the tastes of the herd but vigilant and constantly updated individualism. We consume not to fit in, but to prove, on the surface at least, that we are rock 'n' roll rebels, each one of us as rule-breaking and hierarchy-defying as our heroes of the '60s, who now pitch cars, shoes, and beer. This imperative of endless difference is today the genius at the heart of American capitalism, an eternal fleeing from "sameness" that satiates our thirst for the New with such achievements of civilization as the infinite brands of identical cola, the myriad colors and irrepressible variety of the cigarette rack at 7-Eleven.

As existential rebellion has become a more or less official style of Information Age capitalism, so has the countercultural notion of a static, repressive Establishment grown hopelessly obsolete. However the basic impulses of the countercultural idea may have disturbed a nation lost in Cold War darkness, they are today in fundamental agreement with the basic tenets of Information Age business theory. . . .

Contemporary corporate fantasy imagines a world of ceaseless, turbulent change, of centers that ecstatically fail to hold, of joyous extinction for the craven gray-flannel creature of the past. Businessmen today decorate the walls of their offices not with portraits of President Eisenhower and emblems of suburban order, but with images of extreme athletic daring, with sayings about "diversity" and "empowerment" and "thinking outside the box." They theorize their world not in the bar car of the commuter train, but in weepy corporate retreats at which they beat their tom-toms and envision themselves as part of the great avant-garde tradition of edge-livers, risk-takers, and ass-kickers. Their world is a place not of sublimation and conformity, but of "leadership" and bold talk about defying the herd. And there is nothing this new enlightened species of businessman despises more than "rules" and "reason." The prominent culture-warriors of the right may believe that the counterculture was capitalism's undoing, but the antinomian businessmen know better. "One of the t-shirt slogans of the sixties read, 'Question authority,'" the authors of *Reengineering the Corporation* write. "Process owners might buy their reengineering team members the nineties version: 'Question assumptions.'"

The new businessman quite naturally gravitates to the slogans and sensibility of the rebel sixties to express his understanding of the new Information World. He is led in what one magazine calls "the business revolution" by the office-park subversives it hails as "business activists," "change agents," and "corporate radicals." . . . In television commercials, through which the new American businessman presents his visions and self-understanding to the public, perpetual revolution and the gospel of rule-breaking are the orthodoxy of the day. You only need to watch for a few minutes before you see one of these slogans and understand the grip of antinomianism over the corporate mind:

> Sometimes You Gotta Break the Rules — Burger King
> If You Don't Like the Rules, Change Them — WXRT-FM
> The Rules Have Changed — Dodge
> The Art of Changing — Swatch
> There's no one way to do it. — Levi's
> This is different. Different is good. — Arby's
> Just Different From the Rest — Special Export beer
> The Line Has Been Crossed: The Revolutionary New Supra — Toyota
> Resist the Usual — the slogan of both Clash Clear Malt and Young & Rubicam
> Innovate Don't Imitate — Hugo Boss
> Chart Your Own Course — Navigator Cologne
> It separates you from the crowd — Vision Cologne

In most, the commercial message is driven home with the vanguard iconography of the rebel: screaming guitars, whirling cameras, and startled old timers who, we predict, will become an increasingly indispensable prop as consumers require ever-greater assurances that, Yes! You are a rebel! Just look at how offended they are! . . .

The structure and thinking of American business have changed enormously 10 in the years since our popular conceptions of its problems and abuses were formulated. In the meantime the mad frothings and jolly apolitical revolt of Beat, despite their vast popularity and insurgent air, have become powerless against a new regime that, one suspects, few of Beat's present-day admirers and practitioners feel any need to study or understand. Today that beautiful countercultural idea, endorsed now by everyone from the surviving Beats to shampoo manufacturers, is more the official doctrine of corporate America than it is a program of resistance. What we understand as "dissent" does not subvert, does not challenge, does not even question the cultural faiths of Western business. What David Rieff wrote of the revolutionary pretensions of multiculturalism is equally true of the countercultural idea: "The more one reads in academic multiculturalist journals and in business publications, and the more one contrasts the speeches of CEOs and the speeches of noted multiculturalist academics, the more one is struck by the similarities in the way they view the world." What's happened is not co-optation or appropriation, but a simple and direct confluence of interest.

READING THE TEXT

1. In your own words, define what Frank means by the terms "countercultural idea" (para.1) and its commodification.

2. How does Frank explain the relationship between the countercultural idea and conformity?

3. How were the Beats early progenitors of today's countercultural ideas, according to Frank?

4. In what ways does Frank believe that modern business has co-opted the countercultural idea?

5. How do you characterize Frank's tone in this selection? Does his tone enhance or detract from the forcefulness of his argument?

READING THE SIGNS

1. Analyze some current advertising in a magazine, on the Internet, or on television, determining whether the advertisements employ the countercultural idea as a marketing ploy. Use your observations as the basis for an essay in which you assess whether the countercultural idea and the associated "iconography of the rebel" (para. 9) still prevail in advertising, as Frank suggests.

2. In class, brainstorm a list of today's cultural rebels, either marketing characters or real people such as actors or musicians, and discuss why these rebels are considered attractive to their intended audience. Use the class discussion as a springboard for your own essay in which you analyze how the status of cultural rebels is a sign of the mood of modern American culture.

3. Write an essay in which you agree, disagree, or modify Frank's contention that marketing no longer promotes conformity but, rather, promotes "never-ending self-fulfillment" and "constantly updated individualism" (para. 6).

4. Visit a youth-oriented store such as Urban Outfitters, and analyze its advertising, product displays, exterior design, and interior decor. Write an essay in which you gauge the extent to which the store uses the iconography of the rebel as a marketing strategy.

5. Study a current magazine focused on business or on modern technology, such as *Bloomberg BusinessWeek*, *Business 2.0*, or *Wired*. To what extent does the magazine exemplify Frank's claim that modern business eschews conformity and embraces rebellion and rule breaking? Alternatively, you might analyze some corporate Web sites, preferably several from companies in the same industry. Keep in mind that different industries may have very different corporate cultures; the values and ideals that dominate high tech, for instance, may differ dramatically from those in finance, entertainment, or social services.

YOUR CARD.
YOUR TOWN.
M life
mlife.com

ClearChannel

BROUGHT TO YOU B(U)Y

The Signs of Advertising

A Requiem for Vampires

It could have been a scene from a new TV vampire series. Gathered in a dark forest clearing with a blazing campfire, sexy young vampires party it up, dancing, flirting, climbing trees — you know, doing vampire things. The camera cuts to the interior of an Audi driven by a hip-looking undead party animal who's got the vampire equivalent of liquid refreshments in a cooler on the passenger seat. "The party's arrived," he smirks as he motors into the clearing, pulls out his case of Type O+, and approaches the welcoming crowd.

Now, before you throw down this book in disdain with the conviction that any reference to vampires is just so hopelessly out-of-date, hold on, because a semiotic reading of this television advertisement from Super Bowl XLVI will reveal that that is exactly the point. The ad works precisely on the assumption that its target audience is getting sick of vampires, and it calculates its effect on the "Gotcha!" with which it concludes.

That happens as Mr. Undead Party Animal of 2012 gets out of his Audi with the headlights still on. Immediately, as his friends turn to greet him, they are vaporized by his Audi's light beams. He gets it too. And so we come to the punch line. As the remnants of the vampires and their party gear burn up in the darkness, a message appears on the screen: "Daylight, now in a headlight. Audi LED headlights." This is followed by a hashtag: "#SoLongVampires." End of ad.

The ad, of course, is a joke. But in order to get the joke, you have to be in on its premise. That premise, as calculated by the team that created the ad, is that you are yourself young (late teens to late twenties), that you tweet

157

Discussing the Signs of Advertising

Bring to class a print ad from a newspaper, a magazine, or a commercial Web site and in small groups discuss your semiotic reading of it. Be sure to ask, "Why am I being shown this or being told that?" How do the characters in the ad function as signs? What sort of people don't appear as characters? What cultural myths are invoked in this ad? What relationship do you see between those myths and the intended audience of the publication? Which ads do your group members respond to positively, and why? Which ads doesn't your group like?

---

or at least understand the mechanics of Twitter, and, most importantly, that you know all about the *Twilight / Vampire Diaries* phenomenon and that you are getting sick of it. The whole gag about LED headlights being like daylight turns upon your knowledge that traditional vampires can't stand daylight, which is made funnier by your satisfaction in seeing a bunch of *Twilight*-style vampires getting offed. The hope is that you will connect this satisfaction with Audi automobiles and that the next time you are in the market for a car, you'll pick Audi accordingly.

And Here's the Pitch

The preceding analysis is intended to illustrate how advertisements, too, are **signs** of cultural desire and consciousness. Indeed, advertising is not just show-and-tell. In effect, it's a form of behavior modification, a psychological strategy designed not only to inform you about products but also to persuade you to buy them by making associations between the product and certain pleasurable experiences or emotions that may have nothing to do with the product at all—like sex, or a promise of social superiority, or a simple laugh. Indeed, in no other area of popular culture can we find a purer example of the deliberate movement from objective **denotation** (the pictorial image of a product that appears in an advertisement) to subjective **connotation** (the feeling that the advertiser wishes to associate with the product), thereby transforming *things* into signs.

No one knows for sure just how effective a given ad campaign might be in inducing consumer spending by turning objects into signs, but no one is taking any chances either, as the annual increase in advertising costs for the Super Bowl reveals: At last count a thirty-second spot cost as much as $4 million. And it is the promise of ever-increasing advertising revenues that has turned Google into the darling of Wall Street. As James B. Twitchell has written, America is indeed an "ad culture," a society saturated with advertising.

Exploring the Signs of Advertising

Select one of the products advertised in the "Portfolio of Advertisements" (in this chapter), and design in your journal an alternative ad for that product. Consider what different images or cast of characters you could include. What different **mythologies**—and thus different values—could you use to pitch this product? Then freewrite on the significance of your alternative ad. If you have any difficulty imagining an alternative image for the product, what does that say about the power of advertising to control our view of the world? What does your choice of imagery and cultural myths say about you?

The New Marketing

With all the advertising out there, it is getting harder for advertisers to get our attention, or keep it, so they are constantly experimenting with new ways of getting us to listen. For years now, advertisers who are out to snag the youth market have staged their TV ads as if they were music videos—complete with rapid jump cuts, rap or rock music, and dizzying montage effects—to grab the attention of their target audience and to cause their viewers to associate the product with the pleasures of music videos. Self-conscious irony is also a popular technique to overcome the ad-savvy sophistication of generations of consumers who have become skeptical of advertising ploys.

More recently, a marketing strategy known as "stealth advertising" has appeared in selected locations. For example, companies pay people to do things like sit in Starbucks and play a game on a smartphone; when someone takes an interest, they talk about how cool the game is, and ask others to take their photo with this really cool smartphone—and by the way, they say, isn't this a really cool smartphone? The trick here is to advertise a smartphone without having people actually know they're being marketed to—just what the ad doctor ordered for advertising-sick consumers.

Then there are those stealth ads that appear on such Web sites as BuzzFeed and Yahoo! Interspersed among the actual news headlines are news-sponsored "headlines" that are really advertisements in disguise: advotainment, if you will. By masking the ad in the form of the content for which you went to the Web site in the first place, such a marketing strategy updates for the digital era the television trick of turning commercials into, say, sitcoms to accompany actual sitcoms.

But most profoundly, those with products and services to sell are coming to rely on marketing strategies based on data mining (a polite term for on-line spying) rather than attention getting. That is, by purchasing information about our online behavior from such titans as Facebook and Google, would-be advertisers attempt to determine just which consumers would be most susceptible to their ads. If you post on your Facebook page that you are planning a long trip, for example, you will immediately find airline ads on your screen. If you conduct a Google search for watches, ads for watches suddenly appear.

Many people do not mind this sort of marketing surveillance and in fact regard it as a way of receiving relevant product information more efficiently than the traditional hit-or-miss advertising approach. For such consumers, the convenience offered by online data mining offsets its invasiveness. For others, especially after the revelation in 2013 of the scale of the National Security Administration's phone and Internet surveillance, the corporate invasion of their privacy is more alarming. Whatever your own personal take on the matter happens to be, there is no question that personal privacy has been a major casualty of a digital culture that is mostly underwritten by the advertising revenues that flow from data mining.

As the years pass and the national mood shifts with the tides of history, new advertising techniques will surely emerge. So look around and ask yourself, as you're bombarded with advertising, "Why am I being shown *that*, or being told *this*?" Or cast yourself as the director of an ad, asking yourself what you would do to pitch a product; then look at what the advertiser has done. Pay attention to the way an ad's imagery is organized, its precise denotation. Every detail counts. Why are these colors used, or why is the ad in black and white? Why are cute stuffed animals chosen to pitch toilet paper? What are those people doing in that perfume commercial? Why the cowboy hat in an ad for jeans? Look, too, for what the ad doesn't include: Is it missing a clear view of the product itself or an ethnically diverse cast of characters? In short, when interpreting an ad, transform it into a text, going beyond what it denotes to what it connotes — to what it is trying to insinuate or say.

The Semiotic Foundation

There is perhaps no better field for semiotic analysis than advertising, for ads work characteristically by substituting signs for things, and by reading those signs you can discover the values and desires that advertisers seek to exploit. It has long been recognized that advertisements substitute images of desire for the actual products, selling images of fun, popularity, or sheer celebrity — promising a gratifying association with the likes of LeBron James if you get your next burger from McDonald's. Automobile commercials, for their part, are notorious for selling not transportation but fantasies of power, prestige, and sexual potency.

By substituting desirable images for concrete needs, modern advertising seeks to transform desire into necessity. You need food, for example, but it takes an ad campaign to convince you through attractive images that you need a Big Mac. Your job may require you to have a car, but it's an ad that persuades you that a Land Rover is necessary for your happiness. If advertising worked otherwise, it would simply present you with a functional profile of a product and let you decide whether it will do the job.

From the early twentieth century, advertisers have seen their task as the transformation of desire into necessity. In the 1920s and 1930s, for example, advertisements created elaborate story lines designed to convince readers that they needed this mouthwash to attract a spouse or that caffeine-free breakfast drink to avoid trouble on the job. In such ads, products were made to appear not only desirable but absolutely necessary. Without them, your very survival as a socially competent being would be in question. Many ads still work this way, particularly "guilt" ads that prey on your insecurities and fears. Deodorants and mouthwashes still are pitched in such a fashion, playing on our fear of smelling bad in public. Can you think of any other products whose ads play on guilt or shame? Do you find them to be effective?

The Commodification of Desire

Associating a logically unrelated desire with an actual product (as in pitching beer through sexual come-ons) can be called the **commodification** of desire. In other words, desire itself becomes the product that the advertiser is selling. This marketing of desire was recognized as early as the 1950s in Vance Packard's *The Hidden Persuaders*. In that book, Packard points out that by the 1950s America was well along in its historic shift from a producing to a consuming economy. The implications for advertisers were enormous. Since the American economy was increasingly dependent on the constant growth of consumption, as discussed in the Introduction to Chapter 1, manufacturers had to find ways to convince people to consume ever more goods. So they turned to the advertising mavens on Madison Avenue, who responded with ads that persuaded consumers to replace perfectly serviceable products with "new and improved" substitutions within an overall economy of planned design obsolescence.

America's transformation from a producer to a consumer economy also explains why while advertising is a worldwide phenomenon, it is nowhere as prevalent as it is here. Open a copy of *Vogue*. It is essentially a catalog, where scarcely a page is without an ad. Indeed, advertisers themselves call this plethora of advertising "clutter" that they must creatively "cut through" each time they design a new ad campaign. The ubiquity of advertising in our lives points to an economy in which people are constantly pushed to buy, as opposed to economies like China's, which despite recent rises in consumer interest, continues to emphasize constant increases in production. And desire is what opens the wallet.

While the basic logic of advertising may be similar from era to era, the content of an ad, and hence its significance, differs as popular culture changes. This is why a thorough analysis of a specific advertisement should include a historical survey of ads by the same company (and even from competing companies) for the same product, examining the *differences* that point

Reading Advertising Online

Many viewers watch the Super Bowl as much for the commercials as for the football game; indeed, the Super Bowl ads now have their own pregame public-relations hype and, in many a media outlet, their own postgame analysis and ratings. Visit *Advertising Age*'s report on the most recent Super Bowl (www.adage.com), and study the ads and the commentary about them. What images and styles predominate, and what do the dominant patterns say about popular taste? What does the public's avid interest in Super Bowl ads say about the power of advertising and its role in American culture?

to significance. (The Internet has made this task much easier, as enormous archives of both print and television ads can be found on Web sites such as YouTube and vintageadbrowser.com; a simple ad search entry will produce all sorts of relevant images and information.)

Looking at ads from different eras reveals just what was preoccupying Americans at different times in their history. Advertising in the 1920s, for instance, focused especially on its market's desires for improved social status. Ads for elocution and vocabulary lessons appealed to working- and lower-middle-class consumers, who were invited to fantasize that buying the product or service could help them enter the middle class. Meanwhile, middle-class consumers were invited to compare their enjoyment of the sponsor's product with that of the upper-class models shown happily slurping the advertised coffee or purchasing the advertised vacuum cleaner. Of course, things haven't changed that much since the twenties. Can you think of any ads that use this strategy today? How often are glamorous celebrities called in to make you identify with their "enjoyment" of a product?

One particularly amusing ad from the 1920s played on America's fear of communism in the wake of the Bolshevik revolution in Russia. "Is your washroom breeding Bolsheviks?" asks a print ad from the Scott Paper Company. The ad's lengthy copy explains how your bathroom might be doing so: If your company restroom is stocked with inferior paper towels, it says, discontent will proliferate among your employees and lead to subversive activities. RCA Victor and Campbell's Soup, we are assured, are no such breeding grounds of subversion, thanks to their contracts with Scott. You, too, can fight the good fight against communism by buying Scott towels, the ad suggests.

Populism versus Elitism

American advertising tends to swing in a pendulum motion between the status-conscious ads that dominated the twenties and the more populist approach of decades like the seventies, when *The Waltons* was a top TV series and country music and truck-driving cowboys lent their popular appeal to Madison Avenue. This swing between elitist and populist approaches in advertising reflects a basic division within the American dream itself, a mythic promise that at once celebrates democratic equality and encourages you to rise above the crowd, to be better than anyone else. Sometimes Americans are more attracted to one side than to the other, but there is bound to be a shift back to the other side when the thrill wears off. Thus, the populist appeal of the seventies (even disco had a distinct working-class flavor: recall John Travolta's character in *Saturday Night Fever*) gave way to the elitist eighties, and advertising followed. Products such as Gallo varietal wines, once considered barely a step up from jug wine, courted an upscale market, while Michelob light beer promised its fans that they "could have it all." Status advertising was all the rage in that glitzy, go-for-the-gold decade.

The nineties brought in a different kind of advertising that was neither populist nor elitist but was characterized by a cutting, edgy humor. This humor was especially common in dot.com ads that typically addressed the sort of young, irreverent, and rather cocky souls who were the backbone of what was then called the "New Economy" and is now called "Web 1.0." More broadly, edgy advertising appealed to twentysomething consumers who were coveted by the marketers who made possible such youth-oriented TV networks as Fox and the WB. Raised in the *Saturday Night Live* era, such consumers were accustomed to cutting humor and were particularly receptive to anything that smacked of attitude, and in the race to get their attention, advertisers followed with attitude-laden advertising.

The new millennium has seen an increasing tendency of advertising that focuses on demographically targeted markets. Such *niche marketing* is not new, but it has been intensified both by the growth of digital media and by the number of subscription television sources that cater to an enormous variety of viewer categories. Once upon a time, TV advertisers had only three networks to choose from: ABC, CBS, and NBC (and their affiliated stations). In those days, television ads were constructed to appeal to a relatively undifferentiated (though primarily white and middle class) national audience. Today, with audiences identifying their tastes and even identities through their cable choices and online behavior, advertisers tailor their ads much more specifically, choosing images and strategies designed to appeal to particular demographics and even to particular individuals. This development appears to be breaking up America's "common culture" into an atomized one. What effect this change may be having on our society could prove to be one of the most important semiotic questions of all.

The Readings

Jack Solomon begins the chapter with a semiotic analysis of American advertising, highlighting the ways in which conflicting mythologies of populism and elitism are exploited to push the goods. A paired set of readings by James B.

Twitchell and Steve Craig follows, revealing the elaborate psychological pro-filing schemes by which marketers categorize potential consumers and the gender-coded formulas that can be found in television advertisements. Next, Jennifer L. Pozner lambastes the chauvinistic critics of the Dove "Campaign for Real Beauty," while Gloria Steinem's insider's view of what goes on be-hind the scenes at women's magazines provides an exposé of the often-cozy relationships between magazine content and advertisers' demands. Juliet B. Schor then surveys the ways in which marketers try to turn kids into cool cus-tomers — perhaps somewhat ahead of their actual years — and Joseph Turow explores the brave new world of market spying, explaining how digital tech-nology enables advertisers to target their ads by following you around on the Internet. Julia B. Corbett concludes the readings with a look at marketers who seek to cash in on the "lucrative market of 'green consumers.'" The chapter then presents a "Portfolio of Advertisements" for you to decode for yourself.

READING THE SIGNS

1. The advertisement on page 165 tells a story. What is it? You might start with the title of the ad.

2. To whom is the ad directed? What emotions does it play on? Be sure to provide evidence for your answers. What are the "dearest possessions" the ad refers to?

3. This ad originally appeared in 1914. If you were to update it for a magazine today, what changes would you make? Why?

JACK SOLOMON

Masters of Desire: The Culture of American Advertising

When the background music in a TV or radio automobile commercial is classical, you can be pretty certain that the ad is pitching a Lexus or a Mercedes. When it's country western, it's probably for Dodge or Chevy. English accents are popular in Jaguar ads, while a good western twang sure helps move pickup trucks. Whenever advertisers make use of status-oriented or common-folk-oriented cultural cues, they are playing on one of America's most fundamental contradictions, as Jack Solomon explains in this cultural analysis of American advertising. The contradiction is between the simultaneous desire for social superiority (elitism) and social equality (populism) that lies at the heart of the American dream. And one way or another, it offers a good way to pitch a product. Solomon, a professor of English at California State University, Northridge, is the author of *The Signs of Our Time* (1988), from which this selection is taken, and *Discourse and Reference in the Nuclear Age* (1988). He is also coeditor with Sonia Maasik of both *California Dreams and Realities* (2005) and this textbook.

Amongst democratic nations, men easily attain a certain equality of condition; but they can never attain as much as they desire.
— ALEXIS DE TOCQUEVILLE

On May 10, 1831, a young French aristocrat named Alexis de Tocqueville arrived in New York City at the start of what would become one of the most famous visits to America in our history. He had come to observe firsthand the institutions of the freest, most egalitarian society of the age, but what he found was a paradox. For behind America's mythic promise of equal opportunity, Tocqueville discovered a desire for *unequal* social rewards, a ferocious competition for privilege and distinction. As he wrote in his monumental study, *Democracy in America*:

> When all privileges of birth and fortune are abolished, when all professions are accessible to all, and a man's own energies may place him at the top of any one of them, an easy and unbounded career seems open to his ambition. . . . But this is an erroneous notion, which is corrected by daily experience. [For when] men are nearly alike, and all follow the same track, it is very difficult for any one individual to walk quick and cleave a way through the same throng which surrounds and presses him.

Yet walking quick and cleaving a way is precisely what Americans dream of. We Americans dream of rising above the crowd, of attaining a social summit beyond the reach of ordinary citizens. And therein lies the paradox.

The American dream, in other words, has two faces: the one communally egalitarian and the other competitively elitist. This contradiction is no accident; it is fundamental to the structure of American society. Even as America's great myth of equality celebrates the virtues of mom, apple pie, and the girl or boy next door, it also lures us to achieve social distinction, to rise above the crowd and bask alone in the glory. This land is your land and this land is my land, Woody Guthrie's populist anthem tells us, but we keep trying to increase the "my" at the expense of the "your." Rather than fostering contentment, the American dream breeds desire, a longing for a greater share of the pie. It is as if our society were a vast high-school football game, with the bulk of the participants noisily rooting in the stands while, deep down, each of them is wishing he or she could be the star quarterback or head cheerleader.

For the semiotician, the contradictory nature of the American myth of equality is nowhere written so clearly as in the signs that American advertisers use to manipulate us into buying their wares. "Manipulate" is the word here, not "persuade"; for advertising campaigns are not sources of product information, they are exercises in behavior modification. Appealing to our subconscious emotions rather than to our conscious intellects, advertisements are designed to exploit the discontentments fostered by the American dream, the constant desire for social success and the material rewards that accompany it. America's consumer economy runs on desire, and advertising stokes the engines by transforming common objects — from peanut butter to political candidates — into signs of all the things that Americans covet most.

But by semiotically reading the signs that advertising agencies manufacture to stimulate consumption, we can plot the precise state of desire in the audiences to which they are addressed. Let's look at a representative sample of ads and what they say about the emotional climate of the country and the fast-changing trends of American life. Because ours is a highly diverse, pluralistic society, various advertisements may say different things depending on their intended audiences, but in every case they say something about America, about the status of our hopes, fears, desires, and beliefs.

We'll begin with two ad campaigns conducted by the same company that bear out Alexis de Tocqueville's observations about the contradictory nature of American society: General Motors' campaigns for its Cadillac and Chevrolet lines. First, consider an early magazine ad for the Cadillac Allanté. Appearing as a full-color, four-page insert in *Time*, the ad seems to say "I'm special—and so is this car" even before we've begun to read it. Rather than being printed on the ordinary, flimsy pages of the magazine, the Allanté spread appears on glossy coated stock. The unwritten message is that an extraordinary car deserves an extraordinary advertisement, and that both car and ad are aimed at an extraordinary consumer, or at least one who wishes to appear extraordinary compared to ordinary citizens.

Ads of this kind work by creating symbolic associations between their product and what the consumers to whom they are addressed most covet. It is significant, then, that this ad insists that the Allanté is virtually an Italian rather than an American car; as its copy runs, "Conceived and Commissioned by America's Luxury Car Leader—Cadillac" but "Designed and Handcrafted by Europe's Renowned Design Leader—Pininfarina, SpA, of Turin, Italy." This is not simply a piece of product information, it's a sign of the prestige that European luxury cars enjoy in today's automotive marketplace. Once the luxury car of choice for America's status drivers, Cadillac has fallen far behind its European competitors in the race for the prestige market. So the Allanté essentially represents Cadillac's decision, after years of resisting the trend toward European cars, to introduce its own European import—whose high cost is clearly printed on the last page of the ad. . . .

American companies manufacture status symbols because American consumers want them. As Alexis de Tocqueville recognized a century and a half ago, the competitive nature of democratic societies breeds a desire for social distinction, a yearning to rise above the crowd. But given the fact that those who do make it to the top in socially mobile societies have often risen from the lower ranks, they still look like everyone else. In the socially immobile societies of aristocratic Europe, generations of fixed social conditions produced subtle class signals. The accent of one's voice, the shape of one's nose, or even the set of one's chin immediately communicated social status. Aside from the nasal bray and uptilted head of the Boston Brahmin, Americans do not have any native sets of personal status signals. If it weren't for his Mercedes-Benz and Manhattan townhouse, the parvenu Wall Street millionaire often couldn't be distinguished from the man who tailors his suits. Hence, the demand for status symbols, for the objects that mark one off as a social success, is particularly strong in democratic nations—stronger even than in aristocratic societies, where the aristocrat so often looks and sounds different from everyone else.

Status symbols, then, are signs that identify their possessors' place in a social hierarchy, markers of rank and prestige. We can all think of any number of status symbols — Rolls-Royces, Beverly Hills mansions, even shar-pei puppies (whose rareness and expense has rocketed them beyond Russian wolfhounds as status pets and has even inspired whole lines of wrinkle-faced stuffed toys) — but how do we know that something *is* a status symbol? The explanation is quite simple: When an object (or puppy!) either costs a lot of money or requires influential connections to possess, anyone who possesses it must also possess the necessary means and influence to acquire it. The object itself really doesn't matter, since it ultimately disappears behind the presumed social potency of its owner. Semiotically, what matters is the signal it sends, its value as a sign of power. One traditional sign of social distinction is owning a country estate and enjoying the peace and privacy that attend it. Advertisements for Mercedes-Benz, Jaguar, and Audi automobiles thus frequently feature drivers motoring quietly along a country road, presumably on their way to or from their country houses.

Advertisers have been quick to exploit the status signals that belong to body language as well. As Hegel observed in the early nineteenth century, it is an ancient aristocratic prerogative to be seen by the lower orders without having to look at them in return. Tilting his chin high in the air and gazing down at the world under hooded eyelids, the aristocrat invites observation while refusing to look back. We can find such a pose exploited in an advertisement for Cadillac Seville in which we see an elegantly dressed woman out for a drive with her husband in their new Cadillac. If we look closely at the woman's body language, we can see her glance inwardly with a satisfied smile on her face but not outward toward the camera that represents our gaze. She is glad to be seen by us in her Seville, but she isn't interested in looking at *us*!

Ads that are aimed at a broader market take the opposite approach. If the American dream encourages the desire to "arrive," to vault above the mass, it also fosters a desire to be popular, to "belong." Populist commercials accordingly transform products into signs of belonging, utilizing such common icons as country music, small-town life, family picnics, and farmyards. All of these icons are incorporated in GM's Heartbeat of America campaign for its Chevrolet line. Unlike the Seville commercial, the faces in the Chevy ads look straight at us and smile. Dress is casual; the mood upbeat. Quick camera cuts take us from rustic to suburban to urban scenes, creating an American montage filmed from sea to shining sea. We all "belong" in a Chevy.

Where price alone doesn't determine the market for a product, advertisers can go either way. Both Johnnie Walker and Jack Daniel's are better-grade whiskies, but where a Johnnie Walker ad appeals to the buyer who wants a mark of aristocratic distinction in his liquor, a Jack Daniel's ad emphasizes the down-home, egalitarian folksiness of its product. Johnnie Walker associates itself with such conventional status symbols as sable coats, Rolls-Royces, and black gold; Jack Daniel's gives us a Good Ol' Boy in overalls. In fact, Jack Daniel's Good Ol' Boy is an icon of backwoods independence, recalling the days of the moonshiner and the Whisky Rebellion of 1794. Evoking emotions quite at odds with those stimulated in Johnnie Walker ads, the advertisers of Jack Daniel's transform their product into a sign of America's populist tradition. The fact that both ads successfully sell whisky is itself a sign of the dual nature of the American dream. . . .

Populist advertising is particularly effective in the face of foreign competition. When Americans feel threatened from the outside, they tend to circle the wagons and temporarily forget their class differences. In the face of the Japanese automotive "invasion," Chrysler runs populist commercials in which Lee Iacocca joins the simple folk who buy his cars as the jingle "Born in America" blares in the background. Seeking to capitalize on the popularity of Bruce Springsteen's *Born in the USA* album, these ads gloss over Springsteen's ironic lyrics in a vast display of flag-waving. Chevrolet's Heartbeat of America campaign attempts to woo American motorists away from Japanese automobiles by appealing to their patriotic sentiments.

The patriotic iconography of these campaigns also reflects the general cultural mood of the early to mid-1980s. After a period of national anguish in the wake of the Vietnam War and the Iran hostage crisis, America went on a patriotic binge. American athletic triumphs in the Lake Placid and Los Angeles Olympics introduced a sporting tone into the national celebration, often making international affairs appear like one great Olympiad in which America was always going for the gold. In response, advertisers began to do their own flag-waving.

The mood of advertising during this period was definitely upbeat. Even deodorant commercials, which traditionally work on our self-doubts and fears of social rejection, jumped on the bandwagon. In the guilty sixties, we had ads like the Ice Blue Secret campaign with its connotations of guilt and shame. In the feel-good Reagan eighties, Sure deodorant commercials featured images of triumphant Americans throwing up their arms in victory to reveal — no wet marks! Deodorant commercials once had the moral echo of Nathaniel Hawthorne's guilt-ridden *The Scarlet Letter*; in the early eighties they had all the moral subtlety of *Rocky IV*, reflecting the emotions of a Vietnam-weary nation eager to embrace the imagery of America Triumphant. . . .

Live the Fantasy

By reading the signs of American advertising, we can conclude that America is a nation of fantasizers, often preferring the sign to the substance and easily enthralled by a veritable Fantasy Island of commercial illusions. Critics of Madison Avenue often complain that advertisers create consumer desire, but semioticians don't think the situation is that simple. Advertisers may shape consumer fantasies, but they need raw material to work with, the subconscious dreams and desires of the marketplace. As long as these desires remain unconscious, advertisers will be able to exploit them. But by bringing the fantasies to the surface, you can free yourself from advertising's often hypnotic grasp.

I can think of no company that has more successfully seized upon the subconscious fantasies of the American marketplace — indeed the world marketplace — than McDonald's. By no means the first nor the only hamburger chain in the United States, McDonald's emerged victorious in the "burger wars" by transforming hamburgers into signs of all that was desirable in American life. Other chains like Wendy's, Burger King, and Jack-In-The-Box continue to advertise and sell widely, but no company approaches McDonald's transformation of itself into a symbol of American culture.

McDonald's success can be traced to the precision of its advertising. Instead of broadcasting a single "one-size-fits-all" campaign at a time, McDonald's pitches its burgers simultaneously at different age groups, different classes, even different races (Budweiser beer, incidentally, has succeeded in the same way). For children, there is the Ronald McDonald campaign, which presents a fantasy world that has little to do with hamburgers in any rational sense but a great deal to do with the emotional desires of kids. Ronald McDonald and his friends are signs that recall the Muppets, *Sesame Street*, the circus, toys, storybook illustrations, even *Alice in Wonderland*. Such signs do not signify hamburgers. Rather, they are displayed in order to prompt in the child's mind an automatic association of fantasy, fun, and McDonald's.

The same approach is taken in ads aimed at older audiences — teens, adults, and senior citizens. In the teen-oriented ads we may catch a fleeting glimpse of a hamburger or two, but what we are really shown is a teenage fantasy: groups of hip and happy adolescents singing, dancing, and cavorting together. Fearing loneliness more than anything else, adolescents quickly respond to the group appeal of such commercials. "Eat a Big Mac," these ads say, "and you won't be stuck home alone on Saturday night."

To appeal to an older and more sophisticated audience no longer so afraid of not belonging and more concerned with finding a place to go out to at night, McDonald's has designed the elaborate "Mac Tonight" commercials, which have for their backdrop a nightlit urban skyline and at their center a cabaret pianist with a moon-shaped head, a glad manner, and Blues Brothers shades. Such signs prompt an association of McDonald's with nightclubs and urban sophistication, persuading us that McDonald's is a place not only for breakfast or lunch but for dinner too, as if it were a popular off-Broadway nightspot, a place to see and be seen. Even the parody of Kurt Weill's "Mack the Knife" theme song that Mac the Pianist performs is a sign, a subtle signal to the sophisticated hamburger eater able to recognize the origin of the tune in Bertolt Brecht's *Threepenny Opera*.

For yet older customers, McDonald's has designed a commercial around 20 the fact that it employs a large number of retirees and seniors. In one such ad, we see an elderly man leaving his pretty little cottage early in the morning to start work as "the new kid" at McDonald's, and then we watch him during his first day on the job. Of course he is a great success, outdoing everyone else with his energy and efficiency, and he returns home in the evening to a loving wife and a happy home. One would almost think that the ad was a kind of moving "help wanted" sign (indeed, McDonald's *was* hiring elderly employees at the time), but it's really just directed at consumers. Older viewers can see themselves wanted and appreciated in the ad — and perhaps be distracted from the rationally uncomfortable fact that many senior citizens take such jobs because of financial need and thus may be unlikely to own the sort of home that one sees in the commercial. But realism isn't the point here. This is fantasyland, a dream world promising instant gratification no matter what the facts of the matter may be.

Practically the only fantasy that McDonald's doesn't exploit is the fantasy of sex. This is understandable, given McDonald's desire to present itself as a family restaurant. But everywhere else, sexual fantasies, which have always had an important place in American advertising, dominate the advertising scene. You expect sexual come-ons in ads for perfume or cosmetics or jewelry — after all, that's what they're selling — but for room deodorizers? In a magazine ad for Claire Burke home fragrances, for example, we see a well-dressed couple cavorting about their bedroom in what looks like a cheery preparation for sadomasochistic exercises. Jordache and Calvin Klein pitch blue jeans as props for teenage sexuality. The phallic appeal of automobiles, traditionally an implicit feature in automotive advertising, becomes quite explicit in a Dodge commercial that shifts back and forth from shots of a young man in an automobile to teasing glimpses of a woman — his date — as she dresses in her apartment.

The very language of today's advertisements is charged with sexuality. Products in the more innocent fifties were "new and improved," but everything in the eighties is "hot!" — as in "hot woman," or sexual heat. Cars are "hot." Movies are "hot." An ad for Valvoline pulses to the rhythm of a "heat wave, burning in my car." Sneakers get red hot in a magazine ad for Travel Fox athletic shoes in which we see male and female figures, clad only in Travel Fox shoes, apparently in the act of copulation — an ad that earned one of *Adweek*'s annual "badvertising" awards for shoddy advertising.

The sexual explicitness of contemporary advertising is a sign not so much of American sexual fantasies as of the lengths to which advertisers will go to get attention. Sex never fails as an attention-getter, and in a particularly competitive, and expensive, era for American marketing, advertisers like to bet on a sure thing. Ad people refer to the proliferation of TV, radio, newspaper, magazine, and billboard ads as "clutter," and nothing cuts through the clutter like sex.

By showing the flesh, advertisers work on the deepest, most coercive human emotions of all. Much sexual coercion in advertising, however, is a sign of a desperate need to make certain that clients are getting their money's worth. The appearance of advertisements that refer directly to the prefabricated fantasies of Hollywood is a sign of a different sort of desperation: a desperation for ideas. With the rapid turnover of advertising campaigns mandated by the need to cut through the "clutter," advertisers may be hard pressed for new ad concepts, and so they are more and more frequently turning to already-established models. In the early 1980s, for instance, Pepsi-Cola ran a series of ads broadly alluding to Steven Spielberg's *E.T.* In one such ad, we see a young boy, who, like the hero of *E.T.*, witnesses an extraterrestrial visit. The boy is led to a soft-drink machine where he pauses to drink a can of Pepsi as the spaceship he's spotted flies off into the universe. The relationship between the ad and the movie, accordingly, is a parasitical one, with the ad taking its life from the creative body of the film. . . .

Madison Avenue has also framed ad campaigns around the cultural 25 prestige of high-tech machinery. This is especially the case with sports cars, whose high-tech appeal is so powerful that some people apparently fantasize about *being* sports cars. At least, this is the conclusion one might draw from a Porsche commercial that asked its audience, "If you *were* a car, what kind of car would you be?" As a candy-red Porsche speeds along a rain-slick forest road, the ad's voice-over describes all the specifications you'd want to have if you *were* a sports car. "If you were a car," the commercial concludes, "you'd be a Porsche."

In his essay "Car Commercials and *Miami Vice*," Todd Gitlin explains the semiotic appeal of such ads as those in the Porsche campaign. Aired at the height of what may be called America's "myth of the entrepreneur," these commercials were aimed at young corporate managers who imaginatively identified with the "lone wolf" image of a Porsche speeding through the woods. Gitlin points out that such images cater to the fantasies of faceless corporate men who dream of entrepreneurial glory, of striking out on their own like John DeLorean and telling the boss to take his job and shove it. But as DeLorean's spectacular failure demonstrates, the life of the entrepreneur can be extremely risky. So rather than having to go it alone and take the risks that accompany entrepreneurial independence, the young executive can substitute fantasy for reality by climbing into his Porsche — or at least that's what Porsche's advertisers wanted him to believe.

But there is more at work in the Porsche ads than the fantasies of corporate America. Ever since Arthur C. Clarke and Stanley Kubrick teamed up to present us with HAL 9000, the demented computer of *2001: A Space Odyssey*, the American imagination has been obsessed with the melding of man and machine. First there was television's *Six Million Dollar Man*, and then movieland's *Star Wars*, *Blade Runner*, and *Robocop*, fantasy visions of a future dominated by machines. Androids haunt our imaginations as machines seize the initiative. *Time* magazine's "Man of the Year" for 1982 was a computer. Robot-built automobiles appeal to drivers who spend their days in front of computer screens — perhaps designing robots. When so much power and prestige is being given to high-tech machines, wouldn't you rather be a Porsche?

In short, the Porsche campaign is a sign of a new mythology that is emerging before our eyes, a myth of the machine, which is replacing the myth of the human. The iconic figure of the little tramp caught up in the cogs of industrial production in Charlie Chaplin's *Modern Times* signified a humanistic revulsion to the age of the machine. Human beings, such icons said, were superior to machines. Human values should come first in the moral order of things. But as Edith Milton suggests in her essay "The Track of the Mutant," we are now coming to believe that machines are superior to human beings, that mechanical nature is superior to human nature. Rather than being threatened by machines, we long to merge with them. *The Six Million Dollar Man* is one iconic figure in the new mythology; Harrison Ford's sexual coupling with an android is another. In such an age it should come as little wonder that computer-synthesized Max Headroom should be a commercial spokesman for Coca-Cola, or that Federal Express should design a series of TV ads featuring mechanical-looking human beings revolving around strange and powerful machines.

Fear and Trembling in the Marketplace

While advertisers play on and reflect back at us our fantasies about everything from fighter pilots to robots, they also play on darker imaginings. If dream and desire can be exploited in the quest for sales, so can nightmare and fear.

The nightmare equivalent of America's populist desire to "belong," for example, is the fear of not belonging, of social rejection, of being different. Advertisements for dandruff shampoos, mouthwashes, deodorants, and laundry detergents ("Ring around the Collar!") accordingly exploit such fears, bullying us into consumption. Although ads of this type were still around in the 1980s, they were particularly common in the fifties and early sixties, reflecting a society still reeling from the witch-hunts of the McCarthy years. When any sort of social eccentricity or difference could result in a public denunciation and the loss of one's job or even liberty, Americans were keen to conform and be like everyone else. No one wanted to be "guilty" of smelling bad or of having a dirty collar.

"Guilt" ads characteristically work by creating narrative situations in which someone is "accused" of some social "transgression," pronounced guilty, and then offered the sponsor's product as a means of returning to "innocence." Such ads, in essence, are parodies of ancient religious rituals of guilt and atonement, whereby sinning humanity is offered salvation through the agency of priest and church. In the world of advertising, a product takes the place of the priest, but the logic is quite similar.

In commercials for Wisk detergent, for example, we witness the drama of a hapless housewife and her husband as they are mocked by the jeering voices of children shouting "Ring around the Collar!" "Oh, those dirty rings!" the housewife groans in despair. It's as if she and her husband were being stoned by an angry crowd. But there's hope, there's help, there's Wisk. Cleansing her soul of sin as well as her husband's, the housewife launders his shirts with Wisk, and behold, his collars are clean. Product salvation is only as far as the supermarket. . . .

If guilt looks backward in time to past transgressions, fear, like desire, faces forward, trembling before the future. In the late 1980s, a new kind of fear commercial appeared, one whose narrative played on the worries of young corporate managers struggling up the ladder of success. Representing the nightmare equivalent of the elitist desire to "arrive," ads of this sort

30

created images of failure, story lines of corporate defeat. In one ad for Apple computers, for example, a group of junior executives sits around a table with the boss as he asks each executive how long it will take his or her department to complete some publishing jobs. "Two or three days," answers one nervous executive. "A week, on overtime," a tight-lipped woman responds. But one young up-and-comer can have everything ready tomorrow, today, or yesterday, because his department uses a Macintosh desktop publishing system. Guess who'll get the next promotion?

For other markets, there are other fears. If McDonald's presents senior citizens with bright fantasies of being useful and appreciated beyond retirement, companies like Secure Horizons dramatize senior citizens' fears of being caught short by a major illness. Running its ads in the wake of budgetary cuts in the Medicare system, Secure Horizons designed a series of commercials featuring a pleasant old man named Harry — who looks and sounds rather like Carroll O'Connor — who tells us the story of the scare he got during his wife's recent illness. Fearing that next time Medicare won't cover the bills, he has purchased supplemental health insurance from Secure Horizons and now securely tends his roof-top garden. . . .

The Future of an Illusion

There are some signs in the advertising world that Americans are getting fed up with fantasy advertisements and want to hear some straight talk. Weary of extravagant product claims and irrelevant associations, consumers trained by years of advertising to distrust what they hear seem to be developing an immunity to commercials. At least, this is the semiotic message I read in the "new realism" advertisements of the eighties, ads that attempt to convince you that what you're seeing is the real thing, that the ad is giving you the straight dope, not advertising hype.

You can recognize the "new realism" by its camera techniques. The lighting is usually subdued to give the ad the effect of being filmed without studio lighting or special filters. The scene looks gray, as if the blinds were drawn. The camera shots are jerky and off-angle, often zooming in for sudden and unflattering close-ups, as if the cameraman were an amateur with a home video recorder. In a "realistic" ad for AT&T, for example, we are treated to a monologue by a plump stockbroker — his plumpness intended as a sign that he's for real and not just another actor — who tells us about the problems he's had with his phone system (not AT&T's) as the camera jerks around, generally filming him from below as if the photographer couldn't quite fit the equipment into the crammed office. "This is no fancy advertisement," the ad tries to convince us, "this is sincere."

An ad for Miller draft beer tries the same approach, re-creating the effect of an amateur videotape of a wedding celebration. Camera shots shift suddenly from group to group. The picture jumps. Bodies are poorly framed. The color is washed out. Like the beer it is pushing, the ad is supposed to strike us as being "as real as it gets."

Such ads reflect a desire for reality in the marketplace, a weariness with Madison Avenue illusions. But there's no illusion like the illusion of reality. Every special technique that advertisers use to create their "reality effects" is, in fact, more unrealistic than the techniques of "illusory" ads. The world, in reality, doesn't jump around when you look at it. It doesn't appear in subdued gray tones. Our eyes don't have zoom lenses, and we don't look at things with our heads cocked to one side. The irony of the "new realism" is that it is more unrealistic, more artificial, than the ordinary run of television advertising.

But don't expect any truly realistic ads in the future, because a realistic advertisement is a contradiction in terms. The logic of advertising is entirely semiotic: It substitutes signs for things, framed visions of consumer desire for the thing itself. The success of modern advertising, its penetration into every corner of American life, reflects a culture that has itself chosen illusion over reality. At a time when political candidates all have professional image-makers attached to their staffs, and the president of the United States can be an actor who once sold shirt collars, all the cultural signs are pointing to more illusions in our lives rather than fewer—a fecund breeding ground for the world of the advertiser.

READING THE TEXT

1. Describe in your own words the paradox of the American dream, as Solomon sees it.

2. In Solomon's view, why do status symbols work particularly well in manipulating American consumers?

3. Why, in Solomon's view, has McDonald's been so successful in its ad campaigns?

4. What is a "guilt" ad (para. 31), according to Solomon, and how does it affect consumers?

5. What relationship does Solomon find between the "new realism" (para. 35) of some ads and the paradoxes of the American dream?

READING THE SIGNS

1. **CONNECTING TEXTS** The American political scene has changed since the late 1980s, when this essay was first published. Do you believe the contradiction between populism and elitism that Solomon describes still affects American advertising and media? In an analytic essay, argue your case. Be sure to discuss specific media examples. To develop your ideas, you might consult Thomas Frank's "Commodify Your Dissent" (p. 150).

2. **CONNECTING TEXTS** In television advertising, the most coveted market is the eighteen to forty-nine age group, a cohort that often includes what James B. Twitchell ("What We Are to Advertisers," p. 177) describes as "experiencers"

and "strivers." To what extent do the TV ads you view display a populist or elitist ethos? Or do you find that the ads do not harbor class sensitivity? How do you explain your observations?

3. Bring to class a general-interest magazine (such as *People* or *O: The Oprah Magazine*), and in small groups study the advertising. Do the ads tend to have an elitist or a populist appeal? What relationship do you see between the appeal you identify and the magazine's target readership? Present your group's findings to the class.

4. In class, brainstorm a list of status symbols common in advertising today. Then discuss what groups they appeal to and why. Can you detect any patterns based on gender, ethnicity, or age?

5. Visit your college library, and locate an issue of a popular magazine from earlier decades, such as the 1930s or 1940s. Then write an essay in which you compare and contrast the advertising found in the early issue with that in a current issue of the same publication. What similarities and differences do you find in the myths underlying the advertising, and what is the significance of these similarities and differences?

CREATING CONSUMERS

JAMES B. TWITCHELL
What We Are to Advertisers

Are you a "believer" or a "striver," an "achiever" or a "struggler," an "experiencer" or a "maker"? Or do you have no idea what we're talking about? If you don't, James Twitchell explains it all to you in this selection in which the psychological profiling schemes of American advertising are laid bare. For like it or not, advertisers have, or think they have, your number, and they will pitch their products according to the personality profile they have concocted for you. And the really spooky thing is that they're often right. A prolific writer on American advertising and culture, Twitchell's books include *Adcult USA: The Triumph of Advertising in American Culture* (1996); *Twenty Ads That Shook the World* (2000); *Living It Up: Our Love Affair with Luxury* (2002); *Lead Us into Temptation: The Triumph of American Materialism* (1999), from which this selection is taken; and *Branded Nation* (2004). His most recent book is *Look Away Dixieland* (2011).

Mass production means mass marketing, and mass marketing means the creation of mass stereotypes. Like objects on shelves, we too cluster in groups. We find meaning together. As we mature, we move from shelf to shelf, from aisle to aisle, zip code to zip code, from lifestyle to lifestyle, between what the historian Daniel Boorstin calls "consumption communities." Finally, as full-grown consumers, we stabilize in our buying, and hence meaning-making, patterns. Advertisers soon lose interest in us not just because we stop buying but because we have stopped changing brands.

The object of advertising is not just to brand parity objects but also to brand consumers as they move through these various communities. To explain his job, Rosser Reeves, the master of hard-sell advertising like the old Anacin ads, used to hold up two quarters and claim his job was to make you believe they were different, and, more importantly, that one was better than the other. Hence, at the macro level the task of advertising is to convince different sets of consumers — target groups — that the quarter they observe is somehow different in meaning and value than the same quarter seen by their across-the-tracks neighbors.

In adspeak, this is called *positioning*. "I could have positioned Dove as a detergent bar for men with dirty hands," David Ogilvy famously said, "but I chose to position it as a toilet bar for women with dry skin." Easy to say, hard to do. But if Anheuser-Busch wants to maximize its sales, the soccer mom driving the shiny Chevy Suburban must feel she drinks a different Budweiser than the roustabout in the rusted-out Chevy pickup.[1]

The study of audiences goes by any number of names: psychographics, ethnographics, macrosegmentation, to name a few, but they are all based on the ineluctable principle that birds of a feather flock together. The object of much consumer research is not to try to twist their feathers so that they will flock to your product, but to position your product in such a place that they will have to fly by it and perhaps stop to roost. After roosting, they will eventually think that this is a part of their flyway and return to it again and again.

Since different products have different meanings to different audiences, 5 segmentation studies are crucial. Although agencies have their own systems for naming these groups and their lifestyles, the current supplier of much raw data about them is a not-for-profit organization, the Stanford Research Institute (SRI).

---

[1] Cigarette companies were the first to find this out in the 1930s, much to their amazement. Blindfolded smokers couldn't tell what brand they were smoking. Instead of making cigarettes with different tastes, it was easier to make different advertising claims to different audiences. Cigarettes are hardly unique. Ask beer drinkers why they prefer a particular brand and invariably they tell you: "It's the taste," "This goes down well," "This is light and refreshing," "This is rich and smooth." They will say this about a beer that has been described as their brand, but is not. Anheuser-Busch, for instance, spent three dollars per barrel in 1980 to market a barrel of beer; now they spend nine dollars. Since the cost to reach a thousand television households has doubled at the same time the audience has segmented (thanks to cable), why not go after a particular market segment by tailoring ads emphasizing, in different degrees, the Clydesdales, Ed McMahon, Beechwood aging, the red and white can, dates certifying freshness, the spotted dog, the Eagle, as well as "the crisp, clean taste." While you cannot be all things to all people, the object of advertising is to be as many things to as many segments as possible. The ultimate object is to convince as many segments as possible that "This Bud's for you" is a sincere statement.

The "psychographic" system of SRI is called acronomically VALS (now VALS2+), short for Values and Lifestyle System. Essentially this schematic is based on the common-sense view that consumers are motivated "to acquire products, services, and experiences that provide satisfaction and give shape, substance, and character to their identities" in bundles. The more "resources" (namely money, but also health, self-confidence, and energy) each group has, the more likely they will buy "products, services, and experiences" of the group they associate with. But resources are not the only determinant. Customers are also motivated by such ineffables as principles, status, and action. When SRI describes these various audiences, they peel apart like this (I have provided them an appropriate car to show their differences):

- Actualizers: These people at the top of the pyramid are the ideal of every-one but advertisers. They have "it" already, or will soon. They are sophis-ticated, take-charge people interested in independence and character. They don't need new things; in fact, they already have their things. If not, they already know what "the finer things" are and won't be told. They don't need a new car, but if they do they'll read *Consumer Reports*. They do not need a hood ornament on their car.

- Fulfilled: Here are mature, satisfied, comfortable souls who support the status quo in almost every way. Often they are literally or figuratively retired. They value functionality, durability, and practicality. They drive something called a "town car," which is made by all the big three auto-makers.

- Believers: As the word expresses, these people support traditional codes of family, church, and community, wearing good Republican cloth coats. As consumers they are predictable, favoring American products and rec-ognizable brands. They regularly attend church and Walmart, and they are transported there in their mid-range automobile like an Oldsmobile. Whether Oldsmobile likes it or not, they do indeed drive "your father's Oldsmobile."

Moving from principle-oriented consumers who look inside to status-driven consumers who look out to others, we find the Achievers and Strivers.

- Achievers: If consumerism has an ideal, here it is. Bingo! Wedded to their jobs as a source of duty, reward, and prestige, these are the people who not only favor the establishment but are the establishment. They like the concept of prestige. Not only are they successful, they demonstrate their success by buying such objects as prestigious cars to show it. They like hood ornaments. They see no contradiction in driving a Land Rover in Manhattan.

- Strivers: A young Striver is fine; he will possibly mature into an Achiever. But an old Striver can be nasty; he may well be bitter. Since they are unsure of themselves, they are eager to be branded as long as the brand is elevating. Money defines success and they don't have enough of it.

Being a yuppie is fine as long as the prospect of upward mobility is possible. Strivers like foreign cars even if it means only leasing a BMW.

[And then there] are those driven less by the outside world but by their desire to participate, to be part of a wider world.

- Experiencers: Here is life on the edge — enthusiastic, impulsive, and even reckless. Their energy finds expression in sports, social events, and "doing something." Politically and personally uncommitted, experiencers are an advertiser's dream come true as they see consumption as fulfillment and are willing to spend a high percent of their disposable income to attain it. When you wonder about who could possibly care how fast a car will accelerate from zero to sixty m.p.h., they care.

- Makers: Here is the practical side of Experiencers; they like to build things and they experience the world by working on it. Conservative, suspicious, respectful, they like to do things in and to their homes, like adding a room, canning vegetables, or changing the oil in their pickup trucks.

- Strugglers: Like Actualizers, these people are outside the pale of materialism not by choice, but by low income. Strugglers are chronically poor. Their repertoire of things is limited not because they already have it all, but because they have so little. Although they clip coupons like Actualizers, theirs are from the newspaper. Their transportation is usually public, if any. They are the invisible millions.

As one might imagine, these are very fluid categories, and we may move through as many as three of them in our lifetimes. For instance, between ages 18 and 24 most people (61 percent) are Experiencers in desire or deed, while less than 1 percent are Fulfilled. Between ages 55 and 64, however, the Actualizers, Fulfilled, and Strugglers claim about 15 percent of the population each, while the Believers have settled out at about a fifth. The Achievers, Strivers, and Makers fill about 10 percent apiece, and the remaining 2 percent are Experiencers. The numbers can be broken down at every stage allowing for marital status, education, household size, dependent children, home ownership, household income, and occupation. More interesting still is the ability to accurately predict the appearance of certain goods in each grouping. SRI sells data on precisely who buys single-lens reflex cameras, who owns a laptop computer, who drinks herbal tea, who phones before five o'clock, who reads the *Reader's Digest*, and who watches *Beavis and Butthead*.

When one realizes the fabulous expense of communicating meaning for a product, the simple-mindedness of a system like VALS2 + becomes less risible. When you are spending millions of dollars for a few points of market share for your otherwise indistinguishable product, the idea that you might be able to attract the owners of socket wrenches by shifting ad content around just a bit makes sense. Once you realize that in taste tests consumers cannot tell one brand of cigarettes from another — including their own — nor distinguish such products as soap, gasoline, cola, beer, or what-have-you, it is clear that the product must be overlooked and the audience isolated and sold.

READING THE TEXT

1. What do marketers mean by "positioning" (para. 3), and why is it an important strategy to them?
2. What does the acronym VALS stand for, and what is the logic behind this system?
3. Why do marketers believe that the "product must be overlooked and the audience isolated and sold" (para. 8), according to Twitchell?
4. Why does Twitchell explain that the VALS2 categories are "fluid" (para. 7)?

READING THE SIGNS

1. Write a journal entry in which you identify where you fit in the VALS2 system. Conversely, explain why none of the categories describe you. What is your attitude toward being stereotyped by marketers?
2. In class, discuss whether the categories of consumers defined by the VALS2 paradigm are an accurate predictor of consumer behavior. Use the discussion as the basis of an essay in which you argue for or against the proposition that stereotyping consumer lifestyles is an effective way of marketing goods and services.
3. Study the VALS2 paradigm in terms of the values it presumes. To what extent does it presume traditionally American values such as individualism? Use your analysis to formulate an argument about whether this marketing tool is an essentially American phenomenon.
4. Using the VALS2 paradigm, analyze the consumption habits of the interviewees described in Jon Mooallem's "The Self-Storage Self" (p. 102). Do they fit neatly into the paradigm, or do their patterns of consumption call for a revision of it? Use your findings as the basis of an essay in which you assess the usefulness of the paradigm.
5. **CONNECTING TEXTS**   Twitchell, Stephanie Clifford and Quentin Hardy ("Attention, Shoppers: Store Is Tracking Your Cell," p. 110), and Malcolm Gladwell ("The Science of Shopping," p. 93) all describe marketing research strategies. Read these selections, and write an argument that supports, opposes, or modifies the proposition that marketers have misappropriated research techniques for manipulative and therefore ethically questionable purposes.

STEVE CRAIG
Men's Men and Women's Women

Men and women both drink beer, but you wouldn't guess that from the television ads that pitch beer as a guy beverage and associate beer drinking with such guy things as fishing trips, bars, and babes. Conversely, both men and women can find themselves a few pounds overweight, but you wouldn't know that from the ads, which almost always feature women, as they are intended to appeal to women dieters. In this selection, Steve Craig provides a step-by-step analysis of four TV commercials, showing how advertisers carefully craft their ads to appeal, respectively, to male and female consumers. A professor in the department of radio, television, and film at the University of North Texas, Craig has written widely on television, radio history, and gender and media. His most recent book is *Out of the Dark: A History of Radio and Rural America* (2009).

Gender and the Economics of Television Advertising

The economic structure of the television industry has a direct effect on the placement and content of all television programs and commercials. Large advertisers and their agencies have evolved the pseudo-scientific method of time purchasing based on demographics, with the age and sex of the consumer generally considered to be the most important predictors of purchasing behavior. Computers make it easy to match market research on product buying patterns with audience research on television viewing habits. Experience, research, and intuition thus yield a demographic (and even psychographic) profile of the "target audience." Advertisers can then concentrate their budgets on those programs which the target audience is most likely to view. The most economical advertising buys are those in which the target audience is most concentrated (thus, the less "waste" audience the advertiser must purchase) (Barnouw, 1978; Gitlin, 1983; Jhally, 1987).

Good examples of this demographic targeting can be seen by contrasting the ads seen on daytime television, aimed at women at home, with those on weekend sports telecasts. Ads for disposable diapers are virtually never

e macmillanhighered.com/signsoflife

Are the overt gender codes in classic TV advertising still evident today?

e-readings > **Ford**, *Two-Ford Freedom* [TV commercial] seen during a football game any more than commercials for beer are seen during soap operas. True, advertisers of some products simply wish to have their commercials seen by the largest number of consumers at the lowest cost without regard to age, sex, or other demographic descriptors, but most consider this approach far too inefficient for the majority of products.

A general rule of thumb in television advertising, then, is that daytime is the best time to reach the woman who works at home. Especially important to advertisers among this group is the young mother with children. Older women, who also make up a significant proportion of the daytime audience, are generally considered less important by many advertisers in the belief that they spend far less money on consumer goods than young mothers.

Prime time (the evening hours) is considered a good time to reach women who work away from home, but since large numbers of men are also in the audience, it can also be a good time to advertise products with wider target audiences. Weekend sports periods (and, in season, "Monday Night Football") are the only time of the week when men outnumber women in the television audience, and therefore, become the optimum time for advertising products and services aimed at men.

Gendered Television, Gendered Commercials

In his book *Television Culture* (1987, Chs. 10, 11), John Fiske discusses "gen-   5
dered television," explaining that the television industry successfully designs some programs for men and others for women. Clearly, program producers and schedulers must consider the target audience needs of their clients (the advertisers) in creating a television program lineup. The gendering of programming allows the industry to provide the proper audience for advertisers by constructing shows pleasurable for the target audience to watch, and one aspect of this construction is in the gender portrayals of characters.

Fiske provides the following example:

> Women's view of masculinity, as evidenced in soap operas, differs markedly from that produced for the masculine audience. The "good" male in the daytime soaps is caring, nurturing, and verbal. He is prone to making comments like "I don't care about material wealth or professional success, all I care about is us and our relationship." He will talk about feelings and people and rarely express his masculinity in direct action. Of course, he is still decisive, he still has masculine power, but that power is given a "feminine" inflection. . . . The "macho" characteristics of goal centeredness, assertiveness, and the morality of the strongest that identify the hero in masculine television, tend here to be characteristics of the villain. (p. 186)

But if the programming manipulates gender portrayals to please the audience, then surely so must the commercials that are the programs' reason for being. My previous research (Craig, 1990) supports the argument that advertisers also structure the gender images in their commercials to match the expectations and fantasies of their intended audience. Thus, commercials portraying adult women with children were nearly four times more likely to appear during daytime soap operas than during weekend sports (p. 50). Daytime advertisers exploit the image of women as mothers to sell products to mothers. Likewise, during the weekend sports broadcasts, only 18% of the primary male characters were shown at home, while during the daytime ads, 40% of them were (p. 42). For the woman at home, men are far more likely to be portrayed as being around the house than they are in commercials aimed at men on weekends.

Gendered commercials, like gendered programs, are designed to give pleasure to the target audience, since it is the association of the product with a pleasurable experience that forms the basis for much American television advertising. Yet patriarchy conditions males and females to seek their pleasure differently. Advertisers therefore portray different images to men and women in order to exploit the different deep-seated motivations and anxieties connected to gender identity. I would now like to turn to a close analysis of four television commercials to illustrate some of these differing portrayals. Variations in how men and women are portrayed are especially apparent when comparing weekend and daytime commercials, since ads during these day parts almost completely focus on a target audience of men or women respectively.

Analysis of Four Commercials

In order to illustrate the variation of gender portrayal, I have chosen four commercials. Each was selected to provide an example of how men and women are portrayed to themselves and to the other sex. The image of men and women in commercials aired during weekend sports telecasts I call "Men's Men" and "Men's Women." The portrayals of men and women in commercials aimed at women at home during the daytime hours I call "Women's Men" and "Women's Women." Although there are certainly commercials aired during these day parts that do not fit neatly into these categories, and even a few that might be considered to be counter-stereotypical in their gender portrayals, the commercials and images I have chosen to analyze are fairly typical and were chosen to permit a closer look at the practices revealed in my earlier content analysis. Further, I acknowledge that the readings of these commercials are my own. Others may well read them differently.

Men's Men

I would first like to consider two commercials originally broadcast during   10
weekend sports and clearly aimed at men. (These and the other commercials I will discuss were broadcast on at least one of the three major networks. I recorded them for analysis during January 1990.)

COMMERCIAL 1: ACURA INTEGRA (:30)

MUSIC: Light rock guitar music runs throughout. Tropical elements (e.g., a steel drum) are added later.

A young, white, blond, bespectacled male wearing a plain sweatshirt is shown cleaning out the interior of a car. He finds an old photograph of himself and two male companions (all are young, slender, and white) posing with a trophy-sized sailfish. He smiles. Dissolve to what appears to be a flashback of the fishing trip. The three men are now seen driving down the highway in the car (we now see that it is a new black Acura Integra) in a Florida-like landscape. We see a montage of close-ups of the three men inside the car, then a view out the car window of what looks to be the Miami skyline.

ANNOUNCER (male): "When you think about all the satisfaction you get out of going places . . . why would you want to take anything less . . ."

Dissolve to a silhouette shot of a young woman in a bathing suit walking along the beach at sunset.

ANNOUNCER: ". . . than America's most satisfying car?"

On this last line, the three young men are seen in silhouette knee-deep in the water at the same beach, apparently watching the woman pass. One of the men drops to his knees and throws his arms up in mock supplication. A montage of shots of the three men follows, shots of a deep-sea fishing boat intercut with shots of the first man washing the car. The montage ends with the three posing with the trophy sailfish. The screen flashes and freezes and becomes the still photo seen at the first shot of the commercial. The final shot shows a long shot of the car, freshly washed. The first man, dressed as in the first shot, gives the car a final polish and walks away. The words "Acura" and "Precision Crafted Performance" are superimposed over the final shot.

ANNOUNCER: "The Acura Integra."

This ad, which ran during a weekend sports telecast, has a number of features that makes it typical of many other commercials aimed at men. First, it is for an automobile. My previous research found that 29% of the network commercials telecast in the weekend time period were for cars and other automotive products (compared to only 1% during the daytime sample) (Craig, 1990, p. 36). In our culture, automobiles are largely the male's province, and men are seen by the automotive industry as the primary decision makers when it comes to purchases. Further, cars are frequently offered as a means of freedom (literally so in this ad), and escapism is an important component in many weekend ads (only 16% of weekend ads are set at home compared to 41% of daytime ads) (p. 43).

Second, with the exception of a brief silhouette of the woman on the beach, there are no women in this commercial. Camaraderie in all-male or nearly all-male groupings is a staple of weekend commercials, especially those for automobiles and beer. Again, my earlier research indicates that fully one-third of weekend commercials have an all-adult male cast (but only 20% of daytime commercials have an all-adult female cast) (p. 36).

The escapism and male camaraderie promised in this commercial are simply an extension of the escapism and camaraderie men enjoy when they watch (and vicariously participate in) weekend sports on television. Messner (1987) suggests that one reason for the popularity of sports with men is that it offers them a chance to escape from the growing ambiguity of masculinity in daily life.

> Both on a personal/existential level for athletes and on a symbolic/ideological level for spectators and fans, sport has become one of the "last bastions" of male power and superiority over—and separation from—the "feminization" of society. The rise of football as "America's number-one game" is likely the result of the comforting *clarity* it provides between the polarities of traditional male power, strength, and violence and the contemporary fears of social feminization. (p. 54)

The Acura commercial acts to reinforce male fantasies in an environment of clear masculinity and male domination. Men's men are frequently portrayed as men without women. The presence of women in the commercials might serve to threaten men's men with confusing uncertainty about the nature of masculinity in a sexist, but changing, society (Fiske, 1987, pp. 202–209, offers an extended psychoanalytic explanation of the absence of women in masculine television). On the other hand, the absence of women must *not* suggest homosexuality. Men's men are clearly heterosexual. To discourage any suspicions, the Acura ad portrays three (rather than two) men vacationing together.

It is also at least partly for this reason that the single quick shot in which the woman *does* appear in this commercial is important. She is nothing more than an anonymous object of desire (indeed, in silhouette, we cannot even see her face), but her presence both affirms the heterosexuality of the group while at the same time hinting that attaining sexual fulfillment will be made easier by the possession of the car. Men's men have the unchallenged freedom of a fantasized masculinity—to travel, to be free from commitment, to seek adventure.

Men's Women

COMMERCIAL 2: MILLER BEER (:30)

> We see the interior of a cheap roadside cafe. It is lit with an almost blinding sunlight streaming in the windows. A young couple sits in a far booth holding hands. A young, blond waitress is crossing the room. A silent jukebox sits in the foreground. At first we hear only natural sounds. We cut to a close-up from a low angle from outside the cafe of male legs as they enter the cafe. The legs are clad in blue jeans and cowboy boots.

As the man enters, we cut to a close-up of the blond waitress looking up to see the man. We see a close-up of the man's body as he passes the silent jukebox. As if by magic, the jukebox begins to play the rhythm and blues number "I Put a Spell on You." We see the couple that was holding hands turn in surprise. The man in the booth's face is unlit and we can see no features, but the woman is young with long blond hair. She looks surprised and pulls her hand away from the man's. We cut to an extreme close-up of the waitress's face. It is covered with sweat. As she watches the man pass, a smile appears on her face. She comes over to take the man's order. The camera takes the man's point of view.

MAN: "Miller Genuine Draft."
WAITRESS: "I was hopin' you'd say that."

We see a shot of a refrigerator door opening. The refrigerator is filled with sweating, backlit bottles of Miller beer. We then see a close-up of the man holding a bottle and opening it magically with a flick of his thumb (no opener). A montage of shots of the product amid blowing snow follows this. The sounds of a blizzard are heard.

ANNOUNCER: "Cold filtered. Never heat pasteurized. Miller Genuine Draft. For those who discover this real draft taste . . . the world is a *very* cool place."

On this last line we see close-ups of the woman in the booth and the waitress. Wind is blowing snow in their faces and they are luxuriating in the coolness. The waitress suddenly looks at the camera with shocked disappointment. We cut to an empty seat with the man's empty beer bottle rocking on the table. The music, snow, and wind end abruptly. We see the man's back as he exits the cafe. The final shot is of the waitress, elbow propped on the counter, looking after the man. The words "Tap into the Cold" are superimposed.

When women do appear in men's commercials, they seldom challenge the primary masculine fantasy. Men's women are portrayed as physically attractive, slim, and usually young and white, frequently blond, and almost always dressed in revealing clothing. Since most men's commercials are set in locations away from home, most men's women appear outside the home, and only infrequently are they portrayed as wives. There are almost always hints of sexual availability in men's women, but this is seldom played out explicitly. Although the sexual objectification of women characters in these ads is often quite subtle, my previous content analysis suggests that it is far more common in weekend than in daytime ads (Craig, 1990, p. 34). Men's women are also frequently portrayed as admirers (and at times, almost voyeurs), generally approving of some aspect of product use (the car he drives, the beer he drinks, the credit card he uses).

In these respects, the Miller ad is quite typical. What might have been a simple commercial about a man ordering and drinking a beer becomes an elaborate sexual fantasy, in many respects constructed like a porn film. The attractive, eager waitress is mystically drawn to the man who relieves her bored frustrations with an orgasmic chug-a-lug. She is "hot" while he (and the beer) is "*very* cool." But once he's satisfied, he's gone. He's too cool for conversation or commitment. We never see the man's face, but rather are invited, through the use of the point-of-view shot, to become a participant in the mystic fantasy.

There is, of course, considerable tongue-in-cheek intent in this ad. Males know that the idea of anonymous women lusting after them, eager for sex without commitment, is fantasy. But for many men, it is pleasurable fantasy, and common enough in weekend commercials. The main point is that the product has been connected, however briefly, with the pleasure of this fantasy. The physical pleasure of consuming alcohol (and specifically cold Miller beer) is tied to the pleasurable imaginings of a narrative extended beyond that which is explicitly seen.

One industry executive has explained this advertising technique. Noting the need for "an imaginary and motivating value" in ads, Nicolas (1988) argues that:

> Beyond the principle of utility, it becomes more and more important to associate a principle of pleasure to the value. The useful must be linked to the beautiful, the rational to the imaginary, the indispensable to the superfluous. . . . It is imperative that the image be seductive. (p. 7)

Although some research has documented changes in gender portrayals in 20 television advertising over the past few years (e.g., Bretl & Cantor, 1988; Ferrante et al., 1988), such conclusions are based on across-the-schedule studies or of prime time rather than of specifically gendered day parts. While avoiding portraying women as blatant sex objects is doubtless good business in daytime or prime time, it would almost certainly inhibit male fantasies such as this one, commonly seen during weekend sports. The man's woman continues to be portrayed according to the rules of the patriarchy.

The next two commercials were originally aired during daytime soap operas. They represent Madison Avenue's portrayal of women and men designed for women.

Women's Women

COMMERCIAL 3: WEIGHT WATCHERS (:30)

> The opening shot is a quick pan from toe to head of a young, thin, white woman with dark hair. She is dressed in a revealing red bathing suit and appears to be reclining on the edge of a pool. Her head is propped up with a pillow. She is wearing sunglasses and smiling.
>
> ANNOUNCER (woman, voice-over): "I hate diets . . . but I lost weight fast with Weight Watchers' new program."

We see the same woman sitting at a dining table in a home kitchen eating a meal. She is wearing a red dress. The camera weaves, and we briefly glimpse a man and two small children also at the table. Another close-up of the woman's body at the pool. This time the camera frames her waist.

ANNOUNCER: "And I *hate* starving myself."

We see the same family group eating pizza at a restaurant. More close-ups of the woman's body at poolside.

ANNOUNCER: "But with their new 'fast and flexible' program I don't have to."

Shot of the woman dancing with the man, followed by a montage of more shots of the family at dinner and close-ups of the woman at poolside.

ANNOUNCER: "A new food plan lets me live the way I want . . . eat with my family and friends, still have fun."

Close-up shot of balance scales. A woman's hand is moving the balance weight downward.

ANNOUNCER: "And in no time . . . *here I am!*"

Shot of the woman on the scales. She raises her hands as if in triumph. The identical shot is repeated three times.

ANNOUNCER: "Now there's only one thing I hate . . . not joining Weight Watchers sooner."

As this last line is spoken, we see a close-up of the woman at the pool. She removes her sunglasses. The man's head comes into the frame from the side and kisses her on the forehead.

This commercial portrays the woman's woman. Her need is a common one in women's commercials produced by a patriarchal society — the desire to attain and maintain her physical attractiveness. Indeed, my previous research indicates that fully 44% of the daytime ads sampled were for products relating to the body (compared with only 15% of the ads during weekend sports). In this ad, her desire for an attractive body is explicitly tied to her family. She is portrayed with a husband, small children, and a nice home. It is her husband with whom she dances and who expresses approval with a kiss. Her need for an attractive body is her need to maintain her husband's interest and maintain her family's unity and security. As Coward (1985) has written:

> Most women know to their cost that appearance is perhaps the crucial way by which men form opinions of women. For that reason, feelings about self-image get mixed up with feelings about security and comfort. . . . It sometimes appears to women that the whole possibility of being loved and comforted hangs on how their appearance will be received. (p. 78)

But dieting is a difficult form of self-deprivation, and she "hates" doing it. Implicit also is her hatred of her own "overweight" body—a body that no longer measures up to the idealized woman promoted by the patriarchy (and seen in the commercial). As Coward explains:

> . . . advertisements, health and beauty advice, fashion tips are effective precisely because somewhere, perhaps even subconsciously, an anxiety, rather than a pleasurable identification [with the idealized body], is awakened. (p. 80)

Weight Watchers promises to alleviate the pain of dieting at the same time it relieves (or perhaps delays) the anxiety of being "overweight." She can diet and "still have fun."

A related aspect is this ad's use of a female announcer. The copy is written in the first person, but we never see the model speaking in direct address. We get the impression that we are eavesdropping on her thoughts—being invited to identify with her—rather than hearing a sales pitch from a third person. My earlier research confirmed the findings of other content analyses that female voice-overs are relatively uncommon in commercials. My findings, however, indicated that while only 3% of the voice-overs during weekend sports were by women announcers, 16% of those during daytime were. Further, 60% of the women announcers during daytime were heard in commercials for body-related products (Craig, 1990, p. 52). 25

Women's Men

COMMERCIAL 4: SECRET DEODORANT (:30)

We open on a wide shot of a sailing yacht at anchor. It is sunrise and a woman is on deck. She descends into the cabin. Cut to a close-up of the woman as she enters the cabin.

WOMAN: "Four bells. Rise and shine!"

A man is seen in a bunk inside the cabin. He has just awakened. Both he and the woman are now seen to be young and white. She is thin and has bobbed hair. He is muscular and unshaven (and a Bruce Willis look-alike).

MUSIC: Fusion jazz instrumental (UNDER).
MAN (painfully): "Ohhhh . . . I can't move."
WOMAN: "Ohhhhh. I took a swim—breakfast is on—I had a shower. Now it's *your turn.*"

As she says this, she crosses the cabin and places a container of Secret deodorant on a shelf above the man. The man leans up on one elbow then falls back into bed with a groan.

MAN: "Ahhh, I can't."

She pulls him back to a sitting position then sits down herself, cradling him in her arms.

WOMAN: "Come onnn. You only changed *one* sail yesterday."
MAN (playfully): "Yeah, but it was a *big* sail."

Close-up of the couple. He is now positioned in the bed sitting with his back to her. He leans his head back on her shoulder.

WOMAN: "Didn't you know sailing's a sport? You know . . . an active thing."
MAN: "I just don't get it. . . . You're so together already. . . . Um. You smell great."
WOMAN: "Must be my Secret."

She looks at the container of Secret on the shelf. The man reaches over and picks it up. Close-up of the Secret with the words "Sporty Clean Scent" visible on the container.

MAN: "Sporty clean?"
WOMAN: "It's new."
MAN: "Sounds like something I could use."
WOMAN: "Unnnnn . . . I don't think so. I got it for me."

She takes the container from him and stands up and moves away. He stands up behind her and holds her from behind.

WOMAN: "For these close quarters . . . ?"
MAN: "Well, close is good."

He begins to kiss her cheek.

WOMAN: "I thought you said you couldn't move."

She turns to face him.

MAN: "I was saving my strength?"
WOMAN: "Mmmm."

We dissolve to a close-up of the product on the shelf.

ANNOUNCER (woman): "New Sporty Clean Secret. Strong enough for a man, but pH-balanced for an active woman."

This commercial portrays the woman's man. He's good looking, sensitive, romantic, and he appreciates her. What's more, they are alone in an exotic location where he proceeds to seduce her. In short, this commercial is a 30-second romance novel. She may be today's woman, be "so together," and she may be in control, but she still wants him to initiate the love-making. Her man is strong, active, and probably wealthy enough to own or rent a yacht. (Of course, a more liberated reading would have her as the owner of the yacht, or at least sharing expenses.) Yet he is also vulnerable. At first she mothers him, holding him in a Pietà-like embrace and cooing over his sore muscles. Then he catches her scent — her Secret — and the chase is on.

As in the Weight Watchers commercial, it is the woman's body that is portrayed as the source of the man's attraction, and it is only through maintaining that attraction that she can successfully negotiate the relationship. Although at one level the Secret woman is portrayed as a "new woman"—active, "sporty," self-assured, worthy of her own deodorant—she still must rely on special (even "Secret") products to make her body attractive. More to the point, she still must rely on her body to attract a man and fulfill the fantasy of security and family. After all, she is still mothering and cooking breakfast.

Once again, the product is the source of promised fantasy fulfillment—not only sexual fulfillment, but also the security of a caring relationship, one that allows her to be liberated, but not too liberated. Unlike the women of the Acura and Miller's commercials who remained anonymous objects of desire, the men of the Weight Watchers and Secret commercials are intimates who are clearly portrayed as having relationships that will exist long after the commercial is over.

Conclusion

Gender images in television commercials provide an especially intriguing field of study. The ads are carefully crafted bundles of images, frequently designed to associate the product with feelings of pleasure stemming from deep-seated fantasies and anxieties. Advertisers seem quite willing to manipulate these fantasies and exploit our anxieties, especially those concerning our gender identities, to sell products. What's more, they seem to have no compunction about capitalizing on dehumanizing gender stereotypes to seek these ends.

A threat to patriarchy is an economic threat, not only to men who may   30 fear they will have their jobs taken by women, but also in a more fundamental way. Entire industries (automotive, cosmetics, fashion) are predicated on the assumption that men and women will continue behaving according to their stereotypes. Commercials for women therefore act to reinforce patriarchy and to co-opt any reactionary ideology into it. Commercials for men need only reinforce masculinity under patriarchy and, at most, offer men help in coping with a life plagued by women of raised conscience. Betty Friedan's comments of 1963 are still valid. Those "deceptively simple, clever, outrageous ads and commercials" (p. 270) she wrote of are still with us. If anything, they have become more subtle and insidious. The escape from their snare is through a better understanding of gender and the role of mass culture in defining it.

WORKS CITED

Barnouw, E. (1978). *The sponsor*. New York, NY: Oxford.
Bretl, D. J., & Cantor, J. (1988). The portrayal of men and women in U.S. television commercials: A recent content analysis and trends over 15 years. *Sex Roles, 18*(9/10), 595–609.
Coward, R. (1985). *Female desires: How they are sought, bought and packaged*. New York, NY: Grove.

Craig, S. (1990, December). *A content analysis comparing gender images in network television commercials aired in daytime, evening, and weekend telecasts.* (ERIC Document Reproduction Service Number ED329217)

Ferrante, C., Haynes, A., & Kingsley, S. (1988). Image of women in television advertising. *Journal of Broadcasting & Electronic Media, 32*(2), 231–237.

Fiske, J. (1987). *Television culture.* New York, NY: Methuen.

Friedan, B. (1963). *The feminine mystique.* New York, NY: Dell.

Gitlin, T. (1983). *Inside prime time.* New York, NY: Pantheon.

Jhally, S. (1987). *The codes of advertising: Fetishism and the political economy of meaning in the consumer society.* New York, NY: St. Martin's.

Messner, M. (1987). Male identity in the life course of the jock. In M. Kimmel (Ed.), *Changing men* (pp. 53–67). Newbury Park, CA: Sage.

Nicolas, P. (1988). From value to love. *Journal of Advertising Research, 28,* 7–8.

READING THE TEXT

1. How, according to John Fiske, is television programming gendered?

2. Why is male camaraderie such a common motif in "men's men" advertising, according to Craig?

3. What roles do women tend to play in the two types of commercials aimed at men? What roles do men tend to play in the two types of commercials aimed at women?

4. Why does Craig believe that "a threat to patriarchy is an economic threat" (para. 30)?

READING THE SIGNS

1. In class, discuss whether you agree with Craig's interpretations of the four commercials that he describes. If you disagree, what alternative analysis do you propose?

2. The four commercials Craig analyzes aired in 1990. View some current commercials broadcast during daytime and sports programs. Use your observations as the basis for an argument about whether the gendered patterns in advertising that Craig outlines exist today. If the patterns persist, what implications do they have for the tenacity of gender codes? If you see differences, how can you account for them?

3. Write an essay in which you support, refute, or modify Craig's belief that gendered advertising of the sort he describes is "dehumanizing" (para. 29).

4. Watch TV programs that are not overtly geared toward one gender, such as prime-time scripted drama or network news. To what extent does the advertising that accompanies these shows fit Craig's four categories of gender portrayal? How do you account for your findings?

5. **CONNECTING TEXTS**   Enter the debate over the origins of gender identity: Is it primarily biologically determined or largely socially constructed? Write an essay in which you advance your position; you can develop your ideas by consulting Aaron Devor's "Gender Role Behaviors and Attitudes" (p. 504) and Deborah Blum's "The Gender Blur: Where Does Biology End and Society Take Over?" (p. 511).

JENNIFER L. POZNER
Dove's "Real Beauty" Backlash

It sounds almost like the Macy's Santa Claus advising shoppers to look for something at Gimbel's in *Miracle on 34th Street*, but there you have it: Dove's "Campaign for Real Beauty" is actually telling ordinary girls and women to feel good about themselves. And, for the most part, Jennifer L. Pozner is rather glad it is, even if the Dove ads are still aimed at selling beauty products according to the implicit philosophy that "cellulite is unsightly, women's natural aging process is shameful, and flabby thighs are flawed and must be fixed." No, what angers Pozner are the male media figures who have voiced dismay at Dove's display of women with realistic figures and faces, some of whom dare to be middle-aged. Indeed, for Pozner, it is the commentary of such men that makes the Dove campaign so necessary in the first place. Pozner is executive director of Women In Media & News, and her media criticism has appeared in many national publications.

When it comes to Madison Avenue misogyny, usually it's the ad that's objectionable (hello, *Advertising Week*!), rather than the product itself.

The opposite is true in the latest incarnation of Dove's "Campaign for Real Beauty," which poses a bevy of full-figured babes in bras and boyshorts on billboards throughout New York, Chicago, D.C., L.A., and other top urban markets . . . just in time for the rollout of their new line of "firming cremes."

If the same smiling size sixes (and eights, and tens) were hawking hair dye or shilling for soap, the campaign would be revolutionary — but despite the company's continued and commendable intent to expand notions of female beauty to include the non-skinny and non-white, Dove's attempts are profoundly limited by a product line that comes with its own underlying philosophy: cellulite is unsightly, women's natural aging process is shameful, and flabby thighs are flawed and must be fixed . . . oh, so conveniently by Dove's newest lotion.

The feel-good "women are ok at whatever size" message is hopelessly hampered by the underlying attempt to get us to spend, spend, spend to "correct" those pesky "problem areas" advertisers have always told us to hate about our bodies. As Salon.com's Rebecca Traister put it, the message is "love your ass but not the fat on it."

Yet even though Dove's "Real Beauty" ads play to and subtly reinforce the stereotypes they claim to be exposing, it's impossible not to feel inspired by the sight of these attractive, healthy women smiling playfully at us from their places of billboard honor, their voluptuous curves all the more luscious alongside the bags-of-bones in competitors' campaigns. 5

Gina Crisanti was featured in Dove's campaign.

Unless, of course, you're *Chicago Sun Times* columnist Richard Roeper, who reacted to Dove's "chunky women" with the sort of fear and loathing he should reserve for the cheesy Hollywood schlock he regularly "thumbs up" during his Ebert & Roeper film reviews. "I find these Dove ads a little unsettling. If I want to see plump gals baring too much skin, I'll go to Taste of Chicago, OK?," Roeper ranted, saying that while he knows he should probably praise Dove for breaking away from airbrushed, impossible-to-achieve, youth-obsessed ad imagery, he much prefers to bitch and moan. "When we're talking women in their underwear on billboards outside my living room windows, give me the fantasy babes, please. If that makes me sound superficial, shallow and sexist — well yes, I'm a man."

Unsettling? Try Roeper's implication that all men are just naturally sexist — and that a man who wears gender-based bigotry as a badge of pride has some of the most power in the media to determine which films succeed and which fail. (Remember Roeper's admission next time his thumb goes way up for a flick whose humor rarely rises above cheap gags about sperm as hair gel, or when he pans a promising movie centered around strong female characters.)

Dozens of major media outlets jumped on Roeper's comments as an excuse to run insulting headlines such as "Fab or Flab," with stories exploring the "controversy" over whether Dove's ads are, as *People* put it, "the best thing to happen to advertising since the free sample, or an eyesore of outsize proportions."

The tone of this debate turned nasty, quickly, with women's self-esteem in one camp and men's fragile eyes in another as typified by a second *Sun Times* writer's comments that these "disturbing" and "frightening" women should "put on clothes (please, really)" because "ads should be about the beautiful people. They should include the unrealistic, the ideal or the unattainable look for which so many people strive." Besides, wrote Lucio Guerrero, "the only time I want to see a thigh that big is in a bucket with bread crumbs on it."

From there, print and broadcast outlets featured a stream of man-on-   10 the-street interviews begging Madison Avenue to bring back the starvation-saturated, silicone-enhanced sweeties they'd come to expect seeing on their commutes to work, echoing Guerrero's mean-spirited musings.

Some masked their aesthetic objections under the guise of health concerns: "At the risk of sounding politically incorrect," Bill Zwecker, the balding, paunchy, middle-aged anchor of CBS's local newscast in Chicago, weighed in on his CBS blog, "In this day and age, when we are facing a huge obesity problem in this country, we don't need to encourage anyone—women OR men—to think it's okay to be out of shape." Perhaps this line of attack would have been more convincing if the women in the ads were unhealthily over-weight (they're actually smaller-sized than the average American woman), or if Zwecker was a little more *GQ* and a little less *Couch Potato Quarterly*.

Certainly, these men so quick to demonize "the Dove girls" show no understanding that those "fantasy babes" of traditional ads have a profoundly negative impact on the health of girls and women in America. Advertising has never glorified obesity (though that problem is arguably a byproduct of McDonald's, M&Ms, and other junk food ads), but the industry has equated starvation and drug addiction with women's beauty and value for decades.

The "real beauty" backlash underscores just how necessary Dove's campaign is—however hypocritical the product they're selling may be. What's "unsettling" is not that Roeper, Guerrero, and Zwecker might have to look at empowerment-infused ads targeted to female consumers—it's that men with power positions in the media still think it's acceptable to demand that women be displayed only in the hyper-objectifying images they feel is somehow their due.

READING THE TEXT

1. Why does Pozner believe that Dove's "Real Beauty" ads "reinforce the stereo-types they claim to be exposing" (para. 5)?

2. In Pozner's view, what is the basis of the objections that Richard Roeper and some other male commentators have to the Dove "Campaign for Real Beauty"?

3. Characterize Pozner's tone in this selection, particularly in her comments regarding male critics of Dove's ads. What effect does it have on your response to her essay?

READING THE SIGNS

1. In a creative journal assignment, assume the perspective of one of the Dove "Real Beauty" models, and write a letter in response to Richard Roeper's complaints about the Dove ads.

2. Write an argumentative essay that validates, rejects, or complicates Pozner's claim that "the 'real beauty' backlash underscores just how necessary Dove's campaign is — however hypocritical the product they're selling may be" (para. 13).

3. Write an essay evaluating Richard Roeper's response to the Dove ad campaign. Do you find his response "unsettling" (para. 7), as Pozner sees it, or do you find it simply honest?

4. Write an essay arguing whether ad campaigns such as Dove's "Real Beauty" and Nike's "My Butt Is Big" are indeed revolutionary or are simply a new twist on advertising's tendency to objectify women's bodies.

5. Since Pozner wrote her essay, Dove has embarked on a series of "Real Beauty Sketches," an experiment in which forensic artist Gil Zamora first draws a sight-unseen woman based on her own self-description and then draws the same woman based on a stranger's description of her. The goal of this experiment is to show women that they are "more beautiful" than they assume. Watch some of these sketches on YouTube, and then write an essay in which you critique the videos. How do you think Pozner would respond to them? Do you believe that they are problematic, as she considered the original "Real Beauty" ad campaign to be?

GLORIA STEINEM
Sex, Lies, and Advertising

One of the best-known icons of the women's movement, Gloria Steinem has been a leader in transforming the image of women in America. As a cofounder of *Ms.* magazine, in which this selection first appeared, Steinem has provided a forum for women's voices for more than forty years, but as her article explains, it has not been easy to keep this forum going. A commercial publication requires commercials, and the needs of advertisers do not always mesh nicely with the goals of a magazine like *Ms.* Steinem ruefully reveals the compromises *Ms.* magazine had to make over the years to satisfy its advertising clients, compromises that came to an end only when *Ms.* ceased to take ads. Steinem's publications include *Revolution from Within* (1992), a personal exploration of the power of self-esteem; *Moving beyond Words* (1994); *Outrageous Acts and Everyday Rebellions* (2nd ed., 1995), and *Doing Sixty & Seventy* (2006). Currently a consulting editor for *Ms.*, Steinem continues to combine her passion for writing and activism as an unflagging voice in American feminism.

> Goodbye to cigarette ads where poems should be.
> Goodbye to celebrity covers and too little space.
> Goodbye to cleaning up language so *Ms.* advertisers won't be boycotted by the Moral Majority.
> In fact, goodbye to advertisers *and* the Moral Majority.
> Goodbye to short articles and short thinking.
> Goodbye to "post-feminism" from people who never say "post-democracy."
> Goodbye to national boundaries and hello to the world.
> Welcome to the magazine of the post-patriarchal age.
> The turn of the century is *our turn*!

That was my celebratory mood in the summer of 1990 when I finished the original version of the exposé you are about to read. I felt as if I'd been released from a personal, portable Bastille. At least I'd put on paper the ad policies that had been punishing *Ms.* for all the years of its nonconforming life and still were turning more conventional media, especially (but not only) those directed at women, into a dumping ground for fluff.

Those goodbyes were part of a letter inviting readers to try a new, ad-free version of *Ms.* and were also a homage to "Goodbye to All That," a witty and lethal essay in which Robin Morgan bade farewell to the pre-feminist male Left of twenty years before. It seemed the right tone for the birth of a brand-new, reader-supported, more international form of *Ms.*, which Robin was heading as editor-in-chief, and I was serving as consulting editor. Besides, I had a very personal kind of mantra running through my head: *I'll never have to sell another ad as long as I live.*

So I sent the letter off, watched the premiere issue containing my exposé go to press, and then began to have second thoughts: Were ad policies too much of an "inside" concern? Did women readers already know that magazines directed at them were filled with editorial extensions of ads—and not care? Had this deceptive system been in place too long for anyone to have faith in changing it? In other words: Would anybody give a damn?

After almost four years of listening to responses and watching the ripples spread out from this pebble cast upon the waters, I can tell you that, yes, readers do care; and no, most of them were not aware of advertising's control over the words and images around it. Though most people in the publishing industry think this is a practice too deeply embedded ever to be uprooted, a lot of readers are willing to give it a try—even though that's likely to mean paying more for their publications. In any case, as they point out, understanding the nitty-gritty of ad influence has two immediate uses. It strengthens healthy skepticism about what we read, and it keeps us from assuming that other women must want this glamorous, saccharine, unrealistic stuff.

Perhaps that's the worst punishment ad influence has inflicted upon us. It's made us feel contemptuous of other women. We know we don't need those endless little editorial diagrams of where to put our lipstick or blush — we don't identify with all those airbrushed photos of skeletal women with everything about them credited, *even their perfume* (can you imagine a man's photo airbrushed to perfection, with his shaving lotion credited?) — but we assume there must be women out there somewhere who *do* love it; otherwise, why would it be there?

Well, many don't. Given the sameness of women's magazines resulting from the demands made by makers of women's products that advertise in all of them, we probably don't know yet what a wide variety of women readers want. In any case, we do know it's the advertisers who are determining what women are getting now.

The first wave of response to this exposé came not from readers but from writers and editors for other women's magazines. They phoned to say the pall cast by anticipated or real advertising demands was even more widespread than rebellious *Ms.* had been allowed to know. They told me how brave I was to "burn my bridges" (no critic of advertising would ever be hired as an editor of any of the women's magazines, they said) and generally treated me as if I'd written about organized crime instead of practices that may be unethical but are perfectly legal. After making me promise not to use their names, they offered enough additional horror stories to fill a book, a movie, and maybe a television series. Here is a typical one: when the freelance author of an article on moisturizers observed in print that such products might be less necessary for young women — whose skin tends to be not dry but oily — the article's editor was called on the carpet and denounced by her bosses as "anti-moisturizer." Or how about this: the film critic for a women's magazine asked its top editor, a woman who makes millions for her parent company, whether movies could finally be reviewed critically, since she had so much clout. No, said the editor; if you can't praise a movie, just don't include it; otherwise we'll jeopardize our movie ads. This may sound like surrealism in everyday life, or like our grandmothers advising, "If you can't say something nice, don't say anything," but such are the forces that control much of our information.

I got few negative responses from insiders, but the ones I did get were bitter. Two editors at women's magazines felt I had demeaned them by writing the article. They loved their work, they said, and didn't feel restricted by ads at all. So I would like to make clear in advance that my purpose was and is to change the system, not to blame the people struggling within it. As someone who has written for most women's magazines, I know that many editors work hard to get worthwhile articles into the few pages left over after providing all the "complementary copy" (that is, articles related to and supportive of advertised products). I also know there are editors who sincerely want exactly what the advertisers want, which is why they're so good at their jobs.

Nonetheless, criticizing this ad-dominant system is no different from criticizing male-dominant marriage. Both institutions make some people happy, and both seem free as long as your wishes happen to fall within their traditional boundaries. But just as making more equal marital laws alleviates the suffering of many, breaking the link between editorial and advertising will help all media become more honest and diverse.

A second wave of reaction came from advertising executives who were asked to respond by reporters. They attributed all problems to *Ms.* We must have been too controversial or otherwise inappropriate for ads. I saw no stories that asked the next questions: Why had non-women's companies from Johnson & Johnson to IBM found our "controversial" pages fine for their ads? Why did desirable and otherwise unreachable customers read something so "inappropriate"? What were ad policies doing to *other* women's media? To continue my marriage parallel, however, I should note that these executives seemed only mildly annoyed. Just as many women are more dependent than men on the institution of marriage and so are more threatened and angry when it's questioned, editors of women's magazines tended to be more upset than advertisers when questioned about their alliance. . . .

Then came the third wave — reader letters which were smart, thought- ful, innovative, and numbered in the hundreds. Their dominant themes were anger and relief: relief because those vast uncritical oceans of food/fashion/ beauty articles in other women's magazines weren't necessarily what women

10

Gloria Steinem (left) and Patricia Carbine cofounded *Ms.* magazine.

Angel Franco/New York Times Co./Getty Images

wanted after all, and also relief because *Ms.* wasn't going to take ads anymore, even those that were accompanied by fewer editorial demands; anger
because consumer information, diverse articles, essays, fiction, and poetry
could have used the space instead of all those oceans of articles about ad categories that had taken up most of women's magazines for years. . . .

Last and most rewarding was the response that started in the fall. Teachers of journalism, advertising, communications, women's studies, and other
contemporary courses asked permission to reprint the exposé as a supplementary text. That's another reason why I've restored cuts, updated information, and added new examples — including this introduction. Getting
subversive ideas into classrooms could change the next generation running
the media.

The following pages are mostly about women's magazines, but that
doesn't mean other media are immune.

Sex, Lies, and Advertising

Toward the end of the 1980s, when glasnost was beginning and *Ms.* magazine seemed to be ending, I was invited to a press lunch for a Soviet official.
He entertained us with anecdotes about the new problems of democracy in
his country; for instance, local Communist leaders who were being criticized
by their own media for the first time, and were angry.

"So I'll have to ask my American friends," he finished pointedly, "how
more subtly to control the press."

In the silence that followed, I said: "Advertising."   15

The reporters laughed, but later one of them took me aside angrily: How
dare I suggest that freedom of the press was limited in this country? How
dare I imply that *his* newsmagazine could be influenced by ads?

I explained that I wasn't trying to lay blame, but to point out advertising's media-wide influence. We can all recite examples of "soft" cover stories
that newsmagazines use to sell ads, and self-censorship in articles that should
have taken advertised products to task for, say, safety or pollution. Even television news goes "soft" in ratings wars, and other TV shows don't get on the
air without advertiser support. But I really had been thinking about women's
magazines. There, it isn't just a little content that's designed to attract ads;
it's almost all of it. That's why advertisers — not readers — had always been
the problem for *Ms.* As the only women's magazine that didn't offer what the
ad world euphemistically describes as "supportive editorial atmosphere" or
"complementary copy" (for instance, articles that praise food/fashion/beauty
subjects in order to "support" and "complement" food/fashion/beauty ads),
Ms. could never attract enough ads to break even.

"Oh, *women's* magazines," the journalist said with contempt. "Everybody knows they're catalogs — but who cares? They have nothing to do with
journalism."

————

I can't tell you how many times I've had this argument since I started writing for magazines in the early 1960s, and especially since the current women's movement began. Except as moneymaking machines — "cash cows," as they are so elegantly called in the trade — women's magazines are usually placed beyond the realm of serious consideration. Though societal changes being forged by women have been called more far-reaching than the industrial revolution by such nonfeminist sources as the *Wall Street Journal* — and though women's magazine editors often try hard to reflect these changes in the few pages left after all the ad-related subjects are covered — the magazines serving the female half of this country are still far below the journalistic and ethical standards of news and general-interest counterparts. Most depressing of all, this fact is so taken for granted that it doesn't even rate as an exposé.

For instance: If *Time* and *Newsweek*, in order to get automotive and GM 20 ads, had to lavish editorial praise on cars and credit photographs in which newsmakers were driving, say, a Buick from General Motors, there would be a scandal — maybe even a criminal investigation. When women's magazines from *Seventeen* to *Lear's* publish articles lavishing praise on beauty and fashion products, and credit in text, the cover, and other supposedly editorial photographs a particular makeup from Revlon or a dress from Calvin Klein because those companies also advertise, it's just business as usual.

When *Ms.* began, we didn't consider *not* taking ads. The most important reason was to keep the price of a feminist magazine low enough for most women to afford. But the second and almost equal reason was to provide a forum where women and advertisers could talk to each other and experiment with nonstereotyped, informative, imaginative ads. After all, advertising was (and is) as potent a source of information in this country as news or TV or movies. It's where we get not only a big part of our information but also images that shape our dreams.

We decided to proceed in two stages. First, we would convince makers of "people products" that their ads should be placed in a women's magazine: cars, credit cards, insurance, sound equipment, financial services — everything that's used by both men and women but was then advertised only to men. Since those advertisers were accustomed to the division between editorial pages and ads that news and general-interest magazines at least try to maintain, such products would allow our editorial content to be free and diverse. Furthermore, if *Ms.* could prove that women were important purchasers of "people products," just as men were, those advertisers would support other women's magazines, too, and subsidize some pages for articles about something other than the hothouse worlds of food/fashion/beauty. Only in the second phase would we add examples of the best ads for whatever traditional "women's products" (clothes, shampoo, fragrance, food, and so on) that subscriber surveys showed *Ms.* readers actually used. But we would ask those advertisers to come in *without* the usual quid pro quo of editorial features praising their product area; that is, the dreaded "complementary copy."

From the beginning, we knew the second step might be even harder than the first. Clothing advertisers like to be surrounded by editorial fashion spreads (preferably ones that credit their particular labels and designers); food advertisers have always expected women's magazines to publish recipes and articles on entertaining (preferably ones that require their products); and shampoo, fragrance, and beauty products in general insist on positive editorial coverage of beauty aids—a "beauty atmosphere," as they put it—plus photo credits for particular products and nothing too depressing; no bad news. That's why women's magazines look the way they do: saccharine, smiley-faced, and product-heavy, with even serious articles presented in a slick and sanitized way.

But if *Ms.* could break this link between ads and editorial content, then we should add "women's products" too. For one thing, publishing ads only for gender-neutral products would give the impression that women have to become "like men" in order to succeed (an impression that *Ms.* ad pages sometimes *did* give when we were still in the first stage). For another, presenting a full circle of products that readers actually need and use would allow us to select the best examples of each category and keep ads from being lost in a sea of similar products. By being part of this realistic but unprecedented mix, products formerly advertised only to men would reach a growth market of women, and good ads for women's products would have a new visibility.

Given the intelligence and leadership of *Ms.* readers, both kinds of products would have unique access to a universe of smart consultants whose response would help them create more effective ads for other media too. Aside from the advertisers themselves, there's nobody who cares as much about the imagery in advertising as those who find themselves stereotyped or rendered invisible by it. And they often have great suggestions for making it better.

As you can see, we had all our energy, optimism, and arguments in good working order.

I thought at the time that our main problem would be getting ads with good "creative," as the imagery and text are collectively known. That was where the women's movement had been focusing its efforts, for instance, the National Organization for Women's awards to the best ads, and its "Barefoot and Pregnant" awards for the worst. Needless to say, there were plenty of candidates for the second group. Carmakers were still draping blondes in evening gowns over the hoods like ornaments that could be bought with the car (thus also making clear that car ads weren't directed at women). Even in ads for products that only women used, the authority figures were almost always male, and voice-overs for women's products on television were usually male too. Sadistic, he-man campaigns were winning industry praise; for example, *Advertising Age* hailed the infamous Silva Thin cigarette theme, "How to Get a Woman's Attention: Ignore Her," as "brilliant." Even in medical journals, ads for tranquilizers showed depressed housewives standing next to piles of dirty dishes and promised to get them back to work. As for women's magazines, they seemed to have few guidelines, at least none that excluded even the ads for the fraudulent breast-enlargement or thigh-thinning products for which their back pages were famous.

Obviously, *Ms.* would have to avoid such offensive imagery and seek out the best ads, but this didn't seem impossible. The *New Yorker* had been screening ads for aesthetic reasons for years, a practice that advertisers accepted at the time. *Ebony* and *Essence* were asking for ads with positive black images, and though their struggle was hard, their requests weren't seen as unreasonable. . . .

Let me take you through some of our experiences — greatly condensed, but just as they happened. In fact, if you poured water on any one of these, it would become a novel:

- Cheered on by early support from Volkswagen and one or two other car 30 companies, we finally scrape together time and money to put on a major reception in Detroit. U.S. carmakers firmly believe that women choose the upholstery color, not the car, but we are armed with statistics and reader mail to prove the contrary: A car is an important purchase for women, one that is such a symbol of mobility and freedom that many women will spend a greater percentage of income for a car than will counterpart men.

But almost nobody comes. We are left with many pounds of shrimp on the table, and quite a lot of egg on our face. Assuming this near-total boy-cott is partly because there was a baseball pennant play-off the same day, we blame ourselves for not foreseeing the problem. Executives go out of their way to explain that they wouldn't have come anyway. It's a dramatic begin-ning for ten years of knocking on resistant or hostile doors, presenting endless documentation of women as car buyers, and hiring a full-time saleswoman in Detroit — all necessary before *Ms.* gets any real results.

This long saga has a semi-happy ending: Foreign carmakers understood better than Detroit that women buy cars, and advertised in *Ms.*; also years of research on the women's market plus door-knocking began to pay off. Even-tually, cars became one of our top sources of ad revenue. Even Detroit began to take the women's market seriously enough to put car ads in other women's magazines too, thus freeing a few more of their pages from the food/fashion/beauty hothouse.

But long after figures showed that a third, even half, of many car mod-els were being bought by women, U.S. makers continued to be uncomfort-able addressing female buyers. Unlike many foreign carmakers, Detroit never quite learned the secret of creating intelligent ads that exclude no one and then placing them in media that overcome past exclusion. Just as an African American reader may feel more invited by a resort that placed an ad in *Ebony* or *Essence*, even though the same ad appeared in *Newsweek*, women of all races may need to see ads for cars, computers, and other historically "mascu-line" products in media that are clearly directed at them. Once inclusive ads are well placed, however, there's interest and even gratitude from women. *Ms.* readers were so delighted to be addressed as intelligent consumers by a routine Honda ad with text about rack-and-pinion steering, for example, that they sent fan mail. But even now, Detroit continues to ask: "Should we make special ads for women?" That's probably one reason why foreign cars still have a greater share of the women's market in the United States than of the men's.

• In the *Ms.* Gazette, we do a brief report on a congressional hearing into coal tar derivatives used in hair dyes that are absorbed through the skin and may be carcinogenic. This seems like news of importance: Newspapers and newsmagazines are reporting it too. But Clairol, a Bristol-Myers subsidiary that makes dozens of products, a few of which have just come into our pages as ads *without* the usual quid pro quo of articles on hair and beauty, is outraged. Not at newspapers or newsmagazines, just at us. It's bad enough that *Ms.* is the only women's magazine refusing to provide "supportive editorial" praising beauty products, but to criticize one of their product categories on top of it, however generically or even accurately—well, *that* is going too far.

We offer to publish a letter from Clairol telling its side of the story. In an   35
excess of solicitousness, we even put this letter in the Gazette, not in Letters to the Editors, where it belongs. Eventually, Clairol even changes its hair-coloring formula, apparently in response to those same hearings. But in spite of surveys that show *Ms.* readers to be active women who use more of almost everything Clairol makes than do the readers of other women's magazines, *Ms.* gets almost no ads for those dozens of products for the rest of its natural life.

• Women of color read *Ms.* in disproportionate numbers. This is a source of pride to *Ms.* staffers, who are also more racially representative than the editors of other women's magazines (which may include some beautiful black models but almost no black decisionmakers; Pat Carbine hired the first black editor at *McCall's*, but she left when Pat did). Nonetheless, the reality of *Ms.*'s staff and readership is obscured by ads filled with enough white women to make the casual reader assume *Ms.* is directed at only one part of the population, no matter what the editorial content is.

In fact, those few ads we are able to get that feature women of color—for instance, one made by Max Factor for *Essence* and *Ebony* that Linda Wachner gives us while she is president of Max Factor—are greeted with praise and relief by white readers, too, and make us feel that more inclusive ads should win out in the long run. But there are pathetically few such images. Advertising "creative" also excludes women who are not young, not thin, not conventionally pretty, well-to-do, able-bodied, or heterosexual—which is a hell of a lot of women.

• Our intrepid saleswomen set out early to attract ads for the product category known as consumer electronics: sound equipment, computers, calculators, VCRs, and the like. We know that *Ms.* readers are determined to be part of this technological revolution, not to be left out as women have been in the past. We also know from surveys that readers are buying this kind of stuff in numbers as high as those of readers of magazines like *Playboy* and the "male 18 to 34" market, prime targets of the industry. Moreover, unlike traditional women's products that our readers buy but don't want to read articles about, these are subjects they like to see demystified in our pages. There actually *is* a supportive editorial atmosphere.

"But women don't understand technology," say ad and electronics executives at the end of our presentations. "Maybe not," we respond, "but neither do men — and we all buy it."

"If women *do* buy it," counter the decisionmakers, "it's because they're 40 asking their husbands and boyfriends what to buy first." We produce letters from *Ms.* readers saying how turned off they are when salesmen say things like "Let me know when your husband can come in."

Then the argument turns to why there aren't more women's names sent back on warranties (those much-contested certificates promising repair or replacement if anything goes wrong). We explain that the husband's name may be on the warranty, even if the wife made the purchase. But it's also true that women are experienced enough as consumers to know that such promises are valid only if the item is returned in its original box at midnight in Hong Kong. Sure enough, when we check out hair dryers, curling irons, and other stuff women clearly buy, women don't return those warranties very often either. It isn't the women who are the problem, it's the meaningless warranties.

After several years of this, we get a few ads from companies like JVC and Pioneer for compact sound systems — on the grounds that women can understand compacts, but not sophisticated components. Harry Elias, vice president of JVC, is actually trying to convince his Japanese bosses that there is something called a woman's market. At his invitation, I find myself speaking at trade shows in Chicago and Las Vegas trying to persuade JVC dealers that electronics showrooms don't have to be locker rooms. But as becomes apparent, however, the trade shows are part of the problem. In Las Vegas, the only women working at technology displays are seminude models serving champagne. In Chicago, the big attraction is Marilyn Chambers, a porn star who followed Linda Lovelace of *Deep Throat* fame as Chuck Traynor's captive and/or employee, whose pornographic movies are being used to demonstrate VCRs.

In the end, we get ads for a car stereo now and then, but no VCRs; a welcome breakthrough of some IBM personal computers, but no Apple or no Japanese-made ones. Furthermore, we notice that *Working Woman* and *Savvy*, which are focused on office work, don't benefit as much as they should from ads for office equipment either. . . .

• Then there is the great toy train adventure. Because *Ms.* gets letters from little girls who love toy trains and ask our help in changing ads and box-top photos that show only little boys, we try to talk to Lionel and to get their ads.

It turns out that Lionel executives *have* been concerned about little girls. They made a pink train and couldn't understand why it didn't sell.

Eventually, Lionel bows to this consumer pressure by switching to a photo- 45 graph of a boy *and* a girl — but only on some box tops. If trains are associated with little girls, Lionel executives believe, they will be devalued in the eyes of little boys. Needless to say, *Ms.* gets no train ads. If even 20 percent of little girls wanted trains, they would be a huge growth market, but this remains unexplored. In the many toy stores where displays are still gender divided, the "soft" stuff, even modeling clay, stays on the girls' side, while the "hard" stuff, especially rockets and trains, is displayed for boys — thus depriving both. By 1986, Lionel is put up for sale.

We don't have much luck with other kinds of toys either. A *Ms.* department, Stories for Free Children, edited by Letty Cottin Pogrebin, makes us one of the very few magazines with a regular feature for children. A larger proportion of *Ms.* readers have preschool children than do the readers of any other women's magazine. Nonetheless, the industry can't seem to believe that feminists care about children — much less have them.

• When *Ms.* began, the staff decided not to accept ads for feminine hygiene sprays and cigarettes on the same basis: They are damaging to many women's health but carry no appropriate warnings. We don't think we should tell our readers what to do — if marijuana were legal, for instance, we would carry ads for it along with those for beer and wine — but we should provide facts so readers can decide for themselves. Since we've received letters saying that feminine sprays actually kill cockroaches and take the rust off metal, we give up on those. But antismoking groups have been pressuring for health warnings on cigarette ads as well as packages, so we decide we will accept advertising if the tobacco industry complies.

Philip Morris is among the first to do so. One of its brands, Virginia Slims, is also sponsoring women's tennis tournaments and women's public opinion polls that are historic "firsts." On the other hand, the Virginia Slims theme, "You've come a long way, baby," has more than a "baby" problem. It gives the impression that for women, smoking is a sign of progress.

We explain to the Philip Morris people that this slogan won't do well in our pages. They are convinced that its success with *some* women means it will work with *all* women. No amount of saying that we, like men, are a segmented market, that we don't all think alike, does any good. Finally, we agree to publish a small ad for a Virginia Slims calendar as a test, and to abide by the response of our readers.

The letters from readers are both critical and smart. For instance: Would 50 you show a photo of a black man picking cotton next to one of an African American man in a Cardin suit, and symbolize progress from slavery to civil rights by smoking? Of course not. So why do it for women? But instead of honoring test results, the executives seem angry to have been proved wrong.

We refuse Virginia Slims ads, thus annoying tennis players like Billie Jean King as well as incurring a new level of wrath: Philip Morris takes away ads for *all* its many products, costing *Ms.* about $250,000 in the first year. After five years, the damage is so great we can no longer keep track.

Occasionally, a new set of Philip Morris executives listens to *Ms.* saleswomen, or laughs when Pat Carbine points out that even Nixon got pardoned. I also appeal directly to the chairman of the board, who agrees it is unfair, sends me to another executive — and *he* says no. Because we won't take Virginia Slims, not one other Philip Morris product returns to our pages for the next sixteen years.

Gradually, we also realize our naïveté in thinking we could refuse all cigarette ads, with or without a health warning. They became a disproportionate source of revenue for print media the moment television banned them, and few magazines can compete or survive without them; certainly not *Ms.*, which lacks the support of so many other categories. Though cigarette ads actually inhibit editorial freedom less than ads for food, fashion, and the like — cigarette companies want only to be distant from coverage on the dangers of smoking, and don't require affirmative praise or photo credits of their product — it is still a growing source of sorrow that they are there at all. By the 1980s, when statistics show that women's rate of lung cancer is approaching men's, the necessity of taking cigarette ads has become a kind of prison.

Though I never manage to feel kindly toward groups that protest our ads and pay no attention to magazines and newspapers that can turn them down and still keep their doors open — and though *Ms.* continues to publish new facts about smoking, such as its dangers during pregnancy — I long for the demise of the whole tobacco-related industry. . . .

• General Mills, Pillsbury, Carnation, Del Monte, Dole, Kraft, Stouffer, Hormel, Nabisco: You name the food giant, we try to get its ads. But no matter how desirable the *Ms.* readership, our lack of editorial recipes and traditional homemaking articles proves lethal.

We explain that women flooding into the paid labor force have changed the way this country eats; certainly, the boom in convenience foods proves that. We also explain that placing food ads *only* next to recipes and how-to-entertain articles is actually a negative for many women. It associates food with work — in a way that says only women have to cook — or with guilt over *not* cooking and entertaining. Why not advertise food in diverse media that don't always include recipes (thus reaching more men, who have become a third of all supermarket shoppers anyway) and add the recipe interest with specialty magazines like *Gourmet* (a third of whose readers are men)? 55

These arguments elicit intellectual interest but no ads. No advertising executive wants to be the first to say to a powerful client, "Guess what, I *didn't* get you complementary copy." Except for an occasional hard-won ad for instant coffee, diet drinks, yogurt, or such extras as avocados and almonds, the whole category of food, a mainstay of the publishing industry, remains unavailable to us. Period. . . .

• By the end of 1986, magazine production costs have skyrocketed and postal rates have increased 400 percent. Ad income is flat for the whole magazine industry. The result is more competition, with other magazines offering such "extras" as free golf trips for advertisers or programs for "sampling" their products at parties and other events arranged by the magazine for desirable consumers. We try to compete with the latter by "sampling" at what we certainly have enough of: movement benefits. Thus, little fragrance bottles turn up next to the dinner plates of California women lawyers (who are delighted), or wine samples lower the costs at a reception for political women. A good organizing tactic comes out of this. We hold feminist seminars in shopping centers. They may be to the women's movement what churches were to the civil rights movement in the South — that is, *where people are*. Anyway, shopping center seminars are a great success. Too great. We have to stop doing them in Bloomingdale's up and down the East Coast, because meeting space in the stores is too limited, and too many women are left lined up outside stores. We go on giving out fancy little liquor bottles at store openings, which makes the advertisers happy — but not us.

Mostly, however, we can't compete in this game of "value-added" (the code word for giving the advertisers extras in return for their ads). Neither can many of the other independent magazines. Deep-pocketed corporate parents can offer such extras as reduced rates for ad schedules in a group of magazines, free tie-in spots on radio stations they also own, or vacation junkets on corporate planes.

Meanwhile, higher costs and lowered income have caused the *Ms.* 60/40 preponderance of edit over ads — something we promised to readers — to become 50/50: still a lot better than most women's magazines' goals of 30/70, but not good enough. Children's stories, most poetry, and some fiction are casualties of reduced space. In order to get variety into more limited pages, the length (and sometimes the depth) of articles suffers. Though we don't solicit or accept ads that would look like a parody in our pages, we get so worn down that some slip through. Moreover, we always have the problem of working just as hard to get a single ad as another magazine might for a whole year's schedule of ads.

Still, readers keep right on performing miracles. Though we haven't been 60 able to afford a subscription mailing in two years, they maintain our guaranteed circulation of 450,000 by word of mouth. Some of them also help to make up the advertising deficit by giving *Ms.* a birthday present of $15 on its fifteenth anniversary, or contributing $1,000 for a lifetime subscription — even those who can ill afford it.

What's almost as angering as these struggles, however, is the way the media report them. Our financial problems are attributed to lack of reader interest, not an advertising double standard. In the Reagan–Bush era, when "feminism-is-dead" becomes one key on the typewriter, our problems are used to prepare a grave for the whole movement. Clearly, the myth that advertisers go where the readers are — thus, if we had readers, we would have advertisers — is deeply embedded. Even industry reporters rarely mention the editorial demands made by ads for women's products, and if they do, they assume advertisers must be right and *Ms.* must be wrong; we must be too controversial, outrageous, even scatalogical to support. In fact, there's nothing in our pages that couldn't be published in *Time, Esquire*, or *Rolling Stone* — providing those magazines devoted major space to women — but the media myth often wins out. Though comparable magazines our size (say, *Vanity Fair* or the *Atlantic*) are losing more money in a single year than *Ms.* has lost in sixteen years, *Ms.* is held to a different standard. No matter how much never-to-be-recovered cash is poured into starting a magazine or keeping it going, appearances seem to be all that matter. (Which is why we haven't been able to explain our fragile state in public. Nothing causes ad flight like the smell of nonsuccess.)

My healthy response is anger, but my not-so-healthy one is depression, worry, and an obsession with finding one more rescue. There is hardly a night when I don't wake up with sweaty palms and pounding heart, scared that we won't be able to pay the printer or the post office; scared most of all that closing our doors will be blamed on a lack of readers and thus the movement, instead of the real cause. ("Feminism couldn't even support one magazine," I can hear them saying.)

We're all being flattened by a velvet steamroller. The only difference is that at *Ms.*, we keep standing up again.

Do you think, as I once did, that advertisers make decisions based on rational and uniform criteria? Well, think again. There is clearly a double standard. The same food companies that insist on recipes in women's magazines place ads in *People* where there are no recipes. Cosmetics companies support the *New Yorker*, which has no regular beauty columns, and newspaper pages that have no "beauty atmosphere."

Meanwhile, advertisers' control over the editorial content of women's magazines has become so institutionalized that it is sometimes written into "insertion orders" or dictated to ad salespeople as official policy — whether by the agency, the client, or both. The following are orders given to women's magazines effective in 1990. Try to imagine them being applied to *Time* or *Newsweek*. 65

• Dow's Cleaning Products stipulated that ads for its Vivid and Spray 'n' Wash products should be adjacent to "children or fashion editorial"; ads for Bathroom Cleaner should be next to "home furnishing/family" features; with similar requirements for other brands. "If a magazine fails for ½ the brands or more," the Dow order warned, "it will be omitted from further consideration."

- Bristol-Myers, the parent of Clairol, Windex, Drano, Bufferin, and much more, stipulated that ads be placed next to "a full page of compatible editorial."

- S. C. Johnson & Son, makers of Johnson Wax, lawn and laundry products, insect sprays, hair sprays, and so on, insisted that its ads "*should not be opposite extremely controversial features or material antithetical to the nature/copy of the advertised product.*" (Italics theirs.)

- Maidenform, manufacturer of bras and other women's apparel, left a blank for the particular product and stated in its instructions: "The creative concept of the _____ campaign, and the very nature of the product itself, appeal to the positive emotions of the reader/consumer. Therefore, it is imperative that all editorial adjacencies reflect that same positive tone. The editorial must not be negative in content or lend itself contrary to the _____ product imagery/message (e.g., *editorial relating to illness, disillusionment, large size fashion, etc.*)." (Italics mine.)

- The De Beers diamond company, a big seller of engagement rings, prohibited magazines from placing its ads with "adjacencies to hard news or anti-love/romance themed editorial."   70

- Kraft/General Foods, a giant with many brands, sent this message with an Instant Pudding ad: "urgently request upbeat parent/child activity editorial, mandatory positioning requirements — opposite full page of positive editorial — right hand page essential for creative — minimum 6 page competitive separation (i.e., all sugar based or sugar free gelatins, puddings, mousses, creames [sic] and pie filling) — Do not back with clippable material. Avoid: controversial/negative topics and any narrow targeted subjects."

- An American Tobacco Company order for a Misty Slims ad noted that the U.S. government warning must be included, but also that there must be: "no adjacency to editorial relating to health, medicine, religion, or death."

- Lorillard's Newport cigarette ad came with similar instructions, plus: "Please be aware that the Nicotine Patch products are competitors. The minimum six page separation is required."

Quite apart from anything else, you can imagine the logistical nightmare this creates when putting a women's magazine together, but the greatest casualty is editorial freedom. Though the ratio of advertising to editorial pages in women's magazines is only about 5 percent more than in *Time* or *Newsweek*, that nothing-to-read feeling comes from all the supposedly editorial pages that are extensions of ads. To find out what we're really getting when we pay our money, I picked up a variety of women's magazines for February 1994, and counted the number of pages in each one (even including table of contents, letters to the editors, horoscopes, and the like) that were not ads and/or copy complementary to ads. Then I compared that number to the total pages. Out of 184 pages, *McCall's* had 49 that were nonad or ad-related. Of 202, *Elle* gave readers 48. *Seventeen* provided its young readers with only 51 nonad or ad-related pages out of 226. *Vogue* had 62 out of 292. *Mirabella* offered readers 45 pages out of a total of 158. *Good Housekeeping* came out on top, though only at about a third, with 60 out of 176 pages. *Martha Stewart Living* offered the least. Even counting her letter to readers, a page devoted to her personal calendar, and another one to a turnip, only 7 out of 136 pages had no ads, products, or product mentions. . . .

Within the supposedly editorial text itself, praise for advertisers' products 75 has become so ritualized that fields like "beauty writing" have been invented. One of its practitioners explained to me seriously that "It's a difficult art. How many new adjectives can you find? How much greater can you make a lipstick sound? The FDA restricts what companies can say on labels, but we create illusion. And ad agencies are on the phone all the time pushing you to get their product in. A lot of them keep the business based on how many editorial clippings they produce every month. The worst are products [whose manufacturers have] their own name involved. It's all ego."

Often, editorial becomes one giant ad. An issue of *Lear's* featured an elegant woman executive on the cover. On the contents page, we learn she is wearing Guerlain makeup and Samsara, a new fragrance by Guerlain. Inside, there just happen to be full-page ads for Samsara, plus a Guerlain antiwrinkle skin cream. In the article about the cover subject, we discover she is Guerlain's director of public relations and is responsible for launching, you guessed it, the new Samsara. . . .

When the *Columbia Journalism Review* cited this example in one of the few articles to include women's magazines in a critique of ad influence, Frances Lear, editor of *Lear's*, was quoted at first saying this was a mistake, and then shifting to the defense that "this kind of thing is done all the time."

She's right. Here's an example with a few more turns of the screw. Martha Stewart, *Family Circle*'s contributing editor, was also "lifestyle and entertaining consultant" for Kmart, the retail chain, which helped to underwrite the renovation of Stewart's country house, using Kmart products; *Family Circle* covered the process in three articles not marked as ads; Kmart bought $4 million worth of ad pages in *Family Circle*, including "advertorials" to introduce a line of Martha Stewart products to be distributed by Kmart; and finally, the "advertorials," which at least are marked and only *look* like editorial pages, were reproduced and distributed in Kmart stores, thus publicizing *Family Circle* (owned by the New York Times Company, which would be unlikely to do this kind of thing in its own news pages) to Kmart customers. This was so lucrative that Martha Stewart now has her own magazine, *Martha Stewart Living* (owned by Time Warner), complete with a television version. Both offer a happy world of cooking, entertaining, and decorating in which nothing critical or negative ever seems to happen.

I don't mean to be a spoilsport, but there are many articles we're very unlikely to get from that or any other women's magazine dependent on food ads. According to Senator Howard Metzenbaum of Ohio, more than half of the chickens we eat (from ConAgra, Tyson, Perdue, and other companies) are contaminated with dangerous bacteria; yet labels haven't yet begun to tell us to scrub the meat and everything it touches — which is our best chance of not getting sick. Nor are we likely to learn about the frequent working conditions of this mostly female work force, standing in water, cutting chickens apart with such repetitive speed that carpal tunnel syndrome is an occupational hazard. Then there's Dole Food, often cited as a company that keeps women in low-level jobs and a target of a lawsuit by Costa Rican workers who were sterilized by contact with pesticides used by Dole — even though Dole must have known these pesticides had been banned in the United States.

The consumerist reporting we're missing sometimes sounds familiar. 80 Remember the *Ms.* episode with Clairol and the article about potential carcinogens in hair dye? Well, a similar saga took place with L'Oréal and *Mademoiselle* in 1992, according to an editor at Condé Nast. Now, editors there are supposed to warn publishers of any criticism in advance, a requirement that might well have a chilling effect.

Other penalties are increasing. As older readers will remember, women's magazines used to be a place where new young poets and short story writers could be published. Now, that's very rare. It isn't that advertisers of women's products dislike poetry or fiction, it's just that they pay to be adjacent to articles and features more directly compatible with their products.

Sometimes, advertisers invade editorial pages — literally — by plunging odd-shaped ads into the text, no matter how that increases the difficulty of reading. When Ellen Levine was editor of *Woman's Day*, for instance, a magazine originally founded by a supermarket chain, she admitted, "The day the copy had to rag around a chicken leg was not a happy one."

The question of ad positioning is also decided by important advertisers, a rule that's ignored at a magazine's peril. When Revlon wasn't given the place of the first beauty ad in one Hearst magazine, for instance, it pulled its ads from *all* Hearst magazines. In 1990 Ruth Whitney, editor in chief of *Glamour*, attributed some of this pushiness to "ad agencies wanting to prove to a client that they've squeezed the last drop of blood out of a magazine." She was also "sick and tired of hearing that women's magazines are controlled by cigarette ads." Relatively speaking, she was right. To be as controlling as most advertisers of women's products, tobacco companies would have to demand articles in flat-out praise of smoking, and editorial photos of models smoking a credited brand. As it is, they ask only to be forewarned so they don't advertise in the same issue with an article about the dangers of smoking. But for a magazine like *Essence*, the only national magazine for African American women, even taking them out of one issue may be financially difficult, because other advertisers might neglect its readers. In 1993, a group called Women and Girls Against Tobacco, funded by the California Department of Health Services, prepared an ad headlined "Cigarettes Made Them History." It pictured three black singers — Mary Wells, Eddie Kendricks, and Sarah Vaughan — who died of tobacco-related diseases. *Essence* president Clarence Smith didn't turn the ad down, but he didn't accept it either. When I talked with him in 1994, he said with pain, "the black female market just isn't considered at parity with the white female market; there are too many other categories we don't get." That's in spite of the fact that *Essence* does all the traditional food-fashion-beauty editorial expected by advertisers. According to California statistics, African American women are more addicted to smoking than the female population at large, with all the attendant health problems.

Alexandra Penney, editor of *Self* magazine, feels she has been able to include smoking facts in health articles by warning cigarette advertisers in advance (though smoking is still being advertised in this fitness magazine). On the other hand, up to this writing in 1994, no advertiser has been willing to appear opposite a single-page feature called "Outrage," which is reserved for important controversies, and is very popular with readers. Another women's magazine publisher told me that to this day Campbell's Soup refuses to advertise because of an article that unfavorably compared the nutritional value of canned food to that of fresh food — fifteen years ago.

I don't mean to imply that the editors I quote here share my objections to 85 ad demands and/or expectations. Many assume that the women's magazines at which they work have to be the way they are. Others are justifiably proud of getting an independent article in under the advertising radar, for instance, articles on family violence in *Family Circle* or a series on child sexual abuse and the family courts in *McCall's*. A few insist they would publish exactly the same editorial, even if there were no ads. But it's also true that it's hard to be honest while you're still in the job. "Most of the pressure came in the form of direct product mentions," explained Sey Chassler, who was editor in chief of *Redbook* from the sixties to the eighties and is now out of the game. "We got threats from the big guys, the Revlons, blackmail threats. They wouldn't run ads unless we credited them."

What could women's magazines be like if they were as editorially free as good books? as realistic as the best newspaper articles? as creative as poetry and films? as diverse as women's lives? What if we as women — who are psychic immigrants in a public world rarely constructed by or for us — had the same kind of watchful, smart, supportive publications on our side that other immigrant groups have often had?

We'll find out only if we take the media directed at us seriously. If readers were to act in concert in large numbers for a few years to change the traditional practices of *all* women's magazines and the marketing of *all* women's products, we could do it. After all, they depend on our consumer dollars — money we now are more likely to control. If we include all the shopping we do for families and spouses, women make 85 percent of purchases at point of sale. You and I could:

- refuse to buy products whose ads have clearly dictated their surroundings, and write to tell the manufacturers why;

- write to editors and publishers (with copies to advertisers) to tell them that we're willing to pay *more* for magazines with editorial independence, but will *not* continue to pay for those that are editorial extensions of ads;

- write to advertisers (with copies to editors and publishers) to tell them that we want fiction, political reporting, consumer reporting, strong opinion, humor, and health coverage that doesn't pull punches, praising them when their ads support this, and criticizing them when they don't;

- put as much energy and protest into breaking advertising's control over what's around it as we put into changing the images within it or protesting harmful products like cigarettes;

- support only those women's magazines and products that take us seriously as readers and consumers;

- investigate new laws and regulations to support freedom from advertising influence. The Center for the Study of Commercialism, a group founded in 1990 to educate and advocate against "ubiquitous product marketing," recommends whistle-blower laws that protect any members of the media who disclose advertiser and other commercial conflicts of interest, laws that require advertiser influence to be disclosed, Federal Trade Commission involvement, and denial of income tax exemptions for advertising that isn't clearly identified — as well as conferences, citizen watchdog groups, and a national clearinghouse where examples of private censorship can be reported.

Those of us in the magazine world can also use this carrot-and-stick technique. The stick: If magazines were a regulated medium like television, the editorial quid pro quo demanded by advertising would be against the rules of the FCC, and payola and extortion would be penalized. As it is, there are potential illegalities to pursue. For example: A magazine's postal rates are determined by the ratio of ad pages to editorial pages, with the ads being charged at a higher rate than the editorial. Counting up all the pages that are *really* ads could make an interesting legal action. There could be consumer fraud cases lurking in subscriptions that are solicited for a magazine but deliver a catalog.

The carrot is just as important. In twenty years, for instance, I've found no independent, nonproprietary research showing that an ad for, say, fragrance is any more effective placed next to an article about fragrance than it would be when placed next to a good piece of fiction or reporting. As we've seen, there are studies showing that the greatest factor in determining an ad's effectiveness is the credibility and independence of its surroundings. An airtight wall between ads and edit would also shield corporations and agencies from pressures from both ends of the political spectrum and from dozens of pressure groups. Editors would be the only ones responsible for editorial content — which is exactly as it should be.

Unfortunately, few agencies or clients hear such arguments. Editors often ⁹⁰
maintain the artificial purity of refusing to talk to the people who actually control their lives. Instead, advertisers see salespeople who know little about editorial, are trained in business as usual, and are usually paid on commission. To
take on special controversy editors might also band together. That happened
once when all the major women's magazines did articles in the same month on
the Equal Rights Amendment. It could happen again — and regularly.

Meanwhile, we seem to have a system in which everybody is losing. The
reader loses diversity, strong opinion, honest information, access to the arts,
and much more. The editor loses pride of work, independence, and freedom
from worry about what brand names or other critical words some sincere
freelancer is going to come up with. The advertiser loses credibility right
along with the ad's surroundings, and gets more and more lost in a sea of
similar ads and interchangeable media.

But that's also the good news. Because where there is mutual interest,
there is the beginning of change.

If you need one more motive for making it, consider the impact of U.S.
media on the rest of the world. The ad policies we tolerate here are invading
the lives of women in other cultures — through both the content of U.S. media
and the ad practices of multinational corporations imposed on other countries. Look at our women's magazines. Is this what we want to export?

Should *Ms.* have started out with no advertising in the first place? The odd
thing is that, in retrospect, I think the struggle was worth it. For all those years,
dozens of feminist organizers disguised as *Ms.* ad saleswomen took their
courage, research, slide shows, humor, ingenuity, and fresh point of view into
every advertising agency, client office, and lion's den in cities where advertising is sold. Not only were sixteen years of *Ms.* sustained in this way, with all
the changeful words on those thousands of pages, but some of the advertising
industry was affected in its imagery, its practices, and its understanding of the
female half of the country. Those dozens of women themselves were affected,
for they learned the art of changing a structure from both within and without,
and are now rising in crucial publishing positions where women have never
been. *Ms.* also helped to open nontraditional categories of ads for women's
magazines, thus giving them a little more freedom — not to mention making
their changes look reasonable by comparison.

But the world of advertising has a way of reminding us how far there is ⁹⁵
to go.

Three years ago, as I was finishing this exposé in its first version, I got a
call from a writer for *Elle*. She was doing an article on where women parted
their hair: Why, she wanted to know, did I part mine in the middle?

It was all so familiar. I could imagine this writer trying to make something
out of a nothing assignment. A long-suffering editor laboring to think of new
ways to attract ads for shampoo, conditioner, hair dryers, and the like. Readers
assuming that other women must want this stuff.

As I was working on this version, I got a letter from Revlon of the sort we disregarded when we took ads. Now, I could appreciate it as a reminder of how much we had to disregard:

> We are delighted to confirm that Lauren Hutton is now under contract to Revlon.
>
> We are very much in favor of her appearing in as much editorial as possible, but it's important that your publication avoid any mention of competitive color cosmetics, beauty treatment, hair care or sun care products in editorial or editorial credits in which she appears.
>
> We would be very appreciative if all concerned are made aware of this.

I could imagine the whole chain of women—Lauren Hutton, preferring to be in the Africa that is her passion; the ad executive who signed the letter, only doing her job; the millions of women readers who would see the resulting artificial images; all of us missing sources of information, insight, creativity, humor, anger, investigation, poetry, confession, outrage, learning, and perhaps most important, a sense of connection to each other; and a gloriously diverse world being flattened by a velvet steamroller.

I ask you: Can't we do better than this?   100

READING THE TEXT

1. What does Steinem mean by "complementary copy" (para. 17) and "advertorials" (para. 78)?

2. Summarize the relationship Steinem sees between editorial content and advertising in women's magazines.

3. In Steinem's view, what messages about gender roles does complementary copy send readers of women's magazines?

4. What is the history of response to this article since its initial publication in 1990, according to Steinem?

READING THE SIGNS

1. In your journal, explore whether you believe advertisers infringe on freedom of the press.

2. Steinem asserts that virtually all content in women's magazines is a disguised form of advertising. Test her hypothesis in a detailed analysis of a single issue of a magazine such as *Cosmopolitan* or *Elle*. Do you find instances of complementary copy and advertorials? How do you react as a potential reader of such magazines?

3. Explore whether Steinem's argument holds for men's magazines such as *Maxim* or *GQ*. If you identify differences, how might they be based on different assumptions about gender roles?

4. Bring a favorite magazine to class, and compare it with those chosen by other students. In small groups, study the relationship between ads and articles.

What magazines have the most complementary copy? How can you account for your findings?

5. Steinem asks, "What could women's magazines be like if they were as editorially free as good books?" (para. 86). In a creative essay, write your own response to this question, presenting evidence to support your thesis. If you prefer, you could focus on another type of magazine, such as a young men's publication like *Maxim*, which also links advertising with editorial content.

JULIET B. SCHOR

Selling to Children: The Marketing of Cool

Being cool isn't just an attitude — it's a consumer lifestyle. As Juliet B. Schor describes the situation in this selection from her book *Born to Buy*, the marketing of edgy, sexy, violent, and subversive images of coolness has moved from teen and young-adult advertising to children's advertising. Closely related to what Thomas Frank calls the "commodification of dissent," cool marketing to kids has created a "giant feedback loop," whereby advertisers study youth behavior to see what kids respond to, while the kids study advertisements to see what's cool and what's not. A professor of sociology at Boston College, Schor is the author of numerous books on American consumption, including *The Overworked American: The Unexpected Decline of Leisure* (1993); *The Overspent American: Why We Want What We Don't Need* (1999); *Born to Buy: The Commercialized Child and the New Consumer Culture* (2005); and *True Wealth: How and Why Millions of Americans Are Creating a Time-Rich, Ecologically Light, Small-Scale, High-Satisfaction Economy* (2011).

The Marketing of Cool

Cool has been around for decades. Back in the fifties, there were cool cats and hipsters. In the sixties, hippies and the Beatles were cool. But in those days, cool was only one of many acceptable personal styles. Now it's revered as a universal quality — something every product tries to be and every kid needs to have.[1] Marketers have defined cool as the key to social success, as what matters for determining who belongs, who's popular, and who gets accepted by peers. While there is no doubt that the desire for social acceptance is a central theme of growing up, marketers have elevated it to the sine qua non of children's psyches. The promotion of cool is a good example of how the practices of marketing to teens, for whom social acceptance is even more important, have filtered down to the children's sphere. In a recent survey of 4,002 kids in grades 4 through 8, 66 percent reported that cool defines them.[2] Part of why is that cool has become *the* dominant theme of children's marketing.

Part of the genius of cool is its versatility. Cool isn't only about not being a dork. Cool takes on many incarnations. It can incorporate dork and jock, if necessary. It can be driven by neon or primary colors; it's retro or futuristic, techno or natural. Today, Target is cool. Yesterday it was the Gap. Good-bye Barney. Hello Kitty. By the time you read these words, today's cool will not be. But although cool is hard to pin down, in practice it centers on some recurring themes, and these themes are relentlessly pushed by marketers in the conception and design of products, packaging, marketing, and advertising. At every step, these principles apply.

One theme is that cool is socially exclusive, that is, expensive. In an earlier era, cheap stuff dominated kids' consumer worlds, mainly because they didn't have much money. They bought penny candy, plastic toys, and cheap thrills. In those days, the functional aspects of products were paramount, such as the fact that the toy is fun to play with or the candy tastes good. Social symbolism and status weren't wholly absent, but they were far less important. Now that kids have access to so much more money, status and its underlying values of inequality and exclusion have settled at the heart of the kid consumer culture. Branding expert Martin Lindstrom reports that for tweens, the brand took over from function as the main attraction of products in the 1990s.[3] From video games, to apparel, to that ubiquitous symbol of status, the athletic shoe, kids' products have upscaled, in the process becoming both more unaffordable and more desirable. Gene Del Vecchio, former Ogilvy and Mather executive and author of *Creating Ever-Cool: A Marketer's Guide to a Kid's Heart*, is more candid than most others about the exclusionary nature of cool: "Part of cool is having something that others do not. That makes a kid feel special. It is also the spark that drives kids to find the next cool item."[4] When Reebok introduced its computerized Traxtar shoe, it was banking on a message of "superiority" ("I have Traxtar and you don't"), according to the people who designed the program.[5] The shoe became the top seller in its category, a notable accomplishment given its significantly higher price. Marketers convey the view that wealth and aspiration to wealth are cool. Material excess, having lots of money, career achievement, and a lifestyle to go with it are all highly valued in the marketing world's definition of what's hot and what's not. Living modestly means living like a loser.

Cool is also associated with being older than one's age.[6] Marketers and advertisers take this common desire of kids and play into it in a variety of ways. They put a few older kids in ads that are targeted to younger kids. They have young kids in ads morph into older kids or into adults. They use adult celebrity endorsers for products or brands that kids buy. They depict fantasy worlds in which a young kid sees himself or herself grown up. Cool is also associated with an antiadult sensibility, as ads portray kids with attitude, outwitting their teachers and tricking their parents. Finally, cool is about the taboo, the dangerous, the forbidden other. Among advertisers, *edgy* has been and remains the adjective of the moment — not "over the edge," because that is too dangerous, but "at the edge," "pushing the edge."

Edgy style has associations with rap and hip-hop, with "street" and African American culture. In the 1990s, ads aimed at white, middle-class Americans began to be filmed in inner-city neighborhoods with young black men as the stars. The ads made subtle connections to violence, drugs, criminality, and sexuality — the distorted and stereotypical images of young black men that have pervaded the mainstream media. As Harvard University's Douglas Holt wrote in 1999 in a paper we coauthored, "Street has proven to be a potent commodity because its aesthetic offers an authentic threatening edginess that is very attractive both to white suburban kids who perpetually recreate radical youth culture in relation to their parents' conservative views about the ghetto, and to urban cultural elites for whom it becomes a form of cosmopolitan radical chic. . . . We now have the commodification of a virulent, dangerous 'other' lifestyle. . . . Gangsta."[7]

The story of how street came to be at the core of consumer marketing began more than thirty years ago. Chroniclers of the marketing of "ghetto" point to the practices of athletic shoe companies, starting with Converse in the late 1960s and, more recently, Nike and its competitors. The shoe manufacturers intentionally associated their product with African American athletes, giving free shoes to coaches in the inner cities, targeting inner-city consumers in their research, attaching their brand to street athletics and sociability.[8] They also developed a practice dubbed "bro-ing" by industry insiders, that is, going to the streets to ask the brothers which designs deserve the moniker of cool. Apparel companies, beginning with Tommy Hilfiger, became active in this world, giving rap stars and other prominent tastemakers free samples of their latest styles.[9] While the connection to inner-city life may sound like a contradiction with the idea that cool is exclusive and upscale, it is partially resolved by the fact that many of the inner-city ambassadors of products are wealthy, conspicuous consumers such as rap stars and athletes driving fancy cars and living luxurious lifestyles.

Eventually soft drink companies, candy manufacturers, culture producers, and many others that sell products to teens and kids would be on the street, trying desperately to get some of that ineluctable cool to rub off on their brand. As advertiser Paul Kurnit explains, "What's going on in white America today is [that] the inner city is very much a Gold Standard. We've got lots of white kids who are walking around, emulating black lifestyle."[10] Of course, mere association with ghetto style is not a guarantee of success. Some campaigns have been flat-footed with their mimicry. Others lack basic credibility, such as preppy tennis shoe K-Swiss, which tried to position itself as a street brand. The brands that have been skilled at this approach are those with images that are more plausibly and authentically connected to it.

Although many aspects of African American culture have had a long historical association with cool such as jazz and sartorial styles, as well as a legacy of contributions to popular culture, what's happening now is unique. Never before have inner-city styles and cultural practices been such a dominant influence on, even a primary definer of, popular culture. The process is also no longer one of mainstreaming, in which a cultural innovation from the margins is incorporated into the larger culture. Rather, in the words of Douglas Holt again, "It is now the local, authentic qualities of Street culture that sell. Instead of black cultural products denuded of their social context, it is now primarily the context itself — the neighborhood, the pain of being poor, the alienation experienced by black kids. These are the commodifiable assets." The other new development is the role of large corporations in the movement of styles and cultural forms from the ghetto to the suburb. The process no longer develops through an organic movement as it once did. Instead, cool hunters manage the process of cultural transmission. Another novel aspect is the evolution of a back-and-forth dynamic between the companies and the grass roots, with cool-hunting and street marketing creating what media critics have called a feedback loop.

The feedback loop is a sharp departure from decades past, when consumers blindly followed where advertisers led. In Holt's words, marketers once possessed a monopoly on "cultural authority," in which they set the tone and agenda, and consumers eagerly looked to them to learn what to wear, eat, drive, and value.[11] That cultural authority has virtually disappeared. Its demise can be traced to the backlash against advertising that originally emerged in the 1950s with the popularity of books such as John Kenneth Galbraith's *The Affluent Society* and Vance Packard's *The Hidden Persuaders*.[12] By the 1960s, some of the most successful marketers were those who took their cues from consumers. Since, then, advertisers have increasingly attempted to figure out what people already value and let those findings direct ads. With youth, the process has gone a step further, because they know the advertisers are relying on them, and consciously play to their influence. That's the feedback idea, which has been identified by observers such as Douglas Kellner, Holt, and Douglas Rushkoff. As Rushkoff explains, in a plea to the industry: "It's turned into a giant feedback loop: you watch kids to find out what trend is 'in,' but the kids are watching you watching them in order to figure out how to act. They are exhibitionists, aware of corporate America's fascination with their every move, and delighting in your obsession with their tastes."[13] Although there's a democratic veneer to the feedback loop, that perspective obscures the fact that giant businesses orchestrate, control, and profit from the process. Furthermore, kids are increasingly pulling outrageous and even dangerous stunts to get themselves noticed by the great big marketing machine.

Originally, the marketing of edgy was a teen and young adult development. Now it too has trickled down to the children's market, though with some adjustments. Kid advertisers had to become far more discriminating, screening out what had become an anything-goes ethic. By way of illustration, consider the heroin-chic fashion photography of the mid-1990s, At that time cool hunters routinely included drugs, including hard ones, on their lists of what's hot and what's not. As one now-famous accounting from a cool-hunter publication that appeared in the *New Yorker* had it: "In San Francisco it's Nike, heroin, and reggae; in Chicago, Jungle music, Tag watches, and drugs."[14] Similarly, in kids' ads, violent images are more restricted, although this is less the case in movie ads, video games, and on the Web. The situation is similar with sexuality, exploitative racial imagery, and certain antisocial themes, all of which are prominent in cultural forms for teens and young adults. While going edgy can almost guarantee cool, it can also jeopardize a brand that depends on maintaining its wholesome image. Advertisers calibrate the degree of edginess and strive to go as far as, but not beyond what, a brand's image can tolerate.

Kids Rule: Nickelodeon and the Antiadult Bias

What else is cool? Based on what's selling in consumer culture, one would have to say that kids are cool and adults are not. Fair enough. Our country has a venerable history of generational conflict and youth rebellion. But marketers have perverted those worthy sentiments to create a sophisticated and powerful "antiadultism" within the commercial world.[15]

This trend also has a history. Advertising agencies have been co-opting youth rebellion for years, beginning with Bill Bernbach's embrace of the counterculture in Volkswagen ads in the 1960s, a development insightfully chronicled in Thomas Frank's *The Conquest of Cool*. More recently, the entity most responsible for the commercial exploitation of youth rebellion has been Viacom. The trend began with MTV and its teen audience, as the enormously popular network capitalized on teen desires to separate from and rebel against their parents.[16] MTV allowed teens to immerse themselves in an increasingly separate culture, with its own fashions, language, and attitudes. Over time, some of that sensibility has trickled down to Nickelodeon's younger target.

Nickelodeon was founded in 1979 as a cable network, but it has since become a transcendent brand identity, selling a wide array of products and a relationship with kids. Nickelodeon would eventually dominate children's media. Nickelodeon's audience outpaces all other kid-oriented networks by a wide margin. At 80 percent, its household penetration tops the children's cable networks.[17] As I write these words, it is enjoying its best ratings year ever, surging far above the competition. The Nickelodeon Web site is the number one children's online destination. Its magazines boast 1.1 million subscribers and 6.3 million readers.[18] Nickelodeon is shown in 158 countries. Incredibly enough, given its limited demographic target, Nickelodeon has become one of the nation's most profitable networks.[19] In the process, it has remade children's programming and advertising.

Early on, Nickelodeon earned a reputation for offering quality shows. Its graphics were visually arresting, and the content was fresh. In comparison to the tired world of program-length commercials, that is, shows whose primary purpose is to sell products, Nickelodeon's offerings stood out. The network has also benefited from its recognition that children are a diverse group in terms of race and ethnicity, family type, and age. On the revenue side, Nickelodeon has made hay with the insight that children are a major influence market for parental purchases. A senior executive explained their stance: "The whole premise of our company was founded on serving kids, and what we've found is that when you do good things for kids, it happens to be good for business."[20]

The secret of Nickelodeon's success is its core philosophy: *kids rule.* In 15 everything that they do, Nickelodeon tries to take the child's perspective. The network has positioned itself as kids' best friend, on their side in an often-hostile environment. Donna Sabino, director for research and development at Nickelodeon's Magazine Group, explained the thinking to me: "It's hard to be a kid in an adult world. The adult world doesn't respect kids. Everywhere else adults rule; at Nick kids rule."[21] The Nickelodeon worldview is that childhood has gotten tough. "Kids are experiencing increased pressure for achievement and activity. They don't have enough time for homework, they're oversched-uled." Nickelodeon gives them what they need: "funny, happy, empowering." There are thirteen criteria a program must have to pass muster at the net-work, including good quality, a kid-centered message, humor, and edgy visual design. In theory, these are good criteria. But in practice, when kid-centric and edgy come together, what often results is attitude — an antiauthoritarian us-versus-them sensibility that pervades the brand.

Nickelodeon is not unique in its positioning. The world of children's mar-keting is filled with variants of the us-versus-them message. A prominent example is the soft drink Sprite, one of the most successful youth culture brands.[22] One witty Sprite ad depicted an adolescent boy and his parents on a road trip. The parents are in the front seat singing "Polly wolly doodle all the day," the epitome of unnerving uncool. He's in the back, banging his head on the car window in frustration, the ignominy of being stuck with these two los-ers too much to bear. "Need a CD player?" the ad asks.

A Fruit-to-Go online promotion tells kids that "when it comes to fashion class, your principal is a flunkie." A spot for Sour Brite Crawlers has a group of tween boys in an elevator going into gross detail about how they eat this gummy worm candy, eventually sickening the adults and forcing them to flee. The cre-ators of the spot consider it "a great example . . . where tweens demonstrate their superiority of the situation with control over the adults."[23]

Adults also enforce a repressive and joyless world, in contrast to what kids and products do when they're left in peace. Consider a well-known Starburst classroom commercial. As the nerdy teacher writes on the board, kids open the candy, and the scene erupts into a riotous party. When the teacher faces the class again, all is quiet, controlled, and dull. The dynamic repeats itself, as the commercial makes the point that the kid world, courtesy of the candy, is a blast. The adult world, by contrast, is drab, regimented, BORRRR-inggg.

A study of 200 video game ads produced between 1989 and 1999 revealed a similar approach. Researchers Stephen Kline and Greig de Peuter report themes of boy empowerment through "oedipal rebellion" and rejection of home environments depicted as boring suburban spaces. "Nintendo ads," they write, "often construct the gamer as under siege by the adultified world while promising the young male gamers 'empowerment' and 'control' in an unlimited virtual world."[24] This attitude pervades the company's marketing strategy as well. As one Nintendo marketer explained, "We don't market to parents. . . . We market to our target group, which is teens and tweens. . . . The parental seal of approval, while it is something that we like, it is not something that we actively encourage in our marketing because that might say to the kids that we're boring."[25]

A related theme in some kid advertising is to promote behavior that is annoying, antisocial, or mischievous. There's usually a playful quality to these spots, as in the various ads involving stealing candy at the movies. Julie Halpin of the Gepetto Group explains the strategy they used for Kids Foot Locker: "We wanted to be able to show them the empowerment they could have with the shoes. . . . What's really fun about a new pair of sneakers is a lot of the things that kids do that are really mischievous: squeaking on the floor, giving each other flat tires, writing little messages underneath. . . . Sales during the advertising period were about 34 percent higher than they were the previous year."[26]

Industry insiders and outsiders confirm the antiadultism in much of today's youth advertising. As one marketer explained to me: "Advertisers have kicked the parents out. They make fun of the parents. . . . We inserted the product in the secret kid world. . . . [It's] secret, dangerous, kid only."[27] Media critic Mark Crispin Miller makes a similar point: "It's part of the official advertising worldview that your parents are creeps, teachers are nerds and idiots, authority figures are laughable, nobody can really understand kids except the corporate sponsor. That huge authority has, interestingly enough, emerged as the sort of tacit superhero of consumer culture. That's the coolest entity of all."[28]

Similar trends can be found in programming. Journalist Bernice Kanner notes that "television dads — and to a lesser extent moms — once portrayed as loving and wise are now depicted as neglectful, incompetent, abusive or invisible. Parenthood, once presented as the source of supreme satisfaction on TV, is now largely ignored or debased." It's "parents as nincompoops."[29] After 9/11, Holly Gross, then of Saatchi and Saatchi kid Connection, counseled companies that although "families *are* reconnecting and kids and parents *do* wish for more time together . . . that doesn't mean the tender moments must be shared in *your* marketing communication . . . some parents are just *sooooo* embarrassing." She advises going "parent-free" to market to tweens.[30]

Marketers defend themselves against charges of antiadultism by arguing that they are promoting kid empowerment. Social conservatives, however, see treachery in the ridicule of adults. Wherever one comes down on this debate, it's important to recognize the nature of the corporate message: kids and products are aligned together in a really great, fun place, while parents, teachers, and other adults inhabit an oppressive, drab, and joyless world. The lesson to kids is that it's the product, not your parent, who's really on your side.

Age Compression

One of the hottest trends in youth marketing is age compression — the practice of taking products and marketing messages originally designed for older kids and targeting them to younger ones. Age compression includes offering teen products and genres, pitching gratuitous violence to the twelve-and-under crowd, cultivating brand preferences for items that were previously unbranded among younger kids, and developing creative alcohol and tobacco advertising that is not officially targeted to them but is widely seen and greatly loved by children. "By eight or nine they want 'N Sync," explained one tweening expert to me, in the days before that band was eclipsed by Justin Timberlake, Pink, and others.

Age compression is a sprawling trend. It can be seen in the import of tele- 25 vision programming specifically designed for one year olds, which occurred, ironically, with Public Broadcasting's *Teletubbies*. It includes the marketing of designer clothes to kindergarteners and first graders. It's the deliberate targeting of R-rated movies to kids as young as age nine, a practice the major movie studios were called on the carpet for by the Clinton administration in 2000. It's being driven by the recognition that many children nationwide are watching MTV and other teen and adult programming. One of my favorite MTV anecdotes comes from a third-grade teacher in Weston, Massachusetts, who reported that she started her social studies unit on Mexico by asking the class what they knew about the country. Six or seven raised their hands and answered, "That's the place where MTV's Spring Break takes place!" For those who haven't seen it, the program glorifies heavy partying, what it calls "bootylicious girls," erotic dancing, wet T-shirt contests, and binge drinking.

Nowhere is age compression more evident than among the eight- to twelve-year-old target. Originally a strategy for selling to ten- to thirteen-year-olds, children as young as six are being targeting for tweening. And what is that exactly? Tweens are "in-between" teens and children, and tweening consists mainly of bringing teen products and entertainment to ever-younger audiences. If you're wondering why your daughter came home from kindergarten one day singing the words to a Britney Spears or Jennifer Lopez song, the answer is that she got tweened. Tween marketing has become a major focus of the industry, with its own conferences, research tools, databases, books, and specialty firms. Part of why tweening is so lucrative is that it involves bringing new, more expensive products to this younger group. It's working because tweens have growing purchasing power and influence with parents. The more the tween consumer world comes to resemble the teen world, with its comprehensive branding strategies and intense levels of consumer immersion, the more money there is to be made.[31]

NOTES

[1]For a now-classic account of cool-hunting, see Gladwell (1997), reprinted in Schor and Holt (2000).

[2]A recent survey in which 66 percent of kids say cool defines them is from the KidID survey of JustKid Inc. Data provided to the author and presented by Wynne Tyree at KidPower 2002.

[3]On the shift from function to brand as the main attraction, see Lindstrom (2003), p. 82.

[4]Gene Del Vecchio quote "part of cool" is from Del Vecchio (1997), p. 121.

[5]On Traxtar marketing and its success, see Siegel et al. (2001), pp. 179–190.

[6]On kids wanting to be older than they are, this is what Paul Kurnit had to say in our interview: "Emulation and aspiration work up, but only to a certain point. So if you capture six to eleven year olds, your bull's-eye is probably the eleven year old boy. . . . If you're looking for the eleven year old boy you're probably in a commercial casting a twelve or thirteen year old boy."

[7]Douglas Holt quote on street as a potent commodity is from Holt and Schor (1998).

[8]On sneaker marketing in the inner city, see Vanderbilt (1998), ch. 1.

[9]On Hilfiger, see Smith (1997) and Spiegler (1997).

[10]Paul Kurnit quote from his interview with O'Barr (2001).

[11]On the cultural authority of marketers, see Holt (2002).

[12]On these issues, see Kellner (1998), Holt (2002), and Frank (1997) on the backlash against advertisers and the subsequent marketing of cool.

[13]The feedback loop is explored in the PBS special *Merchants of Cool*, available online at pbs.org/frontline/shows/cool/. Douglas Rushkoff quote from his essay "The Pursuit of Cool: Introduction to Anti-Hyper-Consumerism," available online at http://www.rushkoff.com/essay/sportswearinternational.html.

[14]On cool-hunters' lists of what's hot and what's not, see Gladwell (1997), from which these items are drawn.

[15]For an early recognition of the rise of antiadultism, see Nader (1996).

[16]On the sale of youth rebellion to teens, see Nader (1996), ch. 4 and conclusion.

[17]Nickelodeon's ratings are from *Kidscreen* magazine (2002), p. 33. On weekdays in 2002, Nickelodeon commanded a 2.7 audience share, a full point above the Cartoon Network; on Saturday mornings, its 4.2 share was 1.2 points higher than the number two.

[18]The 1.1 million subscribers and 6.3 million readers from June 2003 data provided by Donna Sabino to the author.

[19]On Nickelodeon's profitability, see Carter (2002). MTV Networks, to which Nickelodeon belongs, earned more than $3 billion in revenue in 2002. The statistic of 158 countries is also from this source.

[20]"Whole premise of our company" quote by Lisa Judson, senior vice president of programming and executive creative director, cited in Hood (2000).

[21]Sabino quote beginning "It's hard to be a kid" and thirteen criteria from interview with the author, July 2001.

[22]On Sprite's success positioning itself as a youth brand, see *Merchants of Cool*, program 1911, *Frontline*. Available at www.pbs.org/wgbh/pages/frontline/shows/cool/etc/script.html.

[23]The Sour Brite Crawlers example is from Siegel et al. (2001), p. 61.

[24]"Nintendo ads" from Kline and de Peuter (2002), p. 265.

[25]Nintendo marketer quote on targeting kids directly is from Kline and de Peuter (2002), p. 266.

[26]Halpin quote from an interview with her at Reveries, available online at http://www.reveries.com/reverb/kids_marketing/halpin/index.html.

[27]"Advertisers have kicked the parents out" quote from Mary Prescott (pseudonym), interview with the author, July 2001.

[28]Crispin Miller quote from *Merchants of Cool* transcript, cited above.

[29]Television dads quote from Kanner (2002), p. 45, and parents as nincompoops on p. 56. See also Hymowitz (1999), ch. 4, for a discussion of antifamilial attitudes in television.

[30]Holly Gross quote from Gross (2002b).

[31]On the idea of the tween and its evolution from earlier categories of sub- and preteen, see Cook and Kaiser (2003).

READING THE TEXT

1. Explain in your own words what constitutes "cool" in children's advertising, according to Schor.

2. How has "street" culture influenced consumer marketing, as Schor explains it?

3. What does researcher Douglas Holt mean by his claim that "the neighborhood, the pain of being poor, the alienation experienced by black kids . . . are the commodifiable assets" (para. 8) exploited in advertising?

4. What does the term "age compression" (para. 24) mean, in your own words?

READING THE SIGNS

1. Perform a semiotic analysis of an advertisement from any medium directed at children. What signifiers in the ad are especially addressed to children? To what extent do you see evidence of "cool marketing"? Consider such details as colors, music, voice track, the implied narrative of the ad, and its characters and their appearance.

2. Conduct an in-class debate over whether advertising to young people should be more strictly regulated. To develop support for your team's position, watch some TV programs aimed at children or teens and the advertising that accompanies them.

3. **CONNECTING TEXTS** Read or reread James B. Twitchell's "What We Are to Advertisers" (p. 177), and write an essay in which you analyze whether Twitchell's assertion that "mass marketing means the creation of mass stereotypes" (para. 1) applies to child or tween consumers.

4. Using Thomas Frank's perspective in "Commodify Your Dissent" (p. 150) as a critical framework, analyze a suite of ads aimed at tweens and discuss the to extent to which the ads "commodify" coolness and edginess. Ads that promote popular clothing, such as jeans, can be especially rich objects of analysis.

JOSEPH TUROW

The Daily You: How the New Advertising Industry Is Defining Your Identity and Your Worth

It's called "data mining": the practice by which such digital media giants as Google and Facebook track every move by Internet users and sell that information to marketers who use it to construct advertisements that are tailor-made for their recipients. In this selection from his book *The Daily You*, Joseph Turow describes how this world of digital profiling and personalized marketing works. If his revelation "creeps you out," Turow explains, you are not alone. The Robert Lewis Shayon Professor of Communication at the University of Pennsylvania's Annenberg School, Turow is the author of many books, most recently *Playing Doctor: Television, Storytelling, and Medical Power* (2010); *Media Today: An Introduction to Mass Communication* (2011); and *The Daily You: How the New Advertising Industry Is Defining Your Identity and Your Worth* (2013).

At the start of the twenty-first century, the advertising industry is guiding one of history's most massive stealth efforts in social profiling. At this point you may hardly notice the results of this trend. You may find you're getting better or worse discounts on products than your friends. You may notice that some ads seem to follow you around the internet. Every once in a while a website may ask you if you like a particular ad you just received. Or perhaps your cell phone has told you that you will be rewarded if you eat in a nearby restaurant where, by the way, two of your friends are hanging out this very minute.

You may actually like some of these intrusions. You may feel that they pale before the digital power you now have. After all, your ability to create blogs, collaborate with others to distribute videos online, and say what you want on Facebook (carefully using its privacy settings) seems only to confirm what marketers and even many academics are telling us: that consumers are captains of their own new-media ships.

But look beneath the surface, and a different picture emerges. We're at the start of a revolution in the ways marketers and media intrude in — and shape — our lives. Every day most if not all Americans who use the internet, along with hundreds of millions of other users from all over the planet, are being quietly peeked at, poked, analyzed, and tagged as they move through the online world. Governments undoubtedly conduct a good deal of snooping, more in some parts of the world than in others. But in North America, Europe, and many other places, companies that work for marketers have taken the lead in secretly slicing and dicing the actions and backgrounds of

Portfolio of Advertisements

READING THE SIGNS

Consider these questions as you analyze the advertisements on the following pages.

1. This ad for the Bose Sound-Link Mini speaker reflects a change in the way that people listen to music. What is that change, and how is Bose responding to it through this ad?

2. This ad for Buffalo Exchange promotes an attitude as well as a lifestyle. What is that attitude, and how does it reflect what Thomas Frank calls the "commodification of dissent"?

3. An ad for a trade organization rather than a particular brand, this pitch for California Walnuts is intended to resemble a certain kind of movie poster. What is the kind of movie alluded to here, and why do you think it was chosen to spearhead this campaign?

4. The United States of America broke away from Britain and its royalist government in 1776, but this ad for Johnson's baby products is cast as an homage to the birth of a child to an heir to the British throne. Why do you think the creators of this ad presumed that such an approach would appeal to American consumers?

5. This ad for Playdead's video game Limbo contains a typical image from the game itself but otherwise very little information as to what the product being advertised is. What is the ad designer taking for granted about the audience for this ad? How might a fan of the game respond differently to the ad than someone unfamiliar with it?

6. This ad for Sanuk sandals contains numerous images, most of which are not of sandals. What are those images, and what do they say about the presumed lifestyles and desires of the target market for the product?

7. This ad contains a mixture of populist and elitist appeals. What are those appeals, and how do they combine to sell watches?

BOSE
Better sound through research

You know when you hear
a song that's the perfect
soundtrack for whatever
you're doing? I love when
that happens. It makes an
ordinary moment feel so...
extraordinary. That's why
wherever we go,

our music
goes with us.

Better sound. From a wireless speaker that fits in the palm of your
hand. The radically different design of this ultra-compact speaker
delivers clear, full sound you simply have to hear to believe. So pick
up a SoundLink® Mini and take your music places it's never been.

Bose.com/Mini | 1.800.699.BOSE

NEW **Bose®**
SoundLink® Mini
Bluetooth® speaker

©2013 Bose Corporation. The _Bluetooth_® word mark is a registered trademark of
Bluetooth SIG, Inc. and any use of such mark by Bose Corporation is under license.

Uniquely you.
buy.sell.trade

BuffaLo
EXCHANGE
New & Recycled Fashion

BuffaloExchange.com
#iFoundThisAtBX

CALIFORNIA WALNUTS

NATURAL DEFENDERS OF THE HUMAN BODY™

The harder you live, the more you need powerful, portable California Walnuts. They're rich in the essential plant-based omega-3 fatty acid ALA.

And the American Heart Association certifies foods, including walnuts, for the contribution they can make to an overall heart-healthy diet.

"Supportive but not conclusive research shows that eating 1.5 ounces of walnuts per day, as part of a low saturated fat and low cholesterol diet and not resulting in increased caloric intake, may reduce the risk of coronary heart disease." (FDA) One ounce of walnuts provides 18g of total fat, 2.5g of monounsaturated fat, 13g of polyunsaturated fat including 2.5g of alpha-linolenic acid – the plant-based omega-3 fatty acid and 3.68mmol of antioxidants.

WALNUTS.ORG   f FACEBOOK.COM/CAWALNUTS   TWITTER.COM/CAWALNUTS

American Heart Association CERTIFIED Meets Criteria For Heart-Healthy Food

Per one ounce serving.
See heartcheckmark.org/guidelines

A parent's love is the same the world over.

Congratulations from our humble family to your royal one.

Johnson's baby

LIMBO
On iPad and iPhone

SANDALS ARE FOR: LAUGHTER, LOVE AND LATE NIGHTS.

YOGA MAT SANDALS

THE LONG TRADITION OF DETROIT WATCHMAKING HAS JUST BEGUN.

WATCHES WILL BE MADE IN DETROIT FOR DECADES TO COME, BUT WE WILL NEVER MAKE THIS ONE AGAIN. RESERVE **THE RUNWELL**, AN EXTREMELY LIMITED SINGLE EDITION OF THE FIRST HANDMADE WATCH FROM THE MOTOR CITY.

SHINOLA.COM

SHINOLA
DETROIT

Where American is made.™

huge populations on a virtually minute-by-minute basis. Their goal is to find out how to activate individuals' buying impulses so they can sell us stuff more efficiently than ever before. But their work has broader social and cultural consequences as well. It is destroying traditional publishing ethics by forcing media outlets to adapt their editorial content to advertisers' public-relations needs and slice-and-dice demands. And it is performing a highly controversial form of social profiling and discrimination by customizing our media content on the basis of marketing reputations we don't even know we have.

Consider a fictional middle class family of two parents with three children who eat out a lot in fast-food restaurants. After a while the parents receive a continual flow of fast-food restaurant coupons. Data suggest the parents, let's call them Larry and Rhonda, will consistently spend far more than the coupons' value. Additional statistical evaluations of parents' activities and discussions online and off may suggest that Larry and Rhonda and their children tend toward being overweight. The data, in turn, result in a small torrent of messages by marketers and publishers seeking to exploit these weight issues to increase attention or sales. Videos about dealing with overweight children, produced by a new type of company called content farms, begin to show up on parenting websites Rhonda frequents. When Larry goes online, he routinely receives articles about how fitness chains emphasize weight loss around the holidays. Ads for fitness firms and diet pills typically show up on the pages with those articles. One of Larry and Rhonda's sons, who is fifteen years old, is happy to find a text message on his phone that invites him to use a discount at an ice cream chain not too far from his house. One of their daughters, by contrast, is mortified when she receives texts inviting her to a diet program and an ad on her Facebook page inviting her to a clothing store for hip, oversized women. What's more, people keep sending her Twitter messages about weight loss. In the meantime, both Larry and Rhonda are getting ads from check-cashing services and payday-loan companies. And Larry notices sourly on auto sites he visits that the main articles on the home page and the ads throughout feature entry-level and used models. His bitterness only becomes more acute when he describes to his boss the down-market Web he has been seeing lately. Quite surprised, she tells him she has been to the same auto sites recently and has just the opposite impression: many of the articles are about the latest German cars, and one home-page ad even offered her a gift for test-driving one at a dealer near her home.

This scenario of individual and household profiling and media customization is quite possible today. Websites, advertisers, and a panoply of other companies are continuously assessing the activities, intentions, and backgrounds of virtually everyone online; even our social relationships and comments are being carefully and continuously analyzed. In broader and broader ways, computer-generated conclusions about who we are affect the media content — the streams of commercial messages, discount offers, information, news, and entertainment — each of us confronts. Over the next few decades the business logic that drives these tailored activities will transform the ways we see ourselves, those around us, and the world at large. Governments too may be able to use marketers' technology and data to influence what we see and hear.

From this vantage point, the rhetoric of consumer power begins to lose credibility. In its place is a rhetoric of esoteric technological and statistical knowledge that supports the practice of social discrimination through profiling. We may note its outcomes only once in a while, and we may shrug when we do because it seems trivial—just a few ads, after all. But unless we try to understand how this profiling or reputation-making process works and what it means for the long term, our children and grandchildren will bear the full brunt of its prejudicial force.

The best way to enter this new world is to focus on its central driving force: the advertising industry's media-buying system. Media buying involves planning and purchasing space or time for advertising on outlets as diverse as billboards, radio, websites, mobile phones, and newspapers. For decades, media buying was a backwater, a service wing of advertising agencies that was known for having the lowest-paying jobs on Madison Avenue and for filling those jobs with female liberal arts majors fresh out of college. But that has all changed. The past twenty years have seen the rise of "media agencies" that are no longer part of ad agencies, though they may both be owned by the same parent company. Along with a wide array of satellite companies that feed them technology and data, media agencies have become magnets for well-remunerated software engineers and financial statisticians of both sexes.

In the United States alone, media-buying agencies wield more than $170 billion of their clients' campaign funds; they use these funds to purchase space and time on media they think will advance their clients' marketing aims. But in the process they are doing much more. With the money as leverage, they are guiding the media system toward nothing less than new ways of thinking about and evaluating audience members and defining what counts as a successful attempt to reach them. Traditionally, marketers have used media such as newspapers, magazines, radio, billboards, and television to reach out to segments of the population through commercial messages. These advertisers typically learned about audience segments from survey companies that polled representative portions of the population via a variety of methods, including panel research. A less prestigious direct-marketing business has involved contacting individuals by mail or phone. Firms have rented lists of public data or purchase information that suggests who might be likely customers.

The emerging new world is dramatically different. The distinction between reaching out to audiences via mass media and by direct-response methods is disappearing. Advertisers in the digital space expect all media firms to deliver to them particular types of individuals—and, increasingly, *particular* individuals—by leveraging a detailed knowledge about them and their behaviors that was unheard of even a few years ago. The new advertising strategy involves drawing as specific a picture as possible of a person based in large part on measurable physical acts such as clicks, swipes, mouseovers, and even voice

commands. The strategy uses new digital tracking tools like cookies and bea-
cons as well as new organizations with names like BlueKai, Rapleaf, Invidi,
and eXelate. These companies track people on websites and across websites
in an effort to learn what they do, what they care about, and who their friends
are. Firms that exchange the information often do ensure that the targets'
names and postal addresses remain anonymous — but not before they add
specific demographic data and lifestyle information. For example:

- Rapleaf is a firm that claims on its website to help marketers "customize
  your customers' experience." To do that, it gleans data from individual
  users of blogs, internet forums, and social networks. It uses ad exchanges
  to sell the ability to reach those people. Rapleaf says it has "data on
  900+ million records, 400+ million consumers, [and] 52+ billion friend
  connections." Advertisers are particularly aware of the firm's ability to
  predict the reliability of individuals (for example, the likelihood they will
  pay their mortgage) based on Rapleaf's research on the trustworthiness of
  the people in those individuals' social networks.

- A company called Next Jump runs employee discount and reward programs for about one-third of U.S. corporate employees. It gets personal
  information about all of them from the human relations departments of
  the companies and supplements that information with transactional data
  from the manufacturers it deals with as well as from credit companies.
  Armed with this combination of information, Next Jump can predict what
  people want and what they will pay for. It also generates a "UserRank"
  score for every employee based on how many purchases a person has
  made and how much he or she has spent. That score plays an important
  role in determining which employee gets what product e-mail offers and
  at what price.

- A firm called The Daily Me already sells an ad and news personalization
  technology to online periodicals. If a *Boston Globe* reader who reads a lot of
  soccer sports news visits a *Dallas Morning News* site, the Daily Me's technology tells the *Dallas Morning News* to serve him soccer stories. Moreover,
  when an ad is served along with the story, its text and photos are instantly
  configured so as to include soccer terms and photos as part of the advertising pitch. A basketball fan receiving an ad for the same product will get
  language and photos that call out to people with hoop interests.

These specific operations may not be in business a few years from now. 10
In the new media-buying environment, companies come and go amid furious
competition. The logic propelling them and more established firms forward,
though, is consistent: the future belongs to marketers and media firms —
publishers, in current terminology — that learn how to find and keep the most
valuable customers by surrounding them with the most persuasive media
materials. Special online advertising exchanges, owned by Google, Yahoo!,
Microsoft, Interpublic, and other major players, allow publishers to auction

and media agencies to "buy" individuals with particular characteristics, often in real time. That is, it is now possible to buy the right to deliver an ad to a person with specific characteristics at the precise moment that that person loads a Web page. In fact, through an activity called cookie matching, . . . an advertiser can actually bid for the right to reach an individual whom the advertiser knows from previous contacts and is now tracking around the Web. Moreover, the technology keeps changing. Because consumers delete Web cookies and marketers find cookies difficult to use with mobile devices, technology companies have developed methods to "fingerprint" devices permanently and allow for persistent personalization across many media platforms.

The significance of tailored commercial messages and offers goes far beyond whether or not the targeted persons buy the products. Advertisements and discounts are status signals: they alert people as to their social position. If you consistently get ads for low-priced cars, regional vacations, fast-food restaurants, and other products that reflect a lower-class status, your sense of the world's opportunities may be narrower than that of someone who is feted with ads for national or international trips and luxury products. Moreover, if like Larry and Rhonda you happen to know that your colleague is receiving more ads for the luxury products than you are, and more and better discounts to boot, you may worry that you are falling behind in society's estimation of your worth.

In fact, the ads may signal your opportunities actually *are* narrowed if marketers and publishers decide that the data points — profiles — about you across the internet position you in a segment of the population that is relatively less desirable to marketers because of income, age, past-purchase behavior, geographical location, or other reasons. Turning individual profiles into individual evaluations is what happens when a profile becomes a reputation. Today individual marketers still make most of the decisions about which particular persons matter to them, and about how much they matter. But that is beginning to change as certain publishers and data providers — Rapleaf and Next Jump, for example — allow their calculations of value to help advertisers make targeting decisions. In the future, these calculations of our marketing value, both broadly and for particular products, may become routine parts of the information exchanged about people throughout the media system.

The tailoring of news and entertainment is less advanced, but it is clearly under way. Technologies developed for personalized advertising and coupons point to possibilities for targeting individuals with personalized news and entertainment. Not only is this already happening, the logic of doing that is becoming more urgent to advertisers and publishers. Advertisers operate on the assumption that, on the internet as in traditional media, commercial messages that parade as soft (or "human interest") news and entertainment are more persuasive than straightforward ads. Publishers know this too, and in the heat of a terrible economic downturn even the most traditional ones have begun to compromise long-standing professional norms about the separation of advertising and editorial matter. And in fact many of the new online publishers — companies, such as Demand Media, that turn out thousands of text and video pieces a day—never really bought into the old-world ideas about editorial integrity anyway. What this means is that we are entering a world of intensively customized content, a world in which publishers and even marketers will package personalized advertisements with soft news or entertainment that is tailored to fit both the selling needs of the ads and the reputation of the particular individual.

The rise of digital profiling and personalization has spawned a new industrial jargon that reflects potentially grave social divisions and privacy issues. Marketers divide people into *targets* and *waste*. They also use words like *anonymous* and *personal* in unrecognizable ways that distort and drain them of their traditional meanings. If a company can follow your behavior in the digital environment—an environment that potentially includes your mobile phone and television set—its claim that you are "anonymous" is meaningless. That is particularly true when firms intermittently add off-line information such as shopping patterns and the value of your house to their online data and then simply strip the name and address to make it "anonymous." It matters little if your name is John Smith, Yesh Mispar, or 3211466. The persistence of information about you will lead firms to act based on what they know, share, and care about you, whether you know it is happening or not.

All these developments may sound more than a little unsettling; *creeped out* is a phrase people often use when they learn about them. National surveys I have conducted over the past decade consistently suggest that although people know companies are using their data and do worry about it, their understanding of exactly how the data are being used is severely lacking. That of course shouldn't be surprising. People today lead busy, even harried, lives. Keeping up with the complex and changing particulars of data mining is simply not something most of us have the time or ability to do. There are many great things about the new media environment. But when companies track people without their knowledge, sell their data without letting them know what they are doing or securing their permission, and then use those data to decide which of those people are targets or waste, we have a serious social problem. The precise implications of this problem are not yet clear. If it's allowed to persist, and people begin to realize how the advertising industry segregates them from and pits them against others in the ads they get, the discounts they receive, the TV-viewing suggestions and news stories they confront, and even the offers they receive in the supermarket, they may begin to suffer the effects of discrimination. They will likely learn to distrust the companies that have put them in this situation, and they may well be incensed at the government that has not helped to prevent it. A comparison to the financial industry is apt. Here was an industry engaged in a whole spectrum of arcane practices that were not at all transparent to consumers or regulators but that had serious negative impact on our lives. It would be deeply unfortunate if the advertising system followed the same trajectory.

Despite valiant efforts on the part of advocacy groups and some federal and state officials, neither government rulings nor industry self-regulation has set policies that will address these issues before they become major sources of widespread social distress. Part of the reason for the lack of action may be that neither citizens nor politicians recognize how deeply embedded in American life these privacy-breaching and social-profiling activities are. Few individuals outside advertising know about the power of the new media-buying system: its capacity to determine not only what media firms do but how we see ourselves and others. They don't know that that system is working to attach marketing labels to us based on the clicks we make, the conversations we have, and the friendships we enjoy on websites, mobile devices, iPads, supermarket carts, and even television sets. They don't know that the new system is forcing many media firms to sell their souls for ad money while they serve us commercial messages, discounts, and, increasingly, news and entertainment based on our marketing labels. They don't realize that the wide sharing of data suggests that in the future marketers and media firms may find it useful to place us into personalized "reputation silos" that surround us with worldviews and rewards based on labels marketers have created reflecting our value to them. Without this knowledge, it is hard to even begin to have broad-based serious discussions about what society and industry should do about this sobering new world: into the twenty-first century the media-buying system's strategy of social discrimination will increasingly define how we as individuals relate to society — not only how much we pay but what we see and when and how we see it.

READING THE TEXT

1. In your own words, describe how digital media agencies' methods to ascertain consumer behavior differ from traditional consumer research strategies used at least twenty years ago.

2. Describe in a paragraph what Turow means by the "advertising industry's media-buying system" (para. 7).

3. According to this selection, how are digitally obtained profiles of individuals and households translated into personalized advertising?

4. Make a list of the advantages and problems of digital marketing strategies.

5. What assumptions does Turow make about his readers' likely responses to his indictment of the digital mining of personal information? How do those assumptions shape your response to his argument?

READING THE SIGNS

1. Write a letter to the hypothetical couple Larry and Rhonda, whom Turow describes as being surprised and bitter about the precise profiling of their household by media marketers. Can you offer any suggestions about how to avoid being so profiled? To develop ideas about possible strategies, consult Gloria Steinem's "Sex, Lies, and Advertising" (p. 197).

2. In class, hold a debate on whether marketers' mining of personal information and creation of specific consumer profiles are advantageous or problematic

for the consumer (do not consider whether this strategy benefits the marketers or their clients). For the former position, your argument might focus on the advantages of customized "content"; for the latter, your argument might focus on the creation of social distinctions and/or privacy concerns. After the debate, write an essay in which you advance your own argument about this question.

3. As Turow explains, the majority of consumers do not realize that their Internet activities are mined for commercial reasons. Write an essay in which you support, oppose, or complicate the proposition that for-profit data miners such as Google should pay, in money or services, users whom they monitor for information that they then sell.

4. In an essay, analyze semiotically the Web site of one of the data-tracking companies that Turow mentions, such as Rapleaf or Next Jump, or the Web site of an online advertising exchange such as those owned by Google and Yahoo! What signs appear on the Web site (especially the home page) that indicate whose interests the company serves?

5. In his conclusion, Turow expresses a desire for "broad-based serious discussions about what society and industry should do about this sobering new world." He continues, "Into the twenty-first century the media-buying system's strategy of social discrimination will increasingly define how we as individuals relate to society — not only how much we pay but what we see and when and how we see it" (para. 16). Write an essay in which you respond to Turow's remarks.

JULIA B. CORBETT

A Faint Green Sell: Advertising and the Natural World

Though "green" marketing and advertising is not as prevalent today as it was in the 1980s and 1990s, advertisers still exploit natural imagery to move the goods. Believing, however, that "the business of advertising is fundamentally 'brown'" and that "therefore the idea of advertising being 'green' and capable of supporting environmental values is an oxymoron," Julia B. Corbett sets out to analyze and categorize the ways in which advertising exploits nature, from treating it as a commodity to presenting nature as something that exists solely for the pleasure of human beings. All these strategies, Corbett concludes, perpetuate "an anthropocentric, narcissistic relationship" with the natural world. In other words, beautiful mountain ad backgrounds do not mean that you should go out and buy an SUV. Julia B. Corbett is a professor of communication at the University of Utah.

In the 1980s, advertisers discovered the environment. When a revitalized environmental movement helped establish environmentalism as a legitimate, mainstream public goal (Luke, 1993), corporate America quickly capitalized on a lucrative market of "green consumers" (Ottman, 1993; Zinkham & Carlson, 1995). Marketers not only could create new products and services, they could also reposition existing ones to appear more environmentally friendly. What resulted was a flood of advertisements that focused on green product attributes, touting products as recyclable and biodegradable and claiming them good or safe for the environment. Increases in this genre were remarkable, with green print ads increasing 430% and green television ads increasing 367% between 1989 and 1990 (Ottman, 1993). The total number of products claiming green attributes doubled in 1990 to 11.4% from the previous year ("Selling green," 1991).

Virtually all of the existing research on so-called green advertising was conducted during this boom. Green advertising was defined by researchers as product ads touting environmental benefits or corporate green-image ads (Banerjee, Gulas, & Iyer, 1995; Shrum, McCarty, & Lowrey, 1995). Researchers also targeted and segmented green consumers (Ottman, 1993) and tested their motivations (Luke, 1993). Green appeals were categorized (Iyer & Banerjee, 1993; Obermiller, 1995; Schuhwerk & Lefkoff-Hagius, 1995) and consumer response to green ads analyzed (Mayer, Scammon, & Zick, 1993; Thorson, Page, & Moore, 1995).

By the late 1990s, advertisers announced the end of the green-ad boom. *Advertising Age* reported that as the country headed into the thirtieth anniversary of Earth Day, green positioning had become more than just a non-issue — it was almost an anti-issue (Neff, 2000). Marketers were launching a whole new class of disposable products from plastic storage containers to dust mops. There was a perceived decline in controversy over anti-green products such as disposable diapers, toxic batteries, and gas-guzzling SUVs (sport utility vehicles). In addition, only 5% of new products made claims about recyclability or recycled content, and the explosion of e-tailing added boxes, styrofoam peanuts, and air-puffed plastic bags to the waste stream. Green product ads in prime-time television, which never amounted to more than a blip, virtually disappeared by 1995, reflecting "the television tendency to get off the environmental bandwagon after it had lost its trendiness" (Shanahan & McComas, 1999, p. 108).

But Shanahan and McComas noted that their study — like virtually all research published during the green-ad boom — did not consider the most prevalent use of the environment in advertising: when nature functions as a rhetorically useful backdrop or stage. Using nature merely as a backdrop — whether in the form of wild animals, mountain vistas, or sparkling rivers — is the most common use of the natural world in advertisements. For all but the most critical message consumers, the environment blends into the background. We know that an advertisement for a car shows the vehicle outdoors and that ads for allergy medications feature flowers and "weeds." The environment per se is not for sale, but advertisers are depending on qualities and features of the non-human world (and our relationship to it) to help in the selling message. When the natural world is so depicted, it becomes a convenient, culturally relevant tool to which meanings can be attached for the purpose of selling goods and services. Although this intentional but seemingly casual use of the environment in advertising is by far the most common, it is the least studied by researchers.

Nature-as-backdrop ads also are notable for their enduring quality. 5 Although the number of ads that focus on product attributes such as "recyclable" may shift with marketing trends and political winds, nature has been used as a backdrop virtually since the dawn of advertising. The natural world was depicted in early automobile ads ("see the USA in your Chevrolet") and Hamms Beer commercials ("from the land of sky-blue water") and continues to be a prominent feature in the advertising landscape. Nature-as-backdrop ads, therefore, provide an important record of the position of the natural world in our cultural environment and, as such, deserve scrutiny.

Advertisements are a special form of discourse because they include visual signals and language fragments (either oral or written) that work together to create messages that go beyond the ability of either individually. This essay undertakes a critical analysis of the symbolic communicative discourse of advertising, viewing nature-as-backdrop ads as cultural icons of environmental values embedded in our social system. When ads present the environment with distorted, inauthentic, or exaggerated discourse, that discourse has the potential to foster inauthentic relationships to nature and influences the way we perceive our environment and its value to us.

Schudson (1989) argued that ads have special cultural power. In addition to being repetitive and ubiquitous, ads reinforce messages from primary institutions in the social system, provide dissonance to countering messages, and generally support the capitalistic structure that the advertising industry was created to support. This essay will discuss how the ad industry developed, how ads work on us, and how ads portray the natural world. It will argue, according to environmental theories such as deep ecology (Bullis, 1996; Naess, 1973), that the "green" in advertising is extremely faint by examining and developing six related concepts:

1. The business of advertising is fundamentally "brown"; therefore, the idea of advertising being "green" and capable of supporting environmental values is an oxymoron.
2. Advertising commodifies the natural world and attaches material value to non-material goods, treating natural resources as private and possessible, not public and intrinsic.
3. Nature-as-backdrop ads portray an anthropocentric, narcissistic relationship to the biotic community and focus on the environment's utility and benefit to humans.
4. Advertising idealizes the natural world and presents a simplified, distorted picture of nature as sublime, simple, and unproblematic.

5. The depiction of nature in advertising disconnects and estranges us from what is valued, yet at the same time we are encouraged to reconnect through products, creating a circular consumption.
6. As a ubiquitous form of pop culture, advertising reinforces consonant messages in the social system and provides strong dissonance to oppositional or alternative messages.

The "Brown" Business of Advertising

1. The business of advertising is fundamentally "brown"; therefore, the idea of advertising being "green" and capable of supporting environmental values is an oxymoron.

Advertisements are nothing new to this century or even previous ones. There are plentiful examples in literature, including the works of Shakespeare, that peddlers have long enticed buyers by advertising (in print or orally) a good's attributes and associated meanings. After World War II, however, advertising found a firm place in the worldview of Americans. According to Luke (1993), after 1945, corporate capital, big government, and professional experts pushed practices of a throw-away affluent society onto consumers as a purposeful political strategy to sustain economic growth, forestall mass discontent, and empower scientific authority. Concern for the environment was lacking in the postwar prosperity boom, at least until the mid-1960s when Rachel Carson sounded the alarm over chemicals and the modern-day environmental movement was born (Corbett, 2001).

To help alert consumers to new mass-produced goods, a new type of 10 show called the "soap opera" was created for the relatively recent phenomenon of television. These daytime dramas were created for the sole purpose of delivering an audience of homemakers to eager manufacturers of household products, including soap. Advertisers realized that advertising on soap operas would help to establish branding, or creating differing values for what are essentially common, interchangeable goods such as soap.

Essentially, advertising was viewed as part of the fuel that would help keep a capitalist economy burning. Capitalism is a market system that measures its success by constant growth (such as the gross national product and housing starts), a system that many environmentalists recognize as ultimately unsustainable. You might even say that advertising developed as the culture that would help solve what some economists view as the central problem of capitalism: the distribution of surplus goods (Twitchell, 1996). Schudson (1989) concluded, "Advertising is capitalism's way of saying 'I love you' to itself." In a capitalist economy, advertising is a vital handmaiden to consumption and materialism. In the words of the author of *Adcult*, Americans "are not too materialistic. We are not materialistic enough" (Twitchell, 1996, p. 11).

The development of mass media, particularly radio and television, played an important role in delivering audiences to advertisers. By the mid-1980s, half of U.S. homes had cable, and the burgeoning number of channels allowed advertisers to target more specific audience segments. Advertisers and media programmers engage in a dance to fill each other's needs, each having a vested interest in constructing certain versions of the world and not others. According to Turow (1999), "the ad industry affects not just the content of its own campaigns but the very structure and content of the rest of the media system" (p. 194). At the same time, media develop formats and tones for their outlets and programming deemed to be most acceptable to the audiences that they hope marketers find most attractive. What this means for programming is that the upscale twenty-something audience — the most appealing segment to advertisers — will find itself represented in more media outlets than older men and women to whom only a small number of highly targeted formats are aimed. According to researchers of the green marketing boom, the segments of the population most committed to the environment do not belong to this twenty-something group (Ottman, 1993).

It is precisely the ability of advertisers and media programmers to tell some stories and not others that gives these entities power. "When people read a magazine, watch a TV show, or use any other ad-sponsored medium, they are entering a world that was constructed as a result of close cooperation between advertisers and media firms" (Turow, 1999, p. 16). Because all media provide people with insights into parts of the world with which they have little direct contact, media representations of the natural world to a largely urbanized population are highly significant. They show us, over and over again, where we belong in the world and how we should treat it. Yet, representations of the natural world are crafted for the sole purpose of selling certain audiences to advertisers.

The close cooperation between advertisers and media firms is understandable given advertising's financial support of media. For newspapers and some magazines, at least 50% of their revenue is from advertising; ad support approaches 100% for much of radio and television. By some estimates, advertisers spent $27 billion on support to television, $9 billion on radio, $46 billion on daily newspapers, and about $7 billion on consumer magazines (Turow, 1999, p. 13).

Given advertising's purpose of selling audiences to advertisers, is it even 15
possible for any form of advertising — whether product ads or nature-as-backdrop ads — to be "green"? Dadd and Carothers (1991) maintained that a truly green economy would require all products to be audited and analyzed from cradle to grave for their environmental effects. Effects could include the resources used and pollution generated in the product's manufacture, energy used to produce and transport the product, the product's role in the economic and social health of the country of origin, investment plans of the company, and final disposal of product.

Applying this standard at the most basic level connotes it is an oxymoron to label marginally useful or necessary products (and the ads that promote them) as "green" or somehow good for the environment. Can an advertisement that encourages consumption of a product (or patronage of a company that produces the product) ever be green with a capital G? In his attempt to reconcile a brown industry with green ideals, Kilbourne (1995) identified three levels of green in advertisements. But even at the lowest level (defined as ads promoting a small "techno-fix" such as biodegradability) the message is still that "consuming is good, more is better, and the ecological cost is minimal" (p. 15). If an ad recognizes finite resources, it nevertheless views the environment purely as a resource, not as possessing intrinsic, non-economic value. Kilbourne concluded that from a purely ecological position, a truly Green ad is indeed an oxymoron: "the only Green product is the one that is not produced" (p. 16). Other researchers have likewise tried to categorize the green in advertisements (Banerjee et al., 1995). Adapting the deep and shallow ecology concepts of Naess (1973) to advertisements, they concluded that very few ads were "deep" — 2% of television and 9% of print — defined by the researchers as discussing environmental issues in depth and mentioning actions requiring more commitment.

However, these attempts to make advertising fit a green framework simply illustrate how ideologically opposed advertising and environmental values are. Because advertising is the workhorse of capitalism and supports continually increased production, it is ideologically contrary to environmentalism, which recognizes that ever-increasing growth and consumption are inherently unsustainable. It matters not whether an ad boasts of recyclability or quietly features pristine mountain meadows in the background; the basic business of advertising is brown. Perhaps the only truly Green product is not only one not produced, but also one not advertised.

Nature as Commodity

2. Advertising commodifies the natural world and attaches material value to non-material goods, treating natural resources as private and ownable, not public and intrinsic.

Have you ever viewed a single advertisement and then rushed out to buy that product? Probably not. That is not the way that advertising generally works on us, especially not for national consumer goods. Advertising scholars argue that ads cannot create, invent, or even satisfy our desires; instead, ads channel and express current desires with the hope of exploiting them.

You may disagree that ads cannot create desires, particularly if you have ever found yourself yearning for a product that six months ago you did not know existed or that you "needed." But even if ads do not greatly corrupt our immediate buying habits, they can gradually shape our values by becoming our social guides for what is important and valued. According to Benton (1995), advertising displays values and signals to people what our culture thinks is important. Advertising is not capable of inventing social values, but it does a masterful job at usurping and exploiting certain values and not others. The prominent (though not monopolistic) role of advertising in the symbolic marketplace is what gives advertising "a special cultural power" (Schudson, 1989). In the words of one scholar, "Advertising is simply one of a number of attempts to load objects with meaning . . . it is an ongoing conversation within a culture about the meaning of objects" (Twitchell, 1996, p. 13).

The rhetorical challenge for an advertiser, then, is to load one product (even though numerous similar ones exist) with sufficient meaning so that the product appears able to express a desire. The natural world is full of cultural meaning with which to associate products, thereby attaching commodity value to qualities that are impossible to own. By borrowing and adapting well-known, stereotypical portrayals of nature, advertising is able to associate water with freshness and purity and weather as fraught with danger. If, for example, an ad wants to attach the value of "safety" to one particular car, it might demonstrate the car's ability to dodge "dangerous" elements of nature, such as falling rocks. On the other hand, if the ad wants to convey a truck's durability, it could just as easily attach a very different meaning to the same resource and say the truck is "like a rock." Neither product guarantees that you can buy safety or durability; both product ads merely expressed a consumer desire for them by associating a non-material good with a material one.

Animals in particular provide cultural shorthand for advertising. Animals, as popular symbols of the nonhuman environment, are a way for advertisers to link the perceived "personality" and stereotyped cultural value of the animal to the product (Phillips, 1996). In car advertising alone, ads compare vehicles to rams, eagles, wolves, cougars, falcons, and panthers. Some ads go so far as to portray the vehicle as an animal itself. An individual needs no direct experience with untamed environs to know what an eagle or cougar represents and is valued for.

The portrayal of animals in advertising need not be authentic or realistic for us to ascertain the value they represent. In a television commercial, two raccoons are peering inside a brightly lit living room window, "singing" a song from *My Fair Lady*. As the camera moves beyond the raccoons into the living room — where it appears the residents are not home — it focuses on the rocker-recliner. The raccoons sing, "All I want is a room somewhere, far away from the cold night air. Warm hands, warm feet . . . ."

In this ad, the rocker-recliner you are enticed to buy has no direct or obvious connection to the natural world, but animals are very much part of the overall persuasive message. We are able to overlook the anthropomorphized singing raccoons because we have enough shared cultural meaning about raccoons and their behavior. We can decipher that these cute, mischievous "bandits" would like to "break in" to this warm room far away from the cold night air and maybe even snooze in that rocker. The intrinsic value of raccoons as a species has been usurped and exploited to demonstrate the comfort and desirability of a certain brand of chair.

Even if the original function of advertising was to market simple products 25 such as soap, advertising now functions to market feelings, sensations, and lifestyles. According to advertisers, the consumption of an object often has more to do with its meaning than with its actual use (Twitchell, 1996). Discrete objects — whether cold medicine or fabric softener — are easier to sell if they are associated with social and personal meaning. The purpose of an ad is not to stress that the product functions properly, but that consumption of it will cure problems (Lasch, 1978), whether loneliness, aging, or even a desire to connect with the natural world. Advertising channels our psychological needs and ambitions into consumptive behaviors (Pollay, 1989). Price (1996) concluded that the success of the store The Nature Company depends "not so much [on] what nature is as what nature means to us" (p. 189).

Take for example a series of print and television ads for a particular SUV that labeled the vehicle as "the answering machine for the call of the wild." The print version tells us that "nature calls out for us" but with the vehicle's leather-trimmed seats, "civilization's never very far away." In television versions, we see the vehicle traveling over rugged terrain (but not the woman driving it) while an answering machine plays numerous messages from a worried mother and boyfriend to the woman who has escaped into the wild.

These ads do not focus on all the ways that this vehicle is superior to all the other very similar SUVs out there. The ads give us no reason to believe that the repair record, safety rating, price, or other important product attributes are somehow superior. Instead, these ads are selling meanings and values associated with the natural world. This product will reconnect you with "the wild," which appears to be missing in your life, and it will help you escape from your troubles and relationships. A rugged environment (yet one somehow made safer and more civilized by this SUV) is portrayed as the best place to find peace and this vehicle will take you there. (An ad for a very different type of product used the same slogan in a different way: "Radio Shack is answering the call of the wild with two-way personal radios." In the ad, "renowned wildlife expert" Jim Fowler uses the radio in a remote-looking location. "No matter where the wild calls you, you'll be ready to answer.")

Some scholars insist that advertising appeals primarily to personal dissatisfactions in our lives and insecurities over the ways and pace in which we live, not to our personal needs. In doing so, ads are carriers of anxiety that serve only to alienate us further (Lasch, 1978). In the SUV ads, the driver is not portrayed as using the vehicle for personal need, but for escape from relationship problems to an environment that is depicted as being free of all problems.

The rhetorical argument of commodification leads us to believe that we can solve problems and dissatisfactions with a purchase. We buy the peace and escape — represented by the wilderness and promised by the product — even though the product is incapable of fulfilling that promise. The intent of advertising, says Pollay (1989), is to preoccupy society with material concerns and to see goods as a path to happiness and a solution to problems (which is very brown thinking). In many of the appeals of nature-as-backdrop ads, the advertisements attempt to associate material goods with nonmaterial qualities that have disappeared from many people's lives, qualities such as solitude, wilderness, lush landscapes, free-flowing water, and clean air. In a print ad for L.L. Bean, we see a man wading across calm, milky blue waters to a small sailboat in early morning light. The caption reads, "Don't mistake a street address for where you actually live." Apparently this man cannot "live" in his everyday life—which we assume takes place in a far less serene setting—but must leave it to achieve qualities it lacks. Yet another SUV ad promises, "Escape. Serenity. Relaxation." Pristine mountain vistas and sparkling waters (usually devoid of people) allow us to romanticize about a life lost or connections broken. When such adventures are tied in such a way to products, that connection materializes a way of experiencing the natural world.

Commodification of what are essentially public resources—like milky   30
blue waters—encourages us to think of resources as private and possessible. Ads may invoke public values of family, friendship, and a common planet as part of their message, but these values are put to work to sell private goods, a very capitalist principle. The satisfaction derived from these goods, even those that appear inherently collective such as water, is depicted as invariably private. This encourages "the promotion of a social order in which people are encouraged to think of themselves and their private worlds" (Schudson, 1989, p. 83), a very anthropocentric and narcissistic perspective. The environment, in many respects, doesn't function well as private space.

For the Pleasure of Humans

3. Nature-as-backdrop ads portray an anthropocentric, narcissistic relationship to the biotic community and focus on the environment's utility and benefit to humans.

Another common feature in advertising appeals that utilize the natural world is self-absorption and narcissism. The word derives from Narcissus, a youth in Greek mythology who fell in love with his own reflection in a pool. The way in which advertising portrays this universal emotional type is as self-absorbed, self-righteous, and dependent on momentary pleasures of assertion. Narcissism in advertising often takes the form of outdoor adventure, as in this print ad: Two pickup trucks are parked on an expansive, rolling sand dune. In the open bed of each truck, a young man in a wet suit appears to be wind-surfing—through the manipulation of computer graphics. Water splashes around them in the air and onto the sand. The caption says the trucks are "built fun tough" and have "gallons of attitude." Of course we know this picture to be fake (although a similar juxtaposition of desert and water exists in human-made Lake Powell), but the picture tells us that these men are in it for the fun, for the adventure.

A narcissist is most concerned with pleasing himself or herself at the expense of others, and if we extend the analogy, at the expense of the environment. In terms of environmental ideology, a narcissist would be anthropocentric, believing that his or her own outdoor pleasure comes before that of

other species and their needs. Ads that show people "conquering" natural elements are expressing me-first anthropocentrism. According to Lasch (1978),
our culture is marked by an exaggerated form of self-awareness and mass
narcissism, finely attuned (with the help of advertising) to the many demands
of the narcissistic self.

Another example is a television ad that shows a young boy working
through the pages of a puzzle book. He reads aloud, "Help the knight reach
the castle," and with his crayon follows the winding path safely past the
dragon to the castle. On the next page he reads, "Help the Jeep Wrangler
reach the fishing hole." "Hmm," he says, grins, and makes a noise like a truck
revving up. He draws a line straight across the puzzle book landscape, across
two mountain ranges, a deep valley, and a patch of quicksand, ignoring the
cleared path. As he smiles smugly, the announcer tells us that a Jeep is "more
fun than you imagine."

Yet another truck commercial begins in a deserted mountain valley at 35
twilight. Next, a gigantic booted foot with a spur crashes to the ground, rever-
berating all in sight. We then see that the foot belongs to a cowboy the size
of Paul Bunyan. The message is that the human is essentially larger than life,
dominating the entire landscape and all within it, as Bunyan did. Such exaggerated domination intentionally positions humans at the top of a pyramid,
instead of belonging equally to a biotic community.

Nature as Sublime

*4. Nature-as-backdrop ads idealize the natural world and present a simpli-
fied, distorted picture of nature as sublime, simple, and unproblematic.*

As much as ads intentionally distort reality (in images such as wind-
surfing in a truck or singing raccoons), they also present reality as it should
be, a reality that is worth desiring and emulating (and owning). If you have
backpacked or camped, you know that slapping mosquitoes, getting dirty,
getting wet, and sweating are often part of the package. Such a real outdoor
experience is unlikely to be depicted in advertisements (unless the product
is for something like insect repellent). Instead, ads subordinate reality to a
romanticized past, present, or even future. "Real" in advertising is a cultural
construct: "The makers of commercials do not want what is real but what
will seem real on film. Artificial rain is better than 'God's rain' because it
shows up better on film or tape" (Schudson, 1989, p. 79). Advertisers do
not intend to capture life as it really is, but intend instead to portray the
"ideal" life and to present as normal and everyday what are actually relatively rare moments, such as a phenomenal sunset or a mosquito-less lake.

A great many nature-as-backdrop ads present the natural world as sublime, a noble place inspiring awe and admiration. As an exercise, my students
draw their interpretation of a sublime place in nature, and invariably, similar elements appear in their pictures: snow-capped mountain peaks towering

above pine trees and a grassy or flower-filled meadow, through which a clear creek or river flows. Sometimes, large mammals such as deer graze in the meadow. Humans are rarely present.

According to Oravec (1996), the sublime is a literary and artistic convention that uses a prescribed form of language and pictorial elements to describe nature, and that in turn encourages a specific pattern of responses to nature. Artistically, sublime representations can include blurring, exaggeration of detail, and compositional elements such as a foreground, middle ground, and frame. Settings are frequently pastoral or wild with varying amounts of human presence. There is a self-reflexive nature to the positioning, with the observer feeling both within a scene and also outside it, viewing the scene (and reflexively, the self) from a higher or more distant (and morally outstanding) perspective.

Oravec (1996) has called the sublime the founding trope in the rhetoric of environmentalism: "Sublimity has remained a touchstone or grounding for our public conception of nature and, through nature, of the environment" (p. 68). As a conventional linguistic device, the sublime represents and encodes our understanding of the natural world. Because the sublime is associated with what is "natural," "the sublime connotes an authenticity and originality that is part of its very meaning; yet like rhetoric itself, it has a long-standing reputation for exaggeration and even falsehood" (p. 69).

The sublime is as much a part of advertising as it is of the artistic and literary realms. Advertising presents the natural world as pristine, simple, and not endangered, yet depictions are always contrived and often created. What appears as real rain is artificial, what looks like a natural wildlife encounter is contrived, and what appears entirely natural was created with computer animation and digital manipulation. The artificial seamlessly approximates the real in the sublime world of advertising.

Numerous vacation advertisements depict people in sublime settings, such as thin and tan couples on pristine white sand beaches, or peacefully cruising under sunny skies amid glaciers and whales. Vacationers in this idealized world never encounter anything other than perfect environmental conditions and enjoy these sublime locations unfettered by crowds.

A host of pharmaceutical ads likewise enlist nature backdrops as rhetoric for the sublime. One ad for an arthritis medication takes place in a pastoral setting assumed to be a park. The sun is shining, the park is empty except for the actors, there is no litter or noise, and even the dogs are exceedingly friendly and behaved. In another ad for what is presumed to be a mood-enhancer, a woman strolls slowly along a pristine, deserted beach in soft light, a contented smile on her face. In these instances, the sublime backdrop doubly represents the sublime state the person will achieve upon taking the medication. Many of these ads rely so heavily on the power of sublime meaning that the actual purpose of the drug is not stated, only assumed.

Other commercials depict the sublime after a product has changed problematic nature into idealized nature. Numerous ads for lawn care products and allergy medications first portray nature in a state of chaos or war, needing to be tamed and brought under control. One television ad for lawn chemicals showed a small army of men and supplies descending from the sky to tame and tackle nature. Some allergy commercials depict the flowers and weeds physically attacking people. But ah, after the product is introduced, unproblematic and peaceful nature returns.

When humans are introduced into sublime scenes, their representation is also idealized. Just as nature is presented as reality-as-it-should-be, people are presented as-they-should-be in a limited number of social roles. Therefore, people in ads are primarily attractive, young or middle-aged, vibrant, and thin, or they are celebrities with those qualities. The environments in which they live, whether inside or outside, are also limited to idealized conditions; no one has dirty houses or unkempt lawns, and no one travels through dirty city streets, encounters polluted rivers, or finds abused landscapes. In the world of advertising, there are no poor people, sick people, or unattractive people, and sometimes there are no people at all. For example, most car ads do not show anyone actually driving the vehicle through the tinted windows, and you hear only the disembodied voice of the announcer. The social roles played by advertising actors are easily identifiable — the businessperson, the grandmother, the teenager — but the actors are anonymous as individual people and portray only social roles tailored to specific demographic categories. The flat, abstract, idealized, and sometimes anonymous world of advertising "is part of a deliberate effort to connect specific products in people's imagination with certain demographic groupings or needs or occasions" (Schudson, 1989, p. 77).

Of course you recognize pieces of this idealized presentation of people and their environments, just as you recognize the utterly impossible pieces — a car parked on an inaccessible cliff or polar bears drinking Coke. We are not stupefied by a natural world that is unrealistic and idealized in advertising: in fact, we expect it.

A Natural Disconnect

5. The depiction of nature in advertising disconnects and estranges us from what is valued, and we attempt to reconnect through products, creating a circular consumption.

Some critics believe that advertising may be more powerful the less people believe it and the less it is acknowledged. According to Schudson (1989), ads do not ask to be taken literally and do not mean what they say, but "this may be the very center of their power" (p. 87). While we are being exposed to those 3,000 ads a day, we may carry an illusion of detachment and think them trivial and unimportant. According to some theories, though, it is very possible to "learn" without active involvement, a so-called sleeper effect. This myth of immunity from an ad's persuasion may do more to

protect our self-respect than help us comprehend the subtleties and implications of their influence (Pollay, 1989). Although we may not think an ad
speaks to us, its slogan may suddenly pop into our vocabulary — just do it, it
does a body good, got milk? We may be unaware and uninvolved in front of
the television, but the message of the ad may prove important at purchase
time. According to Pollay (1989), advertising does more than merely stimulate
wants; it plays a subtle role in changing habits.

Take the habit of drying your clothes, an activity that for many people
throughout the world involves pinning clothes to a line in the backyard or
between buildings. When I was a girl, I loved sliding between clean sheets
dried outside on the clothesline and drinking in the smell. How do many
people get that same outside-smell nowadays? They get it with detergents
and fabric softeners with names like "mountain air" and "springtime fresh"
or with similarly scented dryer sheets. Although perceived convenience and
affordable dryers no doubt helped change our clothes-drying habits, where
did we learn to associate the smell of outdoors with purchased products?
Advertising.

The message in these product ads is that the artificial smell is some- 50
how easier or superior or even just equivalent to the real smell in the natural
world. It not only commodifies something of value from the natural world,
it gradually disconnects us from that thing of value. The more successfully
ads teach us to associate natural qualities such as fresh air with products,
the more disconnected we become from what was originally valued. The
more estranged from the original thing of value, the more we may attempt
to reconnect through products that promise an easy replacement. When we
become so estranged from the natural world that we attempt to reconnect
through products, a circular consumptive pattern is created — which supports
the capitalist economy that advertising was created to support. If advertising
tells us that non-saleable qualities of the outdoors such as fresh air and natural smells are easy to bring inside, need we worry about the condition of the
real world?

Just as advertising can change habits, it can help create rituals and taboos.
A good example of a taboo largely created by advertising is litter. Through
national advertising campaigns begun decades ago, litter was labeled as an
environmental no-no. While cleaning up litter makes for a visually appealing
environment, the automobiles from which the trash is generally tossed cause
far more environmental harm than almost all types of litter.

Advertising also works to create rituals. A ritual is created when we
make inert, prosaic objects meaningful and give them symbolic significance.
Mistletoe means little to us as a parasitic evergreen, but it is loaded with significance as a holiday ritual about kissing. Whales mean more to us as communicative, spiritual symbols of the deep than for their inherent value and
place in ocean ecosystems. Price (1996) concluded that Native American
fetishes and baskets, which have been ritualized by nonnative populations
(and appropriated by advertising), "associate nature nearly interchangeably

with indigenous peoples" (p. 189). In a similar way, once a species or animal has been so ritualized, it precludes a more complete and accurate knowing of it and disconnects us.

Advertising, directly and subtly, idealizes and materializes a way of experiencing the world, including the natural world. It promotes products as the simple solutions to complex dilemmas by tapping into our dissatisfactions and desires. If you feel disconnected to the natural world, you can "solve" that with mountain-scented laundry products, bear fetishes, and whale audiotapes, but these purchases only increase the estrangement. If you need to escape modern life yet want to feel safe and civilized while doing so, you can simply solve that by taking a rugged SUV into the wilderness.

Yet environmental dilemmas are anything but simple, and wilderness is a good example. A print ad features a four-wheel-drive car crossing a sparkling, boulder-strewn stream and announces, "Coming soon to a wilderness near you." In this idealized portrayal, there is no mud being stirred up from the bottom of the stream, no dirt of any kind on the car, and of course, there is no visible driver. But in addition, "wilderness" is a rare commodity that rarely exists "near you," and by its very definition, includes few people and even fewer developed signs of people. In wilderness with a capital W, cars and all motorized equipment are forbidden. Setting aside an area as wilderness involves contentious negotiations and land-use trade-offs. But whether formally designated or not, experiencing wilderness is not the simple matter of materialization and driving a certain kind of car.

Another example of advertising portraying a complex environmental 55 issue as simple and uncomplicated is the depiction of water. We see it babbling down brooks in beverage commercials, refreshing someone in a soap commercial, quenching thirst in ads for water filters and bottled water. Pure, clean, healthy — but simple? More than half the world's rivers are drying up or are polluted. Agricultural chemicals have seeped into many U.S. underground aquifers. Oil, gas, and a host of herbicides and pesticides wash off streets and lawns into waterways. Political and legal fights are waged over dams, diversions, and water rights. A host of bacterial contaminants have threatened water supplies and public health in major U.S. cities, and traces of antibiotics and other prescription drugs have been detected in some municipal water supplies. Clean water is definitely not a simple environmental issue.

Advertising Does Not Stand Alone

6. As a ubiquitous form of popular culture, advertising reinforces consonant messages in the social system and provides strong dissonance to oppositional or alternative messages.

For any societal element to wield power, it must exist in concert with other social institutions in a way that is mutually reinforcing. Advertising is layered on top of other cultural elements and bound up with other institutions, from entertainment and popular culture to corporate America and manufacturing. Each element is heteroglossic, continually leaking into other sectors, with advertising slogans showing up in both casual conversation and political speeches. The very ubiquitousness of advertising — extending beyond regular media buys to include placing products in movies, sponsoring sporting events, and the full-length infomercial — ensures its power and influence in numerous places and institutions.

For an example of this interwoven character of advertising and consumption with other elements of society, consider plastics recycling. We routinely see ads touting how certain products are recyclable or made from recycled items. Currently, the plastics industry is running an advertising campaign that reminds us of all the wonderful ways that plastic contributes to our lives. That means that multiple corporate public relations departments and public relations agencies are involved in getting mileage from the recycling issue. Public relations and advertising personnel have regular contact with media people in both the advertising and editorial sides, and the boundaries between news and advertising functions are becoming increasingly blurred (Stauber & Rampton, 1995). Meanwhile, giant corporate conglomerates have become the norm, putting journalists under the same corporate roof as advertisers and the very companies they attempt to scrutinize. For example, if a television station is owned by General Electric and is also receiving thousands of dollars in revenue from an ad campaign about the value of plastics, there is dissonance — whether acknowledged or not— for those TV reporters covering a story about environmental impacts and energy used to recycle plastic.

The hallowed halls of education are not immune from commercial messages, including those about plastic. Captive youngsters are a tempting market: more than 43 million kids attend schools and even elementary-age children exert tremendous spending power, about $15 billion a year (McNeal, 1994). Ads cover school buses, book covers, and scoreboards, and corporate flags fly next to school flags. The Polystyrene Packaging Council, like other corporations, has supplied "supplemental educational materials" free of charge to K–12 classrooms. Their "Plastics and the Environment" lesson teaches that plastics are great and easily recycled, even though most plastics are not recyclable for lack of markets. Consumers Union evaluated this lesson as "highly commercial and incomplete with strong bias . . . [T]he disadvantages of plastics . . . are not covered" (Zillions, 1995, p. 46). Another critic noted that when teachers use such materials, "American students are introduced to environmental issues as they use materials supplied by corporations who pollute the soil, air, and water" (Molnar, 1995, p. 70).

Beyond communication and education, legal sectors also get involved 60 in advertising claims about recycled and recyclable plastic, and politicians know it is wise to support recycling as a generalized issue. Some municipalities sponsor curbside pick-up programs for plastic, and trash haulers and manufacturers run businesses dependent on recycling plastics. Recycling plastics not only creates new business opportunities, it also is philosophically consistent with a capitalist economy that is based on ever-increasing consumption. After all, the message of recycling is not to reduce or avoid consumption but essentially to consume something again. According to one critic in *Harper's*, oftentimes the new product created from recycled plastics is "the perfect metaphor for everything that's wrong with the idea of recycling plastics. It's ugly as sin, the world doesn't need it, and it's disposable" (Gutin, 1992, p. 56).

The vested interest of so many powerful social institutions makes it that much harder to separate the influence of one from another — such as advertising from news media — and to effect significant social change. It also makes the ubiquitous, repetitive messages of advertising reinforced and in a sense replicated, free of charge. Individuals or groups with oppositional messages about plastics would have to contend with what seems a united front about the place, if not the value, of plastic.

Working Together

Obviously, the six concepts presented here work in concert. Here is one final example of an ad that considers them together.

First, the visual of this television ad: A waterfall flows over the driver's seat of a car and a tiny kayaker (in relation to the size of the car seat) spills down the face of the falls. The scene quickly shifts to the kayaker (full-sized now and paddling away from us) amid glaciers. The next scene takes us into the car's back cargo area — still covered with water — and two orca whales breach in front of the kayaker, who pauses mid-stroke. (In all of these shots, we have never seen the kayaker's face; when he paddles away, his head is covered in a fur-lined parka that looks "native.") The next shot is a close-up of a paddle dipping into water shimmering with the colors of sunset and above the words "Discover Chevy Tahoe." The last scene shows the unoccupied vehicle parked on the edge of a stream in front of snow-covered mountain peaks. The accompanying audio includes Native American–sounding drum beats and a mixed chorus singing a chant-like, non-English song. Over this music, we hear the voice of a male announcer who quotes a passage from John Muir about how a person needs silence to get into the heart of the wilderness away from dust, hotels, baggage, and chatter.

The meanings that these elements convey to us are multiple. Peace, serenity, at-oneness with nature, and a return to a simple yet sublime "native" existence are part of the promise of this vehicle. Native drums, whales, glaciers, paddling through still waters, and even the deep ecologist Muir are powerful, idealized, and ritualized symbols that are employed to market a feeling and a sensation. The seamless juxtaposition of scene both inside and outside the vehicle conveys that nature is transported effortlessly for you to experience these things directly, without leaving the safety and luxury of your car. The vehicle is the commodity to aid your escape to this sublime place, a place depicted as real yet entirely contrived, with kayakers spilling over car seats. The entire promise is one of self-gratification, helping the driver/kayaker travel to this idealized wilderness. Yet, if you truly want to heed John Muir's advice, silence is needed to get into the heart of the wilderness, not a noisy car. Hence if you buy into (pun intended) the vehicle being the solution (and not existing instead in your own life or soul), the result is further estrangement from the very thing desired and valued. Advertising, as a primary support system for a capitalist economy, can only transfer meaning and express latent desires — not deliver on any of these promises.

REFERENCES

Banerjee, S., Gulas, C. S., & Iyer, E. (1995). Shades of green: A multidimensional analysis of environmental advertising. *Journal of Advertising, 24,* 21–32.

Benton, L. M. (1995). Selling the natural or selling out? Exploring environmental merchandising. *Environmental Ethics, 17,* 3–22.

Bullis, C. (1996). Retalking environmental discourses from a feminist perspective: The radical potential of ecofeminism. In J. G. Cantrill & C. L. Oravec (Eds.), *The symbolic earth: Discourse and our creation of the environment* (pp. 123–148). Lexington, KY: University Press of Kentucky.

Corbett, J. B. (2001). Women, scientists, agitators: Magazine portrayal of Rachel Carson and Theo Colborn. *Journal of Communication, 51,* 720–749.

Dadd, D. L., & Carothers, A. (1991). A bill of goods? Green consuming in perspective. In C. Plant & J. Plant (Eds.), *Green business: Hope or hoax?* Philadelphia, PA: New Society Publishers (pp. 11–29).

Fink, E. (1990). Biodegradable diapers are not enough in days like these: A critique of commodity environmentalism. *EcoSocialist Review, 4.*

Gutin, J. (1992, March–April). Plastics-a-go-go. *Harper's, 17,* 56–59.

Iyer, E., & Banerjee, B. (1993). Anatomy of green advertising. *Advances in Consumer Research, 20,* 484–501.

Kilbourne, W. E. (1995). Green advertising: Salvation or oxymoron? *Journal of Advertising, 24,* 7–20.

Lasch, C. (1978). *The culture of narcissism.* New York, NY: W. W. Norton.

Luke, T. W. (1993). Green consumerism: Ecology and the ruse of recycling. In J. Bennett & W. Chaloupka (Eds.), *In the nature of things: Languages, politics and the environment* (pp. 154–172). Minneapolis, MN: University of Minnesota Press.

Mayer, R. N., Scammon, D. L., & Zick, C. D. (1993). Poisoning the well: Do environmental claims strain consumer credulity? *Advances in Consumer Research, 20,* 698–703.

McNeal, J. U. (1994, February 7). Billions at stake in growing kids market. *Discount Store News, 41.*

Molnar, A. (1995). Schooled for profit. *Educational Leadership, 53,* 70–71.

Naess, A. (1973). The shallow and the deep, long-range ecology movement: A summary. *Inquiry, 16,* 95–100.

Neff, J. (2000, April 10). It's not trendy being green. *Advertising Age, 16.*

Obermiller, C. (1995). The baby is sick / the baby is well: A test of environmental communication appeals. *Journal of Advertising, 24,* 55–70.

Oravec, C. L. (1996). To stand outside oneself: The sublime in the discourse of natural scenery. In J. G. Cantrill & C. L. Oravec (Eds.), *The symbolic earth: Discourse and our creation of the environnment* (pp. 58–75). Lexington, KY: University Press of Kentucky.

Ottman, J. A. (1993). *Green marketing: Challenges and opportunities for the new marketing age*. Lincolnwood, IL: NTC Business Books.

Phillips, B. J. (1996). Advertising and the cultural meaning of animals. *Advances in Consumer Research, 23*, 354–360.

Pollay, R. W. (1989). The distorted mirror: Reflections on the unintended consequences of advertising. In R. Hovland & G. B. Wilcox (Eds.), *Advertising in society* (pp. 437–476). Lincolnwood, IL: NTC Business Books.

Price, J. (1996). Looking for nature at the mall: A field guide to the Nature Company. In W. Cronon (Ed.), *Uncommon ground: Rethinking the human place in nature*, (pp. 186–203). New York, NY: W. W. Norton.

Schudson, M. (1989). Advertising as capitalist realism. In R. Hovland & G. B. Wilcox (Eds.), *Advertising in society* (pp. 73–98). Lincolnwood, IL: NTC Business Books.

Schuhwerk, M. E., & Lefkoff-Hagius, R. (1995). Green or non-green? Does type of appeal matter when advertising a green product? *Journal of Advertising, 24*, 45–54.

Selling green. (1991, October). *Consumer Reports, 56*, 687–692.

Shanahan, J., & McComas, K. (1999). *Nature stories: Depictions of the environment and their effects*. Cresskill, NJ: Hampton Press.

Shrum, L. J., McCarty, J. A., & Lowrey, T. M. (1995). Buyer characteristics of the green consumer and their implications for advertising strategy. *Journal of Advertising, 24*, 71–82.

Stauber, J., & Rampton, S. (1995). *Toxic sludge is good for you! Lies, damn lies, and the public relations industry*. Monroe, ME: Common Courage Press.

Thorson, E., Page, T., & Moore, J. (1995). Consumer response to four categories of "green" television commercials. *Advances in Consumer Research, 22*, 243–250.

Turow, J. (1999). *Breaking up America: Advertisers and the new media world*. Chicago, IL: University of Chicago Press.

Twitchell, J. B. (1996). *Adcult USA: The triumph of advertising in American culture*. New York, NY: Columbia University Press.

Zillions: For Kids from Consumer Reports (1995). *Captive kids: Commercial pressures on kids at school*. New York, NY: Consumers Union Education Services.

Zinkham, G. M., & Carlson, L. (1995). Green advertising and the reluctant consumer. *Journal of Advertising, 24*, 1–6.

READING THE TEXT

1. Define in your own words "nature-as-backdrop" ads.

2. How, according to Corbett, did advertising become "part of the fuel that would help keep a capitalist economy burning" (para. 11)?

3. Why does Corbett claim, "commodification of what are essentially public resources—like milky blue waters—encourages us to think of resources as private and possessible" (para. 30)? Why does she think such commodification is problematic?

4. In your own words, define the term "sublime."

5. How can some ads using nature as a backdrop be considered to reflect our narcissism?

6. Why does Corbett have concerns regarding ad campaigns for plastics recycling, which is usually considered an environmentally conscious venture?

READING THE SIGNS

1. In an essay, write your own argument in response to Corbett's speculative question: "Is it even possible for any form of advertising—whether product ads or nature-as-backdrop ads—to be 'green'?" (para. 15).

2. Study some travel magazines, focusing on the advertising. To what extent is nature presented as "sublime" or as a backdrop? Use your observations to demonstrate, refute, or complicate the contention that presenting nature as "unproblematic" can have a dangerous effect on our environmental consciousness.

3. Select a single ad that uses nature as a backdrop, and conduct an in-depth analysis of it. As a critical framework, use the six reasons advertising can be "faint green" that Corbett outlines on pages 238–50.

4. Adopting the perspective of Laurence Shames ("The More Factor," p. 80), write an essay in which you argue whether the "faint green" advertising Corbett describes is an expression of the American desire for "more."

5. Corbett asserts that "attempts to make advertising fit a green framework simply illustrate how ideologically opposed advertising and environmental values are" (para. 17). In class, form teams and debate this assertion. Use the debate as a jumping-off point for your own essay in which you explore your own response.

6. Study advertisements for companies that produce oil, plastics, or chemicals. Do they use nature as a backdrop, as Corbett describes, or is nature presented in a different way? Use your observations to describe and critique the techniques such companies use to present a positive public image. As an alternative, do the same with automobile advertising, focusing on ads for SUVs (you might study a magazine such as *Car and Driver* or consult promotional material on auto companies' Web sites). Or study advertising that promotes alternative-fuel vehicles, such as the Prius, Volt, or Leaf.

VITAMEATAVEGAMIN
FOR HEALTH

VIDEO DREAMS
Television and Cultural Forms

The Walking Dead, Westerns, and the New Westerns

Forget the zombies for a moment and look at the basic setup. Against the backdrop of a lawless wilderness infested with savage killers who can leap to the attack at any moment, *The Walking Dead* centers on a small group of armed men and women as they struggle to survive in a postapocalyptic state of nature. Carrying guns, swords, and bows, they are unrestrained by any regulations in the possession of their weapons and are fully justified by their circumstances in using them whenever they need to.

Jump now to Westeros, the fictional setting of *Game of Thrones*. Here, too, armed men and women inhabit a nearly lawless landscape, with sudden violence a constant presence in their lives, and savage White Walkers (or Others) waiting mysteriously over the border at the far frontier, threatening the outbreak of even-greater mayhem in an ever-violent world.

It would seem to be a big jump between the futuristic *Walking Dead* and the Tolkienesque world of *Game of Thrones*, but these two wildly popular television series share a common significance; namely, a fundamental similarity to the Western, a now more or less defunct television genre that also features armed characters perpetually fighting it out in a lawless frontier. This similarity suggests a potential semiotic **system**, whose **associations** and **differences** can lead us to some cultural insights.

To determine the significance of what are called "the new Westerns," we can begin, as is usually the case with a semiotic analysis, with a survey of the history of the genre to which they belong. One of America's most popular narratives from the latter part of the nineteenth century (when it was consumed

in the form of dime novels, newspaper features, and Western-themed circuses) through the middle of the twentieth (when it inspired a nearly endless
stream of radio programs, TV series, and feature films), the Western originally reflected Americans' pride in their frontier history. The genre was a celebration of the pioneers, settlers, cowboys, and gunslinging lawmen who, as
people used to say, "won the West." Like medieval knights in armor, the Western's armed men on horseback were the heroes of a national mythology, legendary outliers of a rapidly expanding nation.

   This all changed in the later 1960s and the 1970s, when the historical
distortions of the Western became all too clear — when, that is to say, winning
the West came to be seen as a genocidal injustice to the native peoples who
paid the price for American expansion, and former heroes like Wyatt Earp
were revealed to be little more than bullies no better (and perhaps worse)
than their victims. This difference in perception produced a new Western, a
rewriting of the script that replaced the likes of Ben Cartwright of *Bonanza*
with a revisionary George Armstrong Custer in movies like *Little Big Man*
(1970), which retold the battles of Wounded Knee and the Little Big Horn
from the Native American point of view.

   At the same time, the Western's inherent violence was revisited in different ways. On the one hand, Westerns like Sam Peckinpah's *The Wild Bunch*
turned that violence into a metaphor for the upheavals of the sixties, essentially critiquing, not celebrating it. On the other hand, a post–Vietnam War
reaction against violent gunplay resulted in pacified Westerns like *Little House
on the Prairie* and, years later as the genre was sputtering out, *Dr. Quinn, Medicine Woman*. By the new millennium, the television Western was pretty much
finished, with *Deadwood* — a highly unflattering look at the fighters who won
the West — standing as the last gasp of a genre that no longer appealed to
the imagination of an audience who had become more diverse than the traditional Western's fundamentally WASP viewers and had become less interested in the frontier history that spawned the genre.

   But science fiction narratives like the short-lived *Terra Nova* and the
soon-to-be-sequelized *Avatar* reveal that the Western did not so much vanish as evolve to suit newer tastes and ideologies. Like the revisionary Western
Dances with Wolves, *Avatar* reverses the traditional narrative by making the
Na'vi the heroes and the Resources Development Administration (an obvious
metaphor for the Euro-American conquest of the New World) the villains. It's
good versus evil, but this time it's not the cavalry that comes to the rescue
against the "Indians"; it's nature itself rising against an evil civilization.

   This all returns us to *The Walking Dead* and *Game of Thrones*. If *Avatar* is
a Western turned upside down, *The Walking Dead* and *Game of Thrones* are
Westerns turned inside out. Here the frontier is a moral as well as a physical
wilderness, and the battle between good and evil has devolved into little more
than a messy struggle for survival. *The Walking Dead*, particularly, feels like a
kind of National Rifle Association fantasy, in which constantly carrying, and
using, weapons without restriction is not only necessary but justified. We can

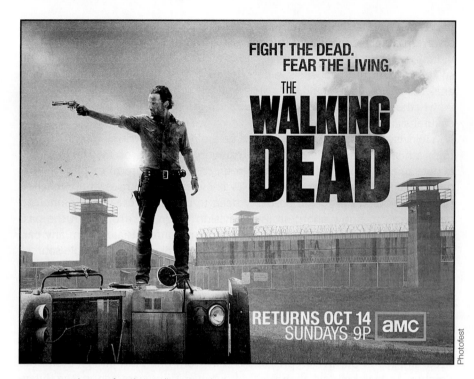

A promotional poster for *The Walking Dead*.

further detect a vicarious wish fulfillment at work, through which audiences can imagine themselves living in a perilous world where they can fight back, with a wild freedom, against the forces that threaten and oppress them.

Such fantasies appeal to a society suffering from an apparently eternal threat of terroristic violence (zombies make good metaphors for ruthless terrorists) and economic malaise. As individuals we may feel helpless in the face of such forces, but as audiences we can find in the new Westerns an imaginary freedom to resist, while at the same time being reassured that everyone else is as badly off as we are. Thus, the new Westerns can be taken as a **sign**, a signifier of a society in distress.

Writing about Television

We begin this chapter with a brief semiotic analysis to show how you can look at television programs in the same way that you can look at any cultural phenomenon: as a series of signs, signifiers of the society that consumes them. But while you might find writing about television familiar from high school assignments in which you were asked to write about a favorite program — perhaps in a summary-writing exercise, a descriptive essay, or an opinion piece on why a particular program is your favorite show — writing semiotic interpretations of TV shows is a different task. Although you still need to rely on your skills in description and summary in writing semiotic analyses of TV, you should put aside your personal opinions of a show (that is, whether you like it or not) to construct interpretive arguments about its cultural significance.

Television offers an especially rich field of possible writing topics, ranging from a historical analysis of a whole category, or genre, of TV programming (as we briefly presented above with respect to the Western) or of a general trend, to an interpretation of a single TV show episode. Whatever approach to television you take, you will probably need to do some research. No one can be expected to know about all the television programs (from both the past and the present) that can be associated with and differentiated from any particular show that you are analyzing, so you should plan to find reliable sources to help you contextualize whatever program you are interpreting.

From Symbols to Icons

When writing about TV, keep in mind that the ubiquity of televised (or digitized) images in our lives represents a shift from one kind of sign system to another. As Marshall McLuhan pointed out over fifty years ago in *The Gutenberg Galaxy* (1962), Western culture since the fifteenth century has defined itself around the printed word — the linear text that reads from left to right and top to bottom. The printed word, in the terminology of the American founder of semiotics, Charles Sanders Peirce, is a **symbolic sign**, one whose meaning is entirely arbitrary or conventional. A symbolic sign means what it does because those who use it have decided so. Words don't look like what they mean. Their significance is entirely abstract.

Not so with a visual image, which does resemble its object and is not entirely arbitrary. Although a photograph is not literally the thing it depicts and may reflect a good deal of staging and manipulation by the photographer, we often respond to it as if it were an innocent reflection of the world. Peirce called such signs "icons," referring by this term to any sign that resembles what it means. The way you interpret an **icon**, then, differs from the way you interpret a symbol or word. The interpretation of words involves your cognitive capabilities; the viewing of icons is far more sensuous, more a matter of vision than cognition. The shift from a civilization governed by the paradigm of the book to one dominated by the image accordingly involves a shift in the way we "read" our world, as the symbolic field of the printed page yields to the iconic field of the screen.

The shift from a symbolic, or word-centered, world to an iconic universe filled with visual images carries profound cultural implications. For while we *can* read visual images actively and cognitively (which, of course, is the whole point of this book), the sheer visibility of icons tempts us to receive them uncritically and passively. Icons look so much like the realities they refer to that it is easy to forget that icons, too, are signs: images that people construct to carry ideological meanings.

The Kids Aren't All Right

Consider, for example, the image of the American family as presented in the classic situation comedies of the 1950s to 1960s. White, suburban, and middle class, these families signified an American ideal that glorified patriarchal authority. Even *I Love Lucy*, a sitcom showcasing Lucille Ball, reinforced masculine privilege through such plotlines as Lucy's attempt to market her own line of "Vitameatavegamin" dietary supplements, an endeavor which, the show implied, was predestined to end in disaster due to female business incompetence. The advent of such "dysfunctional" family sitcoms as *Married with Children*, which undermined *male* authority and competence, thus signified a profound difference, a rejection of the old patriarchal values.

By the turn of the new millennium, this ideological shift had produced such popular series as *Desperate Housewives*, a program that not only adopted a matriarchal rather than patriarchal point of view but also helped to create a new television genre — the "dramedy" — which is neither a comedy nor a drama but is instead a hybrid of the two. And while the show is now in syndication and is no longer producing new episodes, a close look at one of its episodes can reveal just how subversive a TV program can be.

When studying a single episode of a television program, you should consider every potentially significant detail in it — from the appearance and nature of the characters to the settings, plotlines, and dialogue. And as with all semiotic analyses, you should suspend your personal opinions — that is, whether you like a show or not. What you are working toward is a critical analysis, what you think a program's underlying cultural significance may be. This process can also differ from describing what you think the show's explicit

Discussing the Signs of Television

In class, choose a current television program, and have the entire class watch the same episode (either individually as "homework" or together in class). Interpret the episode semiotically. What values and cultural myths does the show project? What do the commercials broadcast during the show say about its presumed audience? Go beyond the episode's surface appeal or "message" to look at the particular images it uses to tell its story, always asking, "What is this program *really* saying?"

message is. Many programs present overt messages, or morals, but what you are looking for is the message beyond the message, so to speak — the implicit, often contradictory, signals the show is sending.

A clear example of this type of double message can be found in "My Heart Belongs to Daddy" (Episode 204 of *Desperate Housewives*). We chose this episode because of its especially sly way of undercutting its own apparently conservative "moral" with a subtle, but powerful, counterpoint. Concluding with a voice-over in which the show's ghostly narrator, Mary Alice, comments on the good things that happen when families have good fathers present, the episode appears to extol the old-fashioned patriarchal vision of the family. But a close reading of the plot reveals something quite different indeed.

You can find a recap of "My Heart Belongs to Daddy" at www.televisionwith outpity.com/show/desperate-housewives/my-heart-belongs-to-daddy/18/. Given the soap-operatic nature of a dramedy like *Desperate Housewives* — the way that any single episode is intertwined with past episodes and never achieves closure in itself — you should research the backstory of a series of this kind before attempting an analysis, as we did prior to our own analysis. But rather than attempting to summarize the highly involved situation in which this particular episode is entwined, we shall treat it as a largely stand-alone story, focusing on three different subplots featuring the behavior of young boys.

These subplots center on the characters of Lynette, Susan, and Bree. Lynette has recently returned to her job in the corporate world because her husband lost *his* job, and she is unhappy about missing time with her young son Parker. Unmarried Susan, for her part, is pursuing a romantic relationship with Mike, who happens to be the secret father of Zach, a homicidal teenage runaway. Zach is looking for Paul, his presumptive father, who has gone missing for reasons of his own. Meanwhile, widow Bree is dating George, and her son Andrew highly resents the relationship since it is so soon after his father's death. Got all that? The show's fans will be aware of the excessively complicated story line that has taken the series to this point, but this will do for our purposes.

Let's begin with Lynette. She isn't simply unhappy; she is driven to tears by Parker's behavior in response to her absence. He has invented an "imaginary friend" whom he calls Mrs. Mulberry and who is embodied in a black umbrella (obviously inspired by *Mary Poppins*) that he carries with him everywhere and insists on sleeping with. When his mother comes in to kiss him good night, Parker rejects her while expressing his deep affection for Mrs. Mulberry. The situation could make us very sympathetic for a child who is going through severe separation anxiety, but he is really nasty about the whole matter. Not only does he callously reject Lynette's sincere attempts to connect with him, but he uses the umbrella to assault his teacher at school, an event that leads to Lynette's having to visit the school principal.

Lynette surreptitiously tosses the umbrella into the trash, but the next morning the trash collector accidentally drops the umbrella in the street. When Lynette comes out shortly thereafter to take Parker (who is protesting that he can't leave until he finds Mrs. Mulberry) to school, she tells him that Mrs. Mulberry has gone on to help another child, but at this moment they both see the umbrella lying in the street. An expression of joy crosses Parker's face, soon to be replaced by one of horror when a car drives by and flattens the umbrella. Lynette looks relieved, as Parker finally turns to his mother for comfort. She's gotten him back, and she's back in control.

Meanwhile, Bree has invited George over for dinner, and Andrew, trying to disgust George and drive him away from his mother, starts telling him about the noises his mother makes during sex. Bree, who is in the kitchen, doesn't hear this, and when George erupts in anger, he is the one who looks bad to Bree as Andrew smirkingly looks on. The audience, however, can see clearly that Bree is being duped. George gets his revenge at a swim meet, carefully planning things so that just at the beginning of Andrew's race, Andrew will look up into the stands to see Bree rapturously kissing George. Andrew jumps out of the pool, runs into the stands, and begins to slug George. Bree erupts at Andrew, to George's great satisfaction. Andrew is subsequently packed off to a camp for troublesome children, and his mother is firmly in control at the end of the episode.

Finally, Susan, who has located the missing Zach, is on the verge of helping him find his "father," Paul, when Zach brings up his continuing romantic feelings for Susan's daughter, Julie. A homicidal near-maniac with a track record of threatening people with guns, Zach is not exactly any mother's idea of a good suitor for her daughter. Susan changes her mind about helping Zach and instead tricks him into leaving the state. As with Parker's shock and Andrew's comeuppance, the situation is presented in such a manner that the audience's sympathy is likely to be with the woman, not the boy. Susan skillfully controls the situation.

To determine a semiotic significance for these details, we need to keep in mind the program's target audience and what is likely to entertain that audience. Remember, commercial television exists to entertain, and analyzing what makes it entertaining is what leads us to its significance. In the case of *Desperate Housewives*, the target audience predominantly consists of women, often mothers, who can especially identify with the parenting difficulties of the women depicted in the program. An episode packed with conflicts with misbehaving boys who have taken control of various situations but who all get a put-down in the end **abductively** points to an existing frustration in the mothers who watch it. The entertainment value lies in the catharsis such viewers may feel in seeing the boys "punished." Now, none of the boys suffers any physical harm (mothers would not be entertained by *that*); the punishment lies in a restoration of maternal power. In each case, the boy's comeuppance leaves the woman in control after she had lost her authority for a while. Evidently, a significant number of American women are feeling such desperation, or the scriptwriters would not have exploited it. Commercial TV exists to attract its audience, not repel it, and *Desperate Housewives* is not a show for young boys.

This episode of *Desperate Housewives* thus sends a signal beyond the explicit message. Recall that the explicit message is, in effect, patriarchal, a declaration of the need for good and strong fathers. But the underlying message, somewhat contradictorily, is matriarchal, presenting the cathartic triumph of women over young males. The potentially subversive significance of this counter-message is masked by Mary Alice's voice-over, which makes the episode appear completely conventional and thus avoids the sort of controversy that could sink a prime-time series. But it is that unconventional, subtle counter-signal in the plot that may account for much of the success of *Desperate Housewives*, an indicator that there are a good many desperate women eager to see their frustrations sympathetically dramatized.

The Flow

Whatever show you choose to analyze, remember why it is on TV in the first place: Television, whether network or cable, is there to make money. It is a major part of our consumer culture, and most of what appears on TV is there because advertisers who want to reach their intended markets sponsor it. The shows that command the highest share of viewers, accordingly, command the highest advertising rates. Producers want their viewers to connect emotionally with their programs—and a main strategy for encouraging this connection involves satisfying viewer fantasies. This is especially striking in teen-addressed shows that feature fashion-model-glamorous actors (often in their twenties) playing adolescents in the awkward years, but it is also true for adult-addressed shows, which invite their viewers to identify with high-status professionals like doctors (*Grey's Anatomy*) and lawyers (*The Good Wife*). Identifying with their favorite characters, viewers will identify with the products they see advertised on the shows—and buy them (or so television sponsors hope).

For this reason, the advertising that accompanies the show is one of the most revealing features in a television program analysis. By paying attention to the ads, you can learn much about the intended audience. Why is the nightly news often sponsored by over-the-counter painkillers? Why is daytime TV, especially in the morning, typically accompanied by ads for vocational training schools? Why are youth-oriented prime-time shows filled with fast-food commercials, while family programs have a lot of car ads?

Your analysis of a single episode of a television program can also usefully include a survey of where the show fits in what cultural studies pioneer Raymond Williams called the "flow" of an evening's TV schedule. Flow refers to the sequence of TV programs and advertisements, from, say, the 5:00 news, through the pre-prime-time 7:00 to 8:00 slot, through prime time and on through to the 11:00 news and the late-night talk shows. What precedes your program? What follows? Can you determine the strategy behind your show's scheduling?

Exploring the Signs of Television: Viewing Habits

In your journal, explore your television-viewing habits and how the way you have watched TV has changed over time. When and why do you usually watch television? Have you transitioned from watching shows with your family or friends to watching them alone on a computer? Do you watch shows when they are broadcast, or do you watch them via Netflix, Hulu, or DVR on your own time? Do you think of watching television as a social activity? If so, write about how the diverse technical options for watching television have complicated this notion. If not, what place does watching television occupy in your life?

Reality Bites

No overview of modern television can be complete without a look at reality TV (RTV), and as with any semiotic analysis, some history is essential. One might say that reality television began in 1948 with Allen Funt's *Candid Camera*, which featured the filming of real people (who didn't know they were on camera) as they reacted to annoying situations concocted by the show's creators. The show's attraction lay in the humor viewers could enjoy by watching other people get into minor jams. There is a name for this kind of humor that comes from psychoanalytic theory: schadenfreude, or taking pleasure in the misfortunes of others, as when we laugh at someone slipping on a banana peel. And we shall see that this appeal from the early days of reality TV is very much a part of the genre's popularity today.

After *Candid Camera* came the 1970s PBS series *An American Family*. In this program, a camera crew moved in with a suburban family named the Louds and filmed them in their day-to-day lives. The Louds were not contestants and there were no prizes to be won. The program was conceived as an experiment in cinema verité to see if it was possible for television to be authentically realistic. The experiment was a bit of a failure, however, as the Loud family members began to act out for the camera. The result was the eventual dissolution of the Louds as a family unit and a general uneasiness about such experiments.

The next and probably most crucial step was when MTV launched *The Real World* in 1992. Like *An American Family*, *The Real World* (and similar programs like *Big Brother*) attempts to be realistic, with its constant camera recording a group of people living in the same house. Unlike *An American Family*, however, *The Real World* is a fantasy that caters to young-adult viewers, who can imagine themselves living in glamorous circumstances and vicariously enjoy the experience of becoming instant TV stars. That there is a certain tampering with reality in *The Real World*, a deliberate selection of participants based upon their appearance and how they can be cast into often-contrived romances as well as conflicts, constitutes a contradiction that differentiates *The Real World* from *An American Family* and leads us to the dawning of the reality revolution.

The astounding success of the inaugural versions of *Who Wants to Marry a Multi-Millionaire?* and *Survivor* established reality TV's full coming-of-age. In both programs, we can see strong traces of what made their pioneering predecessors popular. But through their introduction of a game show element, complete with contestants competing for huge cash prizes, a whole new dimension was added with new layers of significance in an even more **overdetermined** fashion. Reality programs that include a game show dimension offer their viewers the vicarious chance to imagine themselves as being in the shoes of the contestants (after all, anyone in principle can get on a game show) and winning lots of money. There is an element of schadenfreude here as well, if viewers take pleasure in watching the losers in game show competitions. But by adding the real-life element of marriage to the mix, *Who Wants to Marry a Multi-Millionaire?* (and its descendants) has brought an extra dimension of humiliation, not to mention voyeurism, to the genre. It's one thing to be caught on camera during the emotional upheaval of competing for large cash prizes, but it is quite another to be in an erotic competition, and lose, with millions watching you.

While game shows usually feature some sort of competition among the contestants, the *Survivor* series takes such competition to a new level by compelling its contestants to engage in backstabbing conspiracies as they claw their way to the top. (The 2006 season even introduced an element of racial conflict by forming tribes according to race.) It isn't enough for tribe to compete against tribe; there has to be intratribal backbiting and betrayal as well. Such a subtext constitutes a kind of grotesque parody of American capitalism itself, in which the cutthroat competition of the workplace is moved to the wilderness. Not to miss out on a good thing, RTV brought it all back to the office with *The Apprentice*, a show that makes capitalist competition its major theme, while echoing the talent show elements of *American Idol*. Indeed, so successful was the formula that *The Apprentice* would be joined for a while by *My Big Fat Obnoxious Boss*, which really turned the evils of life under capitalism into schadenfreude-laden entertainment.

Voyeurism. Schadenfreude. Dog-eat-dog capitalist competitiveness. Conspicuous consumption. RTV's formula seems to appeal to some of the most primitive and socially disruptive of human instincts, violating taboos in the name of profits (for an example of *real* taboo tweaking, consider the *Jackass* franchise). Indeed, after one of the *Survivor: The Australian Outback* contestants was seriously burned by a fire, commentators wondered whether future installments would have to include the death of a contestant to satisfy their viewers' ever-greater desire for mayhem. But while there has been no such event (to date), reality TV continues to grow, covering every imaginable possible topic (storage container speculation, anyone?). Combining disdain with desire, RTV invites viewers to fantasize that they, too, can effortlessly become rich or famous or beautiful, while sneering at those who—like the people of *Jersey Shore* and *Here Comes Honey Boo Boo*—are put on TV so their audiences can feel better about themselves by feeling superior to them. We've come a long way from the "I'm OK. You're OK." era. Today, it's more like "I'm not OK. You're an idiot."

Real Populists of the U.S.A.

Among the more recent varieties of reality television are programs that focus on fundamentally working-class occupations (*America's Toughest Jobs*, *Ice Road Truckers*, *Deadliest Catch*, and so on). Such programs, with their claim that viewers are being shown what life is like for ordinary working-class people, introduce yet another layer of significance to RTV that can best be explained in relation to the contradictory **mythologies** of American populism and elitism.

America's populist tradition celebrates the common citizen, the ordinary man or woman on the street, "Joe Six-Pack." These are the heroes of our democratic tradition and institutions. Programs like *America's Toughest Jobs* embrace this vision, inviting their viewers to identify with, and celebrate, ordinary people. It is highly significant, however, that *America's Toughest Jobs* lasted only one season, while elitist RTV programs that focus on the lives of wealthy families like the Kardashians or those that appear in one *Real Housewives of . . .* franchise or another seem to go on forever. Ask yourself what the appeal of such shows to their largely nonaffluent audiences might be. What signs do you see that their characters' lives are happy or unhappy, and what are they happy or unhappy about? What fantasies about being a mom at home do these shows encourage? Use your semiotic tool kit to extend the discussion we've started here, not only about these sorts of programs but about any TV show your instructor asks you to analyze.

The Medium Is the Message

In short, there are a myriad of RTV formulas to suit a highly segmented, niche-marketed audience, with a seemingly limitless appetite for programs that appeal to their particular fantasies, desires, interests, and even irritations. But perhaps all reality programming shares a fundamental common denominator that links it to the newer digital technologies that are now reshaping the American consciousness. This is the way that RTV offers ordinary people the chance to enjoy extraordinary media fame and exposure, or, conversely but in a similar fashion, offers at least the illusion of access to the lives of the truly famous. That is, whether you are auditioning for *American Idol* (at virtually impossible odds, of course) or viewing a program like *Duck Dynasty* or voting

---

Reading about TV Online

The Internet has given rise to a number of popular sites for TV criticism and community discussion, including tvworthwatching.com. Using a search engine, find a forum devoted to your favorite TV show and take notes on how the community of fans interacts. What about the show you've chosen most interests fans? What topics are most popular, or most contested? Does the conversation stick to television, or does it veer into discussions of users' personal lives? Are you drawn to participate? Using the forum as a microcosm, reflect on how television might be considered a social adhesive. How do the fans of TV shows use the Web to bond over the show and with one another?

---

on *Dancing with the Stars*, you are touching the big grid of a media-saturated and media-fascinated society. So, too, does your own Twitter feed (or YouTube account, Facebook page, or whatever) give you a place, however small, in a global media environment, even as it allows you to read celebrity tweets (or Facebook pages) and, perhaps, be tweeted back to.

Two sides of the same coin, RTV and social networking are signifiers of the full maturity of the age of **mass media**, an era in which nothing seems to matter unless it can be publicized and broadcast, and fame by any means trumps all other values. With the celebrity as the defining identity for our **mass culture**, both television and the social media made possible by the new technology are shaping a culture in which celebrity access seems to be open to all. Andy Warhol once quipped that in the future everyone would be famous for fifteen minutes, but while that fifteen minutes is still an unrealistic goal for the vast majority of us, reality television, along with its digital cousins, signifies a world where personal publicity or sheer notoriety is not only a means to an end but the end itself, the goal of goals.

The Readings

We begin the readings in this chapter with Nick Serpe's trenchant analysis of such reality television programs as *Repo Games*, *Pawn Stars*, and *Storage Wars*, in which he explores the depths to which RTV will go in a bad economy in order to make money. Claire Miye Stanford and Michelle Dean follow with a paired set of readings that take us to the country, with Stanford analyzing the feminist dimensions of ABC's *Nashville* and Dean critiquing *Here Comes Honey Boo Boo*'s exploitation of that old American stereotype: the redneck hillbilly. Next, Carl Matheson looks at *The Simpsons* — one of TV's longest-running institutions — and explores what happens when self-conscious irony overrides just about everything else that the show may represent, while Natasha Simons unravels the political significance of *Mad Men*, a show that looks quite different depending upon the ideology of the viewer. Jane Hu's nuanced analysis of sex, class, eating, and economics in *Girls* brings out the ambivalences of millennialist life in an era of reduced expectations, and Willa Paskin follows with a critique of the contradictions in *Devious Maids*, a program that at once skewers and celebrates the American dream. Neal Gabler concludes the chapter with his suggestion that having contributed to the atomization of American society, "TV has learned how to compensate for the increasing alienation it seems to induce" by filling its schedule with shows saturated with inauthentic "flocks" of friends and family relationships.

NICK SERPE

Reality Pawns: The New Money TV

When the going gets tough, reality TV gets nasty. Such is the conclusion that Nick Serpe draws in this review of such RTV shows as *Repo Games*, "one of the vilest reality shows in the history of American television," as Serpe puts it. Pulling no punches, Serpe explores the ways in which the Great Recession has been exploited by RTV producers who have found that debt and down-and-outedness make for entertaining fare in such programs as *Pawn Stars* and *Storage Wars*, gritty shows that, like *Repo Games*, reap profits out of other people's losses. Nick Serpe is the online editor of *Dissent: A Quarterly of Politics and Culture*, from which this selection is taken.

Repo Games, one of the vilest reality shows in the history of American television, premiered on Spike in 2011 with no fanfare and a simple premise, delivered in a voiceover intro: "Nobody wants to meet the repo man. But when this repo man comes, you'll get the chance to ditch those late notices for good." A little more than a minute later, we see a man built like a professional wrestler pull up in front of a woman's house, along with a camera crew that rushes into her driveway like a SWAT team. The owner's "REPO REPORT" then flashes across the screen: "Name: Wallace. Age: 44, Vehicle: '96 Dodge Caravan. Intel: Her weave alone will whoop your ass." Heavy metal plays in the background. A tow truck backs in under the van, which Wallace does not appreciate, and then the wrestler, co-host Tom DeTone, proceeds to describe the situation in which Wallace now finds herself: Tom is going to repo her car, but if she can answer three of five trivia questions right, the car will be hers, and fully paid off. The tow rig lifts the back of the car when she gets answers wrong and brings it down when she gets them right. With six family members watching on, Wallace prevails. She dances with Tom and then boasts in the post-game interview, "I ain't going to even fucking look for a job now."

The next contestant, a skinny, shirtless stoner living at his mom's, has a similar message when he wins: "Guess what I learned, America: if you don't pay your bill, somebody else will."

The last contestant, a woebegone fifty-eight-year-old man, grovels when he loses: "Even though I lost, you guys gave me an opportunity to save my car and I appreciate that, because in this time and age not many people would even do that." Tom responds, "Wish you all the best, John, and I wish I could pay off everybody's car. It's just not possible."

Even in "this time and age" — years into a hollow economic recovery built atop an already hollowed-out economy, more than a decade after the ascendance of American reality television — and even given the very low bar of taste set by Spike, I expected to find some online traces of outrage at the cruelty, exploitation, and heavy-handed stereotypes on display in *Repo Games*. All I could find was a commentary in the *American Thinker*, a conservative website, speculating that "the numerous stupid and vulgar contestants" on the show were typical Obama voters. In depicting these people seemingly cast from a Tea Partier's nightmare — the lazy welfare queen, the languid video-gamer mooching off the 'rents, the emasculated, aging white man who "never should've gotten this far" — the show "inadvertently [veered] from goofy entertainment into trenchant social commentary."

Reality television, though almost never considered serious, was seriously   5
considered in its early days, and the attention was mostly negative. Some early precursors, such as MTV's *The Real World* (1992–present), which brought a group of young strangers together under one roof for a few months, earned begrudging respect for their occasionally frank depictions of stigmatized subjects. But the ethical tone and artistic qualities of reality TV seemed to be set by *Who Wants to Marry a Multi-Millionaire?*, a one-night special aired on Fox in February 2000. *Multi-Millionaire* was like a beauty pageant that collided with a high-stakes *Dating Game*: women were paraded on stage for a rich man, seen only in silhouette, who would pick a lucky winner and marry her right then and there. The National Organization of Women denounced the show, as did the bride in numerous interviews. (It turns out that a restraining order had been filed against the man by a former girlfriend, not to mention that he wasn't that rich after all.) The marriage was annulled in April. By the summer, American versions of *Survivor* and *Big Brother*, both European imports, had premiered and won huge audiences. These series featured "normal" people, competing for prizes and for their fifteen minutes of fame. They set the standards — confessional interviews, fierce competition, oblivious narcissism, casting designed to foster conflict, semi-scripted scenes — that would define the genre.

Critics worried about what had opened the reality TV floodgates. Perhaps it was the seductive intimation that anyone could be (briefly) famous — and that the skeptical audience probably deserved it more than the charmless cutthroats who auditioned successfully. Perhaps the viewing public was growing so detached, so impatient with clichés and inured to fictional cruelty, that they hungered for something realer. Maybe we'd watched so much television that we were all acting like TV characters anyway; someone just had to put the cameras in front of us. Or was the rest of TV already so bad that anything novel was welcome?

If you were reading the tea leaves of popular taste, you would find a lot to get upset about. But focusing only on viewers reinforces the idea that TV programming is driven by what consumers want. There's no doubt that reality TV would have remained a very marginal phenomenon without a willing audience, but it wouldn't have spread the way it did — with proliferating subgenres colonizing the whole TV landscape — were it not for the economics of producing these shows. According to Charles B. Slocum, assistant executive director of the Writers Guild of America, West:

In virtually every line of the production budget, reality-based programming is cheaper than traditional programming. Not as much equipment
is needed, and it's cheaper. There is a smaller crew. There are fewer paid
performers. There are fewer sets. The economic role of reality-based programming is to permit a network to cost-average down the price of programming across the entire primetime schedule.

And, as a strike this spring by writers on the show *Fashion Police* brought to
public attention, reality writers are predominantly nonunionized, with wages
and benefits that reflect this fact. Even if entertainment execs weren't terrified of the Internet pushing down their bottom lines, cheap and titillating
programming was a no-brainer.

The cultural panic over reality programming faded as the genre became a permanent and profitable TV fixture. In the meantime, a relatively small group of
intelligent and well-crafted television dramas, from *The Sopranos* to *Breaking
Bad*, became critical darlings, arguably marking the first time the medium has
surpassed mainstream American cinema as an art form.

As a result, more recent developments in reality TV, including some of the
most popular cable shows of the last five years, have attracted less attention.
Critics have taken note of the rise of so-called blue-collar TV — where "blue
collar" means burly fishermen (*Deadliest Catch*) and loggers (*Ax Men*) risking
their lives to take care of their families — and the related "redneck" subgenre,
featuring, for example, Cajuns with thick accents hunting swamp alligators
(*Swamp People*). *Repo Games* also follows people doing their jobs — the co-
hosts are supposedly both actual repo men — but it is part of a different phenomenon: the money-crazed, market-idealizing reality show, immersed in a
funhouse version of the culture of debt and credit.

Although consumer debt was holding the American economy together for   10
decades before the recession laid it bare, these shows are a distinctly post-
recession phenomenon. They thrive on foreclosed property and unpaid bills;
they promote a bargain-basement ethos where everything has a price, and
where discovering and comparing those prices is a source of pleasure. These
shows are competitive in the way that much reality TV is, but the competitions are embedded in actual economic practice. These shows are the popular
idea of the free market, writ small.

Two shows define this subgenre more than any other: *Pawn Stars*, which premiered on the History Channel in the summer of 2009, and A&E's *Storage
Wars*, launched in December 2010. These remarkably formulaic programs set
viewing records on their respective channels and inspired cable TV execs to
run dozens of imitators.

Pawn Stars depicts the goings-on at a Las Vegas pawn shop that caters
both to people making ends meet at the end of the month and to habitual
gamblers. Most of the store's transactions are pawns, offered at the industry's typically high interest rates. Most of the customers depicted on the show,

however, resemble the people who bring heirlooms to *Antiques Roadshow*, if slightly gruffer. And most of the transactions depicted are sales and purchases, not loans. (The producers defend the absence of the typical pawn customer by appealing to the unique character of this pawn shop, to the repeat customers' desire for privacy, and to audience sensibilities.)

In its structure, *Pawn Stars* is in fact a lot like *Antiques Roadshow*, the old PBS standby. Both ride on the fantasy that treasure might be lurking in anyone's attic. But the differences between *Roadshow* and what History Channel executives are calling "artifactual entertainment" are telling. The pawn shop setting (unlike *Roadshow*'s convention hall set-up) tells us that we're here for business, and lends the show at least the pretense of documentary. The PBS series features dozens of experts in various fields, while on *Pawn Stars* the assessors are mainly in the family business: Richard Harrison the patriarch, his son Rick (the show's star), Rick's son Corey, and Corey's friend Austin "Chumlee" Russell. They sometimes call on specialist "friends" in town to assess or restore particular items, and they frequently go to shooting ranges to test antique weapons, such as a nineteenth-century cannon shown on the first episode. *Pawn Stars* also attempts to signify youthfulness (successfully, as evidenced by its high under-thirty-five viewer ratings) with generic hard-rock interludes and souped-up graphics.

Despite its alleged factual and historical content, *Pawn Stars* is character driven. The Harrisons and Chumlee bicker and mock each other more or less constantly, in scenes that seem scripted to varying extents. The arguments are presented as a tough-guy façade covering a warm, family-friendly core. These men make their living by driving down what their customers ask for, but they have to put food on their tables, too, and pay all those employees we don't see on camera. Their homespun manner, their fascination with historical artifacts and the moment of discovery, the fact that we don't see their private homes (a very rare sight in the entire subgenre) or any truly desperate clientele — all of it makes the pawn biz seem like an honest one: usury with a human face. There aren't any complex debt vehicles or international price-fixing scandals at this lender, and the simple profit calculus is literally shown on screen: projected sale price minus purchase price equals projected profit. When the Harrisons and their staff won the National Pawnbrokers Association "Pawnbroker of the Year" award in 2010, the organization claimed they had improved the public image of pawn shops more in one year than the NPA's publicity team had over decades.

On *Storage Wars*, naked economic warfare takes a more central role, 15 but the family unit and flights of whimsy intervene to prevent the characters from looking like complete sociopaths. The show features a husband and wife duo who auction off storage units whose owners are delinquent in their payments. Various characters who want to resell the contents try to intimidate and frustrate each other as they compete for the units. The winners dig through their lockers and assign unverified prices to the items inside. On the first season, there's Dave, a brash man with a secondhand business big enough that he brings a team of men with him to carry off his hauls; Jarrod and Brandi, another husband-and-wife pair, who run a struggling consignment shop; Barry, a dilettante collector who employs various outlandish tricks (for instance, using a little person on stilts) to gain advantage; and Darrell, a perpetually sunburned and doltish man who, along with his son, is on the hunt for the "wow factor." One participant warns that "once we get through those gates, there is [sic] no friends, and there is no professional courtesy. It's every man for himself, and may the best man win," and at the end of each episode, the day's winner is declared according to self-reported profits. But despite the fierce bidding, the show's tone is light-hearted, even ironic.

Pawn Stars and *Storage Wars* launched an entire subgenre, with various epigones on cable channels including TLC, Lifetime, Discovery, Travel, Spike, and of course History and A&E. There are direct franchise spin-offs, such as *Cajun Pawn Stars* and *Storage Wars: Texas*, related shows such as *American Restoration* (which features an antique restorer frequently consulted on *Pawn Stars*), and a host of imitators. On *American Pickers*, two friends travel around the country dropping in on old farmers and hoarders to make on-the-spot deals on salvaged antiques. On *Barter Kings*, the hosts do away with cash altogether, transforming a small and inexpensive item into something grand through a series of in-kind trades with people they meet through Craigslist. Other shows transplant the auction idea into other settings, like *Baggage Battles* (unclaimed luggage at airports), *Container Wars* (unclaimed commercial shipping containers), *Texas Car Wars* (semi-junked hotrods), and *Flip Men* and *Property Wars* (foreclosed houses). On *Picker Sisters* and *Pawn Queens*, there are women.

One of the most notable of the debt-and-credit reality TV shows released in the wake of *Pawn Stars* and *Storage Wars* is *Hardcore Pawn*, truTV's most popular show and the inspiration for its own spin-offs, such as *Hardcore Pawn: Chicago* and the deranged *Combat Pawn*. Although it is clearly an attempt to cash in on the popularity of *Pawn Stars*, the show's producers and writers have set out to differentiate themselves from their relatively staid predecessor. Like the other shows in the subgenre, *Hardcore Pawn* extols the small-business owner, depends on a familial cast to drive the action ("We disagree more than regular employees, but we have each other's back"), and is full of scripted scenes that strain credulity. But *Hardcore Pawn* trades on its grit and volatility. The Harrisons appear to make money by playing with toys, while the Golds have captured the pugilistic atmosphere of *The Jerry Springer Show*, replete with bleeped-out cursing, fights broken up by large security guards, and a stripper pole (all on the first episode).

Despite the obvious fakery, the Detroit pawn shop owned by Les Gold, a third-generation pawnbroker working with his children Seth and Ashley, appears to have real customers who are about as happy as you would expect customers at a pawn shop — let alone a pawn shop in Detroit — to be. And as Les proudly states, "We don't call the experts, we are the experts." The customers lie and get lied to, and they are indeed desperate. "We're not *Antiques Roadshow*," Les told an interviewer, claiming *Hardcore Pawn* shows "how the *other* other half lives," a reverse image *Lifestyles of the Rich and Famous*. (David Paulin, author of the *American Thinker* commentary, explicitly draws a comparison between the people on *Repo Games* and the poor depicted in Michael Harrington's *The Other America*, all of whom he sees as suffering more from a lack of middle-class values than a lack of money.) "The draw that truTV has really focused on was the reality of what goes on in a real pawn shop with real people,"* Gold told an interviewer for the *Detroit Free Press*. Again, its claim to depicting real life is laughable. But the show might actually present what the typical petit bourgeois believes is typical of the working poor, either jocular deference or outrageous hijinks.

Watched in close succession, these cash-crazed shows reveal a number of common tropes. They portray an unforgiving social landscape, where taking risks at others' expense is the way to get ahead. They recommend crude psychological techniques for closing the sale: trick your auction competition into dropping too much money on a bad unit, encourage people selling their goods to name a price before you do, leverage their personal problems to encourage a less-than-ideal trade, and never be afraid to get the better deal. They rely on family and childhood friends to provide some centripetal moral force and invoke "the economy" and "the times" to explain why people are willing to do what they do. They express awe in the face of old, undiscovered, and abandoned riches, and nostalgia for a simpler capitalism. And beneath the veneer of small-town, small-business, conservative ethics, you can find the preening personalities, petty feuds, platitudes, and falsities that have characterized the bulk of reality television.

Some of the suspicious scenes are obvious and expected. Struggling 20 actors are cast into the parts of longtime assistants to the experts; the first "reveal" of a locked-up, foreclosed house begins with a camera already inside; a piece of dialogue is filled with zingers that could only have been written beforehand; transactions that could have taken place online are dramatized on location; shop owners implement harebrained schemes to squeeze a couple extra bucks.

But a lawsuit issued last fall by Dave Hester, possibly the most despised character on *Storage Wars*, after he was fired, charged that producers "salted" storage lockers with rare, expensive, and antique items before they went on the block. Allegedly, some of the items already belonged to the winner before

---

*truTV's motto is "Not Reality. Actuality," and its reality programming is consistently a couple of steps beyond credibility; some of its shows, including another repo show, *Operation Repo*, are filmed like reality shows but feature completely reconstructed scenes. The trajectory of truTV, which used to be Court TV (spell "court" backward, drop the "oc," and you get something like the truth), mirrors a number of other cable channels. The History Channel has dropped its standard historical content in favor of reality fare and picked up a slogan to reflect the change: "History: Made Every Day." TLC, which used to stand for "The Learning Channel," now stands for "TLC," and A&E (previously "Arts & Entertainment") is now just "A&E," presenting "Real Life. Drama."

the sale, and at other times goods were supplied by a large Los Angeles antiques store. The auctions themselves, Hester claims, were often staged, with producers giving extra money to contestants they wanted to win a particular locker. Parts of the far-reaching suit (as of this writing) have been dismissed by the Los Angeles Superior Court, and A&E denies his allegations. But given the unbelievable rate at which bidders find unbelievable items on the show, it's hard to believe that Hester is just making it up. Some committed, online amateur sleuths (like the person behind www.storagewarsisfake.com) have made a cause of finding inconsistencies in this show and other reality-cash programs that back up his claims.

One of the biggest revelations in the lawsuit was an incidental one: at the time the suit was issued, Hester was earning $25,000 per episode, plus numerous bonuses. The real cash was never in buying abandoned storage units, but in making the auctions an exciting venue of social conflict for TV. On online message boards, people claiming to have attended these auctions in the past write that they have given up: huge crowds now show up and lose lots of money in the elusive pursuit of the baseball card collections, rare coins, celebrity memorabilia, and bizarre antiques that frequently pop up on *Storage Wars* and its competitor shows. Others have reported their disappointment upon visiting the Harrisons' pawn shop in Las Vegas, where the main business now appears to be selling *Pawn Stars* tchotchkes.

This isn't to deny that the market in buying foreclosed properties, and in pawning and selling secondhand goods, has boomed in the post-recession years. As Richard Harrison told the *Las Vegas Sun*, "[Y]ou have to understand that 17 to 20 percent of people in the United States don't have an active checking account or any bank affiliation, and this is a place where they can get a loan." The same arguments are made by the booming payday loan industry and others in the quick-cash credit business. They can get away with charging usurious rates — what scholars have called "the cost of being poor" — because they satisfy a need that other institutions, from banks to employers to government programs, aren't meeting.

Are these shows also satisfying a need? Busted-economy reality TV wouldn't exist if it weren't cheap to make, and it may be popular for any number of the scary-seeming reasons that reality TV in general is popular. But it also seems like a coming out for a number of predatory business practices that seem refreshingly frank in the wake of a financial crisis that people are told is too complicated for them to understand. For an audience primed on the language of individual bootstrapping and grave threats to the free market, these shows may seem practically heartwarming.

Rick Harrison made his politics explicit in recent months. In an interview on the *Mark Levin Show*, a program hosted by one of the most popular right-wing radiomen this side of Rush Limbaugh, Harrison assailed the state for not granting him a permit to film a *Pawn Stars* segment on government land (they blamed, falsely, he believed, the sequester for the permit denial) and attacked Obamacare for hurting employers. After beginning to make an interesting if ill-informed point about how small banks were treated poorly by the Obama administration while the big banks were bailed out, Harrison revealed a simpler, more sinister endgame: "We have the government that's down on business, down on business, people with money. I know someone else who did that. His name was Lenin. I mean he blamed the banks, aka the Jews, he blamed the intelligentsia. Let's reeducate everybody."

This sort of statement is a commonplace in right-wing U.S. politics, and, along with Rick Santelli's infamous screed against "loser" homeowners who couldn't keep up with their mortgages, constitutes the worldview of the Tea Party Right: the beleaguered middle against the underclass and its elite allies. But coming from the *Pawn Stars* star, the statement brought to mind an exchange from the film *Repo Man*, Alex Cox's 1984 punk classic. Bud, played by Harry Dean Stanton, tells his repo trainee Otto (Emilio Estevez), "Credit is a sacred trust, it's what our free society is founded on. Do you think they give a damn about their bills in Russia?"

> OTTO: They don't pay bills in Russia, it's all free.
> BUD: All free? Free my ass. What are you, a fuckin' commie? Huh?
> OTTO: No, I ain't no commie.
> BUD: Well, you better not be. I don't want no commies in my car. No Christians either.

These shows and the seedy corner of the economy they depict aren't just about winners and losers, but strivers and failures, the bold and the broken. In this universe, there are simply some people on the right side of the asymmetrical information divide, and others born to be conned. And there is no mutual aid without interest.

READING THE TEXT

1. What reasons does Serpe provide to support his claim that the growth of reality TV was largely *not* audience driven?

2. Summarize in your own words the history of reality TV, as Serpe presents it.

3. What is the appeal of *Pawn Stars* and *Storage Wars*, according to Serpe?

4. What connection does Serpe see between "busted-economy reality TV" (para. 24) and right-wing politics in America, especially the Tea Party variety?

5. How do producers of shows like *Storage Wars* manipulate events to make the program more entertaining and less realistic, according to Serpe?

READING THE SIGNS

1. In class, discuss the tone of Serpe's article. To what extent does that tone enhance or reduce its effectiveness?

2. Watch one of the programs that Serpe discusses, and conduct your own analysis of it. Does the show use any of the "common tropes" (para. 19) that Serpe mentions? Is it a "funhouse version of the culture of debt and credit" (para. 9)?

3. Write an essay in which you support, refute, or complicate Serpe's link between right-wing politics and the popularity of "debt-and-credit" reality TV shows.

4. In the 1950s, the show *Queen for a Day* also focused on people in economic distress. Research *Queen for a Day*, and write an analysis comparing it to a program like *Repo Games*. In what way are the shows similar? How do you account for any differences?

5. **CONNECTING TEXTS** Read Jon Mooallem's "The Self-Storage Self" (p. 102), and compare the real-life lives of self-storage users with the lives of those depicted on reality TV programs like *Storage Wars*. Use your comparison as the basis for an essay in which you argue for the appropriateness of the word "reality" in RTV.

SOUTHERN WOMAN

CLAIRE MIYE STANFORD

You've Got the Wrong Song: Nashville *and Country Music Feminism*

Ever since Tammy Wynette counseled women to "Stand By Your Man" no matter what abuse he dishes out, country music has hardly been noteworthy for its feminist spirit. Such a background makes the country music–themed series *Nashville* all the more remarkable, Claire Miye Stanford argues in her review of the program, which she regards as "one of the most feminist television shows on television." In fact, for Stanford, *Nashville* resists simple political categorization and instead mixes femininity and feminism in the Dolly Parton tradition. Claire Miye Stanford is a freelance writer who has written for *The Millions*, *The Rumpus*, *Good*, and the *Los Angeles Review of Books*, in which this reading first appeared.

Both femininity and feminism have become harder and harder to define in 2013. In regard to the first, there are as many examples of femininity in the world as there are people (not just biological women) who embody them. As for the second, the term "feminism" is now so loaded with meaning, confusion, and incorrect associations that it has become all too common, especially among young women, to disavow the term entirely.

Into this complex terminology, enter Rayna James (Connie Britton) and Juliette Barnes (Hayden Panettiere), the lead characters of ABC's *Nashville*, created by former Nashville resident Callie Khouri. Khouri is a film veteran who wrote 1991's *Thelma & Louise*, a feminist classic that also won her the Academy Award for best original screenplay (typically a heavily male-dominated category). In its first season, the show has explored what it means to be both feminine and feminist in the world of country music and television.

Ultimately, any female-driven television show has to contend with these two concepts — whether that treatment is overt or more indirect, if only because every female-driven show will ultimately contend with the characters' love lives and how they interact with men (since their romantic interests are, almost always, male). But what stands out about *Nashville*, among all female-driven television shows, is that it places these omnipresent questions in unique contexts: professional, rather than personal, in the frame of a highly gendered genre, industry, city, and region.

But can a show that is so ostensibly interested in the "feminine" — in sexual and romantic relationships, in motherhood and daughterhood, in short skirts and spangly tops and big hair — also be feminist? That same question has been asked time and time again about country music itself, long considered a bastion of heteronormative, gendered songs about pick-up trucks. Historically, most feminist ire lands squarely on the shoulders of country music legend Tammy Wynette, and her biggest hit, 1968's "Stand By Your Man," in which Wynette advises the listener to forgive your man and, for that matter, to be "proud" of him, even when he's off having "good times / doing things that you don't understand." Whether these things that "you don't understand" are cheating, boozing, gambling, or other unsavory activities is not entirely clear, but still, Wynette counsels the listener to stand by him "'cause after all he's just a man"; in other words, he can't help it, it's in his Man Nature to mistreat you.

There are countless other songs, less famous than Wynette's, with the 5 same degrading message, but critics keep circling back to "Stand By Your Man" as a kind of shorthand for anti-feminist doctrine in country music, and, to a greater extent, life in general. In 1992, Hillary Clinton referred to the song when responding to allegations of then-presidential-hopeful Bill's extramarital affairs. "I'm not sitting here some little woman standing by my man like Tammy Wynette," she said in a *60 Minutes* interview. (In a whole other layer of feminist rhetoric, Clinton was pressured into apologizing to Wynette only days later by legions of country music fans who said it was an unfair comparison.)

Still, plenty of female country musicians have serious feminist chops, using their lyrics to take on political feminist issues from birth control and abortion to equal pay and spousal abuse. Loretta Lynn's 1975 song, "The Pill," is the first major song to mention oral contraceptives; more recently, Neko Case's 2002 song, "Pretty Girls," examines the judgment that comes with abortion. Other songs — about disappointment in marriage and motherhood, about not being slut-shamed for wearing a short skirt, about hitting your cheating husband upside the head with a cast-iron skillet — are not as overtly political, but still deal with realities of female experience head-on, without conforming to gender norms or social conventions.

Of all female country musicians, Dolly Parton presents the most interesting example of the tension that exists between femininity and feminism.

Her 1980 classic hit, "9 to 5," is set to a catchy beat but makes a political point about being an ambitious woman in a discriminatory workplace. Lesser known, her 1968 song "Just Because I'm a Woman" took on sexual hypocrisy and double standards way before "slut-shaming" was even an established phrase. But these days, Parton is often discounted as an artist—and as a feminist—made into a punch line about breast implants and plastic surgery; even when she is held up as a feminist icon, the argument often comes with a tone of questioning surprise and an acknowledgment that her big hair, big breasts, and tiny waist make her a less-than-obvious feminist heroine.

In their music on the show, both Rayna and Juliette fall firmly in the Dolly Parton camp of female country music star; while their songs are not overtly political or feminist—no abortion or birth control talk here—they are very much about women standing on their own, standing up for themselves, and being respected. Juliette's hits include "Telescope," which warns a cheating lover that she knows full well what he's up to; "Boys and Buses," advising that chasing after boys is a waste of time; and "Undermine," a heartfelt ballad about how it's harder—but more worthwhile—to achieve something on your own than to undermine someone else. Rayna's songs, tinged with more experience, are more downcast, but they, too, advocate for standing one's ground: "Buried Under" tells the story of a woman grappling with finding out her lover's long-buried secrets; in "No One Will Ever Love You," the singer insists that her love is the best love the listener will ever find, and he should accept it.

Of all *Nashville*'s songs, the song that Juliette and Rayna fictionally "cowrote" does the most to situate them within the world of women in country music. Titled "Wrong Song," the song is a fiery duet, addressed to a lying, cheating man, and in classic Rayna/Juliette fashion, it stands up for the woman, saying that she won't stand for that. But "Wrong Song" goes a step further than the usual woman-power advocacy, adding a meta-layer of commentary on country music (and music in general), turning the song into a defiant take on expectations for country music and female narratives in general. The song begins with a series of conditional ifs, setting up the typical country-song scenario—man drinks too much, does foolish thing, woman misses him and forgives him:

> If you think you're gonna hear
> how much I miss you
> If you're needing to feel better 'bout yourself
> If you're waiting to hear me
> say I forgive you
> 'Cause tequila turned you into someone else

The song then slows down, ever so slightly, as it winds up to the chorus, meanwhile deploying the Tammy Wynette shorthand for the disempowered woman, the country music stereotype who stands by her man no matter what he does:

> If you're looking for one more chance
> A little stand by your man

And then there comes the booming chorus, both women's voices coming together for the coup de grace, calling out all those songs before it for so easily forgiving wayward men, and also calling out the listener himself for expecting that they would forgive him, just because they are country music singers, just because they are ladies. If you think you're getting the stereotypical female narrative of passivity and forgiveness (à la "Stand By Your Man"), they tell the listener, then you've got the wrong song and the wrong girl:

> You've got the wrong song
> Coming through your speakers
> This one's about a liar and a cheater
> Who didn't know what he had
> 'till it was gone
> You've got the wrong girl
> Cause I've got your number
> I don't know what kind of spell
> you think I'm under
> This ain't a feel-good,
> 'Everything's fine' sing-along
> You've got the wrong song

This song, this performance, is the epitome of *Nashville* womanhood: active, empowered, and take-charge. But this song is more than just a statement on behalf of the characters. In one catchy chorus, it takes on the music industry and its demands on female artists, and then goes a step further by putting that examination on television, a similar crucible of issues concerning money, sexuality, female image, and power.

As characters, Rayna and Juliette are strong women, still rare on televi- 10
sion, but not impossible to find. As a show, though, *Nashville* — in its unapologetically pure focus on female characters, its self-aware examination of the struggles of female artists, and its critique of male-dominated industries — is one of the most feminist television shows on television.

Still, neither Rayna nor Juliette is a feminist, or, at least, we've never heard them say that they are. *Nashville* has never dropped the F-bomb, surely afraid of alienating part of its audience. As the show goes on, however, and as both Rayna and Juliette give more and more fictional interviews to television talk shows and magazines, the absence of the word "feminist" becomes a more glaring omission; after all, media love to ask women to define themselves in terms of feminism, especially strong, powerful women.

But that kind of definitive stance — feminist or not feminist — doesn't interest *Nashville*. The show is focused on individual characters rather than overarching labels, in showing how strong, powerful women live their strong, powerful lives. There are men on *Nashville*, too, but they are pretty much ineffectual; any success they have comes, directly or indirectly, as a result of their partnerships with the show's various women. Indeed, every woman on the show — not just Rayna and Juliette — is portrayed as a strong woman; they may have their faults, but all of them, from up-and-comer Scarlett O'Connor to Rayna's sister Tandy to more minor characters like the managers and political wives, have ambition, drive, and agency, as well as a self-possessed dignity that leaves no question about who is in control.

There is only one notable exception to this otherwise consistently empowered cast of female characters: the needy, conniving, and man-reliant Peggy Kenter, who has an affair with Rayna's husband and leaks Rayna's subsequent divorce to the tabloids. In both her demeanor and her actions, Peggy appears like a caricature of a helpless female, as if a reminder of all the ghosts of stereotypical soapy female characters past. Peggy is also notably the only character whose situation is presented without a trace of compassion; the show, it would seem, has no sympathy for a woman like Peggy — a woman who belongs in a different kind of world, on a different kind of show.

In fact, even though *Nashville* is billed as a primetime soap, it is much better described as a workplace drama, where the workplace is the country music mainstage. Along with reproductive rights, women's advancement and equal treatment in the workplace is one of the last — and most persistent — issues for feminism, a fact that makes *Nashville*'s portrait of this very particular workplace all the more interesting from a feminist point of view.

As in a workplace drama, we see the way the women express themselves 15 in front of others, but we also see what happens when the stage curtain is pulled back, and how that empowerment translates to both their personal lives and their behind-the-scenes business decisions. And it's in this offstage life that the show truly uses Rayna and Juliette to explore questions of feminism, especially when it looks at the challenges a woman faces when she insists on being in control of her own life.

These challenges are different for Rayna and Juliette, who are at distinct stages in both their career and personal life. For Rayna, married with two daughters, they manifest as a question of how to balance her career ambitions with being a good ("good") mother, daughter, and wife (and eventually ex-wife). Rayna never feels guilty about any of the decisions she makes related to her career; she misses her daughters when she is on the road, but she does not feel guilty or ashamed that she has left them with their (very loving) father. On the flipside, when her father has a heart attack, she flies back to Nashville immediately and says she might have to cancel that night's concert, but those decisions are made without agony, without any drama over where to put family and where to put career. This departure from female guilt over the intersection of professional and domestic priorities is refreshing.

Rayna also faces the challenge of how to stay relevant as a female artist and performer in her forties, an age our society deems over the hill. Again, the show defies the stereotypical storyline — one that might end in a middle-age crisis, substance abuse, or plastic surgery — and gives the character of

Rayna the dignity of a real person, taking on a real professional challenge. Rayna has to work even harder to stay relevant; there is no such thing as resting on laurels, especially for a female celebrity over the age of thirty. And, as always, Rayna rises to the challenge, writing more songs, evolving her sound, taking more risks, going on tour. When faced with a challenge, Rayna does not break down; she steels herself and takes it on, and she succeeds — not by chance or wiles, but by hard work and force of will.

For Juliette — young, hot, and unattached — the challenges are different. More than anything, Juliette wants to be taken seriously: by her record label, by her employees, by her colleagues, by reviewers, by her fans. Her youth is a major part of her problem: her male-dominated world (her boss at the label, her manager, her roadies, her band, the predominately male reviewers) do not want to take her seriously. But, even more problematic for a young woman like Juliette is her attitude. She knows what she wants, and she does what she wants without thinking of the consequences.

Juliette's behavior is not always perfect, but her slips in judgment are exacerbated by her gender and her age, and these mistakes drive the show's examination of social and professional double standards. Were Juliette a man, she would be described as "driven" and "demanding" when she fires her manager or changes her set list at the last minute; instead, since she is a woman, she is seen as irrational. Were she a man, she would be called a "bad boy" for her brushes with the law and her late nights clubbing; since she is a woman, this behavior threatens to ruin her career and her image. When Juliette's ex-boyfriend blackmails her over a sex tape he secretly filmed, the show takes on one of the most gendered celebrity scandals: a sex tape for a male celebrity means almost nothing, but becomes part of a woman's permanent record.

Even when exploring the rivalry between Rayna and Juliette — one of *Nash-* 20 *ville*'s central plotlines — the show treats the women with sophistication and dignity, making it clear from the start that it's a professional rivalry. It would be ideal if all women — or, for that matter, all people — could support each other even in competition, but in the world in which Rayna and Juliette operate, that isn't an option. This kind of competition is particularly endemic to women and particularly brutal, but professional competition transcends gender. Record labels only have so much promotional money to put behind artists; magazines only have so many pages to dedicate to female country music stars. In the plotline that will wrap up this season, Rayna and Juliette are both nominated for Female Country Music Artist of the Year. This turn of events is a brilliant move by the show in that it brings their competition to the forefront.

The show's recognition of this contest — and also the way the rivalry unfolds — again defies the typical portrayal of female envy. The very fact that competition is the major plot point of the show recognizes that women can compete in the first place — that women don't always "play nice," that a woman can want to be number one. Beyond that initial recognition, the rivalry itself is handled with sophistication and dignity. Other than a few snippy comments in the first few episodes when the show was finding its footing, both women are refreshingly direct (the gendered thing to say here would be that they aren't catty) about their relationship. Other than a few offhand statements, neither of them really talks about the other behind her back; when one of them is frustrated or angry at the other, she says so to her rival's face.

Most refreshingly, the competition stays entirely in the professional sphere. When Juliette is confronted with a giant billboard of Rayna's face as a celebrity endorsement, she does not react by commenting on Rayna's appearance or her age; she is pissed, but she is pissed because she wants an endorsement deal and a billboard of her own. When Rayna is forced to fly on Juliette's plane, she is also unhappy, but mostly about the fact that she doesn't have her own jet. Even when Juliette beds Rayna's long-ago love, the story focuses more on both women wanting him as a bandleader and songwriter — in a professional capacity — than a sexual or romantic rivalry.

In fact, in a brilliantly self-aware move, this season's closing plotline about Rayna and Juliette's award rivalry perfectly appropriates real-world media commentary about the show itself. When the show debuted in the fall, *Nashville*'s creator Khouri and stars Connie Britton and Hayden Panettiere both had to spend a lot of time (an inordinate amount of time) telling interviewers that the show was not about a "catfight" between the two women. In a recent episode, as Britton's Rayna and Panettiere's Juliette walked a red carpet together, reporters ask them how it feels to compete and Rayna, echoing Britton's real-life remarks, tells them, "If you're expecting a catfight, you're not going to get it."

Not only does this statement provide a new meta-commentary on female-driven narratives, but also continues the themes established in "Wrong Song" of defying traditional expectations for women, both for the way women act and the way women are represented — and represent themselves. In other words, if viewers come to *Nashville* looking for the same old soapy female tropes — catfights, bitchiness, seduction, backstabbing — then they've got the wrong show.

READING THE TEXT

1. According to Stanford, how do the fictional *Nashville* characters Rayna James and Juliette Barnes compare with real-life country music stars Tammy Wynette and Dolly Parton?

2. Why does Stanford claim that the word "'feminism' is now so loaded with meaning, confusion, and incorrect associations that it has become all too common, especially among young women, to disavow the term entirely" (para. 1)?

3. Summarize in your own words the conventional motifs of mainstream country music. In what ways does *Nashville* depart from the genre's conventions?

4. What does Stanford mean by saying that "Wrong Song" adds "a meta-layer of commentary on country music (and music in general)" (para. 9)?

READING THE SIGNS

1. In class, list on the board the connotations class members attach to the word "feminism." What do you think the sources of these connotations may be? Do you detect any differences between male and female students; if so, how do you account for them?

2. In an essay, argue for your own response to Stanford's question about *Nashville*: "Can a show that is so ostensibly interested in the 'feminine' . . . also be feminist?" (para. 4). As an alternative, focus your argument on a different program that features women characters, such as *Orange Is the New Black*.

3. Using Stanford's critique of femininity and feminism as a critical framework, analyze some songs popularized by current real-life country music artists such as Carrie Underwood or Taylor Swift. As an alternative, conduct a survey of country music lyrics by both male and female performers, and write an essay analyzing the gender politics implicit in these lyrics.

4. Write a semiotic analysis of a music superstar such as Lady Gaga who is overtly political in her public persona and actions. In what ways might your object of analysis reflect "the themes established in 'Wrong Song' of defying traditional expectations for women, both for the way women act and the way women are represented — and represent themselves" (para. 24)?

5. **CONNECTING TEXTS**   Adopting Stanford's perspective, analyze the gender dynamics you see in a different show that focuses on Southern female characters, *Here Comes Honey Boo Boo*. To what extent does this show replicate or defy "the same old soapy female tropes" (para. 24)? To develop your ideas, read Michelle Dean's "Here Comes the Hillbilly, Again" (below).

SOUTHERN WOMAN

| MICHELLE DEAN
Here Comes the Hillbilly, Again

From *The Beverly Hillbillies* to *Hee Haw* to *Duck Dynasty*, Americans have liked television hillbillies. But when *Here Comes Honey Boo Boo* became a surprise TV hit in 2012, things got sticky, causing enough of a "fuss" that Michelle Dean figured she'd better have a look at the show. And in this review for *Slate*, Dean reveals that, to her surprise, she found herself relating to Honey and her family, while at the same time seeing that, like *Jersey Shore* and *Teen Mom*, *Here Comes Honey*

🅔 macmillanhighered.com/signsoflife
How does a vintage TV show mine the hillbilly stereotype for comedy?
e-readings > *The Beverly Hillbillies,* "Getting Settled" [TV episode]

Boo Boo is very much a TV show for our times. This is an era when the increasing gap between the haves and the have-nots has the haves laughing at the have-nots, and the have-nots clinging precariously to the notion that the American dream isn't over for them yet, even when the reality is otherwise. Michelle Dean is an editor-at-large for *Flavorwire* and a writer whose work appears in *Slate*, the *New Yorker*, the *Nation*, and *Hazlitt*.

Somehow America always goes a little off the rails in the allegedly slow month of August, and this year's party is as wild as any. Republicans can't figure out how babies are made; cutting-and-pasting an article from the *New Yorker* into your *Time* column is no longer a fireable offense; and all the way down in McIntyre, Ga., there is a mother who feeds her child a Mountain Dew-and-Red Bull concoction before the 6-year-old gets onstage at beauty pageants. June Shannon, who stars with her daughter Alana "Honey Boo Boo Child" Thompson in TLC's controversial hit *Here Comes Honey Boo Boo*, would have provoked a firestorm even if what she calls "go-go juice" were the only sin she was broadcasting all over Christendom. All that caffeine, pop-culture commentators everywhere clucked, and all that sugar.

Lost in the outrage is just how squarely "go-go juice" fits into America's long tradition of "white trash" entertainment, which for decades has elevated characters like Honey Boo Boo into the nation's objects of fun. The Pepsi Co. borrowed the Mountain Dew brand-name from slang for moonshine; in the 1960s, it was explicitly advertised as a "hillbilly" drink. The campaign's entertaining TV ads, which you can watch on YouTube, were scored by twangy banjos and errant buckshot and plotted around a "stone-hearted gal" who will open her heart to you if you only take a swig. Watching these old videos after an episode or two of *Honey Boo Boo* makes at least one thing clear: The hillbilly has regained the spotlight in American culture.

As Anthony Harkins observes in *Hillbilly: A Cultural History of an American Icon*, one of the hillbilly's signature moves is to peak, popularity-wise, just when Americans sense that things in general are headed south. Its first true zenith came in the depressed 1930s, a handmaiden to the birth of commercial country music. Another arrived in the turbulent 1960s, when *The Beverly Hillbillies* and *Green Acres* and *Hee Haw* were in their prime. (Those are hardly the only examples, of course: It also popped up in the Ma and Pa Kettle films of the 1940s and 1950s and Paul Webb's 1930s *Esquire* cartoons about "The Mountain Boys," among other places.)

Though the term first referred to mountaineers in the Appalachians and the Ozarks, the hillbilly trope spread to cover pretty much all non-urban territory in America, joined by its cousins in cultural iconography, the "redneck" and "white trash." Today, people even apply that last term to residents of certain New Jersey beachfronts, for instance. Yet, as Harkins points out, no matter where an alleged country bumpkin comes from, he will be derided for his crass behavior. And such ridicule has always been politically coded:

The hillbilly figure allows middle-class white people to offload the venality and sin of the nation onto some other constituency, people who live somewhere — anywhere — else. The hillbilly's backwardness highlights the progress more upstanding Americans in the cities or the suburbs have made. These fools haven't crawled out of the muck, the story goes, because they don't want to.

This idea that the hillbilly's poverty is a choice allows more upscale Americans to feel comfortable while laughing at the antics before them. It also pushes some people to embrace the stereotype as a badge of honor. "Guitars, Cadillacs, hillbilly music / It's the only thing that keeps me hangin' on," Dwight Yoakam once sang. For more contemporary examples of reappropriation, you can attend any number of Tea Party rallies. The classist term "redneck," originally coined to indicate those who worked so hard and so long in the sun that they sported sunburns in the designated anatomical location, likewise has been adopted in the name of all that's good and holy. What's more American than a hard day's work?

June Shannon is a reappropriator *par excellence*. One of her signature phrases on *Here Comes Honey Boo Boo* is a call to, as she puts it, "Redneckognize." And yet all the cultural chatter that's attended Honey Boo Boo has been less than affectionate. The word of the day across the media is "apocalypse" — that is, the show is a sign of it. It's not just the caffeine highs, either. It's a family of six chopping up a roadkill deer for dinner, bellyflopping in the mud, and — those with delicate constitutions may want to avert their eyes for this next part — farting *in public*. Even critics who enjoy the show do so from a crouched, defensive posture. People seem to think this has all gone a little too far. Even the *Today Show* is starting to wonder if reality television just might be "exploitative."

I'm not a *Toddlers & Tiaras* fan, so I missed out on Alana's big splash on that show earlier this year. Beauty pageants in general are foreign and noxious to me: I can barely muster the energy to put on lip gloss and mascara. But I watched *Honey Boo Boo* out of curiosity about the fuss, and found myself, somewhat surprisingly, relating to Alana and her milieu. I have fond memories of that Dwight Yoakam song playing softly on my parents' radio as we drove home through the dark from a visit to my grandparents' house in rural Quebec. My family isn't from the South — we're not even from the United States — but I know enough of the land Honey Boo Boo lives in to be dubious of simple accusations of bad parenting and worse morals.

The practices are different, of course, and no, I'm not wild about the caffeine and sugar thing, either. Alana's little-girl grandiosity must become exhausting when experienced in more than 30-minute increments. But the people raising her are clearly aware of your disdain. Shannon can be delightfully funny when she self-consciously plays with her hillbilly image, warning the audience that she's about to "scratch her bugs," or speaking of her beauty routine: "Granted, I ain't the most beautimous out the box, but a little paint on this barn, shine it back to its original condition. 'Cause it shines up like it's brand new."

That's not to say the humor is always comfortable or even funny. Alana's trademark phrases and mannerisms — "a dollar makes me holler," a particular head swivel she does — are informed by racist stereotypes of black women. This ambiguous borrowing from black culture has always been part of the hillbilly trope as well. Early commercial country music borrowed liberally from black folk music. (Hank Williams learned to play guitar, he said, from a black street performer.) And this borrowing often turned into racist mimicry: The Grand Ole Opry included minstrelsy shows in the 1920s and 1930s. Interestingly, the term "white trash" may have been coined by black slaves in the early 19th century to describe poor white people in the South; American attitudes toward poor white people have long been tangled up with "the race problem."

And hillbilly stereotypes have always made it easier for middle-class whites 10 to presume that racism is the exclusive province of "that kind" of person. As Ta-Nehisi Coates has written, "It is comforting to think of racism as a species of misanthropy, or akin to child molestation, thus exonerating all those who bear no real hatred in their heart. It's much more troubling to think of it as it's always been — a means of political organization and power distribution."

As that distribution of power becomes more and more unequal, it's no surprise to see the hillbilly here again — on *Here Comes Honey Boo Boo*, on *Jersey Shore*, on MTV's *16 & Pregnant* and *Teen Mom* franchises. These shows reassure us that our struggle is worth it, all economic evidence to the contrary — if only because *we would never* belly-flop into the mud on cable television. *Here Comes Honey Boo Boo* casts this socio-economic divide in especially sharp relief, since the show is rooted partly in beauty pageant culture, which, in its own idiosyncratic way, indulges the American belief that you can work and spend your way to greatness. If you can afford the entry fees, the glitter, the makeup, the coach, and the stylists, you will be the Ultimate Supreme, as they say in the business. You'll have the sash to prove it.

But tiny, 6-year-old Alana is too crass and happy to get it. She is a terrible pageant queen. Her wigs are always askew, her daisy-dukes ill-fitting, and sometimes she grinds her fake teeth. Those rhinestone-studded bootstraps simply can't pull her up the way she needs them to.

READING THE TEXT

1. What are the typical characteristics of "hillbilly" culture, as you glean them from Dean's description?

2. Dean uses the terms "hillbilly," "white trash," and "redneck," offering some explanations of how they differ. In a chart, tease out the different connotations of these terms, especially as they may be interpreted by people of differing ethnic or socioeconomic groups.

3. According to Dean, how has hillbilly culture appropriated black culture?

4. What does Dean mean by saying that media representations of hillbilly culture are "politically coded" (para. 4)?

5. How do TV programs like *Honey Boo Boo* exploit the impoverished and offer them unrealistic hope for the future, in Dean's view?

READING THE SIGNS

1. Watch an episode of *Honey Boo Boo*, and write an essay in which you agree, disagree, or modify Dean's claim that the program exploits hillbilly, redneck, or white trash stereotypes. As an alternative, do the same analysis on an older TV show that Dean mentions, such as *The Beverly Hillbillies* or *Hee Haw*.

2. **CONNECTING TEXTS** Compare Dean's analysis of the social significance of a show like *Honey Boo Boo* with Nick Serpe's reading of shows like *Repo Games* (p. 268). To what extent do the shows use similar class stereotypes? To develop your analysis, consult Michael Parenti's "Class and Virtue" (p. 361).

3. Dean suggests similarities between *Honey Boo Boo*, a show located in the deep American South, and *Jersey Shore*, a program situated in a mid-Atlantic state. Write an essay in which you evaluate her connection between these programs. Do both use signs of "white-trashiness"? If so, how do they do that? If you see divergences, explain them.

4. Dean suggests that viewing a 1960s Mountain Dew commercial can be enlightening. Watch such an older commercial and then a current ad for Mountain Dew. Analyze them, and in an essay explain how the ads have used, modified, or changed the image of the "hillbilly."

CARL MATHESON
The Simpsons, *Hyper-Irony, and the Meaning of Life*

Don't have a cow or anything, but most comedy, as Carl Matheson points out in this analysis of *The Simpsons*, which first appeared in *The Simpsons and Philosophy* (2001), is based in cruelty. And while Matheson doesn't "mean to argue that the makers of *The Simpsons* intended the show primarily as a theater of cruelty," he does "imagine that they did." At any rate, Matheson suggests, the pervasive irony that makes the program funny should serve as a warning to anyone who believes that this ever-popular cartoon sitcom is a warm endorser of family values. Carl Matheson is a professor in, and chair of, the department of philosophy at the University of Manitoba. He has published essays in the *British Journal of Aesthetics*, the *Journal of Aesthetics and Art Criticism*, and *Philosophy and Literature*.

DISAFFECTED YOUTH #1: Here comes that cannonball guy. He's cool.
DISAFFECTED YOUTH #2: Are you being sarcastic, dude?
DISAFFECTED YOUTH #1: I don't even know anymore.
— "Homerpalooza," Season 7

What separates the comedies that were shown on television fifty, forty, or even twenty-five years ago from those of today? First, we may notice technological differences, the difference between black-and-white and color, the difference between film stock (or even kinescope) and video. Then there are the numerous social differences. For instance, the myth of the universal traditional two-parent family is not as secure as it was in the 1950s and 1960s, and the comedies of the different eras reflect changes in its status — although even early comedies of the widow/widower happy fifties, sixties, and seventies were full of nontraditional families, such as are found in *The Partridge Family*, *The Ghost and Mrs. Muir*, *Julia*, *The Jerry van Dyke Show*, *Family Affair*, *The Courtship of Eddie's Father*, *The Andy Griffith Show*, *The Brady Bunch*, *Bachelor Father*, and *My Little Margie*. Also, one may note the ways in which issues such as race have received different treatments over the decades.

But I would like to concentrate on a deeper transformation: today's comedies, at least most of them, are funny in different ways from those of decades past. In both texture and substance the comedy of *The Simpsons* and *Seinfeld* is worlds apart from the comedy of *Leave It to Beaver* and *The Jack Benny Show*, and is even vastly different from much more recent comedies, such as *MASH* and *Maude*. First, today's comedies tend to be highly *quotational*: many of today's comedies essentially depend on the device of referring to or quoting other works of popular culture. Second, they are *hyper-ironic*: the flavor of humor offered by today's comedies is colder, based less on a shared sense of humanity than on a sense of world-weary cleverer-than-thouness. In this essay I would like to explore the way in which *The Simpsons* uses both quotationalism and hyper-ironism and relate these devices to currents in the contemporary history of ideas.

Quotationalism

Television comedy has never completely foregone the pleasure of using pop culture as a straight man. However, early instances of quotation tended to be opportunistic; they did not comprise the substance of the genre. Hence, in sketch comedy, one would find occasional references to popular culture in *Wayne and Shuster* and *Johnny Carson*, but these references were really treated as just one more source of material. The roots of quotationalism as a main source of material can be found in the early seventies with the two visionary comedies, *Mary Hartman Mary Hartman*, which lampooned soap operas by being an ongoing soap opera, and *Fernwood 2Night*, which, as a small-budget talk show, took on small-budget talk shows. Quotationalism then came much more to the attention of the general public between the mid-seventies and early eighties through *Saturday Night Live*, *Late Night with David Letterman*, and *SCTV*. Given the mimical abilities of its cast and its need for weekly material, the chief comedic device of *SNL* was parody — of genres (the nightly news, television debates), of particular television shows (*I Love Lucy*, *Star Trek*) and of movies (*Star Wars*). The type of quotationalism employed by Letterman was more abstract and less based on particular shows. Influenced by the much earlier absurdism of such hosts as Dave Garroway, Letterman immediately took the formulas of television and cinema beyond their logical conclusions (*The Equalizer Guy*, chimp cam, and spokesperson Larry "Bud" Melman).

However, it was *SCTV* that gathered together the various strains of quotationalism and synthesized them into a deeper, more complex, and more mysterious whole. Like *Mary Hartman*, and unlike *SNL*, it was an ongoing series with recurring characters such as Johnny Larue, Lola Heatherton, and Bobby Bittman. However, unlike *Mary Hartman*, the ongoing series was about the workings of a television station. *SCTV* was a television show about the process of television. Through the years, the models upon which characters like Heatherton and Bittman were based vanished somewhat into the background, as Heatherton and Bittman started to breathe on their own, and therefore, came to occupy a shadowy space between real (fictional) characters and simulacra. Furthermore, *SCTV*'s world came to intersect the real world as some of the archetypes portrayed (such as Jerry Lewis) were people in real life. Thus, *SCTV* eventually produced and depended upon patterns of inter-textuality and cross-referencing that were much more thoroughgoing and subtle than those of any program that preceded it.

The Simpsons was born, therefore, just as the use of quotationalism was maturing. However, *The Simpsons* was not the same sort of show as *SNL* and *SCTV*. One major difference, of course, was that *The Simpsons* was animated while the others were (largely) not, but this difference does not greatly affect the relevant potential for quotationalism — although it may be easier to draw the bridge of the U.S.S. *Enterprise* than to rebuild it and re-enlist the entire original cast of *Star Trek*. The main difference is that as an ostensibly ongoing family comedy, *The Simpsons* was both plot and character driven, where the other shows, even those that contained ongoing characters, were largely sketch driven. Furthermore, unlike *Mary Hartman Mary Hartman*, which existed to parody soap operas, *The Simpsons* did not have the raison d'être of parodying the family-based comedies of which it was an instance. The problem then was this: How does one transform an essentially non-quotational format into an essentially quotational show?

The answer to the above question lies in the form of quotationalism employed by *The Simpsons*. By way of contrast, let me outline what it was definitively not. Take, for instance, a *Wayne and Shuster* parody of Wilde's *The Picture of Dorian Gray*. In the parody, instead of Gray's sins being reflected in an artwork, while he remains pure and young in appearance, the effects of Gray's overeating are reflected in the artwork, while he remains thin. The situation's permissions and combinations are squeezed and coaxed to produce the relevant gags and ensuing yuks. End of story. Here the quotationalism is very direct; it is the source both of the story line and of the supposedly humorous contrast between the skit and the original novel. Now, compare this linear and one-dimensional use of quotation for the purposes of parody with the pattern of quotation used in a very short passage from an episode from *The Simpsons* entitled "A Streetcar Named Marge." In the episode, Marge is playing Blanche Dubois opposite Ned Flanders's Stanley in *Streetcar!*, her community theatre's musical version of the Tennessee Williams play. In need of day care for little Maggie, she sends Maggie to the Ayn Rand School for Tots, which is run by the director's sister. Headmistress Sinclair, a strict disciplinarian and believer in infant self-reliance, confiscates all of the tots' pacifiers, which causes an enraged Maggie to lead her classmates in a highly organized reclamation mission, during which the theme from *The Great Escape* plays in the background. Having re-acquired the pacifiers, the group sits, arrayed in rows, making little sucking sounds, so that when Homer arrives to pick up Maggie, he is confronted with a scene from Hitchcock's *The Birds*.

The first thing that one can say about these quotations is that they are very funny. . . . To see that these quotations are funny just watch the show again. Second, we note that these quotations are not used for the purpose of parody.[1] Rather, they are allusions, designed to provide unspoken metaphorical elaboration and commentary about what is going on in the scene. The allusion to Ayn Rand underscores the ideology and personal rigidity of Headmistress Sinclair. The theme music from *The Great Escape* stresses the determination of Maggie and her cohort. The allusion to *The Birds* communicates the threat of the hive-mind posed by many small beings working as one. By going outside of the text via these nearly instantaneous references, *The Simpsons* manages to convey a great deal of extra information extremely economically. Third, the most impressive feature of this pattern of allusion is its pace and density, where this feature has grown more common as the series has matured. Early episodes, for instance the one in which Bart saws the head off the town's statue of Jebediah Springfield, are surprisingly free of quotation. Later episodes derive much of their manic comic energy from their rapid-fire sequence of allusions. This density of allusion is perhaps what sets *The Simpsons* most apart from any show that has preceded it.

However, the extent to which *The Simpsons* depends on other elements of pop culture is not without cost. Just as those readers who are unfamiliar with Frazer's *Golden Bough* will be hindered in their attempt to understand Eliot's "The Waste Land," and just as many modern-day readers will be baffled by many of the Biblical and classical allusions that play important roles in the history of literature, many of today's viewers won't fully understand much of what goes on in *The Simpsons* due to an unfamiliarity with the popular culture that forms the basis for the show's references. Having missed the references, these people may interpret *The Simpsons* as nothing more than a slightly off-base family comedy populated with characters who are neither very bright

---

[1]I don't mean to say that *The Simpsons* does not make use of parody. The episode currently under discussion contains a brilliant parody of Broadway adaptations, from its title to the show-stopping tune "A Stranger Is Just a Friend You Haven't Met!"

nor very interesting. From these propositions they will probably derive the theorem that the show is neither substantial nor funny, and also the lemma that the people who like the show are deficient in taste, intelligence, or standards of personal mental hygiene. However, not only do the detractors of the show miss a great deal of its humor, they also fail to realize that its pattern of quotations is an absolutely essential vehicle for developing character and for setting a tone. And, since these people are usually not huge fans of popular culture to begin with, they will be reluctant to admit that they are missing something significant. Oh well. It is difficult to explain color to a blind man, especially if he won't listen. On the other hand, those who enjoy connecting the quotational dots will enjoy their task all the more for its exclusivity. There is no joke like an in-joke: The fact that many people don't get *The Simpsons* might very well make the show both funnier and better to those who do.

Hyper-Ironism and the Moral Agenda

Without the smart-ass, comedy itself would be impossible. Whether one subscribes, as I do, to the thesis that all comedy is fundamentally cruel, or merely to the relatively spineless position that only the vast majority of comedy is fundamentally cruel, one has to admit that comedy has always relied upon the joys to be derived from making fun of others. However, usually the cruelty has been employed for a positive social purpose. In the sanctimonious *MASH*, Hawkeye and the gang were simply joking to "dull the pain of a world gone mad," and the butts of their jokes, such as Major Frank Burns, symbolized threats to the liberal values that the show perpetually attempted to reinforce in the souls of its late-twentieth-century viewers. In *Leave It to Beaver*, the link between humor and the instillation of family values is didactically obvious. A very few shows, most notably *Seinfeld*, totally eschewed a moral agenda.[2] *Seinfeld*'s ability to maintain a devoted audience in spite of a cast of shallow and petty characters engaged in equally petty and shallow acts is miraculous. So, as I approach *The Simpsons*, I would like to resolve the following questions. Does *The Simpsons* use its humor to promote a moral agenda? Does it use its humor to promote the claim that there is no justifiable moral agenda? Or, does it stay out of the moral agenda game altogether?

These are tricky questions, because data can be found to affirm each 10 of them. To support the claim that *The Simpsons* promotes a moral agenda, one usually need look no further than Lisa and Marge. Just consider Lisa's speeches in favor of integrity, freedom from censorship, or any variety of touchy-feely social causes, and you will come away with the opinion that *The Simpsons* is just another liberal show underneath a somewhat thin but

[2]For a different view, see Robert A. Epperson, "Seinfeld and the Moral Life," in William Irwin, ed., *Seinfeld and Philosophy: A Book about Everything and Nothing* (Chicago: Open Court, 2000), pp. 163–74.

tasty crust of nastiness. One can even expect Bart to show humanity when it counts, as when, at military school, he defies sexist peer pressure to cheer Lisa on in her attempt to complete an obstacle course. The show also seems to engage in self-righteous condemnation of various institutional soft targets. The political system of Springfield is corrupt, its police chief lazy and self-serving, and its Reverend Lovejoy ineffectual at best. Property developers stage a fake religious miracle in order to promote the opening of a mall. Mr. Burns tries to increase business at the power plant by blocking out the sun. Taken together, these examples seem to advocate a moral position of caring at the level of the individual, one which favors the family over any institution.

However, one can find examples from the show that seem to be denied accommodation within any plausible moral stance. In one episode, Frank Grimes (who hates being called "Grimey") is a constantly unappreciated model worker, while Homer is a much beloved careless slacker. Eventually, Grimes breaks down and decides to act just like Homer Simpson. While "acting like Homer" Grimes touches a transformer and is killed instantly. During the funeral oration by Reverend Lovejoy (for "Gri-yuh-mee, as he liked to be called") a snoozing Homer shouts out "Change the channel, Marge!" The rest of the service breaks into spontaneous and appreciative laughter, with Lenny saying "That's our Homer!" End of episode. In another episode, Homer is unintentionally responsible for the death of Maude Flanders, Ned's wife. In the crowd at a football game, Homer is eager to catch a T-shirt being shot from little launchers on the field. Just as one is shot his way, he bends over to pick up a peanut. The T-shirt sails over him and hits the devout Maude, knocking her out of the stands to her death. These episodes are difficult to locate on a moral map; they certainly do not conform to the standard trajectory of virtue rewarded.

Given that we have various data, some of which lead us toward and others away from the claim that *The Simpsons* is committed to caring, liberal family values, what should we conclude? Before attempting to reach a conclusion, I would like to go beyond details from various episodes of the show to introduce another form of possibly relevant evidence. Perhaps, we can better resolve the issue of *The Simpsons*' moral commitments by examining the way it relates to current intellectual trends. The reader should be warned that, although I think that my comments on the current state of the history of ideas are more or less accurate, they are greatly oversimplified. In particular, the positions that I will outline are by no means unanimously accepted.

Let's start with painting. The influential critic Clement Greenberg held that the goal of all painting was to work with flatness as the nature of its medium, and he reconstructed the history of painting so that it was seen to culminate in the dissolution of pictorial three-dimensional space and the acceptance of total flatness by the painters of the mid-twentieth century. Painters were taken to be like scientific researchers whose work furthered the progress of their medium, where the idea of artistic progress was to be taken as literally as that of scientific progress. Because they were fundamentally unjustifiable and because they put painters into a straitjacket, Greenberg's positions gradually lost their hold, and no other well-supported candidates for the essence of painting could be found to take their place. As a result painting (and the other arts) entered a phase that the philosopher of art Arthur Danto has called "the end of art." By this Danto did not mean that art could no longer be produced, but rather that art could no longer be subsumed under a history of progress toward some given end.[3] By the end of the 1970s, many painters had turned to earlier, more representational styles, and their paintings were as much commentaries on movements from the past, like expressionism, and about the current vacuum in the history of art, as they were about their subject matter. Instead of being about the essence of painting, much of painting came to be about the history of painting. Similar events unfolded in the other artistic media as architects, filmmakers, and writers returned to the history of their disciplines.

However, painting was not the only area in which long-held convictions concerning the nature and inevitability of progress were aggressively challenged. Science, the very icon of progressiveness, was under attack from a number of quarters. Kuhn held (depending on which interpreter of him you agree with) either that there was no such thing as scientific progress, or that if there was, there were no rules for determining what progress and scientific rationality were. Feyerabend argued that people who held substantially different theories couldn't even understand what each other was saying, and hence that there was no hope of a rational consensus; instead he extolled the anarchistic virtues of "anything goes." Early sociological workers in the field of science studies tried to show that, instead of being an inspirational narrative of the disinterested pursuit of truth, the history of science was essentially a story of office-politics writ large, because every transition in the history of science could be explained by appeal to the personal interests and allegiances of the participants.[4] And, of course, the idea of philosophical progress has continued to be challenged. Writing on Derrida, the American philosopher Richard Rorty argues that anything like *the* philosophical truth is either unattainable, non-existent, or uninteresting, that philosophy itself is a literary genre, and that philosophers should reconstrue themselves as writers who elaborate and re-interpret the writings of other philosophers. In other words, Rorty's version of Derrida recommends that philosophers view themselves as historically aware participants in a conversation, as opposed to quasi-scientific researchers.[5] Derrida himself favored a method known as deconstruction, which was popular several years ago, and which consisted of a

[3]See Arthur Danto, *After the End of Art* (Princeton: Princeton University Press, 1996).

[4]Thomas Kuhn, *The Structure of Scientific Revolutions*, second edition (Chicago: University of Chicago Press, 1970). Paul Feyerabend, *Against Method* (London: NLB, 1975). For a lively debate on the limits of the sociology of knowledge, see James Robert Brown (ed.), *Scientific Rationality: The Sociological Turn* (Dordrecht: Reidel, 1984).

[5]Richard Rorty, "Philosophy as a Kind of Writing," pp. 90–109 in *Consequences of Pragmatism* (Minneapolis: University of Minnesota Press, 1982).

highly technical method for undercutting texts by revealing hidden contradictions and unconscious ulterior motives. Rorty questions whether, given Derrida's take on the possibility of philosophical progress, deconstruction could be used only for negative purposes, that is, whether it could be used for anything more than making philosophical fun of other writings.

Let me repeat that these claims about the nature of art, science, and philosophy are highly controversial. However, all that I need for my purposes is the relatively uncontroversial claim that views such as these are now in circulation to an unprecedented extent. We are surrounded by a pervasive crisis of authority, be it artistic, scientific or philosophical, religious or moral, in a way that previous generations weren't. Now, as we slowly come back to earth and *The Simpsons*, we should ask this: If the crisis I described were as pervasive as I believe it to be, how might it be reflected generally in popular culture, and specifically in comedy?

We have already discussed one phenomenon that may be viewed as a consequence of the crisis of authority. When faced with the death of the idea of progress in their field, thinkers and artists have often turned to a reconsideration of the history of their discipline. Hence artists turn to art history, architects to the history of design, and so on. The motivation for this turn is natural; once one has given up on the idea that the past is merely the inferior pathway to a better today and a still better tomorrow, one may try to approach the past on its own terms as an equal partner. Additionally, if the topic of progress is off the list of things to talk about, an awareness of history may be one of the few things left to fill the disciplinary conversational void. Hence, one may think that quotationalism is a natural offshoot of the crisis of authority, and that the prevalence of quotationalism in *The Simpsons* results from that crisis.

The idea that quotationalism in *The Simpsons* is the result of "something in the air" is confirmed by the stunning everpresence of historical appropriation throughout popular culture. Cars like the new Volkswagen Beetle and the PT Cruiser quote bygone days, and factories simply can't make enough of them. In architecture, New Urbanist housing developments try to re-create the feel of small towns of decades ago, and they have proven so popular that only the very wealthy can buy homes in them. The musical world is a hodgepodge of quotations of styles, where often the original music being quoted is simply sampled and re-processed.

To be fair, not every instance of historical quotationalism should be seen as the result of some widespread crisis of authority. For instance, the New Urbanist movement in architecture was a direct response to a perceived erosion of community caused by the deadening combination of economically segregated suburbs and faceless shopping malls; the movement used history in order to make the world a better place for people to live with other people. Hence, the degree of quotationalism in *The Simpsons* could point toward a crisis in authority, but it could also stem from a strategy for making the world better, like the New Urbanism, or it could merely be a fashion accessory, like retro-khaki at the Gap.

No, if we want to plumb the depths of *The Simpsons'* connection with the crisis in authority we will have to look to something else, and it is at this point that I return to the original question of this section: Does *The Simpsons* use its humor to promote a moral agenda? My answer is this: *The Simpsons* does not promote anything, because its humor works by putting forward positions only in order to undercut them. Furthermore, this process of undercutting runs so deeply that we cannot regard the show as merely cynical; it manages to undercut its cynicism too. This constant process of undercutting is what I mean by "hyper-ironism."

To see what I mean, consider "Scenes from the Class Struggle in Spring- 20 field," an episode from the show's seventh season. In this episode Marge buys a Coco Chanel suit for $90 at the Outlet Mall. While wearing the suit, she runs into an old high-school classmate. Seeing the designer suit and taking Marge to be one of her kind, the classmate invites Marge to the posh Springfield Glen Country Club. Awed by the gentility at the Club, and in spite of snip-ing from club members that she always wears the same suit, Marge becomes bent on social climbing. Initially alienated, Homer and Lisa fall in love with the club for its golf course and stables. However, just as they are about to be inducted into the club, Marge realizes that her newfound obsession with social standing has taken precedence over her family. Thinking that the club also probably doesn't want them anyway, she and the family walk away. However, unbeknownst to the Simpsons, the club has prepared a lavish welcome party for them, and is terribly put out that they haven't arrived — Mr. Burns even "pickled the figs for the cake" himself.

At first glance, this episode may seem like another case of the show's reaffirmation of family values: after all, Marge chooses family over status. Fur-thermore, what could be more hollow than status among a bunch of shallow inhuman snobs? However, the people in the club turn out to be inclusive and fairly affectionate, from golfer Tom Kite who gives Homer advice on his swing despite the fact that Homer has stolen his golf clubs — and shoes — to Mr. Burns, who thanks Homer for exposing his dishonesty at golf. The jaded cyni-cism that seems to pervade the club is gradually shown to be a mere conver-sational trope; the club is prepared to welcome the working-class Simpsons with open arms — or has it realized yet that they are working class? Further complicating matters are Marge's reasons for walking away. First, there is the false dilemma between caring for her family and being welcomed by the club. Why should one choice exclude the other? Second is her belief that the Simp-sons just don't belong to such a club. This belief seems to be based on a class-ism that the club itself doesn't have. This episode leaves no stable ground upon which the viewer can rest. It feints at the sanctity of family values and swerves closely to class determinism, but it doesn't stay anywhere. Further-more, upon reflection, none of the "solutions" that it momentarily holds is satisfactory. In its own way, this episode is as cruel and cold-blooded as the Grimey episode. However, where the Grimey episode wears its heartlessness upon its sleeve, this episode conjures up illusions of satisfactory heart-warming resolution only to undercut them immediately. In my view, it stands as a paradigm of the real *Simpsons*.

I think that, given a crisis of authority, hyper-ironism is the most suitable form of comedy. Recall that many painters and architects turned to a consideration of the history of painting and architecture once they gave up on the idea of a fundamental trans-historical goal for their media. Recall also that once Rorty's version of Derrida became convinced of the non-existence of transcendent philosophical truth, he reconstructed philosophy as an historically aware conversation which largely consisted of the deconstruction of past works. One way of looking at all of these transitions is that, with the abandonment of *knowledge* came the cult of *knowingness*. That is, even if there is no ultimate truth (or method for arriving at it) I can still show that I understand the intellectual rules by which you operate better than you do. I can show my superiority over you by demonstrating my awareness of what makes you tick. In the end, none of our positions is ultimately superior, but I can at least show myself to be in a superior position for now on the shifting sands of the game we are currently playing. Hyper-irony is the comedic instantiation of the cult of knowingness. Given the crisis of authority, there are no higher purposes to which comedy can be put, such as moral instruction, theological revelation, or showing how the world is. However, comedy can be used to attack anybody at all who thinks that he or she has any sort of handle on the answer to any major question, not to replace the object of the attack with a better way of looking at things, but merely for the pleasure of the attack, or perhaps for the sense of momentary superiority mentioned earlier. *The Simpsons* revels in the attack. It treats nearly everything as a target, every stereotypical character, every foible, and every institution. It plays games of one-upmanship with its audience members by challenging them to identify the avalanche of allusions it throws down to them. And, as "Scenes from the Class Struggle in Springfield" illustrates, it refrains from taking a position of its own.

However, to be fair to those who believe *The Simpsons* takes a stable moral stance, there are episodes that seem not to undercut themselves at all. Consider, for instance, the previously mentioned episode in which Bart helps Lisa at military school. In that episode, many things are ridiculed, but the fundamental goodness of the relationship between Bart and Lisa is left unquestioned. In another episode, when Lisa discovers that Jebediah Springfield, the legendary town founder, was a sham, she refrains from announcing her finding to the town when she notices the social value of the myth of Jebediah Springfield. And, of course, we must mention the episode in which jazzman Bleeding Gums Murphy dies, which truly deserves the Simpsonian epithet "worst episode ever." This episode combines an uncritical sentimentality with a naïve adoration of art-making, and tops everything off with some unintentionally horrible pseudo-jazz which would serve better as the theme music for a cable-access talk show. Lisa's song "Jazzman" simultaneously embodies all three of these faults, and must count as the worst moment of the worst

episode ever. Given these episodes and others like them, which occur too frequently to be dismissed as blips, we are still left with the conflicting data with
which we started. . . . Is *The Simpsons* hyper-ironic or not? One could argue
that the hyper-ironism is a trendy fashion accessory, irony from the Gap,
which does not reflect the ethos of the show. Another critically well-received
program, *Buffy the Vampire Slayer* is as strongly committed to a black and
white distinction between right and wrong as only teenagers can be. Its
dependence on wisecracks and subversive irony is only skin deep. Underneath the surface, one will find angst-ridden teens fighting a solemn battle
against evil demons who want to destroy the world. Perhaps, one could argue,
beneath the surface irony of *The Simpsons* one will find a strong commitment
to family values.

I would like to argue that Simpsonian hyper-ironism is not a mask for an
underlying moral commitment. Here are three reasons, the first two of which
are plausible but probably insufficient. First, *The Simpsons* does not consist
of a single episode, but of over two hundred episodes spread out over more
than ten seasons. There is good reason to think that apparent resolutions in
one episode are usually undercut by others.[6] In other words, we are cued to
respond ironically to one episode, given the cues provided by many other episodes. However, one could argue that this inter-episodic undercutting is itself
undercut by the show's frequent use of happy family endings.

Second, as a self-consciously hip show, *The Simpsons* can be taken to be   25
aware of and to embrace what is current. Family values are hardly trendy, so
there is little reason to believe that *The Simpsons* would adopt them whole-
heartedly. However, this is weak confirmation at best. As a trendy show, *The
Simpsons* could merely flirt with hyper-irony without fully adopting it. After
all, it is hardly hyper-ironic to pledge allegiance to any flag, including the flag
of hyper-ironism. Also, in addition to being a self-consciously hip show, it
is also a show that must live within the constraints of prime-time American
network television. One could argue that these constraints would force *The
Simpsons* toward a commitment to some sort of palatable moral stance.
Therefore, we cannot infer that the show is hyper-ironic from the lone premise that it is self-consciously hip.

The third and strongest reason for a pervasive hyper-ironism and against
the claim that *The Simpsons* takes a stand in favor of family values is based on
the perception that the comedic energy of the show dips significantly whenever moral closure or didacticism rise above the surface (as in the Bleeding
Gums Murphy episodes). Unlike *Buffy the Vampire Slayer*, *The Simpsons* is
fundamentally a comedy. *Buffy* can get away with dropping its ironic stance,
because it is an adventure focused on the timeless battle between good and
evil. *The Simpsons* has nowhere else to go when it stops being funny. Thus, it's
very funny when it celebrates physical cruelty in any given *Itchy and Scratchy
Show*. It's very funny when it ridicules Krusty and the marketing geniuses who

---

[6]Thanks to my colleague and co-contributor, Jason Holt, for first suggesting this to me.

broadcast *Itchy and Scratchy*. It's banal, flat, and not funny when it tries to deal seriously with the issue of censorship arising from *Itchy and Scratchy*. The lifeblood of *The Simpsons*, and its astonishing achievement, is the pace of cruelty and ridicule that it has managed to sustain for over a decade. The prevalence of quotationalism helps to sustain this pace, because the show can look beyond itself for a constant stream of targets. When the target-shooting slows down for a wholesome message or a heart-warming family moment, the program slows to an embarrassing crawl with nary a quiver from the laugh-meter.

I don't mean to argue that the makers of *The Simpsons* intended the show primarily as a theater of cruelty, although I imagine that they did. Rather, I want to argue that, as a comedy, its goal is to be funny, and we should read it in a way that maximizes its capability to be funny. When we interpret it as a wacky but earnest endorsement of family values, we read it in a way that hamstrings its comedic potential. When we read it as a show built upon the twin pillars of misanthropic humor and oh-so-clever intellectual one-upmanship, we maximize its comedic potential by paying attention to the features of the show that make us laugh. We also provide a vital function for the degree of quotationalism in the show, and as a bonus, we tie the show into a dominant trend of thought in the twentieth century.

But, if the heart-warming family moments don't contribute to the show's comedic potential, why are they there at all? One possible explanation is that they are simply mistakes; they were meant to be funny but they aren't. This hypothesis is implausible. Another is that the show is not exclusively a comedy, but rather a family comedy — something wholesome and not very funny that the whole family can pretend to enjoy. This is equally implausible. Alternatively, we can try to look for a function for the heart-warming moments. I think there is such a function. For the sake of argument, suppose that the engine driving *The Simpsons* is fueled by cruelty and one-upmanship. Its viewers, although appreciative of its humor, might not want to come back week after week to such a bleak message, especially if the message is centered on a family with children. *Seinfeld* never really offered any hope; its heart was as cold as ice. However, *Seinfeld* was about disaffected adults. A similarly bleak show containing children would resemble the parody of a sitcom in Oliver Stone's *Natural Born Killers*, in which Rodney Dangerfield plays an alcoholic child-abuser. Over the years, such a series would lose a grip on its viewers, to say the least. I think that the thirty seconds or so of apparent redemption in each episode of *The Simpsons* is there mainly to allow us to soldier on for twenty-one and a half minutes of maniacal cruelty at the beginning of the next episode. In other words, the heart-warming family moments help *The Simpsons* to live on as a series. The comedy does not exist for the sake of a message; the occasional illusion of a positive message exists to enable us to tolerate more comedy. Philosophers and critics have often talked of the paradox of horror and the paradox of tragedy. Why do we eagerly seek out art forms that arouse unpleasant emotions in us like pity, sadness, and fear? I think that, for at least certain forms of comedy, there is an equally important paradox of comedy. Why do we seek out art that makes us laugh at the plight of unfortunate people in a world without redemption? The laughter here seems to come at a high price. *The Simpsons'* use of heart-warming family endings should be seen as its attempt to paper over the paradox of comedy that it exemplifies so well.

I hope to have shown that quotationalism and hyper-ironism are prevalent, inter-dependent, and jointly responsible for the way in which the humor in *The Simpsons* works. The picture I have painted of *The Simpsons* is a bleak one, because I have characterized its humor as negative, a humor of cruelty and condescension — but really funny cruelty and condescension. I have left out a very important part of the picture, however. *The Simpsons*, consisting of a not-as-bright version of the Freudian id for a father, a sociopathic son, a prissy daughter, and a fairly dull but innocuous mother, is a family whose members love each other. And, we love them. Despite the fact that the show strips away any semblance of value, despite the fact that week after week it offers us little comfort, it still manages to convey the raw power of the irrational (or nonrational) love of human beings for other human beings, and it makes us play along by loving these flickering bits of paint on celluloid who live in a flickering hollow world. Now *that's* comedy entertainment.

READING THE TEXT

1. Write an outline of Matheson's essay, being sure to note how Matheson establishes differences and similarities in relation to other pop culture phenomena. Compare your outline with those produced by the rest of the class.

2. Explain in your own words what Matheson means by "quotationalism" and "hyper-ironism" (para. 2). How do those words relate to the current term "sampling"?

3. What does Matheson mean by "historical appropriation" (para. 17)?

4. Matheson outlines recent intellectual trends in the study of art, science, and philosophy. What are those trends, and what relationship does Matheson find between them and a TV program such as *The Simpsons*?

5. What connection does Matheson see between the "crisis of authority" (para. 15) and hyper-irony?

READING THE SIGNS

1. Write an argumentative essay that supports, challenges, or complicates Matheson's position that "heart-warming family moments" appear in *The Simpsons* "mainly to allow us to soldier on for twenty-one and a half minutes of maniacal cruelty" (para. 28).

2. In class, brainstorm other TV shows and films that are hyper-ironic, and use the list as the basis for your own essay in which you argue whether their popularity is a barometer of the current cultural mood in America or whether it is an aberration.

3. Watch an episode of *The Simpsons*, and analyze the extent to which it supports Matheson's belief that, rather than promoting a moral stance, the show "does not promote anything" (para. 19).

4. Visit a Web site devoted to *The Simpsons*, such as www.thesimpsons.com, and study the comments fans make about the program. To what extent do your observations support Matheson's belief that "those who enjoy connecting the quotational dots will enjoy their task all the more for its exclusivity" (para. 8)?

5. Compare and contrast the humor in *The Simpsons* with that of another TV show such as *Family Guy*. Do the shows appeal to different audiences, and if so, why?

NATASHA SIMONS

Mad Men *and the Paradox of the Past*

Mad Men, a dramatic re-creation of early 1960s America, when the country was poised upon the brink of a cultural revolution but had not quite tipped over yet, is a deeply ambiguous television series. Does it represent an exposé of the bad old days of rampant sexual harassment in the workplace and casual racism, when everyone smoked too much and men called all the shots? Or does the show's appeal lie in nostalgia for a bygone era on the other side of a vast cultural divide? As Natasha Simons observes in this article that originally appeared in the *National Review*, it depends upon who is viewing it. Thus, as Simons notes, "Conservatives and liberals just can't help but see *Mad Men* differently: the former with apprehension, the latter with anticipation." Even the show's creator, Matthew Weiner, seems divided, Simons claims. Basically a liberal, Weiner likes his main character, Don Draper, too much to make it clear just which side he's on. Such is the stuff of which pop culture paradoxes are made. Natasha Simons is an assistant editor at Simon and Schuster.

Mad Men is a show about an unbending generation on the cusp of dissolution; Matthew Weiner, the show's head writer, has often said that the majority of America in the early '60s was still, by and large, living in the domestic '50s. Weiner, a baby boomer, has a conflicted relationship with this time period. Because it is the generation of his parents, he wants to explore it and pore over it; because it's the generation that, through Weiner's specific political prism, reflects a hypocritical façade, he'd like it to form a gangway for the liberation to come. This ambivalence creates a divide in the audience's responses to the show, which tend to fall along political lines.

Conservatives and liberals just can't help but see *Mad Men* differently: the former with apprehension, the latter with anticipation. The show inspires a certain self-satisfaction in the type of viewers who would observe each instance of sexism, racism, and general prejudice as just more foundation for an interpretation many critics have arrived at: "The show explains why the '60s had to happen." Rod Dreher says, "For unreflective liberals, *Mad Men* is only temporarily tragic. It has a happy ending. Deliverance from all this sexism and repression and cigarette smoke draws nigh."

The show, and in particular, the third season, is shot through with references to that impending deliverance. Don Draper says, "New York City is decaying." Paul Kinsey says, "This city has no memory." The World's Fair in New York, given passing lip service on the show, turned out to be a bust, the old-money business class's last hurrah at corralling an innocent kind of fun already beset by the counterculture. Its slogan? "Man in a Shrinking Globe in an Expanding Universe." That's not only a pointed assessment of modern fear, but a wonderful précis of the theme of *Mad Men*. And it's difficult to ignore the ambitious allusions to the prototypical decayed society of ancient Rome, which made a few cameos in the past season. Don's daughter, Sally, reads to her grandfather the beginning of a passage from *The History of the Decline and Fall of the Roman Empire*: "The Praetorian bands, whose licentious fury was the first symptom and cause of the decline of the Roman empire . . ."

The Praetorian guards, of course, were a specially chosen group of soldiers who abused their imperial power over Rome. *Mad Men* depicts a group of men who have great influence over what they consider their particular citizenry — consumers — and their particular emperor — consumerism. By cataloging this group's "licentious" excesses (imbibing during the workday, hiring prostitutes on the company dime, etc.), general indifference to the burgeoning youth counterculture (think: Bertram Cooper's horror at Kennedy's lack of hat), and miring themselves in the past (Roger Sterling's unfortunate minstrel show in "My Old Kentucky Home"), Weiner, consciously or unconsciously, is demonstrating the ways in which America's Old Guard is leading the '50s generation to its end by stubbornly refusing to go forward. Weiner has remarked of that generation of people, "[They were saying,] 'We don't want to be that way. We'd rather fail.'"

Clearly, Don Draper is the starring figure of this collapse. He is the Man in 5 the Grey Flannel Suit, an Ayn Rand–ian allegory of a stoic firmly in the past. He is the prototype '50s representative male, confident in his role without, and in turmoil within. Don is a member of a dying breed who wants to play by the old business rules, and he can barely conceive of the ways in which advertising is inexorably moving (unlike, say, fellow ad man Pete Campbell). He is a relic waiting to be phased out.

But Weiner's flaw is that he loves Don Draper too much to make him that relic, as intended — he is clearly not going to leave Don in the past, if season-four promotional posters are any indication. So the show attempts to imbue him with the sympathy of the audience, despite his stodgy '50s limits —which leads to all sorts of annoying contradictions. Don looks down on Roger for the blackface, yet behaves dismissively toward his own black servant; Don assaults his mistress in a bathroom and demands women not speak to him "like that," despite facilitating his former secretary Peggy's surge upward through the ranks; Don lectures his wife about being a good parent even as he picks up strangers in his car and recklessly partakes of some unidentified drugs. These frustrating contradictions can't simply be chalked up to mere nuance of human character, either; it seems clear that Weiner started out by using Don as an emblem of the '50s, defining him in opposition to the '60s to come.

Which brings us again to the main political schism for viewers of this show: Conservatives and liberals cannot see the inevitability of the '60s the same way. The hedonism, the "licentious fury" set up in these soldiers of such terrible, soul-destroying consumerism, is about to give way to the tortured emoting of Frank O'Hara and reggae-inspired coffee commercials, both of which have been featured in the past few seasons. But conservatives understand that the hedonism is only just beginning. The Me Generation is about to swing into full effect, after which we lose both the unrepentant ambition and

A promotional still from *Mad Men*.

Photofest

charming earnestness of the American Dream — a phrase never to be uttered without a small smirk again.

True, the keeping-up-with-the-Joneses mentality was unsustainable, simply because of the practical problem of the single income that families were expected to fulfill the traditional iteration of the American Dream on. And, often, the unwavering values of the '50s resulted in an outwardly homogenous appearance that left many marginalized parties gasping for air. But the '60s, with their relentless concentration on the self and self-expression, shaped individualistic tendencies in consumers that brought them out of the follow-the-leader consumption of the '50s into a gluttonous consumption merely for selfish purposes. So which is better? And is that really the redemption the show hopes to establish, and what liberal viewers gaze backward and clutch the edges of their seats in anticipation of?

Weiner's chosen narrative posits that our present is much better than the '50s zeitgeist he portrays, but the essential paradox is that he portrays it with so much love and tenderness that it is sometimes impossible to pull out the theme of generational decay. The audience is caught between a mislaid nostalgia for the often sexist and bigoted environment and an equally mislaid moral desire to see it all disappear. As Benjamin Schwarz pointed out in the *Atlantic*, the show invites us to "indulge in a most unlovely — because wholly unearned — smugness."

Mad Men has lost its way a bit; Weiner, wrapped up in adoring his main 10 character and the intricacies of a period he wants to evaporate, has fallen into a quicksand trap, not wanting to move on, despite his obvious political loyalties to the '60s generation. Critics remarked that the pace of *Mad Men* has recently slowed to a ponderous crawl, perhaps to allow Weiner time to languish a while. But he is definitely plunging forward now, having commented in an interview that "It's got to be something different. . . . Life is change." Here's hoping that the fourth season marks that change with the same ambivalence we've seen prior, which would prove Weiner is interested in portraying history with a fair hand. Falling into a rote '60s nostalgia would be wholly unwelcome for a show that has come to be known for its nuance.

READING THE TEXT

1. What significance for *Mad Men* does Simons see in scriptwriter Matthew Weiner's status as a baby boomer?

2. Summarize in your own words the ways in which conservatives and liberals interpret *Mad Men*, according to Simons.

3. What does Simons mean when she says that *Mad Men* character Don Draper "is the Man in the Grey Flannel Suit" (para. 5)?

4. In class, discuss whether Simons is presenting an objective analysis of *Mad Men*, as you would want to do in an academic essay, or whether she betrays a bias favoring or opposing the program. Use this discussion of objectivity as a guide when you write your own essay on the program.

READING THE SIGNS

1. Simons claims that conservatives and liberals interpret *Mad Men* in diametrically opposed ways. Interview at least ten viewers of the program, preferably half who identify as conservative and half who identify as liberal, asking them about their reading of and reaction to it. Use your results to assess the validity of Simons's claim.

2. Write an essay in which you support, refute, or modify Simons's claim that *Mad Men*'s "audience is caught between a mislaid nostalgia for the often sexist and bigoted environment and an equally mislaid moral desire to see it all disappear" (para. 9).

3. Read Sloan Wilson's novel *The Man in the Gray Flannel Suit* (1955). To what extent does *Mad Men* reflect the discontented business culture depicted in that novel, as Simons asserts? Alternatively, read Vance Packard's *The Hidden Persuaders* (1957). Do you find that book to reflect the advertising industry's practices as they are depicted in *Mad Men*?

4. Write a semiotic analysis of a current episode of *Mad Men* that features a diverse cast, focusing on the depiction of nonwhite characters. To what extent do you find those depictions to be realistic or stereotypical? To develop your analysis, consult Michael Omi's "In Living Color: Race and American Culture" (p. 538).

5. Many critics of *Mad Men* focus on the show's depiction of female characters. Drawing on Aaron Devor's "Gender Role Behaviors and Attitudes" (p. 504), write an essay in which you analyze the prevailing mythology of gender roles as the program presents them.

JANE HU

Reality Hunger: On Lena Dunham's Girls

In its own way, *Girls* is a lot like *Friends*, but without the fun, for both programs feature white middle-class young adults coming of age in an era of reduced economic expectations. Still, in Jane Hu's review of *Girls* for the *Los Angeles Review of Books*, it is hard to sort out just how much the series speaks for an entire generation of millennials and how much it speaks for its creator, Lena Dunham, and her more particular milieu. Leaving the matter open for further analysis, Hu points out that for all the talk about sex on *Girls*, there's also an awful lot on food and eating, making for a very different, and ambiguous, kind of hunger games. Jane Hu is a freelance writer who writes for *Slate* and other online publications.

Most reviews of Lena Dunham's new HBO show *Girls* so far have focused on its "realism," which immediately begs questions. If Dunham's show is meant to be realistic, then we're obliged to judge whether it's either refreshingly on target or entirely missing the mark. Do we, the viewers, feel represented and reflected by the conversations and scenarios that *Girls* presents? Or do we feel alienated from them? Do we identify? Or do we feel something in between?

In the promotional trailer for the series, Dunham's character Hannah Horvath sits before her parents and proclaims: "I think I may be the voice of my generation," only to retreat instantly behind the modification: "or at least *a* voice . . . of *a* generation." This line, tagged as the catchphrase of *Girls* in the lead up to its pilot, was received almost as a dare. Someone, finally, was going to take on the challenge of speaking the real and raw truth for recession-era youth! For all its overwhelming narcissism, though, the line also anticipates the mix of recklessness and reluctance that the show cultivates. *Girls* wants to have it both ways: it wants to be both brash and unsure of itself, universal and specific, speaking (when it wants to) for a generation but reserving the right not to specify which one.

Based on the internet chatter, there seems to be a voracious desire to find oneself in *Girls*, implying an urgency to locate a voice for this generation, a generation that understands itself to be diverse. As *The Hairpin*'s Jenna Wortham says about these *Girls*: "They are us but they are not us. They are me but they are not me." The show's representations of race, class, and gender have generated an expansive range of reactions, not least because of the show's monolithic middle-class whiteness. It seems like the one thing anyone can agree on is that, unlike Hannah Horvath, *they* don't eat cupcakes in the bathtub.

But if we're looking for what's truly universal in Dunham's depiction of young, white, upper-middle-class life in New York City, then maybe the cupcake isn't such a bad place to start. Eating is, after all, about as universal as it gets. The overwhelming excitement about and immediate backlash to Dunham's show both seem to suggest a profound hunger on the part of its audience for something nourishing, sustaining, and nutritious, prepared especially for them. This is fitting, because hunger, in all its manifestations, drives *Girls*. As with all lost generations, there seems to be a profound sense of lack among Hannah's friends. Hannah showcases her appetite for attention, sex, and food, none of which prove exclusive to one another.

The first shot of the pilot shows Hannah in an upscale restaurant seated 5 in front of multiple plates of food, inhaling alternating mouthfuls from each plate. Her mother tells her to slow down: "You're eating like they're going to take it away from you." To which Hannah responds (childishly, mid-bite): "I'm a growing girl." For her, eating and talking are inseparable from the process of growing up. Hannah is, in turn, interrupted mid-bite, for her parents have chosen dinner as the opportunity to announce that they will no longer be supporting her unpaid internship in New York, or as her mother describes it, "bankrolling your groovy lifestyle." Shocked and outraged in all of her unself-aware entitlement, Hannah announces to her parents that she cannot see them tomorrow evening since she has a "dinner thing" and then will be "too busy becoming who I am." This scene of furious public ingestion looks forward to a future of relaxed, private digestion: Hannah needs to eat, and then she needs to figure her shit out. Throughout the *Girls* pilot, there is a sense that the world as we know it will slip away if we do not get to — and through — it fast enough. What these *Girls* are running toward, and who they are busy becoming, they have yet to discover. But resources are scarce, and no one is getting younger.

Consuming and facing the reality that there might not be enough left to consume are seemingly incompatible in Hannah's world. When she's let go from her internship after her request for a paying position is denied, Hannah's boss (played by Chris Eigeman, familiar as a privileged slacker from Whit Stillman and Noah Baumbach movies) assures her: "When you get hungry enough, you'll figure it out." To which she responds: "Do you mean like physically hungry or like hungry for the job?" The line is played for comic effect, but it also expresses Hannah's confusion about exactly what she might get hungry for. An appetite, and an appetitive drive, is what Hannah and her fellow *Girls* need in order to "become who they are." If you lack hunger, then you just might be lost. But, then again, you might still be anyway.

No matter: talking and eating will keep us distracted from the object of our hunger. Later on, Hannah tells her roommates in a typically melodramatic moment: "I can last in New York for three and a half more days — maybe seven if I don't eat lunch." The running joke behind these statements is that Hannah's livelihood is not actually at stake (even her roommates roll their eyes during this moment of self-pity) since, when push comes to shove, Hannah's parents could just take back what they said about buying a lake-house and bail her out instead. Yet Hannah's fixation on ingestion is no less real or urgent. Food, as both a metaphoric notion and a real, onscreen substance, is essential to *Girls*. The tentative title of Hannah's memoir-in-progress is, after all, *Midnight Snack*. A title is supposed to be suggestive and representative of a body of work, but really all Hannah's (unfinished) *Midnight Snack* indicates is that she still has not learned how or when to eat like an adult. As for talking, she has only just begun.

The paradox in writing about — or filming — scenes of eating is that any meal is, narratively speaking, a snack, in that it's not an end in itself but a brief interruption of some more crucial ongoing action. Exceptions, such as Louis Malle's *My Dinner with Andre* and Francis Veber's *Le dîner de cons*, only emphasize the latent narrative potential surrounding cultures of eating. Jim Jarmusch's *Coffee and Cigarettes* — a film that strings together vignettes of café scenes — finds the narratability in visualizing a break or snack. Snacks are by definition inessential, unstructured, and irregular: you never know when the next one might come. The snack does not offer satisfaction or closure; in fact, it demands a more responsible future that might justify the present indulgence.

Food is meant to help us fuel up so we can get on with life, but food in *Girls* becomes the very excuse to avoid the mundane reality of growing up.

Scenes of eating, which abound in the pilot, are pauses in the real work that constitutes a bread-earning life. Rather than showcase the necessary regularity of eating, however, *Girls* uses food scenes as a way of driving plot and exploring character development. A meal is an opportunity for Hannah's parents to tell her "No. More. Money." (and, by extension, no more food). When the waiter asks if they would like more of anything, Hannah's mother drives the message home and speaks on her behalf: "No, she's fine." Food is also the gateway to Hannah's method of coping with her new economic status. After twenty-four hours of being financially cut off, Hannah comes home (notably late for her "dinner thing") and drinks a cup of cooked opium leaves upon mishearing that it "tastes like Twix." (It, surprisingly, does not.) Where a proper, scheduled restaurant dinner facilitates Hannah's "final push" into adulthood, she responds by consuming a drug (masked in the form of a drink, or a chocolate bar, or even better, a midnight snack). Characters' motivations and affective responses are, here and elsewhere, displaced onto food.

In terms of development — narrative, character, and otherwise — food is a 10 means to an end. It will bring the girls of *Girls* together, but it also differentiates them. Hannah eats her bathtub cupcake while complaining about her situation (and her body) to roommate Marnie. At the dinner party for their returning friend Jessa, a last-minute invitee occupies a seat at the table that was never meant for her, though this finally matters little as her presence feels inconsequential since she will not eat: "I didn't mean to be rude. I'm just not really into eating this week." Unsurprisingly, further development of this character stops at this sentence.

As pauses, eating is both what keeps us from attaining our ideals, as well as the literal driving force for life, and thus living the good life, itself. For all that is clichéd and flat about the show's glancing portrayal of Joy Lin, the Asian intern who got hired because of her Photoshopping skills, the show establishes common ground between Joy and the rest of the girls through her privileged relationship to food. Her one line in the pilot — "Will you get me a Luna bar, and a SmartWater, and Vitamin Water?" — indexes her socioeconomic status more precisely than it does her racial one. A health bar and two types of bottled water? If Joy can care about what she consumes, it's because, as a skilled and paid employee, she can afford to. As a point of fixation, food becomes an excuse and distraction to keep Hannah from facing up to her imminent shift in financial conditions. Again, the joke is that there is always enough food around to provide a distraction from worries about not having enough food.

The intermingling of appetites for food and for sex in fiction, film, and even television long predates *Girls*. A few examples: François Rabelais's *Gargantua and Pantagruel*, Thomas Mann's *The Magic Mountain*, Marco Ferreri's *La grande bouffe*, *I Love Lucy*, and, like, all of Evelyn Waugh. What makes narrative so directly contingent on physical drives? ("You're tired of eating him out," Hannah tells Marnie about her submissive boyfriend, "because he has a vagina.")

If our culture has mostly neglected food in its discussion of *Girls* thus far, it's got sex pretty well covered. Coinciding with the broadcast of the pilot,

Katie Roiphe wrote an article on submissive sexual appetites for *Newsweek* and, following the premiere, another on the performance of sadomasochistic sex in *Girls* for *Slate*. While many have responded to Roiphe's ideas on female fantasies of sexual domination with appropriate rage, more have received it as mostly dull and uncritical. In comparison to Roiphe's earlier pieces, which seem controversial and infuriating because they struck something about her generation's ideas of modern womanhood, her latest take on heteronormative desire seems to be getting tired. In Troy Patterson's take on *Girls* (also for *Slate*), he both quotes and comments on Roiphe's loss of steam:

> "The movement against date rape is a symptom of a more general anxiety about sex. . . . The crisis is not a rape crisis, but a crisis in sexual identity." I think that Roiphe had a strong point back then. It is unclear to me what she is saying, now, in lamenting the awkward sex of *Girls*. She is lamenting human nature? She is disappointed that non-marital sex still had yet to achieve zipless perfection?

Roiphe's retrograde reading of female desire does not take into account the possibilities of displacement and suppression that could lead to conclusions other than, simply, that women wish to be dominated. *Girls* might really represent a generational shift that diverges from, or at least complicates, Roiphe's concepts of female submission and, more importantly, sexual identity in general that get us talking again. Who is eating whom out anymore in *Girls*?

What is seen as realism in *Girls* is exactly what we would not expect to be able to see in our everyday interactions with others: uncomfortable scenes involving food and sex. Sex is explicitly bad and unsatisfying in *Girls*, but in an unfazed way. Dunham's camera takes us into the bathtub and the bedroom as though she were just narrating another chapter in our shared diary. In the sex scenes between Hannah and her "boyfriend" Adam, *Girls* plays on the expectations of erotic submission but fails to go all the way. Through mimicking, rather badly, the narratives of submissive sex, the show exposes the potential for disengagement and humor in sadomasochism through its overperformance. Indeed, sex for Hannah seems to feed her appetite to analyze her environment. (At one point, mid-thrust, Adam tells Hannah: "Let's play the quiet game.") In turn for the bad pornographic script that Adam feeds her, Hannah responds with her own. She wants to focus on the talk that occurs not just around — but also during — the act of sleeping with another person. When Adam offers Hannah a Gatorade after a particularly unappetizing round of sex for the latter, Hannah pauses then responds: "No thanks I'm good." An exercise in pleasure for Adam means he'll need a snack to replenish; but Hannah not only does not need a drink, her rejection of nutrients also signals an implicit rejection of the sex to which it would be a response. For Hannah, talking is a way of coming to terms with, and owning, her appetites.

These scenes, lurid in their will to show what is unsexy about sex, are 15 outside our ordinary purview, except, as *Girls* seems to suggest, when girls are with their closest female friends. Even when Hannah is having sex with

Adam, there is still a sense that her best friend, Marnie, is there with them as a judgmental third. Sitting back in her apartment, Marnie tells her own boyfriend: "I know exactly where she is. She's off having gross sex with that animal." For all that writers have spoken about *Girls'* appetite for sex — bad or good — these scenes often seem like just another appetite that drives the show's deeper dynamic of female friendship. Men are often only the catalyst through which women connect. Marnie's boyfriend Charlie is, literally, the outsider, who keeps trying to insert himself where he does not belong. He interrupts Marnie conversing with another girl in the bathroom not once, but twice; first sharing the bathtub with Hannah, and again just after Jessa, on the toilet, confesses to being pregnant (he is shooed out with a disgruntled wave of Marnie's hand). "Dude, it's never 'just your girlfriend' in here," Hannah tells Charlie, and really, it seems like he would know this by now. Unlike the men that interrupt Hannah and her girlfriends, however, Dunham's camera is allowed to stay inside with her female protagonists, inviting viewers to become a part of the talk that happens behind closed bathroom doors.

The camera's ability to insert viewers in intensely, even uncomfortably, intimate scenes of female bonding is at the heart of Dunham's art. Unloading your shit is a process that takes place in more than one form, with more than one body, in the bathrooms of *Girls*. Dunham's visualization of these moments of too-closeness is, however, how she prompts moments of visceral identification from her audience. In his article, Patterson compares Dunham's interaction with the camera as

> kind of like an *SNL* player doing body art [. . .] Has any of the commentary around Dunham's use of her nude or naked body in her work bothered to compare her to Tracey Emin, Pipilotti Rist, Vanessa Beecroft, Marina Abramović, or for that matter Matthew Barney?

The cast of *Girls*.

As a type of performance art, Dunham's manipulation of her body engages viewers because she treats her body wholly irreverently. Like Hannah, Dunham has a desire to "take control of her shape," and she does this through bold portrayals of her naked body, in bizarre contortions, on screen. As the person who gets to script, direct, block, and portray her own body, all the arguments about Dunham's resolve to degrade herself fall apart on screen. Viewers might not have a hard time deciding what they think about Hannah's use of her body, but they will have a harder time locating Hannah's, or Dunham's, own take on sex since these acts are never fixed in the sexual identity of one body. Like body art, Dunham's directing of Hannah's body, alongside the psychological characterization she attributes to it, undoes any clear notion of what it is that body is doing and why.

Patterson's placement of Dunham among the pantheon of feminist body artists might, however, be slightly off key, as Dunham, ultimately, communicates her body via a television character. The immediacy of body art is precipitated by the real, physical fact of viewers' confrontation with the live body of the performer before them. What makes *Girls* a piece of art (and entertainment) of its time is precisely its ability to maintain a distance and anonymity from its viewers by virtue of the televisual medium.

The second episode of *Girls* concludes with Dunham lying flat on a gynecologist's table, while she makes a characteristically insensitive, and provocative, remark about her body. Though a large part of *Girls* runs on forcing the audience to contend with Dunham's body, Hannah, in this moment of vulnerability, wants nothing more than to escape her corporeality: "Maybe I'm actually not scared of AIDS. Maybe I thought I was scared of AIDS, but really what I am is . . . wanting AIDS." This is not Ron Athey or Tim Miller, however, whose performance art demanded one's response to the very real, very immediate consequences of AIDS. Like Dunham's treatment of food and sex, AIDS now stands as just another vehicle for her fantasy of escaping the current moment. Dunham goes on to tell her gynecologist that her fear of AIDS is like a *"Forrest Gump"* — that is, a cinematic — type of fear, one that only occurs when you are detached from the real, distanced from the object that prompts this fear. The scene is stunning in its portrayal of Hannah's narcissism, but it also shows Dunham's complete unawareness that her privilege lies in her ability to dramatize disease, starvation, and sexual degradation as forms of liberation.

Though its first season might be scripted, shot and ready to air, *Girls* — like its characters — is still feeling out a precarious situation, trying to find a space of identification for viewers that is neither too insular and restrained nor so expansive and universal that it stops signifying anything meaningful at all. So far the show seems stuck somewhere between its characters' sense of the emergency of the present moment and the magical ability to postpone emergency, seemingly indefinitely, because they have the economic and cultural resources to do so. Talk about *Girls*, too, is coming at us hard and fast in a [20] way that forestalls, rather than forecloses, our developing sense of what it's about. If *Girls* truly resembles performance art, as Patterson suggests, it is in its ability to precipitate lively talk about itself almost instantaneously. Our responses are vital and urgent, but provisional, and we should remember that Dunham's show is still becoming what it is. Writing about *Girls* instantaneously on the internet, however, we might be chewing on a lot — and for a long time — before we get a chance to look down and really examine what it is that we've been digesting. Maybe we're afraid they'll take it away from us.

READING THE TEXT

1. How, according to Hu, does food function as a narrative and thematic leit-motif in *Girls*?

2. What does Hu mean by saying that "*Girls* wants to have it both ways: it wants to be both brash and unsure of itself, universal and specific, speaking (when it wants to) for a generation but reserving the right not to specify which one" (para. 2)?

3. Hu claims that in *Girls* "talking and eating will keep us distracted from the object of our hunger" (para. 7). What, in your own words, does Hu mean by "hunger"?

4. In her final paragraph, Hu says "Our responses [to *Girls*] are vital and urgent, but provisional" (para. 20). How might that comment reflect her own analysis of this TV show?

READING THE SIGNS

1. Both *Girls* and the earlier TV program *Friends* focus on the lives of young people who face economic difficulties living in an urban environment. In an essay, conduct a semiotic analysis of these two shows; you might focus on gender relations, economic forces, or both. What do these shows say about the times in which they appeared? How are they similar and different, and what do any differences signify?

2. Hu quotes *Girls*' protagonist, Hannah, who claims to be "at least *a* voice . . . of *a* generation" (para. 2) in the show's pilot episode. That generation is millennials. For an essay, first interview four or five acquaintances about their view on whether *Girls* indeed reflects the lifestyles and problems of millennials. Use your interviews as the foundation of an essay that argues for, disputes, or modifies the proposition that the show indeed accurately reflects the millennial experience.

3. Research the two articles by Katie Roiphe about *Girls* that Hu mentions. Write an essay in which you support, oppose, or modify Hu's assertion that Roiphe proposes a "retrograde reading of female desire [that] does not take into account the possibilities of displacement and suppression that could lead to conclusions other than, simply, that women wish to be dominated" (para. 13).

4. Hu mentions that commentary about *Girls* often focuses on the show's "realism" and adds, "What is seen as realism in *Girls* is exactly what we would not

expect to be able to see in our everyday interactions with others: uncomfortable scenes involving food and sex" (para. 14). After watching a few episodes of *Girls*, write an argumentative essay in which you take a position on the extent to which the program can be labeled "realistic." Be sure to define how you use the word "realism" in your essay.

5. After quoting commentator Troy Patterson's discussion of *Girls'* cinematography, Hu dubs the program an example of "performance art" (para. 17). Write an essay in which you assess the validity of this claim, being sure to research performance art if you are unfamiliar with the genre.

6. **CONNECTING TEXTS**   Hu claims that *Girls* has been criticized for its "monolithic middle-class whiteness" (para. 3). Adopting the perspective of Michael Parenti (see "Class and Virtue," p. 361), analyze the racial and class dynamics that you see in *Girls*.

WILLA PASKIN

Devious Maids *Skewers the One Percent*

Even when American television sets out to be subversive, it usually ends up celebrating the status quo. Take Lifetime's *Devious Maids*, a semi-soap in the tradition of *Desperate Housewives*, which manages to suggest, in Willa Paskin's words, that "[e]ven if the rich are bitches, . . . we should still aspire to be them." Indeed, the Latina maids who star in the series never seem to leave Beverly Hills, and their plans are to get just as wealthy as the unpleasant women who employ them. It all looks like *workers of the world, move up*, which is hardly the stuff of revolution. Willa Paskin is a staff writer specializing in television for *Salon*, where this selection first appeared.

I was recently having a conversation about working class people and television, and how it has become nearly impossible to find the former on the latter. Sitcoms used to have a blue-collar tradition, from *All in the Family* to *Roseanne*, but in recent years that's been all but abandoned. People on television are usually rich, nearly so, or becoming so. They are typically untroubled by financial practicalities or only marginally bothered by them. Into this desert of class diversity comes Lifetime's cheeky new melodrama *Devious Maids*, premiering Sunday, which features five working class Latina women but still just flickers in and out of class consciousness.

Devious Maids comes from Marc Cherry, the creator of *Desperate Housewives* and a man who clearly believes in sticking to certain naming conventions. Tonally, the shows are very similar: comedic super-soaps about a group of women with a central murder mystery, crazy plot turns, and a knowing, winking tone. The stars of *Devious Maids* are not housewives but Latina domestic servants, all working for crazy rich people in Beverly Hills. In the first minutes of the pilot, a maid, Flora, is murdered by a person unknown. When her employer, a camp character on the order of Cruella De Vil, breaks down, it's not because of the death, but the mess: "My maid was murdered! Who is going to clean all this up?" she screeches.

Soon thereafter, Marisol (*Ugly Betty*'s Ana Ortiz) appears on the scene, eager to find out more about Flora's murder and ingratiate herself with the other women who work nearby. These include the bratty Carmen (*Without a Trace*'s Roselyn Sanchez), an ultra-ambitious singer who has gained employment in a superstar's house, hoping she'll be able to get him to hear her music; Rosie (Dania Ramirez), a kind, widowed nanny working to bring her small son to America from Mexico while she cares for the son of a soap actor (*Melrose Place*'s Grant Show) and his bitchy, selfish wife; and Zoila (*Scrubs*' Judy Reyes) and her daughter Valentina (Edy Ganem), who work in the home of a histrionic woman (soap legend Susan Lucci) and her rich son, who Valentina loves even though her mother insists it will never work out.

Devious Maids has already been accused of perpetuating stereotypes for having all five Latina characters be domestic servants (though I suspect that Marisol, who in a flashback appears to have a maid of her own, is secretly rich), and been defended from these charges by executive producer Eva Longoria. But there's a second-order stereotyping going on of the well-meaning and yet still totally ghettoizing variety, as June Thomas points out in her review for *Slate*. The show is a parade of "Latina maids who are both devious and pure of heart, and of their Caucasian employers, who are all selfish, utterly detestable, entitled snobs." In other words, while the nasty white people get all the ridiculous, over-the-top lines and complicated, knotty emotions, the "good" Hispanic characters are largely straitjacketed into having no fun, imprisoned by their ethical superiority.

Having watched *Desperate Housewives*, I suspect that the goody-two-shoes nature of the Latina characters will be short-lived: Marc Cherry churns through too much plot to leave anyone pristine. Carmen, already, is a straight manipulator on the make not at all interested in being a maid — "you guys know how to be poor," she tells her friend, "I do not." — and willing to use a nice guy to get her way. But for now, the bias toward boring is definitely at work. Cherry should look at *Scandal*, a show in which everyone of every color gets to be troubled and naughty and still expect our sympathy, to see how to improve.

Until then, there is something really fascinating about at least one half of *Devious Maids*' stereotyping: the part that turns it into the "indulge your vitriol for white ladies with too much money" hour. In one scene, Rosie's boss won't let Rosie go see a lawyer about her son's immigration because the boss has a facial appointment she refuses to cancel. Another woman doesn't want to hire Marisol because she has no accent and sounds like "she went to college" and thus appears to have "attitude." Wherever we are, culturally speaking, it appears to be a place where a TV show aspiring to be frothy, escapist and fun can get its dramatic climaxes and moments of triumph from a bunch of rich bitches — whose husbands are, by and large, much, much nicer than them — getting theirs. Gleefully skewering the one percent of obnoxious white ladies — and obnoxious, in the pilot anyway, is the only way they come — must have market-tested just fine.

This is not to suggest that *Devious Maids* has something larger to say about the inequity of American society. This is a TV show about class that does not for one minute want to leave the safe haven of real estate porn. Even if the rich are bitches, the show implies, we should still aspire to be them. *Devious Maids* may star people who have to work for a living, but since three of the five women are live-in maids, we never have to leave Beverly Hills. None of the domestics seem concerned about money. Rosie's efforts to bring her son to America get back-burnered by the second episode. And Carmen and Valentina are pursuing affluence as hard as they can. *Devious Maids* finds a way to have all its stars sitting in lounge chairs by a pool — it may not make sense, but at least it looks like *Sex and the City*. The message of *Devious Maids* is not quite that the rich are no better than anyone else, but that anyone else — in this case, five maids — would make for better rich people than the already rich, which also happens to be one of the guiding fantasies of American life. I think this show, however flawed, just might be a big hit.

READING THE TEXT

1. Summarize in your own words the stereotypes that Paskin sees in the characters featured in *Devious Maids*.

2. In your own words, explain how *Devious Maids* actually endorses the values it seems to satirize, according to Paskin.

3. What parallels does Paskin draw between *Devious Maids* and *Desperate Housewives*?

4. What does Paskin mean by saying that *Devious Maids* engages in both typical stereotypes of Latinas and a "second-order stereotyping" (para. 4)?

READING THE SIGNS

1. **CONNECTING TEXTS** Watch an episode or two of *Devious Maids*, and then write your own analysis of its depiction of class differences. To what extent does your viewing support, undercut, or modify Paskin's claim that the show's message is "not quite that the rich are no better than anyone else, but that anyone else — in this case, five maids — would make for better rich people than the already rich, which also happens to be one of the guiding fantasies of American life" (para. 7). To develop your ideas, consult Michael Parenti's "Class and Virtue" (p. 361).

2. View an episode of *Ugly Betty*, and then write an analytic essay that considers whether that program and *Devious Maids* perpetuate class and racial stereotypes.

3. **CONNECTING TEXTS**   Using Michael Omi's "In Living Color: Race and American Culture" (p. 538) as a critical framework, analyze the racial dimensions that you view in *Devious Maids*. To what extent does the show exemplify his categories of racial stereotyping, such as overt and inferential racism? Given that the show's debut occurred nearly twenty-five years after Omi first published his essay, do you think that the show has moved beyond the stereotypes Omi describes?

4. In class, discuss the merits of Paskin's claim that "gleefully skewering the one percent of obnoxious white ladies . . . must have market-tested just fine" (para. 6). In other words, to what extent do you think that the popularity of a show such as *Devious Maids* might relate to an increasing class division in America? Use your discussion as a jumping-off point for your own essay that addresses Paskin's claim.

5. In the first paragraph, Paskin refers to earlier TV programs that featured working-class characters. Watch an episode of *All in the Family*, *Roseanne*, or *Laverne and Shirley*, and write an essay that compares the depiction of these characters with the maids as Paskin describes them. What ethnic and class differences do you see? How do you explain any such observations?

NEAL GABLER
The Social Networks

Remember *Friends*, that sprightly comedy in which no one ever seemed to be alone? Or *Sex and the City*, wherein busy Manhattan professional women always seemed to have time to share a glass of water and some lettuce? Indeed, even today, wherever you look on television, Neal Gabler notes in this essay that originally appeared in the *Los Angeles Times*, you are certain to see "lots of folks spending the better part of their day surrounded by their friends and family in happy conviviality." Yet oddly enough, this sort of programming is appearing "at a time when it is increasingly difficult to find this kind of deep social interaction anyplace but on TV." Clearly, Gabler suggests, television is providing some sort of compensation for the social atomization that it itself has contributed to, and thus, all the simulated conviviality, while being a pleasant "dream," is "pure wish fulfillment," indeed, rather "phony," and, perhaps, sad. The author of *An Empire of Their Own: How the Jews Invented Hollywood* (1989), *Winchell: Gossip,*

Power and the Culture of Celebrity (1994), *Life the Movie: How Enter-tainment Conquered Reality* (1998), and *Walt Disney: The Triumph of the American Imagination* (2006), Neal Gabler is a well-known analyst and historian of American cinema and popular culture.

With the new television season upon us, here are a few things you are virtu-ally certain to see again and again and again: lots of folks spending the better part of their day surrounded by their friends and family in happy conviviality; folks wandering into the unlocked apartments and homes of friends, family, and neighbors at any time of the day or night as if this were the most natural thing in the world; friends and family sitting down and having lots of tearful heart-to-hearts; Little League games, school assemblies, and dance recitals, all attended by, you guessed it, scads of friends and family.

You're going to be seeing these scenes repeatedly because the basic unit of television is not the lone individual or the partnership or even the nuclear family. The basic unit of television is the flock — be it the extended family of brothers and sisters, grandfathers and grandmothers, nieces, nephews, and cousins, or the extended circle of friends, and, rest assured, it is always a circle. On television friends never come in pairs; they invariably congregate in groups of three or more.

That television has become quite possibly the primary purveyor in Ameri-can life of friendship and of the extended family is no recent blip. Over the last twenty years, beginning with *Seinfeld* and moving on through *Friends*, *Sex and the City*, and more recently to *Desperate Housewives*, *Glee*, *The Big Bang Theory*, *How I Met Your Mother*, *Cougartown*, and at least a half-dozen other shows, including this season's newbies *Raising Hope* and *Better with You*, tele-vision has become a kind of friendship machine dispensing groups of people in constant and intimate contact with one another, sitting around in living rooms, restaurants, and coffee shops, sharing everything all the time. You might even say that friendship has become the basic theme of television, cer-tainly of broadcast television, though cable has its own friendship orgies like *Men of a Certain Age*, *My Boys*, and *It's Always Sunny in Philadelphia*. Friend-ship is what television is about.

What makes this so remarkable is that it has been happening at a time when it is increasingly difficult to find this kind of deep social interaction anyplace but on TV. Nearly a decade ago, Harvard professor Robert Putnam observed in his classic *Bowling Alone* that Americans had become more and more disconnected from one another and from their society. As Putnam put it, "For the first two-thirds of the twentieth century a powerful tide bore Ameri-cans into ever deeper engagement in the life of their communities, but a few decades ago — silently, without warning — that tide reversed and we were over-taken by a treacherous current." It was a current that pulled Americans apart.

Moreover, the current that Putnam observed has, according to more recent studies, only intensified in the last decade. One study found that 5

Americans had one-third fewer nonfamily confidants than they had twenty years earlier, and 25 percent had no one in whom to confide whatsoever. Another study of 3,000 Americans found that on average they had only four close social contacts, but these included family members like one's own spouse. This decline in real friendships may account in part for the dramatic rise of virtual friendships like those on social-networking sites where being "friended" is less a sign of personal engagement than a quantitative measure of how many people your life has brushed and how many names you can collect, but this is friendship lite. Facebook, in fact, only underscores how much traditional friendship — friendship in which you meet, talk, and share — has become an anachronism and how much being "friended" is an ironic term.

Among the reasons Putnam cited for the increasing atomization in American life were economic pressures and anxieties; women entering the workplace in full-time employment by necessity and thus disengaging from their friends and neighbors; metropolitan sprawl, which meant more time spent commuting, greater social segregation, and the disruption of community boundaries; and last but by no means least, the rise of television itself, especially its splintering influence on later generations who have grown up addicted to the tube. It is no secret that watching television is not exactly a communal activity. Rather, we often use it to fill a communal void. But instead of bringing comfort, it seems only to remind us of our alienation. In Putnam's view, based on several studies, "TV is apparently especially attractive for people who feel unhappy, particularly when there is nothing else to do."

It's not that we prefer television to human contact. The laugh track attests that most people don't really want to be alone in front of their TV sets. They want to be part of a larger community. Yet another study indicates that TV provides a sort of simulacrum of community because the relationship between the TV viewer and the people he or she watches on the screen competes with and even substitutes for physical encounters with real people. It is Facebook with hundreds of "friends" but without any actual contact with any of them, only the virtual contact of watching.

But what none of these theories of television has noticed is that TV has learned how to compensate for the increasing alienation it seems to induce. And it compensates not by letting us kill time with "friends" on-screen but by providing us with those nonstop fantasies of friendship, which clearly give us a vicarious pleasure. Watch *Seinfeld* or *Friends* or *Sex and the City* or *Community* or *Men of a Certain Age* — the list is endless — and you'll see people who not only are never ever alone but people whose relationships are basically smooth, painless, uninhibited and deeply, deeply intimate — the kind of friendships we may have had in college but that most of us can only dream about now. How many adults do you know who manage to hang out with their friends every single day for hour after hour?

Or watch the incomparable *Modern Family* or *Brothers and Sisters* or *Parenthood* and you'll see big, happy family gatherings with lots of bonhomie and jokes and an outpouring of love. On the last there seems to be a huge extended family dinner every other night where most families would be lucky to have one such get-together each year at Thanksgiving. And don't forget those school assemblies, already mentioned, which everyone in the family takes off work to attend en masse or the weekend birthday parties where attendance is also compulsory.

One feels a little churlish pointing out how phony most of this intimacy is. 10 After all, these shows, even one as observant as *Modern Family*, aren't about realism. They aren't about the genuine emotional underpinnings of friendship or family, and they certainly aren't about the rough course that almost every relationship, be it with a friend or family member, takes — the inevitable squabbles, the sometimes long and even permanent ruptures, the obtuseness, the selfishness, the reprioritization, the expectations of reciprocity, the drifting apart, the agonizing sense of loneliness even within the flock. These shows are pure wish fulfillment. They offer us friends and family at one's beck and call but without any of the hassles. It is friendship as we want it to be.

For the fact is that we miss the friendships we no longer have, and we know that Facebook or e-mails cannot possibly compensate for the loss. So we sit in front of our television sets and enjoy the dream of friendship instead: a dream where we need never be alone, where there are a group of people who would do anything for us, and where everyone seems to understand us to our very core, just like Jerry and George, Chandler and Joey, Carrie and her girls, or the members of the McKinley High glee club. It is a powerful dream, and it is one that may now be the primary pleasure of television.

READING THE TEXT

1. Summarize in your own words what Gabler means by saying, "The basic unit of television is the flock" (para. 2).

2. How does Robert Putnam's research on friendship in America inform Gabler's argument?

3. Why does Gabler say that "being 'friended' is an ironic term" (para. 5)?

4. How does Gabler use concession to strengthen his argument?

5. In your own words, explain what Gabler means by "simulacrum of community" (para. 7)?

READING THE SIGNS

1. Write an argumentative essay in which you assess the validity of Gabler's claim that "instead of bringing comfort, [television] seems only to remind us of our alienation" (para. 6). To support your argument, you might interview friends or acquaintances about their reasons for watching television.

2. In an essay, analyze an episode of one of the friend-heavy TV programs that Gabler mentions, such as *Desperate Housewives*, *Glee*, or *Modern Family*. To

what extent does it confirm Gabler's assertion that "these shows are pure wish fulfillment" (para. 10)?

3. Write an essay in which you support, oppose, or complicate Gabler's belief that Facebook offers "friendship lite" (para. 5). To develop your ideas, read "Students Addicted to Social Media" (p. 403).

4. **CONNECTING TEXTS** Adopting Gabler's perspective, analyze the friendships and interpersonal relations depicted in Lena Dunham's *Girls*. To what extent do they replicate or deviate from the ones represented in the shows "The Social Networks" discusses? How do you think Gabler would explain any differences you see among these TV shows? To develop your ideas, read Jane Hu's "Reality Hunger: On Lena Dunham's *Girls*" (p. 304).

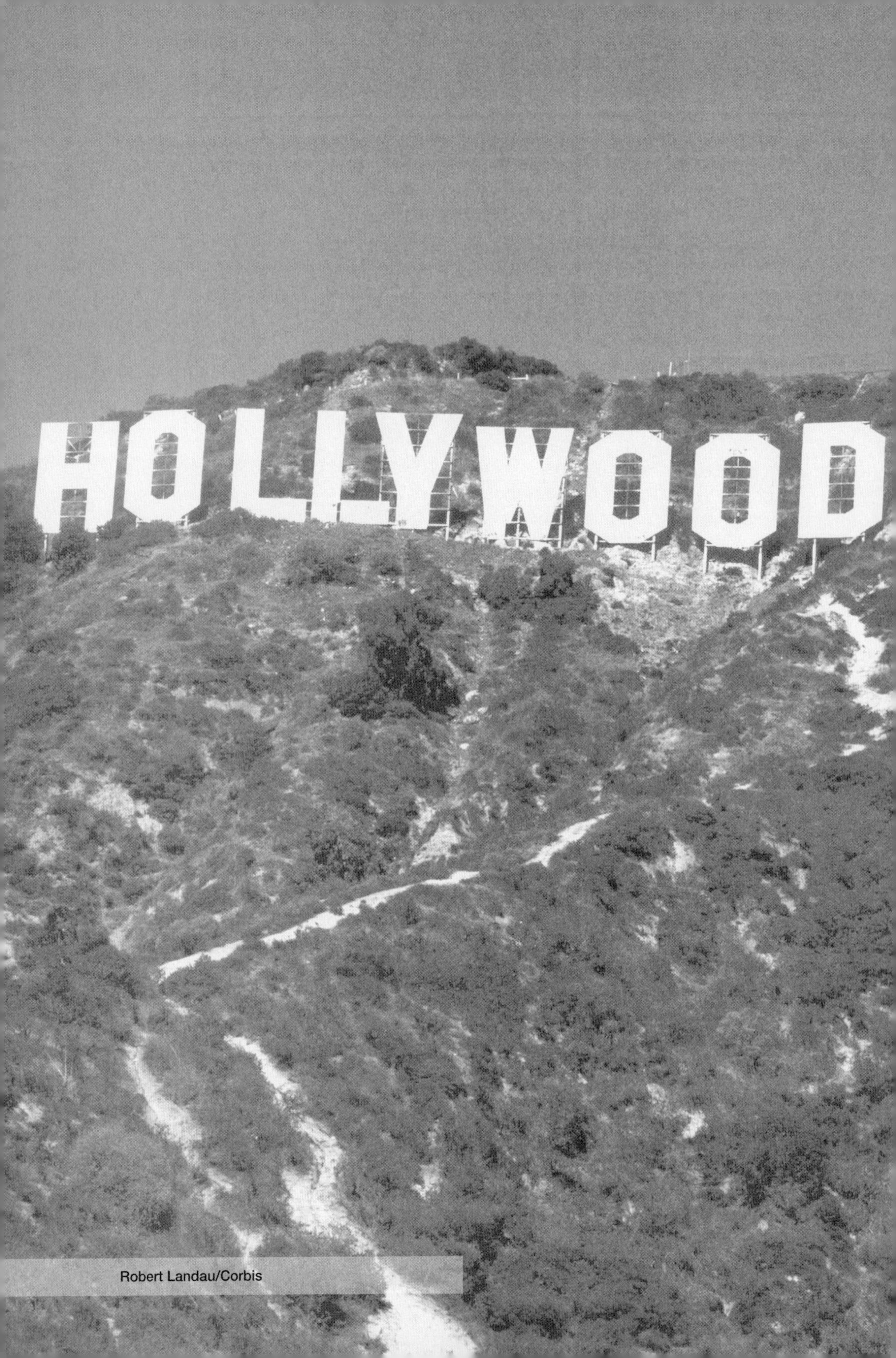

Robert Landau/Corbis

THE HOLLYWOOD SIGN
The Culture of American Film

One Enchanted Evening

By the first half of 2013, *Iron Man 3*, *Man of Steel*, *Oz*, *Star Trek: Into Darkness*, *The Croods*, *Monsters University*, and *World War Z* were, respectively, America's first, second, third, fifth, sixth, seventh, and tenth top-grossing movies. In 2012, the top ten included *The Avengers* (1), *The Dark Knight Rises* (2), *The Hobbit* (5), *Breaking Dawn–Part 2* (6), and *The Amazing Spider-Man* (7). Similarly, in 2011, 2010, 2009, 2008, and so on back to the year 2000, most of the top-grossing movies were, in some way, fantasy or science fiction films, featuring superheroes, vampires, wizards, and whatnot. By contrast, in 1975, the only top-ten movie with a fantasy theme was *Monty Python and the Holy Grail*, which, as a send-up of sword-and-sorcery storytelling, hardly counts. In the previous five years, not a single top-five film could be counted as a fantasy film, unless you include Disney's *The Aristocats* (number 5 in 1970). In the 1960s, the fantasy genre was virtually nonexistent in the box office bonanza sweepstakes (our source for this information is leesmovieinfo.net /WBOYearly).

The turning point seemed to occur in 1977, when George Lucas combined the spirit of J. R. R. Tolkien's *Lord of the Rings* trilogy with the short-lived *Star Trek* television series to create *Star Wars: Episode IV–A New Hope* — a movie that took advantage of new developments in film technology to help transform the old, rather cheesy, B-movie tradition of science fiction into A-list entertainment. From then on, we find an ever-increasing share of Hollywood movie production devoted to fantasy, and, as is so often the case in **semiotic** analysis, such a shift, or **difference**, points to cultural significance.

Here is the key to a semiotic analysis: finding a pattern or detail that stands out and practically begs to be analyzed. The question now is simply: Why have American audiences turned so decisively to fantasy in recent decades? What does this shift tell us?

A full analysis of such a question would take us beyond the scope of this Introduction, but a few **abductive** explanations might be offered. First, in the rise of what traditionally was regarded as a children's genre, we can find a reflection of the evolution of America's youth culture, a culture that places great value upon childhood and adolescence as a period of innocence apart from adult experience (the late J. D. Salinger played a major role in this evolution). Essentially a form of escapism, fantasy plays upon a sense of childhood wonder and enchantment, and in the popularity of fantasy among adult audiences we can accordingly find the desire of adults to escape from the realities of their ordinary lives into an enchanted realm wherein the imagination, rather than reality, reigns.

This desire for enchantment can thus also be seen as a **sign** of a certain cultural disenchantment that has emerged in an era of economic contraction, political dysfunction, social divisiveness, and global terrorism. In such times, it should not be surprising that Americans are seeking not only distractions from the grim realities of their lives but also simple solutions to complex problems that resist real-life resolution. And that is the ultimate fantasy. (See Christine Folch's article on p. 378 for a divergent reading.)

Donald Sutherland as President Snow in *The Hunger Games: Catching Fire*.

Photofest

The Culture Industry

Filmmakers have been providing Americans with entertainments that have both reflected and shaped their desires for over a century. Long before the advent of TV, movies offered viewers the glamour, romance, and sheer excitement that modern life seems to deny. So effective have movies been in molding audience desire that such early culture critics as Theodor Adorno and Max Horkheimer[1] accused them of being part of a vast, Hollywood-centered "culture industry" whose products successfully distracted their audiences from the inequities of modern life and thus effectively maintained the social status quo under capitalism by drawing everyone's attention away from it.

More recent analysts, however, are far less pessimistic. Indeed, for many cultural studies "populists," films, along with the rest of popular culture, can represent a kind of mass resistance to the political dominance — or what is often called the *hegemony* — of the social and economic powers-that-be. For such critics, films can provide utopian visions of a better world, stimulating their viewers to imagine how their society might be improved, and so, perhaps, inspiring them to go out and do something about it.

Whether you believe that films distract us from the real world or inspire us to imagine a better one, their central place in contemporary American culture demands interpretation, for their impact goes well beyond the movie theater or Netflix rental. Far from being mere entertainments, movies constitute a profound part of our everyday lives, with every film festival and award becoming major news, and each major release becoming the talk of the country. Just think of the pressure you might feel to discuss the latest film sensation among your friends. Consider how, if you decide to save a few bucks, not watch the latest hit, and wait for the DVD release or watch it online, you can lose face and be seriously on the social outs. No, nothing is frivolous about the movies. You've been watching them all your life: Now's the time to start thinking about them semiotically.

Interpreting the Signs of American Film

Interpreting a movie or a group of movies is not unlike interpreting a television program or group of programs. Again, you should suspend your personal feelings and aesthetic judgments about your subject. As with any semiotic analysis, your goal is to interpret the cultural significance of your topic, not to give it a thumbs-up or a thumbs-down. Thus, you may find it more rewarding to interpret films that promise to be culturally meaningful than to simply examine your favorite flick. Determining whether a movie is culturally

---

[1]**Theodor Adorno** (1903–1969) and **Max Horkheimer** (1895–1973) authored *Dialectic of Enlightenment* (1947), a book whose analyses included a scathing indictment of the culture industry. — EDS.

Discussing the Signs of Film

In any given year, one film may dominate the Hollywood box office, becoming a blockbuster that captures that public's cinematic imagination. In class, discuss which film would be your choice as this year's top hit. Then analyze the film semiotically. Why has *this* film so successfully appealed to so many moviegoers?

---

meaningful in the prewriting stage, of course, may be a hit-or-miss affair; you may find that your first choice does not present any particularly interesting grounds for interpretation. That's why it can be helpful to consider reasons a particular movie is special, such as enormous popularity or widespread critical attention. Of course, cult favorites, while often lacking in critical or popular attention, can also be signs pointing toward their self-selected audiences and thus are strong candidates for analysis. Academy Award nominees are also reliable as cultural signs.

Your interpretation of a movie or group of movies should begin with a construction of the *system* in which it belongs — that is, those movies, past and present, with which it can be *associated*. While tracing those associations, be on the lookout for striking *differences* from films that are otherwise like what you are analyzing, because those differences are what often reveal the significance of your subject.

Archetypes are useful features for film analysis as well. An archetype is anything that has been repeated in storytelling from ancient times to the present. There are character archetypes, such as the wise old man, which include such figures as Yoda and Gandalf, and plot archetypes, such as the heroic quest, which is the archetypal backbone of films like *The Lord of the Rings* trilogy. All those male buddy films — from *Butch Cassidy and the Sundance Kid* to *Lethal Weapon* to *Men in Black* — hark back to archetypal male bonding stories as old as *The Epic of Gilgamesh* (from the third millennium B.C.E.) and the *Iliad*, while Cruella de Vil from *101 Dalmatians* is sister to the Wicked Witch of the West, Snow White's evil stepmother, and every other witch or crone dreamed up by the patriarchal imagination. All those sea monsters, from Jonah's "whale" to Moby Dick to the great white shark in *Jaws*, are part of the same archetypal phylum, and every time a movie hero struggles to return home after a long journey — Dorothy to Kansas, Lassie to Timmy — a story as old as Exodus and the *Odyssey* is retold.

Hollywood is well aware of the enduring appeal of archetypes (see Linda Seger's selection in this chapter for a how-to description of archetypal scriptwriting), and director George Lucas's reliance on the work of anthropologist Joseph Campbell in his creation of the *Star Wars* saga is widely known. But it is not always the case that either creators or consumers are consciously aware of the archetypes before them. Part of a culture's collective unconscious, archetypal stories can send messages that their audiences only subliminally understand. A heavy dosage of male-bonding films in a given Hollywood season, for instance, can send the unspoken cultural message that a man can't really make friends with a woman and that women are simply the sexual reward for manly men. Similarly, too many witches in a given Hollywood season can send the antifeminist message that there are too many bitches. Conversely, the modification of an archetype, as in the *female*-bonding film *Thelma and Louise*, can signify a feminist emergence.

Repetition with a Difference

Just as movies frequently repeat ancient archetypal character and plot types, they also may refer to other movies and modern cultural artifacts in what is referred to as a **postmodern** manner. Postmodernism is, in effect, both a historical period and an attitude. As a historical period, postmodernism refers to the culture that emerged in the wake of the advent of mass media, one obsessed with electronic imagery and the products of mass culture. As an attitude, postmodernism rejects the values of the past, not to support new values but instead to ironize value systems as such. Thus, in the postmodern worldview, our traditional hierarchical distinctions valuing high culture over low culture, say, or creativity over imitation, tend to get flattened out. What was once viewed in terms of an oppositional hierarchy (origination is opposed to emulation and is superior to it) is reconceived and deconstructed. Postmodern artists, accordingly, tend to reproduce, with an ironic or parodic twist, already-existing cultural images in their work, especially if they can be drawn from mass culture and mass society. Roy Lichtenstein's cartoon canvases, for instance, parody popular cartoon books, and Andy Warhol's tomato soup paintings repeat the familiar labels of the Campbell Soup Company — thus mixing high culture and mass culture in a new, nonoppositional, relation.

To put this another way, the postmodern worldview holds that it is no longer possible or desirable to create new images; rather, one surveys the vast range of available images that mass culture has to offer, and repeats them, but with a difference. Postmodern filmmakers accordingly allude to existing films in their work, as in the final scene of Tim Burton's *Batman*, which directly alludes to Alfred Hitchcock's *Vertigo*, or Oliver Stone and Quentin Tarantino's *Natural Born Killers*, which recalls *Bonnie and Clyde*. Such allusions to, and repetitions of, existing cultural images in postmodern cinema are called *double-coding*, because of the way that the postmodern artifact simultaneously refers to existing cultural **codes** and recasts them in new contexts. The conclusion of *Batman*, for example, while echoing *Vertigo*'s climactic scene, differs dramatically in its significance, turning from Hitchcock's tragedy to Burton's quasi-farce.

Exploring the Signs of Film

In your journal, list your favorite movies. Then consider your list: What does it say about you? What **cultural mythologies** do the movies tend to reflect, and why do you think those myths appeal to you? What signs particularly appeal to your emotions? What sort of stories about human life do you most respond to?

Movies as Metaphors

Sometimes movies can also be seen as metaphors for larger cultural concerns. Consider the grade-B horror flicks of the 1950s, such as the original *Godzilla*. If we were to study only its plot, we would see little more than a cheesy horror story featuring a reptilian monster that is an archetypal kin of the dragons in medieval literature. But Godzilla was no mere dragon transported to the modern world. The dragons that populated the world of medieval storytelling were themselves often metaphors for the satanic serpent in the Garden of Eden, but Godzilla was a wholly different sort of metaphor. Created by Japanese filmmakers, Godzilla was originally a metaphor for the nuclear era. A female mutant creation of nuclear poisoning, Godzilla rose over her Japanese audiences like a mushroom cloud, symbolizing the potential for future mushroom clouds both in Japan and around the world in the Cold War era.

For their part, 1950s American filmmakers had their own metaphors for the nuclear era. Whenever some "blob" threatened to consume New York or

Reading Film Online

Most major films now released in the United States have their own Web sites. You can find them listed online under the film's title or in print ads for the film. Select a current film, find the Web address, log on, and analyze the film's site semiotically. What images are used to attract your interest in the film? What interactive strategies, if any, are used to increase your commitment to the film? If you've seen the movie, how does the site's presentation of it compare with your experience of viewing it either in a theater or on video? Alternatively, analyze the posters designed to attract attention to a particular film; a useful resource is the Movie Poster Page (www.musicman.com/mp/mp.html).

some especially toxic slime escaped from a laboratory, the suggestion that science — especially nuclear science — was threatening to destroy the world filled the theater along with the popcorn fumes. And if it wasn't science that was the threat, Cold War filmmakers could scare us with Communists, as films like *Invasion of the Body Snatchers* metaphorically suggested through its depiction of a town in which everyone looked the same but had really been taken over by aliens. "Beware of your neighbors," the movie seemed to warn. "They could be Communists."

In such ways, an entire film can be a kind of metaphor, but you can find many smaller metaphors at work in the details of a movie as well. Early filmmakers, for example, used to put a tablecloth on the table in dining scenes to signify that the characters at the table were good, decent people (you can find such a metaphor in Charlie Chaplin's *The Kid*, where an impoverished tramp who can't afford socks or a bathrobe still has a nice tablecloth on the breakfast table). Sometimes a director's metaphors have a broad political significance, as at the end of the Rock Hudson/James Dean/Elizabeth Taylor classic *Giant*, where the parting shot presents a tableau of a white baby goat standing next to a black baby goat, which is juxtaposed with the image of a white baby standing in a crib side by side with a brown baby. Since the human babies are both the grandchildren of the film's protagonist (one of whose sons has married a Mexican woman, the other an Anglo), the goats are added to underscore metaphorically (if rather heavy-handedly) the message of racial reconciliation that the director wanted to send.

Reading a film, then, is much like reading a novel. Both are texts filled with intentional and unintentional signs, metaphors, and archetypes, and both are cultural signifiers. The major difference is in their medium of expression. Literary texts are cast entirely in written words; films combine verbal language, visual imagery, and sound effects. Thus, we perceive literary and cinematic texts differently, for the written sign is perceived in a linear fashion that relies on one's cognitive and imaginative powers, while a film primarily targets the senses: One sees and hears (and sometimes even smells!). That film is such a sensory experience often conceals its textuality. One is tempted to sit back and go with the flow, to say that it's only entertainment and doesn't have to "mean" anything at all. But even the most cartoonish cinematic entertainment can harbor a rather profound cultural significance. To see how, let's look at that recurring subject for Hollywood moviemaking concerning a banker who dresses up in a bat costume — yes, a bat suit — in order to fight crime.

Batman: The Dark Knight

There are a lot of *Batman* movies to choose from, of course, including the Tim Burton version we have already referred to. And as we write these words, a new version is in the works that will bring a new actor to the role (Ben Affleck), while the latest version to have hit the theaters so far is still *The*

Dark Knight Rises (2012). We are choosing to present an analysis of a Batman movie from 2008 because that film addresses an especially powerful social dilemma for Americans, a dilemma that will still affect us all into the foreseeable future, making that movie as culturally cogent in the years to come as it was when it first appeared.

We can begin with a movie poster. One of the posters used to advertise *Batman: The Dark Knight* featured the familiar figure of Batman, in full regalia, standing in front of a high-rise office tower whose upper floors are on fire. This image would be immediately recognizable to audiences as alluding to the September 11, 2001, attacks on the World Trade Center and is a key signifier of what was different about this entry into the long history of Batman movies and television shows. As always, this difference is crucial to understanding the cultural significance of the film.

Heath Ledger's Joker provides an especially good figure with which to start. In the early days of the Batman saga, when Batman was still simply a children's comic book hero, the Joker was one of a group of villains who were little more than cartoon clowns. Like Burgess Meredith's Penguin in the 1960s *Batman* television series, the Joker was not really very frightening and mostly out for a fast buck. Ledger's Joker belongs to this system and thus can be associated with all the other Jokers and villains within it. But we can see a striking difference. This Joker is no clown; he is an out-of-control homicidal maniac, and although he robs banks, he most certainly is not motivated by a desire for money. Something else is going on.

Ledger's Joker, of course, was not pulled out of a hat. Before Ledger there was Jack Nicholson, and before Nicholson there was *Arkham Asylum*. That graphic novel introduced a far more disturbing Joker into the system, a psychopath rather than a mere criminal. Jack Nicholson's Joker in Tim Burton's *Batman* surely displayed some of the maniacal energy of the *Arkham* Joker, and he was far more violent and sadistic than any Joker in the past. Still, Nicholson's Joker was motivated by desires that his audience could understand: He wanted money, he wanted power, and he wanted revenge. We see him ruthlessly taking over the organized crime syndicate in Gotham City because he wants to be at its head. His war with Batman is fueled by an earlier duel with the Caped Crusader that left him disfigured for life. We may not be on his side, but we can understand him.

And we can also laugh with him. His epic attack on an art gallery is just plain funny, and his ability to run rings around everyone in Gotham City, especially the news media, makes Nicholson's Joker something like a stand-up comedian — a murderous comedian, but a comedian all the same.

Heath Ledger's Joker is no comedian. He is never funny. Much more importantly, he does not seem to have any motives for his actions. He doesn't want power, as is evident from the fact that while he makes war on the mob, he does not attempt to build his own organization. Rather, he continually murders his own subordinates, along with the mob leaders whose organization he is taking over. And he doesn't want money, which is dramatically symbolized

by his setting fire to a huge pile of cash atop which sits the mob's accountant. He doesn't really seem to want revenge (even his indications that he was cruelly raised — thereby suggesting a possible revenge motive emerging from his childhood — are undercut by later speeches that make it clear that he will say just about anything, no matter how untrue). And he doesn't want sex (Nicholson's Joker had a girlfriend, though she was horribly abused; Ledger's Joker is completely unattached). Basically, all he wants to do is create mayhem and make people suffer as much as possible.

So it is quite a journey from the comic book criminal-clowns of the past to Ledger's Joker. The semiotic question is: What does this journey mean?

The key change here is one of ever-increasing violence. When we look at popular culture more generally, we can find innumerable instances of ever-more-violent entertainment with which the Batman saga can be associated. Consider the difference between the horror films of the 1950s and today's splatter films, or even between Hitchcock's *Psycho* and Van Sant's. And then there's Dexter, who manages to out-Hannibal Hannibal Lecter. The difference lies not only in the enhanced ability to simulate violence in modern moviemaking due to advances in film technology but also in the fact that today's audiences don't want much to be left to the imagination. The more graphically gruesome, the better. What is more, audiences today are attracted to representations of emotional along with physical torture — as seen in such movies as *Hostel*, parts 1 and 2, and the *Saw* franchise, as well as in the way that Ledger's Joker emotionally tortures his victims, such as the civilians on a ferryboat who are forced to choose between the destruction of their boat or that of one carrying a group of criminals being evacuated from a prison.

Does this mean that people are more violent today than in the past or more evil? No, not really. Violence has always been a staple of low cultural entertainment (indeed, for the ancient Romans, violent entertainment was literally violent and not merely a simulation). But Americans have traditionally chosen to restrict the level of violence that they allow in their entertainments. The Hays Code of the 1930s, for example, represented a self-imposed censorship by the film industry, restricting not only the sexual content of movies but their violent content as well. But with the passing of the years those restrictions have been considerably loosened. Why?

As always, the answer is **overdetermined**. Part of it lies in an increasing sophistication in American audiences, who will no longer accept as realistic a highly toned-down representation of violence. In 1950s TV Westerns, for example, when a man was shot at close range by a .45 caliber bullet, audiences were satisfied with a small spot of blood where the bullet entered. Now they want to see what a .45 caliber bullet really does at close range.

But there is another explanation as well. Remember, history shows that the appeal of violent entertainment is universal, which implies that at any time there will be an audience for it. Until relatively recently, American values held that such a desire should not be satisfied, that extremely violent entertainment should not be allowed in a civilized society. So what changed?

Photofest

Jack Nicholson (left) and Heath Ledger (right) had vastly different takes on *Batman* arch-villain the Joker.

Here we might consider a primary contradiction in American culture: the contradiction between America's "spiritual" and "materialistic" values. One side sees that it is better for the spirit to repress our violent proclivities. But the other side sees that a lot of money can be made precisely by catering to those ancient desires. The fact that we can find the materialistic calculation overriding the spiritual principle throughout contemporary popular culture is a striking sign of the power of modern capitalism.

And yet, there is still more. Let's return to the movie poster for *Batman: The Dark Knight*. That poster, as we have seen, was immediately evocative of one of the most violent days in American history; with such violence (and more) to be found in the real world, it should not be surprising to find a demand for its realistic representation in our entertainment. Here the difference between Nicholson's and Ledger's Jokers comes back into play, for Ledger's Joker is very much a reflection of the terroristic violence of our times. Simply stated, Ledger's Joker is a terrorist, and as such he raises an important question that is explicitly presented in the movie—namely, how can a society fight terrorism without becoming terroristic itself?

Batman: The Dark Knight both reflects and addresses this larger cultural dilemma by dramatizing the choices that civilized societies must make when battling enemies who do not seem to respect any limits. Thus, while Batman is willing to break some rules to fight the Joker, he is not willing to kill him when he has him at his mercy (the Joker even anticipates this as he dares Batman to kill him and so become like the Joker himself). Reflecting the dilemma that Americans face when confronted by shadowy organizations like al-Qaeda, *Batman: The Dark Knight* is ultimately a profoundly *political* film that raises questions about the conduct of America's war on terror.

The fact that *Batman: The Dark Knight* contains both "official" and "outlaw" heroes, however, strongly indicates that it does not intend to subvert that war. As Robert B. Ray argues in "The Thematic Paradigm" (included in Chapter 6 of this book), an official hero is someone who serves and protects society from within its institutions. As the district attorney of Gotham City, Harvey Dent is just such a hero. His courageous war on the mob differentiates him from the bumbling and/or corrupt officials in Tim Burton's *Batman*, a difference that reflects the general rehabilitation of official heroes after the 9/11 terror attacks (such television series as the *CSI* franchise, *Criminal Minds*, and any show featuring sympathetic cops, FBI agents, or any other branch of law enforcement are all signifiers of this return to the official hero in popular culture). That Harvey Dent is eventually corrupted to become Two Face does not really contradict this because the audience can see that he has a very strong motive for going "bad," and he is only after those who have hurt him (which much ameliorates his change). What is more, we see plenty of other officials in the movie who are innocent victims of the Joker (for example, the chief of police and a judge), and, in the end, it is Batman who decides that the people of Gotham City *need* an official hero, and so conspires to conceal the truth about Harvey Dent / Two Face and take the blame for Two Face's deeds so that the people will not become overwhelmed with despair and disillusionment.

Batman himself is what Ray calls an "outlaw hero," someone who may serve and protect society, but only on his or her own terms, even if this means breaking the law. Batman is a pure outlaw hero, in that he has no official connection with law enforcement, while figures like Dirty Harry and Jack Bauer (of *24*) are outlaw heroes who work for official law enforcement institutions. Outlaw heroes have been steadily gaining favor over official heroes in American popular culture ever since the cultural revolution of the 1960s, which dethroned most if not all of America's traditional official heroes and replaced them with a variety of outlaw heroes. It was this shift that vaulted Batman over Superman in the 1980s as America's favorite cartoon superhero.

Interestingly, in *Batman: The Dark Knight* the official hero and the outlaw hero are symbolically *combined* when Dent declares during a press conference that *he* is Batman. This union of official and outlaw hero offers a satisfying mediation of the conflict between the two heroic types in the post–9/11 era, when Americans have turned once more to official heroes like police, firefighters, Homeland Security personnel, and soldiers, while not abandoning the outlaw heroes made popular by the cultural revolution.

Thus, the evidence is that *Batman: The Dark Knight* does not represent a metaphoric challenge to the war on terror. Rather, it reassures its audience in troubling times that they have not been abandoned. Heroic men and women are on the case, fighting for the rest of us. It's all rather sentimental and unrealistic — in short, a fantasy — but as a popular expression of American angst and desire in an era of unprecedented conflict, this *Batman* is no mere entertainment. It is a sign of a society desperately in need of cathartic reassurance in times that often seem apocalyptic.

The Readings

Linda Seger's how-to guide for the creation of the kind of archetypal characters that made *Star Wars* one of the most popular movies of all time opens this chapter's readings. A paired set of readings follow, in which Jessica Hagedorn surveys a tradition of American filmmaking that stereotypes Asian women as either tragic or trivial, and Helena Andrews compares the critical reactions to *The Butler* and *The Help*, revealing how complicated attitudes toward race and gender have affected the two films' receptions. Matt Zoller Seitz is next with a critical exposé of cinema's "'Magical Negro': a saintly African-American character who acts as a mentor to a questing white hero." Michael Parenti then takes a social-class-based approach to the codes of American cinema, noting the caste biases inherent in such popular hits as *Pretty Woman*, while David Denby explains in "High-School Confidential" why generations of teenagers flock to all those jocks-and-cheerleaders-versus-the-nerds movies. Michael Agresta surveys the rise and fall of the once-mighty Western, a genre that even *The Lone Ranger* (not to mention Johnny Depp) has been unable to save as America comes to terms with its own history. And Christine Folch concludes the chapter with an analysis of the cultural differences that make sci-fi and fantasy movies all the rage in America but nothing special in India.

LINDA SEGER

Creating the Myth

To be a successful screenwriter, Linda Seger suggests in this selection from *Making a Good Script Great* (1987), you've got to know your
archetypes. Seger reveals the secret behind the success of such Hollywood creations as *Star Wars'* Luke Skywalker and tells you how
you can create such heroes yourself. In this how-to approach to the
cinema, Seger echoes the more academic judgments of such semioticians of film as Umberto Eco — the road to popular success in mass
culture is paved with cultural myths and clichés. A script consultant
and author who has given professional seminars on filmmaking
around the world, Seger has also published *Creating Unforgettable
Characters* (1990), *When Women Call the Shots: The Developing Power
and Influence of Women in Television and Film* (1996), and *Writing
Subtext: What Lies Beneath* (2011).

All of us have similar experiences. We share in the life journey of growth,
development, and transformation. We live the same stories, whether they
involve the search for a perfect mate, coming home, the search for fulfillment,
going after an ideal, achieving the dream, or hunting for a precious treasure.
Whatever our culture, there are universal stories that form the basis for all our
particular stories. The trappings might be different, the twists and turns that
create suspense might change from culture to culture, the particular characters may take different forms, but underneath it all, it's the same story, drawn
from the same experiences.

Many of the most successful films are based on these universal stories.
They deal with the basic journey we take in life. We identify with the heroes
because we were once heroic (descriptive) or because we wish we could do
what the hero does (prescriptive). When Joan Wilder finds the jewel and saves
her sister, or James Bond saves the world, or Shane saves the family from the
evil ranchers, we identify with the character, and subconsciously recognize
the story as having some connection with our own lives. It's the same story
as the fairy tales about getting the three golden hairs from the devil, or finding the treasure and winning the princess. And it's not all that different a story
from the caveman killing the woolly beast or the Roman slave gaining his
freedom through skill and courage. These are our stories — personally and collectively — and the most successful films contain these universal experiences.

🄴 macmillanhighered.com/signsoflife
How do B-movies critique society?
e-readings > **Louis J. Gasnier and Arthur Hoerl,** *Reefer Madness* [film clip]
               George A. Romero and John A. Russo, *Night of the Living Dead*
[film clip]

Some of these stories are "search" stories. They address our desire to find some kind of rare and wonderful treasure. This might include the search for outer values such as job, relationship, or success; or for inner values such as respect, security, self-expression, love, or home. But it's all a similar search.

Some of these stories are "hero" stories. They come from our own experiences of overcoming adversity, as well as our desire to do great and special acts. We root for the hero and celebrate when he or she achieves the goal because we know that the hero's journey is in many ways similar to our own.

We call these stories *myths*. Myths are the common stories at the root of 5 our universal existence. They're found in all cultures and in all literature, ranging from the Greek myths to fairy tales, legends, and stories drawn from all of the world's religions.

A myth is a story that is "more than true." Many stories are true because one person, somewhere, at some time, lived it. It is based on fact. But a myth is more than true because it is lived by all of us, at some level. It's a story that connects and speaks to us all.

Some myths are true stories that attain mythic significance because the people involved seem larger than life, and seem to live their lives more intensely than common folk. Martin Luther King, Jr., Gandhi, Sir Edmund Hillary, and Lord Mountbatten personify the types of journeys we identify with, because we've taken similar journeys — even if only in a very small way.

Other myths revolve around make-believe characters who might capsulize for us the sum total of many of our journeys. Some of these make-believe characters might seem similar to the characters we meet in our dreams. Or they might be a composite of types of characters we've met.

In both cases, the myth is the "story beneath the story." It's the universal pattern that shows us that Gandhi's journey toward independence and Sir Edmund Hillary's journey to the top of Mount Everest contain many of the same dramatic beats. And these beats are the same beats that Rambo takes to set free the MIAs, that Indiana Jones takes to find the Lost Ark, and that Luke Skywalker takes to defeat the Evil Empire.

In *Hero with a Thousand Faces*, Joseph Campbell traces the elements that 10 form the hero myth. In their own work with myth, writer Chris Vogler and seminar leader Thomas Schlesinger have applied this criteria to *Star Wars*. The myth within the story helps explain why millions went to see this film again and again.

The hero myth has specific story beats that occur in all hero stories. They show who the hero is, what the hero needs, and how the story and character interact in order to create a transformation. The journey toward heroism is a process. This universal process forms the spine of all the particular stories, such as the *Star Wars* trilogy.

The Hero Myth

1. In most hero stories, the hero is introduced in ordinary surroundings, in a mundane world, doing mundane things. Generally, the hero begins as a

Star Wars, 1977.

nonhero; innocent, young, simple, or humble. In *Star Wars*, the first time we see Luke Skywalker, he's unhappy about having to do his chores, which consist of picking out some new droids for work. He wants to go out and have fun. He wants to leave his planet and go to the Academy, but he's stuck. This is the setup of most myths. This is how we meet the hero before the call to adventure.

2. Then something new enters the hero's life. It's a catalyst that sets the story into motion. It might be a telephone call, as in *Romancing the Stone*, or the German attack in *The African Queen*, or the holograph of Princess Leia in *Star Wars*. Whatever form it takes, it's a new ingredient that pushes the hero into an extraordinary adventure. With this call, the stakes are established, and a problem is introduced that demands a solution.

3. Many times, however, the hero doesn't want to leave. He or she is a reluctant hero, afraid of the unknown, uncertain, perhaps, if he or she is up to the challenge. In *Star Wars*, Luke receives a double call to adventure. First, from Princess Leia in the holograph, and then through Obi-Wan Kenobi, who says he needs Luke's help. But Luke is not ready to go. He returns home, only to find that the Imperial Stormtroopers have burned his farmhouse and slaughtered his family. Now he is personally motivated, ready to enter into the adventure.

4. In any journey, the hero usually receives help, and the help often comes from unusual sources. In many fairy tales, an old woman, a dwarf, a witch, or a wizard helps the hero. The hero achieves the goal because of this help, and because the hero is receptive to what this person has to give.

There are a number of fairy tales where the first and second sons are sent to complete a task, but they ignore the helpers, often scorning them. Many times they are severely punished for their lack of humility and unwillingness to accept help. Then the third son, the hero, comes along. He receives the help, accomplishes the task, and often wins the princess.

In *Star Wars*, Obi-Wan Kenobi is a perfect example of the "helper" character. He is a kind of mentor to Luke, one who teaches him the Way of the Force and whose teachings continue even after his death. This mentor character appears in most hero stories. He is the person who has special knowledge, special information, and special skills. This might be the prospector in *The Treasure of the Sierra Madre*, or the psychiatrist in *Ordinary People*, or Quint in *Jaws*, who knows all about sharks, or the Good Witch of the North who gives Dorothy the ruby slippers in *The Wizard of Oz*. In *Star Wars*, Obi-Wan gives Luke the light saber that was the special weapon of the Jedi Knight. With this, Luke is ready to move forward and do his training and meet adventure.

5. The hero is now ready to move into the special world where he or she will change from the ordinary into the extraordinary. This starts the hero's transformation, and sets up the obstacles that must be surmounted to reach the goal. Usually, this happens at the first Turning Point of the story, and leads into Act Two development. In *Star Wars*, Obi-Wan and Luke search for a pilot to take them to the planet of Alderaan, so that Obi-Wan can deliver the plans to Princess Leia's father. These plans are essential to the survival of the Rebel Forces. With this action, the adventure is ready to begin.

6. Now begin all the tests and obstacles necessary to overcome the enemy and accomplish the hero's goals. In fairy tales, this often means getting past witches, outwitting the devil, avoiding robbers, or confronting evil. In Homer's *Odyssey*, it means blinding the Cyclops, escaping from the island of the Lotus-Eaters, resisting the temptation of the singing Sirens, and surviving a shipwreck. In *Star Wars*, innumerable adventures confront Luke. He and his cohorts must run to the *Millennium Falcon*, narrowly escaping the Storm-troopers before jumping into hyperspace. They must make it through the meteor shower after Alderaan has been destroyed. They must evade capture on the Death Star, rescue the Princess, and even survive a garbage crusher.

7. At some point in the story, the hero often hits rock bottom. He often [20] has a "death experience," leading to a type of rebirth. In *Star Wars*, Luke seems to have died when the serpent in the garbage-masher pulls him under, but he's saved just in time to ask R2D2 to stop the masher before they're crushed. This is often the "black moment" at the second turning point, the point when the worst is confronted, and the action now moves toward the exciting conclusion.

8. Now, the hero seizes the sword and takes possession of the treasure. He is now in charge, but he still has not completed the journey. Here Luke has the Princess and the plans, but the final confrontation is yet to begin. This starts the third-act escape scene, leading to the final climax.

9. The road back is often the chase scene. In many fairy tales, this is the point where the devil chases the hero and the hero has the last obstacles to overcome before really being free and safe. His challenge is to take what he has learned and integrate it into his daily life. He *must* return to renew the

mundane world. In *Star Wars*, Darth Vader is in hot pursuit, planning to blow up the Rebel Planet.

10. Since every hero story is essentially a transformation story, we need to see the hero changed at the end, resurrected into a new type of life. He must face the final ordeal before being "reborn" as the hero, proving his courage and becoming transformed. This is the point, in many fairy tales, where the Miller's Son becomes the Prince or the King and marries the Princess. In *Star Wars*, Luke has survived, becoming quite a different person from the innocent young man he was in Act One.

At this point, the hero returns and is reintegrated into his society. In *Star Wars*, Luke has destroyed the Death Star, and he receives his great reward.

This is the classic "Hero Story." We might call this example a *mission* or *task* 25 *myth*, where the person has to complete a task, but the task itself is not the real treasure. The real reward for Luke is the love of the Princess and the safe, new world he had helped create.

A myth can have many variations. We see variations on this myth in James Bond films (although they lack much of the depth because the hero is not transformed), and in *The African Queen*, where Rose and Allnutt must blow up the *Louisa*, or in *Places in the Heart*, where Edna overcomes obstacles to achieve family stability.

The *treasure myth* is another variation on this theme, as seen in *Romancing the Stone*. In this story, Joan receives a map and a phone call which forces her into the adventure. She is helped by an American birdcatcher and a Mexican pickup-truck driver. She overcomes the obstacles of snakes, the jungle, waterfalls, shootouts, and finally receives the treasure, along with the "prince."

Whether the hero's journey is for a treasure or to complete a task, the elements remain the same. The humble, reluctant hero is called to an adventure. The hero is helped by a variety of unique characters. S/he must overcome a series of obstacles that transform him or her in the process, and then face the final challenge that draws on inner and outer resources.

The Healing Myth

Although the hero myth is the most popular story, many myths involve healing. In these stories, some character is "broken" and must leave home to become whole again.

The universal experience behind these healing stories is our psychological 30 need for rejuvenation, for balance. The journey of the hero into exile is not all that different from the weekend in Palm Springs, or the trip to Hawaii to get away from it all, or lying still in a hospital bed for some weeks to heal. In all cases, something is out of balance and the mythic journey moves toward wholeness.

Being broken can take several forms. It can be physical, emotional, or psychological. Usually, it's all three. In the process of being exiled or hiding out in the forest, the desert, or even the Amish farm in *Witness*, the person becomes whole, balanced, and receptive to love. Love in these stories is both a healing force and a reward.

Think of John Book in *Witness*. In Act One, we see a frenetic, insensitive man, afraid of commitment, critical and unreceptive to the feminine influences in his life. John is suffering from an "inner wound" which he doesn't know about. When he receives an "outer wound" from a gunshot, it forces him into exile, which begins his process of transformation.

At the beginning of Act Two, we see John delirious and close to death. This is a movement into the unconscious, a movement from the rational, active police life of Act One into a mysterious, feminine, more intuitive world. Since John's "inner problem" is the lack of balance with his feminine side, this delirium begins the process of transformation.

Later in Act Two, we see John beginning to change. He moves from his highly independent lifestyle toward the collective, communal life of his Amish hosts. John now gets up early to milk the cows and to assist with the chores. He uses his carpentry skills to help with the barn building and to complete the birdhouse. Gradually, he begins to develop relationships with Rachel and her son, Samuel. John's life slows down and he becomes more receptive, learning important lessons about love. In Act Three, John finally sees that the feminine is worth saving, and throws down his gun to save Rachel's life. A few beats later, when he has the opportunity to kill Paul, he chooses a nonviolent response instead. Although John doesn't "win" the Princess, he has nevertheless "won" love and wholeness. By the end of the film, we can see that the John Book of Act Three is a different kind of person from the John Book of Act One. He has a different kind of comradeship with his fellow police officers, he's more relaxed, and we can sense that somehow, this experience has formed a more integrated John Book.

Combination Myths

Many stories are combinations of several different myths. Think of *Ghost-* [35] *busters*, a simple and rather outrageous comedy about three men saving the city of New York from ghosts. Now think of the story of "Pandora's Box." It's about the woman who let loose all manner of evil upon the earth by opening a box she was told not to touch. In *Ghostbusters*, the EPA man is a Pandora figure. By shutting off the power to the containment center, he inadvertently unleashes all the ghosts upon New York City. Combine the story of "Pandora's Box" with a hero story, and notice that we have our three heroes battling the Marshmallow Man. One of them also "gets the Princess" when Dr. Peter Venkman finally receives the affections of Dana Barrett. By looking at these combinations, it is apparent that even *Ghostbusters* is more than "just a comedy."

Tootsie is a type of reworking of many Shakespearean stories where a woman has to dress as a man in order to accomplish a certain task. These Shakespearean stories are reminiscent of many fairy tales where the hero becomes invisible or takes on another persona, or wears a specific disguise to hide his or her real qualities. In the stories of "The Twelve Dancing Princesses" or "The Man in the Bearskin," disguise is necessary to achieve a goal. Combine these elements with the transformation themes of the hero myth where a hero (such as Michael) must overcome many obstacles to his success as an actor and a human being. It's not difficult to understand why the *Tootsie* story hooks us.

Archetypes

A myth includes certain characters that we see in many stories. These characters are called *archetypes*. They can be thought of as the original "pattern" or "character type" that will be found on the hero's journey. Archetypes take many forms, but they tend to fall within specific categories.

Earlier, we discussed some of the helpers who give advice to help the hero—such as the *wise old man* who possesses special knowledge and often serves as a mentor to the hero.

The female counterpart of the wise old man is the *good mother*. Whereas the wise old man has superior knowledge, the good mother is known for her nurturing qualities, and for her intuition. This figure often gives the hero particular objects to help on the journey. It might be a protective amulet, or the ruby slippers that Dorothy receives in *The Wizard of Oz* from the Good Witch of the North. Sometimes in fairy tales it's a cloak to make the person invisible, or ordinary objects that become extraordinary, as in "The Girl of Courage," an Afghan fairy tale about a maiden who receives a comb, a whetstone, and a mirror to help defeat the devil.

Many myths contain a *shadow figure*. This is a character who is the opposite of the hero. Sometimes this figure helps the hero on the journey; other times this figure opposes the hero. The shadow figure can be the negative side of the hero which could be the dark and hostile brother in "Cain and Abel," the stepsisters in "Cinderella," or the Robber Girl in "The Snow Queen." The shadow figure can also help the hero, as the whore with the heart of gold who saves the hero's life, or provides balance to his idealization of woman.

Many myths contain *animal archetypes* that can be positive or negative figures. In "St. George and the Dragon," the dragon is the negative force which is a violent and ravaging animal, not unlike the shark in *Jaws*. But in many stories, animals help the hero. Sometimes there are talking donkeys, or a dolphin which saves the hero, or magical horses or dogs.

The *trickster* is a mischievous archetypical figure who is always causing chaos, disturbing the peace, and generally being an anarchist. The trickster uses wit and cunning to achieve his or her ends. Sometimes the trickster is a

40

harmless prankster or a "bad boy" who is funny and enjoyable. More often, the trickster is a con man, as in *The Sting*, or the devil, as in *The Exorcist*, who demanded all the skills of the priest to outwit him. The "Till Eulenspiegel" stories revolve around the trickster, as do the Spanish picaresque novels. Even the tales of Tom Sawyer have a trickster motif. In all countries, there are stories that revolve around this figure, whose job it is to outwit.

"Mythic" Problems and Solutions

We all grew up with myths. Most of us heard or read fairy tales when we were young. Some of us may have read Bible stories, or stories from other religions or other cultures. These stories are part of us. And the best way to work with them is to let them come out naturally as you write the script.

Of course, some filmmakers are better at this than others. George Lucas and Steven Spielberg have a strong sense of myth and incorporate it into their films. They both have spoken about their love of the stories from childhood, and of their desire to bring these types of stories to audiences. Their stories create some of the same sense of wonder and excitement as myths. Many of the necessary psychological beats are part of their stories, deepening the story beyond the ordinary action-adventure.

Myths bring depth to a hero story. If a filmmaker is thinking only about 45 the action and excitement of a story, audiences might fail to connect with the hero's journey. But if the basic beats of the hero's journey are evident, a film will often inexplicably draw audiences, in spite of critics' responses to the film.

Take *Rambo*, for instance. Why was this violent, simple story so popular with audiences? I don't think it was because everyone agreed with its politics. I do think Sylvester Stallone is a master at incorporating the American myth into his filmmaking. That doesn't mean it's done consciously. Somehow he is naturally in sync with the myth, and the myth becomes integrated into his stories.

Clint Eastwood also does hero stories, and gives us the adventure of the myth and the transformation of the myth. . . . Eastwood's films have given more attention to the transformation of the hero, and have been receiving more serious critical attention as a result.

All of these filmmakers — Lucas, Spielberg, Stallone, and Eastwood — dramatize the hero myth in their own particular ways. And all of them prove that myths are marketable.

Application

It is an important part of the writer's or producer's work to continually find opportunities for deepening the themes within a script. Finding the myth beneath the modern story is part of that process.

To find these myths, it's not a bad idea to reread some of Grimm's fairy 50
tales or fairy tales from around the world to begin to get acquainted with various myths. You'll start to see patterns and elements that connect with our own human experience.

Also, read Joseph Campbell and Greek mythology. If you're interested in Jungian psychology, you'll find many rich resources within a number of books on the subject. Since Jungian psychology deals with archetypes, you'll find many new characters to draw on for your own work.

With all of these resources to incorporate, it's important to remember that the myth is not a story to force upon a script. It's more a pattern which you can bring out in your own stories when they seem to be heading in the direction of a myth.

As you work, ask yourself:

Do I have a myth working in my script? If so, what beats am I using of the hero's journey? Which ones seem to be missing?

Am I missing characters? Do I need a mentor type? A wise old man? A wizard? Would one of these characters help dimensionalize the hero's journey?

Could I create new emotional dimensions to the myth by starting my character as reluctant, naïve, simple, or decidedly "unheroic"?

Does my character get transformed in the process of the journey?

Have I used a strong three-act structure to support the myth, using the first turning point to move into the adventure and the second turning point to create a dark moment, or a reversal, or even a "near-death" experience?

Don't be afraid to create variations on the myth, but don't start with the myth itself. Let the myth grow naturally from your story. Developing myths is part of the rewriting process. If you begin with the myth, you'll find your writing becomes rigid, uncreative, and predictable. Working with the myth in the rewriting process will deepen your script, giving it new life as you find the story within the story.

READING THE TEXT

1. How does Seger define the "hero myth" (para. 11)?

2. In your own words, explain what Seger means by "the healing myth" (para. 29).

3. What is an "archetype" in film (para. 37)?

READING THE SIGNS

1. Seger is writing to aspiring screenwriters. How does her status as an industry insider affect her description of heroic archetypes?

2. **CONNECTING TEXTS** Focusing on gender issues, compare Seger's formulation of heroes with Robert B. Ray's in "The Thematic Paradigm" (p. 450). To what extent do Seger and Ray adequately explain the role of women — and men — in movies?

3. **CONNECTING TEXTS**   Review Michael Parenti's "Class and Virtue" (p. 361), and write an essay identifying the myths behind the modern story *Pretty Woman* (1990) or *Juno* (2007).

4. Watch *Titanic* or a segment of the *Lord of the Rings* trilogy, and write an essay in which you explain the myths and archetypal characters the film includes. How might archetypal and mythic patterns explain the film's success?

5. Seger recommends that aspiring screenwriters read Grimm's fairy tales for inspiration. You can find them online. Read some of Grimm's tales, and then write an argument assessing the suitability of such tales as inspiration for films today.

6. Watch one of the *Hunger Games* films, focusing particularly on character types. In an essay, analyze the film's use of archetypes. To what extent does it replicate, reinvent, or otherwise complicate archetypal characters?

GENDER AND RACE IN FILM

JESSICA HAGEDORN

Asian Women in Film: No Joy, No Luck

Why do movies always seem to portray Asian women as tragic victims of history and fate? Jessica Hagedorn asks in this essay, which originally appeared in *Ms.* Even such movies as *The Joy Luck Club*, based on Amy Tan's breakthrough novel that elevated Asian American fiction to best-seller status, reinforce old stereotypes of the powerlessness of Asian and Asian American women. A screenwriter and novelist, Hagedorn calls for a different kind of storytelling that would show Asian women as powerful controllers of their own destinies. Jessica Hagedorn's publications include the novels *Dogeaters* (1990), *The Gangster of Love* (1996), *Dream Jungle* (2003), and *Toxicology* (2011); *Danger and Beauty* (1993), a collection of poems; *Fresh Kill* (1994), a screenplay; and *Charlie Chan Is Dead 2: At Home in the World* (2004) and *Manila Noir* (2013) (as editor).

Pearl of the Orient. Whore. Geisha. Concubine. Whore. Hostess. Bar Girl. Mamasan. Whore. China Doll. Tokyo Rose. Whore. Butterfly. Whore. Miss Saigon. Whore. Dragon Lady. Lotus Blossom. Gook. Whore. Yellow Peril. Whore. Bangkok Bombshell. Whore. Hospitality Girl. Whore. Comfort Woman. Whore. Savage. Whore. Sultry. Whore. Faceless. Whore. Porcelain. Whore. Demure. Whore. Virgin. Whore. Mute. Whore. Model Minority. Whore. Victim. Whore. Woman Warrior. Whore. Mail-Order Bride. Whore. Mother. Wife. Lover. Daughter. Sister.

As I was growing up in the Philippines in the 1950s, my fertile imagination was colonized by thoroughly American fantasies. Yellowface variations on the exotic erotic loomed larger than life on the silver screen. I was mystified and enthralled by Hollywood's skewed representations of Asian women: sleek, evil goddesses with slanted eyes and cunning ways, or smiling, sarong-clad South Seas "maidens" with undulating hips, kinky black hair, and white skin darkened by makeup. Hardly any of the "Asian" characters were played by Asians. White actors like Sidney Toler and Warner Oland played "inscrutable Oriental detective" Charlie Chan with taped eyelids and a singsong, chop suey accent. Jennifer Jones was a Eurasian doctor swept up in a doomed "inter-racial romance" in *Love Is a Many Splendored Thing*. In my mother's youth, white actor Luise Rainer played the central role of the Patient Chinese Wife in the 1937 film adaptation of Pearl Buck's novel *The Good Earth*. Back then, not many thought to ask why; they were all too busy being grateful to see anyone in the movies remotely like themselves.

Cut to 1960: *The World of Suzie Wong*, another tragic East/West affair. I am now old enough to be impressed. Sexy, sassy Suzie (played by Nancy Kwan) works out of a bar patronized by white sailors, but doesn't seem bothered by any of it. For a hardworking girl turning nightly tricks to support her baby, she manages to parade an astonishing wardrobe in damn near every scene, down to matching handbags and shoes. The sailors are also strictly Hollywood, sani-tized and not too menacing. Suzie and all the other prostitutes in this movie are cute, giggling, dancing sex machines with hearts of gold. William Holden plays an earnest, rather prim, Nice Guy painter seeking inspiration in The Other. Of course, Suzie falls madly in love with him. Typically, she tells him, "I not important," and "I'll be with you until you say — Suzie, go away." She also thinks being beaten by a man is a sign of true passion and is terribly dis-appointed when Mr. Nice Guy refuses to show his true feelings.

Next in Kwan's short-lived but memorable career was the kitschy 1961 musical *Flower Drum Song*, which, like *Suzie Wong*, is a thoroughly American commercial product. The female roles are typical of Hollywood musicals of the times: women are basically airheads, subservient to men. Kwan's coun-terpart is the Good Chinese Girl, played by Miyoshi Umeki, who was better playing the Loyal Japanese Girl in that other classic Hollywood tale of forbid-den love, *Sayonara*. Remember? Umeki was so loyal, she committed double suicide with actor Red Buttons. I instinctively hated *Sayonara* when I first saw it as a child; now I understand why. Contrived tragic resolutions were the only way Hollywood got past the censors in those days. With one or two excep-tions, somebody in these movies always had to die to pay for breaking racial and sexual taboos.

Until the recent onslaught of films by both Asian and Asian Ameri- 5 can filmmakers, Asian Pacific women have generally been perceived by Hollywood with a mixture of fascination, fear, and contempt. Most Hollywood movies either trivialize or exoticize us as people of color and as women. Our intelligence is underestimated, our humanity overlooked, and our diverse cul-tures treated as interchangeable. If we are "good," we are childlike, submis-sive, silent, and eager for sex (see France Nuyen's glowing performance as

Liat in the film version of *South Pacific*) or else we are tragic victim types (see *Casualties of War*, Brian De Palma's graphic 1989 drama set in Vietnam). And if we are not silent, suffering doormats, we are demonized dragon ladies — cunning, deceitful, sexual provocateurs. Give me the demonic any day — Anna May Wong as a villain slithering around in a slinky gown is at least gratifying to watch, neither servile nor passive. And she steals the show from Marlene Dietrich in Josef von Sternberg's *Shanghai Express*. From the 1920s through the 1930s, Wong was our only female "star." But even she was trapped in limited roles, in what filmmaker Renee Tajima has called the dragon lady/lotus blossom dichotomy.

Cut to 1985: There is a scene toward the end of the terribly dishonest but weirdly compelling Michael Cimino movie *Year of the Dragon* (cowritten by Oliver Stone) that is one of my favorite twisted movie moments of all time. If you ask a lot of my friends who've seen that movie (especially if they're Asian), it's one of their favorites too. The setting is a crowded Chinatown nightclub. There are two very young and very tough Jade Cobra gang girls in a shoot-out with Mickey Rourke, in the role of a demented Polish American cop who, in spite of being Mr. Ugly in the flesh — an arrogant, misogynistic bully devoid of any charm — wins the "good" Asian American anchorwoman in the film's absurd and implausible ending. This is a movie with an actual disclaimer as its lead-in, covering its ass in advance in response to anticipated complaints about "stereotypes."

My pleasure in the hard-edged power of the Chinatown gang girls in *Year of the Dragon* is my small revenge, the answer to all those Suzie Wong "I want to be your slave" female characters. The Jade Cobra girls are mere background to the white male foreground/focus of Cimino's movie. But long after the movie has faded into video-rental heaven, the Jade Cobra girls remain defiant, fabulous images in my memory, flaunting tight metallic dresses and spiky cock's-comb hairdos streaked electric red and blue.

Mickey Rourke looks down with world-weary pity at the unnamed Jade Cobra girl (Doreen Chan) he's just shot who lies sprawled and bleeding on the street: "You look like you're gonna die, beautiful."

JADE COBRA GIRL: "Oh yeah? [blood gushing from her mouth] I'm proud of it."

ROURKE: "You are? You got anything you wanna tell me before you go, sweetheart?"

JADE COBRA GIRL: "Yeah. [pause] Fuck you."

Cut to 1993: I've been told that like many New Yorkers, I watch movies with the right side of my brain on perpetual overdrive. I admit to being grouchy and overcritical, suspicious of sentiment, and cynical. When a critic like Richard Corliss of *Time* magazine gushes about *The Joy Luck Club* being "a fourfold *Terms of Endearment*," my gut instinct is to run the other way. I resent being told how to feel. I went to see the 1993 eight-handkerchief movie version of Amy Tan's bestseller with a group that included my ten-year-old

Anna May Wong.

daughter. I was caught between the sincere desire to be swept up by the turbulent mother-daughter sagas and my own stubborn resistance to being so obviously manipulated by the filmmakers. With every flashback came tragedy. The music soared; the voice-overs were solemn or wistful; tears, tears, and more tears flowed on-screen. Daughters were reverent; mothers carried dark secrets.

I was elated by the grandness and strength of the four mothers and the luminous actors who portrayed them, but I was uneasy with the passivity of the Asian American daughters. They seemed to exist solely as receptors for

Michelle Yeoh, *Tomorrow Never Dies*, 1997.

their mothers' amazing life stories. It's almost as if by assimilating so easily into American society, they had lost all sense of self.

In spite of my resistance, my eyes watered as the desperate mother played by Kieu Chinh was forced to abandon her twin baby girls on a country road in war-torn China. (Kieu Chinh resembles my own mother and her twin sister, who suffered through the brutal Japanese occupation of the Philippines.) So far in this movie, an infant son had been deliberately drowned, a mother played by the gravely beautiful France Nuyen had gone catatonic with grief, a concubine had cut her flesh open to save her dying mother, an insecure daughter had been oppressed by her boorish Asian American husband, another insecure daughter had been left by her white husband, and so on. . . . The overall effect was numbing as far as I'm concerned, but a man sitting two rows in front of us broke down sobbing. A Chinese Filipino writer even more grouchy than me later complained, "Must ethnicity only be equated with suffering?"

Because change has been slow, *The Joy Luck Club* carries a lot of cultural baggage. It is a big-budget story about Chinese American women, directed by a Chinese American man, cowritten and coproduced by Chinese American women. That's a lot to be thankful for. And its box office success proves that an immigrant narrative told from female perspectives can have mass appeal. But my cynical side tells me that its success might mean only one thing in Hollywood: more weepy epics about Asian American mother-daughter relationships will be planned.

That the film finally got made was significant. By Hollywood standards (think white male; think money, money, money), a movie about Asian Americans even when adapted from a bestseller was a risky proposition. When I asked a producer I know about the film's rumored delays, he simply said, "It's still an *Asian* movie," surprised I had even asked. Equally interesting was director Wayne Wang's initial reluctance to be involved in the project; he told the *New York Times*, "I didn't want to do another Chinese movie."

Maybe he shouldn't have worried so much. After all, according to the media, the nineties are the decade of "Pacific Overtures" and East Asian chic. Madonna, the pop queen of shameless appropriation, cultivated Japanese high-tech style with her music video "Rain," while Janet Jackson faked kitschy orientalia in hers, titled "If." Critical attention was paid to movies from China, Japan, and Vietnam. But that didn't mean an honest appraisal of women's lives. Even on the art house circuit, filmmakers who should know better took the easy way out. Takehiro Nakajima's 1992 film *Okoge* presents one of the more original film roles for women in recent years. In Japanese, "okoge" means the crust of rice that sticks to the bottom of the rice pot; in pejorative slang, it means fag hag. The way "okoge" is used in the film seems a reappropriation of the term; the portrait Nakajima creates of Sayoko, the so-called fag hag, is clearly an affectionate one. Sayoko is a quirky, self-assured woman in contemporary Tokyo who does voice-overs for cartoons, has a thing for Frida Kahlo paintings, and is drawn to a gentle young gay man named Goh. But the other women's roles are disappointing, stereotypical "hysterical females" and the movie itself turns conventional halfway through. Sayoko sacrifices herself to a macho brute Goh desires, who rapes her as images of Frida Kahlo paintings and her beloved Goh rising from the ocean flash before her. She gives birth to a baby boy and endures a terrible life of poverty with the abusive rapist. This sudden change from spunky survivor to helpless, victimized woman is baffling. Whatever happened to her job? Or that arty little apartment of hers? Didn't her Frida Kahlo obsession teach her anything?

Then there was Tiana Thi Thanh Nga's *From Hollywood to Hanoi*, a self-serving but fascinating documentary. Born in Vietnam to a privileged family that included an uncle who was defense minister in the Thieu government and an idolized father who served as press minister, Nga (a.k.a. Tiana) spent her adolescence in California. A former actor in martial arts movies and fitness teacher ("Karaticize with Tiana"), the vivacious Tiana decided to make a record of her journey back to Vietnam.

From Hollywood to Hanoi is at times unintentionally very funny. Tiana 15 includes a quick scene of herself dancing with a white man at the Metropole hotel in Hanoi, and breathlessly announces: "That's me doing the tango with Oliver Stone!" Then she listens sympathetically to a horrifying account of the My Lai massacre by one of its few female survivors. In another scene, Tiana cheerfully addresses a food vendor on the streets of Hanoi: "Your hairdo is so pretty." The unimpressed, poker-faced woman gives a brusque, deadpan reply: "You want to eat, or what?" Sometimes it is hard to tell the difference between Tiana Thi Thanh Nga and her Hollywood persona: The real Tiana still seems to be playing one of her B-movie roles, which are mainly fun because they're fantasy. The time was certainly right to explore postwar Vietnam from a Vietnamese woman's perspective; it's too bad this film was done by a Valley Girl.

Nineteen ninety-three also brought Tran Anh Hung's *The Scent of Green Papaya*, a different kind of Vietnamese memento — this is a look back at the peaceful, lush country of the director's childhood memories. The film opens in Saigon, in 1951. A willowy ten-year-old girl named Mui comes to work for a troubled family headed by a melancholy musician and his kind, stoic wife. The men of this bourgeois household are idle, pampered types who take naps while the women do all the work. Mui is male fantasy: She is a devoted servant, enduring acts of cruel mischief with patience and dignity; as an adult, she barely speaks. She scrubs floors, shines shoes, and cooks with loving care and never a complaint. When she is sent off to work for another wealthy musician, she ends up being impregnated by him. The movie ends as the camera closes in on Mui's contented face. Languid and precious, *The Scent of Green Papaya* is visually haunting, but it suffers from the director's colonial fantasy of women as docile, domestic creatures. Steeped in highbrow nostalgia, it's the arty Vietnamese version of *My Fair Lady* with the wealthy musician as Professor Higgins, teaching Mui to read and write.

And then there is Ang Lee's tepid 1993 hit, *The Wedding Banquet* — a clever culture-clash farce in which traditional Chinese values collide with contemporary American sexual mores. The somewhat formulaic plot goes like this: Wai-Tung, a yuppie landlord, lives with his white lover, Simon, in a chic Manhattan brownstone. Wai-Tung is an only child and his aging parents in Taiwan long for a grandchild to continue the family legacy. Enter Wei-Wei, an artist who lives in a grungy loft owned by Wai-Tung. She slugs tequila straight from the bottle as she paints and flirts boldly with her young, uptight landlord, who brushes her off. "It's my fate. I am always attracted to handsome gay men," she mutters. After this setup, the movie goes downhill, all edges blurred in a cozy nest of happy endings. In a refrain of Sayoko's plight in *Okoge*, a pregnant, suddenly complacent Wei-Wei gives in to family pressures — and never gets her life back.

> "It takes a man to know what it is to be a real woman."
> —SONG LILING in *M. Butterfly*

Ironically, two gender-bending films in which men play men playing women reveal more about the mythology of the prized Asian woman and the superficial trappings of gender than most movies that star real women. The slow-moving *M. Butterfly* presents the ultimate object of Western male desire as the spy/opera diva Song Liling, a Suzie Wong/Lotus Blossom played by actor John Lone with a five o'clock shadow and bobbing Adam's apple. The best and most profound of these forays into cross-dressing is the spectacular melodrama *Farewell My Concubine*, directed by Chen Kaige. Banned in China, *Farewell My Concubine* shared the prize for Best Film at the 1993 Cannes Film Festival with Jane Campion's *The Piano*. Sweeping through fifty years of tumultuous history in China, the story revolves around the lives of two male Beijing Opera stars and the woman who marries one of them. The three characters make an unforgettable triangle, struggling over love, art, friendship, and politics against the bloody backdrop of cultural upheaval. They are as capable of casually betraying each other as they are of selfless, heroic acts. The androgynous Dieyi, doomed to play the same female role of concubine over and over again, is portrayed with great vulnerability, wit, and grace by male Hong Kong pop star Leslie Cheung. Dieyi competes with the prostitute Juxian (Gong Li) for the love of his childhood protector and fellow opera star, Duan Xiaolou (Zhang Fengyi).

Cheung's highly stylized performance as the classic concubine-ready-to-die-for-love in the opera within the movie is all about female artifice. His sidelong glances, restrained passion, languid stance, small steps, and delicate, refined gestures say everything about what is considered desirable in Asian women — and are the antithesis of the feisty, outspoken woman played by Gong Li. The characters of Dieyi and Juxian both see suffering as part and parcel of love and life. Juxian matter-of-factly says to Duan Xiaolou before he agrees to marry her: "I'm used to hardship. If you take me in, I'll wait on you hand and foot. If you tire of me, I'll . . . kill myself. No big deal." It's an echo of Suzie Wong's servility, but the context is new. Even with her back to the wall, Juxian is not helpless or whiny. She attempts to manipulate a man while admitting to the harsh reality that is her life.

Dieyi and Juxian are the two sides of the truth of women's lives in most Asian countries. Juxian in particular—wife and ex-prostitute—could be seen as a thankless and stereotypical role. But like the characters Gong Li has played in Chinese director Zhang Yimou's films, *Red Sorghum*, *Raise the Red Lantern*, and especially *The Story of Qiu Ju*, Juxian is tough, obstinate, sensual, clever, oafish, beautiful, infuriating, cowardly, heroic, and banal. Above all, she is resilient. Gong Li is one of the few Asian Pacific actors whose roles have been drawn with intelligence, honesty, and depth. Nevertheless, the characters she plays are limited by the possibilities that exist for real women in China. [20]

"Let's face it. Women still don't mean shit in China," my friend Mee-ling reminds me. What she says so bluntly about her culture rings painfully true, but in less obvious fashion for me. In the Philippines, infant girls aren't drowned, nor were their feet bound to make them more desirable. But sons were and are cherished. To this day, men of the bourgeois class are coddled and prized, much like the spoiled men of the elite household in *The Scent of Green Papaya*. We do not have a geisha tradition like Japan, but physical beauty is overtreasured. Our daughters are protected virgins or primed as potential beauty queens. And many of us have bought into the image of the white man as our handsome savior: G.I. Joe.

Buzz magazine recently featured an article entitled "Asian Women/L.A. Men," a report on a popular hangout that caters to white men's fantasies of nubile Thai women. The lines between movies and real life are blurred. Male screenwriters and cinematographers flock to this bar-restaurant, where the waitresses are eager to "audition" for roles. Many of these men have been to Bangkok while working on film crews for Vietnam War movies. They've come back to L.A., but for them, the movie never ends. In this particular fantasy the boys play G.I. Joe on a rescue mission in the urban jungle, saving the whore from herself. "A scene has developed here, a kind of R-rated *Cheers*," author Alan Rifkin writes. "The waitresses audition for sitcoms. The customers date the waitresses or just keep score."

Colonization of the imagination is a two-way street. And being enshrined on a pedestal as someone's Pearl of the Orient fantasy doesn't seem so demeaning, at first; who wouldn't want to be worshipped? Perhaps that's why Asian women are the ultimate wet dream in most Hollywood movies; it's no secret how well we've been taught to play the role, to take care of our men. In Hollywood vehicles, we are objects of desire or derision; we exist to provide sex, color, and texture in what is essentially a white man's world. It is akin to what Toni Morrison calls "the Africanist presence" in literature. She writes: "Just as entertainers, through or by association with blackface, could render permissible topics that otherwise would have been taboo, so American writers were able to employ an imagined Africanist persona to articulate and imaginatively act out the forbidden in American culture." The same analogy could be made for the often titillating presence of Asian women in movies made by white men.

Movies are still the most seductive and powerful of artistic mediums, manipulating us with ease by a powerful combination of sound and image. In many ways, as females and Asians, as audiences or performers, we have learned to settle for less—to accept the fact that we are either decorative, invisible, or one-dimensional. When there are characters who look like us represented in a movie, we have also learned to view between the lines, or to add what is missing. For many of us, this way of watching has always been a necessity. We fill in the gaps. If a female character is presented as a mute, willowy beauty, we convince ourselves she is an ancestral ghost—so smart she doesn't have to speak at all. If she is a whore with a heart of gold, we claim her as a tough feminist icon. If she is a sexless, sanitized, boring nerd, we embrace her as a role model for our daughters, rather than the tragic whore. And if she is presented as an utterly devoted saint suffering nobly in silence, we lie and say she is just like our mothers. Larger than life. Magical and insidious. A movie is never just a movie, after all.

READING THE TEXT

1. Summarize in your own words Hagedorn's view of the traditional images of Asian women as presented in American film.

2. What is the chronology of Asian women in film that Hagedorn presents, and why do you think she gives us a historical overview?

3. Why does Hagedorn say that the film *The Joy Luck Club* "carries a lot of cultural baggage" (para. 11)?

4. What sort of images of Asian women does Hagedorn imply that she would prefer to see?

READING THE SIGNS

1. Watch *The Joy Luck Club*, and write an essay in which you support, refute, or modify Hagedorn's interpretation of the film. Alternatively, view another film featuring Asian characters, such as *Better Luck Tomorrow* or *Gran Torino*, or a TV show with an Asian character, such as *The Big Bang Theory*, and use Hagedorn's article as a critical framework to evaluate your choice's representation of Asian characters.

2. **CONNECTING TEXTS** In class, form teams and debate the proposition that Hollywood writers and directors have a social responsibility to avoid stereotyping ethnic characters. To develop your team's arguments, brainstorm films that depict various ethnicities, and then discuss whether the portrayals are damaging or benign. You might also consult Michael Omi's "In Living Color: Race and American Culture" (p. 538).

3. Study a magazine that targets Asian American readers, such as *Tea*, *Hyphen*, or *Yolk*. Then write an essay in which you analyze whether Asian women in the magazine fit the stereotypes that Hagedorn describes, keeping in mind the magazine's intended readership (businessmen, twentysomethings of both sexes, and so forth).

4. **CONNECTING TEXTS** Watch one of the gender-bending films Hagedorn mentions (such as *M. Butterfly*), and write your own analysis of the gender roles portrayed in the film. To develop your ideas, consult Aaron Devor's "Gender Role Behaviors and Attitudes" (p. 504).

5. Few American films have featured Asian characters as protagonists. Watch an exception to this trend, *Harold & Kumar Go to White Castle* (2004), and write a semiotic analysis of the racial depictions in this film. To what extent does this film replicate or avoid the stereotypes Hagedorn discusses?

GENDER AND RACE IN FILM

HELENA ANDREWS

The Butler versus *The Help*: Gender Matters

> Though both movies shared much, including commercial success, *The Butler*, in Helena Andrews's words, was critically "toasted," while "*The Help* was trashed." Finding the critical dichotomy grounded in gender biases that undervalue "women's work" — the lead character in *The Help* is a maid — Andrews situates *The Butler* in a system of recent films featuring black men that give the benefit of the doubt to their lead characters, even as black actresses are still criticized for playing "mammy"-like roles. Helena Andrews is a contributing editor at *The Root*, where this article first appeared, and the author of *Bitch Is the New Black* (2011).

Like many of the films in the "it's complicated" historical-fiction genre, *Lee Daniels' The Butler* uses broad strokes to paint a decidedly unpretty picture — the cinematic equivalent of an Instagram filter.

But despite the artistic liberties and Forrest Gump–like rendering of the life of White House butler Cecil Gaines — based upon the true story of Eugene Allen — in its first week out *The Butler* has seemed to bob and weave past the reflexive reproof such movies usually attract.

Almost immediately, I noticed the stark difference in tone between critical discussion of *The Butler* and another similarly entitled film, *The Help*. Whereas this most recent film, jam-packed with big first names like Oprah, Cuba and Forest, has been toasted, *The Help* was trashed.

Early criticism of *The Help* — starring Viola Davis, who was nominated for an Academy Award for her leading role as Aibileen, a maid — was swift and unrelenting. As part of her publicity blitz in the lead up to the film's release and the ensuing awards season, Davis spent as much time defending her choice to play Aibileen as she did promoting the film.

In an interview with newsman Tavis Smiley—who pointedly told Davis   5
and her co-star, Octavia Spencer, "I want you to win, but I'm ambivalent
about what you are winning for"—Davis had to explain herself.

"The black artist cannot live in a place, in a revisionist place. The black
artist can only tell the truth about humanity, and humanity is messy, people
are messy," said Davis. At this point the actress had had a lot of practice being
on the defense.

"I've been under assault that the maid, the mammy, is a tired image,
to which I respond and have responded that I created a character, a human
being, and this is an important story to tell. It's an important dialogue to
have," said Davis in an interview with the *Wall Street Journal* right before the
2011 awards season.

None of Davis' defensive tactics have been necessary for Forest Whitaker
during the full-court publicity press for *The Butler*.

While on ABC's *The View*, Whitaker said early positive responses to the
film had been "universal." In an interview with the *New York Times*, the actor
was asked about his methods, how he was able to convey his character's
"pride and struggle," and not why he'd decided to take on such a role. *Rolling Stone* film critic Peter Travers asked Whitaker in an interview about the
research involved in playing Cecil Gaines.

So far the most popular sentiment from the film—repeated in several   10
interviews—is the notion that black domestics serving white families were, in
fact, subversive.

"Just by their presence, by their dignity, by their dedication to their work,
they were able to move things forward," explained Whitaker on *Good Morning
America*.

This is a radical shift in thought when applied to the debate about the
lack of nonstereotypical roles in mainstream Hollywood. From Hattie McDaniel onward, the debate about whether or not black actors and actresses (along
with screenwriters, directors and producers) should ever play the roles of the
maid or the butler has been ongoing. Davis couldn't escape the backlash for
her role in *The Help* in 2011, but just two years later Whitaker has.

The most obvious difference between Davis' Aibileen and Whitaker's
Cecil is the characters' gender. Then comes the issue of class and access. Aibileen is a maid in a middle-class enclave in Jackson, Miss., serving up chicken
salad and changing diapers. Cecil is a tuxedoed butler at the most famous
address in the United States, serving tea in fine china to the leaders of the free
world. They both wear the uniform. They both wear two faces.

But Aibileen's world is dominated by women. She does "women's
work"—cleaning, cooking, care-giving. Cecil, though just as invisible, occupies space crowded by men. He's "in service" and "serving his country," as
President Ronald Reagan (played by Alan Rickman) puts it.

I don't think it's too far of a stretch to think that for most—despite the   15
effusive testaments to the legacy of maids delivered by Oprah and the film's
director, Lee Daniels—the role of the maid, no matter how dignified, is still

considered less significant. It's a story that audiences, especially black ones, believe has been told before.

To be fair, *The Help* and *The Butler* are two distinct narratives. The white characters, though presidents and first ladies they may be, are ancillary to Cecil's story. *The Butler* is woven around Cecil's life. By contrast, in *The Help*, Aibileen's story is tightly tied to those of the white women around her, a narrative device that didn't sit well with some because it reinforces the notion that black women's stories cannot stand on their own.

Still, the onslaught of accolades for the recent batch of films starring black men in historically complicated roles, from Jamie Foxx's Django to Whitaker's Cecil and Chiwetel Ejiofor's Solomon Northup in the upcoming *12 Years a Slave*, says something about how films featuring black actresses in similarly uncomfortable roles are perceived. And in a creative landscape where Harriet Tubman gets a "sex tape" instead of a starring role, I'm not sure if it says something good.

READING THE TEXT

1. Summarize in your own words how the critical response to *The Butler* and *The Help* differed, in Andrews's estimation.

2. What does Viola Davis mean by saying, "The black artist cannot live . . . in a revisionist place" (para. 6)?

3. What evidence does Andrews provide to support her contention that attitudes toward gender and class have influenced the different responses to these two films?

4. Define in your own words the "mammy" (para. 6) role in films.

READING THE SIGNS

1. Analyze reviews of *The Butler* and *The Help* (using a site like Rotten Tomatoes), and write an essay in which you support, refute, or complicate Andrews's claims about the critical reception of these films. Alternatively, read reviews of another film focused on African American characters, such as *12 Years a Slave* (2013), and analyze their response to the portrayal of blacks in the film.

2. **CONNECTING TEXTS**   Andrews refers to an ongoing "debate about whether or not black actors and actresses (along with screenwriters, directors and producers) should ever play the roles of the maid or the butler" (para. 12). In an argumentative essay, present your own position in this debate, being sure to ground your claims in an analysis of specific characters. To develop your ideas, read Michael Omi's "In Living Color: Race and American Culture" (p. 538) and Matt Zoller Seitz's "The Offensive Movie Cliché That Won't Die" (p. 356).

3. **CONNECTING TEXTS**   Andrews suggests that attitudes toward class also influenced viewers' responses to *The Help* and *The Butler*. Adopting the perspective of Michael Parenti in "Class and Virtue" (p. 361), conduct your own analysis of how the two films use class-based signs to shape their characters' identities.

Lee Daniels' The Butler

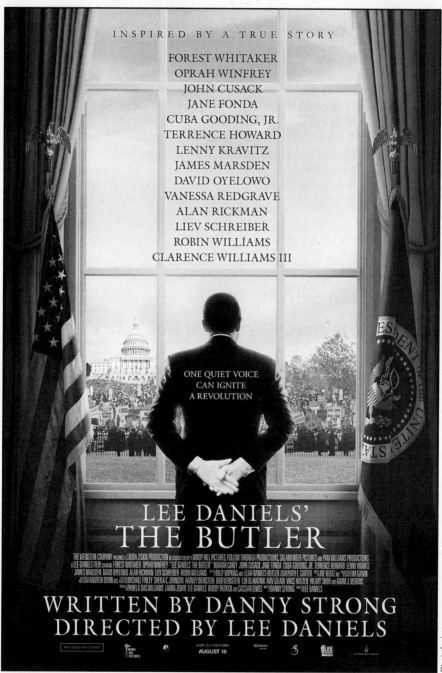

Reading the Signs

1. Based on this poster for *Lee Daniels' The Butler*, how would you characterize the subject matter of this film? Does the poster make you want to see the film? Why or why not?

2. If you have read Helena Andrews's "*The Butler* versus *The Help*: Gender Matters" (p. 352), then you already know a little bit about the plot of this film, the story of an African American White House butler. In your opinion, how is the central figure in the poster (the butler of the film's title) portrayed in the poster? What are we supposed to think about this character from the poster alone?

3. Judging from this poster for *The Butler*, who in your opinion is the intended audience for this film? Why? What elements in this poster appeal to that intended audience?

4. Consider the caption on this poster: "One quiet voice can ignite a revolution." In your opinion, is this caption effective as a teaser? Why or why not? How is the language in this caption designed to stoke interest in the film?

MATT ZOLLER SEITZ
The Offensive Movie Cliché That Won't Die

You've seen a satirical portrayal of him on *The Simpsons*, in the guise of Bleeding Gums Murphy, and he has appeared quite seriously in such movies as *The Legend of Bagger Vance*, *The Green Mile*, and *Legendary*. He's the "Magical Negro": "a saintly African American character who acts as a mentor to a questing white hero" in many recent movies. First identified as such by Spike Lee, as Matt Zoller Seitz observes in this critique of the character, the "Magical Negro" has his roots in such figures as Uncle Remus and Bill "Bojangles" Robinson, and his persistence in American popular culture can be read as a signifier of a larger cultural negotiation in which, Seitz argues, white America, finding itself no longer in complete control of the cultural and political agenda, is trying to strike a "deal." Matt Zoller Seitz is a freelance critic and film editor and the founder of the online publication *The House Next Door*.

"You always know the right things to say," says Cal Chetley (Devon Graye), the high school wrestler hero of *Legendary*, in conversation with Harry "Red" Newman (Danny Glover), a local fisherman.

The hero seems bewildered and delighted as he says this. He's about to compete in an important match, reeling from melodramatic blows. When

Harry shows up out of nowhere to give Cal a pep talk, the stage is set for a *Rocky*-style, go-the-distance ending. But if Cal had thought about Harry in terms of pop culture stereotypes, he could have answered his own implied question: *How come you're always there when I need you, even though I barely know you?* Harry seems to stand apart from the rest of the community, even though he's a familiar and beloved part of it. The only character who speaks to Harry directly is Cal, and their conversations are always about Cal and his well-being. He's such the benevolent guardian angel figure that the cynical viewer half-expects him to be revealed as a figment of Cal's imagination.

He's not imaginary. He's a "Magical Negro": a saintly African American character who acts as a mentor to a questing white hero, who seems to be disconnected from the community that he adores so much, and who often seems to have an uncanny ability to say and do exactly what needs to be said or done in order to keep the story chugging along in the hero's favor.

We have Spike Lee to thank for popularizing this politically incorrect but very useful term. Lee used it in a 2001 appearance at college campuses. He was blasting a then-recent wave of such characters, played by the likes of Cuba Gooding Jr., in *What Dreams May Come* (a spirit guide helping Robin Williams rescue his wife from Hell), Will Smith in *The Legend of Bagger Vance* (a sherpa-on-the-green, mentoring Matt Damon's golfer), Laurence Fishburne in *The Matrix* (Obi-Wan to Keanu Reeves' Luke Skywalker), and Michael Clarke Duncan in *The Green Mile* (a gentle giant on death row whose touch heals white folks' illnesses).

The word choice is deliberately anachronistic — "negro" started to fall out   5 of fashion about forty years ago. But that's why it's so devastating. The word "negro" was a transitional word that fell between the white-comforting "colored" and the more militantly self-determined and oppositional "black." It asked for dignity and autonomy without going that extra step asserting that it existed anyway, with or without white America's approval. "Negro" fits the sorts of characters that incensed Lee. Even though the movies take pains to insist that the African American character is as much a flesh-and-blood person as the white hero, the relationship is that of a master and servant. And not a *real* servant, either: one that really, truly lives to serve, has no life to speak of beyond his service to Da Man, and never seems to trouble himself with doubts about the cause to which he's devoting his time and energy. "How is it that black people have these powers but they use them for the benefit of white people?" Lee asked sarcastically.

The Magical Negro character (or as Lee called him, the "super-duper magical negro") wasn't invented in the 1990s. He's been around for at least a hundred years, accumulating enough examples (from Uncle Remus in *Song of the South* through the clock-keeper played by Bill Cobbs in *The Hudsucker Proxy*) to merit snarky lists, an entry in the urban dictionary, and a detailed Wikipedia page (turns out Stephen King's fiction has been a Magical Negro factory). The term gained an even wider audience when a candidate to chair the Republican National Committee mailed out a song titled "Barack the Magic Negro," with lyrics to the tune of the Peter, Paul and Mary hit. Outraged liberals

Photofest

A scene from *The Green Mile*.

focused on the surface racism encoded in the song title, ignoring the possibility that the song, however lead-footed in its humor, was rooted in something real.

What got lost in the flap over the song was the phrase's relevance to Obama's candidacy: There was (among Democrats, at least) a widespread sense that replacing George W. Bush with the Illinois senator would send a definitive signal that everything was different now, that it was time to rebuild, repair, rejuvenate, and move forward, not just toward a post-Bush society, but a post-racial one. It was an absurd hope, one that Obama himself seemed to resist endorsing at first, only to relent and begin publicly playing up his pioneer status as the first not-entirely-Caucasian man to pursue and then win the Democratic presidential nomination. Frequent *Salon* commenter

David Ehrenstein tackled this subject in a memorable 2007 *Los Angeles Times* piece that called Obama a "magic negro" almost a year before that RNC ditty appeared. Likening Obama to a spiritual descendant of the noble, kind-hearted, often sexless black men portrayed by pioneering leading man Sidney Poitier, he wrote, "Like a comic-book superhero, Obama is there to help, out of the sheer goodness of a heart we need not know or understand. For as with all Magic Negroes, the less real he seems, the more desirable he becomes."

Suffice to say Obama's election triggered a paroxysm of paranoia, insecurity, and rage in roughly half the population (maybe more, if polls on immigration and the Park51 project are to be believed). These flare-ups of privilege (wherein an almost entirely white sector of the populace descended from once-despised immigrants embraces the idea that "we" have to protect or reclaim "our" country from "them") cast retrospective light on the Magical Negro resurgence, which flowered in earnest during the last Democratic administration and has been going full-steam ever since.

Between demographers' projections of a twenty-first-century majority-minority swap, Clinton's unprecedented (un-presidented?) comfort with African American culture (which he made official during the 1992 campaign, in an effective bit of pandering stagecraft, by playing sax on *The Arsenio Hall Show*), and hip-hop's supplanting rock as the country's unofficial national soundtrack, there was a sense, even in the pre-Internet era, that the white man either wasn't in control anymore or soon wouldn't be. Whitey was just going to have to deal.

Things haven't played out quite so simply, of course. In every aspect of 10 quality of life that can be measured, nonwhite folks have always tended to be worse off than whites. That hasn't changed in the aughts, and the recession/depression has hit black men especially hard.

Looking back over the last twenty years' worth of cultural and demographic unrest, the M. N. phenomenon seems a form of psychological jujitsu — one that takes a subject that some white folks find unpleasant or even troubling to ponder (justifiably resentful black people's status in a country that, fifty years after the start of the modern civil rights struggle, is still run by, and mostly for, whites) and turns it into a source of gentle reassurance. Do "they" hate us? Oh, no! In fact, deep down they want "us" to succeed, and are happy to help "us" succeed, as long as we listen well and are polite. That's why Whoopi Goldberg put her life on hold to help Demi Moore get in touch with her dead boyfriend in *Ghost*, and Jennifer Hudson lived to serve Sarah Jessica Parker in the first *Sex and the City* movie. And it's why Danny Glover's character — one of but a few black men in an otherwise white town — takes such a keen interest in the life of a bantamweight high school wrestler who has apparently lived in the same town with Harry his entire life and recognizes him as a local eccentric, yet never bothered to get to know him before now.

People that enjoyed *Legendary* may say I'm being unfair to Harry, that there's more to him than Magical Negro-hood. And yes, it's true, at the end — spoiler alert! — we're told that he's not just a gravel-voiced sweetheart who likes to hang out by the local creek, catching fish and dispensing words of wisdom. He's actually quite influential — not *literally* magical, but nevertheless demi-godlike in his influence over the town and its history. But the specifics of Harry's character don't refute the label; quite the contrary. The revelation of Harry's influence is a nifty trick, one that's common in nearly all movies featuring nonwhite mentor/sidekick/deus ex machina characters. It seems appealing enough in the abstract. But it's weak soup when you look at such a character's role in the totality of the story.

Danny Glover, arguably one of cinema's most versatile and likable character actors, gets to play something close to God (he even narrates the story and turns out to have had a hand in three generations of local lives). But he doesn't get a good scene with anybody but the hero, doesn't get even the intimation of a private life, and barely speaks to anyone in the town that supposedly adores and respects him. Like the clock-tender in *The Hudsucker Proxy*, the HIV-stricken painter/saint from *In America*, and Ben Vereen's characters in *Pippin* and *All That Jazz*, Harry's aura of omnipotence is compensation for being shut out of the movie. It's a screenwriter's distraction that obscures the character's detachment from the heart of the narrative — and the character's essentially decorative nature. Like the hot-tempered black police captain who demands the maverick white detective's badge and the stern black woman judge who dresses down the kooky but irresponsible white heroine and warns her to get her life together, the Magical Negro is a glorified walk-on role, a narrative device with a pulse. The M. N. doesn't really drive the story, but is a glorified hood ornament attached to the end of a car that's being driven by white society, vigorously turning a little steering wheel that's not attached to anything.

Which might be a harsh but accurate metaphor for our current president, come to think of it.

READING THE TEXT

1. In your own words, define the term "Magical Negro" (para. 3). Why is it considered "anachronistic" (para. 5)?

2. What evidence does Seitz offer to suggest that the Danny Glover character in *Legendary* is a Magical Negro?

3. Why did some commentators dub Barack Obama, who was not a cinematic character, a Magical Negro during the 2008 presidential race?

4. Characterize Seitz's tone in this selection. In what ways does it affect your response to his argument?

READING THE SIGNS

1. Write your own interpretation of the representation of African American characters in *Legendary*, *Ghost*, *Sex in the City*, *All That Jazz*, or another film that Seitz refers to. To develop your ideas, consult Michael Omi's "In Living Color: Race and American Culture" (p. 538). To what extent do the characters in the

film you've selected display traits of "overt" or "inferential" racism, as Omi describes those concepts?

2. Both the Magical Negro and the black domestic servant are exaggerated versions of racial stereotypes. In class, compare and contrast these stereotypes. What underlying myths regarding racial difference do they display? Use your discussion to jump-start your own essay about the extent to which these stereotypes perpetuate racial myths. To develop your ideas, read Helena Andrews's "*The Butler* versus *The Help*: Gender Matters" (p. 352).

3. Seitz attributes the recurrence of the Magical Negro stereotype, in part, to concern about changing demographics whereby Caucasians would no longer be the dominant ethnic group in America. Considering today's political landscape, what signs do you see that support or complicate this explanation? Be sure to consider both national voting patterns and movements like the Tea Party.

4. Seitz comments parenthetically that "Stephen King's fiction has been a Magical Negro factory" (para. 6). Read at least one King novel that includes African American characters. Write an essay in which you support, refute, or modify this assertion.

5. Seitz is critical of the Magical Negro stereotype, but it has been argued that this particular representation of African Americans is a positive response to accusations that this demographic group too often is portrayed with overtly negative, violent stereotypes. Write an essay in which you evaluate this argument, taking care to base your claims on an analysis of specific films and characters.

MICHAEL PARENTI
Class and Virtue

In 1993, a movie called *Indecent Proposal* presented a story in which a billionaire offers a newly poor middle-class woman a million dollars if she'll sleep with him for one night. In Michael Parenti's terms, what was really indecent about the movie was the way it showed the woman falling in love with the billionaire, thus making a romance out of a class outrage. But the movie could get away with it, partly because Hollywood has always conditioned audiences to root for the ruling classes and to ignore the inequities of class privilege. In this selection from *Make-Believe Media: The Politics of Entertainment* (1992), Parenti argues that Hollywood has long been in the business of representing the interests of the ruling classes. Whether it is forgiving the classist behavior in *Pretty Woman* or glamorizing the lives of the wealthy, Hollywood makes sure its audiences leave the theater thinking you can't be too rich. Michael Parenti is a writer who lectures widely at university campuses around the country. His publications include *Power and the Powerless* (1978), *Inventing Reality: The Politics of the News Media* (1986), *Against Empire* (1995), *Dirty Truths* (1996), *America Besieged* (1998), *The Culture Struggle* (2006), *Democracy for the Few* (2007), *God and His Demons* (2010), *The Face of Imperialism* (2011), and *Waiting for Yesterday: Pages from a Street Kid's Life* (2013).

Class and Virtue

The entertainment media present working people not only as unlettered and uncouth but also as less desirable and less moral than other people. Conversely, virtue is more likely to be ascribed to those characters whose speech and appearance are soundly middle- or upper-middle class.

Even a simple adventure story like *Treasure Island* (1934, 1950, 1972) manifests this implicit class perspective. There are two groups of acquisitive persons searching for a lost treasure. One, headed by a squire, has money enough to hire a ship and crew. The other, led by the rascal Long John Silver, has no money — so they sign up as part of the crew. The narrative implicitly assumes from the beginning that the squire has a moral claim to the treasure, while Long John Silver's gang does not. After all, it is the squire who puts up the venture capital for the ship. Having no investment in the undertaking other than their labor, Long John and his men, by definition, will be "stealing" the treasure, while the squire will be "discovering" it.

To be sure, there are other differences. Long John's men are cutthroats. The squire is not. Yet, one wonders if the difference between a bad pirate and a good squire is itself not preeminently a matter of having the right amount of disposable income. The squire is no less acquisitive than the conspirators. He just does with money what they must achieve with cutlasses. The squire and his associates dress in fine clothes, speak an educated diction, and drink brandy. Long John and his men dress slovenly, speak in guttural accents, and drink rum. From these indications alone, the viewer knows who are the good guys and who are the bad. Virtue is visually measured by one's approximation to proper class appearances.

Sometimes class contrasts are juxtaposed within one person, as in *The Three Faces of Eve* (1957), a movie about a woman who suffers from multiple personalities. When we first meet Eve (Joanne Woodward), she is a disturbed, strongly repressed, puritanically religious person, who speaks with a rural, poor-Southern accent. Her second personality is that of a wild, flirtatious woman who also speaks with a rural, poor-Southern accent. After much treatment by her psychiatrist, she is cured of these schizoid personalities and emerges with a healthy third one, the real Eve, a poised, self-possessed, pleasant woman. What is intriguing is that she now speaks with a cultivated, affluent, Smith College accent, free of any low-income regionalism or ruralism, much like Joanne Woodward herself. This transformation in class style and speech is used to indicate mental health without any awareness of the class bias thusly expressed.

Mental health is also the question in *A Woman under the Influence* (1974), the story of a disturbed woman who is married to a hard-hat husband. He cannot handle—and inadvertently contributes to—her emotional deterioration. She is victimized by a spouse who is nothing more than an insensitive, working-class bull in a china shop. One comes away convinced that every unstable woman needs a kinder, gentler, and above all, more *middle-class* hubby if she wishes to avoid a mental crack-up.

Class prototypes abound in the 1980s television series *The A-Team*. In each episode, a Vietnam-era commando unit helps an underdog, be it a Latino immigrant or a disabled veteran, by vanquishing some menacing force such as organized crime, a business competitor, or corrupt government officials. As always with the make-believe media, the A-Team does good work on an individualized rather than collectively organized basis, helping particular victims by thwarting particular villains. The A-Team's leaders are two white males of privileged background. The lowest ranking members of the team, who do none of the thinking nor the leading, are working-class palookas. They show they are good with their hands, both by punching out the bad guys and by doing the maintenance work on the team's flying vehicles and cars. One of them, "B.A." (bad ass), played by the African American Mr. T., is visceral, tough, and purposely bad-mannered toward those he doesn't like. He projects an image of crudeness and ignorance and is associated with the physical side of things. In sum, the team has a brain (the intelligent white leaders) and a body with its simpler physical functions (the working-class characters), a hierarchy that corresponds to the social structure itself.[1]

Sometimes class bigotry is interwoven with gender bigotry, as in *Pretty Woman* (1990). A dreamboat millionaire corporate raider finds himself all alone for an extended stay in Hollywood (his girlfriend is unwilling to join him), so he quickly recruits a beautiful prostitute as his playmate of the month. She is paid three thousand dollars a week to wait around his super-posh hotel penthouse ready to perform the usual services and accompany him to business dinners at top restaurants. As prostitution goes, it is a dream gig. But there is one cloud on the horizon. She is low-class. She doesn't know which fork to use at those CEO power feasts, and she's bothersomely fidgety, wears tacky clothes, chews gum, and, y'know, doesn't talk so good. But with some tips from the hotel manager, she proves to be a veritable Eliza Doolittle in her class metamorphosis. She dresses in proper attire, sticks the gum away forever, and starts picking the right utensils at dinner. She also figures out how to speak a little more like Joanne Woodward without the benefit of a multiple personality syndrome, and she develops the capacity to sit in a poised, wordless, empty-headed fashion, every inch the expensive female ornament.

[1]Gina Marchetti, "Class, Ideology and Commercial Television: An Analysis of *The A-Team*," *Journal of Film and Video* 39, Spring 1987, pp. 19–28.

A scene from *Pretty Woman* (1990).

She is still a prostitute but a classy one. It is enough of a distinction for the handsome young corporate raider. Having liked her because she was charmingly cheap, he now loves her all the more because she has real polish and is a more suitable companion. So suitable that he decides to do the right thing by her: set her up in an apartment so he can make regular visits at regular prices. But now she wants the better things in life, like marriage, a nice house, and, above all, a different occupation, one that would allow her to use less of herself. She is furious at him for treating her like, well, a prostitute. She decides to give up her profession and get a high school diploma so that she might make a better life for herself—perhaps as a filing clerk or receptionist or some other of the entry-level jobs awaiting young women with high school diplomas.[2]

After the usual girl-breaks-off-with-boy scenes, the millionaire prince returns. It seems he can't concentrate on making money without her. He even abandons his cutthroat schemes and enters into a less lucrative but supposedly more productive, caring business venture with a struggling old-time entrepreneur. The bad capitalist is transformed into a good capitalist. He then carries off his ex-prostitute for a lifetime of bliss. The moral is a familiar one, updated for post-Reagan yuppiedom: A woman can escape from economic

[2]See the excellent review by Lydia Sargent, *Z Magazine*, April 1990, pp. 43–45.

and gender exploitation by winning the love and career advantages offered by a rich male. Sexual allure goes only so far unless it develops a material base and becomes a class act.[3]

READING THE TEXT

1. According to Parenti, what characteristics are typically attributed to working-class and upper-class film characters?

2. How does Parenti see the relationship between "class bigotry" and "gender bigotry" (para. 7) in *Pretty Woman*?

3. What relationship does Parenti see between mental health and class values in films?

READING THE SIGNS

1. Watch *Wall Street*, *Unstoppable*, or *The Fighter*, and analyze the class issues that the movie raises. Alternatively, watch an episode of *The Apprentice*, and perform the same sort of analysis.

2. Do you agree with Parenti's interpretation of *Pretty Woman*? Write an argumentative essay in which you defend, challenge, or complicate his reading of the film.

3. CONNECTING TEXTS   Read Aaron Devor's "Gender Role Behaviors and Attitudes" (p. 504). How would Devor explain the gender bigotry that Parenti finds in *Pretty Woman*?

4. Watch the 1954 film *On the Waterfront* with your class. How are labor unions and working-class characters portrayed in that film? Does the film display the class bigotry that Parenti describes?

5. CONNECTING TEXTS   Read Michael Omi's "In Living Color: Race and American Culture" (p. 538). Then write an essay in which you create a category of cinematic racial bigotry that corresponds to Parenti's two categories of class and gender bigotry. What films have you seen that illustrate your new category?

[3]Ibid.

DAVID DENBY

High-School Confidential: Notes on Teen Movies

Face it: High school for most of us is one extended nightmare, a long-playing drama starring cheerleaders and football players who sneer at the mere mortals who must endure their haughty reign. So it's little wonder that, as David Denby argues in this *New Yorker* essay from 1999, teen movies so often feature loathsome cheerleaders and football stars who, one way or another, get theirs in this ever-popular movie genre. Indeed, Denby asks, "Who can doubt where Hollywood's twitchy, nearsighted writers and directors ranked—or feared they ranked—on the high-school totem pole?" Nerds at the bottom, where else, like the millions of suffering kids who flock to their films. A staff writer and film critic for the *New Yorker*, David Denby is the author of *The Great Books: My Adventures with Homer, Rousseau, Woolf, and Other Indestructible Writers of the Western World* (1996), *American Sucker* (2003), and *Snark: It's Mean, It's Personal, and It's Ruining Our Conversation* (2009).

The most hated young woman in America is a blonde—well, sometimes a redhead or a brunette, but usually a blonde. She has big hair flipped into a swirl of gold at one side of her face or arrayed in a sultry mane, like the magnificent pile of a forties movie star. She's tall and slender, with a waist as supple as a willow, but she's dressed in awful, spangled taste: her outfits could have been put together by warring catalogues. And she has a mouth on her, a low, slatternly tongue that devastates other kids with such insults as "You're vapor, you're Spam!" and "Do I look like Mother Teresa? If I did, I probably wouldn't mind talking to the geek squad." She has two or three friends exactly like her, and together they dominate their realm—the American high school as it appears in recent teen movies. They are like wicked princesses, who enjoy the misery of their subjects. Her coronation, of course, is the senior prom, when she expects to be voted "most popular" by her class. But, though she may be popular, she is certainly not liked, so her power is something of a mystery. She is beautiful and rich, yet in the end she is preëminent because . . . she is preëminent, a position she works to maintain with Joan Crawford–like tenacity. Everyone is afraid of her; that's why she's popular.

She has a male counterpart. He's usually a football player, muscular but dumb, with a face like a beer mug and only two ways of speaking—in a conspiratorial whisper, to a friend; or in a drill sergeant's sudden bellow. If her weapon is the snub, his is the lame but infuriating prank—the can of Sprite emptied into a knapsack, or something sticky, creamy, or adhesive deposited in a locker. Sprawling and dull in class, he comes alive in the halls and in the cafeteria. He hurls people against lockers; he spits, pours, and sprays; he has a projectile relationship with food. As the crown prince, he claims the best-looking girl for himself, though in a perverse display of power he may invite an outsider or an awkward girl — a "dog" — to the prom, setting her up for some special humiliation. When we first see him, he is riding high, and virtually the entire school colludes in his tyranny. No authority figure — no teacher or administrator — dares correct him.

Thus the villains of the recent high-school movies. Not every American teen movie has these two characters, and not every social queen or jock shares all the attributes I've mentioned. (Occasionally, a handsome, dark-haired athlete can be converted to sweetness and light.) But as genre figures these two types are hugely familiar; that is, they are a common memory, a collective trauma, or at least a social and erotic fantasy. Such movies of the past year [1999] as *Disturbing Behavior*, *She's All That*, *Ten Things I Hate about You*, and *Never Been Kissed* depend on them as stock figures. And they may have been figures in the minds of the Littleton shooters, Eric Harris and Dylan Klebold, who imagined they were living in a school like the one in so many of these movies — a poisonous system of status, snobbery, and exclusion.

Do genre films reflect reality? Or are they merely a set of conventions that refer to other films? Obviously, they wouldn't survive if they didn't provide emotional satisfaction to the people who make them and to the audiences who watch them. A half century ago, we didn't need to see ten Westerns a year in order to learn that the West got settled. We needed to see it settled ten times a year in order to provide ourselves with the emotional gratifications of righteous violence. By drawing his gun only when he was provoked, and in the service of the good, the classic Western hero transformed the gross tangibles of the expansionist drive (land, cattle, gold) into a principle of moral order. The gangster, by contrast, is a figure of chaos, a modern, urban person, and in the critic Robert Warshow's formulation he functions as a discordant element in an American society devoted to a compulsively "positive" outlook. When the gangster dies, he cleanses viewers of their own negative feelings.

High-school movies are also full of unease and odd, mixed-up emotions. 5 They may be flimsy in conception; they may be shot in lollipop colors, garlanded with mediocre pop scores, and cast with goofy young actors trying to make an impression. Yet this most commercial and frivolous of genres harbors a grievance against the world. It's a very specific grievance, quite different from the restless anger of such fifties adolescent-rebellion movies as *The Wild One*, in which someone asks Marlon Brando's biker "What are you rebelling against?" and the biker replies "What have you got?" The fifties teen outlaw was against anything that adults considered sacred. But no movie teenager now revolts against adult authority, for the simple reason that adults have no authority. Teachers are rarely more than a minimal, exasperated presence, administrators get turned into a joke, and parents are either absent or distantly benevolent. It's a teen world, bounded by school, mall, and car, with occasional moments set in the fast-food outlets where the kids work, or in the kids' upstairs bedrooms, with their pinups and rack stereo systems. The enemy is not authority; the enemy is other teens and the social system that they impose on one another.

The bad feeling in these movies may strike grownups as peculiar. After all, from a distance American kids appear to be having it easy these days. The teen audience is facing a healthy job market; at home, their parents are stuffing the den with computers and the garage with a bulky SUV. But most teens aren't thinking about the future job market. Lost in the eternal swoon of late adolescence, they're thinking about their identity, their friends, and their clothes. Adolescence is the present-tense moment in American life. Identity and status are fluid: abrupt, devastating reversals are always possible. (In a teen movie, a guy who swallows a bucket of cafeteria coleslaw can make himself a hero in an instant.) In these movies, accordingly, the senior prom is the equivalent of the shoot-out at the O.K. Corral; it's the moment when one's worth as a human being is settled at last. In the rather pedestrian new comedy *Never Been Kissed*, Drew Barrymore, as a twenty-five-year-old newspaper reporter, goes back to high school pretending to be a student, and immediately falls into her old, humiliating pattern of trying to impress the good-looking rich kids. Helplessly, she pushes for approval, and even gets herself chosen prom queen before finally coming to her senses. She finds it nearly impossible to let go.

Genre films dramatize not what happens but how things feel — the emotional coloring of memory. They fix subjectivity into fable. At actual schools, there is no unitary system of status; there are many groups to be a part of, many places to excel (or fail to excel), many avenues of escape and self-definition. And often the movies, too, revel in the arcana of high-school cliques. In last summer's *Disturbing Behavior*, a veteran student lays out the cafeteria ethnography for a newcomer: Motorheads, Blue Ribbons, Skaters, Micro-geeks ("drug of choice: Stephen Hawking's *A Brief History of Time* and a cup of jasmine tea on Saturday night"). Subjectively, though, the social system in *Disturbing Behavior* (a high-school version of *The Stepford Wives*) and in the other movies still feels coercive and claustrophobic: humiliation is the most vivid emotion of youth, so in memory it becomes the norm.

The movies try to turn the tables. The kids who cannot be the beautiful ones, or make out with them, or avoid being insulted by them — these are the heroes of the teen movies, the third in the trio of character types. The female outsider is usually an intellectual or an artist. (She scribbles in a diary, she draws or paints.) Physically awkward, she walks like a seal crossing a beach, and is prone to drop her books and dither in terror when she stands before a handsome boy. Her clothes, which ignore mall fashion, scandalize the social queens. Like them, she has a tongue, but she's tart and grammatical, tending toward feminist pungency and precise diction. She may mask her sense of vulnerability with sarcasm or with Plathian rue (she's stuck in the bell jar), but even when she lashes out she can't hide her craving for acceptance.

The male outsider, her friend, is usually a mass of stuttering or giggling sexual gloom: he wears shapeless clothes; he has an undeveloped body, either stringy or shrimpy; he's sometimes a Jew (in these movies, still the generic outsider). He's also brilliant, but in a morose, preoccupied way that suggests masturbatory absorption in some arcane system of knowledge. In a few special cases, the outsider is not a loser but a disengaged hipster, either saintly or satanic. (Christian Slater has played this role a couple of times.) This outsider wears black and keeps his hair long, and he knows how to please women. He sees through everything, so he's ironic by temperament and genuinely indifferent to the opinion of others — a natural aristocrat, who transcends the school's contemptible status system. There are whimsical variations on the outsider figure, too. In the recent *Rushmore*, an obnoxious teen hero, Max Fischer (Jason Schwartzman), runs the entire school: he can't pass his courses but he's a dynamo at extracurricular activities, with a knack for staging extraordinary events. He's a con man, a fund-raiser, an entrepreneur — in other words, a contemporary artist.

In fact, the entire genre, which combines self-pity and ultimate vindication, might be called "Portrait of the Filmmaker as a Young Nerd." Who can doubt where Hollywood's twitchy, nearsighted writers and directors ranked — or feared they ranked — on the high-school totem pole? They are still angry, though occasionally the target of their resentment goes beyond the jocks and cheerleaders of their youth. Consider this anomaly: the young actors and models on the covers of half the magazines published in this country, the shirtless men with chests like burnished shields, the girls smiling, glowing, tweezed, full-lipped, full-breasted (but not too full), and with skin so honeyed that it seems lacquered — these are the physical ideals embodied by the villains of the teen movies. The social queens and jocks, using their looks to dominate others, represent an American barbarism of beauty. Isn't it possible that the detestation of them in teen movies is a veiled strike at the entire abs-hair advertising culture, with its unobtainable glories of perfection? A critic of consumerism might even see a spark of revolt in these movies. But only a spark.

My guess is that these films arise from remembered hurts which then get recast in symbolic form. For instance, a surprising number of the outsider heroes have no mother. Mom has died or run off with another man; her child, only half loved, is ill equipped for the emotional pressures of school. The motherless child, of course, is a shrewd commercial ploy that makes a direct appeal to the members of the audience, many of whom may feel like outsiders, too, and unloved, or not loved enough, or victims of some prejudice or exclusion. But the motherless child also has powers, and will someday be a success, an artist, a screenwriter. It's the wound and the bow all over again, in cargo pants.

As the female nerd attracts the attention of the handsomest boy in the senior class, the teen movie turns into a myth of social reversal — a Cinderella fantasy. Initially, his interest in her may be part of a stunt or a trick: he is leading her on, perhaps at the urging of his queenly girlfriend. But his gaze lights her up, and we see how attractive she really is. Will she fulfill the eternal American fantasy that you can vault up the class system by removing your specs? She wants her prince, and by degrees she wins him over, not just with her looks but with her superior nature, her essential goodness. In the male version of the Cinderella trip, a few years go by, and a pale little nerd (we see him at a reunion) has become rich. All that poking around with chemicals paid off. Max Fischer, of *Rushmore*, can't miss being richer than Warhol.

So the teen movie is wildly ambivalent. It may attack the consumerist ethos that produces winners and losers, but in the end it confirms what it is attacking. The girls need the seal of approval conferred by the converted jocks; the nerds need money and a girl. Perhaps it's no surprise that the outsiders can be validated only by the people who ostracized them. But let's not be too schematic: the outsider who joins the system also modifies it, opens it up to the creative power of social mobility, makes it bend and laugh, and perhaps this turn of events is not so different from the way things work in the real world, where merit and achievement stand a good chance of trumping appearance. The irony of the Littleton shootings is that Klebold and Harris, who were both proficient computer heads, seemed to have forgotten how the plot turns out. If they had held on for a few years they might have been working at a hip software company, or have started their own business, while the jocks who oppressed them would probably have wound up selling insurance or used cars. That's the one unquestionable social truth the teen movies reflect: geeks rule.

There is, of course, a menacing subgenre, in which the desire for revenge turns bloody. Thirty-one years ago, Lindsay Anderson's semi-surrealistic *If . . .* was set in an oppressive, class-ridden English boarding school, where a group of rebellious students drive the school population out into a courtyard and open fire on them with machine guns. In Brian De Palma's 1976 masterpiece *Carrie*, the pale, repressed heroine, played by Sissy Spacek, is courted at last by a handsome boy but gets violated—doused with pig's blood—just as she is named prom queen. Stunned but far from powerless, Carrie uses her telekinetic powers to set the room afire and burn down the school. *Carrie* is the primal school movie, so wildly lurid and funny that it exploded the clichés of the genre before the genre was quite set: The heroine may be a wrathful avenger, but the movie, based on a Stephen King book, was clearly a grinning-gargoyle fantasy. So, at first, was *Heathers*, in which Christian Slater's satanic outsider turns out to be a true devil. He and his girlfriend (played by a very young Winona Ryder) begin gleefully knocking off the rich, nasty girls and the jocks, in ways so patently absurd that their revenge seems a mere wicked dream. I think it's unlikely that these movies had a direct effect on the actions of the Littleton shooters, but the two boys would surely have recognized the emotional world of *Heathers* and *Disturbing Behavior* as their own. It's a place where feelings of victimization join fantasy, and you experience the social élites as so powerful that you must either become them or kill them.

But enough. It's possible to make teen movies that go beyond these fixed   15
polarities — insider and outsider, blond-bitch queen and hunch-shouldered nerd. In Amy Heckerling's 1995 comedy *Clueless*, the big blonde played by Alicia Silverstone is a Rodeo Drive clotheshorse who is nonetheless possessed of extraordinary virtue. Freely dispensing advice and help, she's almost ironically good — a designing goddess with a cell phone. The movie offers a sunshiny satire of Beverly Hills affluence, which it sees as both absurdly swollen and generous in spirit. The most original of the teen comedies, *Clueless* casts away self-pity. So does *Romy and Michele's High School Reunion* (1997), in which two gabby, lovable friends, played by Mira Sorvino and Lisa Kudrow, review the banalities of their high-school experience so knowingly that they might be criticizing the teen-movie genre itself. And easily the best American film of the year so far is Alexander Payne's *Election*, a high-school movie that inhabits a different aesthetic and moral world altogether from the rest of these pictures. *Election* shreds everyone's fantasies and illusions in a vision of high school that is bleak but supremely just. The movie's villain, an overachieving girl (Reese Witherspoon) who runs for class president, turns out to be its covert heroine, or, at least, its most poignant character. A cross between Pat and Dick Nixon, she's a lower-middle-class striver who works like crazy and never wins anyone's love. Even when she's on top, she feels excluded. Her loneliness is produced not by malicious cliques but by her own implacable will, a condition of the spirit that may be as comical and tragic as it is mysterious. *Election* escapes all the clichés; it graduates into art.

READING THE TEXT

1. Describe in your own words the stereotypical male and female villains common in teen movies.

2. What does Denby mean by the comment, "Adolescence is the present-tense moment in American life" (para. 6)?

3. What sort of characters are typically the heroes in teen films, in Denby's view?

4. In what ways does a Cinderella fantasy influence teen films?

5. What is the "menacing subgenre" (para. 14) of teen movies?

READING THE SIGNS

1. Using Denby's description of stock character types in teen movies as your critical framework, analyze the characters in a teen TV program, such as *The Carrie Diaries*, *Awkward*, or *90210*. Do you see the same conventions at work? How do you account for any differences you might see?

2. In class, brainstorm a list of current teen films. Then, using the list as evidence, write an essay in which you assess the validity of Denby's claim: "The

enemy [in teen films] is not authority; the enemy is other teens and the social system that they impose on one another" (para. 5).

3. Watch *The Perks of Being a Wallflower* (2012), and write an essay in which you argue whether it can be categorized as a teen film, at least as Denby defines the genre.

4. Denby asks, "Do genre films reflect reality? Or are they merely a set of conventions that refer to other films?" (para. 4). Write an essay in which you propose your own response to these questions, using as evidence your high school experience and specific teen films. In addition, you can consider as evidence teen-based TV programs such as *Glee*.

MICHAEL AGRESTA
How the Western Was Lost — and Why It Matters

The Western, once one of Hollywood's favorite and most reliable film genres, is in trouble. With such highly promoted box-office disappointments as *The Lone Ranger* (2013) and *Cowboys & Aliens* (2011), among others, the Western just isn't what it was. In this analysis of both the genre and the particular example of *The Lone Ranger*, Michael Agresta sets out to determine what happened. The trouble, primarily, is history, because while the Western is all about history, that history, in Agresta's words, has become "embarrassing to us." The conquest of the West was a messy, and racist, process, so toxic a subject that any film that takes it on has to use extraordinary measures (as, for example, transporting it to another planet, like *Avatar*'s Pandora) to save it. Hi-ho, Silver, away! A freelance writer on popular culture and the arts, Michael Agresta has written for such publications as *Slate*, the *Wall Street Journal*, and the *Atlantic*, where this selection originally appeared.

The Lone Ranger's failure at the box office earlier this month not only dealt a blow to mega-budget Hollywood blockbusters, Johnny Depp's career, and Disney. The Jerry Bruckheimer–Gore Verbinski flop — which cost a reported $250 million to make and brought in just $50 million opening on a holiday weekend — also may mark a decisive chapter in the sad story of how the Western was lost.

Since the dawn of film, the Western has been one of the great, durable movie genres, but its audience seems to be finally drying up. *The Lone Ranger* is the third Western to flop in four summers, and the most expensive, capping a trend set by *Cowboys & Aliens* and *Jonah Hex*. (Remember them? Exactly.) Western fans are getting older and whiter with respect to the overall population, and as any Republican political consultant will tell you, that doesn't bode well for the future. Other, newer genres like superhero movies and fighting-robot flicks have cowboy movies outgunned with younger generations and international audiences.

Now the genre finds itself in the ironic position of needing a hero to save it, and quick. If *The Lone Ranger* goes down in history as the last of the big-budget oaters, it'll be a sad milestone for moviemaking — and for America. For a century plus, we have relied on Westerns to teach us our history and reflect our current politics and our place in the world. We can ill afford to lose that mirror now, especially just because we don't like what we see staring back at us.

Westerns provide many timeless pleasures — tough guy heroes, action set pieces on horseback, adventures in magnificent landscapes, good triumphing over evil. It's all there already in arguably the first narrative film ever made, *The Great Train Robbery*.

But to discuss Westerns as if they just boiled down to heroic stories of 5 saving the homestead from savages, tracking the bad guy through the wilderness, or finding the treasure in the mountains would be to miss the real meaning of the genre. Westerns have earned their place at the heart of the national culture and American iconography abroad because they've provided a reliable vehicle for filmmakers to explore thorny issues of American history and character. In the enduring examples of the genre, the real threat to the homestead, we learn, is an economic system that is being rigged for the wealthy, or the search for the bad guy becomes a search for meaning in a culture of violent retribution, or the treasure of the Sierra Madre is a diabolical mirage of the American dream.

Through the past century of Western movies, we can trace America's self-image as it evolved from a rough-and-tumble but morally confident outsider in world affairs to an all-powerful sheriff with a guilty conscience. After World War I and leading into World War II, Hollywood specialized in tales of heroes taking the good fight to savage enemies and saving defenseless settlements in the process. In the Great Depression especially, as capitalism and American exceptionalism came under question, the cowboy hero was often mistaken for a criminal and forced to prove his own worthiness — which he inevitably did. Over the '50s, '60s, and '70s however, as America enforced its dominion over half the planet with a long series of coups, assassinations, and increasingly dubious wars, the figure of the cowboy grew darker and more complicated. If you love Westerns, most of your favorites are probably from this era — *Shane*, *The Searchers*, *Butch Cassidy and the Sundance Kid*, *McCabe & Mrs. Miller*, the spaghetti westerns, etc. By the height of the Vietnam protest era, cowboys were antiheroes as often as they were heroes.

The dawn of the 1980s brought the inauguration of Ronald Reagan and the box-office debacle of the artsy, overblown *Heaven's Gate*. There's a sense of disappointment to the decade that followed, as if the era of revisionist Westerns had failed and a less nuanced patriotism would have to carry the day. Few memorable Westerns were made in the '80s, and Reagan himself proudly associated himself with an old-fashioned, pre-Vietnam cowboy image. But victory in the Cold War coincided with a revival of the genre, including the revisionist strain, exemplified in Clint Eastwood's career-topping *Unforgiven*. A new, gentler star emerged in Kevin Costner, who scored a post-colonial megahit with *Dances with Wolves*. Later, in the 2000s, George W. Bush reclaimed the image of the cowboy for a foreign policy far less successful than Reagan's, and the genre retreated to the art house again.

Under the presidency of Barack Obama, there has been a short-lived Western revival that would seem to match America's tentative new moral authority. If the genre in this era can be said to have a unifying aim, it's to divest itself and its audiences of a strictly white, male, heterosexual perspective on history, and by extension on present day conflicts. *Cowboys & Aliens* is a cynical attempt at a post-racial Western — just take the Indians out of the equation so we can be good guys again! — but with more sincerity. *True Grit*, *Django Unchained*, and now *The Lone Ranger* have all put non-male, non-white perspectives front and center. (Two other notable movies from the past 15 years, the wonderful *Brokeback Mountain* and the awful *Wild Wild West*, also fit this model.) It's worth pointing out, however, that all of these examples (except *Brokeback Mountain*) were directed by white men, and *The Lone Ranger* has Tonto played by an actor with only the slightest claim to American Indian ancestry.

Although end-of-year prestige movies like *True Grit* and *Django Unchained* have broken through to achieve critical acclaim, Oscars, and substantial return on investment, the Obama era has not been kind to newfangled Westerns that aimed for large audiences. Exacerbating the problem is the rejection of cowboy movies by international audiences, particularly the Chinese. So even as filmmakers have become more interested in incorporating a diversity of viewpoints, they have hit against what appears a global demographic ceiling. It's another reason why *The Lone Ranger* will probably be the last attempt to build a true summer tent-pole in the genre.

Nobody likes a weak ending, and this is especially true for cowboy movies. [10] A sad outcome we can accept, even the death of a genre, but at least let our hero meet his challenge, fulfill his destiny, stand his (or her) ground. Watching *The Lone Ranger* slink off into the sunset, it's hard to feel any sense of resolution for the Western.

It's always difficult to diagnose the reason for a movie's success or failure. Did the audience dislike what *The Lone Ranger* tried to do, or the fact that it executed its aims poorly? Since it bombed definitively on opening weekend (long before China got a look at it, too) it seems safest to base conclusions in part on the movie's advertising and the media storylines surrounding its release.

Armie Hammer and Johnny Depp in *The Lone Ranger* (2013).

Three contributing factors stand out. First, there was some coverage of an outcry about racism in Depp's portrayal of Tonto, which conceivably made audiences less comfortable laughing along with the pidgin English. Second, advertising leaned heavily on the association with the *Pirates of the Caribbean* franchise, touting the movie as a family-friendly adventure yarn, but word quickly spread that *The Lone Ranger* was not safe for kids. Finally, the 149-minute runtime can't have helped.

The irony is that the very factors that helped make *The Lone Ranger* a bomb also helped make it much more interesting than typical summer fare. (Mild spoilers follow.) The runtime ballooned because the filmmakers wouldn't dispense with a time-consuming framing story that shows Depp's Tonto, in old-man makeup and a historically inappropriate headdress, wilting away inside a Museum of Natural History–style display called "The Noble Savage in His Native Habitat." The scenes deemed unsafe for children included two graphic depictions of American Indian genocide. The character of Tonto came to the filmmakers with heavy racist baggage, and, rather than tossing him out altogether, they took on the challenge of trying to carry that baggage while walking the tightrope of commenting on a stereotype through the performance of that same stereotype.

This is not to say that any of these bold moves are executed adeptly. The framing story never goes anywhere; the Indian genocide scenes are distastefully incidental to the plot, especially one scene of mass slaughter that provides the heroes cover to get out of a pickle; Depp's winking performance is still fundamentally problematic, as if he or any other white actor had done a modern Mr. Bojangles, blackface and all, and tried to get actual laughs out of it.

Still, in simple terms, *The Lone Ranger* went there. And there. And over there. *The Lone Ranger* did not fail for being timid. In this cautious, sequel-dominated era of summer movies, that's a recommendation in itself. Even if they weren't particularly clever about it, Verbinski and his collaborators deserve credit for engaging critically with the history involved, both the 19th-century Indian massacres and the legacy of racism from the early 20th-century source material.   15

This is also a tribute to the genre. The ground rules of the Western more or less forced Verbinski and company into that treacherous territory. They could make, say, a movie about Caribbean pirates without addressing the slave trade, even though such pirates often held slaves as cargo. That's fine, because pirate movies are about gold, not slaves. Everyone knows that. Westerns, on the contrary, are traditionally about cowboys and Indians, or at least homesteaders and land and railroad barons, the kinds of men who built the cities we live in today.

It's the task of Westerns to address that history, even as decade by decade that history becomes more and more embarrassing to us. In theory, it's a beautiful thing, though in practice it means cowboy movies are easy to bungle, because by now they all take place on contested ground. Every Western must find its own way to reconcile itself to the founding contradictions of America. A certain kind of escapism becomes impossible.

Unless, of course, we stop making and watching Westerns. The genres that currently rule the box office do other things well—sci-fi movies can address the ecological crisis and challenges of new technology, for instance, and superhero movies can provide never-ending glosses on the core myth of American exceptionalism—but none are particularly engaged with history, especially pre–World War II. And none can boast the richness of symbolic language developed by Westerns over the course of a century at the heart of film culture.

It would be a terrible thing to give up on that language, especially now, in the wake of *The Lone Ranger*'s failure. Isn't there anyone, perhaps a female or non-white director, capable of making a great mass-audience Western for the Obama era? Or, if it's too late for that, then for whatever era comes next? If neither, here's hoping that filmmakers will keep trying at the art-house level and on cable television.

The other great theme of the Western, after that of the conquering of native peoples and the establishment of civilization in the desert, is that of loss and of nostalgia for a certain way of life—the early freedoms of the West, the idea of riding across an unfenced landscape, the infinite possibilities of the frontier. That "West," of course, is already gone, fallen, conquered. It has been for decades, even though holding onto some sense of it seems crucial to   20 our identity as Americans. Movie Westerns have been tracking that loss for a century.

Now, as *The Lone Ranger* leaves theaters this month, that sense of loss begins to expand to cowboy movies themselves. The train is leaving the station, and the thing we rely on to help make sense of ourselves in the world is tied to the tracks. Is there a hero on the horizon?

READING THE TEXT

1. Why does Agresta say that the Western has been "a reliable vehicle for film-makers to explore thorny issues of American history and character" (para. 5)?
2. In your own words, trace the history of the American Western, as Agresta describes it.
3. What does the term "American exceptionalism" (para. 18) mean?
4. In what ways have modern Westerns changed the motifs and patterns of classic Westerns?
5. According to Agresta, why was 2013's *The Lone Ranger* a box-office failure?

READING THE SIGNS

1. Watch *The Lone Ranger*, and write an essay in which you take on Agresta's contention that "the very factors that helped make *The Lone Ranger* a bomb also helped make it much more interesting than typical summer fare" (para. 13).
2. **CONNECTING TEXTS**   Watch one of the recent films that Agresta mentions, such as *Django Unchained* (2012) or *Brokeback Mountain* (2005), and write a semiotic analysis of the film's depiction of race relations. To develop your ideas, read Michael Omi's "In Living Color: Race and American Culture" (p. 538).
3. Write a semiotic analysis of *Avatar* (2009). In what ways does it resemble a conventional Western? How does it differ? Alternatively, write an essay that asks the same questions of the TV show *The Walking Dead*.
4. Both Agresta and Christine Folch ("Why the West Loves Sci-Fi and Fantasy: A Cultural Explanation," p. 378) offer cultural explanations for what Americans find most compelling in films. Write an essay in which you synthesize their views, developing your own cultural explanations as well.

CHRISTINE FOLCH

Why the West Loves Sci-Fi and Fantasy: A Cultural Explanation

> Hollywood loves sci-fi and fantasy; Bollywood doesn't. Just why the Indian movie industry (which is the world's largest) is so uninterested in fantasy is an anthropological question that Christine Folch sets out to answer in this *Atlantic* analysis. The key, Folch believes, lies in history, a history that in the West has included a post-Enlightenment reign of scientific rationalism that has led to a general disenchantment with things-as-they-are, which fantasy strives to reverse by "re-enchant[ing] the world." Experiencing a different kind of history without this disenchantment, Indians, Folch suggests, feel no need for cinematic fantasy, so Bollywood doesn't bother much with it. Christine Folch is an assistant professor of anthropology at Wheaton College.

Hollywood's had a long love affair with sci-fi and fantasy, but the romance has never been stronger than it is today. A quick glance into bookstores, television lineups, and upcoming films shows that the futuristic and fantastical is everywhere in American pop culture. In fact, of Hollywood's top earners since 1980, a mere eight have *not* featured wizardry, space or time travel, or apocalyptic destruction caused by aliens/zombies/Robert Downey Jr.'s acerbic wit. Now, with *Man of Steel*, it appears we will at last have an effective reboot of the most important superhero story of them all.

These tales of mystical worlds and improbable technological power appeal universally, right? Maybe not. Bollywood, not Hollywood, is the largest movie industry in the world. But only a handful of its top hits of the last four decades have dealt with science fiction themes, and even fewer are fantasy or horror. American films in those genres make much of their profits abroad, but they tend to underperform in front of Indian audiences.

This isn't to say that there aren't folk tales with magic and mythology in India. There are. That makes their absence in Bollywood and their overabundance in Hollywood all the more remarkable. Whereas Bollywood takes quotidian family dramas and imbues them with spectacular tales of love and wealth found-lost-regained amidst the pageantry of choreographed dance pieces, Hollywood goes to the supernatural and futurism. It's a sign that longing for mystery is universal, but the taste for science fiction and fantasy is cultural.

Cultural differences are fascinating because even as we learn about others, we learn about ourselves. As an anthropologist, I want to flip this conversation: Why are *we* so into science fiction and fantasy? Nineteenth-century

German sociologist Max Weber had a useful theory about this: The answer may be that we in the West are "disenchanted." The world in which we live feels explainable, predictable, and boring. Weber posited that because of modern science, a rise in secularism, an impersonal market economy, and government administered through bureaucracies rather than bonds of loyalty, Western societies perceived the world as knowably rational and systematic, leading to a widespread loss of a sense of wonder and magic. Because reality is composed of processes that can be identified with a powerful-enough microscope or calculated with a fast-enough computer, so Weber's notion of disenchantment goes, there is no place for mystery. But this state of disenchantment is a difficult one because people seem to *like* wonder.

And so we turn to science fiction and fantasy in an attempt to re-enchant   5
the world. Children and childhood retain mystery, and so one tactic has been to take fairytales and rewrite them for adults and here we get the swords and sorcery of modern fantasy. Another strategy was to reinsert the speculative unknown into the very heart of scientific processes. But just because *we* have mined myth for magic — and, remember, even what we define as *myth* would have been called *religion* two millennia earlier (and the very fact that we think those two terms equivalent is also cultural) — does not mean that this fills the same need for wonder elsewhere.

India has developed many of the same features as America: a capitalist economy, an enormous bureaucratic government, and cutting-edge scientific expertise. But its intellectual history is different. Weber's argument is much more nuanced and substantive than the cursory description I have given here, but, in sum, disenchantment is rooted in the intellectual tradition of the 18th-century European Enlightenment with its struggles over the place of religion versus rationality. The aftermath of that contest in the West was to relegate the supernatural mysterious to a lower position than material-based reason. The key point is that this is a particular moment in cultural history, not some necessary and universal stage of human societal "development." Similarly, for that reason, I'd guess Japan's vibrant tradition of the supernatural in its anime, and China's recent taste for American FX spectacles, results from those countries' specific cultural contexts rather than from disenchantment. (And some of the ways the West looks to the non-West for re-enchantment are another, Orientalist can of worms best left for a different day.)

Anyone looking to debunk cultural explanations for the American/Indian sci-fi gap might point out that Hollywood has had the big-budget, dragons-and-droids market flooded for years. Perhaps Bollywood, for commercial reasons, doesn't want to jump in. Average production costs for American superhero blockbusters hover around $200 million these days, and audiences have come to expect the computer-generated spectacle that kind of money buys. But . . . *Star Wars* was made for $11 million in 1977 (less than $40 million now) and 25 percent of *Iron Man 3*'s $200 million budget was Robert Downey Jr.'s salary. Surely there's enough technical expertise and financial muscle in India to digitize a realistic Mars landing when the country's space program is on track to launch a real spacecraft (unmanned) to the red planet this upcoming November.

What about the fact that American blockbusters make tons of money worldwide? For films like *Avatar* and *The Hobbit*, foreign sales equal or exceed domestic U.S. sales. But India, the world's ninth-largest economy and second-most populous country, does not even rank in the top 12 foreign markets for the genre. The list of those markets reads like the attendees of a G-8 summit (plus some key trading partners): the United Kingdom, Japan, France, Germany, Italy, Mexico, Brazil, Spain, South Korea, Russia, Australia, and China. *Avatar* (2009) set the high-water mark for India, where South Asian audiences purchased $24 million worth of tickets—about 10 percent of foreign ticket sales worldwide. But for most science fiction, countries with smaller GDPs than India (Australia, Mexico, South Korea) are higher consumers. Of *Avengers'* (2012) $888 million worldwide, $12 million came from India; *Iron Man 3* is on track with similar numbers; and, to their credit, Indian audiences contributed a paltry $2.8 million to *Transformers 3*'s $434 million. Fantasy fares much worse. *The Hobbit* (2012) made $714 million worldwide; it took home $1.8 million in India. That is barely more than Croatia's $1.4 million.

The simplest conclusion to draw from this is that Bollywood doesn't produce science fiction and fantasy because Indian audiences aren't as keen on it. Local cultural production doesn't just result from economic wherewithal; desires and needs also matter. And desires and needs are cultural. This sometimes feels hard to accept because desires and needs feel so *natural*. Often we think that the way we live is normal and not cultural; this is what anthropologists call "tacit ethnocentrism," when we are not *trying* to be prejudiced, but we have unquestioned assumptions that somehow we are the normal human baseline and others somehow deviate from that.

Hollywood continues to make science fiction and fantasy movies because 10 disenchantment creates a demand for these stories, but disenchantment predates Hollywood. We were journeying ten thousand leagues under the sea or scarcely surviving a war of the worlds before the film industry began. If the uptick of *Hunger Games*–inspired archery lessons and the CDC's humorous-but-practical Zombie Preparedness Guide are any indication, this is not going away any time soon. Re-enchantment delivers something more important than escapism or entertainment. Through its promise of a world of mystery and wonder, it offers the hope that we haven't seen all that there is.

READING THE TEXT

1. Explain in your own words Max Weber's notion of "disenchantment" (para. 4).
2. What is Folch's explanation for why Western film audiences find the supernatural and futurism appealing?
3. According to Folch, what are the cultural reasons Indian film audiences are not "keen on" science fiction and fantasy?

4. What was the Enlightenment, and how did it affect Western consciousness?

5. What does Folch mean by the anthropological term "tacit ethnocentrism" (para. 9)?

READING THE SIGNS

1. Research the last ten years of American movies, and determine how many of the most successful films were fantasies. Use your findings to write your own argument about why fantasy films appeal to American audiences, basing your claims on an analysis of particular movies.

2. Write an essay in which you support, refute, or modify the claim that the rise of fantasy films in America reflects market forces pandering to immature cinematic tastes.

3. Watch a Bollywood film such as *Dhoom 3* (2013), the all-time most popular Indian film, or *Chennai Express* (2013). In an essay, analyze the nature of its appeal to Indian audiences, using Folch's selection as a critical framework. What cultural needs and desires does the film seem to satisfy?

4. Folch claims that "Bollywood takes quotidian family dramas and imbues them with spectacular tales of love and wealth found-lost-regained amidst the pageantry of choreographed dance pieces" (para. 3). In an essay, compare an Indian film like *Devdas* (2002) with an American movie such as *My Big Fat Greek Wedding* (2002). How do the films you select depict family and interpersonal relations? What cultural explanations can you offer for your observations?

PAY ATTENTION WHILE WALKING

YOUR FACEBOOK STATUS UPDATE CAN WAIT.

 Metropolitan Etiquette Authority

THE CLOUD

Semiotics and the New Media

The New Panopticon

In the spring of 2013, an obscure government subcontractor named Edward Snowden blew the cover on the National Security Agency. A hero to some and a traitor to others, Snowden not only created some very odd political bedfellows through his revelation that the NSA had been collecting and storing data for years on every phone call and digital transaction made in America (congressional Democrats joined Libertarians in seeking new NSA restrictions after the leak, while Republicans joined the White House in resisting those efforts), but also indirectly revealed just how deeply digital technology has invaded our lives. Because here was a revelation that put a new edge on the already-widespread knowledge that such digital titans as Google, Facebook, and Apple were mining user data and selling that information to anyone willing to pay for it. It raised to a whole new level the sense that there is a price to pay for all the pleasures and conveniences of the digital age. That price is our privacy, whether it is sold for the benefit of businesses that want to know what we are doing so they can more efficiently market goods and services to us, or given to the government on behalf of national security. And with the arrival of Google Glass, ordinary citizens will be all the more able to invade the privacy of anyone around them, surreptitiously recording and posting to YouTube everything in their path. Thus, one way or another, the new media are transforming America into what the late Michel Foucault called a "Panopticon": a society that is under constant surveillance, like a prison.

And yet, that isn't the way that many, if not most, people see it. Rather—especially for those who have spent their lives within the digital era—their smartphones, tablets, e-readers, laptops, and even desktops are not merely sources of pleasure or convenience; they are necessities, required not only for work, school, and play, but for existence itself. Who cares if someone's watching as long as the connection is still up, and they can remain enveloped in the vast, round-the-clock social network in which no one ever has to be alone? It isn't a Panopticon; it's a global village that's revolutionizing human life all over the world.

So which is it: prison or village? An abuse of power or a triumph of social evolution? Like all technological interventions—such as the automobile or television—that have made an indelible impact on society, digital technology is not easy to assess, but there may be no subject as important to think about semiotically in an era when the new media are expanding into every corner of our lives with a velocity that some think will soon become infinite. Indeed, your analyses of the new media could well begin with questions just like these.

The Global Hive

Grasping the impact of the new media isn't made any easier by the conflicting signals that have been sent by media history itself. In 1962, when Marshall McLuhan launched the modern era of media studies with his groundbreaking book *The Gutenberg Galaxy*, the situation looked pretty straightforward. At the time, television, cinema, radio, and stereos were the dominant electronic media, so it was only natural that McLuhan would focus on the shift he saw taking place from a text, or print-based, culture to an aural and image-based culture. Such a culture would mark a radical change in consciousness, he predicted, a departure from the logical form of thinking fostered by the linear structure of alphabetic writing and a return of sorts to a more ancient oral/visual consciousness in what he was the first to call the "global village."

With the rise of the Internet and related digital technologies, however, McLuhan's predictions have become considerably complicated. While digital technology, too, is an electronic medium saturated with visual images and aural content, it has also brought the (digitally) printed word back into popular culture and consciousness. Indeed, before the full blossoming of the Internet as we know it today, word processing and, subsequently, print-based e-mail, constituted the leading edge of the digital revolution. And with the rise of the blogosphere in the late 1990s, not to mention the online posting of such traditional print media as newspapers, magazines (does anyone remember "zines"?), and fiction (does anyone remember "hypertexts"?) and the rise of texting (often at the expense of telephonic talking), the digital proliferation of print appeared to refute one of McLuhan's most fundamental observations about media history. Indeed, things seemed to be going *back* to Gutenberg.

With the obliteration of MySpace—which in its heyday tended to be plastered with visual imagery and aural content—at the hands of Facebook, which made printed text the dominant feature on the screen "page," this return of the font appeared to be closer to accomplishment. Sure, there was still YouTube, but Facebook was really getting much of the attention.

But while it is far too early to predict the eventual demise of Facebook, a new trend is appearing, a differential shift in the high-speed history of digital culture. This **difference** involves the emergence of such sites as Twitter (still print based but reduced to a kind of digital shorthand) and Tumblr, which, in its presentation of "microblogs," is heavy on uploaded images and light on printed text. Facebook, for its part, has largely supplanted the much more text-based world of the original blogging site, and individual Facebook pages can be filled with photos and videos in a kind of semi-return to the MySpace era. Add the continued popularity of YouTube and the emergence of many other sites, like Instagram, Snapchat, and Flickr, devoted to the uploading of an endless image stream contributed by a ubiquitous arsenal of iPhones, Droids, Galaxys, and other devices, and you have a veritable tsunami of pixels, not fonts.

The ability to upload your own images instantly with the same device that took the pictures has further enhanced the "village-like" nature of the cloud in a socially profound manner as well. We call it "sharing," but it is more than that, because the tendency to post images of your personal experiences even as you experience them is an expression and intensification of what sociologists call the "heterodirectedness" of our culture. A heterodirected society is one in which members live their lives predominantly in relation to others, constantly seeking their approval and recognition. In contrast with the autonomous individualist, who isn't concerned with what others think, the heterodirected person lives his or her life within a social web where everyone is in contact with everyone else, not only sharing with others but ultimately judging them. It is not unlike the premodern experience of small-town or village life, where everyone knew everyone else, but now, thanks to new technologies, the scale is global, with people all over the world living their lives in relation to the often-anonymous others who share their experiences via those tiny digital boxes that they can never seem to put down.

So maybe it is premature to rule McLuhan out entirely. Perhaps the global village has arrived in the form of a global hive, a buzzing crowd of digitally connected Netizens who appear to be unable to let go for a few minutes to concentrate on an actual here-and-now as they hook up with a virtual elsewhere.

Of course, you hardly need to be told about how digital technology has revolutionized the ways in which people communicate with each other and consume entertainment. You really don't need to be told about the latest, and hottest, social networking sites. Indeed, even if we try to identify what those sites are, by the time this book is published that information would be dated, as we discovered when composing the Introduction to our initial chapter on digital technology for the sixth edition of *Signs of Life in the U.S.A.* At that time, MySpace was the eight-hundred-pound gorilla of social networking, with hundreds of millions of mostly youthful members. Facebook was an out-lier, something for some college students in the Northeast and a few adults. But by the time the sixth edition appeared, Facebook had become a world-wide behemoth, and MySpace was on the way out. Even as we prepare the eighth edition of this text, however, Facebook is showing some signs of losing its hegemony, with such sites as Twitter, Instagram, Pinterest, Tumblr, Snap-chat, and Reddit looming large, but we expect that at least some will be old hat by the time this book comes out, and that new names will dominate the Internet, which will, in turn, rise to dizzying heights of popularity and then subside.

So, when considering the semiotics of digital technology and social media, the point is not to identify what's hot and what's not; instead, you should explore the cultural significance of digitality. Consider for a moment the basic setup, the experiential situation of online communication through social media sites. They weren't always called "social media," by the way. In the early days of the Internet, they were called "chat rooms."

Whose Space?

The first chat rooms were rather primitive places. Austere, you might say, with no images, music, or decoration of any kind, just plain text boxes where words materialized as if from out of nowhere. Visiting such places was a bit of an adventure, a pioneering voyage into cyberspace and the uncharted expanses of the electronic frontier.

Until the advent of the now-ubiquitous smartphone and tablet, these excursions were carried out indoors, in homes and offices via stationary desk-top computers. Today, of course, thanks to mobile devices operating within a cloud computing environment, the journey can be taken anywhere — in the street, in the classroom, in a club, in a park, in a restaurant, in an airport — literally everywhere. Yet, either way, via desktop or smartphone, navigating the cloud through an ever-expanding number of social networking sites dis-rupts some very ancient codes governing the use of social space, deconstruct-ing not only the old demarcations between public and private space but the meaning of social experience itself.

Consider for a moment an ordinary public road: It isn't just a ribbon of asphalt; it's a complex structure of codes for pedestrians. These codes tell you that you may walk down the street, but must stick to the side (or sidewalk if there is one), and that it's best to stay to the right to avoid oncoming foot traffic. If there are private houses on the street, you may approach the front door, but you're not supposed to cut through the yard, and you're certainly not allowed to enter without permission. You may enter the public space of a store, shopping center, or post office, but you probably need to pay to enter a museum, and you must pass through a security checkpoint if you are entering a courthouse or an airline terminal.

Now consider your own physical personal space: There, you set the rules. You determine who enters it and what can be done there. You might actually write out the rules that govern your space (as in posting a NO SMOKING sign), but those rules are more likely to be obeyed if you are personally present. Indeed, the most basic personal space rule is that no unauthorized person should be in it when you are absent.

The spaces of everyday life, both public and private, are, in short, packed with codes that we violate or ignore at our peril. These codes all originate in the way that human beings define their territories. A *territory* is a space that has been given meaning through having been claimed by an individual or group of individuals. Unclaimed, unmarked space is socially meaningless, but put up a building or a fence and the uncircumscribed landscape becomes a bounded territory, a human habitat with its own rules for permitted and unpermitted behavior. Anyone unaware of those rules can't survive for long in human society.

But what sort of territory is a social networking site, and what rules govern it? In a sense, it is a place where its users are all hosts and guests simultaneously, with the rules accordingly being quite confusing. A host is hospitable; a guest is polite and follows the host's guidance. But with no one in the cloud being entirely host or entirely guest, things can easily go wrong. You don't insult people in their own homes, but online flaming occurs all too often. Indeed, many sites and forums where people socialize and communicate are described as being like the Wild West — a wide-open space known for its lack of clear rules of conduct and the way in which it challenges traditional conceptions of social space. The result has been a blurring of the traditional lines between the uses of public and private space and, with that, much confusion about how to behave in the essentially public arena of digital communication. Just read responses people make in the feedback or comments sections of popular Web sites like YouTube. Certainly, the old rules about public courtesy no longer apply.

This is one reason so many people flocked to Facebook in the latter half of the first decade of the new millennium. Since everyone is the administrator of his or her Facebook page, it feels like you are in control there, that your Facebook page is like your own home: a private space whose rules you control. But it really isn't. Not only does Facebook periodically change how its privacy protections work, but the company can, and does, overstep those protections all the time in order to sell your information to virtually anyone who wants it, and the company will give it to the government as well. So even though your Facebook page may feel private and controllable, it is actually quite public — as all too many Facebook users have learned to their distress.

Or consider the very common phenomenon of someone (perhaps yourself) in an ostensibly public setting — say, sitting with a group of friends — while engaging in an essentially private activity on a mobile device. Whether texting, tweeting, posting to Instagram, updating your Facebook page, or doing any one of an almost-unlimited number of online activities, you

---

Exploring the Signs of the Cloud

If you have a Facebook page, describe it in your journal and discuss why you designed it as you did. What signs did you choose to communicate your identity, and why? Did you deliberately avoid including some signs? If so, why? If you chose not to join Facebook or another such site, why did you make that choice?

---

have, once again, turned a public social space into a private one, moving back and forth between what were once separate spheres (after all, you can share what you are doing on your Galaxy, or even put it aside for a moment and talk to the people around you) as if there were no difference between them.

Thus, one way or another, the private/public divide is being undone, and the old rules governing the use of social space are becoming obsolete. This is all happening so quickly that not only is it easy to take for granted, but there hasn't been sufficient time to constitute new rules to take the place of the old ones. Given that society cannot function without such codes, this change is of profound social significance, a problem that cannot be addressed without first realizing that it exists.

Tweeting with the Stars

Then there is the disruptive nature of the way that we socialize in the cloud. While the invention of the telephone began the disruption in the nineteenth century, today's social networking greatly magnifies the possibilities of socializing in the absence of anyone being physically present. You can tweet to the whole world, but no one is necessarily listening. You can have thousands of Facebook "friends," without actually meeting any of them. You can even "tweet with the stars," though the chances that any celebrity tweeter will know who you are, or care, are tiny. Often, then, that sense of intimacy with others in the cloud is, in reality, an illusion, especially given the way that people can stage-manage their online profile. How, in such conditions, can you know for certain whether those profiles of "friends" whom you have never met are accurate or true?

Thus, the lack of actual spatial proximity in digital communication produces what could be called a "proxemic disruption" within human history. **Proxemics**, a field loosely related to semiotics, is the study of how we communicate with others in face-to-face situations, including such means as body language, facial expression, and tone of voice. Because these social cues are absent in the cloud, social communication itself is being revolutionized in ways that are not yet entirely clear. Certainly, there has been a loss of civility due to the proxemic disruption, thanks to the lack of the controlling influence of the threat of direct retaliation for rude or insulting behavior that exists in face-to-face communication, while the possibility for misunderstanding has also increased. Indeed, a phenomenon known as "Poe's Law" — which refers to the difficulty of determining whether someone is being ironic or not in the cloud — is a particularly striking example of how the lack of physical contact can lead to less, not more, effective communication, in spite of the apparently limitless opportunities for social interaction that the cloud provides.

What is more, much of the communication that does take place in the cloud is either a form of shorthand (as on Twitter or on microblogging sites like Tumblr) or simply an exchange of pictures. Then there is the fact that those whom you allow to "speak" on your Facebook page more often than not do not speak at all: They just give you a thumbs-up. And if people say anything you don't like, you can silence them. This is profoundly different from traditional communication among peers, which cannot be individually controlled and requires much more complete verbalization. In some ways, then, communication in the cloud has become a highly segregated activity where only those who already agree with each other are allowed to "speak," and they don't have to say much because everyone already agrees.

And yet, the cloud doesn't *feel* exclusive to the innumerable people who "live" there. In fact, it feels all-inclusive, like a vast buzzing hive of closely related "friends." Clearly, part of the appeal of the new media is that they make people feel connected, with family, with friends, and with online communities that may be based on little more than shared interests — instantly postable to sites like Pinterest that encourage the passing around of information like a vast chain letter — but that can be very real communities all the same. Human beings are social animals, after all, but nothing in our genes says that those with whom we socialize have to be physically present. The addictive nature of digital technology, the way that its users suffer something like drug withdrawal when they are deprived of it, is a powerful testimony to the deep appeal of socializing in the cloud. Whether this compelling draw of digital socializing will eventually lead to a whole new definition of "society," a whole new way of relating to other people, is anyone's guess at this point, but there is no doubt that it has become a very effective way of making money for those who control the networks. Which leads us to yet another semiotic question.

Top-Down After All?

Traditionally, the mass media have been structured in a top-down manner, with corporate elites providing passive consumers with the news, entertainments, and products that they consume, along with the advertisements that promote them. But now the top-down news has turned into a bottom-up conversation in which anyone can become a pundit, while newspapers and online news sites invite input from their readers. Broadband Internet access has turned video creativity over to the masses in such a way that you no longer have to be a famous director or producer to present your own television shows or films to a wide audience, and you don't have to be an authorized critic to respond, with YouTube, Rotten Tomatoes, and related sites offering unlimited opportunities to critique what you find there. In short, what was once a passive and vicarious media experience for the mass of consumers is now active and participatory.

Another way of putting this is that until recently our relationship with the mass media has been more or less a one-way street. Those with the power to control the media (TV networks, radio stations, movie studios, newspaper owners, corporate sponsors with advertising dollars to spend) have broadcast their signals to us (TV and radio programs, films, newspapers, and ads), and we have passively received them, without being able to answer back. The late semiologist and sociologist Jean Baudrillard (1929–2007) regarded this situation as one of the essential conditions of postmodern times and used it as a basis for his analyses of contemporary society. But with so much of the mass media now actively eliciting responses from their audiences, and with consumers of the mass media able to create and disseminate their own media content — indeed, now an ordinary news story can be remixed into memes that go viral and become news stories of their own, like the "Bed Intruder Song" in 2010, which turned an interview with the brother of a victim of sexual assault into an international sensation — it certainly appears that something post-postmodern is emerging beyond Baudrillard's perceptions.

But while the new media are definitely opening up channels for democratic communication and expression that previously did not exist, they have also created new elites whose wealth and power depend upon their ability to exploit the mass of people who use the technologies they offer. We have already referred here to the price we all have to pay for personal privacy thanks to the panoptic capabilities of digital technology, but there is also the way that technology tycoons seek to monopolize daily life and shut down older, predigital forms of commerce and professional activity. We're referring here to the assaults on "brick-and-mortar" retailing via online shopping sites, print journalism via online news outlets, and face-to-face education via massive open online courses (MOOCs) as just three prominent examples.

Partly, what has made the creation of the new media elites possible has been the consumer expectation (and demand) that "information should be free." While consumers do not balk at paying for the tangible commodities they purchase online, they do feel that such intangible commodities as education, music, and written texts should be accessible without cost (which is why so many people regarded Aaron Swartz, who hacked into MIT's servers to release copyrighted articles, as a martyr to the open access movement when he committed suicide in 2013). Already trained by commercial TV and radio to expect free content, American consumers were immediately receptive to the similar business models of the new media, taking for granted the free use of online services, not realizing that those services have a cost and that they are not really free at all. Thus, traditional media (like newspapers) that paid for and profited by charging directly for their operation are going out of business, while the new media titans that have found ways to monetize their operations without any direct out-of-pocket costs to consumers are replacing them.

At the same time, once-populist, user-generated sites have tended to become dominated by social and corporate elites very quickly. Twitter is an example. Though it is still a site where anyone can tweet (if he or she is a registered user, that is) and still serves as a premier source of breaking news stories from the people who experience them first, the major news organizations now present news stories in the form of tweets from their reporters in the field; similarly, celebrity tweeters and politicians like Sarah Palin have pretty well hogged vast spaces of Twitterland in recent years.

And so we have a paradox: Top-down has met bottom-up in a cloud that is at once democratic and hierarchical, your space and corporate space. The democratic, user-generated spaces in the cloud are simultaneously revolutionary and business as usual. Users pass around their own content (often not self-created), but they do so on sites that are owned by huge corporations that require registration so that their services can be monetized. Somehow, the future doesn't seem to be what it used to be.

In the famous 1984 Super Bowl commercial that introduced the Macintosh, Apple Computer promised that the future was going to belong to the people, not to rigid, profit-seeking corporate powers. Web 1.0 and Web 2.0 were both built, in large part, by people who believed in this vision of a sort of anticorporate utopia. But that isn't what happened at all. The Macintosh ad, after all, featured a big screen with an image of Big Brother hectoring a room full of hypnotized viewers. Is that so very different from the billions of people who compulsively stare into their digital devices, knowing that those devices are looking back at the behest of corporate elites who want to use their information to profit from, and control, their behavior?

We are all living in the midst of a gigantic social experiment whose significance can be determined only by careful critical thinking. Often uncritically celebrated as a "disruption," the brave new world of digital technology is easy to take for granted, but the profound differences that it has introduced into our lives call for semiotic attention. In its own way, the cloud is the most

---

Discussing the Signs of the Cloud

Critics of online social networking sites have expressed concern that excessive online networking will diminish participants' ability to socialize normally in face-to-face environments. In class, discuss the legitimacy of this concern, drawing upon your personal experiences with social networking.

Reading the Cloud

YouTube allows users to create their own "television" content, yet the site is filled with content taken from other sources, such as television clips, concert footage, and the like. Conduct a survey of YouTube content to estimate the ratio of user-created content to postings of professional performers. Analyze and interpret your results semiotically. What are the implications of your findings for the bottom-up versus top-down debate over Web 2.0 "democracy"?

---

important popular cultural topic you can semiotically analyze. This chapter is designed to prompt you to do that.

The Readings

S. Craig Watkins opens the chapter with a look at today's always turned-on and tuned-in world of digital entertainment, wondering if it isn't all leading to an epidemic of Continuous Partial Attention. The International Center for Media and the Public Agenda and Simon Dumenco follow with a paired set of readings, with the former reporting on experimental data that suggest digital usage may be literally addictive, and the latter looking at the way Facebook "guilts" its inactive users into logging back in as it seeks to maintain its social media supremacy. Next, danah boyd reveals the surprising racial coding that separates rival social networking sites Facebook and MySpace, and that has led to the near demise of the latter. Salvador Rodriguez follows with a personal essay on lost romances that refuse to disappear when it comes to the almost-ineradicable traces they leave on the Internet, while Richard Rushfield blogs on what he sees as social networking overkill — that is, the tendency of the Internet to talk just about any subject to death. Daniel D'Addario's rumination on the way that the word "trolling" has become overused and abused in Internet discourse is next, and Henry Jenkins concludes this chapter with an analysis of the phenomenon that he calls "convergence culture," a world where old and new media come together.

S. CRAIG WATKINS

Fast Entertainment and Multitasking in an Always-On World

Thanks to digital technology, a veritable universe of entertainment is now available to us whenever and wherever we want it. S. Craig Watkins, in this excerpt from his book *The Young and the Digital* (2009), calls this cornucopia of always-on diversion "fast entertainment," focusing here on the multitasking ways of its youthful consumers. But, Watkins warns, "like fast food, fast entertainment is easy to get, all around us, and typically cheap, but not always good for you." Something to keep in mind while studying for finals. S. Craig Watkins is a professor at the University of Texas at Austin, where he teaches in the departments of Radio-Television-Film, Sociology, and the Center for African and African American Studies. His previous books include *Hip Hop Matters* (2005) and *Representing: Hip Hop Culture and the Production of Black Cinema* (1998).

> For the younger generation of multitaskers, the great electronic din is an expected part of everyday life. And given what neuroscience and anecdotal evidence have shown us, this state of constant intentional self-distraction could well be of profound detriment to individual and cultural well-being.
>
> —CHRISTINE ROSEN, Senior Editor of *The New Atlantis*[1]

Laptop computers, mobile phones, and iPods deliver a vast assortment of digital media content in unprecedented speed — now! Today, we can view video clips, listen to our favorite music downloads, squeeze in a game, access user-generated content, or just about anything else in smaller and quicker doses, thus making these digital delights all-pervading and irresistible. A 2007 *Wired* magazine cover story titled "Snack Culture" celebrates the rise of what it calls bite-size entertainment and the emergent world of one-minute media. "We now devour our pop culture," writes Nancy Miller, "the same way we enjoy candy and chips — in conveniently packaged bite-size nuggets made to be munched easily with increased frequency and maximum speed."[2] *Wired* calls it snack culture. I call it fast entertainment — this ever-widening menu of media content that we can consume easily and on the go.

No matter where we are, fast entertainment is generally just a click away. I liken the efficient delivery of digital media content to another staple in the

---

[1]Christine Rosen, "The Myth of Multitasking," *New Atlantis* no. 20 (Spring 2008): 105–10.
[2]Nancy Miller, "Minifesto for a New Age," *Wired*, March 2007.

daily American diet: fast food. Like fast food, fast entertainment is easy to get, all around us, and typically cheap, but not always good for you.

It is hard to know which came first — our appetite for speedy entertainment or the widespread manufacturing and aggressive marketing of it. Mobile technologies are ideal platforms for delivering bite-size media easily and effectively. For much of its early life, fast entertainment was the primary domain of technology companies, Silicon Valley start-ups, and Web entrepreneurs. Known for its user-generated content, a major part of YouTube's success can also be attributed to the creation of a space that supplies an endless stream of short video clips that complement our desire to consume a lot very quickly. Yahoo! is also a favorite online destination to grab a quick video clip, music playlist, or game. Social-network sites allow users to share a wide range of content with their fellow users casually and throughout the day. Come across a funny video and send it to your Facebook friends. Discover a cool new underground hip-hop band and spread the word through MySpace. Nowhere is the hegemony of fast entertainment more evident than in the rise of Apple's iTunes Store, one of the most prolific platforms for delivering digital media content.

In his book *The Perfect Thing: How the iPod Shuffles Commerce, Culture, and Coolness*, *Newsweek* chief technology correspondent Steven Levy explains how the music industry insiders dismissed the idea of selling digital downloads. Apple's CEO, Steve Jobs, told Levy, "When we first approached the labels, the online music business was a disaster. Nobody had ever sold a song for ninety-nine cents. Nobody ever really sold a *song*."[3] When Apple launched the iTunes Store in 2003, the service developed a reputation for delivering digital music downloads quickly, reliably, legally, and cheaply. From day one the iTunes Store was a huge success, reportedly selling 275,000 downloads in its first eighteen hours of operation. By day five, the number of downloads reached one million. In six short years, iTunes went from being nonexistent to surpassing the retail behemoth, Walmart, to become the number one music retailer in the United States.

In 2005 the iTunes Store began offering downloads of music videos and 5 popular television programs for the iPod. Soon after that the store expanded to include movies, podcasts, audiobooks, and games, among other things. Apple's iPhone has been an even bigger hit and distributor of fast entertainment. In just nine months iPhone users downloaded more than one billion applications, many from categories like games, music, and entertainment. Apple's iPod and iPhone made it convenient and cool to carry our entire inventory of media and entertainment in our pocket. No matter if you are at home or on the road, access to your media entertainment library is just a touch of a button away. Technology companies such as YouTube, Yahoo!, and Apple were among the first to superserve our desire to quickly and constantly consume media. After

[3]Steven Levy, *The Perfect Thing: How the iPod Shuffles Commerce, Culture, and Coolness* (New York: Simon & Schuster, 2006), 135.

realizing our desire to consume content on the go and in smaller bites, the old media guard is responding.

From the big music labels to the network television industry, the major media companies are investing, strategically and financially, in fast entertainment by offering up their own versions of bite-size media. In 2007 Sony Corporation and its production studio, Sony Pictures Television, tossed its hat in the fast entertainment ring. The studio announced that it would begin sifting through its massive inventory to produce three-to-five-minute versions of programs that once filled the thirty-minute and hour-length programming slots in the primetime schedule. Sony executives call these tiny TV episodes minisodes. According to the studio, minisodes are not clips but rather full episodes containing a discernible narrative structure consisting of a beginning, middle, and end. The initial roster of miniature programs included old television series like *Charlie's Angels*, *T.J. Hooker*, and *Starsky & Hutch*.

Sony executives characterize the minisodes as campy and fun, but the decision to produce them is a serious response to how young people enjoy their media. In many ways, the creation of three-to-five-minute episodes are influenced by a video-clip culture that is a staple in the online experiences of many young people. From Lime Wire to BitTorrent, the adoption of file-sharing platforms not only alters how the young and the digital consume media content; it also reflects a greater interest on their part to manage, share, and engage content.

One of the more intriguing paradoxes of today's digital media environment is that we consume more and less at the same time. How is this possible? The rise of YouTube, founded in February 2005 by Chad Hurley and Steve Chen, is a great illustration. They launched the video file-sharing site to empower users of social media to do with videos what they were doing with photos — create, manage, and share them with peers. You name it — music videos, sports highlights, news segments, political speeches, user-generated content, clips from television and film — and YouTube users share it. According to comScore, "Americans viewed more than II.4 billion videos for a total duration of 558 million hours during the month of July 2008."[4] Five billion, or 44 percent, of the videos were watched on YouTube. More precisely, 91 million viewers watched a YouTube video, which averages out to about fifty-five videos per person. The average length of a video watched in July 2008: 2.9 minutes. In short, Americans watched a ton of online videos, the vast majority of them short clips. In the digital media age, more equals less.

In addition to consuming less of more, we are constantly consuming. We have evolved from a culture of instant gratification to one of constant gratification. Fast entertainment encourages an insatiable desire to be entertained no matter where we are (at work) or what we are doing (driving a car). While the scientific merits of Internet addiction are still being measured, analyzed, and

---

[4]*YouTube Draws 5 Billion U.S. Online Video Views in July 2008* (Reston, VA: comScore Media Metrix, September 10, 2008), www.comscore.com/press/release.asp?press = 2444.

assessed, one thing is undeniable: the desire for fast entertainment is widespread and voracious. We not only want our media content now, we expect it now. Not that long ago, consuming media on the go was a luxury. Today, it is a standard feature of daily life.

In many ways, the social- and mobile-media lifestyle represents a new cultural ethos and a profound shift in how we consume media — in smaller and steadier portions and on smaller and more mobile screens. Along with changing how we consume media, fast entertainment changes where we consume media. Two developments defined the post-war boom Americans experienced starting around the 1950s: a rapid increase in home ownership and a bustling consumer economy. By the 1950s Americans were furnishing their new homes with all kinds of appliances that helped to establish a more modern and socially mobile lifestyle. Beginning with the radio, the phonograph, and then the television, Americans also filled their homes with media. Over the next half century, Americans participated in a flourishing home-centered media consumer culture that redefined leisure and household life.

Not that long ago we typically left our homes to purchase a wide array of media — music, books, magazines, videocassettes, games, DVDs — and then returned home to enjoy it. Today, however, the reverse is increasingly more common. We collect content from the comfort and convenience of our home, via digital downloads and peer-to-peer networks, to take with us when we leave our home. Throughout the last two decades of the twentieth century, Americans turned their homes into what media technology professor Jorge Schement calls the wired castle. Our homes became the ultimate leisure space. But in an always-on world, any place can be a good place to grab a quick bite of entertainment.

Despite all the euphoria over iTunes, iPods, iPhones, Webisodes, minisodes, minigames, and one-minute media, is the ability to be entertained constantly and no matter where you are really a good thing?

Young people are media rich. They own music players, computers, mobile phones, TVs, and game consoles. Young people's media environment is like a kid who wakes up one day and finds himself in a candy store. Surrounded by so many tasty options, what does he do? Naturally, he devours as much of it as he can, any way that he can. And that is essentially what we are seeing young people do with media. Immersed in a world of media, they use as much of it as they can, any way that they can. Innovative as ever, the one sure way for young people to use all of the media and technology they own is to use it simultaneously. One study, for example, found that American youth report spending about six hours a day with media. If you include the simultaneous use of media, that figure grows to about eight hours a day. Communication scholars refer to this as media multitasking.

We all media multitask. As I work on this chapter, my e-mail box, music player, photo application, and several tabs on my two favorite browsers are all open on my computer screen. But the young and the digital are widely viewed as masterful multitaskers, capable of managing several technologies, screens, and conversations fluidly and simultaneously. They multitask habitually and according to many observers, they also do it instinctively.

Donald F. Roberts, a Stanford University communications professor, has 15 studied the media behaviors of children and adolescents for more than thirty years. Roberts believes that adolescents' multitasking ways began to really take shape as the media in their homes migrated into their bedrooms. With the use of ethnographic techniques, time diaries, and surveys, researchers began building more nuanced portraits of the media environment in American homes in the 1970s. A 1972 study of southern California sixth graders found that 6 percent of the sample had a television in their bedrooms.[5] Since then, the flow of media into children's bedrooms has continued at a steady clip. In his study of media use by youth, Roberts and his colleagues found that no matter if they were especially young, ages two to seven, or older, ages eleven to fourteen, kids in America access a lot of media from their bedrooms.[6]

At least a third of young children, for example, can watch television or listen to music from their own bedroom. Similarly, three-quarters of older children are able to watch TV or play a videogame from the comforts of their bedroom.[7] By the year 2000, about 20 percent of older youth, ages twelve to eighteen, were accessing computers from their bedrooms. Assessing the state of young people's media environment by the start of the new millennium, Roberts writes, "Compared with even a few years ago, the sheer numbers of children and adolescents possessing personal media is remarkable."[8] The movement of media into children's bedrooms creates the context for more frequent, intense, unsupervised, and in the view of some researchers, unhealthy media behaviors.

Until recently the data on media multitasking was extremely limited. How much do young people media multitask? According to a 2006 study by the Kaiser Family Foundation, a lot.

The San Mateo, California–based research unit surveyed a national cross-section of 2,032 school-age kids ages eight to eighteen. In addition, Kaiser analyzed data from a self-selected subsample of 694 respondents who completed a seven-day diary of their media use. Here are some of the study's findings. Children and teenagers spend at least a quarter of their time with multiple media.[9] On a typical day, Kaiser reports, eight in ten school-age children media multitask. Predictably, young people do a lot of their multitasking when they are using a computer. Older children, ages fourteen to eighteen,

---

[5]J. Lyle and H. R. Hoffman, "Children's Use of Television and Other Media," in E. A. Rubinstein, G. A. Comstock, and J. P. Murray, eds., *Television and Social Behavior*, vol. 4, *Television in Day-to-Day Life: Patterns and Use* (Washington, DC: U.S. Government Printing Office, 1972): 129–256.

[6]Roberts and Foehr, *Kids and Media in America*, 42–48.

[7]Ibid., 42–43.

[8]Ibid., 42.

[9]For a detailed assessment of media multitasking among young people, see Foehr, *Media Multitasking Among American Youth*.

multitask more, but by the age of ten, their desire to multitask is strong. Young multitaskers tend to use other media — such as television or music — while on the computer. Even when using the computer is the only activity, it is common for young people to shuffle back and forth between instant messaging, their favorite Web sites, online videos, and games, all while managing a wealth of digital content such as photos and music files.

Tweens and teens are not the only ones multitasking their media. Our surveys and in-depth conversations show that college students are avid users of multiple media too. They multitask with just about every media they use — the Internet, music, television, and books and magazines. A decisive majority, 95 percent, listen to music either most or some of the time when using the computer. Seventy-two percent of our survey respondents said they watch television most or some of the time when using a computer is their primary activity. And when television is the primary activity, 81 percent of our respondents said they use a computer either most or some of the time. That is what Justin, a twenty-one-year-old psychology major, does.

"I multitask the most with the computer and television," Justin explained. 20 When there are commercials he usually goes online. "In that gap of time, I am normally on instant messenger talking to friends."

Twenty-one-year-old Andrea, an advertising major, uses television and the Internet at the same time too. "For me, the television works as background noise and the Internet allows me to be connected at all times," she said. When she gets bored with television, her computer is never too far away. Different media require different cognitive loads. For example, the load needed to listen to music is considered less than the cognitive resources needed to read a book. One thing is consistently clear in our research: among college students, using one media almost always means interacting with other media too.

Multitasking media habits are formed relatively early and right around the time young teens begin to develop their own peer networks, media interests, and greater independence from their parents. Among the young people we met, media multitasking is widely accepted as a fact of everyday life. Johnson, a nineteen-year-old, summed up multitasking this way: "I don't really think about it. It's just something that I've always done." Twenty-two-year-old Justine's multitasking skills are at once typical and amazing. "At one time I can be banking, paying bills, checking my e-mail, Facebooking, e-mailing my parents, talking online to my friends, checking the *TV Guide* on the Internet, and researching possible graduate schools," she said. As one young woman put it when referring to her generation, "Multitasking is easy and natural for us."

She's right. Multitasking for the young and the digital is easy and it certainly appears natural. But a growing body of evidence provokes the question, is media multitasking effective? More important, is it healthy?

When we asked young people why they multitask, the response was consistent: to accomplish more things efficiently. Twenty-two-year-old Brandon said, "I would never get anything done if I did not multitask." Most of us, in fact, multitask as a way to more effectively manage our time. And yet, even as humans continue managing multiple screens, media, and tasks simultaneously, cutting-edge brain research is beginning to confirm what some say is obvious: doing several things at once actually reduces task efficiency and proficiency. There is growing evidence that multitasking may not only slow down the completion of tasks but may also impair our performance. Addressing our incessant desire to multitask in a piece that appears in the *Atlantic*, Walter Kirn writes, "The great irony of multitasking—that its overall goal, getting more done in less time, turns out to be chimerical."[10]

In 2007 a team of psychology professors working from the Human Information Processing Laboratory at Vanderbilt University conducted a series of 25 test trials to assess the brain's capacity to perform multiple tasks. For years brain specialists have suspected that the brain contains a bottleneck function that keeps us from concentrating on two different things at once. Dr. René Marois, one of the principal investigators from the Vanderbilt lab, focuses on the neural basis of attention and information processing in the human brain. More precisely, Marois and his colleagues seek to more fully understand why humans appear unable to execute more than one mental task at a time. Using functional magnetic resonance imaging (fMRI) of the brain, Marois and his colleagues identified what doctors believe is the mechanism that prohibits humans from processing two or more things at the same time, the central bottleneck of information processing.

To determine what happens when we ask our brain to execute two tasks at the same time, the Vanderbilt researchers conducted dual-task trials.[11] In the first task participants were instructed to touch the appropriate button in response to a sound stimulus. In the second task participants were asked to select the appropriate vocal response to a visual stimulus. Compared to the complex information processing that takes place daily, each task in the trials is easy to perform. Hear a sound, push a particular button. See an image, utter a specific word. Easy, right? But the Vanderbilt team made things more interesting and challenging by varying the time interval in between these two simple tasks. In some instances participants were given 300 milliseconds in between tasks, while others were allotted more time, on average about 1560 milliseconds.

Among the test subjects with very little time in between the first and second tasks, there was a statistically significant delay in executing the second task. The experiments along with the brain scanning data from the fMRI provide neural evidence of what researchers call dual-task interference. That is, when we try to process two pieces of information simultaneously, a traffic

---

[10]Walter Kirn, "The Autumn of the Multitaskers," *Atlantic*, November 2007. www .theatlantic.com/doc/200711/multitasking.

[11]Paul E. Dux et al., "Isolation of a Central Bottleneck of Information Processing with Time-Resolved fMRI," *Neuron* 52 (December 21, 2006): 1109–20.

jam ensues in the brain. Conversely, among the subjects allotted more time in between each task, there was no significant delay in their execution of the second task. In addition to executing the trial experiments more efficiently, the subjects with a longer interval between tasks were more likely to push the correct button or execute the right vocal response. In short, subjects with more time in between tasks were much more efficient and proficient. Our brains, it turns out, are not wired to process dual information simultaneously. Results of the study were published in the December 2007 issue of the medical journal *Neuron*.

In the summary section of the peer-reviewed article, the Vanderbilt researchers write, "When humans attempt to perform two tasks at once, execution of the first task usually leads to postponement of the second one." The results of the trial experiments, the doctors maintain, "suggest that a neural network of frontal lobe areas acts as a central bottleneck of information processing that severely limits our ability to multitask."[12]

The significance of these findings extends well beyond medical labs and scientific journals. Multitasking has real-life implications both for our brains and our world. Think about how frequently we multitask throughout the day. In some situations multitasking — say, responding to e-mails while eating lunch — may be quite useful in managing a busy day. In other situations multitasking may be inappropriate and even fatal. That was certainly the case on September 20, 2008, when twenty-five people were killed after Metrolink III crashed head-on with an oncoming Union Pacific freight train in Chatsworth, California. It was the worst California train disaster in fifty years. An investigation revealed that, seconds before the crash, the Metrolink engineer at the helm of the train was sending and receiving text messages. Concentrating on his phone messages meant that he could not focus on his path and a series of warning signals that would have almost certainly prevented the accident.

At this point and time there are as many questions as there are answers 30 when it comes to understanding the neurological implications of multitasking. For instance, some brain specialists believe that constant multitasking may be stretching our neural capabilities beyond their outer limits and subtly changing the machinations of our brain. Studies show that certain regions of the human brain are wired to process information, whereas other regions facilitate our ability to recall information. There is growing speculation in the medical community that young multitaskers may be conditioning their brains to quickly access, manage, and process information while underdeveloping the neural ability to recall and understand the information that they find.

Popular notions of media multitasking are misleading. The person using a computer while watching television and responding to text messages on their phone actually uses one screen at a time. Multitasking involves switching one's attention back and forth from one platform to another. In reality,

[12]Ibid., 1109.

the issue media multitasking raises is not simultaneous media use per se, but rather the ability of humans to pay attention in an always-on, always-connected digital-media environment. Underscoring this very issue, Christine Rosen, senior editor of the *New Atlantis*, writes, "When we talk about multitasking, we are really talking about attention: the art of paying attention, the ability to shift our attention, and, more broadly, to exercise judgment about what objects are worthy of our attention."[13]

Now that anytime, anywhere technology and fast entertainment are pervasive parts of our cultural environment, deciding what to pay attention to is more challenging than ever. Linda Stone, a communication technology thought leader and consultant, believes that the constant efforts by humans to manage our time — a main reason we multitask — should be accompanied by an equally zealous effort to better manage our attention. In an age of multiplying screens, constant connections, and content overload, Stone, a former Apple researcher, believes that humans suffer severe lapses in attention. She even has a name for this particular state of being: continuous partial attention, or CPA. Whether or not humans are genuinely addicted to the Web is still a major source of debate, but one thing is undeniable — managing our attention in a world of anytime, anywhere technology is one of the great challenges of modern life.

Stone makes a distinction between multitasking and CPA. With multitasking, she maintains, "we are motivated by a desire to be more productive and more efficient."[14] We multitask to save time. Conversely, Stone writes, "we pay continuous partial attention in an effort NOT TO MISS ANYTHING." She adds that CPA "is an always-on, anywhere, anytime, anyplace behavior that involves an artificial sense of constant crisis. We are always in high alert when we pay continuous partial attention."[15] CPA describes a familiar yet relatively recent state of being — the constantly tethered to technology lifestyle. No matter if it's sending a text message, responding to e-mails, tagging the latest batch of pictures posted by a friend online, or downloading the latest application for your cool new phone, the digital world is a busy world. The nonstop access to content and comrades via smaller and more mobile screens keeps us on constant alert. Meanwhile, our attention stays on the move, constantly shifting from one task to the next, one conversation to the next, one screen to the next.

Whereas CPA is an increasingly normal state of being, it is not a very healthy state of being. As a result of CPA, Stone argues that "in a 24/7, always-on world, continuous partial attention used as our dominant attention mode contributes to a feeling of [being overwhelmed], over-stimulation and to a sense of being unfulfilled."[16]

Along with understanding the neurological implications of multitasking, 35 we need to understand the sociological implications too. Millions of people talking on their phones while driving make the roads less safe. Multitasking

[13]Rosen, "Myth of Multitasking."
[14]http://continuouspartialattention.jot.com/WikiHome.
[15]Ibid.
[16]Ibid.

while doing homework, a common behavior these days, can contribute to poor academic performance. For robust multitaskers like the young and the digital the stakes are even higher, the outcomes potentially more profound. As Rosen notes, "For the younger generation of multitaskers, the great electronic din" is a common aspect of life. Rosen notes, however, that "when people do their work only in the 'interstices of their mind-wandering,' with crumbs of attention rationed out among many competing tasks, their culture may gain in information, but it will surely weaken in wisdom."[17]

READING THE TEXT

1. In your own words, what do the terms "fast entertainment" and "snack culture" (para. 1) mean?
2. What does Watkins mean by saying, "In the digital media age, more equals less" (para. 8)?
3. Summarize the results of the scientific studies of the brain's ability to handle multiple tasks simultaneously.
4. What does the term "continuous partial attention" mean, according to the article, and why is it "not a very healthy state of being" (paras. 32–34)?

READING THE SIGNS

1. In an essay, write your own response to Watkins's question: "Is the ability to be entertained constantly and no matter where you are really a good thing?" (para. 12).
2. In your journal, explore your own ability to multitask. For you, is multitasking "a fact of everyday life" (para. 22) that makes completing daily activities more efficient? Or do you tend to avoid multitasking and prefer concentrating on one activity at a time? How do you explain your behavioral choices?
3. Write an argumentative essay that supports, refutes, or complicates Watkins's concluding quote from editor Christine Rosen: "When people do their work only . . . with crumbs of attention rationed out among many competing tasks, their culture may gain in information, but it will surely weaken in wisdom" (para. 35).
4. **CONNECTING TEXTS** In an essay, discuss the extent to which University of Maryland students (see "Students Addicted to Social Media," p. 403) who participated in a research study on social media are "addicted" to their electronic toys.
5. **CONNECTING TEXTS** Watkins claims that "we have evolved from a culture of instant gratification to one of constant gratification" (para. 9). Drawing upon Laurence Shames's "The More Factor" (p. 80), write an essay analyzing whether "consuming media on the go" is a twenty-first century extension of "the hunger for more."

[17]Rosen, "Myth of Multitasking."

INTERNATIONAL CENTER FOR MEDIA AND THE PUBLIC AGENDA

Students Addicted to Social Media

It's official: The use of digital technology is addictive, or so concludes a 2010 study by the International Center for Media and the Public Agenda at the University of Maryland. After two hundred University of Maryland students willingly gave up their digital devices for twenty-four hours, journalism professor Susan D. Moeller found them virtually traumatized by the experience. Indeed, as one student wrote, "Texting and IM-ing my friends gives me a constant feeling of comfort. . . . When I did not have those two luxuries, I felt quite alone and secluded from my life. Although I go to a school with thousands of students, the fact that I was not able to communicate with anyone via technology was almost unbearable." Maybe iPhones should come with a warning from the Surgeon General?

American college students today are addicted to media, describing their feelings when they have to abstain from using media in literally the same terms associated with drug and alcohol addictions: *In withdrawal, Frantically craving, Very anxious, Extremely antsy, Miserable, Jittery, Crazy.*

A new study out today from the International Center for Media and the Public Agenda (ICMPA) at the University of Maryland concludes that most college students are not just unwilling, but functionally unable to be without their media links to the world. "I clearly am addicted and the dependency is sickening," said one student in the study. "I feel like most people these days are in a similar situation, for between having a BlackBerry, a laptop, a television, and an iPod, people have become unable to shed their media skin."

The new ICMPA study, "24 Hours: Unplugged," asked 200 students at the College Park campus to give up all media for 24 hours. After their 24 hours of abstinence, the students were then asked to blog on private class Web sites about their experiences: to report their successes and admit to any failures. The 200 students wrote more than 110,000 words: in aggregate, about the same number of words as a 400-page novel.

Without Digital Ties, Students Feel Unconnected Even to Those Who Are Close By

"We were surprised by how many students admitted that they were 'incredibly addicted' to media," noted the project director Susan D. Moeller, a

403

journalism professor at the University of Maryland and the director of the International Center for Media and the Public Agenda which conducted the study. "But we noticed that what they wrote at length about was how they hated losing their personal connections. Going without media meant, in their world, going without their friends and family."

"The students did complain about how boring it was to go anywhere and do anything without being plugged into music on their MP3 players," said Moeller. "And many commented that it was almost impossible to avoid the TVs on in the background at all times in their friends' rooms. But what they spoke about in the strongest terms was how their lack of access to text messaging, phone calling, instant messaging, e-mail, and Facebook, meant that they couldn't connect with friends who lived close by, much less those far away." 5

"Texting and IM-ing my friends gives me a constant feeling of comfort," wrote one student. "When I did not have those two luxuries, I felt quite alone and secluded from my life. Although I go to a school with thousands of students, the fact that I was not able to communicate with anyone via technology was almost unbearable."

The student responses to the assignment showed not just that 18–21-year-old college students are constantly texting and on Facebook — with calling and e-mail distant seconds as ways of staying in touch, especially with friends — but that students' lives are wired together in such ways that opting out of that communication pattern would be tantamount to renouncing a social life.

News: Accessed via Connections with Friends & Family

Very few students in the study reported that they regularly watched news on television or read a local or national newspaper (although a few said they regularly read *The Diamondback*, the University of Maryland student newspaper). They also didn't mention checking mainstream media news sites or listening to radio news while commuting in their cars. Yet student after student demonstrated knowledge of specific news stories. How did they get the information? In a disaggregated way, and not typically from the news outlet that broke or committed resources to a story. "To be entirely honest I am glad I failed the assignment," wrote one student, "because if I hadn't opened my computer when I did I would not have known about the violent earthquake in Chile from an informal blog post on Tumblr."

"Students expressed tremendous anxiety about being cut off from information," observed Ph.D. student Raymond McCaffrey, a former writer and editor at *The Washington Post*, and a current researcher on the study. "One student said he realized that he suddenly 'had less information than everyone else, whether it be news, class information, scores, or what happened on *Family Guy*.'"

"They care about what is going on among their friends and families and even in the world at large," said McCaffrey. "But most of all they care about 10 being cut off from that instantaneous flow of information that comes from all sides and does not seem tied to any single device or application or news outlet."

That's the real takeaway of this study for journalists: Students showed no significant loyalty to a news program, news personality or even news platform. Students have only a casual relationship to the originators of news, and in fact rarely distinguished between news and more general information.

While many in the journalism profession are committing significant resources to deliver content across media platforms — print, broadcast, online, mobile — the young adults in this study appeared to be generally oblivious to branded news and information. For most of the students reporting in the study, information of all kinds comes in an undifferentiated wave to them via social media. If a bit of information rises to a level of interest, the student will pursue it — but often by following the story via "unconventional" outlets, such as through text messages, their e-mail accounts, Facebook, and Twitter.

Students said that only the most specific or significant news events — for example, a medal event at the Olympics — merited their tuning in to a mainstream outlet. Even news events that students cared about were often accessed via their personal interactions. To learn about the Maryland vs. Virginia Tech basketball game, for example, one student told of "listening to someone narrate the game from a conversation they were having on their own phone" (although he would have preferred watching it on TV) and another student told of calling her father to learn more about the earthquake in Chile.

Study Background

The University of Maryland is a large state university campus, and the class, *JOUR 175: Media Literacy*, that undertook this 24-hour media-free assignment, is a "core course" for the entire student body — which means it enrolls undergraduate students across majors. It is, in short, a class of 200 students, characterized by a diversity of age, race, ethnicity, religion, and nationality. According to the assignment, students had to go media-free for a full day (or had to try to go media-free), but they were allowed to pick which 24 hours in a nine-day period, from February 24–March 4. By coincidence that period saw several major news events, including the earthquake in Chile on February 27, and the close of the Vancouver Olympics on February 28.

According to separately obtained demographic data on the student class, 15 75.6 percent of the students in JOUR 175 self-identify as Caucasian/White, 9.4 percent as Black, 6.3 percent as Asian, 1.6 percent as Latino, 3.1 percent as Mixed Race, and 3.9 percent as Other. Students who self-reported themselves as non-American said they were from China, South Korea, Sri Lanka, and Ethiopia. Women outnumbered men, 55.9 percent to 44.1 percent.

44.1 percent of the class reported that their parents or guardians earned over $100,000 or more; 28.3 percent reported that their parents or guardians earned between $75–$100,000; 22 percent reported coming from a household with an income between $50–75,000; and 5.5 percent reported that their families' income was between $25–50,000.

40.9 percent of the students who responded to the demographic survey reported that they were first-year students, 40.9 percent reported that they were sophomores, 11 percent reported that they were juniors, and 7.1 percent reported that they were seniors or beyond. Most students reported their ages as between 18–21; the average class age was 19.5.

When asked about what types of media devices they own, 43.3 percent of the students reported that they had a "smart phone" (e.g., a BlackBerry or an iPhone), and 56.7 percent said they did not.

Prof. Susan Moeller led the study research team, and the six teaching assistants for the course acted as researchers/authors, conducting a qualitative content analysis of the student responses. Those six TAs, all Ph.D. students in the Philip Merrill College of Journalism, were: Ms. EunRyung Chong, Mr. Sergei Golitsinski, Ms. Jing Guo, Mr. Raymond McCaffrey, Mr. Andrew Nynka, and Ms. Jessica Roberts.[1]

READING THE TEXT

1. What are the symptoms of addiction to social media, according to the International Center for Media and the Public Agenda study conducted at the University of Maryland?

2. What can journalists learn from this study?

3. What is the primary reason for the use of digital media for the students in this study?

4. In your own words, how can people's reliance on social media be considered an "addiction"?

READING THE SIGNS

1. Write a journal entry in which you reflect upon your own use of text messaging, social media, and other forms of electronic media. Why do you use such media? Would you consider yourself "addicted"? If you do not use them, or do so rarely, why is that your preference?

2. Conduct a similar experiment in your class, having everyone give up their use of all digital media for twenty-four hours. Then use your course Web site to blog about your experiences (or discuss them in class). To what extent does your experiment replicate the results of the University of Maryland study? If your results differ, how do you account for that difference?

---

[1] The study is available online at http://www.withoutmedia.wordpress.com.

3. Write an essay that assesses students' reliance on text messaging and social media as their primary source for news of the world rather than mainstream news sources. You might base your essay on interviews with acquaintances about which news sources they typically rely on.

4. **CONNECTING TEXTS** In "Fast Entertainment and Multitasking in an Always-On World" (p. 393), S. Craig Watkins asks whether media multitasking is "healthy." In an essay, write your own response to his query, using the University of Maryland study as your evidence.

5. Do some research on the clinical definition of "addiction," and then write an essay in which you argue whether reliance on electronic media can accurately be classified as addictive.

FACING FACEBOOK

SIMON DUMENCO

If We're All So Sick of You, Facebook, Why Can't We Quit You?

The death of Facebook has been highly exaggerated, as Simon Dumenco notes in this essay for *Advertising Age*, and the question is, what accounts for Facebook's continuing success even as its PR tanks? The company's success is no accident, Dumenco proposes, because Facebook actively pursues its dormant users, bombarding them with e-mails designed to get them to log back in, while social media and marketing consultants continue to intone the mantra "You *have* to be on Facebook." And so, the social media behemoth that growing numbers of people love to hate, can moan—all the way to the bank. Simon Dumenco is a media columnist for *Advertising Age*.

Facebook is one of the digital world's great shape-shifters—it's endlessly changed its user interface, its business strategy and (notoriously) its privacy policies over the years—but one thing has remained constant: We all love to complain about it.

In fact, hinting at, or outright predicting, the eventual demise of Facebook has become something of an obsession for a lot of the media. *Business Insider*, for instance, recently ran a post titled. "You Have to Believe This Chart Makes Mark Zuckerberg Slightly Anxious." The graphic came from Kleiner Perkins' Mary Meeker and it plots the results of a survey of 2,000 social-media users, age 12 to 64, who were asked in 2011 and then again in 2012 which social-media products they use. YouTube, Twitter, Google+, LinkedIn,

Pinterest, Instagram, Tumblr, Foursquare and even MySpace all gained. But Facebook actually shrunk a bit.

Though surveys about self-reported media usage obviously should be taken with a grain of salt, the chart still would seem to jibe with data Nielsen released last month, which said that Facebook shed more than 10 million U.S. users from March 2012 to March 2013 — going from 153 million monthly uniques to 142 million.

But wait! For every Facebook-is-in-trouble story, there is, of course, a counter-narrative. As the *Wall Street Journal*'s Tom Gara wrote in response to the Nielsen figures, "While some web traffic numbers might be down, it's a mistake to read this as a peak in usage. The company is undergoing an amazing boom in mobile usage."

And the revenue is following. As my colleague Cotton Delo reported last   5
month, 30 percent of Facebook's first-quarter ad revenue came from mobile ads, up from 23 percent last quarter. The company pulled in $1.46 billion in revenue last quarter, vs. $1.06 billion in the same quarter a year ago.

So, basically: Facebook usage in the U.S. might be down, or maybe it's just flat, but mobile is growing, and revenue is up. Which means, what, exactly? What's missing from our big-picture understanding of Facebook? Some thoughts:

We don't have access to the right data, really.

Speaking of self-reporting, Facebook itself claims "1.11 billion monthly active users as of March 2013." That, of course, includes users who visit Facebook as infrequently as once every four weeks or so — the kind of users who think of Facebook as less of an immersive hangout and more as a sort of monolithic directory that's occasionally useful for tracking people down (because "everyone's on Facebook"). A utility, of sorts.

Facebook's other most recent self-reported start — "655 million daily active users on average in March 2013" — offers a little more insight, but not much. Mainly because Facebook doesn't break that number down country-by-country (though it does concede that "79 percent of our daily active users are outside the U.S. and Canada"). And also because "daily active" . . . well, that covers everyone from the status-updating, picture-posting addict to the time-strapped user who, say, quickly checks her Facebook inbox every morning as a matter of habit.

Facebook stalks people into being "active."   10

You know the Morrissey song "The More You Ignore Me, the Closer I Get"? That's Facebook's modus operandi. If you don't log in for a while, Facebook guilts you into visiting with its vaguely desperate "You have notifications pending" emails, which name-check friends and colleagues who have "posted statuses, photos and more on Facebook." In one recent two-week period, for example, during which I stayed away from Facebook, I got four such emails (on May 19, 23, 28 and 29). In essence, Facebook is using the oldest trick in the digital-marketing book — email — to keep those users who are sick of Facebook from abandoning it entirely.

Facebook's big mobile push lets it be a "must-spend" in a whole new way. But for how long?

"You have to be on Facebook." Self-appointed social-media and marketing "experts" still say that sort of thing, even though it's increasingly clear that Facebook is helpful for certain kinds of products and pretty useless for others.

There's still a lot of experimental marketing spend flooding into social media, but by becoming, almost overnight, a company with significant mobile revenue, Facebook can now also partake of the ongoing mobile-marketing frenzy/paranoia.

Remember, before mobile, before Facebook, there were marketing "experts" who were saying, "You have to be on MySpace." And to rewind to the dawn of digital-marketing time, in the '90s their forebears were saying, "You have to be on AOL." 15

AOL posted some amazing numbers during its go-go years because a lot of marketers really believed the hype about advertising on AOL being almost mandatory. Until, you know, they didn't.

These days, if you're a CMO who has been questioning the "You have to be on Facebook" dogma, well, there's a new faith — "You have to be on mobile" — and continuing to spend on the newly mobile-first Facebook satisfies that imperative.

For the time being, at least.

READING THE TEXT

1. What evidence does Dumenco advance to demonstrate — and complicate — the "Facebook-is-in-trouble" story?

2. In your own words, how does Facebook "stalk" users into remaining constant fans?

3. Characterize Dumenco's tone here. How does it affect your response to his article?

4. What are the implications for Facebook that Dumenco sees in the history of MySpace and AOL?

READING THE SIGNS

1. In class, discuss the validity of Dumenco's opening claim that "we all love to complain about [Facebook]"? Do you think that Facebook receives as much criticism as Dumenco implies? If so, how might Facebook's business practices contribute to that response? If not, why not?

2. Individuals are not the only ones with Facebook pages; big institutions like universities, businesses, and governmental entities have them as well. In an essay, explore the extent to which the ubiquity of such pages pressures people to join Facebook.

3. Facebook has largely replaced the open-to-all world of blogging, which means that much of what once appeared to any viewer in blogs now is visible only to Facebook members. In a contemplative essay, explore the extent to which this restriction limits the exchange of opinion and information.

danah boyd

Implications of User Choice: The Cultural Logic of "MySpace or Facebook?"

Once upon a time, everyone was on MySpace. Or almost everyone. Oh, there was Friendster and Facebook, but Facebook was for networking adults and a few Ivy League college students. Then, suddenly, everyone was on Facebook. Well, not everyone, of course, and in this 2009 study of the shift from MySpace to Facebook, danah boyd explains what happened. Interviewing numerous Facebook users, boyd concludes that a good deal of racial and class snobbery was involved, with Facebook users referring, somewhat shamefacedly, to MySpace as a "ghetto." So maybe the world of social networking isn't really drawing people together after all; it may only be reproducing ancient conflicts and divisions. A researcher at Microsoft Research, a research assistant professor in media, culture, and communication at New York University, and a fellow at Harvard University's Berkman Center, danah boyd specializes in the sociology of the Internet.

Many of us have had our lives transformed by technology. And many of us are also enamored of the transformative potential of technology, which has led us to develop technology and become advocates of technological practices. As we become more enveloped in and by technology, it's easy to feel excited about what's going on. Yet we must also be cautious.

The rhetoric around technology often makes it out to be the great equalizer of society, suggesting that technology can in and of itself make the world a better place. Let's ignore the technological determinist overtones for a moment and note that this rhetoric fails to capture the complex ways in which the actual adoption of technology tends to mirror and magnify a whole suite of societal issues.

It is crucial that we begin accounting for how technology actually reveals social stratification and reproduces social divisions. For decades we've assumed that inequality in relation to technology has everything to do with access and that if we fix the access problem, all will be fine. This is the grand narrative of politicized concepts like the digital divide. Yet, increasingly, we're seeing people with similar levels of access engage with technology in very different ways. And we're experiencing a social media landscape in which participation "choice" leads to a digital reproduction of social divisions, which already pervade society.

Rather than staying in the land of the abstract, let's go concrete with a specific case study: the differential adoption of MySpace and Facebook among American teens. I have been doing ethnographic fieldwork on various aspects of social network sites since 2003. Starting in 2005, I began specifically focusing on the social media practices of American high school–age teenagers. During the 2006–2007 school year, I started noticing a trend. In each school, in each part of the country, there were teens who opted for MySpace and teens who opted for Facebook. There were also plenty of teens who used both. At the beginning of the school year, teens were asking "Are you on MySpace? Yes or No?" At the end of the school year, the question had changed to "MySpace or Facebook?"

In analyzing my data, one can reasonably see this as a matter of indi- 5 vidual choice in a competitive market. There are plenty of teenagers who will tell you that they are on one or the other as a matter of personal preference having to do with features, functionality, design, and usability. For example, Justin (15, Austin) prefers Facebook because of the unlimited pictures while Anindita (17, Los Angeles) likes that MySpace is "more complex" while "Facebook is just plain white and that's it."

Teens will also talk about their perceptions of different sites, about what they think certain affordances mean, or how they perceive the sites in relation to values they hold, such as safety. For example, Cachi (18, Iowa) likes that "Facebook is less competitive than MySpace" while Tara (16, Michigan) thinks that Facebook seems safer.

For all of the technology-specific commentary teens offer, the dominant explanation teens will give to justify their choice has to do with their friends. Simply put, they go where their friends are:

KEVIN (15, Seattle): I'm not big on Facebook; I'm a MySpace guy. I have a Facebook and I have some friends on it, but most of my friends don't check it that often so I don't check it that often.

RED (17, Iowa): I am on Facebook and MySpace. I don't talk to people on MySpace anymore. . . . The only reason I still have my MySpace is because my brother's on there.

In choosing to go where their friends are, teens reproduce preexisting social networks. Yet their choice is not neutral. Teens do not randomly select their friends; they connect with people who are like them. This is the basis of the sociological concept of "homophily," which highlights that "birds of a feather stick together." By the time most teens join MySpace or Facebook, they already know someone who is on the site. They are attracted to the site because of the people there. Thus, the early adopters of the sites and the network effects of adoption fundamentally shaped each site's tenor.

MySpace came out first and quickly attracted urban twenty-somethings. It spread to teenagers through older siblings and cousins as well as those who were attracted to indie rock and hip-hop culture. Facebook started at Harvard and spread to the Ivies before spreading more broadly, first to other colleges, then to companies, then elite high schools, and then the unwashed masses. The first teenagers to hear about Facebook were those connected to the early adopters of Facebook (i.e., the Ivy League–bound). Thus, the desirability of the site spread from people who were heading to college. As the two sites grew, they initially attracted different audiences. But by early 2007, teens were choosing between the sites. And while that choice was driven by friendship, it also reinforced distinctions.

Teens recognize that MySpace and Facebook attracted different populations: 10

KAT (14, Massachusetts): I was the first one of my friends to get a Facebook, and then a lot of people got one afterwards. . . . The people who use MySpace — again, not in a racist way — but are usually more like ghetto and hip-hop rap lovers group. And pretty much everyone else might have a Facebook. But there's some people that aren't that. All the rockers, too, will have a MySpace.

In trying to describe what distinguishes the two groups, Kat chooses words that signal that those on MySpace are from a lower socio-economic background and, most probably, black. This is reinforced both by her apology for the racial connotation of her distinction and also by her reference to a different group of youth defined by music, who are presumably not lumped into the group she marks as "ghetto."

The structure of social relations in the United States is shaped by race, socio-economic status, education, and lifestyle. Given the network-driven adoption of MySpace and Facebook, it is not surprising that the adoption patterns also play out along these lines. What is interesting is what happened when some teens chose to move from MySpace to Facebook.

Social media is faddish. MySpace came first and many teens chose to embrace it. When Facebook came along, plenty of teens adopted it as the "new thing." In doing so, some chose to leave MySpace, while others simply maintained two profiles. Yet Facebook did not simply usurp MySpace. In May 2009 — two and a half years after teens began splitting — comScore reported that MySpace and Facebook had roughly equal numbers of unique visitors. In other words, while a shift did occur, not all MySpace users left for Facebook, and not all who joined after both were available opted for the newer site.

Those teens who left were not abstractly driven by fads; they were driven by their social networks. Thus, the shift that took place was also shaped by race, socio-economic status, education, and lifestyle. Here is where the division solidified, marked by social categories and distinctions:

ANASTASIA (17, New York): My school is divided into the "honors kids" (I think that is self-explanatory), the "good not-so-honors kids," "wangstas" (they pretend to be tough and black but when you live in a suburb in Westchester you can't claim much hood), the "latinos/hispanics" (they tend to band together even though they could fit into any other groups), and the "emo kids" (whose lives are alllllways filled with woe). We were all in MySpace with our own little social networks, but when Facebook opened its doors to high schoolers, guess who moved and guess who stayed behind. . . . The first two groups were the first to go and then the "wangstas" split with half of them on Facebook and the rest on MySpace. . . . I shifted with the rest of my school to Facebook and it became the place where the "honors kids" got together and discussed how they were procrastinating over their next AP English essay.

In choosing between the two sites, teens marked one as for "people like me," which suggested that the other was for the "other" people. Teens — and adults — use social categories and labels to identify people with values, tastes, and social positions. As teens chose between MySpace and Facebook, these sites began reflecting the cultural frames of those social categories. Nowhere is this more visible than in the language of those who explicitly chose Facebook over MySpace.

CRAIG (17, California): The higher castes of high school moved to Facebook. It was more cultured, and less cheesy. The lower class usually were content to stick to MySpace. Any high school student who has a Facebook will tell you that MySpace users are more likely to be barely educated and obnoxious. Like Peet's is more cultured than Starbucks, and jazz is more cultured than bubblegum pop, and like Macs are more cultured than PCs, Facebook is of a cooler caliber than MySpace.

Craig's description focuses on a comparison of MySpace and Facebook to a series of lifestyle brands. Taste identification is a way in which people self-segregate. Yet, as with social networks, taste is highly correlated with race, socio-economic status, and education. Social networks also drive taste; people like what their friends like. Thus, in choosing Facebook, teens were both connecting with their friends and identifying with a particular lifestyle brand.

The mere fact that network effects, shaped by homophily, resulted in a self-segregation of teens across two social network sites should not be particularly surprising. Yet it ruptures a well-loved fantasy that the Internet would be a great equalizer in which race and class would no longer matter. Furthermore, it presents new challenges for those seeking to address the costs of social stratification in American society.

Social network sites are not like e-mail, where it doesn't matter if you're on Hotmail or Yahoo (although there are connotations implied, with AOL conveying a different signal than Gmail). These are walled gardens. Those who use MySpace can't communicate with those on Facebook, and vice versa. So choosing to participate in one but not the other introduces a hurdle for communication across social divisions. This is further magnified when educators and politicians and universities and organizations choose to use social network sites to connect with their students/constituents/customers. Choosing one becomes political, because choosing only one means excluding those who opted for the other. Consider, for example, the universities that are doing all of their high school recruiting through Facebook. Or the public officials who use just one platform to reach all constituents, thinking that everyone is or will be present. It's one thing to make this choice to reach a specific demographic; it's another to do so blindly and think that everyone is at the table simply because people like you are.

We cannot expect to suddenly eradicate inequality from society, and it is not surprising that technology reflects persistent social stratification. In raising these issues, I'm not arguing that technology can or should be the great equalizer. Instead, I want us to all recognize that it is not. The technologies that we build are never neutral — they are infused with the values and ideas of the creators and the actions and goals of the users. Network effects of adoption patterns further shape technology. As people begin to identify with specific technologies, they take on specific frames in society and begin to reflect them in everyday life. Understanding that divisions are taking place does not necessarily mean trying to "fix" them; there are perfectly rational explanations for self-segregating. Rather, recognizing social divisions means being conscious of the underlying factors and vigilant in thinking of the implications.

We can ignore the fact that social divisions are taking place, but in doing   20
so we fail to realize that we shape what's unfolding. We are building systems in which social stratification will be reproduced and reenacted even if we do not design it that way. We often launch our systems first to those who are like us; the early adopters who set the norms are baking specific cultural values into our systems. These values can alienate people who are not like us, and the choices we make can thus reinforce social divisions. We are shaping the public dialogue about these technologies and our attitudes reflect our personal structural positions, often at the expense of people who are not like us. Knowing how the technologies we create mirror and shape society is crucial to being an ethical technologist. Even if we don't know how to tackle large societal issues, the least we can do is be conscious of their presence in the environments we create and respect the choices and attitudes of those who aren't like us.

READING THE TEXT

1. How, according to boyd's research, do digital choices reflect existing social divisions?

2. What is the image of MySpace for such young Facebook users as Kat and Anastasia? How do they view the users of Facebook?

3. What does boyd mean by the word "homophily" (para. 8)?

4. In your own words, how are MySpace and Facebook "walled gardens" (para. 18)?

5. What is the social effect of universities' use of Facebook but not MySpace for recruiting purposes, according to boyd?

READING THE SIGNS

1. In your journal, discuss why you prefer to use MySpace, Facebook, or another social networking site. What is your view of sites that you do not use? If you do not use social networking sites, discuss why you are not attracted to them.

2. Write an essay in which you support, refute, or complicate boyd's claim that Facebook and MySpace reproduce racial divisions in America.

3. Watch the movie *The Social Network*, and write a paper arguing for or against the proposition that the prestige of Facebook's Harvard origins has been a significant cause of its rise in popularity and the decline of MySpace.

4. Conduct a class debate in which you address the proposition that technology "reveals social stratification and reproduces social divisions" (para. 3). To develop your ideas, consult the introduction to this chapter. Use the debate as a jumping-off point for your own essay that responds to this proposition

5. Write a comparative essay that analyzes today's Facebook and MySpace. Do the appearances of the sites continue to reflect teenager Craig's opinion that Facebook "was more cultured, and less cheesy" than MySpace (para. 15)?

SALVADOR RODRIGUEZ

In the Digital Age, Breaking Up Is Hard to Do

If only love were as enduring as the digital archive, but alas, as Salvador Rodriguez reports in this personal attestation to the recalcitrance of the social network for couples who have cut the knot, it isn't so. From shared lists to search engines, Dropbox to Google +, the cloud has got your, and your former significant other's, numbers, and it won't let go. Yes, you can try to delete all traces of your love's labor lost, but it's a painful business, Rodriguez laments, and it's likely that you won't get it all anyway. The best way forward, sometimes, is just to log off for a while. Salvador Rodriguez is a technology writer for the *Los Angeles Times*, where this article first appeared.

It's Valentine's Day, and I'm not celebrating. A few weeks ago my fiancée and I broke up.

It was a difficult breakup, so I immediately stopped following her on Facebook, Twitter and Instagram, and deleted her name from my iPhone address book.

I thought that would be enough to disconnect her from my digital life. But I'm finding out — as many others have in the age of smartphones and social networks — that connecting is easy, but severing ties online is nearly impossible. Take even the basic task of doing an Internet search. When I type in the letter "T" into my Web browser, Google suggests Twitter and just below that it lists my former fiancée's Twitter handle. Other social media platforms serve up similar uncomfortable reminders. It feels like no matter what I do, I run into her online.

Ka-Yuet Liu, a sociologist who studies social networks at UCLA, said I'm not alone. Social networks have taken away some of the controls that we have over our social lives. As soon as we post information, it is forever on the Internet somewhere, she said. That means you can't undo or wipe away a memory by merely pressing the delete button.

Adrian Miller, who runs a Studio City Web branding firm, recently ended   5 a relationship with his longtime girlfriend, leading him to swear off social media so that he can focus his attention on other things. "I just have not looked at Facebook, Twitter, Instagram or any of that, and I'm not going to for another, at least, month," the Los Feliz resident said. "Do something else. Go to a movie, get in the community. At the end of the day, you cannot let social media dictate you or your life."

Miller, 43, said that disconnecting is tough because many people rely on the Internet to manage a great deal of their social lives, so they share too much personal information. He has kept busy working on HeartBreakSecrets .com, a new website he created that gives users who are dealing with break-ups a place to go to write about their experiences anonymously. "Just bleed your heart, tell your story," he said. "Because you don't want to do that on your Facebook page."

But it's not just romantic breakups that can be distressing when it comes to disconnecting. A few years back, Miller left a job under less than friendly terms. In the years before social networking, he would have naturally stopped seeing his former colleagues and hearing about them unless he sought them out. But because he was friends with them on Facebook, Miller said he had to manually delete all of them, one by one. "I just didn't want to deal with any of those people anymore," he said. "I don't want to see their respective timelines and feeds."

Or in my case, efforts by social networks to make it easier for me to connect has made it impossible for me to disconnect from my former fiancée.

After my breakup, when I typed "V" (the initial of my former fiancée's first name) into the Twitter search feature, her profile was the first suggestion that popped up.

When I use Facebook's Messenger app, her name is the first suggestion when   10 I want to start a new chat, even though we're no longer connected on Facebook.

On Spotify, a music streaming service, I was able to delete the playlists I shared with her and unfollow her so I won't see what she's listening to. But I have not been able to block her from seeing what I'm enjoying.

On Dropbox, the cloud storage service, are hundreds of photos of us together shot with my phone that it backed up for me automatically, along with countless other photos. I've stopped trying to go through them and delete them one by one. Google + does the same, and it also stores some GIFs, or short slide shows, of my proposal to her. It will be a while before I browse through my photos on either of these services.

We've been apart for a few weeks now, but the most recent instance of randomly coming across her on the Web was one that was particularly devastating. It came courtesy of LinkedIn, the social network for professionals.

I logged into LinkedIn because I hadn't used the service in a while and I had a ton of notifications that needed attention. I went through dozens of connection requests and was feeling very proud of myself for clearing them out. I finished the last request, and that's when I felt like *Fight Club*'s Tyler Durden had punched me right in the stomach.

"Join V . . . , Dustin and 313 others who have found people they already   15
know," the service said, hoping to keep me on its website a little longer.

When I saw her avatar right below that suggestion, LinkedIn nearly brought me to tears.

READING THE TEXT

1. Why did Rodriguez assume that it would be easy to disconnect his former fiancée from his digital life?

2. How do social media platforms manage to hold on to one's personal information, according to Rodriguez?

3. In your own words, explain what sociologist Ka-Yuet Liu means by saying that "social networks have taken away some of the controls that we have over our social lives" (para. 4).

4. In what ways does Rodriguez's personal tale of a broken relationship shape your response to his selection?

READING THE SIGNS

1. Rodriguez laments that postings on social media sites remain "forever" and that a user has little control over his or her own online content. In class, brainstorm a set of guidelines that people should consider when posting personal or romantic material online. To what extent do class members already follow these guidelines? Why? If the class had difficulty drafting such guidelines, what problems emerged?

2. Snapchat is an app that supposedly avoids the "online forever" problem that Rodriguez describes because it almost instantaneously deletes posts. Study Snapchat, and then write an essay analyzing whether it can indeed protect you from the problems Rodriguez cites and why that protection may be appealing.

3. Interview friends who are active on social media sites about their motivation for posting personal information. Based on your results, to what extent do they acknowledge sociologist Ka-Yuet Liu's claim that "[s]ocial networks have taken away some of the controls that we have over our social lives" (para. 4)?

4. **CONNECTING TEXTS**   Read Rachel Lowry's "Straddling Online and Offline Profiles, Millennials Search for Identity" (p. 500). Assuming the perspective of Lowry's interviewee Mariah Hanaike, write a letter to Rodriguez in which you offer him advice on how to handle the difficulty of stopping a romantic relationship in the digital age.

RICHARD RUSHFIELD

Toward a Unified Theory of How the Internet Makes Everything Terrible

Watching television isn't bird-watching, but you'd be forgiven for thinking it was, with all the tweeting that goes on every time a popular show like *Game of Thrones* airs. And this, Richard Rushfield believes, is too much — too much media frenzy "articulating the frenzy of the mob." It's *Sharknado* out there on the Internet, Rushfield believes, and the only way to stop it is by simply "shutting the hell up." Richard Rushfield is the author of the blog *Rushfield Babylon: Where It All Went Wrong*, in which this plea for a sense of proportion first appeared.

I have nothing bad to say about *Breaking Bad*. I was completely gripped by Sunday night's episode. I've watched it twice and enjoyed it more the second time. I think when the show concludes it is certain to go down as one of the great dramas in TV history. What quibbles I have with the show I recognize as just that — quibbles.

So why on Monday did the Internet make me ashamed to have watched the show, much less to have liked it? Part of the revulsion is no doubt due to some vestigial adolescent need to feel myself ahead of the crowd and just getting cranky when I find my tastes are actually not particularly unique or special.

But beyond that, I think there is something terrifying about the way the Internet turns out for these events and cranks up the GIF, meme, Tweet and think piece machines like some sort of disembodied 4th of July parade. These moments carry a desperation with them; the logical conclusion of the *Bowling Alone* thing, where now living our lives glued to our individual screens cut off from actual human interaction, we are desperate to find ways to march together. I've noticed that these events — awards shows, series premieres, etc. — are becoming bigger and bigger group phenomena. Super Bowl ratings have never been higher. The Grammies for chrissake inch upwards. We want to watch together. In our own homes, in front of our own multiple screens. All to some extent harmless enough. If the world (or the upscale, urban sub-sub-subset of the world) can find some comfort in cheering on an episode of gritty drama together, then good for it for finding some in this cold machine-driven world. But here are the downsides as I see them.

In our desperation to make a community out of watching an episode of a TV show, we pour more of our hopes and desires into that show than any hour of entertainment can bear. We meme the life out of whatever is original and striking about a work within minutes, overexposing it so much it becomes noxious. In olden times, it took years for enough VHS copies of *Scarface* to trickle back to frat houses so that every brother could do a passably awful Tony Montana imitation and make you wince when you heard the real thing. And in the meantime people could talk about the film, consider it, pass judgment and change their mind before the re-use of the film became this world-devouring thing apart from the show itself. Today, "I'm the one who knocks" and "say my name" are reproduced in every form upside down and backwards literally before the show is even over and any hope of a quiet place to take it in is in vain.

The fancy media, instead of calming the crowd, now only stokes the flames. Once they could have put things in perspective, but now they see their job as articulating the frenzy of the mob. What is the good of having a blog or a Twitter account if you're going to be the only corner of this corner of the Internet not enjoying the hooplah? And if you're a professional reviewer and get screeners in advance you can actually get ahead of the mob by declaring an episode the best thing since Euripides before anyone else has even watched it, and hope that your words are printed on banners in the parade.

Frenzied mobs, history has shown us, are not always just about fun, games and watching TV together. Now and then, they can have a dark side. Once we say this is all about us just piling on together for some kind of group ecstatic transformation, that can lead to all kinds of places, and as I have noted in the past, Twitter's less attractive tendency to transform into a lynch mob at the drop of a hat. Its hunger for fresh blood has not in the least abated.

Of late, its hunger has actually become an industry. *Sharknado* represents the Internet now creating material for itself to mock. In olden times again, the camp fun of watching old disaster films was mocking the dead serious overacting and unintentionally hamfisted actions. Now at Twitter's demand, networks are producing intentionally hamfisted and overacted pieces so the Internet can tear them apart. They are even letting us—in a contest—pick the name that we find most mockable. So we pick the thing we most want to rip to shreds, like a school bully making a nerd dress up in the most ridiculous costume, so we can make fun of him for wearing it.

What is the solution? Well, as America's leading anti–First Amendment crusader I have advocated the power and dignity of shutting the hell up many times before. Short of that catching fire, we can pray the Internet continues to be merely annoying and only sporadically dangerous. And short of that, networks that want their shows to be appreciated by the people and not just the subject of a mass spectacle should stop sending screeners to critics. That part of the conversation at least we can put a lid on.

READING THE TEXT

1. What does Rushfield's title signify to you, and why do you think he used this title for this essay?

2. In your own words, why do you think Rushfield objects to the Internet response to an episode of *Breaking Bad*? In what general media trend does he locate this particular incident?

3. Characterize Rushfield's tone in this selection. To what extent does it affect your response as a reader? How do you suppose Rushfield meant his readers to take his essay?

4. Rushfield states, "The fancy media, instead of calming the crowd, now only stokes the flames" (para. 5). Why does he say this?

READING THE SIGNS

1. **CONNECTING TEXTS**   Adopt the perspective of S. Craig Watkins ("Fast Entertainment and Multitasking in an Always-On World," p. 393), and analyze the effect of instant media-generated responses to media products. How would Watkins interpret the plethora of awards shows, premieres, tweet fests, and the like?

2. Rushfield identifies "Twitter's less attractive tendency to transform into a lynch mob at the drop of a hat" and observes that "its hunger for fresh blood has not in the least abated" (para. 6). In an essay, support, refute, or modify Rushfield's criticism.

3. Rushfield claims that today "[w]e want to watch together. In our own homes, in front of our own multiple screens" (para. 3). In an argumentative essay, discuss whether or how this behavior exemplifies a form of digital addiction. To develop your ideas, consult the International Center for Media and the Public Agenda's "Students Addicted to Social Media" (p. 403).

DANIEL D'ADDARIO

Everything Is "Trolling" Now

What is "trolling?" Well, it's rather hard to say, Daniel D'Addario believes, now that we use the word *trolling* so frequently "its meaning seems to evaporate into air." Providing a concise history of the popular Internet term — from how it began to where it went wrong — D'Addario illustrates how a once-useful word can become useless once it gets overused. We can only hope that this article doesn't bring the trolls out. Daniel D'Addario is a staff reporter for *Salon*, in which this article originally appeared.

If everyone is a troll, maybe no one is.

In the past few years, accusations of "trolling" have flown across the Internet fast and furious; recently, the targets have included a *New York Times* feature about the popularity of chopped salads, just about everything *Vice* does, and a cover of *Rolling Stone* featuring Dzhokhar Tsarnaev.

But for a word that's tossed around so frequently, its meaning seems to evaporate into air when grasped at. Trolling is bad. Trolling provokes a reaction, usually negative. Trolling is apparently quite easy to do. But, if only to better gird one's own defenses against it — what *is* trolling?

"I think that it started with a pretty clear definition — which is somebody who goes into a place that shares a particular ideology and says something they don't believe just to get a reaction," said Sady Doyle, a feminist blogger and staff writer for *In These Times*.

"Originally, it was, like, racist Reddit kids going into r/blackgirls — that was old-school trolling, a very specific online behavior," said Matt Buchanan, a tech blogger for the *New Yorker*, referring to the popular message board and clearinghouse for human pathologies in which racist, sexist or homophobic vitriol flowed freely. On Reddit, clearly defined groups sort themselves according to demographics, identity and ideology — a troll would attempt to disrupt these groups, and order as normal. Trolls, as classically defined, could insert themselves into any number of milieus; the classic *New York Times Magazine* piece documenting the state of the troll in 2008 recorded instances like self-defined trolls hacking the Epilepsy Foundation's website in order to fill it with flashing lights, triggers for epileptics. As an action designed to harm and upset a specific group of people, it wasn't exactly a newspaper piece about salad. 5

"It's one of those semi-useful but also dumb Internet words that just kind of means whatever you want it to mean," said Shani Hilton, an editor at *BuzzFeed*. "It's a good shorthand for a kind of thing that's been going on for a long time at more contrarian publications." Consider the case of *Newsweek*, the publication that got attention for splashy covers (like the one featuring a resurrected Princess Diana, aged 50, or the one calling Barack Obama "The First Gay President"). Those were frustrating — so too was *Newsweek*'s online arm the *Daily Beast* publishing a gallery of "magazine controversies" today after spending years trying to provoke. But whose existence or fixed ideas were they upending?

"People have come to use the word 'troll' to mean, 'It made me angry on the Internet,'" said Doyle. "And that's pretty broad. It's a big and noisy Internet."

During the rise of the troll, the Internet was less in the thrall of legacy media than it is today; legacy media outlets, by their very nature, broadcast to a wide audience rather than a narrow and self-selecting community. If the visually striking, provocative and attention-getting *Rolling Stone* cover is trolling, what, then, are the visually striking, provocative and attention-getting covers George Lois designed for *Esquire* in the mid-20th century? (Lois recently told *New York* magazine the cover should "maybe have a devil's tongue or horns. I'm not saying I would do that, but you better do something" — such a visual frippery would, if the media outrage cycle behaved as normal, likely only further elicit calls of trolling.)

"When people accuse publications of trolling," said Doyle, "it's a weird rhetorical move that erases the content and says, 'You made me angry, you must have meant to, I don't need to engage with the content of the article.'"

"It's a cheap shot," said Maria Bustillos, whose recent sympathetic inter- 10
view of a pickup artist on *The Awl* came in for that very criticism. "You have
to come out and say, 'I want to have a productive conversation on this topic.'
And to have to say that is silly. We're all adults. It takes the whole conversation down a notch.

"There's certain writers accused of it, publications accused of it — for
instance, the *Daily Caller* — there's worthy stuff in there in it. It's hard to
believe the whole publication's not worth reading, that it's all trolling. They do
have polemicists, but there's stuff worth reading."

The distinction is important; perhaps a polemicist, a politically minded
columnist whose very purpose is not merely to engage in the world of ideas
but stir the blood of a self-selected few and poke at the other side, can be
a troll. But is it really possible to "troll" when broadcasting to the universe?
If so, perhaps the Internet has evolved too quickly; though we're in a vast
and free-form space, we all still believe we're in walled gardens. When anything upsetting invades that garden, we don't discuss the emotions or ideas
aroused by the image of an alleged terrorist as tousled-haired boy, or reflect
on what it means to live in an age when the variegations of salad-choppings
and -toppings are endlessly debatable among a certain class. We tend to reach
for something a bit more ad hominem.

But perhaps sometimes trolling can be good. Said Bustillos, "Some people
use it as a slur. It's not always meant that way. A lot of people on Twitter use it
to mean 'You're a provocateur.' I'm perfectly happy being called that. It's not
uniformly pejorative."

The distinction Bustillos draws — between a conversation, one that's ultimately productive through the painful process of challenging assumptions, and
the sort of personal, targeted hate that trolling historically had been — is a difficult one for Internet users. It's your Internet. *Everything* seems personal. But,
said Doyle, it's more difficult than accusers think to get people's hackles up.

"I can't ever think of a published piece as trolling," she said. "Someone 15
must have wanted to write this piece enough to commit to a deadline and commit to an editing process. It's a heck of a lot of work to get a couple people
angry. It's not in the best interest of a publication or a writer's career to do that.
But maybe I'm naive."

As for the future, "trolling" may literally be redefined in exactly the way "literally" has (though as Buchanan notes, many Internet-savvy folks are already
using it as a joke, saying anything that even mildly offends them is "trolling").
The term may move from conflating malevolent actions and pageview-
baiting to simply describing the second. "It's the best way to describe it," said
Buchanan, "a certain, compact way of describing! It's why we use German
words. It's such a good descriptor!"

READING THE TEXT

1. According to D'Addario, how has the meaning of the word *troll*, in the context
   of the Internet, evolved?

2. What does D'Addario mean by the term "legacy media" (para. 8)?

3. How does Maria Bustillos distinguish between Internet trolling and criticism delivered in a published piece? How convincing do you find that distinction?

4. What does D'Addario mean when he says, "As for the future, 'trolling' may literally be redefined in exactly the way 'literally' has" (para. 16)?

READING THE SIGNS

1. In small groups in class, compose your own definition of online trolling, being sure to provide specific examples for illustration. Compare the groups' results. Which definitions would you consider accurate and current? Why?

2. Write an essay in which you support, refute, or complicate Maria Bustillos's contention that trolling can have benefits.

3. Visit a political Web site or forum, and study the level of decorum you observe. To what extent do you find that trolling has become the new normal for Internet communication?

4. The comments sections of everything from online news pages and newspapers to YouTube are filled with violent and hostile posts that could be described as "trolling." Write an essay in which you present your own argument for, against, or complicating the proposition that such comments should be moderated.

HENRY JENKINS
Convergence Culture

You're watching *American Idol* and a text message comes in informing you that AmericanIdolWatch.com reports that the guy who sings like Alvin the Chipmunk is outpolling your favorite contestant, so you log in to check the report and then phone in your vote to *American Idol* before "Alvin" can move on to the next level. Though it may seem pretty routine to you, your movement from television screen, to text messaging, to the Internet, to cell phone constitutes a newly emerging mixture of old and new media that Henry Jenkins calls "convergence culture." In this selection from his book of the same title, Jenkins describes the new multi-mixed media and their possible effects on society and human consciousness. A self-avowed fan of the new media, Henry Jenkins is the founder of MIT's Comparative Media Studies Program, and he is currently the provost's professor of communication, journalism, and cinematic arts at the University of Southern California. He is the author of numerous books, including *Textual Poachers: Television Fans and Participatory Culture* (1998), *Convergence Culture: Where Old and New Media Collide* (2006), *The Wow Climax: Tracing the Emotional Impact of Popular Culture* (2007), and *Spreadable Media: Creating Value and Meaning in a Networked Culture* (2013, coauthored with Sam Ford and Joshua Green).

Worship at the Altar of Convergence
— Slogan, the New Orleans Media Experience (2003)

The story circulated in the fall of 2001: Dino Ignacio, a Filipino-American high school student created a Photoshop collage of *Sesame Street*'s (1970) Bert interacting with terrorist leader Osama Bin Laden as part of a series of "Bert Is Evil" images he posted on his homepage. Others depicted Bert as a Klansman, cavorting with Adolph Hitler, dressed as the Unabomber, or having sex with Pamela Anderson. It was all in good fun.

In the wake of September 11, a Bangladesh-based publisher scanned the Web for Bin Laden images to print on anti-American signs, posters, and T-shirts. *Sesame Street* is available in Pakistan in a localized format; the Arab world, thus, had no exposure to Bert and Ernie. The publisher may not have recognized Bert, but he must have thought the image was a good likeness of the al-Qaeda leader. The image ended up in a collage of similar images that was printed on thousands of posters and distributed across the Middle East.

CNN reporters recorded the unlikely sight of a mob of angry protestors marching through the streets chanting anti-American slogans and waving signs depicting Bert and Bin Laden (Fig. 1). Representatives from the Children's Television Workshop, creators of the *Sesame Street* series, spotted the CNN footage and threatened to take legal action: "We're outraged that our characters would be used in this unfortunate and distasteful manner. The people responsible for this should be ashamed of themselves. We are exploring all legal options to stop this abuse and any similar abuses in the future." It was not altogether clear whom they planned to sic their intellectual property attorneys on — the young man who had initially appropriated their images, or the terrorist supporters who deployed them. Coming full circle, amused fans produced a number of new sites, linking various *Sesame Street* characters with terrorists.

From his bedroom, Ignacio sparked an international controversy. His images crisscrossed the world, sometimes on the backs of commercial media, sometimes via grassroots media. And, in the end, he inspired his own cult following. As the publicity grew, Ignacio became more concerned and ultimately decided to dismantle his site: "I feel this has gotten too close to reality. . . . 'Bert Is Evil' and its following has always been contained and

© Reuters/Corbis

FIGURE 1   Ignacio's collage surprisingly appeared in CNN coverage of anti-American protests following September 11.

distanced from big media. This issue throws it out in the open."[1] Welcome to convergence culture, where old and new media collide, where grassroots and corporate media intersect, where the power of the media producer and the power of the media consumer interact in unpredictable ways. . . .

By convergence, I mean the flow of content across multiple media plat- 5 forms, the cooperation between multiple media industries, and the migratory behavior of media audiences who will go almost anywhere in search of the kinds of entertainment experiences they want. Convergence is a word that manages to describe technological, industrial, cultural, and social changes depending on who's speaking and what they think they are talking about. . . .

In the world of media convergence, every important story gets told, every brand gets sold, and every consumer gets courted across multiple media platforms. Think about the circuits that the Bert Is Evil images traveled — from *Sesame Street* through Photoshop to the World Wide Web, from Ignacio's bedroom to a print shop in Bangladesh, from the posters held up by anti-American protestors that are captured by CNN and into the living rooms of people around the world. Some of its circulation depended on corporate strategies, such as the localization of *Sesame Street* or the global coverage of CNN. Some of its circulation depended on tactics of grassroots appropriation, whether in North America or in the Middle East.

---

[1]Josh Grossberg, "The Bert-Bin Laden Connection?" E Online, October 10, 2001, http://www.eonline.com/News/Items/0,1,8950,00.html. For a different perspective on Bert and Bin Laden, see Roy Rosenzweig, "Scarcity or Abundance? Preserving the Past in a Digital Era," *American Historical Review* 108 (June 2003).

This circulation of media content — across different media systems, competing media economies, and national borders — depends heavily on consumers' active participation. I . . . argue here against the idea that convergence should be understood primarily as a technological process bringing together multiple media functions within the same devices. Instead, convergence represents a cultural shift as consumers are encouraged to seek out new information and make connections among dispersed media content. . . .

The term *participatory culture*, contrasts with older notions of passive media spectatorship. Rather than talking about media producers and consumers as occupying separate roles, we might now see them as participants who interact with each other according to a new set of rules that none of us fully understands. Not all participants are created equal. Corporations — and even individuals within corporate media — still exert greater power than any individual consumer or even the aggregate of consumers. And some consumers have greater abilities to participate in this emerging culture than others.

Convergence does not occur through media appliances, however sophisticated they may become. Convergence occurs within the brains of individual consumers and through their social interactions with others. Each of us constructs our own personal mythology from bits and fragments of information extracted from the media flow and transformed into resources through which we make sense of our everyday lives. Because there is more information on any given topic than anyone can store in their head, there is an added incentive for us to talk among ourselves about the media we consume. This conversation creates buzz that is increasingly valued by the media industry. Consumption has become a collective process — and that's what [I mean] by *collective intelligence*, a term coined by French cybertheorist Pierre Lévy. None of us can know everything; each of us knows something; and we can put the pieces together if we pool our resources and combine our skills. Collective intelligence can be seen as an alternative source of media power. We are learning how to use that power through our day-to-day interactions within convergence culture. Right now, we are mostly using this collective power through our recreational life, but soon we will be deploying those skills for more "serious" purposes. . . .

Convergence Talk

Another snapshot of convergence culture at work: In December 2004, a hotly 10 anticipated Bollywood film, *Rok Sako To Rok Lo* (2004), was screened in its entirety to movie buffs in Delhi, Bangalore, Hyderabad, Mumbai, and other parts of India through EDGE-enabled mobile phones with live video streaming facility. This is believed to be the first time that a feature film had been fully accessible via mobile phones.[2]

---

[2]"RSTRL to Premier on Cell Phone," IndiaFM News Bureau, December 6, 2004, http://www.indiafm.com/scoop/04/dec/0612rstrlcell/index.shtml.

Over the past several years, many of us have watched as cell phones have become increasingly central to the release strategies of commercial motion pictures around the world, as amateur and professional cell phone movies have competed for prizes in international film festivals, as mobile users have been able to listen in to major concerts, as Japanese novelists serialize their work via instant messenger, and as game players have used mobile devices to compete in augmented and alternative reality games. Some functions will take root; others will fail.

Call me old-fashioned. The other week I wanted to buy a cell phone — you know, to make phone calls. I didn't want a video camera, a still camera, a Web access device, an MP3 player, or a game system. I also wasn't interested in something that could show me movie previews, would have customizable ring tones, or would allow me to read novels. I didn't want the electronic equivalent of a Swiss army knife. When the phone rings, I don't want to have to figure out which button to push. I just wanted a phone. The sales clerks sneered at me; they laughed at me behind my back. I was told by company after mobile company that they don't make single-function phones anymore. Nobody wants them. This was a powerful demonstration of how central mobiles have become to the process of media convergence.

You've probably been hearing a lot about convergence lately. You are going to be hearing even more.

The media industries are undergoing another paradigm shift. It happens from time to time. In the 1990s, rhetoric about a coming digital revolution contained an implicit and often explicit assumption that new media were going to push aside old media, that the Internet was going to displace broadcasting, and that all of this would enable consumers to more easily access media content that was personally meaningful to them. A best-seller in 1995, Nicholas Negroponte's *Being Digital* drew a sharp contrast between "passive old media" and "interactive new media," predicting the collapse of broadcast networks in favor of an era of narrowcasting and niche media on demand: "What will happen to broadcast television over the next five years is so phenomenal that it's difficult to comprehend."[3] At one point, he suggests that no government regulation will be necessary to shatter the media conglomerates: "The monolithic empires of mass media are dissolving into an array of cottage industries. . . . Media barons of today will be grasping to hold onto their centralized empires tomorrow. . . . The combined forces of technology and human nature will ultimately take a stronger hand in plurality than any laws Congress can invent."[4] Sometimes, the new media companies spoke about convergence, but by this term, they seemed to mean that old media would be absorbed fully and completely into the orbit of the emerging technologies. George Gilder, another digital revolutionary, dismissed such claims: "The computer industry is converging with the television industry in the same sense that

[3]Nicholas Negroponte, *Being Digital* (New York: Alfred A. Knopf, 1995), p. 54.
[4]Ibid., pp. 57–58.

Robyn Beck/AFP/Getty Images

An attendee of the 2014 Consumer Electronics Show tries the Epson Moverio BT-200 smart glasses. Each lens has its own display right in the user's field of vision.

the automobile converged with the horse, the TV converged with the nickel-odeon, the word-processing program converged with the typewriter, the CAD program converged with the drafting board, and digital desktop publishing converged with the linotype machine and the letterpress."[5] For Gilder, the computer had come not to transform mass culture but to destroy it.

The popping of the dot-com bubble threw cold water on this talk of a   15 digital revolution. Now, convergence has reemerged as an important reference point as old and new media companies try to imagine the future of the entertainment industry. If the digital revolution paradigm presumed that new media would displace old media, the emerging convergence paradigm assumes that old and new media will interact in even more complex ways. The digital revolution paradigm claimed that new media were going to change everything. After the dot-com crash, the tendency was to imagine that new media had changed nothing. As with so many things about the current media environment, the truth lay somewhere in between. More and more, industry

[5]George Gilder, "Afterword: The Computer Juggernaut: Life after *Life after Television*," added to the 1994 edition of *Life after Television: The Coming Transformation of Media and American Life* (New York: W. W. Norton), p. 189. The book was originally published in 1990.

leaders are returning to convergence as a way of making sense of a moment of disorienting change. Convergence is, in that sense, an old concept taking on new meanings. . . .

The Prophet of Convergence

If *Wired* magazine declared Marshall McLuhan the patron saint of the digital revolution, we might well describe the late MIT political scientist Ithiel de Sola Pool as the prophet of media convergence. Pool's *Technologies of Freedom* (1983) was probably the first book to lay out the concept of convergence as a force of change within the media industries:

> A process called the "convergence of modes" is blurring the lines between media, even between point-to-point communications, such as the post, telephone, and telegraph, and mass communications, such as the press, radio, and television. A single physical means — be it wires, cables or air-waves — may carry services that in the past were provided in separate ways. Conversely, a service that was provided in the past by any one medium — be it broadcasting, the press, or telephony — can now be provided in several different physical ways. So the one-to-one relationship that used to exist between a medium and its use is eroding.[6]

Some people today talk about divergence rather than convergence, but Pool understood that they were two sides of the same phenomenon.

"Once upon a time," Pool explained, "companies that published news-papers, magazines, and books did very little else; their involvement with other media was slight."[7] Each medium had its own distinctive functions and markets, and each was regulated under different regimes, depending on whether its character was centralized or decentralized, marked by scarcity or plenitude, dominated by news or entertainment, and owned by governmental or private interests. Pool felt that these differences were largely the product of political choices and preserved through habit rather than any essential characteristic of the various technologies. But he did see some communications technologies as supporting more diversity and a greater degree of participation than others: "Freedom is fostered when the means of communication are dispersed, decentralized, and easily available, as are printing presses or microcomputers. Central control is more likely when the means of communication are concentrated, monopolized, and scarce, as are great networks."[8]

Several forces, however, have begun breaking down the walls separating these different media. New media technologies enabled the same content to

[6]Ithiel de Sola Pool, *Technologies of Freedom: On Free Speech in an Electronic Age* (Cambridge, Mass.: Harvard University Press, 1983), p. 23.
[7]Ibid.
[8]Ibid., p. 5.

flow through many different channels and assume many different forms at the point of reception. Pool was describing what Nicholas Negroponte calls the transformation of "atoms into bytes" or digitization.[9] At the same time, new patterns of cross-media ownership that began in the mid-1980s, during what we can now see as the first phase of a longer process of media concentration, were making it more desirable for companies to distribute content across the various channels rather than within a single media platform. Digitization set the conditions for convergence; corporate conglomerates created its imperative.

Much writing about the so-called digital revolution presumed that the outcome of technological change was more or less inevitable. Pool, on the other hand, predicted a period of prolonged transition, during which the various media systems competed and collaborated, searching for the stability that would always elude them: "Convergence does not mean ultimate stability or unity. It operates as a constant force for unification but always in dynamic tension with change. . . . There is no immutable law of growing convergence; the process of change is more complicated than that."[10]

As Pool predicted, we are in an age of media transition, one marked by   20
tactical decisions and unintended consequences, mixed signals and competing interests, and most of all, unclear directions and unpredictable outcomes.[11] Two decades later, I find myself reexamining some of the core questions Pool raised — about how we maintain the potential of participatory culture in the wake of growing media concentration, about whether the changes brought about by convergence open new opportunities for expression or expand the power of big media. Pool was interested in the impact of convergence on political culture; I am more interested in its impact on popular culture, but the lines between the two have now blurred.

It is beyond my abilities to describe or fully document all of the changes that are occurring. My aim is more modest. I want to describe some of the ways that convergence thinking is reshaping American popular culture and, in particular, the ways it is impacting the relationship between media audiences, producers, and content. My goal is to help ordinary people grasp how convergence is impacting the media they consume and, at the same time, to help industry leaders and policymakers understand consumer perspectives on these changes. This has been challenging because everything seems to be changing at once and there is no vantage point that takes me above the fray. Rather than trying to write from an objective vantage point, I describe what this process looks like from various localized perspectives — advertising executives struggling to reach a changing market, creative artists discovering new ways

[9]Negroponte, *Being Digital*.

[10]Pool, *Technologies of Freedom*, pp. 53–54.

[11]For a fuller discussion of the concept of media in transition, see David Thorburn and Henry Jenkins, "Towards an Aesthetics of Transition," in David Thorburn and Henry Jenkins (eds.), *Rethinking Media Change: The Aesthetics of Transition* (Cambridge, Mass.: MIT Press, 2003).

to tell stories, educators tapping informal learning communities, activists deploying new resources to shape the political future, religious groups contesting the quality of their cultural environs, and, of course, various fan communities who are early adopters and creative users of emerging media.

I can't claim to be a neutral observer in any of this. For one thing, I am not simply a consumer of many of these media products; I am also an active fan. The world of media fandom has been a central theme of my work for almost two decades — an interest that emerges from my own participation within various fan communities as much as it does from my intellectual interests as a media scholar. During that time, I have watched fans move from the invisible margins of popular culture and into the center of current thinking about media production and consumption. For another, through my role as director of the MIT Comparative Media Studies Program, I have been an active participant in discussions among industry insiders and policymakers; I have consulted with some of the companies discussed; my earlier writings on fan communities and participatory culture have been embraced by business schools and are starting to have some modest impact on the way media companies are relating to their consumers; many of the creative artists and media executives I interviewed are people I would consider friends. At a time when the roles between producers and consumers are shifting, my job allows me to move among different vantage points. Yet, readers should also keep in mind that my engagement with fans and producers alike necessarily colors what I say. My goal here is to document conflicting perspectives on media change rather than to critique them. I don't think we can meaningfully critique convergence until it is more fully understood; yet if the public doesn't get some insights into the discussions that are taking place, they will have little to no input into decisions that will dramatically change their relationship to media.

The Black Box Fallacy

Almost a decade ago, science fiction writer Bruce Sterling established what he calls the Dead Media Project. As his Web site (http://www.deadmedia.org) explains, "The centralized, dinosaurian one-to-many media that roared and trampled through the twentieth century are poorly adapted to the postmodern technological environment."[12] Anticipating that some of these "dinosaurs" were heading to the tar pits, he constructed a shrine to "the media that have died on the barbed wire of technological change." His collection is astounding, including relics like "the phenakistoscope, the telharmonium, the Edison wax cylinder, the stereopticon, . . . various species of magic lantern."[13]

---

[12]Bruce Sterling, "The Dead Media Project: A Modest Proposal and a Public Appeal," http://www.deadmedia.org/modest-proposal.html.
[13]Ibid.

Yet, history teaches us that old media never die—and they don't even necessarily fade away. What dies are simply the tools we use to access media content—the 8-track, the Beta tape. These are what media scholars call *delivery technologies*. Most of what Sterling's project lists falls under this category. Delivery technologies become obsolete and get replaced; media, on the other hand, evolve. Recorded sound is the medium. CDs, MP3 files, and 8-track cassettes are delivery technologies.

To define media, let's turn to historian Lisa Gitelman, who offers a model 25 of media that works on two levels: on the first, a medium is a technology that enables communication; on the second, a medium is a set of associated "protocols" or social and cultural practices that have grown up around that technology.[14] Delivery systems are simply and only technologies; media are also cultural systems. Delivery technologies come and go all the time, but media persist as layers within an ever more complicated information and entertainment stratum.

A medium's content may shift (as occurred when television displaced radio as a storytelling medium, freeing radio to become the primary showcase for rock and roll), its audience may change (as occurs when comics move from a mainstream medium in the 1950s to a niche medium today), and its social status may rise or fall (as occurs when theater moves from a popular form to an elite one), but once a medium establishes itself as satisfying some core human demand, it continues to function within the larger system of communication options. Once recorded sound becomes a possibility, we have continued to develop new and improved means of recording and playing back sounds. Printed words did not kill spoken words. Cinema did not kill theater. Television did not kill radio.[15] Each old medium was forced to coexist with the emerging media. That's why convergence seems more plausible as a way of understanding the past several decades of media change than the old digital revolution paradigm had. Old media are not being displaced. Rather, their functions and status are shifted by the introduction of new technologies.

The implications of this distinction between media and delivery systems become clearer as Gitelman elaborates on what she means by "protocols." She writes: "Protocols express a huge variety of social, economic, and material relationships. So telephony includes the salutation 'Hello?' (for English speakers, at least) and includes the monthly billing cycle and includes the wires and cables that materially connect our phones. Cinema includes everything from the sprocket holes that run along the sides of film to the widely shared sense of being able to wait and see 'films' at home on video. And

---

[14]Lisa Gitelman, "Introduction: Media as Historical Subjects," in *Always Already New: Media, History and the Data of Culture* (Cambridge, Mass.: MIT Press, 2006).

[15]For a useful discussion of the recurring idea that new media kill off old media, see Priscilla Coit Murphy, "Books Are Dead, Long Live Books," in David Thorburn and Henry Jenkins (eds.), *Rethinking Media Change: The Aesthetics of Transition* (Cambridge, Mass.: MIT Press, 2003).

protocols are far from static."[16] I have less to say about the technological dimensions of media change than about the shifts in the protocols by which we are producing and consuming media.

Much contemporary discourse about convergence starts and ends with what I call the Black Box Fallacy. Sooner or later, the argument goes, all media content is going to flow through a single black box into our living rooms (or, in the mobile scenario, through black boxes we carry around with us everywhere we go). If folks could just figure out which black box will reign supreme, then everyone can make reasonable investments for the future. Part of what makes the black box concept a fallacy is that it reduces media change to technological change and strips aside the cultural levels we are considering here.

I don't know about you, but in my living room, I am seeing more and more black boxes. There are my VCR, my digital cable box, my DVD player, my digital recorder, my sound system, and my two game systems, not to mention a huge mound of videotapes, DVDs and CDs, game cartridges and controllers, sitting atop, laying alongside, toppling over the edge of my television system. (I would definitely qualify as an early adopter, but most American homes now have, or soon will have, their own pile of black boxes.) The perpetual tangle of cords that stands between me and my "home entertainment" center reflects the degree of incompatibility and dysfunction that exists between the various media technologies. And many of my MIT students are lugging around multiple black boxes — their laptops, their cells, their iPods, their Game Boys, their BlackBerrys, you name it.

As Cheskin Research explained in a 2002 report, "The old idea of convergence was that all devices would converge into one central device that did everything for you (à la the universal remote). What we are now seeing is the hardware diverging while the content converges. Your e-mail needs and expectations are different whether you're at home, work, school, commuting, the airport, etc., and these different devices are designed to suit your needs for accessing content depending on where you are — your situated context."[17] This pull toward more specialized media appliances coexists with a push toward more generic devices. We can see the proliferation of black boxes as symptomatic of a moment of convergence: because no one is sure what kinds of functions should be combined, we are forced to buy a range of specialized and incompatible appliances. On the other end of the spectrum, we may also be forced to deal with an escalation of functions within the same media appliance, functions that decrease the ability of that appliance to serve its original function, and so I can't get a cell phone that is just a phone.

Media convergence is more than simply a technological shift. Convergence alters the relationship between existing technologies, industries, markets, genres, and audiences. Convergence alters the logic by which media industries

---

[16]Gitelman, "Introduction."

[17]Cheskin Research, "Designing Digital Experiences for Youth," *Market Insights Series*, Fall 2002, pp. 8–9.

operate and by which media consumers process news and entertainment. Keep this in mind: convergence refers to a process, not an endpoint. There will be no single black box that controls the flow of media into our homes. Thanks to the proliferation of channels and the portability of new computing and telecommunications technologies, we are entering an era where media will be everywhere. Convergence isn't something that is going to happen one day when we have enough bandwidth or figure out the correct configuration of appliances. Ready or not, we are already living within a convergence culture.

Our cell phones are not simply telecommunications devices; they also allow us to play games, download information from the Internet, and take and send photographs or text messages. Increasingly they allow us to watch previews of new films, download installments of serialized novels, or attend concerts from remote locations. All of this is already happening in northern Europe and Asia. Any of these functions can also be performed using other media appliances. You can listen to the Dixie Chicks through your DVD player, your car radio, your Walkman, your iPod, a Web radio station, or a music cable channel.

Fueling this technological convergence is a shift in patterns of media ownership. Whereas old Hollywood focused on cinema, the new media conglomerates have controlling interests across the entire entertainment industry. Warner Bros. produces film, television, popular music, computer games, Web sites, toys, amusement park rides, books, newspapers, magazines, and comics.

In turn, media convergence impacts the way we consume media. A teenager doing homework may juggle four or five windows, scan the Web, listen to and download MP3 files, chat with friends, word-process a paper, and respond to e-mail, shifting rapidly among tasks. And fans of a popular television series may sample dialogue, summarize episodes, debate subtexts, create original fan fiction, record their own soundtracks, make their own movies—and distribute all of this worldwide via the Internet.

Convergence is taking place within the same appliances, within the same 35 franchise, within the same company, within the brain of the consumer, and within the same fandom. Convergence involves both a change in the way media are produced and a change in the way media are consumed.

The Cultural Logic of Media Convergence

Another snapshot of the future: Anthropologist Mizuko Ito has documented the growing pace of mobile communications among Japanese youth, describing young couples who remain in constant contact with each other throughout the day, thanks to their access to various mobile technologies.[18] They

[18]Mizuko Ito, "Mobile Phones, Japanese Youth and the Re-Placement of the Social Contract," in Rich Ling and Per Petersen (eds.), *Mobile Communications: Re-Negotiation of the Social Sphere* (forthcoming). http://www.itofisher.com/mito/archives/mobileyouth.pdf.

wake up together, work together, eat together, and go to bed together even though they live miles apart and may have face-to-face contact only a few times a month. We might call it telecocooning.

Convergence doesn't just involve commercially produced materials and services traveling along well-regulated and predictable circuits. It doesn't just involve the mobile companies getting together with the film companies to decide when and where we watch a newly released film. It also occurs when people take media in their own hands. Entertainment content isn't the only thing that flows across multiple media platforms. Our lives, relationships, memories, fantasies, desires also flow across media channels. Being a lover or a mommy or a teacher occurs on multiple platforms.[19] Sometimes we tuck our kids into bed at night and other times we Instant Message them from the other side of the globe.

And yet another snapshot: Intoxicated students at a local high school use their cell phones spontaneously to produce their own soft-core porn movie involving topless cheerleaders making out in the locker room. Within hours, the movie is circulating across the school, being downloaded by students and teachers alike, and watched between classes on personal media devices.

When people take media into their own hands, the results can be wonderfully creative; they can also be bad news for all involved.

For the foreseeable future, convergence will be a kind of kludge — a jerry-rigged relationship among different media technologies — rather than a fully integrated system. Right now, the cultural shifts, the legal battles, and the economic consolidations that are fueling media convergence are preceding shifts in the technological infrastructure. How those various transitions unfold will determine the balance of power in the next media era. | 40

The American media environment is now being shaped by two seemingly contradictory trends: on the one hand, new media technologies have lowered production and distribution costs, expanded the range of available delivery channels, and enabled consumers to archive, annotate, appropriate, and recirculate media content in powerful new ways. At the same time, there has been alarming concentration of the ownership of mainstream commercial media, with a small handful of multinational media conglomerates dominating all sectors of the entertainment industry. No one seems capable of describing both sets of changes at the same time, let alone show how they impact each other. Some fear that media are out of control, others that it is too controlled. Some see a world without gatekeepers, others a world where gatekeepers have unprecedented power. Again, the truth lies somewhere in between.

---

[19]For a useful illustration of this point, see Henry Jenkins, "Love Online," in Henry Jenkins (ed.), *Fans, Gamers, and Bloggers* (New York: New York University Press, 2005).

Another snapshot: People around the world are affixing stickers showing yellow arrows (http://global.yellowarrow.net) alongside public monuments and factories, beneath highway overpasses, onto lamp posts. The arrows provide numbers others can call to access recorded voice messages — personal annotations on our shared urban landscape. They use it to share a beautiful vista or criticize an irresponsible company. And increasingly, companies are co-opting the system to leave their own advertising pitches.

Convergence, as we can see, is both a top-down corporate-driven process and a bottom-up consumer-driven process. Corporate convergence coexists with grassroots convergence. Media companies are learning how to accelerate the flow of media content across delivery channels to expand revenue opportunities, broaden markets, and reinforce viewer commitments. Consumers are learning how to use these different media technologies to bring the flow of media more fully under their control and to interact with other consumers. The promises of this new media environment raise expectations of a freer flow of ideas and content. Inspired by those ideals, consumers are fighting for the right to participate more fully in their culture. Sometimes, corporate and grassroots convergence reinforce each other, creating closer, more rewarding relations between media producers and consumers. Sometimes, these two forces are at war and those struggles will redefine the face of American popular culture.

Convergence requires media companies to rethink old assumptions about what it means to consume media, assumptions that shape both programming and marketing decisions. If old consumers were assumed to be passive, the new consumers are active. If old consumers were predictable and stayed where you told them to stay, then new consumers are migratory, showing a declining loyalty to networks or media. If old consumers were isolated individuals, the new consumers are more socially connected. If the work of media consumers was once silent and invisible, the new consumers are now noisy and public.

Media producers are responding to these newly empowered consumers 45
in contradictory ways, sometimes encouraging change, sometimes resisting what they see as renegade behavior. And consumers, in turn, are perplexed by what they see as mixed signals about how much and what kinds of participation they can enjoy.

As they undergo this transition, the media companies are not behaving in a monolithic fashion; often, different divisions of the same company are pursuing radically different strategies, reflecting their uncertainty about how to proceed. On the one hand, convergence represents an expanded opportunity for media conglomerates, since content that succeeds in one sector can spread across other platforms. On the other, convergence represents a risk since most of the media fear a fragmentation or erosion of their markets. Each time they move a viewer from television to the Internet, say, there is a risk that the consumer may not return.

Industry insiders use the term "extension" to refer to their efforts to expand the potential markets by moving content across different delivery systems, "synergy" to refer to the economic opportunities represented by their ability to own and control all of those manifestations, and "franchise" to refer to their coordinated effort to brand and market fictional content under these new conditions. Extension, synergy, and franchising are pushing media industries to embrace convergence.

You are now entering convergence culture. It is not a surprise that we are not yet ready to cope with its complexities and contradictions. We need to find ways to negotiate the changes taking place. No one group can set the terms. No one group can control access and participation.

Don't expect the uncertainties surrounding convergence to be resolved anytime soon. We are entering an era of prolonged transition and transformation in the way media operate. Convergence describes the process by which we will sort through these options. There will be no magical black box that puts everything in order again. Media producers will only find their way through their current problems by renegotiating their relationship with their consumers. Audiences, empowered by these new technologies, occupying a space at the intersection between old and new media, are demanding the right to participate within the culture. Producers who fail to make their peace with this new participatory culture will face declining goodwill and diminished revenues. The resulting struggles and compromises will define the public culture of the future.

READING THE TEXT

1. Define in your own words what Jenkins means by "convergence culture," and create a list of current media examples that would constitute that culture.
2. What contradictions does Jenkins find in convergence culture?
3. Explain how convergence culture is both top-down and bottom-up.
4. Describe Jenkins's tone, considering the extent to which it may be neutral or biased. How does it affect your response to the concept of convergence culture?
5. In your own words, define what industry insiders mean by "extension," "synergy," and "franchise" (para. 47), and explain how they apply to the new media.

READING THE SIGNS

1. In your journal, reflect on your own experience with new media. What participatory media do you engage in, and why? If you avoid such media, what are the reasons behind your behavior?
2. Jenkins's claim that "when people take media into their own hands, the results can be wonderfully creative; they can also be bad news for all involved" (para. 39) presents the two outcomes as equally possible. Write an essay in which you support Jenkins's assumption or weigh the outcomes and

decide that one is more likely. If you argue the latter position, what tips the balance in favor of the side you chose?

3. **CONNECTING TEXTS**   Write an essay arguing for or against the proposition that "concentration of the ownership of mainstream commercial media" (para. 41) is turning the Cloud into just another way for the corporate world to make money. To develop your ideas, consult the introduction to this chapter.

4. A significant proportion of the videos on YouTube and similar sites consist of copyrighted material. Write an essay in which you support, oppose, or modify the position that ordinary copyright law should apply to the use of such material on YouTube.

5. Since Jenkins wrote the book from which this selection is taken, Facebook and Twitter have joined cell phones and other media as tools of political revolution — for example, in the revolutions against the governments of Egypt, Tunisia, and Libya in 2011. Picking one such revolution, research how social and other media were used, and write an essay that evaluates the effectiveness of electronic media as a political force.

Navigating On- and Offline Lives

AFP/Getty Images

READING THE SIGNS

1. How often on a daily basis do you encounter stickers, signs, or posters like this one, which asks you to link up some sort of real-world experience with

your social media account? What types of things are you most likely to "like," and why?

2. Think about all the companies, services, and entertainments that you've "liked." What inferences might a stranger make about you based on these "likes"? How do they contribute to a fuller picture of "you" on social media?

3. **CONNECTING TEXTS**   Write an essay in which you argue whether or not signs like this one are a part of what Henry Jenkins calls "convergence culture" (p. 423).

HEROES AND VILLAINS

Encoding Our Conflicts

Saving the World

The first full-fledged hero of written storytelling was Gilgamesh, the legendary king of the Mesopotamian kingdom of Uruk, whose exploits are recounted in the various cuneiform texts that make up *The Epic of Gilgamesh*. Like many superheroes today, Gilgamesh was described as having superhuman strength (indeed, he is more than half divine in his origins), and he was a monster slayer. Many modern readers might question whether Gilgamesh is really the good guy in the story (after all, he is an oppressor of his own people, and his slaying of Humbaba, the guardian of the Cedars of Lebanon, leads to his destruction of the entire forest). Nonetheless, he does defend his city from the Bull of Heaven who has been sent to destroy it, thus becoming the first of many heroes whose job is to "save the world."

Saving the world (or, at least, a city or society) appears to have been a primary duty of ancient heroes, whether the threat came from nature (as symbolized by such figures as Humbaba), from demons (like the mysterious Grendel and his mother), from dragons (a symbol for evil itself in Western society), or simply from enemy warriors (like Goliath). That's still the job description, especially in popular culture, of many modern heroes, who fight monstrous forces of nature (*Jaws*), demons (*World War Z*), dragons (*The Hobbit*), and enemy warriors/nations (*G.I. Joe: The Rise of Cobra*). Whether they operate alone — as what Robert B. Ray, in "The Thematic Paradigm," calls "outlaw heroes" — or from within established social institutions — Ray's "official heroes" — heroes represent the best in us — courage, skill, altruism — defending and protecting their societies against whatever threatens them.

Exploring the Signs of Heroes and Villains

In your journal, jot down four or five fictional heroes whom you admire, then list a similar number of real-life heroes whom you also regard as outstanding. Study your two lists: What traits do they share? What values do these heroes embody, and what do those values reveal about your own worldview? In addition (or as an alternate), do the same with fictional and real-life villains. If you have difficulty creating such lists, explore in your journal why you think that is the case.

Ugly Is as Ugly Does

But saving the world requires someone (or something) to save the world *from*, and in the modern era that is more often a human threat, not a natural or a nonhuman one. This threat is the *villain*, the hero's necessary antagonist, and the history of storytelling is as filled with vivid villains as it is with heroes. They are usually easy to spot, because if the hero is conventionally coded by his or her physical attractiveness (by whatever standard of beauty a society holds), the villain is often simply ugly (equally often a matter of social construction). Consider Sauron and the Orcs in *The Lord of the Rings* versus the cute Hobbits, beautiful elves, and handsome warriors like Aragorn and the Riders of Rohan. Even the two wizards, Gandalf and Saruman, who are superficially similar, can be distinguished: Gandalf is grandfatherly when still gray, distinguished when white; Saruman, on the other hand, has the wrong nose (too long, too hooked) and the wrong fingernails (too long, too pointed). Or take Batman (buff, tall, dark, and handsome) versus Bane (who looks like something out of a WWE promoter's worst nightmare). Or Iron Man versus Mandarin. Luke Skywalker versus Darth Vader (in spite of the family relationship). Glinda, the Good Witch of the North, versus the Wicked Witch of the West. The list is endless.

It's a crude code, of course, and an obvious one, but it is extremely common in popular cultural representation, so common that currently a not uncommon gambit is to deliberately turn it upside down in order to make a point. Take Shrek.

The whole point of the Shrek stories is to reverse the codes of good versus evil and thus expose the social constructions of beauty and ugliness that can lie behind them. Here the hero is literally an ogre, an ugly troll with funny ears, while the villain can be a blond and handsome Prince Charming. Something similar goes on in the *Despicable Me* franchise with the Minions, who, in their apparent amalgamation of Alvin and the Chipmunks with Pac-Man and the Budweiser Ferret, are very cute parodies of the "evil-must-be-ugly" tradition. But the jokes work (and the reversals in *Shrek* and *Despicable Me* are jokes) precisely because they are reversals, transpositions of the usual signs of good and evil in popular storytelling.

The coding of evilness through ugliness and of goodness through beauty is such a universal convention of storytelling that it is often easy to forget that in reality things don't really work out that way. For one, real-life villains are simply human beings, and beautiful people can be evil while unattractive ones can be very good indeed. What is more, in conflicts among human beings, one man's villain is likely to be another's hero, and vice versa. This is usually not a problem in traditional storytelling, which is generally unconcerned with the niceties of moral relativity, but it most certainly is in contemporary narratives, which frequently serve as metaphors for real-world conflicts. Often reflecting an uneasy apprehension that perhaps good and evil aren't so easily distinguished after all, such stories feature a new kind of hero — one who isn't precisely a hero at all.

Enter the Antihero

Such protagonists as *Mad Men*'s Don Draper, *Dexter*'s Dexter, *Breaking Bad*'s Walter White, *The Sopranos*' Tony Soprano, and *The Sons of Anarchy*'s Jax Teller are prominent examples of recent protagonists who embody a *mixture* of good and evil. They commit patently evil acts and are hardly heroes in the ordinary sense of the term, yet they aren't simply villains either. Indeed, even when they are behaving badly, usually there is someone worse in the room, as it were, to make it clear who the *real* villain is. Often referred to as "antiheroes," these characters offer an interesting counterpoint to the hordes of cartoonish superheroes who have cast so large a shadow on contemporary popular culture.

The dichotomy between superheroes and antiheroes can be explained, in part, by the different media in which they typically appear. Cinema tends to be the superhero's prime domain; the antiheroes mentioned above, on the other hand, all come from television — to be more precise, from cable networks, not the traditional commercial TV stations. The distinction is significant, because unlike commercially sponsored television, cable has its own guaranteed revenue stream provided by viewer subscriptions. Unbeholden to commercial sponsors, who are themselves vulnerable to pressure groups and the threat of consumer boycotts, the producers of cable TV series are much freer to experiment with more controversial, complex, and, quite simply, mature story concepts. Thus, they are able to show human beings in all their complexity, mixing good and bad, strength and frailty, vision and blindness, kindness and cruelty.

The movies, on the other hand, lack this freedom, not because they are held hostage to corporate sponsors but because they cost so much to produce in an era when audiences demand all sorts of expensive special effects

---

Discussing the Signs of Antiheroes

Antiheroes, who are most commonly the protagonists of television series and movies, are effectively heroes in that the audience is expected to sympathize with them. In class, discuss the consequences for social behavior when Americans sympathize and identify with deeply flawed (including illegal and psychopathic) behavior on the part of a fictional protagonist (who, by definition, is the focal character who shapes the viewers' emotional responses).

(including, of course, 3-D technology) and high-priced stars. By contrast, cable TV, with its cheaper production costs and — at least initially — relatively cheap actor salaries, is far less expensive and can thus take greater risks than movies can. With so much at stake financially, American moviemakers have increasingly turned to simplistic formulas that are calculated to attract multiple demographics to the theaters. To appeal to adults and children, simple confrontations between handsome heroes and ugly villains are the safest bet, combined with stories taken from already-proven cartoon series and children's books that are also popular with adults (Batman, Spider-Man, Iron Man, the Avengers, the X-Men, Superman, Harry Potter, and so on).

Thus, the rise of the antihero suggests a more nuanced level of understanding in its audience, along with a certain cultural resignation and weariness, fostered by a growing apprehension that no one is perfect and that there is some evil in all of us. At a time when so many ordinary Americans are under stress and finding themselves facing their own temptations to test the boundaries of civil society, popular culture's exploration of the antihero's flawed behavior can be especially enticing. It's as if there were a bit of Walter White in all of us.

At the same time, the popularity of the antihero may also reflect a certain rising cynicism as well, a diminishing interest in old-fashioned morality and a growing fascination with no-holds-barred freedom, because the antihero, who violates the law and does what he wants when he wants and as he wants, is, in effect, an ultra-individualist: exactly the sort of protagonist one might expect to find in an era of widespread libertarian tendencies. Either way, the antihero stands as a signifier of a society that is losing its traditional certitudes and becoming resigned instead to that gray area of moral uncertainty in which pure heroes cannot thrive.

The Capitalist Villain to the Rescue

But the rise of the antihero doesn't mean that the villain has disappeared; indeed, without the villain there is often no story to tell at all. The problem, however, lies in who gets cast *as* the villain, which can be a very sensitive matter indeed. With their long history of racist stereotyping, for example, Hollywood filmmakers are far less likely today to cast nonwhite actors as villains. During the Cold War, the Soviet Union provided a source of villains for many James Bond and other spy films, but that pretty much came to an end with the fall of the Soviet Union. Evil white Southern sheriffs were popular villains in the 1960s to 1970s, while Colombian drug dealers were the villains of choice in many an action flick in the 1980s. And the Mafia has provided a steady stream of Hollywood villains, much to the dismay of many Italian Americans, who see themselves being negatively stereotyped.

In recent years, another kind of villain has stepped up to the plate, one that can be called the "capitalist villain." Unlike a conventional criminal such as a bank robber or murderer, the capitalist villain is not a social outsider: He is an *insider*, a businessman whose crimes are the crimes of corporate capitalism itself. Movies like *Avatar*, *The Lone Ranger*, *Iron Man 3*, and *White House Down* and TV shows like *Arrested Development* and *Sons of Anarchy* feature this new variety of villain. This is not at all surprising in the wake of the Great Recession, an economic catastrophe that continues to brutalize most Americans and is decimating the middle class. While some corporate leaders have expressed irritation that now *they* are being unfairly stereotyped, they have provided what appears to be a convenient source of new villains for entertainment purposes, villains who, as members of the dominant culture, cannot effectively complain that they are being persecuted.

And they are needed, for one way or another, American entertainment today is packed with stories of heroes and villains locked in violent conflict. Such stories point to a society in crisis, a divided people who feel threatened but are unable to agree on the source of the threat. Such a society will be drawn to simplistic stories where the difference between good and evil is obvious (call out the Avengers!) or to more cynical narratives (like *The Walking Dead*) where evil is everywhere and it's "every man for himself." All of which leads to

Lord Business, the capitalist villain of *The Lego Movie* (2014).

Photofest

yet another semiotic question: What has so divided the American people, leading to so many narratives—both fictional and real—involving irreconcilable conflict?

This Is the End of the Innocence

Though often neglected today, America's experience in the Vietnam War was a watershed in American history. Prior to that, Americans had no difficulty identifying who were the heroes in their wars and who were the villains. (Even during the Civil War, Northerners and Southerners alike had no difficulty making this distinction: They simply lined up on different sides.) But Vietnam was different. Unlike World War II, which really did represent a war between the forces of evil and its opponents, Vietnam turned into a moral quagmire. Popular cultural representations of war changed accordingly with movies (and TV series) like *M*A*S*H* serving as metaphors for a conflict that divided America and shook our trust in the American government as well.

In the same era, America also split apart over the effects of a cultural revolution that included the civil rights movement, the women's movement, and sexual liberation. The backlash against this profound disruption in cultural history produced a "silent majority" that had evolved into the Moral Majority by the late 1970s. Ever since, America has been so fractured that a tendency to divide the country into sets of heroes and villains—rather than citizens who happen to disagree—has taken hold.

Just look at some popular news media. On one side, for instance, we have Fox News, and on the other MSNBC. For the fans of Fox News, such current and former MSNBC personalities as Keith Olbermann, Chris Matthews, and Al Sharpton—not to mention politicians like Barack Obama, Hillary Clinton, and Nancy Pelosi—are absolute villains, while such figures as Glenn Beck, Rush Limbaugh, Bill O'Reilly, and Sarah Palin are heroes. Of course, this is exactly reversed for MSNBC fans. The Fox News versus MSNBC conflict is but a microcosm of a larger one whereby Americans apparently can't simply agree to disagree but are inclined to treat all politics as some sort of WWE smackdown or out-and-out war.

What's Red and Blue and Mad All Over?

This split between hostile political ideologies has been directly reflected in national elections that have produced the red-state and blue-state divide, a cultural division that was first officially noted after the 2000 presidential election. At the time, maps color-coded the states that voted Republican in red and the states that voted Democratic in blue. Since then it has become common to refer to "red state" and "blue state" regions of America, with the former generally considered conservative, and the latter liberal or progressive.

Exploring Heroes Online

Visit a Web site that proposes historical heroes, such as "History's Heroes" (http://historysheroes.e2bn.org/), "Heroes of History" (www.heroesofhistory.com), or "100 Greatest Heroes" (www.adherents.com/people/100_heroes.html). Evaluate the choices you find. What criteria does the site seem to use to define a "hero"? Do you agree with the site's judgments? Why or why not? Alternatively, compare two of the sites: What differences in their choices do you find, if any?

Although these terms run the risk of stereotyping, red and blue states do tend to take different sides in relation to America's cultural and ideological conflicts, reflecting their opposing positions on some very fundamental American values. These values include a number of highly contradictory cultural **mythologies** that exist in hostile relation to each other and, consequently, underpin a great deal of the political conflict in America today. Knowing what those contradictions are can be an important step in your analysis of many current tales of heroes and villains.

Three Basic Contradictions

Perhaps the values that especially divide Americans today can be boiled down to three fundamental conflicts over attitudes toward the **body**, toward the **mind**, and toward **community**. Let's take them in order.

MYTHOLOGIES OF THE BODY

Prior to the sexual revolution of the 1960s to 1970s, the prevailing mythology of the body in America could be characterized as one of modesty and repression. Valuing bodily health and hygiene ("cleanliness is next to godliness"), this mythology celebrates sports and recreation but frowns on erotic display and expression. Clearly reflected in Hollywood's Hays Code, which restricted the sexual content of movies from the 1930s onwards, this puritanical streak in the American character led many people to disapprove of the sexual energy of rock and roll in the 1950s and, notoriously, caused broadcasters to film Elvis Presley from the waist up when he first performed on *The Ed Sullivan Show* (they objected to the King's vigorous pelvic gyrations). Within the terms of the mythology, the body's fundamental sexual instincts must be controlled through prohibitions on premarital sex and channeled into state-approved monogamous and procreative marital relationships.

But in the wake of the "Summer of Love" in 1967, a sexual revolution swept America, a revolution that divides sexually repressive red-state and sexually liberated blue-state attitudes to this day. In the view of the new mythology, the body need not be covered up and its instinctive desires need not be constrained — in fact, both body and desire can be commodified and exploited. This transformation is especially apparent in our popular culture, where sexually explicit entertainments and clothing fashions paradoxically reflect not only the triumph of the progressive spirit of the sexual revolution but also the prevalence of the conservative capitalistic profit motive over traditional morality, which once put values above profits. Lady Gaga, who has so successfully commodified her own body, is an apt emblem of this complex contradiction, exemplifying both a capitalistic exploitation of erotic desire and a socially progressive position on sexual freedom. Accordingly, she has become a heroine to some and an object of revulsion to others, like members of the Florida Family Association, who protested her Born This Way tour in 2013.

MYTHOLOGIES OF THE MIND

Closely related to our conflicting mythologies of the body, American attitudes toward the mind, or spirit, divide along a faith versus reason axis. Upholders of a sexually modest and repressive ideology of the body tend to embrace orthodox religious beliefs that put piety of mind above rationality and science. A conflict ingrained within an American history that includes both the theocratic Puritans of the Massachusetts Bay Colony and such Enlightenment nation builders as Benjamin Franklin and Thomas Jefferson, who created America upon the basis of a separation of church and state, this division is expressed in the battle over the teaching of evolution in public schools and in the red-state-tending rejection of scientific research on global warming and climate change. In such an environment, evangelical leaders like Pat Robertson can be heroes to many and villains to others, while scientists like Albert Einstein and Richard Feynman and technology pioneers like Steve Jobs and Elon Musk can be culture heroes.

MYTHOLOGIES OF COMMUNITY

Although you would hardly know it from listening to much of the social conversation these days, America has a history of social altruism — the communitarian ethos that led to the establishment of such entitlements as Social Security, Medicare, and federal and state welfare programs — along with the individualistically grounded libertarianism that underlies the emergence of such political movements as the Tea Party Patriots. The conflict between these two ideologies came to a dramatic head in the battle over the Affordable Care Act ("Obamacare"), which made President Barack Obama a heroic figure to those blue-state Americans who believe in socially guaranteed health care, and an arch-villain to its libertarian opponents, with such red-state politicians as Senator Ted Cruz vying for the hero role among those who shared his opposition to a governmentally organized health system.

Faced with such ideological conflicts, Americans today do not simply argue — they demonize each other, turning opponents into "villains" and supporters into "heroes." They become dragon slayers, as it were, putting all ideological opponents to the sword. Such real-life conflict inevitably makes its way into our popular culture, but there it is often mediated into a less controversial form, as in the movie *Gettysburg*, which treats both Union and Confederate soldiers alike as heroes in order to avoid alienating a large portion of the potential audience, conveniently soft-pedaling the fact that one side was fighting for slavery and the other against it. Or, much more commonly still, popular cultural narratives avoid reality altogether by presenting cartoonish Hitlerian villains who are so obviously evil that the battle against them can be entertainingly uncomplicated and uncontroversial. Thus, while vaguely aware that something is wrong, American audiences can be beguiled into a feeling that problems can be resolved quite simply, and they can be distracted from the uncomfortable fact that in America today, as *Pogo* cartoonist Walt Kelly put it so well many years ago, "we have met the enemy, and he is us."

The Readings

Robert B. Ray's analysis of the "official hero" and "outlaw hero" begins this chapter, providing a solid foundation for the analysis of the complexities of heroism in popular culture. Stevie St. John comes next with her analysis of Wonder Woman, a superhero who in spite of decades of popularity still hasn't had her own feature film. A paired set of readings on a third kind of popular hero — the antihero — follows, with Heather Havrilesky providing an in-depth reading of *Breaking Bad*'s Walter White, and Laura Bennett arguing that the term "antihero" has become an almost-meaningless buzzword. George Packer's "Celebrating Inequality" takes a trenchant look at today's celebrities — an exclusive "superclass" of entertainers, corporate executives, politicians, and a handful of intellectuals, whom Packer finds to be anything but heroic. Then, looking at the villains from three high-profile movies of 2013 — *Iron Man 3*, *White House Down*, and *The Lone Ranger* — Noah Gittell notes the emergence of a new kind of Hollywood villain: the greedy and corrupt businessman. Tim Layden's "A Patriot's Tale" follows, telling the story of a family of New York City firefighters, real-life heroes who risked their lives during the September 11 terror attack on the World Trade Center. And Lorraine Devon Wilke concludes the readings with a critique of what she sees as the overly simplistic, black-and-white assessments of the actions of Edward Snowden, whose embrace as an out-and-out hero by some and denunciation as a villain by others gloss over the broadly gray moral dimensions of his exposure of the NSA.

ROBERT B. RAY
The Thematic Paradigm

Usually we consider movies to be merely entertainment, but as Robert B. Ray demonstrates in this selection from his book *A Certain Tendency of the Hollywood Cinema* (1985), American films have long reflected fundamental patterns and contradictions in our society's myths and values. Whether in real life or on the silver screen, Ray explains, Americans have always been ambivalent about the value of civilization, celebrating it through official heroes like George Washington and Jimmy Stewart, while at the same time questioning it through outlaw heroes like Davy Crockett and Huck Finn. Especially when presented together in the same film, these two hero types help mediate America's ambivalence, providing a mythic solution. Ray's analyses show how the movies are rich sources for cultural interpretation. Robert B. Ray is a professor of English at the University of Florida at Gainesville. His publications include *The Avant Garde Finds Andy Hardy* (1995), *How a Film Theory Got Lost and Other Mysteries in Cultural Studies* (2001), and, most recently, *Walden × 40: Essays on Thoreau* (2011).

The dominant tradition of American cinema consistently found ways to overcome dichotomies. Often, the movies' reconciliatory pattern concentrated on a single character magically embodying diametrically opposite traits. A sensitive violinist was also a tough boxer (*Golden Boy*); a boxer was a gentle man who cared for pigeons (*On the Waterfront*). A gangster became a coward because he was brave (*Angels with Dirty Faces*); a soldier became brave because he was a coward (*Lives of a Bengal Lancer*). A war hero was a former pacifist (*Sergeant York*); a pacifist was a former war hero (*Billy Jack*). The ideal was a kind of inclusiveness that would permit all decisions to be undertaken with the knowledge that the alternative was equally available. The attractiveness of Destry's refusal to use guns (*Destry Rides Again*) depended on the tacit understanding that he could shoot with the best of them, Katharine Hepburn's and Claudette Colbert's revolts against conventionality (*Holiday*, *It Happened One Night*) on their status as aristocrats.

Such two-sided characters seemed particularly designed to appeal to a collective American imagination steeped in myths of inclusiveness. Indeed, in creating such characters, classic Hollywood had connected with what Erik Erikson has described as the fundamental American psychological pattern:

> The functioning American, as the heir of a history of extreme contrasts and abrupt changes, bases his final ego identity on some tentative combination of dynamic polarities such as migratory and sedentary, individualistic and standardized, competitive and co-operative, pious and free-thinking, responsible and cynical, etc. . . .

To leave his choices open, the American, on the whole, lives with two sets of "truths."[1]

The movies traded on one opposition in particular, American culture's traditional dichotomy of individual and community that had generated the most significant pair of competing myths: the outlaw hero and the official hero.[2] Embodied in the adventurer, explorer, gunfighter, wanderer, and loner, the outlaw hero stood for that part of the American imagination valuing self-determination and freedom from entanglements. By contrast, the official hero, normally portrayed as a teacher, lawyer, politician, farmer, or family man, represented the American belief in collective action, and the objective legal process that superseded private notions of right and wrong. While the outlaw hero found incarnations in the mythic figures of Davy Crockett, Jesse James, Huck Finn, and all of Leslie Fiedler's "Good Bad Boys" and Daniel Boorstin's "ring-tailed roarers," the official hero developed around legends associated with Washington, Jefferson, Lincoln, Lee, and other "Good Good Boys."

An extraordinary amount of the traditional American mythology adopted by Classic Hollywood derived from the variations worked by American ideology around this opposition of natural man versus civilized man. To the extent that these variations constituted the main tendency of American literature and legends, Hollywood, in relying on this mythology, committed itself to becoming what Robert Bresson has called "the Cinema."[3] A brief description of the competing values associated with this outlaw hero–official hero opposition will begin to suggest its pervasiveness in traditional American culture.

1. *Aging*: The attractiveness of the outlaw hero's childishness and propensity to whims, tantrums, and emotional decisions derived from America's cult of childhood. Fiedler observed that American literature celebrated "the notion that a mere falling short of adulthood is a guarantee of insight and even innocence." From Huck to Holden Caulfield, children in American literature were privileged, existing beyond society's confining rules. Often, they set the plot in motion (e.g., *Intruder in the Dust*, *To Kill a Mockingbird*), acting for the adults encumbered by daily affairs. As Fiedler also pointed out, this image of childhood "has impinged upon adult life itself, has become a 'career' like everything else in America,"[4] generating stories like *On the Road* 5

---

[1] Erik H. Erikson, *Childhood and Society* (New York: Norton, 1963), p. 286.

[2] Leading discussions of the individual–community polarity in American culture can be found in *The Contrapuntal Civilization: Essays Toward a New Understanding of the American Experience*, ed. Michael Kammen (New York: Crowell, 1971). The most prominent analyses of American literature's use of this opposition remain Leslie A. Fiedler's *Love and Death in the American Novel* (New York: Stein and Day, 1966) and A. N. Kaul's *The American Vision* (New Haven: Yale University Press, 1963).

[3] Robert Bresson, *Notes on Cinematography*, trans. Jonathan Griffin (New York: Urizen Books, 1977), p. 12.

[4] Leslie A. Fiedler, *No! In Thunder* (New York: Stein and Day, 1972), pp. 253, 275.

The "outlaw hero," Davy Crockett, portrayed by Fess Parker.

The Kobal Collection at Art Resource, NY

or *Easy Rider* in which adults try desperately to postpone responsibilities by clinging to adolescent lifestyles.

While the outlaw heroes represented a flight from maturity, the official heroes embodied the best attributes of adulthood: sound reasoning and judgment, wisdom and sympathy based on experience. Franklin's *Autobiography* and *Poor Richard's Almanack* constituted this opposing tradition's basic texts, persuasive enough to appeal even to outsiders (*The Great Gatsby*). Despite the legends surrounding Franklin and the other Founding Fathers, however, the scarcity of mature heroes in American literature and mythology indicated American ideology's fundamental preference for youth, a quality that came to be associated with the country itself. Indeed, American stories often distorted the stock figure of the Wise Old Man, portraying him as mad (Ahab), useless (Rip Van Winkle), or evil (the Godfather).

2. *Society and Women*: The outlaw hero's distrust of civilization, typically represented by women and marriage, constituted a stock motif in American mythology. In his *Studies in Classic American Literature*, D. H. Lawrence detected the recurring pattern of flight, observing that the Founding Fathers had come to America "largely to get *away*. . . . Away from what? In the long

run, away from themselves. Away from everything."[5] Sometimes, these heroes undertook this flight alone (Thoreau, *Catcher in the Rye*); more often, they joined ranks with other men: Huck with Jim, Ishmael with Queequeg, Jake Barnes with Bill Gorton. Women were avoided as representing the very entanglements this tradition sought to escape: society, the "settled life," confining responsibilities. The outlaw hero sought only uncompromising relationships, involving either a "bad" woman (whose morals deprived her of all rights to entangling domesticity) or other males (who themselves remained independent). Even the "bad" woman posed a threat, since marriage often uncovered the clinging "good" girl underneath. Typically, therefore, American stories avoided this problem by killing off the "bad" woman before the marriage could transpire (*Destry Rides Again*, *The Big Heat*, *The Far Country*). Subsequently, within the all-male group, women became taboo, except as the objects of lust.

The exceptional extent of American outlaw legends suggests an ideological anxiety about civilized life. Often, that anxiety took shape as a romanticizing of the dispossessed, as in the Beat Generation's cult of the bum, or the characters of Huck and "Thoreau," who worked to remain idle, unemployed, and unattached. A passage from Jerzy Kosinski's *Steps* demonstrated the extreme modern version of this romanticizing:

> I envied those [the poor and the criminals] who lived here and seemed so free, having nothing to regret and nothing to look forward to. In the world of birth certificates, medical examinations, punch cards, and computers, in the world of telephone books, passports, bank accounts, insurance plans, wills, credit cards, pensions, mortgages and loans, they lived unattached.[6]

In contrast to the outlaw heroes, the official heroes were preeminently worldly, comfortable in society, and willing to undertake even those public duties demanding personal sacrifice. Political figures, particularly Washington and Lincoln, provided the principal examples of this tradition, but images of family also persisted in popular literature from *Little Women* to *Life with Father* and *Cheaper by the Dozen*. The most crucial figure in this tradition, however, was Horatio Alger, whose heroes' ambition provided the complement to Huck's disinterest. Alger's characters subscribed fully to the codes of civilization, devoting themselves to proper dress, manners, and behavior, and the attainment of the very things despised by the opposing tradition: the settled life and respectability.[7]

[5]D. H. Lawrence, *Studies in Classic American Literature* (New York: Viking/Compass, 1961), p. 3. See also Fiedler's *Love and Death in the American Novel* and Sam Bluefarb's *The Escape Motif in the American Novel: Mark Twain to Richard Wright* (Columbus: Ohio State University Press, 1972).

[6]Jerzy Kosinski, *Steps* (New York: Random House, 1968), p. 133.

[7]See John G. Cawelti, *Apostles of the Self-Made Man: Changing Concepts of Success in America* (Chicago: University of Chicago Press, 1965), pp. 101–23.

3. *Politics and the Law*: Writing about "The Philosophical Approach of the 10 Americans," Tocqueville noted "a general distaste for accepting any man's word as proof of anything." That distaste took shape as a traditional distrust of politics as collective activity, and of ideology as that activity's rationale. Such a disavowal of ideology was, of course, itself ideological, a tactic for discouraging systematic political intervention in a nineteenth-century America whose political and economic power remained in the hands of a privileged few. Tocqueville himself noted the results of this mythology of individualism which "disposes each citizen to isolate himself from the mass of his fellows and withdraw into the circle of family and friends; with this little society formed to his taste, he gladly leaves the greater society to look after itself."[8]

This hostility toward political solutions manifested itself further in an ambivalence about the law. The outlaw mythology portrayed the law, the sum of society's standards, as a collective, impersonal ideology imposed on the individual from without. Thus, the law represented the very thing this mythology sought to avoid. In its place, this tradition offered a natural law discovered intuitively by each man. As Tocqueville observed, Americans wanted "to escape from imposed systems . . . to seek by themselves and in themselves for the only reason for things . . . in most mental operations each American relies on individual effort and judgment" (p. 429). This sense of the law's inadequacy to needs detectable only by the heart generated a rich tradition of legends celebrating legal defiance in the name of some "natural" standard: Thoreau went to jail rather than pay taxes, Huck helped Jim (legally a slave) to escape, Billy the Kid murdered the sheriff's posse that had ambushed his boss, Hester Prynne resisted the community's sexual mores. This mythology transformed all outlaws into Robin Hoods, who "correct" socially unjust laws (Jesse James, Bonnie and Clyde, John Wesley Harding). Furthermore, by customarily portraying the law as the tool of villains (who used it to revoke mining claims, foreclose on mortgages, and disallow election results — all on legal technicalities), this mythology betrayed a profound pessimism about the individual's access to the legal system.

If the outlaw hero's motto was "I don't know what the law says, but I do know what's right and wrong," the official hero's was "We are a nation of laws, not of men," or "No man can place himself above the law." To the outlaw hero's insistence on private standards of right and wrong, the official hero offered the admonition, "You cannot take the law into your own hands." Often, these official heroes were lawyers or politicians, at times (as with Washington and Lincoln), even the executors of the legal system itself. The values accompanying such heroes modified the assurance of Crockett's advice, "Be sure you're right, then go ahead."

---

[8]Alexis de Tocqueville, *Democracy in America*, ed. J. P. Mayer, trans. George Lawrence (Garden City, N.Y.: Anchor/Doubleday, 1969), pp. 430, 506. Irving Howe has confirmed Tocqueville's point, observing that Americans "make the suspicion of ideology into something approaching a national creed." *Politics and the Novel* (New York: Avon, 1970), p. 337.

In sum, the values associated with these two different sets of heroes contrasted markedly. Clearly, too, each tradition had its good and bad points. If the extreme individualism of the outlaw hero always verged on selfishness, the respectability of the official hero always threatened to involve either blandness or repression. If the outlaw tradition promised adventure and freedom, it also offered danger and loneliness. If the official tradition promised safety and comfort, it also offered entanglements and boredom.

The evident contradiction between these heroes provoked Daniel Boorstin's observation that "never did a more incongruous pair than Davy Crockett and George Washington live together in a national Valhalla." And yet, as Boorstin admits, "both Crockett and Washington were popular heroes, and both emerged into legendary fame during the first half of the nineteenth century."[9]

The parallel existence of these two contradictory traditions evinced the general pattern of American mythology: the denial of the necessity for choice. In fact, this mythology often portrayed situations requiring decision as temporary aberrations from American life's normal course. By discouraging commitment to any single set of values, this mythology fostered an ideology of improvisation, individualism, and ad hoc solutions for problems depicted as crises. American writers have repeatedly attempted to justify this mythology in terms of material sources. Hence, Irving Howe's "explanation": 15

> It is when men no longer feel that they have adequate choices in their styles of life, when they conclude that there are no longer possibilities of honorable maneuver and compromise, when they decide that the time has come for "ultimate" social loyalties and political decisions — it is then that ideology begins to flourish. Ideology reflects a hardening of commitment, the freezing of opinion into system. . . . The uniqueness of our history, the freshness of our land, the plenitude of our resources — all these have made possible, and rendered plausible, a style of political improvisation and intellectual free-wheeling.[10]

Despite such an account's pretext of objectivity, its language betrays an acceptance of the mythology it purports to describe: "honorable maneuver and compromise," "hardening," "freezing," "uniqueness," "freshness," and "plenitude" are all assumptive words from an ideology that denies its own status. Furthermore, even granting the legitimacy of the historians' authenticating causes, we are left with a persisting mythology increasingly discredited by historical developments. (In fact, such invalidation began in the early nineteenth century, and perhaps even before.)

The American mythology's refusal to choose between its two heroes went beyond the normal reconciliatory function attributed to myth by Lévi-Strauss. For the American tradition not only overcame binary oppositions; it systematically mythologized the certainty of being able to do so. Part of this process

[9]Daniel J. Boorstin, *The Americans: The National Experience* (New York: Random House, 1965), p. 337.

[10]*Politics and the Novel*, p. 164.

involved blurring the lines between the two sets of heroes. First, legends often brought the solemn official heroes back down to earth, providing the sober Washington with the cherry tree, the prudent Franklin with illegitimate children, and even the upright Jefferson with a slave mistress. On the other side, stories modified the outlaw hero's most potentially damaging quality, his tendency to selfish isolationism, by demonstrating that, however reluctantly, he would act for causes beyond himself. Thus, Huck grudgingly helped Jim escape, and Davy Crockett left the woods for three terms in Congress before dying in the Alamo for Texas independence. In this blurring process, Lincoln, a composite of opposing traits, emerged as the great American figure. His status as president made him an ex officio official hero. But his Western origins, melancholy solitude, and unaided decision-making all qualified him as a member of the other side. Finally, his ambivalent attitude toward the law played the most crucial role in his complex legend. As the chief executive, he inevitably stood for the principle that "we are a nation of laws and not men"; as the Great Emancipator, on the other hand, he provided the prime example of taking the law into one's own hands in the name of some higher standard.

Classic Hollywood's gallery of composite heroes (boxing musicians, rebellious aristocrats, pacifist soldiers) clearly derived from this mythology's rejection of final choices, a tendency whose traces Erikson detected in American psychology:

> The process of American identity formation seems to support an individual's ego identity as long as he can preserve a certain element of deliberate tentativeness of autonomous choice. The individual must be able to convince himself that the next step is up to him and that no matter where he is staying or going he always has the choice of leaving or turning in the opposite direction if he chooses to do so. In this country the migrant does not want to be told to move on, nor the sedentary man to stay where he is; for the life style (and the family history) of each contains the opposite element as a potential alternative which he wishes to consider his most private and individual decision.[11]

The reconciliatory pattern found its most typical incarnation, however, in one particular narrative: the story of the private man attempting to keep from being drawn into action on any but his own terms. In this story, the reluctant hero's ultimate willingness to help the community satisfied the official values. But by portraying this aid as demanding only a temporary involvement, the story preserved the values of individualism as well.

Like the contrasting heroes' epitomization of basic American dichotomies, the reluctant hero story provided a locus for displacement. Its most famous version, for example, *Adventures of Huckleberry Finn*, offered a typically individualistic solution to the nation's unresolved racial and sectional anxieties, thereby helping to forestall more systematic governmental measures. In adopting this story, Classic Hollywood retained its censoring power, using it, for example,

[11]*Childhood and Society*, p. 286.

in *Casablanca* to conceal the realistic threats to American self-determination posed by World War II.

Because the reluctant hero story was clearly the basis of the Western, American literature's repeated use of it prompted Leslie Fiedler to call the classic American novels "disguised westerns."[12] In the movies, too, this story appeared in every genre: in Westerns, of course (with *Shane* its most schematic articulation), but also in gangster movies (*Angels with Dirty Faces*, *Key Largo*), musicals (*Swing Time*), detective stories (*The Thin Man*), war films (*Air Force*), screwball comedy (*The Philadelphia Story*), "problem pictures" (*On the Waterfront*), and even science fiction (the Han Solo character in *Star Wars*). *Gone with the Wind*, in fact, had two selfish heroes who came around at the last moment, Scarlett (taking care of Melanie) and Rhett (running the Union blockade), incompatible only because they were so much alike. The natural culmination of this pattern, perfected by Hollywood in the 1930s and early 1940s, was *Casablanca*. Its version of the outlaw hero–official hero struggle (Rick versus Laszlo) proved stunningly effective, its resolution (their collaboration on the war effort) the prototypical Hollywood ending.

The reluctant hero story's tendency to minimize the official hero's role (by making him dependent on the outsider's intervention) suggested an imbalance basic to the American mythology: Despite the existence of both heroes, the national ideology clearly preferred the outlaw. This ideology strove to make that figure's origins seem spontaneous, concealing the calculated, commercial efforts behind the mythologizing of typical examples like Billy the Kid and Davy Crockett. Its willingness, on the other hand, to allow the official hero's traces to show enables Daniel Boorstin to observe of one such myth, "There were elements of spontaneity, of course, in the Washington legend, too, but it was, for the most part, a self-conscious product."[13]

The apparent spontaneity of the outlaw heroes assured their popularity. By contrast, the official values had to rely on a rational allegiance that often wavered. These heroes' different statuses accounted for a structure fundamental to American literature, and assumed by Classic Hollywood: a split between the moral center and the interest center of a story. Thus, while the typical Western contained warnings against violence as a solution, taking the law into one's own hands, and moral isolationism, it simultaneously glamorized the outlaw hero's intense self-possession and willingness to use force to settle what the law could not. In other circumstances, Ishmael's evenhanded philosophy paled beside Ahab's moral vehemence, consciously recognizable as destructive.

D. H. Lawrence called this split the profound "duplicity" at the heart of nineteenth-century American fiction, charging that the classic novels evinced "a tight mental allegiance to a morality which all [the author's] passion goes to destroy." Certainly, too, this "duplicity" involved the mythology's pattern of obscuring the necessity for choosing between contrasting values. Richard

[12]*Love and Death in the American Novel*, p. 355.
[13]*The Americans: The National Experience*, p. 337.

Chase has put the matter less pejoratively in an account that applies equally to the American cinema:

> The American novel tends to rest in contradictions and among extreme ranges of experience. When it attempts to resolve contradictions, it does so in oblique, morally equivocal ways. As a general rule it does so either in melodramatic actions or in pastoral idylls, although intermixed with both one may find the stirring instabilities of "American humor."[14]

Or, in other words, when faced with a difficult choice, American stories resolved it either simplistically (by refusing to acknowledge that a choice is necessary), sentimentally (by blurring the differences between the two sides), or by laughing the whole thing off.

READING THE TEXT

1. In your own words, describe the two basic hero types in American cinema that Ray describes.

2. How do these two hero types relate to America's "psychological pattern" (para. 2)?

3. Explain why, according to Ray, the outlaw hero typically mistrusts women.

4. Define what Ray means by the "reluctant hero" (para. 17).

READING THE SIGNS

1. What sort of hero is Katniss in *The Hunger Games*? Write an essay in which you apply Ray's categories of hero to her character, supporting your argument with specific references to both films in the series.

2. In class, brainstorm on the board official and outlaw heroes you've seen in movies. Then categorize these heroes according to characteristics they share (such as race, gender, profession, or social class). What patterns emerge in your categories, and what is the significance of those patterns?

3. Ray focuses on film, but his categories of hero can be used as a critical framework to analyze other media, including television. What kinds of heroes are the heroes in the program *Sons of Anarchy*? Alternatively, consider a character such as Dexter Morgan in *Dexter*. How might he fit Ray's definitions of a hero?

4. Cartoon television series like *The Simpsons* and *South Park* feature characters that don't readily fit Ray's two main categories of hero. Invent a third type of hero to accommodate such characters.

5. In class, brainstorm a list of female heroes from film and television. Then try to categorize them according to Ray's article. Do the characters easily fit the categories Ray mentions, or do they seem to be mismatches? Do you feel a need to create an additional category? If so, what would it be?

---

[14]Richard Chase, *The American Novel and Its Tradition* (Garden City, N.Y.: Anchor/Doubleday, 1957), p. 1.

STEVIE ST. JOHN

Out of Character: Wonder Woman's Strength Is Her Compassion — What Happened?

At a time when filmmakers are mining the comic book archives for just about any as-yet-unexploited superhero on which to hang a movie, it is odd that Wonder Woman, who has had her own TV series and has been a prominent popular cultural character for decades, is only scheduled to appear in her first feature film in 2016, and even then may not really have the starring role. In this essay exploring the history and significance of Wonder Woman, Stevie St. John invites us to wonder whether a preference for testosterone-charged violence in our superheroes has had something to do with this filmic marginalization of Wonder Woman, who has traditionally been distinctive for her compassionate reluctance to get tough. But now that even Wonder Woman is getting "harder" in the DC comics in which she appears, it remains to be seen which one — violent warrior or compassionate woman — will be featured on the big screen. Stevie St. John is a freelance writer who writes for such publications as *Bitch*, in which this essay first appeared in 2014.

It seems like a given that the best-known and longest-running female superhero would have made it to the big screen by now, especially considering the box-office supremacy of American superhero films in the past decade. Yet while comics fans watched the Dark Knight rise, Captain America soldier forth, and Spider-Man get his own trilogy — twice — Wonder Woman is only now hitting the big screen, and she's not even in the spotlight. The as-yet unnamed 2016 Batman/Superman project will feature Gal Gadot, best known for her work in the *Fast & Furious* series, in the iconic role.

Many hope Gadot will star in her own Wonder Woman film soon, especially because she signed a three-picture deal. But for now it's not clear whether the new film is the prelude to a Wonder Woman project or if she'll just be making a cameo alongside Henry Cavill's Superman and Ben Affleck's Batman.

But it's not just the big picture that has fans apprehensive. Director Zack Snyder isn't exactly known for complex female characters (see: past projects *300* and his *Watchmen* adaptation). "I don't see the director or writers having the desire to grasp the nuances of [Wonder Woman]," says DC Women Kicking Ass blogger Sue, who declined to give her last name due to past issues with online harassment. "And it isn't her story, so I fear she'll be written more as a plot device than a fleshed-out character."

Susie Rantz, PR manager of Geek Girl Con, has similar concerns. "Certainly Wonder Woman has physical strength — but what I always associate more with Wonder Woman is her strength of character. Unlike other superheroes, Wonder Woman always fights for peace. Sometimes that means bringing down the villain, but oftentimes it means unlocking the potential inside every person she encounters." When it comes to the silver screen, Rantz wonders if Wonder Woman will be "physically strong *and* focused on peace, justice, and equality."

And that's what has folks most worried. Like any superhero who's been 5 around for seven decades, Wonder Woman and her alter ego, Diana Prince, have gone through many transformations, carrying with them the expectations of comic-book fans, new readers, and feminists alike. What's always stuck out isn't her physical prowess but her strength as a leader who inspires others and never betrays her beliefs.

"Wonder Woman represents the best of humanity," says Rantz. "She is strong but also compassionate. She elevates the voices of those who are underrepresented. She comes at every situation with an optimism about our human potential, not a preconceived and pessimistic view of an individual. And she is focused on promoting the idea that women should support other women."

It's this essence of her character that fans are afraid will be missing from her long-awaited film debut. And if her recent turn in comics is any indication, their fears are not unfounded.

Certainly Wonder Woman's story in the pages of DC Comics has left many disappointed. In recent story lines, Wonder Woman appears more angry than amused and has a much quicker trigger for when to use physical force. Her original creator, William Marston, didn't arm the Amazon with ropes and chains just for a kinky subtext: He favored them because they were less violent than other weapons, like guns. In the original Wonder Woman stories, villains were usually sent to Reform Island for rehabilitation — inflicting physical harm was generally a last resort.

But in DC's New 52 series, which launched in 2011, Wonder Woman's first appearance comes when a scantily clad woman in peril wakes the slumbering superhero. Although she eventually aids the distressed woman, her first reaction is to swiftly grab and lift the woman by the neck. Later, Wonder Woman smashes a broken wineglass into a villain's hand and draws blood. Notably, it's done in anger, not to deflect an imminent physical threat.

Self-proclaimed "Wonder Woman evangelist" Boston Blake, who gives a 10 Wonder Woman presentation called "The Kink in the Golden Lasso" at fan conventions and academic settings, describes the new series as "all about being stronger, being tougher — not necessarily being wiser." He describes the revamped Wonder Woman as a "butt-kicking piece of ass" — and Snyder's interpretation will likely reflect that as well.

Phil Jimenez, who first became enamored with Wonder Woman through Lynda Carter's 1970s television show, has worked on several superhero titles for both DC Comics and Marvel (credits include *X-Men* and *Spider-Man*). "The

Lynda Carter Wonder Woman was incredibly likable," Jimenez says. "Her great strength [was that] when she walked into a room, you just wanted to be around her. And when she left, you wanted to be a different person. You wanted to be a *better* person."

Jimenez was elated to work on *Wonder Woman* comics between 2000 and 2003, and he coauthored *The Essential Wonder Woman Encyclopedia* (2010). But his take didn't always mesh with what DC Comics envisioned.

Jimenez noticed a shift in the industry shortly after 9/11. As with many depictions of New York in pop culture at the time, several adjustments were made to the art for DC's *Superman*, issue no. 175, published in December 2001. Buildings and falling debris were taken out, as were any deaths shown as the result of the Joker flying a plane into Times Square. Significantly, though, Jimenez's editor asked him to change a scene where Wonder Woman embraces her friend Superman, who is shedding tears for lost lives. Jimenez thought it was "a very Superman/Wonder Woman moment" that "seemed like a genuine expression of these two characters"—but his editor thought it made the Man of Steel look weak. Jimenez fought for the original image and ultimately prevailed, but the art still needed to be adjusted: "He couldn't look fetal; he couldn't cry. He had to look like he was ready for battle, angry—clenched fists, screaming anger, etc."

The impact of 9/11 on comics went further than a single issue: Villains were more likely to be killed than reformed, and superheroes—including Wonder Woman—became "harder."

Terrorism and wars aren't the only factors making modern comics more violent or Wonder Woman's strength more defined by physicality. Jimenez says it's just easier to sell comics with shocking violence than with the complex qualities that originally drew him to Wonder Woman.

Whatever the reason, the New 52 Wonder Woman storyline certainly has a different sensibility—grittier, more violent—than past iterations. Even the titles of the graphic novel compilations of the new series reflect the darker tone: *Blood*, *Guts*, *Iron*, and *War*. More troubling, though, are the changes to Wonder Woman's origin story—a story that's intrinsic to earlier visions of the character and what she stands for. Marston's Paradise Island, the land of Amazons, was a peaceful matriarchy where the Amazons had eternal life, advanced technology, rich natural resources, and no conflict or war. To Marston, these were the results of an all-female society. He assumed the male-wrought ills of society could be ameliorated by women, who possessed innate qualities of love and compassion.

Of course, as KL Pereira writes in "Female Bonding: The Strange History of Wonder Woman" (*Bitch*, no. 33), Marston's version of feminism was "less about advocating gender equality and fighting sexism than it was a variant of the 19th-century temperance movement, which held that women were morally superior to men and, as such, responsible for controlling their appetites."

Still, Marston's Amazon mythology has been important to Wonder Woman's feminist fans for ages. And while there were supernatural aspects to

Marston's Diana, her physical strength, speed, and agility were gained through sheer training. Jimenez says this was "a huge part of the original mythology," and a way to connect to the audience. It told readers that if you worked hard, "you, too, could be a 'wonder woman.'"

But this isn't the case with the comics reboot, says DC Women Kicking Ass blogger Sue. "The writer chose to present [the Amazons] as sirenlike creatures that lured soldiers into sex to get pregnant, murdered them after intercourse, and then traded their boy babies for guns. Not only did [this] radically revamp the Amazons from what Wonder Woman's creator had meant them to be, it revamped them into a set of antifeminist tropes."

Susan Polo, managing editor of TheMarySue.com, a "Girl Guide to Geek   20
Culture," admits that the utopia concept is also problematic—any society built on the idea of exclusion is bound to encounter some trouble—but systematically murdering men and bartering with babies takes it to quite an extreme. "[I'm] really not into the idea of Amazons as [embodying the] greatest fears of the men's rights movement." She has taken the comic off of her pull list.

And instead of a fatherless birth—the original Diana Prince was sculpted out of clay from the Amazons' queen—in the reboot, Diana Prince is another spawn of Zeus, the clay birth a clever ruse to protect her from the jealous rage of Zeus's wife, Hera. She's essentially born out of female rivalry, rather than solidarity. Also, instead of being trained alongside her Amazon sisters, she is trained by Ares, god of war.

Some readers see this as a return to the Greek myth that inspired Marston. However, as Les Daniels explains in *Wonder Woman: The Complete History* (2000), Marston's origin story was itself a subversion of a sexist myth, as "the Amazons in ancient legend and literature . . . were said to be a band of self-mutilating child murderers who launched violent, ultimately suicidal attacks on the social order." The lesson of these older myths was that women should know their place. Daniels concluded that "modern feminists who view Amazons as an ideal may well owe more to comic books than to ancient myths."

Ironically, Marston's subversion of sexist mythology has itself been upended. And the results are hard to reconcile with the ideals that spawned the character and then made her a feminist powerhouse.

As Pereira wrote, male superheroes are "revered for their incredible strength and X-ray vision, their mild-mannered alter egos serve as foils to their super selves . . . making it clear to the reader that no amount of pumping iron or fancy cars could ever transform him into his male hero." Diana Prince, however, "encouraged the women she met to realize that while their talents and hard work were important, a positive attitude and confidence in oneself was what really got the job done."

Of course, Diana Prince has evolved through many eras and identities.   25
After Marston's death in 1947, Wonder Woman was taken up by other writers who didn't quite know what to do with the wasp-waisted Amazon. In

the 1950s, the comics focused largely on Diana Prince's love life with the inept Steve Trevor. And in the late 1960s, she gave up her powers and iconic swimsuit costume for mod dresses. ("Talk about bondage!" quipped comics historian Trina Robbins about this dark era in Diana's history.) Switching to jumpsuit apparel in the '70s, Emma Peel–style, she continued defeating criminals while also running a clothing store.

It was around then that Gloria Steinem picked up the Wonder Woman mantle. "We discovered that she had fallen on very hard times," says Steinem dryly in Kristy Guevara-Flanagan's 2012 documentary *Wonder Women! The Untold Story of American Superheroines*. "We [had to] practically march in the street to get her magical powers back." When Wonder Woman graced the cover of *Ms.* magazine's inaugural 1972 issue, it was also the beginning of a feminist interpretation of her origin story.

A few years later came the debut of the lovably campy TV series anchored by Lynda Carter. Like the Wonder Woman from the original comic pages, Carter's character confidently stood up for what she believed in without taking anything too seriously. In the pilot, she thwarts bank robbers then comments on how silly it is that the police expect her — and not the robbers — to fill out paperwork: "What a country this is!"

Boston Blake, like so many others, fell in love with Carter's portrayal, but laments that her carefree crime-fighting days seem over. "This is a sad time to be a Wonder Woman fan," he says. "We're really divided."

Tim Hanley, whose new book *Wonder Woman Unbound: The Curious History of the World's Most Famous Heroine* traces the development of Wonder Woman's character over the decades, is looking on the bright side. "A comic book read by 30,000 people isn't going to affect the millions of people who know Wonder Woman as an icon of feminism and female empowerment. Her comic-book iterations come and go, but the icon is bigger than any of them."

And while Hanley can see how the New 52 Wonder Woman "would easily 30 fit into the dark, violent, joyless world Zack Snyder created in *Man of Steel*," he doesn't necessarily think the movies will reflect the comics. That being said, "Wonder Woman could be the Pollyanna of superhero comics and Snyder would still make her sexy and violent above all else."

As for a film starring the Amazon princess, The Mary Sue's Susan Polo is hedging her bets. "It's so far in the future and there are so many maybes. . . . I'm not getting excited about it yet."

With a string of false-start Wonder Woman projects dotting pop culture history, it's no surprise that some Wonder Woman enthusiasts have an I'll-believe-it-when-I-see-it attitude. Two TV pilots have been axed: a CW pilot called *Amazon* and an NBC Wonder Woman pilot from David E. Kelley. The highest-profile disappointment was a Wonder Woman film attached to *Buffy the Vampire Slayer* creator Joss Whedon, who told *Rookie* magazine that his version of Wonder Woman would have emphasized her humanity and vulnerability. A goddess on earth, Diana Prince would "look at us and the way we kill each other and the way we let people starve and the way the world is run and she'd just be like, 'None of this makes sense to me.'" Whedon said that through Diana's relationship with Steve Trevor, the film would have focused on "what it's like when you are weak, when you do have all these forces controlling you and there's nothing you can do about it. That was the sort of central concept: [Trevor] teaching her humanity and [Wonder Woman] saying, okay, great, but we can still do better."

Jimenez understands why valuing a female superhero for embodying stereotypically feminine traits might rankle some people. But the fact that Wonder Woman was loving and compassionate was what he always loved about the heroine. "That's not seen as valid anymore," he says. "I think more people should be like that."

READING THE TEXT

1. In your own words, summarize the reasons Hollywood producers have had difficulty in deciding how to present a female hero, as St. John describes them.

2. What does the PR manager Susie Rantz mean in saying, "Wonder Woman represents the best of humanity" (para. 6)? How do you respond to this claim?

3. What impact did the 9/11 terrorist attacks on America have on the comic industry, according to cartoonist Phil Jimenez?

4. Summarize in your own words the history of Wonder Woman, according to St. John.

5. What is the significance of the Amazons, as St. John explains it?

READING THE SIGNS

1. Compare Wonder Woman with another female superhero, such as Catwoman, Elektra, or Emma Frost. To what extent does your choice exhibit either compassion, on the one hand, or a gritty penchant for violence, as many male superheroes do?

2. **CONNECTING TEXTS**   Read or reread Robert B. Ray's "The Thematic Paradigm" (p. 450), and write an essay in which you argue whether Wonder Woman should be categorized as an official or outlaw hero. Do those categories even apply to this character?

3. Cartoonist Phil Jimenez claims that the 9/11 terrorist attacks changed the depiction of violence in cartoons specifically and popular culture more generally. In an essay, explore the extent to which popular culture serves as an accurate sign of political attitudes. Be sure to ground your argument in an analysis of particular media examples.

4. **CONNECTING TEXTS**   To what extent does Wonder Woman reproduce, change, or complicate traditional gender codes? To develop your argument, read or reread Aaron Devor's "Gender Role Behavior and Attitudes" (p. 504).

5. **CONNECTING TEXTS**   Read or reread Mariah Burton Nelson's "I Won. I'm Sorry" (p. 524). Adopting Nelson's perspective, write a response to cartoonist Phil Jimenez's endorsement of female superheroes that embody stereotypical feminine traits.

HEATHER HAVRILESKY
No Sympathy for the Devil

Ever since HBO's *The Sopranos* managed to make millions of viewers identify with a violent criminal who would have been the villain of any conventional crime drama, television producers have been churning out flawed protagonists — like *Mad Men*'s Don Draper and *Breaking Bad*'s Walter White — who, though often called antiheroes in the tradition of Tony Soprano, may simply be doomed and degraded men unworthy of our sympathy. That, at least, is the conclusion that Heather Havrilesky draws in this 2013 assessment of TV's recent crop of flawed protagonists, and if Don Draper and Walter White have been unable to elicit the kind of viewer identification that Tony Soprano did, so be it, Havrilesky believes. As she suggests, that is what real life is all about. Indeed, those who are brave enough to explore the depths have shown that modern television has the potential to reach literary status — to be art as well as entertainment — and that can be a very good thing. Heather Havrilesky is the author of *Disaster Preparedness: A Memoir* (2011) and a journalist who writes for such publications as *Salon* and *Bookforum*.

A moderately bad man knows he is not very good: a thoroughly bad man thinks he is all right.

— C. S. LEWIS

For the past decade, TV has been awash with deeply flawed antiheroes: philandering ad men and pill-popping nurses, meth-cooking chemistry teachers and mob boss suburban dads. But when you launch a show that's centered on an unethical protagonist, how do you keep viewers engaged and invested in that character indefinitely — or at least through six seasons?

Because for every show like *The Sopranos* and *The Shield* that made us cheer for a rotten scoundrel, there were five or six others that failed to engage us. Dark dramedies like *Californication*, *Shameless*, *Weeds*, *American Horror Story*, *Nurse Jackie*, and *Nip/Tuck* have plenty of redeeming qualities — a wicked sense of humor, an irresistible visual style, a delicious knack for realistic marital spats. But the second we determine that our antihero is nothing but an irredeemable loser and/or we conclude that his or her choices will never make a shred of sense, we're lost. Every plot twist feels arbitrary and impossible to care about, like watching Bart Simpson burn his finger over and over again without learning a thing about cause and effect.

Despite Edie Falco's great performance on *Nurse Jackie*, which made Jackie far more likable and believable than she would've been otherwise, it was tough to understand why this very practical woman was popping pills and sleeping around on her perfectly good husband. Eventually it became hard to watch. Likewise, Hank Moody's high jinx on *Californication* were only amusing until his total lack of a soul and somewhat repetitive insistence on deadpan debauchery reduced him to a caricature. The two antiheroes of *Nip/Tuck* navigated their shiny, shallow world with irresistible swagger, but the arrogance and slickness that drew us in were exactly what drove us away in the end. The drama *Dexter*'s perverse sense of humor (its perverse sense of everything, really) kept us in a serial killer's thrall far longer than seemed plausible, but that show's appeal started to crumble once our antihero's antics landed his wife, a reliable source of comic relief, in mortal danger.

But what did we expect from a show about a serial killer? Hugging and learning? Isn't it a little unfair to lose interest in *Dexter* the second it stops looking like a darkly comical revenge fantasy and starts to look more like a gory horror movie featuring a baby in a pool of blood?

Unfair or not, maintaining an audience's interest can require self-restraint 5 in storytelling. Carmela of *The Sopranos* never ended up with her throat slit, and if she did, our feelings about her husband would've been irretrievably altered.

In truth, the likability of any given protagonist represents one of the most subjective assessments you can make about a TV show. Debating how hateful Vic Mackey, Walter White, Nancy Botwin, or Don Draper is can feel like squabbling over whether a tasteless joke is funny or not. Gut checks depend on what's at stake for viewers, how many ethical lapses are tolerable to them, how interesting they find it to watch a person's principles bend and then break, and which personality strengths (and weaknesses) they judge as redemptive, where others are judged as unforgivable.

And as easy as it is to pinpoint when *Weeds* or *Nip/Tuck* stopped commanding our interest, it's a little more thorny when two of the best shows on television, *Breaking Bad* and *Mad Men*, repeatedly grapple with the same problem of character likability.

Breaking Bad presents a particularly fascinating example because its protagonist, Walter White (Bryan Cranston), was never supposed to charm us, enthrall us, or appear remotely heroic. The hard sell of *Breaking Bad* is that it offers up a painfully regular, geeky school teacher who sees himself as a big failure (and he's dying of cancer to boot). Our antihero is *anti-hero* in the literal sense: He is clumsy, stutters, and rarely saves the day. And who better to occupy the role of sidekick than a self-interested, shallow kid like Jesse Pinkman (Aaron Paul)? Jesse is the epitome of a thug: uneducated, naïve, and brutish.

Even though *Breaking Bad*'s pilot was much more comedic than the subsequent series proved to be, an acute sense of the absurd seems to drive the show. Throw in its gorgeous cinematography, its poetic appreciation of little

Photofest

Bryan Cranston as Walter White in *Breaking Bad*.

details (a stuffed animal's eyeball in a swimming pool, a pizza fermenting on a garage rooftop), its unerring grasp of dramatic tension, of nuanced dialogue, of escalating stakes, and you've got one of the strangest, most riveting shows on TV. *Breaking Bad* is so good, in part, because of creator Vince Gilligan's insistence on ignoring every TV convention in the book. What we see on our screen are two essentially unlikable, not very attractive human beings, placed in ethically indefensible situations over and over again, each of which unfolds at an extremely patient pace.

But even as Walt stretches our patience to the breaking point, he never 10 gets to enjoy the spoils of his crimes. Unlike Tony Soprano, who eats and cheats and drinks and indulges his own vanity and self-delusion over and over, Walt is usually focused on digging his way out of one mess or another, trying to win his family back, trying to hide his crimes from them so they never know just how far he's fallen. This fact alone can be exhausting. But if Walt were vain or wasteful, or if any of his choices felt ego-driven at the outset, we'd never stay on his side. He's not appealing enough to pull that off. He's more of a blank slate than a character, someone we can project our own longing or frustration onto.

Slowly over the course of the show, Walter goes from desperate man in a tight spot to a true criminal — killing somewhat blameless people out of convenience. Jesse, on the other hand, proclaims at the start of season three, "I'm the bad guy," but by the end of that season, he's the one trying to convince

Walt not to commit murder. Over the course of the show, Jesse develops from typical scumbag to something else, a lonely guy who's smart enough to know better but who keeps falling short of his best intentions. For all of his flaws, Jesse is usually more sympathetic than Walt, because he's actively trying to connect with other people, even if he does so by falling in love with a manipulative junkie or throwing hundred dollar bills in the air. Walt is troubling because the guilt and moral compass he has at the start of the series melts off him until his choices feel purely pragmatic. But he no longer has a choice. He boards this crazy train and then he can't get off without destroying his entire family.

Because *Breaking Bad* doesn't take pains to show us Walt's vulnerabilities and the root causes of his damage the way *The Sopranos* did with Tony, we rarely feel that much sympathy for the man. We do want him to find a way out of each mess (unlike Dexter, who we sometimes wish would get caught). But we don't look into his eyes and feel heartbroken the way we felt with Tony Soprano. James Gandolfini was a master of showing us Tony's mixed emotions and regrets and guilt, and David Chase served up at least one vivid, guilt-inducing moment per episode (Tony says the wrong thing to Meadow and immediately cringes at his own gall; Tony orders a hit and then can't sleep at night, etc.).

But Walt isn't a giant puppy dog in mob boss clothing. He's not supposed to be lovable. While *Breaking Bad* veers into unrelenting darkness so often that it can be tough to stomach, that's kind of the point. The daring of *Breaking Bad* lies in its insistence on making its protagonists scrape and claw and make awful compromises without any retreat into giant plates of pasta or reassuringly mundane family bickering or self-doubting therapy sessions.

Tony's very relatable vices — laziness, gluttony, adultery — offered the recurring impression of an indulged child who refused to grow up. We were meant to see our own lapses reflected in Tony, and to empathize with him despite his obvious repugnant choices. Our feeling of connection to him was necessary, thanks to how extreme his flaws were. He was vengeful, ego-driven, short-sighted, and sometimes even casually reprehensible, striking people down out of mere convenience. The trick that David Chase pulled off with *The Sopranos* was that he made us feel protective, affectionate love for a bad, bad guy, a guy who wanted to grow but couldn't, a guy who, at the end of the day, just wanted to daydream about the good old days and stuff his face with onion rings. When Tony had a panic attack or missed the ducks in his pool or got beat up or embarrassed, it made us feel terribly sorry for him in spite of ourselves. That's not how we feel about Walter White. But that's not how we're supposed to feel about him.

Just as Walt wasn't designed to occupy the same place in our hearts as Tony Soprano, neither was Don Draper of *Mad Men*. But because Matthew Weiner and the show's other writers take pains to show us why Don does what he does, it's more of a problem when we come away from these character sketches feeling unmoved. In the show's sixth season, Don didn't necessarily make bigger mistakes than he ever had, but his hungry ego and his weaknesses were on full display like never before. Aside from being called a monster by Peggy and assuming the fetal position toward the end of the season, Don didn't register guilt or awareness of his own terrible behavior that often. Even though it may be Weiner's intention to demonstrate the limitations of Don's consciousness, even though *Mad Men* is arguably guided by ideas more than emotions, and Don's shortcomings are meant to embody the shortcomings of not just an entire generation but also late capitalist American society itself, the exercise can grow tiresome when Don is less likable than the writers seem to believe.

That's arguably a minor quibble, considering that *Mad Men* is an ensemble show, and Peggy and Joan and Roger and even Pete continue to draw us in thoroughly despite (and even because of) their flaws. Still, Don's story lines would be more satisfying if the show's awkward attempts to have us understand him — via flashbacks to a not-all-that-sympathetic kid in a whore house — didn't fail about half the time. Weiner and company seemed to assume that we'd tolerate Don's repeated hypocritical behavior in the absence of any hint of how alone he felt in the world. As Don cheated on his second wife, betrayed his new friend, demeaned his new lover, disappointed his co-workers and horrified his daughter, we needed some offsetting moments of feeling sad for him. We needed to see him wishing for something that he couldn't quite have (something other than another man's wife). We needed to see him relying on someone for help (other than the man whose wife he was sleeping with). Instead, we got the same repeating close-up of his perplexed face. In the show's sixth season, the writers set out to make Don the victim, but they accidentally made him the enemy instead.

Maybe it's time to admit that we've been spoiled by Chase, who made Tony sympathetic from the very first episode of *The Sopranos*. Chase tricked showrunners into thinking they could make audiences feel sympathy for a truly awful person. It wasn't as easy as Chase and Gandolfini made it look.

And to be fair, Walter White and Don Draper aren't designed to elicit the same kind of affection that Tony Soprano is. At the end of *The Sopranos,* the show's audience was on the edge of their seats, wondering whether Tony would be killed or not because, by then, for better or for worse, Tony felt like part of the family. When *Breaking Bad* ends with Walt doing something so reprehensible it makes our teeth hurt, or *Mad Men* ends with Don leaping from his office window to his death or leaving his fourth wife for his eleventh secretary, we're unlikely to feel quite as wound up about it. Most likely, Walt will simply continue suffering, and Don will continue to believe his own hero complex despite all evidence to the contrary. These characters were made to disappoint us, even if the shows they occupy rarely do.

We might wish for a prettier picture, or hope for some closure, but redemption is not at the heart of either of these shows, and that's exactly what makes them so mesmerizingly different from more typical, saccharine fare. Neither show is perfect; both Don Draper and Walter White could be humanized more. But as *Breaking Bad* and *Mad Men* enter their home stretches, it might make sense to step back and accept that these are both dark portrayals of doomed men. We're not going to be treated to a heart-warming indie pop ballad as Skyler White drives off into the sunset in a Prius like Claire Fisher on the *Six Feet Under* finale. Instead, we should expect an unnerving ending, and feel grateful that such unapologetically bleak, literary stories now occupy the small screen. Because this picture was never pretty to begin with.

READING THE TEXT

1. How does Havrilesky explain why some TV shows that feature antiheroes succeed and others fail?

2. Havrilesky only implicitly offers her own definition of hero or antihero. Read through her essay, and summarize in your own words the definition of hero/ antihero that seems to govern her selection.

3. Explain in your own words what Havrilesky means by "redemptive" (para. 6).

4. According to Havrilesky, how do TV antiheroes contribute to a more realistic and more artistic entertainment than simple heroes and villains?

5. Explain in your own words the reasons that shows like *Mad Men* and *Breaking Bad* have enjoyed a loyal fan base, while audiences eventually tired of programs like *Nurse Jackie*.

READING THE SIGNS

1. Havrilesky claims that "the likability of any given protagonist represents one of the most subjective assessments you can make about a TV show" (para. 6). In an essay, evaluate the plausibility of this claim, based on a careful analy-sis of a TV show protagonist of your choice. To what extent does "likability" influence an audience's response to a program?

2. Watch a few of the final episodes of *The Sopranos*, and write your own analy-sis of what kind of hero Tony Soprano is. Does your interpretation support, oppose, or modify Havrilesky's analysis of this character? Alternatively, write an analysis of *Breaking Bad* or *Mad Men*, again comparing your reading with Havrilesky's.

3. **CONNECTING TEXTS**   In class, brainstorm a list of current TV shows that feature antihero protagonists. Use the list as the basis of your own essay in which you argue for your explanation for why antiheroes have become so dominant on TV, focusing on your interpretation of two or three programs. How is their dominance a sign of the times? To develop your ideas, consult Laura Ben-nett's "Against Antiheroes" (p. 471).

LAURA BENNETT
Against Antiheroes

> Antiheroes are hot, and Laura Bennett thinks that it's high time we
> stepped back and chilled out a bit about it all. When book agents
> and TV network publicists promote practically everything they've got
> going as antiheroic, and journalists lasso the likes of Edward Snowden
> and Bradley Manning into the antihero corral, this once-useful label
> has become little more than a buzzword, Bennett believes. Maybe it's
> time to retire the term and coin a fresher and more specific word.
> Laura Bennett is an author and designer whose books include *Didn't*
> *I Feed You Yesterday? A Mother's Guide to Sanity in Stilettos* (2010) and
> *Handmade Chic: Fashionable Projects That Look High-End, Not Home-*
> *spun* (2012).

I recently received an email from the publicist for Junot Diaz's *This Is How*
You Lose Her declaring that "the protagonist, Yunior, is also a bit of an antihero, which makes these topics all the more interesting and relatable." There
it was again: antihero, that vague and fashionable word, with its connotation
of middle-aged family men and their shadowy consciences. To be clear, Diaz's
Yunior is not an antihero. He is a vulnerable, likeable protagonist with human
flaws, as most every protagonist in the history of literature has been. But it
was hardly surprising that a publicist, in search of an easy toehold on the
zeitgeist, would deploy the word. Somehow "antihero" has come to represent
an impossibly broad characterological range: from psychopathic drug lords to
well-meaning serial killers to wayward Dominican kids who sometimes mistreat women because of culturally ingrained misogyny.

More than a decade after Tony Soprano cried about ducks and several
weeks before Walter White completes his infernal transformation, this is perhaps the most overused term in all of pop culture. I should clarify that I also
say this in response to myself, as I recently wrote an essay about "Breaking
Bad" that featured "antihero" in the headline. And granted, the TV obsession
with troubled bad boys borders on self-parody. AMC teased its new drama,
"Low Winter Sun," in ways that felt like a comically transparent attempt to
get in on the antihero hype: "Good man. Cop. Killer," the ads proclaimed. But
the sheer volume of antihero references over the past few months seems like
evidence of a current tendency in cultural criticism to rely too heavily on pre-
established archetypes. At this point, "antihero" barely means anything at all.

The recent books *Difficult Men* by Brett Martin and *The Revolution Was*
Televised by Alan Sepinwall, which both chart the golden age of TV drama,
have launched countless essays about our era of antiheroes; TV showrunners themselves have even been characterized as the antiheroes of showbiz.

471

An article in *The American Spectator* was titled "In Defense of the Antihero," though today's antiheroes scarcely need defending. The *Global Post* weighed in on "Snowden, Manning, and the Rise of the American Antihero." Amazon lists some three hundred titles containing the word over the past few years alone.

What, exactly, does "antihero" mean? *Merriam-Webster* traces its first appearance back to 1714 and murkily defines it as "a protagonist or notable figure who is considerably lacking in heroic qualities." Some books on the subject claim that the term has its roots in the idea of the Byronic hero, though this is a far more concrete and specific type: Byron's leading men are melancholic loners with a distaste for authority, struggling to overcome their own dark pasts. In Hollywood, the concept has been around at least since films of the '40s and '50s began exploring the new post-war cynicism, and an action film actually titled "Anti-hero" appeared in 1999. *Britannica* cites as some early antiheroes Satan in *Paradise Lost*, Heathcliff in *Wuthering Heights*, and Don Quixote, none of whom are particularly useful analogues for the wretched, morally bankrupt leading men of cable drama. And the men of HBO and AMC are not as similar in their sinfulness as they have been made out to be. Walter White is by now less an antihero than a straightforward villain, a macho foil for Hank. "Antihero" implies that a character encourages a conflicted sympathy; Walt forfeited our sympathy long ago.

Even Emily Nussbaum — who it should be said, is singularly skilled at [5] inventing her own critical archetypes, à la the "Hummingbird theory" — wrote a piece on "Sex and the City" that identified Carrie as the "first female antihero," the one frustrating bit of an otherwise lovely essay. Carrie could be irksome as a character, but "Sex and the City" was defensive of its protagonist in a way that "Breaking Bad" and "The Sopranos" never were, permitting Carrie to be abrasive and vain only to rein her in at the last minute with a pat, chastened ending; the other shows pushed us to see just what it would take to sever our emotional attachment to their protagonists, while Carrie's reprehensibility was always a learning experience. It is hard to deny that seeing "antihero" applied to Carrie provides a quick, simple thrill of analytical recognition. But in the end, it confuses more than it reveals.

Over-reliance on buzzwords is not specific to pop culture — academia is an echo chamber of scholars responding to and recasting each others' jargon — but the world of online cultural coverage is so breakneck and ephemeral that the pressure to find quick reference points is particularly intense. So instead of describing a phenomenon on its own terms, the impulse is to locate it in relation to some other, louder phenomenon, to riff on an old paradigm instead of devising a new one. Another similarly abused term is "manic pixie dream girl," coined by Nathan Rabin in a 2007 *A.V. Club* essay, which has had an absurdly long half-life, applied to every female, free-spirited weirdo to cavort across our screens.

This one even engendered spin-off archetypes: A lengthy essay in *Grantland* identified the new trend of the "manic pixie dream guy." (To name a few: the boys of One Direction, Ben Wyatt of "Parks and Recreation," Joseph Gordon-Levitt, and Ryan Gosling.) An article in *Flavorwire* announced the arrival of the "nerdy doormat dream girl." It's hard to blame critics for feverishly trying to come up with formulations that stick, an impulse rooted in the sorry Internet-age assumption that every concept must be crammed into some neat, buzzy category in order to be understood amid a sea of fruit-fly attention spans. But the result is a narrowness of interpretation, a critical culture of shortcuts. If Yunior is an antihero and Ryan Gosling is a manic pixie dream guy, it's probably time to retire these phrases for good.

READING THE TEXT

1. Trace the evolution of the term "antihero," as Bennett describes it.
2. What reasons does Bennett provide for her proposal to abandon the word "antihero"?
3. In your own words, explain what Bennett means when she claims that critics have "an impulse rooted in the sorry Internet-age assumption that every concept must be crammed into some neat, buzzy category in order to be understood amid a sea of fruit-fly attention spans" (para. 7).
4. Characterize Bennett's tone in this selection. How does it affect your response to her ideas?

READING THE SIGNS

1. Write an essay that supports, rejects, or modifies Bennett's claim that the term "antihero" is being overused. You might use as evidence some reviews of films or TV programs that purportedly include antihero protagonists. If you agree with her, explain why; if not, propose your own explanation for why antiheroes are part of today's cultural zeitgeist.
2. Read one of the texts focused on antiheroes that Bennett mentions in paragraph 3. Analyze its use of the term, and in an essay discuss whether Bennett's indictment of the term is valid, overblown, or something else.
3. **CONNECTING TEXTS** Bennett briefly notes the history of antiheroes in film and literature. Adopting the perspective of Linda Seger in "Creating the Myth" (p. 334), write an essay that evaluates the proposition that antiheroes are an enduring character archetype that deserves its nomenclature.

GEORGE PACKER

Celebrating Inequality

Are celebrities heroes? No, not at all, George Packer suggests, but in tough times like today's, when the gap between the rich and the poor yawns ever wider, celebrities loom larger on the social horizon than they do in more equitable times, overshadowing the rest of us. And we're not just talking about entertainers. Indeed, as Packer quips in this 2013 essay for the *New York Times*, "Our age is lousy with celebrities"; they include bankers, computer engineers, real estate developers, media executives, journalists, politicians, scientists, and even chefs. And as the new celebrity deities gobble up whatever opportunities are left in America, Packer believes, America itself is turning backward to the days of the Jazz Age and Jay Gatsby. So, meet the new celebrity gods; same as the old celebrity gods — or "something far more perverse." George Packer is a staff writer for the *New Yorker* and the author of numerous books, including *The Assassins' Gate: America in Iraq* (2006) and the National Book Award–winning *The Unwinding: An Inner History of the New America* (2013).

The Roaring '20s was the decade when modern celebrity was invented in America. F. Scott Fitzgerald's *The Great Gatsby* is full of magazine spreads of tennis players and socialites, popular song lyrics, movie stars, paparazzi, gangsters and sports scandals — machine-made by technology, advertising and public relations. Gatsby, a mysterious bootlegger who makes a meteoric ascent from Midwestern obscurity to the palatial splendor of West Egg, exemplifies one part of the celebrity code: it's inherently illicit. Fitzgerald intuited that, with the old restraining deities of the 19th century dead and his generation's faith in man shaken by World War I, celebrities were the new household gods.

What are celebrities, after all? They dominate the landscape, like giant monuments to aspiration, fulfillment and overreach. They are as intimate as they are grand, and they offer themselves for worship by ordinary people searching for a suitable object of devotion. But in times of widespread opportunity, the distance between gods and mortals closes, the monuments shrink closer to human size and the centrality of celebrities in the culture recedes. They loom larger in times like now, when inequality is soaring and trust in institutions — governments, corporations, schools, the press — is falling.

The Depression that ended Fitzgerald's Jazz Age yielded to a new order that might be called the Roosevelt Republic. In the quarter-century after World War II, the country established collective structures, not individual monuments, that channeled the aspirations of ordinary people: state universities, progressive taxation, interstate highways, collective bargaining, health insurance for the elderly, credible news organizations.

One virtue of those hated things called bureaucracies is that they oblige everyone to follow a common set of rules, regardless of station or background; they are inherently equalizing. Books like William H. Whyte's *The Organization Man* and C. Wright Mills's *White Collar* warned of the loss of individual identity, but those middle-class anxieties were possible only because of the great leveling. The "stars" continued to fascinate, especially with the arrival of TV, but they were not essential. Henry Fonda, Barbara Stanwyck, Bette Davis, Jimmy Stewart, Perry Como, Joe DiMaggio, Jack Paar, Doris Day and Dick Clark rose with Americans—not from them—and their successes and screw-ups were a sideshow, not the main event.

Our age is lousy with celebrities. They can be found in every sector of society, including ones that seem less than glamorous. We have celebrity bankers (Jamie Dimon), computer engineers (Sergey Brin), real estate developers/conspiracy theorists (Donald J. Trump), media executives (Arianna Huffington), journalists (Anderson Cooper), mayors (Cory A. Booker), economists (Jeffrey D. Sachs), biologists (J. Craig Venter) and chefs (Mario Batali).

There is a quality of self-invention to their rise: Mark Zuckerberg went from awkward geek to the subject of a Hollywood hit; Shawn Carter turned into Jay-Z; Martha Kostyra became Martha Stewart, and then *Martha Stewart Living*. The person evolves into a persona, then a brand, then an empire, with the business imperative of grow or die—a process of expansion and commodification that transgresses boundaries by substituting celebrity for institutions. Instead of robust public education, we have Mr. Zuckerberg's "rescue" of Newark's schools. Instead of a vibrant literary culture, we have Oprah's book club. Instead of investments in public health, we have the Gates Foundation. Celebrities either buy institutions, or "disrupt" them.

After all, if you *are* the institution, you don't need to play by its rules. Mr. Zuckerberg's foundation myth begins with a disciplinary proceeding at Harvard, which leads him to drop out and found a company whose motto is "Move fast and break things." Jay-Z's history as a crack dealer isn't just a hard-luck story—it's celebrated by fans (and not least himself) as an early sign of hustle and smarts. Martha Stewart's jail time for perjury merely proved that her will to win was indomitable. These new celebrities are all more or less start-up entrepreneurs, and they live by the hacker's code: ask forgiveness, not permission.

The obsession with celebrities goes far beyond supermarket tabloids, gossip Web sites and reality TV. It obliterates old distinctions between high and low culture, serious and trivial endeavors, profit making and philanthropy, leading to the phenomenon of being famous for being famous. An activist singer (Bono) is given a lucrative role in Facebook's initial public offering. A patrician politician (Al Gore) becomes a plutocratic media executive and tech investor. One of America's richest men (Michael R. Bloomberg) rules its largest city.

This jet-setting, Davos-attending crowd constitutes its own superclass, who hang out at the same TED talks, big-idea conferences and fund-raising galas, appear on the same talk shows, invest in one another's projects, wear one another's brand apparel, champion one another's causes, marry and cheat on one another. *The New Digital Age*, the new guide to the future by Eric Schmidt and Jared Cohen of Google, carries blurbs from such technology experts as Henry A. Kissinger and Tony Blair. The inevitable next step is for Kim Kardashian to sit on the board of a tech start-up, host a global-poverty-awareness event and write a book on behavioral neuroscience.

This new kind of celebrity is the ultimate costume ball, far more exclu-   10
sive and decadent than even the most potent magnates of Hollywood's studio era could have dreamed up. Their superficial diversity dangles before us the myth that in America, anything is possible — even as the American dream quietly dies, a victim of the calcification of a class system that is nearly hereditary.

As mindless diversions from a sluggish economy and chronic malaise, the new aristocrats play a useful role. But their advent suggests that, after decades of widening income gaps, unequal distributions of opportunity and reward, and corroding public institutions, we have gone back to Gatsby's time — or something far more perverse. The celebrity monuments of our age have grown so huge that they dwarf the aspirations of ordinary people, who are asked to yield their dreams to the gods: to flash their favorite singer's corporate logo at concerts, to pour open their lives (and data) on Facebook, to adopt Apple as a lifestyle. We know our stars aren't inviting us to think we can be just like them. Their success is based on leaving the rest of us behind.

READING THE TEXT

1. In your own words, trace the evolution of the celebrity from the 1920s to the post–World War II era to today, as Packer describes it.

2. What does Packer mean when he asserts that today a celebrity "evolves into a persona, then a brand, then an empire, with the business imperative of grow or die" (para. 6)?

3. Why does Packer consider today's celebrities their "own superclass" (para. 9)?

4. What relation does Packer find between the plethora of celebrities today and economic conditions?

5. Why does Packer say that America today is returning to the ethos of the Jazz Age (or, perhaps, becoming even worse)?

READING THE SIGNS

1. In class, discuss the meanings of the terms "celebrities" and "heroes." Using that conversation as a starting point, write an essay that argues for your own definition of the two terms, taking care to delineate distinctions between them. Be sure to ground your discussion in real-life examples of both categories, as Packer does in his essay.

2. As Packer mentions, one kind of current celebrity is the person who is "famous for being famous" (para. 8). In class, brainstorm a list of current such celebrities and discuss what they have in common. Use this discussion to jump-start your own essay on what this sort of fame signifies about the values and worldview of modern America.

3. Write an essay in which you support, refute, or complicate Packer's claim that "this new kind of celebrity is the ultimate costume ball. . . . Their superficial diversity dangles before us the myth that in America, anything is possible" (para. 10). To develop your ideas, consult the introduction to this chapter.

4. Select one of the recent celebrities whom Packer mentions, such as Martha Stewart or Bono, and research the public relations surrounding the individual. Use your findings to endorse, refute, or modify Packer's contention that "these new celebrities are all more or less start-up entrepreneurs, and they live by the hacker's code: ask forgiveness, not permission" (para. 7).

5. In your journal, ruminate about which celebrities you admire and why. Then, in an essay, subject one or two of your choices to Packer's critique of today's celebrities. Do they survive his accusation that they "have grown so huge that they dwarf the aspirations of ordinary people, who are asked to yield their dreams to the gods" (para. 11)? Alternatively, if you do not admire any celebrities, write an essay in which you explain why, basing your comments on examples of particular "celebrity monuments of our age" (para. 11).

NOAH GITTELL

The Lone Ranger *Seals It: America's New Favorite Villain Is a Rich Guy*

Even as life gets better and better for the CEO class, its image gets worse and worse. Indeed, as Noah Gittell observes in this 2013 movie review for the *Atlantic*, it appears that corrupt business executives are taking over as the villain of choice in Hollywood blockbusters. This shouldn't be too surprising, given the role of big business in the making of the Great Recession, and so, in a fairly typical irony of entertainment logic, a good way of making money for large corporate studios like Disney and Sony is to make movies about greedy corporations. Go figure. Noah Gittell is the editor of the blog *Reel Change*.

Writer Ian Fleming is known to have once said, "Once is happenstance. Twice is coincidence. Three times is enemy action." If that's the case, three recently released Hollywood films — *Iron Man 3*, *White House Down*, and now *The Lone Ranger* — show that American moviegoers and moviemakers have identified a new enemy of the moment, and it doesn't come from overseas. These would-be summer blockbusters convey a leftward turn in thinking about the militarization and the War on Terror. The real enemy, Hollywood seems to be telling us, is within.

In discussing the progressive politics of *The Lone Ranger*, most critics have focused on the depiction of Native Americans, and with good reason. Over the history of the American Western, Native Americans have often been depicted as faceless savages whose efforts to defend themselves were merely obstacles to America's Manifest Destiny. Some cinematic efforts have been made to subvert this convention (*The Searchers* and *Dances with Wolves* are probably the most famous examples), but *The Lone Ranger* takes things a step further, making Tonto and John Reid (who will become the eponymous hero) dual protagonists. There is room for debate on this; some critics still feel that Depp's performance, with its use of "red face" and halted speaking style, is dehumanizing, but the increased role for Tonto is at least a step in the right direction.

This depiction of Native Americans in *The Lone Ranger* actually serves an even deeper revision of the genre, as it posits war as the underlying oppressor in American society. Here's how it's done: In making Tonto and Reid equals, the filmmakers are able to give them a mutual enemy. This is Cole (Tom Wilkinson), a railroad magnate trying to lay tracks from Texas to California. A treaty between the U.S. and the Indian tribes has prevented him from building on tribal lands, so he makes it look like the Comanches — Tonto's tribe — have broken the agreement, thus opening up their land for train travel. The turn of events will lead to war — and Indian genocide at the hands of the U.S. Cavalry. But who could make a fuss over the survival of an indigenous people when there are American dollars to be made?

It comes across like a Western as told by Howard Zinn, a shocking change for a genre that has leaned conservative in all things. Unlike previous Westerns, in which Indians were seen as an obstacle to American economic expansion, the historical perspective inherent in *The Lone Ranger* shows the same story from the other side and suggests that American business interests were the driving force behind the Indian massacres. There may be a lot of professors at liberal arts colleges who agree, but you'll be unable to find that point of view in more than a couple of movies through the Western's long history.

This may be a new perspective for its genre, but a variant of it has been 5 amazingly common in other summer blockbusters, particularly those released *this year*. And its implications hit far closer to home than the events of the 19th century. You can learn a lot about a film's values from examining the motivations of its villains, and you can learn a lot about a society — or at least what Hollywood thinks society wants to hear — when it produces three mainstream movies in a few months that give its villains the exact same motivation. *Iron Man 3*, *White House Down*, and *The Lone Ranger* span cinematic categories—respectively, we have a comic-book film, a political action thriller, and a Western—but each of their stories portrays war, and implicitly the War on Terror, as caused by corporations and greed.

In *Iron Man 3*, we are introduced to an Osama Bin Laden–like terrorist named the Mandarin (played by Ben Kingsley), who is carrying out attacks on American military bases. But halfway through the film, we learn—spoiler alert—that the Mandarin is just a decoy character dreamed up by a scientist to provide cover for his experimentation on war veterans. The film's writer/director Shane Black explained this major plot twist as "a message that's more interesting for the modern world, because I think there's a lot of fear that's generated toward very available and obvious targets, which could perhaps be directed more intelligently at what's behind them." The *Iron Man* franchise laid the groundwork for this subtext from its first film, which featured Jeff Bridges as a greedy arms dealer who was arming a Taliban-like terrorist group to drive sales.

White House Down shows just how deeply this notion of villainy has taken root, particularly in contrast to past entries in its genre. The film initially offers a smorgasbord of motivations for its team of villains who hold the White House hostage—one is a white supremacist, and another is a disgruntled ex-soldier—but it ultimately shines a light on the collusion between corrupt government officials and defense contractors who are trying to launch a war in the Middle East to keep their coffers filled with money from government contracts. Again, the War on Terror is shown to be nothing more than a scheme by profiteers, not an ideological struggle and certainly not a necessary war. In explaining the issue to his buddy, President Sawyer (Jamie Foxx) even calls those profiteers out by name. "You ever hear of the military-industrial complex?" We have now, Mr. President.

It is quite a contrast to *Die Hard*, the 1988 action classic to which *White House Down* is most often compared. That film employed German thieves as the source of its terrorism, which fit nicely amid the Reagan era's popular support for increased defense spending to fend off a Communist threat. Similar films like *Air Force One* ("*Die Hard* in the president's plane") or *Toy Soldiers* ("*Die Hard* in a prep school") also address the fight against terrorism, but in their pre-9/11 mind-set, the villains are foreigners with clear-cut political goals.

Though people often forget it, Westerns are also war movies, as they take place during the American-Indian Wars of the 18th and 19th centuries. So it should be no surprise that *The Lone Ranger* uses the same moral template as *Iron Man 3* and *White House Down*. With the stated goal of becoming the wealthiest man in America, Cole launches a battle that seems a stand-in for all of the violence between American settlers and Indian populations. The message we leave with is that both U.S. soldiers and foreign enemies are pawns in the rich man's eternal quest to get even more for himself.

READING THE TEXT

1. Why does Gittell claim that *The Lone Ranger* presents "American business interests" (para. 2) as the real villain of the film?

2. What characteristics do the villains share in the three films Gittell discusses?

3. What historical conditions have led to the rise of the "rich guy" as a new kind of villain?

4. Gittell claims, "You can learn a lot about a film's values from examining the motivations of its villains, and you can learn a lot about a society — or at least what Hollywood thinks society wants to hear — when it produces three mainstream movies in a few months that give its villains the exact same motivation" (para. 5). In what way is he voicing a fundamental semiotic principle in this statement?

READING THE SIGNS

1. Gittell and Michael Agresta ("How the Western Was Lost — and Why It Matters," p. 372) discuss the genre of movie Westerns as a sign of American attitudes and mythologies. In an essay, compare and contrast their treatment of the Western. How do you account for any differences you might observe?

2. Gittell acknowledges that the three films he analyzes belong to rather different cinematic genres: "a comic-book film, a political action thriller, and a Western" (para. 5). In an essay, explore the extent to which this generic diversity strengthens, weakens, or complicates his argument about "a new enemy of the moment" (para. 1). Does this generic diversity make his argument seem more universal or less plausible? To support your argument, refer to current films that present moneyed American corporate interests as the villain.

3. **CONNECTING TEXTS**   Watch *The Wolf of Wall Street* (2013), focusing your analysis on the protagonist Jordan Belfort. In an essay, write a semiotic analysis of his character. Is he the sort of "rich guy" villain Gittell describes? Or might he be better described as a hero or an antihero? To develop your ideas, read or reread Robert B. Ray's "The Thematic Paradigm" (p. 450).

TIM LAYDEN

A Patriot's Tale

With so many superheroes, antiheroes, outlaw heroes, and ultra-villains running around in American entertainment, one might well wonder whether there are any real, *ordinary* heroes left. So, if you're looking for some real-life heroes, you could start with the Andruzzi brothers — Marc, Billy, and Jimmy — New York City firefighters who were right in the thick of it when the World Trade Center towers were attacked and destroyed on September 11, 2001. Though their brother Joe, a former NFL player, is a lot better known, Tim Layden profiles the firefighting brothers — "official heroes," in Robert B. Ray's terms — here. (As the founder of the Joe Andruzzi Foundation, which provides funding for cancer research and cancer patients, Joe has been no slouch as a real-life hero either.) Tim Layden is a writer for *Sports Illustrated.*

The Andruzzis grew up the best kind of brothers, four boys wedged into two small bedrooms in their Staten Island home, loving and fighting, best friends and worst enemies. They spent long Saturday afternoons at the Little League field and Sundays at home, eating their mother's ritual macaroni and meatballs. They handed down paper routes and school clothes through four mini-generations. They were the sons of a New York City cop who sometimes worked three jobs at once to keep them all in parochial school, and their neighborhood was filled with the children of policemen and firefighters. Fathers were sometimes hurt or lost in the line of duty; that was part of life. Many sons would follow the same path.

Three of the Andruzzi boys became New York City firemen. Jimmy, 30, was first, graduating from the academy in October 1995. Billy, the oldest, at 32, first worked as a case manager for the New York City welfare department, but when he saw how much Jimmy loved his job, he joined the firefighting ranks in the summer of '99. The baby, Marc, 24, finished eight weeks of academy training in early September and is a "probie," beginning the probationary period that precedes graduation. "Their father was a cop, and now three sons are in the fire department," says their mother, Mary Ann, with a look of pride in her eyes. "My boys love to help people."

Joe, 26, would be the odd one. He kept growing long after his 200-pound brothers stopped, played football as an offensive lineman at Southern Connecticut State and clawed his way into the NFL as an undrafted free agent in 1997, making the roster of the Super Bowl champion Green Bay Packers. Despite three knee surgeries, he is the starting right guard for the New England Patriots, a 6'3", 315-pound contradiction of weekday calm and Sunday mayhem. "If I didn't play football, I would be teaching special education," says Joe. "I'm the black sheep, I guess. I wouldn't be a firefighter."

Still, he admires his brothers as much as they do him. "What's important is that my brothers are happy in what they do, and I know they are," says Joe. "A lot of people hate their jobs. I know my brothers are excited when they go to work. I'm excited when I get up on Sunday morning and know I've got a game to play. And I know they're excited when they go into a building to put out a fire." Nonetheless, he fights guilt over the opulence made possible by his profession. "I see them driving old cars, scrounging for second jobs," says Joe of his siblings. "The wage difference, it doesn't feel right for what they do."

Joe was in a dentist's chair on the morning of Tuesday, Sept. 11, when he 5
heard a radio report of a fire at the World Trade Center. He rushed back to his
house in North Attleboro, Mass., with his wife, Jen, and their children, Hunter, 3,
and Breanna, 17 months, and they watched coverage of the attacks. Both towers were still standing but soon would fall. Joe knew that Jimmy was stationed
in lower Manhattan (Engine 5, on East 14th Street). "I was thinking Jimmy
could be in the middle of all that," says Joe. "I knew he had to be close. My
heart was in my throat." Five hours passed before Joe learned that his brothers
were all safe and that Jimmy had, indeed, been terrifyingly close to death.

On the day after the disaster, Joe sleepwalked through meetings and practice in preparation for a game at Carolina that he hoped would not take place.
"I was there, but not really there," he says. When the NFL announced the next
day that its games were canceled, Joe drove to Staten Island. Late last Friday
afternoon he was sitting in the living room of his parents' modest split-level
house when Jimmy walked through the door and stopped at the entrance to
the room. He raised his right hand and held his thumb and index finger less
than an inch apart, wordlessly demonstrating the margin of his survival as his
lip trembled and his eyes watered. Both men began to cry, and they embraced
in the center of the room, sobbing for longer than either could ever remember.

On the morning of the attack, Jimmy was scheduled to work a nine-to-six
shift, but firefighters all know that means showing up at eight. Just after 8:30
Jimmy and his squad were called to a smoky apartment on East 19th Street.
Food left on a stove. They put out the fire and, as they climbed back onto the
truck, heard a jet screaming overheard. Awfully low, they said to one another.
Seconds later, the engine radio sounded. *Engine 10, Ladder 10, a plane has
hit Tower 1 of the World Trade Center.* Engine 10 is in the shadow of the twin
towers; firefighters from that company saw the first plane hit. Engine 5, fresh
from the kitchen fire, was not far away. Within minutes the two companies
were at the base of Tower 1, the first building that was struck.

Five days later Jimmy Andruzzi sat on a couch in his parents' living room,
unshaven, wearing denim shorts and a white T-shirt. His brothers, Joe and
Billy, sat nearby. Their father, Bill, 13 years retired from the police force, was
on his way home from his sales job. Their mother was in the kitchen, making the Sunday macaroni and meatballs, seeking blessed routine even as
a newspaper lay open on a table showing pictures of dozens of the missing,
many of them friends of the Andruzzis.

In a soft voice Jimmy described the events of Sept. 11.

"We're on the rig, and we look up and see the first tower burning, and my 10
buddy, Derek Brogan, says to me, 'We're going to the biggest disaster in the
history of New York City.' Once we're there, we're thinking about the proto-
col for a high-rise: command post in the lobby, another command post three
floors below the fire. They told us the bottom of the fire was on the 79th floor.

We're in the lobby when we hear another huge explosion. I figured out later that was the second plane hitting. I'm thinking, When we practice terrorist scenarios, they always tell us, 'First responders will be casualties.' The building is shaking, and nobody wants to go up now. They tell us, 'Engine 5, go with Engine 10 to 79. Put that fire out.' So we go up the stairs, me and Derek and Manny Delvalle and Gerard Gorman and Eddie Mecner and Lieutenant Bob Bohak. That's what we do. We put out fires.

"People are coming down the stairs. They're saying, 'You guys are so brave, thank you, thank you.' The stairwell is narrow — one line going up, another line going down. At the ninth floor Derek's getting chest pains. The lieutenant tells him to stop, but he keeps going. We're carrying 160 pounds of equipment, and it's hot. We get to the 23rd floor, and Derek is worse. The lieutenant radios for oxygen and tells the cops who bring up the oxygen to bring Derek back down. We start up again, maybe four more floors before we hear the biggest, loudest, most intense sound I've ever heard in my life. I didn't know at the time, but that was Tower 2 coming down. We thought it was our building coming down or a huge bomb. I figured I was dead right there. That's it.

"Lieutenant Bohak says, 'Drop your hoses and get out! Right now! Out!' We start running down the stairs, and it's all black smoke. [Here Jimmy begins to sob loudly.] We're leaving all those firemen behind, and they're still going up. All those guys, those guys, going up, but we had to leave. Those poor guys. . . . [He pauses to compose himself.] We get to the fourth floor, and the door out of the stairwell to the lobby is locked. I feel this rumble, like thunder, and the walls start cracking and the beams are bending. Some guy, not a firefighter — God bless him, he was an angel — points out another door, and we got through that into the lobby. I ran out into the street and kept going, and the whole building came down, maybe 45 seconds behind me. All those firemen got killed, and I'm alive because Derek got chest pains and because my lieutenant told us to get out and that guy was on the fourth floor. [Long pause as he begins crying again.] It's not supposed to happen. Terrorists aren't supposed to fly jet planes into a building full of innocent people, and the World Trade Center isn't supposed to fall down. It's just not supposed to happen."

Firefighters have two families: one at home, one at the station house. "My brothers, they're blood," says Jimmy. "But the guys in the station house, they're my brothers too. Everybody knows everything about everybody else. You know who's got a new girlfriend, you know whose kids are sick. The guys with seniority, they get all the respect. The probies, they get all their balls broken a lot. Thin skin doesn't play in the station house."

When Jimmy exited onto the street that Tuesday morning, he found that among his group from the stairwell, only Delvalle was missing. Five days later he was still missing, along with Engine 5 lieutenant Paul Mitchell, who was off duty at the time of the crash but rushed to the site to help. They were two of the more than 300 New York City firefighters lost in the disaster, equal to more than a third of all previous casualties in the department's history. "Probably 100 of them were friends of mine," says Jimmy, who has worked at four station houses in his six-plus years with the department. "That's true of a lot of guys."

At the core of this immeasurable disaster, the missing firefighters were 15 at once heroes and victims, symbols of bravery and tragedy. It will be years before their ranks fully recover the experience and skill that was lost. Two days after the towers fell, Jimmy joined the thousands of firemen and other volunteers searching through the rubble for survivors and bodies. Standing atop a pile of twisted steel and compacted concrete, he felt another rumble, similar to what he had felt 48 hours earlier. He ran from the pile in terror and promised not to return soon.

His brothers Billy and Marc have done multiple shifts on what rescue and recovery workers have come to call "the mountain," their name for the pile of rubble that had been the tallest buildings in the city. "I hate to say that it's hard to appreciate what it's like down there," said Billy on Sunday, "but television does not do justice to how terrible it is."

The previous evening he had held a fellow firefighter's ankles as the man reached deep into the wreckage and scooped intestines out of a detached torso for DNA identification. In another place he picked up a single tooth. "By the end of my shift down there, I smelled like death," he said, and then he too began to cry.

On a cool, crystal-clear Sunday morning, Joe went with Jimmy to the Engine 5 station house, a three-story building that is one of the oldest firehouses in the city. He found tough men, scarred but battling for their sanity. "There were guys there who said they'd been crying for three days and it was time to stop," Joe said later. They were also worried about Jimmy, who had taken things harder than most. "They said he's not back yet," said Joe. "They said he needs more time. I hope it helps him to talk about it."

Joe sat on the steps of his mom and dad's home. A soft breeze ruffled the American flag on the front of the house. Inside, the table was set for dinner. Soon Joe would return to Massachusetts to begin preparing for this Sunday's game against the New York Jets in Foxboro. Football business. "Regular game week," said Joe.

Normalcy beckons, but reaching it will take longest for those survivors 20 who were closest to the flame.

READING THE TEXT

1. How does Joe Andruzzi characterize himself in comparison to his brothers?

2. Describe the organization and narration of events of this article. To what extent do they work to create an emotional impact on the reader?

3. Layden begins the article not by describing his main subject, the firefighter heroes, but by focusing on their football-player brother. What effect does this opening have on you as a reader?

4. In your own words, explain why Layden sees the firefighters missing in the wreckage as having symbolic status.

READING THE SIGNS

1. **CONNECTING TEXTS** Well over a decade has passed since the September 11, 2001, terrorist attacks, and press coverage devoted to police, firefighters, and other rescue workers is now limited to the 9/11 anniversary. In class, discuss whether these workers still have the heroic status they were granted in the immediate aftermath of the attacks. Reflect on your class discussion, and write an essay in which you explore whether America's devotion to its heroes is deep-rooted and genuine or, alternatively, subject to trends. To develop your ideas, consult Lorraine Devon Wilke's "Snowden's a Hero, Obama's a Villain" (below).

2. In class, brainstorm a list of students' personal heroes, and then analyze the results. What areas of life do they hail from (politics, sports, entertainment, medicine, military, and so forth)? To what extent do students mention "ordinary" people, like the 9/11 rescuers, who found themselves in extraordinary circumstances? Use the results as the basis for an essay in which you argue for your own explanation of the criteria Americans use to identify heroes.

3. In an essay, present your own argument in response to this question: How do the identities of real-life heroes compare with those of fictional heroes? To develop your ideas, consult the introduction to this chapter and any of the readings in this chapter; be sure to base your argument on specific examples, both human and fictional.

LORRAINE DEVON WILKE
Snowden's a Hero, Obama's a Villain

Heroes and villains tend to be locked in simple black-and-white binary pairs, the one being defined by the other. But that is precisely the problem, Lorraine Devon Wilke argues, when considering such real-life antagonists as Edward Snowden and the Obama administration. Because if you think that Snowden is a hero for spilling the beans on the NSA, then you are likely to think that Obama must be a villain, but the whole matter is rather more complicated than that, with a whole lot of gray to go around. It's time to grow up, Wilke suggests, and stop demanding clear-cut distinctions between not-so-clear-cut opponents. Lorraine Devon Wilke is an actor, a singer-songwriter, and a columnist for the *Huffington Post*, where this selection first appeared.

As the long and winding road of Edward Snowden's journey continues to play out, trending opinions seem to be keeping pace with his ever-so-fluid travel itinerary. Back in the early days, fist-pumpers on both sides of the political divide — or, rather, *all* sides (we mustn't forget libertarians in this chorus) — were uncharacteristically joined in the certainty that he was a hero, a brave whistleblower who blew the lid off nefarious back-room dealings done to the detriment of Americans and countries the world over. Never mind that the dealings he was denouncing were largely protected by existing law, his hero status was cemented in a cultural climate that frames most things within the palette of black and white, good guys and bad guys. Gray area, nuance, intent between the lines, even fact or truth, are pushed aside for the extreme of belief.

To believe Edward Snowden, to define him as a hero, one must conversely believe that Obama and his administration are villains, as, it seems, Snowden supporters, by and large, do. Of course, swiping Obama et al. with the brush of tyranny has become a convenient meme; we've had "scandals" and conspiracy theories of every ilk occupying our attention, with calls for impeachment and various other forms of mass hysteria, none of which have resulted in much more than wide-ranging and colorful news cycles and a lot of noise that ultimately became deflective and distracting.

But that's where we are as a country: black-and-white thinking, a mode of perspective that comes with grand presumptions that we all know *all* the truth about everything, even things we couldn't possibly know all the truth about. But we make that presumption because we're Americans; we're arrogant and entitled.

When I hear opinionated movie stars and college professors encouraging people not to vote based on their purportedly deep knowledge and arcane understanding of the details and minutia of policies and decisions made behind closed doors of the White House and other government institutions, I can't help but wonder how they got the inside track on an inside track they could not possibly have an inside track to. And yet . . . they speak as if they do. They're little Zeligs, magically present when presidents make globally impacting decisions or ponder the right moves regarding national security. They *know*. Because they're Americans and they just . . . well . . . *know*! And with that mysterious know-it-all knowledge, they put a black hat on the president and others and we're told not to vote for the lot of 'em.

We've got citizens who "just know" the World Trade Center was brought   5
down by Bush and Cheney, that Michael Hastings was blown up by the FBI,

macmillanhighered.com/signsoflife
What happens when you try to map the superhero genre onto real-life dangers?
e-readings > United States Immigration and Customs Enforcement,
iGuardians [video]

that Obama is secretly out to confiscate ALL guns, and that the illuminati is running the whole damn show anyway. You can't argue with this thinking because it's stated in unequivocal black and white; it allows for no persuasion, no debate, no logic. Because it's not based on fact; it's based on conjecture, presumption, guessing, and . . . just knowing.

We are quite knowledgeable, we arrogant, entitled Americans.

As for Snowden, while large numbers "just knew" the truth about him — that he was a hero, that he saved the world by exposing the over-reaching surveillance of the NSA; that he should be honored, protected and deified along with other truth-seeking whistleblowers — other Americans, the less black-and-white thinkers, took a more circumspective view. They said, "Let's wait and see how this all plays out before we jump on any bandwagons," and as they took their reflective, patient pose, they were sometimes maligned by those who'd already made up their minds. Liberals went after liberals, Republicans (who wanted so desperately to side with any side sided against Obama) started in-fighting over exactly *what* Snowden was, and even libertarians got squeamish at the revelations that Snowden was dumping info at the doorsteps of less-than-friendly governments.

Now as his fans carry on about an angry South America inviting him in and Glenn Greenwald of *The Guardian* continues to front for his boy, the black and whiteness of it all is getting a bit muddied.

A recent *Huffington Post* / YouGov poll reveals for the first time a slip in the "hero" numbers:

According to the new poll, 38 percent of Americans think that Snowden,   10 a former contractor for the National Security Agency, did the wrong thing, while 33 percent said he did the right thing. Still, 29 percent of Americans remain unsure about Snowden's actions.

Much of the drop in support for Snowden's actions since the earlier poll appears to have taken place among Republicans, who were divided, 37 percent to 37 percent, on whether Snowden did the right thing in the previous poll, but in the latest poll said by a 44 percent to 29 percent margin that he did the wrong thing.

Ah . . . red staters stirring a little gray into the mix. Fascinating.

In a compelling piece at *Addicting Info* titled "Have We All Been Fooled by Edward Snowden?," the writer references some illuminating information that frames his motivations as less noble than some would have us believe. In public chat rooms, long before he hit the front pages, he made clear his deep disdain for Obama, his support of Ron Paul, his Second Amendment fanaticism, his (truly vile) revulsion about seniors sucking off Social Security; his antipathy for the *New York Times* for "reporting classified shit" (ironic, isn't it?!), followed by put-downs of Wikileaks (his current BFFs) and his support of Bush's warrantless wiretapping. Yes. Really. I know . . . getting grayer all the time. I urge you to read the whole article; the chats alone are worth the click.

Edward Snowden, the hero, the whistleblower, the do-gooder doing good for the good of America seems to have been a very different fellow not all that long ago. What are we to make of that? My first impulse is to say, "Like everything that happens in life, we are to watch, listen, pay attention, open our minds, get past our partisan impulses, and wait for enough information to arrive at an intelligent, fact-based opinion." Turns out that's my second impulse too.

Because there's very little that comes in true black and white. That we   15 Americans persist in believing that, demanding that others believe in that, indicates a sort of cultural arrested development . . . like children who only see in broad strokes of good or bad (no child believes Daddy can be dastardly). Most people — those we hate, those we love and all those in between — have at least some shades of gray. We've just got to be willing to see past the black and white to notice.

READING THE TEXT

1. How does the scandal surrounding Edward Snowden's revelation of NSA practices complicate the definitions of "hero" and "villain" in this case, according to Wilke?

2. Why does Wilke say, "That's where we are as a country: black and white thinking, a mode of perspective that comes with grand presumptions that we all know *all* the truth about everything, even things we couldn't possible know all the truth about" (para. 3)?

3. How does Wilke connect reactions to the Edward Snowden case to modern conspiracy theories?

4. Wilke states that, in reaction to Edward Snowden, "liberals went after liberals, Republicans . . . started in-fighting over exactly *what* Snowden was" (para. 7). According to Wilke, why did people react this way?

READING THE SIGNS

1. In class, discuss writing strategies you can use both to avoid black-and-white thinking and to present a more nuanced argument that recognizes shades of gray. Use your findings to evaluate an op-ed piece in a general-interest newspaper (such as the *Washington Post* or the *New York Times*) or, alternatively, an opinion piece on a pointed political site such as Fox News.

2. When this selection first appeared in the *Huffington Post*, some bloggers responded that Wilke herself could be accused of black-and-white thinking, while others praised her nuanced view. In an essay of your own, evaluate the evenhandedness of her essay.

3. In an essay, argue for your own evaluation of the Edward Snowden affair, taking heed of Wilke's admonition that we consider "at least some shades of gray" (para. 15). Alternatively, do the same for a different polarizing debate, such as same-sex marriage.

4. Write an essay supporting, refuting, or complicating the proposition that making the hero-villain dichotomy "grayer" can risk a lack of commitment and moral indecisiveness.

5. In class, brainstorm non-gray distinctions of political heroes and villains. Then use your results to analyze a current topic that tends to invite dichotomous responses (consider, for instance, the split between Fox News and MSNBC supporters), using fan comments as evidence.

You are not yourself

MY SELFIE, MY SELF

Ma(s)king Identity in the New Millennium

Who Are You?

You are not your self-portrait, but if you are at all like tens of millions of other people who own smartphones, it is quite likely that you have presented yourself to the world by way of a digital image taken, quite literally, at arm's length: your selfie. And since that image has the power to define who you are to an incalculable number of people the world over, you probably took a good deal of care in constructing it before posting it to Instagram or Snapchat or Facebook or wherever. "Here I am," says your selfie. "This is me, my unique self." But, in truth, a selfie cannot tell anyone much about who you are, and, paradoxically enough, one selfie really looks quite like another, often featuring the same poses and facial expressions framed within the strict limits imposed by a tiny camera held less than two feet from your face. So you have to go beyond your selfie to let other people know who you are, but that's a lot more difficult, isn't it? Who are you, anyway?

We like to think, especially in America where individualism is such a prized **mythology**, that our identity is completely within our control, autonomous and self-constructed. But it isn't that simple, because a large part of who you are is shaped socially and externally from your many experiences in life. Your social class, for example, influences what life experiences you may (or may not) have had, and these experiences play a strong role in shaping your consciousness and sense of self. Your race, too, has a powerful effect; because humans have not yet created a post-racial society, the way people treat you is affected by your ethnicity and influences how you identify yourself. And your gender and sexual orientation, too, can profoundly affect your experience and identity.

It is easy to forget the ways our identities began to be constructed in childhood, and all human cultures have their ways of influencing that process. Such institutions as family, religion, and education, for example, all tell you who you are and what you should expect of life. But in an entertainment culture like that of contemporary America, popular culture has emerged as an equally potent shaper of individual identity and desire.

Just think of all those children's television programs you may have watched even before you could walk or talk. When America's (and, increasingly, the world's) children spend hours in front of a TV set (which has been called "the great pacifier"), watching programs whose plots and characters subtly communicate to them how to behave — from appropriate gender roles to appropriate professional careers — the role of popular culture in shaping personal identity can be enormous. And at the same time that children are exposed to all that television, they are also absorbing a great deal of advertising. These ads are carefully constructed not only to shape children as consumers when they grow up but also to "brand" them as consumers of the products they see advertised, in the expectation of a lifetime of brand loyalty. Much the same can happen with kiddie flicks, which so often inculcate traditional social norms even as they dazzle young viewers' eyes with today's technological wizardry.

The products you consume in your youth can also have a powerful effect on your sense of identity. Your favorite clothing fashions, for example, are not only personal forms of expression but **signs** of your identification with the various youth cohorts who share your tastes. In a sense, using consumption as a badge of your identity can be considered a form of self-stereotyping (have you ever summed someone up as a "skater" or a "geek"?), but if we are the ones adopting the signs, it doesn't feel like stereotyping. The difference is the belief that we have a choice in the matter, and the desire for the freedom to choose our own identities is especially prevalent in America today. Consider, for example, some recent challenges to the gender codes that have traditionally defined our identities as gendered subjects.

Gender Codes

A **gender code** is a culturally constructed system that prescribes the appropriate roles and behaviors for men and women in society. Assuming both a continuity between your biological sex and your gender awareness or identity, as well as a normative heterosexual orientation, such codes tell you how to conduct yourself as a male or a female: *Boys don't cry; girls wear makeup. Boys are aggressive; girls are passive. Boys play sports; girls are cheerleaders. Men go out to work; women stay at home and raise children.* The list is long, and it has shaped your gender identity since your birth.

But challenges by transgender people to the assumption that biological sexual identity determines psychological gender identity have disrupted the authority of the traditional codes, leading to a multiplicity of possible identities that can be chosen rather than received. The popularity of such reality TV programs as *RuPaul's Drag Race* is a striking sign of this disruption of the old gender codes, for here we find a transgender performer whose flamboyant defiance of traditional gender behavior — which would have once subjected him to social marginalization — has made him both popular and successful.

Similarly, disruptions of the heteronormative assumptions that have traditionally governed sexual identity are also changing the cultural landscape. The success of television programs like *Modern Family*, the increasing number of athletes and politicians coming out to their fans and constituents, and the growing number of Americans who endorse same-sex marriage all signify an emerging acceptance of the freedom to differ from mainstream notions of sexual identity and desire.

But this is not to say that traditional gender codes have disappeared from popular culture. They are still very much at work and are particularly evident in advertising campaigns. Consider, for example, a current campaign for Axe grooming products. Denotatively, Axe is simply a perfume, but since the traditional gender codes specify that perfume is a woman's product, the marketing of Axe fragrances tries to connote a hypermasculine identity for its male consumers. Thus, like Brute before it, Axe products are given a name traditionally associated with such masculine-coded traits as violence and aggression. One famous Axe ad featured a swarm of passionate women running frantically toward a beach where a single man stands dousing himself in Axe fragrance, reinforcing the gender-coded belief that an unmarried man should "score" as often as possible (a woman who behaves in the same way can be called all kinds of unpleasant names).

Similarly, products (especially cosmetics) aimed at women play up the traditional gender-coded prescription that a woman's primary concern, and role, in life is to attract the gaze of a man — that is, to look beautiful. This is so glaringly obvious in women's magazines that it has stimulated its own

Exploring the Signs of Gender

In your journal, explore the expectations about gender roles that you grew up with. What gender norms were you taught by your family or the media, either overtly or implicitly? Have you ever had any conflicts with your parents over "natural" gender roles? If so, how did you resolve them? Do you think your gender-related expectations today are the same as those you had when you were a child?

backlash in the well-known Dove "Campaign for Real Beauty." But, while the campaign does feature more ordinary models than do other beauty product ads, it does not abandon the focus on physical attractiveness that the traditional code demands — and, it might also be pointed out, the same company that constructed the Dove campaign is also behind the Axe line of products.

Maybe things haven't changed so much after all.

Postfeminist or Third Wave?

The continuing tendency of American popular culture to tell girls and women that their primary identities lie in their ability to be sexually attractive to men through endless images of eroticized female bodies presents a particular challenge to cultural theory. For, given the attempts of the feminist movement in the 1970s to challenge such messages — which are reflections of what journalist Ariel Levy has called a "raunch culture" — the current era might seem to be more postfeminist than feminist when it comes to female identity in America. That is, some of the current signs (for instance, the notorious performance of Miley Cyrus at the 2013 VMA ceremony) suggest that America may have abandoned feminist goals and reverted to the most conservative of gender-coded prescriptions.

But it may not be that simple, because it is also the case that traditional gender codes insist that female sexuality must be tightly controlled by male masters, whereas for many women who embrace what is often called third wave feminism, the confident display of their sexuality is actually empowering rather than degrading, a taking charge rather than a knuckling under — an attitude that was behind the immense popularity, among women, of the TV hit *Sex and the City* and many similar books, movies, and TV series, like *Girls*. Thus, third wave feminists regard themselves as representing an evolution within the women's movement itself, not a movement away from it, arguing that being proud of her body and using it to get what she wants is part of a woman's empowerment and a valid identity choice. More traditional feminists are not persuaded by this argument, however, and point out that, by focusing their attention on their bodies rather than their minds, women may subject themselves to the tyranny of a youth-worshipping culture that will reject them once they are past the peak of their sexually appealing years. It is no accident that the vast majority of the images of women we see in popular culture are of very young women. There are a lot more Betty Boops than Betty Whites.

The Space for Race

Despite claims that race is no longer a significant factor in American life, with some commentators insisting that America has reached a "post-racial" condition in which race no longer matters, plenty of evidence shows that racial identity is still a profound, and often painful, part of American identity formation and politics. One only needs to look at the national obsession with the 2013 trial for Trayvon Martin's killing (itself a kind of inverse reproduction of the fascination with the O. J. Simpson trials of the 1990s) to see this. And while some see the election of Barack Obama as evidence that America has finally gotten beyond race, the sometimes-hysterical reaction against the first black American president has been widely interpreted as being racially motivated.

Even within the context of a popular culture that includes such race-transcending stars as Denzel Washington, Halle Berry, and Beyoncé, racial identity—especially when it appears in the form of racial stereotyping—continues to be a major issue in American entertainment. Having endured long histories of negative stereotyping in Hollywood, African Americans, Asian Americans, Native Americans, and Latin Americans can still find themselves being stereotyped by directors and scriptwriters who by now presumably should be aware of the problem. Complaints about the character Jar Jar Binks in the *Star Wars* saga, for example, were based upon a perception that it perpetrated a derisive stereotype of Afro-Caribbean culture, while even *Avatar*, with its sympathetic depiction of a nonwhite society under siege by white invaders, has been compared to *Dances with Wolves* as yet another example of a stereotypical story in which a group of nonwhites needs a white hero to lead them. In 2013, Disney's box-office failure with *The Lone Ranger* was also attributed, at least in part, to its revival of the always racially problematic character of Tonto.

But while the representation of race in popular culture is still a politically potent topic, certain changes in racial identity itself are altering the landscape. With increasing numbers of Americans identifying themselves as being of mixed race (while President Barack Obama identified himself as "Black, African Am or Negro" on his 2010 census form, he could have chosen "mixed race" as well), the traditional racial categories, like those of gender, are in a state of flux. Indeed, even the term "minority" is becoming obsolete in a country that will have no racial majority by midcentury. Such a demographic shift will have a profound effect on racial consciousness in America, an effect whose traces will be increasingly visible in popular culture in the years to come, shaping and reshaping Americans' sense of who they are.

Discussing the Signs of Race

Demographers predict that, by the middle of the twenty-first century, America will no longer have any racial or ethnic majority population. In class, discuss what effects this may have on Americans' sense of this country's history, culture, and identity.

The Great Divide

More subtly, but arguably just as profoundly, your social class also shapes your identity. But unlike such identifying categories as race and gender, class has historically been underplayed, even denied, as a component in American life. Obscured by the mythology of the American dream, which promises an opportunity for upward social mobility, class has been the great blind spot in American history ever since Michel-Guillaume-Jean de Crèvecoeur (an eighteenth-century French aristocrat who wrote glowingly of his experiences in America) declared that America was a land of economic equality that had transcended Europe's great gulf between rich and poor.

The inability of Americans to recognize the role that social class plays (and has always played) in their lives was dramatically altered in the wake of the Great Recession that broke over America like a tidal wave after the near-meltdown of our economy in 2008. Movements like Occupy Wall Street, which has famously divided America into "the 99 percent" and "the 1 percent," have finally brought class to the forefront. But the class divide that such twenty-first-century movements have brought to popular attention has been growing for a far longer time than merely the past few years. Indeed, we can trace it back to at least the 1970s, when the historic post–World War II expansion of the American middle class hit the skids thanks to the stagflation economy that beset the country after the Vietnam War. Since that period, the real wages of most Americans have scarcely grown at all.

But in the 1980s, thanks to a combination of the Reagan-era tax cuts for the wealthy and the restructuring of the American economy from an industrial to a postindustrial one, the wealth of America's top earners skyrocketed. This is when the 1 percent versus the 99 percent divide that the Occupy movement refers to originated, and this divide represents a profound disruption of what Americans have always thought themselves to be. For America has always considered itself a land of equality: That principle has been a key part of our national identification. But in the past forty years or so, that belief has been seriously challenged by the reality of a class divide that is changing the identity of America itself.

But so pertinacious are cultural mythologies that the America of vast class differences is still not very visible in popular culture. The movie *Batman: The Dark Knight Rises* certainly alluded to the class divide in 2012, but, as a number of critics noted at the time, it characterized the class revolution of Bane and company as brutally terroristic, thus potentially undermining those with a serious desire to promote class equality. Generally, one can argue that while American popular culture is eager to present itself as progressive about race and gender, it is not so eager to reveal the effects of class inequality — which is not so very surprising when so many members of the entertainment industry belong to that 1 percent.

Be Whatever You Want to Be

Race, class, and gender form a triad of identifiers that are especially prominent in cultural studies. But plenty of evidence in popular culture suggests that American youth are not terribly preoccupied with them. For one, these forms of identification are based in demographic categorization, while the signs are indicating that millennials are more concerned with their own highly individual identities as expressed through the self-constructions that appear on social networking sites from LinkedIn to Facebook, Instagram to Snapchat, Twitter to Tumblr, and everything in between and beyond. In short, in the world of the selfie, the emphasis is on self-advertising, not demographic classification. And this opens up a whole new territory in identity formation.

On the Internet, you can be pretty much what you want to be. From online gaming sites (like World of Warcraft) where you can adopt a host of identities, to the Facebook profiles where you can present to the world an idealized version of your life, the Internet has revolutionized the traditional restrictions on identity formation. With no one able to see you in person, you can adopt whatever personae you like, exchanging identities as if you were changing your clothes. Such freedom to present yourself in whatever way you like has been a fundamental appeal of the Internet from its beginnings.

But just as the Internet creates the opportunity for self-making, it also offers users the possibility of disguise — a masked *non-identity* that seems

Science fiction fans wear elaborate costumes at the annual Comic-Con convention.

AP Photo/Denis Poroy

to unleash some of our most antisocial tendencies. Just read the comments that follow online news stories, YouTube videos, or just about anything on the Internet. You will find the same aggression, vile language, flame wars, and hate and hostility, no matter what the topic. This "keyboard courage" is made possible by the anonymity that the Internet confers upon its users, who feel emboldened to say things that they would not say face-to-face because non-virtual society has ways of policing itself that the Internet does not (a lot of rude comments on the Internet would get their posters punched out if delivered in person; others would get them fired).

Paradoxically, then, the Internet offers to its users a kind of non-identity in its offer of anonymity. And since identification is also a form of social control (think of your driver's license — it is your ID, and without it you cannot legally drive your car or board a commercial airplane), the outbursts that fill the Internet are signifiers not only of all the conflict out there but also of a resentment against the restrictions that come with social identity. Such resentment bears a close relation to that fundamental American mythology of individualism, which can be found at work so often in American culture, for it is our individualism that guides our cherishing of our liberty. The possibility of escaping identity, of having a non-identity, offers an immense freedom — even if that freedom is expressed only as a license to rant in public.

The Supermarket of IDs

But let's look again at your ability to construct your own online identity. You pay a price for the self-making you can do on the Internet. As you advertise yourself, the social networking site on which you do so is mining your data to sell to others who want to advertise to you. Rather than setting up your own Web page — which is what people did in the Internet's early days — you build your social networking identity upon mass-produced platforms that offer ease and convenience in exchange for your life details. Ironically, your identity is a commodity for sale, and you sold it without even knowing it.

In short, identity itself has become a commodity in America. The mining of our private information can be very disturbing to members of a society

---

Reading Identity Online

Many Internet sites are devoted to the culture of a particular ethnicity, gender, or cultural subgroup. Visit several such sites and survey the breadth of information available within them. Is there any information that you wish would appear online but could not find? Do you find any material problematic?

in which individualism and independence are so highly valued, but it is routinely shrugged off by consumers who are pleased to have advertising tailored to their online profiles. This isn't very surprising in a consumer culture wherein people have been trained from the cradle to *identify* themselves as consumers.

And so we come full circle to what it really means to live in a consumer society and why the study and understanding of popular culture, so much of which is involved with consumption, is important. Although one American tradition, a mythology that goes back to the roots of this nation, clings desperately to a sense of individualism within a mass culture, another more recent development — the advent of consumerism — is taking that all away. And if that worries you, just look online: At fearandclothing.com, you can buy a T-shirt that reads "I'm Not a Number." The shirt refers to a popular television program from the 1960s: *The Prisoner*.

The Readings

Rachel Lowry opens the readings with a news feature on millennials who "may be suffering from an identity crisis" due to the difference between their online profiles and their more authentic, and private, selves. In a paired set of readings, Aaron Devor analyzes gender roles and the ways men and women manipulate the signs by which we traditionally communicate our gender identity, while Deborah Blum suggests that biology *does* play a role in gender identity and that we can best understand the gender gap by looking at both the cultural and the physiological determinants of human behavior. Kevin Jennings follows with a personal memoir that chronicles his struggles with growing up gay in conflict with his family's traditionalist construction of male heterosexual identity. Next, Mariah Burton Nelson's essay on the predicament of women athletes points out the cultural contradictions that women must negotiate when they enter the world of competitive sport, while Alfred Lubrano offers a reflection on the personal disruptions in moving out of the working class into a new middle-class identity. Michael Omi's historical survey of racial stereotyping in American entertainment provides an essential foundation for the analysis of race in popular culture, and Dani McClain's journalistic exploration of "the intersection of blackness, gender expression and sexual orientation" unveils the risks incurred by LGBTQ African Americans. Then, Theresa Celebran Jones calls for more mixed-race representation on television, celebrating Nickelodeon's *Sanjay and Craig*, an animated series about a mixed-race boy and his "best friend/talking pet snake." And Aymar Jean Christian concludes the chapter with an argument that the era of "post-identity" television — that is, shows that play down demographic differences and specificities — is coming to an end, as new programs like *Girls*, *The Misadventures of Awkward Black Girl*, *Buppies*, and *Afro City* make race, gender, and sexual orientation explicit topics for TV and online entertainment.

RACHEL LOWRY
Straddling Online and Offline Profiles, Millennials Search for Identity

> It's hard to know who you really are when everyone counsels you to market yourself on such social networking sites as LinkedIn and Facebook, which is pretty much the fate of most of the people who belong to the generation of millennials. And so, as Rachel Lowry reports in this feature for *Deseret News*, a lot of millennials, who have spent their entire lives with digital technology and self-hyped social networking profiles, have begun to wonder just who their authentic selves really are. Sometimes it's best just to find some time to be alone, but that's not easy to do when you're online all the time. So maybe it's time to turn that smartphone off, once in a while, so you can look for yourself. Rachel Lowry is a magazine editor for *Graphis*.

Twenty-year-old Mariah Hanaike waits in the disconcerting silence of a temporary employment agency lobby in Redwood City, Calif. Though the interview has not yet begun, Hanaike said she knows she is being scrutinized before she shakes the hand of a potential employer. "You know the person you're going to meet is somewhere close in the building preparing for you, maybe by looking you up on Facebook or Googling your name, possibly reading an embarrassing entry about you on your mom's blog or being surprised to not find you on LinkedIn," said Hanaike. "I can't just be myself where and when I want because anything I do has the potential to end up on some site somewhere where anyone can look at it and judge. I feel like I need to water down who I am."

Millennials, the term given for those born between 1980 and 2000, may be suffering from an identity crisis as they search for their authentic self. According to a recent online study, one out of four millennials say they can only be their true self when alone. As today's twenty-somethings create online identities to market themselves professionally, as well as socially, some fear that the disparity between the two can prevent a young person from finding authentic self-definition.

Living Life Publicly

As today's younger generation navigates the transition to adulthood, reconciling between online and offline identities can be difficult.

Nearly 25 percent of all millennials say they can only be their true self when alone, Belgium researcher Joeri Van den Bergh found. In his book,

Millennials: How Cool Brands Stay Hot, Branding to Generation Y, Van den
Bergh argues that authenticity is key for brands to connect with millennials.
"The key concept behind authenticity is to stay true to yourself, so we wanted
to know when Millennials stay true to themselves," he said.

Van den Bergh asked 4,056 people, ages 15 to 25, when they felt they 5
were or weren't being authentic online or offline, with friends, parents, partners or employers. Identity, he found, was strongly influenced by the back-and-
forth of these two spheres. "Millennials are pre-wired to achieve and create
success stories in their lives," Van den Bergh said. "They would rather blow
up some stories or pretend they are having fun on Instagram and Facebook
than admit they had a boring night out to the friends and immediate social
circle." This can alter authenticity in identity, Van den Bergh found. Only half
of the millennials surveyed believe themselves to be authentic and real. "[It's]
a response to the social society in which private moments are rare and everything is transparent and in the open on social media," Van den Bergh said.

For Victor Ruiz, 25, a student at Utah State University, social media perpetuates the problem. "We live in a capitalist society," Ruiz said. "People don't
want to be singled out, especially in a negative way, so they will try to make
themselves look better and good to impress. They would try to make their
online pages look as though they are living the American dream and not
expose weakness." It's a "fluffy portrayal of reality," said 27-year-old Angie
Rideout, a hairstylist in Salt Lake City. "It shows what we value, how we spend
our time and who we spend our time with."

If you don't participate online, you risk being uninvolved and out of
touch, said Hanaike, who is also attending LDS Business College in Salt Lake
City. "Nobody will show you to others for you, so you will be voiceless and
unseen." Hanaike said online media can be detrimental to her offline identity.
"I am perfectly capable of representing myself without a domain name or
URL," she said. "But I do not have that option. My freedom is definitely being
infringed upon. I can't just be myself where and when I want because literally
anything I do has the potential to end up on some site somewhere where anyone can look at it and judge."

Twenty-three-year-old Braden Bissegger, a student at LDS Business College,
agrees. "You're required to define yourself to be involved: Build a Facebook
page and Twitter account and post your thoughts and show the world who you
are," Bissegger said. "But what if that's inaccurate? What if we are all purporting to be something we're not? Yes, we are certainly in an identity crisis."

Linking In

Hanaike is one of 80 million millennials, ages 18 to 24, in the U.S., many of
whom are competing for the job market, according to a 2010 U.S. Census
Bureau report. How to get a leg up? Many say self-promotion through online
media can be huge. "It's standard procedure for hiring managers to check

out your Facebook, Twitter and LinkedIn profiles," wrote Jenna Goudreau in a recent *Forbes* article. "Simply sifting through job postings and sending out applications en masse was never a good route to success, and is even less so now," wrote Phyllis Korkki, an employment editor for the *New York Times.* "One of the most important questions that many job seekers can ask these days is this: How searchable am I?"

Professional self-branding and social networking is necessary no matter 10 what the economy looks like, according to David Lake, a 25-year-old marketer in Lindon. "When tools like these are available you can either keep up with the times and use them for your benefit, or you can let others take advantage of the opportunity," Lake said. "The days of a paper resume and a blind interview are over. With social media platforms and personal websites, interviewers can know a lot about who you are before the interview even starts."

For many millennials, however, self-branding can bleed into narcissism or the creation of a false persona. "It is upsetting to think that an employer can base their decision to hire me on who I appear to be on online media. That is not the person that they are hiring," said Hanaike. "I don't want to appear narcissistic when I talk to a potential employer," said Duncan Purser, 25, a student of managerial financial accounting. "But with the way applying for jobs goes in today's technological work, you have to promote yourself and continually go for presence."

Thoren Williams, a 22-year-old studying accounting at LDS Business College, agrees. "If you don't update your LinkedIn when applying for jobs, your personality doesn't come through on social media platforms and it can seem as if you don't have one," Williams said. "Potential employers may assume they know what type of an employee you would be because they've checked out your resume on LinkedIn."

It's almost necessary to be a little bit narcissistic, Hanaike said. "If you want to get noticed, or if you want someone to see your qualifications, you have to show them, lest you get swept away with the tide." For Hanaike, this can lead to a disparity between online and offline identity.

Reconciling Identities

So how do you reconcile the two identities and maintain a true center?

For Mutual Leonard, a 29-year-old actuarial analyst living in Salt Lake City, 15 culture can be a strong source of identity. "Mormons with pioneer heritage, for example, say 'My grandmother walked across the plains. I'm not giving up my religion for anything. This is my identity.'" Leonard said culture prepares youth for adulthood, preparing boys to be men through priesthood duties in a church, or hunting for your first kill as initiation into a tribe. "Psychologically, you need that kind of a thing," he said, noting that identity requires an outward focus. "You will establish identity as soon as you focus on something beyond yourself."

Katie Greer, a nation-wide Internet and technology safety trainer, recommends tolerance. "I could follow someone's entire day online, seeing when they wake up, eat, what they wear and the traffic they hit," said Greer. "Perhaps we should lift our eyes from our screens more often and live the lives we are purporting." Reconciliation, Greer said, requires creating an identity worth owning up to online. "I'm 30 years old and it's really bizarre to think of all the things in my life that have formed my identity: Soccer, politics, clubs, sports, friends," Greer said. "I worked really hard to prove who I was, for myself, my friends, my family, the colleges I've applied to. Can I just put all that effort into saying I am something I'm not online? It's kind of like cheating." The things today's twenty-somethings do can later define you, Greer warned. Being cautious about what one posts online can avoid false labels and assumptions.

Millennials, themselves, are learning how to create a consistent identity across the many platforms before them. "I meet people who seem to be in a sort of fog because they are so focused on Facebook and getting likes," Bissegger said. "But then I've also seen many people who are not trying to boast or brag about themselves, but trying to show how they are contributing to something or giving of themselves and social media is one of their most effective platforms." In fact, those who are able to see social media as a means of getting beyond yourself are the ones who are confident in their identity, Hanaike said. "We've been given a lot of crap, as millennials, but if we want our future to be something significant and if we want our lives to be great, we have to have self-confidence," she said. "It takes a certain level of self-awareness to think I am going to provide something for the community and the world that no one else is, so that I can do the best job of doing this. That is the antithesis of an identity crisis."

For David Lake, the two platforms can actually enhance one's identity both online and offline. "Facebook and other social networks give a voice and confidence to many people that didn't previously have either of those things," Lake said. "They might be shy or naturally lacking in confidence. Now that they have a stage to project their voice, we really get to see who those people are."

READING THE TEXT

1. Summarize in your own words Lowry's explanation for why millennials feel that they are losing touch with their essential selves.

2. What does researcher Joeri Van den Bergh mean by saying, "Millennials are pre-wired to achieve and create success stories in their lives" (para. 5)?

3. Why does interviewee Mutual Leonard claim that culture can ground one's sense of identity?

4. In your own words, explain how concerns about future job prospects can affect millennials' profiles on social network sites such as Facebook and LinkedIn.

READING THE SIGNS

1. In a journal entry, describe how you might have profiled yourself on a social network site. Did you try to "improve" your self-image, or did you just describe yourself as accurately as you could? Then consider why you chose that profile. If you have not constructed a social network profile, discuss why you preferred to avoid that venue.

2. In an essay, explore how the job-related stress that Lowry discusses supports or deviates from the proposition that social media controls our lives more than users control social media. As evidence, you might interview some upper-division students who are contemplating entering the job market and ask them about their social media profiles.

3. Lowry suggests that millennials feel pressured by job counselors, teachers, and parents to use social media to market themselves. But young people are also influenced by their peers. In an essay, evaluate the influence adults and peers have on engagement with social media. In your essay, you should base your analysis on interviews with social media users, perhaps analyzing how they behaved in high school and in college.

4. **CONNECTING TEXTS**   Both Lowry and Salvador Rodriguez ("In the Digital Age, Breaking Up Is Hard to Do," p. 415) write journalistic accounts, based on individuals' experiences, to elucidate ways that online communication can be problematic. As brainstorming, first synthesize the ways that Facebook and other sites have affected millennials' sense of and projection of identity. Then use your thoughts to support an essay in which you argue your own position on how social media affect millennials' sense of identity. For further ideas, consult "Students Addicted to Social Media" by the International Center for Media and the Public Agenda (p. 403).

PERFORMING GENDER

AARON DEVOR

Gender Role Behaviors and Attitudes

"Boys will be boys, and girls will be girls": Few of our cultural mythologies seem as natural as this one. But in this exploration of the gender signals that traditionally tell what a "boy" or "girl" is supposed to look and act like, Aaron Devor shows how these signals are not "natural" at all but instead are cultural constructs. While the classic cues of masculinity — aggressive posture, self-confidence, a tough appearance — and the traditional signs of femininity — gentleness, passivity, strong nurturing instincts — are often considered "normal," Devor explains that they are by no means biological or psychological necessities. Indeed, he suggests, they can be richly mixed and varied, or to paraphrase the old Kinks song "Lola," "Boys can be girls and girls can be boys." Devor is professor of sociology, former dean of graduate studies, and the founder and academic director of the Transgender Archives at the University of Victoria and author of *Gender Blending: Confronting the Limits of Duality* (1989), from which this selection is excerpted, and *FTM: Female-to-Male Transsexuals in Society* (1997).

Gender Role Behaviors and Attitudes

The clusters of social definitions used to identify persons by gender are collectively known as "femininity" and "masculinity." Masculine characteristics are used to identify persons as males, while feminine ones are used as signifiers for femaleness. People use femininity or masculinity to claim and communicate their membership in their assigned, or chosen, sex or gender. Others recognize our sex or gender more on the basis of these characteristics than on the basis of sex characteristics, which are usually largely covered by clothing in daily life.

These two clusters of attributes are most commonly seen as mirror images of one another with masculinity usually characterized by dominance and aggression, and femininity by passivity and submission. A more evenhanded description of the social qualities subsumed by femininity and masculinity might be to label masculinity as generally concerned with egoistic dominance and femininity as striving for cooperation or communion.[1] Characterizing femininity and masculinity in such a way does not portray the two clusters of characteristics as being in a hierarchical relationship to one another but rather as being two different approaches to the same question, that question being centrally concerned with the goals, means, and use of power. Such an alternative conception of gender roles captures the hierarchical and competitive masculine thirst for power, which can, but need not, lead to aggression, and the feminine quest for harmony and communal well-being, which can, but need not, result in passivity and dependence.

Many activities and modes of expression are recognized by most members of society as feminine. Any of these can be, and often are, displayed by

---

[1]Eleanor Maccoby, *Social Development: Psychological Growth and the Parent-Child Relationship* (New York: Harcourt, 1980), p. 217. Egoistic dominance is a striving for superior rewards for oneself or a competitive striving to reduce the rewards for one's competitors even if such action will not increase one's own rewards. Persons who are motivated by desires for egoistic dominance not only wish the best for themselves but also wish to diminish the advantages of others whom they may perceive as competing with them.

🄴 macmillanhighered.com/signsoflife
Is gender a learned performance?
e-readings > Sut Jhally, *The Codes of Gender* [documentary film clip]

persons of either gender. In some cases, cross-gender behaviors are ignored by observers, and therefore do not compromise the integrity of a person's gender display. In other cases, they are labeled as inappropriate gender role behaviors. Although these behaviors are closely linked to sexual status in the minds and experiences of most people, research shows that dominant persons of either gender tend to use influence tactics and verbal styles usually associated with men and masculinity, while subordinate persons, of either gender, tend to use those considered to be the province of women.[2] Thus it seems likely that many aspects of masculinity and femininity are the result, rather than the cause, of status inequalities.

Popular conceptions of femininity and masculinity instead revolve around hierarchical appraisals of the "natural" roles of males and females. Members of both genders are believed to share many of the same human characteristics, although in different relative proportions; both males and females are popularly thought to be able to do many of the same things, but most activities are divided into suitable and unsuitable categories for each gender class. Persons who perform the activities considered appropriate for another gender will be expected to perform them poorly; if they succeed adequately, or even well, at their endeavors, they may be rewarded with ridicule or scorn for blurring the gender dividing line.

The patriarchal gender schema currently in use in mainstream North American society reserves highly valued attributes for males and actively supports the high evaluation of any characteristics which might inadvertently become associated with maleness. The ideology underlying the schema postulates that the cultural superiority of males is a natural outgrowth of the innate predisposition of males toward aggression and dominance, which is assumed to flow inevitably from evolutionary and biological sources. Female attributes are likewise postulated to find their source in innate predispositions acquired in the evolution of the species. Feminine characteristics are thought to be intrinsic to the female facility for childbirth and breastfeeding. Hence, it is popularly believed that the social position of females is biologically mandated to be intertwined with the care of children and a "natural" dependency on men for the maintenance of mother-child units. Thus the goals of femininity and, by implication, of all biological females are presumed to revolve around heterosexuality and maternity.[3]

Femininity, according to this traditional formulation, "would result in warm and continued relationships with men, a sense of maternity, interest in caring for children, and the capacity to work productively and continuously

---

[2]Judith Howard, Philip Blumstein, and Pepper Schwartz, "Sex, Power, and Influence Tactics in Intimate Relationships," *Journal of Personality and Social Psychology* 51 (1986), pp. 102–9; Peter Kollock, Philip Blumstein, and Pepper Schwartz, "Sex and Power in Interaction: Conversational Privileges and Duties," *American Sociological Review* 50 (1985), pp. 34–46.

[3]Nancy Chodorow, *The Reproduction of Mothering: Psychoanalysis and the Sociology of Gender* (Berkeley: U of California P, 1978), p. 134.

in female occupations."[4] This recipe translates into a vast number of proscriptions and prescriptions. Warm and continued relations with men and an interest in maternity require that females be heterosexually oriented. A heterosexual orientation requires women to dress, move, speak, and act in ways that men will find attractive. As patriarchy has reserved active expressions of power as a masculine attribute, femininity must be expressed through modes of dress, movement, speech, and action which communicate weakness, dependency, ineffectualness, availability for sexual or emotional service, and sensitivity to the needs of others.

Some, but not all, of these modes of interrelation also serve the demands of maternity and many female job ghettos. In many cases, though, femininity is not particularly useful in maternity or employment. Both mothers and workers often need to be strong, independent, and effectual in order to do their jobs well. Thus femininity, as a role, is best suited to satisfying a masculine vision of heterosexual attractiveness.

Body postures and demeanors which communicate subordinate status and vulnerability to trespass through a message of "no threat" make people appear to be feminine. They demonstrate subordination through a minimizing of spatial use: People appear feminine when they keep their arms closer to their bodies, their legs closer together, and their torsos and heads less vertical than do masculine-looking individuals. People also look feminine when they point their toes inward and use their hands in small or childlike gestures. Other people also tend to stand closer to people they see as feminine, often invading their personal space, while people who make frequent appeasement gestures, such as smiling, also give the appearance of femininity. Perhaps as an outgrowth of a subordinate status and the need to avoid conflict with more socially powerful people, women tend to excel over men at the ability to correctly interpret, and effectively display, nonverbal communication cues.[5]

Speech characterized by inflections, intonations, and phrases that convey nonaggression and subordinate status also make a speaker appear more feminine. Subordinate speakers who use more polite expressions and ask more questions in conversation seem more feminine. Speech characterized by sounds of higher frequencies are often interpreted by listeners as feminine, childlike, and ineffectual.[6] Feminine styles of dress likewise display

[4]Jon K. Meyer and John E. Hoopes, "The Gender Dysphoria Syndromes: A Position Statement on So-Called 'Transsexualism,'" *Plastic and Reconstructive Surgery* 54 (Oct. 1974), pp. 444–51.

[5]Erving Goffman, *Gender Advertisements* (New York: Harper, 1976); Judith A. Hall, *Non-Verbal Sex Differences: Communication Accuracy and Expressive Style* (Baltimore: Johns Hopkins UP, 1984); Nancy M. Henley, *Body Politics: Power, Sex and Non-Verbal Communication* (Englewood Cliffs, N.J.: Prentice, 1979); Marianne Wex, *"Let's Take Back Our Space": "Female" and "Male" Body Language as a Result of Patriarchal Structures* (Berlin: Frauenliteraturverlag Hermine Fees, 1979).

[6]Karen L. Adams, "Sexism and the English Language: The Linguistic Implications of Being a Woman," in *Women: A Feminist Perspective*, 3rd ed., ed. Jo Freeman (Palo Alto, Calif.: Mayfield, 1984), pp. 478–91; Hall, pp. 37, 130–37.

Rearing children is work typically done by women, but not always.

subordinate status through greater restriction of the free movement of the body, greater exposure of the bare skin, and an emphasis on sexual characteristics. The more gender distinct the dress, the more this is the case.

Masculinity, like femininity, can be demonstrated through a wide variety 10 of cues. Pleck has argued that it is commonly expressed in North American society through the attainment of some level of proficiency at some, or all, of the following four main attitudes of masculinity. Persons who display success and high status in their social group, who exhibit "a manly air of toughness, confidence, and self-reliance" and "the aura of aggression, violence, and daring," and who conscientiously avoid anything associated with femininity are seen as exuding masculinity.[7] These requirements reflect the patriarchal ideology that masculinity results from an excess of testosterone, the assumption being that androgens supply a natural impetus toward aggression, which in turn impels males toward achievement and success. This vision of masculinity also reflects the ideological stance that ideal maleness (masculinity) must remain untainted by female (feminine) pollutants.

Masculinity, then, requires of its actors that they organize themselves and their society in a hierarchical manner so as to be able to explicitly quantify the achievement of success. The achievement of high status in one's social group requires competitive and aggressive behavior from those who wish to obtain it. Competition which is motivated by a goal of individual achievement, or egoistic dominance, also requires of its participants a degree of emotional insensitivity to feelings of hurt and loss in defeated others, and a measure of emotional insularity to protect oneself from becoming vulnerable to manipulation by others. Such values lead those who subscribe to them to view

[7]Joseph H. Pleck, *The Myth of Masculinity* (Cambridge, Mass.: MIT P, 1981), p. 139.

feminine persons as "born losers" and to strive to eliminate any similarities to feminine people from their own personalities. In patriarchally organized societies, masculine values become the ideological structure of the society as a whole. Masculinity thus becomes "innately" valuable and femininity serves a contrapuntal function to delineate and magnify the hierarchical dominance of masculinity.

Body postures, speech patterns, and styles of dress which demonstrate and support the assumption of dominance and authority convey an impression of masculinity. Typical masculine body postures tend to be expansive and aggressive. People who hold their arms and hands in positions away from their bodies, and who stand, sit, or lie with their legs apart — thus maximizing the amount of space that they physically occupy — appear most physically masculine. Persons who communicate an air of authority or a readiness for aggression by standing erect and moving forcefully also tend to appear more masculine. Movements that are abrupt and stiff, communicating force and threat rather than flexibility and cooperation, make an actor look masculine. Masculinity can also be conveyed by stern or serious facial expressions that suggest minimal receptivity to the influence of others, a characteristic which is an important element in the attainment and maintenance of egoistic dominance.[8]

Speech and dress which likewise demonstrate or claim superior status are also seen as characteristically masculine behavior patterns. Masculine speech patterns display a tendency toward expansiveness similar to that found in masculine body postures. People who attempt to control the direction of conversations seem more masculine. Those who tend to speak more loudly, use less polite and more assertive forms, and tend to interrupt the conversations of others more often also communicate masculinity to others. Styles of dress which emphasize the size of upper body musculature, allow freedom of movement, and encourage an illusion of physical power and a look of easy physicality all suggest masculinity. Such appearances of strength and readiness to action serve to create or enhance an aura of aggressiveness and intimidation central to an appearance of masculinity. Expansive postures and gestures combine with these qualities to insinuate that a position of secure dominance is a masculine one.

Gender role characteristics reflect the ideological contentions underlying the dominant gender schema in North American society. That schema leads us to believe that female and male behaviors are the result of socially directed hormonal instructions which specify that females will want to have children and will therefore find themselves relatively helpless and dependent on males for support and protection. The schema claims that males are innately aggressive and competitive and therefore will dominate over females. The social hegemony of this ideology ensures that we are all raised to practice gender roles which will confirm this vision of the nature of the sexes. Fortunately, our training to gender roles is neither complete nor uniform. As a result, it

[8]Goffman; Hall; Henley; Wex.

is possible to point to multitudinous exceptions to, and variations on, these themes. Biological evidence is equivocal about the source of gender roles; psychological androgyny is a widely accepted concept. It seems most likely that gender roles are the result of systematic power imbalances based on gender discrimination.[9]

READING THE TEXT

1. List the characteristics that Devor describes as being traditional conceptions of "masculinity" and "femininity" (para. 1).

2. What relationship does Devor see between characteristics that are considered masculine and feminine?

3. How does Devor explain the cultural belief in the "superiority" (para. 5) of males?

4. How, in Devor's view, do speech and dress communicate gender roles?

READING THE SIGNS

1. In small same-sex groups, brainstorm lists of traits that you consider to be masculine and feminine, and then have each group write its list on the board. Compare the lists produced by male and female groups. What patterns of differences or similarities do you see? To what extent do the traits presume a heterosexual orientation? How do you account for your results?

2. Study the speech patterns, styles of dress, and other nonverbal cues communicated by your friends during a social occasion, such as a party, trying not to reveal that you are observing them for an assignment. Then write an essay in which you analyze these cues used by your friends. To what extent do your friends enact the traditional gender codes Devor describes?

3. **CONNECTING TEXTS** Study a popular magazine such as *Vanity Fair*, *Rolling Stone*, or *Maxim* for advertisements depicting men and women interacting with each other. Then write an essay in which you interpret the body postures of the models, using Devor's selection as your framework for analysis. How do males and females typically stand? To what extent do the models enact stereotypically masculine or feminine stances? To develop your essay, consult Steve Craig's "Men's Men and Women's Women" (p. 182).

4. **CONNECTING TEXTS** Devor argues that female fashion traditionally has restricted body movement while male styles of dress usually allow freedom of movement. In class, discuss whether this claim is still true today, being sure to consider a range of clothing types (such as athletic wear, corporate dress, party fashion, and so forth). To develop your ideas, consult Mariah Burton Nelson's "I Won. I'm Sorry" (p. 524).

[9]Howard, Blumstein, and Schwartz; Kollock, Blumstein, and Schwartz.

DEBORAH BLUM

The Gender Blur: Where Does Biology End and Society Take Over?

There's an old argument over whether nature or nurture is more important in determining human behavior. Nowhere is this argument more intense than in gender studies, where proponents of the social construction of gender identities are currently exploring the many ways in which our upbringing shapes our behavior. But after watching her two-year-old son emphatically choose to play only with carnivorous dinosaur toys and disdainfully reject the "wimpy" vegetarian variety, Deborah Blum decided that nurture couldn't be all that there was to it. Exploring the role of biology in the determination of human behavior, Blum argues that both nature and nurture have to be taken into account if we are to understand gender differences. A Pulitzer Prize–winning professor of journalism at the University of Wisconsin at Madison, Blum is the author of several books, including *Sex on the Brain: The Biological Differences between Men and Women* (1997), *Ghost Hunters: William James and the Search for Scientific Proof of Life after Death* (2006), and *The Poisoner's Handbook: Murder and the Birth of Forensic Medicine in Jazz Age New York* (2010).

I was raised in one of those university-based, liberal elite families that politicians like to ridicule. In my childhood, every human being — regardless of gender — was exactly alike under the skin, and I mean exactly, barring his or her different opportunities. My parents wasted no opportunity to bring this point home. One Christmas, I received a Barbie doll and a softball glove. Another brought a green enamel stove, which baked tiny cakes by the heat of a lightbulb, and also a set of steel-tipped darts and competition-quality dartboard. Did I mention the year of the chemistry set and the ballerina doll?

It wasn't until I became a parent — I should say, a parent of two boys — that I realized I had been fed a line and swallowed it like a sucker (barring the part about opportunities, which I still believe). This dawned on me during my older son's dinosaur phase, which began when he was about two-and-a-half. Oh, he loved dinosaurs, all right, but only the blood-swilling carnivores. Plant-eaters were wimps and losers, and he refused to wear a T-shirt marred by a picture of a stegosaur. I looked down at him one day, as he was snarling around my feet and doing his toddler best to gnaw off my right leg, and I thought: This goes a lot deeper than culture.

Raising children tends to bring on this kind of politically incorrect reaction. Another friend came to the same conclusion watching a son determinedly bite his breakfast toast into the shape of a pistol he hoped would blow away — or at least terrify — his younger brother. Once you get past the guilt part — Did I do this? Should I have bought him that plastic allosaur with the oversized teeth? — such revelations can lead you to consider the far more interesting field of gender biology, where the questions take a different shape: Does love of carnage begin in culture or genetics, and which drives which? Do the gender roles of our culture reflect an underlying biology, and, in turn, does the way we behave influence that biology?

The point I'm leading up to — through the example of my son's innocent love of predatory dinosaurs — is actually one of the most straightforward in this debate. One of the reasons we're so fascinated by childhood behaviors is that, as the old saying goes, the child becomes the man (or woman, of course). Most girls don't spend their preschool years snarling around the house and pretending to chew off their companion's legs. And they — mostly — don't grow up to be as aggressive as men. Do the ways that we amplify those early differences in childhood shape the adults we become? Absolutely. But it's worth exploring the starting place — the faint signal that somehow gets amplified.

"There's plenty of room in society to influence sex differences," says 5 Marc Breedlove, a behavioral endocrinologist at the University of California at Berkeley and a pioneer in defining how hormones can help build sexually different nervous systems. "Yes, we're born with predispositions, but it's society that amplifies them, exaggerates them. I believe that — except for the sex differences in aggression. Those [differences] are too massive to be explained simply by society."

Aggression does allow a straightforward look at the issue. Consider the following statistics: Crime reports in both the United States and Europe record between ten and fifteen robberies committed by men for every one by a woman. At one point, people argued that this was explained by size difference. Women weren't big enough to intimidate, but that would change, they predicted, with the availability of compact weapons. But just as little girls don't routinely make weapons out of toast, women — even criminal ones — don't seem drawn to weaponry in the same way that men are. Almost twice as many male thieves and robbers use guns as their female counterparts do.

Or you can look at more personal crimes: domestic partner murders. Three-fourths of men use guns in those killings; 50 percent of women do. Here's more from the domestic front: In conflicts in which a woman killed a man, he tended to be the one who had started the fight — in 51.8 percent of the cases, to be exact. When the man was the killer, he again was the likely first aggressor, and by an even more dramatic margin. In fights in which women died, they had started the argument only 12.5 percent of the time.

Enough. You can parade endless similar statistics but the point is this: Males are more aggressive, not just among humans but among almost all species on earth. Male chimpanzees, for instance, declare war on neighboring troops, and one of their strategies is a warning strike: They kill females and infants to terrorize and intimidate. In terms of simple, reproductive genetics, it's an advantage of males to be aggressive: You can muscle your way into dominance, winning more sexual encounters, more offspring, more genetic future. For the female — especially in a species like ours, with time for just one successful pregnancy a year — what's the genetic advantage in brawling?

Thus the issue becomes not whether there is a biologically influenced sex difference in aggression — the answer being a solid, technical "You betcha" — but rather how rigid that difference is. The best science, in my opinion, tends to align with basic common sense. We all know that there are extraordinarily gentle men and murderous women. Sex differences are always generalizations: they refer to a behavior, with some evolutionary rationale behind it. They never define, entirely, an individual. And that fact alone should tell us that there's always — even in the most biologically dominated traits — some flexibility, an instinctive ability to respond, for better and worse, to the world around us.

This is true even with physical characteristics that we've often assumed   10 are nailed down by genetics. Scientists now believe height, for instance, is only about 90 percent heritable. A person's genes might code for a six-foot-tall body, but malnutrition could literally cut that short. And there's also some evidence, in girls anyway, that children with stressful childhoods tend to become shorter adults. So while some factors are predetermined, there's evidence that the prototypical male/female body design can be readily altered.

It's a given that humans, like most other species — bananas, spiders, sharks, ducks, any rabbit you pull out of a hat — rely on two sexes for reproduction. So basic is that requirement that we have chromosomes whose primary purpose is to deliver the genes that order up a male or a female. All other chromosomes are numbered, but we label the sex chromosomes with the letters X and Y. We get one each from our mother and our father, and the basic combinations are these: XX makes female, XY makes male.

There are two important — and little known — points about these chromosomal matches. One is that even with this apparently precise system, there's nothing precise — or guaranteed — about the physical construction of male and female. The other point makes that possible. It appears that sex doesn't matter in the early stages of embryonic development. We are unisex at the point of conception.

If you examine an embryo at about six weeks, you see that it has the ability to develop in either direction. The fledgling embryo has two sets of ducts — Wolffian for male, Muellerian for female — an either/or structure, held in readiness for further development. If testosterone and other androgens are released by hormone-producing cells, then the Wolffian ducts develop into the channel that connects penis to testes, and the female ducts wither away.

Without testosterone, the embryo takes on a female form; the male ducts vanish and the Muellerian ducts expand into oviducts, uterus, and vagina. In other words, in humans, anyway (the opposite is true in birds), the female is the default sex. Back in the 1950s, the famed biologist Alfred Jost showed that if you castrate a male rabbit fetus, choking off testosterone, you produce a completely feminized rabbit.

We don't do these experiments in humans — for obvious reasons — but there are naturally occurring instances that prove the same point. For instance: In the fetal testes are a group of cells, called Leydig cells, that make testosterone. In rare cases, the fetus doesn't make enough of these cells (a defect known as Leydig cell hypoplasia). In this circumstance we see the limited power of the XY chromosome. These boys have the right chromosomes and the right genes to be boys; they just don't grow a penis. Obstetricians and parents often think they see a baby girl, and these children are routinely raised as daughters. Usually, the "mistake" is caught about the time of puberty, when menstruation doesn't start. A doctor's examination shows the child to be internally male; there are usually small testes, often tucked within the abdomen. As the researchers put it, if the condition had been known from the beginning, "the sisters would have been born as brothers."

Just to emphasize how tricky all this body-building can get, there's a peculiar genetic defect that seems to be clustered by heredity in a small group of villages in the Dominican Republic. The result of the defect is a failure to produce an enzyme that concentrates testosterone, specifically for building the genitals. One obscure little enzyme only, but here's what happens without it: You get a boy with undescended testes and a penis so short and stubby that it resembles an oversized clitoris.

In the mountain villages of this Caribbean nation, people are used to it. The children are usually raised as "conditional" girls. At puberty, the secondary tide of androgens rises and is apparently enough to finish the construction project. The scrotum suddenly descends, the phallus grows, and the child develops a distinctly male body — narrow hips, muscular build, and even slight beard growth. At that point, the family shifts the child over from daughter to son. The dresses are thrown out. He begins to wear male clothes and starts dating girls. People in the Dominican Republic are so familiar with this condition that there's a colloquial name for it: *guevedoces*, meaning "eggs (or testes) at twelve."

It's the comfort level with this slip-slide of sexual identity that's so remarkable and, I imagine, so comforting to the children involved. I'm positive that the sexual transition of these children is less traumatic than the abrupt awareness of the "sisters who would have been brothers." There's a message of tolerance there, well worth repeating, and there are some other key lessons, too.

These defects are rare and don't alter the basic male-female division of our species. They do emphasize how fragile those divisions can be. Biology allows flexibility, room to change, to vary and grow. With that comes room for error as well. That it's possible to live with these genetic defects, that they don't merely kill us off, is a reminder that we, male and female alike, exist on a continuum of biological possibilities that can overlap and sustain either sex.

Marc Breedlove points out that the most difficult task may be separat- 20 ing how the brain responds to hormones from how the brain responds to the *results* of hormones. Which brings us back, briefly, below the belt: In this context, the penis is just a result, the product of androgens at work before birth. "And after birth," says Breedlove, "virtually everyone who interacts with that individual will note that he has a penis, and will, in many instances, behave differently than if the individual was a female."

Do the ways that we amplify physical and behavioral differences in childhood shape who we become as adults? Absolutely. But to understand that, you have to understand the differences themselves — their beginning and the very real biochemistry that may lie behind them.

Here is a good place to focus on testosterone — a hormone that is both well-studied and generally underrated. First, however, I want to acknowledge that there are many other hormones and neurotransmitters that appear to influence behavior. Preliminary work shows that fetal boys are a little more active than fetal girls. It's pretty difficult to argue socialization at that point. There's a strong suspicion that testosterone may create the difference.

And there are a couple of relevant animal models to emphasize the point. Back in the 1960s, Robert Goy, a psychologist at the University of Wisconsin at Madison, first documented that young male monkeys play much more roughly than young females. Goy went on to show that if you manipulate testosterone level — raising it in females, damping it down in males — you can reverse those effects, creating sweet little male monkeys and rowdy young females.

Is testosterone the only factor at work here? I don't think so. But clearly we can argue a strong influence, and, interestingly, studies have found that girls with congenital adrenal hypoplasia — who run high in testosterone —

Shoppers gather at the opening of an American Girl doll store in Colorado.

Andy Cross/Getty Images

tend to be far more fascinated by trucks and toy weaponry than most little girls are. They lean toward rough-and-tumble play, too. As it turns out, the strongest influence on this "abnormal" behavior is not parental disapproval, but the company of other little girls, who tone them down and direct them toward more routine girl games.

And that reinforces an early point: If there is indeed a biology to sex differ- 25 ences, we amplify it. At some point — when it is still up for debate — we gain a sense of our gender, and with it a sense of "gender-appropriate" behavior.

Some scientists argue for some evidence of gender awareness in infancy, perhaps by the age of twelve months. The consensus seems to be that full-blown "I'm a girl" or "I'm a boy" instincts arrive between the ages of two and three. Research shows that if a family operates in a very traditional, Beaver Cleaver kind of environment, filled with awareness of and association with "proper" gender behaviors, the "boys do trucks, girls do dolls" attitude seems to come very early. If a child grows up in a less traditional family, with an emphasis on partnership and sharing — "We all do the dishes, Joshua" — children maintain a more flexible sense of gender roles until about age six.

In this period, too, relationships between boys and girls tend to fall into remarkably strict lines. Interviews with children find that three-year-olds say that about half their friendships are with the opposite sex. By the age of five, that drops to 20 percent. By seven, almost no boys or girls have, or will admit to having, best friends of the opposite sex. They still hang out on the same playground, play on the same soccer teams. They may be friendly, but the real friendships tend to be boy-to-boy or girl-to-girl.

There's some interesting science that suggests that the space between boys and girls is a normal part of development; there are periods during which children may thrive and learn from hanging out with peers of the same sex. Do we, as parents, as a culture at large, reinforce such separations? Is the pope Catholic? One of my favorite studies looked at little boys who asked for toys. If they asked for a heavily armed action figure, they got the soldier about 70 percent of the time. If they asked for a "girl" toy, like a baby doll or a Barbie, their parents purchased it maybe 40 percent of the time. Name a child who won't figure out how to work *that* system.

How does all this fit together — toys and testosterone, biology and behavior, the development of the child into the adult, the way that men and women relate to one another?

Let me make a cautious statement about testosterone: It not only has 30 some body-building functions, it influences some behaviors as well. Let's make that a little less cautious: These behaviors include rowdy play, sex drive, competitiveness, and an in-your-face attitude. Males tend to have a higher baseline of testosterone than females — in our species, about seven to ten times as much — and therefore you would predict (correctly, I think) that all of those behaviors would be more generally found in men than in women.

But testosterone is also one of my favorite examples of how responsive biology is, how attuned it is to the way we live our lives. Testosterone, it turns out, rises in response to competition and threat. In the days of our ancestors, this might have been hand-to-hand combat or high-risk hunting endeavors. Today, scientists have measured testosterone rise in athletes preparing for a game, in chess players awaiting a match, in spectators following a soccer competition.

If a person — or even just a person's favored team — wins, testosterone continues to rise. It falls with a loss. (This also makes sense in an evolutionary perspective. If one was being clobbered with a club, it would be extremely unhelpful to have a hormone urging one to battle on.) Testosterone also rises in the competitive world of dating, settles down with a stable and supportive relationship, climbs again if the relationship starts to falter.

It's been known for years that men in high-stress professions — say, police work or corporate law — have higher testosterone levels than men in the ministry. It turns out that women in the same kind of strong-attitude professions have higher testosterone than women who choose to stay home. What I like about this is the chicken-or-egg aspect. If you argue that testosterone influenced the behavior of those women, which came first? Did they have high testosterone and choose the law? Or did they choose the law, and the competitive environment ratcheted them up on the androgen scale? Or could both be at work?

And, returning to children for a moment, there's an ongoing study by Pennsylvania researchers, tracking that question in adolescent girls, who are being encouraged by their parents to engage in competitive activities that were once for boys only. As they do so, the researchers are monitoring, regularly, two hormones: testosterone and cortisol, a stress hormone. Will these hormones rise in response to this new, more traditionally male environment? What if more girls choose the competitive path; more boys choose the other? Will female testosterone levels rise, male levels fall? Will that wonderful, unpredictable, flexible biology that we've been given allow a shift, so that one day, we will literally be far more alike?

We may not have answers to all those questions, but we can ask them, and we can expect that the answers will come someday, because science clearly shows us that such possibilities exist. In this most important sense, sex differences offer us a paradox. It is only through exploring and understanding what makes us different that we can begin to understand what binds us together. 35

READING THE TEXT

1. What effect do Blum's opening personal anecdotes have on the persuasiveness of her argument?

2. What evidence does Blum offer to support her contention that males are naturally more aggressive than females?

3. How does testosterone affect human behavior, according to Blum?

4. In Blum's view, how do the cultural choices that humans make, such as engaging in sports or other competitive activities, affect hormone balances?

READING THE SIGNS

1. In your journal, reflect on the way your upbringing shaped your sense of appropriate gender behavior.

2. **CONNECTING TEXTS**   Blum's selection challenges the common cultural studies position that gender behavior is socially constructed. Write an essay in which you defend, qualify, or reject Blum's point of view. To develop your ideas, consult Aaron Devor's "Gender Role Behaviors and Attitudes" (p. 504) and Kevin Jennings's "American Dreams" (p. 519).

3. Write an essay describing how you would raise a boy to counteract his stereotypical tendencies to aggressive behavior. Alternatively, describe how you would raise a girl to avoid the common stereotypes associated with females.

4. Visit the library, and investigate recent research on the possible genetic basis for homosexuality. Then write an essay in which you extend Blum's argument for the biological basis of gendered behavior to sexual orientation.

5. **CONNECTING TEXTS**   Read or reread Lorraine Devon Wilke's "Snowden's a Hero, Obama's a Villain" (p. 485), focusing on her plea that we avoid black-and-white thinking. In an essay, analyze Blum's approach to argumentation: To what extent does her selection satisfy Wilke's notion of a balanced argument?

Gender Identity Online

READING THE SIGNS

1. In February 2014, Facebook made headlines when it expanded its number of gender categories to more than fifty, including "pangender," "gender fluid," and "transgender." This photo shows Facebook software engineer Brielle Harrison demonstrating the new options for gender identity, and the original caption for this photo indicated that she planned to switch her identifier to "Trans Woman." How does such a move by Facebook challenge traditional ideas of gender identity?

2. Visit your Facebook page and explore these gender identity labels yourself. Pick a few and research them. How do they differ from one another? Why do you think Facebook chose to add so many fine variations in gender identity for users to choose from?

KEVIN JENNINGS
American Dreams

When Ellen DeGeneres became the first television star to come out of the closet on prime-time TV, gay men and lesbians around the country celebrated what appeared to be a major step forward for one of America's most marginalized communities. But the firestorm of protest that also attended Ellen's coming-out equally demonstrated just how far homosexuals have to go before winning full acceptance into American society. In this personal narrative (first published in 1994) of what it means to grow up gay in America, Kevin Jennings reveals the torment endured by a child forced to conceal his difference from everyone around him, especially his own parents. With years of self-denial and one suicide attempt behind him, Jennings shows how he eventually came to accept himself as he is and in so doing achieved his own version of the American dream. Kevin Jennings is founder of the Gay, Lesbian, and Straight Education Network (GLSEN) and author (with Pat Shapiro) of *Always My Child: A Parent's Guide to Understanding Your Gay, Lesbian, Bisexual, Transgendered, or Questioning Son or Daughter* (2003). His most recent book is *Mama's Boy, Preacher's Son: A Memoir* (2007). He is the assistant deputy secretary for the Office of Safe and Drug-Free Schools at the U.S. Department of Education.

When I was little, I honestly thought I would grow up to be the president. After all, I lived in a land of opportunity where anyone, with enough determination and hard work, could aspire to the highest office in the land. I planned to live out the American Dream.

I realized, however, that something was amiss from an early age. I grew up in the rural community of Lewisville, North Carolina, just outside the city of Winston-Salem. As you might guess from the city's name, Winston-Salem, Winston-Salem makes its living from the tobacco industry: It was cigarettes that propelled local conglomerate RJR-Nabisco to its status as one of the world's largest multinational corporations. Somehow this rising tide of prosperity never lapped at our doors, and the Jennings family was a bitter family indeed. Poor whites descended from Confederate veterans, we eagerly sought out scapegoats for our inexplicable failure to "make it" in the land of opportunity. My uncles and cousins joined the Ku Klux Klan, while my father, a fundamentalist minister, used religion to excuse his prejudices — against blacks, against Jews, against Catholics, against Yankees, against Communists and liberals (basically the same thing, as far as he was concerned), and, of course, against gays. Somehow the golden rule of "Do unto others as you would have them do unto you" never made it into his gospel. Instead, I remember church services filled with outbursts of paranoia, as we were warned about the evils of those whom we (incorrectly) held responsible for our very real oppression. I grew up believing that there was a Communist plot undermining our nation, a Jewish conspiracy controlling the banks and the media, and that black men — whom I unself-consciously referred to as "niggers" — spent their days plotting to rape white women. In case this seems like a history lesson on the Stone Age, please consider that I was born in 1963 and graduated from high school in 1981. Hardly the ancient past!

My father's profession as a traveling minister never left much money for luxuries like college tuition. Nevertheless, my mother was determined that I, her last chance, was going to make good on the Dream that had been denied to her and to my four older siblings — that one of her children would be the first member of our extended family ever to go to college. Not that it was going to be easy: my father died when I was eight, and my mother went to work at McDonald's (the only job she could get with her limited credentials). Every penny was watched carefully; dinner was often leftover quarter-pounders that she didn't have to pay for. I'm the only person I know who sees the Golden Arches, takes a bite, and thinks, "Mmm, just like Mom used to make!"

Throughout high school, I was determined to make it, determined to show my mother — and myself — that the American Dream really could come true. I worked hard and got ahead, earning a scholarship to Harvard after I had remade myself into the image of what I was told a successful person was like. Little did I realize at that point the price I was paying to fit in.

The first thing to go was any sign of my Southern heritage. As I came into ⁵ contact with mainstream America, through high school "gifted and talented" programs and, later, at college in Massachusetts, I began to realize that we Southerners were different. Our home-cooked meals — grits, turnip greens, red-eye gravy — never seemed to show up in frozen dinners, and if a character

LGBTQ protestors march in favor of ordaining and consecrating the Rev. Gene Robinson, the first openly gay Bishop in the Anglican church.

on television spoke with a Southern accent, that immediately identified him or her as stupid or as comic relief. As the lesbian writer Blanche Boyd put it:

> When television programs appeared, a dreadful truth came clear to me: Southerners were not normal people. We did not sound like normal people . . . [and] what we chose to talk about seemed peculiarly different also. I began to realize we were hicks. Television took away my faith in my surroundings. I didn't want to be a hick. I decided to go North, where people talked fast, walked fast, and acted cool. I practiced talking like the people on television. . . . I became desperate to leave the South.

Like Blanche Boyd, I deliberately erased my accent and aped the false monotone of television newscasters. I never invited college friends home to North Carolina for fear they might meet my family and realize they were worthless, ignorant hicks — which is how I'd come to view those whom I loved. I applied to colleges on the sole criterion that they not be in the South. I ran as far from Lewisville, North Carolina, as I could.

But there were some things about myself I could not escape from or change, no matter how hard I tried — among them the fact that I am gay.

I had always known I was gay, even before I had heard the word or knew what it meant. I remember that at age six or seven, the "adult" magazines that so fascinated my older brothers simply didn't interest me at all, and I somehow knew that I'd better hide this feeling from them. As I grew older and began to understand what my feelings meant, I recoiled in horror from myself. After all, my religious upbringing as a Southern Baptist had taught me that gay people were twisted perverts destined for a lifetime of eternal damnation.

Being as set as I was on achieving the American Dream, I was not about to accept the fact that I was gay. Here is where I paid the heaviest price for my Dream. I pursued what I thought was "normal" with a vengeance in high school, determined that, if the spirit was weak, the flesh would be more willing at the prospect of heterosexuality. I dated every girl I could literally get my hands on, earning a well-deserved reputation as a jerk who tried to see how far he could get on the first date. I attacked anyone who suggested that gay people might be entitled to some rights, too, and was the biggest teller of fag jokes at Radford High. But what I really hated was myself, and this I couldn't escape from, no matter how drunk or stoned I got, which I was doing on an almost daily basis by senior year.

That was also the year I fell in love for the first time, with another boy in my class. It turned out he was gay, too, and we made love one night in late May. I woke up the next morning and realized that it was true—I really was a fag after all. I spent that day trying to figure out how I was going to live the American Dream, which seemed impossible if I was homosexual. By nightfall I decided it *was* impossible, and without my Dream I couldn't see a reason why I'd want to be alive at all. I went to my family's medicine cabinet, took the new bottle of aspirin out, and proceeded to wash down 140 pills with a glass of gin. I remember the exact number—140—because I figured I could only get down about ten at one swallow, so I carefully counted out fourteen little stacks before I began. Thanks to a friend who got to me in time, I didn't die that night. My story has a happy ending—but a lot of them don't. Those moments of desperation helped me understand why one out of every three gay teens tries to commit suicide.

At Harvard, the most important lessons I learned had little to do with Latin 10
American or European history, which were my majors. Instead, I learned the importance of taking control of my own destiny. I met a great professor who taught me that as long as I stayed in the closet, I was accepting the idea that there was something wrong with me, something that I needed to hide. After all, as my favorite bisexual, Eleanor Roosevelt, once said, "No one can make you feel inferior without your consent." By staying closeted, I was consenting to my own inferiority. I realized that for years, I had let a Dream—a beautiful, seductive, but ultimately false Dream—rule my life. I had agreed to pay its price, which was the rejection of my family, my culture, and eventually myself. I came to understand that the costs of the Dream far outweighed its rewards. I learned that true freedom would be mine only when I was able to make my own decisions about what I wanted out of life instead of accepting those thrust upon me by the Dream. Since I made that realization, I have followed my own path instead of the one I had been taught was "right" all my life.

Once I started down this new path, I began to make some discoveries about the society in which I was raised, and about its notions of right and wrong. I began to ask many questions, and the answers to these questions were not always pleasant. Why, for example, did my mother always earn less than men who did the same exact work? Why did I learn as a child that to cheat someone was to "Jew" them? Why was my brother ostracized when he fell in love with and later married a black woman? Why did everyone in my family work so hard and yet have so little? I realized that these inequalities were part of the game, the rules of which were such that gays, blacks, poor people, women, and many others would always lose to the wealthy white heterosexual Christian men who have won the Presidency forty-two out of forty-two times. Those odds—100 percent—are pretty good ones to bet on. No, I discovered that true freedom could not be achieved by a Dream that calls on us to give up who we are in order to fit in and become "worthy" of power. Holding power means little if women have to become masculine "iron ladies" to get it, if Jews have to "Americanize" their names, if blacks have to learn to speak so-called Standard English (though we never acknowledge *whose* standard it is), or if gays and lesbians have to hide what everyone else gets to celebrate—the loves of their lives.

Real freedom will be ours when the people around us—and when we ourselves—accept that we, too, are "real" Americans, and that we shouldn't have to change to meet anyone else's standards. In 1924, at age twenty-two, the gay African American poet Langston Hughes said it best, in his poem "I, Too":

> Tomorrow,
> I'll be at the table
> When company comes.
> Nobody'll dare
> Say to me,
> "Eat in the kitchen,"
> Then.
> Besides,
> They'll see how beautiful I am
> And be ashamed—
> I, too, am America.

By coming out as a gay man and demanding my freedom, I realize that I have done the most American thing of all. And while I have come a long way since the days when I dreamed of living in the White House, I have discovered that what I'm fighting for now is the very thing I thought I'd be fighting for if I ever became President—"liberty and justice for all."

READING THE TEXT

1. According to Jennings, how did his Southern upbringing influence his goals for the future?
2. Why did Jennings feel he had to eschew his Southern heritage?
3. In what ways did Jennings deny to himself his sexual orientation, and why did he do so?
4. In your own words, trace the evolution of Jennings's understanding of the American dream as he grew up.
5. What is the relationship between the excerpt from Langston Hughes's "I, Too" and Jennings's story?

READING THE SIGNS

1. In your journal, write your own account of how you responded to normative gender codes as a high school student. To what extent did you feel pressure to conform to or to renounce traditional expectations — or to do both?

2. Jennings describes his early attempts to deny his sexual orientation. In class, discuss how other minority or underprivileged groups — ethnic minorities, women, the disabled — sometimes try to erase their identities. What social and cultural forces motivate such self-denial? Use the discussion as a springboard for an essay in which you explore why one might be motivated to do so.

3. In class, brainstorm two lists: films or TV shows that reinforce heterosexuality as normative and those that present homosexuality positively. Then compare your lists. What conclusions do you draw about popular culture's influence on American gender codes?

4. In his conclusion, Jennings states his desideratum: "Real freedom will be ours when the people around us — and when we ourselves — accept that we, too, are 'real' Americans, and that we shouldn't have to change to meet anyone else's standards" (para. 12). Research the current status of efforts to legalize same-sex marriage, and write an essay in which you make an argument about the extent to which Jennings's goal has been realized.

MARIAH BURTON NELSON
I Won. I'm Sorry.

Athletic competition, when you come right down to it, is about winning, which is no problem for men, whose gender codes tell them that aggression and domination are admirable male traits. But "how can you win, if you're female?" Mariah Burton Nelson asks, when the same gender codes insist that women must be feminine, "not aggressive, not victorious." And so women athletes, even when they do win, go out of their way to signal their femininity by dolling themselves up and smiling a lot. Beauty and vulnerability seem to be as important to today's female athlete as brawn and gold medals, Nelson complains, paradoxically contradicting the apparent feminist gains that women athletes have made in recent years. A former Stanford University and professional basketball player, Mariah Burton Nelson is the author of six books, including *We Are All Athletes* (2002) and *Making Money on the Sidelines* (2008). She is vice president for innovation and planning at ASAE: the Center for Association Leadership. This piece originally appeared in *Self* magazine.

When Sylvia Plath's husband, Ted Hughes, published his first book of poems, Sylvia wrote to her mother: "I am so happy that HIS book is accepted FIRST. It will make it so much easier for me when mine is accepted. . . ."

After Sylvia killed herself, her mother published a collection of Sylvia's letters. In her explanatory notes, Aurelia Plath commented that from the time she was very young, Sylvia "catered to the male of any age so as to bolster his sense of superiority." In seventh grade, Aurelia Plath noted, Sylvia was pleased to finish second in a spelling contest. "It was nicer, she felt, to have a boy first."

How many women still collude in the myth of male superiority, believing it's "nicer" when boys and men finish first? How many of us achieve but only in a lesser, smaller, feminine way, a manner consciously or unconsciously designed to be as nonthreatening as possible?

Since I'm tall, women often talk to me about height. Short women tell me, "I've always wanted to be tall—but not as tall as you!" I find this amusing, but also curious. Why not? Why not be six-two?

Tall women tell me that they won't wear heels because they don't want 5 to appear taller than their husbands or boyfriends, even by an inch. What are these women telling me—and their male companions? Why do women regulate their height in relation to men's height? Why is it still rare to see a woman who is taller than her husband?

Women want to be tall enough to feel elegant and attractive, like models. They want to feel respected and looked up to. But they don't want to be so tall that their height threatens men. They want to win—to achieve, to reach new heights—but without exceeding male heights.

How can you win, if you're female? Can you just do it? No. You have to play the femininity game. Femininity by definition is not large, not imposing, not competitive. Feminine women are not ruthless, not aggressive, not victorious. It's not feminine to have a killer instinct, to want with all your heart and soul to win—neither tennis matches nor elected office nor feminist victories such as abortion rights. It's not feminine to know exactly what you want, then go for it.

Femininity is about appearing beautiful and vulnerable and small. It's about winning male approval.

One downhill skier who asked not to be identified told me the following story: "I love male approval. Most women skiers do. We talk about it often. There's only one thing more satisfying than one of the top male skiers saying, 'Wow, you are a great skier. You rip. You're awesome.'

"But it's so fun leaving 99 percent of the world's guys in the dust—oops," 10 she laughs. "I try not to gloat. I've learned something: If I kick guys' butts and lord it over them, they don't like me. If, however, I kick guys' butts then act 'like a girl,' there is no problem. And I do mean girl, not woman. Nonthreatening."

Femininity is also about accommodating men, allowing them to feel bigger than and stronger than and superior to women, not emasculated by them.

Femininity is unhealthy, obviously. It would be unhealthy for men to act passive, dainty, obsessed with their physical appearance, and dedicated to bolstering the sense of superiority in the other gender, so it's unhealthy for women too. These days, some women are redefining femininity as strong, as athletic, as however a female happens to be, so that "feminine" becomes synonymous with "female." Other women reject both feminine and masculine terms and stereotypes, selecting from the entire range of human behaviors instead of limiting themselves to the "gender-appropriate" ones. These women smile only when they're happy, act angry when they're angry, dress how they want to. They cling to their self-respect and dignity like a life raft.

But most female winners play the femininity game to some extent, using femininity as a defense, a shield against accusations such as bitch, man-hater, lesbian. Feminine behavior and attire mitigate against the affront of female victory, soften the hard edges of winning. Women who want to win without losing male approval temper their victories with beauty, with softness, with smallness, with smiles.

Serena Williams at Wimbledon.

AP Photo/Noah Berger

In the fifties, at each of the Amateur Athletic Union's women's basketball championships, one of the players was crowned a beauty queen. (This still happens at Russian women's ice hockey tournaments.) Athletes in the All-American Girls Baseball League of the forties and fifties slid into base wearing skirts. In 1979, professional basketball players with the California Dreams were sent to John Robert Powers' charm school. Ed Temple, the legendary coach of the Tennessee State Tigerbelles, the team that produced Wilma Rudolph, Wyomia Tyus, Willye White, Madeline Manning, and countless other champions, enforced a dress code and stressed that his athletes should be "young ladies first, track girls second."

Makeup, jewelry, dress, and demeanor were often dictated by the male coaches and owners in these leagues, but to some extent the players played along, understanding the trade-off: in order to be "allowed" to compete, they had to demonstrate that they were, despite their "masculine" strivings, real ("feminine") women. 15

Today, both men and women wear earrings, notes Felshin, "but the media is still selling heterosexism and 'feminine' beauty. And if you listen carefully, in almost every interview" female athletes still express apologetic behavior through feminine dress, behavior, and values.

Florence Griffith-Joyner, Gail Devers, and other track stars of this modern era dedicate considerable attention to portraying a feminine appearance. Basketball star Lisa Leslie has received more attention for being a model than for leading the Americans to Olympic victory. Steffi Graf posed in bikinis for the 1997 *Sports Illustrated* swimsuit issue. In a Sears commercial, Olympic basketball players apply lipstick, paint their toenails, rock babies, lounge in bed, and pose and dance in their underwear. Lisa Leslie says, "Everybody's allowed to be themselves. Me, for example, I'm very feminine."

In an Avon commercial, Jackie Joyner Kersee is shown running on a beach while the camera lingers on her buttocks and breasts. She tells us that she can bench-press 150 pounds and brags that she can jump farther than "all but 128 men." Then she says: "And I have red toenails." Words flash on the screen: "Just another Avon lady." Graf, Mary Pierce, Monica Seles, and Mary Jo Fernandez have all played in dresses. They are "so much more comfortable" than skirts, Fernandez explained. "You don't have to worry about the shirt coming up or the skirt being too tight. It's cooler, and it's so feminine."

"When I put on a dress I feel different—more feminine, more elegant, more ladylike—and that's nice," added Australia's Nicole Bradtke: "We're in a sport where we're throwing ourselves around, so it's a real asset to the game to be able to look pretty at the same time."

Athletes have become gorgeous, flirtatious, elegant, angelic, darling—and the skating commentators' favorite term: "vulnerable." Some think this is good news: proof that femininity and sports are compatible. "There doesn't have to be such a complete division between 'You're beautiful and sexy' and 'you're athletic and strong,'" says Linda Hanley, a pro beach volleyball player who also appeared in a bikini in the 1997 *Sports Illustrated* swimsuit issue. 20

Athletes and advertisers reassure viewers that women who compete are still willing to play the femininity game, to be cheerleaders. Don't worry about us, the commercials imply. We're winners but we'll still look pretty for you. We're acting in ways that only men used to act but we'll still act how you want women to act. We're not threatening. We're not lesbians. We're not ugly, not bad marriage material. We're strong but feminine. Linguists note that the word "but" negates the part of the sentence that precedes it.

There are some recent examples of the media emphasizing female power in an unambiguous way. "Women Muscle In," the *New York Times Magazine* proclaimed in a headline. The *Washington Post* wrote, "At Olympics, Women Show Their Strength." And a new genre of commercials protests that female athletes are NOT cheerleaders, and don't have to be. Olympic and pro basketball star Dawn Staley says in a Nike commercial that she plays basketball "for the competitiveness" of it. "I need some place to release it. It just builds up, and sports is a great outlet for it. I started out playing with the guys. I wasn't always accepted. You get criticized, like: 'You need to be in the kitchen. Go put on a skirt.' I just got mad and angry and went out to show them that I belong here as much as they do."

Other commercials tell us that women can compete like conquerors. A Nike ad called "Wolves" shows girls leaping and spiking volleyballs while a voice says, "They are not sisters. They are not classmates. They are not friends. They are not even the girls' team. They are a pack of wolves. Tend to your sheep." Though the athletes look serious, the message sounds absurd. When I show this commercial to audiences, they laugh. Still, the images do depict the power of the volleyball players: their intensity, their ability to pound the ball almost through the floor. The script gives the players (and viewers) permission not to be ladylike, not to worry about whether their toenails are red.

But in an American Basketball League commercial, the Philadelphia Rage's female basketball players are playing rough; their bodies collide. Maurice Chevalier sings, "Thank heaven for little girls." The tag line: "Thank heaven, they're on our side."

Doesn't all this talk about girls and ladies simply focus our attention on 25 femaleness, femininity, and ladylike behavior? The lady issue is always there in the equation: something to redefine, to rebel against. It's always present, like sneakers, so every time you hear the word *athlete* you also hear the word *lady* — or feminine, or unfeminine. It reminds me of a beer magazine ad from the eighties that featured a photo of Olympic track star Valerie Brisco-Hooks. "Funny, she doesn't look like the weaker sex," said the print. You could see her impressive muscles. Clearly the intent of the ad was to contrast an old stereotype with the reality of female strength and ability. But Brisco-Hooks was seated, her legs twisted pretzel style, arms covering her chest. But in that position, Brisco-Hooks didn't look very strong or able. In the line, "Funny, she doesn't look like the weaker sex," the most eye-catching words are funny, look, weaker, and sex. Looking at the pretzel that is Valerie, you begin to think that she looks funny. You think about weakness. And you think about sex.

When she was young, Nancy Kerrigan wanted to play ice hockey with her older brothers. Her mother told her, "You're a girl. Do girl things."

Figure skating is a girl thing. Athletes in sequins and "sheer illusion sleeves" glide and dance, their tiny skirts flapping in the breeze. They achieve, but without touching or pushing anyone else. They win, but without visible signs of sweat. They compete, but not directly. Their success is measured not by confrontation with an opponent, nor even by a clock or a scoreboard. Rather, they are judged as beauty contestants are judged: by a panel of people who interpret the success of the routines. Prettiness is mandatory. Petite and groomed and gracious, figure skaters — like cheerleaders, gymnasts, and aerobic dancers — camouflage their competitiveness with niceness and prettiness until it no longer seems male or aggressive or unseemly.

The most popular sport for high school and college women is basketball. More than a million fans shelled out an average of $15 per ticket in 1997, the inaugural summer of the Women's National Basketball Association. But the most televised women's sport is figure skating. In 1995 revenue from skating shows and competitions topped six hundred million dollars. In the seven months between October 1996 and March 1997, ABC, CBS, NBC, Fox, ESPN, TBS, and USA dedicated 162.5 hours of programming to figure skating, half of it in prime time. Kerrigan earns up to three hundred thousand dollars for a single performance.

Nearly 75 percent of the viewers of televised skating are women. The average age is between twenty-five and forty-five years old, with a household income of more than fifty thousand dollars. What are these women watching? What are they seeing? What's the appeal?

Like golf, tennis, and gymnastics, figure skating is an individual sport 30 favored by white people from the upper classes. The skaters wear cosmetics, frozen smiles, and revealing dresses. Behind the scenes they lift weights and sweat like any serious athlete, but figure skating seems more dance than sport, more grace than guts, more art than athleticism. Figure skating allows women to compete like champions while dressed like cheerleaders.

In women's figure skating, smiling is part of "artistic expression." In the final round, if the competitors are of equal merit, artistry weighs more heavily than technique. Midori Ito, the best jumper in the history of women's skating, explained a weak showing at the 1995 world championships this way: "I wasn't 100 percent satisfied. . . . I probably wasn't smiling enough."

The media portray female figure skaters as "little girl dancers" or "fairy tale princesses" (NBC commentator John Tesh); as "elegant" (Dick Button); as "little angels" (Peggy Fleming); as "ice beauties" and "ladies who lutz" (*People* magazine). Commentators frame skaters as small, young, and decorative creatures, not superwomen but fairy-tale figments of someone's imagination.

After Kerrigan was assaulted by a member of Tonya Harding's entourage, she was featured on a *Sports Illustrated* cover crying "Why me?" When she recovered to win a silver medal at the Olympics that year, she became "America's sweetheart" and rich to boot. But the princess turned pumpkin shortly after midnight, as soon as the ball was over and she stopped smiling and started speaking. Growing impatient during the Olympic medal ceremony while everyone waited for Baiul, Kerrigan grumbled, "Oh, give me a break, she's just going to cry out there again. What's the difference?"

What were Kerrigan's crimes? She felt too old to cavort with cartoon characters. Isn't she? She expressed anger and disappointment — even bitterness and bad sportsmanship — about losing the gold. But wasn't she supposed to want to win? What happens to baseball players who, disappointed about a loss, hit each other or spit on umpires? What happens to basketball players and football players and hockey players who fight? Men can't tumble from a princess palace because we don't expect them to be princesses in the first place, only athletes.

Americans fell out of love with Kerrigan not because they couldn't adore 35 an athlete who lacked grace in defeat, but because they couldn't adore a female athlete who lacked grace in defeat.

Female politicians, lawyers, and businesswomen of all ethnic groups also play the femininity game. Like tennis players in short dresses, working women seem to believe it's an asset to look pretty (but not too pretty) while throwing themselves around. The female apologetic is alive and well in corporate boardrooms, where women say "I'm sorry, maybe someone else already stated this idea, but . . ." and smile while they say it.

When Newt Gingrich's mother revealed on television that Newt had referred to Hillary Clinton as a bitch, how did Hillary respond? She donned a pink suit and met with female reporters to ask how she could "soften her image." She seemed to think that her competitiveness was the problem and femininity the solution.

So if you want to be a winner and you're female, you'll feel pressured to play by special, female rules. Like men, you'll have to be smart and industrious, but in addition you'll have to be "like women": kind, nurturing, accommodating, nonthreatening, placating, pretty, and small. You'll have to smile. And not act angry. And wear skirts. Nail polish and makeup help, too.

READING THE TEXT

1. Summarize in your own words the contradictory messages about appropriate gender behavior that women athletes must contend with, according to Nelson.

2. Nelson begins her article with an anecdote about poet Sylvia Plath. How does this opening frame her argument about women in sports?

3. What is the "femininity game" (para. 7), in Nelson's view, and how do the media perpetuate it?

4. What sports are coded as "feminine," according to Nelson, and why?

READING THE SIGNS

1. Watch a women's sports event on television, such as an LPGA match, analyzing the behavior and appearance of the athletes. Use your observations as

evidence in an essay in which you assess the validity of Nelson's claims about the contradictory gender role behaviors of female athletes.

2. If you are a female athlete, write a journal entry exploring whether you feel pressure to act feminine and your responses to that pressure. If you are not a female athlete, reflect on the behavior and appearance of women athletes on your campus. Do you see signs that they are affected by the femininity game?

3. Obtain a copy of a magazine that focuses on women's sports, such as *Sports Illustrated Women*, or visit an online magazine such as sportsister.com or womensportreport.com. Analyze the articles and the ads in the magazine, noting models' and athletes' clothing, physical appearance, and speech patterns. Using Nelson's argument as a critical framework, write an essay in which you analyze whether the magazine perpetuates traditional gender roles or presents sports as an avenue for female empowerment.

4. Interview women athletes on your campus, and ask them whether they feel pressured by the femininity game. Have they been accused of being lesbians or bitches simply because they are athletes? Do they feel pressure to be physically attractive or charming? Do you see any correlation between an athlete's sport and her responses? Use your observations as the basis of an argument about the influence of traditional gender roles on women athletes at your school.

ALFRED LUBRANO

The Shock of Education: How College Corrupts

One of America's most fundamental contradictions lies at the heart of the American dream itself. That is, America's promise of social mobility compels those who begin at the bottom to leave behind their origins in order to succeed, which entails giving up a part of oneself and leaving one's home behind. It can be a wrenching transition, and in this reflection on what it means to achieve the dream, Alfred Lubrano describes the strain of moving between two worlds, relating both his own experiences moving from working-class Brooklyn to an Ivy League school and those of other working-class "straddlers" who moved into the middle class. The son of a bricklayer, Lubrano is a journalist and National Public Radio commentator. He is the author of *Limbo: Blue-Collar Roots, White-Collar Dreams* (2004), from which this selection is taken.

College is where the Great Change begins. People start to question the blue-collar take on the world. Status dissonance, the sociologists call it. Questions arise: Are the guys accurate in saying people from such-and-such a race are really so bad?

Was Mom right when she said nice girls don't put out? Suddenly, college opens up a world of ideas — a life of the mind — abstract and intangible. The core blue-collar values and goals — loyalty to family and friends, making money, marrying, and procreating — are supplanted by stuff you never talked about at home: personal fulfillment, societal obligation, the pursuit of knowledge for knowledge's sake, and on and on. One world opens and widens; another shrinks.

There's an excitement and a sadness to that. The child, say Sennett and Cobb, is deserting his past, betraying the parents he is rising above, an unavoidable result when you're trying to accomplish more with your life than merely earning a paycheck.[1] So much will change between parent and child, and between peers, in the college years. "Every bit of learning takes you further from your parents," says Southwest Texas State University history professor Gregg Andrews, himself a Straddler. "I say this to all my freshmen to start preparing them." The best predictor of whether you're going to have problems with your family is the distance between your education and your parents', Jake Ryan says. You may soon find yourself with nothing to talk to your folks or friends about.

This is the dark part of the American story, the kind of thing we work to hide. Mobility means discomfort, because so much has to change; one can't allow for the satisfactions of stasis: You prick yourself and move, digging spurs into your own hide to get going, forcing yourself to forget the comforts of the barn. In this country, we speak grandly of this metamorphosis, never stopping to consider that for many class travelers with passports stamped for new territory, the trip is nothing less than a bridge burning.

Fighting Self-Doubt

When Columbia plucked me out of working-class Brooklyn, I was sure they had made a mistake, and I remained convinced of that throughout most of my time there. My high school was a gigantic (4,500 students) factory; we literally had gridlock in the halls between classes, kids belly to back between history and English class. A teacher once told me that if every one of the reliable corps of truant students actually decided to show up to class one day, the school could not hold us all. (We were unofficially nicknamed "the Italian Army." When our football guys played nearby New Utrecht, which boasted an equivalent ethnic demographic, kids dubbed the game the "Lasagna Bowl.") Lafayette High School roiled with restless boys and girls on their way to jobs in their parents' unions or to secretaries' desks. How could you move from that to an elite college?

At night, at home, the difference in the Columbia experiences my father and I were having was becoming more evident. The family still came together

---

[1] Richard Sennett and Jonathan Cobb, *The Hidden Injuries of Class* (New York: Alfred A. Knopf, 1972), 131.

for dinner, despite our disparate days. We talked about general stuff, and I learned to self-censor. I'd seen how ideas could be upsetting, especially when wielded by a smarmy freshman who barely knew what he was talking about. No one wanted to hear how the world worked from some kid who was first learning to use his brain; it was as unsettling as riding in a car with a new driver. When he taught a course on Marx, Sackrey said he used to tell his students just before Thanksgiving break not to talk about "this stuff at the dinner table" or they'd mess up the holiday. Me mimicking my professors' thoughts on race, on people's struggle for equality, or on politics didn't add to the conviviality of the one nice hour in our day. So I learned to shut up.

After dinner, my father would flip on the TV in the living room. My mom 5 would grab a book and join him. And I'd go looking for a quiet spot to study. In his autobiography, *Hunger of Memory: The Education of Richard Rodriguez*, the brilliant Mexican-American Straddler, writer, and PBS commentator invokes British social scientist Richard Hoggart's "scholarship boys," finding pieces of himself in them. Working-class kids trying to advance in life, the scholarship boys learned to withdraw from the warm noise of the gathered family to isolate themselves with their books.[2] (Read primarily as a memoir of ethnicity and—most famously—an anti–affirmative action tract, the book is more genuinely a dissertation on class. At a sidewalk café in San Francisco, Rodriguez himself tells me how often his book is miscatalogued.) Up from the immigrant working class, Rodriguez says in our interview, the scholarship boy finds himself moving between two antithetical places: home and school. With the family, there is intimacy and emotion. At school, one learns to live with "lonely reason." Home life is in the now, Rodriguez says; school life exists on an altogether different plane, calm and reflective, with an eye toward the future.

The scholarship boy must learn to distance himself from the family circle in order to succeed academically, Rodriguez tells me. By doing this, he slowly loses his family. There's a brutality to education, he says, a rough and terrible disconnect. Rodriguez says he despised his parents' "shabbiness," their inability to speak English. "I hated that they didn't know what I was learning," he says. He thought of D. H. Lawrence's *Sons and Lovers*, and of Paul Morel, the coal miner's son. Lawrence is a model for Rodriguez, in a way. Rodriguez remembers the scene in which the son watches his father pick up his schoolbooks, his rough hands fingering the volumes that are the instruments separating the two men. Books were establishing a disharmony between the classroom and Rodriguez's house. Preoccupation with language and reading is an effeminacy not easily understood by workers. "It sears your soul to finally decide to talk like your teacher and not your father," Rodriguez says. "I'm not talking about anything less than the grammar of the heart."

---

[2]Richard Rodriguez, *Hunger of Memory: The Education of Richard Rodriguez* (New York: Bantam Books, 1983), 46. Rodriguez himself quotes from Richard Hoggart, *The Uses of Literacy* (London: Chatto and Windus, 1957), chap. 10.

Myself, I studied in the kitchen near the dishwasher because its white noise drowned out the television. As long as the wash cycle ran, I could not hear Mr. T and the A-Team win the day. I did not begrudge my father his one indulgence; there wasn't much else that could relax him. He was not a drinker. TV drained away the tumult and hazard of his Columbia day [he was a bricklayer]. My own room was too close to the living room. My brother's small room was too crowded for both of us to study in. You never went in your parents' bedroom without them in it, inviting you. When the dishes were clean and the kitchen again too quiet to beat back the living room noise, I'd go downstairs to my grandparents' apartment. If they were both watching the same TV show on the first floor, then the basement was free. Here was profound and almost disquieting silence. I could hear the house's systems rumble and shake: water whooshing through pipes, the oil burner powering on and off, and the refrigerator humming with a loud efficiency. Down in the immaculate redwood-paneled kitchen / living room, which sometimes still smelled of the sausages and peppers my grandfather may have made that night (my grandparents cooked and ate in their basement, something that never seemed unusual to us), I was ninety minutes from my school and two floors below my family in a new place, underscoring my distance from anything known, heightening my sense of isolation — my limbo status. I read Homer, Shakespeare, and Molière down there. I wrote a paper on landscape imagery in Dante's *Inferno*. In my self-pitying, melodramatic teenager's mind, I thought I had been banished to a new, lonely rung of hell that Dante hadn't contemplated.

By 11 p.m., I'd go back upstairs. My mother would be in bed, my father asleep on his chair. I'd turn off the TV, which awakened my dad. He'd walk off to bed, and I'd study for a couple more hours. His alarm would go off before 5 a.m., and he'd already be at Columbia by the time I woke up at 6:30. That's how our Ivy League days ended and began. When my father was done with Columbia, he moved on to another job site. When I was done with Columbia, I was someone else. I'd say I got the better deal. But then, my father would tell you, that was always the plan. . . .

Macbeth and Other Foolishness

Middle-class kids are groomed for another life. They understand, says Patrick Finn, why reading *Macbeth* in high school could be important years down the road. Working-class kids see no such connection, understand no future life for which digesting Shakespeare might be of value. Very much in the now, working-class people are concerned with immediate needs. And bookish kids are seen as weak.

Various education studies have shown that schools help reinforce class. 10 Teachers treat the working class and the well-to-do differently, this work demonstrates, with the blue-collar kids getting less attention and respect. It's no secret, education experts insist, that schools in poorer areas tend to employ teachers who are less well-trained. In these schools, the curriculum is test-based and uncreative. Children are taught, essentially, to obey and fill in blanks. By fourth grade, many of the children are bored and alienated; nothing in school connects to their culture. Beyond that, many working-class children are resistant to schooling and uncooperative with teachers, experts say. They feel pressure from other working-class friends to not participate and are told that being educated is effeminate and irrelevant. Educators have long understood that minority children have these problems, says Finn. But they rarely understand or see that working-class white kids have similar difficulties. "So we're missing a whole bunch of people getting screwed by the education systems," he says.

In our conversations, Finn explains that language is a key to class. In a working-class home where conformity is the norm, all opinions are dictated by group consensus, by what the class says is so. There's one way to do everything, there's one way to look at the world. Since all opinions are shared, there's never a need to explain thought and behavior. You talk less. Language in such a home, Finn says, is implicit.

Things are different in a middle-class home. There, parents are more willing to take the time to explain to little Janey why it's not such a good idea to pour chocolate sauce on the dog. If Janey challenges a rule of the house, she's spoken to like an adult, or at least not like a plebe at some military school. (Working-class homes are, in fact, very much like the military, with parents barking orders, Straddlers tell me. It's that conformity thing again.) There is a variety of opinions in middle-class homes, which are more collaborative than conformist, Finn says. Middle-class people have a multiviewed take on the world. In such a home, where one needs to express numerous ideas and opinions, language is by necessity explicit.

When it's time to go to school, the trouble starts. The language of school — of the teachers and the books — is explicit. A child from a working-class home is at a huge disadvantage, Finn says, because he's used to a narrower world of expression and a smaller vocabulary of thought. It's little wonder that kids from working-class homes have lower reading scores and do less well on SATs than middle-class kids, Finn says.

In high school, my parents got me a tutor for the math part of the SATs, to bolster a lackluster PSAT score. That sort of thing happens all the time in middle-class neighborhoods. But we were setting precedent among our kind. Most kids I knew from the community were not taking the SATs, let alone worrying about their scores. If you're from the middle class, you do not feel out of place preparing for college. Parents and peers help groom you, encourage you, and delight in your progress. Of course, when you get to freshman year, the adjustments can be hard on anyone, middle-class and working-class kids alike. But imagine going through freshman orientation if your parents are ambivalent — or hostile — about your being there, and your friends aren't clear about what you're doing.

It was like that for my friend Rita Giordano, forty-five, also a journal-   15
ist, also from Brooklyn. Her world, like mine, was populated by people who
thought going from 60th to 65th Streets was a long journey. So when Rita
took sojourns into Greenwich Village by herself on Saturday mornings as a
teenager, she made sure not to tell any of her friends. It was too oddball to
have to explain. And she'd always come back in time to go shopping with
everyone. She couldn't figure out why she responded to the artsy vibe of the
Village; she was just aware that there were things going on beyond the neighborhood. When it came time for college, she picked Syracuse University
because it was far away, a new world to explore. That bothered her friends,
and she'd have to explain herself to them on trips back home. "What do you
do up there?" they asked her. "Don't you get homesick?" Suddenly, things
felt awkward among childhood friends who had always been able to talk. "It
was confusing to come home and see people thinking that you're not doing
what they're doing, which meant you're rejecting them," said Rita, a diminu-
tive, sensitive woman with large, brown eyes. "'Don't they see it's still me?' I
wondered. I started feeling like, how do I coexist in these two worlds, college
and home? I mean, I could talk to my girlfriends about what color gowns their
bridesmaids would wear at their fantasy weddings. But things like ambition
and existential questions about where you fit in the world and how you make
your mark—we just didn't go there."

And to make matters more complicated, there was a guy. Rita's decision
to go to Syracuse didn't sit well with the boyfriend who was probably always
going to remain working class. "In true Brooklyn fashion, he and his friends
decided one night they were going to drive four hundred miles to Syracuse to
bring me back, or whatever. But on the way up, they totaled the car and my
boyfriend broke his leg. He never got up there, and after that, the idea of him
bringing me to my senses dissipated."

Another Straddler, Loretta Stec, had a similar problem with a blue-collar
lover left behind. Loretta, a slender thirty-nine-year-old English professor at
San Francisco State University with delicate features and brown hair, needed
to leave the commotion of drugs and friends' abortions and the repressed religious world of Perth Amboy, New Jersey, for the calm life of the mind offered
by Boston College. The only problem was Barry. When Loretta was seventeen, she and Barry, an older construction worker, would ride motorcycles
in toxic waste dumps. He was wild and fine—what every working-class girl
would want. But Loretta knew life had to get better than Perth Amboy, so she
went off to Boston. Barry and she still got together, though. They even worked
on the same taping crew at a construction site during the summer between
Loretta's freshman and sophomore years. But the differences between them
were growing. All the guys on the job—Barry included—thought it was weird
that Loretta would read the *New York Times* during lunch breaks. "What's with
that chick?" people asked.

By the time Loretta returned to Boston for her second year, she knew
she was in a far different place than Barry. The working class was not for her.

Hanging around with this guy and doing construction forever — it sounded awful. "I was upwardly mobile, and I was not going to work on a construction crew anymore," Loretta says. She tried to break it off, but Barry roared up I-95 in a borrowed car to change her mind. Loretta lived in an old Victorian with middle-class roommates who had never met anyone like Barry. When he showed up with a barking Doberman in tow, she recalled he was screaming like Stanley Kowalski in *A Streetcar Named Desire* that he wanted Loretta back. The women became terrified. Loretta was able to calm first Barry, then her roommates. Afterward, the couple went to listen to some music. In a little place on campus, a guitar trio started performing a Rolling Stones song. Suddenly, Barry turned to Loretta and began scream-singing about wild horses not being able to drag him from her, really loud, trying to get her to see his resolve. "People were wondering who was this guy, what's his deal?" Loretta says. "It pointed out the clash between my new world and the old. You don't do stuff like that. It was embarrassing, upsetting, and confusing. I didn't want to hurt him. But I knew it wasn't going to work for me." They walked around campus, fighting about things coming to an end. At some point, she recalls, Barry noticed that a college student with a nicer car than his — Loretta can't remember exactly what it was — had parked behind his car, blocking him. Already ramped up, Barry had a fit and smashed a headlight of the fancy machine with a rock. There Loretta was, a hundred feet from her campus Victorian, newly ensconced in a clean world of erudition and scholarship, far from the violence and swamps of central Jersey. Her bad-boy beau, once so appealing, was raving and breathing hard, trying to pull her away from the books, back down the turnpike to the working class.

"That was really the end of it," Loretta says. "I couldn't have a guy around who was going to act like that. He was wild and crazy and I was trying to make my way." Barry relented, and left Loretta alone. They lost touch, and Loretta later learned that Barry had died, the cause of death unknown to her. It was such a shock.

READING THE TEXT

1. What is your response to Lubrano's title, and why do you think he chose it for his essay?
2. Summarize in your own words the difference between Lubrano's high school and college experiences.
3. What does Richard Rodriguez mean by saying, "There's a brutality to education" (para. 6)?
4. Why did Lubrano avoid discussing his Columbia University experiences with his family?
5. How does child rearing differ in blue-collar and in middle-class families, in Lubrano's view? What evidence does he advance to support his claims?

READING THE SIGNS

1. In your journal, reflect on the effects — positive or negative — that attending college may have had on your relationship with your family and high school friends. How do you account for any changes that may have occurred?

2. In an argumentative essay, support, challenge, or complicate Gregg Andrews's statement that "every bit of learning takes you further from your parents" (para. 1).

3. Write a synthesis of the personal tales of Lubrano, Loretta Stec, and Rita Giordano. Then use your synthesis as the basis of an essay in which you explain how their collective experiences combine to demonstrate Lubrano's position that "for many class travelers with passports stamped for new territory, the trip is nothing less than a bridge burning" (para. 2).

4. Interview students from both blue-collar and middle- or upper-class backgrounds about the effect that attending college has had on their relationship with their family and high school friends. Use your findings to support your assessment of Lubrano's position that college can create divisions between blue-collar students and their families but that it tends not to have that effect on other classes.

5. Analyze Lubrano's use of evidence and quotations. Who is quoted directly? Who is quoted indirectly? What sources and experts are consulted? Use your observations for support in an argumentative essay in which you analyze what Lubrano's article implies about expertise and authority.

MICHAEL OMI

In Living Color: Race and American Culture

Though many like to think that racism in America is a thing of the past, Michael Omi argues that racism is a pervasive feature in our lives, one that is both overt and inferential. Using race as a sign by which we judge a person's character, inferential racism invokes deep-rooted stereotypes, and as Omi shows in his survey of American film, television, and music, our popular culture is hardly immune from such stereotyping. Indeed, when ostensibly "progressive" programs like *Saturday Night Live* can win the National Ethnic Coalition of Organizations' "Platinum Pit Award" for racist stereotyping in television, and shock jocks such as Howard Stern command big audiences and salaries, one can see popular culture has a way to go before it becomes color-blind. The author of *Racial Formation in the United States: From the 1960s to the 1990s* (with Howard Winant, 1986, 1994), Michael Omi is a professor of comparative ethnic studies at the University of California, Berkeley.

In February 1987, Assistant Attorney General William Bradford Reynolds, the nation's chief civil rights enforcer, declared that the recent death of a black man in Howard Beach, New York, and the Ku Klux Klan attack on civil rights marchers in Forsyth County, Georgia, were "isolated" racial incidences. He emphasized that the places where racial conflict could potentially flare up were "far fewer now than ever before in our history," and concluded that such a diminishment of racism stood as "a powerful testament to how far we have come in the civil rights struggle."[1]

Events in the months following his remarks raise the question as to whether we have come quite so far. They suggest that dramatic instances of racial tension and violence merely constitute the surface manifestations of a deeper racial organization of American society — a system of inequality which has shaped, and in turn been shaped by, our popular culture.

In March, the NAACP released a report on blacks in the record industry entitled "The Discordant Sound of Music." It found that despite the revenues generated by black performers, blacks remain "grossly underrepresented" in the business, marketing, and A&R (Artists and Repertoire) departments of major record labels. In addition, few blacks are employed as managers, agents, concert promoters, distributors, and retailers. The report concluded that:

> The record industry is overwhelmingly segregated and discrimination is rampant. No other industry in America so openly classifies its operations on a racial basis. At every level of the industry, beginning with the separation of black artists into a special category, barriers exist that severely limit opportunities for blacks.[2]

Decades after the passage of civil rights legislation and the affirmation of the principle of "equal opportunity," patterns of racial segregation and exclusion, it seems, continue to characterize the production of popular music.

The enduring logic of Jim Crow is also present in professional sports. In April, Al Campanis, vice president of player personnel for the Los Angeles Dodgers, explained to Ted Koppel on ABC's *Nightline* about the paucity of blacks in baseball front offices and as managers. "I truly believe," Campanis said, "that [blacks] may not have some of the necessities to be, let's say, a field manager or perhaps a general manager." When pressed for a reason, Campanis offered an explanation which had little to do with the structure of opportunity or institutional discrimination within professional sports:

> [W]hy are black men or black people not good swimmers? Because they don't have the buoyancy. . . . They are gifted with great musculature and various other things. They're fleet of foot. And this is why there are a lot

---

[1]Reynolds's remarks were made at a conference on equal opportunity held by the Bar association in Orlando, Florida. *The San Francisco Chronicle* (February 7, 1987). Print.

[2]Economic Development Department of the NAACP, "The Discordant Sound of Music (A Report on the Record Industry)," (Baltimore, Maryland: The NAACP, 1987), pp. 16–17. Print.

of black major league ballplayers. Now as far as having the background to become club presidents, or presidents of a bank, I don't know.[3]

Black exclusion from the front office, therefore, was justified on the basis of biological "difference."

The issue of race, of course, is not confined to the institutional arrangements [5] of popular culture production. Since popular culture deals with the symbolic realm of social life, the images which it creates, represents, and disseminates contribute to the overall racial climate. They become the subject of analysis and political scrutiny. In August, the National Ethnic Coalition of Organizations bestowed the "Golden Pit Awards" on television programs, commercials, and movies that were deemed offensive to racial and ethnic groups. *Saturday Night Live*, regarded by many media critics as a politically "progressive" show, was singled out for the "Platinum Pit Award" for its comedy skit "Ching Chang," which depicted a Chinese storeowner and his family in a derogatory manner.[4]

These examples highlight the *overt* manifestations of racism in popular culture — institutional forms of discrimination which keep racial minorities out of the production and organization of popular culture, and the crude racial caricatures by which these groups are portrayed. Yet racism in popular culture is often conveyed in a variety of implicit, and at times invisible, ways. Political theorist Stuart Hall makes an important distinction between *overt* racism, the elaboration of an explicitly racist argument, policy, or view, and *inferential* racism, which refers to "those apparently naturalized representations of events and situations relating to race, whether 'factual' or 'fictional,' which have racist premises and propositions inscribed in them as a set of *unquestioned assumptions*." He argues that inferential racism is more widespread, common, and indeed insidious since "it is largely *invisible* even to those who formulate the world in its terms."[5]

Race itself is a slippery social concept which is paradoxically both "obvious" and "invisible." In our society, one of the first things we notice about people when we encounter them (along with their sex/gender) is their *race*. We utilize race to provide clues about *who* a person is and *how* we should relate to her/him. Our perception of race determines our "presentation of *self*," distinctions in status, and appropriate modes of conduct in daily and institutional life. This process is often unconscious; we tend to operate off of an unexamined set of *racial beliefs*.

[3]Campanis's remarks on *Nightline* were reprinted in *The San Francisco Chronicle* (April 9, 1987). Print.

[4]Ellen Wulfhorst, "TV Stereotyping: It's the 'Pits,'" *The San Francisco Chronicle* (August 24, 1987). Print.

[5]Stuart Hall, "The Whites of Their Eyes: Racist Ideologies and the Media," in George Bridges and Rosalind Brunt, eds., *Silver Linings* (London: Lawrence and Wishart, 1981), pp. 36–37. Print.

Racial beliefs account for and explain variations in "human nature." Differences in skin color and other obvious physical characteristics supposedly provide visible clues to more substantive differences lurking underneath. Among other qualities, temperament, sexuality, intelligence, and artistic and athletic ability are presumed to be fixed and discernible from the palpable mark of race. Such diverse questions as our confidence and trust in others (as salespeople, neighbors, media figures); our sexual preferences and romantic images; our tastes in music, film, dance, or sports; indeed our very ways of walking and talking are ineluctably shaped by notions of race.

Ideas about race, therefore, have become "common sense"—a way of comprehending, explaining, and acting in the world. This is made painfully obvious when someone disrupts our common sense understandings. An encounter with someone who is, for example, racially "mixed" or of a racial/ethnic group we are unfamiliar with becomes a source of discomfort for us, and momentarily creates a crisis of racial meaning. We also become disoriented when people do not act "black," "Latino," or indeed "white." The content of such stereotypes reveals a series of unsubstantiated beliefs about who these groups are, what they are like, and how they behave.

The existence of such racial consciousness should hardly be surprising. 10 Even prior to the inception of the republic, the United States was a society shaped by racial conflict. The establishment of the Southern plantation economy, Western expansion, and the emergence of the labor movement, among other significant historical developments, have all involved conflicts over the definition and nature of the *color line*. The historical results have been distinct and different groups have encountered unique forms of racial oppression—Native Americans faced genocide, blacks were subjected to slavery, Mexicans were invaded and colonized, and Asians faced exclusion. What is common to the experiences of these groups is that their particular "fate" was linked to historically specific ideas about the significance and meaning of race.[6] Whites defined them as separate "species," ones inferior to Northern European cultural stocks, and thereby rationalized the conditions of their subordination in the economy, in political life, and in the realm of culture.

A crucial dimension of racial oppression in the United States is the elaboration of an ideology of difference or "otherness." This involves defining "us" (i.e., white Americans) in opposition to "them," an important task when distinct racial groups are first encountered, or in historically specific periods where preexisting racial boundaries are threatened or crumbling.

Political struggles over the very definition of who an "American" is illustrate this process. The Naturalization Law of 1790 declared that only free *white* immigrants could qualify, reflecting the initial desire among Congress to create and maintain a racially homogeneous society. The extension of

[6]For an excellent survey of racial beliefs see Thomas F. Gossett, *Race: The History of an Idea in America* (New York: Shocken, 1965). Print.

eligibility to all racial groups has been a long and protracted process. Japanese, for example, were finally eligible to become naturalized citizens after the passage of the Walter-McCarran Act of 1952. The ideological residue of these restrictions in naturalization and citizenship laws is the equation within popular parlance of the term "American" with "white," while other "Americans" are described as black, Mexican, "Oriental," etc.

Popular culture has been an important realm within which racial ideologies have been created, reproduced, and sustained. Such ideologies provide a framework of symbols, concepts, and images through which we understand, interpret, and represent aspects of our "racial" existence.

Race has often formed the central themes of American popular culture. Historian W. L. Rose notes that it is a "curious coincidence" that four of the "most popular reading-viewing events in all American history" have in some manner dealt with race, specifically black/white relations in the south.[7] Harriet Beecher Stowe's *Uncle Tom's Cabin*, Thomas Ryan Dixon's *The Clansman* (the inspiration for D. W. Griffith's *The Birth of a Nation*), Margaret Mitchell's *Gone with the Wind* (as a book and film), and Alex Haley's *Roots* (as a book and television miniseries) each appeared at a critical juncture in American race relations and helped to shape new understandings of race.

Emerging social definitions of race and the "real American" were reflected in American popular culture of the nineteenth century. Racial and ethnic stereotypes were shaped and reinforced in the newspapers, magazines, and pulp fiction of the period. But the evolution and ever-increasing sophistication of visual mass communications throughout the twentieth century provided, and continue to provide, the most dramatic means by which racial images are generated and reproduced. 15

Film and television have been notorious in disseminating images of racial minorities which establish for audiences what these groups look like, how they behave, and, in essence, "who they are." The power of the media lies not only in their ability to reflect the dominant racial ideology, but in their capacity to shape that ideology in the first place. D. W. Griffith's aforementioned epic *Birth of a Nation*, a sympathetic treatment of the rise of the Ku Klux Klan during Reconstruction, helped to generate, consolidate, and "nationalize" images of blacks which had been more disparate (more regionally specific, for example) prior to the film's appearance.[8]

In television and film, the necessity to define characters in the briefest and most condensed manner has led to the perpetuation of racial caricatures, as racial stereotypes serve as shorthand for scriptwriters, directors, and actors. Television's tendency to address the "lowest common denominator" in order

---

[7]W. L. Rose, *Race and Religion in American Historical Fiction: Four Episodes in Popular Culture* (Oxford: Clarendon, 1979). Print.

[8]Melanie Martindale-Sikes, "Nationalizing 'Nigger' Imagery through *Birth of a Nation*," paper prepared for the 73rd Annual Meeting of the American Sociological Association (September 4–8, 1978) in San Francisco.

to render programs "familiar" to an enormous and diverse audience leads it regularly to assign and reassign racial characteristics to particular groups, both minority and majority.

Many of the earliest American films deal with racial and ethnic "difference." The large influx of "new immigrants" at the turn of the century led to a proliferation of negative images of Jews, Italians, and Irish which were assimilated and adapted by such films as Thomas Edison's *Cohen's Advertising Scheme* (1904). Based on an old vaudeville routine, the film featured a scheming Jewish merchant, aggressively hawking his wares. Though stereotypes of these groups persist to this day,[9] by the 1940s many of the earlier ethnic stereotypes had disappeared from Hollywood. But, as historian Michael Winston observes, the "outsiders" of the 1890s remained: "the ever-popular Indian of the Westerns; the inscrutable or sinister Oriental; the sly, but colorful Mexican; and the clowning or submissive Negro."[10]

In many respects the "Western" as a genre has been paradigmatic in establishing images of racial minorities in film and television. The classic scenario involves the encircled wagon train or surrounded fort from which whites bravely fight off fierce bands of Native American Indians. The point of reference and viewer identification lies with those huddled within the circle — the representatives of "civilization" who valiantly attempt to ward off the forces of barbarism. In the classic Western, as writer Tom Engelhardt observes, "the viewer is forced behind the barrel of a repeating rifle and it is from that position, through its gun sights, that he receives a picture history of Western colonialism and imperialism."[11]

Westerns have indeed become the prototype for European and American [20] excursions throughout the Third World. The cast of characters may change, but the story remains the same. The "humanity" of whites is contrasted with the brutality and treachery of nonwhites; brave (i.e., white) souls are pitted against the merciless hordes in conflicts ranging from Indians against the British Lancers to Zulus against the Boers. What Stuart Hall refers to as the imperializing "white eye" provides the framework for these films, lurking outside the frame and yet seeing and positioning everything within; it is "the unmarked position from which . . . 'observations' are made and from which, alone, they make sense."[12]

Our "common sense" assumptions about race and racial minorities in the United States are both generated and reflected in the stereotypes presented

[9]For a discussion of Italian, Irish, Jewish, Slavic, and German stereotypes in film, see Randall M. Miller, ed., *The Kaleidoscopic Lens: How Hollywood Views Ethnic Groups* (Englewood, N.J.: Jerome S. Ozer, 1980). Print.

[10]Michael R. Winston, "Racial Consciousness and the Evolution of Mass Communications in the United States," *Daedalus*, vol. III, No. 4 (Fall 1982). Print.

[11]Tom Engelhardt, "Ambush at Kamikaze Pass," in Emma Gee, ed., *Counterpoint: Perspectives on Asian America* (Los Angeles: Asian American Studies Center, UCLA, 1976), p. 270. Print.

[12]Hall, "Whites of Their Eyes," p. 38. Print.

by the visual media. In the crudest sense, it could be said that such stereotypes underscore white "superiority" by reinforcing the traits, habits, and predispositions of nonwhites which demonstrate their "inferiority." Yet a more careful assessment of racial stereotypes reveals intriguing trends and seemingly contradictory themes.

While all racial minorities have been portrayed as "less than human," there are significant differences in the images of different groups. Specific racial minority groups, in spite of their often interchangeable presence in films steeped in the "Western" paradigm, have distinct and often unique qualities assigned to them. Latinos are portrayed as being prone toward violent outbursts of anger; blacks as physically strong, but dim-witted; while Asians are seen as sneaky and cunningly evil. Such differences are crucial to observe and analyze. Race in the United States is not reducible to black/white relations. These differences are significant for a broader understanding of the patterns of race in America, and the unique experience of specific racial minority groups.

It is somewhat ironic that *real* differences which exist within a racially defined minority group are minimized, distorted, or obliterated by the media. "All Asians look alike," the saying goes, and indeed there has been little or no attention given to the vast differences which exist between, say, the Chinese and Japanese with respect to food, dress, language, and culture. This blurring within popular culture has given us supposedly Chinese characters who wear kimonos; it is also the reason why the fast-food restaurant McDonald's can offer "Shanghai McNuggets" with teriyaki sauce. Other groups suffer a similar fate. Professor Gretchen Bataille and Charles Silet find the cinematic Native American of the Northeast wearing the clothing of the Plains Indians, while living in the dwellings of Southwestern tribes:

> The movie men did what thousands of years of social evolution could not do, even what the threat of the encroaching white man could not do; Hollywood produced the homogenized Native American, devoid of tribal characteristics or regional differences.[13]

The need to paint in broad racial strokes has thus rendered "internal" differences invisible. This has been exacerbated by the tendency for screenwriters to "invent" mythical Asian, Latin American, and African countries. Ostensibly done to avoid offending particular nations and peoples, such a subterfuge reinforces the notion that all the countries and cultures of a specific region are the same. European countries retain their distinctiveness, while the Third World is presented as one homogeneous mass riddled with poverty and governed by ruthless and corrupt regimes.

While rendering specific groups in a monolithic fashion, the popular cultural imagination simultaneously reveals a compelling need to distinguish

---

[13]Gretchen Bataille and Charles Silet, "The Entertaining Anachronism: Indians in American Film," in Randall M. Miller, ed., *Kaleidoscopic Lens*, p. 40. Print.

and articulate "bad" and "good" variants of particular racial groups and individuals. Thus each stereotypic image is filled with contradictions: The blood-
thirsty Indian is tempered with the image of the noble savage; the *bandido*
exists along with the loyal sidekick; and Fu Manchu is offset by Charlie Chan.
The existence of such contradictions, however, does not negate the one-
dimensionality of these images, nor does it challenge the explicit subservient
role of racial minorities. Even the "good" person of color usually exists as a
foil in novels and films to underscore the intelligence, courage, and virility of
the white male hero.

Another important, perhaps central, dimension of racial minority stereo- 25
types is sex/gender differentiation. The connection between race and sex has
traditionally been an explosive and controversial one. For most of American
history, sexual and marital relations between whites and nonwhites were
forbidden by social custom and by legal restrictions. It was not until 1967,
for example, that the U.S. Supreme Court ruled that antimiscegenation laws
were unconstitutional. Beginning in the 1920s, the notorious Hays Office, Hollywood's attempt at self-censorship, prohibited scenes and subjects which
dealt with miscegenation. The prohibition, however, was not evenly applied in
practice. White men could seduce racial minority women, but white women
were not to be romantically or sexually linked to racial minority men.

Women of color were sometimes treated as exotic sex objects. The sultry Latin temptress — such as Dolores Del Rio and Lupe Velez — invariably
had boyfriends who were white North Americans; their Latino suitors were
portrayed as being unable to keep up with the Anglo-American competition.
From Mary Pickford as Cho-Cho San in *Madame Butterfly* (1915) to Nancy
Kwan in *The World of Suzie Wong* (1961), Asian women have often been seen
as the gracious "geisha girl" or the prostitute with a "heart of gold," willing to
do anything to please her man.

By contrast, Asian men, whether cast in the role of villain, servant, sidekick, or kung fu master, are seen as asexual or, at least, romantically undesirable. As Asian American studies professor Elaine Kim notes, even a hero such
as Bruce Lee played characters whose "single-minded focus on perfecting his
fighting skills precludes all other interests, including an interest in women,
friendship, or a social life."[14]

The shifting trajectory of black images over time reveals an interesting
dynamic with respect to sex and gender. The black male characters in *The
Birth of a Nation* were clearly presented as sexual threats to "white womanhood." For decades afterward, however, Hollywood consciously avoided portraying black men as assertive or sexually aggressive in order to minimize
controversy. Black men were instead cast as comic, harmless, and nonthreatening figures exemplified by such stars as Bill "Bojangles" Robinson, Stepin
Fetchit, and Eddie "Rochester" Anderson. Black women, by contrast, were

[14]Elaine Kim, "Asian Americans and American Popular Culture," in Hyung-Chan Kim, ed.,
Dictionary of Asian American History (New York: Greenwood, 1986), p. 107. Print.

divided into two broad character types based on color categories. Dark black women such as Hattie McDaniel and Louise Beavers were cast as "dowdy, frumpy, dumpy, overweight mammy figures"; while those "close to the white ideal," such as Lena Horne and Dorothy Dandridge, became "Hollywood's treasured mulattoes" in roles emphasizing the tragedy of being of mixed blood.[15]

It was not until the early 1970s that tough, aggressive, sexually assertive black characters, both male and female, appeared. The "blaxploitation" films of the period provided new heroes (e.g., *Shaft*, *Superfly*, *Coffy*, and *Cleopatra Jones*) in sharp contrast to the submissive and subservient images of the past. Unfortunately, most of these films were shoddy productions which did little to create more enduring "positive" images of blacks, either male or female.

In contemporary television and film, there is a tendency to present and equate racial minority groups and individuals with specific social problems. Blacks are associated with drugs and urban crime, Latinos with "illegal" immigration, while Native Americans cope with alcoholism and tribal conflicts. Rarely do we see racial minorities "out of character," in situations removed from the stereotypic arenas in which scriptwriters have traditionally embedded them. Nearly the only time we see young Asians and Latinos of either sex, for example, is when they are members of youth gangs, as *Boulevard Nights* (1979), *Year of the Dragon* (1985), and countless TV cop shows can attest to. 30

Racial minority actors have continually bemoaned the fact that the roles assigned them on stage and screen are often one-dimensional and imbued with stereotypic assumptions. In theater, the movement toward "blind casting" (i.e., casting actors for roles without regard to race) is a progressive step, but it remains to be seen whether large numbers of audiences can suspend their "beliefs" and deal with a Latino King Lear or an Asian Stanley Kowalski. By contrast, white actors are allowed to play anybody. Though the use of white actors to play blacks in "black face" is clearly unacceptable in the contemporary period, white actors continue to portray Asian, Latino, and Native American characters on stage and screen.

Scores of Charlie Chan films, for example, have been made with white leads (the last one was the 1981 *Charlie Chan and the Curse of the Dragon Queen*). Roland Winters, who played Chan in six features, was once asked to explain the logic of casting a white man in the role of Charlie Chan: "The only thing I can think of is, if you want to cast a homosexual in a show, and you get a homosexual, it'll be awful. It won't be funny . . . and maybe there's something there."[16]

Such a comment reveals an interesting aspect about myth and reality in popular culture. Michael Winston argues that stereotypic images in the visual media were not originally conceived as representations of reality, nor were they initially understood to be "real" by audiences. They were, he suggests,

[15]Donald Bogle, "A Familiar Plot (A Look at the History of Blacks in American Movies)," *The Crisis*, Vol. 90, No. 1 (January 1983), p. 15. Print.

[16]Frank Chin, "Confessions of the Chinatown Cowboy," *Bulletin of Concerned Asian Scholars*, Vol. 4, No. 3 (Fall 1972). Print.

ways of "coding and rationalizing" the racial hierarchy and interracial behavior. Over time, however, "a complex interactive relationship between myth and reality developed, so that images originally understood to be unreal, through constant repetition began to *seem* real."[17]

Such a process consolidated, among other things, our "common sense" understandings of what we think various groups should look like. Such presumptions have led to tragicomical results. Latinos auditioning for a role in a television soap opera, for example, did not fit the Hollywood image of "real Mexicans" and had their faces bronzed with powder before filming because they looked too white. Model Aurora Garza said, "I'm a real Mexican and very dark anyway. I'm even darker right now because I have a tan. But they kept wanting to make my face darker and darker."[18]

Historically in Hollywood, the fact of having "dark skin" made an actor or   35
actress potentially adaptable for numerous "racial" roles. Actress Lupe Velez once commented that she had portrayed "Chinese, Eskimos, Japs, squaws, Hindus, Swedes, Malays, and Japanese."[19] Dorothy Dandridge, who was the first black woman teamed romantically with white actors, presented a quandary for studio executives who weren't sure what race and nationality to make her. They debated whether she should be a "foreigner," an island girl, or a West Indian.[20] Ironically, what they refused to entertain as a possibility was to present her as what she really was, a black American woman.

The importance of race in popular culture is not restricted to the visual media. In popular music, race and race consciousness have defined, and continue to define, formats, musical communities, and tastes. In the mid-1950s, the secretary of the North Alabama White Citizens Council declared that "Rock and roll is a means of pulling the white man down to the level of the Negro."[21] While rock may no longer be popularly regarded as a racially subversive musical form, the very genres of contemporary popular music remain, in essence, thinly veiled racial categories. "R & B" (Rhythm and Blues) and "soul" music are clearly references to *black* music, while Country & Western or heavy metal music are viewed, in the popular imagination, as *white* music. Black performers who want to break out of this artistic ghettoization must "cross over," a contemporary form of "passing" in which their music is seen as acceptable to white audiences.

The airwaves themselves are segregated. The designation "urban contemporary" is merely radio lingo for a "black" musical format. Such categorization affects playlists, advertising accounts, and shares of the listening market. On cable television, black music videos rarely receive airplay on MTV, but are

[17]Winston, "Racial Consciousness," p. 176. Print.

[18]*The San Francisco Chronicle* (September 21, 1984). Print.

[19]Quoted in Allen L. Woll, "Bandits and Lovers: Hispanic Images in American Film," in Miller, ed., *Kaleidoscopic Lens*, p. 60. Print.

[20]Bogle, "Familiar Plot," p. 17.

[21]Dave Marsh and Kevin Stein, *The Book of Rock Lists* (New York: Dell, 1981), p. 8. Print.

confined instead to the more marginal BET (Black Entertainment Television) network.

In spite of such segregation, many performing artists have been able to garner a racially diverse group of fans. And yet, racially integrated concert audiences are extremely rare. Curiously, this "perverse phenomenon" of racially homogeneous crowds takes place despite the color of the performer. Lionel Richie's concert audiences, for example, are virtually all-white, while Teena Marie's are all-black.[22]

Racial symbols and images are omnipresent in popular culture. Commonplace household objects such as cookie jars, salt and pepper shakers, and ashtrays have frequently been designed and fashioned in the form of racial caricatures. Sociologist Steve Dublin in an analysis of these objects found that former tasks of domestic service were symbolically transferred onto these commodities.[23] An Aunt Jemima–type character, for example, is used to hold a roll of paper towels, her outstretched hands supporting the item to be dispensed. "Sprinkle Plenty," a sprinkle bottle in the shape of an Asian man, was used to wet clothes in preparation for ironing. Simple commodities, the household implements which help us perform everyday tasks, may reveal, therefore, a deep structure of racial meaning.

A crucial dimension for discerning the meaning of particular stereotypes and images is the *situation context* for the creation and consumption of popular culture. For example, the setting in which "racist" jokes are told determines the function of humor. Jokes about blacks where the teller and audience are black constitute a form of self-awareness; they allow blacks to cope and "take the edge off" of oppressive aspects of the social order which they commonly confront. The meaning of these same jokes, however, is dramatically transformed when told across the "color line." If a white, or even black, person tells these jokes to a white audience, it will, despite its "purely" humorous intent, serve to reinforce stereotypes and rationalize the existing relations of racial inequality. 40

Concepts of race and racial images are both overt and implicit within popular culture — the organization of cultural production, the products themselves, and the manner in which they are consumed are deeply structured by race. Particular racial meanings, stereotypes, and myths can change, but the presence of a *system* of racial meanings and stereotypes, of racial ideology, seems to be an enduring aspect of American popular culture.

The era of Reaganism and the overall rightward drift of American politics and culture has added a new twist to the question of racial images and meanings. Increasingly, the problem for racial minorities is not that of misportrayal, but of "invisibility." Instead of celebrating racial and cultural diversity, we

[22]*Rock & Roll Confidential*, No. 44 (February 1987), p. 2. Print.
[23]Steven C. Dublin, "Symbolic Slavery: Black Representations in Popular Culture," *Social Problems*, Vol. 34, No. 2 (April 1987). Print.

are witnessing an attempt by the right to define, once again, who the "real" American is, and what "correct" American values, mores, and political beliefs are. In such a context, racial minorities are no longer the focus of sustained media attention; when they do appear, they are cast as colored versions of essentially "white" characters.

The possibilities for change — for transforming racial stereotypes and challenging institutional inequities — nonetheless exist. Historically, strategies have involved the mobilization of political pressure against an offending institution(s). In the late 1950s, for instance, "Nigger Hair" tobacco changed its name to "Bigger Hare" due to concerted NAACP pressure on the manufacturer. In the early 1970s, Asian American community groups successfully fought NBC's attempt to resurrect Charlie Chan as a television series with white actor Ross Martin. Amidst the furor generated by Al Campanis's remarks cited at the beginning of this essay, Jesse Jackson suggested that a boycott of major league games be initiated in order to push for a restructuring of hiring and promotion practices.

Partially in response to such action, Baseball Commissioner Peter Ueberroth announced plans in June 1987 to help put more racial minorities in management roles. "The challenge we have," Ueberroth said, "is to manage change without losing tradition."[24] The problem with respect to the issue of race and popular culture, however, is that the *tradition* itself may need to be thoroughly examined, its "common sense" assumptions unearthed and challenged, and its racial images contested and transformed.

READING THE TEXT

1. Describe in your own words the difference between "overt racism" and "inferential racism" (para. 6).
2. Why, according to Omi, is popular culture so powerful in shaping America's attitudes toward race?
3. What relationship does Omi see between gender and racial stereotypes?
4. How did race relations change in America during the 1980s, in Omi's view?

READING THE SIGNS

1. In class, brainstorm stereotypes, both positive and negative, attributed to specific racial groups. Then discuss the possible sources of these stereotypes. In what ways have they been perpetuated in popular culture, including film, TV, advertising, music, and consumer products? What does your discussion reveal about popular culture's influence on our most basic ways of seeing the world?
2. **CONNECTING TEXTS**   Using Omi's essay as your critical framework, write an essay in which you explore how the film *12 Years a Slave* (2013) may reflect or

[24]*The San Francisco Chronicle* (June 13, 1987). Print.

redefine American attitudes toward racial identity and race relations. Alternatively, watch *Malcolm X*, *Mi Familia*, or another film that addresses race relations.

3. Study an issue of a magazine targeted to a specific ethnic readership, such as *Essence*, *Ebony*, *Latina*, *or Jade*, analyzing both its articles and advertising. Then write an essay in which you explore the extent to which the magazine accurately reflects that ethnicity or, in Omi's words, appeals to readers as "colored versions of essentially 'white' characters" (para. 42).

4. Omi claims that "in contemporary television and film, there is a tendency to present and equate racial minority groups and individuals with specific social problems" (para. 30). In class, brainstorm films and TV shows that have characters that are ethnic minorities; pick one example and watch it. Does Omi's claim apply to that example, or does it demonstrate different patterns of racial representation?

5. Watch the film *Avatar*, and then, using Omi's categories of "overt" and "inferential" racism, write your own analysis of the race relations in this movie.

DANI McCLAIN

Being "Masculine of Center" While Black

The U.S. Census form asks questions about your race and gender, but it presumes that such questions (especially with respect to sex) invite straightforward either/or answers. But what if you are a black female whose gender expression is "masculine of center": that is, male in manner and dress? This is the identity situation that Dani McClain investigates in this report, interviewing women whose masculine-of-center identities lead to hostility and even threats toward them in a world where "black or white" and "male or female" are the norm, with little space for the queer space between. Dani McClain is a fellow with the Nation Institute and a writer for such publications as the *Miami Herald*, *The Root*, *AlterNet*, and *On the Issues*.

The weekend after the George Zimmerman verdict came down, Erica Woodland of Oakland stayed close to home. She could identify with the righteous anger expressed at the protests. But rather than join in, she canceled plans with family, postponed a trip to the laundromat and limited outings to work and the grocery store. "I decided for my own safety, I need to stay in the house," Woodland recalls. "I knew I could be putting myself at risk for anything."

The possibility of being targeted by police or by a fearful, overzealous civilian on account of her race was one consideration for Woodland, who is black. But so was gender. She describes herself as masculine of center, which means that her way of expressing herself—clothes, mannerisms—falls toward that side of the spectrum. It also means that like many of the black men and boys at the center of the recent conversation advanced by everyone from President Obama to Questlove, she's been profiled as criminal or suspicious. "We walk through the world and some of us pass as male," Woodland, 33, says. "We get left out of this conversation."

Somewhere at the intersection of blackness, gender expression and sexual orientation is a heightened risk for harassment and bias-driven violence. According to National Coalition of Anti-Violence Program's 2012 report on hate violence, LGBTQ people of color are nearly twice as likely as their white counterparts to experience physical violence. Last year, nearly three-fourths of anti-LGBTQ homicide victims were people of color and just over half were black.

People who are perceived as feminine—including femme lesbians and trans women—are certainly at risk, as the case of CeCe McDonald brought to national attention last year. But trans men and masculine of center women experience discrimination and harassment in ways that often map more clearly to mainstream narratives about black men. Chai Jindasurat, co-director of organizing and advocacy at the New York City Anti-Violence Project, says this shows up most clearly in the context of police interactions. "They're stopped, searched and arrested, and sometimes they experience police violence as a result of that," says Jindasurat, whose organization is part of a New York City coalition working to address this problem. "It's a combination of both identities that contribute to that disproportionate impact of violence."

Police can be a threat, but more often aggression comes from strangers 5 in public places. In situations where an offender is unknown, nearly three-fourths of assailants are strangers, followed by police at 24 percent, according to the Anti-Violence Project report. Morgan Willis says she's been confronted by random aggressors at bars, in subway cars and on sidewalks. But there's one demographic she tries her best to steer clear of in public spaces: white, intoxicated men in groups. "It's a group of the most powerful people in the world who are not in their right mind and who feel empowered to do whatever they want," says Willis, 29. "Not only do I have to be extremely cautious with my safety; I end up feeling like if for some reason whatever happens escalates to violence, I'm going to get in trouble."

Willis lives in Detroit and works with a collective of masculine of center people called Bklyn Boihood. She said experience has led her to believe that any official first responder or bystander would side with her attackers or otherwise fail to support her safety or version of events. "They're going to be the ones that walk away and I'm going to have to start a campaign online to get people to acknowledge that something actually happened."

Something along those lines unfolded in Oakland five days after the Zimmerman verdict was announced. Veteran community organizer Malkia Cyril says she was verbally and physically attacked outside a downtown bar after she accidentally backed her car into a parked motorcycle. That bar had had its windows smashed by protestors responding to the verdict earlier in the week, and tensions in the neighborhood were high. None of which excuses what unfolded after Cyril got out of her car to assess the damage.

One of the bar's employees, a white man named Issa Eismont, admits he called her a "bitch" and stood in front of her car door, blocking her from being able to reenter. After hearing the crash, he approached the scene and thought she was trying to flee the scene, he said. Cyril says she was also called a "dyke" and "stupid" by bystanders in the crowd that gathered, many of whom were white and male, according to Cyril and another witness. Cyril says a black male employee of the bar pushed and restrained her. Of her version of events, that employee — who was off-duty at the time and would only give his first name as Marcus — told me a week later, "I'm not going to dispute anything. I kind of forgot about what happened."

But Cyril hasn't, and she has ideas about why a simple auto accident escalated so quickly to insults and physical aggression. "They were reading me as a butch. They were reading me as a black woman. They were reading me as a masculine woman," Cyril, 39, says. "The combination of those things is why they felt they could be so physical toward me."

She eventually exchanged insurance information with the bike's owner 10 and continued on to her original destination — a panel on media portrayals of black masculinity. And later that night, she shared her account of what happened with her more than 3,000 Facebook friends and named the bar in question. By the next day, the bar's owner issued a public apology on its own Facebook page and Eismont had reached out to Cyril to apologize.

This kind of online organizing around individual incidents matters, and so do more systemic efforts to shift perceptions and institutions. Jindasurat of the Anti-Violence Project mentions a public awareness campaign run out of the Washington, DC, Office of Human Rights and a legislative campaign advanced by New York City's Communities United for Police Reform as bright spots.

But two groups doing some of the most innovative work in the country with trans men and masculine of center women of color are actually focused inward rather than on advocacy. Willis, of Bklyn Boihood, says that collective is more interested in building community than in confronting head-on the harassment and violence that many in her community consistently face. "If this happens 100 times, I don't have the energy to articulate and to make this call to arms and action 100 times," Willis says. "A lot of times it doesn't feel valuable to take to task something that's happening all the time everywhere." Woodland, who is field building director at an Oakland-based national organization called Brown Boi Project, expresses a similar belief that her energy is better spent shifting the culture of privilege within masculine of center communities of color than on challenging the broader culture. Still, she acknowledges that someone needs to organize in response to the violence, the threats and the humiliations.

"Because we are always responding to events, we don't have any healing going on," Woodland says. "How do we reframe the conversation, first for ourselves?"

READING THE TEXT

1. Summarize in your own words what the term "masculine of center" means.
2. What does McClain mean by "mainstream narratives about black men" (para. 4)?
3. What experiences do black women who appear male have in the black community, as McClain describes them?
4. Why do some members of the masculine of center community devote their energies to in-group politics rather than engaging with mainstream America?

READING THE SIGNS

1. In an essay, evaluate the term "masculine of center." To what extent does it adequately describe the women profiled in McClain's selection? If you think the term is inadequate, can you suggest and defend your own term?
2. **CONNECTING TEXTS**   As of this writing, Facebook has more than fifty categories for a user's gender identification. Study that list, and use it as a basis for an essay in which you explore the traditional binary distinction of male/female. Do you think the traditional distinction or Facebook's categories are more valid? How does Facebook's list complicate the traditional definitions of gender identity? To develop your ideas, consult Aaron's Devor's "Gender Role Behaviors and Attitudes" (p. 504) and Deborah Blum's "The Gender Blur: Where Does Biology End and Society Take Over?" (p. 511).
3. **CONNECTING TEXTS**   While discussing two rather different groups, both McClain and Mariah Burton Nelson (p. 524) describe the experiences of women who violate conventional norms surrounding gender identity. Drawing upon both selections, write an essay in which you analyze the experiences of both groups of women. If you find differences, how do you account for them? What reasons can you advance for the response to such women?
4. McClain says that "LGBTQ people of color are nearly twice as likely as their white counterparts to experience physical violence" (para. 3). Research the National Coalition of Anti-Violence Program's studies on the causes of such violence. Use your results as the basis of an essay that proposes your own argument about how gender and ethnic identities affect people's attitudes toward others.
5. Central to McClain's essay is the notion of "intersectionality," or the idea that race, gender, and sexuality considered together provide a clearer picture of particular needs and issues facing minority groups. Research this term, and write an essay in which you discuss why advocates might favor this model over others. Use examples from the essays in this chapter.

THERESA CELEBRAN JONES

Sanjay and Craig: *Nickelodeon's Hilarious New Mixed-Race Heroes*

With more and more Americans identifying as "mixed race," one might expect that television would be filled with mixed-race characters. But while that hasn't happened yet, Theresa Celebran Jones has been happy to find such Nickelodeon offerings as *Sanjay and Craig*, a children's program featuring an Anglo-Indian boy and his pet snake. In fact, Jones observes, if you are looking for progressive racial programming, preschool shows like *Sesame Street* and *Yo Gabba Gabba* are the best places to look, but avoid tween sitcoms. Theresa Celebran Jones is a columnist for *Hyphen: Asian America Unabridged*.

We need more mixed-race families and kids on television. Nickelodeon is leading the way.

Surely by now you've all heard about the Cheerios commercial featuring a biracial family that received a depressing amount of racist backlash. To refresh your memory, the ad was a pretty benign spot that merely featured a white mother, a black father, and a crazy adorable mixed girl talking about cereal. It was beloved by many, but ended up being a pretty decent barometer for the current state of race relations in America — and it was surprising only to the people who don't have to deal with race on a daily basis (namely white people).

Like it or not, mixed-race families are an ever-growing reality in America. Asian Americans have struggled for a long time (and we continue to struggle) to show there is a demand to see people like us on television, and the controversy over the Cheerios ad shows the fight for mixed-race families is just beginning. The controversy of the Cheerios ad (as well as its Streisand effect) demonstrated the potential for success when you simply show a good-looking mixed-race family on television. The backlash from the ad was disheartening to be sure, but then I discovered Nickelodeon's new show, *Sanjay and Craig*.

Let me first acknowledge that kids' television is generally a mixed bag when it comes to race. Shows for the preschool set (*Sesame Street*; *Yo Gabba Gabba*; *Ni Hao, Kai-Lan*; *Dora the Explorer*) are usually great at being inclusive and reflecting diversity, while, for some reason, tween sitcoms (*iCarly*, *Victorious*, *Jessie*) tend to be the worst offenders when it comes to perpetuating racist stereotypes. Cartoon shows for older kids lie somewhere in the middle, but seem to have the most creative leeway and therefore the most potential for debunking stereotypes.

Enter *Sanjay and Craig*. The show follows the hijinks of a boy (Sanjay) and   5
his best friend / talking pet snake (Craig). In the first episode, Sanjay and Craig
sneak into a hospital disguised as doctors to watch a butt transplant being
performed, and end up performing the butt transplant themselves. Not much
is made of Sanjay's background in the first episode, so I had to watch it twice
to make sure, but I'd picked up that Sanjay's father is Indian, his mother is
white, and she's a surgeon.

Naturally, my five-year-old thought the episode was hilarious, and the
show earned her stamp of approval. The hugeness of the mixed-race family
was entirely lost on her, which may speak to how well the show is written.

That being said, the show is really only groundbreaking in its featuring a
mixed-race family without making it A Big Deal, and is otherwise pretty standard kid fare, fairly indistinguishable from *Adventure Time* or *Regular Show*.
Watching the show gave me a similar feeling to watching *Better Luck Tomorrow* for the first time — it was simply refreshing to see POCs tell a normal
story without having to comment on race. I loved what I saw and I hope the
show continues on for multiple seasons, but I can't say it's the most original
show I've ever seen.

And I think it's important to note that the show's creators are white, and
while it would be nice to have more Asian American representation in all
parts of the production process, it does go to show that it's really not that difficult for white writers to create a normal damn television show that features
people of color that are three-dimensional characters and not just racist caricatures, or simply as vehicles for teaching white people lessons about race.

READING THE TEXT

1. Why do you think Jones says that white people "don't have to deal with race
    on a daily basis" (para. 2)?
2. What does Jones mean by the "Streisand effect" (para. 3)?
3. Jones comments that *Sanjay and Craig* features mixed-race characters "with-
    out making it A Big Deal" (para. 7). Why is this important, according to Jones?
4. Why does Jones find it significant that *Sanjay and Craig*'s creators are white?

READING THE SIGNS

1. Watch an episode or two of *Sanjay and Craig*. Relying on your observation
    of specific details of those episodes, write an essay in which you defend,
    oppose, or modify Jones's assumption that the program eschews typical eth-
    nic stereotypes and "features people of color that are three-dimensional char-
    acters and not just racist caricatures" (para. 8).
2. **CONNECTING TEXTS**   Read or reread Jessica Hagedorn's "Asian Women in Film:
    No Joy, No Luck" (p. 343). Adopting Hagedorn's perspective on the depiction
    of Asian characters in media, assess Jones's selection and its approval of the
    way *Sanjay and Craig* represents Asian characters.

3. Write an essay that demonstrates, refutes, or complicates the proposition that *Sanjay and Craig* represents a positive, subtler representation of racial identity in mass media. To develop a historical context for your argument, read or reread Michael Omi's "In Living Color: Race and American Culture" (p. 538).

AYMAR JEAN CHRISTIAN
The End of Post-Identity Television

> For a while, if you went by television casting strategies, racial and gender identity appeared to be disappearing as anything of significance in popular TV shows like *Grey's Anatomy*. But in more recent years, with shows like *Girls* and *The Misadventures of Awkward Black Girl*, TV and Web TV may be leaving the "post-identity era," Aymar Jean Christian believes, and that's a good thing, especially in a time of LGBTQ emergence. Identity still matters, Christian argues, and that's a positive, he concludes. Aymar Jean Christian is an assistant professor in Northwestern University's School of Communication. His writings have appeared in such publications as *Continuum*, *Transformative Works and Cultures*, *Newsweek*, the *Washington Post*, the *Wall Street Journal*, and *Bloomberg BusinessWeek*.

Nothing ever "ends" in culture — and nothing is ever new. Conditions change. Culture changes, sometimes.

Still, it does feel like a certain era is ending. That era might be called the post-identity era, which, in television, had its prime in the 2000s. "Post-identity" here refers to the casting of characters without focusing on cultural difference — the much-discussed trifecta academics like to call "race, gender, sexuality" (almost always in that order, for some reason).

What's Happening

Years ago when *Grey's Anatomy* premiered, much was made about creator Shonda Rhimes' open casting strategy: characters written black were cast Asian, vice versa, and every which way. The idea was the characters were written broadly, and their races were essentially interchangeable, at least for the beginning of the show. For shows about women and GLBT-identified individuals, this meant writing characters who were either feminist (working women) or post-feminist (freed from the burden of labor, think *SATC*) archetypes. For gays, it meant presenting them as "normal" or "just like you" — married, with kids, or wanting kids. (For more on this, see Suzanna Walters' *All the Rage* and Douglas' *Enlightened Sexism*.)

All of this, was, really, fine. Television reflected our ideals, the belief that our differences had melted away, that we'd learned how we're all, fundamentally, the same. (I've tried to find something redeeming in this idea.) This was particularly true of broadcast networks, who tried to grab mass audiences as cable networks heavily invested in scripted programming.

But in reality, people do feel, recognize and debate cultural differences. If 5 *Survivor* didn't bust that myth, recent television shows — online and on-air — have certainly put it into question.

The Economics of Identity Television

With more and more cable channels creating television, the need to hit a niche has steadily increased. Smaller niches mean smaller audiences and production budgets, but also more creative freedom for producers and auteurs. It's been happening for well over a decade, but we're hitting a crucial turning point — maybe.

So we get *Girls*. We've had plenty of great shows and women and gender politics — *Mary Tyler Moore*, *Roseanne*, *Murphy Brown*, and, yes, *Sex and the City*, many referenced in the *Girls* pilot — but *Girls* arrives at a moment when the need to be "frank" about gender and class is not only necessary, but possible. *Girls* is the television show as thesis statement: it's a critical work about a very, very specific type of woman. Its super-niche focus on upper-middle-class young women allows it to hone in on the minutiae of growing up as an educated girl in the warped US economy. It's uncomfortable. It allows — arguably, encourages — viewers to despise its privileged leads, something only a few critics have decided to do.

When Chuck Lorre obnoxiously lamented the surfeit of lady comedies on TV, what he was really talking about was the explicitness with which these shows address "gender problems": *2 Broke Girls*, *Girls*, *Whitney*, *Parks and Recreation*, *30 Rock*, *Enlightened*, *New Girl*, *Awkward.*, *Web Therapy*, *Don't Trust the B — in Apartment 23* and *Up All Night* are all saturated with story lines about the complications of being a professional woman today. Some of them even manage to approach some realism (*Girls* wins there, hands down). Because unlike in TV's leading procedurals — *The Closer*, *Rizzoli & Isles*, *The Good Wife*, etc. — most women aren't able to conquer the workplace with such elegance and ease.

Down the Long Tail, to the Web

The market for explicitly lady comedy is strong on TV right now, and many of the shows are doing well. One only need look at FX's interest in web comedy hit *Broad City* — one of many borough-centric web shows — to see the trend is in full swing.

But you'd be missing half the story if you stopped there. Look to the 10 incredible success of *The Misadventures of Awkward Black Girl*, and you'll notice basically every non-white-straight-dude is hankering for shows that speak intimately to their lives. With hundreds of thousands of fans, *Awkward Black Girl* is an incredibly well-written show. Like *Girls*, it gets at the ambivalences and complications of gender and race today, and does so in ways perhaps too explicit for TV. It uses the words "bitch" and "nigga" liberally, and explicitly calls out racism and prejudice with humor.

"But, as was demonstrated by some of the Shorty Award tweets, some people can't get past the 'black' in the title. The bewilderment that our show not only exists, but that it could actually be good is indicative of how mainstream media thinks. I'm pretty sure none of the people tweeting that I'd only get three-fifths of my award had even seen an episode of our show, but they were 100 percent positive that it couldn't be as good as whatever it is someone who didn't look like me produced," creator Issa Rae wrote in *xojane*.

If "black" in *ABG* has been a problem — too explicit for a postracial age — it might not be for longer. Before it announced its 2012 programming slate, which includes its first scripted programs, BET got interested in *Single Black Female*, a Gabrielle Union–vehicle now called *Being Mary Jane*.

Web producers have no such restrictions, and of the scores of black, gay, and Latina series, a number call out race outright, like BET's first web show, *Buppies*, *Afro City* (which built a fan base before its first episode even aired) and the new *Unwritten Rules*, about a black woman navigating a white workplace. Jane Espenson's *Husbands* might be inspired by *The Honeymooners* or *I Love Lucy*, but there's no question it's gay, gay, gay. Gayer, it seems, than most of gay television, whose characters are nestled in straight shows like *Modern Family* and *Glee*. (Indeed, NBC has in development a Sean Hayes–starrer that's basically the same thing.) Indie shows like *Gay's Anatomy*, *The Real Girl's Guide to Everything Else*, *Drama Queenz*, and *Two Jasperjohns* are much more nuanced and grounded examinations of being gay-identified than most of what's on TV.

Of course, things change slowly. Logo for its part is moving away from gays to the broader category of women. And aside from *Girls*, few of these shows are particularly challenging or bracing, in the way that series like *Roseanne* and *All in the Family* shook up audiences decades ago. For that matter, class remains a bit of a third rail, particularly in shows without white guy leads.

Why?

In politics, we're debating contraception, stay-at-home moms and a wom- 15 an's right-to-choose. In crime, we're grappling with two chilling alleged hate crimes. And that's just the tip of the iceberg.

Quite simply, we, or the media, have been forced to realize that identity matters — still. It may not be the 1960s, but if you're watching *Mad Men*, it's starting to look a little familiar.

It helps that we have a glut of media outlets today, including tons of blogs for pretty much every interest. Niche, implicitly social media have been integral to pushing awareness to the fore.

We're starting a new decade! And the one thing we know about culture is: anything can change.

READING THE TEXT

1. In your own words, what does Christian mean by "post-identity" television?

2. How has the increasing number of TV channels and the rise in niche marketing, especially on cable, changed the character of programs aired, in Christian's view?

3. Explain what Christian means by saying "*Girls* is the television show as thesis statement" (para. 7).

4. According to Christian, how have TV shows evolved in their depiction of black, gay, and Latina characters?

READING THE SIGNS

1. **CONNECTING TEXTS** Write an essay that supports, refutes, or complicates Christian's assumption that mass media have entered a "post-identity" phase in which they are less inclined to rely on conventional categories of gender, ethnicity, sexual orientation, and other demographics. To develop your ideas, consult the introduction to this chapter, in addition to the other readings in this chapter.

2. Christian says that "*Girls* is the television show as thesis statement" (para. 7). In an essay, argue for, against, or complicate his view of *Girls*. To develop your ideas, consult Jane Hu's "Reality Hunger: On Lena Dunham's *Girls*" (p. 304).

3. **CONNECTING TEXTS** Write an essay in which you propose your own explanation for why "post-identity" TV shows that feature black characters tend to receive short shrift from both viewers and critics. To develop your argument, consult Michael Omi's "In Living Color: Race and American Culture" (p. 538).

4. Use Christian's essay as a critical lens to analyze one or two high school teen movies, as David Denby does in "High-School Confidential: Notes On Teen Movies" (p. 366). To what extent have such films embraced the "post-identity" phase that Christian proposes? How do you explain your findings?

5. As a capstone essay, review the selections in this chapter, along with the introduction to this chapter. Synthesize your response to these readings, and write an essay in which you make an argument about the extent to which America has indeed become a post-identity culture.

GLOSSARY

abduction (n.)   A form of logical inference, first proposed by Charles Sanders Peirce, by which one seeks the most likely explanatory hypothesis or cause for a phenomenon. For example, the most likely explanation for the fact that in teen horror movies the first victims of the murderous monster are the cheerleader and the football player is that the majority of the teen audience enjoys the imaginative revenge of seeing snooty high school types done in.

archetype (n.)   A recurring character type or plot pattern found in literature, mythology, and popular culture. Sea monsters like Jonah's whale and Moby Dick are archetypes, as are stories that involve long sea journeys or descents into the underworld.

canon (n.)   Books or works that are considered essential to a literary tradition, as the plays of Shakespeare are part of the canon of English literature.

class (n.)   A group of related objects or people. Those who share the same economic status in a society are said to be of the same social class: for example, working class, middle class, upper class. Members of a social class tend to share the same interests and political viewpoints.

code (n.)   A system of **signs** or values that assigns meanings to the elements that belong to it. Thus, a traffic code defines a red light as a "stop" signal and a green light as a "go," while a fashion code determines whether an article of clothing is stylish. To *decode* a system is to figure out its meanings, as in interpreting the tattooing and body-piercing fads.

commodification (n.)   The transforming of an abstraction or behavior into a product for sale. For example, selling mass-produced hamburgers

as an expression of rule-breaking defiance and individualism. See also
hypercapitalism.

connotation (n.)   The meaning suggested by a word, as opposed to its
objective reference, or **denotation**. Thus, the word *flag* might connote
(or suggest) feelings of patriotism, while it literally denotes (or refers to)
a pennant-like object.

consumption (n.)   The use of products and services, as opposed to their
production. A *consumer culture* is one that consumes more than it produces. As a consumer culture, for example, America uses more goods
such as computers and stereos than it manufactures, which results in
a trade deficit with those *producer cultures* (such as China) with which
America trades.

context (n.)   The environment in which a **sign** can be interpreted. In the
context of a college classroom, for example, T-shirts, jeans, and sneakers
are interpreted as ordinary casual dress. Wearing the same outfit in the
context of a job interview at an investment bank would be interpreted as
meaning that you're not serious about wanting the job.

cultural studies (n.)   The academic study of ordinary, everyday culture
rather than **high culture**. See also **culture**; **culture industry**; **mass culture**; **popular culture**.

culture (n.)   The overall system of values and traditions shared by a group
of people. Not exactly synonymous with *society*, which can include
numerous cultures within its boundaries, a culture encompasses the
worldviews of those who belong to it. Thus, the United States, which is
a multicultural society, includes the differing worldviews of people of
African, Asian, Native American, and European descent. See also **cultural
studies**; **culture industry**; **high culture**; **mass culture**; **popular culture**.

culture industry (n.)   The commercial forces behind the production of **mass
culture** or entertainment. See also **cultural studies**; **culture**; **high culture**; **mass culture**; **popular culture**.

denotation (n.)   The particular object or class of objects to which a word
refers. Contrast with **connotation**.

discourse (n.)   The words, concepts, and presuppositions that constitute
the knowledge and understanding of a particular community, often academic or professional.

dominant culture (n.)   The group within a **multicultural** society whose
traditions, values, and beliefs are held to be normative, as the European
tradition is the dominant culture in the United States.

Eurocentric (adj.)   Related to a worldview founded on the traditions and
history of European culture, usually at the expense of non-European
cultures.

function (n.)   The utility of an object, as opposed to its cultural meaning.
Spandex or Lycra shorts, for example, have a functional value for cyclists
because they're lightweight and aerodynamic. On the other hand, such
shorts are a general fashion item for both men and women because of

their cultural meaning, not their function. Many noncyclists wear spandex to project an image of hard-bodied fitness, sexiness, or just plain
trendiness, for instance.

gender (n.)   One's sexual identity and the roles that follow from it, as determined by the norms of one's culture rather than by biology or genetics. The assumption that women should be foremost in the nurturing of
children is a gender norm; the fact that only women can give birth is a
biological phenomenon.

high culture (n.)   The products of the elite arts, including classical music, literature, drama, opera, painting, and sculpture. See also **cultural studies**;
culture; **culture industry**; **mass culture**; **popular culture**.

hypercapitalism (n.)   Introduced by Jeremy Rifkin, hypercapitalism refers
to a society in which the values of capitalism, especially the profit motive
and the commodification of experience, have come to override all other
values.

icon (n.), **iconic** (adj.)   In **semiotics**, a **sign** that visibly resembles its refer-
ent, as a photograph looks like the thing it represents. More broadly, an
icon is someone (often a celebrity) who enjoys a commanding or representative place in popular culture. Michael Jackson and Madonna are
music video icons. Contrast with **symbol**.

ideology (n.)   The beliefs, interests, and values that determine one's interpretations or judgments and that are often associated with one's social
class. For example, in the ideology of modern business, a business is
designed to produce profits, not social benefits.

image (n.)   Literally, a pictorial representation; more generally, the identity
that one projects to others through such things as clothing, grooming,
speech, and behavior.

mass culture (n.)   A subset of **popular culture** that includes the popular
entertainments that are commercially produced for widespread consumption. See also **cultural studies**; **culture**; **culture industry**; **high
culture**.

mass media (n. pl.)   The means of communication, often controlled by the
culture industry, that include newspapers, popular magazines, radio,
television, film, and the Internet.

multiculturalism (n.), **multicultural** (adj.)   In American education, the
movement to incorporate the traditions, history, and beliefs of the United
States' non-European cultures into a traditionally *monocultural* (or single-
culture) curriculum dominated by European thought and history.

mythology (n.)   The overall framework of values and beliefs incorporated
in a given cultural system or worldview. Any given belief within such
a structure — like the belief that "a woman's place is in the home" — is
called a *myth*.

overdetermination (n.)   Originally a term from Freudian psychoanalytic
theory to describe the multiple causes of a psychological affect, overdetermination more generally describes the multiplicity of possible

causes for any social phenomenon. Combined with abductive reasoning, overdetermination is a key element in **semiotic** interpretation. See also **abduction**.

politics (n.)   Essentially, the practice of promoting one's interests in a competitive social environment. Not restricted to electioneering; there may be office politics, classroom politics, academic politics, and sexual politics.

popular culture (n.)   That segment of a **culture** that incorporates the activities of everyday life, including the consumption of consumer goods and the production and enjoyment of mass-produced entertainments. See also **cultural studies**; **culture industry**; **high culture**; **mass culture**.

postmodernism (n.), **postmodern** (adj.)   The worldview behind contemporary literature, art, music, architecture, and philosophy that rejects traditional attempts to make meaning out of human history and experience. For the *postmodern* artist, art does not attempt to create new explanatory myths or **symbols** but rather recycles or repeats existing images, as does the art of Andy Warhol.

proxemics (n.)   The study of human uses of space in interactions with other humans, including body language, facial expression, distance between subjects, gestures, and so on.

semiotics (n.)   In short, the study of **signs**. Synonymous with *semiology*, semiotics is concerned with both the theory and the practice of interpreting linguistic, cultural, and behavioral sign systems. One who practices *semiotic analysis* is called a *semiotician* or *semiologist*.

sign (n.)   Anything that bears a meaning. Words, objects, images, and forms of behavior are all signs whose meanings are determined by the particular **codes**, or **systems**, in which they appear.

symbol (n.), **symbolic** (adj.)   A **sign**, according to semiotician Charles Sanders Peirce, whose significance is arbitrary. The meaning of the word *bear*, for example, is arbitrarily determined by those who use it. Contrast with **icon**.

system (n.)   The **code**, or network, within which a **sign** functions and so achieves its meaning through its associational and differential relations with other signs. The English language is a sign system, as is a fashion code.

text (n.)   A complex of **signs**, which may be linguistic, imagistic, behavioral, and/or musical, that can be read or interpreted.

Acknowledgments

Michael Agresta, "How the Western Was Lost—And Why It Matters" from the *Atlantic*. Copyright © 2013 The Atlantic Media Co., as first published in The Atlantic Magazine. All rights reserved. Distributed by Tribune Content Agency, LLC. Reprinted with permission.

Helena Andrews, "*The Butler* vs. *The Help*: Gender Matters" from *The Root*. Copyright © 2013 by Helena Andrews. Used by permission. All rights reserved.

Laura Bennett, "Against Antiheroes" from *The New Republic*, Aug. 17, 2013. Copyright © 2013 by The New Republic. Reprinted with permission.

Deborah Blum, "The Gender Blur: Where Does Biology End and Society Take Over?" from *Utne Reader*, Sept./Oct. 1998. Copyright © 1998 by Deborah Blum. Used by permission. All rights reserved.

danah boyd, "Implications of User Choice: The Cultural Logic of 'MySpace or Facebook?'" from http://interactions.acm.org, Vol. 16, Issue 6, Nov./Dec. 2009. Reprinted by permission of the author. http://interactions.acm.org/content/?p = 1302.

Patti S. Caravello, "Judging Quality on the Web" by Patti Schifter Caravello, UCLA Research Library. Reprinted with permission.

Aymar Jean Christian, "The End of Post-Identity Television" from tvisual.org. Copyright © 2012 by Aymar Jean Christian. Reused with permission of the author.

Stephanie Clifford and Quentin Hardy, "Attention, Shoppers: Store Is Tracking Your Cell" from the *New York Times* online, July 14, 2013. Copyright © 2013 by The New York Times. All rights reserved. Used by permission and protected by the Copyright Laws of the United States. The printing, copying, redistribution, or retransmission of this Content without express written permission is prohibited. http://nytimes.com.

Julia B. Corbett, "A Faint Green Sell: Advertising in the Natural World" from *Enviropop: Studies in Environmental Rhetoric and Popular Culture*, eds. Mark Meister & Phyllis K. Japp, pp. 81–94. Copyright © 2002 by Mark Meister & Phyllis K. Japp. Reproduced with permission of ABC-CLIO, LLC.

Steve Craig, "Men's Men and Women's Women: How TV Commercials Portray Gender to Different Audiences" from *Issues and Effects of Mass Communication: Other Voices* by Steve Craig. Reprinted by permission of the author.

Daniel D'Addario, "Everything Is 'Trolling' Now" from *Salon*. This article first appeared in Salon.com, at http://Salon.com. An online version remains in the Salon archives. Reprinted with permission.

Michelle Dean, "Here Comes the Hillbilly, Again" from *Slate*. Copyright © 2012 The Slate Group. All rights reserved. Used by permission and protected by the Copyright Laws of the United States. The printing, copying, redistribution, or retransmission of this Content without express written permission is prohibited.

David Denby, "High-School Confidential: Notes on Teen Movies" published by the *New Yorker*, May 31, 1999. Copyright © 1999 by David Denby. Reprinted by permission of the author.

Aaron Devor, "Gender Role Behaviors and Attitudes" from *Gender Blending: Confronting the Limits of Duality* by Aaron Devor. Copyright © 1989 by Indiana University Press. Reprinted with permission of Indiana University Press.

Simon Dumenco, "If We're All So Sick of You, Facebook, Why Can't We Quit You?" from *Advertising Age*, June 10, 2013. Copyright © 2013 by Simon Dumenco. Reprinted with permission.

Christine Folch, "Why the West Loves Sci-Fi and Fantasy: A Cultural Explanation" from the *Atlantic*. Copyright © 2013 The Atlantic Media Co., as first published in The Atlantic Magazine. All rights reserved. Distributed by Tribune Content Agency, LLC. Reprinted with permission.

Thomas Frank and Matt Weiland, "Commodify Your Dissent" published as "Why Johnny Can't Dissent" in the *Baffler*, 1997. Copyright © 1997 The Baffler Literary Magazine, Inc. Reprinted with permission.

Neal Gabler, "The Social Networks" from the *Los Angeles Times*, Oct. 17, 2010. Copyright © 2010 by the Los Angeles Times. Reprinted with permission.

Copyright Laws of the United States. The printing, copying, redistribution, or retransmission of this Content without express written permission is prohibited.

Mariah Burton Nelson, "I Won. I'm Sorry." Was originally published in *Self* Magazine, 1998. Reprinted by permission of the author.

Anne Norton, excerpts from *Republic of Signs*. Copyright © 1993 by the University of Chicago. Reprinted by permission of the University of Chicago Press.

Michael Omi, "In Living Color: Race and American Culture" from *Cultural Politics in Contemporary America*, ed. Ian Angus and Sut Jhally. Copyright © 1989 by Michael Omi. Reprinted by permission of the author.

Michael Parenti, "Class and Virtue" from *Make-Believe Media: The Politics of Entertainment*, 1st ed., by Michael Parenti. Copyright © 1992 by Wadsworth. Reprinted by permission of Wadsworth, a part of Cengage Learning, Inc. Reproduced by permission. www.cengage.com /permissions.

Willa Paskin, "*Devious Maids* Skewers the One Percent." This article first appeared in Salon. com, at http://Salon.com. An online version remains in the Salon archives. Reprinted with permission.

Jennifer L. Pozner, "Dove's 'Real Beauty' Backlash" from *Bitch: Feminist Response to Pop Culture*, Issue 30, Fall 2005. Copyright © 2005. Reprinted by permission of the author.

Robert B. Ray, excerpts from "Formal and Thematic Paradigms" from *A Certain Tendency of the Hollywood Cinema 1930–1980*. Copyright © 1985 Princeton University Press. Reprinted by permission of Princeton University Press.

James A. Roberts, "The Treadmill of Consumption," pages 95–101 from *Shiny Objects* by James A. Roberts. Copyright © 2011 by James A. Roberts. Reprinted by permission of HarperCollins Publishers.

Salvador Rodriguez, "In the Digital Age, Breaking Up Is Hard to Do" from the *Los Angeles Times*, published Feb. 13, 2014. Copyright © The Los Angeles Times. Reprinted with permission.

Richard Rushfield, "Toward a Unified Theory of How the Internet Makes Everything Terrible" from http://rushfieldbabylon.com. Copyright © 2013 by Richard Rushfield. Reprinted by permission of the author.

Juliet B. Schor, "Tony the Tiger to Slime Time Live: The Content of Commercial Messages in Children's Advertising" from *Born to Buy: The Commercialized Child and the New Consumer Culture* by Juliet Schor. Copyright © 2004 by Juliet Schor. All rights reserved. Reprinted with permission of Scribner Publishing Group.

Matt Zoller Seitz, "The Offensive Movie Cliché That Won't Die" first appeared in Salon.com, at http://Salon.com. An online version remains in the Salon archives. Reprinted with permission.

Linda Seger, "Creating the Myth" from *Making a Good Script Great*. Copyright © 1987 by Linda Seger. Reprinted by permission of the author.

Nick Serpe, "Reality Pawns: The New Money TV" from *Dissent Magazine*, Summer 2013. Copyright © 2013 by Nick Serpe. Reprinted with permission of the University of Pennsylvania Press.

Laurence Shames, "The More Factor" from *The Hunger for More: Searching for Values in an Age of Greed*. Copyright © 1989 by Laurence Shames. Reprinted by permission of the Stuart Krichevsky Agency, Inc.

Natasha Simons, "*Mad Men* and the Paradox of the Past" from *National Review* online, July 19, 2010. Reprinted by permission of the publisher.

Jack Fisher Solomon, "Masters of Desire: The Culture of American Advertising" from *The Signs of Our Time* by Jack Fisher Solomon. Copyright © 1988 by Jack Solomon. Used by permission of Jeremy P. Tarcher, an imprint of Penguin Group (USA) Inc.

Gloria Steinem, "Sex, Lies, and Advertising" from *Ms.* Magazine, July/August 1990. Copyright © 1990 by Gloria Steinem. Reprinted by permission of the author.

Stevie St. John, "Out of Character" from *Bitch Magazine*, Summer 2014, Issue 63. Copyright © 2014 by Bitch Media. Reprinted with permission.

"Students Addicted to Social Media—New UM Study," Apr. 21, 2010, http://www.newsdesk
.umd.edu/sociss/release.cfm?ArticleID=2144. Reprinted with permission, Susan D. Moeller,
"24 Hours: Unplugged" study.

Joseph Turow, "Introduction" from *The Daily You: How the New Advertising Industry Is Defining Your Identity and Your Worth* by Joseph Turow. Copyright © 2012 by Joseph Turow.
Reprinted by permission of Yale University Press.

James B. Twitchell, "What We Are to Advertisers" from *Lead Us into Temptation: The Triumph
of American Materialism* by James B. Twitchell. Copyright © 1999 by James B. Twitchell.
Reprinted by permission of the author.

S. Craig Watkins, "Now! Fast Entertainment and Multitasking in an Always-On World" from *The
Young and the Digital* by S. Craig Watkins. Copyright © 2009 by S. Craig Watkins. Reprinted
by permission of Beacon Press, Boston.

INDEX OF AUTHORS AND TITLES

MICHAEL THOMAS FORD

1308-94-020

LOOKING FOR IT

KENSINGTON BOOKS
www.kensingtonbooks.com

KENSINGTON BOOKS are published by

Kensington Publishing Corp.
850 Third Avenue
New York, NY 10022

ISBN 0-7582-0408-6

First Hardcover Printing: August 2004
First Trade Paperback Printing: December 2005
10 9 8 7 6 5 4 3 2 1

Printed in the United States of America

1308-94-020

For John Scognamiglio,
who waited

the world is big
the world is bad
but I will find the beauty
I see a vision in my head
I am looking for it now
oh, I am looking for it
oh, I am looking for myself

ACKNOWLEDGMENTS

Thanks and love, as always, to the man who takes care of business and so much more, the divine Mitchell Waters. And for listening, nagging, commiserating, and tolerating: Jill Terry and Christian Muncy, Robrt Pela, Katherine Gleason, Nisa Donnelly, Michael Rowe, Michael Elliott, Jennifer Williams, Lynn Brown, Maureen McEvoy, Stephanie Krmpotic, Mike Lever, Vince Smith, Laura O'Heir, and most especially, Patrick, Roger, and Andy.

CHAPTER I

"Another fireman. That makes five." John Ellison took a sip of his vodka tonic and regarded the man in the yellow slicker and red plastic helmet with an air of weary disdain. "You'd think they'd at least try not to look like overgrown kindergartners."

Mike Monaghan, preoccupied with trying to remember the order the nun waiting at the other end of the bar had just given him, nodded absentmindedly as he poured gin over the ice in a glass, neatly popped the caps from two Rolling Rocks, and searched beneath the counter for the bottle of vermouth. *Damn it, Paulie,* he thought, silently cursing the barback whose duty it was to set up before the evening rush. *Why can't you ever put things back where they belong?*

"I know this is the Engine Room, and I'm sure they think they're being very clever, but can't they show a little more imagination?" said John.

"Actually, engine rooms are on ships and submarines, not in fire stations," Mike remarked as he grabbed a pile of napkins to hand to the nun along with his drinks. "Technically, they should be dressed as sailors."

"That makes it even worse," said John, draining his glass. "Not only are they unoriginal, they're ignorant."

"Well, it was very original of *you* to come as Mr. Rogers," Mike told him, eyeing the blue cardigan John had buttoned almost all the way up. "I know I definitely want to be your neighbor."

"Fuck you," John shot back. "For your information, this is what all self-respecting high school science teachers wear."

"The stuff of teenage boys' wet dreams," joked Mike as he took John's empty glass and refilled it.

"What have I missed?"

A man took the seat next to John at the bar. Leaning over, he kissed John quickly on the mouth.

"Nothing," said John. "Just the annual Halloween Faggot Parade and Masquerade Ball."

"Russell, I don't know how you live with this bitter queen," Mike said. Anticipating the request he knew was coming, he poured a rum and Coke and slid it to the man who had just joined them.

Russell took the drink, lifted it to his lips in salute, and took a deep swig before replying. "I'm just with him for the sex," he said, earning a laugh from Mike and a roll of the eyes from John.

"How was the sale?" asked John, changing the subject.

Russell groaned. "Three hundred overweight women all insisting they were size fours," he said wearily. "I barely made it out alive."

"Oh, the perils of retail," said John.

"I didn't even have time to come up with a costume," said Russell.

"Thank God," John told him, sounding relieved. "There are enough cowboys, Batmen, and lumberjacks here to recreate an episode of *Let's Make a Deal.*"

"Actually, I think those lumberjacks are lesbians," Mike teased. "And since you're asking, I'll take what's behind door number two."

Russell laughed. "You don't have to be so uptight," he said to his lover. "Halloween is supposed to be fun."

John snorted. "Excuse me if I'm a little tired of this nonsense. All day long I had to teach chemistry to children dressed as gangbangers and hookers," he said. "Not that *every* day isn't like that."

"You should have gone as Grand Master J," suggested Mike. "Pimp Daddy of the science lab. You could show them how to make their own street drugs. That would get them interested in chemistry."

"I don't see you in a costume," John retorted. "If you think this is so much fun, how come you're not dressed in some inane getup?"

"I *am* in costume," Mike said. "Can't you tell? I'm a straight guy."

Russell laughed as John shook his head. Mike, noticing a ghost waving a ten-dollar bill at him, excused himself to attend to the customer.

"Can we go now?" John asked Russell.

"Go?" Russell said. "They're just about to start the drag show."

"That's exactly why I want to go," said John. "I've got a splitting headache, and being here isn't helping."

Russell looked down into his drink. "Yeah," he said quietly. "We can go. Let me say good night to Mike."

John stood up. "I'll be outside," he told his partner.

As John pushed his way through the crowd toward the door, Russell finished his drink and set the empty glass on the bar. He caught Mike's eye and waved.

"You're leaving?" asked Mike, coming over and automatically sweeping the empty glass into the plastic tub beneath the counter.

Russell sighed. "Her majesty has a headache."

"So send him home by himself," suggested Mike.

Russell shook his head. "It's okay," he said. "I'm pretty beat anyway. I'll see you later."

Mike nodded and watched as Russell left. Russell and John had been coming into the bar regularly for the six years Mike had worked there, and still he hadn't figured out what kept them together. One of these days, he thought, he'd unravel the mystery. But tonight wasn't the night. Tonight he had too much else to do.

He turned his attention to the customers lined up three deep at the bar. Within moments he was busy mixing drinks, his hands finding the bottles, ice, and wedges of lime as his mind ticked off the orders: three martinis for Wonder Woman, a shot of Jack Daniels and a Cosmo for the scarecrow, and a Budweiser for the devil with the wicked smile. Then he was on to a new set of faces and the next round.

"What's an old queen have to do to get a sidecar around here?"

"Simon!" Mike said, leaning across the bar to kiss the cheek of the man addressing him. He eyed the old-fashioned black dress and powdered wig Simon was wearing. "What are you supposed to be?" he asked as he began putting together the sidecar.

"What did I just say?" asked Simon primly. "I'm an old queen."

Seeing Mike's confusion, Simon shook his head. "You children have no sense of history," he said. "Victoria. I'm Queen Victoria."

Mike nodded. "Oh," he said. "I get it."

Simon took his sidecar and handed Mike a five. "Don't feel badly about not knowing," he said. "Someone else complimented me on my Zsa Zsa Gabor costume. There are, I'm afraid, disadvantages to being the oldest one in a room."

Behind Simon a drag queen sporting a pink-sequined dress, enormous breasts, and a beehive hairdo that added a good two feet to her height stepped onto the small stage that had been erected for the evening. Taking up a microphone, she flashed a red-lipped smile, batted her false eyelashes, and addressed the crowd.

"Happy Halloween!" she shouted. "Welcome to the Engine Room. So, what will it be tonight, tricks or treats?"

"Tricks!" shouted the crowd.

The crowd around the bar thinned as people turned to watch the show. Simon pulled out a stool and sat down. "She got that from Walter, you know," he said to Mike.

Mike knew. He'd heard Simon's stories about Walter many times. Everyone in the bar had, particularly in the year since Walter had died.

"He was so lovely," Simon said, speaking to no one in particular. "So beautiful."

Mike looked at Simon's face. Caked with makeup, it reminded him of a crumbling painting. How old was Simon, he wondered? Surely he must be almost seventy. And Walter had been even older. Mike, picturing Walter, tried to imagine the wrinkled little man with the white mustache who'd worn corduroy trousers and neatly pressed plaid shirts dressed in drag.

"I remember the first time I saw him," Simon said. "It was at a party given by my friend Harold Carver. We didn't have a bar to go to back then, but Harold was wealthy and had a big house in Saratoga. Every weekend we went there. Escaped, really. From our lives. One weekend someone brought Walter along as a guest. Friday night he made his entrance to dinner dressed in a beaded gown, and I fell in love with him."

Simon looked at Mike and smiled, the pancake makeup on his cheeks cracking and flaking off. "I know it all sounds terribly fey," he said. "But he wasn't playing at being a woman. It was just his way of having fun." Simon sighed deeply. "It all seems so much easier now, doesn't it? We have our bars, and parades, and we're on television for everyone to see. People talk about how terrible it was back then, how we had to hide who we were. But they forget that it was also magical. We had our own secret world. Maybe we were afraid sometimes, but we weren't unhappy."

Simon looked down into his glass. "We weren't unhappy," he repeated. "Not then."

"Would you like another one?" Mike asked him, nodding at the empty drink. "It's on the house."

Simon shook his head. "Thank you, but no. One makes me maudlin. Two will make me positively morose. I think I should probably take myself home before I become a spectacle."

"You're going to miss the costume contest," Mike told him.

"That is a misfortune I will have to live with," Simon said, standing up. "I pray that I am up to it."

He waved away the change Mike had placed on the bar. Mike pocketed it as Simon turned and melted into the crowd. With only a few customers waiting, Mike enjoyed the relative quiet. The drag show was in full force, but he was able to block it out. It was a trick he'd developed during years of bartending in places whose clientele favored the cover of blaring music over the ability to communicate with those around them. He simply tuned the noise out, losing himself in his work or his thoughts.

He observed the action from within this sphere of artificial silence, surrounded by the chaos that was Halloween at the Engine Room but at the same time removed from it. As he straightened the bottles and restocked the napkins, he watched the faces of the patrons. Many of them he recognized, but others were strangers to him. This was to be expected. The Engine Room was one of only three gay bars in a two-hour radius. The towns of upstate New York had many charms, but the availability of entertainment for the queer community was not one of them.

Oddly, this was one of the things that appealed to Mike about life in Cold Falls. He'd lived in larger cities, Albany and Syracuse for several years and a brief three-month stint in Buffalo one summer, but he preferred the quieter atmosphere of the smaller towns. Not that Cold Falls was merely a flyspeck on the map of New York State. An hour north of Utica, it shared with that city a history and economy based in brewing. Founded a hundred years earlier, Cold Falls Ale continued to be the bar's best seller, beating out Coors and Budweiser by almost three to one. An image of the falls that gave the town its name graced the label, and the brewery's motto—"Give me a cold one"—was regularly shouted out by customers, each of whom Mike rewarded with a friendly laugh suggesting that it was the first time he'd heard such cleverness.

He didn't mind. He liked his customers. Like the town itself, they had quickly become familiar to him, until he knew their faces and names in the same way that he knew the most recognizable of Cold Falls' landmarks: the brewery, the falls, the statue of the town's lone celebrity (Cuthbert Applewhite, a dairy farmer who had distinguished himself in 1892 by preventing an assassination attempt against presidential candidate and former fellow upstate New Yorker Grover Cleveland during a campaign stop, and who after Cleveland had secured his second, improbable, term in office had been awarded a medal of distinction that he wore for the rest of his life, even when mucking out the barn).

In addition to their names, Mike knew their stories as well. He fell easily into the time-honored role most bartenders held along with their ability to mix drinks, that of father confessor and unpaid therapist. The tips he received were just as often tokens of appreciation for the advice he dispensed as they were for the strength of his cocktails, even if all he'd done was nod sympathetically during a patron's rambling, boozy dissection of a recent breakup.

Stories. It was all about stories. Everyone had one, and almost everyone wanted to tell it. All he did was listen to them, and for that his customers were thankful. He was like a book they were writing, recording the events of their lives in his head. Maybe, he thought occasionally, one day he would write them all down. But who, he asked himself, would want to read it? To whom would the individual stories of heartbreak and joy be of any interest besides those who told them? It was, Mike thought as he washed and dried a wineglass, one of the less appealing characteristics of human beings, the ability to be completely uninterested in the lives of those around them while desperately longing for someone to pay them attention.

A burst of cheering made him look up. On the stage, the beehived drag queen was putting a crown on the head of a muscular man half-heartedly dressed as a pirate, the primary clues to his identity being the patch on one eye and the stuffed parrot somehow affixed to his shoulder. Apart from these props he was nearly nude, which Mike assumed was the reason for his popularity.

"How about showing us your Jolly Roger?" the drag queen teased, shamelessly pawing the pirate's chest as the crowd roared.

"Can I get a cold one?"

Mike looked away from the action to see a skeleton standing at the bar. He wore a black turtleneck and pants painted with crude representations of bones. His hair was slicked back and his face, too, was painted black and white to resemble a skull. His eyes were misshapen white spots above a ghostly mouth, and the overall effect was unsettling.

"Great costume," Mike remarked as he pulled a beer from the ice-filled chest and handed it to the man.

"Thanks," came the short reply. "How much?"

"Two bucks," answered Mike.

Three dollar bills were slapped on the bar. Then the skeleton man turned away, scanning the crowd.

Mike took the money, putting two of the bills into the register and adding the third to the rest of his tips. The man, he guessed, wasn't one of the regulars, otherwise he wouldn't have had to ask the price of a beer, which hadn't changed in well over a year. Probably he was one of the visitors who came in only on nights like this, when they could hide behind the anonymity of a costume. Maybe there was a wife at home, perhaps a kid or two. Mike saw a lot of guys like that. They came to the Engine Room from other small cities, driving an hour or more to ensure invisibility while they spent a night living other lives.

Usually he saw them only once, but sometimes they showed up at regular intervals. Apart from their nervousness and unfamiliarity, they were easy to spot. Often they forgot to remove their wedding rings. He glanced at the left hand of the skeleton man. It was bare. Still, that meant nothing. Not all of them were married, of course. Some were simply afraid of who they were.

The man moved away, out of Mike's sight. Looking for something, Mike thought. He was looking for something. They all were. That's why they came there.

CHAPTER 2

What was it with faggots that they liked to dress up like women? Pete Thayer stared at the drag queen standing on the stage. He was rambling on and on, grinning at everyone and throwing his hands all over the place. Pete couldn't stand to look at his face, painted up like a clown's. Someone needed to take the queen out back and show him how a real man acted.

That was the problem with fags; they wanted to be women. Not all of them, but most of them. That's why so many of them were wearing dresses or girly costumes. Even the ones dressed as men were trying too hard to look masculine, hiding their sissiness behind military uniforms and football player getups. But Pete knew that once the clothes came off, the masculinity would fall with them to the floor of the bedroom, discarded like so much make-believe.

He took a swig of his beer and leaned against the wall. His eyes scanned the bar, looking for anything to relieve his boredom. The possibilities were few and far between. There was a cowboy by the pool table who wasn't too bad, and at the back of the room a guy dressed as a baby wearing nothing but a diaper. The costume was a turnoff, but the guy at least had a hairy chest and didn't seem too swishy.

Pete decided to give the baby a shot and started walking toward him. Halfway there he found his way blocked by a guy in a devil outfit. The devil looked him up and down and smiled.

"Nice costume," he said.

Pete nodded. He wasn't in the mood to talk.

"That paint sort of glows," the devil continued. "Is it fluorescent?"

"Yeah," said Pete curtly. Fluorescent? Who the hell cared? It was paint. He'd grabbed the bottle from the back room at the shop. The costume was a last-minute thing, pulled together in about ten minutes.

"You should have won a prize," the devil said, grinning broadly. "It's really cool."

Behind the devil Pete saw the baby getting ready to leave with someone dressed as Dorothy from *The Wizard of Oz*. He quickly looked for the cowboy, but he, too, was gone.

"Can I buy you a drink?" the devil asked him.

Pete looked at the guy. He was shirtless, like the baby, although his chest was smooth. But at least it was well muscled. His skin was painted red. On his head was perched a set of horns, and he had a goatee. He was wearing red boxer briefs and black work boots. He would do.

"I have a better idea," Pete said. "Why don't you and I take a little trip to hell."

The devil looked at him, confused.

"Let's get out of here," Pete explained.

The devil nodded. "Oh," he said. "I get it. Funny. Well, I'm sort of here with some friends. I should—"

"Okay," Pete interrupted. "No problem."

He turned to go, but the devil grabbed his arm. "I guess I could leave a little early," he said.

"Then let's go," Pete told him.

He walked toward the door, knowing the devil would be right behind him. They always were, predictable as Monday morning. As the door of the Engine Room closed behind him, the devil was there beside him.

"I'm Mark," the devil said.

"Dan," Pete told him. "Where's your car?"

"Over here."

Pete followed Mark to his car, waiting for Mark to unlock it and then getting in. When they were inside, Mark leaned over and tried to kiss him. Pete put his hand on the back of Mark's head and pushed it down to his crotch instead.

Mark's fingers fumbled with Pete's zipper, pulling it down and reaching inside. Unrestrained by underwear, Pete's dick slid out easily. A moment later Mark's mouth was sliding up and down it hungrily and

Pete was growing hard. He leaned back, shut his eyes, and lost himself in the warmth of the mouth that serviced him.

When he felt himself begin to come, he said nothing. His load exploded into Mark's mouth and he felt Mark gag for a moment before swallowing hard. When he was done, Pete pulled his softening cock from Mark's mouth and zipped up. He opened the car door and got out, leaving Mark looking up at him with a puzzled expression.

Pete shut the door quickly, blotting out the sight of Mark's face with its smeared red makeup and the horns hanging askew. He walked briskly away from the car toward the one he'd driven to the bar. It wasn't his; it belonged to a customer from the shop. He would never drive his own car to a fag bar. It was too recognizable.

He got into the borrowed car and left the parking lot. He was home within fifteen minutes, where he parked the car in the garage and shut the door. Once safely inside the house, he went to the bathroom, where he turned the shower on, stripped off his painted clothes, and stuffed them into the small garbage can beneath the sink.

The water was too hot, but he left it that way. It would help wash away the dirt. Maybe, he thought vaguely as he soaped himself, it would also kill anything the queer's mouth had left on his dick. He scrubbed his skin hard with a washcloth, wiping away the oily drugstore makeup he'd bought to create his skeleton face. He watched it run down his body and into the drain, a milky stream that ran clear after several minutes. Still he scrubbed, making sure he was rid of any lingering taint. You could never be too careful.

Turning the water off, he stepped from the shower and dropped the washcloth into the trash on top of the clothes. Grabbing a towel from the hook behind the door, he dried himself and walked into his bedroom. He flopped onto the bed and reached for the remote on the bedside table.

The TV came on with a click. Another push of a button set the tape inside the VCR whirring, and a moment later the image of a big-breasted blonde getting fucked from behind filled the screen. Pete stared at the TV, idly playing with himself while the girl's partner, an unattractive but hugely endowed man, thrust in and out of her pussy. The girl's tits jiggled and her lipsticked mouth was open in an expression of ecstasy as squeaky little "ohs" and "yeahs" filled the air.

After a few minutes the camera moved in, moving behind and

above the couple to focus on the pink folds between the girl's legs. The man pulled his cock out and rubbed the swollen head against the girl's asshole. Pressing it against the pinkish-brown pucker, he slid inside her, the length of him disappearing between her cheeks.

Pete lay back and spread his legs. His cock angled across his belly, untouched, as he wet a finger and slid it beneath his balls and began to rub his asshole. His eyes were fixed on the dick that was pounding the girl's butt. It moved in and out with increasing force, stretching her wide. The skin was slick and shiny with lube. He wondered what it felt like for the girl to have such a thing inside her.

He'd fucked a girl like that once. Like the girl in the film, she'd had blond hair and store-bought tits. He'd met her at a party. Fourth of July, maybe. He couldn't remember. What he did remember was how he'd been fucking her from behind and suddenly wondered what it would feel like to stick his piece in her ass. Without asking, he'd done it. She was so drunk she hadn't even really noticed, groaning a little at first and then going right back to mumbling some foul-mouthed crap she apparently thought was sexy.

He'd blocked out her voice, concentrating on how tight her ass felt around him. He'd come quickly, before he was ready, and it had made him angry. He'd left the girl on her hands and knees, pulling on his jeans and leaving before she could ask him where he was going.

What would it feel like to have something as big as a cock in your ass? He slid his finger inside himself, poking gently. Just a finger hurt a little. He couldn't imagine what a dick must feel like. Especially one as big as the one on his TV screen. Christ, it had to be a good ten inches long. His own was eight. He knew because he'd measured it once just for the hell of it. Eight inches. Man, those faggots loved his big cock. They always said so when they sucked him off.

He'd never fucked a guy. Some of them had wanted him to, but he wouldn't do it. Who knew what kind of shit you could get from that. Not that the idea didn't have some appeal. The girl—what was her name, Amy? Kelly?—had been virgin tight. Probably a guy wouldn't be, though, especially some queer who'd been plowed by everything he could get in there.

He slid more of his finger inside himself. His ass tightened around him and he felt his balls give a jump. He moved in and out a little, fucking his own ass. In the film the guy was pulling almost all the way out and slamming back in. The head of his dick would appear for a moment, the girl's asshole almost closing. Then he would push back into her, his balls slapping against her as he nailed her.

Pete added a second finger to the first, gritting his teeth as he stretched himself open. How did those fags stand it? He was about to pull his hand away when suddenly his ass relaxed, as if something had stopped resisting and opened up. The pain ebbed and his fingers were simply surrounded by heat. He could almost feel the blood pounding in his ass.

He started to fuck himself with his hand, matching the motions of the guy in the movie. With his free hand he gripped his cock tightly. He imagined fucking the girl. His fist was her ass, tight around his dick. She was moaning as he pumped her. He was giving it to her hard, the way he liked it.

Behind him was a guy. Maybe the man in the film, maybe someone else. A cock was pressing against his asshole, pushing its way inside. As he fucked the girl, he too was getting fucked. He closed his eyes and imagined it, the three of them rocking together on the bed, his dick and the other guy's moving in tandem, sliding in and out like the pistons of an engine. It was like they were both fucking the girl, the other man's dick connected to Pete's inside.

He heard loud moans and opened his eyes. On the screen the man had pulled his dick out of the girl's ass and was spraying a thick load over her back. Pete pumped himself harder and came too. His ass tightened around his fingers and he erupted with a shout. Cum splattered across his chest in thick drops, leaving behind a pearly trail caught in the dark hair of his stomach.

He pulled his hand away from his ass and reached for a T-shirt on the floor. He used it to wipe the stickiness from his skin, then tossed it back on the floor. The TV was shut off and he was left in the darkness of the room, looking up at the ceiling.

He reached for the pack of Marlboros on the bedside table. Pulling one free, he flicked his lighter to life and lit it. The smoke felt good as he drew it into his lungs, a cloudy darkness that surrounded his thoughts. The end of the cigarette glowed redly in the dark like a star.

He exhaled, blowing the smoke into the air. He lifted his fingers to his nose and inhaled the scent of himself. It clung to his skin, thick and ripe, like the smell of leaves in the fall. Is that what he smelled like inside? He had expected it to be different, dirtier. But it wasn't; it was rich and dark, like the smoke that fell over him like invisible rain.

He licked a fingertip, expecting to taste something sour. Again he was surprised. The taste that met his tongue was nothing like that. Instead it had a sweetness to it. He sucked on his finger, drawing it inside. Minutes ago it had been inside his ass, filling him. Now he was tasting himself. He was both repulsed and thrilled by the act. He thought about the times when girls had sucked him after he'd pulled his cock from their pussies. Watching them lick their own juices from his skin, he'd wanted to fuck them all over again.

He was no girl, though, he told himself. He didn't get fucked. His fantasy had been about something else. What, he wasn't sure and didn't want to think too much about. It was just something that had popped into his head, that was all. He'd just wondered what it might feel like. Nothing more. And now he knew.

He removed his finger and took a long drag on his cigarette, blotting out the taste in his mouth with the bitter kiss of tobacco. In a few minutes he would get up and wash his hands. He would use lots of hot water and soap, just like his mother had made him do when he was littler. "You can't be too careful," she'd always said as she watched him to make sure he didn't just run his hands under the tap to fool her.

"You can't be too careful." He repeated the phrase out loud. It was the guiding principle of his mother's life, and like a good boy, he followed it himself. Well, mostly. He suspected his mother wouldn't approve of certain aspects of his life. But still, he was careful.

He'd almost totally forgotten about his encounter with Mark earlier in the evening, but now the guy's face came to him. He recalled the red skin, the two little horns.

"You got a blowjob from the devil," he told himself. He laughed. The idea was so ridiculous he couldn't help but find it funny. After all, he was a nice Catholic boy. He'd done altar service, gone through CCD, all that crap. Sometimes he still went to Mass, at least on holidays or when his mother demanded he accompany her. What would Father Fitzpatrick think about his former altar boy getting a knob job from Satan? Maybe he was a cocksucker himself, although Pete doubted it. Despite the recent rash of abuse revelations, he could honestly say that Father Fitzpatrick had never once done anything like that to him or, as far as he knew, any of his friends.

Maybe he would stop by the church tomorrow, he thought. It was, after all, All Saints' Day. He could light a candle for his grandmother. It had been a while since he'd done that. His mother would like it if he did.

He stubbed out his cigarette in the ashtray and got up. Going into the bathroom, he turned on the water in the sink and began to scrub.

CHAPTER 3

"You are no longer strangers and sojourners, but fellow citizens with the saints and members of the household of God."

Father Thomas Dunn looked out at the congregation. There were a surprising number of them given that it was six o'clock on a rainy Wednesday morning. Then again, most of them were elderly. They had nothing else to do, nowhere else to be. The chance that they'd spent the previous evening trick-or-treating or attending Halloween parties was remote. Probably they'd locked themselves in their houses and turned off the porch lights to discourage any children who might come around.

It was an unkind thought, and he admonished himself for having it. The members of Saint Peter's Episcopal Church were, for the most part, kind people. In the ten months that he'd been there, most of them had invited him to dinner at least once. Several had even attempted to interest him in their unmarried daughters, offers he'd so far managed to sidestep. They came to the church, and to him, because they were searching for something that presumably they found there.

He refocused on the service, uttering the words of the Confession of Sin. "Beloved, we have come together in the presence of Almighty God our heavenly Father, to set forth his praise, to hear his holy Word, and to ask, for ourselves and on behalf of others, those things that are necessary for our life and our salvation. And so that we may prepare ourselves in heart and mind to worship him, let us kneel in silence, and with penitent and obedient hearts confess our sins, that we may obtain forgiveness by his infinite goodness and mercy."

Obediently, the people knelt with a muted rustling of papers and the rasping of the wooden prayer benches against the floor. He imagined he heard elderly joints creaking in the cold confines of the old stone church, echoing dimly off the ceiling high above them where spiders swung like tiny many-eyed angels and trapped in their webs the prayers that floated heavenward.

"Most merciful God, we confess that we have sinned against you in thought, word, and deed, by what we have done, and by what we have left undone." The words of the confession came easily, burned into his memory by daily repetition until they had become almost meaningless. "We have not loved you with our whole heart; we have not loved our neighbors as ourselves. We are truly sorry and we humbly repent. For the sake of your Son Jesus Christ, have mercy on us and forgive us; that we may delight in your will, and walk in your ways, to the glory of your Name. Amen."

Standing, he lifted his hand toward the people.

"Almighty God have mercy on you, forgive you all your sins through our Lord Jesus Christ, strengthen you in all goodness, and by the power of the Holy Ghost keep you in eternal life. Amen."

They stood once more, looking at him expectantly. He smiled and felt a collective sigh ripple through the sanctuary as the newly forgiven sank into their seats.

"The Lord is glorious in his saints. Come let us adore him."

He led them through the reading of the Psalm, only half listening as their mingled voices followed his in the call-and-response. When it came time for the reading of the first lesson, he relinquished his place at the pulpit to George Edderly, who removed a pair of bifocals from the pocket of his red flannel shirt before beginning to read in a shaky voice.

"A reading from Ecclesiasticus. 'Let us now sing the praises of famous men, our ancestors in their generations . . .' "

The old man's voice faded into the background as Father Dunn stared at the pattern of the carpet beneath his feet. It was a pattern of vines and flowers, red and purple on a blue background. He chose one particular vine and attempted to follow it with his eyes, but when it circled around itself and became entwined with the petals of a rose, he grew confused and lost interest.

"The word of the Lord."

The ending of the reading brought him back to the moment. Along with everyone else in the church, Father Dunn gave the familiar response. "Thanks be to God."

Another lesson, this one from Revelation, was read by Jenny Parish. A pretty young woman, her clear, pleasant voice bespoke of the terrible things that would come when the angel of the Lord arrived on the day of judgment to open the final seal and release pestilence across the land. Jenny described these events as if she were reading out loud a birthday card from a dear friend, and Father Dunn was reminded of the newscasters who announced the most gruesome of disasters with shining teeth and smiling faces.

Following a reading of the Gospel According to Saint Matthew, it was time for the sermon. Here, able to break away from the rigid bones of the service's prescribed format, Father Dunn grew more lively. He loved the church's traditions and rituals, but sometimes they felt to him like a tether keeping him neatly within a circle whose dimensions had been described by someone else. He knew he was supposed to see them more as a set of exercises, the repetition of which cleansed his soul and brought him closer to God. More and more often, however, the collar signifying his obedience to his faith seemed to be choking him.

In his sermons, though, he was free to fly. The church could offer suggestions—and did—regarding appropriate themes, but ultimately it was up to him to create something that would connect with the hearts of his parishioners. And this morning the topic was remembering the dead. He arranged the notes he'd jotted down the evening before and began.

"When I was very small, I remember sitting in front of the television one Sunday night watching Walt Disney's *Fantasia*. Although I liked the dancing hippos and Mickey Mouse as the beleaguered sorcerer's apprentice, I'm afraid overall I found it a little boring. At least until the sequence set to Mussorgsky's 'Night on Bald Mountain.' Watching the mountain come to life, turning into a demonic figure in whose clawed hand danced imps born of the flames, I was fascinated. And when the frantic last notes of the piece blended into the soothing opening tones of Schubert's 'Ave Maria' and the demon was banished by first the sun and then the candles carried by the mysterious pilgrims walking through the woods, I was mesmerized."

He paused, thinking back to that night, to how he had felt staring at the TV screen from his place on the living room floor.

"I had no idea then that what I was watching was the visualization of the ongoing battle between the sacred and the profane. All I knew was that I was held, spellbound, by the music and the feelings it stirred in me. I think, really, it was Walt Disney who set me on the road to the priesthood."

A ripple of laughter greeted his comment. But he was serious. Even at the age of seven or eight, he knew he had discovered something deeply magical, something he couldn't put into words. He understood that the composers of the music and the animators of the film had also been unable to put what they felt into words, and so had brought their experiences to life in notes and images. When he later discovered God and the Church, the feeling was the same. Faith, he had learned that night in front of the flickering television, was most glorious when it was most untouched by reason.

"Today is the Feast of All Saints," he continued. "Last night was All Hallows' Eve. The sacred and the profane. One is a night of mischief, of goblins and ghosts and witches. The other is a day of remembering the spirits of those who have passed on. And that's what I would like each of you to do today. Remember those who are gone from you, those women and men who touched your lives and helped shape who and what you are."

He let this notion sink in. He knew each person in the church was now thinking of names, seeing faces in their minds, remembering moments of love and anger, joy and sorrow. An image came to him as well, but he pushed it away, saving it for later.

"One day all of us will be gone," he continued quickly. "Who will remember us then? Whose lives are we touching with our actions? When ten, twenty, fifty years from now other bodies are occupying the pews in which you sit and another priest is standing in my place, will they remember us fondly or with pain? As you go about your day today, take time both to remember and to be mindful. Thank those people in your life whom you appreciate, reflect on how your actions affect others, and recall the people—the saints of your life—who are no longer here. We are all of us saints in the making. When it's time for us to be remembered, make it be with gladness and love."

He gathered his notes together, slipping them inside his Book of Common Prayer. The church's old, faithful organ lurched to life as the first notes of "Who Are These Like Stars Appearing" filled the air. It was a lovely hymn, one of the priest's favorites, and he sang along loudly.

"Who are these like stars appearing, these before God's throne who stand? Each a golden crown is wearing; who are all this glorious band?"

Again he was reminded of his childhood, although for much different reasons. The words of the hymn made him think of the Swedish supergroup ABBA. He'd had a poster of the band, pulled from the pages of *Tigerbeat,* in his room when he was thirteen or so. The four members were dressed in white satin jumpsuits, lit softly so that they seemed to glow. With their shiny hair and smiling faces, they'd seemed angelic to him. Now, every time he sang the first line of this hymn, he saw that poster in his mind. It was oddly appropriate, he thought: Agnetha, Bjorn, Frida, and Benny as sweet-voiced, Nordic saints of God.

As the last note faded away, he recited a Prayer of Saint Chrysostom before bestowing the Benediction. "May the God of hope fill us with all joy and peace in believing through the power of the Holy Ghost. Amen."

And it was over.

He descended from the pulpit and made his way down the center aisle of the church to the doors, where he took up his position to await the departing congregation. He always felt a bit like a flight attendant at this point, and once or twice he'd been tempted to greet someone with, "We know you have a choice of religions and we thank you for choosing the Episcopal Church for your worship needs. Come again. Buh-bye."

Instead he shook hands and smiled, listened to earnest praise for his sermons and to requests for prayers. He learned the names and faces of the regulars and attempted, mostly successfully, to commit to memory their various ailments, children, occupations, and assorted other bits and pieces of personal information that, when repeated back, created a sense of belonging.

Today the line of well-wishers was mercifully short. Early-morning services, particularly midweek, were not the popular events that

Sundays were. It took only ten or fifteen minutes for hands to be patted, pleasantries exchanged, and promises to see one another again in
four days made. Then he was alone.

He shut the doors against the rain and entered the church. Empty,
it seemed even colder, and he shivered beneath his robes. He hurriedly blew out the candles that had been lit to provide the illusion of
warmth and left the sanctuary for the cozier environment of his own
house.

The rectory was behind the church. Erected sometime after the
church itself, it was made not of stone but of brick, a simple two-story
house in which the keeper of Saint Peter's could be contained. He had
inherited the furnishings of the previous priest, who had retired to
Florida and left behind a surprisingly tasteful array of sofas, tables, and
other items necessary for housekeeping. Father Dunn liked the house
very much, and felt both comfortable and safe within its walls.

Once inside he went to the second-floor room that was his study.
There was a fireplace there, a twin to the one in the living room directly below, and he'd lit a fire that morning before going to the
church. The air was warm, and a cheerful light flickered over the walls.
He sank into the well-worn leather chair in front of the fire and closed
his eyes.

Away from his duties, from the requirements of his position and the
watchful eyes of the faithful, he finally allowed himself to be a man and
not merely a priest. He permitted himself to remember. And what he
remembered was a face, a handsome face with bright blue eyes, an in-
fectious smile, and cheeks hollowed by approaching death.

Joseph's face had not always been ravaged. It had once been beautiful, was beautiful even as death closed its wings around him and carried him away. The sickness stole his life but not his soul, and he
remained a great, shining presence even as the last breath slipped
from him.

There was a photograph of him and Joseph on the mantle, but he
didn't need to open his eyes to see it. He'd memorized every part of it
in the years since Joseph's death. As the sound of his voice and the
touch of his fingers had become harder and harder to recall with absolute certainty, Thomas had relied more and more on the few photographs he had of his friend for his memories.

Friend. The word was so inadequate. But what else had Joseph been to him? Teacher. Mentor. Inspiration. He'd been many things. Lover? No, not that. Never that, even if Thomas had sometimes wanted it more than anything. Almost anything. God had always come between them, an irony of the cruelest sort since it was God who had brought them together in the first place.

Thomas had come to see Joseph as his greatest gift and his greatest trial. His temptation in the desert, perhaps. It was Joseph who had forced him to explore his heart's capacity to love, but ultimately he'd had to make a choice between that love and his love for the church. In the end it was God who had won the battle for his affections.

Joseph had never pressed him on the issue, had never, in fact, even discussed it with him except in the vaguest of terms. They'd both been too shy. And when Thomas's decision had been made, it was done in secret, behind the closed doors of his heart.

Even during the months of Joseph's illness and death, when Thomas visited often, they never spoke of those things. Nor did they speak of the cause of the illness, Joseph because it didn't matter to him and Thomas because he feared that he had in some way caused it, or at least failed to prevent it, by making the choice he had.

Thomas opened his eyes. Joseph looked back at him from the photo, his eyes forgiving everything. It was indeed the face of a saint, and gazing at it, Thomas began to weep for his sins.

CHAPTER 4

"Don't drive so fast. The road is wet."

Stephen Darby glanced over at his mother. She was wrapped in her thickest wool coat, her hands in her lap, fingers clasped tightly together. As they rounded a turn, one hand flew out to grip the handle of the door, as if Gail Darby's sheer force of will was the only thing that kept the vehicle from careening over the yellow divider line and into a tree. When they were safely around the bend, she let go and gave a sigh.

Stephen ignored her. His mother was an adept at sighing—perhaps the foremost practitioner of the art—but he'd long ago grown immune to her powers. Well, mostly. After all, she had used guilt to get him to take her to Saint Peter's before dawn, all so she could see Father Dunn. He suspected she had a crush on the priest, as she did on almost any man who embodied what she found lacking in her husband and her sons.

"I read the other day that when the brakes are wet, it takes five times as long to stop in the event of an accident," his mother said.

"Really?" answered Stephen. "Where did you read that?"

He deliberately stepped on the brakes, making the car jolt. His mother's hands immediately went to the dashboard, and he saw her pump her tiny foot, as if she controlled an invisible brake.

"I don't remember," she said breathlessly. "Somewhere. Maybe in *Reader's Digest*."

"Mmm-hmm." Stephen stifled a smile. He knew his mother was lying. For heaven's sake, she didn't even have a driver's license. Yet she wouldn't let that stop her from dispensing driving advice, no more than not having degrees in law or medicine could persuade her that she wasn't an expert on every possible legal situation or malady. She frequently invented facts and then insisted on their veracity, despite all proof to the contrary.

"You can learn a lot from the *Reader's Digest*," Gail Darby said sagely.

"What did you think of the service today?" Stephen asked her, anxious to talk about anything other than the redeeming value of the world's most-read magazine.

"I thought it was lovely," his mother answered, nodding her head approvingly. "Very appropriate. Father Dunn is a marvelous priest."

"Better than Father Rogan?" Stephen asked maliciously. He knew his mother had doted on the former priest to an extreme, going so far as to invite him to almost every holiday with their family.

"We'll see," replied Mrs. Darby primly. Her thin lips were pressed tightly together as she peered through her glasses at the road ahead, as if watching for oncoming obstacles.

"Will he be coming to Thanksgiving?" Stephen teased.

His mother shot him a look of reproach. "Don't get smart," she said.

"I wouldn't think of it," Stephen told her.

He turned onto the street where his parents lived. Actually, where the whole family lived, in three houses one beside the next. His brother, Alan, occupied the first of them with his wife and three children. His parents had the middle house, where they'd lived since their wedding day forty years ago and where Alan and Stephen had grown up. On the other side, like a familial bookend, was Stephen's house. He lived there alone.

He pulled into the driveway of his parents' house and followed his mother as she walked into the garage. None of the Darbys used their front doors. They were, for all practical purposes, purely ornamental, something on which to hang Christmas wreaths and other seasonal decorations.

They entered into the kitchen, where they found Martin Darby seated at the round table. A newspaper was spread out in front of him and he was staring at it intently. A half-eaten bowl of oatmeal had been pushed to one side, along with a crumpled napkin and a glass of orange juice.

"What's a seven-letter word for 'solid foundation'?" he asked irritably.

Stephen thought for a moment. "Bedrock," he said.

Mr. Darby looked at his crossword, scowling. "No, it has to have a U in it."

Stephen looked over his father's shoulder at the clue. "It's not 'solid,' it's 'salad,' " he said. "And the answer is lettuce."

Mr. Darby's pencil worked its way across the page. "I hate it when they have these cutesy clues," he said. "Why can't they just say what the hell they mean?"

"Because then it wouldn't be any fun," Stephen told him. "That's the whole point."

His father looked at him. "The point is to finish the damn thing."

"Stop swearing," Mrs. Darby said as she went to the refrigerator and opened it. "Stephen, what do you want for breakfast?"

"Oh, nothing," he told her. "I've got to get to work."

His mother looked at him blankly. "You work at home," she said.

Stephen nodded. "And it's still work," he said. "Just because I don't put on a suit and go to an office doesn't mean it's not a real job."

"I didn't say that," said Mrs. Darby. "Don't put words in my mouth. Now, do you want an omelette or scrambled eggs?"

"Why does he get eggs when I had to eat oatmeal?" complained Martin.

"Because I didn't have a heart attack last year," Stephen reminded him.

"Don't get smart," Mr. Darby said gruffly.

"Scrambled eggs or omelette?" Mrs. Darby asked, her voice rising.

"Time to go," Stephen said, standing up. He went to his mother and gave her a kiss on the cheek, then waved to his father. "See you two later."

"You need to eat something!" his mother called after him as he left.

He got into the car, drove the twenty feet to his own driveway, and parked again. Unlike his parents, he did not enter his house through the garage, which was detached. Rather, he walked to the rear of the house and entered there, into a small laundry room where he kept muddy shoes and the recycling. There he hung up his coat before continuing on into the kitchen.

Gathering eggs, butter, and cheese from the refrigerator, he made himself an omelette. When it was done, he sat at the table, a mirror image of the one in his parents' house, and he ate his breakfast from the same plates he'd eaten from as a child. They'd been given to him when his brother, into whose hands they'd first passed, married and received as a wedding present a new set of dishes. Stephen used them without a trace of sentimentality.

When he was finished eating, he washed and dried the dishes he'd dirtied and put them away. Then he entered the downstairs bedroom that functioned as his office and looked at his work for the day. The files he needed were stacked neatly to one side of his computer. Each one contained a tangle of receipts, bills, and assorted other financial debris, the accumulations resulting from his clients' monetary transactions.

Accounting suited him. Numbers were truthful things, completely incapable of deception, and he loved them. True, they could be made to lie, but their intrinsic nature was one of absolute honesty. Left to their own, they would always reveal the truth, and even if that truth was ugly, it was undeniable.

People, on the other hand, were something of a mystery to him. They were influenced by motivations, and seemingly irrational needs, and other things he found troubling and difficult to comprehend. Often, they wished to see anything other than the truth. He saw this frequently in the reactions his clients gave him to the financial truths he set before them. Unable to accept that they did not, in fact, have enough money to send a child to college or retire, they appeared wounded, as if the numbers had somehow betrayed them despite all of their goodwill and encouragement.

Stephen tried to be understanding, but usually he was simply embarrassed for them. He left them with the numbers and with suggestions for remedying their situations as practically as possible, excusing himself as soon as was polite so as to relieve himself of the contamination of their worry. He filed the encounters away in neatly labeled folders, arranged alphabetically by last name.

His own family was well taken care of. He saw to their finances, and knew that his parents would not have to worry about their golden years and that the concerns his two nephews and one niece would have regarding higher education would be gaining acceptance to the schools of their choosing. Everything else was the responsibility of the numbers, and in those he had unwavering confidence.

He sat at the desk and opened the first folder. Within moments he was lost in the rapture of expenses and receipts, his fingers flying over balance sheets and the keys of his calculator clicking as he added and subtracted, bringing order to chaos. When the phone rang an hour later, he looked at it, annoyed.

"Hello?"

"Good morning. It's Russell. I'm calling to remind you about tonight."

"Dinner," Stephen said. "Seven, right?"

"Seven," Russell repeated. "And look good. There's someone I want to introduce you to."

"Russell—" Stephen began.

"Don't start," Russell interrupted. "It's for your own good."

"But—"

"Be there at seven," Russell concluded, hanging up.

Stephen set the phone down and stared at it. His routine had been disturbed, now he was worried, and worry upset him because it was unnecessary. Why was Russell insisting on introducing him to someone? He hadn't asked for such a thing. Why would Russell assume it would be welcome?

He thought for a moment of canceling, of coming up with a plausible excuse to neatly remove himself from the situation. But he disliked lying. Besides, apart from this new surprise, he was looking forward to seeing Russell and John again. He had few friends, and his meeting with the couple had been a happy accident. Referred to Stephen by a teaching colleague of John's, they had come to him for help with their taxes earlier in the year. He had been impressed by John's organization and both intrigued and frightened by Russell's utter disregard for what others thought about him. When they'd invited him out socially, he'd surprised himself by accepting.

Since then they'd become friends. The subject of Stephen's romantic leanings had never been raised; Russell had just assumed and Stephen hadn't contradicted him. Almost immediately, Russell had made it his mission to find Stephen a suitable partner. So far Stephen had been able to put him off. Now, however, it seemed he was cornered.

He tried to forget about it, to lose himself in his work. But the numbers refused to cooperate, and finally he pushed the papers away and leaned back in his chair. Who was this person that Russell had selected for him? On what had he based his decision? They'd never discussed what Stephen was looking for.

And was he looking for anything? Even he wasn't sure what the answer to that question was. Being alone suited him. It prevented complications and made his life easier to manage. Adding someone else to the equation would mean making changes. Still, perhaps it was what he needed.

Romantic attachment was not something he'd permitted himself much of. In high school he'd seldom dated apart from the annual ritual of the prom. Even then, he'd attended with girls he'd befriended in his classes. There had been the awkward kiss or two, but little more. Once, during a long night of studying for a college midterm in statistical analysis, a study partner had unexpectedly professed her love for him and offered to prove it by allowing him to make love to her. He had tried, but the experiment had been a failure and he'd excused himself, citing exhaustion and concern for his grade point average.

He'd been more receptive to the handful of men with whom he'd had infrequent encounters, beginning with a friend in middle school who during a sleepover one weekend suggested they see whose penis was bigger, a proposal that had led to overly enthusiastic discussions of which girls at school they found attractive and culminated with their briefly touching one another's erections before retreating to the safety of their sleeping bags. There had been others since then, mostly in college, where experimentation of that sort was less significant and where he was assured some measure of anonymity due to the sheer size of the student population at the state school he attended.

In the decade since he'd returned to Cold Falls with his diploma in hand, he'd had less than half a dozen partners. Never had he brought anyone home, certain as he was that somehow his parents would find out and demand to know what exactly he thought he was doing. Nor could he stay over at someone else's house, as the absence of his car from the driveway would be sure to raise questions he was unprepared to answer.

The computer had become his way out. There, in the chat rooms he frequented sporadically, he was able to connect. There he could do the things he wanted to do with the men he wanted to do them with. It mattered little to him that they weren't real, or at any rate not physically present. In some ways he preferred that. When he and his partner were done, he simply logged off and was back in his own safe world where his longings couldn't disrupt things.

But tonight he would be faced with a real man, a person who would expect him to interact, presumably, using more than porn film dialogue. The idea of it made breathing difficult. His fingers drummed nervously on the desktop and he stared blankly at the screen. What would he say?

Instinctively, he opened his web browser and typed in an address. Moments later he was scrolling through the names of the men who were waiting, like him, in cyberspace for someone to come along. BoyBlue. GIJoe. JockStrp. Bi9Hrd. So many for being so early in the morning. They read like a menu of sexual appetizers. Some of them he recognized. Some he'd followed into private rooms. He breathed deeply. He was on familiar ground. They were just names. There was no one behind them, no one looking at him and judging. It was all make-believe.

A small window popped open on his screen. He looked at the message from JacknDude: Hey there. Looking for some fun?

Fun. Is that what he was looking for? No, but if that's what his correspondent wanted to call it, he didn't care. He put his hands on the keyboard and began to type.

CHAPTER 5

"Are they hitting it off?"

Russell paused, the pepper on the cutting board only half diced, as he waited for John's answer.

"I don't know," his lover said testily as he took two glasses from the cupboard. "Would you please stop trying to play matchmaker?"

Russell resumed chopping. "Greg is a nice guy," he said. "He's exactly what Stephen needs."

"How do you know what Stephen needs?" John asked. "Have you even asked him?"

Russell scraped the bits of pepper into the salad bowl. "There are some things you don't need to ask," he said. "Besides, I don't think he knows what he needs."

John picked up the drinks he'd poured and turned to leave. "Your obsession with arranging other people's lives is rivaled only by your obsession with rearranging our living room furniture," he said.

"Very funny," Russell answered. "But as I recall, you didn't know you needed me when we met."

"True," John said. "It took a great deal of convincing."

He left the kitchen. When he was gone, Russell set down the knife in his hand and took a long sip from the wineglass on the counter. So far, everything was going well. The roast was almost done, the pie had turned out beautifully, and with a little luck his attempt at setting Stephen up with Greg might just come off.

Then why don't I feel better about it all? he asked himself.

He knew why. It was John. Or rather, it was he and John. More and more he felt as if they simply occupied the same space, orbiting around one another without ever really connecting. They did the same things they'd been doing for seven years, but something had gone from the relationship. The happiness and confidence he'd once felt had been drained away, a slow, almost imperceptible leaching away of joy that hadn't become truly apparent until there was almost nothing left.

Now, though, he felt it strongly. He tried not to. He tried to go on as he always had, pretending that everything was going well and pushing his worries aside. Whenever he felt the prodding of insecurity, he banished it with an attempt at creating merriment, with an evening at the movies, a foray into a new and quickly abandoned interest, or a dinner party.

It was normal, he told himself. Relationships weren't designed to be perpetually exciting. He and John weren't newlyweds. They had a routine, a way of doing things that had developed over the years. That's what couples did. It's what his parents had done. It's what everyone did. He couldn't expect fireworks every day.

Probably, he thought, he was just depressed. He had to admit that work hadn't been particularly exciting either. Maybe a new job would help. And he *was* in middle age, he reminded himself. At forty-three, it was about time he had some kind of emotional crisis. It was practically expected. Hadn't his father come home with a new sports car one day around his own fortieth birthday? Russell, then fifteen, remembered the exasperated sigh his mother had let out upon seeing it roll into the driveway. But his father had been in noticeably better spirits for a long time afterward.

"See," he told himself firmly. "All you need is a Lexus and you'll be fine."

He picked up the salad bowl and headed for the dining room. As he passed from the kitchen, he forced the gloomy thoughts away and greeted his guests with a beaming smile.

"I hope you're all hungry," he said cheerfully as he placed the salad on the table and took his seat across from John. "What have I missed out here?"

"I was just asking John how the two of you met," Greg told him as he put some salad onto his plate.

"Oh, heavens," Russell answered. "It was at a Pride parade in Albany. I was living there and John was visiting some friends for the weekend."

"Under protest," John added.

"Parades aren't his thing," Russell explained. "But they'd dragged him along and I was there cheering for my friends on the gay chorus float."

"I asked him to stop shouting in my ear," John told Greg and Stephen.

"And I told him to get over himself," said Russell. "Then I left. But later that night I went to a party with my friends, and it turns out some of them knew some of the guys John was visiting, so we ran into each other again."

"Literally," said John. "He spilled a drink on me."

"Actually, I sort of threw it at him," Russell admitted. "He was complaining about the Dykes on Bikes who had led the parade, and he was ruining the mood."

"They were shirtless," John said sharply. "They were the only thing the newspeople focused on, and it made us all look like a bunch of perverts. And you never told me you *threw* that drink at me."

"It wasn't really throwing," Russell said quickly. "It was more like dropping. Anyway, we got into a big fight and somehow or other we ended up in bed back at my place. That was seven years ago."

"Opposites attracting," Greg said. "Kind of like *The Way We Were*. I think it's sweet."

"We dated long-distance for a year. Then John got the job here and we decided to move in together."

Greg picked up his wineglass. "I'd like to make a toast," he said. "To John and Russell. You guys are the kind of couple I want to be when I find the right guy."

The four men picked up their glasses and clinked them together. As he took a drink, Russell glanced across the table at John. His lover, busy picking at a spot on his shirt, didn't look at him.

"It must be amazing finding someone you can be with forever," Greg said.

Russell nodded. "Everyone should get to experience it," he said.

"Maybe if the morons who run this country wake up and legalize gay marriage, more of us will," Greg remarked.

"The only thing gay marriage would do is make a lot of money for gay divorce lawyers," John joked.

"Stephen, do you have many gay couples as clients?" Russell asked, ignoring his partner.

"Not really," Stephen said, wiping his mouth on his napkin. "Maybe two or three."

"Stephen is an accountant," Russell told Greg. "He does our taxes."

"What do you do?" Stephen asked Greg.

"I'm in men's underwear," Greg told him.

Seeing the blank look on Stephen's face, Greg and Russell laughed.

"It's a retail joke," Russell explained. "Greg is the manager of men's furnishings at Carter-Beane. You know, socks, underwear, pajamas."

"Oh," Stephen said, nodding. "Now I get it."

"I used to be in handbags," said Greg. "But after a while you just can't look at another Chanel clutch."

"I bet," said Stephen.

"Have you lived in Cold Falls a long time?" Greg inquired of Stephen.

"All my life," Stephen told him. "I went to Cold Falls Central School from kindergarten through twelfth grade. I didn't leave until I went off to college."

"And you came back?" said Greg. "That was brave."

"Not really," Stephen said. "My family lives here."

"Mine live in Pruitt, Kentucky," Greg told him. "Population sixteen, and fifteen of them are directly related to me. I got out as soon as I could."

"How'd you end up here?" asked Stephen.

"God hates me," Greg said. "Just kidding. I actually don't mind it here too much. The real answer is that I was transferred here from a store in Ohio. They offered it to me in the middle of February, and frankly, anything is better than Ohio in February."

"Except Pruitt, Kentucky, apparently," John remarked.

"Exactly," Greg said, ignoring the sarcastic tone of John's comment.

"Well, I wouldn't be here except that the children of Cold Falls Central School are in desperate need of scientific education," John said drily. "Stephen, I don't know how you ever graduated from such a place knowing anything."

"Actually, my chemistry teacher ended up shooting himself in the head in the boys' bathroom," Stephen replied. "Mr. Keller. It turned out he had a huge gambling debt."

"Is that what I have to look forward to?" John said aloud. "At least it would end my misery."

"I'll go get the pot roast," Russell announced. "Stephen, could you give me a hand with the salad plates?"

The two men disappeared into the kitchen, where the dirty plates were deposited in the sink. As Russell ran hot water over them, he asked, "So, what do you think of Greg?"

"He seems nice," Stephen said.

Russell dried his hands and turned his attention to the roast. "Nice as in okay, or nice as in you wouldn't mind going out on a date with him?"

"A date?" Stephen repeated. "That hadn't even occurred to me."

"Not a good sign," remarked Russell as he carved the meat. "I'll take that as a not-interested."

"No," said Stephen. "I just mean that . . . I don't know that . . . ."

Russell looked at the young man. "Sweetie, you need to get a life," he said kindly. "You can't just sit around with old people all the time."

"I don't!" Stephen protested. "I go out. I do stuff."

Russell sighed. "When's the last time you had a date?"

Stephen shrugged his shoulders. "I don't know," he said.

"Have you ever *had* a date?" asked Russell.

"Of course I've had dates," said Stephen.

"I mean real dates," Russell continued. "At a restaurant, or a movie, or God forbid, the symphony."

"I don't have time," Stephen said vaguely.

"Like hell you don't," said Russell. "You have nothing but time. And you need someone to spend it with." He spooned the roasted potatoes and carrots into a bowl. "Now, I don't mean to get all Auntie Mame on you or anything, but I do know a thing or two about this particular subject, and I know that you are in desperate need of a love life. So take my advice, and if you like that young man sitting across the table from you, you ask him out before you leave here tonight. Now serve."

He pushed the bowl of vegetables into Stephen's hands and pushed him toward the door, following behind with the sliced roast. The two of them entered the dining room and placed the food on the table. Russell dipped back into the kitchen and returned with several more small bowls, which he added to those already there.

"This all looks—and smells—fantastic," Greg told Russell as they passed the food around. "Do you like to cook?" he asked Stephen as he handed him the platter of meat.

"Not really," said Stephen. "Mostly I eat at my parents' house or throw something in the microwave."

"I love cooking," Greg said. "But it's not much fun cooking for yourself. It's nicer to have someone to cook for."

Russell glanced over at Stephen, who was chewing a mouthful of food, oblivious to the obvious invitation Greg had just thrown his way. The boy really was being most uncooperative, and he couldn't understand why.

"So, tell me what the best part of being in a long-term relationship is," Greg asked, surprising him.

"Stability," John said before Russell could answer. "You always know where your life is going. No surprises."

"Russell?" Greg said.

Russell thought. Stability? Is that what he meant to John, a life that was always the same? It made him sound practical and dependable, like a dog or a good winter coat. There was nothing romantic about stability, nothing to tug on the heartstrings or send the senses reeling.

"I guess the best part is not having to wonder who you'll have sex with next," Russell said.

John's head snapped up and he looked at his lover with a startled expression. Russell calmly stabbed a carrot with his fork and put it in his mouth as Stephen and Greg looked from one partner to the other.

"I mean, you know how it is," Russell continued. "When you're single, you always have to worry about the sex thing every time you're with someone new. Will he be good? Will I be good? What if it's too big or too small? Once you partner up, you always know what you're getting. You don't have to wonder if he's freaked out by rimming or hates the taste of cum or whatever."

John was still starring at him, stunned. Russell swallowed the food in his mouth and put his fork down.

"Now, who wants dessert?" he asked brightly.

A moment later he was standing in the kitchen. John was behind him, fuming.

"I can't believe you said that," he hissed. "That was so rude."

"What?" Russell asked. "You mean I surprised you? I'm sorry for not being stable enough for you."

"What are you talking about?" said John irritably.

Russell whirled around and faced him. "You make me feel like a couch," he said.

"What?" John said again, looking even more confused.

"A couch," Russell repeated. "Or old socks, or, or, or something else dependable and boring and predictable." He started to cry.

"I have no idea what's going on here," said John.

"Neither do I!" Russell said, wiping the tears from his face and staring at his partner. He felt as if he was seeing John clearly for the first time, and he was terrified to discover that his lover's face now bore almost no resemblance to that of the man he'd fallen in love with.

He longed for John to take him in his arms, to hold him and comfort him and tell him that everything would be fine. He waited, the seconds stretching out interminably as John looked at him. Then John cleared his throat.

"I'll take the cake out," he said. "You come out when you've calmed down a little."

CHAPTER 6

"How long have you lived here?"

Mike looked at the man sitting in front of him at the bar. The guy was on his third drink—vodka tonics—in an hour, and his face was showing the signs of drunkenness. Not that he'd looked all that great before he'd started drinking. He'd come in right at four, moments after Mike unlocked the front door, not even bothering to brush the snow from his coat. He hadn't moved since, and a small puddle had formed on the floor around him as the snow had melted in the heat of the room.

"Couple of years," Mike told him. He never got too specific with customers, especially ones he didn't know. The man's face was new to him, and he didn't like what he saw. There was a sadness behind the unfocused eyes and reddened nose, a weariness that spoke of long hours spent in other bars, looking for one thing and avoiding another.

"Nice place to live?" the man tried again.

Mike shrugged. "Depends what you like," he said. "It suits me." He thought about asking the man if he wanted another drink, then decided against it. The last thing he needed was a drunk passed out on his floor.

"I used to live in a place like this," the man told him, pushing an ice cube around his half-full glass with his finger. "Couldn't wait to get out. Bunch of small-town hicks with small-town minds."

"Where'd you go?" Mike asked him. He didn't care what the answer was, but since the man seemed intent on taking up his time with the conversation, he thought he might as well play along. He had nothing else to do until the happy hour rush started.

"Oh, here and there," the man told him, waving his hand around vaguely. "Any big city I could find. Anywhere that wasn't like this place. New York. Chicago. Even Amsterdam for a year."

"And what brings you here now?"

"Business," the man told him, taking a swig from his glass. "Had to fly into Albany, drive up to Syracuse, and now I'm going back again. I needed a pit stop, and this hole was listed in my Damron guide."

"I take it we're not what you're used to," Mike commented.

"I don't mean nothing by it," said the man apologetically. "It's just that being here depresses me. Reminds me of what I ran away from."

"I guess you'll be glad to get back home then," said Mike.

The man drained his glass and set it on the bar. "That's the kicker," he said as he zipped his coat and stood up. "What I found out in all those big cities was that everywhere's the same. You trade the trailers for condos, the blue collars for white ones, it doesn't matter. Only difference is that in a big city it's easier to convince yourself that things are better. If you can keep that up long enough, you make yourself believe it."

He gave Mike a final nod and turned to go. Mike watched him walk unsteadily toward the door, waiting for him to push open the portal onto the snowy night before pocketing the bills the man had left behind for his tip.

The snow was something of a surprise. Usually the cold held off until the end of November, making its grand entrance just in time to create a winter wonderland and get everyone in the mood to face Christmas. But the cold had come early this year, the temperatures dropping overnight and the dawn rising on a landscape whose sharp edges were blunted by powdery wrapping. Now it was a world of plows and rock salt, mittens and scarves.

Mike, for one, was pleased that winter had arrived ahead of schedule. He liked the shorter days and the nights that came early and stayed late. Inside the Engine Room, it didn't matter if the sun was shining anyway. His was a world lit by neon beer signs and low-wattage bulbs. It was warm, an escape from the cold where men gathered for company to stave off both their loneliness and the darkness. Seeing the place packed that evening, Mike thought pleasantly of long-ago days when men crowded into similarly shadowed taverns and alehouses as the frigid winds tore at the world.

Those men spoke to one another of things that occupied their lives, of the sea and whales, farms and flocks. The men in the Engine Room talked of much different things: Cher and *Queer as Folk,* their boring jobs and equally boring love lives. But wasn't it in many ways the same? Hadn't they just traded in their mugs of ale for Cosmos in delicately stemmed glasses, their weather-aged faces for eyes bathed in Clinique?

Mike laughed to himself. It was a ridiculous analogy. But he liked it anyway. No, most of the men who were now coming in and filling the bar with their voices were not exactly the hearty adventurers their ancestors might have been. Yet didn't they rub the cold from their hands the way those men might have? Didn't they, too, find brotherhood in one another?

He was stretching again. He sighed. Where was the adventure in the world? He looked around at the men holding their drinks and chatting about nothing. Didn't they want something more? Didn't they want to *do* something?

He was bored, and he knew it, and that irritated him. His customer with the tired face had been right—everything really was the same. But no, he told himself, he didn't really believe that. There *were* different people to meet and places to see. There was something beyond the WELCOME TO COLD FALLS, NY sign that was planted out on the highway running into town. It was they who chose to stay there, safe within the familiar world. They. He. He had chosen to stay there.

"Mike! Give me a cold one!"

A familiar face greeted him, and he brushed his thoughts away. He would, he knew, lose himself in the patterns of a Friday night at the Engine Room, dive headlong into the currents of chatter, and distract himself with filling orders and making change.

Right up until two o'clock in the morning, that's what he did. And when the final customer was sent to his car, the door was locked, and the cleanup guys were washing the place down, Mike headed out the back door to his waiting pickup.

He drove with the windows down, the chill air filling the cab of the truck, sweeping over his body and escaping through the passenger side window. He felt it cleansed him, carried away the smell of smoke and alcohol that permeated his T-shirts every night and seemed to leave behind a layer of grime he could feel clinging to his skin. He hated touching his own face before he had a chance to shower.

It was still snowing. Although not as heavy as it had been earlier, it still fell steadily, forming an ocean of swirling flakes through which the headlights of the truck cut two thin golden paths. The road had been plowed hours before, and now the tracks of the cars that had passed through since then were almost filled up again.

He turned on the radio and suddenly Hank Williams was sitting beside him, so lonesome he could cry. Mike turned the volume up until Hank's voice drowned out the sound of the windshield wipers with their scratchy click-click-click. It was just himself, Hank, and the snow. The only part of the world that existed was the few feet Mike could see ahead of him; everything else fell away into blackness. Contained in this circle of snow and wind and light, he continued down the road.

He crested a hill and began the descent down the other side. As he neared the bottom, he saw, too late, the blinking red and yellow eyes of a car's hazard lights. Then a face emerged from the snow, eyes tightened against the glare of his headlamps, and arm raised to cover the face.

Mike's foot pressed the brake to the floor and the truck slid, first sliding to the right and then, as he turned the wheel, spinning around completely. The world became a blur of black and white, turning in slow motion until the truck came to a stop with a dull thud and Mike was thrown back against his seat.

His first thought was that he'd hit the figure in the snow. But as his head cleared and he was able to look outside, he saw that he had simply ended up in a bank left behind by a plow. His engine had stalled, but the lights still glowed brightly against the snow and there didn't seem to be any damage.

He opened the door and stepped gingerly to the ground, testing his bones. Everything seemed to be working just fine. Reassured, he walked to the rear of the truck and looked back up the road. The car still sat there, twenty feet away, its hazards unnaturally cheerful. A shadow detached itself and ran toward him.

"Are you okay?"

He couldn't see the face, but the voice was distinctly male.

"Yeah, yeah, I'm fine," Mike said. "But what the fuck are you doing parked in the middle of the road?"

The man came closer, stepping into the light so that Mike could finally see him. He peered at Mike through glasses flecked with snow. His dark hair, too, was capped by a white frost.

"I'm so sorry," he said. "My car just stopped, and I couldn't push it anywhere. I don't have my cell phone with me and—"

"It's okay," said Mike. "We're both fine, right? You just gave me a scare."

The man sighed visibly. "It's so cold," he said, glancing up at the sky and putting his hands in his pockets. Then he looked at Mike, wearing just a T-shirt under his open jacket. "Aren't you cold?" he asked.

"Let's take a look at your car," said Mike. "Do you have any idea what's wrong?"

"I'm not exactly mechanical," the man told him as he fell into step beside Mike. "Are you?" he asked hopefully.

"We'll find out," answered Mike.

They reached the car and Mike opened the door. The keys were still in the ignition. He turned them and the car's interior lights burst into life.

"The battery's not dead," Mike said.

He tried to start the engine. The car gave a sad little cough before relapsing into silence. He tried again and got the same result. He was about to get out and look beneath the hood when his gaze fell on the fuel gauge. The needle was deep in the red zone.

"When's the last time you filled this thing up?" he asked the man, who was standing beside the car and looking at him anxiously.

"Filled it up? Oh, I guess a week or so ago maybe."

"Well, you should have done it tonight. You're out of gas."

"Out of gas?" the man repeated. "Really?" He leaned in and stared at the gauge Mike was pointing to. "Oh, I see."

"There's not a gas station in town open this time of night," Mike told him. "Best thing to do is push the car to the side of the road, leave it here, and hope the morning plow doesn't think it's a drift that needs clearing."

He got out, gently pushing the man with the car door.

"I'll push," Mike told him. "You steer."

The man got in and Mike stepped behind the car. Placing his hands on the trunk, he pushed hard. The car didn't budge.

"Is your foot on the brake?" Mike called out.

"Yes," the man shouted back.

"Take it off," Mike ordered, shaking his head.

He pushed again. This time the car rolled forward easily. The man guided it as far to the side of the road as it would go and stopped. Mike dusted off his wet hands and walked to the driver side window.

"Come on," he said. "I'll give you a lift home. You can come back for the car in the morning."

The man got out, locked the car, and followed Mike to his truck. Once inside, Mike turned the key and was relieved to hear his engine rumble to life. He turned up the heater, which rewarded him with breaths of warm air.

"I'm Mike, by the way," he told his passenger.

"Thomas," the man said. "Thanks for stopping to help."

Mike laughed. "I didn't have a lot of choice," he replied.

Thomas smiled. "I guess you didn't," he said. "Thanks anyway."

"So, where are we going?" Mike asked him.

Thomas looked at him blankly.

"Where do you live?" Mike clarified.

"Oh, right," said Thomas. "Saint Peter's Episcopal Church."

"You live in a church?"

"Not in it," Thomas said. "Behind it. I'm the priest there."

Mike looked sideways at him. For the first time he noticed the white collar peering out from the neck of the man's black jacket.

"What were you doing out this time of night?" he asked.

"One of my parishioners is sick," Thomas told him. "She probably won't live to see Thanksgiving."

Mike nodded, not knowing what to say. Just the idea that there was a priest in his truck was a bit unnerving. He wasn't sure why, really. The man seemed nice enough. But he and religion didn't have much to do with one another, and he preferred to keep the whole thing at arm's length.

"Well, we'll have you back at the church in no time," said Mike.

"I really didn't expect anyone to come along so late," the priest told him. "It's something of a miracle that you did."

"I work late hours," Mike explained. "I was on my way home."

Almost immediately he regretted telling the priest that, as he knew the question it would raise. Sure enough, a moment later Thomas asked, "What do you do?"

Mike hesitated. Should he tell the priest the truth? It probably wouldn't go over very well. But why did he care, anyway? He didn't owe the guy anything. He was irritated with himself for even thinking it mattered what the man thought of him.

"I'm a bartender," he said. "At the Engine Room."

He waited for the priest to say something disapproving. Much to his surprise, Thomas said, "So we're in the same line of work."

Mike looked at him, confused. "How so?"

"Well," Thomas said, "we both minister to people. They come to us because they need something. I'm sure you've had to sit through more than one confession or request for advice. Am I right?"

Mike grinned. "Yes," he said. "You're right."

"Not that I have much experience with bars, mind you," the priest continued, "but I think they have quite a bit in common with churches. People gather there to be part of a community. They look for something they don't find elsewhere."

"You're an interesting priest," said Mike.

"Am I?" Thomas said. "I wonder."

The two of them settled into silence as Mike drove through the snow. Ten minutes later he pulled into the driveway of Saint Peter's. When the truck came to a stop, Thomas turned to him.

"Thank you again for your help," he said.

"No problem," said Mike. "Just don't forget to pick up your car tomorrow. Call any garage and they'll be able to get some gas to it."

Thomas nodded. "I will," he said. "And perhaps one of these days you'll come by and see what it is I do."

Mike laughed. "Tell you what," he answered. "If you come see me at work, I'll come see you." The idea of the priest setting foot in the Engine Room was as ridiculous as him setting foot in a church.

"I just might take you up on that offer," Thomas said as he got out and shut the door. "But for now, good night."

Mike waved at the priest and pulled away. Again he thought about Thomas standing in the middle of a bunch of queens at the bar. He laughed. *What I wouldn't give to see the look on his face*, he thought as he headed home.

CHAPTER 7

He wished he'd worn the rubber boots.
The snow was deeper than he'd expected, and with every step, his feet became more and more damp. He should have known better, he told himself. Walter would have scolded him. "I told you so," he would have said, his voice filled with reproach and love.

At least he'd remembered the scarf. It was red, the only flash of color against the white snow and the black of his greatcoat. The scarf was Walter's last gift to him, finished only days before the end. Unable to sleep, he'd stayed up all night knitting furiously, as if the clicking of the needles staved off death's arrival. When finally it was done, he'd given it to Simon, saying, "It's going to be cold. You're going to need this."

And he had needed it. In the days following Walter's death, he had refused to take it off, wearing it wrapped around his throat like a noose. It had absorbed his tears, soaking them up as they coursed down his cheeks. He saw it as a relic, a holy remnant left behind by the most glorious angel he'd ever known.

Eventually he had been able to take it off, to hang it first on the hook beside the kitchen door where his and Walter's coats hung beside the dog's leash, and then, months later, to take it down and put it in a drawer. He'd taken it out at the first sign of fall, but not until that morning had he put it on.

Immediately the memories of the year before had come back, as if his tears had locked them into the fabric of the scarf and putting it around his neck had released them once more. He smelled the scent of Walter's room, the odor of flowers covering up the acrid stench of decay. He saw again his lover's withered body, consumed by cancer until he resembled a doll made of sticks. But always his blue eyes had sparkled, always they had lit up for Simon, until the moment when they closed forever and Simon had been left holding Walter's lifeless hand in his own.

Death had surprised him with its quickness. Despite the length of Walter's decline, the ending had come as a shock. Nine months he had been ill. It had taken as long for the cancerous cells to multiply and devour him as it took other, less treacherous, cells to bond and bring a new life into the world. How strange it was, the power of those infinitesimal building blocks, to both build up and tear down. Where one blossomed, another took back. What, he wondered, determined their temperament? Why was one body blessed and another cursed?

He'd asked himself those questions while Walter was dying, attempting to make sense of it all. Instead, he should have been preparing himself for the cold rain of grief that came upon him at the very moment of Walter's passing. He'd thought about it, of course, but only in the vaguest of terms. Walter would die. Walter would be dead. Walter would be buried.

But the real pain came not from the death, but from the absence. The death he could handle, had handled, with as much grace as he could muster. The absence, however, was unbearable. One moment they had been together; the next Simon had been alone. There was no gradual transition, no soothing possibility of return. There was simply aloneness.

He had adjusted. He'd had no choice. At first his mind refused to accept the truth, and he'd wandered aimlessly around his house as friends helped him deal with the mundane chores of arranging the funeral, informing relations and other concerned parties, and handling the legal affairs. He had pretended that he was simply organizing a party, a party at which Walter would be the guest of honor.

But afterward, when the funeral was over and the friends had gone home, leaving him in an empty house, he had come face to face with the emptiness Walter had left behind when his spirit had flown. Gone was the warmth of his laughter and the strength of his love, and without them Simon was a ghost. He haunted himself, moving from room to room in search of the past. He sat on the bed, the red scarf around his neck, and wept himself dry. And still it did no good. Still every night he went to bed alone and woke up to a coldness no amount of hot water could ease from his bones.

A year had gone by, and with the turning of the seasons, things had become more bearable. Spring, with its renewing of life, had reawakened in Simon a desire to live. Summer's sun had returned the warmth to his blood. And now he had arrived back at fall more or less intact.

He came to the gravestone and stopped. He'd visited Walter many times in the months following his burial, but he had not been there since late summer. He felt slightly guilty about that, as if he'd stood his lover up, left him waiting, alone, wondering what had happened. This, though, was the important day, the anniversary, and he had come. He stood, looking down at the ground.

"Hey there," he said. "How have you been?"

He reached out and brushed some of the snow from the top of Walter's stone, the way he would have brushed it from his shoulder had they been walking together. His fingertips lingered on the stone for a moment before he pulled his hand back and placed it in the pocket of his coat.

"I guess you want to hear about what's been going on," he said. "Not much, I'm afraid. You haven't missed a thing. Clancy's started barking at the mailman. I don't think he hears very well anymore. Sort of like me, right?"

He smiled to himself, imagining Walter's response to that. He'd almost brought Clancy with him, but the old pug hated the snow and preferred to spend his days curled up on the couch in the spot Walter had once occupied.

He had brought something else, however. In the big pocket of his coat was a CD player. He took it out and held it in his hands.

"It's Brahms," he said. "*The German Requiem.* Only it's in English, Shaw's translation. I tried the original and it was just too much."

He placed the tiny earpieces into his ears and hit the play button. The voices of the Mormon Tabernacle Choir filled his head. He himself would have preferred Mozart, but Walter had always had an affinity for Brahms, frequently quoting the composer's well-known remark, "I never laugh on the inside." Despite Walter's love of life, he'd been fascinated with the darkness that could descend upon even the happiest of souls. Brahms had been one of his favorites, a man who composed soothing lullabies through which ran the merest hint of nightmare. He had listened to Brahms endlessly in the last months, until Simon had found himself humming entire movements even when he was far from the house.

He'd discovered the *Requiem* several months after Walter's death. It was in the CD player Walter had used at night, when he needed the solace of music but didn't want to disturb Simon's sleep. While finally cleaning out the things from Walter's bedside table, Simon had opened the player and seen the CD. At first its significance had escaped him, but when he went to locate the case for the disc, the symbolism had become clear—Walter had been listening to the music of death.

He'd waited another few weeks before putting the disc into the stereo and playing it for himself. He'd wept through the entire performance, sitting on the couch stroking Clancy's head as his body shook. The music, even in the original German, seared his heart. When later he'd bought an English translation and actually understood the words, he'd cried anew.

Now he shut his eyes and listened as the Mormon Tabernacle Choir sang for his dead lover. He knew Walter would appreciate the irony of the notoriously homophobic Mormons serenading him. Besides, the music was heavenly, the soprano soloist angelic. The performance transcended any differences of belief, the orchestra and singers merely acting as conduits for the music.

He stood before Walter's grave, the snow falling gently around him, and he listened for some time. He felt neither cold nor weariness. His feet, wet beyond caring, were numb. All that mattered was his being there, sharing the moment with Walter. Brahms's exquisite creation was the bridge between them, a soaring golden arch across which the worlds of the living and the dead were united.

Half an hour passed, or more. When the choir began to sing the first notes of "How Lovely Is Thy Resting Place," Simon opened his eyes. Removing the earphones from his ears, he placed the still-playing CD in the snow atop Walter's grave.

"Good night, sweet prince," he said softly, then turned to go.

The walk back to the car was mercifully short. Only when he tried to insert the key into the lock did he realize how truly cold he was. His fingers hesitated, and he had to blow on them to get them to bend.

Once inside the car, he sat with the heater at full strength until he felt capable of holding the wheel.

When he reached home, the first thing he did was remove his wet shoes and socks. His toes, like his fingers, refused to feel anything but cold for a long time, despite being wrapped in dry wool socks and slippers. A mug of coffee did its bit to revive his frigid interior, however, and soon he was feeling less like an icicle and most definitely like a sixty-five-year-year-old man who had stayed out in the cold for too long a time.

He sat down on the couch, where he was joined by Clancy, who snuggled into his lap and almost immediately went to sleep. Simon sat, rubbing the dog's ears and listening to him snore. He missed Walter. He missed holding him, and touching him. He missed hearing his breathing as he slept and his singing as he moved throughout the house, forever rearranging furniture and cleaning up.

They were supposed to have grown old together. That had always been the plan. Whenever Simon had thought about his life, he'd always imagined it continuing on and on forever, Walter accompanying him hand in hand. He'd thought about death, of course, but never the specifics of it. They would both die, naturally, but he'd secretly hoped it would be together, in a car accident or even in their sleep.

Now he was left to grow old alone. He supposed to many people he already *was* old. At sixty-five, he was far older than most of the men he knew. Certainly he was far beyond being attractive to them. He knew this, and accepted it. Old gay men were not, in the general scheme of things, hot properties. They could be funny. They could dispense advice. If they were very good, they might be allowed to pay someone younger and more handsome for the privilege of touching his body. But they were not supposed to desire any more than that. It was in poor taste. They'd had their chances, and it was expected that they would now relinquish the rights and privileges of love to those coming up behind them.

No one, in the year since Walter's death, had asked him if he ever thought about finding another partner. It was as if a tacit understanding existed that he had been given his years of happiness and was now supposed to live the remainder of his life comforted by memories. He had cooperated, he knew, by assuming the role of the grieving husband. He had waited the appropriate amount of time and then reappeared at the Engine Room, where he'd been greeted warmly and given a seat of honor at the bar.

But it wasn't enough. Perhaps it was selfish, but he wanted more of what he'd had with Walter. He knew that he'd been given more than most people ever had in a lifetime, but still his heart longed to be filled with the sweet ache of love.

He stood, Clancy sliding gently from his lap and stretching out across the sofa cushion. Leaving the dog there, Simon went upstairs and into the bedroom he'd shared with Walter for more than forty years. Bit by bit, Walter's presence had faded from the room, leaving behind only a faint reminder, like the roses on the wallpaper they'd spent one whole weekend hanging almost thirty years ago. His clothes and personal effects were gone, given to charity or put into boxes and stored in the attic.

But something still remained, something that couldn't be seen or touched or smelled. It was a feeling, a lingering memory that often was difficult to grasp on to but which came into sharper focus whenever Simon entered the room. Here, in the place where they'd spent their most intimate times, he felt closer to Walter than he did anywhere else in the world.

Pictures of him and Walter were placed around the room, images capturing them at various stages of life. The oldest was taken at the party where they'd met, a now yellowing photograph depicting two handsome young men, their arms thrown around one another's shoulders. The most recent had been taken a few months before Walter's death. Walter, overly thin but still smiling, sat in bed while Simon stood beside him.

The beginning and the end, Simon thought as he looked around. And everything in between. He was living in a room of memory, a sacred vault where the life he and Walter had created could be safely stored. Here he felt most alive, here where the heart they'd shared continued to beat softly and steadily.

He removed his clothes, letting them fall to the floor. Standing in front of the full-length mirror that covered the back of the closet door, he looked at his body. His belly was slack, the skin of his arms wrinkled. The muscles he'd once possessed had softened, and the hair on his chest had grayed.

Still, Walter had found him sexy. They had found one another sexy.

Making love for the last time, a week before Walter's cancer had made it impossible for him to do anything other than breathe and speak in short sentences, they had been as enamored of one another as they had been on that first night.

Simon held his penis in his hand, gently massaging it. It was funny how the cock never aged. While other parts of their bodies had begun to suffer the vagaries of age, his and Walter's dicks had remained forever eighteen. Even when various medications and health issues made erections difficult, they had managed. When Simon had taken Walter into his mouth and closed his eyes, he had tasted exactly what he'd tasted four decades earlier, and when he entered Walter, perhaps more cautiously than in those days, he was greeted with the same embracing warmth.

How he'd enjoyed making love with Walter. They'd known everything about one another, and even after years together the smell, taste, and feel of his lover's body against his had been a revelation. Each time they'd come together had made him long for more.

He was hard now, thinking about Walter. His hand moved gently up and down the length of his cock as he lost himself in a daydream. They were in bed. It was afternoon. The sun streamed in the windows and the sheets, hopelessly tangled, hung off the bed. The two of them, sweaty and deeply in love, rolled atop the bed, arms and legs a puzzle.

How old were they? Twenty-one? Fifty-seven? It didn't matter. In his dream they were ageless. All that mattered to him was that they were together, their hands caressing one another, their mouths pressed together.

He came unexpectedly, his body convulsing joyfully as he cried out half in pleasure and half in anguish at having his dream end so suddenly. He reached out, hoping to feel warm flesh beneath his fingers. Instead he touched the cold, smooth surface of the mirror.

He opened his eyes. The mirror was spattered with the results of his orgasm. Behind the milky stain his body was reflected back at him, his rapidly softening cock still held in his hand. Suddenly his knees felt weak. He fell to the floor, kneeling in front of the mirror. He was now level with the streaky smears, his face obscured by the net of pale liquid. The joy he'd felt at the moment of climax had disappeared along with his erection.

Putting his face in his hands, he cried.

CHAPTER 8

"Gina's pissed off again because you didn't give her the Lancôme counter."

Russell looked up from his desk to see Greg standing in the doorway.

"Thanks for the warning," he said. "I'll be sure to be busy doing inventory all day."

Greg sat down in the chair across from Russell.

"What's the matter?" he asked. "You don't seem your usual perky self. In fact, you haven't seemed yourself for a while. Is something wrong?"

Russell put down the order sheets he was going over. Things were very wrong, but he was doing his best to pretend that they weren't. So far, it had been working. But now, with Greg sitting in front of him looking at him with such sympathy, he cracked.

"I moved out," he said.

"Out?" Greg repeated.

"Out of the house," Russell said, his voice hitching. "Away from John."

Greg's eyes went wide. "You moved out?"

Russell nodded toward the door of his office. "Close it," he said.

Greg did as he was asked. Once they were alone, he let out a deep breath, trying to hold back the tears that were forming in his eyes. *I won't cry,* he told himself. *I won't cry.* It had become his new mantra.

"So, what happened?" Greg asked him. "You guys seemed fine at dinner."

Russell laughed. He'd been anything but fine at dinner. After his breakdown in the kitchen, he'd pulled it together enough to sit through the meal without letting on that he was falling apart inside. He'd smiled and nodded, and even said one or two funny things that had made everyone laugh.

Then, after dessert was over and Stephen and Greg had taken their leave, he'd come undone again. Standing over the kitchen sink, he'd burst into tears as John had stood, bewildered, in the doorway looking at him. Finally Russell had turned the water off, turned to John, and announced that he was moving out.

"We need a break," Russell told Greg. "I need a break."

"But what's wrong with the relationship?" Greg inquired.

Russell leaned back in his chair and ran his hands over his face. "That's just it," he said. "I don't know. It's more like what's right with it."

"Do you still love him?" Greg said.

Russell nodded.

"And does he still love you?"

"He says he does," Russell answered.

"Then it's about sex," Greg declared emphatically.

"It's *not* about sex," Russell countered.

"Well, it's got to be about something. You don't just move out after, what is it, seven years? Where did you go, anyway?"

"I'm staying with a friend."

"A friend, or a *friend*," Greg asked, emphasizing the last word meaningfully.

"No, it's not like that," Russell told him. "I'm not having an affair. It's a woman. Cheryl."

"Cheryl from furniture?" Greg said.

Russell nodded. "She has an extra room."

"Have you talked to John since you left?"

"A couple of times," Russell said. "Actually, we're supposed to have lunch in forty-five minutes. I don't honestly know what to say to him. He just doesn't get it."

"No offense, but it sounds like you don't either," said Greg.

"I know, I know," Russell said, shaking his head. "I think I just need some time away from him to figure stuff out. I can't think straight when I'm around him."

"Seven years is a long time," Greg suggested.

"Don't say it," Russell told him before Greg could continue.

"Well, it is."

"I know it is. And there's no reason a gay relationship can't go on for a lot longer than that."

Greg nodded. "I'm not saying it can't. I'm just saying that sometimes the, you know, magic, wears off after a while."

"What's the longest you've ever been with someone?" Russell asked him.

"A couple of months," Greg admitted.

"Get back to me when it's been a couple of years," Russell said.

"I know it's different," Greg continued, waving a hand at him. "I know the fireworks turn into something else and blah, blah, blah. Believe me, I hope I find out. But sometimes relationships just run their course."

Russell shook his head. "I just can't think like that," he said sadly. "I can't. If I let myself think that, then it's all been for nothing."

"I don't know what to tell you," Greg said.

"You don't have to tell me anything," Russell reassured him. "I appreciate you just listening to me. You don't know what it's been like not being able to say anything to anyone. I've barely slept in two weeks. I screwed up these reports three times."

"Let me know if there's anything I can do," Greg told him. "In the meantime, I'll keep Gina out of your hair. There's a sweater display out there that's going to need total refolding."

Russell laughed. "Thank you," he said. "Hey, what about you? Have you heard from Stephen?"

Greg shook his head. "Shot down again," he said. "I've left him two messages."

Russell sighed. "I just don't get him," he said. "I could tell he liked you."

"And I liked him," said Greg. "But as we both know, that's not always enough."

Greg stood up. "Time to straighten out the boxer briefs," he said. "And just about time for your lunch."

Russell looked at his watch. Greg was right. He was due to meet John in fifteen minutes.

"You look fine," Greg said.

Russell blushed. "I feel like I'm going on a date," he said. "It's so stupid."

"You're just nervous," Greg told him.

"I'm beyond nervous," said Russell. "This is the first time we've been face to face since I left."

"It's John," Greg reminded him. "Just talk to him."

Russell nodded. Greg opened the office door and left. Russell waited a minute, put on his coat, and left. Minutes later he was in his car, heading for the restaurant he'd suggested for his meeting with John. Much too quickly, he was there. He scanned the parking lot for John's car, saw it, and felt a wave of nausea sweep over him.

He almost left, but he knew that wouldn't change anything. Finally he calmed his nerves and got out of the car. He walked quickly into the restaurant, found John seated at a table near the back, and walked over.

"Hey," he said, sliding into the bench across from John. "Sorry I'm late."

"You're always late," said John emotionlessly. "I'm used to it."

"Sorry," Russell said again.

He picked up the menu and pretended to look at it. It didn't matter what he ordered; he wasn't going to eat much of it anyway. That's why he'd picked Panda Garden; it was easier to make Chinese food look as if you'd eaten it.

"I don't know why they call this place Panda Garden," he said, his voice tight. "Why would pandas have a garden?"

"Russell, I didn't come here to talk about the name of the restaurant," John said.

Russell closed the menu and put it down. He picked up the packet of wooden chopsticks next to his plate and fidgeted with them. "Right," he said.

John was just looking at him, not saying anything. Russell felt like one of his lab experiments. He wondered what results Russell was expecting from this particular test.

"How have you been?" he asked finally.

"How do you think I've been?" John replied.

"Why do you always answer me with another question?" said Russell defensively. "Why can't you ever just say what you're thinking?"

"You just answered me with two questions," John retorted. "But to answer your original one, I've been fine."

"Fine," Russell repeated. Had he really been fine? How fine could someone be whose partner of seven years had snapped and walked out on him? He looked at John. His hands were folded on the table in front of him and his face was expressionless. He looked as cool as he probably did every day when he faced a room full of students who couldn't care less about what he had to say to them.

"I'm really sorry," Russell said. "I know this is weird."

Again John said nothing. Russell tried to think of something else to say, anything to break the awful silence. He was saved by the fortunate arrival of the waitress to take their order.

"Sweet and sour chicken," Russell said dutifully, listening as John requested beef with broccoli. When the waitress had disappeared, he began again. "I'm sorry about leaving."

"Why?"

He looked at his partner. "What?"

"I asked you why," John repeated. "Why are you sorry?"

"Because it was a shitty thing to do," Russell said. "I just left you there with no explanation."

"But you're not sorry you left."

It was a statement, not a question, and Russell wasn't sure what to say to it. Finally he said, "No, I'm not sorry about the leaving, just about how I did it. I needed to leave."

"Fair enough," John said. "Can you tell me why?"

That was the million-dollar question. Russell looked down at his paper placemat. It was printed with the signs of the Chinese Zodiac. Out of habit, he searched for his birthday and saw that he was born in the Year of the Tiger. John, a year older, was an Ox. He looked at the description for the Tiger and saw that in the love section it said "Most incompatible with the Ox." He moved his plate to cover the image and looked at John again.

"I know you're confused," he said carefully. "I'm confused too. I just feel like things aren't right."

"Things," said John. "You mean our relationship. You don't have to be vague."

"And you don't have to be so fucking scientific all the time."

John's head snapped up and he looked at Russell in surprise.

"I'm sorry for saying it like that," Russell said. "But that's part of the problem. I feel like I'm one of your students. When you talk to me, it's like I'm sitting in one of your lectures."

John said nothing. His fingers idly played with the silverware, straightening the fork and knife until they were perfectly parallel. Russell waited for a response from him, but it was clear none was forthcoming.

"It's like we live in a lab," Russell continued. "Our lives are sterile, perfectly planned, boring."

"So you're bored with me," said John, nodding as if he'd figured out the solution to an equation. "It's time to move on."

"No," Russell said. "I didn't say that."

The waitress reappeared, carrying their lunches, and they each looked away as she set them down. When she left, neither moved to begin eating. Finally, John spoke.

"Russell, ever since I've known you, you've flitted from one thing to another," he said evenly. "You have a new interest every week. First it was photography, then it was gardening. Last year it was yoga, for Christ's sake. You're like a little boy sometimes, always looking for a new toy."

Russell felt himself blushing with anger. The tone in John's voice was exactly the one he hated hearing, the one that made him feel small and silly.

"I can't help it if you don't know what you want," John continued. "Maybe if you had a real job . . ."

"I do have a real job," Russell said, trying to control his voice. "Just because you don't think what I do is important doesn't mean it isn't. And I happen to be very good at what I do, but you wouldn't know that because you never ask."

John sighed and opened his mouth.

"And don't talk to me like a child," Russell continued. "I'm not one. I'm an adult. I'm your partner and I'm your equal."

"I don't think this is getting us anywhere," said John. "Maybe we should just do it some other time."

"You're not running away from this," Russell told him. "You're not walking out just because you're too embarrassed to talk about something other than formulas and reactions and the goddamned Periodic Table. You're going to sit there and talk about *us*. That's what's real, John, not your precious science."

The waitress, passing by, paused and gave them a big grin. "Everything all right?" she asked, eyeing their untouched plates.

"Fantastic," Russell told her, smiling. Giving him a bewildered look, she moved on to the next table.

"I do know why I had to leave," Russell said. "Sitting here with you right now, I know why. I had to leave because I was suffocating. I was constantly holding my breath, afraid to say anything in case it would upset you. I was running out of air."

"I never asked you to do that," said John.

Russell nodded. "You're right, you didn't. But you demanded it by the way you acted. You made me afraid to speak."

"You make me sound like a monster," said John.

"Not a monster," Russell said softly. "Just someone who wasn't paying attention."

He reached across the table and took one of John's hands in his. John looked around nervously and made an attempt to pull away. Russell gripped his fingers tightly.

"See," he said. "You're always afraid. Afraid of what people will think. Afraid of what people will know about you. But John, I feel like I don't even know who you really are, or that you know who I am."

He could feel the tension in John's hand. He knew his lover very badly wanted to put his hand in his lap, where it would be safe from the prying eyes of the other patrons. None of them were even giving the men a second look, but Russell knew that John's heart was racing a mile a minute, fueled by the fear of discovery.

"Can I bring you anything else?"

The waitress's voice startled Russell. He looked up just as John, with tremendous effort, pulled his hand away and stuck it under the tablecloth, out of her sight.

"No," Russell said. "I think we're done."

CHAPTER 9

Pete pulled into the parking lot of the Paris Bookstore and Cinema and cut the engine. A dozen other cars were already there. In the dark it was difficult to tell if any of them were recognizable, but it didn't matter anyway. There was no reason he shouldn't be at the Paris. It wasn't a fag place, even if some of the men who came there weren't completely interested in the variety of porn offered for sale inside. Most of Pete's buddies had been there, some regularly, and there was no shame in it.

He got out and walked through the lot to the door. In deference to their clientele's privacy, the Paris had wisely placed the entrance at the rear of the building, invisible to curious passersby on the street. Not that many people drove by it without purpose. The bookstore was located in one of the city's more run-down areas. Anyone going there would be going there for a reason.

Pete opened the door and entered. A hallway lined with video booths offering five minutes of video time for a quarter led to the interior, and he walked by these quickly, noting that they were all unoccupied. Inside, the Paris resembled a remodeled fast-food establishment, which in fact it was. In better times it had been a Red Lobster restaurant, a barn-like building painted bright red, where families gathered to feast on all-they-could-eat popcorn shrimp and crab legs. Now the windows were boarded up, the tables removed and replaced by shelves filled with videos, magazines, and sex toys. Where the kitchen and storage areas had once been, a small theater now resided, reached by passing through a faded velvet curtain.

Pete looked around the main room. A handful of men wandered

around, reading the backs of video boxes and flipping through magazines. Behind a cash register a bored-looking kid with bad skin and a nose ring watched cartoons on a snowy black-and-white television, ignoring the middle-aged man who perused the display of lubricants and rubber vaginas housed behind the counter's glass front.

The crowd was the usual, a mix of young blue-collar types in dusty work clothes, sad-looking men whose wives thought they were at the store picking up ice cream for dessert, and the occasional older man. Each type had their own way of behaving. The younger guys looked without reservation, opening magazines and flipping through them to see which images of overly enhanced breasts and spread, pink-lipped vulvas most excited them. Pete knew most of them would find something fairly quickly, buy it, and leave, taking it home to enjoy with a couple of beers.

The older men, too, were unembarrassed about their activities. Too old to attract actual partners, they were searching for an alternative. Most shunned the magazines and videos, going for the more tactile offerings of the fake pussies and rubber lips made for replicating the experience of a blowjob. They openly fondled the toys, not caring who knew what they desired.

It was the men in between who were secretive, the ones with wedding bands and the thick middles of the married and settled. They moved awkwardly, dressed in their corduroys and ill-fitting sweaters, going from one rack to another as if they were merely searching the shelves of the local video store for something to take home to the kids. These were the men who longed for something they couldn't have, Weary of their bland wives with their sagging breasts, sensible haircuts, and demands for help with the chores, they wanted to lose themselves in the fantasies promised by the magazines and tapes. They looked at the girls who looked back with eager eyes and open mouths and thought about the lives they once dreamed of having, the lives the young men around them still dreamed of and the older men knew would never come.

These were the men Pete despised the most. He despised them for their air of sad desperation and their shame. He despised them for their irritating way of holding the magazines open just enough to peek inside, as if they were fooling anyone. And mostly he despised them for the way they reminded him of his father. In their faces he saw the defeat he saw in his father's face, the look of resignation to a life that was the same day after day, an acceptance of what they had achieved as being the most they would ever have. They'd given up, and he hated them for it.

Having noted the possibilities, he walked toward the velvet curtain. He wasn't wasting time in the outer room, which as far as he was concerned, was simply there to provide a pretense for those too timid to venture directly into the Paris's darker regions. That was where the real appeal of the establishment lay.

Behind the curtain the room was shadowy, and Pete paused to allow his eyes to adjust. On the far wall a porn film was projected, a grainy image of a woman giving a blowjob. The cock was as tall as Pete was, and the woman's red-lipped mouth moved up and down it energetically as the penis's owner gripped her blond hair tightly.

Like the main room, the theater held less than a dozen men. They sat scattered throughout the theater, slumped in the seats. Below the slurping of the woman on the screen, Pete heard the faint groan of tired springs, the telltale sign that one or more of the audience were busily whacking off along with the action.

In the dark it was difficult to tell what the occupants of the theater looked like, but he didn't care. He never hunted; he let them come to him, and decided when they were near enough to see whether they would be allowed to have what they wanted. Sometimes, if they were lucky, he would take them into one of the private booths that lined the hallway out front.

He chose a seat halfway down a row in the middle of the theater. The rows in front of and behind him were empty, meaning he could avoid the glances of anyone he didn't want to have watching him. Sitting, he leaned back and tested the seat's give. Unlike most of the theater's chairs, it didn't let out an audible groan, which pleased him.

He turned his attention to the action on the screen. The blowjob was still going on, the man's cock shiny with spit as the woman, using her hand now, attempted to bring him to orgasm. Pete looked at the man's nuts, enlarged to the size of beach balls, each hair visible in their magnified state. They bounced vigorously as the woman jerked the man off. Then the man came, a fountain of cum shooting from his dick and hitting the woman in the face.

The scene did nothing for him, and he was glad when it ended and a new one began. In this one, two men were fucking a woman in a living room. One man sat on an impossibly ugly orange couch, legs spread, as the woman knelt on the floor between them and sucked him off. Behind her, knees buried in the white shag carpet that covered the floor, the second man was busily pumping himself in and out of her.

Pete felt his dick begin to stiffen inside his pants. Reaching down, he unbuttoned the fly of his jeans and placed his hand inside, squeezing the swelling head of his cock. He kept his eyes on the screen as he played with himself, watching the two pricks filling the woman's mouth and pussy. The men seemed connected through her, almost as if they were making love to one another, using her simply as a conduit for their union.

He was distracted by some motion taking place to his left. Glancing over, he saw that he had been joined in his row by someone else. Instinctively, he put his cock back in his pants, not wanting to advertise his arousal if his potential partner turned out to be undesirable.

The man looked young, which was a good sign. But in the dark it was difficult to tell. Pete had been fooled before. Still, it was light enough that he could see that he wasn't being approached by one of the old trolls who frequently tried to use the darkness as a cover for their wizened faces.

The man looked at him and nodded briefly before turning his attention back to the screen. Pete waited to see what he would do. On the far wall, the trio had changed positions. The man from the couch now lay on his back on the snowy carpet, his legs pulled up. The woman sat astride him, facing him and riding his cock. Somehow, the other man had managed to insert his dick into her ass, so that she was being entered simultaneously by both men.

Pete took a chance, freeing his cock once more and stroking it openly. He didn't know if the man beside him was watching or not; the scene had excited him beyond caring. His eyes focused on the two dicks, so close they were almost touching as they slid in and out of the woman's eager holes.

He sensed the movement of shadows and realized that the man in his row had gotten up and moved over into the seat beside his. That was all right. He glanced over and was pleased by what he saw reflected in the light from the projector. He was indeed young, and not that it mattered, but he wasn't bad-looking either.

The man looked at Pete, then down at the cock in Pete's hand. Tentatively, he reached out and touched it. Pete let him, feeling fingers close around his shaft. He leaned back and let the other man take over the job of getting him off.

The motion of the man's hand combined with the images on the wall, blending into one continuous sensation. Pete became one of the participants in the film. He felt the warmth of the woman's ass surround him, sensed the tightness of her. More than that, he felt the other man's cock moving in time with his. He felt its thickness against his own as they pressed together somewhere inside her. Their dicks were one united organ, tying them together so tightly that their heartbeats became one.

Too soon, the men in the film came. Pete was not ready, and when the clip suddenly faded out, he was left frustrated and disappointed. He needed more of what he'd felt watching it. He wanted to be back there, entwined with another man. He needed the release.

"Let's get out of here," he whispered to the man, who was still jerking him off.

The man released him and stood up. Pete tucked his still-hard dick into his pants and followed as his partner exited the theater. Stepping into the brightly lit main room, he barely looked at him as he led him down the hallway and into a private booth, first making sure that no one was watching them.

It was a tight fit. The booths were designed to hold one person. The two of them were close together, almost touching. Pete fumbled in his pocket for some quarters and plunked them into the video machine. A film began, but he ignored it. He knew what he wanted, and he needed the video only as background noise.

He unbuttoned his pants and pushed them down. Immediately, the man dropped to his knees and began sucking. But that's not what Pete wanted. He pulled the man up.

"I want to fuck you," he whispered.

The man hesitated. Pete turned him around in the small space and reached for the buttons of his jeans. He found them and pulled them open, tugging the man's pants and underwear down. He pressed his cock against the man's ass.

"You want me to fuck you, don't you?" he asked.

The man said nothing, but didn't pull away. Pete spit into his hand

and slicked his cock. Pressing the head between the man's asscheeks, he pushed forward until he felt himself begin to enter the guy's hole.

"Slower," the man said, the first word he'd spoken.

Pete ignored him, pushing himself inside. The tightness was intoxicating, and he couldn't wait. He felt the man tense and he pushed harder, breaking through the resistance.

The man cried out and Pete put a hand over his face, covering his mouth as he started to fuck him. It was so warm, so tight. He felt the man pressing back against him as he fucked him. He wanted Pete's cock inside him, wanted to be used by him.

The man was groaning through Pete's hand. That was better. That was what he wanted to hear. He removed his hand so he could hear his moans. He felt his balls slapping against the man's ass and fucked him harder. The man had braced himself against the door of the booth, and Pete used this leverage to push deep inside him.

"I'm gonna fill your ass with cum," he told the man.

"No," the man gasped. "Not inside me. Pull out."

Pete ignored him. He could feel himself about to explode, and he couldn't stop. He gripped the man's waist and steeled himself for the release.

"I said pull out," the man said again. "I don't want to get anything."

The man lurched forward, dislodging Pete's cock. Pete came, but instead of emptying himself into a warm ass, he saw his load shoot out and splatter against the wall. His partner was hurriedly trying to pull his own pants up.

"What the fuck?" Pete said, looking down at his still-twitching cock.

"I said not to come inside me," the man said. "I don't want to get AIDS."

"You think I have AIDS?" Pete said angrily. "You think I'm some sort of dirty fag? You're the one who was getting fucked, faggot."

The man was trying to unlock the door so he could leave. Pete grabbed his hand and twisted it, making the man cry out.

"Shut up, faggot," Pete ordered. "Tell me you wanted it."

The man let out another cry as Pete squeezed his hand again.

"Tell me you wanted it, fag," he repeated.

The man tried to pull away. Pete hit him, his fist connecting with the man's nose. His head flew back and smacked against the door with a crack. Pete saw blood begin to flow from the man's nose as he raised his hands to cover his face.

Seeing the fag try to hide made him even angrier. Why wouldn't he fight back? He hit him again, this time in the mouth. He felt the man's lip split, felt warm blood on his fingers. The man groaned.

"Help," the man called out softly. "Somebody help."

Hearing his cry, Pete was shocked back to reality. What was he doing? He pulled up his pants. Shoving the man out of the way, he unlocked the booth and looked outside. No one had heard anything.

The man had crumpled to the floor, holding his face. Before he could cry out again, Pete dashed for the door at the end of the hall. He hit the door and flew out into the night, not looking back. His car seemed impossibly far, miles away, as he ran through the parking lot, praying that no one saw him.

He reached the car. He seemed to have hundreds of keys in his hand, none of which would open the door. But then it was open and he was sliding into the driver's seat. He looked anxiously at the door to the theater, expecting at any moment to see people running out, looking for him. But no one came.

The engine started and he tore out of the lot, not even bothering to turn on his headlights.

CHAPTER 10

"What can I get you?"

"Cranberry juice and tonic."

Mike, who had been busy cleaning up the bar, looked up to see who his customer was. When he saw the smiling face of Father Thomas Dunn looking back at him, he stopped. The last person he'd expected to see at the Engine Room on a Saturday night was the priest.

"I told you I just might stop by," Father Dunn said.

"You sure did," Mike said as he put together the priest's drink.

Father Dunn looked around the bar. Mike wondered what he was thinking. Surely he had to know now that it was a gay bar. Probably he was wishing he'd never stepped foot inside. Mike was wishing the same thing. He really hadn't expected the priest ever to show up, and now that he had, Mike was more than a little embarrassed.

"Looks like I came on a good night," Father Dunn said, noting the packed room.

On the bar's stage, two drag queens were lip-synching to ABBA's "Take a Chance on Me," their bewigged heads bobbing in unison. *Thank God they're not wearing the nun outfits,* Mike thought as he handed Father Dunn his drink.

"You're surprised I'm here," the priest said.

"A little," Mike answered. "Okay, a lot."

"I wanted to thank you for helping me out the other night, and I figured my staying up late on a Saturday night was a lot more likely than your getting up early on a Sunday morning."

Mike laughed. "You're probably right about that," he said. "I'm not much of a morning person."

Father Dunn took a sip of his drink. Watching him, Mike realized he was dressed in ordinary clothes.

"You're in disguise," he said jokingly.

"Pardon?" the priest said.

"Your clothes," Mike explained. "You're not wearing your priest outfit."

Father Dunn nodded. "I didn't want to scare anyone," he said. "Besides, the Episcopal Church pretty much lets us make up our own dress code. I only wear the suit when I'm working."

"I didn't mean to make fun of you or anything," said Mike.

Father Dunn raised a hand. "It's not a problem," he said. "Besides, I sort of like the idea of being in drag."

Mike wasn't sure what to make of the man standing across the bar from him. He wasn't like any priest he'd ever met. Not that he'd met very many, but still, Thomas Dunn seemed like a normal guy. If Mike didn't know about his occupation, he wouldn't have seemed any different from the men standing around him, oblivious to the fact that there was a man of God in their midst.

"So, how do you normally spend your Saturday nights?" Mike asked him.

"Well, usually I go over the notes for my sermon," the priest told him. "Then I flog myself a little, pray for a couple of hours, and wait for a vision."

Mike stared at him.

"Now I'm the one who's kidding," Father Dunn said after a moment. "See, priests can have a sense of humor too."

Mike nodded. "Point taken," he said. "Hang on. I'll be right back."

He went to the other end of the bar to attend to some customers. When he came back, he found Father Dunn engaged in conversation with a young man.

"So I told that bitch to give me back my Cher CDs and get the fuck out," the man was saying to the priest.

Mike closed his eyes and groaned. *I should never have left him alone.*

"And did he?" Father Dunn asked.

"Damn right he did," his companion said. "I don't care whose cock he sucks, but you don't fuck with my Cher CDs."

"Apparently not," replied the priest.

"How are we doing here?" Mike asked.

"I need another voddy," the young man told him. He looked at the priest. "Can I get you another?"

"Thank you, but no," Father Dunn said. "I'm afraid it's a school night for me."

The young man nodded absentmindedly, looking around the bar. Mike gave him his drink, took his money, and prayed he would leave. To his relief, the guy saw someone he knew across the room and took off, leaving Father Dunn alone.

"Sorry about that," said Mike. "I didn't mean to leave you alone so long."

"It's all right," the priest told him. "This is—fun—for me. As you can imagine, I don't get out all that much."

"You're not freaked out by it?" asked Mike.

"Why should I be?" Father Dunn said.

Mike shrugged. "I guess I'm just not used to the idea of priests hanging around gay bars."

"This is a *gay* bar?" the priest said, suddenly looking around with a terrified expression.

Mike started to say something, then stopped when he realized that Father Dunn was laughing.

"I wasn't sure you knew," said Mike.

"I didn't when I came in," admitted the priest. "But I figured it out pretty quickly."

Mike wasn't sure how to continue the conversation, and there were customers trying to get his attention. He wanted to talk to Father Dunn some more, but he had work to do.

"I should let you go," the priest said, seeming to sense his dilemma. "I just wanted to come by and say thank you. Besides, I have church in the morning."

"It's good to see you," Mike told him. "Thanks for coming."

"My pleasure," said Father Dunn. "And now I'll expect to see you in my congregation one of these days."

"If you can come here, I think I can manage getting up early one Sunday out of the year," said Mike.

The priest stood up and buttoned his coat. "I look forward to it," he said. "Good night."

Mike smiled. "Good night, Father," he said.

"Thomas," Father Dunn said. "We don't want anyone to get the wrong idea now."

"Thomas," Mike said.

They nodded goodbye and Thomas left. Mike watched until he was out the door, then turned to the men clamoring for drinks. The visit from the priest had been unexpectedly pleasant. And he hadn't seemed at all bothered by the whole gay thing. *He's an interesting man,* Mike thought as he began filling glasses with ice and alcohol.

Driving home in his car with a full tank of gas, Father Thomas Dunn was thinking the very same thing. He'd surprised himself by going to the Engine Room. He hadn't planned on doing anything of the sort. As he'd told Mike, he'd been sitting in his study, going over his notes, when suddenly he'd been seized by a desire to find the man who had helped him, to see him again. He had no logical reason for doing so, but the need had been overwhelming.

Now, making his way down the same road on which he and Mike had met a week before, he feared he knew why. Seeing Mike, he had felt a tugging at his heart, an unreasonable pulse of joy that had both shocked and embarrassed him. He'd gone to the bar only with the intention of thanking the man for assisting him; instead he had discovered that he'd been unconsciously engaging in a fantasy, imagining that Mike would be as happy to see him.

He hadn't known that the Engine Room was a gay bar. That it was made everything even worse. It would have been easier to go there and find Mike surrounded by giggling women anxious for his attentions. Knowing he wasn't so inclined created an impossible situation.

He couldn't let himself go there. He'd done it once and it had almost killed him, may, in fact, have killed the very one he had wanted more than anything to save. He'd sworn he would never do it again, would never open himself up to the possibility of such pain and anguish.

Besides, it was foolish, the daydream of a child. He could not allow himself to entertain even the passing thought. He had to drive it from his mind, focus on the work to which he'd dedicated his life. To deviate from that would be to fail both himself and God, God who made it possible for him to be strong.

He drove home and hurried into the house, relieved to be back in the safety of his familiar world. As he stood in his living room, however, he sniffed the air and realized that he'd carried home with him the smells of the bar. Breathing them in, he was taken back to the ride in Mike's truck. He closed his eyes, remembering the proximity of Mike's body to his, the comfort of the warm cab and the sound of the music coming from the radio.

He needed to rid himself of the memories. Going upstairs, he stripped his clothes off and dumped them into the basket inside his closet. Naked, he padded to the bathroom and turned on the hot water, waiting until the bathroom began to fill with steam before stepping into the tub. He sank into the uncomfortably warm water, letting it close over him until he was immersed in it, only his head left free of the tiny, lapping waves.

The water cleansed him. He felt it stripping away the coat of shame he'd wrapped himself in on the way home, tearing it from his body with soothing fingers and leaving him new. He lowered himself even more, allowing the water to close over his face, until he was wholly baptized in the cleansing heat. He held his breath, not wanting to leave the protected womb of the bathtub until he was forced to by his need for air. The longer he stayed, the more cleansed he would be.

He felt his chest begin to ache, and against his will, he sat up. Fresh air streamed into his lungs as he inhaled deeply. The warm water rushed away from him, replaced by the colder air, and he longed to sink again into the water. But it was tainted now, dirty, and he had to get out of it.

He stood up, grabbing a towel and wrapping himself in it as he opened the drain and watched the water run out. He felt better now that he had rid himself of the bar's touch, more himself. He would sleep now, and in the morning he would get up and minister to his congregation. All would be well again.

Returning to his bedroom, he dressed in pajamas and pulled back the covers of his bed. Sliding between the sheets, he got in and laid his head on the pillow. He was where he belonged, in the place he never should have left. Outside he heard the wind howling, but in his house he was protected from everything—the cold, the wind, the world.

He fell asleep quickly, weary from the evening's events and from staying up several hours past his usual bedtime. As he drifted off, his

conscious mind shutting itself up tightly and the other, more dangerous, part of himself taking wing, the room fell away and he found himself in another room, in another place, in another time.

It was Joseph's room, the one in which he'd spent his last days.
Knowing he had little time left, he'd demanded to be taken from the
hospital and allowed to die in his own room. The doctors, knowing
nothing could be done to stop the inevitable, had acquiesced.

It was night, and the room was lit only by a small lamp on the table
beside Joseph's bed. Joseph himself was sleeping, his hands atop a
book that had fallen open across his chest. Looking at him, Thomas
thought perhaps he was not sleeping at all, that he had arrived at the
very moment following Joseph's last breath. For this was how they had
found him, a copy of Dylan Thomas's collected poems beneath his
hands.

But as he watched, Joseph stirred, his eyelids fluttering softly and
then opening. His eyes, at first unfocused, turned to Thomas and
cleared. Joseph smiled.

"You came," he said. His voice was quiet, like a child's. He tried to
sit up, pushing against the mattress with hands that dangled from impossibly thin wrists.

Thomas went to him and helped him sit, propping pillows behind
his back. He sat on the edge of the bed, not knowing if it was real or
not. It held him. Joseph, too, seemed very much alive. Thomas could
smell the scent of sickness about him.

"I waited up for you, but I must have fallen asleep," Joseph said.
"What time is it?"

Thomas looked around. There were no clocks in Joseph's room,
nothing outside the windows to indicate the hour.

"It's late," he said.

"I was reading Thomas again," Joseph said, closing the book. "I
know you think he's depressing, but I can relate."

"How are you feeling?" Thomas asked him. Joseph's face was
drawn, the lesions on his cheeks dark purple islands against the pale
sea of his skin.

"Like someone who's dying," Joseph answered.

"Don't say that," said Thomas. "It's morbid."

"It's the truth," Joseph said. He sighed. "Every time I start to fall
asleep, I wonder if it's the last time."

"Joseph, please," Thomas pleaded. "I can't."

Joseph took his hand, his twig-like fingers clasping Thomas's. "It's all right," he said. "I'm ready."

"But I'm not," Thomas said.

Joseph laid his head back against the pillows. "It's not your fault," he said. "I know you think it is."

Had Joseph really said that to him that night? He couldn't recall now. No, he was sure he hadn't. But this dream Joseph was right—he did blame himself.

"If only I could have . . ." His voice failed him and he fell into silence.

Joseph squeezed his hand, making Thomas look into his eyes. Despite the sickness, his eyes were alert, untroubled by the disease that raged behind them.

"It isn't your fault," he said. "I chose my own path."

"But I wanted to love you," Thomas whispered, barely able to get the words out.

"I know you did," said Joseph. "But it still wouldn't have saved me."

Thomas fought back tears. Joseph was wrong. He *could* have saved him, if only he'd allowed himself to follow his heart. If he had, Joseph would never have looked elsewhere for what Thomas couldn't give to him.

"Stop," Joseph said. "We don't have much time. Don't waste it on tears. Listen to me."

Thomas wiped his eyes and calmed himself. Again he looked at Joseph. The light in his eyes was failing, growing dim. He seemed less substantial, lighter, as if he were dissolving into ether. Thomas thought he could see the bed through his body.

"Stop hiding," Joseph said. "Let someone in besides God."

Thomas could no longer feel Joseph's fingers in his. He was disappearing. He grasped at the fading image, his hands meeting nothing.

CHAPTER II

"You fell on the ice?"

Stephen nodded. His mother was reaching for the bandages on his face. He pulled away. He didn't want her touching him.

"You should sue that supermarket," his father said. "For negligence. They should have cleared that sidewalk."

"It was just an accident," said Stephen. "I slipped is all. I should have been more careful."

"Why didn't you call us from the hospital?" Mrs. Darby asked her son.

"I didn't want to bother you," said Stephen. "Besides, I'm fine."

"A broken nose and thirty-six stitches is *not* fine," said his mother. "You should have called."

Stephen was sitting on the sofa in his parents' house. He almost wished he'd just stayed at the hospital. At least there the nurses hadn't kept asking him what had happened. They'd taken his story about falling on the sidewalk at the supermarket at face value, not even asking how he'd managed to drive himself to the emergency room with one eye almost totally shut and hands covered in blood. They'd simply stitched him up and sent him on his way.

He was relieved at their lack of interest. He'd had enough trouble getting out of the Paris Cinema without incident. Hearing his calls for help, several people had discovered him lying on the floor in the hallway. They'd been helpful, offering to take him to the hospital, but he had refused. He just wanted to be away from there, away from the memory of what had occurred. As soon as he could, he'd retreated to his car.

"That must have been a huge patch of ice," his brother said. "You look like shit." Alan was standing in the doorway, eating directly from a carton of ice cream he'd snagged from the fridge. Mrs. Darby looked at him.

"Stop swearing," she said. "And get a dish."

"I think I should just go home and sleep for a while," said Stephen. "The hospital gave me some pain pills. I'll take a couple of those."

"You're not going anywhere," his mother told him. "We'll put you in your old room."

Stephen started to protest, but his mother simply took him by the hand and pulled him to his feet. He knew better than to fight with her when she was like this, so he allowed her to lead him down the hallway to the bedroom he had shared with Alan for most of his life.

Little had changed in the room since first Alan and then Stephen had left it for college. Their twin beds still sat on either side of a shared bedside table. Posters of sports and music figures fifteen years out of fashion adorned the walls. Even the books on the bookshelf remained the same.

"It's like a museum in here," Stephen said as his mother gently pushed him onto his old bed.

"Take off your shoes," she said.

He bent to untie the laces, his head throbbing so badly he almost blacked out. He almost asked his mother to do it for him, but he knew she would enjoy it too much. Willing the pain away, he pulled his shoes off and then collapsed onto the bed.

"Give me the pills," his mother ordered. "I'll get you a glass of water."

Stephen took the plastic bottle from his shirt pocket and handed it to her. His mother left the room. Forcing himself to sit up, he pulled back the bedspread and got into bed, not bothering to remove his clothes. He'd at least changed before coming over to tell his parents about his alleged accident, throwing the blood-spattered T-shirt and jeans into the trash in the garage. He couldn't stand even to look at them, and after handling them, he'd washed his hands repeatedly, convinced there was blood staining his skin.

He couldn't decide which was worse, his nose or his mouth. They'd injected something into his lips to make them numb while they sewed them up, and he guessed its effects were lingering, because there was only a dull ache there. One of his teeth seemed loose, too, but the doctor who had examined him thought perhaps it would be fine if he just left it alone. But his nose, his nose definitely hurt. Protected by a metal splint and crisscrossed with white tape, it looked like the nose of a hockey player after a particularly nasty fight.

He tried not to think about what had happened. As far as he was concerned, he really had slipped on some ice outside the A&P and landed on his face. The reality was too dreadful to recall. Every time he relived even a second of it, he felt a terrible churning in his stomach. No, he had not been beaten up. He had fallen. On the ice. Outside the A&P.

His mother returned with his pills and a glass of water. Taking them from her, he gratefully swallowed the two little blue tablets, following them with a long drink.

"It says you should take them with food," his mother said. "I'll get you something."

She left again. Stephen waited for her to return. He could feel the pills in his stomach, swirling around. How long would it take them to kick in? He wanted to sleep, to sleep and to forget everything.

His mother came back with a bowl, which she handed to him.

"It's applesauce," she said.

Applesauce. The sick food of his childhood, the cure-all for everything from fevers to measles, earaches to broken bones. It was the only time his mother ever gave it to the boys. He associated it with pain and nausea, but also with the comfort of being taken care of. And she had sprinkled cinnamon on top.

He spooned some of the applesauce past his battered lips. It tasted odd, metallic, most likely a by-product of the anesthetic and medication he'd been given. But it was sweet enough for him to stomach, and he swallowed eagerly. Just as it had in childhood, it calmed his stomach, made him feel as if everything would be all right in a couple of days.

"Now get some rest," his mother told him. "When you wake up, I'll make you some dinner."

Stephen nodded. His mother left, shutting the bedroom door behind her. Alone in his old room, he almost felt okay. And really, he wasn't that badly hurt. In time, everything would heal, and no one had to know that he had really been beaten by a man whom he wouldn't let come in his ass.

He put the bowl of applesauce down, suddenly feeling as if he might vomit. He hadn't told the nurses or doctors about his ass, about the pain that burned there. He couldn't. Why had he done it? Why had he let someone do that to him in the first place? It was stupid, he knew it, foolish to let someone fuck him without a rubber.

Even more disturbing to him were his reasons for being at the theater in the first place. He had never gone there before, but he had wondered about it, wondered what went on inside the dark place where men congregated. He could imagine, and he wanted to know.

Then there was Greg. He had called, left messages that Stephen had been unable to return. Several times he had picked up the phone, intending to dial the number he had written on the pad beside the phone. But each time he had hung up and instead turned to his computer, finding release in the faceless rooms in which he felt most at home.

But always Greg had been in the back of his mind. Stephen liked him. He was attracted to him. He knew he should pick up the phone and call, suggest dinner or a movie. But he knew, too, that he wouldn't do it. Greg was not a onetime event; he was someone Stephen could see himself being with. And that couldn't happen. Not now. Not when his life was so complicated.

Still, the need to touch someone else had become overwhelming, and he'd found himself pulling into the Paris Cinema parking lot and going inside, where he knew men were waiting for him. Then he'd found one, one who seemed willing to give him what he wanted, to connect with him momentarily without the need for knowing names or even faces. Without complications.

That in itself had been enough for him to let down his guard. And for a time it had been much as it was in his chat room fantasies, at least until he'd realized what the man intended to do to him. Then he'd tried to stop it, and it had all fallen apart.

That's what he got, he told himself, for not being content with what he had. It's what happened to bad little boys who strayed from the path. He'd wandered into the forbidden woods and come face to face with the wolf itself, the vicious beast disguised as a woodsman. He had failed to see the sharp teeth and wicked eyes, too enchanted to notice the claws ripping his flesh.

It didn't matter now. It was all over, and he would never again go in search of what he didn't need. He would change. He would make his life as safe as it could possibly be, protect himself from harm in whatever way he had to. No one would ever hurt him again.

He slept then, drugged into oblivion. He did not dream, and when he felt someone shaking him, he only reluctantly rose up through the dark clouds of sleep and opened his eyes. His mother had returned, and she was not alone.

"Stephen?" she said. "Stephen, wake up. Someone is here to see you."

As his sight cleared, Stephen saw that the figure he'd taken to be his father or brother was instead someone unknown to him, a figure in a blue uniform and hat.

"Mr. Darby?" the officer said. "I'm Officer Chenoweth. Could I speak to you for a minute?"

Stephen looked at his mother, as if she were somehow the reason for the policeman's presence in his room. She looked back blankly, her eyes worried.

"Sure," Stephen said groggily. "Just let me get up."

"You can stay there, sir," Officer Chenoweth said. "Mrs. Darby, would you mind leaving us alone?"

"Stephen?" Mrs. Darby said. "Is everything all right?"

"It's fine, Mom," said Stephen. "I'm sure Officer Chenoweth just has to ask me some questions about the accident."

Mrs. Darby nodded, eyeing the policeman suspiciously as she left the room. When she was gone, the officer looked at Stephen.

"Those are some nasty injuries," he said.

"How did you find me?" Stephen asked him.

"The hospital gave me your address," Officer Chenoweth told him. "I was knocking on your door and your father saw me. He told me you were here."

"I don't understand," Stephen said. "Why would the hospital call the police just because I fell on some ice? I don't plan on suing the store or anything, if that's what they're worried about."

"The hospital didn't call us," said Officer Chenoweth. "We called the hospital."

Stephen looked at him, still not comprehending. "About me?"

"About an attack on someone at the Paris Cinema," the officer answered. "They called and said a man had been beaten by another patron and left, refusing medical attention. In such cases we routinely
call the hospitals to see if anyone has come into the emergency rooms
with injuries that might fit the description. Yours did."

Stephen shut his eyes, not knowing what to say next. Could he get
into trouble for not reporting the incident? He didn't see how. It was
his choice to leave, and he hadn't started the fight. But the police didn't
know that. If he admitted to being the one who was attacked, there
would be a lot of other questions he would be expected to answer.

"I wish I could help," he said. "But I just slipped on some ice."

"You weren't at the Paris Cinema?" Officer Chenoweth asked.

Stephen shook his head. "I don't even know what it is," he said.

The policeman nodded. "It's an adult bookstore," he said. "You're
certain you've never been there?"

"I think I'd remember something like that," Stephen said.
"Especially if someone clocked me while I was in it."

"Okay then," Officer Chenoweth said. "I'm sorry to bother you. I
was hoping you were the guy."

"Why's that?" Stephen asked.

"Because we think we have the guy who beat him up," the officer
said. "Someone saw him driving away and got his license plate number. We ran it and got a name and address."

"You caught the guy?" Stephen said, forgetting that just moments
ago he had denied all knowledge of the incident.

"We're talking to him now. But the only one who saw him was the
victim, and without a positive ID, we can't do anything."

Stephen almost blurted out the truth, stopping himself as the door
opened and his mother looked in. Seeing her face, he gritted his teeth.

"I almost wish I was your man," he said to Officer Chenoweth. "This
guy sounds like a real jerk."

Officer Chenoweth nodded again. "Thank you anyway," he said. "I
hope you're feeling better soon. Watch out for that ice."

"Will do," Stephen said as the policeman left, walking by Mrs. Darby
and saying, "I can let myself out, ma'am. Sorry for the intrusion."

"What did he want?" Mrs. Darby inquired of her son.

"He thought I might know something about a crime he's investigating."

"Crime?" his mother parroted. "What would you know about a crime?"

"Nothing, Mom," Stephen said. "He had me confused with somebody else."

"I should say so," Mrs. Darby said, coming to sit beside him on the bed. "You and your brother were never a bit of trouble."

She put the back of her hand on Stephen's head, the way she had when he was little and she wanted to see if he had a fever. Her skin was cool and dry, like paper.

"You need to sleep some more," she said, as if she could somehow sense this by touching him. "That officer shouldn't have disturbed you."

Stephen said nothing. He was thinking about what Officer Chenoweth had told him. Had they really located the man who had attacked him? What if he had agreed to identify him? He wasn't sure he would even be able to recognize him. He'd only seen him in the light for a short time, and even then he'd been trying to remain as inconspicuous as possible. He remembered short brown hair, a muscular build, rough hands. He remembered the way the man's cock had felt entering him, the way his voice had sounded in his ear. And he remembered the crack of bone against bone.

None of these memories would serve him well in a lineup. He could hardly tell the police that he didn't recognize his attacker because he'd met him in the dark, had seen him mostly from the back. He certainly couldn't ask them to have the suspects drop their pants and show their cocks.

He imagined the questions they would ask him. What were you doing there? Why did he attack you? Do you frequently let strangers fuck you in seedy porn theaters, Mr. Darby, and don't you think maybe you were asking for it when you let him stick his dick up your ass? Don't you think that maybe men who let other men fuck them in the ass deserve to get smacked around a little when they change their minds?

No, he couldn't face questions like that. He had been right to lie to the policeman. Besides, if anyone should decide whether or not this man was prosecuted, it should be him. He, after all, was the one with the broken face.

His mother was stroking his hair, rubbing his forehead and humming. He closed his eyes and pushed all the troubling thoughts from his mind. She would take care of him. She would make him feel better. Everything would be all right again. He just needed to sleep.

CHAPTER 12

"Do you believe in God?"

Simon sipped his drink and thought for a moment before answering Mike's question. "I'm too old not to," he said. "At my age you need to keep all your options open."

"I'm serious," Mike said. "Do you?"

Simon sighed. "What's gotten into you?" he asked.

"I've just been thinking about it lately," Mike answered.

"And what have you decided?"

"I don't know," Mike admitted. "My mother used to drag us to church when we were kids, but I stopped going when I was old enough to have better things to do. I haven't thought about it much since then."

"So why now?" asked Simon.

"No special reason," said Mike evasively. "Maybe just the time of year and all. You still haven't answered my question."

"Yes," Simon said.

"Yes what?" said Mike.

"Yes, I believe in God," Simon told him. "I believe that there is an omnipotent being who created us all and who moves us about like figures on a chess board, manufacturing dramas for his amusement and laughing at us when we behave in ridiculous ways."

Mike fixed him with a look.

"What?" Simon said. "You asked me and I've told you."

"You don't really believe that we're toys for some invisible force that lives up in heaven," Mike said.

"Don't I?" Simon replied. "No, well, I suppose I don't really. That was the God I was raised to believe in, however. I'm afraid we parted on bad terms shortly after he discovered that I liked other boys."

"What do you believe about him now?"

Simon paused again, thinking. "I believe that God—if he exists at all—is what we want him to be. The true God is unknowable, and so we dress him in costumes that make him visible to us. Then we come up with a lot of very silly rules that we attribute to him and tell everyone that if they don't follow those rules, they can't be part of the gang."

"That's oversimplifying religion a little, don't you think?" said Mike.

"Religion *is* simple," Simon answered. "It's the religious who make it complicated. Everybody wants to be right."

"Okay, then, how do you see God?" Mike continued.

"I'll need another drink if we're going to continue this conversation," said Simon. "And this one is on you."

Mike laughed, taking Simon's glass and refilling it. Simon took it back and stirred the ice cubes before speaking again. When he did, his voice was serious.

"Walter was raised Catholic," he told Mike. "He loved the church. He went to Mass every week. I never understood how he could, given what the Pope and his boys have to say about us sodomites. But every Sunday he'd be up and ready for the early service. He tried to get me to come with him, but I wanted none of it, so while he toddled off to church, I stayed home and pondered how I'd managed to marry such a fool."

Mike smiled, knowing Simon was being his usual teasing self. He'd seen Simon and Walter together many times, and knew the deep affection and respect they'd had for one another.

"Normally I could forgive him this eccentricity," Simon continued. "But one night we were watching television and the then-Archbishop of New York was on, Cardinal O'Connor. This was in the midst of the plague, mind you, and several of our old friends had succumbed to the virus. And there was that hateful man talking about how AIDS was God's punishment on homosexuals. I turned to Walter and said, 'That's the God you visit every week.' It was a cruel thing to say, but I was angry."

"What did Walter say?" asked Mike.

"Nothing," said Simon. "He got up, went to the stereo, and put a CD in. It was Bach's *Saint Matthew Passion*. He let it play while I sat, not understanding. Then he said to me, '*That* is the God I visit every week.' "

"I don't get it," Mike said.

"He meant the God behind the music. The inspiration. Not what men had turned God into, but the God behind everything. Think about it. The most beautiful art, music, even architecture—most of it was inspired by a devotion to the divine."

"Maybe because they were sick of painting cows and building huts," Mike remarked.

Simon ignored him. "In every civilization, the greatest achievements in the arts were celebrations of the gods," he said. "The Egyptian pyramids. The Aztec temples. The Sistine Chapel. The compositions of Handel. The works of Milton and Donne and many, many others. All created because the artists were attempting to understand God in some form. Imagine the power of the force that could inspire such things."

"It still doesn't prove that God *exists*," Mike insisted. "Just that people want him to."

"And that's why it's called faith," countered Simon. "You have faith, you believe, against all reason. If it could all be proven, what value would your faith have? It's easy to believe in things that can be seen, or touched, or measured. But believing in the face of all the evidence, that takes more heart than most of us have."

"It sounds as if Walter converted you," said Mike.

"No," Simon replied. "He still never got me to go with him. But I did understand him better after that, and I confess that in comparing myself to him, I found myself wanting. I envied him his ability to believe."

"I think it's all about a fear of death," Mike said. "I think people want to believe that there's something better out there."

"Possibly," Simon agreed. "But does it really matter if they think that?"

Mike nodded. "Sure," he said. "Then religion is just a safety net. You sin, you say you're sorry, and God makes everything okay. You see it all the time with these evangelists who steal money, screw around, and break all the rules they set for everyone else. Then they say they're sorry, God forgives them, and six months later they're doing it all over again. It's just bullshit."

Simon shrugged. "Perhaps it is," he said. "One day we'll all find out."

"That's another thing I resent," Mike said angrily. "They tell you that you don't have a choice. You either believe in God and go to heaven or you don't believe in him and you go to hell. What the fuck kind of options are those? What if I don't want to go to heaven? What if I just want to die and be done with it?"

"For someone who's never been interested in God, you seem to be awfully interested in him now," Simon remarked.

Mike waved a hand at him. "It's nothing," he said. "It's just this guy."

"Oh," Simon said. "Now this is getting interesting."

"No," said Mike. "It's not like that. I picked up this priest the other night."

Simon arched his eyebrows, only half feigning the shock.

"Bad choice of words," Mike said, noting the expression. "I literally picked him up. He had car trouble and needed a ride."

"Go on," Simon encouraged him.

"Well, he came in here the other night to say thank you."

"In *here?*" Simon said incredulously.

Mike nodded. "He's a strange guy. Not strange weird, but strange interesting. He invited me to come to his church."

Simon nodded. "Hence the whole God thing. I see now. Well, my boy, you don't have to believe in God to go see your priest friend."

"No, I know I don't," Mike said. "It just got me thinking is all."

"Tell me more about this priest," Simon said. "Is he humpy?"

"No!" Mike exclaimed. "He's a priest."

"Devotion to God does not preclude humpiness," said Simon.

"I guess he's good-looking," Mike said. "In a priest kind of way. I hadn't really thought about it."

Simon said nothing, watching Mike's face. He could tell the young man was thinking about it now, and he was fairly certain he knew what conclusion Mike was coming to.

"Anyway, I'm not going to go," Mike said. "I mean, what's the point?"

"What's the point of anything?" Simon suggested.

"What are you two talking about over here? You look so serious."

Mike and Simon greeted Russell, who took the seat beside Simon, giving him a peck on the cheek.

"Mr. Monaghan and I were discussing the nature of God," Simon told Russell.

"And what did you decide?" Russell asked, taking the drink Mike had poured for him.

"We decided to postpone our verdict until after our deaths," said Simon.

Russell nodded. "Cheery," he said. "What shall we talk about next, the thrill of stomach cancer?"

"How about what's going on with you and John," suggested Mike.

"That will take another couple of these," said Russell, holding up his glass.

"Where is your other half?" Simon asked.

"Long story," Russell said. "The short version is that we're on a break."

"Any progress?" Mike inquired.

"We tried to talk on Wednesday," said Russell. "It didn't go very well."

"Why does no one tell the old auntie what's going on anymore?" said Simon, sounding hurt.

"I assumed you knew," Mike said apologetically. "You usually know everything that goes on around here."

"I haven't really talked about it with many people," Russell told Simon. "It's sort of embarrassing."

"That's why you *have* old aunties," Simon reminded him. "If you can't talk to us, who can you talk to?"

"Not John, apparently," said Russell. "I don't know what I'm going to do."

"What do you want to do?" asked Mike.

"I don't know," Russell told him. "I wish he would at least talk to someone about what he's feeling, but he's basically just disappeared. None of our friends have seen him."

"Have you considered that perhaps that's because he thinks of them as your friends?" said Simon.

Russell looked at him. "But they're not just my friends."

"Not as far as you're concerned," Simon explained. "But maybe in his mind they are. Does he have any friends he sees apart from you?"

"Just the other teachers at school," said Russell. "And they're all straight. He only talks to them about work."

"There you go," Mike said.

"But he could talk to you guys," Russell protested. "Or to Stephen, or . . ." He stopped talking, realizing that there really weren't many people in John's life apart from the friends Russell had made for them.

"He's probably just sitting in the house waiting for something to happen," Mike said.

"Thanks," Russell told him. "Now I feel a lot better."

"I'm just saying," said Mike.

"He wouldn't talk to anyone anyway," Russell said defensively. "That's part of his problem. He doesn't talk."

"He probably doesn't know what to say," Simon said.

"He just has to tell me what he feels," replied Russell. "What's so hard about that? How can he not know what he feels?"

"Shall we go back to the God conversation?" asked Mike. "It might be easier."

"I've got to figure something out," Russell continued, ignoring him. "I either have to go back home or find somewhere else to stay. Cheryl's been great, but I think we're starting to get on each other's nerves."

"Come stay with me," Simon said.

Russell looked at him. "Really?"

"As I said earlier, what are old aunties for?" said Simon. "I have a big old house with just me and Clancy in it. You're more than welcome."

"Thanks," Russell said. "I think I'll take you up on that."

"You can move in tomorrow," Simon said, patting him on the back. "Just in time for Thanksgiving week."

Russell groaned. "I don't even want to think about Thanksgiving," he said. "Work is going to be hell until after the New Year, and this whole thing with John . . ." Again his voice trailed off. Mike and Simon saw his shoulders begin to shake.

"All right," Simon said, putting his arm around Russell and pulling him close. "We can't have that. Mr. Monaghan, what are your holiday plans?"

Mike shook his head. "I don't have any," he said. "Apart from being here in the evening."

"In that case, you are both invited to my house for Thanksgiving dinner," announced Simon. "It will be a family affair."

Russell cleared his throat. "Can I invite John too?"

"You may invite anyone you like," said Simon.

"In that case, I may bring a guest as well," Mike said.

"It will be a full house then," Simon said happily, already planning the menu in his head.

CHAPTER 13

"Mr. Ellison?"

John looked up from the copy of *Scientific American* he was reading to find a policeman standing in the doorway of the teachers' lounge.

"Yes?"

"Could I speak with you for a moment, sir? In private."

John looked around at his colleagues, all of whom were looking from him to the officer. He put the sandwich he'd been eating down on the table and wiped his hands on his napkin. Ignoring the glances of his fellow teachers, he stood and followed the policeman into the hallway.

"What's this about?" he asked when the door was shut.

"Are you the owner of a 2001 Pontiac Grand Am?" the officer inquired. "License plate HEJ-387?"

John nodded. "That's my car," he answered. "At least, it's registered to me. Why?"

"Were you driving the vehicle this past Friday evening?"

John shook his head. "No," he said.

"Does anyone else have access to the vehicle?"

"Just myself and my partner," John answered.

"Your partner?"

"Yes," John said. "It's registered in my name, but he's the one who drives it. I have another car that I use."

The policeman was looking at him strangely. "Your partner is a man?" he asked.

John felt himself reddening. He was annoyed at the cop for asking him such personal questions, especially when he still didn't know why they were being asked.

"Would you please tell me what's going on?" he said, rather than answering the officer's question.

"Do either yourself or your partner frequent the Paris Cinema?"

"What's that?" asked John irritably. "A movie theater? Sure, we go to the movies. I don't know if we've ever been to that one or not though. You'd have to ask Russell."

"Russell?" the man said.

"My partner. Russell Harding."

Again the policeman wrote on his pad. He looked at John. "Was your partner driving the car on Friday evening?"

"I don't know," John answered.

"You don't know if he was driving the car?"

"We aren't exactly living together at the moment," John said reluctantly.

"May I ask why?"

"No, you may not," John said sharply. "Look, I've been very patient here. Now unless you tell me why you've shown up at my place of work to ask me a lot of very personal questions, I'm going to have to ask you to leave."

"Please try to remain calm, sir," the officer said. "Your car may have been involved in an incident at the Paris Cinema on Friday evening. We're just trying to figure out what happened."

"I guess it's possible that Russell could have been at a theater on Friday night," said John. "But you'd have to ask him. I'm sure you can reach him at work."

The officer closed his pad and nodded. "I'll do that," he said. "If I need anything else, I'll let you know."

John nodded and started to go back in the lounge, but the officer stopped him.

"One more thing," he said. "Are either yourself or Mr. Harding acquainted with a gentleman by the name of Stephen Darby?"

"He's our accountant," John said. "What does he have to do with this?"

"Probably nothing at all," the policeman said. "Good afternoon, Mr. Ellison."

John watched the cop leave, then opened the lounge door and

went inside. All eyes were on him as he entered, but he said nothing. He simply sat down, picked up his sandwich, and resumed eating his lunch. He could feel the stares of the people around him, but he wasn't going to give them the satisfaction of knowing what the policeman had asked him.

He was grateful when the bell for the next period rang, giving him an excuse to leave the room. He knew it was all a big mistake. Still, he was bothered. Along with everything else that was going on, he didn't need to be publicly humiliated in front of his coworkers.

He went to his classroom. Twenty overactive juniors greeted him, talking loudly. Their voices grated on his nerves. He wished they would all just shut up. They were always talking, always making noise. He shut the door to the classroom and took his place behind the desk.

"All right," he said loudly. "Let's get started."

"Hey, Mr. Ellison, what was that cop talking to you about in the hallway earlier?"

John looked up to see who had spoken. Eddie Jessup, the school's star quarterback and resident class clown, was grinning at him. All the other students, too, were now staring openly at him, waiting for his answer. Leave it to Eddie, he thought, to be wandering around the halls when he shouldn't have been.

"Considering the grade you currently have in this class, Mr. Jessup, I think you should concentrate on the material for today's lab, and not on things that are of no concern to you."

A loud "ooh" swept through the room as the other students looked at Eddie and laughed. Eddie, incapable of embarrassment, grinned even more broadly.

"You all have the assignment for the lab," John said, trying to regain a little of the control he'd just lost. "Please get together with your lab partner and begin. I'll be observing your work."

The students got up and immediately resumed talking. For once he didn't tell them to stop. As long as they left him alone, he didn't care what they did. As they filed into the rear of the classroom to start their experiments, he sat behind his desk and began grading their last round of homework.

He picked up his red pencil and put it down again. Why was all of this happening? Things had been going along just fine until Russell had become irrational and announced he was leaving. It had been almost three weeks since that morning and he still didn't understand what was going on. And now the unsettling visit from the policeman. Why, he wondered, couldn't things just go back to the way they were?

He found himself thinking about his car. It was possible they had the wrong vehicle, of course. Mistakes happened. Even if they did indeed have the right car, what kind of incident could Russell have been involved in?

No, it was ridiculous. He went back to grading, making it through half of one paper before the questions returned. Why had the policeman mentioned Stephen Darby's name? What could he possibly have to do with the matter of the car? It seemed completely coincidental. But was it? Was it possible that somehow Russell and Stephen were indeed involved in whatever had occurred?

Russell and Stephen. He'd never thought of it before, but now that he had, he wondered if perhaps he'd overlooked the obvious. Russell had insisted during their lunch that there was no one else. Had he been lying? He himself had said that Stephen needed someone in his life.

He put the pencil down. Was Russell having an affair? Is that what the sudden changes were about? It made sense. It was logical. There was cause and effect. These things he could understand. Suddenly in his mind the pieces all came together, the formula unfolding clearly and unmistakably. Russell had left him because he was in love with Stephen.

"Mr. Ellison, was this stuff supposed to crack the test tube?"

John glanced at the shattered tube being held out by Stacey Koopman. Green goo oozed from it and dripped onto the floor. Stacey, looking at him wide-eyed behind her safety goggles, held it away from her as if it were a poisonous snake.

"You just added it too quickly," John told her. "Clean it up. And you're in charge. I have to go do something."

Stacey looked at him, puzzled, as he took his coat from the rack by the door and put it on. He left her standing there, praying she wouldn't let anyone burn down the school, and walked quickly down the hallway and out of the building.

It was irresponsible, he knew, but he had to do it. He had to see if his theory was correct. If so, it would answer all the questions he had, and although it would mean the end of everything, at least he would

have something tangible to deal with. At least he wouldn't be left wondering.

He drove as quickly as he could to Stephen's house. He couldn't
ask Russell; Russell would be too inclined to spare him the truth. But
Stephen, Stephen was a practical man, like himself. Stephen would understand that he needed to know.

He pulled into the driveway. Stephen's car was there. He got out
and walked to the door before he could convince himself that what he
was doing was irrational. He rang the doorbell, hearing it echo somewhere inside the house. A moment later he heard Stephen's voice ask
who was there.

"Stephen, it's John," he said. "John Ellison. I need to talk to you."

The door opened and Stephen peered out. John, seeing his face,
stepped back. "My God, what happened?"

"I had a little accident," said Stephen. "Come on in."

He opened the door wider and John entered the house. He couldn't
keep from looking at Stephen's face, which was swollen and bruised.

"It looks a lot worse today," Stephen said. "The doctor says it means
it's healing."

"How did it happen?" John asked again.

"It was stupid," Stephen said. "I fell on some ice. It was just a dumb
accident. So, what can I do for you? Do you have a financial question,
or is this a social call?"

John had momentarily forgotten the purpose of his visit to
Stephen. Seeing his face, he suddenly felt like an idiot. The poor man
was clearly in a bad way, and now John was just going to make things
even worse by demanding to know if he was having an affair with
Russell.

"This is going to sound really crazy," he said slowly. "I guess you
know Russell and I are having some problems."

"No," Stephen said. "I didn't know that. I'm sorry."

"You didn't know?" John asked. "Russell didn't tell you."

Stephen shook his head. "I haven't spoken to him since your
party," he said. "Things have been kind of crazy with work and all."

John rubbed his head. Suddenly his perfectly constructed theory
was revealing its weaknesses. If Stephen was telling the truth, then he
was right back where he started.

"You weren't with Russell on Friday night?" he asked.

"No," Stephen said.

"And you weren't at the Paris Cinema?" John continued.

Stephen hesitated. "No," he said. "I wasn't."

John sighed. "I'm really sorry," he said. "I'm really sorry I bothered you. I should go."

"Why would you think I was with Russell on Friday?" asked Stephen.

"It's a long story," answered John. "I just thought maybe you were with him, that's all."

"At the Paris Cinema?" Stephen said.

John nodded. "I don't even know where that is, do you?"

Stephen shook his head. "Are you okay?" he asked John.

"I'm fine," John told him. "I'm really sorry for bothering you, Stephen. I should get back to the school. I hope you feel better soon."

"And I hope everything works out with you and Russell," Stephen said. "Give him my best."

"I will," John said. "Thanks."

Safely ensconced in his car, he sat and thought. Something, somewhere, wasn't making sense. Maybe Stephen didn't know about him and Russell. Maybe he and Russell weren't having an affair. But Stephen knew *something*. He could tell that Stephen was uncomfortable talking to him. There was something he wasn't saying.

There was only one other thing to do. He started the car and started driving toward the mall.

CHAPTER 14

"The car's out back, right where I parked it."

Buck Iverson led Officer Wayne Chenoweth, John Ellison, and Russell Harding around the side of the garage to his lot. The Grand Am was sitting exactly where he'd left it on Friday afternoon, parked in between Doreen Baker's 1996 Toyota Celica with its dented fender and Trace Grueland's Jeep 4X4 that was awaiting new shocks. All three cars were covered in snow.

"I'm sorry it's taking so long, Mr. Harding. Like I told you, I had to order the heating coil."

"It's okay, Buck," Russell told him.

"You say someone was driving the car on Friday night?" Buck asked the police officer.

"Someone reported seeing it, yes," replied Officer Chenoweth. "Can you show me where you keep the keys to these vehicles?"

Buck took them back inside and indicated a box in the shop where a tangle of car keys nested.

"That's not very secure," remarked the officer. "Anyone could come in here and take those."

"We lock 'em up at night," said Buck defensively. "Someone would have to break the lock off to get at those keys."

"And you're the only one with access to the box."

"Me, Pete, and Ronnie," Buck answered.

"Can I speak to those men?" asked Officer Chenoweth,

"Ronnie's gone up north to visit his wife's folks for the holiday," Buck said. "Been gone since last week. Pete don't come in until later."

"Do you have an address for him?"

Buck nodded. Officer Chenoweth took out his pad and wrote it down as Buck recited it. "Pete's a good kid," he told the officer when he was done. "Can't imagine him taking a customer's car for a joyride."

"Let's hope he didn't," the policeman said. "Thanks for your time."

Russell and John walked with Officer Chenoweth out to his car. They'd followed him from the mall, where he'd gone to question Russell about his whereabouts on Friday evening. John had come in just as Russell was explaining that the car had been at Iverson's Auto Body since Friday morning, suffering from a problem with the heating system. After an awkward couple of minutes, the cop had suggested they all go over to the garage together to substantiate Russell's story.

"What do you think?" Russell asked him now.

Chenoweth looked at him and shrugged. "Your guess is as good as mine. I'll talk to this Thayer kid and see what I can find out. I'll let you know."

The two men thanked the officer and he departed, leaving them standing together.

"Come on," John told Russell. "I'll drive you back to the store."

They got into John's car and drove away from the garage, neither saying anything for several blocks.

"This is weird," Russell said finally.

"Very," agreed John.

"They must just have the wrong car," said Russell.

"Probably," John said.

"Did that cop really come see you at school?"

John nodded.

"And you left your class to come tell me?"

John hesitated. He hadn't told Russell the full reason for his appearance at the store, mainly because he didn't want Officer Chenoweth to hear, but also because he was feeling more and more stupid about the whole thing.

"That was nice of you. Thanks."

John shrugged. "You would have done the same thing," he said.

"Still," Russell said. "Thanks."

"Did he ask you about Stephen?" John inquired.

"Stephen?" Russell said. "Why would he ask me about Stephen?"

"He asked me if either of us knew Stephen Darby," John told him.

"That doesn't make any sense," remarked Russell.

"I didn't think so either," John said.

"I haven't spoken to Stephen in weeks," Russell continued. "I keep meaning to call him."

"I saw him today," John said.

"Really?" Russell asked. "Where?"

"I, um, went to his house," John told him.

Russell turned and regarded him oddly. "You're just full of surprises today," he said. "Why on earth would you go to Stephen's house?"

"I just thought it was odd that Officer Chenoweth brought up his name," John said, more or less truthfully. "So I went over there."

"How is he?" asked Russell.

"He banged up his face," John said. "He fell on the ice."

"Did he have any idea why the police would be asking about him?"

"No," John said, not mentioning that he'd never actually told Stephen that the police were asking about him.

"It's all too bizarre," Russell said. "And now I'll have to stay late to make up the time. This sale is going to be the death of me."

"You love it," said John.

"Excuse me?" Russell countered.

"You love it," John said. "You're never as happy as when there's some big crisis."

"What's that supposed to mean?" Russell demanded.

"It's true," John said. "Whenever you have a big sale to deal with, you get all giddy."

"Giddy?" Russell said, offended. "I do not get giddy."

"Okay," John said. "Whatever you say. But you do."

"All right," Russell said after a minute. "Maybe I do get a little excited. But it's the only time I really feel important."

They'd arrived at the mall. John pulled into a spot outside the Carter-Beane Department Store. "This is your stop," he said.

"Thanks again," Russell said as he prepared to leave.

"When are you coming home?"

Russell looked at him, surprised at the outburst. John was watching his face, waiting for an answer. Russell swallowed hard.

"Not yet," he said. "I need some more time."

John turned away and nodded.

"Simon is having everyone over for dinner on Thursday," Russell said. "You're coming, right?"

John said nothing. Russell leaned over and kissed him on the cheek. "I want you there," he said.

Again John was silent. Russell waited for a minute, hoping he would say something—anything—to break the awful silence. Finally he put his hand on John's arm.

"Be there at noon," he said. "You don't have to bring anything."

He got out of the car and walked quickly toward the store entrance. He didn't want to watch John leave. For a brief moment, sitting there talking, everything had seemed normal. And that was the problem. He had too easily slipped back into the old routine, the old way of thinking. It had all been so familiar, and he had welcomed it like an old friend. Also, John's question had thrown him off guard. It had been a peace flag, he knew, John's way of saying he was sorry. But Russell doubted his lover even knew what he was apologizing for, and until he did, it meant nothing.

Across town, Officer Wayne Chenoweth was pulling up to the home of Pete Thayer. He was on a wild-goose chase, he knew. For Christ's sake, he didn't even have a victim, at least not one who would come forward. But things were slow, and following up the leads on the Paris Cinema incident beat the hell out of writing traffic tickets. Not that he cared all that much about someone getting roughed up at a porno theater. Guys who went there were asking for trouble anyway, as far as he was concerned.

He walked up to the door and knocked three times. When there was no answer, he knocked again. Finally he was rewarded. The door opened and he was looking at a young man dressed in faded jeans and nothing else.

"Sorry, man, I was in the john," the kid said. "What can I do for you?"

"Are you Pete Thayer?"

The man nodded. "Hey, if this is about those tickets . . ." he began.

"Mr. Thayer, may I come in?"

"Oh, sure," Pete said. "Don't mind the mess."

Officer Chenoweth stepped into a living room cluttered with clothes, pizza boxes, and empty beer cans. It wasn't the worst he'd seen by far, but the disarray didn't improve his opinion of Pete Thayer. In his experience, people's houses reflected a lot more than their taste in furniture.

"I'll make this quick, Mr. Thayer. What were you doing Friday night?"

"Friday?" Pete said. He rubbed his hair, as if trying to recall. "I guess I was here watching television. Some movie on the Sci-Fi channel about aliens invading Los Angeles."

"So you weren't out riding around in a Grand Am you borrowed from the garage where you work?"

Normally Wayne Chenoweth preferred the subtle approach, but he'd discovered that sometimes hitting fast produced the best results.

"Fuck, no," Pete Thayer said. "I'd never borrow a car from the lot. Ask Buck."

"I did," replied the officer. "He told me you're the only other person in town besides himself with access to the key box."

Pete nodded. "Yeah," he said. "But I wouldn't do something like that."

"I guess you wouldn't be inclined to beat the hell out of someone at the Paris Cinema either then," Chenoweth said.

Pete Thayer looked at him, dumbstruck. "No," he said. "No, I didn't do that. Why? Who said I did?"

Officer Chenoweth shook his head. "Nobody," he said casually. "Just asking. Thanks for your time, Mr. Thayer."

"That's all you came here to ask me?" Pete asked as the officer went to the door.

"That's all," Chenoweth answered. "Unless there's something else you'd like to tell me."

Pete shook his head. The officer nodded at him and walked down the steps, not saying anything. It was always better to leave them wondering if they'd really seen the last of him. Besides, he'd gotten his answer. Thayer was lying. Not that it mattered. Without a victim he still didn't have anything to bring the kid in on.

Inside the house, peering out from behind a curtain, Pete Thayer watched him go. His heart was only now starting to slow down. He couldn't believe he'd made it through the conversation without puking. His stomach was twisted into tight knots of anxiety.

How had they found him? Someone must have seen him leaving the parking lot, and they'd traced the car. Jesus Christ. All because he'd punched some faggot in the face. Had the queer gone to the police? He found that hard to believe. What would he tell them, that he was getting his ass fucked in a porno theater and things had gotten a little too rough for him? The cops would laugh him out of the station.

No, if the guy had gone to the police, they would have him sitting in a jail cell answering questions. They wouldn't just send someone to his house to nose around. He might not be the smartest tool in the shed, but he knew something about how the cops worked, especially small-town cops like whatever his name was. Chen-something.

Still, he'd need to be careful. Hopefully if he just laid low, it would all blow over. He just had to hope that little fag didn't decide to shoot his mouth off. He'd also have to stay away from the Paris, not that it would be any big hardship or anything. There were always queers who wanted to suck his cock. He could find them lots of places.

The more he thought about it, the madder he got. Who did that faggot think he was? He was the one who came after Pete. He was the one who grabbed his cock and started playing with it. He was the one who followed Pete into the booth. Hadn't he let Pete fuck him? Hadn't he wanted his ass fucked hard? It wasn't Pete's fault he hadn't asked about a rubber. And then all that shit about not wanting to get fucking AIDS? If anyone should have been worried about it, it should have been *him.* Who knew what the pansy had crawling around in his ass.

Yes, he'd deserved the beating. Maybe it would teach him a lesson, teach him not to be a goddamned cocktease. He was like those girls who went down on you and then bitched when you came in their mouths. They were all a bunch of cockteases, every last one of them. They should be fucking thankful to get a taste of his cum.

He looked at the clock. Buck would be expecting him at the shop soon. He needed to calm down, come up with some story about how dumb the whole situation was, how funny it was that someone had reported a car driving around when they—Buck and Pete—knew damn well it had been sitting in the lot all weekend. Yes, they'd laugh about how fucking stupid people could be sometimes.

He went into the bathroom and started the shower. Everything was going to be fine. He just had to play it cool. They didn't have anything on him, couldn't prove he'd used the car or been to the Paris. He was home free.

He got into the shower and began soaping himself. He wondered how badly he'd beaten the fag up, anyway. He'd hit him pretty hard, and there had been some blood. But he couldn't have done too much damage. After all, he'd only hit him because of what he'd said.

That part had gone all wrong. But the stuff before it, that had been good. The fag's ass had been tighter than any pussy he'd ever had his cock in. Warm and tight. If he hadn't fucked everything up talking his AIDS shit and trying to pull away, it would have been perfect. If he'd just let Pete finish.

He closed his eyes and thought about how it had felt. His fist closed around his stiffening dick, the soapy water gliding under his fingers. Yeah, it had felt like that: hot and tight and sweet.

He pumped harder, remembering, and waited for his reward.

CHAPTER 15

"Would you mind saying the blessing, Father?"

Thomas, seated across the table from Simon, nodded. It was an occupational hazard, always being the one asked to say grace. He'd long ago learned not to refuse; no one else would volunteer to do it, fearing they would make a mess of it in front of the professional. He accepted the responsibility with good humor, assuming the role of Man of God like some sort of holy superhero identity.

"Heavenly Creator," he began. "Thank you for this opportunity to come together and celebrate those things with which you have blessed us: friends, family, health. We share our joy with one another and with you. Amen."

"That was short and sweet," Mike remarked when Thomas finished. "My father used to go on for a good five minutes. Of course, he only said grace once a year, so I suppose he had to save it all up for the occasion."

"A good prayer gets to the point," Thomas said, laughing. "God has no more time to waste than we do."

He still couldn't quite believe he was sitting at a table with five gay men on Thanksgiving. He'd been surprised and delighted to get a phone call from Mike earlier in the week, asking him if he had any plans for the holiday. He did have plans, an invitation from one of his parishioners to join her and her family, but he'd told Mike he was free. After accepting the invitation to dinner with Mike and his friends, he'd called his original hostess and complained of a fever and chills. He'd thrown in a hacking cough for good measure, knowing that above all else Posey Severing feared sickness. She'd readily accepted his regrets and promised to send over a plate with her husband.

And now here he was, surrounded by men he didn't know, invited by a man he knew only slightly. How ironic, he thought as he looked around. It was the church that preached welcoming the stranger. But now he was the stranger, accepted by men some in the church would have turned away.

"I don't want to hear any griping about lumps in the gravy," Simon said as he began passing bowls around. "Russell wanted me to buy *canned* gravy, but I wouldn't hear of it. So if you get lumps, too bad. At least this is the real stuff."

"He had me whisking that stuff all morning," Russell countered, holding up his wrist and letting it dangle. "I think it's broken."

"Please," Mike teased. "Your wrist has always been like that."

"Do you see what I have to put up with?" Russell said plaintively to Thomas. "He's like that kid in *The Sound of Music*. Kurt. What did he tell Maria he was?"

"Incorrigible," Simon answered. "Thomas, you'll have to excuse these children. They're not always this much trouble. I think they're acting out because we have a guest."

"I feel honored," Thomas said. "When I was a kid, my mother always made my sister and me be on our best behavior for company. It was terribly dishonest, since we never behaved at any other time."

"I don't think I've ever met a priest," said Greg. Invited by Russell, he sat beside Mike on one side of the table while John and Russell sat across from them. Thomas and Simon occupied the positions of honor on either end.

"It's not like I'm the Archbishop of Canterbury," Thomas said. "I'm just a priest."

"This bunch doesn't get out much," John told him, spooning cranberry sauce onto his plate and passing the bowl to Thomas.

"What's it like being celibate?" Greg asked.

The others looked at Greg in shock, then began laughing.

"What?" Greg asked. "It's a perfectly reasonable question."

"No, my dear boy, it is not," Simon said.

"But since you've asked it—" Russell said mischievously.

"Episcopal priests aren't required to be celibate," Thomas said, trying not to smile. "Only the Catholic ones."

"But only if you're married, right?" Greg prodded.

Thomas nodded. "That's correct."

"Are you married?"

"No," said Thomas, buttering a roll. "I'm not."

"Well, then—" Greg said triumphantly.

"If you continue with this line of questioning, you will get no pie," Simon said firmly.

Greg started to say something else but Simon held up a warning finger. "No pie," he said sharply.

Greg settled into reluctant silence while the others laughed. Thomas began eating. He was having a remarkably good time, even if Greg's questions had hit uncomfortably close to home. He glanced at Mike, wondering if he, too, was curious about Thomas's romantic experience.

"What time do you have to be at the bar tonight?" Russell asked Mike.

"Four," Mike replied. "I got Luke to open up for me so I could get another two hours off."

"I don't see why they can't just stay closed," John commented.

"Money," Mike said. "The place is packed on holidays. Guys either don't go home or they do go home and want to forget about how awful it was."

"You make it sound like every gay man has a horrible relationship with his family," said John.

"You don't see any of us flying off to visit ours," Mike argued.

"That's not because we don't like them, though," John said. "It's because they're too far away."

"Mine aren't that far," Greg said. "I just can't stand being around them on holidays. All my siblings are married, and all they do is ask me when I'm going to be next."

"They don't know?" Russell said, sounding surprised.

"Please," Greg said. "My father is an ex-Marine. They don't have gay sons, especially in Kentucky."

"Don't they ask about your life?" Simon inquired.

"We talk about the weather and about my parents' dog," Greg

replied. "Then I tell them I have to go because someone is beeping in. It works for us."

"My family doesn't mind at all," said John.

"That's because you never actually talk about it," Russell said to him. "They know, but they don't ask." He looked around the table. "Not once in seven years have they sent a Christmas card addressed to both of us. It's always just to him."

"That's just efficient," John said testily.

"Then how come when your mother calls and I answer, she immediately asks to speak to you?" asked Russell.

"She has nothing to talk to you about," John said.

Russell made a noncommittal noise in response, stabbing a piece of turkey and putting it in his mouth. He and John ate in silence, not looking at one another.

"What about you, Mike?" Thomas asked, trying to redirect the focus in the room. "Where's your family?"

"Dead," Mike told him simply.

"I'm sorry," Thomas said. "I didn't mean to—"

"It's okay," said Mike before the priest could apologize. "It was a long time ago. A car crash."

"You don't have any relatives?" Greg asked.

Mike shrugged. "Some cousins somewhere, I guess. We never really associated much with them. No brothers and sisters."

"You have us," Simon said brightly from his end of the table. "And that's family enough for anyone."

Thomas returned to his food, every so often sneaking a look at Mike. He couldn't imagine not having any family. Although he didn't often see his sister or parents, he was comforted to know that they were out there, reachable if he needed him. To not have that, to be all alone, he couldn't imagine it.

Can't you? A voice echoed in his head. Joseph's voice. *Can't you imagine what it's like to be alone?* He willed the sound away. It wasn't the same, he told himself. It wasn't the same at all.

Besides, he had all he needed. He had his church, his congregation, his God. They were his family. They cared about him, loved him. That was enough for anyone, more than enough for him.

The remainder of dinner went by smoothly. The talk turned to movies and pop culture, things Thomas knew little about. He was content to sit and listen, to lose himself in the playful banter that flew back and forth across the table. It surprised him that the men seemed so unselfconscious in his presence. He wondered what he represented to them, whether they saw him as something alien to their world or just another dinner guest. If so, they showed no signs of it. They talked freely, and even when the subject turned to subjects normally not discussed in front of clergy—such as the relative appeal of the asses of George Clooney and Russell Crowe—they didn't refrain from lively debate.

After the promised pie had been served up and eaten, Simon stood up. "I should start on the dishes," he said.

"Oh, no, you don't," Mike told him, standing up himself. "You already did too much work. I'll do the dishes. You just sit."

"I'll help you," Thomas said quickly.

Mike looked at him. "You're sure? You don't have to."

"I know I don't have to," Thomas told him as he stacked several pie plates on top of one another. "I want to. It's the least I can do."

He and Mike carried the dishes into the kitchen while the other men scattered to the living room to sit and let their dinners settle. Simon had already taken care of most of the cooking dishes and utensils, so the pile of plates, silverware, and glasses needing their attention wasn't so daunting.

"Wash or dry?" Mike asked, turning on the sink.

"How about dry?" Thomas suggested.

Mike nodded. He added soap to the water streaming from the faucet, and soon the sink was filled with bubbles. Mike dunked a plate into the water and scrubbed it with a cloth.

"I hope we weren't too much for you," he said as he cleaned the plate with circular motions.

"Not at all," Thomas told him as he took the proffered dish and wiped it dry. "It was actually refreshing. Usually people hide who they really are around me."

"Not this group," said Mike. "Sometimes I wish they would."

"They all seem very nice," Thomas remarked.

Mike nodded. "They are," he said.

"I sensed a little tension between John and Russell," Thomas said.

"They're going through a hard time right now," Mike told him. "Russell's trying to—find himself, I guess."

"He's not alone there," said Thomas. "I see people like that every day."

"I guess priests are sort of like unofficial therapists," Mike said as he dropped a handful of forks into the sink.

"In my case I'm an actual therapist," Thomas informed him. "A psychologist, to be exact."

"Really?" Mike said, looking at him with new respect. "And here I thought you were just . . ." His words trailed off as he returned to the dishes.

"Just a priest?" Thomas said, completing Mike's sentence.

"I didn't mean it that way," Mike apologized.

"I know what you meant. It's okay. Besides, it's not like I have a practice or anything. When I decided to enter the priesthood, I pretty much closed the book on that chapter of my life, at least in an official capacity. But you'd be surprised what people tell their priests."

"Who am I to talk?" Mike said. "I pour drinks for a living."

"But you like doing it, don't you?"

Mike shrugged. "It's a job," he said. "I guess I like it. I've been doing it for long enough. Do you like being a priest?"

The question took Thomas aback. "Yes, I like it very much."

"Who would have thought that you'd be having Thanksgiving dinner with me and my friends?" Mike continued, apparently satisfied that Thomas was telling him the truth.

"The Lord works in mysterious ways," Thomas said, assuming a mock-serious tone.

"So do Volkswagen Jettas," Mike said. "At least when you forget to put gas in them."

"I won't make that mistake again," said Thomas, laughing. "Thanks to you." He paused for a moment. "I guess I have you to thank for several wonderful events in my life lately, don't I?"

"Hey, like you said, the Lord works in mysterious ways. Maybe I'm really one of those angels he was always sending to bring people good news."

"Maybe you are," Thomas said, drying the last of the spoons.

"How long have you been in Cold Falls?" asked Mike.

"Just under a year," Thomas said.

"And before that?"

"I was the Assistant Rector at The Church of the Epiphany in Burlington, Vermont, for three years. Would you like the rest of my résumé?"

"I think that's good," said Mike. "You're hired."

"So when will I see you in church?" Thomas asked. "I came to see you, and now here I am again. I think it's your turn."

"I don't know," Mike said, wringing out the dishrag before tackling a bowl that had held stuffing. "God and I, we don't really have a lot to say to each other."

"You don't have to come to see God," Thomas told him. "You could come to see me."

"Wouldn't the big guy get jealous?" Mike teased.

"I can handle him," said Thomas. "He's not as tough as people say he is."

Mike laughed, almost dropping the bowl he was rinsing. Thomas caught it. For a moment their hands touched, Mike's underneath Thomas's, supporting it. Then Thomas pulled the bowl away, drying it hurriedly.

"I haven't been to church since my parents' funerals," Mike said, picking up another dish.

"How long ago was that?"

"Fifteen years the end of next month," said Mike instantly, as if the number were burned into his memory. "New Year's Eve. They were killed by a drunk driver." He handed the dish to Thomas. "Ironic, huh?"

"That you're a bartender?" Thomas said, getting his meaning. "Not really. A shrink might say you're trying to understand the enemy. Or trying to save the world because you couldn't save your parents."

"Maybe," Mike said.

"I noticed you didn't have any wine at dinner," Thomas said carefully.

Mike shook his head. "I don't drink," he said. "I used to, a lot after the accident. Then one day I woke up, dumped everything down the drain, and haven't touched it since."

Thomas finished drying. He looked at the pile of clean dishes, the result of their teamwork. Then he looked at Mike. "You get more and more interesting," he said.

Mike dried his hands on a towel. "Not really," he said. "I'm just an ordinary guy with an ordinary life. There are a lot more interesting people out there."

Not in my world, Thomas thought as Mike led the way out of the kitchen, shutting the lights off behind them.

CHAPTER 16

Stephen stepped inside his house and locked the door behind him with a sigh of relief. He'd escaped. Almost a week at his parents' house with his mother looking after him had quickly become monotonous. Several times he'd insisted that he felt well enough to return to his own bed, but each time his mother had taken his temperature and declared that he still had a fever. What a fever had to do with a broken nose, he didn't know, but to his protestations his mother had simply said, "I read it in the *Reader's Digest*." Confronted with the power of the most widely read magazine in the world, he'd given up and stayed in bed.

But now he'd broken free. Busy with cleaning up after the Thanksgiving dinner, his mother had barely noticed when he'd said good-bye and left, taking his pills with him. He knew she'd call as soon as she was done tucking the leftovers into their Tupperware beds and putting them to sleep in the refrigerator, but he just wouldn't answer. His father would keep her from actually coming over. He hoped.

It was good to be in his own house. He missed his bed, and his privacy. He was feeling immensely better than he had been a week earlier. His lip was healing nicely, and his nose hurt only on the few occasions when he'd had to sneeze. Other than that, the pills had kept him in a state of mild euphoria while his body had healed itself.

He walked into the office. Luckily, not much happened around Thanksgiving, and he wasn't facing a mountain of work he would have to catch up on. Still, he hadn't checked his e-mail in a long time. There might be something there requiring his attention. He sat down at his desk, turned the computer on, and waited for it to run through its warm-up of beeps and whirs. When it was done, he signed on.

His mailbox, like his desk, was almost empty once he deleted the seventy-three messages promising him a bigger dick and the best teen lesbian sex on the Net. There was an e-mail from Russell, asking how he was, and a couple from his bank, but otherwise he was free of any pressing correspondence. He was about to sign off when an instant message box popped up. He looked at it. HrdAtWrk: Hey, buddy. It's been a while.

HrdAtWrk. It certainly had been a while. What was it, two or three months? Stephen couldn't remember exactly. He did recall that it had been toward the end of summer, an unpleasantly humid night when he hadn't been able to sleep. He'd encountered HrdAtWrk in a chat room. The guy had said he was in his office and needed a break. They'd had a good session.

He typed a message back: Still hard at work? It was completely un-original, but it would do.

The response came back instantly: Always. U?

Stephen looked at the screen. Suddenly he was very much aware of the fact that he hadn't jacked off in a week. He'd thought about it once or twice, but the idea of doing it in his old bed, while his parents were asleep down the hall, sent his erections screaming. Even when he was thirteen and horny as hell, he'd been able to do it only if they were out of the house.

Now, looking at the box on his screen, a week's worth of need came crashing down on him. He felt his cock jump and thought, *Why the hell not?* He typed a message back to his online buddy: Ready when you are.

While he waited for HrdAtWrk to start, he quickly removed his clothes. Naked, he leaned back in his desk chair. The leather felt good against his bare skin, and it was warm enough in the room that he didn't feel at all cold. His balls rested between his spread legs, and he idly played with his cock, waiting.

HrdAtWrk: Feel like something different 2nite?

Different? What did he mean by different? Stephen had no idea. Sure, he wrote. What do you have in mind?

HrdAtWrk: I'm going to tell you a story.

Stephen gave a short laugh? A story? It was different all right. But if this guy wanted to tell him a story, that was okay by him. I like bedtime stories, he typed back.

HrdAtWrk: You're driving home. You're speeding. You see a cop car in your rearview mirror. The lights are flashing.

Stephen pictured it. He was in his car. It was early evening. Summer. He had the window down. Maybe he was going a little fast, but not too much. Not enough to worry about. Suddenly something in the rearview mirror caught his eye. Lights. Red and blue. But surely they couldn't be for him? He was only going five miles over the limit. But the car pulled right up behind him.

HrdAtWrk: A cop gets out and walks toward you. He asks to see your license and registration.

Stephen opened the glove compartment of his car, searching for the red AAA folder that held his proof of insurance and his registration card. A map of New York fell out.

"I know it's right here," he told the cop, who was watching him through the window. He was a young man, handsome, with stern eyes and a square jaw. The name tag on his uniform read CAFFREY.

Stephen found the folder and opened it, retrieving the card. He handed it to the waiting officer.

"License, too, sir," Caffrey said.

Stephen pulled his wallet from his back pocket and took his license out. The cop took it in one gloved hand and looked at it.

"Mr. Darby, do you realize that you were speeding?"

"No," Stephen said. He felt himself blushing. "Well, I mean I knew I was going a *little* fast, but—"

"You're either speeding or you're not, Mr. Darby. There's no in between. Do you understand?"

"Yes, sir," Stephen said.

HrdAtWrk: Officer Caffrey takes your license back to his car. He gets in and sits there. You wait, wondering what he's doing. Then he gets out and comes back.

Officer Caffrey put his hand on the door. "Would you step out of the car, Mr. Darby?"

Stephen looked at him, not comprehending.

"Step out of the car, Mr. Darby."

"But—"

"Now," the officer said.

Stephen did as he was told. Opening the door, he stepped out and stood up. Officer Caffrey turned him around and spread Stephen's legs by placing a knee between them and shoving. Taking one wrist, he held it behind Stephen's back. Stephen felt the cold kiss of metal on his skin.

"What—" Stephen began.

Officer Caffrey pulled his other wrist back and cuffed it. "I need you to get in my car, sir," he said.

"Am I under arrest?" Stephen asked as he stumbled forward, Caffrey's hand hard on his back.

The cop said nothing as they walked to the cruiser. He opened the back door. "Get in."

Stephen ducked and slid into the rear of the patrol car. A wire screen separated it from the front. The black leather seats smelled faintly of polish.

HrdAtWrk: The cop gets in after you and shuts the door.

As the door shut, Stephen noticed that the car's windows were tinted. No one could see in. He looked nervously over at the policeman as he locked the doors.

"Now, let's talk about your difficulty with obeying the rules."

Officer Caffrey leaned back, spreading his legs. Stephen could only stare at him, not understanding what was going on. The cop put one leather-gloved hand in his crotch and squeezed.

"I think you need to be taught a lesson about respect for the law," he said.

Slowly, the cop pulled the zipper on his uniform pants down. Stephen watched as he reached inside the open fly and pulled out his cock. Long and thick, it rose up from a tangle of dark hair. Caffrey's gloved hand slid up and down it slowly.

HrdAtWrk: The cop leans forward and pulls your head down.

The fat head of Caffrey's dick hit Stephen in the mouth. With his hands cuffed, he had a difficult time balancing, but he forced himself up and opened his mouth. His lips closed over the swollen head and he tasted the salty flavor of Caffrey's skin. The cop, his powerful hand on Stephen's head, pushed him down.

Stephen choked as several inches of thick cop meat slid into his throat. He felt his air cut off, and inhaled through his nose. Caffrey ignored his distress, rising up to shove more of his cock into Stephen's mouth. Stephen felt his nose press against the rough hair of the officer's crotch.

"That's right," Caffrey said. "Take it all."

Stephen moved back up the cop's dick, leaving just the head in his mouth. His throat ached from being penetrated, but the taste left behind by Caffrey's cock lingered, and he wanted more of it. He ran his tongue around the head of his cock, teasing him.

"You like that, don't you?" Caffrey said.

Stephen answered him by going down on him again. This time it was easier. The cop's tool slipped into his throat easily, wet with his spit. Stephen slid up and down it, feeling every inch as it passed over his tongue and lips.

HrdAtWrk: The cop holds you by the hair, feeding you his prick.

Caffrey's fingers pulled at Stephen's hair, holding him in place. He raised his hips a little at a time, each movement pushing more of himself into Stephen's mouth.

"Tell me how bad you want it," he ordered.

Stephen, unable to speak, looked up into the cop's face. His dark eyes were cold, hard. He looked at Stephen with a mixture of lust and hatred.

"Tell me," Caffrey repeated. "Do you want my cop cum in your mouth?"

Stephen nodded. Caffrey rewarded him by shoving himself roughly into Stephen's throat. Stephen expected to feel him shoot his load, but instead the officer pulled out again.

"My cum is too good for your fucking mouth," he said. "Now get up."

He fumbled with his belt, pulling it open and lowering his pants. Freed from the confinement of the uniform, his cock stood up from his belly. His big balls hung over the edge of the seat. He reached for the belt at Stephen's waist, pulling it open as well.

"Sit up," he demanded.

HrdAtWrk: He pulls your pants down.

When Caffrey saw Stephen's hard cock jutting up from between his legs, he reached over and squeezed it painfully. Stephen let out a moan.

"You like it rough, do you?" the cop asked. "Sit on me."

He leaned back, putting his hands behind his head. He'd unbuttoned his shirt so that it hung open. His chest was covered in light brown hair that swirled around his pecs and down his belly.

Stephen straddled him as best he could, kneeling on the seat and trying to keep his balance. He was facing Caffrey, the head of his erect cock touching the cop's chest. The feel of his hair on Stephen's sensitive dickhead made Stephen shudder.

Caffrey spit into one gloved hand and used it to wet his cock. He spit again, this time rubbing one finger between the cheeks of Stephen's ass. His finger probed roughly at Stephen's asshole, then pushed inside. Stephen gasped.

"My cock is next," Caffrey informed him as he removed his finger. "Fuck yourself with it."

Trembling, Stephen lowered himself until he felt the tip of Caffrey's dick against his hole. Steeling himself, he sat, feeling himself spread open. He closed his eyes.

"Look at me!" Caffrey barked.

Stephen's eyes flew open. He looked into the cop's face as he inched more of him inside his burning asshole. It hurt like hell, but he wasn't going to let Caffrey know that. He kept going until he felt himself resting on Caffrey's thighs.

HrdAtWrk: You start to move up and down his thick tool.

His cock was being dragged through the fur on Caffrey's chest. The sensation was almost unbearable, riding the edge between pleasure and pain. Also, he had started to leak precum, and the cop's chest was wet with it, little swirls of hair sticking up in moist tangles.

"Fuck yourself, faggot," Caffrey said.

Stephen's face burned red at the slur, but somehow it made him even more excited. He lifted himself up on Caffrey's dick and then pressed back, filling himself. Caffrey put his hands on Stephen's ass, gripping them painfully. He slapped one cheek hard with his gloved hand.

"I said fuck yourself, cocksucker," he growled.

Stephen moved faster. Caffrey's prick filled him again and again. He was getting close himself, but he knew that if he came, it would be a mistake. Caffrey would punish him for it somehow.

"Do you want my load in your faggot ass?" asked Caffrey.

Stephen nodded.

"Say it, then," Caffrey told him. "Tell me to fill your faggot ass with my cum."

"Fill my faggot ass," Stephen said softly.

"Louder!" Caffrey said, slapping his ass again.

"Fill my faggot ass with your cum, sir," Stephen said.

Caffrey leaned back and arched upward. Stephen felt the cock inside him swell, then twitch. Caffrey groaned and thrust into Stephen several more times as he unloaded in his ass.

HrdAtWrk: He pulls out and orders you to lick him clean.

Stephen couldn't control himself. His cock exploded in a blast of warmth as his body shook with the joy of release. He saw Caffrey's chest covered in the proof of his inability to control himself, and he immediately felt shame come over him. Yet still his body quivered, the electricity taking control of his motions.

He felt Caffrey's hand connect with the side of his face. His head flew sideways, the sting of the slap soaking into his skin. But still the joy washed over him.

"Goddamn faggot," Caffrey said. "Now you're really in trouble."

Stephen opened his eyes. A trail of rapidly cooling cum trickled down his stomach, dotting the hair around his cock with sticky pearls. He'd come a lot. His hand was covered with it, and the leather of his chair was spotted in places.

He looked at the computer screen. HrdAtWrk had signed off. The instant message box still remained, however, his last message flashing red: Thanks. See U around.

He reached over and pulled some tissues from the box on his desk. Wiping himself off with one hand, he clicked the instant message box shut with the other. *Yeah,* he thought. *See you around.*

He turned the computer off and stood up. It was time for another pill. He was starting to feel the pain too much.

CHAPTER 17

"I think this is the best time," Simon said, stretching his feet and letting out a contented sigh. "The afterglow, so to speak."

Russell stretched. "I agree," he said. "And it was great. Thanks."

"What is a house for," Simon replied "if not to fill it with friends."

They were in the living room, Simon lying on the couch and Russell sitting in one of the armchairs, Clancy on his lap. The log in the fireplace was burning low, filling the room with its glow. The guests had all left an hour earlier, and now the two men were enjoying the comfort of a house that still retained the feeling of warmth generated by the company they'd shared.

"Do you ever wish you weren't gay?" Russell asked.

Simon, who was on the verge of nodding off, opened his eyes and regarded the younger man. Russell was staring into the fire intently.

"No," Simon said. "I don't. Why would I?"

Russell sighed. "I don't know," he said. "Sometimes it just seems like it would be easier."

"Easier," Simon said, "or just more convenient?"

"Isn't it the same thing?"

"No," replied Simon. "What you mean is that you think being straight would make your life more convenient because you'd be more like the rest of the world."

"Wouldn't it?" asked Russell. "Don't you ever get tired of being in the minority?"

"Sometimes, of course," Simon answered. "But this is who I am."

"How did you and Walter do it?" said Russell. "Figure out your relationship, I mean."

"Figure it out?" Simon said. "What was there to figure out? I loved
him and he loved me."

"But it's not that easy," Russell protested. "You can love someone
more than anything in the world and still not be able to make things
work."

Simon groaned. "You make it so hard," he commented.

"Who does?" Russell said defensively. "Me?"

Simon shook his head. "All of you," he said. "All of you who think
there's some secret formula to life. I blame it on gay liberation."

"What are you talking about?" asked Russell. "Gay liberation? Who
says that anymore?"

"I do," said Simon. "And it's true. Ever since everyone started running around waving signs and demanding attention, things have been
complicated."

"So you're saying we should all have just shut up and stayed in the
closet?" demanded Russell.

Simon put another pillow beneath his head so that he was half sitting up. "What I'm saying is that it used to be so uncomplicated. Do
you know how many friends I had when I was your age who had been
together for years and years? Couples found one another and stayed
together because we needed one another. Nowadays you just flit from
person to person as your mood changes."

"That's not true about everyone," Russell said.

"No, it's not," said Simon. "But most people don't value marriage
anymore."

"Marriage?" said Russell. "We can't even get married."

"I don't mean that legal nonsense," Simon argued. "I mean the notion itself. Do you know we used to hold weddings when I was young?
Long before any of you thought about asking the courts for permission."

"Where?" Russell asked him.

Simon waved his hands. "In our homes," he said. "Wherever we
wanted to. Walter and I attended many weddings. We got married ourselves."

"What?" Russell exclaimed. "You never mentioned that."

Simon got up and walked over to one of the many bookshelves that lined his walls. He scanned the rows for a moment and then pulled out a photograph album. He carried it back to the sofa, where he sat and put it on his lap. Russell joined him.

Simon opened the album. The first page was filled with faded black-and-white photographs. Simon flipped past them. Several pages later he stopped and pointed to a shot showing a couple dressed for their wedding. The bride wore a short white dress, the groom a smart tuxedo. They smiled at the camera, holding hands.

"Those are our friends Emma and Patience," he said.

"Those are two women?" Russell said. He peered more closely at the photo and saw that, indeed, the groom's face was feminine in features.

"We didn't call her Patience," Simon informed him. "She was Hank."

Russell laughed. "She makes a good-looking guy."

"Yes, she did," said Simon.

"When was this taken?"

Simon thought for a moment, doing the math in his head. "Nineteen fifty-nine," he said. "Hank died a few years ago."

"And Emma?" Russell inquired.

"She lives in Florida," said Simon. "With another widowed friend of ours."

"Do you have any pictures of you and Walter?" asked Russell.

Simon turned a few more pages, watching the faces of friends passing before him like leaves in the wind. So many of them were gone now. He missed them. A few he still spoke to by telephone from their homes scattered around the country, but more and more the days passed without hearing a voice from the old days. Every so often he would receive word that another one had passed, that their numbers were dwindling.

He came to the page he was looking for and stopped. He hadn't looked at these photos in some time. For years he'd been meaning to take them out, have them enlarged, perhaps, so that he could display them. Walter had wanted that. But Simon had never gotten around to it, and after Walter's death he hadn't been able to bring himself to do it.

"That's you and Walter?" said Russell.

Simon nodded. The first photograph showed the two of them,

both dressed in dark suits, standing on the porch of a house. Subsequent ones showed them surrounded by friends, big smiles on their faces as they congratulated the couple.

"Who did the ceremony?" Russell wanted to know.

"We took turns," Simon said. "It didn't really matter. We were doing this for ourselves, not for God or the state."

"I had no idea this sort of thing happened," said Russell.

"Every generation thinks they invented being gay," Simon replied. "The past is not something most young people care to learn about."

"But this is important stuff," said Russell. "This is our lives."

"No, it was *our* lives," Simon corrected him. "You have your own."

"But don't you see?" Russell said. "If we had these kinds of role models, it would give more of us hope that we could do it too."

Simon closed the album and set it on the coffee table. He understood what Russell was saying, but he knew it wasn't entirely true. Explaining why was going to be difficult.

"We did this," he said, "because we wanted to prove we could do it. It was a noble idea. But it was also flawed."

"What do you mean?" Russell asked.

Simon weighed his words carefully. "As much as we would have denied it, we were in some ways attempting to copy the world around us," he explained. "I said that we did it for ourselves, and that was true. But also we were doing it because it made us feel better about who we were. It gave us a sense of normalcy."

"And that's bad?" said Russell.

"Not necessarily," Simon continued. "But some of us were fooled by the notion that we were indeed becoming more like everyone else. When we discovered that this wasn't true, it was very difficult to handle."

"You're contradicting yourself," Russell countered. "First you tell me your relationships were so much better. Now you're telling me they were harder."

"I'm saying that sometimes our expectations were unrealistic. When we told ourselves that the world might be kinder to us because we looked more like those around us, we discovered too often that this was not true."

"So now we're back to staying in the closet," Russell declared impatiently.

Simon closed his eyes. How could he make the young man understand? It had been wonderful then, but also terrible sometimes. He
wanted Russell to know what it had been like, to know why, despite
everything, he wouldn't trade those years for anything in the world.

"Hope has to come from inside," he said finally. "It has to be something you find in your heart, not something you take from others.
Walter and I created our own hope. We knew we belonged together.
We knew we needed one another. Even when it was terribly, terribly
hard, we knew that. No one can guarantee that something is going to
work. No piece of paper, or ceremony, or promise. When you come to
a place where you have to decide to leave or stay, the only thing that
will keep you there is knowing that it's where you belong."

He looked at Russell. He was staring at the photo album and nodding silently. He turned and looked into Simon's face.

"You're right," he said. "I've been looking for something to tell me
what to do, something to help me make a decision. But I just have to
make it."

"Walter left me once," Simon told him, surprising himself. He'd
never told anyone the story of their one separation.

"Why?" asked Russell.

"He thought I was having an affair," Simon said.

"Were you?"

Simon shook his head. "No," he said. "But I wasn't showing him
enough interest. He panicked and assumed the worst."

"Is that what I'm doing?"

"Do you think John is having an affair?"

Russell shook his head. "John? No. I almost wish he was. Then I'd
have something to point a finger at."

"But you're not happy?"

"No," Russell admitted. "I'm not at all happy. I love him. I love him
more than anything. But something just isn't there. I just can't figure it
out."

"Is it something missing in him, or is it something missing in you?"
asked Simon quietly.

"Me?" Russell said. "I told you, I love him more than anything."

"Maybe that's the problem," said Simon. "Maybe you need to love
yourself more than you love him."

"Great," Russell said. "He thinks I don't love him enough and you think I love him too much. I feel like fucking Goldilocks. This one's too hard; this one's too soft. How do I find the one that's just right?"

"Two halves can only make a whole when those halves are already complete in themselves," Simon said.

Russell looked at him blankly. "What the hell does that mean?"

"It means don't expect either John or your relationship to make you feel good about who you are," Simon explained. "You need to be happy all by yourself."

"Where do you get this stuff?" Russell asked him.

"Dr. Phil," Simon answered. "There's not a lot to do around here in the mornings but watch *Oprah*."

He waited a moment to see if Russell would catch on that he was joking. Russell just nodded, however, apparently thinking about what Simon had said.

"What is it you want from your life?" Simon asked him after a minute had passed.

"That's just it," said Russell. "I thought I had it. I like my job. I like my partner. But it's just not coming together somewhere."

"Find the missing piece and you'll find your answer," said Simon. He knew it wasn't what Russell wanted to hear, but he also knew it was the truth.

"Are you happy with your life?" Russell asked him.

"No," Simon said. "I'm not." Again, he knew it wasn't what Russell wanted to hear, but again, it was the truth. He wasn't going to lie just to make his friend feel better. "I do not like being alone."

"You have all of us," Russell said kindly.

Simon put a hand on Russell's knee and squeezed. "And I love you all dearly," he said. "But it's not the same as having someone to share your life with."

"I guess we both need something more," Russell said. He looked thoughtful. "I'll make a deal with you."

"What kind of deal," Simon asked suspiciously.

"By New Year's both of us have to do something about getting what we want," said Russell. "If we haven't, we'll spend the rest of our lives together."

Simon laughed. "I think I'd be getting the better half of that deal," he said.

"Come on," Russell said. "I'm serious. Not about living together forever, but the other part. I'll figure out what it is I want and you'll look for someone you can date."

"Date," Simon repeated. "It sounds so modern. It's a lovely idea, Russell, but I think maybe I'm too old for that kind of challenge."

"So you're giving up?"

"No," Simon answered. "I'm waiting patiently."

"Now you're the one avoiding the issue."

"Really," Simon said with exasperation. "Where do you think I'm going to meet someone around here?"

"You're not going to if you don't look," Russell said. "That's why we're making this deal. By New Year's Eve I will have figured out what to do about John and you will have gotten a date for the big party we're going to have."

"Party?" Simon asked. "What party?"

"The one we're throwing to celebrate our success," said Russell.

Simon groaned. "You're too much," he said. "I don't think—"

"Say yes," Russell interrupted.

"But—"

"Say yes."

"Fine," Simon capitulated. "Yes. Yes, I will agree to make a complete fool of myself for your amusement."

"Excellent," Russell said cheerfully. "It's settled then."

He leaned over and kissed Simon on the cheek. "And now I'm going to bed. You've worn me out."

"It's been a long time since anyone's said that to me," Simon joked.

"With a little luck, it won't be the last," Russell told him as he stood up. "I'll see you in the morning."

Simon waved good night. "I'm going to sit here for a while longer."

Alone in his living room, he looked into the flames, thinking about Russell's suggestion. New Year's Eve was what, about five weeks away? Would he be able to find someone to ask out by then? It was a silly notion. He was sixty-five, hardly what the men he saw at the Engine Room were interested in. Even the ones who were closer to his age were looking for partners many years their juniors. He was last year's model, worn out and dented. Who was going to want him?

What would Walter think of the deal he'd made? He smiled to himself, imagining the look his lover always gave him whenever he mentioned some plan Walter thought was overly ambitious.

"You're right," Simon said out loud. "I'm an old fool. So perhaps it's time I acted like one."

CHAPTER 18

"I can't believe you've never done this," Mike said.

Thomas, panting and sweating, stopped to catch his breath. "How am I doing for my first time?"

"Not bad," said Mike. "You need to get your legs moving more, though. Really push."

Thomas looked down at his skis. He thought he *was* pushing. His thighs and calves ached, and they'd been out for only twenty minutes. If he pushed any more, he'd have a heart attack.

"The good news is that we're going downhill now," said Mike. "You can just coast. But remember to bend your knees."

"Bend the knees," Thomas echoed. "Got it."

Mike poled ahead and began his descent down the gentle slope. Thomas sent up a silent prayer and followed after him, trying to keep his skis in the tracks made by Mike's. He dutifully bent his knees as his rate of speed increased, but still he felt wobbly. He was glad they were only cross-country skiing. He supposed trying to attempt downhill maneuvers would result in his death.

He made it to the bottom of the hill, where the ground flattened out and his speed decreased. Ahead of him, Mike turned to watch his progress.

"That was perfect," he told Thomas as the priest skied up behind him. "Ready for another one?"

"Does it mean going *up* first?"

"Afraid so," said Mike, plunging a pole into the snow and setting off. "Come on. Trust me, it will be worth it."

Thomas had his doubts. The notion of skiing, as it turned out, was much easier than the actual doing of it. When Mike had suggested a day of outdoor activity, it had seemed like a novel way to spend an afternoon. Now, though, he was wondering if he'd be able to walk when it was all over. His muscles hadn't had such a workout in years.

He doggedly plodded after Mike, managing to keep up as they tackled another hill, this one, thankfully, smaller than the first. And despite how tired he felt, he was having a good time. For one thing, it was absolutely gorgeous. They'd had another storm, and everything was sparkling in the afternoon sun. The snow was dry and powdery, swirling in billowy wisps across the ground. They were skiing through a valley, and on either side a forest surrounded them, walls of green reaching up to the sky. The peaceful quiet was interrupted only by their occasional conversation and the chirping of the birds that foraged in the tree branches, cocking their heads and staring with small, dark eyes at the intruders in their world.

"How often do you do this?" Thomas asked as they crested the hill and paused again to rest.

"Whenever I can," answered Mike. "It's one of the advantages of having an early and long winter."

He must have legs like iron, Thomas thought to himself, immediately blocking out the mental image that had formed in his mind of Mike's legs. He'd been troubled enough by his thoughts of late; he didn't need to add to the problem by picturing Mike naked.

Still, he wondered in spite of himself, what *would* Mike look like beneath his clothes? The only men he'd ever seen naked, besides the boys in his high school gym class, were other priests, and then only in the seminary locker room. His frame of reference for what constituted male physical beauty was limited mostly to religious paintings of Christ preparing for his crucifixion. Those came in either the emaciated version or the well-muscled version, or Scrawny Jesus and Musclebound Jesus, as Joseph had referred to them once as he looked over a book of Christian-themed art.

Given Christ's occupation as a carpenter, Thomas believed he probably would have tended to the latter body type, although perhaps not to the ideal portrayed by many of the painters and sculptors. Their visions of him verged on the sexual. Then again, so did much of religious art, what with all its saints in ecstasy and whatnot. Devotion to religion had long been the favored outlet of expression for the sexually frustrated, and the intermingling of the two came as no shock, particularly to someone who had intimate knowledge of the religious life. Undoubtedly, there was something about Jesus that brought out the erotic in artists. Probably, Thomas thought, it was not a coincidence that so many of them were rumored to be queer.

Mike didn't resemble Jesus in any way, of course. But Thomas had some idea of what he might look like out of his winter coat and ski pants. He could picture Mike, his captivating smile flashing as he pulled a sweater over his head. He could imagine him stepping out of a shower, his hair tousled. He could see—

He drove Jesus, and Mike, from his mind before he went too far. He needed to concentrate on his balance, as he was having difficulty keeping his skis in the ruts left behind by Mike. Twice he had slipped out of them and almost fallen. Only by catching himself with his poles had he avoided doing a face plant in the snow.

They skied for another half hour without saying more than a few words. Then, just as Thomas thought there was no way he could handle another hill, Mike came to a stop. A large boulder sat in the middle of the field, completely out of place, as if an alien ship had come along and dropped it there for some secret purpose.

"Isn't this thing strange?" said Mike, bending down to undo the bindings of his skis. "I discovered it a few years ago."

"Who put it here?" Thomas asked, copying Mike and releasing the clips that held his boots in place.

"Your buddy," Mike answered.

Thomas looked at him, not understanding.

"God," said Mike as he shucked the backpack he'd been carrying from his shoulders and pointed to the rock. "Actually, a glacier left it behind when it made this valley, but it's sort of the same thing, right? Climb on up."

Thomas put his foot on a small outcropping and pulled himself up to the top of the rock. Its surface, warmed by the sun, was free of snow. It was also flat. He sat down and watched as Mike climbed up beside him.

"What's in the pack?" asked Thomas.

"Lunch," said Mike. "But we don't have to eat it if you're not hungry."

"Oh, I'm hungry," Thomas said quickly. "But I didn't know lunch came with the outing."

"This is a full-service operation," Mike said, unzipping the pack and pulling out two brown bags. "I just hope you like peanut butter and jelly."

"It's my favorite," Thomas said, accepting the bag Mike held out. "Thanks."

"There are also a couple of Power Bars in here," said Mike, opening his bag and taking out the sandwich. "And water."

Thomas bit into the sandwich, tasting peanut butter and strawberry jam. It was the most delicious thing he'd ever tasted. His stomach growled its appreciation as he chewed.

"It's beautiful up here," he told Mike.

"I come here in the summer, too," said Mike. "Actually, I come out here all year round. It's a great place to think. On a clear night the stars spread out and it's like being on your very own planet."

"The universe in the palm of God's hand," Thomas said thoughtfully."

"Did you make that up?" Mike inquired.

"Me? No. Sylvia Tressier did."

Mike raised an eyebrow. "Who?"

Thomas smiled. "An eighteenth-century mystic. She wrote about experiencing nature in its purest form. My favorite is her description of standing in a thunderstorm naked. At those moments she said she knew that the entire universe was held in the palm of God's hand."

"She sounds like my kind of girl," Mike remarked.

"She wasn't the church's," Thomas told him. "They called her a pagan."

"I've noticed you guys do that a lot," said Mike.

"Hey, I wasn't there," Thomas said jokingly. "Don't blame me. Besides, that was the Catholics."

"Ah," Mike said, nodding. "Nothing like a lifelong rivalry to bring out the bitterness."

Thomas laughed. "Some of my best friends are Catholics."

"And some of my best friends are straight," replied Mike. "I guess we're both sort of fraternizing with the enemy here, aren't we?"

"Enemy?" said Thomas. "I don't understand."

"You and me," said Mike. "The church and the sinner, the saved and the unsaved."

"Oh," Thomas said uncomfortably. "I guess I hadn't thought about it like that."

"Really?" Mike asked. "It never crosses your mind that you've been spending time with a gay guy?"

"That's not important to me," Thomas said quickly. "You're just you. I'm just me. I could just as easily ask you if it ever crosses your mind that you've been spending time with a priest."

"Every day," said Mike. "Don't tell me you don't think about it."

"I don't," Thomas lied. He felt a heavy weight descend on his shoulders as he spoke. Suddenly, he didn't feel so much like eating.

"You're a better man than I am," Mike said, patting him on the back.

Thomas didn't reply. He took a long drink of water, trying to clear the block that had formed in his throat. Mike, seemingly oblivious, continued to eat his sandwich.

"Can I ask you something?" Thomas asked when he was able to speak again.

"Shoot."

"Have you ever had a, you know, partner?"

Mike didn't answer right away. Thomas was afraid he'd somehow offended his friend by asking. He was on the verge of apologizing when Mike answered him.

"Once," he said. "Before I moved to Cold Falls. It wasn't a long thing, only about three years."

He stopped talking. Thomas wondered if it would be impolite to ask more. He didn't want Mike to think he was prying. But another part of him desperately wanted to know.

"What was his name?" he asked tentatively.

"Jim," Mike said. He said the name without either fondness or anger, giving Thomas no clue as to how he felt about the man.

"He was a bartender too," Mike continued. "We worked at the same place. I had a rule about never dating customers, so I figured my only option was to date another bartender."

"You're joking," said Thomas.

Mike shook his head. "Dating customers is a big mistake," he said. "A lot of your tips depend on customers thinking you're available. Having a jealous boyfriend hanging around puts a real cut in your take.

Besides, when you break up, either the bar loses a customer or you lose a job. But another bartender gets how it is, so it's okay."

"I had no idea it was so complicated," Thomas joked.

"Jim and I got along really well," said Mike. "Until the end."

"Can I ask what happened?" Thomas assumed the story would have something to do with an affair, a lapse of judgment involving a customer, perhaps.

"He was an addict," answered Mike. He'd finished his sandwich. Now he balled up the baggie it had been wrapped in and stuffed it into the paper sack. "Not street drugs. Prescription."

"I'm sorry," said Thomas, starting to wish he'd never asked.

"He was using them the whole time we were together," Mike said. His voice had taken on a new tone, one that made Thomas sad to hear. "It turned out he was trading some doctor free drinks at the bar for prescriptions. Vicodin. Demerol. Anything that would get him high."

"How did you find out?"

"One night he crashed his car into a lamp post," said Mike. "He was conscious enough to have the hospital call me. When I got there, the doctor told me blood tests had shown abnormally high levels of narcotics in Jim's blood. I told them they were crazy. But the more I thought about it, the more it added up. I guess I'd been ignoring the signs. That night I went to his place and did a little looking around. I found garbage bags filled with empty pill bottles in one of his closets."

"So you broke things off?" said Thomas as Mike looked off into the distance.

"I confronted him," Mike said. "At first he told me that he was just selling the drugs to other people. Believe it or not, for a minute that actually made me feel better. But deep down I knew it wasn't the truth. So then I decided to save him. I convinced him to go from the hospital to rehab. I went with him to a couple of NA meetings. He seemed to be doing everything right. But he wasn't. He'd started using again as soon as he was out of the hospital."

Thomas was listening intently. Although their stories were dissimilar in many ways, he could relate to a lot of what Mike was saying. He badly wanted to tell him about Joseph, but he couldn't bring himself to do it. So he sat and listened as Mike finished his tale.

"We stayed together for a year after that," said Mike. He gave a little half laugh. "Looking back, I can't believe I was so stupid. A year." He shook his head sadly. "What an idiot. Anyway, finally I had enough of the broken promises, the worrying, the waiting up for the next phone call from the hospital or the police. One Saturday morning after he hadn't come home all night, I packed up my truck and left."

"Did you ever see him again?"

"No," said Mike. "No one knew where I went, so he had no way of reaching me. That's when I came here. He could be dead for all I know. He might be better off if he was."

Thomas looked up at the bright blue sky. Tattered bits of cloud chased one another across the azure field, the sun peering through them and turning them into ghosts. How strange it seemed to him that anything horrible could go on beneath such a sky. The story Mike had just told him saddened him deeply. He felt for both Mike and Jim, for different reasons.

"That's strange," Mike said, drawing Thomas's attention back to him. "Usually people tell *me* their sob stories."

"Well, this time it was your turn."

"What about you?" asked Mike. "Any tragic tales of love you need to get off your chest?"

Thomas looked up at the sky again, letting the sun dazzle his eyes. There was so much he wanted to tell Mike. But he knew he wouldn't. He turned to his friend. He knew Mike would accept the terrible lie he was about to tell.

"I've never been in love," he said.

CHAPTER 19

"Look at the tits on that one."

Pete turned to see what Ronnie Boudreaux was staring at. Behind them, leaning against the pool table, a blonde with big breasts and bigger hair was talking to some girlfriends. The girls, noticing Pete and his friends staring at them, giggled and turned away.

"Man, she wants you," Ronnie told Pete. "She's been staring at you all night."

Pete's buddies hooted. Having downed at least three beers apiece, they were feeling no pain. The jokes had been flying back and forth, and all of them were in the mood for a little fun.

"Bet she could suck the chrome off a fender," Gary Pitt said, putting his mouth over his beer bottle and feigning a blowjob. "Bet she'd suck the suds down too."

Pete took a sip of his own beer before replying. "Give her a couple more drinks and I bet she'd do all of us."

The comment earned him another round of laughs from his friends and a high-five from T.J. Donnley. Ronnie, shaking his head, said, "Man, if my wife heard us talking this shit, she'd never let me out of the house."

"Just 'cause she won't go down on you's no reason to be a ball buster," T.J. taunted him.

Ronnie flipped his middle finger at T.J. The guys crowed, knowing they'd hit upon one of Ronnie's sore spots. His wife, Julie, was a great woman, but she hated giving head. He'd made the mistake of telling them all about it one drunken night, and they'd never let him forget.

"Dude," T.J. said, leaning forward as if he were about to share a secret. "I was with this girl last week, biggest fucking tits you've ever seen. I mean porn star big. And she wanted me to titty-fuck her. Man, it was like fucking an ass, these things were so huge."

"You're full of it," Gary said.

"Like shit I am," T.J. said angrily. "I met her at the High Spot over in Herkimer. She took me back to her place. It was fucking amazing."

"Bet that one would like a titty fuck from Pete," said Ronnie, cocking his head toward the girl at the pool table.

"Cool it," Pete said.

"What's the matter?" Ronnie asked. "You giving up on chasing pussy or something?"

"Maybe he's turned queer on us," Gary said.

"Fuck you," Pete spat back. "I'm just not into her."

"I'd be into her," said T.J. He made a circle with his finger and thumb and poked another finger through the hole.

Pete laughed, but inside he was fuming. Fucking Gary, he thought. What kind of shit was that, asking if he'd turned queer? He knew it was just a joke; they all called each other queers whenever they were acting stupid. Still, it pissed him off. Maybe he *should* bang the blond chick, just so they'd all shut the fuck up.

"Another round, boys?"

Pete looked up at Sherrie, the Briar Patch's lone waitress. She was collecting their empty bottles and placing them on the tray in her hand. She swept up the wet napkins and added them to the pile.

"Sure," Pete said. "Bring it on."

Sherrie nodded and walked away. Pete, sensing an opportunity to reclaim his reputation among his buddies, followed her with his eyes. "Now there's an ass I'd like to get into," he said.

"No shit," T.J. seconded. "I've been after her forever. That girl won't give it up for nothing."

"Probably a dyke," Gary remarked.

"Hey," T.J. said. "That's fine with me, as long as she lets me watch."

Sherrie came back a moment later with four Buds. As she put them on the table, Pete, looking at Gary across the table, made a V with his fingers and held it to his mouth. His tongue flicked back and forth lewdly in the opening. Gary tried not to crack up as Sherrie asked if she could get them anything else.

"No thanks, honey," Ronnie said, also trying to hide the big smile that was crossing his face. "That'll do it."

When the waitress left, the boys let out a roar, wailing with laughter. Pete's spirits had lifted considerably. He felt like one of the gang again, one of the guys. He could mix it up with the best of them, he told himself. There was nothing the matter with him.

They sat through two more rounds, bullshitting about nothing. This was what Pete liked, a night out with the boys. His friends were pretty damn cool, he told himself. Regular guys. He could easily sit there all night with them, just talking shit and drinking. Except that right now he had to take a major piss.

"Be right back," he said, standing up. He was a little unsteady on his feet, but putting his hand on the back of his chair steadied him.

"Going to the can?" T.J. asked. "I'll come with you."

The two of them made their way through the bar, attempting not to look as intoxicated as they really were. As they passed the table where the blonde and her friends were now sitting, T.J. gave them a nod. "Evening, ladies."

When he and Pete burst into the men's room, they were laughing. Pete was high on the feeling of camaraderie. "Man, you crack me up," he told T.J. as they lined up at the two urinals.

T.J. unzipped his pants. A moment later Pete heard the heavy sound of his piss hitting the water in the urinal. As he held his own dick, releasing what seemed to be a gallon of pee, he quickly glanced to his left.

T.J.'s cock was big. Even soft it hung low. He held it casually between his thumb and forefinger, aiming the head into the bowl. His other hand was on the wall, supporting him. His eyes were closed. Pete kept staring. The piss poured from T.J.'s prick in a thick stream. T.J. had unbuttoned his Levi's, and in the V formed by the blue denim Pete could see the blond hair of his stomach, the heavier patch around his cock.

T.J. finished and groaned. "That felt good," he said. He shook his cock, a few final drops flying into the urinal. Then he tucked his prick away and buttoned up.

Pete, staring at the wall, finished up as well. He hurriedly zipped up and flushed, not looking at T.J. Going to the sink, he washed his hands thoroughly, trying not to think about what he'd seen. But the image of T.J.'s cock, his hand gently caressing it, was burned into his mind.

Back at the table, he tried to blot the image out with the help of another beer. His head was swimming. He'd had too much. But still he hadn't been able to rid his head of his thoughts. They were still there, teasing. He kept stealing glances at T.J., thinking about what he'd seen. He needed to do something else to banish them, something that would bury them deep and keep them there. He stood up.

"Are you leaving, man?" Gary asked.

Pete shook his head. "I'm going to get myself some pussy," he said, grinning wickedly.

Turning away from his friends, he walked over to where the blonde and her friends were sitting. He stopped beside her and put his hand on her shoulder. She looked up.

"Hey," Pete said. "How are you?"

"Fine," the girl said. Her friends tittered.

"I couldn't help but notice how good you look tonight," Pete told her, giving her a smile.

The girl looked at her friends, who laughed some more. Pete ignored them, focusing all of his attention on the blonde. He knew his buddies were all watching him, waiting for him to score.

He considered his options. The girl had been drinking. She was probably just looking for an excuse to get busy with him. He decided to go for it.

"How'd you like to go somewhere with me and party?" he asked.

The girl seemed to consider his offer for a moment. "No thanks," she said.

Pete looked at her, the smile still on his face. He'd heard her wrong.

"I said no thanks," the girl repeated, this time in a less-friendly tone. "Now would you mind leaving us alone?"

Pete blinked. The girl and all her friends were looking at him. He sensed three other pairs of eyes behind him, taking in the situation. He removed his hand from the girl's shoulder and turned away without saying a word. As he walked back to his table, he saw his friends preparing to give him a hard time.

"Sherrie's not the only dyke around here," he said before they could start in on him. "That cunt's as frigid as a Buffalo winter."

Gary, T.J., and Ronnie smirked but said nothing. Pete's anger radiated from him, and his friends felt it. Pete snatched his jacket from the back of his chair and put it on.

"I'll see you guys later," he said.

He stormed out of the bar, ignoring the table of girls, who teasingly called good night to him as he passed them. Outside, he stopped to take a cigarette from his jacket pocket and light it. He blew a cloud of smoke up at the moon. *Fucking bitches,* he thought. *Who the fuck did they think they were fucking with?*

He got in his car. It took him several tries to get the key into the ignition, but on the third attempt he did it. He pulled out of the parking lot with a squealing of tires and headed for the highway.

Halfway home he saw the lights of the lone truck stop on that stretch of the road. Consisting of nothing more than public rest rooms and a couple of picnic tables—now covered with snow—it was rarely used except by teenagers needing a place to party late at night. And, Pete knew, men looking for some action. Although he'd never been there himself, he'd heard stories about the place ever since he was in high school. Tucker Flatley, when they were sixteen, claimed to have been offered a blowjob by an older man while stopping there to smoke a joint. Pete hadn't believed him then, thinking queers lived only in New York and San Francisco, but he'd never forgotten the story.

The parking lot of the rest stop was deserted save for one lone car, parked directly in front of the rest room, its lights dark. Probably it was just a couple of horny teenagers going at it, Pete thought. Still, he found himself pulling off the road and coming to a stop next to the car. Looking at its windows, he saw that they were empty and unclouded. The car was empty.

He got out, still not quite able to stand without swaying, and looked toward the men's room door. It was closed, but from underneath he saw a line of light extended out to the frozen sidewalk. He walked toward the door and pushed, hearing it bang against the inside wall from the force of his entry. If anyone was inside, they definitely would know he was coming.

The room smelled like piss and dirt. Probably, he thought, it was cleaned only occasionally. And it was cold. His breath formed clouds in the unheated air as he walked toward the sinks that lined one wall, the mirrors over them cracked and covered with filmy streaks, residue splashed there by patrons using the little tubs of pink soap to wash their hands after relieving themselves.

To the right of the sinks there was a row of urinals, five of them side by side with no dividers. A single stall was situated at the far end, its door closed. Beneath the door he could see a pair of shoes.

He walked to the farthest urinal, the one closest to the stall. The walls of the stall were made of some kind of hard plastic, and someone had made a small hole in the wall at waist height. He'd seen such a thing before. Fag Holes, he and his friends called them. Queers looked through them, hoping to get a glimpse of the cocks of the men who used the urinal outside. He couldn't imagine anyone taking the time necessary to drill such a hole through solid plastic. It was the act of someone desperate. But that's what fags were, wasn't it? Desperate and pathetic.

The shoes inside the stall shifted, scraping on the dirty floor. Pete wondered if the guy inside was making himself comfortable, peeping through the hole to get a look at who had come in. *I'll give him a show,* he thought as he undid his pants and pulled his dick out.

Standing at the urinal, he first pissed. Then, his bladder once more empty, he slowly stroked his cock to hardness. He made sure to keep the action in line with the hole in the stall wall. The occupant had made no further noise, and Pete was pretty sure he wasn't there to take a shit. There had been none of the usual movement, no unrolling of toilet paper, no sounds or smells of elimination. No, whoever was in the stall was there for other purposes.

Pete saw one shod foot slip halfway out of the stall. Slowly, the toe was raised and lowered, tapping the floor. Pete ignored it, forcing the faggot to give him more proof of what he wanted. It came a moment later, when the foot emerged farther and tapped again, three times. Then Pete heard the sound of the stall's metal lock being pulled back. Behind him, the door swung inward.

He pushed it open, looking inside. Sitting on the toilet was a middle-aged man. His brown hair was graying at the temples, and he wore the generic gold-rimmed glasses typical of men his age. His brown corduroy pants had been pulled down, and his winter jacket was open, revealing a faded blue button-down shirt and an undershirt beneath it. Only his thighs and upper legs were bare, spread to allow him access to his erect penis, which was short and perfectly undistinguished. The hand wrapped around it featured a gold wedding band on its ring finger.

The man looked at Pete, saying nothing. He just held on to his dick as he stared at the cock in Pete's hand. Pete pumped it a few times, seeing the man's face twitch in anticipation. Then Pete stepped closer, until his crotch was right in the man's face, and slapped his mouth with his cock.

"Suck it, fag," he said.

The man's mouth opened, eagerly accepting Pete's tool. He sucked anxiously, inexpertly, his tongue flicking the head. Pete put a hand behind the man's head and pulled him toward him. He gagged, unable to take the thickness of Pete's cock, but Pete held him there until he calmed down. Then he began fucking the man's mouth.

He didn't look at the man. Instead, he thought about T.J., about his big cock and blond hair. It was T.J. servicing him, running his tongue along the length of Pete's cock. It was T.J. sitting there, jerking off while he waited for Pete to come in his mouth.

He shot, filling the warm mouth with his load. He felt the man swallow, choking. When he was done, he pulled away. The man looked up at him. Cum dribbled from the corner of his mouth.

"What?" Pete said. "What are you looking at?"

The man continued to stare at him. He was pulling on his own dick, his hand moving frantically up and down. He had started to breathe more heavily, filling the stall with puffs of air. Then he groaned. A spray of white shot from between his legs, covering the floor beneath him.

Pete looked down and saw that some of the man's load had landed on his boot. With a shudder of repulsion he glared at the man. "Clean it off," he ordered.

The man reached for the toilet paper dispenser.

"Lick it off," Pete said.

The man looked at him. Pete grabbed him by the collar and pulled him off the toilet. He fell awkwardly to his knees, his bare ass scraping the edge of the toilet. He was kneeling in his own cum, as well as the accumulated dirt of the stall's previous patrons.

"Lick it up, faggot," Pete said again.

The man, clearly shaken, leaned forward, his hands on the filthy floor. Bending his head, he licked at Pete's boot, removing the offending stain. When he was done, he looked up at Pete again, as if waiting for a critique of his work.

Pete spit on him, the liquid spattering the man's glasses and mouth. "Goddamned fag," he said.

He exited the stall, leaving the queer sitting on the floor. His buzz was starting to wear off, and he was going to be sick. Outside the men's room door it hit him, a wave of nausea rising up from his stomach. He leaned over and puked, the contents of his stomach landing on the hood of the fag's car. Three more times he heaved, emptying himself completely until he was only retching. The mess on the car's hood steamed. He recoiled from the smell.

Let the queer wash it off, he thought as he got into his own car. *It serves him right.*

CHAPTER 20

"Look at the tits on that one."

Mike looked up. His friends were gawking at a well-muscled man who had just entered. Immediately he'd shed his jacket, revealing a white tank top underneath. Now he was cruising the room, obviously enjoying the attention he was getting.

"He must be freezing," Greg said. "It's twenty degrees out there."

"If his nipples are any indication, he is indeed quite chilly," remarked Simon.

"I couldn't look like that if I went to the gym for six hours a day," Russell lamented.

"You could if you injected as many steroids as he probably does," said Mike, comforting him.

"I'd do it if I thought I'd get a body like that," Russell told him. "In a heartbeat."

"Yes, and your dick would shrink to the size of a peanut," said Greg.

"Who says it isn't already the size of a peanut?" Russell replied. He looked at Simon. "Maybe you should ask him out for New Year's."

Mike and Greg looked at the two of them. "What's going on on New Year's?" asked Mike.

"Simon and I just have a little bet going," Russell informed them. "He has to find a date, and I have to decide if I'm getting divorced."

Mike eyed Simon. "You agreed to this?"

"Under protest," Simon answered, sighing. "It was the only way to get him to leave me alone. He was impossibly tenacious."

"I think it's a great idea," said Greg. "I wish I had a date for New Year's."

"Would you like to be mine?" Simon inquired.

"No," Russell said firmly. "It can't be a friend. It has to be a real date."

"What makes you think Greg isn't interested in me as more than a friend?" Simon asked. "Perhaps he finds me wildly attractive."

"That's true," Mike said. "I've seen the way he looks at you."

"Simon, perhaps we should tell them," Greg said seriously. He looked at the other two men. "Simon and I have been seeing each other for some time. We didn't want you to know."

"Nice try," Russell said. "I happen to know you have the hots for that new stock boy. Gina told me all about it."

"Cunt," Greg hissed, then grinned. "But I can't help it. Have you seen him?"

"Body of death," Russell informed Mike and Simon. "And the most beautiful face. Unfortunately, he also has the most hateful gum-popping girlfriend you've ever seen."

"Why do all the hunky straight boys have girlfriends from hell?" Greg whined.

"To keep them away from queens like you," Mike told him. "Stick with your own kind."

"I've been trying," Greg said. "It's not exactly like this place is crawling with eligible fags."

"And you want *me* to find one?" said Simon, addressing Russell.

"Tits is going into the men's room," Greg said, getting their attention. "Russell, come on."

Taking a protesting Russell by the hand, he dragged him toward the men's room. Mike and Simon watched them go.

"Greg is good for him," Mike said to Simon. "I haven't seen Russell have fun in a long time."

The two of them locked eyes. "Are you thinking what I'm thinking?" Simon asked.

"Could be," answered Mike. "It would make sense."

"Hmm," Simon said cryptically as he sipped his drink.

"Did you really promise him you'd find a date for New Year's?"

Simon groaned. "It seemed like a good idea at the time."

"I think it's an excellent idea," said Mike. "Russell's not the only one who hasn't had fun in a while."

"I'm old," Simon replied. "I'm not supposed to have fun. I'm supposed to wither quietly and make way for the young ones."

"Bullshit," Mike said. "You know better than that."

"Yes, I do," Simon said. "Unfortunately, the rest of the world doesn't seem to agree with me."

"Do you have anyone in mind for this little endeavor?" Mike asked.

"Not a one," said Simon. "I was rather hoping a likely candidate would simply drop out of the sky onto my porch. So far, the gods have not indulged that request. But I am hopeful."

Mike laughed. "You'll find someone," he said. "And what exactly are these big New Year's plans?"

"That has yet to be determined," said Simon. "I'm assuming there will be festivities here?"

"The usual," said Mike. "Drag queens, tiaras, and noisemakers all around. You guys are more than welcome."

Before Simon could express his opinion on the matter, Russell and Greg returned. They were giggling like children, laughing so hard they could barely speak.

"What happened in there?" Mike asked them.

Russell held his fingers up, barely an inch of space between the thumb and forefinger. "Peanut dick," he said, causing Greg to launch into a new round of convulsive hysterics.

"You should have seen Russell," he said. "He couldn't stop staring at it."

"It's just so *small,*" Russell said. "I couldn't help it."

"He saw us laughing at it," Greg said.

"Well, that's what he gets for letting people get a look at that thing," said Russell. "He should keep it in his pants if he doesn't want anyone to know."

"That's why the tits are so big," Mike said. "He thinks no one will notice his tiny tool."

"Tiny is right," Greg said. "That thing belongs on a two-year-old."

"Now that that pressing matter is settled," Simon said, "we were discussing the options available to us for New Year's Eve."

"I told Simon you guys can always come here," said Mike. "I have to work anyway, and I'd appreciate the company."

"Sounds good to me," said Russell. "I'll see what John has in mind."

"Are you two getting along better?" Mike inquired.

Russell nodded. "We are," he said. "We're sort of dating again, taking it slow."

"Has he put out yet?" Greg asked him.

"If you must know, we're not doing the sex thing," Russell told them. "I told him I thought we needed to start over. I have to give him credit, he's really trying."

"Don't look now," Mike announced, "but Tinky Winky is heading this way."

The man with the big chest approached the bar, standing right next to Greg. "Jack Daniels," he said. "Neat."

As Mike poured the man's drink, he watched his friends out of the corner of his eye. Russell and Greg were trying very hard not to laugh, while Simon was pretending he didn't know them. Mike turned back to the man, handing him his drink.

"That's a little short, isn't it?" the man said.

Mike shot Russell and Greg a look as they hid their faces behind their hands. "I'll top it off for you," he told his customer.

The man gave him exact change and left with his drink. Russell and Greg, their eyes streaming with tears, pounded their fists on the bar as Mike capped the bottle of Jack and returned it to its place on the shelf.

"A little short?" Greg howled. "A little short? Honey, I've seen bigger worms in the bottom of a tequila bottle."

"Getting back to the topic of holidays," Simon said. "Since our Thanksgiving was such a success, shall we plan something for Christmas?"

"I'll be in Kentucky," Greg said, sounding dismally unhappy. "My mother called and laid a guilt trip on me a mile long. The only way to get her to hang up was to agree to come. So I'll be spending two glorious days in redneck heaven."

"I'll be here, and John doesn't go anywhere, either," Russell said.

"I'm in," chimed in Mike.

"How about your boyfriend?" Russell asked Mike.

"Boyfriend?"

Russell put his hands together and looked heavenward, attempting to assume a pious expression. Getting the hint, Mike took a swipe at him with his bar towel.

"Knock it off," he said. "Besides, he's probably doing something. That is the big day for the church, you know."

"Ask him anyway," said Simon. "I found him to be delightful."

"Okay," Mike said. "I'll ask him."

"Did you know Jesus was actually born in March?" Greg said, taking a handful of peanuts from the bowls Mike was setting out and popping them into his mouth.

They all looked at him.

"Why do you know that?" Russell asked.

Greg shrugged. "It's just one of those useless bits of trivia I have floating around in my head, like how many Oscars Bette Davis won or something."

"Actually, he's correct," said Simon before anyone could contradict Greg. "Historical evidence does suggest that Christ was born in March."

"Then why do we celebrate Christmas?" asked Russell.

"In order to make Christianity more acceptable to the pagan communities they wanted to control, the church simply inserted religious holidays over the existing pagan ones," Simon explained. "December was the time for celebrating Yule, or the return of the light. By substituting the Christ child for the sun, they provided a neat compromise. The pagans could continue to celebrate their holidays and the church could gradually wipe out the heathen traditions. It was really very clever on their part, so successful that even most Christians don't realize that the trees they put up each year are, in fact, symbols of pagan rebirth."

"Leave it to religion to fuck up something good," Russell said, shaking his head. "Is there anything they haven't gotten their fingers into? They should just wipe out all the churches and start again."

"We'd just fuck it up all over again," Mike said.

Russell nodded. "Maybe," he said. "But at least this time *we* would be in charge. We could make heterosexuality a sin and see how they like it."

"This conversation has gotten kind of heavy," Greg said. "Can we talk about Teeny Peeny again?"

"You started it," Russell accused him. "You and that stuff about Jesus being a Pisces instead of a Capricorn."

"Whatever," said Greg. "Let's get back to the tits. Do you think he's a top or a bottom?"

"Bottom," Mike and Russell said in unison.

"With a dick like that?" Russell added. "I certainly hope so."

"I don't know," said Greg. "I think he *thinks* he's a top, but really he wants someone to bend him over and give him a good, hard ride."

"It sounds to me like *you* want to give him a good, hard pounding," Mike told Greg.

Greg grinned. "He does have a great ass," he said.

"Oh, for the love of God," said Russell. "If you tell me you're going to try to pick that man up, I'm going to have to reconsider being your friend."

"I didn't say I wanted to marry him," Greg objected. "I just said he had a great ass."

"Go," Russell said, shooing Greg away as if he were a pesky dog. "You've already decided you're going to, so just go. But when you get him home and he says he wants to put that little thing of his in your butt, don't say we didn't warn you."

Greg stood up. "I'll see you boys in a little while," he said, marching off in search of his quarry.

"Can you believe that?" Russell asked Mike and Simon. "What on earth would possess him to go after that?"

"He's a man," Simon said knowingly. "And he's had several drinks. If successful, he will indeed regret it in the morning. We have all of us bedded someone we later regretted."

"Even you?" Mike asked, interested.

"Even me," answered Simon. "My friend Patrick used to call them Monets."

"Monets?" Russell repeated. "I don't get it."

"False impressionism," Simon clarified. "Good from far, but far from good. Every gay man has a few Monets in his romantic gallery."

"I have more than a few," Russell admitted. "But even I wouldn't go after Mr. Tits."

"It sounds to me like you're a little bit jealous," Mike teased.

"Of Greg?" Russell exclaimed. "Please."

Mike and Simon looked at one another. Simon nodded. Russell, noticing the exchange, looked horrified. "You guys think I have it bad for Greg?"

"We've just noticed that the two of you seem to get along awfully well," Mike said. "That's all."

"I am *not* interested in Greg," Russell declared. "Not at all."

"But he does have a great ass," said Mike.

"Doesn't he—" Russell began, stopping when he saw the huge grin on Mike's face. "You asshole," he said, trying hard to sound angry.

Giving Simon a wink, Mike took Russell's empty glass and refilled it. "This one's on the house," he said as he handed it back. "Bottoms up."

CHAPTER 21

Thomas looked at the faces staring back at him. They were waiting for him to tell them something. Some of them fidgeted in their seats, scratching their heads or noses; others looked around the room, completely ignoring him. This, he knew from experience, was the toughest kind of audience for a minister. He was going to have to be good.

"Can anyone tell me why Mary and Joseph were going to Bethlehem?" he asked.

Several hands shot up. He picked one at random. "Yes, Alexa?"

"It was their vacation," the little girl said confidently. "We go to visit my grandma at Christmas. Probably they were going to visit Jesus's grandma."

"That's not why they were going," a boy beside her said. "They went because of the centipede. Isn't that right, Father Dunn?"

The boy, Hamish McTooney, looked at Thomas triumphantly. Thomas wasn't sure what to tell him. The centipede? Where on earth had the child gotten such an idea? Thomas didn't want to make him feel foolish, but he was at a loss for words.

"What's a centipede?" someone else asked, sparing Thomas for the moment.

"It's when people count you, stupid," Hamish said knowingly.

Suddenly Thomas understood. "I think what Hamish means is a *census,*" he said, ignoring for a moment the fact that Hamish had insulted the asker.

"Right," said Hamish. "That."

"Hamish is correct that a census is a counting of people," Thomas continued. "Mary and Joseph were going to Bethlehem because there was a census going on. They went there to be counted."

"Why did they have to go to Bethlehem to get counted?" asked Lily Parsick. "Couldn't they do it by telephone?"

"They didn't have telephones back then," Thomas explained.

The children all nodded, as if this made perfect sense to them. Thomas thanked God that there were some things five-year-olds took at face value.

"Mary and Joseph went to Bethlehem to take part in the census," he said. "And when they got there, they tried to find a room at an inn. But there weren't any to be found."

He waited for one of the kids to ask why they hadn't made a reservation. Apparently, this small detail escaped them completely, however, because they remained quiet.

"Finally they found someone who would let them stay in his stable," Thomas said.

"We have a stable," Jeb Ritner said brightly. "We keep horses in it."

"There were horses in this stable, too," Thomas said quickly, sensing that some of the other children were about to discuss in detail the contents of *their* stables. "And cows, sheep, and donkeys. There were lots of animals. Mary and Joseph made a bed in the straw, and that's where Mary gave birth to Jesus."

The children stared at him. One yawned. He'd just come to the climax of his story, and they couldn't have cared less.

"Did the donkeys lick him?" Alexa asked. "My grandma has a donkey and it licked me once."

"Probably a donkey did lick Jesus," Thomas assured her. "And later, the shepherds and the three wise men came to see him. Do you know how they knew he was there?"

The children shook their heads as one.

"An angel told them he was there. And the wise men followed a star."

"And the wise men brought him presents," Hamish said suddenly, as if he'd just remembered it. "Gold and something."

At the mention of presents, the class perked up considerably. Thomas knew they were envisioning their own ideas of what constituted acceptable Christmas gifts, and he wasn't about to divest them of their notions. It was easier this way.

"So that's what our pageant is going to be about," he said cheerfully. "And all of you are going to be in it. What do you think about that?"

"Can I be Mary?" Alexa asked immediately.

Thomas looked over at Mrs. Evelyn Siggs, their Sunday school teacher. She rolled her eyes and came to his rescue.

"You all are going to be shepherds, angels, and animals," she said enthusiastically. "The older classes will be the other roles."

"But I want to be Mary," Alexa insisted.

"Maybe next year," Mrs. Siggs said kindly.

Alexa mulled over this news. "Then can I be a pig?" she asked.

"Yes," Mrs. Siggs said, beaming. "You can be a pig. And you all get to sing 'Silent Night' as part of the angel choir."

Gladdened by this news, Alexa immediately began snorting. The other children followed her cue, making various animal noises. The room filled with bleating, mooing, oinking, and assorted other sounds, all of which sounded decidedly odd coming from a bunch of rosy-cheeked first graders.

"It's like this every year," Mrs. Siggs told Thomas. "Thanks for coming to talk to them. It makes them feel important."

"I hope the next bunch is easier," Thomas told her. "It's the teen class."

"They'll just be surly," Mrs. Siggs assured him. "And secretly all the girls will want to be Mary. They always do."

Thomas left her with her charges and exited the room. The smaller children had their Sunday school sessions in the church's basement, while the older ones were upstairs. He went up and walked into the room where they were meeting with Saint Peter's music director and de facto pageant organizer, Gavin Bettelheim. In his sixties, Gavin was a portly, bearded man who favored music many in the congregation found slightly depressing. But his skill as an organist and his ability to draw moving performances from the choir were unchallenged, and he had been a fixture at the church for coming on three decades.

"Ah, Father Dunn," Gavin said as the priest entered the room. "I was just telling these young people about my plans for this year's pageant."

The young people in question were a dozen teens ranging in age from eleven to seventeen. None of them looked particularly enthusiastic about the idea of being in a nativity pageant, and a few seemed to be on the verge of mutiny.

"He wants us to sing in *German*," one of the girls wailed.

"It's Brahms!" Bettelheim said, exasperation strangling his voice. "It's supposed to be sung in German."

"No one will even know what it means," the girl argued.

"No one *cares* what it means," said the director. "They'll all be too busy looking at the shepherds wearing their fathers' bathrobes."

The group retreated into sullen silence, the girls folding their arms over their chests and the boys looking off into the distance. Looking at them, Thomas was thankful to be free of the years when acne and a fragile sense of self rendered every interaction with an adult a potential for disaster. He took the fuming music director aside.

"Gavin, how about if I talk to them alone for a while," he suggested. "I'll see if I can warm them up to the idea of the whole thing."

"Thank you," Bettelheim said. "Maybe they'll listen to you. Do you know one of them dared to suggest that we perform 'Winter Wonderland'?"

Thomas rewarded him with a look of shared disappointment in the musical tastes of the church's youth. Gavin, casting a final, disapproving glance in the direction of his mutinous actors, walked off, muttering to himself.

"So," Thomas said once the man was gone. "What seems to be the problem here?"

They all began talking at once, the air clotting with their competing complaints. Thomas held up his hands to silence them. "Why don't we all sit down."

They sat. He took a chair and placed it in front of them, so that he was the focal point for their attention. Once they were settled, he tried again.

"I know this pageant stuff isn't exactly cool," he said. "When I was your age, I had to do them, and every year I got stuck being a wise man because I was the tallest."

This revelation earned him a reluctant laugh from the kids. He knew they were having a hard time imagining a priest who didn't want to be in a Christmas pageant, but he was telling the truth.

"Mr. Bettelheim is right about parents coming to see their kids,"

Thomas continued. "This is more about them than it is about you guys. And there are a bunch of little kids downstairs mooing and clucking their heads off. They can't wait for Christmas Eve to get here. Do they care that this is supposed to be about the birth of Christ? No. They just want to be in a play. They look up to you guys, just like you probably looked up to whoever was in your shoes when you were five. So what do you say? Will you stop giving Mr. Bettelheim a hard time?"

"It's just so dumb is all," said a boy seated in the front. Tall and thin, with shaggy hair and a pimple-scarred chin, he reminded Thomas of himself at the same age.

"What do you mean, Rick?" he asked.

"The whole thing," Rick said, pushing his hair away from his eyes. "Mary being a virgin. The wise men coming. Come on. It would have taken them months to get there. The whole thing is just a big story."

The other kids looked at him with a mixture of respect and horror. Then, as if their minds were connected on a subconscious level, they turned to see what Father Dunn's reaction was going to be. Thomas could tell they expected him to be angry at the young man's attack on the nativity story.

"I can't vouch for Mary's virginity," Thomas said. "And you're right that the elements of the Christmas story have been sort of pushed together for the sake of convenience. But the basic message holds true. Christmas celebrates the birth of the one who saved the world, the birth of hope. The rest of it is just, well, wrapping paper."

The teenagers looked at him as if he'd just declared the Bible to have been written by Stephen King. Probably, he thought, they'd never heard anyone question the absolute truth portrayed in the gospel. He himself had always been taught that the birth of Christ happened exactly as it was depicted in nativity plays across the world. It wasn't until he was in seminary that he had started to question things.

He remembered, suddenly, a Christmas Eve spent with Joseph. It was before Joseph's diagnosis, before they knew that he was carrying death inside him. They were in seminary, halfway through their second year, and neither had the money to go home for the holidays. Instead, they decided to spend them together.

They'd taken the train from Boston to New York on the afternoon of December twenty-fourth, planning on attending the midnight service at the Cathedral of Saint John the Divine. Both adored the towering church, with its cavernous central nave and its smaller side chapels, each dedicated to the memory of a different group of people: poets, freedom fighters, those claimed by AIDS.

It was snowing when they exited the subway that had taken them uptown. Running up the steps to the cathedral's huge wooden front doors, they'd paused inside, entranced by the glow of hundreds of candles that had been lit by visitors to the church. Their light rose up, somehow filling the emptiness of the ceiling high above them. All around them, people shuffled in respectful silence.

Waiting for the service to begin, they had wandered through the various chapels, looking at the tokens left behind by earlier pilgrims. The AIDS chapel, in particular, was decorated with gifts in memory of those who had died: notes written with trembling hands, photographs of the dead, inexplicable talismans (impossibly large high-heel shoes, the sheet music for "In the Still of the Night," a Barbie), and other mementos whose individual meanings were lost on Thomas and Joseph but whose accumulated effect was numbing.

Thomas, in particular, had been anxious to leave that particular chapel. Joseph, sensing his unease, had shepherded Thomas into the cathedral's gift shop. There, among the gargoyle replicas, CDs of sacred music from around the world, and displays of soaps and (most perplexing) snow globes containing miniature plastic cathedrals, Thomas had discovered a Christmas tree decorated with a multitude of ornaments. He had been particularly drawn to the figure of an angel. Unlike its blond cousins, it had black hair streaming out over a dress of deepest purple dotted here and there with gold. Its wings were like those of a bird, and in its hands was a candle, as if it were lighting the way for its brethren.

Hearing the sounds of music heralding the start of the service, they had rushed back to the nave and taken their seats. Thomas, caught up in the service, barely noticed when Joseph excused himself to use the bathroom.

Only later, as they were sitting, exhausted and blissful, on the train back to Boston early on Christmas morning, did Joseph reach into the pocket of his coat and produce a small bundle, which he handed to Thomas with a "Merry Christmas." Inside was the angel.

"I saw you looking at it," Joseph said. "You had the most beautiful look on your face."

He'd then leaned over and kissed Thomas, lightly, on the cheek. Thomas, holding the angel in his hands, had felt a moment of absolute hope and joy. At the time he'd thought it was a response to the holiness of the day and the lingering effects of his time spent in the cathedral. Only later, when it was too late, had he realized the true cause of his happiness.

"Father Dunn?"

Thomas looked up and saw the wondering faces looking at him. How long had he sat there, silent, in front of them? It felt as if he'd been lost in thought for hours, but surely it could only have been a minute.

"Right," he said, trying to remember what they'd been talking about. "So, as you can see, it . . . it . . ." He had no idea what he was saying. The kids were looking at him with expressions of increasing puzzlement. Then he remembered. Christmas. The pageant. Jesus.

"It may be just a story," he said quickly. "Who knows. But people like stories, and they're expecting a pageant, so just do it, all right?"

The teens looked at one another. For a moment Thomas thought they might demand to know just what it was he thought he was doing being a priest. Instead, they nodded.

"Sure," Rick said as the others murmured their assent. "It's cool."

After a moment a girl in the back raised her hand. "Can I be Mary?" she asked shyly.

CHAPTER 22

The phone rang. Stephen ignored it. Probably it was one of his clients, calling to ask where their monthly statements were. They'd been leaving messages for the past two weeks, at first mildly puzzled, then concerned, and now just plain upset. He didn't even play the recordings anymore, letting them pile up until the machine, its electronic stomach bloated, vomited them away. The blinking eye of the message light was nothing more to him than an angry red beacon warning him to stay away. He was happy to oblige.

He opened the bottle of pills that now sat continuously on his desk and took two, washing them down with Diet Coke. The combination was vile, but he'd long ago stopped tasting anything. It was all cardboard to him. He ate resentfully, because his body demanded it, chewing absentmindedly and filling his mouth until whatever can he'd opened was empty.

He made regular appearances at his parents' house, out of necessity, and had managed to convince them that everything was fine. He answered his mother's questions, accompanied her on the occasional errand, and was in every way the dutiful son. As soon as possible, he returned to his house and to the computer.

The computer. It had become his refuge. There, logged into a chat room, he could forget about himself. He was no longer Stephen Darby. He was PoundCk. It was a silly name, but it amused him with its combination of sweetness that after a moment's thought took on another, darker meaning. As PoundCk he prowled the various rooms, sometimes just looking, sometimes joining in, always searching.

Ever since his encounter with HrdAtWrk, he had waited for another meeting with him. But although he remained logged on at all hours and checked his buddy list constantly, he had yet to run into him again. He contented himself with other men, attempting to create with them the thrill he had experienced at the hands of his faceless partner. Sometimes he came close, but afterward he felt the disappointment of having settled for second best.

He couldn't explain, had he been asked, what it was about HrdAtWrk that called out to him. It was something he feared, a seed of darkness that, once planted within him, had blossomed into a need that gnawed at his heart. He thought almost constantly about the leather-gloved hands, the excitement he'd felt in being forced to serve the cop. He knew it was a fantasy, but it didn't matter. It existed in his head. It was real enough. And it was safe.

He never looked at his face. The bruises, midway through their healing process, had turned an ugly purplish-yellow. His lip, too, was a deep purple, and it was becoming evident that he would carry a scar there. He occasionally caught an accidental glimpse of himself in some shiny surface—the side of the toaster, a pane of glass, even the back of the spoons he dipped into the cans of chili and cold pasta he consumed. For a moment he would stare at the distorted, monstrous visage, not recognizing it as his own. Then, realizing that he was seeing his own reflection, he would look away in disgust and shame.

He knew he was a monster. Only a monster would do what he'd done. Only a monster deserved what he'd received. Only a monster could live a life of furtive searching for something so cancerous. After many hours of thinking through his experience, he'd come to understand this. Since then, an uneasy peace had settled around him. He knew what he was, even if he couldn't face that thing directly in a mirror. He knew that, soon, he would have to try to slay the monster.

Until then, he searched. The pills helped him. They silenced the voices that told him to get into the shower, to get dressed, to return to his old life. They told him the truth, that he was destined to remain in the darkness, a pawn to be used for the pleasure of others. Each time he felt the pain returning, he held some of them in his hand, looking down at them as if beholding the secrets of the universe. He marveled that so much solace could be contained in the tiny spheres.

He no longer knew or cared what time it was. The clocks, like the answering machine, were meaningless. The hands swept around in an endless bid for his attention, but he ignored them. He measured his days by the appearance of familiar names on his computer screen. He'd memorized their habits and patterns: who favored the morning, who was on only during his lunch hour, who came out in the small hours of the morning.

These were his landmarks, the signposts by which he traveled. Although his destination remained out of sight, he moved ever onward. Thankfully, the pills did little to dull his sexual appetite. He was almost constantly hard, his hand never far from his waiting cock. Touching it reassured him. Coming was more refreshing than sleep. He jerked off half a dozen times in a single session at his desk, sometimes accompanied by someone in another room, sometimes alone, thinking about the back of the police car. The trash can, and now the floor, was littered with crumpled wads of tissue, the paper hardened into perverse origami by his dried seed.

But still there was no sign of his dark knight. That's how he had come to imagine HrdAtWrk, a figure cloaked in shadow, sent to draw him deeper into the world he longed to live in. Only he could take Stephen by the hand and take him down the dim-lit alleys and dangerous byways of his own mind. Only he could show him the way.

And then, one night as he was battling the call of sleep and forcing his eyes open by staring at the blinking cursor on his computer screen, a miracle occurred. Hearing the familiar ding that signaled the arrival of a message, he turned his gaze to the box and saw there the name he had been waiting for.

HrdAtWrk: U R up late.

Stephen stared at the words until they blurred. He was afraid to blink, lest he open his eyes and discover that he had only imagined the message.

HrdAtWrk: U there?

He reached for the keyboard and typed back a response: Hello. It was the only word he could bring himself to write.

HrdAtWrk: Up 4 some fun?

Stephen's hands trembled as he tried to compose himself. His fingers twitched anxiously as he replied: Anything you want.

He held his breath, awaiting his master's response. He was captive, a bird held in the hands of a hunter. All thought stopped, and he heard only the beating of the blood in his head and in his cock.

HrdAtWrk: U R walking home late at nite. You pass a house, and in the window you see a naked man. He's hard.

Stephen closed his eyes and began to dream. He was on a street. It was past midnight. He was walking quickly, wanting to get out of the darkness and into the safety of his house. The houses around him were dark, asleep, the occupants safe in their beds.

In one house, though, a light glowed. Noticing it, he stopped and looked up. There, on the second floor, someone stood in the window. A man. He was naked, his powerful body illuminated by the moonlight. His hand moved up and down a long, thick cock.

Ashamed, Stephen tried to turn away. But something about the man held his gaze. It was then that he realized that the man was looking back at him. His eyes met Stephen's, and Stephen felt his heart stop.

HrdAtWrk: He motions for you to come up to him.

Stephen walked to the front door of the house. About to knock, he instead tried the handle. At his touch the door swung open into darkness. He saw a stairway, the top lit with pale light that tumbled down the steps, growing fainter until at the bottom it was only a flicker.

He knew the man was waiting for him up the stairs. He knew that he still had a chance to turn and leave. Instead he shut the door behind him and took the first step.

At the top, he looked into a bedroom. The man had turned to face him. He was even more beautiful and terrible than Stephen had realized. His thick legs were spread wide, his balls hanging down between them. The muscles of his chest rose and fell as his hand continued to squeeze his cock. He looked at Stephen and sneered.

"What do you want, faggot?"

Stephen licked his lips, unable to speak.

"Well? Tell me or get out."

Stephen choked on his words. "I want to suck your cock."

The man laughed. "Then get over here and do it," he said.

Stephen walked toward him and dropped to his knees. The man's dick taunted him, waving in front of his face as the man moved it back and forth. It was impossibly large. He knew there was no way he would be able to take it in.

The man's hand flew out and hit him in the cheek. He gasped, surprised at the shock of it.

"Suck it," the man ordered.

Stephen opened his mouth and obeyed. The man showed him no mercy, stuffing himself into Stephen's throat. Stephen accepted it, knowing that his only purpose was to do as he was told. He sucked greedily, lapping at the flesh that filled his mouth.

After a few minutes the man pulled out of his mouth.

"Stand up," he said.

Stephen scrambled to his feet, anxious to please his master. He found himself being spun around.

"Drop your pants."

He did, exposing his ass to the man behind him. Then he felt a push and he found himself sprawling facedown on the bed.

"On your hands and knees."

He assumed the demanded position, legs spread. He sensed the man behind him, and waited to feel his cock pressing against his ass. Instead, he felt a finger slide inside him.

"You want your faggot ass fucked?"

"Yes, sir," he said.

The man slapped his ass hard, making Stephen cry out in pain.

"You don't deserve to have me fuck your ass, faggot. Do you?" He slapped Stephen's ass again.

"No!" Stephen bleated, biting his lip.

"That's right. You don't. But maybe I'll fuck it anyway if you take what I'm going to give you."

Stephen didn't understand. Then he felt a second finger add itself to the first. His asshole stretched open as the man spread it. A third finger went inside him.

Suddenly, he understood. The realization filled him with horror. But it was too late. It had begun, and he had no choice. He felt the man's hand squeeze together momentarily, and then a burst of pain shot through his insides as he was penetrated by the thick, hard fingers.

"What a good faggot," the man said. "Your ass was made for this, wasn't it, fag? Made for using by real men."

"Yes, sir," Stephen gasped.

The man pulled on Stephen's balls, making the erection between Stephen's legs slap against his stomach.

"I'm making you hard, aren't I, faggot? Your fag dick is all stiff over me."

"Yes, sir."

The man pulled his fingers out, leaving Stephen empty.

"Tell me you want the whole thing, faggot."

"I want it, sir."

The hand returned. This time the man pushed into him quickly. Tears came to Stephen's eyes as he was invaded. He'd never known such pain. Yet he welcomed it, accepted it as his punishment for opening the door. He felt the man's fingers curl into a fist inside him and push forward. He had become a puppet, controlled from the inside by the man's hand and will. He was his to do with as he pleased.

"You're mine, faggot. Do you understand that?"

Stephen nodded.

"I can do what I want with you. I could kill you if I wanted to. Do you understand?"

Again Stephen nodded. The man pulled on Stephen's balls again until he cried out for mercy.

"Answer me when I ask you a question, faggot. Do you want me to fuck you now?"

"Yes, sir," said Stephen, eyes blinded by tears of pain. "Please fuck me, sir."

He felt the man's hand retreat. He moaned, not for the relief but because he wanted more. He was dirty, a whore, and he knew it.

"Here's what you want, faggot," the man said as he shoved his cock into Stephen's ass. "Milk my cock."

Stephen let out a moan of joy. He was once again complete. With the man's cock inside him, he was fulfilling his purpose in the world. He pushed himself back, impaling himself on the thick tool. He felt the man's balls smack against his own.

Suddenly he felt something cold against his neck. The man had leaned forward, was holding a knife against the soft surface of Stephen's skin. The edge bit into him.

"Keep fucking yourself, faggot," the man told him. "Don't stop or I'll open you up."

The man held the knife there as Stephen continued to move back and forth, the two of them rocking together. With each push, Stephen felt the blade threaten to peel back his skin. He felt the hot breath of his master on his neck, felt himself enveloped by the muscles of the man's body as it covered his.

"You fags deserve to die," the man said. "Don't you?"

"Yes," Stephen whispered, afraid anything else would result in his being cut.

"You like having a real man's cock in your ass," the man said. "You like being a filthy faggot for me, don't you?"

"Yes, sir."

"You want me to come in your useless ass, don't you?"

Stephen tried to nod. The man tightened his grip on Stephen's throat. "Beg me to come in your ass."

"Please, sir," Stephen said as loudly as he could. "Please come in my ass."

The blade pressed against Stephen's neck as the man thrust several times, quickly and mercilessly. He let out a groan of triumph.

"Ooh," he said as the first wave shook him. "Take it, faggot."

Stephen felt himself blacking out as the man's arm tightened like a vise around his throat.

"Take my fucking load."

Stephen's vision faded. He tried to breathe.

"Fucking faggot," the man yelled as he gave one final pump. Then he pulled out. He released Stephen, who collapsed onto the bed, gasping for breath.

The man got off the bed. Picking up Stephen's pants, he threw them at him.

"You're lucky I didn't kill you," he said, holding up the knife he'd used and snapping it shut. "Now get the fuck out before I change my mind."

Stephen jumped to his feet and fled. As he ran down the stairs, he put his hand to his throat. Where the knife had touched his skin, it burned as if he'd been branded.

The blinking of the computer brought him out of his reverie.

HrdAtWrk: See U soon.

He put his hand to his neck. Closing his eyes, he could feel the knife there, waiting to open him up and reveal his true self.

"See you soon," he whispered.

CHAPTER 23

The Cold Falls Public Library had once been a grand building. Now it was a faded, tired, old lady, the victim of a shrinking budget and a decline in interest on the part of the very people she had been built to serve. Still, Simon loved her. Every Monday for the past fifteen years he had arrived there shortly after ten o'clock, carrying the three (or sometimes four) books he'd taken away the previous Monday. These he returned at the library's enormous wooden front desk before venturing into the stacks in search of new reading material.

Until her death in October, the head librarian had been a woman named Millie St. John. She'd held that post during all the years Simon had been coming to the library. Ancient even to Simon's aging eyes, Millie had been a small, shriveled woman with the face of an applehead doll and a mind that contained the whole of the universe. Not surprisingly, she'd read voraciously, and on each of Simon's visits she'd had one or two suggestions as to books he might enjoy. Only rarely had she been mistaken.

Millie had passed away in her sleep. She'd been discovered, according to local legend, with a copy of William Faulkner's *As I Lay Dying* open on her chest. Whether this was or was not true, what was true was that Millie had somehow during her lifetime amassed a small fortune, all of which she'd bequeathed to the library with the stipulation that it be used to renovate the building and pay the salary of her replacement.

Although the renovations had yet to begin, the replacement had been found. Alistair Wainwright had arrived in November from Potterton, Missouri. Not as small as Millie St. John, he was nonetheless not a large man. Compact, Simon had called him when describing him to Russell. Buttoned-down. He wore sweater vests over starched white shirts and oiled his hair. Despite his age (he was perhaps in his early fifties, Simon guessed), he seemed to have stepped out of a 1940s black-and-white film into the real world.

Alistair's taste in reading material was not as extensive as Millie's had been. More refined, he favored the classics, where Millie had been far more egalitarian, as likely to recommend the latest John Grisham novel as she was to suggest *To Kill a Mockingbird* or *Cannery Row.* Alistair accommodated the tastes of his clientele by purchasing the latest best sellers, but his interest in their reading habits stopped short of encouraging their interests in Anne Rice and Danielle Steel.

Simon had introduced himself to Alistair on his first Monday visit following the new librarian's arrival. Alistair, looking at the books Simon deposited in the return box (Anthony Trollope's *Barchester Towers,* a volume of Virginia Woolf's diaries, and a battered copy of Mark Twain's *The Innocents Abroad*), had sensed a kindred spirit and marked Simon as someone to watch. Simon, in turn, had been relieved that Millie had not, as he'd feared, been replaced by someone right out of library school who would try to revive interest in reading by holding Oprah-esque book discussions.

On this particular Monday, Simon had brought with him for return Mark Helprin's *Winter's Tale* and Truman Capote's *The Thanksgiving Visitor,* both of which he'd enjoyed before but been inspired by the season and the recent snowstorms to revisit. After stamping his feet to remove as much of the attached snow as he could, he duly placed the books in the return box.

"As good as you remembered?" Alistair asked him.

"As good and better," replied Simon. "Helprin should be taken to court for not producing another book in so long. And Capote, well, what can I say? Every one of these so-called wunderkind writers should write a quarter as well as he did."

Alistair chuckled. "I wonder what he'd think of chick lit," he mused.

"Chick lit?" asked Simon.

Alistair held up a copy of a book he'd just finished installing library coding labels on. *"Boyfriend in the Shop,"* he said drily. "Apparently it's about a woman who has it up to here with her imperfect boyfriend. She opens an agency where women can bring their equally unsatisfying men and have them turned into the ideal mates. It is, I am assured by *Library Journal,* destined to be an enormous hit with women from seventeen to seventy. I bought three."

Simon looked at the cover, a vibrant cut-paper collage. The author's name occupied the entire top half. He had never heard of her.

"I have a waiting list for it," Alistair said, giving the book a sour glance. "If you want it, you'll have to wait until February."

"However will I cope?" asked Simon.

"Maybe this will be some comfort," said Alistair, reaching under the counter and producing another book, which he slid across the desk to Simon.

"The new Wallis Simpson biography!" Simon exclaimed. "I didn't even know it was out."

"It's not," Alistair told him. "I received an advance copy from a librarian friend who had an extra. The perks afforded those of us who tend to books for a living may be few, but they're mighty."

"I'm indeed indebted," Simon said happily, opening the book and running his hand over the virgin page. "If there's anything that makes the season bright, it's the reopening of an old scandal."

"I understand Wallis comes across as quite the shrew in this one," Alistair commented. "According to the author, the poor king never stood a chance once she got her claws into him."

Simon gave a murmur of pleased agreement. "The bitch of all bitches," he said. "Quite a woman."

Alistair laughed. "Keep it as long as you like," he said. "I can't imagine anyone else will be asking for it."

Simon closed the book. "Thank you," he said. "And now I will go into the forest and see what other tasty nuts I can gather."

He left Alistair affixing labels to the other new books and entered the library's stacks. Although the city budget of Cold Falls had always been stingy in the funds it bestowed upon the library, Millie had used them wisely. Like a homemaker forced to feed a family of six on a husband's meager salary, she'd cut corners here and stretched resources there, managing during her tenure to acquire a collection that would have impressed any serious reader of literature, had more than a handful existed in the town.

Simon, being one of the few who appreciated Millie's abilities, wandered leisurely among the tall wooden shelves. He seldom came to the library with any particular goal in mind. He preferred to rely on serendipity, the accidental stumbling upon of the perfect book for the perfect time. In this way he was never disappointed. Whatever he took home with him accompanied him because it spoke to him at the time.

Today, though, his mind was occupied with other thoughts. Christmas was only two weeks away, and New Year's Eve a week beyond that. He hadn't yet had even a vague thought as to who might be his date on that night. That wasn't entirely true. He *had* thought in passing about several of the men from the Engine Room. But that had been more in the way of fantasizing than it had been anything he could seriously consider. The men he'd considered were, he knew, much too young. Even if they were to say yes, he wouldn't know what to do with them. Although their physical charms might be considerable, he was old enough and wise enough to know that at some point the intellectual inequities would wear on his patience and result in ugliness.

He had never been one to celebrate youth. Always he had looked forward to being older. Now that he'd arrived, he saw no need to wish he could turn the clock back. The only benefit he could see to being, say, fifty again was that Walter would still be alive. Apart from that, he liked who he had become.

The problem, of course, was finding someone else who appreciated what he'd become. He realized that he was something of a rarity among gay men, an older man who preferred the company of older men. He was familiar with the other variety, the men who longed for the smooth skin of men half their age. He didn't look unkindly upon such men. He understood them. They didn't want to die. They wanted to embrace youth and, by doing so, perhaps slow their own inevitable decline.

It was the same, he believed, as straight men who left their wives for women younger than their daughters, a kind of male survival instinct that revealed itself in pitiful displays of romantic desperation. Still, as long as there were young women and men willing to play along, it would continue to happen. And who cared, really, if people wanted to make fools of themselves. Maybe some of them were even happy together. You never knew what slaked the heart's thirst.

What he wanted, though, was something different. He wanted someone who would help him not forget his age but revel in it. He wanted someone with whom to share the moments of his life that most pleased him, the small everyday occurrences that brought him joy precisely because he was old enough not to take them for granted. He wanted someone who would understand those things.

He looked at the spines of the books he was surrounded by, thinking about their authors. So many of them, he knew, had been both sustained and destroyed by their relationships. He thought of Sylvia Plath and Ted Hughes, perhaps the most brilliant and pathetic of all literary unions. How they'd tortured one another, but also how they'd inspired each other to greatness. He thought, too, of Shirley Jackson and her husband, academic Stanley Hyman. Hyman had encouraged Jackson to write when her own family told her it was folly, had fueled some of her greatest work. But he'd also destroyed her sense of self-worth with his affairs and bitterness, despite Jackson's determination to portray him in her work as the kindest of men.

There were more positive examples, of course. Percy and Mary Shelley. Robert and Elizabeth Barrett Browning. Gertrude Stein and Alice B. Toklas. He and Walter, too, had worked so well together because they complemented one another. Could he find that again? Part of him felt he was too old. He wasn't prepared to make the concessions he'd made in his younger years. He was set in his ways. Could he find someone willing to fit himself into that world?

He sighed. It was a depressing train of thought. Even more depressing, though, was the notion that his only option was solitude. Was that all that was offered to a man his age, particularly a gay man? He thought of his aunts, his mother's sisters, and how as their husbands had died off one by one, the newest widow had moved into a house with the others, until after the death of the last husband (Simon's father), the four of them had comprised a perfectly contented quartet that lived out the remainder of their years with only one another for company.

Had they really been willing to give up on romance, he wondered? He didn't entertain the question of sex. Romance was what he truly missed, those moments of togetherness when both partners knew that the other wanted nothing more than to be there. Hadn't his aunts and his mother longed for such times? They hadn't, after all, been much older than he was now. Some had been even younger. As a boy, he'd never wondered about their lives, seeing them only as sources of birthday gifts and pinched cheeks, not as women—or even people—

who might have personal needs. Now, though, he found himself experiencing an unexpected kinship with those women, most of whom had continued living on after their husbands for nearly twenty years. Surely at some point during that time they had yearned for what they'd lost.

He looked at the book in his hands. Even the ill-starred romance of American divorcee Wallis Simpson and the disgraced Edward VIII had been possessed of a kind of magic, an all-encompassing enchantment that drove them to stay together despite the fact that it had cost Edward a kingdom. What, Simon had often wondered when reading about the affair, had Edward seen when he looked into Wallis's eyes? A handsome and powerful man with many mistresses, he had given them all up for her, even when she tired of him and moved on to other lovers, one of whom, an heir to the Woolworth fortune, was homosexual.

That kind of unhealthy devotion Simon feared. As much as he'd loved Walter, he knew he would have left at the first sign of decay in the relationship. Thankfully, theirs had been a thriving union, even when it was sometimes difficult. That's what he longed for again.

He was tired of looking for something to read. The Simpson biography would have to be his lone treasure for the week. Standing there among the books, he was feeling more and more alone. Finding one that would bring him joy reminded him of the difficulty he was having in finding someone to spend his time with. Like the Simpson book, he decided, the right one would simply have to come into his life by chance.

He walked back toward the desk, preparing to check out. Alistair was still there, carefully taping the identifying labels to the spines of the books, methodically stamping the name of the library onto the inside covers. He seemed perfectly content, at home among the odds and ends of his craft.

Alistair, Simon thought suddenly. *It could be Alistair.*

He stopped in the middle of the room, looking at the man behind the desk. It had never occurred to him before to consider Alistair as a potential partner. Now, looking at him, he wondered why? He was old enough. He was handsome. And certainly they shared mutual interests. Simon looked at him closely. Yes, he could see it.

Nervously, he approached the desk. Alistair, looking up, smiled and put down his stamp. "What did you find this week?"

"Just this," said Simon, setting the book down.

Alistair picked it up. "That's not like you," he said. "Have we run out of books that interest you?"

"No," Simon said as he took his wallet from his pocket and removed his library card. "What with all the holiday fuss and bother, I don't think I'll have much time for reading this week."

He hesitated, not sure how to say what he wanted to. It had been many, many years since he'd asked someone out. Walter had been the last, and Simon couldn't even remember how he'd done it.

"Do you have any New Year's Eve plans?" he blurted out, surprising himself.

"I usually just stay in," Alistair said as he stamped Simon's book and placed the checkout card in the file on his desk. "How about you?"

"Oh, I think I'm going to get together with some friends," Simon answered. "If you're free, you're welcome to join us."

"That might be fun," Alistair said. "We don't know many people in town. It would be nice to meet some."

"We?" repeated Simon, a sinking feeling growing inside of him.

"My wife and I," Alistair said. "Meg."

"Meg," Simon said. "Excellent. Well, let me confirm that everything is still on, and I'll let you know next week."

"I'll see you Monday," Alistair told him.

Simon hustled out into the cold, hoping the frigid air would explain away the redness he knew was coloring his face. *How could I have been so stupid?* Married. Why had he assumed that Alistair was gay? "Probably because he's named Alistair," he said out loud. "And he works in a library."

He was ashamed of himself, both for making such stereotypical assumptions, but more for his apparent inability to distinguish a straight man from a queen. What chance did he stand if he couldn't even do that?

"Maybe you've been out of the game too long," he told himself as he hurried for home.

CHAPTER 24

"Holy shit, they look like rabid monkeys."

Russell and Greg peered over the stack of Estée Lauder gift boxes, looking toward the front doors of the store. Outside, a group of women waited impatiently in the early-morning snow. Every so often one of them tried one of the doors, rattling it loudly to see if perhaps the woman who'd tried before her simply hadn't done it correctly.

"Are you ready for this?" Russell asked.

"I'd feel better if I had a taser," replied Greg. "They look totally out of control."

"This place will be declared a disaster area by seven forty-five," said Russell. "The Red Cross will have to be called in."

It was seven twenty-five. In five minutes, Russell would walk to the front doors and open them, launching the store's before-Christmas sale. With only two shopping weekends before the holiday, they had decided to lower their prices in an attempt to save the season, which so far had been dismal. Now, circulars and credit cards in hand, fifty agitated women waited for their chance to snatch up as many bargains as they could possibly carry.

"Remember," Russell told the assembled staff, "keep your heads down and watch out for flying objects. Everyone ready?"

The staff, eyes wide with terror, nodded. Although several of them were veterans of the Christmas madness, most of them were green. This would be their first, and in some cases last, holiday retail experience. Russell had assigned each of the old-timers a group of virgins to command. Greg he'd put in charge of menswear, where he was overseeing three very nervous young recruits who stood beside their Polo,

Nautica, and Calvin Klein posts, fidgeting with their name tags and sending up silent prayers to their gods.

Russell took a deep breath and walked to the door. The women, sensing the imminent opening of the store, began clamoring with excitement. Their eyes were glassy with the thrill of the hunt, already scanning the store visible through the glass for 30% off signs.

Russell paused before inserting the key in the lock. He turned and nodded at the leaders he was counting on to keep things more or less under control. They nodded back. He pushed the key in and turned, feeling the bolt slide free. An instant later he felt a rush of cold air as the doors flew inward and coated bodies swarmed past him.

The group of women dispersed as they each ran for the section that interested them the most. Many headed for the perfume counter, where they began spritzing the air with abandon, trying out the different scents. Others made for shoes and women's apparel. But by far the majority of them made a beeline for menswear, determined to find gifts for the husbands, brothers, boyfriends, uncles, and sons in their lives.

Russell stepped out of the throng, protecting himself behind a mannequin. Almost immediately the entranceway was turned into a slushy, slippery mess as hundreds of booted feet dragged melting snow inside. He prayed no one would slip and become injured, as had happened recently at a Kmart when overzealous shoppers had practically stampeded through the store to get their hands on Hokey-Pokey Elmo dolls advertised for sale at only $17.99. All he needed was one mother with a broken ankle to make his Christmas bonus fly away.

As the flow of women slowed to a trickle, he risked coming out from behind his hiding place and taking a walk through the store. One of the many advantages he enjoyed as manager was that he didn't actually have to ring any customers up. Although he was frequently subjected to questions from angry shoppers as to the lack of sizes and colors of various articles that they wanted, he didn't have to contend with the temperamental registers and all that accompanied such transactions. He was free to roam and take in the carnage that was ensuing around him.

Ladies shoes was abuzz with excitement. The two staffers who had been assigned this particularly treacherous duty were scurrying in and out of the stock room, their arms piled high with boxes, as women in stockinged feet flitted from shelf to shelf, finding yet more styles they simply had to try on. It would be a good day in shoes, Russell though happily.

Menswear, as expected, was a war zone. Already the neatly folded Polo displays were in disarray, shirts thrown open and left for dead by rapacious hands. One harried-looking clerk was attempting to perform triage on them, roughly folding them and piling them back in their places, but it was hopeless. As quickly as he got them fixed up, someone swooped down to undo his work.

"It's okay," Russell whispered to him as he walked by. "Just keep them off the floor. We'll straighten them out after the first wave leaves."

There would be no distinct "waves"—no ebb and flow—and he knew it, but he had to give the poor young man some hope of respite or he would quickly be overwhelmed. The truth was that they were in for a continuous flood of shoppers. And it would only get worse as the weeks went on. The closer Christmas came, the more of their minds consumers lost. Bedeviled by Christmas cheer, they would go into a frenzy, attempting to manufacture the perfect holiday with the help of wallets stuffed with plastic cards. They would fill the coffers of Carter-Beane with holiday bounty, only realizing the extent of their folly when the bills came in January. By then it would be too late. Returns were not accepted after twenty-one days.

He witnessed the first fight of the day moments later. Two women had both grabbed the last spruce plaid Pendleton flannel shirt, size XXL. Probably they both wanted it for an overweight husband who would hate it because the wool flannel made him itch. He would wear it once to please her and then relegate it to the rear of the closet, where both of them would quickly forget about it.

For the moment, though, the shirt was the most prized possession in the store, and the women were arguing over it like hyenas worrying a particularly meaty chunk of zebra. Each of them had half of the shirt in her hands. Their voices rose above the general din as they attempted to establish dominance.

"I saw it first," said one, her piggy face worked up into an agonized grimace.

"I got to it first," argued the other, who was attempting to maintain her hold on several other items while struggling valiantly with the Pendleton.

Russell was steeling himself to intervene when he saw Greg walk briskly toward the combatants. He watched as Greg laid a hand on each woman's arm and said soothingly but firmly, "Ladies, why don't I take this in the back and see if maybe we don't have another one."

The women glared at one another as Greg smiled at them. Then, apparently calmed by his attention, each let go. Greg took the shirt, smoothed it out, and folded it over his arm.

"I'll be right back," he said.

The women stood several feet apart, arms across their chests and not looking at one another. A minute later Greg returned, another identical shirt in his hands. He handed each woman one of the shirts. Smiling, they went their separate ways.

"Good work," Russell said as Greg came over, rolling his eyes. "I thought we were going to have bloodshed on our hands."

"I told the boys to keep a couple of each size in the back in the event of emergencies," Greg explained. "That way they think we've worked a miracle." He nodded in the direction of the bathrobes. "Speaking of which, I sense trouble in pajama land. I'll see you later."

Russell gave him a pat on the back as he walked away. As he watched Greg go, he thought back to what Simon and Mike had said the other night at the bar about his being jealous when Greg had shown interest in someone. At the time it had seemed ridiculous. After all, wasn't he the one who had tried to set Greg up with Stephen? Wasn't he the one who told everyone what a great catch Greg would be for the right guy? Why, he had made finding Greg a boyfriend practically his mission.

Then why, he asked himself, had he been so annoyed when Greg had pursued the man at the Engine Room? He still didn't know whether or not Greg had been successful. He'd left before Greg had, and he hadn't asked him since what had or had not occurred. Greg hadn't volunteered any information, either. Normally they talked about everything. Why was this one area of discussion apparently off-limits?

As he watched Greg assisting a woman who was searching for something among the boxer briefs, he forced himself to reassess his

feelings about his friend. Did he perhaps have more than a passing interest in him? All the while he'd been doggedly looking for someone
for Greg, had part of him been hoping Greg wouldn't find anyone and
turn his attentions closer to home?

Something had been holding him back from completely reconciling with John. Although their times together had been pleasant, he
still didn't feel ready for a full reunion. He was still living with Simon.
No date had been set for his return to the house he shared with John,
even though John had asked him several times if he was coming
home.

Was Greg the thing standing between him and his relationship? He
considered the possibility. They got along famously. They shared interests and sensibilities. And Greg *was* attractive. Although he'd never
considered him in a sexual way, now that he entertained the notion,
Russell found that it wasn't unappealing. Maybe he owed it to himself
to give Greg a chance.

"Mr. Harding? I need your help."

His thoughts were interrupted by the arrival of a young woman
with panic-stricken eyes, her alarm made even more visible by the co-
pious amounts of shadow and liner she wore. She resembled a disqui-
eted raccoon. Russell waited for her to tell him what the problem was.

"We advertised a one-ounce bottle of the new Elizabeth Taylor perfume, but all we have under the counter are after-bath splashes. I have
a lot of angry people over in fragrances."

Russell put his hand on the girl's shoulder and steered her back to
her station. As they approached, he saw the remaining fragrance clerk
point in his direction. Immediately, the women at the counter turned
upon him, outrage in their countenances.

"Now then, what seems to be the problem?" he said cheerfully.

Half an hour later, after soothing ruffled feathers with rainchecks
and coupons good for an additional 40% off any item in the store,
Russell retreated to the safety of the staff break room. There he found
a handful of his employees, looking worse for wear, slumped in the
hard plastic chairs that surrounded the room's lone table. Most looked
shell-shocked. One was sniffling, apparently on the verge of tears.

"Just keep thinking happy thoughts," Russell joked. "And remember, it could be worse. It could be December twenty-sixth."

A collective groan went up from the troops. December 26, better known as I Don't Have My Receipt Day, was even worse than the pre-Christmas debacle. By then a third of the staff would have quit, swearing never to work in retail again. The rest would band together to fight the hordes who came in the day after Christmas, worn-out and irritable, to return or exchange much of their Christmas take. It was a tedious time, but it at least signaled the end of the holiday season, and if an employee survived it, Russell was almost guaranteed of having her or him the following year.

Russell retrieved a cup of coffee from the much-used machine in the corner. He was seated at the table, stirring cream and sugar into the coffee, when Greg came in. Getting his own cup, he sat down opposite Russell and let out a sigh.

"Halftime," he said wearily.

"What's the score?" Russell inquired.

"Home team is ahead," answered Greg. "But just barely. We're going to need reinforcements."

"How about this," Russell said. "I'll take you to dinner tonight."

Greg brightened. "Now you're talking," he said. "It's a date."

Russell was quiet for a moment. He was hesitant to bring up personal matters in the company of his employees, but most of them had left the room shortly after his appearance. The only one there besides himself and Greg was the girl with the raccoon eyes, who was gazing dazedly off at nothing and paying no attention to their conversation.

Finally he spoke. "Speaking of dates, I never asked you how things went with the guy from the bar."

Greg sipped his coffee before answering. "What guy?" he asked.

Russell cupped his hands over his chest, symbolizing breasts.

"Tits?" Greg said. "You know, we talked a little."

"Just talked?" asked Russell.

Greg grinned. "Maybe a little more than that."

Russell nodded. "Good for you," he said, feigning approval. "It's about time you had some fun."

"I wouldn't exactly call it fun," said Greg. "More like fast food."

"Fast food?" Russell repeated, not getting his meaning.

"Yeah," Greg said. "You know how every so often you just need a Big Mac? That's sort of how it was. I wouldn't want it every day or anything, but that night it hit the spot."

Russell nodded, finally understanding and wishing he didn't. He couldn't help but picture Greg with the man, and it made his stomach churn unpleasantly. What had they done? He immediately pushed the question out of his mind. It wasn't any of his business what they'd done. Besides, he really didn't want to know.

"You took off pretty fast that night," Greg said. "I didn't even see you leave."

"I was sort of tired," said Russell. "It was a long day."

"I thought maybe you were horrified by my sluttiness," Greg said, laughing.

"Why would that bother me?" Russell said quickly.

"I don't know," admitted Greg. "It's just that sometimes when you see people in a new light, it can be a shock. You've never really seen me do something like that."

"It's okay," said Russell. "Really. You're a big boy. You can do what you want."

"But?" asked Greg.

"But what?" Russell retorted.

"You're holding something back," Greg said. "I can tell."

Russell looked down into his coffee cup. "I just think you could do way better."

"Oh, I know I could," Greg said. "But have you seen anyone better banging down my door? I haven't. If you know of someone, I'd love to meet him."

Russell looked up. "I think I might," he said quietly.

"Really?" Greg said. "Who is he?"

Russell started to speak, but was interrupted by someone rushing into the break room. A panting, anxious-looking young man confronted him.

"Russell? There's a woman out there hyperventilating in the handbags. I think she's going to pass out. We can't get her to let go of the Dooney and Bourke she's got her hands on."

Russell looked at Greg. "We'll talk about this tonight over dinner," he said as he got up.

CHAPTER 25

"Thanks for letting me crash here, man."

Pete turned on the lights as he and T.J. entered the house. "No problem," Pete said.

They stood in the kitchen and shook the snow from their coats. Outside, a new storm was raging. It had come unexpectedly, starting while they were inside the Briar Patch downing some beers after work. By the time they'd left, just after ten o'clock, there was a foot of snow covering their cars and the world was a blurry swirl of white. Although a plow had come through and dutifully pushed the snow to the side of the road, eager flakes had swept in to take the place of their vanquished comrades. Driving was treacherous, and even in their inebriated condition, the men had recognized that trying to go too far would be foolish. Pete had suggested that T.J., who lived the farthest away of all of them, and who had the least reliable car, stay the night with him.

They hung their coats up. T.J. sat down on one of the kitchen chairs and unlaced his work boots, pulling them off and placing them to the side, where the melting snow could collect on the linoleum. Pete, following his lead, did the same before walking to the refrigerator and opening it.

"Want a beer?" he asked, scanning the largely empty interior.

"Sure," answered T.J.

Pete pulled out two beers and handed one to T.J., who twisted the top off and took a deep sip. He wiped his mouth with the back of his hand.

"I'm gonna put on something dry," Pete said. "You want some sweats or something?"

T.J. held up a hand. "I'm good," he said.

"Why don't you turn on the TV," Pete suggested. "I'll be out in a minute."

He went into this bedroom while T.J. got up and headed for the living room. He heard the television go on, the sound of voices filling the room with background noise. Setting his beer down, he stripped out of his jeans, the cuffs of which were uncomfortably damp from walking through the snow. He pulled a pair of sweats from a dresser drawer and pulled them on. Almost immediately he felt more relaxed.

Picking up his beer, he went into the living room. T.J. was sitting on the couch, his feet propped up on the coffee table. He was staring at the TV screen, and when he heard Pete enter the room, he looked at him and grinned.

"Nice tape collection," he said.

Pete glanced at the television. On the screen a porn film was playing. A redhead was bent over a couch, getting fucked hard by a man wearing a UPS uniform. His cock stuck out of the fly of the uniform pants. The redhead, who was wearing a string of pearls that bounced against her breasts as she got plowed, was holding on to the sofa cushions with long, red-lacquered nails.

"I guess that's what they mean by special delivery," T.J. joked.

Pete said nothing. He must have left the tape in the VCR, he thought. It was a stupid thing to do. Normally he kept the porn tapes in his bedroom, but he'd felt like jacking off in the living room the night before, so he'd moved in there. After he came, he totally forgot to take the tape out.

He had no idea how to explain the tape's existence to T.J. He felt he should say something, but any excuse he could come up with for why the tape was in there sounded ridiculous. So he just stood there, watching the redhead get reamed.

T.J. didn't seem to care why the tape was there or what Pete was doing with it. He continued to watch, sipping his beer and every so often giving a little laugh as the redhead made a particularly impassioned face or the man smacked her ass. Pete glanced at him, wondering what he was thinking, afraid to ask. Finally, he took a seat on the couch, as far away from T.J. as he could get.

"Man, I wish women liked that as much in real life as they do in these things," he remarked. His voice was a bit slurred, and when Pete looked over at him, he saw that T.J.'s eyes were slightly closed.

The man in the film pulled out and came, spraying jism on the woman's back. When he was done, he zipped up and tipped his cap to her before leaving the room. T.J. laughed again, seemingly at nothing. Pete took a drink from his beer bottle and waited to see if T.J. would tire of the video or let it play out.

The film continued and T.J. made no move to turn it off. He left the remote where it was on the coffee table, apparently content to watch porn. His feet were crossed at the ankle and his beer bottle was nestled in his crotch. His head rested against the back of the couch.

On the screen a new scene was under way. In this one a woman in an office answered a telephone. As she took the call, the man from the earlier scene entered, carrying two large boxes, which he set on the floor beside her desk. He waited for her to finish her phone call.

"Delivery for Mr. Smith," he said in a monotone as he held out a clipboard. "Can you sign for them?"

The girl, a brunette with her hair in a bun and severe glasses that made her look matronly, smiled coyly. "Sure," she said in a squeaky voice. "Do they need any special handling?"

It was typical bad porn film dialogue, but it didn't matter. The talking was just an excuse for what came next. As Pete watched, the man stepped behind the desk and reached for the woman's glasses. Off they came, revealing a pretty face. The girl did her part, unzipping the delivery man's pants and pulling out his already-hard cock. Her red-lipped mouth closed around it as she began giving him head.

The man's dick was in close-up. Pete stared at it, watching the woman's mouth caress it sensuously. The man's balls, large and smooth, banged against her chin as she took him all the way in. His big head, slick with her spit, seemed to fill her whole mouth as she sucked on it eagerly.

Pete was suddenly aware of an uncomfortable feeling in his crotch. He realized then that he'd become hard. His cock was pressing up against the fabric of his sweatpants, making the material tent out obviously. He pressed down on his prick, trying to hide his erection, and looked nervously at T.J.

His friend was paying no attention. But one hand was in his own crotch. His fingers moved slowly, as if he was gently massaging himself. In the other hand he held his beer, taking periodic sips.

The man had removed his uniform shirt. His bare chest was covered in thick, dark hair. He had also undone the woman's bun, removing the clip that held it in place so that her hair tumbled over her shoulders. Her shirt, too, was open, her breasts exposed.

"Look at those fucking tits," T.J. said appreciatively.

The hard-on in Pete's pants wasn't going away. He did his best to cover it up, but the head of his dick was threatening to push past the waistband. He tried willing it down, but he knew it was no use.

The girl in the film dropped to her knees and continued to suck the man's cock. He gripped her hair as he fucked her face, while she wrapped her hands around his ass. The camera, positioned underneath them, showed the man's big tool in glorious detail as it moved in and out.

Pete risked another glance at T.J. His hand was moving more steadily, and it was obvious that he was hard too. His cock swelled hugely beneath the material of his jeans, pushing down the side of his leg. Pete could see its outline clearly, and he knew T.J. must be incredibly uncomfortable with his dick confined that way.

"Look at her take that thing," T.J. said as the girl deep-throated her partner. "That's fucking amazing. How come I always get the chicks who choke?"

Pete laughed nervously. The tension in the room was thick, and he didn't know what to do. What he wanted to do was lean over and touch T.J., feel his cock, maybe even take it out and do what the girl was doing. He remembered how it had looked that night in the men's room, so long and thick. What did it look like hard? He wanted to know. But he couldn't bring himself to move his hand from his lap and into T.J.'s.

T.J. made the decision for him. Draining his beer bottle, he set it on the coffee table and looked at Pete. "I'm beat," he said drunkenly. "Shall I just crash on the couch?"

Pete thought quickly. "Nah, we can share the bed," he said. "It's big enough. This couch sucks for sleeping."

He expected an argument from T.J., but his buddy just nodded. "I'm gonna take a piss," he said, standing up.

Pete avoided looking at T.J.'s crotch. With his friend in the bathroom, he turned the tape off and went into the bedroom. Before T.J. could come back, he shucked off his sweatpants and got into bed in just his boxers. A minute later T.J. appeared. Without saying anything, he removed his clothes and got into bed on the other side, also wearing just his underpants.

"Man, I am wiped out," he said, yawning loudly as he turned off the light. "See you in the morning, dude."

Pete rolled away from him and shut his eyes. His mind, dulled by the beer, refused to sink into oblivion. He kept picturing T.J., holding his cock and pissing. His own hard-on still refused to back down. His hand snuck down past the elastic waistband of his boxers and wrapped around his cock.

Next to him, T.J. seemed to have fallen asleep immediately. He snored roughly, deep inhalations and exhalations that filled the room with his rumbling. He was on his back, arms at his sides. Pete could sense him less than a foot away.

He turned onto his back, terrified that T.J. would be awakened by his movements. When the snoring continued unabated, Pete slowly moved his foot to the left. When it came in contact with T.J.'s, he held his breath. Again, T.J. didn't move.

Pete's cock was aching as he stroked it. He felt the first stickiness seep from the head, coating his fingers. He used this to slick his skin, making his movements silkier, more intense. Was T.J. still hard, he wondered?

He couldn't hold back. Moving painfully slowly, he let his left hand move beneath the sheet toward his sleeping buddy. When he felt the first touch of T.J.'s skin, he stopped. His heart beat in his chest madly, and at any moment he expected to feel the viselike grip of T.J.'s hand around his wrist as he demanded to know what the hell Pete thought he was doing.

But no resistance came. Pete moved his hand higher, feeling the rough hair of T.J.'s belly beneath his fingers. His skin was warm, his stomach moving up and down as he breathed deeply. Pete allowed himself to put his hand flat against T.J.'s stomach, feeling the muscles of his abdomen.

He moved south, and shortly after his fingertips dipped into the indentation of T.J.'s navel, he felt the tip of T.J.'s cock brush his hand through the thin cotton of the boxers he wore. He was still hard. Pete's balls gave a jerk as he realized he was touching T.J.'s rod, and he had to pause to calm himself down.

His mind racing, he pushed his fingers through the fly of T.J.'s boxers. He opened his hand and cupped the head of T.J.'s cock in his fingers. It was hot, and as his fingers closed around it, he felt it twitch. Now he couldn't stop. He slid his hand down T.J.'s shaft, feeling the thickness of it. He moved all the way down, until his fingers met thick hair. Then he went back up, jerking T.J. off in time with the movements on his own dick.

T.J.'s snoring slowed, and Pete sensed him move. His legs opened slightly, and he pressed himself up into Pete's hand. But still he didn't wake, didn't open his eyes. Could he, Pete wondered, really be asleep? Did he think he was dreaming, his subconscious continuing the film they had been watching?

He didn't care. Touching T.J.'s cock, he wanted more. He couldn't be content to just hold it in his hand. The heat radiating through his palm was so intense he felt he might burn himself. He wanted to taste it.

Rolling toward T.J., he ducked his head beneath the sheet. There, under the covers, the world was hot and stuffy. He smelled the scent of sweat and oil from their skin. He felt the warmth emanating from their bodies. Holding his cock in his hand, he bent toward T.J. His cheek brushed against hair as he moved his mouth to the waiting cock.

He pulled T.J.'s cock out, maneuvering it through the opening in his shorts. Parting his lips, he closed them around the head of T.J.'s dick. He tasted heat and salt. He remained still for a moment, just feeling the way T.J. filled his mouth. His tongue gently circled the crown of T.J.'s cock and dipped into the slit at the center.

He couldn't believe he had another man's dick in his mouth. At the same time, he was overcome by the excitement of it. His fingers around T.J.'s shaft, he pushed more of him into his throat. He felt his airway become blocked as the head filled it, and for a moment he didn't know what to do. Then he realized he could breathe through his nose, and he continued on.

Above him, T.J. moaned in his sleep. Pete, emboldened, pressed closer to him and began moving his head up and down T.J.'s dick, sucking him off. He imitated what he'd seen the women in porn films do, using his hand to jerk T.J. off as his mouth worked on his head.

He felt he must be dreaming. He was blowing his best friend, taking his cock like some hungry bitch who couldn't get enough of the big prick between T.J.'s legs. He sucked the fat head and stroked the shaft, wanting to feel T.J. come. He wanted to taste his load.

When T.J. did come, it was in thick jets that spurted into Pete's throat. The musky taste of T.J.'s cum filled him as the sticky liquid gushed from his balls. Pete swallowed greedily as more and more of it erupted from T.J.'s cock. He waited until the last throb died away, then gently squeezed the remaining drops of cum from T.J.'s shaft, milking it with his hand. Reluctantly, he let the softening dick slide from between his lips. Taking one last sniff of the rich smell that came from between T.J.'s legs, he rolled back to his side of the bed.

T.J. grunted in his sleep and turned away from Pete, throwing one arm over himself like a child snuggling deeper into his blankets. Alone, Pete lay in the darkness, tasting the cum that coated his tongue and throat and remembering what T.J.'s cock had felt like in his mouth. What had he done? He'd sucked off another guy. He'd blown T.J.

The mattress shook gently beneath him as he jerked himself off. It didn't take long. Within minutes his hand filled with heat as he came, hard. He gritted his teeth to keep from crying out, and when his orgasm subsided, he wiped his load off on his sweatpants.

Suddenly the excitement he'd felt was replaced by shame and horror. The taste in his throat no longer aroused him; it sickened him. He'd done something terrible, something he couldn't allow himself to consider. Beside him, T.J. slept on, oblivious. But Pete knew—would always know—what he'd done. Every time he looked at T.J., he would be reminded of how he'd lowered himself, how he'd become like one of the faggots whose mouths and asses he'd used. He had become one of them.

He was drunk, he told himself. It was the alcohol that had made him forget himself. That was all. He'd done a lot of stupid things while drunk, hadn't he? This was simply one of them. He had to put it out of his mind, forget everything. He would sleep, and in the morning it would never have happened.

He closed his eyes and willed himself to sleep. His beer-soaked mind obliged him, drawing the dark curtain of exhaustion over his eyes. But as he drifted down into the obliterating blackness, he began to dream, and in his dream he saw himself kneeling before T.J. Kneeling and waiting.

CHAPTER 26

"I'm starting to think that all it does here is snow."

Mike, looking out the window at the continuing blizzard, laughed. "Sometimes it feels that way." He handed Thomas a mug of cocoa and sat down at the kitchen table opposite him.

"I guess this means skiing is off?" Thomas asked.

"We could do it," Mike said. "But it wouldn't be much fun. I suggest we find something else to do."

"And what do you have in mind?" said Thomas. "Making snow angels? Tobogganing?"

"I was thinking more like putting up a tree."

"I'm intrigued," Thomas said.

"I know it's a little late in the game for a tree," Mike admitted. "But there are still five days left before Christmas, and suddenly I'm feeling sort of festive."

"May I ask what brought this on?" Thomas inquired.

"I saw *It's a Wonderful Life* on NBC last night," said Mike. When Thomas gave him a doubting look, he fessed up. "Okay, I just need a little Christmas spirit."

"That's a good enough reason for me," Thomas told him. "I'm in."

"Good. As soon as you're done with that hot chocolate, we'll head out."

"Head out?" Thomas said skeptically. "That sounds suspiciously like what you said when we went skiing."

"What?" Mike said innocently. "It will be fun. Trust me."

Half an hour later, bundled up in their winter coats against the heavily falling snow, the two men were trudging through the snow, making their way through a field of pine trees. Mike carried a saw in one hand.

"I thought we were just going to go to a lot and pick one up," Thomas said as he lifted one booted foot out of the snow. "I didn't realize we were going to track one down."

"Lot trees are for sissies," Mike informed him. "Real men hunt their own."

They stopped and examined several trees, all of which Mike rejected for various reasons. Finally, on the ninth try, he declared the tree they were standing in front of acceptable.

"Hold the trunk while I saw," he told Thomas.

A couple of minutes later the two of them were walking back to the truck, a beautiful evergreen pulled along behind them. The tree cut a wide swath through the snow, covering up their footprints.

"I feel like we're bringing our catch back to the tribe," Thomas remarked as they reached the road and heaved the tree into the back of the truck.

"It's not quite the same thing as a buffalo," Mike commented as they climbed into the truck. "But it's more fun when you get your own. My father used to take me out to get one every year."

Back at Mike's house, they unloaded the tree and shook the snow from its branches before taking it into the garage, where Mike set it in a bucket of warm water.

"This relaxes the branches," he told Thomas when he seemed puzzled by the bucket. "We'll bring it inside in an hour or so."

Once in the house, they shed their coats and went into the living room. Mike lit a fire, and then he and Thomas rearranged the furniture to make room for the tree in front of the big window that looked out on the house's front yard.

"I'll be right back," Mike told Thomas, disappearing down the stairs leading to the cellar.

Thomas waited, warming himself in front of the fireplace. He'd quickly come to enjoy the days spent with his friend. Particularly now that the holidays were upon them, it felt good to have people he enjoyed around him. Christmas was one of the most hectic times around any church, and Saint Peter's was no exception. Although he'd been able to bring about a truce in the matter of the upcoming nativity pageant, there were still a million things occupying his mind, chief among them the memories of Joseph that had been coming back to him more and more strongly.

"Here we are," Mike said, interrupting Thomas's thoughts.

Thomas turned to see Mike, his arms laden with a stack of cardboard boxes. The boxes seemed very old, and were covered in a thick layer of dust. When Mike set them down, the dust rose into the air, settling onto the floor.

"What's in them?" Thomas asked.

"Decorations," answered Mike. "The ones we had when I was a kid. I've been lugging them around all these years, but I've never opened them."

"Never?" asked Thomas, surprised.

Mike shook his head. "Christmas hasn't meant much to me since my folks died," he said quietly. He looked up at Thomas. "But I think it's time to change that."

He sat on the couch and pulled one of the boxes toward him. Hesitating, he reached out and pulled the flaps open. He reached inside and took out a smaller box. Lifting the lid, he revealed a dozen blown-glass ornaments, each one shaped like a fruit. Pears, apples, blackberries, strawberries, peaches, and lemons—two of each—were nestled in cocoons of fragile tissue paper.

"I haven't seen these in fifteen years," Mike said softly as he picked up one of the peaches and let it dangle in front of his face. The pale pink globe was frosted with white, its leaves a brilliant green. "My mother loved these things. I always thought they were silly."

He gazed upon the ornament with an expression of sadness. Looking at it, he couldn't help but picture his mother as she trimmed the tree. Her face radiated happiness as she found the perfect spot for each one, creating a scene of Christmas magic. As a boy, Mike had enjoyed helping her, feeling privileged whenever she allowed him to handle one of the more delicate ornaments. As he'd grown older, the tree had become less and less important to him, and he'd been content to let his mother decorate it more or less alone. Now, beholding the peach, he regretted ever letting a single year go by when he didn't join his mother in her annual ritual.

He put the peach down and returned to the box. This time he lifted out a plastic star. Plain to the point of ugliness, it was three-dimensional, with a hole in the bottom. Mike held the star in his hands and stared at it, not saying a word.

"What is it?" Thomas asked him finally.

Mike held it up, his finger inserted into the hole so that the star stuck up from his hand. "A tree topper," he explained. "My mother bought it the first Christmas she and Dad were married. They didn't have much money, and she saved up for it. I think originally it had a light inside of it and it glowed, but somewhere over the years that broke or fell out. I never understood why she wanted something so ugly on top of the tree. One year I decided to surprise her with a new one. But when she saw it on top of the tree, she started crying. I didn't get it. Not until a long time after."

"It was her tradition," Thomas said, looking at the battered star and seeing it through the eyes of Mike's mother.

Mike nodded. "It reminded her of that first year together. But when you're thirteen, you're too stupid to understand things like that."

He put the star down and sighed. "Let's get that tree," he said. "Before I change my mind."

Together they carried the tree in and set it into a stand Mike dug out of another box. After positioning it several ways, they finally decided on one and stepped back. The tree reached almost to the ceiling, its graceful branches spreading out and filling the room with its scent.

"Lights first," Mike said, removing several boxes of newly purchased lights from a bag. "That was always my father's job. I guess it's mine now."

With Thomas's help, he'd soon encircled the tree with the strings of lights. When Mike plugged them in, the tree burst into color, twinkling all over in red, green, yellow, and blue. Even dressed in just the lights, the tree took on an air of jollity, enlivening the room with its spirit.

"I don't suppose you have any Christmas music," Thomas asked.

Mike regarded him coolly. "Do I look like I would have Christmas music?" he asked.

"Sorry," Thomas apologized. "I thought maybe Madonna had a holiday album or something."

Mike grinned. "Congratulations," he said.

"For what?"

"That's the first queeny thing I've heard you say," Mike told him.

Thomas blushed. "I was just kidding," he said. "I didn't mean—"

"Relax," Mike interrupted. "I'm giving you a hard time. As it so happens, I did pick up some CDs at the mall the other day."

"You really do have the Christmas spirit," Thomas told him as Mike went to the stereo cabinet and returned with a handful of discs.

"Hey," Mike said, "if you're going to do it, you might as well go all out. We've got Christmas albums by Ella Fitzgerald, Louis Armstrong, Etta James, the Andrews Sisters, and Elvis. Which do you want to hear?"

"Elvis," Thomas answered immediately. "Classic."

"These were all records my parents played," said Mike as he slipped the CDs into the stereo. A minute later Elvis started in on "Blue Christmas."

"I'll have a blue-ew-ew-ew-ew-ew-ew Christmas," Mike sang, imitating the King's background singers. "That was always my part. My father sang the lead."

Thomas looked at the boxes of ornaments that were spread out on the coffee table. "Where do we start?" he asked.

Mike picked up an ornament, a red wooden bird painted with white and blue decoration. "Anywhere you like," he answered Thomas.

As Elvis sang, they trimmed the tree. One by one the ornaments went on and the boxes were emptied. In addition to the birds and the fruit, the tree was hung with glass pinecones, angels, several Santas, and assorted elves, stockings, gingerbread men, and stars. When the last of them was placed on the only bare branch remaining, Mike took up his mother's beloved plastic star and, using a chair to reach the uppermost branch, placed it atop the tree.

"And there we are," he said as he stepped down and surveyed their handiwork. "My first Christmas tree since the accident."

"It's a beautiful one," Thomas said. Instinctively, he put his arm around Mike and gave him a hug.

"Thanks," Mike said. "For helping. For coming over. For everything."

He turned to look at Thomas. Thomas, looking into his friend's eyes, felt suddenly unable to move. He stood there, his hand still on

Mike's waist, while Mike stared into his face. Neither said anything. Thomas could feel his heartbeat speed up, until it was pounding so loudly he was sure Mike could hear it as well.

"Have yourself a merry little Christmas."

The sound of Ella Fitzgerald's unmistakable voice floated through the silence. Still, neither Mike nor Thomas moved. It was as if the snowstorm outside had somehow swept them up in its embrace and frozen them in time.

Then Mike leaned forward. Thomas closed his eyes as their lips met. He felt the softness of Mike's mouth on his. Mike's arms went around him, pulling him in closer. Thomas felt strong hands on his back. He kissed Mike back, his hands tentatively reaching up and finding a place against the small of Mike's back.

Too soon, Mike pulled away. He looked at Thomas with an expression of surprise and embarrassment. He let him go and stepped away.

"I'm so sorry," he said, his voice halting. "I didn't mean to do that. Oh, God. I'm really, really sorry."

Thomas put a hand to his mouth, touching the place where Mike's lips had pressed against his. The warmth lingered. He looked at Mike, not able to put into words what he was feeling.

"That was so stupid," Mike continued. "I don't know what I was thinking. I mean, I know you're not—"

"I am," Thomas said.

Mike's mouth stayed open but he said nothing as he stared at Thomas.

"I am," Thomas said again. "I always have been."

Mike blinked. Thomas stepped toward him and took his hands in his own. "I'm gay," he said, thinking perhaps Mike hadn't understood. "And it's okay." He breathed deeply, trying to calm his emotions. "And it's okay."

This time it was he who kissed Mike. And this time neither of them pulled away. Their mouths found one another, tongues pressing against one another. Their arms held one another close, both afraid to let go. Ella's voice serenaded them as they embraced.

When finally they parted, it was Thomas who spoke first. "I guess this is a year of firsts for a lot of things," he said.

Mike, still holding his hand, sat down on the couch, pulling

Thomas down with him. "What's happening here?" he asked. "Are you saying that all this time . . . ?" He looked at Thomas, his question left unfinished.

Thomas nodded. "It's hard to explain," he said. "I'm not even sure I *can* explain it, at least not right now. But you have to understand, I wasn't trying to fool you or your friends or anyone. Well, perhaps myself, but no one else."

Mike rubbed his thumb along the side of Thomas's hand. "Is it true you've never been with anyone?" he asked.

Thomas nodded. "No one," he answered. "I know what you're thinking," he continued. "Another closeted priest. But that's not really it. I—"

"That wasn't what I was thinking at all," Mike interrupted.

Thomas regarded him wonderingly.

"I was thinking that I've never met anyone like you," Mike said softly. "All of this," he said, nodding at the tree, "I did it all because of you."

"Me?" Thomas asked.

Mike nodded. "I didn't understand why, but you made me want to feel alive again," he said, then he laughed. "I thought I was nuts, wanting to spend time with a straight guy. A straight priest. But it didn't matter. I just liked being around you. It never even occurred to me that maybe I was . . ."

"That you were what?" asked Thomas when Mike looked away.

Mike lifted his head. His eyes were damp. "That maybe I was falling in love," said Mike.

CHAPTER 27

The shortest day of the year dawned bleak and gray, as if winter, sensing the eventual loosening of its grip on the world, was trying to obliterate the sun once and for all. The sky remained perpetually dark, clouds obscuring the heavens. Snow fell steadily. There was no hint that, soon, the periods of light would begin to lengthen by several minutes a day as the wheel of the year turned once more.

Stephen Darby didn't know that it was the first official day of winter. Inside his house, a perpetual chill had taken hold many days earlier. In his kitchen, dishes were piled high in the sink. His bedroom floor was littered with discarded clothes. He had some time ago gotten down to his last pair of clean underwear, which he'd now been wearing for six days straight.

Had he bothered to look in a mirror, he wouldn't have recognized himself. Although his bruises were mostly healed, his face hardly resembled the one he'd had before encountering Pete Thayer at the Paris Cinema. Where once he had been handsome, now he was haunted. His eyes were dull, his skin ashen. His hair, uncut and unwashed, hung limply over his forehead. His beard had grown in, covering his cheeks and chin with a patchy forest of reddish-brown.

When the phone rang, Stephen stared at it. It had been ringing a lot lately, but he generally ignored it. There was no one he wanted to hear from, no one who had anything to say to him that was of any importance. Even his family seemed to exist only in the distant past. He'd made a few calls to them, convinced them that he was busy with work and perhaps battling a slight case of the flu. His mother, thankfully, was preoccupied with her usual holiday plans, the undertaking of which outweighed her customary need to oversee every aspect of her son's life. She had left him alone after extracting a promise from him to appear at her annual holiday party, to be held on December twenty-first.

The date was circled on the calendar that hung above Stephen's desk, but it meant little to him. He wasn't sure what day it was, nor did he care. Whenever he had begun to care, even a little, he had taken a couple of pills and retreated into the dull safety of their embrace. There, nothing mattered. He liked it that way.

Now he heard his mother's voice emanating from the depths of the machine. "Stephen? It's your mother. I wanted to remind you that the party is tonight. I want you here by seven o'clock. Oh, and don't forget to bring a gift for the Secret Santa exchange."

Secret Santa. Hearing the words, Stephen laughed. "Secret Santa," he said out loud, enjoying the way the words felt on his tongue, the nonsensical sound of them when they were uttered. "Secret Santa," he said again. "Secret Santa. Secret Santa. Secret Santa."

He laughed again, loudly. What the fuck was a Secret Santa? What did it have to do with him? Nothing, he told himself. Absolutely nothing. It was just something his mother liked to say, another one of her endless, boring topics of conversation, like her perpetually sore back or Stephen's inability to find a wife. Secret Santa. He wondered if she'd read about *that* in the goddamned *Reader's Digest.*

He erased her message. If she wanted him to show up for her goddamned party, he would. Maybe he'd show up dressed exactly as he was, in stained underpants and an old T-shirt. Maybe he'd just walk in like that, a big fucking bow tied around his neck. "Merry Christmas, Mom," he heard himself say. "Merry Fucking Christmas."

He checked the computer screen again. Still nothing from HrdAtWrk. It had been two weeks, two long weeks since he'd heard from him. What was wrong, he wondered? What had he done to drive his master away? He'd been a good boy, hadn't he? He'd done everything that was asked of him. He'd allowed his master to take out his rage on him, to use him the way he deserved to be used. Wasn't that enough?

He lived in front of the computer. Not having heard from his dark lover, and forsaking all others, he'd resorted to searching the web for the next best thing. He'd discovered in his endless wandering several sites that had interested him, places where he could find images that recalled his times with his faceless tormentor. He sat for hours staring at pictures of men who, like him, deserved to be mistreated. He saw their bodies, bound and beaten, their faces twisted in pain as men stronger than they were used them for their pleasure.

These pictures had become the dreamscape of his life. Looking at them, he replaced the bodies of the men in them with his own, super-imposed his features over theirs. Soon he was looking at himself, his own body bruised and broken as the man who now controlled his mind ordered him to degrade himself for his amusement. It was his wrists that were tied behind him as a stream of piss, hot and wicked, slashed across his face. It was his back covered in the welts of his master's whip, his chest puckered with the brand of a white-hot iron that seared a mark of shame into his flesh.

He knew he should be ashamed of himself, ashamed of the thoughts that filled his head and the desires that ate at his soul. And he was ashamed. He had no right to exist in the world, at least not the world around him. He didn't belong there. That world was for normal men, men who could hold their heads high and walk with pride. He was not one of those men. He was something small and frail, bent and twisted by a poison that ran through his veins and intoxicated him with its sweetness. He should, he knew, be strong enough to resist it, but he couldn't. He was weak.

It was this poison that had befogged his mind and raised the voice that had told him to go to that place, that place where he'd allowed himself to be taken. It was this poison that made him half a man, inca-pable of wholeness. He had let it taint him, and now it was eating him alive.

He fumbled for the bottle on his desk. His fingers found it, knock-ing it over. The pills scattered across the surface of the desk, a rain of small blue tablets. The sound echoed loudly in his ears, and for a long horrible moment he saw the pills tumbling off of the desk and into nothingness. His heart stopped as he imagined the loss of them, and he pawed at the desk anxiously, trying to prevent the pills from run-ning away from him like bugs from the light. He trapped them beneath his palm, where they lay still. When he was sure they wouldn't scurry out of his reach, he lifted his hand and nervously scooped the pills back into the bottle.

He held the bottle up, measuring the remaining number. He

sighed. There were enough to last him for some time. *Unless . . .* The thought returned to him. It had first come a few days before, interrupting his fantasies with its teasing voice. *Unless . . .* He'd ordered it away, terrified by its suggestion. But it had come back, wheedling and coaxing. Each time he screamed at it to shut up, it obliged, but only for a time. Now the periods of its silence were growing shorter and shorter, and it was growing stronger, more insistent.

Unless you take all of them.

He put his hands to his ears, trying to shut the voice out. But it came from within, and now that it had had its say, it felt its power. *Unless you take all of them,* it said again. *All of them. All at once. Unless you take them all.*

He shook his head. No, he wouldn't listen to the voice. It lied. It had lied to him about the pleasures that awaited him in the theater. It had lied to him about the pleasures waiting for him in the arms of men. All it knew how to do was lie. He couldn't trust it.

"Go away!" he shouted, trying to drown it out.

The voice laughed quietly. *Not this time,* it said. *Not anymore. You believed me once. Believe me again.*

"No!" Stephen yelled. He reached for the bottle, took three pills, and popped them into his mouth. His glass of Diet Coke was empty so he chewed, grinding the pills to powder beneath his teeth. The taste was foul, sharp, and metallic, but he didn't stop. Producing some spit, he swallowed. The paste stuck in his throat and he coughed, bringing most of it back up. He swallowed again, harder, and the pills entered his system. He breathed more easily.

What are you waiting for?

Stephen looked up. He'd heard the voice of the dark man, the one he longed for. He looked around the room. Where was he?

What are you waiting for, faggot?

"Where are you?" he called out.

The room behind him was empty. He ran into the hall, peering into the darkness. It, too, was barren. His feet slipped on the wooden floor as he went from room to room, searching. Finally he ended up in the bedroom. The blinds were drawn against the pale light outside, and the sheets on the bed were a tangled nest. A stale smell emanated from them.

Why aren't you on your knees, cocksucker?

Stephen turned around, searching wildly for the man who spoke to him. He found only shadows. Perhaps the man was hiding within them. Perhaps he would emerge to take Stephen in his hands, to use him as he needed to be used.

On your knees!

The voice was harsh, commanding. Stephen was forced to obey it. He dropped to his knees, landing on the floor with a sharp crack of bone on wood. Pain bit at him but he ignored it. He looked up hopefully, waiting.

What is it you want, faggot?

Stephen shook his head, unwilling to speak. He knew what he wanted, but he couldn't say it.

Tell me what you want.

The voice bristled with anger. Stephen trembled, expecting at any moment to feel the slap of a hand across his face, the kick of a boot in his stomach. Anticipating it, he began to cry.

Laughter rang through the room. It came from all around him, mocking and jeering, echoing in his head. It was cruel, cold, and hard.

What a joke you are, the voice said, spitting the words at him. *You're not a man. You're nothing. Nothing. You're a worthless rag for me to wipe up my cum with.*

The tears fell from Stephen's eyes, dropping to the floor. He wiped at his eyes with his hands, trying to stanch the flow. He was disgracing himself, he knew.

Don't bother trying, the voice said. *You're like all the rest of the faggots. Weak. Diseased. Good for nothing. Aren't you?*

Stephen shook his head. He was all those things. He was useless. He had no reason to deny it. The evidence was against him, and he knew it. Didn't his body carry the proof of his weakness? Didn't his mind contain the seeds of disease? Everything the voice said was true.

What am I going to do about you?

The voice spoke not to Stephen but to itself, as if his master was considering what punishment to dole out next. Stephen considered praying for mercy, begging for another chance to prove himself. But somehow he knew that point had been passed. He had failed miserably, and whatever his fate was to be, it was what he deserved.

Maybe I should have you go next door and tell your mother what you've been doing, the voice said thoughtfully.

"No," Stephen whispered.

No? And why not? Shouldn't she know what kind of son you really are? Shouldn't she know what it is you dream about doing? Wouldn't that make her happy?

"No," Stephen said again. "Please, no."

The voice laughed at him. *Look at the little faggot, begging me not to tell his mommy what he really is. Why don't you want her to know? Would she be disappointed in you? Would she be ashamed?*

"Yes," Stephen said, choking back a sob. "Yes." He thought of his mother, seeing him on the floor of the Paris Cinema. He saw her eyes troubled with confusion, wondering what her baby boy was doing there, his pants around his feet, his shame on display for the whole world to see. No, he couldn't let her know. She could never know.

Would it break their hearts? asked the voice, as if its owner had read Stephen's thoughts. *Would it kill them to know that their boy had become a cocksucker? That he wasn't a real man?*

It would kill them, Stephen thought hopelessly. It would destroy them. He'd always been the good son, the one who never caused any trouble. They had always told him how proud they were of him. But they wouldn't be proud if they knew. They would think they had failed.

And you can't be who you are, the voice reminded him. *You can't go on like this.*

Again Stephen knew that the voice spoke the truth. He couldn't live like this, always searching, always looking for men who would use him. He couldn't stay in the shadows forever. Someday he would have to come out from the safety of the world he'd been living in, and then he would be revealed for what he was. Then it would all come crumbling down.

There is one way, the voice said, sounding for a moment like it truly cared about him. *There is one thing you can do, one way to make sure they never find out.*

Stephen looked down. Somehow the bottle of pills was in his fist. Had he carried it with him? Had he clung to it through everything? He didn't remember doing so, but there it was. He shook the bottle and heard the reassuring rattle of the pills inside.

There are enough, the voice told him. *More than enough.*

Stephen sobbed. He was wracked with pain. His whole being ached. All he wanted was for it to stop.

Go on, faggot, the voice said, sounding more like the man he remembered. *Do what I tell you. You're good at that.*

Stephen nodded, tears blinding him. He looked around the room and saw a glass sitting on the table beside his bed. He crawled toward it, unable to get to his feet. The weight of his burden was pressing down on him, unbelievably heavy. He felt it like a booted foot between his shoulder blades, crushing him to the floor.

He reached the glass and grabbed it. It was still half full. He took a sip. The soda inside was flat and warm, all life sapped from it. He had no idea how long it had been sitting there. He set the glass on the floor and opened the bottle of pills, dumping them into his hand. His fingers closed around the pile, holding it close.

In the other room the phone rang, startling him. He glanced at the clock on the bedside table. It was seven o'clock. He knew the call was from his mother, wondering where he was.

Finish it, the voice said insistently. *She'll be here soon.*

Yes, he thought, she would be there soon. When he didn't answer, she would be there to see what was keeping him. Perhaps she would send his father or his brother. He was running out of time.

He opened his fist. The pills looked small and insignificant, like candy. He put half of them into his mouth.

Now swallow, faggot. Swallow like a good boy.

Stephen obeyed. He took a swig of the stale soda and let it carry the pills down his throat. He repeated the process again, swallowing the remainder of the pills. When they were down, he took another drink.

He didn't feel any different, not at first. Then a warmth began to creep over him, a comforting blanket that shrouded him in darkness and quieted his heart. His eyes grew heavy. He heard the glass in his hand fall to the floor with a dull thud. He felt warmth against his leg.

Where was the man? Had he gone? Stephen looked around, trying to find him. He wanted to see him one last time, feel his touch. But where was he? Stephen felt alone, and for the first time he was frightened.

What's wrong, fag?

The voice returned, nearer now. The man crouched behind him, just out of sight. Stephen tried to turn his head to see him, but found himself unable to move.

What's the matter? Isn't this what you wanted?

The voice was taunting him. He could see the man watching him, his mouth twisted into a cruel grin. He felt strong hands close around his throat, cutting off his air. He didn't bother to fight. This *was* what he wanted. It was what he'd wanted when he'd gone into the darkness with the man at the theater. It was what he wanted now. It was what he deserved.

He closed his eyes and allowed his dark master to do what he would.

CHAPTER 28

"Are you okay?"

Russell nodded. "It's just sort of, you know, weird."

"I know," Greg agreed. He played with his fork for a moment, then set it down on the table. "Let's just pretend this is a first date," he said.

"It is a first date," said Russell.

"I mean a real one," Greg said. "Let's pretend we don't know much about one another. Someone—a mutual friend—has set us up."

Russell sat back in his chair. "Okay," he said. "That could work."

"Great," Greg said. "I'll start. So, Russell, what do you do?"

"I'm the store manager for the Carter-Beane over at the Stonesgate Mall," Russell answered.

"Really?" replied Greg. "What a surprise. I'm a manager in menswear at Carter-Beane. I'm surprised I've never run into you."

Russell laughed. "Maybe this won't work after all," he said.

"Just go with it," Greg encouraged him.

"Do you like your job?" Russell asked, trying to think of questions he might ask a date. It had been so long since he'd been on one, he wasn't sure how to do it.

"I do," Greg answered confidently. "But our store manager is kind of uptight."

"Sounds like a drag," suggested Russell.

"I think he just needs to have a little more fun," Greg said. "He's been sort of unhappy lately. What about you? Do you enjoy your work?"

"Most of the time," said Russell. "Some of my employees can be difficult sometimes."

"Maybe you need to discipline them," Greg said suggestively.

Russell laughed. "Let's talk about something else," he said. "What do you like to do?"

"I'm really into oral," Greg said cheerfully, as if answering an interview question. "If we're talking anal, I can go both ways but I usually prefer being on the bottom. As for rimming—"

"I meant hobbies," Russell said, interrupting him.

"Those aren't hobbies?" said Greg.

Russell picked up his knife and pointed it at his companion. "This was your idea," he said. "Play nice."

"All right," said Greg. "Seriously. I like to read, go to movies, concerts, that sort of stuff. I'm not really into sports, although I watch a little baseball in the summer. I'm not much into politics, either, but I voted in the last election."

"Who for?" Russell inquired.

"The guy who lost," said Greg. "Now tell me about you."

"I like to cook," Russell told him. "I'm also into reading and movies. I think I like concerts. It's been a couple of years since I went to one. Don't like sports at all."

"What about your last relationship?" Greg asked. "What happened?"

"That's not fair," Russell said.

"Sure it is," countered Greg. "I ask all my dates that question."

Russell sighed deeply. "I don't know," he said reluctantly. "I guess we just weren't a good match."

"How long were you together?"

"Seven years," Russell said.

"That's a long time to not be a good match," suggested Greg.

Russell took a sip of wine from the glass next to his plate. "Yes," he said simply, "it is a long time."

"Well, I think anyone would be lucky to have you as a partner," Greg said.

Russell put his glass down. "Thank you," he said gratefully. "How about you? Any past loves I should know about?"

"I had a huge crush on Kevin Costner when I was seventeen," Greg answered. "Nothing to speak of since then. A guy here and there, but never for long."

"Trouble committing?" asked Russell.

"Just never found anyone worth committing to," said Greg.

The conversation ebbed as their food arrived. Once the waiter had gone, they began eating. Feeling more comfortable now that he had something to do with his hands, Russell continued the game.

"Are you looking to settle down?" he inquired. "Or are you just interested in something casual?"

"Well, you really get right to it, don't you?" replied Greg. "No wonder all your dates run screaming."

"When you're my age, you don't have time to waste," Russell joked. "I like to know where things stand."

Greg slowly chewed a mouthful of pasta before answering. "Why don't we see how things go?" he said.

Russell looked at him. Greg's expression was serious, and Russell knew they were no longer just playing. Greg meant what he said.

"Okay," Russell said. "We'll see how it goes. How's it going so far?"

Greg nodded his head, grinning. "It's going great," he replied.

The remainder of dinner was easy and relaxed. The two men talked about nothing and everything, from their childhoods to their favorite flavors of ice cream. When the check came, Russell was feeling better than he had in a long time. Although the whole date scenario was sort of artificial, he really did feel as if he were getting to know a potential partner better. There was a sense of anticipation about his interactions with Greg, a fluttering in the stomach that he realized he hadn't experienced since his first dates with John.

"So," Greg said when the check had been paid. "Want to come back to my place?"

Russell hesitated. He hadn't thought about how far their date might go. It had been difficult enough suggesting to Greg that maybe they could consider taking their relationship in a different direction. That had been an awkward conversation, one that had taken most of an evening and a bottle of wine to get out. But once he had, Greg had been surprisingly receptive to the notion. Now, almost a week later, they were at another crossroads. Russell looked at Greg, who was waiting for an answer to his question.

"Sure," he answered. "Let's do that."

They got into their cars and Russell followed Greg out of the restaurant parking lot. As he drove behind him, his thoughts raced from one thing to another. What was he doing? Was he really going to maybe sleep with Greg? He hadn't been with anyone but John since they'd started dating seriously. If he did sleep with Greg, did it mean that he and John were officially over? He hadn't, of course, mentioned his date with Greg to John. He hadn't mentioned it to anyone, not even Simon or Mike. But if they started having sex, didn't that obligate him to tell people?

Again he hesitated. He could simply turn the car around and head back to Simon's house. He could call Greg and apologize, tell him that things were moving too quickly. Greg would understand. They could go back to being just friends.

But he didn't turn around. He followed Greg all the way to his house, pulling into the driveway behind him and parking. He hesitated only slightly before opening the door and getting out of the car. Greg waited for him, and together they walked to the front door.

"Here we are," Greg said as he unlocked the door and opened it. He held out his hand, motioning for Russell to enter ahead of him.

The door shut. Russell turned to look at Greg. For a moment they stood there awkwardly, just staring at one another. Then they were kissing. Russell wasn't even sure who had moved first. One moment they were standing with a foot or more of space between them, the next they were entwined in one another's arms.

As they kissed, they fumbled with the buttons of each other's coats, trying to open them with eager fingers. Russell thought, incongruously, of two overeager children in snowsuits bumping against one another. He felt clumsy, silly, like a little boy. He pulled away from Greg and took a breath.

"What's the matter?" Greg asked.

"I just need to slow down a little," Russell told him.

Greg nodded. "Why don't we start with getting these coats off?" he suggested.

Free of their coats and scarves, they faced one another again. Greg stepped forward and kissed Russell. This time, Russell let himself melt into the kiss. Greg's kisses were different than John's. His mouth was softer, his movements more intense. He used his hands to draw Russell to him, held him with a commanding presence that Russell found arousing.

"Let's go upstairs," Greg said when they parted for a moment. He took Russell's hand, and Russell, not objecting, followed him up the stairs.

Greg walked inside the bedroom, still holding Russell's hand. Russell paused in the doorway, looking in. Beyond Greg he could see the bed, the quilt that covered it pulled back a little at the top. He knew that if he stepped over the threshold, he would be making a decision that could change his life forever.

Greg was waiting for him. His eyes were soft, inviting. His fingers held Russell's in a loose grip. He was leaving the decision to stay or go up to Russell. Russell stepped forward.

Greg led him to the bed. Not speaking, he reached for the buttons on Russell's shirt and slowly undid them, pulling Russell's shirt off and dropping it to the floor. He followed it with his own shirt, then reached for the buckle of Russell's belt.

Moments later they stood in just their underwear. Greg embraced Russell, pulling him toward him. Russell felt the smooth skin of Greg's torso pressed against his own, sensed a hardness at his crotch as they kissed. After hesitating a moment, he slid his hands down Greg's back.

Greg pushed him backward, lowering him to the bed. He was between Russell's legs, and now the bulge in his shorts was undeniable. Russell felt the stiffness of Greg's erection pressing against his own growing dick. He closed his eyes as Greg moved his mouth down to his chin and then to his neck.

Greg kept going, his tongue tracing a lazy path down Russell's neck to his chest. There Greg's mouth paused, his teeth biting gently at Russell's nipple. Russell tensed at the slight pain, then relaxed as Greg replaced teeth with the softness of his warm lips.

Russell was uncertain what to do. His lovemaking with John had quickly fallen into a predictable pattern during the first months of their relationship. John preferred things to go in an orderly fashion, seldom straying from his favored activities of mutual masturbation and the occasional blowjob. He found anal sex messy and distasteful, and the few times Russell had convinced him to try it, the experiment had ended badly. Since then Russell had satisfied himself with what John was capable of.

Greg, unlike John, seemed intent on exploring all the possibilities available to two men making love. When he reached Russell's crotch, he tugged his underwear down and off. Russell's cock, feeling harder than it had in many months, jutted up at an angle. Greg ignored it for the time being, preferring to attend to Russell's balls. He nibbled and sucked on them, letting first one and then the other roll around on his tongue.

When his tongue descended into the crack of Russell's ass, Russell inhaled sharply. When he felt his asshole gently spread and Greg's tongue enter him, he cried out despite himself. Hearing him, Greg probed more deeply. Russell gasped, overcome by the sensation. His cock jerked of its own accord as his body was wracked with spasms of excitement.

Greg continued to fuck him with his tongue, alternately moving in and out and then pausing to languidly circle the perimeter of the opening to Russell's ass. Russell, never having had such attention paid to his butt, pushed his head back against the pillows and prayed it would never end.

When it did, he looked down, disappointed, to see Greg moving back up between his legs. This time he stopped at Russell's cock, gently taking the head in his mouth and sliding down it. Russell's dick was encased in warmth, and again his head went back against the pillows. He lost himself in the movements of Greg's mouth. Then Greg moved onto the bed, turning so that he was straddling Russell's body. Russell opened his eyes to see Greg's prick hanging above his face.

He reached for it, feeling its thickness in his hand. As Greg continued to suck him, he returned the favor. For the first time in seven years he tasted a cock other than John's. He took as much as he could into himself, relishing the rich smell and the way Greg slid against his lips and tongue.

As he was sucking, he felt Greg release his cock and move back to his asshole. This time Greg slipped a finger inside. Russell groaned, Greg's cock deep in his throat, and pressed against the finger that played with him. Greg, taking the cue, fucked him more forcefully. When Russell couldn't stand the teasing any longer, he let Greg's cock fall from between his lips.

"Do you have a rubber?" he asked.

Greg rolled off him and reached for the drawer of his bedside table. Opening it, he pulled out a condom and a small bottle, which he set on the table. As Russell watched, he ripped open the foil packet and removed a rubber, which he quickly rolled down the length of his dick. Then he squirted the contents of the bottle into his palm.

Kneeling between Russell's legs, he slid his finger back inside him.

Russell felt the lube on Greg's finger slick his hole. Greg massaged him for a minute, loosening him up. Then Russell felt the head of Greg's dick pressing against him. He tried to relax.

When Greg entered him, his mouth opened in a silent cry. Seeing it, Greg slowed down, giving Russell time to adjust to him. Then he resumed his progress until Russell felt Greg's balls slapping gently against his ass.

Greg began to move in and out, slowly fucking him. He pushed Russell's legs back. Russell, looking up at him, wavered between laughing and crying. Greg's cock felt wonderful. But Russell also felt guilty. Instead of Greg's face, he saw John's. He was looking down at Russell, confused. Russell wanted to reach up and stroke his cheek, tell him that everything was okay.

But it wasn't okay. He was making love with another man. As good as it felt, as much as he wanted it, something was missing. He'd hoped that doing this with Greg would make him feel whole; instead, it was tearing him apart all over again.

"I can't," he whimpered.

Greg, not hearing him, continued to fuck him.

"Stop," Russell said more loudly.

Greg slowed down. "Does it hurt?" he asked.

Russell sat up. Greg pulled out of him and knelt between his knees, concern on his face. "Are you okay?"

Russell shook his head. "No," he said, an overwhelming sadness building up inside him as he looked at Greg and felt his heart breaking all over again. "I'm not."

CHAPTER 29

"Well, here we are again."
Simon looked down at Walter's grave. Someone had, not surprisingly, taken the CD player since his last visit. A new layer of snow had covered the stone, and the lower half was almost completely obscured by a small drift that had been pushed up against the marker by the wind.

"I don't know how you stand it out here," Simon said, addressing the stone as he pulled his coat more tightly around him. "It's not precisely balmy."

He had brought a bouquet of flowers, red roses that he'd paid dearly for at a shop downtown. He bent down and stuck their stems in the snow. The roses, defying the cold, bobbed their blood-red heads against the wind. It was a futile battle, but Simon admired their defiance.

"I'm sorry," he said, again addressing Walter's resting place.

He waited a moment, as if perhaps Walter's voice would creep up from the grave and answer him. He half expected it to, and when he heard nothing, he was vaguely disappointed.

"I'm sorry for thinking that I could replace you," he tried again. "It was a silly notion. I suppose it's what I get for listening to those young men. They don't understand, really, what we had together. And I can't blame them. They haven't yet had it themselves."

He was talking quickly, letting his thoughts pour out. He'd been thinking about what he was going to say ever since he'd walked away from the library after making such a fool of himself. He owed Walter an apology, an explanation for his behavior. Now that he was standing there, giving it, he felt better.

"I'm an old man," he continued. "An old man who had the great fortune of sharing a life with someone he loved. That's enough for me. I've been selfish. But I miss you, Walter. Oh, how I miss you."

A tear slipped from his eye and fell to the snow. Simon sniffed, trying to prevent any further crying. It was too cold for crying. The moisture froze in the corners of his eyes, painful stabs of iciness that hurt when he blinked.

"You should have seen me," he told Walter, hoping that talking would prevent any additional weeping. "You would have laughed. I know you would have laughed. Didn't you always say that I could never tell one of our kind? Well, it seems you were right."

He looked around him. The cemetery, draped in white, was asleep, its dead nestled safe in their earthen beds. Someday, Simon knew, and perhaps not too many years off, he would join them. He looked at the plot beside Walter's. It was empty, bought at the same time and reserved for him. He remembered the day Walter had brought him the brochure and suggested it. How old had they been then? He counted back. They had been in their thirties. Death had seemed an impossibility, although both of them had already buried their parents and a number of friends.

Simon had laughed at Walter's morbidity, agreeing to purchase the plots in order to maintain peace in the house. He had drawn the line at choosing headstones, however, believing that it could only tempt fate. Walter, unusual for him, had acquiesced. It wasn't until Walter's death years later that Simon discovered that Walter had selected his stone in secret. At the time, Simon had been thankful rather than angry, relieved to have one less decision to make on his own.

He had not yet chosen his stone. Although he appreciated Walter's thoroughness in planning for his inevitable passing, he himself couldn't entertain thoughts of his own funeral. Looking at the blank plot of land beside Walter's grave, however, he couldn't help but feel a small sense of peace knowing that there was a place for him beside his lover. It was sentimental, he knew, but the knowledge that they would be together forever made the idea of dying slightly more bearable.

He knew too many couples who had been separated in death, first by the passing of one or the other, and then later by the family who cared little about the partner with whom the deceased had shared his life. He and Walter, at least, would be reunited in death. He had no belief that they would meet again, walking the world as ghostly lovers or existing as some kind of ectoplasmic energy. Dead was dead, and he was content to become fodder for whatever plant or insect life wished to use his decaying body for its purposes. But he would do it while lying next to the man who had captured his heart, with whom he'd spent the majority of his life.

As he stood, thinking these thoughts, a cardinal detached itself from a nearby branch and landed atop Walter's gravestone. Cocking its head, it looked with interest at Simon. Its black eyes sparkled and it ruffled its crimson feathers, fluffing itself up against the cold. Simon regarded the bird with interest. Cardinals had been Walter's favorites. He had often sat at the window watching them forage in the seed he scattered under the trees behind the house for them.

"What?" Simon said to the bird. "Are you supposed to be some kind of a sign? Because I don't believe in signs."

The bird tipped its head at him, but made no move to fly away. It rubbed its beak against the stone and shuffled from foot to foot. Simon crossed his arms over his chest.

"Walter, did you send this bird to me?" he asked. "If so, I think you've been badly influenced by your friends on the other side. Parlor tricks are beneath you."

The bird chirped loudly. Simon waved a hand at it, shooing it away. The bird ignored him.

"Walter, I'm cold," Simon said, half addressing the bird without meaning to. "I'm going to go home now, where I will sit in front of our fireplace with Clancy on my lap and grow old without any further attempts to be twenty-one again."

The cardinal leaped into the air, flapping its wings. It flew at Simon, who put his arm up to block the attack. But the bird flew by him, landing on a stone some way off. It continued to look at him.

"You are a bird," Simon said loudly. "A bird and nothing more. Go away."

The bird chirped.

"Please go away," Simon repeated. "Leave me in peace."

He stared at the cardinal, expecting it to leave. He was irritated, both by the bird's stubbornness and by his own inability to just turn and leave it there. He looked again at Walter's gravestone, a feeling of annoyance growing inside him.

"Fine," he said. "I'll play your game, but I don't believe for a minute that this bird has anything to do with you. I am simply humoring you, you old bastard."

He walked toward the cardinal. When he was a few feet from its resting spot, it took off again, flying to another stone. Resigned to his role as the pawn in whatever was occurring, Simon followed it. Each time he grew near, the bird continued on. It was leading him down the main road that ran through the cemetery, away from the parking lot where his car waited and deeper into the world of the dead.

He followed the bird as it flew around a bend in the road. The wind had picked up, and the snow was blowing against him. Even with his hands pushed deep into the pockets of his coat, he was chilled. He was too old to be out in weather such as this. He should, he knew, just turn around and walk as quickly as he could back to the car. There he could warm himself and forget about the foolish notions that had taken hold of him.

Growing angry, he decided to do exactly that, the bird be damned. He turned, determined to go, but found himself buffeted on all sides by the wind. It had picked up the snow and was twirling it around him, blinding him. He had no idea which direction he was facing; all was whiteness and cold. He put his hands up to his face, suddenly very afraid. He opened his mouth and cried out in fear.

The snow stopped. He felt the wind die away immediately, and he no longer felt the sting of the snow on his skin. The cold remained, but it was tolerable. He lowered his hands and looked around him, searching for the bird. It had gone.

"Hello, Simon."

He blinked. Standing not more than a dozen feet from him was a young man, a young man with familiar features. He was dressed in brown pants and a blue shirt. His features were strong, his eyes bright. He wore no coat.

"Walter?"

His lover was there. But it wasn't the Walter of those last days; it was the Walter of forty years ago, Walter the way he was when he and Simon had first met. Simon stared at his handsome, youthful face, not believing.

"Where's your coat?" he asked incongruously.

Walter laughed. "Look around you," he said.

Simon did. The snow had gone, and in its place summer reigned. The sun shone down from a clear sky, and all around him the grass was fresh and green. Daisies nodded their bright faces in the pleasant breeze that blew. The tombstones, too, were gone. He and Walter were standing instead in a spreading field that seemed to have no end.

"What happened to the snow?" Simon asked.

Again Walter laughed. "You know I was never one for the winter," he said as he walked toward Simon. "Summer was my time."

Simon regarded his lover with wonder and suspicion. Walter, stopping just in front of him, reached out and touched him. Simon flinched. Walter touched him again, this time leaving his hand on Simon's chest. Simon felt the pressure there, as real as the sun on his face and the scent of the grass.

"Walk with me," Walter said.

He took Simon's hand, his fingers curling around Simon's. They were warm, beating with blood. Simon held on to them tightly, afraid that if he let go, Walter would float away from him.

"The roses are beautiful," Walter said. "Thank you."

Simon said nothing. He didn't know how his lover had come to be with him, how the world had changed in the blink of an eye, but he wanted to do nothing that would end it.

"It's all right, Simon," Walter told him. "This is my world. Look at yourself."

Simon did as Walter told him. When he beheld his own figure, he was again shocked into stillness. Like Walter, he had grown young. His body was once more strong. He no longer felt the weight of age, the tiredness of his years. The skin of his hands was smooth, the hair on his arms dark. He felt his face and discovered there the softness of youth.

"This is how I remember us," said Walter. "Forever young. Do you remember how it was that summer, Simon? Do you remember what it was like to be two men in love?"

"I remember," Simon answered. "I remember looking at you and knowing that everything was all right with the world. I remember sleeping beside you and being afraid of nothing."

Walter smiled at him. "It was wonderful," he said. He looked into his lover's eyes. "I want you to have that again, Simon."

Simon's face fell as sadness filled his heart. He was looking into Walter's eyes, and in them he saw nothing but love. Yet what he was saying hurt Simon deeply.

"I can't," he said softly. "No."

Walter nodded. "You can," he said. "And you must. I want you to."

"I'm too old," Simon protested. "Too tired to start again."

"You're not," Walter insisted. "You have all the time in the world, even if it's only a day, a month, a year. Don't spend what you have left living with only my memory."

"I miss you," Simon said. "I miss you every day of my life."

"And I miss you," echoed Walter. "That will never change. But it's not a reason to stop living."

"I am living," Simon objected. "I have friends. I—"

"You need more than friends," said Walter.

Simon looked away from him. He knew Walter's words were supposed to comfort him, but they were tearing his heart to pieces.

"Why can't I stay with you?" he asked sadly.

Walter didn't answer. He merely looked at Simon with his great dark eyes. Simon, lost in them, realized suddenly that Walter was fading. His touch was becoming lighter, insubstantial. Simon grabbed at his hands.

"No!" he said plaintively.

Walter continued to diminish, his body growing less and less visible. Simon could see grass through his shirt, sky in the hole where his face had been. He was breaking up, the pieces swept away in the breeze.

Simon grabbed at the air around him, trying to resurrect Walter, to pull him back. His hands found nothing, though, and he was left twirling around, searching blindly for some remaining scrap of his lover. When his fingers found nothing, he buried his face in his hands.

"Are you okay, mister?"

Simon felt a pull on his sleeve. Looking through his fingers, he saw a little boy staring up at him.

"Are you lost?"

Simon lowered his hands. He was standing in the graveyard. Snow was falling. He patted himself. He was once again dressed in his coat. And he felt the heaviness of age once more in his bones.

The boy continued to look at him. Simon smiled at him. "I guess I am a little lost," he said.

"Walter?" A woman's voice echoed through the air. Simon looked up to see a young woman walking toward them. "Walter?" she called out again. "What are you doing?"

Simon turned, half expecting to see his lover standing behind them. But there was no one. He and the boy were alone.

"Walter," the woman said as she reached them. "Where did you run off to?"

"Nowhere," the boy said indignantly. "I was right here."

The woman looked up at Simon and gave him a small smile. "I'm sorry if he was bothering you," she said. "I was putting a wreath on my husband's grave. He must have wandered off."

"I didn't wander," Walter insisted. "I said I was right here."

Simon smiled at the young woman. "It's all right," he said. "Walter was helping me find my way, weren't you, Walter?"

"That's right," Walter said brightly. "I was helping him."

"I was visiting a loved one of my own," Simon explained to the woman. "I'm afraid I got a little bit turned around. I'm sorry about your husband."

The woman nodded. "It's been nearly two years," she said. "But the holidays are always hard."

"Yes," Simon agreed. "They are hard."

The woman looked up. "You have to go on, though, don't you," she said, not speaking directly to Simon. "You have to live your life."

"Can we go?"

Walter was tugging on his mother's hand impatiently.

Simon looked at the boy and his mother. "Thank you for your help, Walter," he said.

The boy nodded, his interest in Simon waning. His mother took his hand and the boy smiled broadly, having achieved his aim.

"Merry Christmas," the woman said to Simon.

"Merry Christmas to you too," replied Simon. It seemed an odd thing to say to someone he'd met in a graveyard, and he almost laughed at the absurdity of it. But the young woman didn't seem to notice the peculiarity of the moment.

Simon watched as Walter and his mother walked in the opposite direction from him. When they were out of sight, he turned and made his way back toward his car. He still wasn't certain what had happened to him there in the cemetery. He wasn't one to believe in ghosts or visions. Still, he'd experienced something. Whether it was a momentary delusion or something else, he wasn't sure.

But did it really matter? As he passed Walter's grave, he gave it a final look. If millions of people could believe that angels appeared to announce the birth of God's son to a virgin, what was one dead queen coming back for a few minutes to deliver a message to his lover? Thinking about it, he felt himself grow lighter. A warmth spread through him, banishing the cold. He began to sing.

"God rest ye merry gentlemen," he sang out to the surrounding graves.

Laughing at his little joke, he returned to the world of the living.

CHAPTER 30

The interior of Saint Peter's Church glowed with the light of numerous candles. The electric lights had been shut off for the evening, and the church was filled with a festive air as the children rushed to and fro, getting ready for the pageant. A handful of adults were there to keep them in line, but by and large their attempts at keeping the confusion to a minimum were unsuccessful.

Father Dunn stood at the rear of the church, silently praying that none of the scampering sheep and angels would tip over a candle and catch something on fire. The church was made primarily of stone, but there were draperies and pews and all manner of other things that could easily combust should an errant flame touch them. Still, despite his low-level worry, he was as enchanted by the beauty of the evening as everyone else.

Christmas Eve services always had their own special magic to them. This particular night the weather was lending a hand, contributing a light snowfall, just enough to be pretty but not enough to raise concerns about driving. The church was filled with people, many of whom Thomas had never seen before. The Once-a-Yearers, he and Joseph had called them, those who made an annual appearance, always at Christmas or Easter, never to be seen again. Thomas didn't care why they were there, though. He had much to be thankful for on this Christmas, the full pews being just one of them.

He looked out into the crowded parking lot, searching for a sign of Mike. He had promised he would come, and Thomas was looking forward to seeing him. But so far he hadn't come, and it was nearing time for the pageant to begin.

"Father, five minutes."

He turned to see the anxious face of Gavin Bettelheim looking at him, his brows knitted up in worry. He knew the music director's nerves were on edge, so when he spoke, he kept his voice low and soothing.

"I'll be ready, Gavin," he said. "And I saw your dress rehearsal this afternoon. It's going to be wonderful. Everything's going to be fine."

Gavin, reassured, brightened considerably. Clutching a roll of sheet music, he turned and hurried off in pursuit of some rogue choristers who had gone by, giggling into the sleeves of their robes.

"Are we on time?"

A figure stepped inside and Mike's face was lit up. Thomas, seeing him, resisted an urge to kiss him. Instead, he took Mike's hand and held it for a long moment. "You're right on time," he said.

"I brought some friends," Mike told him. "I hope that's okay."

Thomas was delighted to see that Simon, Russell, and John were coming up the steps behind Mike. Thomas greeted each of them warmly and ushered them inside.

"We're about to start," he said. "I'm afraid the back row is the only one with any room in it."

"That will be perfect," Simon whispered to Russell as they went in. "This way we can escape if it becomes too much to bear."

Thomas, too excited about having Mike there, failed to notice the lack of enthusiasm. After making sure his friends were situated, he strode up to the front of the church and ascended to the pulpit.

"Good evening," he said. The church grew silent as the murmurings stopped and everyone looked toward the front. "Welcome to Saint Peter's and our Christmas Eve service. Instead of our usual service, tonight we're presenting the children of Saint Peter's in a pageant celebrating the season."

Thomas nodded at Gavin, who was sitting in the first row. As Thomas stepped down and walked to the back of the church to take his seat beside Mike and the others, the music director stood up and walked over to stand in front of the assembled choir of young people. Dressed as angels, they wore white robes and had rings of golden tinsel on their heads. The youngest ones played with the hems of their costumes, looking out at the audience in search of their parents' faces.

Gavin held up his hands. When he brought them down again, the singers launched into "It Came Upon a Midnight Clear." At the same time, a group of fifth graders, dressed as shepherds, emerged from the darkness, herding in front of them several small children wearing sweatshirts glued all over with cotton balls. Seeing them, the audience laughed. One of the sheep bolted, making for her mother in the front row, but was stopped by a keen-eyed shepherd, who collared her and dragged her back into place.

The singers' voices faded out as one of the boys stepped from the back row and took center stage. "And an angel of the Lord appeared unto the shepherds keeping watch over their flocks by night," he said, his voice carrying throughout the church. "Unto you is born this night a savior, which is Christ the Lord."

The shepherds stared at the angel for a moment before filing off-stage. The angel chorus resumed singing as the shepherds were replaced by the three wise men, each dressed in an elaborate robe and long fake beard. One of them carried a telescope, through which he looked into the distance.

"And a star appeared unto them," a voice from the darkness informed the audience. "A sign that in the city of David a child had been born. And then did they set out upon a journey."

The wise men followed the shepherds into the darkness. In the last row, Simon leaned over. "I believe I smell a Tony," he said drolly.

Thomas, sitting beside Mike, reached over and took his hand. As Mike accepted it, Thomas felt a surge of joy fill him. Ever since telling Mike about himself, he'd been happier than he ever had been. The burden he'd been carrying around for so long had been lifted from him. He didn't know what road his life would take now, but he felt confident that everything would be all right. As he sat in the darkness of the church, listening to the greatest story of hope ever told, he understood how the shepherds and the wise men might have felt hearing the words of the angel of the Lord. He, too, had received wonderful news, and his heart resonated with the impact of the message.

At the front of the church a new scene was unfolding. Mary and Joseph, looking tired from their journey, arrived in Bethlehem, seeking shelter. The choir serenaded them with "Oh, Little Town of Bethlehem" as the invisible narrator told of their fruitless search for a room. When finally they found an innkeeper willing to give them space in his barn, the blue-robed Mary seemed genuinely relieved to sit down on the hay bales put there to represent the stable.

"And there, in a stable surrounded by horses, cows, and sheep, she gave birth to the Christ child and laid him in a manger."

"I can't wait to see this part," Mike whispered to Thomas, who stifled a laugh.

The birth was discretely handled, as Mary reached into her robes and removed a baby doll, which she placed in its makeshift bed as the congregation, unable to contain itself, applauded gently. Mary, blushing, bent down to attend to the newborn's needs.

A rustling behind them caused the five men to turn around. There, standing in the vestibule, were the shepherds and wise men. They peered into the sanctuary, awaiting their cue to enter. When it came, in the form of the angel choir's rendition of "Away in a Manger," the shepherds darted forward, filling the aisle between the pews with bleating sheep as they made the long pilgrimage through the church. They were followed in short order by the three wise men, who marched solemnly to their signature tune as they carried their gifts of gold, frankincense, and myrrh, which they laid around the manger as Joseph and Mary nodded appreciatively.

The entire nativity scene having been assembled, the tiniest angels enjoyed their moment in the spotlight, warbling "Silent Night" in various keys and tempos. When they were finished, Gavin turned to the congregation. "Will you now join the angel choir in singing some carols," he instructed them.

Thomas opened the program tucked into the hymnal rack in front of them and held it so that Mike could share it with him. As the first notes of "O Come, O Come, Emmanuel" began, he listened to Mike's voice, a deep, rich sound that melted into his own. On Mike's other side, John, Russell, and Simon formed a trio, their voices fainter but no less important to Thomas. Surrounded by his friends, he looked toward the nativity scene and was almost overcome by the emotions running through him.

He wished Joseph could see him now, see how far he'd come since those days when the very thought of revealing himself to anyone filled him with terror and shame. How had he ever convinced himself that God, in his infinite capacity to love, would turn away from him for reflecting that same ability? How had he not seen, as Joseph had even in his sickness, that to truly serve God he was obligated to welcome life in all its complexity, all of its contradictions?

Now, viewing a children's pageant, he realized the truth. God could not be contained within the teachings of any church, was not waiting to sit in judgment of him. He had been judging himself based on false assumptions, on what he feared others might find wanting in himself, and in the process he had failed in his duty to the one he professed to serve. But no more. Whatever it brought, he was going to live as the man he was. The thought thrilled him, and as he sang, his voice rose up in joy.

Gavin led them in several more carols. Throughout the singing, Thomas held on to Mike's hand, not wanting to let go. But as the final words of "O, Holy Night" faded away, he let go. "I'm on," he told Mike as he stood and walked to the front of the church.

He looked out at the people seated before him. A serenity had settled over the church, a peace and warmth that radiated from the faces looking back at him. In the last row, Mike, Simon, John, and Russell were watching him.

"As our children have shown us tonight, the message of Christ's birth is one of love and wonder," he said. "Hold this message in your hearts as you celebrate the season. Thank you for joining us tonight. As our angel choir sings for us one more time, please join us in the hall for refreshments. May the peace of the Lord and the blessing of the Spirit be with you and yours."

The congregation gathered itself up as the older angels dutifully followed Gavin's direction of the much-debated Brahms piece. Thomas, giving them an appreciative nod, descended into the mass of people making their way to the adjacent hall. He was stopped several times by those wishing to give him holiday greetings, but eventually he made it back to Mike and the others.

"I guess we'll go," Mike said. "We'll see you later at Simon's, though, right?"

"Go?" Thomas asked. "Why?"

Mike looked at the people streaming past them. "You know," he said. "It's not like we belong here."

"Yes, you do," said Thomas firmly. "Now get in there and eat some cookies."

Mike looked back at John, Russell, and Simon for their reaction.

"I, for one, would love some eggnog," said Simon.

"Cookies sound great," Russell seconded.

"I guess we're staying," Mike told Thomas.

"I'll see you in there in a minute," Thomas said happily. "I have some priest stuff to do."

Thomas disappeared into the sea of departing figures, leaving them to find their way into the hall. Mike followed the crowd, and moments later the men found themselves standing beside a table heaped high with cookies, fudge, and candy. They each got a glass of punch and a small plate of goodies and stood to one side, munching and observing the people around them.

"Do you think they know we're from the dark side?" Simon asked.

"What makes you think some of them aren't queer?" Russell said.

"Can you say 'queer' in a church?" joked Mike as he nibbled on a cookie.

"You can, and I'm sure some of them are," John announced firmly.

The others looked at him in surprise.

"What?" he said as he popped a piece of fudge into his mouth. "They're *Episcopal,* for Christ's sake. The entire church owes its existence to the fact that Henry the Eighth wanted a divorce so he could marry Anne Boleyn and the Pope wouldn't give it to him. They're practically founded on deviance."

"While not entirely true, that's essentially correct," Simon opined. "Although 'deviance' is perhaps not the word I would use."

"What would you say?" Russell asked him.

"I prefer 'openness,' " Simon answered. "Both in mind and in sexuality. It is true that gays are quite prominent in the church now, although not everyone is happy about it."

"There's a shock," remarked John. "Religious people not liking us."

"Spoken like a true scientist," Simon said, patting him on the back.

Before they could continue the conversation, they were confronted by a beaming woman dressed from head to toe in red. She carried a plate of cookies, and she smiled at them broadly. "I don't believe I've seen you here before," she said.

"It's our first time," Mike told her.

"Well, welcome to Saint Peter's," the woman said. "I'm Beth-Ann Milliman. I'm in charge of the deaconesses."

"It's nice to meet you," said Mike.

"Are you here alone, or are your wives with you?" Beth-Ann inquired.

Mike looked at his friends for help. Simon stepped forward and smiled at Beth-Ann. "I'm afraid we're all single gentlemen," he said.

"Not all of us," John said.

Simon gave a small smile. "That's right," he said. "I forgot. Mr. Harding and Mr. Ellison are companions."

Beth-Ann looked at John and Russell with a perplexed look, not comprehending. "You're friends?" she said.

"That's right," Russell replied. "Special friends."

"Well, we're happy to have you here," Beth-Ann said after a moment. "I hope we'll see you again."

"Oh, I think you just might," Simon said. "We're quite taken with your pastor."

Before Beth-Ann could respond to the remark, Thomas appeared.

"Father Dunn," Beth-Ann said, sounding relieved. "We were just talking about you. These gentlemen—"

"Could you excuse us for a moment, Beth-Ann?" Thomas said, taking Mike's arm and pulling him away.

"What's going on?" Mike asked when they were away from the crowd. "You look like you've seen a ghost."

"I just spoke with one of our members who knows the Darby family," Thomas said.

"Stephen?" Russell said. "I've been calling him all week, but he never answers."

"He's in the hospital," Thomas said.

"Is he all right?" asked Russell.

Thomas shook his head. "He's alive," he said, "but he's not all right. He overdosed on pain pills."

"What?" Russell said. "Why would he do that?"

"I don't know," said Thomas. "It was probably accidental. But it sounds like he's pretty badly off."

"We have to go see him," Russell said. "Right now."

"We can't," Thomas told him. "He can't have visitors. Not until tomorrow."

Russell looked at the plate in his hand. "What a way to spend Christmas," he said sadly. "Poor guy."

"I'm sure he'll be fine," John said, putting his arm around Russell and pulling him close.

"This sort of puts a damper on things, doesn't it?" Mike said softly.

"It's still Christmas Eve," Thomas reminded him. "And we're all still together."

"That's true," said Simon cheerily. "And tomorrow we will all have Christmas dinner together. As a *family,*" he added, stressing the last word.

Thomas looked around the room. "I should go mingle," he said. He turned to Mike. "See you later?"

"Come over when you're done here," Mike told him. "We'll wait up for Santa."

"I'll see you boys tomorrow," Thomas said to the others. "Merry Christmas."

When Thomas was gone, Mike put his plate and cup on the table. "Shall we?" he asked.

They left the hall and went out into the night. The snow was still falling, and over the church the moon shone pale and round against the sky.

"All is calm, all is bright, indeed," Simon said as they walked to their cars and prepared to head for home.

CHAPTER 31

"And may all your Christmases be bright."

Pete stared dully at the television. On the screen some teenage pop singer he didn't recognize was singing. Dressed in a white fur coat, she stood surrounded by dancers dressed as carolers. Fake snow tumbled from somewhere above her, littering the stage. The girl beamed, flashing impossibly white teeth.

"Fuck you, bitch," Pete said. He changed the channel. An animated Rudolph pranced across the screen, his nose glowing red. Pete banished him with another press of the remote button, replacing the reindeer with a talking snowman. He ran quickly through some of the other channels. Even goddamned MTV was showing Christmas videos.

He threw the remote down in disgust and reached for the bottle on the table. Pouring a healthy shot of Jack Daniels into the glass in his hand, he drank deeply. The whiskey burned his throat, but after a quarter of a bottle he was used to it. Besides, whiskey was the quickest way to get into a festive fucking mood, wasn't it?

He'd just had Christmas Eve dinner at his mother's house, putting up with her annoying cheerfulness. She'd made too much food, as usual, and the neighbors who stopped by had barely put a dent in it. Pete had stayed as long as necessary, promising to come back in the morning to open presents, then headed home to escape the merriment.

His buddies were all with their own families, doing whatever it was they did to celebrate the holiday. Pete wished it was all over, so life could return to normal. The last couple of weeks had been totally fucked up, what with having to shop for presents for his mother and endure the craziness that came with the holiday season. He couldn't wait for New Year's. Then they'd have a real party. It was going to be at his place this year, and he had plans.

But New Year's was a week away, and right now he had nothing to do but drink and wait for it all to end. There weren't any good movies on. Christ, he thought, he might as well turn the TV off and go to bed. But he wasn't tired. He was just bored. There had to be something to do, some way to amuse himself.

He thought about putting in a porn tape. But ever since the night T.J. had stayed over, he'd been unable to get off from looking at porn. Whenever he tried, he remembered what had happened and felt sick to his stomach. Nothing had happened, he corrected himself, as he had been all week. Nothing. He'd dreamed it all. If anything *had* happened, it would mean he was something he most definitely was not. Only someone like that could do the things he'd dreamed he'd done to T.J. that night.

Then why was T.J. acting all weird, he asked himself. Why hadn't T.J. called or stopped by? Why had he hurried out the next morning when they'd woken up, saying he had to get home to do something? Why hadn't he looked Pete in the eye when he'd said goodbye?

It was nothing, Pete told himself. T.J. had just been in a hurry. And he'd been busy. He'd come around again soon enough. He'd be there for the New Year's party, along with Gary, Ronnie, and everyone else he was inviting. They'd all be there, and they'd have an amazing fucking time. He wouldn't think about that night ever again.

Maybe, he thought, he'd invite the girl he'd been introduced to at the bar the other night, the one who'd looked like she wanted him to do her right there on the table. What was her name? Carolyn. That was it. Carolyn. Pretty face. Nice tits. He'd thought about fucking her, taking her out to his car and screwing her in the backseat. Maybe he'd give it to her good on New Year's, ring in the year with a good hard bang.

He drained his glass and refilled it. He was feeling better. The bullshit he'd been thinking about T.J. wasn't anything to worry about. It was just something he'd imagined, that was all. A really bad fucking dream. He hadn't actually put his mouth on another guy's tool. Only queers did that shit.

He wouldn't mind having a mouth on *his* dick, though, he thought.

He hadn't had his cock sucked in a long time. Not since the faggot at the rest stop. He could use a good blowjob. It would relax him. He'd be able to sleep.

But where would he find someone to blow him on Christmas Eve? Nobody was going to be hanging out in a men's room or a truck stop looking for cock tonight. They'd all be home, even the faggots. They had to take a break sometime, he guessed. They couldn't spend every night on their knees.

He laughed at the image in his mind, a queer on his knees sucking off Santa Claus. It was funny. He pictured Santa's big hairy belly hanging out while some fag pulled on his dick. "You want Santa to come down your chimney?" he imagined old Nick saying.

He stood up, his head swimming a little. Maybe he could find some action after all. Maybe there were some desperate homos sitting around with nothing better to do than give his prong a wash. Taking the bottle of Jack with him, he went into his bedroom and to the computer that sat on his makeshift desk. He'd bought it to play video games and burn CDs on, but he'd discovered it had other uses as well. He sat in front of it and signed on to his online service.

He'd discovered the chat rooms accidentally while poking around his Internet service. He'd been surprised to see rooms with names like BiM4M and M4MJONow. The first time he'd entered such a room, nothing had been going on. It wasn't until a little window appeared on his screen and someone asked him if he wanted to get off that he'd understood. Even then, it had taken some time for him to really get into the game. He'd spent a long time just sitting in rooms, looking at the profiles of other users, waiting for people to approach him.

Finally he'd made up his own profile. It was largely the truth, with a few important details changed. And it seemed to work. Guys liked him. They sent him pictures of themselves, faceless images of them with their hard cocks in their hands. He never sent one back, but it didn't seem to matter. They never turned him down. They always did what he asked them to.

He usually limited himself to rooms with generic titles: M4MJocks, MilitaryM4M, StrtM4JO. But lately he'd been looking at other rooms, ones where men met to meet in real life. He'd never ventured into one, afraid of identifying himself geographically. More and more often, though, he'd found himself wondering what he might find in

M4MUpstateNY. Would there be anyone from Cold Falls, anyone near enough to actually come over and drain his balls or, better, let him come to him? He found the idea exciting, but also terrifying. What if he should encounter someone he knew? Someone like T.J.?

That would never happen, of course. T.J. was no more queer than he was. Still, he'd been cautious. Fucking around with people he couldn't see was one thing; meeting them in the flesh was different. But he couldn't deny the attraction of it. He'd had some hot times with his electronic buddies, with one in particular. He wondered idly what had happened to the guy. What had his name been? Pound-something? Cake? It had struck Pete as a stupid name. But the guy had been into anything. They'd fooled around a couple of times.

Maybe he'd run into pound cake tonight, but he doubted it. Even if he did, he wasn't interested in online play. Having accepted the idea, he now had his heart set on real live action. That is, if he could find any. He still had his doubts that there would be anyone within a two-hour drive of Cold Falls.

He found the list of rooms and searched for M4MUpstateNY. There it was. According to the listing, there were twenty-three people in it. Jesus Christ, didn't faggots take a break even on Christmas? He logged himself in and looked at the list of members. The names were all new to him. Apparently none of them ever ventured into the rooms he frequented.

He clicked on a couple of profiles that sounded promising, but rejected them for one reason or another. Finally, toward the bottom of the list, he came across one that caught his eye: CldFllsGy. Selecting it, he read the details. The man indeed claimed to be from Cold Falls. The rest was immaterial. Pete opened an instant message box and typed a query: Looking for some fun?

He waited impatiently for a response. In his experience, if people didn't reply quickly, they were busy with someone else. He had no interest in reeling someone in; he wanted a hungry one. When a window popped open, he raised a fist in triumph.

CldFllsGy: What's up?

Pete continued the direct approach with his reply: My cock. Want 2 suck it?

He poured himself some more Jack and downed it. His foot tapped against the floor impatiently. What the fuck was taking so long? Either the fag was interested or he wasn't. A ding broke the silence as the answer came back: Pic?

"Fuck a pic!" Pete muttered. He wrote back: No. Got 8 thick and cut. Big balls.

It took very little time for CldFllsGy to get back to him. Where R U? he asked.

Pete knew he had him. They always went for the big cock. And in his case, he wasn't lying. He felt his dick stiffen as he wrote back to his quarry: Cold Falls 2.

It was a risk, he knew. Cold Falls wasn't that big a place, and although it was unlikely, it was possible he was talking to someone who would recognize him. But now he was anxious to have his dick sucked. Besides, he wasn't the one looking to be the cocksucker. He wasn't the fag here. He had nothing to be ashamed of.

CldFllsGy: Come to my place?

A few more exchanges later and Pete had the address. He told CldFllsGy he'd be there in fifteen minutes and grabbed his jacket. He knew he probably shouldn't be driving, but it wasn't far, and he'd be careful.

Right on time, he pulled into the driveway of the house whose address he'd scrawled on the scrap of paper. Decorated with Christmas lights, it looked like all the other houses on the street. But unless someone was fucking with him, waiting inside was a queer who was going to do exactly what Pete told him to do.

He got out and walked to the door. He rang the bell and waited. A few moments later the door opened and he found himself looking at a guy not much older than he was. He was dressed in jeans and a T-shirt.

"I'm Greg," he said. "Come on in."

Pete stepped inside and the queer shut the door. The house was nice, nicer than Pete's. It looked like the fag made some money. The furniture was new and it all looked kind of expensive. From somewhere the sound of a woman singing a Christmas song floated into the foyer. Pete noticed that Greg wasn't wearing shoes, probably so he wouldn't track anything onto the clean floors. Fuck him. Pete wasn't about to take his boots off for any faggot.

"Quite a way to spend Christmas Eve, huh?" Greg said. He was just standing there, looking Pete up and down. It made Pete sick to see the queer sizing him up. He was lucky Pete was going to let him suck him off.

"Just another night," Pete said surlily.

"Yeah," Greg answered. "I guess it is. So, you want a drink?"

"No," Pete said. "Let's get to it."

Greg nodded. "Whatever you want," he said. His words seemed a little dulled, and Pete noticed for the first time a mostly empty bottle of vodka on the coffee table. Apparently he wasn't the only one who'd been drinking.

Greg walked into the living room and Pete followed him. Greg motioned to a leather armchair. "Make yourself comfortable," he said. "Do you mind if I leave Barbra on? She kind of sets a mood, you know?"

"Whatever," Pete said. He assumed the fag was talking about the crappy music that was playing. He didn't care if it stayed on or not. He undid his belt buckle and pushed his jeans down. His cock sprang free and stood out from his crotch. He saw Greg eye it greedily. *That's right,* Pete thought. *And you're going to take it all.*

He sat down in the chair, spreading his legs. He grabbed his dick and stroked it a few times, giving Greg a good view. The queer came over and stood in front of him, looking down. What the fuck was he waiting for?

"Suck it," Pete said.

Greg lowered himself to his knees. Looking into his face, Pete realized that he was drunker than he'd seemed at first. He knelt there, swaying slightly as he stared at the cock in front of his face.

Pete grabbed him by the hair and pulled him down. His dick hit Greg in the face and he opened his mouth, clumsily putting the head of Pete's dick between his lips. When he slid forward, his teeth scraped the sides of Pete's cock.

"Jesus Christ!" Pete said. "Watch it!"

Greg looked up at him, the head of Pete's cock still between his lips. He seemed unable to move. Then he started to cry. He let Pete's dick slip from his mouth and sat back on his heels, bawling like a little kid.

"What the fuck is wrong with you?" Pete asked, growing angry.

Greg shook his head. "Just go," he blubbered. "Go."

"Not until you blow me," Pete said.

"Get out," Greg said, his voice rising. "I don't want you here."

Pete grabbed the queer by the neck and pulled him back toward him. He tried to shove his cock in the man's mouth. "Suck it!" he yelled. "Suck my fucking cock!"

Greg pushed against him, forcing himself away. He sprawled on the floor. "I was supposed to be home," he said quietly. "For Christmas. Then my father called and said he didn't want me there. He didn't want his faggot son to come home." He looked up at Pete with drunken eyes. "I just wanted to be with someone tonight," he said. "That's all. I didn't want to be alone."

"Fuck you," Pete said. He didn't care what the fag wanted, or why he was home alone on Christmas Eve. This wasn't about him. It was about what Pete wanted. He stood up and advanced toward Greg. If the faggot wouldn't suck him off voluntarily, he was going to get what he wanted by force.

He grabbed Greg by the shirt, holding him in place. With his other hand, he whipped the queer's face with his cock, smacking him in the mouth.

"Suck it, faggot," he ordered. "Suck it now."

Greg pushed him away. Pete, enraged, brought his fist down against Greg's face. He heard the queer cry out as his nose crunched. He was just like the cocksucker at the theater, too weak to fight back. Pete hit him again.

He continued to hit, bringing his fist down again and again. At first Greg made an attempt to protect his face, but after a minute he went limp. Blood dripped from his face onto the floor. Seeing it, Pete let the man go and he slumped to the floor. Pete kicked him in the stomach.

"Get up!" he screamed. "Get your faggot ass up!"

Greg didn't move. Pete kicked him again. He felt something snap. Why wasn't the faggot trying to protect himself? Why was he letting Pete beat the shit out of him?

Because it's what he wants, a voice said. *It's what he wants you to do to him.*

Pete knew it was true. All the queers who'd ever sucked him off, that's what they'd wanted, wasn't it? The fag at the theater, the one at the truck stop. They all wanted him to use them. Well, he'd give this one what he wanted.

He continued to kick Greg, watching the blood spatter and enjoying the soft thuds his boot made against the queer's chest. Finally, his anger drained enough that he saw how much blood there was, he stopped. Through the foggy haze that enveloped him, he saw that he had to leave. He'd done what he'd needed to, and the fag had gotten what he wanted. Their meeting was over.

He left Greg on the floor and walked to his car. Turning the radio up, he put the car into gear and pulled away, leaving the front door open. From inside the house, Barbra Streisand wished the world peace on earth.

CHAPTER 32

At eleven o'clock on Christmas Day, Mike Monaghan unlocked the back door of the Engine Room and stepped inside. Flipping a switch, he brought to life the garlands of twinkling lights that had been strung throughout the bar's main room. Another flip of another switch turned on the bar's sound system, and holiday music filled the air. Mike, standing in the middle of the bar and looking around, had never felt more depressed.

He had been woken up shortly after five by a kiss on the cheek from Thomas, who had spent the night. Rubbing the dreams from his eyes, he'd managed a mumbled "Merry Christmas" as Thomas had dressed and prepared to go to church, where he was presiding over a morning service. Mike, watching him dress, had wished the two of them could spend the morning together. But each had the needs of their followers to attend to, and so they had parted.

Mike had slept awhile longer, enjoying the warmth of the bed and the memory of Thomas's body lying next to his. They'd yet to make love, or even to be naked with one another. But twice they'd shared a bed, sleeping with arms around one another, one's back pressed against the other's stomach. Mike was certain that at some point during their nightly cycles of dreaming, during the shifting of positions that occurred in the deepest stages of sleep, erect cocks had undoubtedly butted against unsuspecting bodies, fingers had unconsciously fallen upon and stroked exposed skin, but for all practical purposes their relationship was as yet unconsummated.

Without ever having discussed it, they were waiting. For what or when, exactly, Mike wasn't sure. He knew only that the time had not yet come. Until it did, he and Thomas were exploring one another, talking and questioning and finding in one another something that delighted them equally. They were like children who, distanced from the world around them by illness, or difference, or the watchful eye of a nervous parent, had spent long hours staring from a bedroom window, watching others at play and longing for a special playmate. Now, having discovered one another, they were caught up in the innocent joy of discovery.

With the realization that he was falling in love with Thomas had come, however, a reawakening of a fear Mike had tried to bury. Along with the excitement of finding someone with whom he felt comfortable had come a flicker of doubt, a tiny nagging worry that it would never last. He had tried to ignore the feeling, but it had been persistent, returning again and again despite his best efforts to push it away. Nothing lasted forever. The freshest emotions would eventually sour. Even the most solid of foundations hid fault lines that, once disturbed, would result in crumbling. It had happened to him before, first with his family and then with Jim. He was not someone who was destined for happiness.

When he was with Thomas, he was able to pretend that the enchantment would last, that the golden light that seemed to surround them at all times would never succumb to the shadows of doubt. But when he was alone, his strength waned, and the demons of worry pounced upon him, pinching at him mercilessly and whispering to him of failure. There was no reason to believe, they said, that things would be different this time. Why should they be?

Because Thomas was different, he argued. Because he was kind, and because he wasn't demanding anything. True, the demons countered in their ugly, hypnotic voices, but there were also many things standing in the way, not the least of which was Almighty God. How, they asked, did Mike think he would be able to stand up to such competition? And even if he should win that battle, how would he fill the hole left in Thomas's heart afterward?

They were right, of course. He knew that. Even if he and Thomas did fall in love, where would it lead them? Would Thomas forsake his church for a man he loved? Would he turn his entire world upside down to pursue a life he'd never even let himself imagine, to become someone he freely admitted he'd always been terrified of?

"You had to go and fall for a priest," Mike said out loud to the empty room. "You couldn't settle for a drunk or a tweaker; you had to find one who's addicted to God. There's no twelve-step program for that."

He walked behind the bar and looked around. The Christmas lights were reflected in the glass of the bottles, tiny, bright stars of color shining against a clear vodka sky. The whiskey glowed warmly, promising forgetfulness. The glasses, lined up like soldiers awaiting deployment, gaped at him with open mouths.

In less than an hour the bar would begin to fill with men seeking solace from the events of the morning. Either having no family or having too much family, they would come in from the cold, leaving outside the memories of strained holiday rituals. With bottles of beer and glasses clinking with the sounds of swirling ice cubes, they would rid themselves of the ghosts of Christmases past and present, until everything around them blurred and the interiors of their heads filled with dizzying warmth. And Mike, like some kind of modern-day Marley, would aid them on their journeys with the tip of a bottle, the squeeze of a lime. Standing behind the bar, he would watch the spectacle play out as it did after every holiday, the participants gamely waltzing through the familiar moves. Sugarplum fairies, indeed.

He couldn't do it. Not again. He was tired of the same old show, weary of the unhappiness and the forced camaraderie he helped perpetuate. Yes, some of the men who came to the Engine Room were his friends. Some of them he cared about, and some cared about him. But by and large the men who gathered there were strangers to one another. They knew, sometimes, one another's names, perhaps a few small details about each other's lives. Just enough to convince them that they were friends.

But that was all. Seldom did their curiosity about one another extend any further than finding out more, unless perhaps it was to seek out the answers to questions answered in the bedroom: How big was he? Did he give it or take it? What secret desires did he have? These things they might display some interest in knowing, might even spend some time and effort into researching, but once they had their answers, the spotlight of their curiosity quickly panned to another face, another crotch, another distraction.

None of them were looking for anything real. They might tell themselves they were, but they lied. Mike had seen enough during his years in various bars to know that ultimately they were simply prisons, cells in which condemned men waiting to die spent their time. Oh, they always hoped for a pardon, for someone to come along and release them from whatever held them there. And sometimes, briefly, they were granted a reprieve. But almost always they came back after a time, looking even wearier than they had before they left. Over time they grew accustomed to their fate, until finally, accepting it, their faces acquired a resignedness that masqueraded as contentment.

Mike looked in the mirror behind the bar. Unblinking, he examined his face closely. Had it changed? Had the years yet taken their toll? It was the eyes that told the story. In the beginning they shined brightly, darting here and there like rabbits crossing a field as they tried to take in everything at once. Gradually they slowed and grew dull as the field of vision narrowed, as the spirit that lit them up from within was drained, until finally they looked out at the world as dull, dirtied windows clouded over with the grime of disappointment.

Did he have eyes like that? He leaned forward and looked closely. No, he hadn't yet come to that point. He was simply tired. Despite the rest he found with Thomas in his bed, his face bore the marks of sleeplessness. He was growing older. The Engine Room, its patrons, were slowly draining him of his soul. How long until it was gone completely? A week? A month? A year?

It wasn't their fault. He understood that. They needed the bar, and the bar needed them. And it wasn't all bad. There was happiness contained in the walls, a sense of place and belonging that kept everything from falling in on itself. But the balance was delicate, and more and more he felt himself tipping the wrong way. He'd been there too long, spent too many hours among the lost and the directionless.

"How about a shot of Christmas cheer?"

Mike turned and saw his first customer of the day. Ernie Cheddum. Ernie walked to the bar and sat down, undoing his coat. Underneath he wore an unflattering burgundy sweater patterned all over with white snowflakes.

"From my mother," he said, noticing Mike looking at the sweater. "I wear it home from her house and then never put it on again."

Mike continued to stare at Ernie's sweater. The snowflakes had begun to move, swirling around and around in front of his eyes, becoming a blinding storm. Through the falling flakes he saw Ernie looking at him with sad eyes.

"It's not *that* ugly," he said. "Now how about that shot?"

Mike reached for a bottle of scotch and set it on the counter in front of Ernie. "It's on the house," he said as he walked from behind the bar and toward the front door.

"Thanks," said Ernie as he poured himself a glass. "Where are you going?"

"Dale will be in in fifteen minutes," Mike said. "Tell him I took the day off."

Ernie watched, confused, as Mike rushed out the door. Climbing into his truck, he started it and pulled out of the parking lot, fishtailing as the truck's rear tires skidded on the ice. Driving as quickly as he could on the slick road, he raced toward Saint Peter's. When he arrived, he pulled up in front of the rectory, got out, and walked to the door. Not bothering to knock, he went inside.

"Thomas?" he called out as he went from room to room.

"Up here."

He heard Thomas's voice, puzzled, calling to him from the house's second story. Bounding up the stairs, he discovered the priest in his bedroom.

"What's wrong?" Thomas asked. "I was just getting ready to go over to Simon's."

Mike stood in the doorway, staring at Thomas. He had apparently just stepped out of the shower. A white towel was wrapped around his waist, and his torso was bare. His hair, still damp, was playfully unkempt. Suddenly Mike recalled one of his early fantasies about Thomas: Thomas getting out of the shower, his hair wet, just as it was now.

"Tell me it will be okay," he said.

Thomas looked at him. "What will be okay?" he asked.

"Me," Mike said. "You. This. Us. Everything. Tell me it won't all fall apart."

Thomas bit his lip, thinking. He regarded Mike for what seemed like far too long. "It will be okay," he said.

Mike shook his head. "Not good enough," he said. "You don't sound convinced."

Thomas crossed his arms over his chest and leaned against the door frame. "I can't promise," he said. "Nobody can. All I can tell you is that I want it to be okay."

"But how do you know?" asked Mike. "How do you know we won't wake up one morning and it will all be over?" He looked at Thomas, feeling his heart struggling not to break. "I'm tired of running," he said.

Thomas stepped forward and held out his arms. "Then come home," he said.

Mike went to him. Thomas's arms closed around him, pulling him close. Mike smelled soap and honey.

"I don't know what's going to happen," Thomas whispered softly. "I've been running too, and I don't know what happens when you finally stand still. Maybe everything you've been running from comes crashing into you. Maybe you fall down and have to get back up again. I don't know. But whatever it is, we'll find out together."

Mike leaned back and looked into his eyes. They were bright, unclouded. Thomas smiled at him. "What?"

"You're so beautiful," Mike said.

He leaned in and kissed Thomas. This time, he didn't pull away when he was done. Instead, he kissed Thomas again, more deeply. His hands went to the towel and pulled it free. It fell to the floor, and for the first time his hands touched the smooth globes of Thomas's bare ass. His fingers ran over warm skin as he pressed himself against Thomas and felt naked muscle meet him.

They moved toward the bed, neither breaking contact. Thomas tugged Mike's shirt from his jeans and helped him pull it over his head. Shoes, socks, and pants followed, until both were undressed. Then they were on the bed, Thomas on his back and Mike atop him, their bodies sliding against each other.

Mike, a veteran of numerous encounters with different men, now felt as if he'd never touched another man before. Thomas, who hadn't, felt each finger, each kiss, each pressing of flesh against flesh, with breathtaking intensity. When his hands, wandering over Mike's body, followed the line of hair down his belly and felt for the first time the thickness of his cock, the heaviness of his balls against his palm, his mouth opened in a cry of delight.

His reaction was repeated moments later when Mike, lowering

himself between Thomas's thighs, took Thomas's dick into his mouth. He was surrounded by warmth as Mike slid up and down the length of him, tugging at the head of his cock, toying with his balls. When Mike wet a finger and slid it up inside him, Thomas clutched the sheets beneath him.

Mike continued to work Thomas's cock with his mouth as he gently eased him open. Thomas, his head spinning with each new sensation, anticipated what was coming and welcomed Mike's fingers. When they retreated and Mike positioned himself, pushing Thomas's knees back slightly, Thomas held his breath, waiting.

Mike went slowly, proceeding only when Thomas was ready. With only the moisture of his own mouth to ease his entry, he knew he had to take it easy. But his desire for Thomas made it difficult, and when finally his stomach pressed against the cheeks of Thomas's ass and he knew he could go no farther, he began to move in and out with more speed. Beneath him, Thomas breathed heavily, not in pain but with excitement. Mike, looking into his face, saw there an expression of rapture.

Thomas's legs went around Mike's waist, pulling him deeper. Feeling himself enveloped by Thomas's thighs, Mike leaned down, kissing him while continuing to pump his hips. Thomas's tongue met his, probing, and Mike felt the hardness of Thomas's cock as it was sandwiched between them.

When he felt himself getting close, he leaned back and pulled out. Holding his dick against Thomas's, he jerked them both the rest of the way. With his balls slapping against Thomas's he came, crying out as a thick jet of cum shot from his swollen head and rained down on Thomas's chest. Thomas was right behind him, his cock pulsing repeatedly as he emptied himself along the length of Mike's dick. Sticky wet heat slathered Mike's fingers and he continued his strokes, their combined loads slicking their still-hard shafts.

Mike continued to hold Thomas against him as they softened, not wanting to let go. Bending down, he stretched himself along the length of Thomas's body, the cum on their bodies cementing them together. Bound like this, they kissed for a long time as the glow of orgasm wrapped them in its cocoon. When they finally parted, Mike rolling over to lie beside Thomas, it was with contented sighs. They remained like that for a long time, holding hands and lost in their thoughts. After a few minutes Thomas rolled onto his side and peered down at Mike.

"Well?" Mike said. "Was it worth waiting for?"

Thomas grinned. "Oh, yeah," he said. "I just have one question?"

Mike raised his eyebrows, waiting.

"Is it as much fun being on top?"

"Why?" Mike asked suspiciously.

Thomas took Mike's hand and guided it down between his legs, where his cock was beginning to swell to life again. "Because I'd really like to find out," Thomas said as he lowered his head toward Mike's crotch.

CHAPTER 33

"What have you two been up to?"

Mike and Thomas exchanged a glance then looked at Simon. He was standing in the doorway of his house, while they waited on the front step, holding a green bean casserole and several bottles of wine. Neither of them answered the question.

"Well?" Simon said, crossing his arms over his chest.

"It's freezing out here," said Mike. "Let us in."

Simon shook his head. "Not until you tell me what's been going on."

"What makes you think we've been up to anything?" Mike asked.

"Please," replied Simon. "You're redder than Rudolph's nose, and this one has a grin on his face a mile wide. You've been very bad little boys, haven't you?"

"Will there be coal in our stockings?" Thomas asked.

"I think your stockings have been filled with much more interesting things," Simon answered primly. "Now get inside before I catch my death of pneumonia."

Thomas and Mike hurried in, where they were greeted by Russell, who hugged them both and said, "You're late. What happened, couldn't get out of bed?"

"Why does everyone think we were doing something?" Thomas asked, trying to sound irritated and doing a very poor job of it.

"You *were* in bed!" Russell exclaimed as John emerged from the kitchen.

"Where's Greg?" Mike asked as he handed Simon the wine and took his coat off. "I hear he decided to stay here after all. How come?"

"He's not here yet," Russell told him, "and don't try to change the subject."

"There is no subject to change," said Mike.

"Like hell there isn't," protested Russell. "So, are you two officially an item now? Won't you get burned at the stake or something?" he added, addressing Thomas. "I mean, isn't it illegal for priests to be queer?"

"There are people in the church who aren't wild about the idea of gay priests, true," Thomas said, taking a seat on the couch.

"That's the understatement of the year," remarked Simon as he returned with wineglasses and one of the bottles Mike and Thomas had brought over. "Look what happened in New Hampshire when Robinson was made a bishop. You'd have thought a serial killer had been installed at Canterbury."

"What is the official position on the subject?" asked John, taking a seat across from Thomas.

Thomas sighed. "The Episcopal Church recognizes that God's children come in many different forms," he said as he took a sip of wine.

"Seriously," Mike said, "what do they have to say about it?"

Thomas held his glass in his hand, staring down at it. "That depends on who you ask," he said. "Different parishes have different views."

"But there must be *some* official opinion," Russell pressed.

Thomas gave a small laugh. "Officially, we welcome everyone," he said. "Unofficially, we would prefer that our priests not talk about what they may or may not do in the privacy of their bedrooms."

"Don't ask, don't tell," John summarized.

"Something like that," said Thomas. "Bishop Robinson's consecration caused a stir primarily because he lives openly as a gay man with his partner."

"And if he stayed in the closet?" asked Mike.

Thomas shrugged. "Who knows? Maybe nothing. The point is, he *isn't* in the closet, and that's what upsets people. Many people in the church are perfectly willing to accept gay people in theory. It's when they actually dare to *be* gay people that there's a problem."

"Love the sinner, hate the sin," Simon said tersely. "Isn't that what so many of our religious leaders are fond of saying when it comes to this particular discussion?"

"It's an easy way around what a bishop of mine used to refer to as the 'Gay Problem.' You can be a homosexual, you just can't engage in homosexuality. At least not if you don't want to make God throw up."

"How magnanimous," quipped Simon as he cut a piece of cheese and placed it on a cracker.

"When you think about it, it's sort of like what the Catholic Church asks of its clergy," Thomas said. "You can have a sexual identity, you just aren't allowed to ever act upon it. The idea is that by fighting temptation, you become stronger spiritually."

"Meanwhile, three quarters of them are sticking their dicks in altar boys' behinds," said Russell.

"It seems to put being gay on a par with, say, alcoholism or drug addiction," Simon mused.

"Really, I think the majority of people in the church really don't care what anyone does in bed," said Thomas. "But the ones who do make such a noise about it that we're forced to make it an issue."

"Which brings us back to where we started," Mike said. "What does this mean for you?"

"Honestly? I don't know," answered Thomas. "I'm trying not to think too far ahead."

"A sensible plan," Simon told him, raising his glass. "In the meantime, welcome to our little family."

"I always thought your were a fag," said Russell, earning him a slap on the arm from John. "What? I did. I'm sorry if the rest of you have defective gaydar. Besides, do you think it's an accident that his car broke down and Mike helped him? No. It was fate."

"The meeting with Mr. Monaghan does seem to be rather providential," agreed Simon.

Thomas looked at Mike. "God works in mysterious ways," he said.

"Speaking of Mr. Monaghan," John said, "shouldn't you still be at work?"

"I sort of took a leave of absence," Mike said. "A mental health break."

"The two of you are filled with surprises this afternoon," said Simon. "What's next?"

"Dinner, if Greg ever gets here," John said, looking at his watch. "Do we know what's keeping him?"

"He's always late," Russell said. "I'm sure he'll be here in a few minutes." He stood and picked up the cheese plate. "I'll go get some more crackers," he said.

"I need a refill," said Mike, looking down at his empty glass. "I'll come with you."

"Check on the ham while you're in there," Simon told them.

Mike followed Russell into the kitchen. As Russell fussed with the cheese and crackers, Mike opened the oven. Satisfied that the ham was taking care of itself, he went to the refrigerator and refilled his glass with iced tea. He drank some and leaned against the counter, watching Russell.

"Want to tell me what's wrong?"

"Nothing's wrong," Russell said, a little too quickly. He sliced some Gouda and placed it on the plate. "Why?"

"You seem edgy," explained Mike. "Are things not working out with John?"

"It's not John," answered Russell, unwrapping some brie. "It's Greg."

"Greg?" Mike repeated.

Russell nodded as he fanned crackers around the edge of the plate. "Remember how you and Simon were teasing me about him a few weeks ago?"

"Yeah," Mike said. "When you got so bent out of shape about him chasing after that trick."

"Well, you were right," said Russell. "Sort of, anyway. I was upset about it. So I thought maybe he and I should, you know . . ."

"Really?" Mike said, surprised, as Russell let the sentence hang, unfinished, between them. "You and Greg?"

"Quiet," Russell ordered, looking toward the kitchen door. "Anyway, it didn't happen. I couldn't do it."

"Why?"

"It just didn't seem right," said Russell, cleaning up the cheese wrappers and dropping the knife he'd been using into the sink. "It's hard to explain. Anyway, he said it was okay, but I think maybe he was angry at me. When he said he was staying here for Christmas, I invited him to come with us last night, but he said he had other plans."

"Maybe he did," Mike suggested.

"It was the way he said it," Russell said. "I think he'd been drinking. And now he's not here."

"I'm sure he'll show up," said Mike reassuringly. "You have too much drama in your life."

"Said the man sleeping with the priest," Russell countered.

"Good point," admitted Mike. "And now probably the man with no job."

"You think they'll fire you for skipping out?"

"Even if they don't, I don't think I can go back," said Mike. "I think it's time to move on."

"To what?" asked Russell.

"Who knows?" replied Mike. "Whatever's next. I haven't thought a lot about it."

Russell looked at him curiously. "Don't run away from him," he said.

"Away from who?" Mike asked.

"Thomas," Russell said. "You're thinking about it. I see it in your face."

Mike laughed. "I'm not running anywhere," he said.

Russell said nothing, but he fixed Mike with a hard look. "You'd better not be," he said as he picked up the cheese plate and turned toward the door.

They returned to the living room, where in their absence Simon and John had gotten into a heated discussion. Thomas, looking bewildered, was sitting quietly on the couch, listening to them.

"What are you girls yakking about in here?" asked Russell as he put the plate on the coffee table. "More church talk?"

"Your lover had the audacity to say that Gwyneth Paltrow is the new Audrey Hepburn," Simon said indignantly. "That stick of a girl wishes she were half as talented as Audrey was."

"Remember that pink dress she wore when she won the Oscar?" said Russell. "She looked so glamorous."

"She looked like an emaciated peppermint stick," Simon said caustically.

"Why is it all you old queens get so angry whenever anyone suggests that a new star is as good as one of your beloved divas?" asked John. "It's so annoying. I'm sorry Bette and Joan and whoever are dead and gone, but get over it."

"I will not get over it," Simon insisted, only half joking. "These new girls have no idea what being a star means. They think they can put on a British accent or play someone with a handicap and that makes them special."

"Unlike Bette Davis, who made a career out of accents and handicaps," John retorted.

"Welcome to gay Christmas," Mike said to Thomas as he sat down. "This little spat will be followed by an hour-long debate on the best way to moisturize."

"Here's an idea," Russell said suddenly. "How about presents?"

The Gwyneth versus Audrey argument came to an end as Simon and John grudgingly agreed to postpone the discussion to a later time. Russell, his excitement restored by the prospect of gifts, acted as delivery man, handing out presents from a pile sitting beneath the tree he and Simon had put up earlier in the week. He read the names on the tags and handed them round.

"And here's one for you," he said as he presented Thomas with a parcel wrapped in red paper and tied with a green bow.

"I'm afraid I didn't get you anything," Thomas said, sounding embarrassed.

"Don't worry," Russell reassured him. "You have until New Year's to make up for it."

"But now you have to make it *really* good," Mike whispered to him. "Otherwise you'll hear about it all year long."

Thomas pulled at the bow on the package. It came off easily, and was soon followed by the paper. Inside was a Carter-Beane box. And inside the box was a scarf. It was cashmere, deep red, and very soft. As he fingered the material, Thomas looked around and saw the others looking down at or holding up the same scarf, in different colors.

"I know, it's a cop-out," Russell said. "But it's been a rough month."

"Can we exchange them?" Mike asked, laughing as Russell threw a bow at him. He wrapped his dark blue scarf around his neck. "This is great," he said. "Thanks."

"Am I the only one who actually got gifts?" Russell asked, looking around at his friends.

"You are not," Simon said. "Mine, however, are upstairs, hidden from the prying eyes of nosy young people. I'll return momentarily."

He stood up and left the room, leaving the others to discuss the possible contents of the boxes he would be returning with.

"I hope it's not homemade jam, like last year," Mike said quietly.

"Or fruitcake," added John. "Remember those?"

They laughed. Then, turning serious for a moment, Mike turned to Russell. "Are you going to see Stephen later?"

Russell nodded. He looked at John. "Will you come with me? I'm sure he'd like to see you."

John hesitated. "I don't know," he said. "He's more your friend."

"He's *our* friend," Russell said.

Before John could answer him, there was a knock on the door. Russell stood up. "It's probably Greg," he said.

He threw open the door, exclaiming, "It's about time, you bitch!"

Officer Wayne Chenoweth regarded him with an expression of shock mixed with irritation. He had been called away from his own family's Christmas to deal with the matter at hand, and his wife had been none too happy to be left alone with two hyperactive children and a pile of new toys, most of which either made noise or required assembly. But he quickly masked his annoyance and addressed Russell Harding for the second time in as many months.

"What are you doing here?" Russell asked, confused.

"You're a friend of Greg Mihalski, is that correct?" the officer asked him.

Russell nodded. "Yes," he said.

"Mr. Mihalski was attacked last night," Officer Chenoweth continued.

"Oh, my God," Russell said. "Is he okay?"

"He was beaten quite severely," answered the cop. "Apparently he has no family in the area, but he gave me this address and told me I would find some of his friends here."

"That's right," Russell said, nodding.

"Could I come in?" the policeman asked.

"I'm sorry," Russell said. "Of course."

He stepped aside and allowed the officer to come in. As Wayne Chenoweth entered the foyer, Simon was coming down the stairs. He was carrying an armload of presents and had put a Santa hat on his head. When he saw the uniformed man standing in the hallway of his house, he stopped.

"I assume," he said, looking from Officer Chenoweth to the distraught expression on Russell's face, "that you have not come bearing tidings of comfort and joy."

CHAPTER 34

The fourth floor of Mercy Hospital—recently rechristened the Binny Sellwidge Houghton Memorial Wing, after the wife of a local auto dealership owner who, moved by the staff's treatment of his spouse of fifty-three years during her three-month battle with and subsequent death from cirrhosis of the liver, had donated slightly more than one million dollars in her memory before discovering at her funeral that for more than half of their marriage his beloved helpmate had been carrying on an adulterous affair with his best friend—smelled, as all hospitals do, of disinfectant and decaying flowers. The fluorescent lights spraying the linoleum-tiled floor with their harsh glare did little to boost its appeal; nor did the grim-faced nurses and orderlies who paced the halls in thick-soled shoes, clipboards in their hands and eyes on the clock, counting the minutes until they could go home.

Nobody liked working the Christmas shift. It was when the suicides came calling, the alcoholics and manic-depressives who, driven to the brink of distraction by the holidays, decided to finally do something about it. They seldom succeeded, and consequently became the problem of the women and men who had been such a boon to Binny Sellwidge Houghton in her final days. They tended to their charges with barely disguised irritation, administering (and sometimes withholding) pain pills, inserting thermometers, and doling out tiny paper cups of gelatin colored red and green in celebration of the season.

It was into this world that Mike, Simon, Thomas, John, and Russell entered, rising up from the lobby past Floors 2 (Obstetrics and its twin, Pediatrics) and 3 (Cardiac Care and Oncology) to 4, and stepping

out of the stuffy confines of the elevator and into the twilight realm of
General Services. There were housed all those who failed to fit neatly
into any specific category, those whose bodies, while not entirely well,
were not being attacked by anything precisely nameable, like lym-
phoma, or suffering from something definite, like a torn ACL or broken vertebrae. In the rooms of General Services lay those afflicted with
more general ailments: labored breathing, mysterious rashes, gashes
and punctures and scrapes that necessitated looking after but failed to
merit the vigilant guarding demanded by more serious injuries and
more virulent diseases. Floor 4 was a zoo of the mildly distressed,
which accounted somewhat for the lack of interest shown by the employees who staffed it. Had their charges been touched by more exotic
maladies, they perhaps would have displayed more enthusiasm for
their care, thus truly earning the favorable, if inaccurate, opinion of
their attentions shown by Mr. Jerry "The Cadillac King" Houghton, who
had apparently visited the ward on one of their infrequent good days.

"I hate hospitals," Russell said as the five men walked down the
hallway, searching for Room 448.

"Nobody likes hospitals," countered John. "That would be like enjoying pain."

"Tell that to the leather guys," said Mike as they came to an intersection. Rooms 401–425 stretched off to their left, while a right-hand
turn would take them to 426–450. A small waiting area existed in the
middle, an oasis of vinyl-upholstered chairs and out-of-date magazines
in the midst of sickness.

"We probably shouldn't all go in at once," Russell said.

"We'll wait here," Simon suggested, looking doubtfully at the garish
orange chairs. "In Shangri-la."

Russell nodded. "I'll be back in a little bit," he said.

Leaving the others to thumb through old issues of *Redbook,*
People, and *U.S. News and World Report,* he walked quickly down the
hall to the end, where he found the door to Room 448 and peered in.
Greg was the lone occupant, barely recognizable beneath a mask of
bandages and bruises. The television mounted on the wall across from
the bed blared tinny Christmas carols courtesy of the smiling performers on the screen. An untouched tray of food sat on the table beside
the bed.

Unsure whether Greg was awake or not (his swollen eyes seemed

to be stuck halfway between open and closed), Russell stepped inside.
"Hey," he said.

Greg turned to look at him. He attempted to smile, his face distorting and reflecting the pain he felt from the effort. Instead, he lifted
one hand in greeting. Russell walked closer, trying not to register
shock at Greg's appearance. In addition to the darkening bruises,
there was dried blood on his face, a splint on his nose, stitches in both
upper and lower lips, and a cast on his right arm. Beneath the sheet,
unseen by Russell but felt acutely by Greg, were four broken ribs and a
mosaic of additional contusions. There were deeper wounds as well,
invisible but even more painful.

Russell stopped at the side of the bed, unsure of how to proceed.
He didn't want to touch Greg, fearing hurting him, and he didn't know
what to say. Finally, Greg solved the dilemma by speaking himself.
"Sorry I missed dinner."

Russell smiled. If his friend was joking, perhaps things weren't as
bad as they looked. He reached out and touched Greg's hair. Greg
flinched only slightly. Russell pushed the hair out of his eyes.

"Want to talk about it?"

Greg turned his head to the side, presenting Russell with a cheek
the color of a rotting plum. "Santa showed up with some nasty elves,"
he said. "I guess I was on the naughty list."

He turned back to look at Russell. Tears were slipping from the slits
of his eyes. "I did something really stupid," he said softly.

Russell knew the basics. Chenoweth had told them. From the
rough story Greg had given the officer, Russell had pieced together
the rest. "Was it someone from the bar?" he asked.

Greg shook his head. "Online," he said.

Russell sat down in the chair positioned beside the bed. He took
Greg's hand and held it gently, careful not to disturb the IV taped to
the back. Locating the remote on the bedside table, he turned the television off, silencing the overly joyful carolers.

"This wasn't your fault," he said.

Greg closed his eyes completely, the bruised lids shielding him
from Russell. He didn't say anything, but Russell could see his chest
shaking.

"Greg, this guy is crazy. He was looking for someone to hurt. I
wouldn't be surprised if he's done it before."

He paused, hearing his own words. Done it before. He looked at Greg's face, the eyes still closed. It was eerily familiar. Suddenly an image of Stephen, his nose bandaged, his skin mottled with broken blood vessels, flashed across his mind. Stephen, who at that very moment was lying in a room two floors above them, whom Russell had planned on visiting when he was done in Greg's room.

He said nothing to Greg about his thoughts. Instead, he stroked his hand, waiting for the shaking to stop. When it did, Greg opened his eyes. "I didn't want to be alone," he said. "That's all."

"You're not alone," Russell told him. "You've got us."

Greg looked at him, the tears in his eyes obscuring the pupils, distorting them as if Greg were looking up from underneath the water. "But I don't have you," he said. "That's why I couldn't spend Christmas Eve with you."

And suddenly Russell understood. Despite his carefree attitude about their aborted date, Greg *had* wanted something to happen. He had wanted Russell, and when Russell had pulled away, it had wounded him deeply. Russell saw that now. He looked at Greg's damaged face and saw that, on some level, he was responsible for it.

"I'm so sorry," he whispered, his throat refusing to let the words out fully.

They sat, looking at one another. Russell could think of nothing else to say, and he prayed Greg would be likewise silenced. He didn't want to talk about the things he was thinking and feeling. He didn't want to believe that he in any way had had a hand in Greg's attack. He had been sitting in a church, watching children dressed in their fathers' bathrobes play at being angels and shepherds. He had been far away. But perhaps he had been closer than he knew.

A nurse interrupted the moment, entering the room with a heavy tread and glancing suspiciously at the two men holding hands. She looked briefly at Greg's chart, saw what was written there, and came to her own conclusions.

"It's time for Mr. Mihalski's medication," she said, her voice flat and authoritative. "He needs to rest now."

Russell glared at her but, seeing her expression, said nothing. Although he resented her intrusion, he also welcomed the opportunity for escape. He looked at Greg and once again touched his hair.

"We'll be back later," he said. "Try to sleep."

"Oh, he'll sleep," said the nurse, producing a hypodermic needle, which she inserted into one of the ports in the IV standing beside the bed. "I don't think he'll be having any more visitors tonight."

She finished the injection, the pale fluid in the needle's barrel mixing with the clear liquid in the IV tube. Russell watched the oily-looking stream float down the tube toward Greg's hand, promising unconsciousness. He gave Greg's fingers a final squeeze and left the room.

Back in the waiting area, his friends had quickly tired of reading yesterday's news and were sitting uncomfortably. Seeing Russell appear, they brightened considerably.

"How is he?" Mike asked.

"Not good," said Russell. "He's pretty wrecked."

"Did he say anything about who did it?" inquired John.

Russell hesitated. Answering the question would possibly bring additional ones, ones he wasn't sure he could answer honestly, especially with John present. But these were Greg's friends, too, and they deserved some explanation. He opted for an edited version.

"Let's just say a date didn't go very well," he said.

Simon let out a groan, while Mike, Thomas, and John shook their heads.

"What was he thinking?" John said angrily.

"It wasn't his fault!" Russell snapped. "He didn't ask for this to happen."

"Did he even know the guy?" asked John. "Or was it just some trick he picked up somewhere?"

Russell faced him. "What difference does it make?" he said. "What are you saying?"

"I'm saying that when you go home with guys you don't know, that . . ." John stopped, looking down at the floor.

"What?" Russell demanded loudly. "That you deserve what you get?" He glared at his lover, anger growing inside him until it exploded. "This is exactly your problem," he said. "You're the most goddamned judgmental person I've ever met. And you know what? You can go fuck yourself. You think you're so perfect? Then why are you so fucking unhappy, John?"

He turned and walked away from them. Mike, running after him, reached out for his elbow. Russell pulled away, but he stopped. He leaned against the wall, not looking back to where John and the others stood.

"You know he didn't mean it," said Mike.

"No," Russell said, "he meant it. He always means it, and I'm tired of making excuses for him." He took a breath before continuing. "Greg is in there because of me."

"What?"

Russell nodded. "He did it because of what happened between us," he explained.

"No," Mike said, taking Russell by the shoulders and making him look at him. "No. That's not why he did it. It may have played a small part, but it's not the whole reason."

"Does it really matter how much it had to do with it?" asked Russell.

"You can't take responsibility for this," Mike said.

"There's something else," said Russell. "I think Stephen might have been attacked too."

"I thought he fell on the ice," Mike said.

"That's what he told everyone," Russell said. "But when I looked at Greg in there, it was like looking at Stephen. I think maybe he was lying."

"Shit," said Mike, running his hands through his hair. "Should we tell the cop?"

Russell shook his head. "Not until I talk to Stephen," he said. "I'm going to go up there now. Can you ask Thomas to come with me? Stephen knows him from church, and it might help."

Mike nodded. "What about John?"

"One casualty at a time," answered Russell. "I'll be back as soon as I can."

He walked to the elevators as Mike returned to the other men. As Russell waited for Thomas, he thought about John. The truth was, he had no idea what he was going to do about him. He pushed that problem to the back burner of his mind, though, as Thomas arrived.

"Mike said you want my help. What can I do?"

As they walked toward the elevators, Russell briefed Thomas on his theory. By the time the doors opened and they stepped once more into the tiny metal box, on their way to the sixth floor and the Psych Ward, the priest was up to speed.

Finding Stephen was easy; they had only to look for the worried faces of his parents and brother. The Darbys were clustered outside of Room 613, having been shooed away by a nurse who could have been the twin of the one in Greg's room. Russell and Thomas approached them.

"Father Dunn," Mrs. Darby said when she saw Thomas. "Thank you for coming."

"How's Stephen doing?"

"The doctor tells us he'll be all right," Mrs. Darby said. "Thank God. He took too many of his pills. It was an accident."

"I'm sure it was," Thomas said kindly. "May we see him?"

Mrs. Darby glanced briefly at Russell, then nodded. "You can go in," she said.

Thomas and Russell entered the room as the nurse emerged, brushing by them without a look as she moved on to her next duty. Thomas deftly shut the door, giving them some privacy from Stephen's family.

Stephen himself was, like Greg, in bed and hooked up to an IV. Unlike Greg, he seemed awake and alert. Seeing Thomas, he gave him a small smile. Then, seeing Russell behind him, he looked confused.

"We met in the gift shop," Russell joked.

"You two know each other?" asked Stephen.

Thomas nodded. "It's a funny story," he said. "We'll tell you all about it."

"But first we need to talk," said Russell.

CHAPTER 35

On the morning of December 26, Wayne Chenoweth pulled up to the house on Meridan Street and got out. He was in no mood for any shit, and when he knocked on the door of the house, he did it without gentleness. When the door was opened by a sleepy-eyed Pete Thayer, Chenoweth wasted no time pushing his way by the kid and into the house, where he produced the handcuffs from his belt and, turning his suspect around, affixed them to his wrists.

"Peter Thayer, you're under arrest for the assault and battery of Stephen Darby and Gregory Mihalski. You have the right to remain silent."

As he read Pete the rest of his rights, the kid, as they all did, protested.

"What the fuck? I didn't do anything! I don't even know those guys you just said."

"Mr. Thayer, if you want to keep talking, you are free to do so," said Officer Chenoweth. "I advise you, however, to shut the hell up until you can consult with your attorney. Now walk."

He left the house, pushing Pete ahead of him. He knew that in just a T-shirt and jeans, the kid was probably freezing, but he didn't give a damn. It wasn't his job to make sure he was comfortable; it was simply his job to bring him in. Let the asshole complain to his lawyer if he was cold.

Pete continued his professions of innocence as Wayne drove back to the station. The officer only half listened as the demands to be let go slowly faded away, replaced, again predictably, by attempts at gaining sympathy.

"I didn't try to kill anyone, man," he said.

Chenoweth stared straight ahead, not replying, but his eyes watched Pete's reflection in the rearview mirror closely. The young man was leaning against the window, his forehead pressed to the glass. The cop had seen hundreds of men, and a few women, do exactly what Pete Thayer was doing. Everything looked different from inside a squad car. Thayer, he knew, was looking at the world with new eyes.

"I didn't do anything!" Pete shouted, a final act of bravado before hanging his head. Sometimes they kicked the back of the seat for emphasis, but Pete left this particular flourish out.

Chenoweth had a choice. He could let Thayer talk himself out and hope he got the truth from him at the station in a formal interrogation, or he could push him a little and see if maybe he'd pop right there in the car. The former would be more by the book, but there were advantages to getting it over with.

"You hate fags, right?" he asked.

Pete looked up. Chenoweth, still watching him in the mirror, saw his eyes dart back and forth as he thought about how to answer the question.

"Fags," Chenoweth said again. "You don't like them, right?"

Pete shook his head. "Who said anything about fags?"

Chenoweth laughed, a light chuckle designed to create an air of friendliness. "Come on," he said. "Those two guys you clocked. You didn't know they were queers?"

He saw Pete hesitate. Answering the question would mean he had to admit to the crimes. Not answering was the smart thing to do. Chenoweth would bet his entire week's paycheck he knew which choice Thayer would make.

"No," Pete said. "I don't like fags."

Bingo. Chenoweth nodded his head, as if agreeing with Thayer. More buddy bonding. They were going to be good pals, he and Pete Thayer. He turned his head and glanced at Pete. "Me neither. Fucking pansies are always calling up the station complaining about getting picked on. State says we have to deal with them. Hate crimes, they call them."

Pete grunted, as if indicating that the fairies were indeed wasting Wayne Chenoweth's very valuable, taxpayer-financed time. Yes, it was a real goddamned shame that the Cold Falls Police Department had to involve themselves in the affairs of a bunch of fruits, just because they weren't capable of defending themselves.

"So you roughed up a couple of queers," Chenoweth continued. "What'd they do, try to get in your pants? Wouldn't surprise me."

He saw Pete studying the back of his head, calculating the risk he was about to take. Again, Chenoweth figured the odds were in his favor.

"So what if I did?" Pete said. "I'm allowed to protect myself, right?"

"Absolutely," Chenoweth said heartily. "Someone tries to feel you up or something, no one's going to blame you for popping them a couple of times."

"Right," Pete said, sounding hopeful. "If I was just trying to keep them away from me, no one can say I was doing anything wrong. They can't just put their hands on you, right? Not if you don't want them to."

"Hey, it works for the ladies when they cry rape," Chenoweth said. "What's good for the goose, you know."

Pete was nodding, a smile forming on his face. His eyes had brightened, and Chenoweth could practically hear the ungreased wheels of his mind clunking along as he saw what he thought was a way out. He decided to give Thayer one last push.

"So that's what happened, right? Couple of fags tried getting sweet with you and you had to push them away?"

Pete started to speak, then stopped. Chenoweth held his breath, waiting for him to crumble. *Come on,* he thought. *Just tell me you did it.*

"No, man, I didn't do nothing," Thayer said.

Chenoweth cursed him silently. Now they were going to have to do it the hard way.

"I don't like fags, man, but I didn't hit nobody," Thayer said. "Wouldn't blame whoever did, though. Like you said."

Yeah, Chenoweth thought, *like I said.*

He pulled into the station parking lot and into the space reserved for his car. Getting out, he opened the rear door and helped Pete Thayer out. Together they walked into the station. Half an hour later, after letting the kid make his phone call, he showed Thayer to a cell and left him there to stew.

Pete, sitting on the cell's cot, stared at the wall opposite him and waited. He congratulated himself on catching on to the cop's trick in the car before he got into any more trouble. He'd been so freaked out that he'd almost let it happen, but he'd stopped himself at the last minute. He had his dad to thank for that. Good old dad, who'd always managed to get him to reveal his sins by making Pete think he was on his side. "So you broke a window. No big deal. What happened, you playing ball in the house? Shit, I did that a million times when I was your age."

Pete had fallen for it time and again, and every time he'd paid dearly for believing that, for once, his father really did understand where he was coming from. After each confession, though, had come punishment: a mouth full of soap, a stick on the backside, a week with no TV. Eventually he'd wised up and stuck to flat-out denials. In his experience, that always worked best. Unless they had proof, all they had to go on was your word against the other guy's.

The cop—the stupid fucking doughnut-eater—had claimed they did have proof. Witnesses. Maybe they did; maybe they didn't. He didn't know, and he didn't really care, either. If they were going to nail him, he was going to make damn sure they worked hard to do it. He wasn't going to give them any fucking help.

He tapped his foot nervously, making the springs of the cot squeak like surprised mice. Where was Ronnie? He'd used his one call to phone his buddy, asking him to come down to the station and bail him out. He'd done it once for Ronnie when he'd been picked up for driving after a few too many beers, so Ronnie owed him one. Pete wished he'd hurry up. Being in the cell made him feel like an animal. Plus, he was fucking cold. The goddamned cop hadn't even let him put on a jacket. He wondered idly if maybe he could sue them for something because of that.

Eventually his anxiety turned to weariness and he dozed, his dreams sketchy and troubled, a disjointed narrative in which he was pursued by something he couldn't see. The projectionist in his head, asleep on the job, failed to keep the image in focus, so that Pete ran through shadowy hallways that shook beneath his feet. His hands went out to steady himself, but the walls retreated from his touch and he fell, feeling the hot breath of his pursuer on his neck as teeth like razors closed around his throat.

He woke up when he heard someone calling his name. In the first moments of wakefulness, he thought he was fourteen, in his own bed, being told by his father to get downstairs for breakfast before he missed the goddamned school bus. Shaking his head, he looked for his clothes before realizing he was dressed, a grown man, and looking out at the face of Wayne Chenoweth, who glared at him from behind the bars.

"Get up," he said as he unlocked the door.

Pete followed the cop down the hallway and back to the front desk of the station. Ronnie stood there, his hands in the pockets of his coat. Pete went to him and gave him a rough hug.

"Thanks, man," he said.

"No problem," Ronnie said. "Let's get out of here."

"Mr. Thayer," Wayne Chenoweth said as he slid Pete's personal possessions to him across the counter, "we'll be seeing you again."

Pete resisted an urge to flip him off, taking his wallet and leaving with Ronnie. It wasn't until he was safely locked inside Ronnie's car that he allowed himself the joy of giving Officer Wayne Chenoweth and the entire Cold Falls Police Force the finger. He did so gleefully, waving his extended third digit around wildly and yelling, "Suck my cock, you fat-assed pieces of shit."

"You owe me twelve hundred bucks," Ronnie said, pulling onto the road. "What the fuck did you do?"

"Nothing," Pete said. "It's total bullshit. I'll pay you back, don't worry."

"At twelve hundred bucks, it must be pretty major bullshit," said Ronnie.

"They think I beat up a couple of homos," Pete told him.

"Did you?"

"Nah," answered Pete. "They've got me mixed up with someone else. What the hell would I be doing around fags?"

"How the fuck do I know?" Ronnie said, turning on the radio. "I'm just asking."

"Like I said, they've got the wrong guy."

"Just make sure you get me that money," said Ronnie. "Julie'll have a shit fit if she finds out I took it out of the bank."

"You'll have it tomorrow, buddy," Pete assured him.

That was the extent of the conversation about the matter. Ten minutes later Ronnie dropped Pete off at his house, and after a quick handshake, he was off. Pete went inside, locked the door behind him, and breathed freely for the first time since opening the door and seeing Wayne Chenoweth standing on his stoop.

The first thing he did was take a shower to wash the jail smell off his skin. Then, dressed in clean clothes, he retrieved a beer from the fridge and sat down in the living room to think. He lit a joint (thank God the cop hadn't searched the house) and drew the comforting smoke into his lungs. He wasn't in the clear yet. Despite almost convincing even himself that he hadn't done anything, he *had* given the two queers a pretty good thrashing. And even if they did deserve it, he knew they'd try to make him out to be the bad guy, the one with the problem, all because he'd taught some cocksuckers a lesson.

He was surprised they'd even told the cops what had happened. That just proved how pathetic they were, running to the police when they couldn't take care of themselves. If they were really men, they'd handle things themselves. Then again, he reminded himself, if they were real men, they wouldn't be faggots.

It had to be the second one, he thought, the one he'd visited on Christmas Eve. He must have gone crying to the cops and that asshole with the badge probably played detective, putting two and two together and thinking he'd see if he could get Pete to crack. That was the only possibility. He'd never given the fruit his real name. The cop—Chenoweth—must have remembered him from the incident at the porn theater, must have had a hunch the two things were connected.

Well, they were, but that didn't mean shit if they couldn't prove it. To do that, they'd have to get both the faggots to ID him as the one who'd knocked their lights out. That would mean admitting they'd wanted to suck his cock, and then who would look bad? Not him. Not Pete Thayer. He was just a regular guy minding his own business. It was those stupid fairies who had gone gay on him, trying to get at his dick. Nobody with half a brain would blame him for trying to keep them away.

Yes, in order to nail him, the cops would have to get the fags to testify against him. And that, he was pretty sure, would never happen. He took another drag on the joint, the mellowing effects of the grass spreading through him. He was already feeling better. Things weren't all that bad. He just had to keep playing it cool, keep reminding himself that he hadn't done anything wrong. It was those two queers who should be ashamed of themselves, who should be worrying about what was going to happen to them.

He wondered if he still had the second guy's address, if he'd kept the scrap of paper he'd written it down on. Not that it mattered; he was pretty sure he remembered where he lived. Maybe, he thought, he'd pay the queer another visit, put another scare into him. That might keep him from talking any more.

He chugged his beer, letting the alcohol mix with the pot, knowing it would make everything smooth as silk. He thought about going back to the fag's house, knocking on his door. "Hi," he'd say. "Remember me? Your friendly neighborhood ass-kicker? How about we follow up on that conversation we had a few nights ago? How about I just step inside and show you a few more samples?"

He laughed, imagining the expression on the queer's face. Would he scream? Would he call for help? Or would he drop to his knees and beg, beg Pete not to hurt his pretty face? Maybe even beg to suck his cock again. And this time Pete would make sure he finished what he'd started.

Pete slid his hand into his pants. His cock was getting hard. He closed his eyes and imagined the faggot, on his knees, begging Pete not to hurt him. He pictured grabbing the queer by the hair, forcing his cock into his mouth. He felt himself slide into his throat.

He unzipped his pants and pulled his dick out. Holding the joint in his mouth, he imagined what he would do if he got another chance to teach that faggot what a real man was made of.

CHAPTER 36

The classical music section at the Sam Goody's in Stonesgate Mall was not what could be called extensive, but Simon had managed to find a handful of purchases, mostly things he already had on vinyl (vinyl—it sounded so old-fashioned, like galoshes, or the croup) and wanted to replace. He was particularly excited about finding Jonas Starker's recordings of the Bach cello suites, which he loved but which he hadn't listened to since scratching one of the albums. This had set him on a Bach tear, and he'd picked up several other CDs of the composer's work. He planned on spending the evening listening to them and trying to forget about the unpleasant events of the past two days.

He was standing, looking at a cardboard cutout and wondering why someone called Marilyn Manson would want to have such unpleasant photographs of herself displayed in public, when he noticed someone else intently perusing the classical selections. Something about the man's face was familiar, and after a moment he realized that he was looking at the director of the nativity pageant he'd attended at Saint Peter's. The man was flipping through the discs, his brow furrowed. Then, unexpectedly, he looked up and straight into Simon's face. Faced with either turning away or acknowledging his own stare, Simon chose the latter. He nodded. The man nodded back.

"I was at your concert on Christmas Eve," Simon said. "Lovely."

The man laughed roughly. "I'm not sure if that's quite the word for it. Passable is more like it. But thank you."

"I was particularly taken by the Brahms piece," Simon continued. He thought suddenly of Walter, and looked down.

"Really?" the man said. He walked closer to Simon.

"Brahms was a favorite of my late partner," Simon explained.

"He's one of my favorites as well." He held out his hand. "I'm Gavin Bettelheim."

"Simon Bird."

"I don't think I've ever seen you at Saint Peter's."

"I'm not a regular attendee," explained Simon. "I was there with some friends."

Gavin looked at the CDs in Simon's hand and his face lit up. "You got the Starker!" he said. "That's what I came in for. I saw it the other day while I was on my way out. I was sure nobody else would ever even notice it, so I didn't rush back."

"And here I stumbled upon it completely by accident," Simon said. "Here. It's rightfully yours."

"I couldn't," Gavin said as Simon held the box out to him.

"Your face says that you could," said Simon. "I insist."

"In that case, I accept," Gavin said happily, taking the CD. "Thank you so much. I've been looking forward to listening to these. I'm afraid my old albums don't sound quite as good as they did in the glorious days of hi-fi."

"Just what I was thinking earlier," Simon told him. "I'm afraid my old turntable is soon to go the way of the dinosaurs."

Gavin laughed. "Say, what are you doing for lunch?"

"Nothing whatsoever," said Simon.

"Then let me take you," Gavin said. "It's the least I can do in exchange for making you relinquish the Starker."

Simon nodded. "All right, then. I think that's a very fair trade."

After checking out, the two men walked into the mall. Filled with teenagers celebrating the week off from school, the cavernous space rang with voices as the kids moved through the shopping center in tight little knots, like sticking with like. Boys in baggy clothes stared at girls in too-tight jeans, trying to look as cool and uncaring as they could. The girls, in turn, ignored them completely, all the while praying that their hair and makeup were doing their part to ensure admiring glances.

"Amazing, isn't it?" Gavin remarked, nodding toward a gaggle of young women trying as hard as they could not to acknowledge three boys who had just turned to watch them walk by. "In ten years they'll have babies of their own and will be complaining to one another about how their husbands never pay them any attention."

"What do you think they'd do if they knew that now?" Simon mused.

"Become lesbians?" Gavin suggested.

Simon shook his head. "Then they'd have cats and complain that their *lovers* aren't paying them any attention."

Gavin laughed loudly, earning a contemptuous glare from the very girls they were joking about. He put his hand over his mouth.

"They can't imagine what two such unforgivably old people could possibly find to laugh at," said Simon as they arrived at one of the several chain restaurants scattered throughout the mall.

"Is this all right?" Gavin asked, nodding at the garish neon sign welcoming them to T.G.I. Friday's. "Given our other options, I think it's the best of the lot."

"I'm game if you are," said Simon, walking into the restaurant and facing the chipper host, a young woman wearing a red and white striped apron and what seemed to be about ten thousand pins of various kinds.

"Welcome to Friday's," she said. "I'm Patty. How many of you are there?"

"I believe the most accurate estimate is about one in ten," Simon said.

The girl wrinkled her brow.

"Two," Simon said.

Picking up two menus, Patty led them to a booth at the rear of the restaurant. Simon was relieved to see that there were no tables of teenagers in sight. Apparently, the section he and Gavin were being placed in was reserved for everyone who didn't fit neatly into the restaurant's preferred demographics.

"Your server will be right with you," said Patty, giving them one last smile before running off, her ponytail bouncing jauntily.

"I think I'll have whatever she had," Gavin said drily.

Simon, looking over the menu, nodded. He was enjoying Gavin's sense of humor, and even if the choice of luncheon location wasn't one he would normally make, it had an air of fun about it. After the previous two days, fun was something he very much needed to experience. As he perused the lists of salads and burgers, chicken-fried steaks and spaghetti bowls, he couldn't help but think about Stephen and Greg. He felt terrible about what had happened to the two young men, but was unsure how he could help them. Since Monday he had remained largely in the background as Russell, more distracted than usual, had raced around the house, making calls and assisting the police in speaking with Greg and Stephen. The resulting arrest of the man responsible for hurting them had only intensified Russell's agitation, particularly when the suspect was freed on bail, and finally Simon had simply removed himself from the house for a day out.

"What can I get for you fellows today?"

Simon looked up and saw Patty's twin beaming at him. So similar was she to the peppy hostess that he had to look twice at her apron (no buttons, he noticed) to make sure she hadn't reappeared. But in addition to the absence of decoration on her apron, this girl's name tag read ALICIA.

"I'll have the chicken caesar and a bowl of the French onion soup," Gavin told the girl, who scribbled furiously on a pad in her hand, as if any second the order would flee from her memory.

"And you?" she asked Simon.

"I think the roast beef sandwich, please."

"Fries?"

"Why not?" Simon answered, earning a bob of the head from Alicia as she noted it on her pad. "And an iced tea, if you would."

"Make that two iced teas," Gavin said.

Alicia frowned as she crossed out Simon's single tea and wrote a two next to it. Then she collected their menus. "Thanks, guys," she said as she trotted off, apparently to join Patty.

"How many of them do you think there are?" Gavin asked. "And do they manufacture them just to work in T.G.I. Friday's across the country?"

"I think it's just us," Simon answered. "Everyone under twenty looks the same to me."

"I know," said Gavin. "My daughter is thirty-five, and I can't believe it. I still remember changing her diapers."

"You have a daughter?" Simon said, surprised. He had assumed that

Gavin was gay. *That's what you get for making assumptions about men who like classical music and direct church choirs,* he chided himself. And what did he expect? After the disaster with the fellow in the library, he should, he thought, know better than to trust his first impressions.

"There's a granddaughter as well," Gavin continued. "She's almost twelve."

"You and your wife must be very proud," Simon said.

"We are," agreed Gavin. "I'm not sure they're so proud of *me,* but that's another story."

"I love stories," Simon told him.

Gavin stroked his beard, as if thinking about how to begin. "I'm gay," he said. Then he laughed. "I'm sorry. That sounds so dramatic. It's just that I heard what you said to the girl—what's her name?"

"Patty."

"Patty. When we came in. About the whole one in ten thing. I assumed you meant that you're gay."

"I did," Simon assured him.

"Thank God," Gavin said. "I was afraid maybe I was going to make a fool of myself."

"By telling me you're gay?"

"It's just that I haven't told all that many people. Outside of my family, that is."

"This does sound like a good story," said Simon as Alicia arrived with their drinks and Gavin's soup.

Gavin waited until she was gone before continuing. "I was married for a long time," he said. "Twenty-five years."

"Good Lord," Simon remarked. "Didn't you know?"

Gavin poked his spoon through the melted cheese covering his soup. "I had some suspicions," he said. "But I was happy. At least I thought I was. Then I fell in love for the first time. I mean really fell in love. I loved my wife, but I realized I was never *in* love with her. Unfortunately, the person I fell in love with was one of my students at the college where I taught music. There was an affair, I felt guilty and broke it off, he went first to my wife and then to the dean."

"How awful for you," said Simon.

"It was," Gavin said. "I can't blame him, though. He was young. I should have been more responsible." He paused. "In the end I lost them both, plus my job. That's when I moved here, to start over."

"And now?" Simon asked. "Do you speak to your ex-wife and daughter?"

"I do. It took a long time, but now we can talk. I think Deborah is still hoping a miracle will occur and Marjorie and I will get back together."

Simon hesitated before asking his next question. "And is there anyone in your life now?"

"No," Gavin said. "After what happened with Ben, I largely turned off my romantic needs. I threw myself into composing. That's how I spend most of my time now, when I'm not orchestrating Christmas spectaculars for the good folks at Saint Peter's."

Again Alicia interrupted, this time with the salad and sandwich. "Can I get you anything else?" she asked, smiling so wildly that Simon almost ordered something just to please her. But he refrained, and soon the girl was gone again.

"What about you?" asked Gavin. "Are you with anyone?"

Simon chewed a fry before answering. He knew from experience that talking about a dead lover could quickly turn maudlin, and he didn't want that to happen. He decided to give Gavin the short version of his story. The longer one could wait for another time.

"I had a lover for many years," he said. "He passed away last year."

"I'm sorry," Gavin said. "You must miss him."

"I do," said Simon. "But I have the memories, and I have the life we made together."

"I wonder sometimes what my life would have been like if I'd understood myself better when I was young."

"Your life isn't over," Simon reminded Gavin.

Gavin shrugged. "I'm fifty-five," he said. "It's not exactly beginning."

"You might be surprised," Simon told him. He thought for a moment before continuing. "What are you doing New Year's Eve?"

"Probably going to some very boring party held by some of the church people," Gavin answered. "Charades and eggnog all around."

"No," Simon said firmly. "You're going to come to my house."

"But I won't know anyone."

"You'll know me," Simon said. "And again, you might be surprised," he added, thinking about Gavin's reaction to seeing Thomas among a group of gay men.

Gavin speared some lettuce and looked at it. "All right," he said. "But only because I feel I still owe you for giving up the Starker."

"After Sunday night you may consider the debt fully repaid," said Simon. He was now thinking about his bet with Russell. Did Gavin count as a date? He wasn't certain of the definition, but decided that he was close enough. In fact, he thought as he looked across the table at Gavin, he was better than a date. He was a new friend.

"So, you really liked the pageant?" Gavin asked.

"I especially enjoyed the magi," said Simon. "Their adoration of the Christ child is unparalleled in the history of the theater."

Gavin accepted the remark with good humor. "I know it's not Shakespeare in the Park or anything, but it's good for me," he said. "Saint Peter's became a home for me when I first moved here. There are a lot of wonderful people there."

"I met some of them the other night," Simon said. "One in particular. Beth-Ann, I believe her name was."

Gavin responded with a roll of his eyes. "Don't hold her against the rest of us. She's special."

"I believe she, Patty, and Alicia would get along famously," Simon suggested. "Perhaps we should invite her to lunch next time?"

"I'd rather we kept it to just the two of us," Gavin said.

Simon looked up. Gavin smiled shyly and returned to his salad, leaving Simon to wonder what, exactly, he'd meant by that.

CHAPTER 37

Stephen opened his eyes. Without moving his head from the pillow, he traced the pattern of the ceiling tiles above him with his eyes. Although at first the tiles all appeared to be completely alike, a closer inspection revealed that every other one had been set into the plastic grid of the support beams facing the alternate direction of its neighbors. The differences in the patterns were subtle, but obvious once you knew what to look for. He had been counting them for hours, and was now fairly certain that the sky of his room consisted of four hundred and twenty-six tiles, although it may have been as few as four hundred and eighteen or as many as four hundred and sixty-eight. He'd counted several times and come up with different numbers, a situation he attributed to the fact that he was floating in and out of sleep.

He was, in fact, in withdrawal. He knew this because his doctor, a young man with beautiful black eyes and the equally beautiful name of Ashak Vinpasa, had told him that he was. He had also given Stephen something to help with the worst of the symptoms, but it had not tamed all of them, and as a result, Stephen's body had reacted by going to sleep. This in itself was not so bad; when he was asleep, he had only to contend with the troubling dreams, most of which involved his running from some large, invisible, but completely terrifying monster.

It was being awake he had difficulty with. When he was awake, he remembered what he'd done. Worse, he remembered that his family was there with him, awaiting an explanation. So far all they'd been told by Dr. Vinpasa was that Stephen had consumed far too many pills and needed to rid his body of the lingering toxic effects. They had not yet been told that the pills had initially been consumed over a period of weeks, and that the final handful had been nothing more than a chaser to bring things to an end.

He wished he had died. That first moment of awakening, when he'd heard someone calling his name and, thinking it was the voice of his dark master, swam up through the haze of death to answer, had been enormously disappointing. Instead of the face of an angel, he'd found himself staring into the eyes of a man named David Farris, one of two EMTs assigned to the ambulance that had answered the 911 call Alan Darby, sent to his brother's house to see what was keeping him, made after finding Stephen unconscious. David Farris's partner, Heidi Winterton, had existed only as a disembodied voice calling out random numbers that buzzed like bees in Stephen's head. They had been his vital stats, and they had not been good.

But under David and Heidi's care, he had survived, and his next memory was of having a tube shoved up his nose and down his throat so that the poison he'd fed himself could be sucked out. The purging had worked, and now he was in a hospital bed, still alive and counting ceiling tiles to prevent himself from thinking too much while the final traces of chemicals worked their way through his skin like worms boring into rotten wood.

Losing count of the tiles, he thought instead of his visit from Russell and Father Dunn. He still had difficulty believing that it hadn't been a dream as well. The effects of the pills had been lingering, and at first he'd assumed he was hallucinating. But Russell and Thomas (he had insisted that Stephen call him by his given name) had been very much real, as had their questions. Stephen had initially continued to deny the origin of his injuries, once again mentioning the ice, the slipperiness, the fall. Then Russell had told him about Greg, who lay two floors down, taking the first steps on the path down which Stephen had so blindly stumbled. He'd recalled Greg's smiling face from dinner, his kindness, and the unreturned phone calls. Perhaps if he'd had the courage to dial Greg's number, neither of them would be where they were.

Father Dunn's—Thomas's—role in the visit had been unclear at first, and when it was explained to him how the priest was connected to both Greg and to himself, Stephen found it difficult to believe what he was told. But Thomas had assured him that what he was saying was indeed the truth, and finally Stephen's barriers had come down. He'd agreed to speak to the police. When, an hour later, Wayne Chenoweth had come in and sat at Stephen's bedside, Stephen related the events of his visit to the Paris Cinema as quickly as he could, never looking at the officer's face.

He had no idea what would happen next. He'd been told that he would likely have to identify his attacker, perhaps testify at a trial. The idea filled him with cold dread. He imagined a jury looking at him as he spoke, as he admitted to willingly following his attacker into a dark booth. He saw his mother's face, her hands covering her eyes as he confessed to wanting to suck another man's dick, felt his father's shame as his son declared to the world that he had allowed someone to fuck him in the ass. He heard his brother's muttered curses, and once more he wished he had died.

"Knock, knock."

He looked toward the door, where his mother was walking in carrying a stuffed bear and yet another bouquet of flowers. As she placed both on the dresser with the other flowers, she chatted steadily.

"These are from the Roepers," she informed him, rearranging the daisies. "And the bear is from your Aunt Sally. I don't know why. I guess she thinks you're still seven. But it was a nice thought, so don't forget to thank her when you see her. Your father and your brother are working on the car—it keeps stalling when you put it into second—but they'll come by later. I cleaned your house this morning. I can't believe you let it get to such a state. It's snowing again, so probably . . ."

Stephen tuned her out. He knew she was talking because she was still upset. It's what she did, had always done ever since he was a kid. Hearing her babble on was soothing in a strange way, a kind of maternal white noise that drowned out other, more troubling, thoughts. He closed his eyes and let her words surround him like rain.

"And the dog just would *not* stop barking. I don't know what he thought was out there. A fox, maybe. Your father saw one last week. But probably it was just a jay. They're all over the suet since the temperature dropped. Oh, the racket they make when a squirrel comes around." There was a pause in the flow, and Stephen opened his eyes. His mother was standing very close, looking down at him.

"What?" he said, startled.

"Nothing," his mother said, turning away.

"You were checking to see if I was alive, weren't you?" Stephen said.

"No, I wasn't."

Stephen sighed. He knew she was lying.

His mother went to one of the vases of flowers and began moving the blooms around. "I never asked you, did you have a nice chat with Father Dunn the other night? And who was that with him? He said he knew you, but I haven't seen him before."

Here we go, Stephen thought. He knew he could tell his mother anything and she would believe it. But he also knew that eventually she was going to find out what he'd really talked to Father Dunn about, and what he'd told Officer Chenoweth.

"Mom, come here," he said.

Mrs. Darby turned, a carnation in her hand. "What do you need, dear?"

"Just come sit down for a minute. I want to talk to you."

His mother placed the flower back with the others and walked to the bed. She sat and placed her hands in her lap, one resting on top of the other.

"About what happened," Stephen began.

"It's all right," Mrs. Darby said. "You took too many pills. It happens all the time. Why, Liz Taylor—"

"Mom, it wasn't an accident," Stephen interrupted.

His mother's mouth shut and she shook her head. "No. You just took too many. The directions were very unclear. I told your father we should think about suing the hospital."

"I took them on purpose."

Mrs. Darby ruffled herself like a hen, shaking her head and pulling herself deeper into her sweater. "Nonsense. Why would you do that? It would kill you."

"That's exactly the point, Mom. I wanted to die."

Mrs. Darby's face registered confusion. Her mouth, the lipstick applied too heavily, was a flat line. She regarded Stephen as if he'd suddenly announced that he was going to launch himself into space on a homemade rocket, or perhaps run for president of the United States.

"Don't be ridiculous."

"Mom, listen to me. This isn't easy for me to say. I tried to kill my-self."

"Why on earth would you do such a thing?"

Stephen couldn't look at her when he answered. "I didn't want you to be ashamed of me."

"I'm your mother. I would never be ashamed of you."

Stephen felt tears form in his eyes. Everything was so simple for his mother, so black and white. He was her son, and she loved him. But she had no idea who he was, what he was. She had no idea that he was about to blow her neat and tidy world into a billion pieces.

"Mom, I'm gay," he said before the words could lock themselves inside his mouth.

There was no answer. He could hear his mother breathing, not a foot away from him, but she said nothing. He felt his heart begin to race, beating wildly inside his chest as the seconds stretched out into an unbearable quiet. Nor could he open his eyes to see his mother's face.

"What do you mean?" she said finally.

Stephen forced his eyes open and looked at her. She hadn't moved. Her hands were still in her lap, although now one hand was stroking the other nervously. She fingered her wedding band, turning it around as she waited for him to answer her.

"I'm gay," he said again. He knew no other way of putting it. Surely his mother didn't need for him to tell her what made someone gay, what particular interests and activities defined who he was. "I like men," he added.

His mother nodded her head. "Oh," she said.

"I don't want to be this way," Stephen told her. "I don't want you to be ashamed of me."

"Why would I be ashamed of you?" Mrs. Darby said sharply. "Why would you ever think that? You're my child."

Stephen looked away. Seldom in his life had his mother surprised him, but she had now. He'd expected her to cry, or yell, or at the very least run from the room. But she continued to sit quietly, watching him.

"Listen to me," Mrs. Darby said after a moment. "I know you and your brother think I'm a silly old woman, and I suppose I am. But I am also your mother. There is nothing you could ever do to make me stop loving you. When I look at you and Alan, I see the babies I held in my arms when they were born. And I want those babies to grow up healthy and safe and happy. That's all."

When he turned to look at her, Stephen saw that now his mother *was* crying. But they weren't tears of anger or disappointment, they were the tears of a mother who saw her younger child in pain, pain she could do nothing to relieve. She continued to look at him as the drops rolled down the lines of her face.

"I love you, Stephen," she said. "Whoever you are."

Stephen didn't know what to say to her. He had underestimated his mother, failed to understand the capacity of her heart for acceptance and love. She was right; he had seen her as a silly woman, one whose life consisted of immaterial events and unimportant thoughts. He saw now that he had been wrong about her.

"How did you get so smart?" he asked, his voice cracking.

His mother wiped her eyes. *"Reader's Digest,"* she said.

There was more he needed to tell her, but now wasn't the time. Later she would find out about how he'd been beaten up, and why. For now it was enough that she knew the truth about him. But having told his mother, Stephen now realized something else: He couldn't take it back. He had committed himself to this identity of his. Now that he'd come out, staying in was not an option.

This, almost more than telling his mother, was the real burden. His thoughts flashed suddenly to the nights spent in front of the computer screen, searching for someone to wring desire from his heart. Was that all there was for him? Was the dark man right about him; was he nothing more than a rag to be used by others?

He didn't want that. He didn't want to spend his life in darkness, constantly looking for faces in the shadows, waiting to feel a hand on his neck. He didn't want to live on his knees, looking up into the face of someone who wanted only to destroy him.

"What are you thinking about?"

His mother's voice broke through his thoughts. He couldn't tell her what he was thinking. She had done enough for him. His fears were something he was going to have to shoulder himself. And he would shoulder them, if only because he wanted his mother to be proud of him.

"I was just thinking about what Dad and Alan are going to say," he told her. Although not precisely true, it was a question he had been asking himself.

"You leave those two to me," his mother said. "I can handle them."

Stephen laughed. "You're something else," he said.

His mother smiled at him, arching an eyebrow. "And don't you forget it."

CHAPTER 38

Thomas stared at the notes on his desk, rubbed his temples, and sighed. His sermon wasn't going well at all. He picked up the piece of paper and reread the first line. "On this last day of the year, as we look forward to the next, I want to talk about new beginnings."

He let the paper drop to the desk and groaned. It was awful. But so were the dozen or so other opening lines he'd written and rejected. He pawed through the discarded scraps of paper, hoping maybe one of them would contain a gem he could reconsider, or at least something that didn't sound like a greeting card.

It almost seemed providential, the fact that December 31 fell on a Sunday. His last sermon of the year would also be his opportunity to tell his congregation about himself. He would start the next year as a new man. He hadn't thought beyond that. Several things could happen. Although there was nothing in the church laws that necessitated his stepping down from his position, if his parishioners were uncomfortable attending Saint Peter's under his leadership, he would have to consider removing himself from the pulpit. At the moment, simply thinking about living his life openly was difficult enough; he had no interest in forcing change upon a small-town parish.

And then there was Mike. Thinking about him, Thomas couldn't help but smile. Their meeting had completely altered the course of his life. It was hard for him even to remember what things had been like six weeks earlier, before the snowstorm, before his car trouble, before he'd first sat in the cab of Mike's truck. Since then, his world had been turned on its head. But rather than feeling disoriented, he saw more clearly than ever before in his life.

Sitting back in his chair, he looked at the photo of him and Joseph. How would his life have been different, he wondered, if he'd allowed himself to love Joseph? Where would he be now? What would he be doing? Would he have been able to fill the need Joseph sought to fill in his encounters with other men, the couplings that had resulted in his sickness and, eventually, his death? Would Thomas's love have been enough to save the bright, kind, and funny man who had first stirred his heart?

Joseph's face looked back at him, revealing nothing. Thomas studied it, pondering the questions. He knew he would never have the answers. Wondering what might have been was a game without end. He could go around and around, and still he would be no closer to knowing.

"How's it going, preacher man?"

Mike, entering the study, put his hands on Thomas's shoulders and squeezed. Feeling the strong pressure of his fingers, Thomas relaxed. Mike leaned down and kissed him on the top of the head.

"Not so well," Thomas told him. "This sermon just isn't coming together."

"Anything I can do to help?"

"Write it for me?" Thomas suggested.

"Sorry," Mike answered. "I was never very good at writing. But if you want me to get up there and demonstrate how to make the perfect cocktail, I'll have them eating out of my hand."

"That might work," said Thomas. "They're Episcopalians. They love cocktails."

Mike took a seat in the room's other chair. "Seriously, are you really going to come out to them?"

Thomas nodded. "I have to," he said. "Not just for them, but for me. How can I claim to be their spiritual leader and not be honest with them?"

"It seems to work for the guys on TV," said Mike. "They just ask everyone to forgive them when they get caught."

"Exactly my point. I don't want anyone saying I'm hiding who I am."

"Suppose they don't like who you are. Then what?"

"Then we open a B and B and I learn how to make waffles," Thomas said. "I don't know. This is all I've ever been."

"Then you'd better make sure that sermon is damn good," Mike suggested. "Because I've tasted your waffles, and they suck."

"While we're on the subject of the future, have you given any more thought to yours?" Thomas inquired. Mike hadn't returned to the Engine Room since walking out earlier in the week.

"I was thinking it might be fun to be a porn star."

"Too old," said Thomas.

"Ouch."

"You qualify in every other way, if it's any consolation."

"I'd take that as a compliment, but I know you don't have anything to compare me to," Mike said. "No, I've actually been thinking that maybe it's time I finished my degree."

"You never told me you started one."

"It's one of the many dark secrets of my past," Mike teased. "Actually, I did one year of a teaching program when I was working in Syracuse. I was going to teach high school English."

"Why didn't you finish?"

Mike sighed. "Oh, you know," he said. "There was this guy."

"Jim."

Mike nodded. "It was kind of hard to work, go to class, *and* clean up after him. Then I left and just never got around to getting back to it."

Thomas looked at Mike for a moment, tilting his head to the side.

"What?" said Mike.

"I'm just trying to picture you holding a copy of *The Great Gatsby* and discussing the symbolism of the color yellow."

"I'll have you know my lesson plan for *The Scarlet Letter* had them on their feet," said Mike. "Smart ass."

"Could you really see yourself in front of a class every day?"

Mike nodded. "I think I could. I mean, it can't be any harder than standing behind a bar for eight hours a night listening to a bunch of drunks."

"High school students don't tip you because they think you're cute, though," Thomas remarked.

"I hear some of them do," said Mike, grinning.

Thomas wadded up a piece of paper and threw it at him. He looked out the window at the snow, which had begun to fall again, then back at Mike. "What do you think you'd be doing right now if you hadn't stopped that night?"

Mike looked at his watch. "It's eight forty-five. I'd be pouring drinks and listening to Miss Minnie Skirts and Miss Fellatio Hornblower work their way through 'Any Man of Mine.'"

"And you'd rather be here with me?"

"Hard to believe, isn't it?"

"You've really changed my life," said Thomas.

"No more than you've changed mine."

"I guess the person we really have to thank is Margaret Sorenson."

"Who?"

"Margaret Sorenson," Thomas repeated. "The old woman I was visiting the night I ran out of gas."

Mike nodded. He'd forgotten about the errand that had called Thomas out in the middle of a winter night. "We'll send her flowers," he suggested.

"It wouldn't do much good," Thomas said. "She died a couple of days later. Stomach cancer."

"Thank God she held on long enough to get you out of the house."

"Speaking of getting out of the house, I'm sending you home," Thomas said. "I've got to get this sermon written, and I'll never do it if you keep distracting me."

"Who's distracting you?" Mike said innocently as he got up and went over to Thomas's chair. Kneeling, he looked up with wide eyes. "Forgive me, Father, for I have sinned."

"Out," Thomas said, stifling a laugh. "Get thee behind me, Satan."

"Behind you?" said Mike. "That's exactly what I had in mind."

"Out!" Thomas said again.

Mike stood up. "Okay," he said. "I'm going. But call me later. You can read me your sermon."

"Deal," Thomas said, accepting the kiss Mike gave him. "Now get out."

Mike left Thomas with his notes, heading downstairs to grab his coat before going out to his truck. The falling snow was light and dry. There wouldn't be much accumulation, and what did hang around wouldn't interfere with driving. It was the perfect winter night, pretty without being inconvenient, and it made him happy.

He got into the truck and turned on the radio. The Dixie Chicks started singing "Landslide" to him as he drove out to the road. " 'I took my love, I took it down,' " he sang along softly along with Natalie Maines. " 'I climbed a mountain and I turned around.' "

The truck hummed along as he made his way down the road. He wasn't quite ready to go home, and decided to take a drive around town. When he came to the place where he had almost crashed into Thomas and ended their relationship before it had even begun, he slowed down to take a look. It was just a stretch of road, a dip at the bottom of a hill with nothing at all remarkable about it. Yet passing through it in the still of one cold, snowy night had completely altered the course of his life.

He was past the spot and halfway up the hill even before he completed the thought in his head. Just a few seconds was all it took. Just a few seconds, and the whole universe could shift to one side or another, throwing you off your feet and send you tumbling in a new direction. It was amazing.

The truck crested the hill and kept going. The Dixie Chicks were replaced by Tim McGraw. Mike tapped his fingers on the wheel, thinking about what was in the refrigerator at home and wondering if he should stop at the store before calling it a night. He was mentally running through the contents of his freezer when he passed the Engine Room.

Out of habit, he glanced at the parking lot. It was half full. Not bad for a Thursday night. The bar would be busy, especially since Dale was on his own. Mike felt a twinge of guilt when he thought about how he'd just walked out. But it happened all the time in bars. People quit. Usually you never heard from them again. Dale would find someone else.

On an impulse, he swung the wheel and turned into the lot, taking the first spot he came to. Leaving the engine running, he sat and looked at the bar. The sign over the door blinked in red and white, the "M" in Room dimmer than the rest of the letters, so that the name resembled some offbeat children's show about trains. The building itself was nondescript, cinder blocks painted black. Why were so many gay bars painted black? Maybe because it made them blend in with the night, helped them disappear, like so many of the men who walked through their doors.

It was only four walls and a roof with a sign over the door. Before it had become the Engine Room, it had been a VFW. Before that, an Agway farm supply store (and before that, nothing but a rough set of plans drawn by Roy Dimpler on the back of a piece of paper taken from his desk at Dimpler & Sons Construction). The building itself had no identity; it was what went on within it that gave it a purpose.

For six years the building had given Mike a purpose as well. It had been his home, his refuge. The men who came in and out of its front door had been his family; a dysfunctional one, perhaps, but a family nonetheless. He had met Russell, John, and Simon there. He had re-built his life, one night at a time, until finally the memories of Jim had become pale ghosts that haunted him only when he awoke in the middle of the night, forgetting that he was alone.

If he felt guilty for abandoning Dale, he felt guiltier about abandoning the bar itself. Now, looking at it, he felt almost as if he were looking at the face of an ex-lover. The Engine Room, more than any other place in Cold Falls, had welcomed him in, allowed him to escape inside its doors and heal, safe from the world outside. Within it was a world in which he, and men like him, were able to live as they wanted to.

But like an ex-lover, he and the bar had outgrown one another. He no longer needed it. Staying together would only keep him in one place, endlessly treading water. It was time to let go and move on. He wished it well, wished its other lovers—the ones who still came to find comfort in its arms—well.

He wondered how many of the men who came to the bar truly understood their relationship with the place, knew why it was, apart from the obvious reasons of alcohol and the possibility of sex, they returned again and again. Probably not. Probably they wouldn't know unless it was taken from them. He imagined a giant, invisible hand reaching down and picking the building up, lifting the roof and walls up into the sky so that the people within were left standing amid the drifts of snow. He pictured the surprised faces of the patrons as they looked around, drinks in hand, trying to figure out what had happened. He saw the drag queens, wigs catching the snowflakes in their blue and purple curls, fluttering their impossibly long lashes as they stared up at the heavens.

Hopefully they would never have to experience such a thing. Hopefully their little world would continue to exist and they would continue to visit it as often as necessary. But for him the journey was ended. There were other worlds to explore, and while someday he might pay this one a return visit, it would be only as someone passing through.

Saluting the bar, he pulled out of the lot and drove toward home, leaving the other travelers to keep searching after whatever it was they were looking for. He hoped they found it.

CHAPTER 39

"Thanks for coming over, dude."

Pete closed the front door as T.J. came into the house. He was glad to see his buddy. The past few days had been difficult ones. Although Ronnie had been cool about his arrest, not everyone had. Word had somehow gotten around (Pete suspected Julie Boudreaux), and a couple of customers had told Buck they didn't want Pete working on their vehicles. On Wednesday afternoon Buck told him to take some time off until things blew over. He'd spent the past forty-eight hours in the house, watching television, drinking, and convincing himself that he was the one being attacked. Finally, he'd called Ronnie, T.J., and Gary to see if they wanted to go to the Briar Patch. Gary hadn't picked up, and when Julie answered instead of Ronnie, Pete hung up on her. Only T.J. had been home.

"So, what's the plan?" Pete asked. "Want to head over to the bar?"

"Nah," T.J. answered. "I thought we could just hang out here."

"Shit, man, I've been in this house for two fucking days. I want to get out."

T.J. nodded. "I hear you," he said. "But I'm not so sure you should be out on the town, if you know what I mean."

"Why not?"

"Dude, you know people are talking," said T.J.

"Let them talk," Pete snapped. "What the hell do I care? I didn't do nothing."

"Come on, Pete," T.J. said, looking down. "Everybody knows you did it, man. For Christ's sake, you used a car from the shop."

"What the fuck are you talking about?"

T.J. looked at him. "Well, you did, right?"

"No," Pete said. "No."

T.J. continued to look at him. Pete, agitated, walked around the living room. If even his friends didn't believe him, how the hell was he going to convince anyone else of his innocence? Suddenly, the confidence he'd been feeling began to crumble. He sat on the couch and hung his head.

"Hey," T.J. said. "It's no big deal."

Pete stared at him. "No big deal? Right. Tell that to the cops. They think it's a big fucking deal."

"They just want to scare you, man. What's the worst that could happen?"

"I could go to jail," Pete said.

"You're not going to jail for beating up a couple of fags," said T.J. "Most you'll get is probation."

"You think so?" Pete asked.

"Shit, yeah," said T.J.

"What about what people are saying? What about Buck?"

"Screw Buck. So a couple of customers are freaked out. They'll get over it."

Pete nodded. T.J. was right; people would get over it. He was worrying for nothing. The knot that had gripped his stomach loosened, and he relaxed a little. He just had to chill, take it easy. A couple of weeks and no one would even remember that he'd been arrested.

"Got any beer?" T.J. asked.

"In the fridge," said Pete. "Grab me one too."

T.J. disappeared, returning a minute later with two cold Buds. He handed one to Pete and sat down on the couch. Holding up his bottle, he clinked it against Pete's. "You cool?"

Pete took a deep swallow of beer. "Yeah," he answered, picking up the television remote. "I'm cool. Thanks."

He turned on the set and flipped to the cable menu, looking for a movie. "How about *Die Hard?*" he suggested, and when T.J. shrugged, he turned to the channel and sat back.

For two hours they watched Bruce Willis fight his way out of a building overrun with terrorists. Every half an hour or so, one or the other of them would make a trip to the kitchen and come back with two more beers, until the coffee table was littered with them. Pete had sunk into a comfortable haze, his thoughts fleeting and unfocused. Mainly he just stared at the screen, imagining himself in the building with Bruce. Man, he'd blow the shit out of those terrorists if he had the chance.

When the movie ended and the credits began to roll, Pete got up to take a piss. He'd been holding it in for a while, and he badly needed to go. "You pick the next movie," he told T.J., tossing him the remote.

He went into the bathroom, unzipped, and let his stream fly. Christ, how many beers had he had? He peed for what seemed like forever, his bladder spitting out an endless flow of urine. Finally, he felt it end. Squeezing out the last few drops, he tucked himself away and flushed.

"What's on?" he called out to T.J. as he went to the kitchen for more beer and then headed back to the living room.

"Nothing good was on, so I got one of your videos," T.J. called back.

When Pete entered the room, he saw that Pete had gone into his bedroom and picked up one of his porn tapes. A muscular guy with a shaved head and massive cock was sitting on a couch, stroking himself. Seeing him, Pete wanted to throw up. T.J. had found one of the movies he'd ordered online, a bisexual film called *Switch Hitters*. He'd watched it once and put it away, telling himself he'd only gotten it because the girl on the cover had such hot tits.

"You don't want to see this, dude," he told T.J. "It sucks." He reached for the remote in T.J.'s hand, but his friend pulled it away.

"I want to see what happens," said T.J.

Pete handed him a beer. Maybe if he got him drunk enough, he thought, he could convince T.J. to turn it off.

"Look at that fucking thing," said T.J. as the man in the film smacked his hard dick against his stomach. "Jesus H. Christ."

Knowing there was no arguing with T.J., Pete took his place on the couch and watched through half-lidded eyes as another guy entered the room. Apparently the first man's roommate, he wore only boxer shorts, and seemed surprised to find his buddy sitting on their couch, his tool in his hand.

"What are you doing?" the man asked.

"I couldn't sleep," the guy with the shaved head answered, speaking as if reading a cue card held off camera. "This beats counting sheep."

The roommate looked down at his friend's huge prick. "Need some help?"

"Sure."

The second man sank to his knees and took his roommate's cock in his mouth. Pete closed his eyes. Why did it have to be a scene with two guys? What the hell was T.J. going to think? He waited for an exclamation of disgust to come. When it didn't, he opened his eyes and looked over at T.J.

T.J. was looking at the screen, seemingly unmoved by the two men going at it. After a moment he looked over at Pete. "Feel like helping me out?"

Pete laughed, thinking that T.J. was mimicking the dialogue in the film.

"Come on, dude," T.J. said, looking down. Pete followed his gaze down and saw that T.J.'s hand was rubbing his obviously hard cock.

Pete shook his head. "I'm not into that," he said.

T.J. laughed. "Like shit. You were into it the other night."

Pete was silent. It was the first mention T.J. had ever made of what had happened between them. Pete had almost convinced himself that it had never even happened. T.J. took a swig from his beer bottle and squeezed his crotch again.

"Nothing happened," Pete said.

T.J. responded by unbuttoning his jeans, exposing the head of his cock. Pete stared at it.

"You know you want it," T.J. said, milking his prick with his hand so that a glistening drop of precum escaped from his piss slit. "Come on."

"T.J., man, I'm not like that," said Pete. "I don't know what you think—"

"What do you think Ronnie and Gary would think if I told them how you put the moves on me while I was sleeping?" T.J. interrupted. "Think they'd believe nothing happened?"

Pete felt as if he'd been slapped. He looked at T.J., his mouth open, not believing what he'd heard.

"Come on, Pete. I don't give a shit. Just do it."

T.J. shucked his jeans down so that his lower half was bare. His cock stretched toward Pete as T.J. scratched his balls with one hand. Pete swallowed.

"Do it, dude."

Slowly, Pete leaned down toward T.J.'s dick. Halfway there, T.J.'s hand came down on his neck, forcing him the rest of the way. Pete felt the thick, warm head of T.J.'s cock against his mouth and opened to it. T.J. groaned.

"That's it," he said.

Pete took as much as he could into his mouth. T.J.'s hand was insistent, pushing him farther down until he started to choke. Still T.J. pushed. Pete resisted, but his buddy's touch was firm, and finally he had to just relax and let T.J. fill him. He felt the rough hair of T.J.'s belly against his nose, smelled sweat and manliness.

"I bet you've been thinking about my cock ever since you sucked it, haven't you?" T.J. said.

Pete, unable to respond, moved his mouth up and down T.J.'s shaft. T.J.'s hand never left his neck, working like a piston to control Pete's movements. Pete's throat began to burn as it was scraped by the thick head. T.J. continued to talk, his voice droning in Pete's ears.

"Suck that big prick," he said. "Suck it nice and slow."

He continued to imitate the dialogue coming from the television set, where the man on the couch was receiving the same treatment from his roommate that Pete was providing for T.J.

"Oh, yeah," T.J. growled. "Milk my fucking balls, faggot."

Pete recoiled at the word. Had T.J. just called him a fag? Pushing against T.J.'s grip, he raised his head. "What did you say?"

"Suck my cock," T.J. replied, trying to push him back down.

Pete pulled away. "I'm not a fag."

T.J. looked at him and laughed. "Tell it to my dick," he said, reaching out and grabbing Pete's T-shirt, pulling Pete toward him.

Pete pushed against him, freeing himself. "Knock it off."

T.J.'s eyes went dark. "Suck my fucking cock," he said.

"Get out," Pete ordered. "Get the hell out of here."

Before he knew what was happening, T.J. had tackled him. Pete was thrown to the floor as T.J. landed on top of him. He felt his hard cock pressing against his stomach. Then T.J. was straddling his chest, pinning his arms down. The head of T.J.'s cock was placed against Pete's lips.

"Suck it," T.J. said, his voice hard.

Pete turned his face away, but T.J. forced it back. He slapped his dick against Pete's lips. "I said suck it."

"Fuck you," Pete said. "Get the fuck off me."

"Okay," T.J. said. "I guess you want it in another hole."

He got off Pete, who tried to scramble away. But T.J. overpowered him, holding him around the waist as if they were wrestling. Pete felt T.J. fumbling with the zipper of his jeans, then felt them pulled down. T.J. pushed forward, and Pete found himself flat on his face. T.J.'s weight held him there, his face pressed into the carpet.

"Is this what you want?" asked T.J. as Pete felt his cock press against his asshole. "You want my dick in your ass?"

T.J. pushed into him and Pete yelled into the carpet as pain ripped through him. He felt as if he were being split in two as T.J. kept going, filling his butt. Pete tried to buck him off, but his motions simply drove T.J. deeper.

"That's it," T.J. said. "That's what you want, isn't it?"

He lay on top of Pete, his thighs pressing against Pete's, his hips moving up and down as he fucked Pete's ass. His breath was hot against Pete's ear, the smell of beer foul in Pete's nose. His hands gripped Pete's wrists, holding him prisoner.

"Your ass is fucking tight," T.J. said, moaning.

Pete closed his eyes tightly, trying to will the hurt away. He felt sick, his ass on fire and his stomach clenched as he attempted to ease the fresh bursts of pain that came with each thrust of T.J.'s invading tool. Even worse, he was hard as a rock, his own cock pressed tightly against his belly, scratching against the carpet. How could he be hard? He was in pain, ashamed. Yet there it was, evidence to him of how right T.J. was.

T.J. increased his thrusts, pounding Pete's ass. Pete could sense his breathing getting heavier, faster. Then there was a loud moan and T.J. shuddered. Pete felt his cock twitch, and knew that T.J. was coming in his ass.

"Fuck," T.J. said simply as he finished. He pulled out and got up. Pete, rolling over, looked up at him. T.J. was pulling his jeans back up.

"How about you help me out now?" Pete said, gripping his still-hard cock in his fist.

T.J. shook his head. "I'm not a queer," said T.J. "Sorry, man. You're the cocksucker."

Pete could only look at him, a mixture of rage and fear flooding through him. T.J. was getting dressed as if nothing had happened, as if he hadn't just held Pete down and fucked him.

"Don't worry," T.J. said as he picked up his beer and drained the rest of it. "I'm not gonna tell Ronnie and Gary. This will be our little secret. You take care of me when I need it and we'll be fine."

Pete was on his knees, standing up and pulling his jeans up, covering himself. He couldn't believe what T.J. was saying. All he could do was watch as T.J. put his jacket on.

"I'll see you later," said T.J., going to the front door and opening it. "Thanks for the beer."

He left, the door shutting behind him. Pete stared at it. Then he looked at the empty beer bottle T.J. had left behind. Picking it up, he threw it as hard as he could at the door.

"Fuck you!" he shouted. "Fuck you! I'm not a faggot!"

He collapsed, falling to his knees. The pain inside him poured out as he cried, hot tears filling his eyes. "I'm not a faggot," he repeated. "I'm not a faggot."

CHAPTER 40

"If anyone else moves into this house, I'm going to have to get a hotel license."

Simon puttered around the guest room, straightening Greg's pillows and opening the curtains. Greg, propped up in bed, watched him.

"You're making me dizzy," he said.

"That's the medication," Simon replied. "Which reminds me, it's time for your pills. I'll go get you some applesauce."

"Applesauce? Thanks, Mom."

"Just for that, I'll make it cod liver oil."

"Do they even make that anymore?"

"Unfortunately for the cod, yes," Simon said. "And for you, too, since I just opened a new bottle. My mother used to make me take a tablespoon of the stuff every morning. It's hardly appetizing though quite health-promoting."

"I'll stick with the applesauce," said Greg. "Thanks. And thanks for letting me stay here."

"Well, we couldn't have you sitting in that hospital another week, could we?" Simon replied. "I'm happy to have you."

"Sorry for ruining Christmas for everyone," Greg said.

Simon waved away the remark. "You didn't ruin it for anyone, except possibly for yourself."

"How's the patient?" Russell, fresh from work, poked his head in.

"The patient is doing just fine, thank you," said Simon. "I was just on my way down to the kitchen to get him a little something."

"Want me to get it?"

"You stay here and keep him company," Simon ordered. "I'll be the candy striper."

As Simon left, Russell came in and sat on the edge of the bed.

"So, honey, how was the office?" Greg asked.

"Slow. Everybody asked about you. I told them you were in an accident. By the way, you look like shit."

"I feel like shit," Greg said. "But I feel a lot better now that I'm out of that hospital room. Thanks for covering for me."

"Well, you *were* in an accident," Russell said. "You can make up the details later."

"I don't suppose getting beat up by rough trade is covered under workers' comp, is it?"

Russell laughed. He was glad to see that Greg's sense of humor seemed to be coming back, especially as there was something they needed to talk about.

"Listen," he said. "About what you said that day, about not having me—"

"I was drugged out of my mind," said Greg. "Forget about it."

Russell shook his head. "I don't want to forget about it," he said. "I want to talk about it. I want you to know that you really mean a lot to me. I'm sorry I couldn't—you know." He stopped, embarrassed, and looked away.

"Get it up with me?" Greg suggested.

Russell laughed despite himself. "Yeah, that," he said. He looked at Greg's bruised face. "Did you really get together with that guy because of me?"

"Not just because of you," Greg said. "I've been lonely for a long time. Sometimes I look for people to help me through it."

"The guy from the bar," Russell said, more to himself than to Greg.

"Him. Whoever. It doesn't usually matter. Sometimes I just need to touch someone. Are you disappointed?"

Russell took Greg's hand. "You're a wonderful man," he said. "And you deserve somebody special. No, I'm not disappointed."

"That's funny," said Greg. "Because I am. I should have known better. Christ, I never even asked for a picture of the guy before he came over. How pathetic is that?"

"We've all done it in one way or another," Russell reassured him.

"You're not the first gay man to pick up the wrong guy, and you certainly won't be the last. It's what we *do*," he added dramatically.

"That doesn't make me feel better," Greg informed him. "But thanks for trying."

Russell released his hand. "The right one is out there," he said. "You just have to keep looking for him."

"Couldn't you just find him for me?"

"I thought I had," Russell said.

"Stephen?" said Greg. "Did he really run into the same guy I did?"

"It looks like it."

"That's too creepy."

"It's a small town," Russell told him.

"At least we have more in common now," said Greg. "It will give us something to talk about if I ever see him again."

"He'll be here tomorrow night for the party," said Russell.

Greg laughed. "My party face is in the shop," he said. "I think I'll stay up here."

"You at least have to come down for midnight," said Russell. "Otherwise we'll all come up here."

"We'll see," Greg told him.

"Will you leave that poor boy alone?" Simon said, coming in with a tray. "He's supposed to be resting."

"I was just leaving," said Russell. "It's time to get out of these clothes."

He left Simon and Greg and went to his own room, at the other end of the hall. He'd been living with Simon for over a month, and he'd come to think of the house as his home. But with Greg's arrival, he was reminded that his home was somewhere else, in another house, where John was living alone while Russell made up his mind about what he wanted from his life. And he knew he had to do it soon, if only to keep from losing his bet with Simon.

He went into his room and shut the door. Removing his tie, he quickly unbuttoned his shirt and hung it up. His pants followed, folded neatly and placed over the back of the chair beside his dresser. He was pulling on jeans and a T-shirt when there was a knock on the door. He opened it to find Simon standing there.

"Are you decent?" Simon asked.

286 Michael Thomas Ford

"Am I ever?" Russell answered, opening the door all the way.

Simon stepped into the room and shut the door.

"Is it that serious?" Russell asked, sitting on the bed and pulling on fresh socks.

"Gravely," said Simon. "I want to talk to you about the party tomorrow."

"You had to shut the door for that?"

"I don't want to disturb our patient," said Simon.

"Right," Russell said, not believing a word of it.

"All right, if you must know, I need some advice," said Simon. "Dating advice, if you will?"

"Dating?" Russell said.

Simon nodded. "It appears that I may have accomplished the goal you set for me."

"You got a date for tomorrow?" exclaimed Russell. "Way to go!"

"Shh," Simon hissed, motioning for Russell to keep it down.

"What's the big secret?" Russell asked. "This is great. Who is it?"

"I'd prefer to keep at least that much to myself until I'm sure this is an actual date," said Simon.

"You're not sure?"

Simon sighed. "It's been a very long time," he said. "Forgive me if I'm a little out of practice."

"Okay," said Simon. "What can I help you with?"

Simon looked discomfited. He cleared his throat. "This safer sex business," he began.

Russell gave a hoot and clapped his hands. Once again Simon, glancing at the door as if Russell's voice would penetrate the oak and sail down the hallway, motioned for him to keep it down. Russell, grinning, composed himself.

"As I said, it's been a very long time," Simon said. "Things have changed. I understand there are—things—one needs to be concerned about."

"Sure," Russell nodded. "That's true. But rubbers pretty much take care of that. Do you swallow?"

"Do I what?" Simon asked.

"Swallow," Russell repeated. "You know, when you give head."

Simon blushed deeply. "Well, I suppose I . . . I don't . . . Good heavens."

"It's okay," said Russell. He patted the bed beside him. "Come sit down. We'll start at the beginning."

Simon went to the bed and obediently sat. "I feel like a fool," he said.

"Don't," Russell told him. "I'm glad you came to me instead of believing what all your friends tell you."

Simon glared at him. "If you're going to mock me, I can just ask Mike."

"I'm sorry," Russell apologized. "This is just so after-school special. Besides, I'm never going to have kids, so let me have some fun."

"Very well. But just stick with the basics. I *have* been with a man before, as you know."

"Right. So, what did you and Walter used to do? I mean, did you, you know, engage in anal intercourse?"

"Oh, for the love of God," Simon said. "I'm not your grandfather. You can say 'fuck.' "

"All right, did you and Walter fuck?"

"Yes," Simon answered.

"And who did the fucking?"

"Well, me mostly," Simon explained. "Walter was never very comfortable doing that. He said it made him feel like an overeager terrier."

"Good," said Russell. "So you're usually a top. What about rimming?"

"Rimming?"

"Sticking your tongue in someone's ass," Russell elaborated.

"Can you do that?" asked Simon.

"Don't tell me you and Walter never did."

"It never occurred to us," Simon told him.

"Well, if you're going to try it, just remember that you can get hepatitis and a bunch of other stuff that way."

"This is all starting to sound a little hazardous," Simon said. "Perhaps I should just forget about it."

"Relax," said Russell. "I just want you to consider the possibilities. Chances are you'll be fine. Has this guy been around a lot?"

"I don't think so."

"Good, then he's probably low-risk. Still, if you're going to fuck him, you should use a rubber. Have you ever used one?"

Simon shook his head. "We didn't worry about such things then," he said.

"It's no big deal," Russell said. "Just make sure you don't use any oil-based lube."

"Lube," Simon repeated, as if memorizing a grocery list.

"Lubricant," said Russell, sensing his confusion. "Don't use anything like baby oil, or Vaseline. You want something water-based."

"Where would one purchase something like that?" Simon ventured.

"At the drugstore," answered Russell. "Right by the condoms. It's a brave new world," he added, seeing Simon's surprise at hearing this news.

"When I was a boy, condoms were kept in a locked case in the pharmacy," he said. "You had to ask the druggist for them. I remember my father purchasing some once. The clerk wrapped them in brown paper. For the longest time I thought they must be some kind of candy that he was taking home to surprise my mother."

"Well, I guess they sort of were," said Russell. "But don't worry, you can walk into any store and get them. If you want, I'll do it for you."

"I think I can manage, thank you."

"Okay, well, that's pretty much all there is to it. You just roll it on your pecker and go to town."

"And they're used for both?"

"Both what?"

"Fucking," Simon said, "and the other." He pointed to his mouth.

"That's your call," said Russell. "Most people think sucking someone off without a rubber is pretty safe. But definitely for the fucking."

Simon nodded. "I feel fully prepared," he said. "Thank you for your help."

"You really going to do it with this guy?"

"If I do, you will be the first to know," Simon said.

"Good for you," Russell said, putting his arms around Simon's shoulders. "Really. Walter would want you to find someone."

"Yes," Simon replied. "He would. But I must say, the prospect of starting all over again with someone new is a trifle frightening."

"Tell me about it," Russell said. "I've been thinking about that a lot lately."

"Have you come to any decision about John?"

Russell sighed. "Yes," he said. "And then an hour later I change my mind."

"Where are you right now?"

"In the middle," said Russell. "Smack dab in the middle."

"May I offer you some unsolicited advice?"

"Hey, you sat through my condom talk," Russell said. "It's the least I can do."

"When people are fearful, they shut the world out. They make themselves safe by lashing out at anything they perceive as a threat."

"You mean John? What does he have to be afraid of?"

"You'll have to ask him that," said Simon. "I don't know."

"Why do I always have to be the one to ask?" Russell protested. "Why can't he be the one to take the first step?"

"Maybe he doesn't know how."

"So I have to help him? Why should I?"

"Because you love him," Simon said.

"You sound more sure of that than I am."

"That's because I'm on the outside looking in," Simon said. "It gives me an advantage. Besides, I loved a man for forty-three years. I recognize it when I see it."

"I don't know," said Russell. "It got really hard. I couldn't stay there."

"But the question is, can you go back?"

Russell leaned his head on Simon's shoulder. "Do I have to answer that right now?"

"No," Simon said. "You have until tomorrow at midnight, remember?"

"Can we talk about condoms some more? That's easier for me."

"I think we've covered that," answered Simon. "But I do have a couple of questions about this rimming thing."

CHAPTER 41

At a few minutes past ten on the morning of New Year's Eve, Simon walked through the doors of a CVS pharmacy and stopped. He scanned the helpful signs hung over each row detailing the contents of that aisle's shelves: FEMININE NEEDS, SHAMPOO, PAPER PRODUCTS. What heading, he wondered, would condoms come under? Finally he located it: FAMILY PLANNING. Such a name, he thought with amusement. How coy. Did heterosexual men really sheath their penises to prevent pregnancy? He'd almost forgotten, having come to regard condoms as the province of gay men. Didn't women simply take a pill, or stuff something inside themselves? Did they really leave such an important task up to the men who sweated and panted on top of them? It seemed barbaric.

He walked down the aisle, hoping he looked inconspicuous. A young woman, an employee, was the only other occupant of the row. She was looking intently at tubes of hemorrhoid cream, arranging them into neat stacks. Simon nodded at her in passing and continued on. The condoms were at the very end of the aisle, isolated from the aspirins and cold remedies, like exotic animals in a zoo. He stopped in front of them.

The condoms were in boxes, a rainbow of colors hung on thin metal arms. Scanning the offerings, Simon realized with some dismay that things were not going to be as simple as Russell had led him to believe. There seemed to be an endless array of options: ribbed, colored, and—was he reading correctly?—flavored. A multitude of descriptions assailed him. Reservoir tip. Super-thin. Ultra-Last. Spermicidal. (How violent, he thought. As if trapping the poor sperm weren't enough,

now they needed to be eradicated completely, like unwanted ro-
dents.) There were condoms with bumps, condoms made from the
skin of lambs, condoms for men with extra length and girth and for
men with reduced length and girth (did anyone buy the latter?).

As the length of time he spent looking at the condoms increased,
he grew more and more nervous. He decided to delay his decision by
first locating the promised lubricant Russell had assured him would be
nearby. This proved to be true. There was a small shelf devoted to the
slippery stuff. Again, he discovered that this necessary accessory to
lovemaking came not in one generic form, but in different permuta-
tions. Fortunately, there were only a handful of them, unlike the condoms, which seemed to mutate constantly, creating newer and more
perplexing varieties of themselves even as he tried to decide which
ones to purchase.

He read the information on the bottles. Recalling Russell's edict to
stick with things water-based, he searched for the words. This narrowed his options to three. The first product guaranteed him a feeling
of "skin on skin." The second claimed to produce a sensation of heat.
The third promised nothing, its label generic, almost clinical. Comforted
by its modesty, he chose it with a sense of relief.

He turned back to the condoms. Again their myriad voices clam-
ored at him, each entreating him to give it a try. He was about to just
take one at random when a voice interrupted his thoughts.

"Are you looking for something in particular?"

Shaken, he turned to see the young woman he'd greeted earlier
standing beside him. Apparently having completed her hemorrhoid
cream duties, she had come down to assist him. Now she stood, her
head cocked, waiting for him to answer. He tried to make the bottle of
lubricant in his hand disappear as he composed himself.

"My grandson," he said, thinking quickly. "I'm purchasing him
some—of these," he concluded, indicating the boxes of rubbers. "He's
sixteen," he added as an afterthought.

"That's so cool of you," said the girl, not much older than that herself.

"Thank you," Simon said. "I'm afraid they're slightly more complicated than they were when I was your age."

The girl laughed. "No problem," she said. She reached for a light
blue box. "My boyfriend likes these."

Simon accepted her suggestion thankfully, not even looking at the box. "I'm sure these will be excellent," he said.

"Can I help you find anything else?"

"No. That will be all."

"Okay, then. Have a great day."

Simon hurried away from her, grateful to have the ordeal over with. He was still reeling from the girl's complete lack of embarrassment. Had she really told him that she and her boyfriend were intimate with one another? It seemed inconceivable. Then again, he thought, he had concocted an imaginary grandson as cover for his own needs. Which of them should be ashamed?

In the checkout line he experienced another brush with ignominy when he found himself sandwiched between an elderly woman purchasing numerous cans of cat food and a weary mother with two young children in tow. He placed the condoms and lube on the counter, where they waited between the tins of Friskies and a bottle of Tide and two Snickers bars for the clerk to ring them up. He felt the eyes of all concerned on him, and resisted the urge to blurt out the story about his grandson.

Mercifully, he was able to pay without incident. The clerk barely looked at him as he handed over some bills and accepted his change. When asked if he needed a bag, Simon answered firmly that he did, and moments later he was outside. Clutching his purchases in his hands, he got into his car and sped away, imagining the clerk and the harried mother discussing the foolish dreams of old men as the children devoured their candy bars.

Walking into his house twenty minutes later, he hid the bag beneath his jacket, as if he were smuggling pornography or contraband into his own home. When he entered the kitchen and found Greg in there, standing in front of the refrigerator and peering inside, he was glad he had.

"What are you doing?" he asked. "You're supposed to be in bed."

"All of my nurses deserted me," Greg said, taking out a Tupperware container and opening it.

"Where's Russell?"

"He went out about an hour ago," Greg answered, opening the container and sniffing the contents. "He said he'd be back this afternoon to help you get ready for the party."

"Well, I want you back in bed," Simon ordered. "Go on. I'll bring you some lunch in a little while."

"This is fine for now," Greg said, grabbing a spoon from the dish drainer.

"Take it upstairs," Simon told him. "I have a lot to do for this evening."

"Yes, ma'am," said Greg, walking as quickly as he could out of the kitchen.

Simon waited until he heard Greg clomping around upstairs before going up himself. He snuck by Greg's open door and disappeared into his own bedroom, shutting and locking the door. He went to the bed and sat. Taking the paper bag out from beneath his jacket, he removed the bottle of lube and the box of condoms and looked at them. The box sported a picture of a laughing man and woman. The words "More Pleasure!" were stamped across the bottom in red.

"More pleasure than what?" Simon asked out loud.

Setting aside the lube, he opened the box and dumped the contents into his hand. Six wrapped rubbers tumbled out, landing on his palm. They were encased in plastic. He picked the top one up and the others came with it, falling out behind like the tail of a kite. He dangled the half-dozen little plastic-wrapped packages before him, watching them swing back and forth. Taking hold of the last one, he tore along the perforated edge, separating it from the chain. Collapsing the remaining five back into one another, he put them into the box and put it next to the lubricant on his bedside table.

Tearing the packet in his hand open, he pulled out the condom inside. He was surprised to see that it was a pale brown in color; he had expected it to be blue, like the box. It was wrinkled and damp, like a baby bird or the discarded skin of a large insect. Simon looked at it with distaste, imagining putting such a thing on his penis.

Standing, he lowered his trousers and underwear before sitting down again. His cock hung between his legs, hardly aroused. Holding the condom in one hand, he played with himself with the other, attempting to coax an erection out of his flaccid member. It stubbornly refused to cooperate, so he shut his eyes and tried to think of something exciting. The first image that came to him was Walter, and he rather guiltily pushed it aside. That was the past; he wanted to concentrate on the future.

He could think of nothing else. It had been so long that he had no frame of reference for his own desires, for what stirred him apart from the memories of his lover. Frustrated, he stroked himself harder, as if he could force the blood to flow into his soft tissues. This only resulted in making him sore, and finally he fell back on the bed, annoyed and tired, and stared at the ceiling.

Downstairs, the doorbell rang. Thankful for the reprieve, Simon got up and pulled his pants up. Tossing the still-unused condom onto the bedside table, he left the room and went to answer the door. Assuming it to be one of the boys coming over to help with party preparations, he was surprised instead to find Gavin standing outside.

"I hope I'm not bothering you," Gavin said. "I was going to the market and thought I'd stop by to see if you needed anything for tonight."

"How very kind," said Simon. "I think we've got everything covered, but why don't you come in."

He showed Gavin into the house. Gavin, looking around, said, "I didn't interrupt anything, did I? I wouldn't want to keep you from whatever you were doing."

"Believe me," Simon said, taking Gavin's coat, "you didn't."

"Your house is fantastic," Gavin remarked.

"Walter and I completely redid it," said Simon. "The previous owners had painted all the woodwork in this room a hideous green. It took months to get it all off. Would you like to see the rest of the house?"

Gavin nodded, and Simon began the tour. After the lower level, he took him up the stairs to the second floor. Peering into Greg's room, he found him asleep, so he pulled the door shut and moved on to the other rooms.

"And this is the master bedroom," he said, showing Gavin into his room.

"The moldings are lovely," Gavin remarked. As he turned around, his gaze fell upon the bedside table and lingered. Following it, Simon saw the discarded condom, the bright blue box, the bottle of lube. The paper bag from which all had been extracted lay crumbled beside the pillows.

"I should explain that," said Simon. "I—"

"It's all right," said Gavin quickly. "Really. I understand. I didn't know you were expecting anyone."

"Oh, no," Simon protested. "I wasn't expecting anyone. I was . . . practicing."

Gavin looked at him. "Practicing?"

"Oh, dear," Simon said. "That wasn't quite what I meant. I mean, it *was,* but it sounds so lurid somehow." He was babbling, he knew, and it only increased his embarrassment. "It's just that I've never worn a— I thought that perhaps if I *tried* one before we—" He stopped as Gavin's eyes widened. "Not that I assumed you would want to," said Simon, trying to save the moment.

Gavin looked again at the condoms, then back at Simon.

"This is very awkward," Simon said sheepishly. "If you want to go, I don't blame you at all."

Gavin shook his head. "No," he said. "I don't want to go."

"You don't?"

Gavin picked the condom up. "Shall I show you what to do with it?"

Simon was at a loss for words. But Gavin made them unnecessary as he came to him and put his arms around Simon's waist. They stood, looking at one another for a moment. Then they were kissing. Simon felt the roughness of Gavin's beard against his face. For a moment he hesitated at the unfamiliar sensation. Walter's skin had always been so smooth. But it wasn't Walter he held in his arms. Walter was gone. But Gavin was right there, his mouth warm against Simon's. Simon kissed him back.

Moments later, their clothes were on the floor. Simon was surprised at the quickness of it, but once it began, he found himself caught up in the excitement. He removed his pants and shirt, hesitating only a moment before adding his underthings to the pile. Gavin, too, had stripped, and they stood, naked, looking at one another.

Gavin's body was soft. His stomach, covered in dark hair, formed a pouch over his waist. His cock hung beneath it, nestled in a thicket of hair. His balls, heavy and fat, swung beneath it. He kept his glasses on, examining Simon through them.

Simon looked down at himself, back at Gavin. They were hardly young, hardly what most would consider specimens of beauty. But in Gavin he saw something lovely. They were two men in their later years, with lived-in bodies that had experienced much. Anticipating Gavin's touch, Simon found himself stiffening.

Gavin reached out, wrapping his fingers around Simon's lengthening cock. "Come here," he said, pulling Simon toward him, and toward the bed.

They fell together, arms and legs entwining as they kissed once more. Simon ran his hands over Gavin's body, felt Gavin's roaming over his. His hardness increased, and he pressed himself against Gavin. Gavin responded by spreading his legs, so that Simon was lying between them. Simon sensed Gavin's dick, equally hard, against his stomach.

He moved down, his mouth kissing Gavin's chest, then his stomach. When he came to Gavin's cock, he paused, looking at it. Short and thick, it was the opposite of what Walter's had been, the narrow smoothness of his lover replaced by something denser, weightier. Simon took it in his hand and felt how it filled his fist. He held it while he leaned down and surrounded the head with his lips. He had always enjoyed sucking Walter's cock. Now he took Gavin's into his mouth.

His fingers worked their way between Gavin's buttocks as he sucked him, searching for the tender center. There was hair, and heat, in the veldt of Gavin's ass. He pulled his feet up toward his waist, spreading himself so that Simon could see what his fingers were stroking. There, beneath the plump sack of his balls, his pucker waited.

Simon rubbed a fingertip around the wrinkled eye, probing gently. Then, thinking about his conversation with Russell, he bent down and flicked his tongue against it. Gavin groaned, pushing against him. Simon applied more force, and felt the tip of his tongue penetrate the opening. His cock twitched as an unfamiliar thrill radiated through him.

"Here."

He looked up and saw that Gavin was handing him the bottle of lubricant. He took it and squeezed some onto his palm. This he rubbed into Gavin's asshole, sliding a finger inside. Gavin was tight, and Simon felt his finger pinched comfortably.

"Let me put it on you," Gavin said, and Simon saw that he was holding the rubber.

Gavin sat up. Taking the bottle from Simon, he poured some lube onto his hand and used it to slick Simon's cock. The sensation was intense, and for a moment Simon thought he might come. But then

Gavin released him, and the threatened climax retreated. Then he felt Gavin's hand again, this time rolling the condom down the length of his prick. When he looked down, Simon saw that he was encased in the rubber.

"That's it?" he asked.

Gavin laughed. "That's it," he said. "Go to town."

He lay back again and spread his legs. Simon, his heart racing, positioned the head of his cock against Gavin's slicked hole and pressed in. He watched Gavin's face as he entered him. At first slightly tense, the muscles of Gavin's mouth softened as Simon patiently proceeded, until finally he was all the way in and Gavin seemed relaxed and ready.

He moved in and out slowly, enjoying the smoothness and the warmth. Gavin, reaching down, stroked himself as Simon fucked him, his arm moving in time with Simon's thrusts.

"You're going to make me come," Gavin said after a few minutes.

"Good," Simon answered. "Because so am I, and I didn't want to be rude."

Humor was replaced moments later by heavy breathing as first Gavin and then Simon climaxed. A spray of cum blasted from Gavin's cock as Simon gripped his thighs, pushing himself deep. Simon shook with the force of his own orgasm, filling the rubber with his load. When he was done, he slipped out of Gavin and pulled the rubber off. He rolled onto his side beside Gavin, his cock flushed and sticky.

"I hope you don't think I'm easy," he said as he put his hand on Gavin's chest.

"I do," Gavin answered. "But it's okay. I like easy."

They rested in silence. Simon closed his eyes. Lying beside only the second man he'd made love to since meeting Walter, he felt as if it were his very first time. He felt young again, filled with the thrill of having accomplished something very grand and important.

"What are you thinking?" Gavin asked him.

Simon propped himself up on his side and looked down into Gavin's face. "That it's going to be a very good year," he answered.

CHAPTER 42

"Fuck you, Dick Clark."

Pete gave the TV the finger. Dick Clark, ignoring him, continued to beam. What the hell was wrong with that guy, anyway? Wasn't he, like, eighty years old? Pete had been watching him since he was a kid. Every New Year's until he was old enough to go out with his friends.

He should be out with his friends now, he thought. Instead he was home, sitting in just his boxer shorts alone, stoned, and drunk, watching goddamned Dick Clark and a bunch of bands nobody gave a shit about count down to the new year. Fucking T.J. It was all his fault. Pete couldn't even think about it. Whenever he did, he got so mad he thought about killing T.J. He'd even gone out to the garage and found the gun, the one his father used to keep on the top shelf of his closet, underneath girlie magazines and the flannel shirts he wore when he went hunting. When Pete wanted to impress his buddies, he used to take them into his parents' bedroom and show them the gun.

The gun had passed to him after his father's death from a heart attack. His mother hadn't wanted it in the house anymore, and so Pete had taken it. Now it sat on the coffee table. Beside it was a box of bullets, dug out of one of the boxes stacked against the garage's far wall.

He picked the gun up and examined it. A classic Colt pistol, its surface gleamed a steely blue-black. It was heavy, substantial, a gun meant for business. His father had spent hours polishing it, telling Pete stories about the lawmen and bandits of the Old West who had carried similar weapons: Wyatt Earp, Billy the Kid, Jesse James. Later, when Pete was older, he'd taken him into the woods and shown him how to hold the piece, how to aim and pull the trigger. Once he had allowed him to actually shoot it. The recoil had nearly knocked Pete off his nine-year-old feet, but he had never forgotten the thrill of feeling the bullet lock in the chamber, the excitement of pulling the trigger, hearing the gun roar, and a split second later, seeing the empty beer can he'd targeted fly into the air, its metal skin ripped open.

He imagined taking aim at T.J., pointing the Colt at his shit-eating grin, and pulling the trigger. He saw T.J.'s head fly into a million pieces, the grin disappearing. He laughed. Wouldn't T.J. shit his fucking pants? They'd see who the fucking faggot was then.

"The new year will be here in half an hour, folks. And you'll see it right here."

Pete lowered the gun. Dick Clark was talking to some chick with pink hair. Behind them, a bunch of assholes jumped up and down, waving at the camera. Dick ignored them. He was asking the girl, who had just finished lip-synching her latest hit, how it felt to have the number one record in the country.

Pete picked up the joint he'd been working on and took a toke on it. He blew the smoke out at Dick Clark's face. That's what Dick needed to do; he needed to get high. Then maybe the stick up his ass wouldn't bother him so much. Then maybe he could actually act like he wasn't so damn old and tired.

Pete laughed, pointing the Colt at Dick's head. He imagined pulling the trigger. Blam. With one shot, Dick's head would disappear. "No more Rockin' New Year's Eve for you, asswipe," Pete said to the television.

He put the joint down and picked up a beer. "How about a cold one?" he shouted at the set as he toasted Dick with his beer. He chugged it, draining the half of the bottle that was left. When it was gone, he opened his mouth and belched, tasting pot and Cold Falls Ale.

Dick disappeared and a commercial came on. Burger King. Suddenly he remembered that he was hungry. He'd been drinking since early afternoon, but he hadn't eaten anything since a bowl of Frosted Flakes at breakfast. He decided to see what there was in the kitchen.

He stood up, and immediately sat back down. The room swayed around him. He laughed. "You are majorly fucked up," he told himself. "Majorly."

He tried again. This time he was prepared for the swaying sensation, and managed to keep standing. Moving slowly, he made his way down the hall to the kitchen. It, too, was swaying. The refrigerator seemed impossibly far away. He wasn't sure he'd be able to get there before falling down.

He did, though, but when he pulled the door open, he discovered that the only things inside were more beer and a jar of pickles. He took both out. The beer he set on the counter; the pickles he opened. He reached in and pulled one out, putting it in his mouth. It was sour. Dill. He took one bite and threw the rest of the pickle in the sink. The smell was making him sick.

He put the jar down and took up the beer, twisting the top off and dropping it on the floor. He took a long sip, killing the pickle taste in his mouth. Afterward, he felt much better, although his head was starting to throb. He needed to get back to the couch.

He made it, largely by feeling his way along the hallway wall. Once he was sitting down, though, he was all right. Sitting was good; it was standing up that was tricky. He could sit all night, sight and drink and smoke and fucking ring in the New Year all on his goddamned own.

He considered picking up the phone and calling Ronnie or Gary, but he knew they'd be out. Then he thought about calling T.J. "Hey, faggot," he heard himself say. "Hey, you fucking cocksucker. Why don't you come over here and suck my goddamned cock?"

Laughter poured from him. That's what he should do. Or maybe he should go over to T.J.'s house, go over and knock on the door. When T.J. answered, he would pull the gun out and give him a scare, make him get on his knees and tell Pete what a faggot he was. Tell him how sorry he was for thinking *Pete* was the queer.

Even better, maybe he'd get T.J. on his knees and make him suck his cock. Hold the gun against his head while he pumped his dick in and out of T.J.'s mouth. He'd like that. He'd like seeing T.J. cry like a baby while he shot a load in his mouth.

He picked the gun up again. Holding it in both hands, he closed his eyes and imagined T.J. on the floor. He would make him strip first, so that he was naked. Then he'd hold the end of the gun at T.J.'s temple, right above his eye. He'd hold it there while T.J. took his cock in his mouth, while he put his hand on the back of T.J.'s head and buried his dick in his throat.

"Oh, yeah," he said. "You like that, don't you?"

He slid his hand into his boxers. His dick, fighting the alcohol and pot swirling through his blood, was getting hard. He played with it while he continued his fantasy. He pressed the barrel of the Colt against his own cheek, the steel cool on his skin. He traced the line of his jaw with it while he thought about T.J.'s mouth on his prick.

"That's the way," he whispered, his fingers gripping T.J.'s hair.

The barrel of the gun met his lips. He opened his mouth, darting his tongue into the opening. He tasted the bitter tang of metal. The gun tapped against his teeth. He closed his lips around it, sucking.

"Are you a faggot?" he asked T.J. "Are you a good little cocksucker?"

He moved the gun in and out of his mouth as he pulled his boxers down and off. Nude, he lay back on the couch, putting his feet up on the coffee table. He stroked himself. The fingers of one hand gripped the handle of the Colt; the fingers of the other gripped his dick.

"And now we're just fifteen minutes away from the dropping of the ball!"

Dick Clark's voice cut through the haze of his fantasy. Pulling the gun from his mouth, Pete pointed it at the TV and pulled the trigger. He saw the screen shatter. Smoke fanned out from the place where Dick's head had been. His arm stung.

He looked at the gun, then at the remains of the television. Apparently there had been a bullet in it. For a moment he was shaken. Then he began to laugh. He'd killed fucking Dick Clark. Put a bullet right through his big plastic head. It was pretty goddamned funny, when he thought about it.

He touched the barrel of the gun. It was warm. He put it to his lips, feeling the heat transfer from the steel to his skin. The acrid smell of powder filled his nose.

"That could have been you," he pictured himself telling T.J. as the two of them stared at what was left of the television. "That could have been your head instead of Dick's."

T.J., looking at the TV, begged him to stop. Pete responded by getting on his knees, so that he and T.J. were face to face. He traced the outline of T.J.'s face with the gun's barrel while T.J. shook, trying not to cry. He ran it down T.J.'s neck, circled one of his nipples, and continued down his belly until he reached his cock. It was hard.

"What's this?" he asked T.J.

T.J. shook his head. Pete put the end of the barrel beneath T.J.'s balls, lifting them up. He pressed the gun into the soft place beneath T.J.'s nuts. His balls fell on either side of the barrel, brushing Pete's fingers.

"Am I making you hard, T.J.?" he asked. "Do you like this?"

He opened his eyes and saw that he had the Colt beneath his own balls. The barrel, having cooled, bit into his skin with its cold teeth. He pushed up, pressing his balls tightly against the base of his cock. Then, slowly, he let the end of the barrel slip down.

Moving behind T.J., he placed the barrel of the gun between the cheeks of his ass. "On your hands," he ordered.

T.J. dropped forward, supporting himself on his hands. His ass was before Pete, exposed and unprotected. Pete spread the cheeks with his hand. T.J.'s asshole stretched open. Pete spit on it, beads of saliva catching in the hair on T.J.'s thighs and balls. He pointed the gun at T.J.'s hole.

"Do you want me to fuck you?" he asked.

T.J. whimpered. Pete jabbed him with the gun. "Do you want me to fuck you?" he repeated.

"Yes," T.J. said almost inaudibly.

"Because you're a faggot?" Pete asked.

T.J. nodded.

"Say it. Tell me what you are."

"I'm a faggot," said T.J.

Pete pushed the barrel of the gun into T.J.'s asshole, watching the pink lips part and swallow the steel shaft. He kept pushing until the gun was buried to the chamber inside T.J.'s butt.

"Shall we find out if there are any more bullets?" he asked. "What do you think about that, faggot?"

T.J. didn't answer. He was crying. His head was down, and his body shook. Watching him, Pete felt himself come. Again his eyes opened. The Colt was between his own legs. He had spread them, and the gun, held upside down, was inside him. It wasn't T.J. he was fucking, but himself. The long shaft of the Colt was inside him, where T.J. had once been, and his hand was covered in his own stickiness.

"T.J. isn't the faggot," he said. "You are."

There. He'd said it. He *was* queer. T.J. was right. He had wanted T.J.'s cock, and when he'd gotten it, he'd taken it all in his ass. He was just like the men he despised, a pathetic cocksucker. And like them, he deserved what he got.

He pulled the gun from his ass and brought it to his face. Again he placed it in his mouth. He ran his tongue over it, tasting himself on the barrel. He felt for the trigger. Was there another bullet left? What if there was? It no longer mattered to him. He'd discovered what he was. His cock, still hard, told him. T.J. had told him. He was a faggot, a queer, a cocksucker.

His finger found the trigger. Trembling, he pulled back on it. He heard the mechanism within the Colt start to click, felt the chamber rotate into place. In his mind he saw T.J. look up at him, grinning, and then his soul was flying across the sky.

CHAPTER 43

"How did your father take the news?"

Stephen dipped a cracker into the bowl on the table. "Pretty well," he told Russell. "I think when my mother said she had something to tell him about me, he assumed she was going to tell him I had some fatal disease."

"What about Alan?"

"Him I'm not so sure about. He's been a little distant."

"He'll come around," Russell said. "It took my brother a while too. I think they're convinced that it must be hereditary and that they've got it too."

Stephen laughed. "Wait until they find out about Father Dunn," he said. "Then they'll really think it's spreading."

"Did you go to Saint Peter's this morning?"

Stephen nodded. "It was amazing," he said. "Thomas stood up there and came out to the entire congregation. You could have heard a pin drop when he was finished. Then my mother stood up and started clapping. It was like the ending to one of those John Hughes films, where the geeky girl gets a standing ovation. Except that no one else stood up."

"Ouch," Russell said. "Did anyone leave?"

"A couple of people. But basically we just went on with the service as if nothing had happened, like the good WASPs we are. I'm sure the fallout, if it happens, will take a while."

"And what about you? How are you feeling about everything?"

"Embarrassed," Stephen said. "Stupid. Like a fool. Pick one."

"Don't," Russell said. "You made a mistake. It's over. Now it's time to get on with your life."

"I know," Stephen said. "My new shrink said the same thing. But it's scary."

"That's why you've got friends. We've all been there."

"So why do we always seem to feel like we're the only ones?"

"It's the gay drama gene," Russell said. "I'm afraid you're stuck with it."

Stephen, laughing, dropped his cracker on the floor.

"What's so funny?"

Russell and Stephen looked up to see Greg standing beside the couch. Stephen, who hadn't yet seen him since his run-in with Pete Thayer, stared at his battered face in shock.

"That bad?" Greg asked.

Russell stood up. "I'm going to help Simon in the kitchen," he said, motioning for Greg to take his place. "You boys sit and chat."

Greg took his place on the couch as Russell left. "I hear we went out with the same guy," he said. "We should have compared notes."

"Are you okay?"

"Do I look okay?" Greg said. He put his hand on Stephen's leg. "I'm sorry. I don't mean to be bitchy. It's how I'm dealing with this."

"That's better than my way, I guess," Stephen remarked.

They looked at each other, then laughed.

"We're pretty pathetic, huh?" said Greg.

"You are," Stephen said. "I'm fine."

"Asshole," Greg joked. He took Stephen's hand and held it, neither of them speaking for a while.

"I should have called you," Stephen said finally.

"Yeah, you should have," Greg agreed, nodding his head.

"Is it too late?"

"I don't know," Greg said. "I've sort of been seeing this hot guy. He's got a little anger management problem, but I think we can work it out."

Stephen hesitated a moment, then shook his head. "Now who's the asshole."

"That's enough name calling, children," Simon said as he appeared with a tray of food. "Don't make me send you to your rooms before midnight."

"Where are the rest of the guys?" Greg asked.

"On their way," answered Simon as he fussed with arranging the food.

"By the way, your date's a cutie," Greg remarked. "And from all the noise I heard coming from your room this afternoon, he's a tiger in the sack. Or was that you doing all the grunting?"

Simon, a flush of red moving from his neck and up his face, concentrated on a dish of olives. "You were supposed to be having a nap," he said.

"I was," said Greg. "All the banging woke me up."

"What banging?" asked Russell, entering with another tray, this one filled with glasses of champagne. Gavin was behind him, a plate of deviled eggs in one hand and a bowl of chips in the other.

"There was no banging," Simon said firmly, giving Greg a sharp look. "Greg thought he heard something. It was probably squirrels in the attic."

"No," Greg said. "It sounded more like something getting nailed. Hard."

Simon, blushing afresh, turned away. "I have to attend to something in the kitchen," he said. "Gavin, would you help me, please?"

"What was that about?" Russell asked, nabbing a chip.

"Simon's got a boyfriend," Greg said in a singsong voice.

Russell looked at him, then at the retreating figures of Simon and Gavin. He looked back at Greg. "No," he said. "Really?"

"Well, I don't know if you can call him a boyfriend yet. I guess technically he's still just a trick. But they're pretty cute together, aren't they?"

Russell, thinking back to his conversation with Simon, suddenly had a mental image of him and Gavin, naked. "You go, old boy," he crowed.

The doorbell rang. Excusing himself, Russell went to answer it. Mike, Thomas, and John all stood outside when he opened the door.

"It's about time," he said. "We were starting to think we wouldn't see you until next year."

"I had a call from the bishop," Thomas explained as they came in.

"And what's your excuse?" Russell asked John. "Did you have a call from the bishop too?"

"Worse," John answered. "My mother. She says hello."

"Hmm," Russell said. "So, what did the bishop have to say?" he asked Thomas.

"Apparently word travels fast," said Thomas as they made their way into the living room. "One of my beloved parishioners phoned him as soon as he or she—he didn't tell me who it was—got home and informed him that Saint Peter's was under attack by sodomites."

"It makes us sound like a football team," Russell said. "The Cold Falls Sodomites. We should have T-shirts made up."

"Yes, well, the bishop wasn't exactly thrilled to be the last one to know," Thomas continued. "He and I are having a meeting on Wednesday."

"What's this I hear about sodomites and football?" asked Simon, returning to the room with Gavin, whose flushed face suggested that Simon had told him that their afternoon tryst was no longer a secret.

"It's our new team," Greg told him. "We're playing the Packers on Sunday. Hopefully our tight ends will score."

"Get to your room!" Simon said as Greg laughed. "Now!"

"What do you think the bishop will say?" Russell asked Thomas, who had settled into one of the armchairs.

Thomas shook his head. "I have no idea," he said. "It could go either way. He was pretty annoyed, and he hasn't been supportive of gay clergy in the past. But he's the one who suggested me for the post, so we'll see."

"In the meantime, we're going to have a good time tonight," said Mike, standing behind Thomas and putting his hands on his shoulders. "Right?"

"Right," Thomas agreed.

"Then I suggest we begin the festivities," said Simon. He picked up a glass of champagne and handed it to Thomas. "And for you some sparkling cider," he said, handing a second glass to Mike.

"I wonder how this would mix with my medication," Greg mused, holding a glass up and looking at it.

"Trust me, not well," said Stephen, taking it from him. "Have some cider instead."

"We haven't even had a date yet, and already you're nagging me," Greg told him. "Is this how it's going to be?"

"Good for you," Simon said to Stephen. "Someone needs to keep that one under control."

"John?" Russell said, holding a glass out to his partner, who was standing apart from the others, looking out a window.

"No, thanks," John said. "I'm sticking to cider too. I'm driving."

"One glass isn't going to turn you into a falling-down drunk," Russell said. "Have a little fun."

John looked at the glass Russell was holding out to him.

"Besides," Russell said, "I'll make sure you get home in one piece."

John looked up at him. "What do you mean?"

"My bags are packed," Russell told him.

"You're coming home?"

"If you want me to."

John nodded. "I want you to," he said.

"But we both need to make some changes," Russell said. "It can't be like it has been. We need to meet somewhere in the middle."

"I'll try," said John.

Russell shook his head. "That's not good enough," he said. "You have to want this too."

"I do want it."

"Tell me why?"

John looked confused. He stood for a moment, looking at Russell without saying a word. Then he cleared his throat. "I need you," he said haltingly. "When I thought you were gone for good, I tried to imagine my life. I couldn't. It was just blank."

He took his glasses off and absentmindedly wiped them with his shirt. Russell recognized it as a sign that he was trying to work out a problem in his head. He waited. John put his glasses back on.

"I love you, Russell. I love you more than anything in this world. I guess I don't always know how to say that, but I do."

"You did pretty well just now," said Russell. "And I love you, too."

He held out the glass of champagne once more. This time, John reached out for it. Their fingers touched.

"Thank you," John said, taking the glass.

"Hey, you two, join the party," Mike called.

They went back to the others. Greg had resumed throwing out veiled references to Simon and Gavin's earlier activities, and the innuendoes were flying. Simon, attempting to turn the conversation away from himself, was vainly trying to interest the men in a game of charades.

"And after that, we can roll hoops down the road," said Greg.

"I despise you," Simon told him, trying not to laugh. "You're a hateful little boy."

"You have to be nice to me, though," said Greg. "I'm recovering."

"Much too quickly," Mike suggested, sending them all into fits of laughter.

For the next two hours they talked, ate, and drank, the conversation flowing from one topic to the next like a leaf traversing the rapids of a stream. The eight of them formed ever-changing configurations as the night progressed, sometimes sitting in groups of three or four, others times breaking into pairs as they followed divergent paths of discussion. Always they came back together at some point, sharing and laughing before heading off in new directions.

Finally, as midnight neared, Mike looked at his watch and realized that they were about to miss the transition from the old to the new year. "Hey, boys," he called out. "Get your glasses ready."

They converged from their respective locations. Empty glasses were filled, and as Mike looked at his watch, he began the countdown. "Ten," he said, raising his glass. "Nine."

His cup was joined by seven others, all held aloft. "Eight. Seven. Six." Their voices mingled as, together, they sent the old year on its way. "Five. Four. Three. Two. One."

A collective "Happy New Year!" went up as glasses were clinked together and the ritual kissing began. When they'd gone fully around the circle, Mike put his arm around Thomas and held his glass up again.

"To friends old and new," he said. "And to seeing everyone again same time next year."

EPILOGUE

The waters of Lake Hinckley glistened black and cool in the late June sun. Mike, standing on the dock that stretched out into the lake, took the stone he'd picked up on the shore and skimmed it across the surface. It jumped four times, finally sinking beneath the water.

"Not bad," Thomas remarked. He was sitting on the dock's edge, his feet dangling in the water. "Bet I could get five, though."

"You're all talk," said Mike. "I'll believe it when I see it."

"Later," said Thomas. "I'm enjoying just sitting."

"Chicken," Mike teased.

"What time is it?"

Mike checked his watch. "Almost three," he said.

"We should go soon," said Thomas. "I have to finish my sermon for tomorrow."

"Why do you always put them off until Saturday night?"

"I guess I work best under pressure," said Thomas, laughing. "Why do you always put off your lesson plans until Sunday night?"

"Because I'm a lazy fuck," said Mike.

"Don't forget, we're having dinner with Simon and Gavin tonight too."

"Please tell me Gavin isn't making one of his weird concoctions," Mike said. "I don't know how he's managed not to poison Simon yet."

"I don't think Simon would notice," said Thomas. "He likes everything Gavin makes."

"Is it just us?"

"Maybe John and Russell," Thomas answered. "Greg and Stephen have other plans."

"I can't believe they're actually still together," Thomas remarked, shaking his head. "They're so different."

"And we aren't?" Mike countered. "Besides, don't they sort of have to stay together after what happened? You couldn't write an ending like that."

Thomas stared out at the water. "I know it sounds awful," he said, "but I still feel bad for that Thayer kid. Can you imagine what must have been going on in his head to do that?"

Mike sat beside him. He put his bare feet in the lake, welcoming the coolness on his skin. "He was looking for something," he said, thinking about Pete Thayer and how he'd blown his brains out rather than face trial for what he'd done. "Who knows what it was."

"We're all looking for something," Thomas said. "All of us."

Mike lay his head on Thomas's shoulder, nuzzling his neck. "And some of us are lucky enough to find it," he said.

In novels such as **Last Summer** *and* **Looking for It,** *Michael Thomas Ford has honestly and lovingly explored the intimate details of gay men's lives, from hot sex and lasting relationships to friendship and the search for family. Now he's crafted his most extraordinary novel yet, a powerful saga of three friends and lovers whose story spans decades and whose bonds have finally come* **Full Circle.**

History professor Ned Brummel is living happily with his partner of fifteen years in small-town Maine when he receives a phone call from his estranged friend—Jack—telling him that another friend—Andy—is very ill and possibly near death. It is news that shatters the peace of his world for many reasons. And as Ned boards a plane to Chicago on his way to his friend's bedside, he embarks on another journey into memory, examining the major events and small moments that have shaped his world and his relationships with these two very different, very important men.

Growing up together through the restrictive 1950s and confusing '60s, Jackson "Jack" Grace and Ned took solace in their love for each other. But once they arrive at college in 1969 and meet handsome farm boy Andy Kowalski, everything changes. Despite Andy's apparent heterosexuality, both Jack and Ned fall hard for him, straining their close friendship. Soon, the three men will become involved in a series of intense liaisons and bitter betrayals, coming together and flying apart, as they alternately hurt, love, shape, and heal one another over the course of years. From the heady, drug- and sex-fueled days of San Francisco in the wild seventies to the haunting spectre of AIDS in the eighties and the righteous activism of the nineties, their relationship transforms and grows, reflecting the changes going on around them. Now, together again in the most crucial and intimate of settings, Ned, Jack, and Andy have another chance to confront the damage of the past and embrace the bonds of friendship and love that have stood the test of time.

Full Circle is a wonderfully moving chronicle of three friends that is also an unflinching, triumphant celebration of the power of gay friendships, of the deep bonds forged despite strong obstacles, and of the love that is ultimately the most important thing we can ever share.

**Please turn the page for an exciting sneak peek at
FULL CIRCLE
coming in June 2006!**

PROLOGUE

"Ned, it's Jack."

I open my eyes and look up into the shadows that fill the ceiling over the bed. Rain is falling, drumming on the roof, and vaguely I make a mental reminder to clean the gutters before the storm arrives in full force as promised by the weatherman on the evening news. Tomorrow, perhaps, after I finish grading the stack of freshman essays sitting on my desk in the next room. If I can find the ladder in the mess that is the barn.

Beside me, Thayer rolls onto his back and breathes deeply. As usual, he's somehow managed to pull most of the quilt around himself so that he's cocooned in warmth. I both admire and resent his ability to sleep so fully, like a child. Or a dog, I think, as on his smaller bed beside ours Sam imitates Thayer, stretching his big paws and sighing contentedly.

How old is Sam now? I count back, ticking off the years. Eleven? No, I correct myself. Twelve. Twelve years since Thayer and I returned home from the Banesbury County Animal Shelter with him sitting between us on the seat of our pickup, nose raised hopefully as he sniffed the air for the scent of home. Even then his paws had been enormous, hinting at the great lumbering beast he was soon to become.

Twelve years. How did they slip by so quickly, turning the lively puppy we couldn't keep away from the pond behind the house into the gray-muzzled fellow who now spends most of the hours asleep in a pool of sun on the porch? What have they done, too, to Thayer and myself? Somewhere in that rush of days we've slipped from our forties into our fifties, our hair graying and our bodies beginning to betray us in small ways—eyesight that proves more and more unreliable, muscles that complain more than they used to about getting the chores done. My last birthday was number fifty-six, and Thayer will catch up to me in less than a month's time.

We are all of us—men and dog—growing old together. Older, Thayer says whenever I mention the unstoppable advancement of time. Not old. "We'll never be *old*," he says defiantly, kissing me on top of my head where my hair is thinning. "And you shouldn't worry so much," he tells me. "It's burning a hole in your head, like a crop circle."

This eternal optimism is one of the many things I love about this man, my partner for nearly fifteen years. He is the antidote to my suspicion that the world is forever on the brink of calamity, teetering perilously between salvation and destruction, ready to tumble headlong toward annihilation at the merest push. He saves me from myself on a daily basis. And he bakes the sweetest apple pie I have ever tasted. What he sees in me I don't know and am afraid to ask, in case thinking about the answer finally makes him see what a fool he's been to stick around.

And what of Jack? Has Jack aged along with the rest of us? I can't help but wonder. Although I'm trying desperately to distract myself from thinking about him, he intrudes, pushing his way in as he always has, as if he belongs in the room simply because he wants to be there. It's how he's always approached the world. I know from far too much past experience that now that he's settled in, he won't go away, so I give in and pull back the covers.

The wood floors of our old farmhouse are cool beneath my feet and groan softly as I walk from the bedroom, down the hallway, and into my office. Sitting at my desk, I turn on the lamp and surround myself with a circle of light. Pushed back, the drakness retreats through the window. The rain seems to dilute the blackness, and through the thinning night I see the outline of the barn. Beyond it is the pond, and beyond that the blueberry bushes and, finally, the woods. This is the place I call home, the place where until Jack's phone call I believed that I was safe from the past.

"Ned, it's Jack." And just like that, the ground fell away beneath my feet. Even now, hours later, I still feel as if I'm tumbling through the air, waiting to hit the ground.

I open one of the desk's drawers and remove an envelope.

Yellowed with time, it's addressed to a house I no longer live in, on a street thousands of miles away, in a city I left long ago without looking back. Inside is a card decorated with a Christmas scene and signed with a hastily scrawled signature. Tucked into the card are two photographs.

I don't know why I've kept either the card or the photos. I'm not by nature a sentimental man, a trait that confounds Thayer, a hopeless romantic who still has the flowers I gave him on our first date, dried and stored in a box somewhere in the attic. I don't believe in cataloging my past, surrounding myself with reminders of people and places. What I want to remember I keep in my head.

But I've held on to these, although until Jack's call I hadn't looked at them in a very long time, and had to unearth them from a box of old tax returns and unfiled articles in my closet. Now, seeing them for the first time in many years, I'm reminded of something a photographer friend once told me. The only subjects that photograph completely naturally, she said, are children and animals. "The rest of us are afraid the camera will see us for who we really are."

In the first photograph, Jack and I are children, probably four or five years old. We're dressed in nearly identical outfits—cowboy costumes complete with hats and little pistols. Jack is waving his gun at the camera and beaming, while I look at the gun in my hand with a perplexed expression, as if concerned that at any moment it might go off.

As I look at the boys Jack and I once were, I can't recall the occasion for the cowboy getups. It's one of the many childhood moments that have disappeared from the files of my memory like scraps of recycled paper. Without the photographic evidence, I'd be unable to prove its existence at all. But there we are, the two of us, captured forever as we appeared in that one brief moment in time.

The occasion of the second photograph I remember more fully. It was a birthday party for a mutual friend. This time Jack and I are men nearing forty. It was one of the last times I saw him. Once again, Jack is smiling for the camera while I look away, caught in profile. Gone are the cowboy outfits, and there are no guns in our hands, but something much more dangerous separates us. A man. Andy Kowalski.

Andy stands between Jack and me. We flank him, like guards, although neither of us touches him. Andy regards the photographer with disinterest, his handsome face perfectly composed as if he is alone in front of a mirror. Once again I think of animals and children and how they lack the fear of being betrayed by the camera. Andy Kowalski is something of both.

These two photographs, taken decades apart, roughly mark the beginning and the end of my relationship with Jack. With Andy, too, although our time together was only half as long. Both friendships were laid to rest when I came to Maine to start my life over again, when I left behind everything I knew and everything I was, to become something else.

But the past has apparently decided not to stay buried. Jack's call has opened a door I thought to be long shut and locked. Now it stands open, waiting for me to walk through. When I look beyond it, though, all I see is a room filled with dusty boxes, boxes best left unopened.

"Hey."

Thayer's voice, soft and sleepy as it is, startles me. He comes into the office and puts his hands on my shoulders.

"What are you doing up so early? When I woke up and you weren't there, I thought maybe my mama was right after all and the Rapture had come and Jesus had swept you into his bosom. I was afraid you'd left Sam and me to face the army of hell all on our own."

"Somehow I think I'm the last one Jesus would sweep into his bosom if he came back," I tell him. "And even if he did, I think you and Sam would do just fine against Satan and his hordes."

"Sam maybe," says Thayer, leaning over my shoulder. "He's a tough old boy. But I'd be the first one on my knees letting 'em brand me with the Number of the Beast."

He picks up the photographs. "Who are these handsome gentlemen?"

I sigh. Although he knows the basic outline of my life's story, Thayer has heard very few of the details, not because I fear knowing them would change how he feels about me, but simply because I've never felt the need to tell them.

"That is a long and complicated tale," I answer.

"Well, apparently it's interesting enough that it got you out of bed. And now I'm up, too, so I think it's only fair that you tell me," Thayer says. "I'll go put the coffee on."

He leaves me alone with the photos and with the memories that are starting to push their way into my thoughts. Do I really want to tell him about Jack and Andy? Can I even remember it all and make some sense of it? I teach history to my students, but my own is one I'm not sure that I'm completely qualified to relate. I fear that given my role in the events, I'm an unreliable narrator. At best, my memories are tarnished by years spent trying to erase them, so that what remain are faded, possibly beyond recognition.

Still, I find that part of me wants to tell the story. Maybe, I think, it will help me decide what to do about what Jack has called to tell me. More likely it will simply resurrect old ghosts. Either way, Thayer is waiting downstairs with coffee, and I find that I can no longer sit up here alone.

I leave the photos behind and descend the creaky staircase to the first floor. The smell of coffee scents the air, and the kitchen is comfortingly lit. The doorway glows, and through it I see Thayer setting two mugs on the table. Sam has followed him downstairs and has stretched himself out on the floor. His tail thumps against the worn planks as I enter and sit down, and then he closes his eyes and settles back into sleep.

"All right," Thayer says, sitting down across from me, "start talking."

CHAPTER I

For many reasons, August of 1950 was not a pleasant time to be nine months pregnant, particularly for my mother, Alice Brummel. The war in Korea, less than two months old, weighed heavily on the minds of Americans everywhere, and my mother was no exception. Worried that there might be rationing , she'd taken to buying large quantities of things like bread, sugar, and coffee, all of which she stored in the basement along with bottles of water and extra blankets, which she fully expected to need when the North Koreans began running rampant through Pennsylvania and it became unsafe to venture outdoors unarmed.

When she wasn't stocking up on emergency supplies, she was contending with my father, Leonard Brummel. Unlike his wife, my father felt that the whole Korean business would be settled swiftly and efficiently by the superior war-waging power of the good old U.S. of A. Unconcerned for his own safety, he was therefore free to focus instead on the war raging between his beloved Philadelphia Phillies and everyone else in major league baseball.

The summer of 1950 belonged—as far as the entire baseball-loving population of Pennsylvania was concerned—to the team that had been dubbed the Whiz Kids. Young, cocky, and with the talent to back up their attitude, the Phillies had stormed to the front of the National League thanks to the work of guys like Andy Seminick, Granny Hamner, Dick Sisler, and Robin Roberts. These resident gods of Shibe Park were my father's sole interest during those hot, sticky days, and every evening he came home from his insurance salesman job, settled into his favorite chair with a bottle of Duke beer, and listened to the night's game on the radio.

My mother was not without a sympathetic ear, however. As luck would have it, her best friend and next door neighbor, Patricia Grace, was also pregnant. Like my father, Patricia's husband, Clark, was also unavailable for support, but not because he was in love with a baseball team. Clark Grace, who didn't know an earned run average from a double play, was a scientist—a physicist—and suddenly much in demand by the military. He was currently spending most of his time in Washington, working on something he described vaguely to his wife and neighbors as "a possible new fuel source made from hydrogen."

With their husbands otherwise occupied, Alice and Patricia spent most of their time together. As their bellies swelled in tandem, they spent the mornings playing cards while lamenting their sleeplessness, their hemorrhoids, and the utter unattractiveness of maternity clothes. Out of concern for the welfare of the country, they were careful to limit themselves to two cups of coffee and four Lucky Strikes apiece, not wanting to take more than their share. In the afternoon they did their shopping at DiCostanza's grocery store and, if Clark was staying in Washington, made dinner together in Alice's kitchen, leaving a plate in the refrigerator for Leonard before going downtown to see a movie or sit in the park. If Clark was home, dinners would be made and eaten separately, but as soon as Leonard was ensconced in front of the radio and Clark in his study, the two women would be out the screen doors of their kitchens and on their way.

Given this closeness, it was no surprise when both Alice and Patricia went into labor within minutes of one another. On a particularly torpid Thursday afternoon, while searching for potential ingredients to put into the fruit salad recipe they'd clipped out of the *Ladies' Home Journal* earlier in the day, Patricia was in the process of thumping a honeydew melon to test its freshness when she felt a wetness on her legs and realized to her dismay that her water had broken right there in the produce section and that her good shoes were most likely soiled beyond repair. Turning to alert Alice, she discovered her friend looking at the apple in her hand with an astonished expression that suggested that she, too, was engaged in something more significant than simply admiring the quality of the fruit.

Moments later they were on their way to Mercy Hospital, Alice at the wheel of the Nash Rambler Leonard had purchased for her to use in May but which she'd rarely taken out of the driveway. Patricia, in the

322   Michael Thomas Ford

passenger seat, clutched the door handle and called out directions. By the time they reached the hospital, both women were breathing heavily and barely able to remember their names to give to the attending nurse. It wasn't until they were installed in beds next to each other and receiving simultaneous injections of sedatives that they realized they'd forgotten to inform their husbands of their impending fatherhood.

As it turned out, there was no immediate hurry. Both women would be in labor for some hours, giving Leonard and Clark time to arrive at the hospital and take up stations in the waiting room, where they sat nervously and passed the hours waiting to hear their names called. For Clark the call came shortly before midnight, when a nurse arrived to tell him that he was the proud father of a healthy baby boy. He had hardly finished receiving congratulations from Leonard when another nurse appeared to announce that the second birth had occurred at exactly one minute after twelve.

And so it was that Jackson Howard Grace was born on August the 10th and I was born on August the 11th. As for my name, had it been up to my father it would have been Phillip, for obvious and unfortunate reasons. My mother, however, stood her ground and I became Edward Canton Brummel. My father's disappointment at this turn of events faded later in the year when the Phillies won the National League pennant for the first time since 1915 in a nail-biter that came down to the last game on the final day of the season and a 4–1 win against the favored but despised Brooklyn Dodgers. And although they subsequently lost the World Series to what my father referred to for the rest of his life only as "that other team from New York," he continued to view his Whiz Kids as the greatest team in baseball history.

The next several years passed quietly, as Jack and I did the requisite growing up and our parents duly noted every coo and giggle, every burp and bowel movement, each more glorious than the last. Our days were spent together, as were most holidays, our grandparents living far enough away that regular visits were difficult. Our mothers even dressed us aike, so that we were often mistaken for brothers, despite Jack having his mother's fair hair and blue eyes and me having inherited my father's darker looks.

Thankfully, my mother's preoccupation with the North Korean army waned as it became apparent that although the war was not going to end as quickly as my father had believed, it was highly unlikely that our small house was going to become the base of operations for Kim Il-sung's militia. And once it did end, in the summer of 1953, she and Patricia celebrated by throwing Jack and me a third birthday party complete with matching cakes and a pony upon whose back we were posed for numerous photographs.

In an age where most of us move fairly frequently to accommodate changes in schooling, employment, romantic involvement, or just plain boredom, it seems inconceivable that both my family and Jack's remained in the same houses for more than fifty years. Yet they did, and for the two of us it meant that neither knew a time without the other. From the time I can remember, Jack was there, as present and as constant as the sun.

The differences between us first emerged when we were old enough to begin talking. Jack discovered early on that adults found him charming and irresistible when he spoke, a trait he was quick to use to his advantage. I, on the other hand, preferred to remain quiet, observing the world around me and trying desperately to find in it some sense of order that would explain the reasons things happened the way they did. Our mothers joked that while Jack's first word was "more" mine was "why".

These contrasting personalities extended to the ways in which we explored our surroundings, beginning with the shared lawn between our two houses and extending in larger and larger circles to include first our street, then the neighborhood, and eventually the whole town. Where Jack threw himself headlong into life, expecting someone to be there should he happen to fall and assuming that everything would be okay, I hesitated before every step. Jack wouldn't hesitate to climb a tree or attempt riding a bike, and even when he fell or scraped a knee he laughed, delighted at the many ways in which the world could surprise him. I was more likely to be the one encouraging hesitation, to which Jack's reply was always a playful, "You worry too much."

Our partnership had benefits for both of us that extended beyond the simple joys of friendship. As we advanced in school, my studiousness meant that I was able to help Jack with his assignments, which held little interest for him. He, in turn, was the buffer between myself and the social world of public school. Shy and awkward around other children, I dreaded the daily social interactions that Jack took for granted, in fact looked forward to. Popularity came natural to him, where for me it was almost completely unimaginable. Yet due to my association with him, I was spared a number of humiliations that otherwise would have assuredly befallen me. In the cafeteria, I always had a place at his side, and when the time came for choosing teams for kickball, I was always Jack's first pick.

Whether Jack was aware of what he was doing for me, I don't know. I think for him it was simply a matter of my being his best friend, and he was doing for me what best friends did for one another. Certainly we never spoke of it, any more than we spoke about how I did his math problems and helped him cheat on the occasional test. It was just the way things were, and the way they continued to be as year followed year.

I recall having only one fight with Jack during this time, during the summer we turned nine. It was over superheros. We were in Jack's bedroom, sprawled on his bed reading the latest issues of our favorite comics, which we'd just picked up from the drugstore along with an assortment of sour drops and licorice. Turning the pages of his *Superman* comic, Jack posed the question of who would win in a battle between Superman and Batman. "I mean, if one of them was a bad guy," he clarified.

"Batman would win," I said without hesitation.

"Batman?" Jack asked, clearly ready to disagree.

"Sure," I said. "He's smarter. Superman is strong and all, but he's not as smart as Batman."

"You don't have to be smart to win a fight," Jack told me, shaking his head. "What a dope. Everyone knows it's more important to be strong than smart."

"What do you know?" I shot back, suddenly angry and not sure why.

"Don't get sore at me," said Jack, surprised at my outburst. "I just said Superman could beat up Batman."

"He could not!" I shouted. "Take it back."

I felt myself shaking. I stood up, hands balled at my sides. "Take it back!" I said again.

Jack sat up and looked at me as if I was some new creature he'd never encountered before.

"No," he said stubbornly. "I'm not taking it back."

I threw myself at him, all fists and anger. He fell back on the bed, momentarily caught off guard. I was on top of him, pinning him with my knees. I raised my hand to hit him, but stopped. He was looking at me with a confused expression, making no attempt to cover his face or otherwise protect himself. I felt my heart beating wildly in my chest as I struggled to understand what I was doing. Beneath me, Jack's body rose and fell as he breathed, waiting to see what I would do.

I scrambled off the bed and stood in the middle of the room, glaring at my friend. Jack didn't move. The comic book was crumpled at his side, the pages torn. At my feet, Batman's face looked up at me. My cheeks burned with shame and lingering rage.

"You go to hell!" I told Jack.

His mouth fell open. Although Jack was proficient at cussing, I'd never sworn before, and the shock of hearing it must have taken him by surprise as much as my attack had. I could sense that I'd grown some in his estimation, and the knowledge thrilled me.

I turned and ran from his room, unable to look at him. Back in my own room, I shut the door and threw myself on my bed. Tears came hot and thick as I sobbed, letting out the emotions that roiled inside of me. Suddenly I didn't know who I was or what I was feeling. The world had turned upside down, throwing me off balance in a way that at the same time filled me with both fear and excitement. In Jack's room, for just a moment, our roles had been reversed, and for the first time I'd seen that perhaps neither of us was exactly what we appeared to be.

Eventually I slept, and when I woke it was to hear my mother calling me for supper. I went down and joined her and my father at the table, where I ate my meatloaf and green beans silently while my parents talked to one another about their days. When I was done, I asked to be excused and slipped out the screen door to the backyard.

Jack was there, as I'd known he would be, sitting on the back steps of his house. He was holding a Mason jar in his hands and looking at a firefly he'd caught. I went over and sat next to him.

"Hey," he said.

"Hey."

"Want to sleep over tonight?" he asked.

I nodded, watching the firefly blink on and off and wondering if its light would burn my fingers if I touched it.

"Sure," I told Jack.